PREFACE.

Multitudes of books have been published upon life on the sea. These almost invariably are collections of only one of its many phases—its disasters. A few narratives of this kind are undoubtedly attractive; yet he who attempts to read a series of only such, will discover, as he progresses, that his interest gradually weakens, until thoroughly palled, he casts the book from him, half unread, in disgust at its absence of variety.

In these pages we have endeavored to present all that goes to form the life of the mariner, and in the natural connection to give descriptions of the hardships and perils, even unto death, in its most appalling forms, to which that life is peculiarly exposed. These are combined with personal narratives, the most attractive of all compositions, for they reveal to us not only the events themselves in the minutest particulars, but excite intense sympathy by the disclosures of the thoughts and emotions which influence the minds and the hearts of the narrators.

To most of us who have never been "far at sea," the revelations of those whose lives have been passed upon the deep, are invested with a peculiar interest, from their novelty, and from their instruction in human conduct, under circumstances so foreign to our own experience. The great truth illustrated by this is, that man is the same everywhere; and, furthermore, we possess in these incidents in the lives of our fellow-men, and the action of the same upon their characters, that which enlarges our own range of thought, and better prepares us for the performance of those duties which fall within our own peculiar sphere.

In preparing this work, we have had constantly in view the heavy responsibility which all incur who issue books, lest sentiments should be advanced and revelations unfolded of an evil tendency. While we have endeavored to excite, it has only been by the legitimate exercise of the varied emotions to which our common humanity is susceptible, and this is rarely otherwise than beneficial to our nature.

CONTENTS.

The Perilous Voyage of Captain Norwood, an Officer of the Army of Charles the First, and the sufferings endured by himself and Companions, on a Desert Island, on the Coast of Virginia.............................. 9

Seven Years of a Sailor's Life, among the Savages of the Caroline Islands .. 35

Successful Resistance of Three Sailors against several thousand Savages.... 58

Paddock's Narrative of Bondage among the Arabs, detailing the Sufferings of the Master and Crew of the Ship Oswego, upon the Coast of South Barbary 61

The Abandonment of Alexander Selkirk, a Scottish Sailor, on the Island of Juan Fernandez, where he dwelt in solitude for several years 113

Ethan Allen's Narrative of his Captivity on board of British Vessels, in the Revolutionary War 133

Incidents in the War with Tripoli.. 149

The Chase of the United States Frigate Constitution by a British Squadron.. 161

Description, by an English Sailor Boy, of the Battle between the American Frigate United States, and the British Frigate Macedonian, together with his subsequent Adventures in the American Naval Service during the War. 166

The Extraordinary Sufferings of Donald Campbell, who, being shipwrecked, fell into the hands of the cruel Hyder Ali 181

The Captivity of Thomas Andros, since Pastor of the Church at Berkeley, Mass., on board the Old Jersey Prison-Ship 195

A Sailor's Story of what he saw and suffered in the Naval Service of the United States, in the War of the Revolution............................ 211

The Narrative of the Mutiny of the Bounty, with the escape of Captain Bligh, and his Perilous Voyage of near four thousand miles, in an open boat, to the Island of Timor, together with the fate of Fletcher Christian, the Leader of the Mutineers, and the final Settlement of the latter at Pitcairn Island, in the Pacific Ocean 233

How they Live on board of an American Man-of-War; being the Experiences of a Sailor in the United States Navy.................................. 261

Narrative of an Old English Sailor, yet living, related by himself, in a Style of amusing Simplicity, which shows vividly the many vicissitudes which form Life Experiences on the Ocean 285

Destruction of the Ocean Steamer Arctic, by collision with the Vesta, a French Propeller, on the Banks of Newfoundland, on Wednesday, the 27th of September, 1854, by which disaster more than three hundred persons perished 323

The Lost Russian Sailors, who were abandoned on the Desert Island of East Spitzbergen: to which is added the Narrative of the Misfortunes of the Crew of the Russian Ship St. Peter 341

Experiences of a Naval Officer, as given by Captain Basil Hall, of the Royal Navy.................................. 357

Narrative of a Sailor among Savages, being the Adventures of John R. Jewett, Survivor of the Crew of the Ship Boston, during a Captivity of nearly Three Years, among the Savages of Nootka Sound, by whom his Comrades were massacred 387

Adventures of Philip Ashton, of Massachusetts, who was taken by Pirates, escaped from them, and dwelt for sixteen months in solitude on a Desolate Island 419

Shipwreck of the French Frigate Medusa; as related by Mademoiselle Picard; added to which is the Narrative of two of the Officers, who shared the unspeakable miseries of a raft full of her Sailors and Passengers, who were reduced to the necessity of feeding upon the Corpses of their Companions. 433

The Story of Robert Drury, a Sailor Boy, who was Shipwrecked, Captured, and held in Slavery for fifteen years, by the Savages of Madagascar 469

Incidents in the Life of a Yankee Sailor, as detailed by William Nevens, in his Forty Years at Sea.................................. 493

Adventures of a Slave-Trader, who was engaged, for many years, in the African Slave-Trade 521

Convict Life in Australia. How they get there, and what they get when there, together with a Narrative of Convict Life in Norfolk Island, the place for those too bad for Botany Bay.......... 551

The Horrors of a Fire at Sea, as shown by the account of the Burning of the Prince, a French Vessel, Related by Lieutenant Fonda, one of her Officers. 571

A Sailor's Life and Duties 577

Scenes on a Man-of-War in a Hurricane.......... 581

A Man Overboard.......... 589

Narrative of the Mutiny on the Somers, a brig-of-war in the American Naval Service—Alexander Slidell Mackenzie, commander—and of the Execution of Spencer, Cromwell and Small 591

Abstract of American Nautical Laws 606

Men and Things in the Navy of the United States, as described by the Rev. Charles Rockwell, late Chaplain in the American Naval Service. 609

THE PERILOUS VOYAGE

OF

CAPTAIN NORWOOD,

AND THE HARDSHIPS ENDURED BY HIMSELF AND COMPANIONS ON A DESERT ISLAND ON THE

COAST OF VIRGINIA.

THE month of August, A. D. 1649, being the time I engaged to meet my two comrades, Major Francis Morrison, and Major Richard Fox, at London, in order to a full accomplishment of our purpose, to seek our fortunes in Virginia, pursuant to our agreement, the year before, in Holland, all parties very punctually appeared at the time and place assigned; and were all still in the same mind, fully bent to put in practice what we had so solemnly agreed upon. It fell out to be about the first day of September, A. D. 1649, that we grew acquainted, on the Royal Exchange, with Captain John Locker, whose bills upon the posts made us know he was master of a good ship, (untruly so called,) the Virginia Merchant, burden 300 tons, of force thirty guns or more. We were not long in treaty with the captain, but agreed with him for ourselves and servants, at six pounds a head, to be transported into James river: our goods to be paid for at the current price.

About the fifteenth day, we were ordered to meet the ship at Gravesend, where the captain was to clear with his merchants, and we to make our several payments; which, when we had performed, we staid not for the ship, but took post for the Downs, where, with some impatience, we expected her coming there. About the sixteenth, we could see the whole fleet under sail, with a south-west wind; which, having brought them to that road, kept them there at anchor, until our money was almost spent at Deal. September 23d, the wind veered to the east, and we were summoned, by signs and guns, to repair on board. We had a fresh, heavy gale for three days, which cleared us of the channel, and put us out of soundings. With this propitious beginning, we pursued our course for about twenty days, desiring to make the Western Islands; at which time the cooper began to complain that our water-cask was almost empty; alleging, that there was not enough in hold for our great family, (about three hundred and thirty souls,) to serve a month. We were now, by all accounts, near the Western Islands; Fyal was that we were likely first to see, and our captains resolved to touch there to supply this defect, as the most commodious port for our purpose.

The day-break of October 14th, showed us the peak of that island. As soon as we had saluted the castle, and returned, for being civilly answered, Captain John Tatam, our countryman, did the same from aboard his goodly ship, the St. John. The English merchants, from the town, came on board our ship, and gave us a very civil welcome. Of them, one Mr. Andrews, invited me, with my two comrades, to refresh ourselves with fruit and meat, such as the islands produced. Our captain dined with us at his house, and so did Captain Tatam, who, in like courteous manner, engaged us all to dine on board his ship the next day. We visited the peach-trees for our dessert, of which I took, at least, a double share: a little before the time of dinner, Captain Tatam had sent his boats to bring us on board his ship, and it was well for us he did so, our ship's long-boat having been staved in pieces the night before, by the seamen's neglect, who had all tasted so liberally of new wine, by the commodiousness of the vintage, that they lay up and down, dead drunk, in all quarters, in a sad pickle. The loss of our long-boat, as it was likely to make our watering tedious, and chargeable to the owners, so did it expose us to the hazard of many inconveniences and perils, in the whole course of our voyage. Our captain led the van into Tatam's boat, which brought us safe on board the John. At our arrival, we were welcomed with a whole tier of guns, and with a very kind aspect in the captain. He gave us excellent wines to drink before dinner, and, at our meat, as good of other sorts, for concoction. There was a handsome plenty of fish and fowl, several ways cooked, to relish the Portuguese and English palates. While we were caressed in this manner on ship-board, the seamen on shore continued in their debauchery, with very little advance of our dispatch; the getting water was so tedious in itself, for lack of our boats, and so full of delays, by drunken contests of ours with the islanders, and with themselves; that, after some days stay upon the island, when our captain resolved to sail away, he found the ship in worse condition for liquors, than when we came on shore. For if we got a new supply of water, the proportion was hardly enough to balance the expense of beer, that was spent in the time we got in.

It was about the 22d of October, that we took leave of our landlord and Fyal. We had a store of black pigs for fresh meat, and I carried peaches without number. We parted with an easterly wind, a top-sail gale, which soon brought us into a trade wind, that favored us at fifty or sixty leagues in twenty-four hours, till we came to the height of Bermudas. The gale continued fair till November the 8th; then we observed the water changed; and heaving the lead, we had thirty-five fathoms of water, which was joyful news. Our want of all things necessary for human life made it so. Toward break of day, weary of my lodgings, I visited Mate Putts on the watch; and would have treated him with brandy, but he refused that offer, unless I could give him tobacco, which I had not. He said it was near break of day, and he would look out to see what change there was in the water. No sooner were his feet upon the deck, but with stamps and noise he calls up the seamen, crying out, "All hands aloft! breaches on both sides! all hands aloft!"

The seamen were soon on deck with this dismal alarm, and saw the cause thereof; but instead of applying their hands for their preservation, through a general despondency, they fell on their knees, commending their souls, as at the last gasp. The captain came out at the noise to rectify what was amiss; but seeing how the case stood, his courage failed. Mate Putts, a stout seaman, took heart again, and cried, "Is there no good fellow that will stand to the helm, or loose a sail?" But among all the ship's crew, there were but two fore-mastmen that would be persuaded to obey commands; viz: Thomas Reaisin and John Smith, men of innate courage, who, for their good resolution, on that and divers other occasions in the various traverses of this voyage, deserve to have their names kept in lasting remembrance. One of them got up and loosened the fore-topsail, to put the ship, if possible, in steerage way, and under command; the other stood to the helm, and he shifted it in a nick of time; for the ship was at the point of dashing on the starboard breach: and, although in the rest of the voyage, she was wont to be blamed for the ill quality of not feeling the helm, she did, in this important instance, redeem her credit, and fell round off for our rescue from that danger. But the joy of this escape lasted but a moment, for no sooner was she fallen from that breach, but another on the larboard bow was ready to receive her.

The ship's crew, by this time, reproached by the courage of Reaisin and Smith, were all at work; and the helm shifting opportunely, she fell off again as before. The light of the day, which now broke forth, discovered our condition to be altogether as perilous as possible; for we now saw ourselves surrounded with breaches. Scarce any water, like a channel, appeared for a way to shun them. In this sad condition, the ship struck ground, and raised such a war of water and sand together which fell on the main chains, that now all hopes of safety were laid aside; but the ship being still afloat, and the seamen, all of them now under command, nothing was omitted for our preservation that was in their power.

Tom Reaisin, seeing the ship go ahead, in the likeliest water for a channel, and ordering the helm accordingly, heaved the lead; and after a little further advance in that new channel, wholly against his hopes, he had a good deal of water more than the ship drew, which soon mended upon us; the next cast of the lead, affording eighteen or twenty feet. We stood to this channel, and the light of morning enabling the quarter-masters to con the ship, we were, by this miraculous mercy of God, soon clear of the breaches at Cape Hatteras, and got out to sea. No sooner was the ship freed of this danger, and got a little into the offing, but the seamen, like so many spirits, surveyed each other, as if they doubted the reality of the thing, and shook hands like strangers, or men risen from the other world; and did scarce believe they were what they seemed to be—men of flesh and blood. As they recovered force, they made what sail they could, to stand to leeward.

The gale came fresh at north-west, and this fresh gale did soon grow up to a violent storm, which increased to so great a rigor, separating us from the land at the rate of eight leagues a watch, merely with our fore-courses; insomuch that the master thought it necessary to stop that career; and, in order thereunto, he did advise with his officers, to bring the ship about, to furl up sails, and to try with the mizzen. The mountainous, towering, north-west seas that this storm made, were so unruly, that the seamen knew not how to work the ship about. We were already at a great distance from land, and something must be done to hinder our running off at that excessive rate. The first thing they did, was to lower the mainyard, to give some ease to that mast, by laying it on the ship's waste. Our great difficulty was how to deal so with the foresails, that the ship might work about with safety, or, at least, with as little hazard as possible. All hands were too little to haul the sheet close, in order to bring the ship about. Many great seas were shipped, as she came to work through the trough of the sea; among the rest, one chanced to break upon the poop, where we were quartered, and that with so sad a weight, that we guessed a ton of water, at least, did enter the tarpaulin, and set us all on float who were in the round-house. The noise it made by discharging itself in that manner, was like the report of a great gun, and put us all in a horrible fright, which we could not soon shake off. This shock being past, the ship about, and our fore-sail hauled, we now lay trying with our mizzen.

I cannot forget the prodigious number of porpoises that did that evening appear about the ship, to the astonishment of the oldest seaman in her. They seemed to cover the surface of the sea, as far as our eyes could discern; insomuch that a musket-bullet, shot at random, could hardly fail to do execution on some of them. This the seamen would look upon as of bad portent, predicting ill weather; but in our case, who were in present possession of a storm, they appeared too late to gain the credit of foretelling what should come upon us in that kind. The seas thus enraged, and all in foam, the gale still increasing upon us; the officers on the watch made frequent visits to the round-house, to prepare the captain for some evil encounter, which this mighty tempest must bring forth; and their fears proved reasonable; for, about the hour of ten or eleven, our new disasters did begin with a crash from aloft. All hands were summoned up with loud cries, that the fore-topmast was come by the board; not alone, but with the fore-masthead broken short off, just under the cap. This was a sore business, and put all to their wits' end, to recover to any competent condition. Mate Putts was then on the watch, and did not want his apprehensions of what did soon ensue, which, in all likelihood, was to end in utter perdition; for, about the hours of twelve or one at night, we heard and felt a mighty sea break on our foreship, which made such an inundation on the deck, where the mate was walking, that he retired back with all diligence, up to his knees in water, with short ejaculations of prayer in his mouth, supposing the ship was foundering, and at the last gasp. This looked like a stroke of death in every seaman's opinion. The ship stood stock still, with her head under water, seeming to bore her way into the sea. My two comrades and myself, lay on our platform, sharing liberally in the consternation. We took a short leave of each other, men, women and children; all assaulted with the fresh terror of death, made a most dolorous outcry throughout the ship; while Mate Putts, perceiving the deck almost freed of water, called out aloud for hands to pump. This we thought a lightning before death; but gave me occasion, as having the best sea-legs, to look out, and learn the subject of this astonishing alarm; which proved to arise from no less cause than the loss of our forecastle, with six guns, and our anchors, (all but one that was fastened to our cable,) together with our two cooks, whereof one was recovered by a strange providence.

This great gap, made by want of our forecastle, did open a passage into the hold, for other seas that should break there, before a remedy was found out to carry them off; and this made our danger almost insuperable. But it fell out, propitiously, that there were divers land-carpenter passengers, who were very helpful in this distress; and, in a little time, a slight platform of deal was tacked to the timbers, to carry off an ordinary sea; in the present strait we were in, every moment of this growing tempest, cutting out new work to employ all hands to labor The bowsprit, too heavy in itself, having lost all stays and rigging that should keep it steady, swayed to and fro, with such bangs on the bows, that at no less rate than the cutting it close off, could the ship subsist. All things were in miserable disorder, and it was evident our danger increased upon us. The stays of all the masts were gone, the shrouds, that remained, were loose and useless, and it was easy to foretell, our main-topmast would soon come by the board. Tom Reaisin, who was always ready to expose himself, with an ax in his hand, ran up with speed to prevent that evil; hoping thereby to ease the mainmast, and preserve it: but the danger of his person in the enterprise was so manifest, that he was called down again; and no sooner was his foot upon the deck, but what was feared came to pass with a witness. Both main and topmast all came down together, and, in one shock, fell all to the windward clear into the sea, without hurt to any man's person.

Our mainmast thus fallen to the broadside, was like to incommode us more in the sea than in her proper station; for the shrouds and rigging, not losing the hold they had of the ship, every surge did so check the mast, whose butt-end lay charged to fall perpendicular on the ship's side, that it became a ram to batter and force the plank; and was doing the last execution upon us, if not prevented in time by edge-tools, which freed the ship from that expected assault and battery. Abandoned, in this manner, to the fury of the raging sea; tossed up and down without any one regarding the loss of another; every man expecting the same fate, though in a different manner. The ceilings of this hulk, for it was no better, were, for the same cause, so uneasy, that, in many tumbles, the deck would touch the sea, and there stand still, as if she would never make another. Our mizzenmast only remained, by which we hoped to bring the ship about in proper season, which now lay stemming to the east. In this posture we passed the 10th and 11th days of November. The 12th, in the morning, we saw an English merchant, who showed his ensign, but would not speak with us, though the storm was abated, and the season more fit for communication. We imagined the reason was, because he would not be compelled to be civil to us. He thought our condition desperate, and we had more guns than he could resist, which might enable us to take what he would not sell or give. He shot a gun to leeward, stood his course, and turned his hoof upon us. Before we attempted to bring the ship about, it was necessary to refresh the seamen, who were almost worn out with toil and want of rest, having had no leisure of eating set meals for many days. The passengers, overcharged with excessive fears, had no appetite to eat; and, which was worst of all, both seamen and passengers were in a deplorable state as to the remaining victuals, all like to fall under extreme want; for the storm, by taking away the forecastle, having thrown much water into the hold, our stock of bread was greatly damaged; and there remained no way to dress our meat, now that the cook was gone: the incessant tumbling of the ship, as has been observed, made all such cookery wholly impracticable. The only expedient to make fire between decks, was by sawing a cask in the middle, and filling it with ballast; which made a hearth to parch peas, and boil salt beef. Nor could this be done, but with great attendance, which was many times frustrated by being thrown topsy-turvy, in spite of all circumspection, to the great defeat of empty stomachs. The seas were much appeased the 17th day, and divers ships saw, and were seen by us, but would not speak with us; only one, who kept the pump always going, for having tasted too liberally of the storm, he was so kind as to accost us. He lay by till our wherry, the only surviving boat that was left us, made him a visit. The master showed our men his leaks, and proposed, that ours would spare him hands to pump, in lieu of anything he could spare for our relief. He promised, however, to keep us company, and give us a tow to help to weather the Cape, if occasion offered. But this was only a copy of his countenance; for in the night we lost each other, and we never heard more of him, though he was bound to our port.

November 13th. The weather now invited us to get the ship about with our mizzen; and having done so, the next consideration was how to make sail. The foremast, all this while, as much as was of it, stood its ground; and as it was without dispute, that a yard must, in the first place, be fixed to it, so was it a matter of no small difficulty how to advance to the top of that greasy, slippery stump; since he that would attempt it could take no hold himself, nor receive any help for his rise by other hands. This was a case that put all the ship's crew to a non-plus. But Tom Reaisin, a constant friend at need, that would not be baffled by any difficulty, showed, by his countenance, he had a mind to try his skill to bring us out of this unhappy crisis. To encourage him the more, all passengers promised and subscribed to reward his service, in Virginia, by tobacco, when God should enable us so to do. The manner of Tom Reaisin's ascent, was thus: among the scattered parcels of the ship's stores, he had the luck to find about half a dozen iron spikes fit for his purpose. His first onset was to drive one of them into the mast, almost to the head, as high as he could reach, which being done, he took a rope of about ten feet long, and having the same in a block or pulley, so as to divide it in the middle; he made both ends meet in a knot upon the spike, on both sides of the mast, so that the block, falling on the contrary side, became a stirrup to mount upon for driving another spike in the same manner: and thus, from step to step, observing the best advantage of striking with his hammer in the smoothest sea, he got aloft, and drove cleats for shrouds to rest upon, and was soon in a posture of receiving help from his comrades, who got a yard and sails, with other accommodation, such as could be had; and thus were we enabled, in a few hours time, to make some sail for our port. The mainyard, that in the storm had been lowered to the waist, to lie out of harm's way, was now preferred to the place of a mainmast, and was accordingly fitted and accoutered, and grafted into the stump of what was left in the storm, some eight or ten feet from the deck. It was a hard matter to find out rigging answerable to that new-fashioned mast and yard. Topgallant sails and yards were most agreeable for his equipage, and was the best part of our remaining stores. The seas grew every moment smoother, and the weather more comfortable, so that, for awhile, we began to shake off the visage of utter despair, as hoping ere long to see ourselves in some capacity to fetch the Cape. We discovered another ship bound to Virginia, who as frankly promised to stand by us, the wind at N.N.W. We did what could be done by a ship so mangled, to get the weather gauge of Cape Henry, conceiving ourselves to the southward of Cape Hatteras; but, by taking an observation on a sunshiny day, we found ourselves carried by a current, we knew not of, to the windward, much beyond our dead reckonings, and allowances for sailing; insomuch, that when we thought we had been to the southward of the Cape, we found ourselves considerably shot to the north of Achomat; and that in the opinion of Mate Putts, who was as our north star.

We passed this night with greater alacrity than we had done any other since we had left Fyal; for Mate Putts, our trusty pilot, did confidently affirm, that if the gale stood, there would be no question of our dining the next day within the Capes. This was reasonable news: our water being long since spent; our meat spoiled or useless: no kind of victuals remaining to sustain life, but a biscuit cake a day for a man; at which allowance there was not a quantity to hold out many days. In the dark time of the night, in tacking about, we lost our new comrade, and, with much impatience, we expected the approaching day; the wind N. W. The morning appeared foggy, as the wind veered to the east, and that covered and concealed the land from our clearer sight: howbeit, we concluded, by Mate Putt's computation, we were well to the northward of the Capes. Many times he would mount the mizzentop for discovery, as the weather seemed to clear up; and would espy, and point at certain thum-works of trees, that used to be his several landmarks, in most of the twenty-two voyages he had made to that plantation. Under this confidence he made more sail, the daylight confirming him in what he thought right. All the forenoon we lost the sight of land, and marks by trees, by reason of the dark fogs and mists that were not yet dispelled; but as soon as the sun, with a north-west gale, had cleared all the coast, which was about the hours of two or three o'clock, Mate Putts perceived his error from the deck, and was convinced that the thum-works of trees he had seen, and relied on for sure landmarks, had counter points to the South Cape, which had misguided him; and that it was the opening of the bay, which made the land at distance, out of sight.

This fatal disappointment, which was now past human help, might have met an easy remedy, had our sails and rigging been in any tolerable condition to keep the windward gauge, for we had both the Capes in our sight. But, under our circumstances, it was vain to endeavor such a thing; all our equipage, from stem to stern, being no better than that of a western barge; and we could not lie within eleven or twelve points of the wind. Defeated thus of lively hopes we had the night before entertained, to sleep in warm beds with our friends in Virginia, it was a heavy spectacle to see ourselves running at a round rate from it, notwithstanding all that could be done to the contrary. Nothing was now to be heard but sighs and groans through all that wretched family, which must be soon reduced to so short allowance as would just keep life and soul together. Half a buiscuit cake a day, of which five whole ones make a pound, was all we had to trust to. Of liquors there remained none to quench thirst; Malaga served rather to inflame and increase thirst, than to extinguish it. The gale blew fresh toward night, and made a western sea, that carried us off at a great rate. Mate Putts, extremely abashed to see his confidence so miserably deluded, grew sad and contemplative, even to the moving compassion in those whom his unhappy mistake had reduced to misery. We cherished him the best we could, and would not have him so profoundly sad, for what was rather his misfortune than his fault The wind continued many days and nights to send us out into the ocean; insomuch, that until we thought ourselves at least a hundred leagues from the Capes, the north-west gale gave us no truce to consider what was best to do. All little helps were used by topgallant sails, and masts placed where they could be fixed, to keep the windward tack; but, for want of borolins and other tackle to keep them stiff to draw, every great head sea would check them in the wind, and rend, and tear them in pieces; so that it was an ordinary exercise with us to lie tumbling in the sea, a watch or two together, driving to leeward, while the broken sails were in hand to be repaired.

November 19th. To give us a little breathing, about the nineteenth day, the wind shifted to the east, but so little to our avail, the gale so gentle, and the seas made against us like a strong current, that, with the sail we were able to make, we could hardly reckon the ship shortened the way, but that she rather lost ground. In less than two watches, the gale faced about; and if we saved our own by the change, it was all we could pretend unto. Our mortal enemy, the north-west gale, began afresh to send us out to sea, and to raise our terrors to a higher pitch. One of our pumps grew so unfixed, that it could not be repaired; the other was kept in perpetual motion; no man was excused to take his turn that had strength to perform it. Among the manifest perils that threatened every hour to be our last, we were in mortal apprehension that the guns, which were aloft, would show us a slippery trick, and some of them break loose, the tackle that held them being grown very rotten; and it was another providence they held so long, considering how immoderately the ship rolled, especially when the sails were mending that should keep her steady, which was very near a third part of our time, while we plied to the windward with a contrary gale. To prevent this danger, which must befall when any one gun should get loose, Mate Putts found an expedient; by a more than ordinary smooth water, and by placing timber on the hatchway, to supply the place of shrouds, he got them safe in hold which tended much to our good, not only in removing the present danger, but by making the ship, as seamen say, more wholesome, by having so great a weight removed from her upper works into her center, where ballast was much wanted. But the intolerable want of all provision, both of meat and drink, jostled the sense of this happiness soon out of our minds; and to aggravate our misery yet the more, it was our interest to pray that the contrary gale might stand; for, while the westerly wind held, we had rain-water to drink, whereas at east the wind blew dry. In this miserable posture of ship and provision, we reckoned ourselves driven to the east, in less than a week's time, at least two hundred leagues, which we despaired ever to recover without a miracle of Divine mercy. The storm continued so fresh against us, that it confounded the most knowing of our ship's company in advising what course to take. Some reckoned the ship had made her way most southerly, and, therefore, counseled we should put ourselves in quest of the Bermuda Islands, as the nearest land we could hope to make; but that motion had great opposition in regard of the winter season, which would daily produce insuperable difficulties, and give greater puzzle in the discovery of it than our circumstances would admit. Backward we could not go, nor forward we could not go, in the course we steered; it followed then, of course, that we must take the middle way; and it was resolved, that, without further persisting in endeavoring to gain our port by a close hale, we should raise our tackle, and sail tardy for the first American land we could fetch, though we ran to the leeward as far as the coast of New England.

While this determination was agreed and put in practice, the famine grew sharp upon us. Women and children made dismal cries, and grievous complaints. The infinite number of rats, that all the voyage had been our plague, we now were glad to make our prey to feed on; and, as they were ensnared and taken, a well-grown rat was sold for sixteen shillings, as a market-rate. Nay, before the voyage ended, (as I was credibly informed,) a woman, great with child, offered twenty shillings for a rat, which the proprietor refusing, the woman died. Many sorrowful days and nights we spun out in this manner, till the blessed feast of Christmas came upon us, which we began with a very melancholy solemnity; and yet, to make some distinction of times, the scrapings of the meal-tubs were all amassed together to compose a pudding. Malaga sack, sea-water, with fruit and spice, all well fried in oil, were the ingredients of this regale, which raised some envy in the spectators; but, allowing some privilege to the captain's mess, we met no obstruction, but peaceably enjoyed our Christmas pudding.

My greatest impatience was of thirst, and my dreams were all of cellars, and taps running down my throat, which made my waking much the worse by that tantalizing fancy. Some relief I found very real, by the captain's favor in allowing me a share of some butts of small claret, he had concealed in a private cellar for a dead lift. It wanted a mixture of water for qualifying it to quench thirst; however, it was a present remedy, and a great refreshment to me. The westerly wind continued to shorten our way to the shore, though very distant from our port; but this did not at all incline us to change our resolution of sailing large for the first land; it rather animated and supported us in our present fatigue: the hopes of touching land was food and raiment to us. In this wearisome expectation, we passed our time for eight or nine days and nights, and then we saw the water change color, and had soundings. We approached the shore the night of January 3d, with little sail; and as the morning of the fourth day gave us light, we saw the land, but in what latitude we could not tell; for that the officers, whose duty it was to keep the reckoning of the ship, had for many days past totally omitted that part; nor had we seen the sun a great while, to take observations, which, though a lame excuse, was all they had to say for that omission. But, in truth, it was evident that the desperate state of the ship, and hourly jeopardy of life, made them careless of keeping either log or journal; the thoughts of another account, they feared to be at hand, made them neglect that of the ship as inconsiderable.

About the hours of three or four in the afternoon of the twelfth eve, we were shot in fair to the shore. The evening was clear and calm the water smooth; the land we saw nearest was some six or seven English miles distant from us; our soundings twenty-five fathoms in good ground for anchor hold. These invitations were all attractive to encourage the generality, especially the passengers, to execute what had been resolved on for the shore; but one old officer, who was husband for the ship's stores, while there were any, would not consent, on any terms, to trust the only anchor of any service that was left us for preservation out of his sight at sea. His arguments to back his opinion were plausible; as, first, the hazard of losing the only anchor by any sudden storm, bringing with it a necessity to cut or slip, on which every life depended; secondly, the shortness of the cable, very unfit for anchoring in the ocean; and thirdly, the weakness of the ship's crew, many dead and fallen overboard; and the passengers, weakened by hunger, dying every day on the decks, or at the pump, which, with great difficulty, was kept going, but must not rest.

Against the old man's reasoning, was urged the very small remains of biscuit, to our short allowance, which would hardly hold a week; the assurance of our loss by famine, if we should be forced to sea again, by a north-west storm; and the greatest possibility of finding a harbor to save our ship, with our lives and goods, in some creek on the coast. These last reasons prevailed upon the majority against all negatives; and when the anchor was let loose, Mate Putts was ordered to make the first discovery of what we might expect from the nearer land. He took with him twelve sickly passengers, who fancied the shore would cure them, and carried Major Morrison on shore with him. In four or five hours time, we could discover the boat returning with Mate Putts alone for a setter, which we looked upon as a signal of happy success. When he came on board, his mouth was full of good tidings; as, namely, that he discovered a creek that would harbor our ship, and that there was a depth of water on the bar, sufficient for her draught when she was light; that there was excellent water; (a taste whereof Major Morrison had sent me in a bottle;) that the shore swarmed with fowl; and that Major Morrison staid behind in expectation of the whole ship's company to follow.

I opened my ears wide to the motion, and promoted the design of our landing there with all the rhetoric and interest I had. The captain was no less forward for it, hoping thereby to save the lives of the passengers that remained; and, that he might not wholly rely on Mate Putts' judgment, in a matter wherein he was most concerned, he embarked with me in the wherry, with a kinsman of his, and some others; and the seamen were glad of my help to put the boat to shore, my hands being very well seasoned at the pump by taking my turn for many weeks, at the rate of three hours in twenty-four. My passionate desires to be on shore, at the fountain head, to drink without stint, did not a little quicken me; insomuch, that the six or seven miles I rowed on this occasion, were no more than the breadth of the Thames at London, at another time, would have been toilsome to me. In our passage to the shore, the darkness of the evening made us glad to see the fires of our friends at land, which were not only our beacons to direct us to their company, but were also a comfortable relief to our chilled bodies when we came near them, the weather being very cold, as it ever is; the wind blowing north-west on that coast. As soon as I had set my foot on land, and had rendered thanks to the Almighty for opening this door of deliverance to us, after so many rescues, even from the jaws of death at sea, Major Morrison was pleased to oblige me beyond all requital, in conducting me to the running stream of water, where, without any limitation of short allowance, I might drink my fill. I was glad of so great liberty, and made use of it accordingly, by prostrating myself on my belly, and setting my mouth against the stream, that it might run into my thirsty stomach without stop. The rest of the company were at liberty to use their own methods to quench their thirst; but this I thought the greatest pleasure I ever saw on earth.

After this sweet refreshment, the captain, myself, and his kinsman, crossed the creek in our wherry, invited thither by the cackling of wild fowl. The captain had a gun charged; and the moon shining bright in his favor, he killed one duck of the flock that flew over us, which was roasted on the stick out of hand by the seamen, while we walked on the shore of the creek for further discovery. In passing a small stream, we trod on an oyster-bank, that happily furnished us with a good addition to our duck. When the cooks had done their parts, we were not long about ours, but fell on without using the ceremony of calling the rest of our company, which would have been no entertainment to so many—the proverb telling us, "The fewer the better cheer." The bones, head, legs and inwards were agreed to be the cooks' fees; so we gave God thanks, and returned to our friends without making boast of our good fortunes.

Fortified with this repast, we informed ourselves of the depth of water at the bar of the creek, in which the captain seemed satisfied, and made shows, in all his deportment, of his resolution to discharge his ship there, in order to our safety. Toward break of day, he asked me in my ear, if I would go back with him on board the ship. I told him no; because it would be labor lost, in case he would persist in his resolution to do what he pretended; which he ratified again by protestations, and so went off with his kinsman, who had a large, coarse, cloth gown, I borrowed of him to shelter me from the sharpest cold I ever felt. No sooner had the captain cleared himself of the shore, but the day-break made me see my error in not closing with his motion in my ear. The first object we saw at sea, was the ship under sail, standing for the Capes, with what canvas could be made to serve the turn. It was a very heavy prospect to us, who remained, we knew not where, on shore, to see ourselves thus abandoned by the ship; and more, to be forsaken by the boat, so contrary to our mutual agreement. Many hours of hard labor and toil were spent before the boat could fetch the ship; and the seamen, whose act it was to set sail without the captain's order, (as we were told after,) cared not for the boat, while the wind was large to carry them to the Capes. But Mate Putts, who was more sober, and better natured, discovering the boat from the mizzentop, lay by till she came with the captain on board.

In this amazement and confusion of mind, that no words can express, did our miserable, distressed party condole with each other, on our being so cruelly abandoned, and left to the last despairs of human life, or, indeed, of ever seeing more the face of man. We entered into a sad consultation what course to take; and having, in the first place, by united prayers, implored the protection of Almighty God, and recommending our miserable state to the same Providence which, in so many instances of mercy, had been propitious to us at sea: the whole party desired me to be, as it were, the father of the distressed family, to advise and conduct them in all things I thought might most tend to our preservation. At the same time I quitted the ship, my servant, Thomas Harman, a Dutchman, did at parting, advertise me, (for I left him on board to look to my goods,) that in the bundle I ordered to be carried with me on shore, I should find about thirty biscuit cakes, which he, by unparalleled frugality, had saved out of his own belly, in the great dearth and scarcity we lived in. The thoughts of these biscuits entering upon me at the time I was pressed to accept this charge, I thought myself obliged, in christian equity, to let every one partake of what I had; and so, dividing the bread into nineteen parts, which was our number, perhaps I added the fraction to my own share.

It was, to the best of my remembrance, upon the 5th day of January, 1650, that we entered into this method of life, or rather into an orderly way into our graves; since nothing but the image of death was represented to us. But that we might use our utmost endeavors to extract all the good we could out of those evil symptoms that every way seemed to confound us, I made a muster of the most able bodies for arms and labor; and, in the first place, I put a fowling-piece into every man's hand that could tell how to use it. Among the rest, a young gentleman, Mr. Francis Cary by name, was very helpful to me in the fatigue and active part of this undertaking.

All our woodmen and fowlers had powder and shot given them, and some geese were killed for supper. Evening came on apace, and our resolution being to stay one night more in these quarters, I sent my cousin, Cary, to head the creeks, and make what discovery he could, as he passed along the shore, whether of Indians, or any other living creatures, that were likely to relieve our wants or end our days.

My cousin Cary was not absent much above an hour, when we saw him return in a contrary point to that he sallied out upon. His face was clouded with ill news he had to tell us, namely, that we were now residing on an island without any inhabitants, and that he had seen its whole extent, surrounded, as he believed, with water deeper than his head; that he had not seen any native, or anything in human shape, in all his round; nor any other creature beside the fowls of the air, which he would, but could not, bring unto us. This dismal success, of so unsuccessful a nature, startled us more than any single misfortune that had befallen us and was like to plunge us into utter despair. We beheld each other as miserable wretches sentenced to a lingering death, no man knowing what to propose for prolonging life any longer than he was able to fast. My cousin, Cary, was gone from us without notice, and we had reason, from what followed, to believe he was under the conduct of an angel; for we soon saw him return with a cheerful look, his hands carrying something we could not distinguish by any name at a distance; but, by nearer approach, we were able to descry they were a parcel of oysters, which in crossing the island, as he stepped over a small current of water, he trod upon to his hurt; but laying hands on what he felt with his feet, and pulling it with all his force, he found himself possessed of this booty of oysters, which grew in clusters, and were contiguous to a large bank of the same species, that was our staple subsistence while we remained there. While this very cold season continued, great flights of fowl frequented the island—geese, ducks and curlieus; and some of every sort we killed and roasted on sticks, eating all but the feathers. It was the only perquisite belonging to my place of preference to the rest, that the right of carving was annexed to it; wherein, if I was partial to my own interest, it was in cutting the wing as large and full of meat as possible, whereas the rest was measured out, as it were, with scale and compass. But, as the wind veered to the southward, we had greater warmth and fewer fowl; for they would then be gone to colder climates. In their absence we were confined to the oyster-bank, and a sort of weed, some four inches long, as thick as house leek, and the only green (except pines) that the island afforded. It was very insipid on the palate, but being boiled with a little pepper, of which one had brought a pound on shore, and helped with five or six oysters, it became a regale for every one in turn.

In quartering our family we observed the decency of distinguishing sexes. We made a small hut for the poor weak women to be by themselves. Our cabin for men was of the same fashion, but much more spacious, as our numbers were. One morning, in walking on the shore by the seaside, with a long gun in my hand, loaded with small shot, I fired at a great flight of small birds, called oxeyes, and made great slaughter among them, which gave refreshment to all our company. But this harvest had a short end; and as the weather, by its warmth, chased the fowl to the north, our hunger grew keener upon us; and, in fine, all the strength that remained unto us was employed in a heartless struggle to spin out life a little longer; for we still deemed ourselves doomed to die by famine, from whose sharpest and most immediate darts, though we seemed to be rescued for a small time, by meeting these contingent helps on shore, yet still we apprehended (and that on too great probability) they only served to reprieve us for a little longer day of execution, with all the dreadful circumstances of a lingering death: for the south-west winds, that had carried away the fowl, brought store of rain, which, meeting with a spring-tide, our chief magazine, the oyster-bank, was overflown; and, as they became more accessible, our bodies also decayed so sensibly, that we could hardly pull them out of the muddy beds they grew on; and from this time forward we rarely saw the fowl; they now grew shy, and kept aloof when they saw us contriving against their lives. Add to this, our guns, most of them unfixed and out of order, and our powder much decayed; insomuch, that nothing did now remain to prolong life, but what is counted rather sauce to whet, than substance to satisfy the appetite. I mean the oysters, which were not easily gotten by our crazy bodies, after the quantity was spent that lay most commodious to be reached, and which had fed us for the first six days we had been on the island.

Of the three weak women before mentioned, one had the envied happiness to die about this time; and it was my advice to the survivors, who were following her apace, to endeavor their own preservation by converting her dead carcass into food; as they did to good effect. The same counsel was embraced by those of our sex. The living fed upon the dead; four of our company having the happiness to end their miserable lives on Sunday night, the —— day of January. Their chief distemper, it is true, was hunger; but it pleased God to hasten the exit by an immoderate access of cold, caused by a most terrible storm of hail and snow, at north-west, on the Sunday aforesaid, which not only dispatched those four to their long homes, but sorely threatened all that remained alive, to perish by the same fate. Great was the toil that lay on my hands, as the strongest to labor, to get fuel together sufficient for our preservation. In the first place, I divested myself of my great gown, which I spread at large, and extended against the wind, in lieu of a screen, having first shifted our quarters to the most calm, commodious place that could be found, to keep us as much as possible from the inclemency of that prodigious storm. Under the shelter of this traverse, I took as many of my comrades as could be comprehended in so small a space; whereas, those who could not partake of that accommodation, and were unable to make provision for themselves, were forced to suffer for it; and it was remarkable, that notwithstanding all the provision that could possibly be made against the sharpness of this cold, either by a well burning fire, consisting of two or three loads of wood, or shelter of this great gown to the windward, we could not be warm. That side of our wearing clothes was singed and burnt, which lay toward the flames, while the other side, that was from the fire, became frozen and congealed. Those who lay to the leeward of the flame could not stay long to enjoy the warmth so necessary to life, but were forced to quit and be gone, to avoid suffocation by the smoke and flame.

When the day appeared, and the sun got out to dissipate the clouds, with downcast looks and dejected, the survivors of us entered into a final deliberation of what remained to be done on our parts, beside our prayers to Almighty God, to spin out a little longer time of life, and wait a further Providence from heaven for our better relief. There were still some hands that retained vigor, though not in proportion to those difficulties we were to encounter, which humanly did seem insuperable. Major Morrison, on whose counsel I had reason to rely most, was extremely decayed in his strength, his legs not being able to support him. It was a wonderful mercy that mine remained in competent strength, for our common good, which I resolved, by God's help, to employ for that end to the last gasp. In this last resolution we had to make, I could not think on anything worthy my proposal, but by an attempt to cross the creek, and swim to the main, which was not above a hundred yards over; and, being there, to coast along the woods to the south-west, which was the bearing of Virginia, until I should meet Indians, who would either relieve or destroy us. To fortify me for this expedition, it was necessary that some provision should be made for a daily support to me in this my peregrination. Our choice was small; our only friend, the oyster-bank, was all we had to rely on, which, being well stewed in their own liquor, and put up in bottles, I made no doubt, by God's blessing, but that two of them, well filled, would suffice to prolong my life, in moderate strength, until I had obtained my end. To accomplish this design, my cousin Cary labored hard for oysters, hoping to make one in the adventure.

January 14. About the ninth day of our being in the island, I fell to my oyster cookery, and made a progress that very day. When in the heat of my labor, my cousin Cary brought me word, that he had just in that instant seen Indians walking on the main. I suspended my cookery out of hand, and hastened, with all possible speed, to be an eye-witness of that happy intelligence; but with all the haste I could make, I could see no such things, but judged it a chimera that proceeded from some operation in my cousin's fancy, who was more than ordinary of a sanguine nature, which made him see as it were, by enchantment, things that were not, having many times been deluded, as I judged, by the same deception.

Defeated in this manner of my hopes to see Indians, without the pains of seeking them, I returned to my work, and continued at it till one bottle was full, and myself tired; therefore, that I might be a little recreated, I took a gun in my hand, and, hearing the noise of geese on the shore, I approached them privately, and had the good fortune to be the death of one. This goose, now in my possession, without witnesses, I resolved to eat alone, deducting the head, bones, guts, etc., which were the cooks fees, hoping thereby to be much the better enabled to swim the creek, and perform the work I had upon my hands. I hung my goose upon the twist of a tree, in a shrubby part of wood, while I went to call our cook, with his broach and a coal of fire, to begin the roast. But when we came to the place of execution, my goose was gone all but the head, the body stolen by wolves, which, the Indians told us after, abound greatly in that island.

The loss of this goose, which my empty stomach looked for with no small hopes of satisfaction, did vex me heartily. I wished I could have taken the thief of my goose, to have served him the same kind, and to have taken my revenge in the law of retaliation. But that which troubled me more, was an apprehenson that came into my mind, that this had been the effect of divine justice on me, for designing to deal unequally with the rest of my fellow-sufferers, which I thought, at first blush, looked like a breach of trust; but then again, when I considered the equity of the thing, that I did it merely to enable myself to attain their preservation, and which otherwise I could not have done, I found I could absolve myself from any guilt of that kind. Whatever I suffered from this disappointment, the cook lost not all his fees; the head and neck remained for him on the tree. Being thus overreached by the wolf, it was time to return to my cookery, in order to my sally out of the island for I had little confidenee in the notice frequently brought me, of more and more Indians seen on the other side, since my own eyes could never bear witness of their being there. The next morning, being the ninth or tenth of our being there, I fell to work afresh, hoping to be ready to begin my journey that day; and, being very busy, intelligence was brought that a canoe was seen to lie on the broken ground to the south of our island, which was not discovered till now since our being there; but this I thought might be a mistake, cast in the same mold of many others, that had deceived those discoverers, who fancied all things real according to their own wishes. But when it was told me that Indians had been at the poor women's cabin in the night, and had given them shellfish to eat, that was a demonstration of reality beyond all suspicion. I went immediately to be informed from themselves, and they both avowed it for truth, showing the shells, the like whereof I never had seen; and this I took for proof of what they had said. The farther account that these women gave of the Indians, was, that they pointed to the south-east with their hands, which they knew not how to interpret; but imagined, by their several gestures, they would be with them again to-morrow. Their pointing to the south-east was like to be the time they would come, meaning nine o'clock to be their hour, where the sun will be at that time.

This news gave us all new life, almost working miracles among us, by making those who desponded, and totally yielded themselves up to the weight of despair, and lay down with an intent never to rise again, to take up their beds and walk. This friendly charitable visit of the Indians also put a stop to my preparations to seek them, who had so humanely prevented me, by their ways, seeking to preserve and save our lives. Instead of those preparations for my march, which had cost me so much pains, I passed my time now in contriving the fittest posture our present condition would allow us to put on, when these angels of light should appear again with the glad tidings of our relief; and the result was, that every able man should have his gun lying by his side, loaded with shot, and as fit for use as possible, but not to be handled unless the Indians came to us like enemies, which was very unlikely, the premises considered, and then to sell our lives at as dear a rate as we could. But if they came in an amicable posture, then would we meet them unarmed, cheerfully; which the Indians like, and hate to see a melancholy face. Scouts were sent out to the right and left hands, without discovery of anybody all the forenoon; and then, considering our case admitted no delay, I began to resume my former resolution of swimming to them that would not come to us. But how wholesome soever this counsel might seem in itself, it was most difficult to be put in practice, in regard of the cold time.

The northerly wind, that in these climates blows very cold in the heat of summer, much more distempers the air in the winter season, (as our poor comrades felt that Sunday night to their cost,) and sent so cold a gale upon the surface of water in the creek I was to pass, that, in the general opinion of all concerned, it was not a thing to be attempted, and that if I did, I must surely perish in the act. I was easily persuaded to forbear an action so dangerous; and the rather, because I verily believed the Indians would bring us off, if our patience would hold out.

About the hour of two or three o'clock, it pleased God to change the face of our condition for the best; for while I was busy at the fire in preparations to wait on them, I discovered the Indians, who had placed themselves behind a very great tree; their faces wore most cheerful smiles; they were without any kind of arms, or appearances of evil design; the whole number of them, perhaps twenty or thirty in all, consisting of men women, and children; all that could speak accosting us with joyful countenance, shaking hands with everyone they met. The words, "ny tap," often repeated by them, made us believe they bore a friendly signification, as they were soon interpreted to signify, my friend. After many salutations, and "ny taps," interchanged, the night approaching, we fell to parley with each other; but performed it in signs more confounded and unintelligible than any other conversation I ever met withal; as hard to be interpreted as if they had expressed their thoughts in the Hebrew or Chaldean tongues. They did me the honor to make all applications to me, as being of largest dimensions, and equipped in a camlet coat, glittering with galoon lace of gold and silver. The ears of Indian corn they gave us for present sustenance, needed no other interpreter to let them know how much more acceptable it was to us than the sight of dead and living corpses, which raised great compassion in them, especially in the women, who are observed to be of a soft, tender nature. One of them made me a present of the leg of a swan, which I ate as privately as it was given me; and thought it so much the more excellent by how much it was larger than the greatest limb of any fowl I ever saw.

The Indians stayed with us about two hours, and parted not without a new appointment to see us again the next day, and the hour we were to expect them, by their pointing to the sun, was to be at two o'clock in the afternoon. I made the chief of them presents of ribbon, and other slight trade which they loved, designing, by mutual endearment, to let them see it would gratify their interest, as well as their charity, to treat us well. Ha-na haw, was their parting word, which is, farewell; pointing again to the place where the sun would be at our next meeting. We took leave in their own words, Ha-na haw. The going away of the Indians and leaving us behind, was a separation hard to be borne by our hungry company, who, nevertheless, had received a competent quantity of corn and bread to keep us till they returned to do better things for our relief. We did not fail to give glory to God for our approaching deliverance; and the joy we conceived in our minds, in the sense of so great a mercy, kept us awake all the night, and was a cordial to the sick and weak, to recover their health and strength. The delay of the Indians coming next day, beyond their set time, we thought an age of tedious years. At two o'clock we had no news of them; but, by attending their own time, with a little patience, we might see a considerable number of them, men, women, and children, all about our huts, with recruits of bread and corn to stop every mouth. Many of them desired beads, and little truck they use to deal in, as exchange for what they gave us, and we as freely gave them what we had brought on shore. But to such of us as gave them nothing, the Indians failed not, however, to give them bread for nothing.

One old man of their company, who seemed, by the preference they gave him, to be the most considerable of their party, applied himself to me, by gestures and signs, to learn something, if possible, of our country, and occasions of the sad posture he saw us in, to the end that he might inform his master, the king of Kickotank, on whose territories we stood, and dispose him to succor us as we had need. I made return to him, in many vain words, and as many significant signs as himself had made to me, and neither of us one jot the wiser. The several nonplusses we both were at in striving to be better understood, afforded so little of eaification to either party, that our time was almost spent in vain. It came at last into my head, that I had long since read Mr. Smith's Travels through those parts of America, and that the word Werowance, a word frequently pronounced by the old man, was, in English, the king. That word, spoken by me, with strong emphasis, together with the motions of my body, speaking my desires of going to him, was very pleasing to the old man; who, thereupon, embraced me with more than common kindness, and by all demonstrations of satisfaction, showed that he understood my meaning. This one word was all the Indian I could speak, which, like a little armor well placed, contributed to the saving of our lives. In order to what was next to be done, he took me by the hand, and led me to the seaside, where I embarked with himself and one more Indian, in a canoe, that had brought him there; which the third man rowed over to that broken ground, where, not long before, we made discovery of a canoe newly laid there; and, as they told us, was lodged there on purpose to be ready for our transport, at such time as they thought fit to fetch us off: and the reason of their taking me with them, was to help to launch this weighty embarkation, which was very heavy for its proportion; as being made of the body of an oak or pine, some twenty-two feet in length, hollowed like a pigs' trough, which is the true description of a canoe. The manner of its being put into motion is very particular: the laborers, with long brooms, place their feet on the starboard and larboard sides of the boat, and with this fickle footing do they heave it forward.

The canoes being fitted to take us in, and waft us to the main, I made a fair muster of the remnant we had to carry off; and found we wanted six of the number we brought on shore; viz. four men and two women. Five of those six, we knew were dead; but missing one of our living women, we made the Indians understand the same; who as readily made us know that she was in their thoughts, and should be cared for, as soon as we were settled in our quarters. In passing the creek that was to lead us to an honest fisherman's house, we entered a branch of it to the southward, that was the road to it. The tide was going out, and the water very shoal; which gave occasion to any one that had a knife, to treat himself with oysters all the way. At the head of that branch, we were able, in a short time, to discover that haven of happiness, where our most courteous host, with a cheerful countenance, received and entertained us. Several fires were kindled out of hand, our arms and powder were laid up in safety, and divers earthen pipkins were put to boil, with such varieties as the season would afford. Everybody had something or other to defend and save them from the cold; and my obligation to him, by a peculiar care that he had of me, exceeded all the rest; I had one entire side of the fire, with a large platform to repose on, to myself, furs and deer-skins to cover my body and support my head, with a priority of respect and friendly usage; which, to my great trouble, I was not able to deserve at his hands, by any requital then in my power to return.

I can never sufficiently applaud the humanity of this Indian; nor express the high contentment that I enjoyed in this poor man's cottage, which was made of nothing but mats and reeds, and bark of trees fixed to poles. It had a loveliness of symmetry in the air of it, so pleasing to the eye and refreshing to the mind, that neither the splendor of the Escurial, nor the glorious appearance of Versailles, were able to stand in com petition with it. We had a boiled swan for supper, which gave plentiful repast to all our upper mess. Our bodies thus refreshed with meat and sleep, comforted with fires, and secured from all the changes and inclemencies of that sharp, piercing cold season, we thought the morning, though clad in sunshine, did not come too fast upon us. Breakfast was liberally provided, and soon set before us, our arms faithfully delivered up to my order for carriages; and thus, in readiness to set forward, we put ourselves in a posture to proceed to the place where the king resided. The woman left behind at the island, had been well looked to, and was now brought off to the care of her comrade that came with us; neither of them in a condition to take a journey: but they were carefully attended and nourished in this poor man's house till such time as boats came to fetch them to Virginia; where they soon arrived in perfect health, and lived (one, or both of them,) to be well married, and to bear children, and to subsist in as plentiful a condition as they could wish. In beginning our journey through the woods, we had not advanced half a mile, till we heard a great noise of men's voices directed to meet and stop our further passage. These were several Indians, sent by the king to order us back to our quarters. The good-natured king being informed of our bodily weakness, and inability to walk through the woods to his house on foot, (which might be about four miles distant from our setting out,) had a real tenderness for us, and sent canoes to carry us to the place nearest his house by the favor of another branch of the same creek: and to the end we might take no vain steps, as we were going to do, and exhaust our strength to no purpose, these Indians made this noise to stop us. We entered the canoes that were manned and lay ready to receive us. We had a pleasant passage in the shallow water, and ate oysters all the way: for although the breakfast we had newly made, might well excuse a longer abstinence than we were like to be put to, our arrear to our stomachs was so great, that all we swallowed was soon concocted and our appetite still fresh and craving more.

Having passed this new course for some three English miles in another branch of the creek, our landing place was contrived to be near the house of the queen, then in waiting. She was a very plain lady to see, not young, nor yet ill-favored. Her complexion was of a red white, but the measures of beauty in those parts where they are exposed to the scorching sun from their infancy, are not taken from red and white, but from colors that better lie upon their tawny skins. The beauty of this queen's mind, which is more permanent than that of color, was conspicuous in her charity and generosity to us poor starved weather-beaten creatures, who were the objects of it. A mat was spread without the house, upon the ground, furnished with pone, hominy, oysters, and other things. The queen made us sit down and eat, with gestures that showed more courtesy than majesty; but spoke as hearty welcome as could in silence be expected: and these were the graces that, in our opinion, transcended all other beauties in the world; and abundantly supplied all defects of outward appearances in the person and garb of the queen.

When this collation of the queen's was at an end, we took leave of her majesty, with all the shows of gratitude that silence knew how to utter. We were now within half an hour's walk of the king's mansion which we soon discovered by the smoke, and saw it was made of the same stuff with the other houses from which we had newly parted, namely, of mat and reed. Locust posts sunk in the ground at corners and partitions, were the strength of the whole fabric. The roof was tied fast to the body with a knot of strong rushes that grow there, which supplied the place of nails and pins, mortices and tenants. The breadth of this place was about eighteen or twenty feet; the length about twenty yards. The only furniture was several platforms for lodging, each about two yards long and more; placed on both sides of the house, distant from each other about five feet; the space in the middle was the chimney, which had a hole in the roof over it, to receive as much of the smoke as would naturally repair to it: the rest we shared among us, which was the greatest part; and the sitters divided to each side, as our soldiers do in their corps de guarde. Fourteen great fires, thus situated, were burning all at once. The king's apartment had a distinction from the rest; it was twice as long, and the bank he sat on was adorned with deer skins finely dressed, and the best furs of otter and beaver that the country produced. The fire assigned to us was suitable to our number; to which we were conducted, without intermixture of any Indians, but such as came to do us offices of friendship. There we were permitted to take our rest, until the king pleased to enter into communication with us. Previously to which he sent his daughter, a well-favored young girl of about ten or twelve years old, with a great wooden bowl full of hominy, which is the corn of that country, beaten and boiled to mash. She, in a most obliging manner, gave me the first taste of it; which I would have handed to my next neighbor after I had eaten; but the young princess interposed her hand, and taking the bowl out of mine, delivered it to the same party I aimed to give it, and to all the rest in order. Instead of a spoon there was a well shaped muscle-shell that accompanied the bowl. About three hours after this meal was ended, the king sent to have me come to him. He called me Ny a Mutt, which is to say, my brother; and compelled me to sit down on the same bank with himself, which I had reason to look upon as a mighty favor. After I had sat there about half an hour, and had taken notice of many earnest discourses and repartees betwixt the king and his crotemen, (so the Indians call the king's council,) I could plainly discover, that the debate they held was concerning our adventure and coming there. To make it more clear, the king addressed himself to me, with many gestures of his body; his arms displayed in various postures, to explain what he had in his mind to utter for my better understanding. By all which motions I was not edified in the least, nor could imagine what return to make by voice, or sign, to satisfy the king's demand, in anything that related to the present straits of our condition. In fine, I admired their patient sufferance of my dullness to comprehend what they meant, and showed myself to be troubled at it: which being preceived by the king, he turned all into mirth and jollity, and never left till he made me laugh with him, though I knew not why.

I took that occasion to present the king with a sword and long shoulder belt, which he received very kindly; and, to witness his gracious acceptance, he threw off his mach coat, or upper covering of skin, stood upright on his bank; and, with my aid, accoutered his naked body with his new harness, which had no other apparel to adorn it, beside a few skins about his loins to cover his nakedness. In this dress he seemed to be much delighted; but to me, he appeared a figure of such extraordinary shape, with sword and belt to set it off, that he needed no other art to stir me up to laughter and mirth, than the sight of his own proper person. Having made this short acquaintance with the king, I took leave, and returned to my comrades. Several Indians of the first rank followed me to my quarters, and used their best endeavors to sift something from us that might give them light into knowing what we were. They sought many ways to make their thoughts intelligible to us; but still we parted without knowing what to fix upon, or how to steer our course in advance of our way to Virginia. In this doubtful condition, we thought it reasonable to fall upon a speedy resolution what was next to be done on our parts, in order to the accomplishment of our voyage by land; which we hoped, by the divine aid, we might be able to effect, after a little more refreshment, by the plenty of victuals allowed us by the king; who was no less indulgent and careful to feed and caress us, than if we had been his children. Toward morning we were treated with a new regale, brought to us by the same fair hand again. It was a sort of spoon meat, in color and taste not unlike to almond milk, tempered and mixed with boiled rice.

Major Morrison, who had been almost at death's door, found himself abundantly refreshed and comforted with this delicacy. He wished the bowl had been a fathom deep; and would say, when his stomach called on him for fresh supplies, that if this princess royal would give him his fill of that food, he should soon recover his strength. Our bodies growing vigorous with this plenty, we took new courage, and resolved, as many as were able, to attempt the finding out of Virginia. We guessed the distance could not be great, and that it bore from us S. by W. to S W. Our ignorance of latitude we were in, was some discouragement to us; but we were confident, from what the seamen discoursed, we were to the southward of the Menados, then a Dutch plantation, now New York: fair weather and full stomachs made us willing to be gone. To that end we laid out for a quantity of pone; and, for our surer conduct, we resolved to procure an Indian to be our pilot through the wilderness; for we were to expect many remoras in our way, by swamps and creeks, with which all those coasts abound. The king remarking our more than ordinary care, to procure more bread than amounted to our usual expense, gathered thence our designs to leave him, and shift for ourselves. To prevent the rashness and folly of such an attempt, he made use of all his silent rhetoric to put us out of conceit of such design; and made us understand the peril and difficulty of it, by the many obstacles we must meet with. He showed us the danger we should expose ourselves unto, by rain and cold, swamps and darkness, unless we were conducted by other skill than we could pretend to. He pointed to his fires and shocks of corn, of which he had enough; and made it legible to us in his countenance, that we were welcome to it. All the signs the king made upon this occasion, we were content to understand in the best sense; and taking for granted our sojourning there was renewed to another day, we retired to our quarters.

About midnight following, the king sent to invite me to his fire. He placed me near him, as before; and, in the first place, showing me the quarters of a lean doe, newly brought in, he gave me a knife to cut what part of it I pleased; and then pointing to the fire, I inferred I was left to my own discretion for the dressing of it. I could not readily tell how to show my skill in the cookery of it, with no better ingredients than appeared in sight; and so did no more but cut a collop, and cast it on the coals. His majesty laughed at my ignorance; and to instruct me better, he broached the collop on a long skewer, thrust the sharp end into the ground, (for there was no hearth but what nature made,) and turning sometimes one side, and sometimes the other, to the fire, it became fit, in a short time, to be served up, had there been a dining-room of state, such as that excellent king deserved. I made tender of it first to the king, and then to his nobles, but all refused, and left it to me, who gave God and the king thanks for that great meal. The rest of the doe was cut up in pieces, stewed in a pipkin, and then put into my hands to dispose of among my company.

Before I parted, the king attacked me again, with reiterated attempts to be understood; and I thought by these three or four days' conversation, I had the air of his expression much more clear and intelligible than at first. His chief drift, for the first essay, seemed to be a desire to know which way we were bound, whether north or south. He took up a stick, with which he made divers circles by the fireside; and then holding up his finger to procure my attention, he gave to every hole a name; and it was not hard to conceive, that the several holes were to supply the place of a sea chart, showing the situation of all the most noted Indian territories that lay to the southward of Kickotank. That circle that was most southerly, he called Achomack, which though he pronounced with a different accent, I laid hold on that word with all the demonstrations of satisfaction I could express; giving him to understand, that was the place to which I had a desire to be conducted.

The poor king was in a strange transport of joy to see me receive satisfaction; and forthwith caused a lusty young man to be called to him, to whom, by the earnestness of his motions, he seemed to give ample instructions to do something for our service; but what it was, we were not yet able to resolve. In two or three days' time, seeing no effect of what he had so seriously said, we began again to despond; and therefore resumed our former thoughts of putting ourselves in a posture to be gone; but the king seeing us thus ready at every turn to leave him, showed in his looks a more than ordinary resentment; still describing (as he could) the care he had taken for us, and the impossibility of accomplishing our ends by ourselves; and that we should surely faint in the way, and die without help, if we would not be ruled by him. He showed me again his stores of corn; and made such reiterated signs, by the cheerfulness of his countenance, that we should not want, while we had such a plenty, as made us lay aside all thoughts of stirring till he said the word. But as oft as he looked or pointed to the coast of Achomack, he would shake his head, with abundance of grimaces, in dislike of our design to go that way till he saw it good we should do so. I was abundantly convinced of our folly, in the resolution we were ready to take of going away, without better information of the distance from Achomack, and the way that led to it; and having so frank a welcome where we were, we resolved to stay till the king should approve of our departure; which he was not able to determine, till the messenger came back, that he had sent to Achomack; who, it now seemed more plainly, was dispatched upon my owning that place to be our home; though we knew it not from any cause we could rely upon, before we saw the effect.

While we lived in this suspense, the king had a great mind to see our firearms, and to be acquainted with the use and nature of them. That which best pleased his eye, I presented to him, and showed him how to load and discharge it. The king's eldest son, of about eighteen years of age, was hugely enamored with our guns, and looked so wistfully on me, when he saw what wonders they would do, that I could not forbear presenting him with a birding-piece. Some of our company, who knew that by the laws of Virginia, it was criminal to furnish the Indians with firearms, gave me a caution in this case: but I resolved for once to borrow a point of that law. For though it might be of excellent use in general, yet as our condition was, I esteemed it a much greater crime to deny those Indians anything that was in our power, than the penalty of that law could amount to. Father and son abundantly gratified in this manner, the king thought himself largely requited for the cost we put him to in our entertainment. I taught his son to shoot at fowls, to charge his gun and clean it: insomuch, that in a few minutes, he went among the flocks of geese, and firing at random, he did execution on one of them to his great joy; and returned to his father with the game in his hand with such celerity, as if he had borrowed wings of the wind.

About three o'clock this afternoon (January 24) the king was pleased, in great condescension, to favor me with a visit; a favor which I may, without vanity, assume to myself, and my better habit, from the many particular applications that he made to me, exclusive of the rest of the company. He thought I was too melancholy, (for the Indians, as has been observed, are great enemies to that temper,) and showed me by his cheerful looks, what humor he would have me put on. He came at this time, attended by his young daughter, who had done us the good offices before mentioned; and having first, by kind words and pleasant gestures, given us renewed assurance of hearty welcome, he singled me out, and pointed with his hand to a way he would have me take; but whither, or to what end, I was at liberty to guess. Upon that he produced his little daughter, for my conductress to the place to which I should follow her, wherever she would lead me. The weather was excessively cold, with frost; and the wind blowing very fresh upon my face, it almost stopped my breath. The late condition I had been in, under a roof, with great fires and much smoke, conduced to make me more sensible of the cold air; but in less than half an hour, that pain was over. We were now in sight of the house to which we were bound, and the lady of the place, who proved to be the mother of my conductress, was ready to receive us, and to show me my apartment in the middle of her house which had the same accommodation to sit and rest upon, as before has been described in other instances. The lusty rousing fire prepared to warm me, would have been a most noble entertainment of itself; but attended, as it was quickly, with good food for the belly, made it to be that complete good cheer, I only aimed at. A wild turkey, boiled with oysters, was preparing for my supper, which, when it was ready, was served up in the same pot that boiled it. This queen was also of the same mold of her majesty, whom we first met at our landing-place. Somewhat ancient, in proportion to the king's age, but so gentle and compassionate, as did very beautifully requite all defects of nature. She passed some hours at my fire, and was very desirous to know the occasion that brought us there, as her motion and the emphasis of her words showed; but I had small hopes to satisfy her curiosity therein, after so many vain attempts to inform the king in that matter. In fine, I grew sleepy, and about nine o'clock every one retired to their quarters, separated from each other by traverses of mat; which, beside their proper virtue, kept the ladies from any immodest attempts, as secure as if they had been bars of iron

As the day peeped in, I went out and felt the same cold as yesterday, with the same wina, N. W. I was not forward to quit a warm quarter, and a frank entertainment; but my young governess, who had her father's orders for direction, knew better than myself what I was to do. She put herself in a posture to lead the way back from whence we came, after a very good repast of stewed muscles, together with a very hearty welcome, plainly appearing in the queen's looks. My nimble pilot led me away with great swiftness, and it was necessary so to do; the weather still continuing in that violent sharpness, nothing but a violent motion could make our limbs useful. No sooner had I set my foot in the king's house to visit my comrades, but a wonderful surprise appeared to me in the change of every countenance; and, as every face did plainly speak a general satisfaction, so did they with one voice explain the cause thereof, in telling me, the messengers of our delivery were arrived, and now with the king. I hastened to see those angels, and addressing myself to one of them in English habit, asked him the occasion of his coming there? He told me his business was to trade for furs, and no more; but as soon as I had told him my name, and the accidents of our being there, he acknowledged he came under the guidance of the Kickotank Indian (which I imagined, but was not sure the king had sent,) in quest of me and those that were left on shore. He had been sent by the governor of Virginia's orders to inquire after us, but knew not where to find us till the Indian came to his house. He gave me a large account of the ship's arrival, and the many dangers and difficulties she had encountered before she could come into James River; where she ran ashore, resolving there to lay her bones. His name was Jenkin Price: he had brought an Indian of his neighborhood with him, that was very well acquainted in those parts, for our conduct back to Achomack, which Indian was called Jack.

The king was very glad of this happy success to us, and was impatient to learn something more of our history than hitherto he had been able to extract from signs and grimaces. Jenkin Price, with his broken Indian, could make shift to instruct Jack to say anything he pleased; and Jack was the more capable to understand his meaning, by some sprinklings of English, that he had learnt at our plantations. Betwixt them both, they were able to satisfy the king in what he pleased to know. Jack told them, of himself, what a mighty nation we were in that country, and gave them caution, not to embezzle any goods we had brought with us, for fear of an after reckoning. I wondered, upon this serious discourse he had with the king, to see guns, and stockings, and whatever trifles we had given, offered to be returned; and being told the reason of it, by Jenkin Price, I was very much ashamed of Jack's too great zeal in our service; which, though it proceeded from a principle of honesty and good morality in him, we were to consider that our dearest lives, and all that we could enjoy in this world, were, next to divine Providence, owing to the virtue and charity of this king; and therefore, not only what they had in possession, but whatever else he should desire, that was in my power, would be too mean an acknowledgment for such high obligations. I took care to let them know that I had no hand in the menace by which Jack brought them to refund what they had got of us: the right understanding whereof increased our good intelligence, and became a new endearment of affection between us.

By better acquaintance with these, our deliverers, we learned that we were about fifty English miles from Virginia. That part of it where Jenkin governed, was called Littleton's Plantation, and was the first English ground we expected to see. He gave me great encouragement to endure the length of the way, by assuring me, I should not find either stone or shrub to hurt my feet through my thin soled boots; for the whole colony had neither stone or underwood. Having thus satisfied my curiosity, in the knowledge of what Jenkin Price could communicate, we deferred no longer to resolve how and when to begin our journey to Achomack.

The Indian he brought with him (who afterwards lived and died my servant) was very expert, and a most incomparable guide in the woods we were to pass, being a native of these parts; so that he was as our sheet anchor in this our perigrination. The king was loth to let us go till the weather was better tempered for our bodies; but when he saw we were fully resolved, and had pitched upon the next morning to begin our journey, he found himself much defeated in a purpose he had taken, to call together all the flower of his kingdom, to entertain us with a dance; to the end that nothing might be omitted on his part for our divertisement, as well as our nourishment, which his territory could produce. Most of our company would gladly have deferred our march a day longer, to see this masquerade: but I was wholly bent for Achomack, to which place I was to dance almost on my bare feet; the thoughts of which took off the edge I might otherwise have had to novelties of that kind.

When the good old king saw we were fully determined to be gone the next day, he desired, as a pledge of my affection to him, that I would give him my camlet coat; which he vowed to wear, while he lived, for my sake. I shook hands, to show my willingness to please him, in that or in any other thing he would command; and was the more willing to do myself the honor of compliance in this particular, because he was the first king, I could call to mind, that had ever showed any inclination to wear my old clothes. To the young princess, that had so signally obliged me, I presented a piece of twopenny scarlet ribbon, and a French tweezer-case, that I had in my pocket, which made her skip for joy; and to show how little she fancied our way of carrying them concealed, she retired apart for some time, and, taking out every individual piece of which it was furnished, she tied a snip of ribbon to each, and came back with scissors, knives, and bodkins, hanging at her ears, neck and hair. The case itself was not excused, but bore a part in this new dress; and, to the end we might not part, without leaving deep impressions of her beauty on our minds, she had prepared on her fore-fingers, a lick of paint on each; the colors (to my best remembrance) green and yellow: which, at one motion, she discharged on her face; beginning upon her temple, and continuing it, in an oval line downwards, as far as it would hold out.

Early next morning we put ourselves in a posture to be gone. Major Morrison was so far recovered, as to be heart-whole; but he wanted strength to go through so great a labor as this was likely to prove. We left him, with many others, to be brought in boats that the governor had ordered for their accommodation; and with them, the two weak women, who were much recovered by the good care and nourishment they received in the poor fisherman's house.

Breakfast being done, and our pilot Jack ready to set out, we took a solemn leave of the good king. He inclosed me in his arms with kind embraces, not without expressions of sorrow to part, beyond the common rate of new acquaintances. I made Jack pump up his best compliments, which at present was all I was capable to return to the king's kindness; and so, after many *hana haes*, we parted. We were not gone far, till the fatigue and tediousness of the journey discovered itself in the many creeks we were forced to head, and swamps to pass, (like Irish bogs,) which made the way at least double what it would have amounted to in a straight line: and it was our wonder to see our guide Jack lead on the way, with the same confidence of going right as if he had had a London road to keep him from straying. Toward evening we perceived smoke, an infallible sign of an Indian town, which Jack knew to arise from Gingo Teague. We went boldly into the king's house, by advice of his brother of Kickotank, who was also a very humane prince. What the place and season produced, was set before us with all convenient speed; which was enough to satisfy hunger, and to fit us for repose. I was extremely tired with this tedious journey, and it was the more irksome to me, because I performed it in boots, my shoes being worn out, which at that time were commonly worn to walk in; so that I was much more sleepy than I had been hungry. The alliance I had newly made at Kickotank, did already stand me in some stead; for that it qualified me to a lodging apart and gave me a first taste of all we had to eat; though the variety was not so great as I had seen in other courts.

I passed the night till almost day-break in one entire sleep; and when I did awake, not suddenly able to collect where I was, I found myself strangely confounded to see a damsel placed close to my side, of no meaner extract than the king's eldest daughter; who had completely finished the rape of all the gold and silver buttons that adorned the king of Kickotank's coat, yet on my back. When I was broad awake, and saw this was no enchantment, like those trances which knights-errant use to be in, but that I was really despoiled of what was not in my power to dispense withal; I called for Jack, and made him declare my resentment, and much dislike of the princess's too great liberty upon so small an acquaintance; which made me have a mean opinion of her. Jack showed more anger than myself, to see such usage by any of his country; and much more was he scandalized, that one of the blood-royal should purloin. But the king, upon notice of the fact, and party concerned in it, immediately caused the buttons to be found out and returned, with no slight reprimand to his daughter, and then all was well; and so much the better by the gift of such small presents as I was able to make to the king and princess. Breakfast was given us, and we hastened to proceed on our journey to Achomack. We reckoned ourselves about twenty-five miles distant from Jenkin's house, and I resolved, by God's help, that night to sleep there. But the distance proving yet greater than had been described, and my boots teazing me almost beyond all sufferance, I became desperate, and ready to sink and lie down. Jenkin lulled me on still with words that spurred me to the quick; and would demonstrate the little distance between us and his plantation, by the sight of hogs and cattle; of which species the Indians were not masters. I was fully convinced of what he said; but would, however, have consented to a motion of lying without doors on the ground, within two or three flights shot of the place, to save the labor of so small a remainder.

The close of the evening, and a little more patience, through the infinite goodness of the Almighty, did put a happy period to our cross adventure. A large bed of sweet straw was spread ready in Jenkin's house for our reception, upon which I hastened to extend and stretch my wearied limbs. And being thus brought into safe harbor by the many miracles of divine mercy, from all the storms and fatigues, perils and necessities to which we had been exposed by sea and land, for almost the space of four months; I cannot conclude this voyage in more proper terms, than the words that are the burthen of that Psalm of Providence,

"O that man would therefore praise the Lord for his goodness, and for his wondrous works unto the children of men!"

Our landlord, Jenkin Price, and conductor Jack, took great care to provide meat for us; and there being a dairy, and hens, we could not want. As for our stomachs they were open at all hours to eat whatever was set before us; as soon as our wearied bodies were refreshed with sleep. It was on Saturday, the —— day of January, that we ended this our wearisome pilgrimage, and entered into our king's dominions at Achomack called by the English, Northampton County; which is the only county on that side of the bay, belonging to the colony of Virginia, and is the best of the whole for all sorts of necessaries for human life.

SEVEN YEARS

OF A

SAILOR'S LIFE,

AMONG THE

SAVAGES OF THE CAROLINE ISLANDS.

"In or about the year 1826, I shipped"—says O'Connell, an English sailor, in the story of his life—"at Sydney, New South Wales, in the bark John Bull, whaler, Capt. Barkus. After we had been from Sydney about four months, we put in at the Bay of Islands, New Zealand. Bishop Marsden, at that time on a visit to New Zealand, from his residence at Paramatta, put on board of us a missionary, who was appointed to Strong's Island, one of the Caroline Archipelago, with his wife and daughter. We were to cruise among the islands toward Japan, with the intention to reach the shores of Japan at a particular season, when whales were supposed to frequent the sea of Japan. At eight months out, we had taken about eight hundred barrels of oil, and were endeavoring to make Strong's Island, to leave our passengers. At nightfall, we had made no land, but knew from observation and the ship's log, that we were within a days' sail of our destination. We were bowling along under easy sail, the wind on our quarter, when, at about eight o'clock in the evening, the vessel struck on a concealed coral reef, which is not laid down on the charts. Capt. Barkus was, as usual, drunk on the hen-coop when the vessel struck. In the presence of the master, the mates can assume with success no authority which it is his peculiar province to exercise; consequently, with a drunken, stupid sot for a master, every one followed the promptings of his own experience or inclination. The boats were lowered; but notwithstanding the necessary precipitation with which we prepared to leave the vessel, the boat in which I escaped was furnished with provisions and arms, and we were able, also, to take away some ammunition, and little portable articles. In the boat with myself were five seamen, and the wife and daughter of the missionary. He was in the boat with the captain. In the four boats the whole crew escaped from the vessel. For five or six hours, we kept together; but, when the morning dawned there was only one of the other boats discernable, and that but faintly a long distance astern, as we crested a wave'

The sufferings of the ladies engrossed more of our care than our own situation, We had a sail in our boat, and kept her away before it, both because of the comparative comfort of such a course, and our indifference as to what point we stood for. As I sat steering, I folded the shivering, sobbing daughter to my body with my left arm, while two of my shipmates assisted in protecting her by placing themselves on each side. The mother was similarly cared for by the other seamen. We tendered them parts of our clothing, but could not persuade or induce them to accept anything of the kind. Oh, such a horrid night! The women had much more to endure than ourselves, for, beside the natural weakness of their frames, and the delicacy which is woman's suffering in misfortune, as her ornament in prosperity, they suffered acute pain from the excoriation they had received in descending to the boat by the davit-tackles: the salt-water rendered poignant the smarting pain of their wounds. But in all their affliction, they bore holy testimony to the efficacy of that religion whose messengers they were. If ever true practice, as well as profession of religion, existed, it was exemplified in this family. On shipboard, before our misfortune, the discreet and feeling manner in which they strove to impress upon rude sailors the truths of religion, had convinced all of their *sincerity*, at least. In the boat we had more affecting proof. They prayed frequently and fervently, and there were none to scoff.

Broiling heat succeeded the chills of night; the wind abated, and at noon we were becalmed—dying with heat and fatigue, upon a sea whose dead swell was so tranquil, that its glassy slimy smoothness was not ruffled. Toward night, we had a breeze again, through the night the wet chills, and the same heat and calm upon the next day. After two days' and three nights' exposure, the daughter died about ten o'clock on the third day. For some hours before, she had been apparently unconscious of her situation: she had talked in her wanderings of her father, of her home, and of the island to which she was destined on an errand of mercy: the happy end of her pilgrimage was attained without the toil to which she had in her youth devoted herself to reach it. The mother was, by suffering, so far bereft of sensibility, that the death of her child hardly moved her. She scarcely appeared to understand us when we informed her of it; or, if she did, the announcement was received with a sort of delirious joy. With as much attention to the forms of civilized society, as our situation would permit, we committed the body to the ocean. We at first intended to wrap the corpse in our sail; but the prudence of a portion of the crew, who objected to exposing the living to save a form for the dead, prevailed. The mother, in her weak state, hardly uttered a comment, and in a few hours followed her daughter. Her body was also consigned to the deep.

Upon the next morning after these melancholy duties to the two martyrs to religion, we made the land. We had been in the boat three days and four nights, but, rejoiced as we were to make the land, no immediate prospect of profiting by it appeared, for it was circled with a coral reef, in which it was past noon before we discovered an opening. Effecting a passage, we entered a smooth basin of water, and saw hundreds of canoes launching and putting off to us. They would approach within a short distance, then suddenly retreat, and at length commenced showering stones, arrows, and other missiles upon us. We threw ourselves in the bottom of the boat, and when they had satisfied themselves that we could or would offer no resistance, they were emboldened to make a rush upon the boat, which they towed to the beech. After we were landed, they stripped us of our clothing, and took everything out of the boat, whale-irons, tubs, muskets, etc. The boat was then hauled upon the beach, and our company, six in number, were led to the canoe-house.

We were seated in the center of the house, upon mats; and yams, bread-fruit, plantains, bananas, fish, bits of cold game of some sort, were brought to us. The building was filled in every chink by natives, seated; the men with crossed legs, like Turks, and the women on their heels. A constant buzz of conversation ran through the assembly, each talking to his next neighbor, and gesticulating vehemently. The interjection, or sound, indicative of pleasure or surprise among the Indians, is a cluck, and of this sound there was abundance, but we were at that time at a loss how to interpret it. Parties of two or three would come down to where we sat, walking with their bodies bent almost double. They took hold of our persons very familiarly, women and men, and gave frequent clucks of admiration at the blue veins which were marked through our skins on parts of the bodies which had not been usually exposed to be bronzed by the sun. My comrades feared the Indians were cannibals, and that this examination was to discover whether we were in good roasting case a horrible supposition, which was strengthened by the building of two or three wood fires, covered with small stones. Their fear was so excessive, that they gave themselves up as lost; but as I had been somewhat acquainted with the manners of the inhabitants of other islands, I reasoned, from the apparent good humor of these people, that they intended us no harm.

In a sort of desperate feeling of recklessness, I determined to try the experiment of dancing upon our savage audience. I proposed it to my comrades, and they endeavored to reason me out of what they esteemed criminal, thoughtless conduct, in the view of a horrid death. The prospect was none of the most agreeable, certainly; but I was determined on my experiment, despite their remonstrances. I accordingly sprung to my feet, and took an attitude ; a cluck of pleasure ran through the savages, and one of them, readily understanding my intention, spread a mat for me. I struck into Garry Owen, and figured away in that famous jig, to the best of my ability and agility, and my new acquaintances were amazingly delighted thereat. There was no loud acclamation, but anxious peering and peeping over each other's shoulders, the universal cluck sounding all over the house. Before my dance was finished, the cause for which the fires were built became apparent, to the no small relief of my comrades. It was ascertained that the roasting preparations were made, not for us, but for some quadrupeds, which we afterward found were dogs. Other preparations, such as the pounding of jago, roasting of game, etc., were making for a feast. In three or four hours all was ready. After my dance was concluded, we were separated from each other, each of us making the nucleus of a group of natives, who could not sufficiently admire and examine him. Food was sent us, and jago. Of the latter I could not drink; it was unpleasant in taste, and a very strong narcotic in effect.

We were now all completely reassured; the conduct of the natives to us was all that uncultivated kindness and hospitality could prompt. For three or four days it was with us a continual feast, islanders crowding from all directions to see the white strangers. Upon the fourth day after our landing, there was an arrival of a fleet of canoes, the head and other chiefs. We were again inspected by the new-comers, and it was my fortune to be selected, with my shipmate, George Keenan, by the principal chief. The other four of my comrades were also appropriated; and our property, and the articles we brought on shore in the boat, were also divided.

On the morrow, my new friend, or master, or owner—I do not know exactly how he considered himself—left the island upon which we landed, taking with him Keenan and myself. Eight or nine hours carried us to his island, where new feasting and *lionizing* awaited us. A grand feast celebrated the return of the chief to his house, at which I repeated the Irish jig which had taken so well upon my first landing. I have no doubt that in my heels was found the attraction which led the chief to select me from among my comrades. Upon the next day after his return, he restored to George and me our "ditty bags," the only property I had preserved from the wreck. In that bag, were two odd volumes of Jane Porter's Scottish Chiefs, and a little shaving-glass.

The shaving-glass did not survive long. While it lasted, I kept it sacred to the eyes of the island aristocracy, never permitting plebeian gazers access to it. I carried it with me on all my rounds of visits to the chiefs, and the exclamations of those who were favored with a peep at the magic glass, were amusing enough. As many as could look in at once, would peep over each other's shoulders, twisting their features into the most grotesque expressions, and *clucking* with delight. They imagined the reflection of their visages was caused by spirits behind the glass; consequently, some awe was mingled with their delight. It is, however, a curious fact for the student of mental philosophy, that their respect for those genii did not prevent their destroying the frame of the glass, one day in my absence, and scraping off the quicksilver, to detect the spirits in their hiding-place, and meet them all at once!

We had been about three days at our new residence, when some of the natives began showing us their tattooed arms and legs, and making signs not entirely intelligible to us at first, though their meaning became afterward too painfully marked. On the fourth or fifth day, George Keenan and myself were put on board of a canoe, with six natives. They paddled a short distance along the shore of the island, and then turned into a creek, wide at the mouth, but soon narrowing till there was not room for two canoes abreast. At length we reached a hut on the banks of the creek, landed, and entered it, directed by our conductors, who remained outside. No person was there to receive us, and for half an hour George and I busied ourselves in guesses and speculation as to the end to which all this was tending.

At length our suspense was relieved—ended, I should say—by the arrival of five or six women bearing implements, the purpose of which we were soon taught. George was made to sit in one corner of the room, and I was seated in another, half the women with me, and the residue with my comrade. One of my women produced a calabash of black liquid; another took my left hand, squeezing it in hers, so as to draw the flesh tight across the back. Then a little sliver of bamboo was dipped in the liquid and applied to my hand, upon which it left a straight black mark. The third beauty then produced a small flat piece of wood, with thorns pierced through one end. This she dipped in the black liquid, then rested the points of the thorns upon the mark on my hand, and, with a sudden blow from a stick, drove the thorns into my flesh. One needs must when the devil drives, so I summoned all my fortitude, set my teeth, and bore it like a martyr. Between every blow my beauty dipped her thorns in the ink. I was too much engaged in my own agreeable employment to watch my comrade, but George soon let me hear from him. He swore and raved without any attention to rule; the way he did it was profane, but not syntactical or rhetorical. He wished all sorts of bloody murder and plagues to light upon his tormentors, prayed that the islands might be earthquake-sunken, hoped forty boats' crews, from a squadron of armed ships, would land and catch the blasted savages tormenting the king's subjects. All this availed nothing but to amuse the women; and even I could not forbear a smile at his exclamations. The operators suspended this work to mimic him—mocked his spasmodic twitches of the arms and horrid gestures. He was a standing butt for it long afterward, and when the natives wished to revile him, they would act the tattooing scene, ending with the exclamation, "Narlic-a-Nutt mucha purk,"—Narlic-a-Nutt (his name) is a coward; "Jim Aroche ma coo mot,"—Jim Chief brave!

After my executioner had battered my hand awhile, she wiped it with a sponge. I hoped she had finished; but no! She held my hand up, squinted at the lines, as a carpenter would true a board, then she commenced again, jagging the thorns into places where she thought the mark was imperfect. The correction of the work was infinitely worse than the first infliction. In about an hour and a half the hand was finished, and the women left us, taking away their tools. Before they left us, however, they smeared the tattooed part with cocoa-nut oil, and then patted pulverized coal upon it. This was repeated often, till there was a thick crust of coal and oil, completely concealing the flesh. The healing properties of charcoal are familiar to chemists. The reader has noted, perhaps, that it will delay the putrefaction of butcher's meat; and, indeed, some over economical housewifes know how to restore tainted meat by an application of it. The women gone, something was sent us to eat, and we flattered ourselves that our punishment for the day was over. However, the afternoon brought a fresh bevy of these tender ladies, who continued operations upon the left arm. At night we were pointed to some mats and informed that we must sleep there.

On the next morning the gout-puffed hand of the canon of Gil Blas would not have been a circumstance in size to mine; though the color of my flesh, maturated, and grimed with charcoal, hardly looked so aristocratic as a delicately swelled, gouty limb. Another squad of these savage printers followed our breakfast. George was outrageous in his protestations, and howled and gesticulated earnestly against a repetition; and I did not spare entreaty. The prayer of his petition was granted, but my reluctance availed nothing. For a reason of which I then knew nothing, they made gestures that I *must* stand it—there was no escape. George was let off, but not without unequivocal expressions of disgust at his cowardice and effeminacy. He was indeed incapable of enduring it; his blood was bad; but physical disability, among all savages, is quite as much a disgrace as a misfortune.

After finishing the left, operations were commenced upon my right arm. It is unnecessary to go into details; eight days were occupied in the process upon different parts of my body. My legs, back, and abdomen, were marked also, and to enable them to operate I was compelled to lay extended upon a mat. The hair upon my body was twitched out with sea-shells—a process which was performed as expeditiously upon my person as the same ground can be cleared of pin-feathers on geese by a dextrous cook. I often thought I should die of these apparently petty, but really actually painful inflictions. George was compelled to remain with me, not only during the eight days the tattooing was going on, but for the month afterward that I was obliged to remain at this hut for my flesh to heal. During this time the application of the oil and charcoal was continually repeated, till I resembled in skin, if not in shape, the rhinoceros.

I had supposed that my tattooing was over, but I had not been ashore three hours, before, by the chief's direction, one of his daughters prepared to mark me still more. She tattooed a ring upon my right breast, another upon my left shoulder, and two about my right arm. This was but the prick of a needle to the extensive printing business which had been prosecuted upon my body at the tattoo-house, and I made no complaint. The feasting continued during the day; many dogs barked their last;

jago in abundance was mauled to express its juice; and my comrade for his fife, and myself for my heels, were in excellent odor with the natives. I enjoyed this much better than my comrade; fell into the spirit of it, and danced like mad upon every visit from strangers; George supplying the music, and the spectators clucking, or breaking out into an unsurpressed laugh of delight. George's music saved him much contumely which he would otherwise have received for his cowardice in the tattoo-house.

So wore the second day. It was not until night that I began to suspect to what it all tended. At night I learned that the young lady who imprinted the last mentioned marks upon my arm and breast was my wife! that last tattooing being part of the ceremony of marriage. Upon the third morning my bride led me away to the bath, and the day was spent in feasting and dancing, as upon the two days preceding; only that the third, being the climax, was more of a day of rejoicing than the two preceding. There was, however, no quarreling or disturbance, no uproar or disorder. The liquor expressed from jago is a tremendously powerful narcotic, and drinking it in large quantities produces deep and stupid sleep. George also was provided with a wife; but his unwillingness to submit to the process of tattooing wedded him to a woman of no rank. She however, proved a good woman to him. My father-in-law was Ahoundel-a-Nutt, chief of the island of Nutt, and the most powerful chief on the group of islands inclosed by the reef, set down on the charts as one island, Ascension, but called by the natives Bonabee. He did not have the grace to give me a separate establishment however, for, during the whole time I remained upon the island, I resided under the same roof with him. He gave me his own name, Ahoundel, but I was oftener called Jem-aroche. George Keenan's island name was Narlic.

I never had more reason to complain of my wife than the majority of people in civilized countries have. She was only about fourteen years of age, affectionate, neat, faithful, and, barring too frequent indulgence in the flesh of baked dogs, which would give her breath something of a canine odor, she was a very agreeable consort. During my residence upon the island she presented me with two pretty little demi-savages, a little girl, and a boy, who stands a chance, in his turn, to succeed his grandfather in the government of the island.

Although my father-in-law never permitted me a house distinct from his, but kept me as one of his own household, with a host of other connections—a knight of his majesty's bedchamber—for there was no division wall in the hut, and I slept on a mat next him; my wife's dower in canoes, Nigurts, (slaves,) and other Caroline personal property, with the improvement of real, was far from inconsiderable. She assumed a task new to her, and one of course which she could have had no idea of before—that of an instructress in the language. I was a tolerably apt scholar, but my teacher had a very critical ear, and the least deviation from the island pronunciation created vast merriment both for her and others present.

My wife accompanied me in my walks and in my canoe excursions, always at my side, and looking up to me affectionately. Her father, who was a practical joker, contrived, in the excursions in which he accompanied us during the lengthened honeymoon, to pop upon places where he knew that, although my name and fame had preceded me, the residents had never seen me. He would direct me to enter a house suddenly, with a howl, and strike an attitude. It would invariably send all the occupants, usually women, flying out at every place of egress. The sight of Ahoundel on the outside, enjoying a hearty laugh, would remove fear, and this rude method of introduction supplied both parties, the visitors and the visited, with rare amusement. Imagine the effect which would be produced on a party of American or European ladies by the sudden apparition of an Albino under such circumstances, and you will have some idea of the fright of the islanders.

To excursions without him Ahoundel was very averse. He would, in answer to my inquiries about the other islands, tell me they were inhabited by cannibals, and assure me, that if I ventured away from him I should certainly be eaten. George and I, if we took excursions, did so in a canoe borrowed of fishermen, because we could not launch our own unperceived. Afraid of being eaten, our trips were at first confined altogether to Nutt, the island upon which we resided; circumnavigating it, and paddling up the creeks. When we were near a settlement, George would take his fife and make its shrill notes echo in the still valleys and mountains. "Narlic! Narlic! Narlic! Narlic!" we would soon hear the natives shouting, as they came running down to the creek side, "Narlic, cudjong! cudjong!" Cudjong was the name which the natives had bestowed upon George's fife. The shore would soon be lined with breathless listeners, and while I kept the canoe just in motion enough to avoid the banks, George would play some of his sweetest tunes. We were always invited to land, and usually did so. As soon as I left the boat came my turn; I was besieged to dance, and as I always refused to land except when intending to astonish the natives with a reel which might have passed for clever, even

—"at the fair of nate Clogheen,"

I usually complied with their request.

There is one species of fish universally held sacred by the islanders, a species of eel, inhabiting the fresh water. Keenan and myself had resided upon Nutt, and eaten at many feasts, beside the regular domestic fare, but in all this eating no eels had furnished their share. To our inquiries why this fish enjoyed such a peculiar and universal exemption, the only answer had been "Major-howi!" This we knew was a partial defense for all fish, and not being aware that the respect for eels was more strenuously insisted upon than that shown their cousins, the dwellers in salt water, we determined upon indulging ourselves in a feast upon them; taking the precaution, however, not to invite any of our copper friends to be of the party.

We selected for the occasion a fine night, and with elbowed sticks poked the fish out of the water at a sudden bend in a brook. Unlike the ells which were used to being skinned, these were not so much as used to being caught, and having enjoyed an immunity from the snares of the fisher, from time immemorial, our trouble was in avoiding to take too many, rather than in catching enough for our purpose. Building a fire and broiling them in an unoccupied house, we had a sit down alone, and demolished them with an appetite which was not abated by the circumstances under which we feasted—the wise man having recorded his opinion that "stolen waters are sweet." Our feast finished, we wiped our mouths, and returned to our island friends with all the conscious rectitude of rogues undiscovered.

We had neglected the precaution of concealing the bones, and, with an aptitude for detecting sin like that which characterizes some civilized people, some of the natives recognized in the bones the fragments of the forbidden fish. Our first intimation of the discovery was taken from seeing the natives repairing to the house, and, not at first understanding the reason of it, we fell in upon the tide. When we reached the hut, we found men, women and children, kneeling, or completely prostrate, beating their breasts, and rocking to and fro, or rolling on the floor. Of the noise they made, we had been, of course, apprised by our ears before we reached the house, and had concluded that some accident or sudden death was the reason of the outcry. Nothing was there however—no broken bones but the bones of the eels; the pyramid of which, as George and I had left it, might indeed have caused cries of surprise that two persons could have left such testimonials of appetite; but as the aspect of affairs looked like an expression of something more than surprise, we esteemed it prudent to keep our own counsel. For two or three days was the lamentation continued; it flew from place to place and from hut to hut; on every side was weeping and lamentation. George and I thought we saw some looks indicative of suspicion, and when the bones were fairly buried by the chief's orders, and the hubbub ceased, we felt relieved from a load of fear which had been sufficient to give us a distaste for eels; which operated better for their safety, as far as we were concerned, than all the acts passed by the legislature of Massachusetts have done for the shad and alewives in Taunton River.

Upon one occasion, when I was sick, a journey was projected, as was the usual course with invalids. I, however, refused to be cured in such a way, preferring ease and quiet. All the preparations having been made for the journey, it was taken without me. I thought my wife might have had the grace to remain at home with her sick spouse, but she chose to accompany her father. Upon her return I had pretty well recovered, and I welcomed her by taking my wedding gift—a few blue beads—from her basket, and breaking them between two stones, before her eyes. As soon as I had done the mischief, Laowni ran from the house to a stone in the edge of the water, where she sat down and commenced crying like an infant. I followed, and endeavored to pacify her, but it was of no use. The only answer she made was to kick like a spoiled child. The tide flowed in, till she was in water to her elbows; then I was enabled to coax her away, but still she ceased not bellowing for her beads. If I had bitten off her finger, it would certainly have grieved her less. At night I went to sleep and left her weeping. She had refused to eat, though fish and the most delicate bits of a murdered puppy had been offered her. Happening, however, to awake at midnight, I detected her solacing her grief, not, like Mrs. Oakley, on boiled chickens, but like a delicate savage, on a dog's drumstick. I said nothing, thinking the return of her appetite was a good omen; but when I waked again in the morning, clouds and darkness still sat upon the countenance of Laowni.

The day long she wore the same sulks, giving me an occasional look of anything but affection, but not vouchsafing a word. At night I took George with me, and instead of sleeping in the canoe-house, which was then Ahoundel's quarters, went to his house proper. There we built a small fire for its light, and just as we had propounded to each other the sage conclusion that his Majesty of Nutt and family were not in the best humor, we were surprised with a visit from that dignitary himself, accompanied by a native who was particularly indebted to me for detecting him in stealing my knife, and two others, all armed with spears. Without saying a word they sat down at a little distance, biting their nether lips, as is always their custom when vexed or in a passion. I spoke to them, and inquired the reason of the visit, but received not a word in answer George shivered beside me like a leaf, though I assured him he need fear nothing, as the visit was undoubtedly intended solely for me. At length our agreeable state of suspense was relieved by the appearance of Laowni, who beckoned them outside, and we saw nothing more of them. It was two or three days afterward before the reconciliation between myself and wife was completed, as I took it upon me, upon the most approved civilized plan, to become sulky when she relented. This lesson, however, taught me better than to trifle again seriously with the property or comfort of a wife, whose father might inflict summary punishment upon me without being amenable for it to any power. Such I afterward ascertained was the intention of the visit. Ahoundel left the canoe-house with a determination to put me to death, and it was the intercession of Laowni, who followed the party, that saved me Upon the whole, the adventure had a good effect. Ahoundel respected the courage with which I faced him, though God knows it was as much in outward seeming as genuine; and respected the firmness which led me to maintain my ground, even after the threat of death.

After I had some time resided with these savages, I happened accidentally to feel a sick man's pulse. This was noted by the observant natives, and I was called upon to explain what it meant, and why I did it. I gave them the best illustration in my power, beating time to show them how fast the pulse should beat, and telling them that anything faster or anything slower was "no good." The beating of the pulse at the wrists was a remarkable discovery to them; all the old women, and indeed all the young, made a dive at the wrists of every one when first suspected of ill health. Once on the scent, they followed it, and detected the throbbing of the temples; so if there was not room enough at the wrists for all examiners, a portion would settle on his head. It was really amusing to see how like civilized people they could ride a hobby to death. Inquiries ceased. As phrenologists are said to read a man's whole character without other data to proceed upon than the external developments upon his head, so the native professors of the new art of pulse-feeling wished only to find rest for the finger on the patient's body. He or she would find rest only when the tormentors were asleep; the sleep of the patient being of too little consequence to interrupt the medical examinations of the thousand friends.

An islander sick is an object ghastly enough. His original sallow face is smeared until it is resplendent in ghastliness. The accompanying objects, the gloomy visages of the attendants, and their howling and moaning, give such scenes a character gloomy as the most inveterate old lady lover of sorrow, rendered doubly sorrowful by exaggeration and anticipaiton, could desire. If possible, I was always called to pronounce whether a patient would live or die; and, by caution in pronouncing judgment, and care in forming it, my word, as I gained experience, was considered, with the islanders, life or death to the patient. By a favorable opinion, confidently pronounced, I question not I saved many lives, as the natives would redouble their efforts when hope was encouraged, and the patient's imagination, thus relieved, would assist the recovery.

With these people, after George and I had become habituated to their customs, and learned to appreciate their character, we resigned ourselves to circumstances, and were content, in the absence of almost all hope of escape, to be happy. In about a year from our arrival, Ahoundel grew a little less cautious about our wandering; a forced remission of care, as we had become too well acquainted with the people to believe them all cannibals. Still he insisted upon our being frequently in his company The difficulty with Laowni, detailed in a preceding page, my father-in-law's conduct, in which he was, I suspect, instigated by Namadow, left my situation not quite so pleasant as before. Ahoundel seemed inclined to repair his harshness with over affection, and it was with much difficulty George and I obtained permission to leave Nutt even for twenty-four hours.

Outside the reef which bounds Bonabee, the island we were upon, are two other islands, one called by the natives Hand, about twenty miles distant; the other Pokeen, about sixty miles distant. The latter, called on the charts Wellington Island, is inhabited; Hand is not. The inhabitants of Wellington Island resemble those of Bonabee, except that they are addicted to cannibalism, a practice which is unknown on Bonabee, except, perhaps, so far as tasting an enemy's heart goes. Keenan and myself visited it once, and found it bounded by a reef, through which there is but one passage. We were detained by a storm longer than we bargained for, being weather-bound ten days. Upon Wellington Island we remained nearly six months.

I did not believe, till my visit, that the natives of Wellington Island were cannibals; then I had ocular demonstration. It seemed with them an ungovernable passion, the victims being not only captives, but presents to the chiefs from parents, who appeared to esteem the acceptance of their children, for a purpose so horrid, an honor. Shortly after our return from Pokeen, or Wellington Island, our four comrades, Johnson, Brayford, Thompson and Williams, paid us a visit, as had been their occasional custom. At these meetings we sparred, danced, sung, and conversed in English, relating to each other our various experience and discoveries in the language of the people, and their character.

Upon this occasion my comrades proposed to George and me that we should leave Nutt, and spend a twelvemonth with them, dividing the time with the different chiefs with whom they were quartered, and devoting the first month to an excursion from island to island. This proposal was eagerly embraced by us. I had frequently expressed to Ahoundel a wish to the same effect, giving as a reason my weariness of the monotony of an abode upon one island, but he uniformly refused his consent. My visit to Wellington Island was protracted, by the strength of the north-east trades, much beyond his pleasure, and, although I was an involuntary absentee, and of course not liable to blame, that long absence had so proved the need of my presence to him, that it made him averse to my going from his sight: a fatherly solicitude that was horribly annoying. Knowing, therefore, the certain answer to an application for leave of absence, I determined to take liberty without. What I fancied a good opportunity soon offered. Ahoundel and his whole household, and connections, launched the canoes for an excursion or visit. I was excused from the party on account of the presence of my friends, who declined accompanying Ahoundel. When they were fairly off, we stepped into the canoe, but had hardly got under weigh, when a rascally native, who had evidently been watching us, shoved his canoe off, and paddled before us like lightning, shoving, or rather poling his canoe over the shallows, and working like a windmill in a gale with his single paddle in the deep water. When he reached a creek or inlet, into which we knew Ahoundel had turned, he shot up the opening, and we began to see his intention, and the meaning of the hoobooing he had kept up as he preceded us.

In a few moments we saw the canoes of Ahoundel in pursuit. We used paddles and sail, and cracked on, esteeming it more a frolic than anything else. As we had the start, and the canoes of the island differ but little in speed, it was nearly two hours before they had neared us enough to be within hailing distance. They then commenced fair promises if we would stop, offering us fish, and bread-fruit, and yams, and using all the logic of persuasion of which they were capable. Still we cracked on; but Ahoundel's canoe at length shoved alongside of us, upon the weather or outrigger side, and we gave up the race as useless. My friend Namadow was the first to lay hold of the outrigger, and gave us the first intimation of their rough intentions, by endeavoring to capsize us. We hung to windward to trim the boat, and finding his strength ineffectual to upset it, he had the brazen impudence to climb on the platform with the intention to board us. In the heat of the moment I administered a settler with my fist, which knocked him into the water. Then half a dozen of the Indians laid hold of our outrigger at once, and esteeming it useless to struggle against such odds, we all jumped out of the canoe. Others of Ahoundel's fleet had by this time gathered around us, and the Indians commenced beating us with the flat sides of the paddles whenever we showed our heads. Our canoe was smashed to smithereens, and my comrades were allowed to climb into others in the fleet, without much beating; indeed, they were assisted in; but I did not fare so well. Ahoundel made frequent feints with his spear, and so did others, but not one was thrown, nor had any person any such murderous intention; as I afterward learned their orders were to frighten and beat, but not to hurt: a consoling circumstance, of which I had not then the benefit, but considered myself a case. During all this time my father-in-law was upbraiding me with my ingratitude, reminding me of my rank, connections, wife, and the benefits he heaped upon me. I protested my purpose was only to make an excursion with the intention to return. The paddle pounding had ceased after the first rude attack, and this conversation was carried on, or rather his scolding, while I was eyeing the spears, and dodging, in anticipation of the expected blows. I made several attempts to climb into Ahoundel's canoe, but my particular friend, who had by this time been fished out of the water, rapped my fingers with his paddle as soon as they clasped the gunwale. The fleet, which had received additions from Nutt, of people who came out from curiosity, seeing the fray, now turned toward Nutt again; and Jem Aroche, Moonjob as he was, was fain to crawl into the canoe of a native, and return to the house of his father. My shipmates accompanied me, and Ahoundel, satisfied that I should not repeat my attempt to escape, proceeded on his excursion. I should have mentioned, that no women accompanied our pursuers, as the precaution was taken to set them ashore before the boats started in pursuit.

Three or four days passed before Ahoundel and his party returned. During that time I had ample opportunity for reflection, and came to the conclusion, that, considering the stealthy circumstances under which I left Nutt, the chief had reason for his jealousy of me. Nay, I could not help acknowledging to myself that my punishment was not altogether undeserved, as my treatment of my father had, to say the least, been unhandsome. When the party returned, Laowni immediately sought me upon landing, as she had heard vague rumors of my adventure, and was not sure that I was not killed. She was overjoyed to see me, rubbed her nose against mine, threw herself on my neck, and fairly wept tears of joy at my safety. Ahoundel himself made a sort of half apology, and excused himself by recapitulating the suspicious circumstances against me Laowni was clamorous in her complaints of my treatment, and even appealed to her father by asking him how he would like such usage if he was a stranger in London.

Laowni questioned all the particulars of the attack out of me, and worked herself into such a rage with Nomadow, the friend who struck my hand, that she ran up to him, and struck him with her codjic, or small wooden knife. It was a severe blow, too, she dealt him, doing her savage notions of friendship more credit than her sex. He had no refuge but flight, and the others, who had been busiest in abusing me at the time of the encounter, noticing the reconciliation with Ahoundel, did not afterward venture into the canoe-house when I was present, till they imagined they had propitiated me with presents. Ahoundel was much better pleased with Laowni's attack upon Nomadow than I was. He called her "brave" for it; not exactly to her face, but as any father among us would rather commend than regret the pranks of a spoiled child; for such was Laowni, his only daughter. Nomadow was so severely wounded by her, that his death, occurring within a couple of months, was attributed to the combined effects of his bodily injury and his shame at being punished by a woman.

Our shipmates lengthened their visit some days after their capture under the apparently suspicious circumstances of running away with George and me. Ahoundel had the justice to present them with a new canoe, the civility; to invite them to prolong their visit, and the delicacy to restore their property so soon after the explanation, that their visit could not seem a detention forced by the lack of means to escape. Not the least interesting among our occupations and amusements on the island was conversation with the natives, and watching the avidity with which they swallowed whatever we told them, and the dexterity with which they applied the information thus gained to the improvement of their arts; always excepting when it interfered with such part of their customs as were based on their religion. It was a practice with us to impress their minds with an idea of the power of the chiefs of England and America. We told them of musketry and of cannons, but never, with the guns in our hands, could convince them that those guns were the death-dealing engines, of which, from tradition, they had some idea. Our powder was all spoiled in the boat, before we landed.

In illustrating geography to my adult scholars, I drew, upon bark, a rough skeleton outline of America, large, a small spot for England, and to show them the comparative size of their own islands, a small dot. This, however, would not suffice to make them understand, till they inquired how many day's journey it required to go round America and England. To the first I assigned an indefinite time, very, very long—too many days to be counted. My inquirers would cluck, cluck, in astonishment. England (not to let her appear too insignificant) I bounded by a year's traveling, the name England comprising the three kingdoms. They would then revert to their own speck in the ocean, almost incredulous to the statement that other inhabited spots so much exceeded it in size.

Some months after this, we were informed that Wajai-a-Hoo, the chief of a neighboring island, had declared war against Ahoundel-a-Nutt, on account of my marriage. It appeared that Laowni was promised to him previous to my arrival. The daughter never much affected the match, as Wajai was old, and the husband already of something like a dozen. It may be to her disgust for that union, quite as much as to my own good looks, that I owed my marriage to her. Be that as it may, Ahoundel, after stating the case, asked me if I was willing to fight; and as I saw no honorable mode of escape, and am a native of a country whose boys have no very decided aversion to a bit of a row, I consented; but George showed the white feather, and positively refused.

Preparations were immediately set on foot to visit him, and "carry the war into Africa," by answering Wajai's challenge at his own door. Natives to the number of about fifteen hundred were mustered, from Nutt and two contiguous small islands, called Hand and Param. Each canoe was furnished with smooth stones, which were stowed in the bottom, and each native was furnished with a sling, a spear, a bow and arrows, and war-club. The spears are from five feet to eight in length, and barbed with the back bone of a fish, preserving five or six joints, with the protruding bones, like arrow barbs. The clubs are made of heavy wood and notched, about eighteen inches or two feet in length. The natives were dressed in their best savage articles of adornment, their heads dressed with flowers, but no paint was put upon their flesh, except the everlasting smearing with cocoanut oil and curry.

The day and place had been appointed with all the circumstance of a duel, or rather of an ancient joust at arms, with the exception that there was no stipulation or limitation as to force on either side; each party bringing all the strength he could muster. Treachery sometimes occurs in island warfare, and attacks by surprise are made; seldom, it is true, but often enough to induce those who are aware that they have enemies to be on their guard. This engagement with Wajai was, however, a fair fight, preceded by a challenge and its acceptance, and of course Wajai was prepared to receive us, though with an inferior force.

His canoes were ranged in the water, in front of his settlement, and as soon as we were near enough to distinguish features, our chief, Ahoundel, and Wajai sprung simultaneously to their feet, upon the platforms of their canoes, and flourishing their spears, set up a shout of defiance, the conches blowing an accompaniment. The inferior chiefs upon both sides then rose and joined in the cry, and the engagement commenced with hurling the stones with slings. The stones are seldom less than a pound in weight, and are thrown with tremendous precision, the parties being from thirty to forty yards apart. Several canoes were broken and sunk on both sides, and many men killed. The stones exhausted, arrows and spears followed; the parties nearing each other, till the battle was canoe to canoe, and hand to hand. The natives would seize each other by the hair, and thrust with a small wooden spear or lance, without barbs, and cut the flesh with sharp shells. In the onset Wajai was killed by one of the party in our canoe. A shout of joy on one side, and a murmur of grief on the other, suspended the battle a moment; but it was soon renewed with unabated fierceness. At length we forced a landing, and the vanquished or broken foe, failing to prevent it, also sprung on shore, and disputed every inch of ground, to the very doors of their houses. The land engagement was fought with the jagged spears and the short war-clubs. It may be necessary here to state that direct thrusts are seldom made with these spears; they are generally used for striking, and inflict mangling wounds in the flesh. The clubs which are worn in the belt, like a North American Indian's tomahawk, are the last resort, but are never hurled.

An hour and a half of hard fighting brought us to the estate of Wajai. The women had long before deserted the houses, taking with them such of their effects as they could conveniently transport, and the men, fairly overpowered, fled to the interior. No attempt had been made to take prisoners on either side, and the fugitives were not pursued. The natives of Bonabee, never slaughter in cold blood after a foe ceases to resist. Our party plundered the houses of whatever movables were left, set fire to them, and, returning to the beach, broke up the canoes of the foe, and taking with us the spears, mats, and other plunder, we returned to Nutt. We brought back such of our own dead as we could find, and the body of Wajai and other chiefs, who fell upon the other side.

For the credit of a people whose character is generally humane, for uncultivated savages, I should rejoice to stop here; but the truth compels me to speak of a custom differing so entirely from their usual character, that I am at a loss to account for it. Upon the next day after our return there was a feast held. The usual preparations of jago and dog venison were made, and the bodies of Wajai and his chiefs were burned; but previously to the entire consumption of the bodies by fire, the heart of Wajai was taken out, and presented to the chiefs on a large plantain leaf Whether it was eaten, or even tasted, I cannot say, as I was not present at the disgusting ceremony. The presumption, however, is, the eating the hearts of the chiefs killed in war is a custom with them. Of this I can speak only so far as I have spoken, having had but one opportunity for ascertaining. No other part of the body than the heart was eaten, and that rather as a ceremony than a gratification.

It was in the early part of the month of November, 1833, that I discovered a vessel from Nutt; the first vessel that I am positive of having seen while on the island of Bonabee. My comrades often said they saw vessels, and I frequently imagined that I did, but none approached near enough for us to distinguish their class. It was about sunrise in the morning when I first discovered her, and I called up George immediately. We ran to the top of the nearest hill, and anxiously watched her, as well as the mist and occasional rain would permit, for it was a dull morning. After we had satisfied ourselves that it was a European or American vessel, we ran down to the chief and informed him that there was a vessel in the offing, and that we wished to board her. He was not half so much elated at receiving the information as we were in imparting it. He eyed me some moments. "What!" said he, "a ship? No, no." I repeated my assurance, and led him to the hill. My wife and the whole household followed. George and I bounded about for joy, skipping up the hill, as if our feet could not serve us fast enough. The pace of our companions offered something of a contrast; they were still incredulous, and my wife and father were evidently hoping against the truth of my discovery, as they saw in my joy anything but a pleasant indication of my feelings respecting remaining upon the island. I pointed out the vessel, and satisfied them that it was not, as they supposed, and hoped it might be, a native war-canoe. I repeated my request for a canoe, assuring Ahoundel that I would make the vessel "*moondie*," literally, "*sit down*," or come to an anchor. At the canoe-house, whither Ahoundel, Laowni, my children, and others, followed me, Ahoundel granted his unwilling consent that I should go off to the vessel, following it up with questions, while Laowni anxiously watched the expression of my face for an answer. "Do you love your wife? your children? Do you love them much, very much? Will you certainly return?" To all this I answered yes, yes; and my heart smites me now, as I recollect the gratified expression of my wife's countenance upon receiving the assurance. A large canoe was prepared to launch, but the tide was out. We were obliged to wait for it two full hours! Oh the impatience we felt! the snail-like progress of time! Knowing perfectly well, had we been cool, the time of the tide, still we could not avoid running down every ten minutes to look. Meanwhile I prepared a quantity of tortoise shell, yams, bread-fruit and cocoanuts, to take off to the captain. We watched the vessel—she tacked and stood off—our hopes fell—she stood back again—we were reassured—she hove to, and we were happy, till we recollected we were tide-bound.

At length the tide served us to launch the canoe. Ahoundel and Laowni accompanied me to the boat, the former reminding me of my promise to bring him trinkets, the latter melancholy, and half doubting that she should see me again. There was a fleet of some dozen canoes beside mine. I was accompanied by Keenan, a young chief, and two natives. We went outside the reef, and had neared the vessel so that we could distinguish the men on her decks, when the native who had the steering oar let the canoe get into the trough of the sea. There was a tremendous sea on, and it was carelessness on my part, to let the paddle go from my hand; the consequence of getting the canoe broadside on to the sea was, that we were swamped. As is usual with the natives, we all jumped overboard, two taking the outrigger side and the others striving to bail out the canoe. There was, however, too much sea running, and all endeavors to bail the boat proved futile, while the tide and the swell were drifting us toward the reef. The young chief, who was quite a lad, made no ado, but cutting away the twine fastenings with his fish-shell knife, stripped the board off the outrigger, laid his breast across it, and paddled away like a dog, for the reef. Seeing no alternative, I disengaged the pole which formed the fore-and-aft part of the outrigger, and, with one of the natives, made also for the reef, with the pole beneath our breasts. As we reached the crests of the waves I could see the vessel, and the other more fortunate canoes every moment getting nearer to her. The very dress of the men on the vessel's deck was distinguishable. And here, in the very sight of the first white men, except our shipmates, that we had seen for years, George and I were apparently devoted to death, before we could exchange a word with them. I should have mentioned, that before leaving the canoe I fastened my mat to the mast and waved it, but the vessel's crew, imagining us natives, paid no attention to the signal. George, with one of the natives, remained with the canoe, contrary to my advice, as he insisted that a native of the island must know better how to conduct in an emergency like this than I could. In a few moments I heard him hailing, beseeching me for God's sake to wait for him to overtake me. The native who was my companion objected, and for a moment I listened to the Indian and paid no attention to the cries of my friend. My better feelings, however, prevailed, and I waited for my ship mate, who reached us panting with exertion, and seized the outrigger just as he was nearly exhausted. I had trembled for him, but it was impossible to turn back and face tide and surf. One moment and I caught a glimpse of his head on the top of a wave, the next he was invisible. My joy at the relief from suspense which his arrival gave was second only to his at reaching us.

We had by this time reached the surf. Taught by former experience, I watched the rollers, and when I saw one coming let go of the outrigger, faced the sea, and clasped my hands over my head. Down it came upon us, but my hands and arms broke the force of the water, and I was driven down, but emerged again, many feet nearer the reef. My companions, George and the native, followed my direction and example, and we rose nearly together. The outrigger was thrown upon the ledge at the second or third roll, and had we clung to it we should have been dashed to pieces among the rocks, by the force with which we should have been driven. The young chief had reached the ledge before us, and between our forced plunges we could see him encouraging us by swinging his mat. After being thus swamped five or six times we reached the rocks, more dead than alive, and crawled where the water had least force. Here, taking the pole of the outrigger, which, as before stated, had preceded us, I attached my mat to it, and made signals of distress. On board the schooner they paid no heed to it, although she stood at one time almost within hail of us. Taking us for natives, and supposing us used to such mishaps, her master thought we could manage for ourselves; had he, however, been inclined to assist us, no boat would have lived in the surf. We were two or three hours on the reef before we were discovered by the natives; then some fishing canoes came to us from the inside, where the sea was comparatively nothing, and the reef approachable, and took us off. One of the party, the native who remained with the canoe, was drowned, his body being picked up a day or two afterward among the rocks which formed the reef.

Upon reaching Nutt, Ahoundel was astonished with the story of our escape. The young chief described our conduct to him, and his astonishment was increased, that two white men should prove better or more fortunate swimmers than a native fisherman. We were weakened, and bruised, and sore, as the reader will readily conceive; but our bodily suffering was forgotten in our mental anxiety, as the last light of day showed us the schooner standing off shore. Would she return? The night long we passed in anxious doubt, and were out with the dawn to look for the sail. At length I saw her, just a speck. Heavens! how my heart leaped! A half hour more and the tide was right. The vessel, standing in, was now fairly visible, and, prepared with a fresh load of tortoise shell and provisions, with George and two natives for companions, I set sail again. As we went out by the reef, we were forcibly reminded of our escape of the preceding day, by a fleet of canoes which were paddling as near the reef as they dared, in search of the body of the drowned man. When we reached the schooner she was hove to, with her boarding nettings up, and her men mustered, with boarding pikes and muskets in hand, or at hand. Two or three other canoes got along side at the same time that we did, and others were coming off. Upon the day before no natives had been allowed to board the vessel, though a barter traffic for yams and bread-fruit was opened between the canoes and those on board the vessel. We passed under her stern, and I read the name, "Spy, of Salem." She was brig rigged forward, and schooner aft. Passing round to her weather bow, I sung out, "Shipmates, throw us a rope's end, will you?" There was a bustle on deck, a buzz of surprise, but no answer, and in a moment I heard somebody exclaiming, "Captain, the *natives* on this island speak English!" The anxiety to get a peep at us through the boarding netting was now redoubled, forward and aft. One of the men, after much hesitation, threw us a rope, and the captain came to the gangway and asked us on board, requesting us to keep the natives in the canoe, which we did. The captain did us the honor to ship the side-ladder for us, and George and I needed no second invitation to come on deck, but, taking up the tortoise shell with us, directed the natives to pass up the yams. To my first question the captain answered that the name of the island was Ascension, the group being laid down as one island on the chart. He inquired particularly into our story, and proceeded, while he did so, to offer us, with a sailor's hospitality, a rummer of grog. It was the first I had tasted for years, of course, and a bare swallow of it burned my throat, flushed my face, and played the deuce with my head altogether. Poor George was even worse flabbergusted than I was.

In answer to Captain Knight's inquiries, I assured him of the peaceable character of the islanders, and that there was abundance of tortoise shell and beche le mer for commerce, and yams, bread-fruit, water, and wood, for provision upon the islands. In a short time Captain Knight expressed a willingness that I should permit my natives to come on board, and we dropped the canoe astern. Other natives were not so fortunate; they huddled about the vessel, and, coveting iron, strove to pull out the iron work under the chains with their hands. The schooner filled away again, and we stood off with a fleet of canoes in tow, dashing and plashing through the water, their outriggers foul of each other, and getting continually carried away. I dined on board, with George, at the cabin table. The condiments of my own furnishing, with the salt provisions, ship bread, and butter, of the ship's stores, furnished a more savory meal than I had sat down to for many a day. I undertook to pilot the Spy inside the reef to an anchorage, at Captain Knight's request. At four or five o'clock in the evening she came to an anchor in the harbor of Matalaleme. By the natives who went that night to Nutt, I sent Ahoundel a large broadax and an adz, and to Laowni I sent beads, red kerchiefs, and other trinkets; while George and I remained on board, afraid to trust ourselves on shore again.

In the morning the vessel was again surrounded by canoes, and Captain Knight purchased of the natives, through me as an interpreter, tortoise shell and other articles, and one canoe, which he purposed to carry away as a curiosity. This was dropped astern and fastened by a rope to the counter. In about two hours from the time of purchasing some of the natives slipped into it, and before we were aware were making off with it, induced probably by some island superstition. Captain Knight immediately fired upon the thieves, and, lowering a boat, sent some men in pursuit; but it would have been impossible to have overtaken them, even if the water had not been too shallow in places for the keel of the boat. Captain Knight now began to fear that the natives intended to take his vessel, although George and I assured him to the contrary, and told him that their worst fault was an irresistible propensity to thieve, where they saw articles they so earnestly coveted. We represented to him that harsh treatment might bring about the very event he dreaded, and that, at any rate, the next vessel which came within their reach would suffer for his conduct. Still he was nervous, agitated, and acted like one beside himself, begging me to prevent treachery and keep the natives quiet. Instead of acting like a discreet person, which had he done, he might have lain at Matalaleme weeks, with profit, he blowed out the brains of a native who was climbing in at the cabin windows, and threw out the body. Luckily for Captain Knight, the murdered man was a common man, so that the dissatisfaction of the natives amounted only to a murmur; had he been a chief, the capture of the vessel and murder of the crew would have atoned for his death. It did not seem long to intimidate them, but after they had clamorously inquired of me the cause of his death, and I told them it was for thieving, they seemed, in a measure, satisfied that it was just. During the time that the Spy lay at Matalaleme no natives were permitted to come upon her deck, but stood in the chains, and in their canoes. No chiefs of note came off to the vessel at all—a precaution adopted by their friends, I presume, and in accordance with the habits and policy of the people; else so simultaneous a measure could not have been carried out by all the islands. In a short time after the native was shot in the cabin, a small swivel was hoisted into the foretop, charged with nails, slugs, and musket balls. Every fresh arrival of canoes put Captain Knight in additional perturbation; he had commenced hostilities, and even I began to have fear for the consequences. Constant persuasion, and even the exercise of authority, was necessary on my part, to prevent a rush upon the vessel, by the natives. At about ten in the morning the Spy got under way, and Captain Knight ordered his crew to fire upon the natives, and even wished Keenan and myself to take arms against people who had for five years been our friends and protectors. We flatly refused. The musket shots were answered by occasional stones hurled from the canoes, none of which took effect, save one, which struck the mate; but from being spent, or some other cause, it injured him but slightly. During all the time the number of the canoes about us rather increased than diminished, and I was in continual conversation and parley with the natives. They complained of the treatment of the Aroche tic-a-tic (petty chief) of the vessel. I answered that I was not to blame for it, and appealed to them for the fact that I had not taken up arms against them. I was anxious that a good report of my conduct should be carried back to Ahoundel.

As we beat out—for the wind was against us—fleet after fleet of the canoes, nothing daunted by the death of the few natives who had fallen, put off for us, from various parts of the group. The echo of a musket report in the harbor of Matalaleme, was of itself startling. It rang from rock to rock, and from hill to hill, probably for the first time; that generation of the islanders, at any rate, knew nothing of the use or character of firearms. Captain Knight's perplexity was doubled by his want of that knowledge of the harbor which was necessary to safe conduct of his vessel.

The sight of a fresh fleet putting off toward us made Captain Knight desperate. He sent a hand with a match into the foretop, clewed up the sail, and sent the charge of the swivel among the thickest of the fleet. I saw several natives drop like dogs over the sides of their canoes. There rose a howl of mingled rage and defiance among the survivors; but the cruel expedient answered the purpose—the natives fell back, and though they followed us far outside the reef, it was at a great distance. In the passage through the reef we narrowly escaped getting on the rocks. Had the vessel been wrecked, the lives of all on board would have answered the death of the natives. The crew of the next American or English vessel which touches at the island of Ascension will probably be sacrificed in revenge, should they fall, by any inadvertence, into the power of the islanders.

The shot from the foretop was not repeated. The mast was strained, and the sailor who officiated as gunner came down the backstays by the run, protesting he would not again fire the swivel. Nothing which occurred during my connection with the islands affected me so unpleasantly as the butchery of my friends by Captain Knight. Knowing perfectly the language and character of the people, I knew that, until they were roused to revenge by the death of the native, no thought of farther mischief than theft was entertained by them. This might easily have been guarded against by mild means; at any rate, the course taken did not answer

I proposed to Captain Knight, as we entered the harbor, that the vessel should lay there a month or six weeks, informing him of the quantities of beche le mer which I proposed to cure for him, taking the requisite tools from the vessel. I did not expect that anything but peace and good fellowship between the natives and the crew of the vessel would grow out of the visit; but the hasty and cruel conduct of Captain Knight marred it all. I was grieved at the death of the the natives; but I was astonished at the effrontery with which Captain Knight called upon us to fire upon our friends. We told him we were anxious to get away from the island, but that we should prefer to be set on shore again, rather than purchase our freedom by such an abuse of friendship.

Fairly out of the harbor of Matalaleme, the deportment of Captain Knight materially changed toward us. He was no longer the supplicant for intercession with the natives, but the master, imposing his authority upon us in every possible manner. In about fourteen days we made Guam, one of the Marian Islands, where Captain Knight would have left us, but the authorities would not permit it. By the way, I should have mentioned that the ship's cook was set ashore at Matalaleme, with his own consent, and I directed the natives into whose canoe he stepped to carry him to Ahoundel, and treat him well, for my sake. Whether he, and the four comrades whom I left upon the islands, did not fare worse for Captain Knight's conduct, I had no means of ascertaining; but must do the natives the justice to express the opinion, based upon a knowledge of their character, that they have too much benevolence and perception of right and wrong to abuse known friends for the conduct of strangers, though those strangers were of their color and language.

After leaving Guam, I had some altercation with Captain Knight, which resulted in no very agreeable consequences to myself. During the whole passage I had been sick, from a cold, exhaustion, fatigue, and derangement of my whole system, from the change of diet. Under my right arm was a large and very painful swelling. One night I had the watch from eight to twelve, the first two hours of which I spent on the topgallant yard, upon the lookout. When I came down I laid myself on the forecastle by the heel of the bowsprit, exhausted, and in agony from the swelling under my arm. Captain Knight came forward, and at the first intimation I had of his proximity was a kick. "What business have you here asleep, sir?" I pleaded my weakness and ill health, and the suffering I had already endured by the lookout at the masthead. He collared me, and I returned his grasp with interest; he freed himself from me, went aft, and returned with a brace of pistols in his hand, threatening to shoot me. I told him to do it; that I was tired of life, and would willingly die. He then let me alone for the night, and indeed we had no more words, but he hove to near the first land we made, lowered the boat, and ordered me into it. George insisted upon accompanying me, to which Captain Knight at first objected, but afterward consented. He then sent the second mate and two men with directions to leave the two Irish villians (he used a worse word) anywhere—on a rock, or a sand-bank, but not to bring them on board again. This was in the straits of Barnardino. Upon reaching the shore we found bullocks grazing, but saw no house, or shelter of any kind, and persuaded the second mate to take us back. He did so, and upon returning to the vessel told the captain that he could not drive us from the boat, but that we insisted upon coming back.

We were taken on board, and the vessel filled away again. I very foolishly, as the event proved, threatened Captain Knight that I would represent to the authorities at Manilla his treatment of the Indians at Ascension, and his abuse of me. Upon arrival at that port he anticipated me, making all sorts of charges against us, as runaways from punishment at New Holland, pirates who strove to cause the capture of his vessel by the Indians, and mutineers on board. Upon being boarded by the captain of the port at Manilla, just as we thought we had reached the end of our vexations and were in a way to return home, we were agreeably surprised by a present of leg safety-chains, and were placed, ironed, in the bows of the captain of the port's barge.

Captain Knight soon came down over the side, and seated himself under the awning in the stern sheets, with the captain of the port, the quarantine and custom-house officers; and as we sat, we could perceive we were the objects of the conversation. We bore this *talking at*, some time in silence, but tiring of it, I requested George to play his flute; which, by the way, as a memento of his residence on Ascension, he had taken care to keep with him. Accordingly he struck up St. Patrick's Day in the Morning, Garry Owen, and divers other merry Irish tunes, to the astonishment and edification of the boatmen, and, after awhile, to the amusement even of the officers in the stern sheets. We were pulled in this way alongside half a dozen vessels which had just entered the harbor, and endured the gratification of being pointed out to their crews as felons:—a story we took every opportunity to contradict. The feelings of the sailors were, of course, with us, and their half-expressed and doubtful sympathy was grateful, when all the rest of the world were disposed to frown.

After being paraded in this way about the harbor for half a day, we were landed, and marched with military honors up the street. We had reached a church—were famished with hunger, having eaten nothing since morning, and faint with exposure to the heat of a broiling sun. "Is it vespers you are taking us to? Well, prayer after fasting." The captain of our escort pointed to the opposite side of the street, and there, fronting the church, stood a less agreeable resort for sinners; one, like the church, not always sought voluntarily—the calabozo. They had the impoliteness to fasten the door at our backs when we entered.

Upon entering, we found ourselves in a sort of reception room, more convenient for its purposes than genteel, or elegantly furnished. It was separated from the rest of the prison by an iron grating, through which the friends of the prisoners conversed with them. Through this grating we saw a large hall, tenanted by prisoners, but were ourselves passed up a flight of stone steps, communicating with the second story. At the end of the room opposite the entrance was an altar and crucifix; and we were curious as to what was coming when we were led toward it. The marvel ceased, however, when a door near the crucifix was opened, and we were ushered into the jailor's office, and requested to favor him with our autographs in his album. This done, we were returned into the common hall, and an allowance of rice served out to us.

All this time we had no precise knowledge of the charges made against us, although we knew it was something in which Captain Knight had a hand. Upon the next day the interpreter, who, by the way, had honored us with his company until he saw the key safely turned upon us, paid us a visit. From him we learned what the reader has already been informed, that there were three distinct charges, either of which was sufficient to authorize the affectionate care taken of us; namely, piracy, escape from Botany Bay, and mutinous conduct. We inquired whether we should have a trial, and how soon; to which he replied, that we probably should. Of Capt. Knight we saw nothing, after leaving him at the landing, except one day, when he passed the prison, and I took the liberty to hail him by name, adding sundry expletives and titles, more applicable and graphic than melodious and beautiful. Days passed, and as a sort of desperate amusement, I commenced writing letters of complaint, and sending them out, directed to any English or American resident whose name I could learn. The rial a day, which was allowed us from some source I never could precisely learn what, to provide our provender, was, after awhile, taken off, and we were served with rice daily, and, once or twice a week, beef and fish.

Sailors, many of whom visited us, were in the frequent practice of making us small presents. With the money thus obtained, we sent and purchased bread and meat, but the eyes of Argus were necessary to prevent too frequent verification of the proverb, "many a slip 'twixt cup and lip." Even after our bit of meat was in the pot with the rice, and we were superintending its cooking, some dextrous Chinese thief would whip it out with his chop-sticks, if our eye strayed from it one moment. Each of the prisoners is obliged to prepare his own food, in a portion of the prison set apart for that purpose.

All sorts of ingenious modes of punishment were practiced upon the prisoners for misdeeds while there. It would almost seem the Chinese ingenuity of torture, tempered by a little more regard for humanity than the officers of his Celestial Majesty possess. Stocks, confining the culprit in all sorts of positions, many of which were as ludicrous as uncomfortable, clogs, irons, and collars, and devices, the description of which would tire, were in continual exercise. Flogging was going on all day, but the poor devils of Chinese came in for more than a proportionate share of it, and the blows were laid on with more hearty good-will, as they were heretics.

To give variety to our life, we had an occasional opportunity of seeing a tenant in the pillory, opposite the prison. Here, too, during the time we lay in jail, we saw two or three executions, done in a manner to which the Turkish bowstring is tender mercy. I shall spare the reader the description of a method of strangulation the most horrible possible; only remarking, that in a country where the office of the executioner is so directly instrumental to the death of the criminal, and his duty so cruel and protracted, it is no wonder that even criminals, the most debased, despise the hangman.

At the rear of the prison ran a river or canal. On the opposite bank stood a church, and near this lay what appeared to us a pile of human bones. When I tired of watching the passengers in the street in front, I looked out upon the church, and noted that no Catholics passed it without making a genuflection. At night, the spot was marked by a taper burning before the image of some saint, and I found myself frequently looking toward that church. I wondered if, among the bones there preserved upon consecrated ground, there lay the relics of any person so much the sport of fortune as myself, who had fallen, unwept and unattended, in a strange land. During no period of my residence upon the Carolines had I felt so utterly dispirited and forsaken, as I did, at times, in the prison at Manilla. I had made repeated applications for trial, besieged every person whose address I could learn with letters; the only effect of which was to bring two English merchants to the prison, to tell us that, as we came in an American vessel, as part of her crew, they could do nothing for us. The American consul, and Mr.

Sturgis, an American resident, visited us in about a week after our committal.

We were not without amusement. George had brought his violin and flute, of course, and I had not forgotten the exercise of my heels. Then, in the various assemblage, there was ample amusement in watching the different disposal of time, according to character. The Chinese were most of them merchants, in a small way, vending tobacco, betel, and other "notions," as a Yankee would say, and there is no better word in the world. Stock in trade was not wanting, while there was a chance to exercise their expert fingers in tricks of sleight-of-hand. Others would operate as barbers, tailors—they had a thousand resources for busy idleness. Spanish blood showed itself in games of chance—cards, draughts, dominoes—and the parties would sit as gravely and intently engaged as if they had been recreating in the palace of a grandee. An occasional industrious one wove hats; and cooking their pilau was the periodical occupation of all hands.

I indulged in an occasional game of draughts with one of my fellow-prisoners, a Spaniard. It did very well, till, one day, he tried to cheat me out of the game. The stake was not worth quarreling about, but it was the point of pride. We wrangled, I collared him, and was reported. As a punishment, I was ordered into the lower prison, and George, my shadow, was moved with me. This apartment, sacred to the lowest rogues, was by no means so light and pleasant as the upper one. There is a choice, even in prisons.

Here I resumed the amusement of dispatching letters; continuing it until, one day, the deputy jailor came to me with orders to put me in close confinement. I resisted, and in the scuffle was severely bruised, and my rigging dismantled. Preparatory to my solitude, and to give me food for reflection during its continuance, I was seized down to a bench and beaten with cowhides. Upon entering the cell which was to be my temporary residence, I found that the happiness of entire solitude was to be denied me, and was compelled to accept the society of a Spanish officer, who was waiting transportation to Cadiz, and trial for murder upon his own confession.

Previous to my committal to the cell, two attempts were made to compel me to ship on board vessels, one of which was the Dash, an American brig or barque, I have forgotten which. She was bound to the Fejees; but, as I had already had enough of the Pacific Ocean, I peremptorily refused to sign articles, and was remanded to prison. The other was a Spanish vessel, and I declined, in terms more positive than polite, to go in her. The American consul gave me a rating for annoying the residents with letters, and for refusing to go away by the opportunities he provided for me. After these adventures I was confined in the cell, as before stated, and could not, in my own mind, avoid connecting them as, at least, partial cause and effect.

The burden of my complaint had been the delay of a trial. Why was no attempt made to substantiate the charges made against me? Why no opportunity given me to disprove them? The treatment I endured would have been adequate punishment for any crime short of willful murder. Beaten, half-starved, and worse than all, thrust, ironed, into a noisome cell with a murderer; a portion of the time bolted to the floor of that cell, and upon three successive Sabbaths paraded with my room-mate to prayers, before all the prisoners, who classed me with the murderer; and all this without the show of any reason, or the pretense of it. No *formal* charge was ever made, or, if made, was ever prosecuted. Upon our egress from the prison, Mr. Sturgis gave George and me five dollars, and the consul procured us a passage to Macao in a Spanish ship.

The prison was a miniature Pandemonium—a little hell, where the worst passions and propensities of the brutal officers who managed it had license unrestrained. I have been fastened in a position painful of itself, my legs extended and arms confined, while two brutes administered flagellation with heavy cowhides. In the struggle which preceded my being thrust into the dungeon, my body was so completely denuded of clothing, that, in the cold, damp cell, I was fain thankfully to accept the comfort of a portion of the mat of the miserable felon who was the occupant of the cell with me. Even the sorry privilege of perambulation about my narrow quarters was, during a portion of the time, denied me. Heavy irons upon my feet, bolting them about three feet apart, were connected with a chain to my left arm, compelling me to keep the arm straight by my side, when I stood erect. The bolt between my legs was, during about a week of the three I spent in the cell, fastened to a ring-bolt in the floor. The food served me there was a miserable pittance of half-boiled rice, floating in three times the quantity of water necessary to cook it. This, with two small broiled fish, was barely sufficient to sustain my miserable existence. Never, during my life, did I so utterly despair as when confined in this horrid hole, seeing no person except my convict companion, save when, upon the Sabbath, I walked in my irons to the altar, to see the institutions of religion profaned in a place where its dictates were utterly set at naught. For all this, decency would seem to require, at least, the form of an examination upon the charges preferred by Capt. Knight; but no such form, to give my confinement a color of justice, ever took place. Upon my liberation, the Spy had been sold, and Capt. Knight had left Manilla. His unsupported word had been sufficient to throw me into the power of these demons, and, careless of my fate, he left me there. The inquiry may be made, why, if my confinement was so irksome, I did not gladly embrace the first opportunity to escape from it. To this I answer, that the worst part of my punishment did not take place till after I had so refused, and that my principal reason for refusing was my unwillingness to leave George, unfriended, in a prison. We had been together so long, and had become so endeared to each other by a participation in good and ill fortune, that to separate was even more painful than to endure the worst that the prison would inflict. I knew that no constitution, even the most iron, could long bear up under the hard usage and scanty food; the records were before me in the names of British and American citizens carved on the guard-bed. Under many of these, survivors had written the date of the death of the persons who cut them there; and the mate of the Spanish vessel in which I left Manilla, who was an American, and had himself been a prisoner in Manilla, informed me that he had known many instances where foreign sailors had fallen victims to the combined ill effects of the climate and the prison.

Arrived at Macao, we were thence sent to Canton. At Canton, we were objects of curiosity, and were visited by merchants and others connected with the English Factory; our tattooing examined, and our story of shipwreck and residence on the Carolines was repeated two or three times a day, during the week we remained there. Through those gentlemen, the owners, and others interested in the John Bull, probably, heard of the loss of that vessel, if it had not before been published by our shipmates who took the other boats. Of the fate of any except those who escaped in the boat with us, I have never heard a syllable. It may be that they found their way to other islands in the Pacific, and it may be that they perished at sea.

SUCCESSFUL RESISTANCE OF THREE SAILORS AGAINST SEVERAL THOUSAND SAVAGES.

THE story of O'Connell well illustrates the superiority of even one civilized man over multitudes of his savage fellow-men. By means of this superiority, the European, or American, cast upon a barbarous shore, will often, indeed, will commonly, secure assistance and support from those who must respect his greater intelligence, and will desire to profit by his acquired knowledge, both so much superior to their own. Most of the instances of the slaughter of sailors or travelers by the barbarians of Oceanica, which have come to our knowledge, have evinced either great imprudence or criminal conduct on the part of these victims of savage fury. The following account of the successful contest of three English sailors with a large tribe of cannibal assailants, while it illustrates the superiority of civilized weapons and civilized courage and skill, seems also to show that this was a case of unprovoked assault of disappointed rage, upon brave and innocent men.

Mr. Dillon was an officer of the ship "Hunter," commanded by Captain Robson, who had made many voyages to the Fejee Islands, and enjoyed a certain influence with the natives, from having interested himself in their dissensions and contests. Bonassar, the chief of Wailea, in particular, was his friend.

The nineteenth of February, 1813, the Hunter came to anchor in the Bay of Wailea, opposite a small river which leads to the village, lying at half a league distance from the shore, and situated upon an elevated spot.

When Robson had fairly established himself in the harbor, he received a visit from his old friend Bonassar, who told him that, in his absence, fortune had turned against him, and that the tribes which had once submitted were again in revolt, and had called to their aid other and more powerful tribes, which had caused a bloody and disastrous war. Bonassar expressed the hope that the visit of his old friend would help to improve his affairs, and insinuated that the necessity of defending the court would prevent the natives from going to the mountains to gather sandal-wood for the Hunter, unless the captain would come to his assistance against his enemies. Bonassar's welcome to his friend was, in other respects, not less cordial nor frank than usual. At this time, a number of European sailors, either deserters or shipwrecked on the island, were in the service of several of the chiefs, well treated, and made much of by their savage friends.

Captain Robson sought to evade the urgency of Bonassar, but was, at length, over-persuaded by the promise of a supply of sandal-wood, and lent him twenty musketeers, three small boats, and a cannon carrying two-pound ball. Accompanied by an army of three or four thousand savages, they made an attack on the hostile island of Nanpakob, which was soon conquered, and the dead bodies of its inhabitants, cut limb from limb, and rolled in green leaves, were roasted with the taro-root, to furnish a feast to the victors. Robson had fulfilled his part of the contract, but Bonassar would not comply with his promise. Under diffeient pretexts, the loading was delayed, and, finally, the natives ceased to come aboard, fearing they might be seized and kept as hostages.

This made Robson furious, and he attacked the fleet of Bonassar, and captured fourteen of his vessels. Subsequently he made a more general attack, with the intention of entirely destroying the military power of the Fejee chief. In this engagement the fatal mistake of separating his men into small detachments was made, which gave the cunning savages an opportunity to cut them off in detail, by means of crafty ambuscades. When a retreat became necessary, the small party to which Dillon belonged was under the command of Normon, the mate, who fell, pierced by a lance, leaving the command to him. Everything then looked desperate to the party, and nothing seemed left but to sell their lives as dearly as possible, when Dillon perceived, in the midst of the plain, an isolated rock, abrupt and inaccessible, a kind of fortress placed there for their safety—a rampart of nature's making, to whose summit the arrows of the natives could hardly reach. To see this refuge, to point it out to his companions, and to direct his steps toward it, was but the work of a moment. Dillon established himself in this aerie, with Savage, Burhart, Duprey and Wilson, Europeans, and a Chinaman, named Luis. The rest of the detachment had been killed, and Duprey himself was pierced with a lance, beside having four arrow-wounds in his back. Fortunately for these poor fellows, the rock, accessible only on a single side, was easy to defend.

Meanwhile, the fury of the savages became a little calmed, and a parley was agreed upon. Among the prisoners taken by Robson, and carried on board the Hunter, was a brother of the high priest of Vai-Tea. To this priest, Dillon proposed an exchange of the savages, in confinement, for him and his companions, which was agreed to, and Duprey was sent on board, together with the priest, to perfect the arrangement. Meantime, the chief of the Fejeeans approached the base of the rock, and sought to entice the Europeans from their posts. To all their promises, Dillon turned a deaf ear, and counseled his companions to do the same. But one of them, Savage, who had lived among them for several years, trusting in their good faith, descended the rock, and placed himself under the protection of Bonassar, who welcomed him with great seeming cordiality. This induced Luis, the Chinese, to do the same, and to claim the protection of one of the chiefs to whom he had formerly rendered several services. Thinking that with these two examples, Dillon would be induced to come down, they renewed their solicitations, but in vain. Then throwing off their mask, the savages raised a great cry, seized Savage, plunged his head in a ditchful of water, and speedily dispatched him, while a blow from another of the murderers made an end of the Chinese. Dismembered and roasted, these poor fellows were soon eaten under the eyes of Dillon.

There now remained upon the rock, only Dillon, Burhart, and Wilson—three men against many thousand assailants. Thinking they now should have it their own way, the savages recommenced the attack with new fury. Burhart, a skillful marksman, shot twenty-seven of the assailants in twenty-nine shots. Dillon also dispatched a large number. Wilson confined himself to loading the muskets of his two companions. Soon the outside of their citadel became encumbered with dead bodies, when the savages, fearful of provoking almost certain destruction, ceased further attack, for the present, trusting that the darkness of night, or hunger, would, sooner or later, deliver their victims into their hands.

Then scenes of horrible cannibalism were practiced under the eyes of the Europeans. The limbs of their dead companions were drawn from the fire, and divided among the tribes, who devoured them with horrible ferocity; but occasionally ceasing their repast to taunt Dillon and his companions, with the assurance that to-morrow they also would be roasted and eaten. To Dillon's threat, that if they were killed, the native prisoners on board would likewise be killed, the cannibals only answered, "Bah! bah! Captain Robson may eat our friends if that will do him any good; but we will eat you there to-morrow, any how."

When night came, their situation was painful in the extreme. They had but seventeen cartridges left, and the first attack of the savages must deliver them into the hands of their pitiless enemies. None of them were willing to be taken alive by these feeders on human flesh, and were about agreeing to destroy their own lives, when, for a moment, their hopes were raised by seeing a boat put off from the Hunter, and steer directly for the land. But what was their amazement and regret, when they saw that the commander had committed the unpardonable fault of releasing the whole number of prisoners, thus cutting off all chance of escape for them. What motive could now induce the natives to spare them, when all fear of reprisals had been taken away?

"A little afterward," says Dillon, in his narrative of these events, "the released prisoners came to me without arms, led on by their priest, who said that Captain Robson had sent a case of cutlery, and other things, to the chiefs, as our ransom, to whom we were also ordered to surrender our arms. The priest added, that, in case we complied, he would conduct us safely to our boats. To all this, I replied, that while a breath of life remained in me, I would deliver my musket to nobody: it was my own property, and I should hold on to it, certain that if I gave it up, I should be treated as my dead companions had been. Failing with me, the priest turned to Martin Burhart, and sought to persuade him to acquiesce in his proposal. At this moment the idea entered my head to make a prisoner of the priest, and either to kill him, or to obtain my liberty in exchange for his. Seizing a gun, I presented it at the priest, threatening to kill him if he attempted to escape, or if any of his party made the least movement toward attacking us, or to hinder in any way our retreat. I then ordered him to march for the boat in a direct line, menacing him with instant death, if he disobeyed. He did as he was directed, and while traversing through the crowd of savages, he exhorted them to be quiet, and do no harm, for if they assailed us, we would kill him, which would bring down upon them the wrath of the gods in the clouds, who, irritated at their disobedience, would cause the ocean to swallow up them and their island. The natives obeyed his orders, and sat down, while we marched toward the boat. When near the landing, the priest stopped short, refusing to stir another step, and saying we might kill him if we wished. I threatened him, but without effect. He said our object was to take him on board our ship, in order to torture him. As we had no time to lose, I ordered him to stand still, while we, marching backward, with our guns all pointed at him, soon reached one of our boats. We were scarcely embarked, before a cloud of arrows and stones darkened the air, but we soon found ourselves beyond the reach of their bows and slings."

PADDOCK'S NARRATIVE

OF

BONDAGE AMONG THE ARABS,

DETAILING THE SUFFERINGS OF THE MASTER AND CREW OF THE SHIP OSWEGO, UPON THE

COAST OF SOUTH BARBARY.

On the 8th of January, 1800, says Captain Judah Paddock, in his narrative, I left New York in the Ship Oswego, of Hudson, of which I was the commander, with a cargo of flaxseed and staves on freight, bound to Cork. Our passage out was very rough, but we arrived there in 24 days. After lying a few days and finding nothing better to employ the ship in, I concluded to ballast her and go to the Cape de Verd Islands, and take a load of salt, skins etc., for New York. While the ship was preparing for the voyage, I was able to collect about 1200 Spanish dollars, besides 600 dollars in gold. While in Cork we had heard of several instances of vessels being robbed on the coast of Spain, by vessels bearing the French flag. The truth of these reports I will leave, but thought if they were to rob me of the 1200 dollars it should require some time to find them. Accordingly I took a small keg, just large enough to contain the money, at my lodgings, and packed it snug. At a late hour in the evening, everything being prepared, I took the keg on board while all were asleep but my officers; unheaded a barrel of beef, took one half out, put the keg in the middle of the barrel, filled it up again, stowed it away along side the keelson, and put the other provisions over it as they were before. None of our crew knew anything of this transaction till some time after we were wrecked.

On the 22d of March, a fine breeze at N. N. W. and fair weather, we put to sea. In the afternoon, while arranging my papers, it occurred to my mind that we had a man on board who had not signed the shipping articles, and, sending for him down, and presenting them for signing, he, to my astonishment, refused, by saying he did not belong to the ship, and knew better than to sign any such articles. I ordered him out of the cabin, and, sending for the mate, I told him his man, as I called him, refused signing the shipping articles. The mate was exceedingly provoked at it. We sent for the man again, and he making use of the same language, I threatened to put him ashore on the first place we should stop at, and as he still persisted, we sent him out of the cabin a second time, declaring he should be put on board the first British ship of war that we should fall in with.

I will now relate the story of that man's being in the ship. A few days before sailing from Cork, I went on board the ship, and saw a stranger at the caboose; on asking the mate who he was, he informed me he came on board the day before, as ragged and dirty as he ever saw a man, and begged to work his passage home; that he pitied his condition, gave him some pieces of clothing, and put him to the caboose, and had found him a good cook. I suspected he was some runaway sailor, and told the mate to put him ashore, and went myself below. As soon as the fellow found he was to be landed, he came below, and begged very hard to go to America, saying he was very poor, that the times were so hard he could not get a living in the country he came from, and that he had no family nor friends: he really appeared an object of pity. I told him I suspected he was some runaway sailor or soldier; he denied that he had ever been either. I then concluded to let him remain a day or two on board, more especially as the mate pleaded so hard for him. When I went on shore, I mentioned the circumstance to some of my friends who had seen him on board, and thought he was to be pitied, and that I had better take him. I have been more particular in stating this thing, in order to prepare the reader for what will be related concerning that fellow hereafter.

Nothing material happened from the time of our leaving Ireland to the 3d of April, being then twelve days from land; and having had moderate and variable gales with fine weather, and also several opportunities to ascertain the exact variation of the compass, we had every reason to believe our reckoning was right. Toward night of this day, as I was sitting in the cabin, and reflecting on our situation as to our passage track, etc. I was led to look over my reckoning again, feeling some uneasiness that I cannot easily describe. When the boy brought our tea down I took up my books and papers, and gave him the table, and as soon as his things were arranged I sent him to call the mates; it was now near dark; he returned, and said the mates were forward at work, and could not come yet. I drank some tea, and laid down with my clothes on, thinking to go on deck at 8 o'clock, which was near at hand. Having been hard at work all the day, I was somewhat fatigued, and unexpectedly fell asleep. I awoke at the sound from striking four bells; was on my feet feeling for my hat, and with no light burning, when I heard an unusually loud noise. The first thought that struck me, was of a man being overboard. Before getting out of the gangway I distinctly heard those forward crying out, Breakers Breakers right ahead! and several of the crew were running aft. I saw nothing, nor did I look forward, but ran to the helm to put it up; too late, for it was hard down, or nearly so. I put my hand on the tiller-head, and bore it hard to the rail, when, in a moment, the ship flew to, head to the wind, our yards being a little pointed or braced. By this time all hands were on deck, and a number aft, to haul round the after yards. We were on the point of hauling, when I discovered her to fall off. At that moment we hauled up the mizzen, she having such quick stern way with the helm yet down, the main and mizzen topsail kept shivering or edging to the wind; the jib and fore staysail sheets being hauled flat, she fell off remarkably quick, every man using his greatest exertions. When she began to gather headway, the helm righted with the wind at least two points on the starboard quarter, wanting not more than once her length of coming round, heading off shore; at that moment she struck tremendously heavy, all the cabin windows came in, and part of the sea came over the taffle rail. She struck twice more in the hollow of the two next seas, and floated, running perhaps three or four times her length, and struck again, and stopped with every sea breaking over us, no land in sight, and we seemingly swallowed up by the raging ocean foaming terribly around us. Her stern soon drove round, so as to bring the sea on our beam, and at every thump she rolled off, with her gunwale near to the water. By this time we saw the land at no great distance from us.

We had now recovered a little from our fright, when I desired the men to go into the hold and shovel the ballast in shore, to prevent her rolling off; in the meantime those of us left on deck braced our yards as hard aback as could be done, to keep her on. In half an hour, with the assistance of the sails and by shifting the ballast, she had beat up so high on the rocks as to lay pretty still; yet every sea rolled some part of it on deck. Before as much of the ballast was shifted as I wished, one of our men came on deck in great haste, and informed me that the ship was sinking, the water coming in amain: it was some time before I could convince him, that though she might be filling, she could not sink any lower, being already on the rocks.

We were in this situation some short time, saying very little to each other, standing by the mizzen mast and holding to the rigging that was hanging all around us, when two or three of our men came aft, and asked me on what coast we were stranded? I told them my fears were that we were on the coast of Barbary, but I had a faint hope that it was one of the Canary islands; that daylight only would determine it, and we must be patient for its approach. It was now about midnight. One of them told me that those forward thought the ship would go to pieces before morning. I used every argument in my power to convince him of their error, telling him the ship was sound, and as strong as wood and iron could make her; that she never had a cargo in her before this one; that she had been employed in the whale fishery from the time she was new, and had never been overstrained. He returned forward only for a short time, when several of them came aft, and proposed to go ashore: that proposal made me shudder. I told them it would, from every appearance, be present death to attempt it, as we now had a considerable view of the hideous rocks within, and could plainly see the impracticableness of ascending them, and that another important point to be considered was, in case they should land in safety, the boat would be dashed to pieces; that she was a very large long-boat, new, and never afloat; that in her, with a temporary deck, which could be made in a few hours, we all might either land there, or go to any other place we should choose; and that if we were on the coast of Barbary, it would be absolutely necessary for us to have a craft to get to the Canaries or some other place, having no reason to expect much mercy from the natives of that country.

This reasoning I thought would have a good effect, and so it seemed at first, for all was quiet. But very soon a new proposition came, and that was to cut away the masts, as by their standing there would be danger of the ship's coming to pieces; and they told me if I would consent to have them cut away, they would stay till morning. I ordered my second mate to take the carpenter's ax from the tool-chest on deck and begin cutting away. When I saw the mast was about half cut off, I told one of them to get into the mizzen chains and cut the lanyards and let them go. He got into the chains and cut one lanyard, and raised himself up very deliberately and said, "It is all —— nonsense, we will go ashore." As grating as that expression was, prudence forbade my making a reply, or noticing it. They all assembled again under the lee of the long-boat, the officers excepted, and held a council. We soon saw them getting up the boat-tackles to the fore and main yards. I began then to reason with them upon the impropriety of that measure, when the only reply I heard, was, "We are in duty bound to take care of ourselves, and not stay here and drown." I went aft to my mates, who had said but very little during the time we had been in this situation, and asked them their opinion of the measure that was about to be pursued. If I recollect aright, my second mate, who was a good young man, said he should prefer staying by the ship. On the contrary, the chief mate, without hesitation, said it was his opinion that we should take the boat, and land; that he had once been shipwrecked in the West Indies; when choosing to stay by the wreck rather than to leave it, he very narrowly escaped death, and had then made up his mind, that, in a like situation, he would always leave the wreck the first opportunity: yet that, in the present case, seeing how anxious I was to stay by the wreck, he, although of the contrary opinion himself, would have been silent if I had prevailed on the crew to have stayed. He was an excellent seaman, a firm determined man, and had kept our men under the best discipline.

Matters by this time were all settled. Go ashore, was the word; the tackles were soon on the yards, and the boat hoisted out. So great was the haste on leaving the ship, that neither provisions nor water were put in: I hove in one trunk, and took my gold, which had been always under my pillow. So, off we pushed, and rowed toward the land, and the nearer it we gained, the more hideous was the appearance. We succeeded at last in reaching the rocks, when two men jumping out, without the boat's rope, the under-tow was so strong that it carried the boat half way back to the ship, where she was placed broadside to the sea, and was near filling. Our oars were so well plied the second time, that we soon reached the rocks again, when two men having the rope, jumped on them, and were assisted by the first two, who had acted before out of fear, rather than from any unfeelingness toward their shipmates; and now assisted to hold the boat in a situation for us all to get safe on the rocks; which done, every one with all his strength, hauled the boat as far up as possible. We then crawled over those slippery rocks, perhaps from ten to twelve feet high, to a sand bed, a little beyond which appeared a high hill, upward of a hundred feet in altitude. There we wrung the water from our clothes, and walked the sand some time, when my mates and myself ascended this sand hill; it being dark, we could see nothing, nor did we expect to see anything except the light of fire. After walking a little while on this mountain of sand, we descended again to the place where our men had remained, who had forgotten their cares in sound sleep. As to ourselves, we walked the sand all that night, bemoaning our condition, being pretty well assured that we were in no other place than the coast of Barbary. The ship was in sight, with all sails standing; the wind blew very fresh about four points on shore, and we thought it probable that her masts would go by the board before morning; a light was burning in the cabin.

On the morning of the 4th of April, as soon as the day began to dawn. I ascended the high mountain of sand, and there remained till near sunrise. What could I see? A barren sand, without either tree or shrub, or the least appearance of vegetation, dreary in every respect; and at a distance back, a long range of mountains extending east and west. Turning my view toward the ocean, and beholding the ship lying in the surf with her sails aloft, while thirteen of my shipmates were standing together before my eyes! I laid myself down on the sand, and gave vent to my grief by a flow of tears.

As soon as I had composed myself a little I descended, and joined my crew, who were waiting with the greatest anxiety to know what I had seen. When I had related my tale, and giving my opinion as to our hopes of the future, we began to devise means to get back to our ship. Upon examining our long-boat, we found her garboard streak was staved and shattered for several feet, and that a hole in another plank had been broken through by the sharp corner of a rock and that she lay from ten to fifteen feet below where it was possible to repair her; while a fine yawl of sixteen feet was hanging in the tackles over the stern of the ship. The poor fellow who, the night before, was the ringleader in the project for landing at all events, was now the first to exclaim; "Had we done as the captain advised us, we should now have been in a situation to go anywhere in so fine a boat as this!" Upon which, I took occasion to caution him and all the others against disobedience; there being then no greater proof necessary than that before their eyes to convince them all of the error they had committed.

Our first object was to get back to the ship for a supply of provisions and water, and also of spars and tackles to raise the long-boat for repairs; we feeling in hopes that all could be effected before any discovery of us should be made by the natives. Marks of horses and asses were visible on the beach, but, from appearances, it had been some considerable time since they had been there. One of our sailors said he could swim to the ship, which was at a distance of not more than a hundred yards. He made many attempts, but failed; the difficulty was in getting beyond the breakers. The next attempt was made by black Sam, who, after two or three hard efforts, succeeded in getting through the breakers, but his strength was so much exhausted that he sunk. Next, two or three of our men went in, following the undertow, or recession of the surf; then they plunged in and seized hold of Sam, and found no difficulty in returning, as the first surf hove them all up together, and those on the shore helped them out. He was entirely helpless and apparently almost gone· we laid him on the rocks, face down, and by moderately rolling and moving him he was made to discharge much water from his mouth, and in a few hours recovered so far as to walk a little. Several others attempted it, but all their attempts proved abortive.

The next plan was to make a raft, in order to pole off to the outer side of the breakers. Timber for that purpose was not lacking, as many parts of a wreck were lying along shore, as far each way as the eye could discern. We took part of the lower yard of a heavy ship, along with some pieces of small spars, enough for our purpose, and lashed them together with the boat's rope; when the second mate, a very strong man, and two good sailors, with each an oar for a pole, launched them off. However, after a fair trial, we found it impossible to gain the ship. I was then about taking my turn to swim, and to gain the ship by a method I had seen practiced by the Portuguese at Madeira, when they went off shore merely for their amusement; that was, to follow the receding water as low as possible, and dive or dart through the breaker, and when once got without, the difficulty was surmounted. But my mate, after observing to me that we were all so weak with fatigue and want of water, that if we did not board the ship very soon we never should at all; he proposed trying himself the experiment first, and, in case of failure, that I should make the last trial. Accordingly he stripped and followed down, and in less than five minutes from the time of starting he was at the ship.

It was not late in the afternoon, and a general rejoicing took place. The rudder was unhung, which served very well as a bridge for him to pass on to the cabin windows, where he entered her. As soon as he had quenched his burning thirst he came on deck, made the deep sea-line fast to an oar, and darted it ashore; and that served as a hauling-line for others to get off by; three went off by it, with directions how to pass our goods on shore Having a cask of whale line on deck, I ordered a single block to be made fast to the mizzen topmast head, and through it rove this line, sending the end ashore, and keeping the bite on deck.

They scuttled the water-casks in the hatchway, which were found floating in the hold; filled all the jugs and kegs, and put what bread was found between decks in bags, and run them aloft by this line; as they veered we hauled: by keeping a taut line our goods were landed dry. The whole of the provisions saved by us consisted of about forty pounds of bread, a small quantity of potatoes and onions, and a bag of Indian corn; our other dry provisions were in the lower hold and destroyed by the salt water. Being placed high on the rocks, we succeeded in landing everything perfectly dry which would be injured by the wet. In the same manner we landed our clothes, beds, etc., together with a spare foresail for a tent. In that affair of landing our goods we committed an act of imprudence which I cannot forbear mentioning as a caution to others who may be unfortunately placed in the like circumstances. The mate sent, among other things, my case, containing six gallons of equal parts of rum, gin, and brandy, and a hamper of port wine and porter. At the moment, I did not think it any harm to have this liquor sent ashore: but more of this matter in its place.

A little after sunset our men landed in the yawl, leaving a rope fast to the ship with one end to the shore. In the meantime, having erected our tent, we boiled some meat, and had a good supper prepared. At eight o'clock we divided ourselves into watches, and set the watch, who were to sit or stand outside of the tent, and be relieved every two hours, with orders, in case of any person or persons approaching, to wake us up in the tent, and, if possible, to secure them without noise. All things being arranged, my mates and myself concluded to begin early in the morning, and to land every article that should be necessary for repairing the boat, which we thought might be repaired in two days so as to be ready for our departure; as we had new canvas sufficient for putting on her a canvas-deck supported by carlings or beams. It was late before we went to sleep. At daylight, on the 5th, the watch called all hands, and we went to work. A little before breakfast I took a turn on the hill with my glass. The sun shone on the mountains, which made a very handsome appearance. I had a strong desire to know whether there were any inhabitants there; if there were any, the chance, I thought, was very much against our getting off before being discovered. I mentioned this thing to my mates, who, with me, thought well of sending a man on that errand. One soon volunteered to go; and as soon as breakfast was over he took a bottle of water and two cakes of bread, and started, with orders to keep a bright lookout, and in case he discovered any persons, to conceal himself from their view, and return as soon as he could. We had a compass on shore, by which we found that the shore lay due east and west; and ten or twelve miles westward of us a Cape projected into the sea in a very square bluff.—Not knowing where we were, I proposed for one man to walk westward and survey that Cape, intending to get the altitude of the sun at noon, to ascertain our latitude, and if from where we saw the bluff the land shaped southerly, he should follow it along as far as only to give time to return at night. I thought if that was Cape Nun, he would find Nun river.

This second man was soon ready to start, with the same stock of provisions and water, and bearing the same orders as the first one. By this time we had commenced landing the carpenter's tools, and the materials for raising the boat, etc. Every man seemed disposed to do his duty freely, but so many little accidents happened that we got along very slowly: what was done before dinner did not amount to much, nor did we think of a quadrant, our minds being occupied about things of more importance. In the afternoon we progressed considerably well, and by night we were prepared to commence repairing the boat, which was to be begun the next morning. Some time before night, with the glass I saw a person on the beach, a long way to the westward, and soon made him out to be our man; it being then at least three hours sooner than I had expected him. As he approached nearer, I discovered that he walked quick; and fearing some bad news, I went on to meet him. As soon as we were near enough to speak to each other, I asked him what was the matter with him, for he really looked frightened. He asked me if I knew what kind of people inhabited this country. I told him I did not, but was apprehensive they were the Arabs. He said, they are man-eaters! Upon asking him how he knew it, he replied, about twelve miles from us is that Cape you see there: I went on it, and there I saw a heap of human bones, and near them a fire had been made within a few days; and adding, the Lord have mercy on us! he began to weep. In a short time he collected himself, when I told him I did not believe these people were man-eaters, though the fire near human bones certainly indicated something like it, and that if he told the story in the tent I should despair of getting away; that our people would fall into a state of despair, and nothing would be done. He made me a solemn promise not to mention anything of the kind, and I believe he was true to that promise.

After this, we returned to the tent, where our people were all assembled, waiting for supper. We observed that Pat had as much to say as any of them, and that, ever since we landed, he had taken some liberties unbecoming a man in his station, and unsuitable to the gloomy condition we were in.—I examined the liquor-case, and found it had not been opened since noon, when each man had a small allowance of rum. After supper, and near dark, we went upon the hill, to look out for the man who had been dispatched to the mountains, and stayed about the place till quite dark, but had no sight of him. We became very uneasy about him; some were of the opinion that he had been devoured by wild beasts, and others that he had found inhabitants on the mountains who detained him. This talk lasted half an hour, and we then returned to the tent, where we all joined in conversation on the subject of our departure; every one agreeing that the long-boat might be nearly ready in one day more, if every exertion were made; and of that I had no reason to doubt. The next topic of discourse was concerning the parts of the wreck, which we had noticed to be lying along shore. The man from the Cape said he had seen almost every part of a ship, in his way to and from the Cape, and had observed particularly that the iron had been taken from the wood; that circumstance we also had noticed in viewing the yards, cross-trees, etc., which lay within our ship. We all concluded that the event of that shipwreck could not have been a long time past, as the blacking on the yards was not entirely chafed off.

At dawn of day on the 6th, we found no person on the watch; when, upon examining into this matter, it was found that Pat and one of the Danes had been called at twelve to watch till two; and that those appointed to watch from two to four had not been called. This discovery immediately led us to the two most unfeeling of mortals, Pat and the Dane, who were found behind the tent, and in such a condition as to be unfit to be talked to. Upon which, without the least hesitation, I took my case out of the tent, and turned each bottle up-end down: then I opened the hamper, and destroyed every bottle of wine and porter; doing this in the presence of all, when only one dissented, and he a very sober man. Thus was ended, as I thought, every opportunity for intoxication in our company. We all, excepting the two sleepers, commenced our labor, rigging tackles, erecting shears, etc., in order to raise the boat. In the meantime, I took a lookout on the hill for our absent man, but saw nothing of him, and returned to the tent, and called all hands to breakfast, which was prepared without the assistance of Pat, who had risen, and taken a copious draught of water; after which he joined the party, declaring most solemnly that neither he nor his watchmate had tasted a drop of liquor that night. All the reply was, a round of such vulgar sailors' blessings as are commonly bestowed on such occasions. Thinking that a thing of the kind could not happen with us again, I judged it most prudent to quiet the men, by telling them that although a great crime, it was not an unpardonable one; that our situation demanding all our strength, we had none to waste in altercations, and so must make the best of it.

I found, during the morning, that most of the crew thought it advisable to give the two delinquents a little corporal punishment; but in a moment as it were, our attention was called to viewing a strange track of man. When we retired from breakfast, the person who had been at the Cape the day before, discovered the track of a man without shoes, and calling to one of our men, he asked him if any of them had been barefooted yesterday; and was answered in the negative. Upon hearing that question and the answer, I went to him, and soon was convinced that we had been visited the night before. We followed the tracks of two men: they had come down the hill from the southwest, and walked round to the mouth of the tent, and, after going around the tent, had returned by the way they came, walking back over the hill nearly in the same line they had come in. I followed them beyond the hill near a quarter of a mile, conjecturing it likely that they were in ambush, but found it not so, from the shape of the track; for as soon as they got over the hill they ran, which appeared by their steps being longer, and the impression of their feet in the sand deeper. What makes their getting off undiscovered the more remarkable, they had a dog with them, and we had a hog lying on the sand before the tent. Had the dog barked, some of us must have heard it. So again, had the watch done their duty (as probably they would, if there had been no liquor in the tent) they would have seen those men approaching, and giving us notice of it, we might have secured them, and kept them in confinement; that would have doubled our diligence, and in one day more we might have been at sea.

It was now nine o'clock, and our man for the mountains still missing. We called all hands together upon this gloomy occasion. Our poor sailors sat silent at this meeting; without uttering a word, they all looked up to me as their counselor. I observed to them that the two men who had discovered us would probably return in a short time with such numbers as would overpower us, and then might do with us as was most for their interest, or as best suited their caprice; that, according to my calculation, if the Cape we saw was Nun, our distance to St.-Cruz, on a straight line, was not more than a hundred and eighty miles; and allowing one fourth part for going in such a serpentine line, as we had reason to expect, we might reach there in ten days by easy marches; and that five bottles of water and twenty biscuits a man would support nature; more than which we could not take with convenience. Every one agreed to the plan immediately, and to take our chance of meeting with obstructions on the way; and the matter being settled, all as one set to work at making knapsacks. While that was going on, I took one man with me and buried in the sand all our muskets, powder, shot, etc. Some of the sailors objected to that measure, by saying we might have occasion for our guns to shoot the wild beasts that might annoy us. But I told them that a musket of ours seen by an Arab might cost us our lives, as it would carry a hostile appearance at least, and that in our warmth we might be led to make an improper use of our weapons. They at last pleaded for a pistol. I, however, buried the whole, and laid a stone over the place.

By this time the man from the mountains made his appearance, coming along shore from the eastward, and when he joined us we were nearly ready for a march: we all stopped our business to hear his story. He said he had traveled at least fifty miles, had ascended the mountain, but had made no discovery of much consequence. He made a hearty breakfast while one of his shipmates was fixing a knapsack for him.

During all the time the arrangement was making I was left ignorant as to what part of the luggage I should carry myself. The sailors had agreed among themselves that I should walk unencumbered, and that my part of the burden should be borne by them. When informed of this, I concluded to carry my spyglass and umbrella, and a copper teakettle full of water to be used first, and some chocolate and sugar in my pockets, to use in case we should be so fortunate as to find water on our journey When it was announced that we were all ready for a march, I changed my clothes, put on a pair of fine worsted stockings, a pair of new corduroy pantaloons, a pair of new half boots, a new linen shirt and neck handkerchief, a silk vest, a nearly new superfine broadcloth coat, and a new beaver hat; a gold watch I took along with me, and also put in my pocket gold of the value of 600 dollars. This done, I called my men to me, and gave them the remainder of my clothing. Black man Jack had previously taken some fine shirts into his pack for me, which he did without my knowledge or direction. When they had all helped themselves with the best of my clothing left in the trunk, they discovered two pieces of tabinet in the bottom of it, and asking me what it was, I told them it was two gown-patterns which I had bought in Ireland for my wife, and that it was best to let it alone, for they had luggage enough already. Jack, who was at a little distance from the trunk, on discovering the matter we were talking about, rushed forward, and got hold of the pieces, saying, "*Master my mistress shall wear these gowns yet.*" I told him he had already too much to carry, and that his mistress would never see those patterns "*She shall, master, depend on it,*" replied Jack, "*they are too pretty to leave here;*"—and he packed them up. Little did I then think my wife would ever see either of those pieces; but she did, and that same tabinet she has occasionally worn to this day. When nearly ready for a start my mate wrote up the log-book and I finished my journal; corn was put in the place for the hog to eat, and water to drink. All things were now prepared, and we on the point of moving, when one of the sailors said, "Let us depart under flying colors;" the others joined him, and we were detained till they had erected a pole on the hill, and hoisted a very handsome ensign.

At about ten o'clock, we started on our march. After a fatiguing walk of two hours, over a deep road in one of the valleys, we all sat down to rest ourselves. I took that opportunity to furnish every man with one and the same story to tell in case we should be separated. This I thought necessary, because contradictory accounts given by us would be likely to expose us to greater sufferings than we might have to endure if the stories of us all should prove consistent with each other. Accordingly we agreed to say that the ship was the Oswego, of Liverpool, bound from Cork to the Cape de Verd islands after a load of salt, and from thence to New York: and to give our names as they were, and all call ourselves Englishmen. I told them the reasons for substituting Liverpool for New York as the home of our ship, and for calling ourselves Englishmen instead of Americans, were, that the English had a considerable trade on that coast, particularly at Mogadore; that some of their ships I had known to have loaded at St. Cruz; that I never had heard of but one American vessel trading there; that, without doubt, the English had a consul both at St. Cruz and Mogadore, and perhaps at other places on the coast. Moreover, I enjoined it upon them, in case of separation, that it should be the study of every one to learn the language of those we should fall among, to give notice to any Christian when an opportunity offered for the safety of the whole. I cannot but think the English reader, considering the forlorn condition I was in, will excuse my claiming the protection of his flag, by assuming a false national name.

We dined on dry bread. One of our sailors having a leg of boiled salt pork, I persuaded him to throw it away, as it would increase his thirst. We each took from the copper teakettle a small tumbler of water, which we had already begun to know the value of. About two o'clock we began our march eastward on the hard sand; and traveled till after sunset, when we had a quiet sleep till morning. On the third day's march, and for some reason which I do not recollect, one man and myself were left a little behind, or did not start with the rest; they were a quarter of a mile ahead when we started. The man was the same one who had been sent to view the Cape which we had taken for Nun. We did not take their track, but to shorten the distance, went a little northward. About fifty yards from some uninhabited cabins he saw a pile of human bones on our left, and exclaimed, "O Lord protect us; look at these bones! now do you believe I saw human bones at the Cape?" We stopped only for a minute, when, within ten feet of us, there was a pile of human bones. Having but an imperfect view of them, I can only say there were many; to speak safely, I should think as many as could be contained in a hogshead. Yet, considering the agitation of mind I was in, it would be nothing strange if the quantity were three times as great, or but half so great as it appeared to me.

Our men were still at some distance ahead, which gave to us two an opportunity to converse together concerning that and other things which we had seen. He told me he had not mentioned what he had seen at the Cape to any one but myself, and that his opinion as to the cause of the bones being there was not altered; "and now," said he, "this is, to my mind, a confirmation of the fact that we are among cannibals, as in several places about these huts there have been fires, but not recently." Our distance from the ship, by calculation, was now fifty miles. We soon fell into a quiet sleep, and were awoke by nothing else but the changing of the watch. It so happened that Pat and the Dane were on the watch; those two who had done us so much injury, and, in the opinion of several at least, prevented us from getting away in our boat, by their being drunk and asleep when we were discovered by the two Arabs spoken of before, who otherwise might have been secured. At the dawn, on the eighth, we were awakened by an unusual noise, which started the whole crew. The cause of it was soon obvious enough; the two watchmen were quarrelling about the other drink. Strange as it may appear, Pat had carried a bottle of gin in his pack, which, on a former examination, had passed very well for water, the color being the same; all along until this time those watch-mates were equally concerned in the fraud. Pat was now too drunk to stand; the other not so drunk, and his story we got, which was as follows: —When they robbed the case on the beach, they put away in the sand one bottle, over and above what they had drank, and when we filled our packs at the ship, he (the Dane) managed it so as to put that bottle in Pat's knapsack, and Pat promised to keep it until we should arrive at a place where we might drink plenty of water, and while on this watch, Pat said they could finish it without being discovered. They opened the pack (a deed which had never been allowed except all were present) and took out the gin, and along with it a bottle of water, and sipped out of each awhile; so thirsty they were in sipping, in about equal portions, that Pat finished the water, and they then took out another bottle of water. By this time the operation of the gin was so powerful that Pat challenged the whole to himself. A battle ensued; and, in their struggle for the gin, they overset the half-packed knapsack on the rocks, and broke several bottles: the noise that this made awoke us all. Judge of our consternation, having before this not the least idea of any liquor being in our camp.

Pat was very drunk: the Dane said he had advised him not to take the bottle out at that time, but to wait till we should find water; but Pat insisted that the gin was his, and he would take a drink, and give him one, and then put it up again; that the taste of the gin created thirst, which before was very severe, and was what tempted them to steal a little water, intending himself to drink only a little, and then put all away again; that Pat swore he would finish it, and drink as much as he had a mind to; and that when remonstrance was in vain, he (the Dane) thought he would drink too, but declared he was very sorry for it. Our men were so exasperated, I did believe if I had not been there Pat would have been stoned to death, and that there was not one of them but would have been willing to cast the first stone. This was the second grand offense; and they all declared it was more than ought to be borne by human beings. I was left alone to plead Pat's cause; and it was merely to save his life that I did it, for I confess my feelings were wrought up to a high pitch against that most unprincipled and unfeeling rascal: yet if any violence had been done him, I should have been censured by the community as the supposed cause of it. Had I been otherwise situated with the crew, or in the same situation as the rest of them, it is very probable that Pat would have fared badly, but not worse than his deserts. Pat was too drunk to stand, and after waiting an hour for him to come to himself, a motion was made at last, and carried without a dissenting voice, to take away what little of water and bread there was left in his knapsack, and march off and leave him. I then proposed to them to leave him his share of each; but being overpowered by numbers, we took our departure, and left the poor object lying on the ground to die a martyr to gin. We had proceeded not more than a quarter of a mile when I prevailed on them to stop, and one of them returned back with me, and we took him up, one under each arm, and lugged him along to our company, whose wrathful dispositions toward him were not in the least abated. I told them it would be less cruel to murder him on the spot than to leave him to linger out his but few days in misery. They remained inflexible: whereupon one of them gave me a part of his history, which they had had from himself on the passage, a little before we were wrecked; this was it:—In 1799, and the beginning of 1800, he commanded a company, consisting of those who were called the Insurgents; he boasted of having destroyed, by cutting their throats, a number who adhered to the king's party; that at one time, he and his company, in a dark night, murdered indiscriminately a number of persons whom they had caught in a house, "and —— them," he said, "I would have done more had I had it in my power;" these murderous deeds he had committed in the neighborhood of Wexford, in Ireland.

When this horrid tale was ended, they said, this fellow deserves all the punishment that we can inflict upon him; and at the same time the countenance of every man of them was, on that occasion, so clearly marked with revenge, that I thought Pat's case was desperate. He by this time was able to walk. All this morning had been lost to us, and what was more to be lamented, was the loss of a great part of our water; we, however, commenced our march, keeping near to the foot of the mountain. On this morning I heard more murmuring among our men than all of it put together that had been since our landing; and the whole of this, as I thought, was to be attributed to Pat's conduct. After dragging along very slowly till noon, and seeing several fresh tracks on the sand, all heading westward as before, we became more and more in fear of meeting the natives, and ascended to the top of a sand hill to take some little refreshment, and to look out for travelers, the weather being extremely hot, with a very light breeze. We ate a little bread, and drank but a little water; so great was our thirst the appetite craved but little food. Every moment discovered more discontent; and, with a view to get a return of harmony in our little camp, so much disturbed the night before, I proposed for us all to take a nap. It was agreed to: I then had the handle of my umbrella stuck into the sand, and as it was large it served as a canopy for the heads of five or six of us. The most of them fell asleep in a few minutes. My own anxiety was too great for me even to slumber. I lay till two o'clock, and then awoke them, who appeared all to have been refreshed.

The first object with me was to prepare and march forward; but there appeared a kind of backwardness to making preparations for our departure, such as had been uncommon in like cases, and it was attended with indistinct murmuring. I had not the least conception of the cause, till a little hurrying on to his work of one of the leaders in it—the same man who had been spokesman in the affair of cutting away the masts, getting away the long-boat, etc. He looked me full in the face, and with an audible voice spoke to me these words, as near as I can recollect: "We have been now three days since leaving the wreck; we get along very slow, and in a very few days our water will all be spent, and then it will be too late to go back to the wreck where there is plenty of it, and we are determined to go no further."

One of the men observed to me, that if he could only find a living spring of cool water, he should be willing to lie down by it and die there with hunger; that the value of water he had never known before. Another said, in any other case he would be willing to follow me; but as it now was, he could not consent to go another step, and die in the burning sands, which were almost insufferable to his feet. After spending a whole hour in this most painful of all debates, they, nearly all as one, were agreed to go back to the place where there was plenty of water, and take their chance of what might follow. Whereupon I advised them all to go back, and in case the natives were not come down, to use every exertion to repair the boat to be ready for sailing; and I said to them that I would go on myself, and if I should find people friendly to us, I had money enough to hire camels, and would send for them. No sooner was this said than the black man Jack (who had been sitting silent before) said to me, "Master, if you go on, I will go too." That was settled. I thought we could travel to St. Cruz in five days at furthest. Every pack was opened for making a division of the water; the rest all agreeing that we should take a larger proportion than themselves. At that moment Sam, the other black man, said, "If you go, Jack, I too will go." That being settled, we proceeded on in making the division of water; bread seeming scarcely thought of, so thirsty were we all. When the bottles were all counted, there appeared only two bottles and a half to a man, which showed that nearly half had been destroyed or lost. Before the division or apportionment of the water had been gone through with, Pat solicited permission to join me, which I then refused to grant him. Upon which, my mate took me aside, and observed to me, that if I would not take him along, he must surely suffer death; that they were so exasperated against him, that he (the mate) could not be able to prevent their taking away his life; that he knew what had been their standing with each other for some time, and was not willing to be implicated with others in the acts of violence that might be committed upon the body of that man. I now saw that poor Pat would be in a bad situation if I were to go off and leave him; and from that consideration alone was I induced to accept of his company.

We parted at about five o'clock, and among my little company not a word was uttered for more than half an hour. About half past six I saw a movement ahead, and so sudden was my stop, that the man next behind me, not observing it, was near throwing me down. In a moment we were all huddled together. I said to them, *Hide yourselves: men ahead!* As we were veering off from the foot-path, those ahead saw us, and stopped; we were then about a quarter of a mile from each other. With my glass I saw them looking steadfastly at us. Their number appeared to us greater than it really was, and as we thought they were looking at us to ascertain our number, we placed ourselves in a situation to be counted by them. We stood in that hopeless situation for more than ten minutes, not knowing nor thinking what steps to take. Jack said to me, "Master, let us run." I told him to stand still, for running would be useless, and I believed our enemies only wanted to know our strength in order to approach us. If you altar your position, said I, that may lead to our ruin; but if you will stand firm, I will go to them alone and know our fate. They were all agreed to do as I had bidden them. When I had advanced only a few paces, one of them called out, "If they kill you, what shall we do?" I only replied, be quiet.

I now walked moderately toward these barbarians, with my umbrella under one arm, and the spyglass in my hand. The nearer I approached them, the more frightful they appeared, but I knew it could answer me no good purpose to stop. When I was within a hundred yards of them, they all, as with one motion, dropped their packs, hove off their outer garments, and made toward me in a swift run. As soon as they had come within a few yards, I held out my right hand in token of friendship. Of that they took no notice, but passed by me as swift as it could be possible for men to run. My poor shipmates stood motionless; and when the monsters were come near enough to grasp them, their attack began. While I was walking toward them, in a quick pace, I perceived my three companions were down on the ground, and the ferocious barbarians at work upon them with their daggers, which glittered in the sun. As they were passing by me I saw a dagger, or long knife, hung to each of their necks. While beholding the horrid sight of their attack, I could think of nothing else than that they were plunging their daggers to the hearts of my poor companions, whose groans and cries I distinctly heard. When I was come within thirty yards I stopped, and looked at them, with no other expectation but that my own turn would come next, after finishing the diabolical work they were then about. In that deplorable situation I remained for near a quarter of an hour, when, to my great surprise, they all arose on their feet; my men with their packs off, and half naked. I then called to my men, and asked them if they were wounded; they answered no. Upon which I was convinced their daggers were made use of in cutting away the straps that secured their knapsacks, which they did not know a quicker way to come at.

Before they had paid any attention to me they ripped open the packs, each of them striving to have the greatest share in the spoil. Having accomplished this, one of them came within a few yards of myself, and stopped, and after viewing me very attentively, he walked partly round to get a side view. I could not perceive his motives for keeping that distance, as I had shown no signs of an intention to defend myself. We were both in those attitudes respecting each other, for a few minutes, and till one or two more of those frightful beings were making toward me with the like caution. Upon that he sprung at me, tiger-like; my watch chain, which was of gold, exciting his first attention. No sooner had he got hold of that than the others, seven in all, with the utmost fury seized hold of the watch, and partly turned the fob inside out; when one of them, with the dagger in his right hand, cut off the fob, and, through his great haste he, with the same stroke, cut my pantaloons. In a moment from this I was the undermost; the whole seven being upon me, each with his dagger drawn. The gold they soon found, and took it, pocket and all. Being unacquainted with our dress, it took them longer, by ten times, to obtain the plunder found on me, than I should have been in giving it up: add to this, they tore and cut my clothes badly. All this time the spyglass and umbrella lay by me on the spot where I had dropped them at the beginning of their attack. After this mauling was gone through with, they let me up again, when one of them examined the spyglass, and another the umbrella; thinking, I have no doubt, that this glass, which probably was the first thing of the kind they had ever seen, was a defensive weapon, and that made them so cautious about attacking me. They asked us many questions, which we did not understand, repeating over several times the same words, particularly the words *Sapena*, *Rais*, etc. These words we soon after found out the meaning of. Their figure, and ferocious look, to say nothing of their behavior, were as savage, and even exceeded in savageness, anything that I ever have read in narratives of voyages.

After that dreadful time was over, my burning thirst seemed more intolerable than before, and as the bottles of water that had been thrown out of our knapsacks were then lying on the ground, I took up one of them, drew the cork, drank it dry; and after that, my thirst being not yet quenched, I took up another, and had already drank two thirds of it, when one of those savage men ran to me, and struck the bottle from my mouth, and it rolled so far away that I could not reach it again. During this sitting of theirs, they appeared to be consulting together as to what they should do with us. At length, about sunset, they came to us, and asked us many questions, wanting, as far as we could understand them, to know the number of us. By making marks on the ground, we informed them that our number amounted to ten; not meaning for them to include ourselves in that number. They wished to know if the rest of our crew had guns; and by the shake of the head, we answered, they had not. Their next inquiry was of the place where lay our ship, which they called Saffina, or, at least, we understood it so. We pointed westward; and then pointing to me, they asked me if I were Rais, or Rice, which I understood to mean captain or master. As well as I could make myself understood, I answered their question in the affirmative. Finally, they inquired for money, and we endeavored to make them believe there was none in the ship. When they had gathered from us all this information, they talked with one another a few minutes, and then, as fast as they could, they gathered all the luggage together except the water, and made it up in the best manner the time would admit of, loaded it into our hackled knapsacks, and gave each of us a load. It was now the dusk of the evening, and we were, as we supposed, from fifty to sixty miles from the ship when they gave the word Bomar, which signifies, Go on.

With the word Bomar there came a blow, and a push forward. They endeavored to get us on a run, and for that purpose beat us cruelly; it was cruel indeed to force us on faster than a moderate walk, extremely fatigued as we were when we started. My companions, to save me from those cruel beatings, managed it so as to fall into the rear in order to get me ahead, and so take the blows themselves; but the Arabs discovering that management, put a stop to it. Thus driven on, we continued to travel, as I should judge, till ten or eleven o'clock, when, through extreme fatigue, I fell on my face in the sand, and no sooner did my companions see it, than they fell also; upon which our beating was increased to such a degree that I thought we should never rise more. After allowing us a short rest, it seemed that they meant to make up for lost time; the word Bomar was oftener repeated, followed, of course, with stripes. As that was the first time I had ever carried a pack, and as mine was heavier than any of the rest, the endurance of the toil came harder, perhaps, to me than to my companions. Jack perceived it, and without my once complaining of the burden I was compelled to bear, he, having the lightest one, and being much the stoutest man, proposed to me that we should exchange packs. Accordingly we stopped for that purpose; but our drivers were as much bent against that arrangement as we were for it. Jack told them, by signs, that he was the stoutest man, but they insisted that we should go on as we were; and while that litigation was at the highest, we both dropped our packs, and the exchange was made by us, but not without our smarting under the lash.

After this, they pushed us on again with all speed. We soon found out their object; six of our men being in sight on the plain about two miles off. We were goaded on by the two men who had us in their charge, and our thirst was so burning that we waddled along as fast as we could, in hopes of getting some water from our men. Those Arabs were within half a mile of our men before they were seen by them; they ran at least five times as fast we could get along. The moment our men saw them they stopped, expecting, from a view of their ferocious looks, and of the guns in their hands, that their own time was short; and having yet some water left, they drank every drop of it before the Arabs got hold of them. In an instant they were all down upon the ground, and thought themselves destined to slaughter; just as myself and my little company had thought of ourselves, when we were in the like circumstances. By the time they were stripped of their treasure, and had got up, we were near them, when there was, with them, a general rejoicing; their seeing us alive giving them hopes. As soon as we could be heard, we cried out for water, and being answered there was none, we dropped down, not thinking it possible for us to live. We lay groaning, and crying out for water, and at the same time our limbs were in excruciating pain from fatigue; the merciless barbarians hen gave us what remained in the skin, which was not enough to wet our throats. At last they got us all ten together, which they (the Arabs) supposed, from what I had told them the day before, was our whole number. It appeared from the story of my mates, that, upon parting with us. they had calculated to walk nearly all the night; that four of the men would not agree to that, as they had rather sleep, and therefore lay down for that purpose. The mates thought, that though we did not see nor hear each other, yet we must have been very near those four men about midnight.

This matter being settled, the word Bomar sounded again in our ears; such melodious voices I never heard before nor since. I do not mean to be understood that their voices were charming as respected ourselves. We cried for water, they forced us up; we pointed to the ship, in hopes they would go there, and let us get along as fast as we could. It was now about noon; the sun beat down with such extreme heat that the sand was almost insufferable. We marched on, and saw nothing till we were on the hill, within fifty rods of the ship. Everything was taken away except our hog, which lay dead, and blasted, and noisome to the smell; shot, no doubt, by the Arabs, the very day we left the wreck. The yawl lay on the rocks, with her oars in her, just as she was left; the foresail was cut off as high up as a man could reach if standing on the bellfry. They must have passed off to her by swimming. While our captors were busying themselves with filling their skins with brackish water from an old well they had dug out of the bank, our four poor fellow-sufferers made their appearance on the hill. They looked down with astonishment, having had no knowledge of our bondage, nor of the Arabs being at that place. One of the Arabs got sight of them, and gave a yell. Upward of fifty of those ruffians ran up the hill, and took them down, and stripped them of their luggage. Those four were permitted to talk with us while we stayed, which was about half an hour. Poor fellows! they wept bitterly upon being told that we were to depart and leave them, with but little hopes of our ever seeing one another again in this world of trouble. At the sound of the word Bomar, we took of one another an affectionate leave, promising that whoever of us should happen to be redeemed from our bondage, he, or they, would endeavor to obtain the redemption of the rest. Not one of us, while continuing to breathe the breath of life, can yet have forgotten, or will ever forget, that trying moment. Poor Pat was reminded, before we parted, of his having been the cause of our distress. He was prudent enough to make no reply. At sunset the remaining ten of us, along with seven Arabs, ascended the hill again, and for the last time; but whither or where going, that was our first and deepest concern.

After this they dispatched off one of their men, who took to the westward, on the run. Within about an hour he returned, and another along with him, who had a camel. On the camel they loaded all the luggage, gave out the word Bomar, pointed eastward, and cried out, *Swearah.* The word Bomar was very familiar to our ears; the word Swearah was new to us They turned the camel eastward, which to us was a matter of great joy, as that was the only direction from which we could derive any hope of relief. That sudden hope, or rather shadow of hope, infused in us such a general joy, that every one seemed to show some considerable degree of animation; whereas we had been utterly dejected before. We continued our journey all that night. When the sun was about an hour high we made a halt in a valley formed by two sand-drifts. We were extremely tired, having walked all the night without sleep or rest. About ten o'clock, an Arab that had left us at daylight, joined us again, bringing with him about half a bushel of sweet berries, and a brute animal, such as we could not name. It was about the size of a half-grown goat; the head, skin, and legs, they took off immediately; after which they opened their game, quartered it, laid it on the sand, covered it over with hot sand, and made a fire upon it with some dry sticks. They reached the guts, just as they were, for us to eat. We were very hungry, but did not suffer so much from hunger as from thirst. This food being warm and moist, we chewed the guts, after sucking off the fat; little thinking it was to be our last meal for five days. The meat was soon cooked, and being in expectation of getting a share of it, we privately buried the remaining part of the guts in the sand. We begged earnestly for water, but they took no notice of it. After they had devoured their meal of meat and sand mixed up together, they hove us the bones, on the whole of which there was not a single ounce of meat.

We then renewed our journey, traveling all day. Toward night we each of us got about one pint of the sweet berries; they were about the seize of whortleberries, the stone or pit being in quantity full three-fourths of the whole. We ate them, stone and all, for the stones were not hard to our teeth. We dug for water, but found none. At dark we got about half a gill each of the water from the sack; that drink finished it, and we lay down. The Arabs tied up the left fore-leg of the camel, and let him go. As to feed, there was none. The night was very cold, the contrast there between night and day being very great. Jack and myself lay close to the man who had claimed us both, and when I thought him asleep, I softly hauled the blanket partly off him upon myself. The moment he missed it, he gave me a hard thump with his fist, and it was a long time before I got clear of the pain which the blow occasioned. Great as our sufferings were, sleep at last closed our eyes.

On the morning of the eleventh, we were awoke at dawn of day by the Arabs at their prayers. Prayers being over, the camel that lay near us was loaded, and we were obliged to march, distressed as we were with hunger and thirst, and every one of us making the outcries of misery. One of our sailors discovered at that time that he had in his pocket a small potato, of the size of a large walnut; half of that he privately gave me, and I thought nothing ever tasted to me more pleasant. After marching a short time, the leader, my master, called out, Umbar — sit down. We soon obeyed, and when seated, they took a little meal which had been concealed from our view, and ate it. We expected some small share, but got none. My master looked very sternly at me: at that moment he got sight of my sleeve-buttons, and caught me by the wrist. I saw what he was after, and gave them up as soon as I could unbutton my sleeves. Till this time I had not been deprived of any of my wearing apparel, except what was in my sailor's packs. He then ordered me to strip, and necessity obliged me to comply. My coat, waistcoat, shirt, and neck handkerchief, were taken from me, and laid by his side. I begged hard for my clothes, or some part of them, but to no effect: the piece of bread happened to be in the pocket of my pantaloons. Soon after this a general search of us took place. My fine shirts, which the sailors had on them, were all taken away; whereas those who fortunately had only their own shirts on, which were coarser, and some of them not white, were permitted to wear them. After this business was over, we re-commenced our march, my clothes lying upon the back of the camel. At that time I was eating my biscuit, or rather grinding it to powder between my teeth; in fact, the power of swallowing was lost to me. This was the first time I ever had in my mouth any food which I could not, after chewing it, convey to my stomach; now I found it could not be done for the want of fluid or moisture in my mouth and throat. My mouth was so parched up that the biscuit could render me no service; not the least morsel found its way down; every particle was discharged, or blown from the mouth, whenever the upper and lower jaw opened.

As soon as the burning sun had retired a little behind the mountains of sand, we were spurred on with greater haste. When it had sunk beneath the horizon, the fresh wind cooled the earth, which became even cold before dark. Negro Sam, as he was walking by my side, asked me if I was cold. I told him I was. He then took off his blue jacket, and reached it to me, and I put it on. After this he complained to his master that *he* was cold; whereupon his master came to me in anger, probably thinking that I had taken the jacket from Sam by demanding it of him Sam made him understand that I was not to suffer. He (the Arab) then gave Sam my coat, and when it was quite dark we exchanged coats, and I got my own again. This evening's walk was worse than anything we had before experienced. About nine o'clock, we all ascended a mountain, I should suppose from two to three hundred feet high, over craggy rocks; at every step our joints seemed to be dislocating. When we were on the top of the mountain, the Arabs called out, Shrub bezef. We knew that shrub was water, and concluded that bezef was plenty. That sound cheered us all. The camel, which on our march was always driven ahead, started off at full trot, and all the Arabs after him, except one, who brought up our rear. The descent of this mountain was ten times worse than the ascent; our feet slipping or giving way at almost every step, it being too dark to pick our road. We found it, indeed, almost too much to be borne, and nothing but the hopes of finding water could have kept us from sinking under our troubles and sufferings.

When we were nearly half way down the mountain, we began to smell something, which could be compared to nothing I could think of but bilge water in the hold of a ship; the nearer we approached it, the stronger was the smell. Before we had come to the water, the camel had drank of it, as also had all the Arabs except the one in our rear, who, taking a wooden bowl from one of his companions, dipped up the water and drank it. From him I took the bowl, dipped it full, and drank every drop. My mates being by my side, called out, "Captain, you will kill yourself!" The bowl contained at least a gallon, and some said five quarts. Several others of us drank as much as I did myself. The reader may be astonished at our taking down such a quantity at a draught, and much more so, when he is informed that the water was so putrid that the smell of it reached from a quarter to half a mile; and that when drinking it, we found it as thick as common gruel used in sickness. After all the rest of us had been satisfied, I took another drink, of at least a quart, and then some others, if not all, mended their draught; when we all lay down by the side of the pond, and slept finely; I think I never enjoyed a finer night's sleep in all my life. This day's travel we computed at thirty-five miles. One of our men, who had been used to driving a team, thought our calculation was moderate.

At dawn of day, on the twelfth, we were awoke, as usual, by the voices of the Arabs saying their prayers. When these were over, they began to load the camel, which appeared almost double the size he was of the preceding evening. He refused to drink this morning. Toward evening, we saw, for the first time, some small shrubs, appearing like our dwarf thorn bushes. The camel seized hold of the tops and little branches, which he ate with avidity; they were dry, so that in breaking them with our hands we could discover very little moisture within the bark. Such as they were, we chewed the twigs, but could not expect any sustenance from them. As soon as the camel had eaten what they thought proper, we were driven on again. The sun was hot, and we were near perishing, when on a sudden two of them started, and ran off in a north-eastern direction, we dragging ourselves along after them. As soon as they had ascended one of the hillocks, we discovered that they were much engaged, appearing to be gathering something from the face of the earth. We doubled our diligence, and soon came to the place, and, to our astonishment, we found about a quarter of an acre of ground thinly covered with barley in the milk, of about eighteen inches in height. The Arabs all fell to work to gather and eat; we followed their example, and the grain being full of milk, we were able in a few minutes to raise moisture enough in our mouths and throats to aid us in swallowing.

The next two days of our miserable lives, were spent in traversing a desolate country, without food or water, and with a burning sun striking down upon our naked bodies. About noon of the fifteenth, upon our ascending a rising ground, we beheld, at no great distance, a large number of tents, to which we were marched in apparent triumph. As soon as we had approached to within about a hundred yards of those tents, we were ordered to sit down, and were surrounded with men, women, and children, to the number of from seven hundred and fifty to a thousand. The crowd around us prevented all circulation of the air, so that we were nearly suffocated, and at the same time were ready to perish with thirst, and all begging for water, our masters being out of sight. After suffering for half an hour in this horrid situation, we perceived a great bustle on the outside of the assembly that surrounded us, the cause of which we were not long at a loss for. The loud noise drew nearer and nearer to us, till, very soon, to our astonishment, we heard a voice inquiring in plain English, "*Where are they? Where are they?*" It was not a dream. A young man, once white, got through the crowd at last. It was an English youth of about nineteen, his skin deeply burnt with the sun, without hat or shoes, and his nakedness covered with only a few rags. The first words uttered to us by this frightful looking object were "*Who are you? My friends! my friends!*" the tears running down his cheeks. I would have risen to salute him, but was too feeble. He sat down by my side; we all shook hands with him, and began our conversation. We told him who we were, and he in return gave us an account of himself; the Arabs meanwhile interrupting him every now and then, to get our tale of him. In turn, he satisfied them who had inquired of him where we were wrecked, how much money and goods we had on board, where it was now, how much those mountaineers (as they called our owners) had got, and so on. George, for that was his name, freely informed us as to himself, that he was the steward of a ship called the Martin Hall.

of London, cast away upon that coast more than a year before; that one of the crew was killed by the natives, and the captain he supposed was drowned; that part of the crew had been marched back, in a south-east direction, to a place they called Elic; that another part had been carried to Swearah, and there ransomed; that four of them yet remained among the wandering Arabs, who had been very cruel to them; that none of them but himself belonged to the tribe he was in; that two boys were not far off; one other boy he had not heard from lately, but believed he was distant not many days' march. "This," said George, "is all I can tell you about our poor unfortunate crew, but I have no doubt that some of them have been murdered, for I heard they did not find a ready sale for all that were carried to Elic, and that our sailors became turbulent there, and a quarrel ensued; the Arabs themselves acknowledged that several of our men were wounded in the fray: but these cursed monsters will lie like dogs, and there is no believing them; what makes me think they were murdered, I have lately heard that some of their shoes and hats have been seen in that neighborhood." This story of George excited our utmost attention, though it was frequently interrupted by the Arabs during the whole of the time.

Hitherto not a drop had been given us to drink, and George now told the Arabs that we were suffering with thirst; but it only made them laugh. Upon this, he started on through the crowd, and brought us about two quarts of milk and water. This we divided, I believe very equally, by each of us sipping a little, and then reaching it to his next neighbor. That delicious beverage occasioned such warm expressions of gratitude as I had never heard before; each of us, in his own style, ejaculating his thanks to poor George, and then to our Father in heaven. Though the quantity was small, still, by taking it in that way, every drop felt in our famished stomachs as a cordial. No sooner had the inquisitive Arabs drawn off from us, than I inquired of George where Swearah was? He said he never could learn, the Arabs having always evaded answering that inquiry, and seemed angry whenever he put the question to them; but he believed it was Mogadore. He then asked me about the coast where the English had their trade; observing to me that some of the Arabs often journeyed eastward, and after an absence of two or three weeks, returned with certain English manufactures, such as combs, loooking-glasses, beads, scissors, knives, powder, guns, and so on. I replied, as St. Cruz was nearer, and a port where a trade was carried on by European nations, I rather thought that *that* must be Swearah. He said he had never heard them so much as name St. Cruz; and I answered it was the Portuguese name, and, by inquiring, he might find out what the Arabic name was. George appeared very much delighted with our company, and no doubt had hopes that we might be the means of his ransom from slavery. Speaking of the ones who then had us in their keeping, he said to me, "These fellows do not belong here to our tribe, nor anywhere hereabouts; they were here about ten or twelve days ago; I remember them very well; they got supper here, and went off the next day, traveling westward; they are hunters, and poor dogs, depend upon it. I will find out where they belong, and let you know. Come," he says, "let us go to the tents, and I will beg some meal and water for you; and, if my old master will let me stay with you till night, I shall be glad. I was watching his flock, and when you had arrived, he sent for me, and put some one else there in my place." We all rose up, and on our approaching the tents, George called out, "There is our chief! he has been gone these three weeks, and

I suspect he is from Swearah." He (the chief) came hastily to us, and inquired who we were; and was told by George that he and ourselves were all brothers. The old man looked smilingly on this occasion, and George told him we were suffering for victuals. He replied, "They shall have some boiled meal directly." By this time the whole male part of the tribe were assembled round their chief; and George, understanding the Arabic, learned from what was said, that he was from Swearah. After George had collected from his master all the information he could upon that subject, he told us the men that were our enslavers were hunters; that they belonged to a degraded tribe of Arabs, distant four days' journey, pointing to the south-east, and about one day's journey from Elic; and that they were about to start off the next morning for their home, and take us along with them. We all as one declared ourselves unable to go further, and that we had rather die on the spot than attempt to advance another step. I told George that when these hunters had first found us they appeared to have made up their minds to put us to death, or at least showed signs of such an intention, by re-priming their guns, etc. At that moment the hunters were engaged in conversation with many of the tribe, and George, to satisfy himself as to that matter, went and spoke with them about it. The old man, who appeared to be the head one of the gang, acknowledged that at the time of plundering us, it was their intention to destroy our lives, but, on reconsideration, he said to them they had better let us live, in order that we might pilot them to our wreck, and after *that* they could dispose of us as best suited them.

By this time the chief, whose name was Ahamed, and who had been engaged elsewhere for some time, came to see us again, bringing with him another English boy, named Jack; he was about thirteen or fourteen years old, covered with rags and vermin; he spoke the Arabic perfectly. We talked to the chief through him as an interpreter, for a short time, and then, having found that I was what they called Rais, he took me and Jack away to a little distance from all the rest of the company, in order to find out where we had buried our money and goods. Upon my telling him that we had neither, he refused to believe it. I told him our ship was bound for the Cape de Verds for a load of salt; that that article was very cheap there; that what money those hunters had taken from us was sufficient for purchasing a load for our ship. This story of mine he seemed not to believe; he thought that all ships carried either money or goods, or both, and he had learned from the hunters who brought us on, that the Arabs at the ship found nothing in her but sand. The sand I told him was ballast, and that a ship could not sail without ballast. Neither did he believe that. He then said, if I would tell him where our money was he would buy us all of these men, and feed us well at his tent; and after the tribe's leaving the wreck, which would be shortly, as he judged from having learned that they would soon burn her for the sake of her iron; that then he would go down and take away the buried treasure, and return and carry us to Swearah. I judged it most prudent to persist in my first story, thinking if I should tell him there was money in a beef barrel, it could do us no good, but probably harm, as it might have led off this chief, and one of us with him perhaps, to the wreck, when, in all probability, he would find her in ashes. When we were about parting, it being then in the evening, I entreated him to buy us all, and told him he would be well paid for all his expense and trouble.

I returned to the place our men were at, where I found Larra a fine mulatto boy, one that George had spoken to me about, aged nearly sixteen years. He understood about as much Arabic as George, but neither of them near as much as Jack. He, Jack, (said the two other boys to me,) always joins with the Arabs in their prayers, and is more an Arab than a Christian, and you must be guarded against him, for he is a little treacherous lying rascal, and ever prefers the company of these devils here to ours, and has made mischief among us, and if he and ourselves quarrel together, they always take Jack's part, and that makes him the more saucy. I was glad to find out Jack's character so early. George and Larra stayed with us till near midnight; by them I found that whenever the Arabs came home after their journeyings, they used to talk of Consul Gwyn, tasher Court, tasher Jackson, tasher Foxcroft, and others. The word *tasher* I concluded must mean merchant; and the proper names being English, I only wanted to know where Swearah was, to make out a story that might carry with it some marks of truth.

Before we got a delicious breakfast, we were visited by most of the tribe, who made their observations concerning our worth, rating some of us at something considerable, and others at nothing at all, but concluded that we were of no great value taken altogether. On the contrary, the men that had us for sale praised us up, saying we were as good as any Christian dogs they had ever seen. Some time about ten o'clock next morning, George and Larra who had been every moment watching the motions of the Arabs, came in haste, to inform us we were all for sale, and that some were actually sold; observing that Rais and the blacks, as well as several others, remained unsold, their price being too high. Larra entreated me to go to their sale and plead for myself, and mentioned that boy Jack had a great deal to say about us there. I thought it best, however, to remain quiet awhile. He (Larra) continued begging me to go, and said if I were to be carried off, there would be no chance of a ransom for George and himself. After the sale was partly, or mostly gone through with, Ahamed came to me, bringing Jack along with him, as an interpreter, and taking me aside, he asked me if I had any friend in Swearah? I told him I had a number of friends there. "Have you," said he, "ever been there yourself?" I answered, Yes. "Who do you know there?" I answered Consul Gwyn, and a number of merchants, Court, Jackson, Foxcroft, and some others, English, French, and Spaniards. "What sort of a man is Consul Gwyn?" said he to me. Being determined to make no mistake, I answered generally, he is a good man. This vague answer did not satisfy him, and he told me I must describe him. As I thought our all depended upon my correctness in this particular, I felt embarrassed, and he discovered my embarrassment; when, collecting myself a little, I told him it was some years since I had seen the Consul, but, according to the best of my recollection, he was about my own height, but rather fatter. Turning to Jack, he says, "That is all right," and locking his fingers together, off at a distance from his own, he says, "His belly is so big." This fiction of mine Jack believed as much as Ahamed.

Ahamed then asked me what I would give him over and above what the Consul would give, if he should buy me? I answered, if he would buy us all, and then set his price, I would think on it. Upon this he said to me, "The mountaineers will not sell the blacks at any price, for they are as good travelers as themselves; they are men that you Christian dogs have taken from the Guinea country, a climate that suits them best, and you were going there to get more of them, and are worse than the Arabs, who enslave you only when it is God's will to send you on our coast."

Never, I must confess, did I feel a reproach more sensibly—that a great many wearing the Christian name did force away from their homes, and carry into perpetual slavery, the poor African negroes, and thereby made themselves worse than Arabs, I well knew was but too true. However, standing on my own defense, I said, in reply, that was not our business: to which boy Jack answered, "It was *our* business;" and in that he spoke the truth, for the ship he belonged to was engaged in the Guinea trade.

The chief demanded of me again, that I should say how much I would give him; but at last he set the price himself, by counting over his fingers till he came to the number forty. I was at a loss to know what it signified, when Jack told me he supposed it meant dollars. I agreed to it, and that, in addition to the sum mentioned, I would give each of his two wives a looking-glass, comb, beads, and some other things. The next thing with him was the security. I told him my word was sufficient, and that I had no other security to give. He then asked Jack in what manner a Christian took an oath? It was some time before Jack understood the question, and not until he was told by him that a Mohammedan swore by his own beard; and by the prophet. Jack then said to him, "A Christian swears by the Bible, and that oath he holds inviolable." Jack went on to compare the Bible to the Alcoran. As no Bible was to be come at, I told him I could make oath as well without the Bible as with it; and this satisfying him, I then, with an audible voice, called my Maker to witness, that as soon as we should be ransomed in Swearah, I would, in addition to what the Consul should pay for our ransom, give him forty dollars, and for his two wives two small looking-glasses, two combs, two pair of small scissors, each a large bunch of beads, and a knife for himself, and as much tobacco as he could smoke all the way back. When this was gone through with, he asked Jack if he believed me. He told him our God was the same as his God, and he might depend on my oath being held as sacred by me, as his own oath would be held by himself. Thus the matter ended, after we had been detained about it for a full hour. Ahamed then went to the mountaineers, and finished the bargain for us all, except the two blacks, for they would not part with them. How the purchase was paid, or in what, we never could find out. This evening the boy Jack paid us a short visit, when Larra advised him to be more with us, and not keep company so much with the Arabs. To this Jack replied, he could have as much meal as he wanted while with them, and that he, Larra, was always quarreling whenever he was with him. Larra now saw the necessity of courting his friendship. Whenever they two talked together about London, Jack used to reproach his own mother there, telling Larra that she was a bad woman, and he did not wish ever to see her again. All this I thought made against us, as it gave room to mistrust Jack of being inclined to the side of the Arabs; I therefore urged upon both of them the necessity of their harmonizing for our general safety and welfare.

On the eighteenth, in the morning, there appeared an uncommon stir in the tribe. The horses were brought up, and rigged out in great style; all was glee, male and female running from tent to tent; our English boys were in as great surprise as ourselves. For the sake of information, Larra and George went after Jack, who of course was knowing to the cause of this great muster. Jack was not to be found then, but soon after the little villain came, and informed us there was to be a wedding that day: this quieted our minds. Upon this time he and Larra fell into familiar discourse between themselves as follows.

Jack. You, Larra, know Afdallah, that fellow that murdered his wife about two weeks ago.

Larra. Oh, yes, I remember all about it.

Jack. Well, he is going to marry that short, thick, yellow girl, that lives in that tent there; you know who I mean.

Larra. Oh, yes, I know her.

This conversation between the two boys, excited in me a curiosity to know the story of that murder, and Larra related it to me. "About two weeks ago," said Larra to me, "this fellow went into his tent, and asked his wife where his knife was. She told him she had lent it to such a one, naming a man belonging to the tribe. Do you not know, he said, that you have no business to meddle with anything belonging to me? She acknowledged she had not; that she was sorry if it had displeased him, and would go immediately and fetch the knife back. He made no other reply to her than by saying, I will see if I cannot have a wife who will obey my commands better; I always told you not to meddle with anything of mine. Having a club in his hand, he struck her upon the breast; she fell, and he continued to maul her as long as there was any breath in her body. Neither man nor woman went near them, although her cries and screams were heard through the whole tribe. That evening," continued Larra, "we went to the funeral, and observed what was done there. The women measured her length, her breadth across her arms, and her whole thickness, with as much exactness as they could, and then they dug a grave to fit her, digging it no deeper than the measure of her breadth, and put her in sideways, all naked; then the women, standing upon the body, trod it down with their feet, till the upper part of it was just level with the surface of the earth; after which, they all fell to gathering stones to cover the body with, so as to prevent its being removed by the wild beasts."

I asked Larra what followed in regard to the murderer. The account he gave me was this:—"The next day after the murder was committed, the chief assembled all the principal men of the tribe to examine into the case. The murderer was called before the council, and heard in his own defense; he voluntarily related the facts as they were, and was then dismissed for a few minutes. Upon this, the chief, who always speaks first in such cases, gave his opinion. "Afdallah," says Ahamed to his counselors, "has not acted agreeably to the law; he should first have complained to me of the disobedience of his wife, and if she should persist therein, he would then have been at liberty to punish her according to his pleasure. For breaking the law in not making his complaint beforehand to me, he is worthy of punishment; wherefore, my sentence is, that he be fined four sheep, seeing his flock is small, and that those sheep be dressed for our supper to-night." Larra added, "the murderer was sent for, his sentence was pronounced, and he, without uttering a word, had his flock brought up, killed the four sheep, and the company ate them—and we, you know," added he, addressing himself to Jack, "got the heads." After Larra had gone through with his story, I desired him to look out for the bride and the bridegroom. He went to the place where the tribe was assembled, a few rods south of our tent, where he found the women pre-preparing the bride for her nuptials: and soon after they all made their appearance. We then walked toward the crowd, taking a circuit round their rear, full as nigh them as it was prudent for us to approach. The couple stopped, fronting a man who officiated in the capacity of a priest; e read over to them a passage engraved on a board, taken originally from the Alcoran, and joined their hands, using a ceremony of words that we could not distinctly hear, by which pronounced them husband and wife.

A tent had been previously prepared by the bridegroom; on it was displayed a white flag or fly; he took his bride, who had been blindfolded by the priest, with a piece of cloth tied over her eyes, led her to his tent, sat her down on a mat, and said to her, "You are at home." Then he left her, and returned to the place where the ceremony was performed, and had a white cloth, in the form of a turban, tied round his head; after which he joined with the company, in their singing, shouting, and firing of guns; most of the company taking part in this merriment. When night came, the whole company went to his tent, but none of them entered it, not even himself; instead of which, they formed in a circle in the front of it, where was prepared a great feast, consisting of boiled meal and milk, along with several sheep, cooked and eaten without spice or salt. Their feasting continued till after midnight, when the company having retired, the bridegroom visits his spouse, takes off her blind, shows himself to her by the light of the fire, to satisfy her that there is no mistake as to the identity of his person, and then blinds her again, and retires. She continues in this condition of utter darkness for the term of one week. During the whole of this week, after the first day, all the women that choose it visit her; one of their number is appointed to cook the victuals, and perform all the other domestic duties, until the spouse is brought out to the light of day, when she beholds, as her husband, a capricious vagabond, and a bloody monster, for the least deviation from whose mandate she is liable to suffer death.

On the morning of the 22d, Ahamed, and with him half a dozen of the tribe, came to our place of residence, and brought along about two yards of red flannel, and inquired if any one of us was a tailor? adding, we were to march on the next morning, and must make Jack some clothes. Overjoyed by that piece of information, we, by means of sending Jack for them among the tribe, were furnished with scissors, thread, and needles—not indeed equal to what are used at *our* tailors' shops; the thread was too large for the needle, but by singling it we made out with our sewing, though but badly. In a few hours, however, Jack was rigged up with a red jacket and trowsers; but, unexpectedly to us, the little fellow despised them, and would rather have had his old rags again. The time now hung very heavy on us all, and we were wishing for to-morrow. Toward night we found out, for the first time, to whom in reality we severally belonged, and also discovered by Jack that we had often been bought and sold among them. As hitherto they had had no labor for us to perform, they had thought it immaterial whether we should know or not, how we were disposed of among themselves, or who of them in particular were our owners. It now appeared that we eight, together with the three English boys, were owned by about twenty of these Arabs; and as to myself, I perceived I was in the hands of the most unfeeling vagabond in the whole tribe.

George, who had been occupied for several days past in keeping his master's herds and flocks, came to us this evening, and told us his master had been uncommonly good to him for the last day or two; and now, says he, I am to have as much meal for to-morrow as I can eat. We informed him that we were to march off for some place or other the next morning. That, said he, is a mistake, for my master told me you were to remain here several days, and that when you go, I shall go too. Poor George, however, was left behind. The next morning, to wit, the 23d, Ahamed told us we were to travel on to his field of grain, where he should be with us in a week's time. On we went, and the only object we regretted parting with was hapless George ; him I pitied from my heart.

We were already fancying ourselves half redeemed, when my new master began to let me know I must obey him in particular. He was one of the most ugly looking rascals among the whole tribe, and his conduct was no better than his looks. We had been traveling together all the day, before we could learn to which of them each of us belonged. The difficulty of our learning it of them, was owing to their ignorance of arithmetic, and their inability to inform us that we had been disposed of in joint shares ; for instance, five of them owning three of us. As our course was northerly, we had hopes of soon seeing the seacoast. Late in the afternoon we came in sight of tents, which, as they were placed in a valley, we had approached near before we discovered them. We came toward them, undiscovered till within about a hundred yards, when we all sat down on a sand hill, excepting our principal man, who was Ahamed's brother, and he stood up for some time before any of the people of the tents perceived him. No sooner did they see him and us, than there seemed among them a great stir, which was made, no doubt, by their looking for their chief. Soon, however, there came to us a venerable looking old man, mostly dried up, who accosted our chief man thus:—"Where are you from? where bound? are these the Christian dogs I have heard so much of? what are you going to do with them?"—and so on. The answers were—"We are from the edge of the desert," pointing south-west ; "we belong to the tribe of Ahamed ; we are bound to such a place," pointing north-east, "to cut our grain ; these Christians that you see are going along with us, and when the harvest is over we shall make a market of them." "All well," says the old man, "come along with me and sup, and stay the night ; you are welcome."

The venerable looking old Arab having pronounced his cordial invitation, on we marched ; and by this time the whole tribe was out, men, women, and children. They all, even the children, had something to say of us ; but we were now become so used to the scurrilous language of such people, that we paid no attention to it, but seated ourselves among their tents on the sand. We begged for water, having had but very little of it all that day, and our stock being now exhausted. We had eaten only once, if eating it may be called, for that meal consisted of a little raw barley-flour wet up pretty thin, so as to be drank rather than eaten ; this we swilled down clean, and licked the bowl : the whole quantity for us eleven was what might be a full meal for one large pig. Our appetites were very keen, and this swill tasted good to us, and lay well on our stomachs, as did everything else that we had eaten or drank. Many a time, and even hundreds of times, had we cause to return thanks to God for this great blessing—a good appetite for whatever food or drink we could find, and a good digestion of it.

Soon after we had made a stop at this place, the chief, and many of his tribe, formed a circle, and began their chat, accompanied with the pipe. When finding themselves short of tobacco, I heard my name, *Rais*, called aloud, and upon my looking toward them, the master of my mates made a sign to me that they had no tobacco, by putting his finger in the bowl of the pipe. This application was made to me in particular, because at the beginning of our journey, I had been appointed tobacco carrier. There was about a pound of tobacco, rolled up snug, and put in a small skin, about the size of a cat's, and which was made in the manner of an old fashioned pouch; this I reached to him, and taking out as much of it as filled his pipe, he returned it to me. Their conversation was on general subjects. Larra, agreeably to the arrangement previously made between him and me, was listening to it, but could gather nothing of interest relative to our future destiny. Indeed they frequently spoke of us, but in such a manner as often reminded me of the old adage, Listeners seldom hear any good of themselves. That saying was verified here completely—the heads of their discourse concerning us were, that we were a poor, miserable, degraded race of mortals, doomed to the everlasting punishment of hell-fire after death, and in this life fit only for the company of dogs; that our country was so wretchedly poor, we were always looking out abroad for sustenance; and ourselves so base as to go to the Coast of Guinea for slaves to cultivate our land, being not only too lazy to cultivate it ourselves, but too stupid to learn how to do it; and finally, that if all the Christians were obliged to live at home, their race would soon be extinct; that those belonging to Christian countries, being dependent on the other countries for almost everything necessary to support nature with, they make for sale such things as guns, powder, knives, and so on, all which the world might do well enough without; and then they barter these things away to people abroad for the necessaries of life.

Upon the 24th, uncommonly early in the morning, we started away, in an east-north-east course, and traveled very fast for travelers in our condition. Before nine o'clock in the morning, we had become very thirsty, as well as hungry. We had taken along with us no water, and but little meal; and while we were begging for water, or for victuals, they snarled out to us, Cooly mackan, shrub mackan—no victuals, no drink—and hurried us along. By eleven o'clock, the heat of the sun was almost insufferable; we sat down only for a few minutes, and then were driven on again. We were fast approaching a rocky mountain lying on our right, appearing to be at least two hundred feet in height. We perceived where this mountain, seeming to have broken asunder, formed two separate hills, with a valley between them; and when we were at no great distance therefrom, some of the Arabs left us and ran ahead, while others were forcing us on as fast as possible. When we came abreast of this valley, to our astonishment we saw a reservoir of water, and the Arabs who had started ahead of us drinking at it. We soon got to it, and when came our own turn, which of course was the last, we drank no small quantity, and all of us sat down at our drinking place. The Arabs then mixed together some raw meal and water, and ate of it; after which they gave us some, and on it we made a sumptuous breakfast about noon, having eaten nothing before from the time of our scanty supper, that is in fifteen hours. When we were about to leave this place, which we all regretted to leave so soon, one of them took the bowl that we had been drinking out of, and rubbed the inside of it over with sand, and put it bottom upward upon a stone which had been left projecting out, just on the inside of the doorway; and no doubt it was left there for that purpose. Then commenced our march, yet not before they had gone through with their long prayers, which in a great measure consisted of thanksgiving for the benefits of that fountain.

On the morning of the 26th, we were awakened earlier than usual, no signs of day being then visible in the firmament. Immediately after the prayers were over we started on, when the north star was still in sight; our course was from north-east to east-north-east. Thirst and hunger were sufferings not new to us, but their cravings were now severe indeed

About noon we saw a dwelling, built of stone; on approaching which, we found it contained a very large family, or rather several families. Under the wall we seated ourselves, and were viewed by them all; and had the mortification (if mortified we could be by anything they could say) of hearing the same kind of remarks upon us, that had been made before from time to time, after our leaving Ahamed's tribe. We however got of them some boiled meal, the remains of the Arabs' breakfast, and in it was a little butter; it was to us a rare dish, though a very scanty one, being not more than enough for two men. At a small distance from this house was a piece of barley, of about ten acres. This was the first inhabited building that might be called a house, which we had seen since our landing, and this was the first considerable piece of barley either grown or growing. There was also here a little garden, in which we saw some fine looking pompions and onions, but could get none of them. Upon leaving this place, we ascended a high hill, covered with barley; on the summit, we discovered at a great distance off, the sea, and as that was the element we were so much accustomed to, the sight of it seemed to infuse joy into every breast. The Arabs pushed us on till near sunset, when we were brought to, and were informed that we now were on the ground belonging to Ahamed, and that the piece of grain that now lay before us was his. Upon viewing it, I thought it contained at least one hundred acres, but as I had not been accustomed to measuring land, I might have been wide from the mark in my calculation; though, at any rate, it was the largest field of grain I ever saw. Our Arabs informed us that we were to stay with them there till that grain was cut and secured; and now, said they, we will see what Christians can do. I told Larra there was some management for us to attend to on this occasion; that if we were to go to work, and do our best, it would be the means of perpetuating our slavery. He was of the same opinion. I then exhorted all my men to make it seem to these Arabs as if they were unused to that kind of labor, and that if they should be compelled to work, they must take care, while at it, to do their employers no good; telling them that the obtainment of our ransom would depend upon our strict adherence to this plan—and upon that point we were all agreed.

Early on the moning of the 27th, the sickles that they brought with them were made ready, and all hands of us were ordered out to work. On hearing my name in particular called, I told them I never had cut grain, nor had ever done any work of the kind; that I was a shipmaster, and had been learned nothing else. For this I received their curses and threats, but with a determination not to heed them. In the meantime Larra said to me, "they are determined to try you; I heard them say, if Rais works, his men will, for he is the head devil among them." I told Larra he might tell them from me, that I would not work, that I was in their power, and they might do with me as they pleased; that Ahamed had promised to carry us all to Swearah, for the purpose of our being ransomed there, and I had pledged myself to make him full compensation for all his expenses and trouble. To this they replied, that Ahamed had ordered them to make us work till the grain was cut and secured, and if I would not work they would shoot me. The boy Jack was present, and interposed, by observing he heard them say, if I would not begin, and my men follow me, they would put *me* to death *first*, and the others should share the same fate. I told Jack to tell them they might do as they pleased; I would take my chance in regard to the consequences of my refusal. I do not wish to make myself appear in this case as the man to brave all dangers. The fact was, both myself and my crew were at that time reduced to mere skeletons, with fatigue of body and troubles of mind, all which made life the less desirable to us; and beside, I thought there would be less danger of their threats being put in execution on account of the absence of Ahamed.

This controversy lasted an hour, and they got my men into the field at last. Some of them could handle a sickle as well as themselves; one of whom (being the man I was fearful would be of the most service to them) I told to cut his own fingers, as if by accident. They all understood my meaning, and it was not long after my men had been dragged into the field, before I found they were doing very well, I mean *well* for our own purposes. Some by accident, and some intentionally, perhaps, cut their fingers and hands with their sickles, and made loud complaints; while others, who were gathering up the grain for binding, did it in such a wasteful manner that their work was a real damage to the owner. Upon this the Arabs took away the sickles from those of them that had been reaping, and set them to hauling the grain up by the roots. They did so, but laid it in the worst form that was possible. By managing things in this way, they beat the Ishmaelites, and got the victory. Our poor fellows suffered very much for a short time; but at last they were all driven out of the field, when we all assembled together at the place where the reapers had begun their business. Being myself strongly impressed with the belief that our obstinacy in this case was the only way to obtain our freedom, I thought it my duty to exhort them all to stand firm in the resolution we had taken. I was the more thoroughly convinced of the necessity of this course of conduct, by two circumstances; the one was, there were at that time immense fields of standing grain, which required a great many laborers, and the other circumstance was, the plague, as I had repeatedly heard, had swept off the inhabitants, which made laborers scarce. Hence I concluded that if we should make ourselves serviceable to our oppressors, we should be kept by them, at least long enough to answer their present purpose, and, perhaps, several of us for life.

Soon after the Arabs had started off to their work the second time, Pat was missing. We all wondered (for none of us could tell) what had become of Pat. In about two hours he returned, marvelously changed in looks, and especially as to his bulk; for he had eaten such a quantity of *stirabout*, as he called it, that his body, about the waist, was swollen to double the size it was when he left us. His story was this; while there was going on with us the conversation about working in the barley-field, he took himself off, first going round a little knoll, then keeping himself in a valley till he thought he was far enough off to be out of his taskmasters' view, and finally ascending the highest hill then in sight, where he saw a large house in the next valley, and the men, at that instant, going from it into the grain-field. As soon as he could do it with safety, he descended the hill, and when near the house, he saw the women, and stopped. They looked at him, and, probably having a knowledge of our being in the neighborhood, were not alarmed. He durst not approach them nearer, for fear of giving alarm to the men. In that situation, he thought to draw their compassion toward him by making to them signs of hunger; but that was of no avail. Whereupon he mounted a large stone, and fell to singing and dancing. This took with them; in a moment, as it were, they all came about him, women and children, some bringing him milk and others stirabout. He ate all that was first brought him, and craved more, which they continued to furnish him with as long as he danced and sung, and that was as long as he could eat and move. After his jig was over, he took as much with him as he could carry in his hands and left them, and came back by the way he went, undiscovered by the Arabs of the other sex.

Some of our men were desirous of trying their luck by the same means, but thinking it imprudent, I dissuaded them from it. Having all that day received nothing to eat, and anticipating, as we then did, another cold night's lodging, we all fell to work (as loose stones were plenty there,) and built a stone wall, three or four feet high, and perhaps ten feet long, as a lee to defend us from the cold of the night-wind. We had it nearly completed as the Arabs came in sight; when each dropping his sickle, they ran to us in a great passion, abused us as usual, and not only hove our wall down, but threatened us with severe beatings in case we should presume to set ourselves about that work again. In vain did we remonstrate against this cruel treatment of theirs, in not only keeping us without food and drink, but exposing us unsheltered to the cold night-winds; it was in vain we told them we could not live under such extreme hardships. Their only reply was, "go to work, and then you may eat." And again, it was in vain to tell them that we could not work on the land, that the sea was our element. They were deaf to all we could say, and not the least relief would they afford us. At length they went to their work again, and when once out of sight, we feeling our situation to be truly distressing, held a sort of council, to devise what steps were necessary to be taken by us before it should be too late. A part of us no doubt had some inclination to go into the field to work; but at last we were unanimously of the opinion that our best plan was to move off to the eastward in a body, and abide its consequences. Things being thus arranged, I took the lead, and all the rest followed. We had proceeded about eighty rods from the field when they discovered us, and, in a moment, each dropping his sickle, they ran for their guns, and seizing these weapons, they ran after us, calling aloud for us to stop. We paid no attention to them, but moved on as fast as possible. The hindermost one got a knock from a musket, as several of the rest of us did after him, and, finally, we were stopped, and held a parley with them. They threatened us with death, but we were now past the fear of that; our lives had become burthensome to us, by means of our sufferings, and of our ceaseless dread of perpetual slavery. They ordered us back, but we refused, at all hazards, pleading, earnestly and repeatedly, the promise made to me by Ahamed. When they found we would not go back, they said we should be put where they could always find us, and then marched us on. After we had walked through the fields about two miles, we came to a large habitation; there we were stopped, under the walls, when one of them went in at the gateway. As the gate was open, the whole of the residents there soon came out to look at us, and the *stuff* that was made use of by their tongues, it is not only improper to mention, but indecent. However, with a woman who occupied an inner room, a bargain was made, that she should keep us till Ahamed should come, at a given sum, by the day. This matter being settled, the Arabian reapers returned to their field. We soon found that a part of this establishment belonged to Ahamed, and that Salear, which was the name of the woman, was his sister.

During our stay here we were visited every day by one or more of our masters, the reapers, who, when going back, never omitted, as I can recollect, to give our keepers a charge not to let us ramble abroad, for fear, as they said, of notice of it being given to some one who they suspected would, in such case, rob them of their property, by stealing us away. On the 29th of April, we having then been two or three days in this horrible place, Ahamed arrived here, bringing with him Bob, another English boy, belonging to the Martin Hall. The poor boy was reduced to a mere skeleton. There was such a rejoicing between him and the other two boys, his shipmates, as it would be difficult to describe. They fawned around him, and asked him twenty questions in the time he could answer one. We mixed with them, and heartily partook of their joy—at this happy meeting even Ahamed seemed pleased. Bob said it must have been six months since he had heard a word from any of the crew, and he had supposed them all dead.

The next morning, Ahamed appearing in a little better humor than the evening before, I asked him when he intended to carry us to Swearah? He answered, as soon as his barley should be all cut and secured, all which was nearly done already. Upon this, he soon went off, and returned to us again about noon, and with him came several Arabs, to whom, as it seemed, he was selling tobacco. As I was much attached to tobacco, I begged him for a small piece to chew. He refused at that time, but a little piece he gave to Larra, who put it in his mouth, which displeasing Ahamed, he said, "Christians are bad in everything; tobacco is made to smoke, and nobody but a Christian dog would eat it."

On the morning of the first of May, I took a seasonable opportunity to mention to Ahamed, that as his grain was all secured, he now would be at leisure to march us on to Swearah. Salear being present at the time, she told her brother that I had promised to send her on from that place a looking-glass, a comb, and a large handkerchief. He looked at me with a smile, and asked me if I really intended to give her the things she mentioned? I told him I did; and, moreover, that I would give her some beads and rings for her fingers. "Now I believe you," replied Ahamed; "you shall go soon, and you shall ride the horse I bought for Bob, as Bob," added he, "is growing stronger every day." Salear, since the time I had promised her some presents from Swearah, had been a little more accommodating toward me. In the dusk of the evening, I found Ahamed with her, and the boy Jack sitting by their side, and I ventured to place myself among them. She reminded me of the promise I had made her, of the glass, and those several other things which the women there so highly value; and I at the same time solemnly declared to her that I would fulfill that promise. Upon this, Ahamed made some inquiries of me with regard to the manufactories of my own country, which I answered as well as I could; and I took the liberty to tell him how much better he would be treated than we had been, if by accident he should be thrown on our shore; that in such an event, instead of being held in bondage, and sold from tribe to tribe, our Sultan would have him conducted back to his native country in safety; whereas he still held us in slavery, and several persons had been here already in order to purchase us for market in the interior; and all this, notwithstanding he could get a great price for our ransom from our Consul, who was distant only a few days journey.

He heard me out, and then warmly retorted upon me as follows: "You say, if I were in your country, your people would treat me better than I treat you: there is no truth in you; if I were there, I should be doomed to perpetual slavery, and be put to the hardest labor, in tilling your ground; you are too lazy to work yourselves in your fields, and therefore send your ships to the negro coast; and in exchange for your useless trinkets, with which you cheat the poor negroes, you take away ship loads of them to your country, from which never one returns; and had your own ship escaped our shore, you yourself would now be taking off the poor negroes to everlasting slavery." After this unpleasant discourse was ended, we sat silent for some time, and then Ahamed said to me, "In a day or two we shall be ready to depart."

On the morning of the third of May, we were awakened early, and found them all in a hurry at preparing for a departure. At about eight o'clock, we took our leave of this horrid place, when Salear followed us out of the yard, and, with her last farewell, bawled out to me, "Rais, remember my things." To which I brieflly answered, *I should not forget her:* nor did I ever forget her, nor ever shall I. She was about the ugliest looking woman I ever saw; about four feet and six inches high, squab, or thick round, ill shaped, petulant, crabbed, savagely ferocious, and all this in the very worst sense of the words. Her dress was nothing but a nearly worn out haick, which she wrapped around her, so as to extend from considerably above her knees to considerably below her breasts, which were enormously large. Her cheek-bones were high, her eyes small and black, her color that of dark copper; her teeth were fine, and were the only clean thing we discerned about her. We all had reason enough to remember her. Forget *you!* no, no, Salear, I can never forget *you.* I mounted the old horse that had been bought for Bob, and we took the foot-path leading down the valley. By noon Bob complained of fatigue, and could not keep up with the company, and to him I gave up the old horse, and made out myself to get along tolerably well on foot.

At dusk we got into a good path, and were walking along very moderately, Ahamed, Jack, and myself, ahead of the rest, when the old man said, if he got as much money for us as he ought, he should be rich. I replied to him, that he should be well paid, and that no danger was to be apprehended on that score. After a few minutes silence, he accosted me in the following manner: "There is no confidence to be placed in Christians; for whenever they come on shore on our coast, and are not immediately discovered by us, they bury their money in the sand, as you yourself have done, to prevent it from falling into the hands of the true believers. This can do you no good, and it is our property. We pray earnestly to the Almighty God to send Christians ashore here; he hears our prayers, and often sends us some good ships; and if you did as you ought to do, we should have the full benefit of them." I then asked him if it ever happened that the crews of the ships coming ashore there had all perished, or been destroyed? To that question he answered, "It *has* happened, and it was the will of God. If they had been spared, they would have secreted their treasure, whereas by destroying the whole of them, we got all they had." After this, he went on to relate to me the following story: "Once," said Ahamed, "there came ashore a very large ship. It being some time before the crew were discovered, they had landed all their property, and had covered themselves with their sails. When they were discovered, a small tribe went down to take them into their possession, but they fired at our men, and some of them they killed. Exasperated by being fired at by such dogs, they fell upon them furiously, and many were killed on both sides. Our men, finding the enemy so strong, fell back, and sending up for help, another tribe went down. They now endeavored to show to the enemy by signs, that to themselves belonged the property, and they must give it up. But not being able to come to an understanding with these men by signs, so as to obtain what they had with them in that way, they drew up toward them in order to take it by force. As soon as our men came within gun-shot, they were fired at by them; the fire was returned, and all fought hard, but our men, not being able to get at them with their long knives, were repulsed the second time. They then sent up again, and I, getting information of it, went down, with all my fighting men. There were now three tribes of us, and we had more men than the Christians; and as my tribe was the largest, the command of the whole was given to me. We got down in the night, and having been running for three days, I thought it best not to attack them till the morning, judging that when they should see our numbers they would yield to us. At daylight I saw them, and made signs to them to lay down their arms, upon which their camp seemed all in confusion. At the moment we were prepared to attack them they formed themselves in a close body, and began to march off eastward. We formed ourselves in three divisions, according to our tribes, and the chief of each tribe led on his own men. My tribe, together with one of the other two, got in their front, and the remaining tribe was on their side. We all began our attack at once, and, after fighting a long time, we had killed half of those dogs, and then the remnant left alive laid down their arms. We now all dropped our guns, and fell upon them with our long knives, and every one of them we killed; and their whole number we found to be upward of five hundred.

"After we had gone through with slaughtering them, we stripped them all, and left their bodies lying on the ground, and went back to the ship, and found that they had landed great quantities of goods. In the ship we found guns, iron, sails, powder, and many other things valuable to us; they had in the ship large guns, such as they have, you know, upon the walls of Swearah. When we had collected all these things together, and burnt the ship, we sent for our camels, and carried them home, and sold them about the country. We got a great deal of booty, but we lost more than a hundred of our men killed in battle." When he had done, I asked him if they had landed casks, and whether they had built stone huts, and covered them with their sails, and several other questions I put to him relative to what we had seen near the harbor. He remained silent till he had heard me through, and then turned me off with this short answer—"that is none of your concern." Nevertheless, I ventured to inquire of him as to the time when that affair happened. But his reply to me was the same as before, nor could I ever afterward get one word more from him about it. Whenever I attempted it, he would turn to Jack, and ask him what it was *for* that I wanted to know concerning that matter? Upon inquiry, I found that Jack had never heard this story before, nor had either of the two other English boys. For myself, I was fully satisfied that the crew of the frigate which was wrecked on that coast not very long before, had all been murdered, and all my companions in misfortune were of the same opinion.

The fourth and fifth of May, we rose early, and traveled late; always suffering under our privations, but meeting with no adventures of consequence. On the sixth of May, so early in the morning that the stars were still visible in the sky, we proceeded on in a south-east course. About sunrise we discovered that the ground ahead was very black, and could not conjecture the cause; but we soon came to it, and found there a swarm of locusts traveling southward. The edge, or side of them, was as straight as a line; they were thicker than they could all stand together on the ground; so numerous were they that they crawled over one another's backs, all struggling hard to get along. The feet of our camel crushed them at every step, and at every step their blood gushed out in a manner shocking to behold; the moment the camel lifted up his foot, his footstep was filled with living locusts crawling over the carcasses of the crushed ones. Whether we looked to the north or to the south, we could see no end to them; they covered the ground for about half a mile in width; the eastern side of them was as straight as the western. We saw no straggling ones, nor did they fly; they were about three inches in length, and we concluded that they were young ones that had not the use of wings. This was the only swarm of locusts that we saw. All the while we were passing over them, the Arabs were muttering over something to themselves.

Not long after we changed our course to the east-north-east, when I had an opportunity of talking with Ahamed, and I endeavored to convince him (of what I had often tried in vain to convince him before) that there was not the least doubt but the Consul would be happy to see us, his brethren, in Swearah, and would immediately pay for our ransom; that it was not *his* money which would be paid for us, but money belonging to our Sultan, who always took care of his subjects. Ahamed's reply was, "If I were sure of *that*, you should have your freedom in a few days." As we advanced the country appeared better; the soil, and the fields of grain, nearly resembled what we had seen before; the land, whenever we had an opportunity to examine it, appeared a fine gravel; the trees were more common, and, in many places, were some small groves, also many fig trees, though with but little fruit. Very soon after we came to a place where a great number of tents were struck. We viewed them, and found, by our Arabs, that the inhabitants had mostly died of the plague, and that when the tribe became reduced to a very few, those few survivors took all the furniture and turned it upside down, hauled out the tent poles, and let the whole fall to the ground, where it remained untouched ever after; that such was their law, that when a whole family died of that disease, no one might take their bowl to dip with, even though he were perishing for water, nor could their flocks be taken possession of by any process, but were left to run at large, till some one unknowing to whom they had belonged, takes them under his own keeping, and makes proclamation of it for a given time, after which, if none should have appeared to claim them, they are to belong to the present possessor. Upon our removing but a few rods from this scene of desolation, we discovered their garden, and getting over the fence, each of us took away a pompion, and was eating of it with greediness, when the Arabs perceiving it, they with great haste deprived us of all that we had not yet swallowed, which was but a little, for we had nearly eaten a raw pompion each. The curses they so liberally heaped upon us for this offense were but little regarded. One of the boys lagged behind, and got one large piece which had been taken from us, a share of which fell to me, and it tasted really well. Late in the afternoon we came to a tribe of about fifty tents, where we stopped.

The Arabs were well received here, but as to ourselves, nowhere had we been so much ridiculed. The were not sparing of their vile epithets, so common to these people, who had ever viewed us as a poor degraded set of beings, hardly fit to live in the world. The women were foremost in insolence and abuse, and their children not far behind them. Here we got water, aud a little raw meal. Ahamed here bought three asses, to assist us along in our journey; one he gave me, and the other two were used among us alternately, as the needs of our men required. On the morning of the eighth, we started on early. The women ridiculed us as we passed along, and bawled out to us, "You swinish looking dogs, go to your own country, we do not want you here." Those of us who rode on the asses were behind the rest, and after us in particular these women ran, and in a few minutes dismounted us, taking the asses away, and laughing immoderately all the time. We cried out for help, and the Arabs discovering the sad plight we were in, came back to us, and, with much persuasion, regained for us our beasts, at the same time blaming us for being behind. There was now in our view a large town, or city, covering, I should suppose, two or three acres of ground. The walls appeared from ten to twenty feet high; on the north side was a large breach in the wall; the Arabs were looking at it, and talking about it, while Jack and myself were both sitting on the animals we rode, and Ahamed perceiving us looking that way, asked Jack if there were such large cities in England? The boy told him there were much larger ones there. Upon which Ahamed went on to say, this city was destroyed, and every soul put to death; that he was at the siege, with all his tribe, and he exultingly added, "we spared none, not even the children!" I asked him the cause of that massacre; to which he replied, "It contained bad men; wicked men, who feared not God, and did not live like true mussulmen."

About noon we took a short turn to the left, over a high hill, and there we saw the sea, and, in a valley not far distant, a great number of tents. No sooner did we see these tents, then Ahamed called out to us, in Arabic, "There is my brother! you shall now have enough to eat." We approached to within the usual distance, and all sat down except Ahamed. As soon as the two brothers met, each put his right hand upon the head of the other, then each kissed his right hand, and then they shook hands; and all this before a word was uttered by either of them. When this ceremony was finished, the chief then says to his near kinsman, "Dear brother, are you well? from whence are you? where are you going? how did you leave your children?" and, last of all, he inquires, "how are your wives?" To this Ahamed answers, "Dear brother, I am directly from home; I am bound off to find a market for these Christians; my children are all well; one of my wives is sick; we have traveled a long way to-day without food; these Christian dogs have been complaining of hunger, and I promised them they should have victuals enough upon our arrival here." The other then says, "All is well; to-night they shall have as much as they can eat; go to my tents." This was a strange sight; two brothers, after a long absence, meeting together, going through as much ceremony as if they were utter strangers, gravely and steadfastly looking one another full in the face, and with eyes seemingly so piercing as to pry into the depths of each other's hearts:—all this was very singular, and at the same time there appeared in it something of dignity or grandeur.

I took this opportunity to beg for victuals, and Ahamed's brother told me he had ordered his wife to cook for us as much as we could eat, and that it was now boiling; he then left us. As soon as he was gone, one of the boys went to his tent, and found, sure enough, a pot boiling. Our hunger was so great that every minute seemed to us an hour. At last, being informed that our meal was cooked, one of our boys went for it, and found one potful only; *that* was turned out into a large bowl, and brought us boiling hot. We could not wait for it to cool, but instantly began to eat it, hot as it was. Reader, if you have ever seen a hog run his nose into a trough of hot swill, and observed the queerness of his behavior upon it, you may figure to yourself the appearance we made while eating this meal in our tent. We soon found the bottom of the bowl, and scraped it out clean with our fingers.

When this bowl was finished, the two brothers came to our tent, and asked us if we had had enough? The boys answered, We have had but one potful, and that is not half enough. He turned from us, and went to his tent, which was not ten paces off, and, in a very moderate tone of voice, spoke to his wife thus: "Did I not tell you to boil for these Christians both pots?" She replied, "You did, but I thought one was as much as they deserved." Without uttering another word, he took up a heavy club, and struck her over the breast. She fell, and he continued to beat her till we could no longer hear her groans. Ahamed stood motionless. We besought him to intercede with his brother for her, but he shook his head, and said nothing. When this old man had done beating his wife, he called to a woman in the next tent, and ordered her to boil a pot of meal for us, and added, "I will see if my orders cannot be obeyed." Upon this, he, together with Ahamed, walked back to the place where the men of his tribe were sitting on the ground, and he seemed as little discomposed as if he had been beating a dog. I sent in one of the boys to see if she was dead, who stayed some time, and I heard him talking there with the woman that was cooking. When I had called him back, he said she was still alive, that her head was considerably swollen, and that her neck and breasts were bruised very much; and that the women there observed, "She will die soon, and to-night we will bury her."

Presently our pot of *stirabout* was done, and she, the cook, called one of the English boys to bring away the bowl. He went, and took it to our tent, where we agreed to let it cool, the craving of our appetite being now somewhat allayed. The boy found the wounded woman still alive, but said she was much more swollen than when he had seen her before. When this food was so far cooled as to be eatable, we fell to, and ate the whole, and sent the bowl back to the tent, with a message, in these few words, *We have had enough.* The old chief, I suppose, saw the bowl returned, and he and Ahamed came and inquired of us if we had had enough; and, after being answered affirmatively, he walked to his tent, and, with apparent indifference, asked the women if his wife was dead. Receiving for answer that she was not dead, but could not live long, he and Ahamed both went back again to the other men.

On the morning of the ninth, we were slow about moving; and did not start till sunrise. At the moment of our departure I sent one of the boys to see whether the woman, so cruelly beaten by Ahamed's brother, was living or dead. He returned, and said they could perceive life in her yet, but he was told by the one that had cooked for us the day before, that she was almost gone, and would die very soon; that she was swollen to a great size. I think it beyond doubt that she died that very morning. As we advanced, the country looked still better and better; the grain-fields seemed alive with reapers; it was not uncommon for us to see forty or fifty of them in a single field. About noon, when we were upon one of the highest of these hills, Ahamed cried out thrice, as loud as he could hallo, "St. Cruz! St. Cruz! St. Cruz!" and then, pointed to me a space where the mountains of the Atlas were fallen away, I could plainly discern what appeared to me a white speck, which he said was St. Cruz. Ahamed now seemed very lively, as did also most of the rest of them. When an opportunity was left me to question him, I asked him what the distance was to St. Cruz, and whether any Christian ships were there? To this he replied, that St. Cruz was in sight, and not far off, that there were no ships there, nor had been for a long time; that all the ships went to Swearah. *That is Mogadore,* said I to him. "Yes," he answered, "you call it so; were you ever there?" Yes. "Were you ever at St. Cruz?" No. "Who do you know in Swearah?" Consul Gwyn, tasher Court, Jackson, Foxcroft, and many others, some French, and some Spaniards. Turning to Ahamed, who was all attention to this conversation, he said to him, "He has been at Swearah, and has friends there." He then concluded with asking me if Consul Gwyn had money enough to ransom so many of his brothers? Without hesitation, I told him he could ransom ten times our number if they were brought to him; and I endeavored to make him understand that the Consul did not pay this money from his own purse, but it was money belonging to our Sultan, who placed it at his disposal for that purpose, and, in case that he (the Consul) should at any time be short of money, it was only for him to borrow of the rich merchants till our Sultan should send him more. This explanation of mine seemed to be satisfactory to him, and our conversation was here closed. On the morning of the tenth, we were awakened by the sound of the voices of the Arabs at prayer. We saw no appearance of any habitation till near night; and having traveled over heavy sand, and the weather extremely hot, we suffered for water, but none could be found. At length Ahamed told us we should soon come to a small tribe of his acquaintance, and there we should fare well. It was beginning to be dusk, when, on our rising a hill, we saw St. Cruz, which did not appear twenty miles off, though in that we were mistaken.

At about eight o'clock we arrived at the tribe which Ahamed had spoken of, which consisted of about thirty. We got here but a poor supper, which consisted of a little raw meal and bad water. When we lay down to sleep, we found ourselves watched in a manner little different from what had been usual, the Arabs lying on the outside of us. We slept not well: being not far from the sea, and the wind blowing strong all the night, we lay extremely cold. We had one comfort, however, and a very great one; we now were beginning to think ourselves nearly out of danger, and *that* rendered our sufferings the more tolerable. The length of this day's travel must, as we thought, have exceeded thirty miles. On the morning of the eleventh, we started on half an hour before daylight, and took a south-east course, and traveled fast. At the dawn of day we saw St. Cruz far on our left. About noon, we found we were at least eight miles from the town, and were hidden from it by some high sand-hills on our front. Here we discovered a few huts a little on our right, and the Arabs proposed to go to them; while we, on the contrary, begged hard to go directly on to St. Cruz, at which we might arrive in two or three hours. Their demur about proceeding directly forward, gave us considerable uneasiness. The Arabs at last gave us peremptory orders to march to the huts, and did it with apparent anger; and, as we were not sure of our being then within the emperor's territory, it was a dictate of prudence that we should obey.

I soon found an occasion of talking with Ahamed, and asked him when we were going on? at the same time reminding him that we had been here two hours, and were pretty well refreshed. He looked me full in the face, and piercingly, as if he could read my heart, and asked me what was my haste? I pretended I was not in much haste, and told him it was much more comfortable traveling now than it was in the morning, as the sun was fast lowering, and the wind blowing fresh, and we felt ourselves very much refreshed. He said to me, "Not long ago you were hungry, and since that you have had nothing considerable to eat; and now, hungry as you are, you are desirous to march off, though there are two pots of victuals boiling for you." At the moment of Ahamed's leaving me, a fellow, on a gray horse, came galloping down the hill on the other side of the river. We all huddled round him, and distinctly heard him say, "Well, I see you are determined to carry these slaves to Swearah;—I heard from there yesterday, and intended to have seen you last night; but you took the lower road, and so I missed you: this morning I heard of you, and intended to have seen you before you had crossed this water—however, it is not too late yet. You may now rest assured that the Consul will not ransom these Christians. But a few days ago, an old man, a friend of mine, came directly from Swearah;—he told me he saw several Christian slaves in that town, whom the Consul refused to ransom, and that the Arab who carried them to that market could get no pay for them at all; but if you will only re-cross the river in time, you may sell every one of your slaves at a place south of here, and which is within three days' march. The plague has taken off so many of our men, that there are not enough of them left to cut and harvest such abundant crops as our God in his goodness hath bestowed upon us, and these men I know can soon learn to work."

Our Arabian masters said but little in reply to this harangue, but with us there was a general vociferation against it. At no time before this, had we dared to interfere in their conversation; but now we were driven to extremities, and pleaded as for our lives. The English boys took the lead: speaking to them in Arabic, they refuted all that the fellow had advânced; and they asserted that I was well known in Swearah, and had friends there enough to redeem us all. In this condition of horrid suspense we were left for half an hour, when Ahamed came back, and told us that none of our masters had consented to sell to the fellow, except the owner of Hussey, my mate, and that he (Hussey's master) had agreed to sell him, and return home himself. I tried to find out the price he was sold for, but could not. My poor companion, Hussey, shed tears in abundance, and the rest of us appeared in great distress. As to Ahamed, all he said on the occasion was, "I cannot help it." After a short silence, my mate put on his manly resolution, and said, "Let it be so; I must go, but our separation will be very short; I will be in St. Cruz in the morning." To part with him in this manner was more than we could bear. Boy Jack was not to be trusted, but as he understood the Arabic much better than either of the other boys, I thought it best to make use of him as my mouth; accordingly I directed him to go to Hussey's master, and tell him if he would not part with that man, I would pledge my honor that the Consul should give more than the price he had sold him for, and that over and above this I would make him a present on our arrival at Mogadore. In this case, though, perhaps, in but few others, Jack did his duty faithfully, and the bargain was broken off; not, however, till after Ahamed, the mate's master, and myself, with Jack for our interpreter, had had a long talk on the subject. At sunset, our chapman re-crossed the river, and rode away over the hill, and out of our sight, in as great a rage as it was possible for a barbarian or savage to show.

On the morning of the twelfth, the sun was fully up before we had got fairly under way. For several miles, and to within two or three miles of St. Cruz, we pursued the downward course of the river, and then we turned to the right, in a direction for that city, which had a formidable appearance. It was situated on the peak of a very high hill, formed by nature for defense, and on the side that met our view were embrasures or guns; it was natural for us to conclude that this was the emperor's frontier town. When we had come within two or three hundred yards of the lower town, we saw a man skipping down over the rocks, and advancing toward the lower town with great speed, having a gun in his hand. As soon as he had come within call, he ordered us to stop ; we all stopped at a little distance from the nearest houses, and he demanded of us who we were. On receiving from the Arabs an answer to this question, he demanded the name of our chief. To which Ahamed answered that he was chief, and he gave him his name, and my name was called for next. Upon which he said to me, "You are to appear before the governor immediately." My bosom swelled with joy at these words. I called to Larra, and bade him follow me. I forgot my inability to jump, and to run, and how, in my feeble and emaciated condition, I made the ascent so quick, is beyond my power to tell. When we had arrived at the gate of the battery, which was in a very short time, Larra observed to me, "Captain, the water *runs* off your face," which was a circumstance that I had not perceived before. We entered, I directly following the soldier, Larra next, and Ahamed last.

In this room of refuge, where we had so happily arrived at last, were sitting on a bench three well-looking men, of much lighter color and stouter frame than the Arabs, and one of them was holding in his hand a long spyglass. They ordered us to sit down, and we did so; seating ourselves in the middle of the room, which was probably from twelve to sixteen feet square, while Ahamed (not chief now) squeezed himself up in one corner. Looking, as I did, all around the room, I saw a door back of us that was shut. We sat silent, for near a quarter of an hour, these men all the time fixing their eyes upon us. At last, Larra breaking silence, asked me if I thought any one of these men was the governor. I told him I thought he was not there. Then one of them asked me in English if I were an Englishman? and upon my replying that I was, he said, "You and the boy both look like Spaniards." I answered him, including Larra with myself, we are English. Speaking very slow and distinctly, he asked me to what part of England our ship belonged? where we were bound, and what after? how large a ship she was? how many poles she had? what goods were on board? and how much money we had with us? In answer to these queries, I told him the ship belonged to Liverpool, was bound to the Cape de Verd islands for a load of salt, that she was a considerably large ship, but not very large, that she had three poles, (masts,) had no goods, and but a little money, barely enough to buy a load of salt. He asked me if there was no salt in Liverpool? I told him we had large quantities of it there, but that the salt which we were going after was of another kind, made in a hot climate by the heat of the sun, and that we were to carry it to a foreign country, far away to the westward, where it was worth more money than the Liverpool salt. "Well," he said, "the next time you come along this coast keep further off; ships with three poles should not come so near; formerly, when we had trade at St. Cruz, the large ships always laid off a great way from shore." At that moment we heard a noise without, when the Moor that had been questioning me, instantly says, "The governor is coming." As he entered the room, I arose, and addressed him in English, just as I should have done if he had understood that language, the Moor in the meantime interpreting to him what I said. He returned my salutation, and invited me to sit down, which I did.

He was a stout, portly, well-looking man, about six feet high and nearly fifty years old, of a light copper color, with a short bushy beard, and wore a clean white haick, and neat morocco slippers; his pleasing, manly look prepossessed me in his favor; all his questions to me were pertinent and distinct. The Moor told him in Arabic the substance of the interrogations which he had put to me, and then the governor went on to ask me himself several questions about my shipwreck, the cause of it, the time it happened, and whether the Arabs there present had any of the gold that I had lost After I had, by and through Larra, answered all these questions to his satisfaction, he asked me how this Arab (Ahamed) had treated me? Without waiting for a reply, he continued on, and said, "These Arabs are all a set of thieves, robbers, and murderers, and from time immemorial they have been at war with the Moors as well as with all others within their reach, and if they have not treated you well, I will keep you here a few days, when I shall be going myself to Swearah, and will take you along with me and deliver you up to the Consul." Ahamed trembled, as I could plainly perceive. I then answered the question he had put to me regarding our treatment by Ahamed, telling him that Ahamed and his companions had bought us of a hunting party, and had paid a considerable sum for us, and had not treated us so well as perhaps they ought, but I had no doubt they would do better in this respect for the time to come, and being so near Swearah, I preferred going on with them. He then asked if I was hungry? I am both hungry and very thirsty, was my reply. Upon this he turned to the soldier that stood behind him, and ordered some drink for me, telling him not to be long after it. In a few minutes he returned, with some sweet milk mixed with water, of which we drank freely. I was about to reach the kettle to Ahamed, but the governor forbade it, saying, "*That fellow don't drink from my kettle.*" The kettle was of copper, and scoured to a high polish. After Larra had drank, I set it down, and then came the victuals. It was a dish of coscoosoo, which is a favorite dish with Moors; on it lay a whole quarter of a fat goat, the sight of which astonished me. The quantity of food in this dish was greater than our whole company of eleven had eaten for three days together. The smell was to us as deliciously fragrant as can possibly be described. I looked at it for some time, when the governor and Larra both speaking to me at the same moment, said, "Captain why do you not eat?" The truth was, I was afraid to eat; for so keen was my appetite, that had I fully gratified it with feeding on such an excellent dish, I do believe, empty as my stomach then was, it would not only have been the means of my going no further, but would have killed me outright. When we began to eat, all their eyes were fixed upon us. I ate in a manner as sparing as I could possibly bring myself to, and finding Larra inclined to be ravenous, I repeatedly told him not to eat like a hog. One of the Moors who understood that expression, interpreted it to the governor, who laughed heartily, which did not, however, disturb Larra at all, but he still bolted it down with all speed. In the dish lay a knife, with which I cut off some of the meat, and ate it, and drank a little milk and water, and so quitted it, while feeling nearly as hungry as when I had begun. At first the governor urged me to eat more, but when I mentioned to him the state of my stomach, he said, "You have been prudent."

The governor was absent about half an hour, when he came to the door, with nearly a dozen thin loaves of bread, which he reached to me, and I do think they were the whitest I ever saw. I took them, and stowed them away about me, and returned him thanks for this noble present. He took the street, and walked back to the battery, which probably was his audience chamber. There he addressed himself to Ahamed in these words: "You

I command to take these Christians to Swearah, and deliver them over to their Consul without any unnecessary delay; in three days after this you are to arrive there; use them in the best manner you possibly can; and now depart." The governor was standing when he uttered this mandate. Ahamed was sitting when I left him, nor had he, according to Larra's account, stirred an inch since that time; but upon hearing the orders of the governor, he fell upon his knees, or rather advanced on them, up to the governor, and kissed the hem of his garment. When I joined the men who had been my companions in distress, I found them feasting sumptuously; they had fine, white, fresh loaves of bread, with dry dates and water, set before them, and no doubt by the governor's order. Instantly upon my appearance, every one of them was desirous of knowing from me what reception I had met with; but so overcome was I at our good fortune, that I could only tell them we were safe. We were then all life and spirits, thanking God for our deliverance thus far. The Arabs with the camels had been detained by the governor's order, as a party connected with us, and they were in great haste to proceed on. We were very quickly provided with such kinds of saddles, or riding-seats, as could be procured, which were mean at best. Some us had none, but luckily for myself, I got some rubbish quilted on behind the hump, so high as to form a tolerable seat.

When it was near noon of the second day after we had left St. Cruz, we met with six or eight men together, who were traveling westward. Whether they were Arabs or Moors we did not know; in some respects these two kinds of people appear alike; their color does not differ a great deal, and some of the wild Arabs shave their heads like the Moors. Our Arabs had some talk with these travelers, which none of us took notice of, as our minds were at rest as regarded our reaching Swearah. They separated, and we walked on, and presently Ahamed seemed to be agitated with something, and muttered to himself as he went along, but none of us regarded it. At length, while he, Larra, and myself, were close together, he broke out in a passion, and expressed himself thus: "I swear by my beard (taking hold of it with his hand) I will carry you no further than that house," pointing to one that was near by. "I have heard, by a man I can believe, the Consul will not ransom any more Christians, and I am sorry I ever brought you here; by the expense of my purchasing you of the mountaineers, and the provision I have made for you, you have destroyed all my substance. You told me the Consul would redeem you, and now I find I am cheated, and you shall go no further."

Larra, with all dispatch, interpreted to me this complaint and threat of Ahamed, and added, "he has taken the oath that is most sacred among the Mohammedans,"—meaning his swearing by his beard. By this time we had arrived at the gate of a large dwelling, and we were marched into the yard, which contained perhaps half an acre; in the rear of which was a small cabin about twelve by twenty feet. Having arrived at this prison of ours, Ahamed said to me, "Here you are to remain until the money for your ransom be paid down." I attempted to reason with him, but he, and all the rest of them, were as cross as curs.

The Arabs were now very peevish, and what seemed to occasion their uncommon peevishness at this time, they could not devise what measures to take with us. We suspected they were trying to collect strength to get us back into their own territory. Soon after this, a lusty Moor with a clean haick and morocco slippers, whom we suspected to be a magistrate, came into the yard. He approached us, calling out Christiano, as usual, and speaking to the Arabs; and, according to my arrangement in the morning, I accosted him in the following words—We are here in the Sultan's territory, held by these Arabs, and from your hands we ask justice. Your Sultan and our Sultan are on the most friendly terms. We ask nothing from these men but our freedom, which we are willing to pay for; they have been told that our Consul is unable to pay a sufficient ransom for us all, but in that they have been misinformed. To keep us here starving will never help them."

After I had gone through with what I had to say, he asked me if I could write? I answered that I could. He then turned to the Arabs, who had heard our talk, and proposed to them to let me write a letter, and have it sent to the Consul, adding, "You will know then whether the stories they have told you be true or false." The Arabs consented that I should send a letter if I would hire a Moor to carry it, which I agreed to. Accordingly a man was sent for, who demanded four dollars for that service, and I promised to pay it. Upon this, he said he would be ready as soon as he could get his horse, and that would be as soon as I could write my letter. A sheet of paper, a reed, (by the way, the Moors always use reeds for pens,) and some ink, were immediately procured for me, and a large flat stone was my writing-table. Our good Moor lent me a sharp knife, with which I made a tolerable pen. Ahamed sat opposite to me. It was agreed upon that Ahamed should dictate my letter, and I called for Larra to interpret it, but he insisted that Jack should be the interpreter, to which I consented. Ahamed began to dictate, and did it in short sentences, and I wrote about as fast as he spoke, but not a single sentence of what he told me to write. The substance of what he dictated to me was, that myself and crew were down in the country, held captives by the Arabs, who would not carry us to Swearah till our redemption money was sent them in advance; that agreeably to our contract, for which they had my solemn pledge of honor, our ransom was to be four hundred dollars for each of us, and forty dollars over and above for myself; that the men who held us captives had been kind to us, but were unable to give us much to eat; that we were very sickly, and needed help immediately, and that the bearer would bring the money, and the Consul might send a man to see it paid.

I directed my letter to the British Consul at Mogadore, or any other humane man into whose hands it might fall, and stated in it that we were a short day's march eastward of St. Cruz, and, according to my calculation, seventy miles south-west of Mogadore, but that I was unable to name the place we were at; that we had been wrecked on the coast of Barbary; that my crew here were eight in number, and that beside we had with us three of the Martin Hall's crew; that we were in a suffering condition, and that the Arabs here were devising means to get us back, beyond St. Cruz, to a region where we should be doomed to drag out our existence in barbarian slavery; and finally, that I wished the bearer might be detained till he could release us, since, in the event of his returning without the money, we should be dragged back before aid could be afforded us, adding my belief that he had a full knowledge of these merciless savages, and would take such measures for us as humanity should dictate. When I had done writing my letter, the Arabs, very unexpectedly, ordered me to read it. My mate, who was looking over my shoulder, seeing my embarrassment, said to me, "Read on, you can do it well enough"—and luckily for me, I made out to read it to their satisfaction. Ahamed then told Jack to read it, and well knowing he could not, I reached him the letter, and Jack, upon looking at it, said it would do very well, as also said our old friend the Moor. Though I had folded the letter up before the Moor was ready to start, yet he demanded some tobacco in addition to his stipulated pay, saying I had detained him too long. *That* I promised, and then had to open the letter and write *tobacco* at the bottom. Now he thought it would do, and said he would return on the third day. We all went to the gate to see him off, and he started upon a full gallop, on a fine bay horse, and was very soon out of sight. The Moors departed. My excellent friend, the Moor, said to me, "You now will soon gain your freedom," and left us, after I had returned to him my cordial thanks for his kindness to us. We all now returned to our lodging-place, rejoicing at this most flattering prospect of soon obtaining our freedom.

In a single hour these hopes of ours were blasted. To our astonishment the Moor came running into the yard, with the letter open in his hand. Upon our going out of our cabin to know the cause of his return, he told us he had ridden but a little way when he met with one of his acquaintances, who desired to know where he was bound, and on what business; and, upon his telling him, he wanted to see the letter, which having examined, he said it was good for nothing. We, on our part, contended that the letter was a good one. In the meantime our faithful friend came to us, in apparent anger, and demanded the cause of our messenger's return; and being told the story of it by the Arabs, and I still insisting upon it, that the letter was good, he took our part, and said the man who had examined it was a liar, and then walked out of the yard. Soon after I took Larra with me, and we went to Ahamed, who was sitting under the wall of our enclosure. I told him he was acting contrary to his own interest in thus detaining us here, and recommended it to him to send on some man or other with the letter which the Moor had brought back, assuring him that immediate attention would be paid to that letter on its arrival at Swearah. Ahamed replied, "That letter is good for nothing." Let me me read it to you again, said I to him. "No," he answered, "that will do no good, for it sha'n't be sent on again." After a little pause, he asked me if I would send a man up for the money? I readily told him I would if he would send a man and horse with him. This proposition he agreed to, and the arrangement made between us was satisfactory to all the Arabs.

Our two envoys were moving toward the gate, when our friendly Moor met them, and demanded to know whither they were bound. "They are bound to Swearah," replied Ahamed, "to bring the money for the ransom of these Christians." The Moor then told them to stop, and they did so, and he addressed himself to Ahamed as follows: "Are you so ignorant as to suppose the Consul will believe the story you are about to send him? depend upon it, he will not. I know him, and know that he is a wise man. If you should send Rais, he would believe him, and the money would be in safe hands." Then turning to me, he said, "Is it not so?" I told him this was a plan of their own forming, and that I had consented to it from a belief that any kind of efforts to obtain our freedom would be better than to stay here and not act at all. Ahamed, looking me full in the face, said, "Will you go?" Yes, I answered. "Will you pay the expenses?" I gave him the same answer. "Well," he rejoined, "I will go also, provided you will return with me in case you can't get the money." That I promised to do. "We must have two horses," he said, "and take turns to ride." I agreed to it; and also agreed with the same Moor that we had engaged before, to furnish another horse, for the additional pay of four dollars and a knife. Accordingly another horse was provided in haste, and in the meantime Ahamed was much engaged with his companions the Arabs. As to my men, they came round me, rejoicing that the time of our deliverance was so near at hand.

About four o'clock of our second day's travel, my two companions suddenly disappeared, while descending a steep sand-hill, and the next moment my horse took down the same hill, when, in an instant, there opened to my view the sea, and the town of Mogadore far on the right, and only a few miles distant from it three large brigs lying at anchor. Here the two men made a full stop, and Ahamed said to me, "Do you know that place? See the ships there!" So great were my emotions at this sudden change of my condition, that I was quite overcome, and lost even the power of speech. When they saw the tears gushing profusely from my eyes, they laughed, I suppose at my weakness; for the Arabs consider weeping as beneath the dignity of a man, though not disgraceful in a woman. These men stood till I had collected the manly part, and then asked me if I knew the place, and the ships, and what nation they belonged to? I told them the place was Mogadore, and I had no doubt but the ships belonged to my own country. Here we made a stop, and Ahamed said that we could not enter the town, because its people were asleep. I made use of all the Arabic I was master of to persuade him to go on, but to no purpose; he refused in plain terms, by saying, we must turn back to the buildings only a few rods behind us, where was a considerable collection of dwellings walled in. About nine o'clock I was conducted into my apartment. After I had laid down in this agreeable resting-place, for such it was to me, the Moors flocked all round me, as many as the room could hold, and many others stood without the doorway Their conversation seemed wholly on the occurrences relating to our shipwreck, the situation we were in, in the desert, the money we had cost them, and the disposition of our masters to restore us to our brothers in Swearah. Our visitors told him there was no danger but the Consul would pay for my ransom; "True," they said, "he was not so rich as Court, Jackson, and some others there, but he was good. After listening to their conversation a long time, and being very weary, I fell asleep, but was soon awakened by the smell of broiled beef, on which the Arab and the Moor, with six or eight beside, were feasting sumptuously. As soon as their meal was finished, mine was brought me, which was a wonderful mess for one man, though the quantity was not quite so great as had been given me by the governor of St. Cruz. What was now set before me consisted of about three pounds of beef-steak broiled, about three pounds of hot bread from the oven, sixteen hard boiled eggs, and half a pound of butter. As I was beginning, Ahamed said to his company, "Now see him eat." I first broke the bread, and ate a little of it; I pulled some of the meat to pieces, and ate of that about two ounces; I broke an egg, and finding it hard boiled, laid it down, and after eating moderately of the bread, and a little butter, I left off, while my appetite was still craving strongly for more. I then broke open a small loaf of bread still warm, and put a little butter on the inside of it, to be laid between my mats, under my head, and, all this done, I gave up the dish. They asked me why I did not eat, and if I were sick? I told them I was not sick, and gave them to understand that eating more plentifully might injure me. Upon which they took the dish to themselves, and ate all I had left, except the broken egg, and what I had polluted with my fingers; not only this did they reject, but they carefully scraped off the butter on the side

I had taken it from. I fell asleep before they had dispersed, and awoke a little before daylight. It was in vain that I urged Ahamed to go on; he objected to it, that the Consul was asleep. After the sun was considerably up, Ahamed, at my repeated solicitations, brought me the horse, and I mounted, and took along the beach, near the edge of the sea, where the ground was firm for traveling. We were soon at the city gate, and were detained there but a few minutes, just to give time for Ahamed to answer several questions that were put to him; which done, we were permitted to enter. As soon as we had passed through the gate, I looked around me, and devoutly exclaimed, O Lord, protect me within these walls! Having turned round several corners, into narrow straight streets, we came at last to a very large double door, at which Ahamed knocked several times, but received no answer. I asked him if this was the Consul's? But before he had time to reply, a man came running up to us, and inquired of me, in good English, who I was? Upon my telling him, he says, "Come along with me, and I will show you the way to the Consul's We soon came to the Consul's door, on which I gave three distinct knocks, when its latch was raised, and the door I pushed open, which led me into the yard that was in the center of the buildings. Hearing men talking above, and there being a stone stairway on the left, I ascended, and at the head of the stairs I saw six or eight well-looking sailors, who, the moment they got their eyes on me, rushed forward, knowing of course that I was a shipwrecked seaman. After bidding me welcome, in their peculiar way, their inquiry of me was, if I had seen any of the Martin Hall's crew? and when I told them that three of that crew were with my men, and that another of them I had seen, who had been left with the wild Arabs, their joy on the occasion was expressed in their own way, but was as sincere no doubt as if they had expressed it in the most refined language. When these emotions had a little subsided, I asked for the Consul, and one of them, after telling me he was asleep, ran to his door, and called out, "Mr. Gwyn, Mr. Gwyn, an English captain is here from the Arab coast, and the Arabs with him."

I heard him answer something, and in one minute open came his door, and he presented himself to me with nothing on but his shirt and breeches. Never can I forget the cordial reception he gave me. "My good friend," he said, "how happy am I to see you! Wait a little till I dress myself." He returned, leaving me with the sailors, who I found were of the Martin Hall's crew. They all huddled around me, like so many children around an adored parent, asking the same questions over and over again. Soon the venerable old gentleman, Consul Gwyn, came to us, dressed, and in a truly friendly manner shook hands with me the second time, and then said, "Come with me, my breakfast is ready." While I was following him to his room, he made a stop, and asked me to what part of England my ship belonged? Upon this I told him that I had been carrying on a piece of deception, but which I believed had injured no man; that I had all along called myself an Englishman, with a view of gaining my freedom, as I was fearful there was no American Consul here; and that in fact I was an American, belonging to the State of New York, and my ship also belonged there. He paused but a moment only, when he said, "Very well; you are a Christian, and that is enough." I hastily asked him if I were safe from the Arabs? He answered, "Yes, you are in no danger." I will do everything in my power for you, but I am poor, and cannot advance money for your ransom; but beyond doubt there are gentlemen here who will do it." I told him I was in fear of my men being dragged back to tne country of the Arabs: upon which he called for Ahamed, who, with the Moor, was sitting by the kitchen door, and interrogated him as to the place where my men were ; and after he had described it in the same manner that I had, he told him to go and bring the whole of them up. Ahamed, in reply, inquired of the Consul if he would pay the ransom for us, together with all that I had promised him beside?

The Consul then, directing his discourse to me, asked me what I had promised? whereupon I went on to tell him every promise I had made in that case, and he interpreted it to Ahamed, who acknowledged that my statement was correct; and the Consul said to him "Very well, that shall all be paid." He also immediately paid off the Moor, and I added to it a bunch of good Virginia tobacco. The Consul, now addressing himself to Ahamed, said, "I order you to return to our men, and before the night of the third day, do you make your appearance before the gates of this city, together with all my brothers that are in your keeping." "I will do it," replied Ahamed, "if you will pay me my price for their ransom, and not otherwise; for Rais," pointing to me, "assured me that if I would come here with him, he would return with me, and carry the money with him, and pay it there." "The money," replied the Consul to him, "shall not be paid there, but here. I never did, nor ever will pay money for my brothers until I can see them; and as to the price, I must see them before my mind can be made up with respect to it." Ahamed continued to urge his claim till the Consul, becoming a little impatient, called his servant, and said to him, "Go to the governor, and tell him from me, that ten of my brothers are on this side of St. Cruz, in possession of the Arabs, who refuse to bring them up; and that I demand of him twenty soldiers to be dispatched for them immediately." Ahamed attentively listened to these orders, and before the servant had reached the street door, he begged that he might be called back, and promised to go himself, and bring the men on; accordingly he set off without delay. It was after he had gone, that the Consul told me the story which I have now related.

As my fears with regard to the safety of my men were by no means at an end, I mentioned those fears to the Consul. "Quiet your mind," he replied to me, "I have been here in this town for more than thirty years, and have ransomed from slavery a number of British subjects: I know what kind of people I have to deal with, and I know their language." After this the Consul proposed to me to walk out with him, in order to see about the ransom of myself and my crew. We went to the house of William and Alexander Court, and found these gentlemen on the terrace roofs of their dwelling. When I had made them acquainted with the object of our visit, and solicited them to advance a sufficient sum for the ransom of myself and crew, they manifested a desposition to relieve us, spoke in the highest terms of our Consul-General at Tangier, and told me we had an agent in the Road, and advised an immediate statement of our situation to him.

We spent the afternoon and the evening at the Courts , and returned home to Consul Gwyn's house at eleven. Soon I fell into a fine sleep, but after a short nap, I awoke, utterly insensible of my situation. Having lost all recollection of being at Mogadore, I sprung from my bed, nor did I conceive where I was, till I had walked across the room and looked out of the window into the yard. It was like a dream. I got my shoes, rolled the blanket round me, and walked the room for two hours. After wearying myself, I laid down again, and slept till morning, and arose very much refreshed. The Consul had now made his appearance, at an hour earlier than usual. According to his custom, he called upon his servant for breakfast, but, before it was ready, we had a long conversation together, relative to the situation I was in.

After breakfast, we repaired to the counting-house of the two Courts, who instantly agreed to pay our ransom. They provided for me a courier to carry a letter to the Consul-General, and to that gentleman I wrote an account of my situation, stating to him all the particulars, and requesting him to point out to me the course I should pursue—observing that I considered myself subject to his direction. If I recollect aright, the courier, who went on foot in preference to riding, was to have thirty dollars for this service, and was to return in twenty-four days. He accomplished the undertaking by the time agreed on, and brought me an answer from that worthy character, couched in such tender and soothing language, as made an impression on my mind, which time can never efface. His congratulations with me on my release from cruel bondage, and his thanks to the Courts for their humane interference in my behalf, seemed spontaneously to have flowed from the warmest of hearts. It was on the afternoon of the twentieth or twenty-first, when, from the terrace, I discovered my men. I went out to meet them, and the English sailors all followed me. As soon as we had come together, I hastily told them we were all safe; that though we had no American Consul here, we had friends enough. Joy was seen in every countenance. We all marched off together to the Consul's house, where their names and ages were all taken down; and having received a message from the governor, ordering us to repair to the Battery gate, we all went to it. Consul Gwyn was asked a few questions concerning us, the first of which was, whether we were Englishmen? He replied, we were not, but, what was the same thing, we were his brothers, and he wished to ransom and keep us. The governor asked me a few questions, particularly as to the place where we were wrecked, how many of our men had been left in the hands of the Arabs, and so forth. He then turned to the Arabs, and told them to bring all the Christians up as soon as they were wrecked, and not suffer them to perish in the desert; which injunction the Arabs promised to obey—and the governor then dismissed us.

As soon as we had left the Battery, we went to the two Courts, who provided a room to lodge our men in; and our next attention was about our ransom. William, the younger of the two brothers, had been in this country for many years, and was well acquainted with the language, and with the nature and dispositions of the Arabs; and with him we had a long conference relative to the amount of the sum that should be paid for our ransom. "Giving a great ransom," said he, "for Christian captives, and showing a strong desire to relieve them, is what has always had a direct tendency to retard their deliverance; for when the Arabs find that a great price is given for Christian slaves, their avarice is excited, and their rich men buy them up to speculate upon. There have been instances," continued he, "when, it being known that a large sum was offered for a certain number of Christians, they were bought up for the purpose of speculation, and the purchaser having come up here, and then getting a better offer, returned home, sold them to other speculators, who kept them for a still greater price, and detained them so long that some of them died of hard usage and of grief." On the other hand, he said, if their ransom was very small, the inducement to bring them would be alike small; and he therefore thought it best to pursue a middle course. The Arabs were constantly at our heels for their pay, and were full of promises to bring on our other men. The Consul and myself left them, and went to dine with a very respectable English merchant by the name of Jackson.

When we returned home, after dinner, I found Ahamed waiting for me. He had become very much alarmed, for he had just found out that we were not Englishmen, but belonged to another country. I suspect that Jack had told him of this, with a view to alarm him, and create dissatisfaction in his mind. I confessed the fact, but through the same boy Jack I explained to him, that though we were inhabitants of another country, yet we were the same kind of people with the English. "You may see yourself," I told him, "that we speak the same language, and that my friends here, as I told you before in the desert, take the same care of me as if I were an Englishman, and tasher Courts you may depend will pay you off to-morrow." But notwithstanding what I said, he went away with the appearance of some jealousy that a trick was to be played upon him. The next morning I arose very early, and after walking upon the terrace for an hour, I took a walk to the market-place, Where I luckily met with a Mogadore Jew, whom I had seen at my friend Jackson's. While I was talking with him, Ahamed hove in sight, walking toward us quickly. I told the Jew that the Arab coming was Ahamed, and begged of him to act as my interpreter with him, which he readily consented to do. We sat down under a wall, and there talked together an hour, and, during that time, I fully explained to Ahamed the particulars as to what country I belonged, how it became separated from the government of England, the harmony subsisting between the two countries, and the cause of my telling him that I was English. Ahamed heard me with the greatest attention, so that it seemed as if every word was imprinting itself in his mind ; and after I had done he replied, "You did very right in telling me that story, for if you had said that you were not English, but from some other country, we should have had nothing to do with you, as not expecting that anybody would pay your ransom, and, in that case, the mountaineers would have carried you back to their homes, and there you must have died:" he added, "what you have now told me, accounts for tasher Courts employing themselves in this matter, and I hope they will do justice to us." Upon my telling him that that would be done, he asked me to name my country again, which I did several times, but he could not pronounce it well, though he came near it, calling it *Amerk*. Finally, he asked me if I had not forgotten my promises to his wives, and to Salear? A Moor's shop being directly opposite, I borrowed a little money of the Jew, and went directly to it, and bought every little article that I had promised, and some other things beside, the whole costing, I believe, three dollars. Ahamed was remarkably well pleased with them, and hastened off, as I supposed, to his comrades.

After this interview with the Arab, I returned home, where I found the Consul waiting breakfast for me. At the table the conversation was confined to our ransom, about which I felt very uncomfortable, as the amount of it might affect our men who were yet behind. The Consul recommended it to me to leave it with the two Courts to act according to their own judgments, saying they were both judicious men, and that William understood well these sort of people, and their language. Agreeably to his advice, I kept at home, and the Courts paid them off, with such an amount as they thought proper. The Arabs craved more of course. As soon as this business was settled, Ahamed came to my room, and acknowledged the receipt of all that I had promised him, but blamed the

Courts (whom I thought blameless) for not giving a higher ransom for us. Being one day at my friend Jackson's table, at dinner, the Consul sick at home the while, and none there but we two, a good-looking Moor, or Jew, (I cannot recollect which,) came in, having business with Jackson. He took a seat along side of him, and for some time they both seemed much engaged in conversation, in the Arabic. When their business seemed to be gone through with, he (the stranger) looked very attentively toward me, and began a conversation, of which, I found, from a few words I caught, that I was the subject, but could not conjecture as to the scope of it. They both laughed heartily, and, in conclusion, Jackson turned to me, and asked me if I had in my ship a keg of dollars in a barrel of beef? I answered yes ; and then he rehearsed to me this man's story, as follows: "As I was down the Arab country on business, (said this Moor, or Jew,) I heard of the wreck of a ship, and I concluded to go to it, thinking there might be an opening for a speculation. When I had arrived, I found there two or three hundred Arabs, the whole of those Arabs that first took possession of the wreck and crew having gone into the interior to sell their plunder and slaves. As to the cargo, they informed me there were no goods, but that they found in the bottom of the ship an *earth*, which they did not know the use or value of, but thought, as it was in a ship, it must be valuable somewhere, and they wished me to look at it. I did so, and I found that they had divided it into little heaps, of which each of them had one to his share. On seeing this, I laughed at them heartily, and told them it was ballast, and of no more value than the sand they stood on. They were mortified in the extreme, and said they had been at work for several days in getting it ashore, and that in small quantities, as they had to *dive* for every pound of it. They told me they had got out most of the salted provisions, and were then finishing that job. About ten barrels of the salted provisions were then lying on the beach, which they were dividing, allowing one barrel to a certain number of men.

When the barrels were opened for a subdivision, such of them as contained pork were rejected with abhorrence, and their owners were greatly mortified ; but every barrel of beef was divided among its joint owners by pieces. One of them, as he was taking the pieces out of one of the barrels, came to a keg, standing endwise, which was so heavy that he could not lift it by its hoops. This exciting curiosity, and many of them, by turns, trying to lift it, in the confusion the barrel was overset, and the keg rolled out of it. They soon got a stone and stove it to pieces, and, in so doing, the dollars flew out, the noise of which rallied together the whole gang, and it was then with them, catch who can. Each contended for his share so ferociously, and their cimeters were employed with such effect, that a great number were severely wounded, and some, it was thought, would die of their wounds. There being some barrels yet unopened, they all, as one, stove them to pieces, with stones, and searched them for more dollars, and, upon their finding none, a party swum to the ship, and searched there for more barrels, but in vain. The right owners of the barrel containing the dollars claimed the whole of them; upon which a council was called, and the chief presided; their pleas were able on both sides, but as I came off soon, I did not learn the result."—Thus ended this stranger's story, as given me by my friend Jackson, and thus it fared with my hidden treasure.

A very lamentable instance of apostacy took place at Mogadore while I was there, and with one of the Martin Hall's boys. The boy Jack, of whom I have so frequently made mention, was often missing from the

Consul's house, and whenever some one was sent in search of him, he was found in some Moorish house, evidently preferring their company The Consul used to admonish him, and point out to him the evil tendency of keeping such company, but all to no purpose. At last he was missing a whole night, and in the morning following he was found in the company of several Moors, one of whom claimed him as his adopted son; and, at the same time, Jack declared that he had embraced the Mohammedan faith, that he had been circumcised, and had gone through their other ceremonies, and he claimed protection from the one whom he called his adopted father. This information was carried to the Consul, who was in much trouble on the occasion. One way only was left to reclaim or recover him out of their hands, and that was to make an application to the governor for that purpose, and accordingly an application was made. The governor's reply was, "You shall have all the indulgence that our laws permit, which is this: examine the boy in my presence, from day to day, for three successive days, and if you can within that time persuade him to return to his former religion, you may receive him back; otherwise, as he has voluntarily come among us, and gone through our ceremonies, we are in duty bound to retain him." The boy being sent for, and examined by the Consul, who did it in the Arabic language, he declared that he loved and esteemed his adopted father; that he had become a Mohammedan, and would never change from it. After the Consul had finished his part of the examination, the governor commenced, by asking Jack why he had changed his faith? His reply was, he did it because he believed the condition of the Mohammedans was preferable to that of the Christians; that if he should continue in the religion he was then of, he should see God, and be saved; whereas the Christians were all to be damned. This lesson had, beyond doubt, been given him by his adopted father. The governor then asked him if he knew the prayers, and the meaning of them? He declared that he did, and went on to repeat them. Finally, he asked him if he understood the prayer of Ramadam? He said he did, and repeated it, without missing a word, though it is a very long one. The governor then dismissed him, and after he was gone, observed to the Consul, "The boy is safe." The Consul continued every day throughout the afore-mentioned term of three days, in his endeavors to reclaim the boy, but at last was obliged to let him go. This story I had from Consul Gwyn's own mouth at the time. When the three days had expired, a great rejoicing took place, a grand procession was formed, and boy Jack, mounted on a horse, moved round the city in great style, the followers singing and shouting in a merry mood, gratified with the grand acquisition they had made, in bringing a poor ignorant Christian boy into the saving light of Mohammedanism! I saw Jack frequently afterward, but he always avoided me when it was in his power, and not only me, but all those belonging to the two other crews.

One day about this time, while Consul Gwyn, John Foxcroft, and myself, were sitting together, engaged in conversation, a wild Arab, and one of the worst-looking kind, came up stairs, with a bundle, and wished to know if the Consul would buy some handsome cloth he had. In unrolling the bundle, out rolled the two gown patterns of tabinet, which I had bought for my wife in Cork. The thoughts of my wife, and of the poor black man who had taken the patterns in his pack, saying, "*Mistress shall have these yet*," rushed so powerfully on my mind, and excited such violent emotions, that I could not refrain from turning aside, and giving vent to my anguish by a flow of tears. Foxcroft proposed to buy the dark colored piece for his wife, and called her in; the Consul, on the contrary, took a fancy to the light colored piece, for waistcoat patterns. While Foxcroft's wife was making her observations upon the tabinet, I told her the price of it in Ireland, and that I had bought there the two pieces for my wife. Upon which the two gentlemen immediately offered to relinquish the bargain to me, but being short of cash, I declined it, and desired them to proceed in the purchase. Each took a piece, and paid the Arab for it, according to my recollection, two dollars. I did not expect to hear or see any more of it; but the next morning, in taking out a clean shirt from my trunk, I discovered that some person had been to it, and, upon examination, I found that the light colored gown pattern had been placed at the bottom in such a manner as might prevent me from discovering it. It is needless to mention what took place respecting it, afterward; suffice it to repeat, my wife got her gown, and wears it to this day.

Some time about the middle of July, a Portuguese schooner arrived from Lisbon, chartered by the house of the Bulkleys of that place. She brought some goods suitable for that market, in order to take in a return cargo of the products of this country, and was consigned to the house of William and Alexander Court. The schooner was loaded with dispatch, with what skins had been procured for her, and as to the rest, was filled with wheat. She being the first vessel that was to sail, I engaged our passage to Lisbon in her. When she was nearly ready for departure, the Consul sent for Pat, who had left our men's lodging-place long before, and was harbored by a countryman of his in town, a cooper by trade: he sent for him to inform him that he was to go with us to Lisbon. Pat refused to come, and sent word back that he durst not go with us, for that the mate and some others of our crew had threatened to kill him whenever they had him in their power. The Consul desired me to speak to him, and tell him he must go. I did so; but he declared that he was afraid of his life, and had no doubt but we would destroy him before he could reach Europe. My promises to the contrary had no good effect upon him, and he remained behind. When the time had come for us to leave the port, (I think it was the twenty-seventh of July,) our stores having been all previously put on board, and notice being sent to the governor, we, with all our baggage, accompanied by the Consul and many of my Mogadore friends, went to the beach. Our captain, who was an easy, slow kind of man, declined going to sea before the next morning, although the wind was fair, and the weather fine. His accommodations were small, but yet they were very comfortable, nor was he wanting in disposition to render our situation pleasant. I could not persuade him to go to sea till the afternoon, when we got under weigh and left the port, going round to the west of Mogadore island. The vessel was a very dull sailer, and the winds being moderate and light, we had been at sea twenty days when we made the rock of Lisbon, right ahead, with a fair wind.

On the twenty-seventh of September, in the morning, according to the best of my recollection, we were examined by the health officer, and permitted to land. After we had gone through with some little ceremony at an office at Belem, we were once more at our liberty on a Christian shore. A captain Hand, of Charleston, was at Belem with his boat, who gave me a passage to Lisbon, where we arrived about eleven o'clock. I immediately visited the American Consul, who treated me with great kindness, and sent a servant to show me to my lodgings, where I had scarcely got seated, when a gentleman accosted me to know who I was.

On my telling him of my situation, which was done with great brevity he asked me if I wished to go home? and, upon my answering that I did, he said to me, "I have a good ship which will be ready to sail for Baltimore in two days; in her you are welcome to a passage." His kind offer I readily accepted, and told him I would call on our Consul, who had offered me money, and to furnish my stores. His reply was, "My good Sir, I did not offer you a half-way passage; my stores are all laid in, of which you are to partake with me; go on board as soon as you please." I could scarcely find words to reply to this generous man His name was Norman, and his ship was the Perseverance, of Baltimore; she was a fine coppered ship, of 340 tons. I now furnished myself with some thick clothes, and repaired on board the Perseverance. I think we left the river Tagus on the second or third of October. Although our ship was a fast sailer, yet by reason of our having had either light or contrary winds, we did not arrive at Baltimore till about the eighteenth of November. I arrived at Hudson, among my dear friends and relatives, after an absence of one year, to a day; that is to say, from the first of December 1800, to the first of the same month, 1801.

THE ABANDONMENT

OF

ALEXANDER SELKIRK.

A SCOTTISH SAILOR, ON THE ISLAND OF JUAN FERNANDEZ, WHERE HE DWELT

IN SOLITUDE FOR SEVERAL YEARS.

ALEXANDER SELKIRK, the undoubted original of Defoe's celebrated character, Robinson Crusoe, was born in the year 1676, in the village of Largo, on the southern coast of the county of Fife in Scotland. The name of Selkirk (or Selcraig, which was the old mode of spelling it,) is not an uncommon one in the village, the population of which now considerably exceeds two thousand.

John Selkirk, the father of Alexander, was a thriving shoemaker, who lived in a house of his own—which has since been pulled down—at the west end of the town. He appears to have been a man of strict temper, respected for his steady and religious character, and, like the majority of Scottish parents at that time, a severe disciplinarian in his family. The name of his wife was Euphan Mackie, also, it would seem, a native of Largo, and reported by tradition to have been the very contrast of her husband in her parental conduct—as yielding and indulgent as he was rigorous. In the case of Alexander, however, there was a special reason why Mrs. Selkirk should prove a kind and pliant mother. Not only was she considerably advanced in years at the time of his birth, but, by a chance not very common, he was her seventh son, born without an intermediate daughter, and therefore destined, according to an old Scottish superstition, to come to great fortune, and make a figure in the world. Mrs. Selkirk firmly believed this, and made no doubt that her son Sandie was to be the great man of the family. He was therefore her pet; and the greater part of her maternal care, in respect to his education, consisted in confidential discourses with him by the fireside, when the rest of the family were absent, and in occasional consultations how they should screen some little misdemeanor from the eyes of his father.

Young Selkirk was a clever enough boy, and quickly learned all that was taught at the school of his native town. Beside reading, writing, and arithmetic, he is said to have made considerable progress in navigation—a branch of knowledge likely to be of some repute in Largo, not only on account of its being a seacoast town, with a considerable fishing population, but also in consequence of its having been the birthplace and property of Sir Andrew Wood, a distinguished Scottish admiral of the preceding century, whose nautical fame and habits must have produced considerable impression on it. At all events, whether owing to the ideas he received at school, or to the effect on his mind of the perpetual spectacle of the sails in Largo Bay, and of his constant association with the Largo fisher men, Selkirk early determined to follow a seafaring life. Either out of a disposition to let the boy have his own will, or as thinking the life of a sailor the likeliest way to the attainment of the great fortunes which she anticipated for her son, his mother favored his intention; his father, however, opposed it strenuously, and was anxious, now that his other sons were all settled in life, that his youngest should remain at home, and assist him in his own trade. This, and young Selkirk's wayward and obstinate conduct, seem to have kept him and his father perpetually at war; and a descendant of the family used to show a walking-stick which the old man is said to have applied to the back of his refractory son, with the affirmation, "A whip for the horse, a bridle for the ass, and a rod for the fool's back." Notwithstanding the boy's restless character, respect for his father's wishes kept him at home for a considerable time: a father's malediction being too awful a thing for even a seventh son to brave with impunity.

The first thirteen years of Selkirk's life coincide with the hottest period of the religious persecutions in Scotland. He was about three years of age at the time of the assassination of Archbishop Sharp, which took place at not a very great distance from Largo; and the chief subject of interest, during his boyhood, in Fife, as in the other counties of Scotland, was the position of the church, then filled by Episcopalian and indulged clergy, greatly to the disgust of the people. What part old Selkirk and his family may have taken during the time when it was dangerous to show attachment to Presbytery—whether they professed themselves Covenanters, or whether, as is more probable, they yielded a reluctant attendance at the parish church—cannot be ascertained; but the following entry in the parish records of Largo, referring to the year 1689, immediately after the revolution had sealed the restoration of Presbytery in Scotland, will show that if they did attend the parish church, it was not out of lukewarmness to the popular cause, or affection for the established clergyman:—"Sabbath—— 1689.—Which day, the minister being obstructed in his duty, and kept out of the church by a great mob, armed with staves and bludgeons, headed by John Selkirk, divided what money there was among the poor, and retired from his charge." John Selkirk, who thus signalized himself by heading the mob for the expulsion of the conforming clergyman, was the eldest brother of our hero, who, however, is reported himself to to have testified his enthusiasm by flourishing a stick with the other boys.

One of the first youths in Largo to experience the stricter discipline of Presbytery, whose restoration he had celebrated, was Alexander Selkirk. His high spirits, and want of respect for any control, led him, it would appear, to be guilty of frequent misbehavior during divine service; for under date the twenty-fifth of August, 1695, is the following entry in the parish records:—"Alexander Selcraig, son of John Selcraig, elder, cited to appear before the session for indecent conduct in church." This seems to have been more than our hero, now in his nineteenth year, could submit to. The elder's son to appear before the session, and be rebuked for laughing in church! Within twenty-four hours after this terrible citation the young shoemaker was gone; he had left Largo and the land of kirk-sessions behind him, and was miles away at sea. When the kirk-session met, they were obliged to be content with inserting the following paragraph in the record:—"August twenty-seventh.—Alexander Selcraig called out—did not appear, having gone to sea." Resolved, however, that he should not escape the rebuke which he had merited, they add, "Continued until his return."

The return which the kirk-session thus looked forward to, did not take place for six years, during which we have no account of Selkirk's adventures, although the probability is, that he served with the buccaneers, who then scoured the South Seas. To have persisted in calling the young sailor to account for a fault committed six years before, would have been too great severity. The kirk-session, accordingly, do not seem to have made any allusion to the circumstance which had driven him to sea; but it was not long before a still more disgraceful piece of misconduct than the former brought him under their censure. The young sailor, coming home, no doubt, with his character rendered still more reckless and boisterous than before by the wild life to which he had been accustomed at sea, was hardly a fit inmate for a sedate and orderly household, and quarrels and disturbances became frequent in the honest shoemaker's cottage. In the spring of 1702, Selkirk seized an opportunity of going to England; and a short time afterward we find him engaged to proceed with the celebrated Dampier on a buccaneering expedition to the South Seas.

The object of Dampier's voyage was either to capture some of the Spanish vessels, which annually carried to the old world the products of the gold and silver mines of the new, or to seize and put to ransom some of the cities of the Spanish Main. Beside his own vessel, the "St. George," Dampier had with him the "Cinque Ports," commanded by Captain Stradling, on board of which Selkirk acted as sailing-master. After several months of ill-luck and misfortune, the two commanders quarreled, and finally agreed to separate—Selkirk remaining with the latter.

For three months the Cinque Ports kept cruising along the shores of Mexico, Guatemala, and Equatorial America, like a villainous vulture watching the horizon for its prey. No ships, however, appeared to reward the greedy activity of the crew; and at length, in the end of August, Stradling resolved to turn southward, and make for Juan Fernandez, to take in provisions and refit. Meanwhile, as was natural among so many men of savage character cooped up idle in a vessel, all was dissension on board. Stradling and Selkirk especially were, to use a common phrase, at daggers-drawing; now in loud and angry dispute below, now scowling sullenly at each other on deck. Selkirk resolved to leave the vessel as soon as an opportunity offered. Accordingly, when, the beginning of September, they came in sight of Juan Fernandez, two men, left by Dampier on a previous occasion, who had been living on the island since the beginning of March—made their appearance, healthy and strong as ever, and delighting their old companions with an account of how they had spent the seven months of their solitary reign, eating fruit in abundance, chasing goats, and hunting seals, the idea flashed across his mind that he would take their place, and, leaving the vessel to sail away without him, remain the possessor of Juan Fernandez. By what process of imagination he flattered himself that such a life would be agreeable; whether he finally adopted his resolution in a fit of unthinking enthusiasm, such as sometimes leads to strange and whimsical acts, or whether his differences with Stradling, and his disgust with his situation on board the Cinque Ports, were really such that escape by any method seemed advisable, cannot now be known; but at all events, the conclusion was, that when the vessel was ready to leave the island, Selkirk signified his intention of remaining. Stradling made no objections; a boat was lowered, Selkirk descended into it with all his effects, three or four men rowed him ashore under the direction of the captain, the crew of the Cinque Ports looking on from the deck. Selkirk leaped on the beach, his effects were lifted out after him by the sailors, and laid in a heap; they shook hands with him heartily, the captain standing in the boat, and bidding them make haste. The sailors jumped in, and the boat was pushed off. Poor Selkirk! he had felt a bound, an exultation of spirit at the moment of stepping on shore; but now, as the boat was shoved off, and the men sat down to the oars with their faces toward him, pride, anger, resolution, all gave way; the horrors of his situation rose at once to his view, and rushing into the surf up to the middle, he stretched out his hands toward his comrades, and implored them to come back and take him on board again. With a jeering laugh the brutal commander bade him stick to his resolution, and remain where he was, adding that it was a blessing for the crew to have got rid at last of so troublesome a fellow. The boat accordingly went off to the ship, and in a short time the Cinque Ports was out of sight. Selkirk remained on the beach beside his bundles, gazing after her till it grew dark.

Juan Fernandez, the island on which our poor Scotchman was thus cast ashore, is situated in latitude 33 degrees 40 minutes south, and longitude 79 degrees west, about four hundred miles west of the coast of Chili. The name is properly applied to a group of islands consisting of two larger and a few smaller; and the name now given to that inhabited by Selkirk, and which is the largest of the group, is Mas-a-tierra. The island was first discovered in 1572, by a Spanish navigator, who conferred on it his own name of Juan Fernandez; and for a short time it was inhabited by a small colony of Spaniards, who ultimately abandoned it, however, to settle on the mainland. Afterward, as we have already seen, it became a resort of such buccaneering vessels as required, during their cruises on the west coast of America, to put in to some safe harbor to victual and refit. Once or twice, by accident, the island had become the residence of a castaway buccaneer, who was afterward picked off by a passing ship. Thus, says a voyager whom we shall have yet to quote more at large, "Ringrose, in his account of the voyage of Captain Sharp and other buccaneers, mentions one who had escaped ashore on this island out of a ship, which was cast away with all the rest of the company, and says he lived five years alone, before he had the opportunity of another ship to carry him off. Captain Dampier also talks of a Mosquito Indian that belonged to Captain Watlin, who, being a hunting in the woods when the captain left the island, lived there three years alone, till Captain Dampier came hither in 1684, and carried him off." Whatever amount of truth there may be in these particular statements as to Juan Fernandez, it is certain that Selkirk's solitary residence on this island was by no means the first instance of the kind. It does not appear to have been an uncommon thing for a buccaneer in those days to be either cast ashore on a desert island by the chances of shipwreck, or to be purposely left upon one by his captain out of savage ill-will, or as a punishment for mutinous conduct. Perhaps, if the records of old voyages were thoroughly searched, instances might be found of the kind as extraordinary as Selkirk's, if not more so. The magic touch, however, of the hand of a genius has conferred a celebrity on the history of the Fifeshire mariner which distinguishes him from all other Crusoes.

To proceed with our description of Juan Fernandez. The island is of an irregular form, from ten to twelve miles long, and about six broad, its area being about seventy square miles—somewhat less than that of the island of Bute. "The south-west side," says the voyager already quoted, "is much the longest, and has a small island about a mile long lying near it, with a few visible rocks close under the shore. On t[illegible] side begins a ridge of high mountains, that run across from the south-west to the north-west of the island; and the land that lies out in a narrow point to the westward appears to be the only level ground in it. On the north-east side it is very high land, and under it are the two bays where ships always put in to recruit. The best bay is all deep water, and you may carry in ships close to the rocks, if occasion require. The wind blows always over the land, and at worst along shore, which makes no sea. Near the rocks there are very good fish of several sorts, particularly large crawfish under the rocks, easy to be caught; also cavalloes, gropers, and other good fish, in so great plenty anywhere near the shore, that I never saw the like but at the best fishing season in Newfoundland. Pimento is the best timber, and most plentiful on this side of the island, but very apt to split, till a little dried. The cabbage-trees abound about three miles into the woods, and the cabbage is very good; most of them are on the top of the nearest and lowest mountains. The soil in these hills is of a loose black earth; the rocks are very rotten, so that, without great care, it is dangerous to climb the hills for cabbages; beside, there are abundance of holes dug in several places by a sort of fowls called puffins, which cause the earth to fall in at once, and endanger the breaking of a man's leg. Our summer months are winter here. In July snow and ice are sometimes seen; but the spring, which is in September, October, and November, is very pleasant. There is then abundance of good herbs, as parsley, purslain, etc. To these descriptions, written about the year 1712, we may add an extract from the account given in Lord Anson's voyages in 1741, in order that our readers may have a pretty distinct idea of the appearance of the island, which, for four years and a half, was to be the home of Selkirk. "The woods," says the author of Anson's voyages, "cover most of the steepest hills, and are free from all bushes and underwood, offering an easy passage through every part of them; and the irregularities of the hills and precipices in the northern part of the island trace, by their various combinations, a number of romantic valleys, most of which have a stream of the clearest water running through them, tumbling in cascades from rock to rock. Some particular spots occur in these valleys where the shade of the contiguous woods, the loftiness of the overhanging rocks, and the transparency and frequent falls of the streams, present scenes of wonderful beauty."

For many days after the departure of the Cinque Ports, Selkirk remained lingering about the spot where he was put ashore, unable to abandon the hope that Stradling would relent and come back for him. His constant occupation was gazing out into the sea. As soon as morning dawned he began his watch, sitting on his chest; and his deepest grief was when the evening came on, so that he could see no longer. Sleep came upon him by snatches, and against his exertions to remain awake. Food he did not think of, till extreme hunger obliged him; and then, rather than go in search of the fruits and game which the woods afforded, he contented himself with the shell-fish and seals' flesh, which he could obtain without removing from the beach. The sameness of the diet, the want of bread and salt, and the sinking sickness of his heart, caused him to loathe his food, so that he ate but at long intervals. Weary, and with aching eyes, he lay down at night, leaning his back against his bundles, listening to the crashing sound of rocks frequently falling among the woods, and to the discordant bleating of the shoals of seals along the shore. The horrors of his situation were augmented during the dark by superstitious alarms. Amid the murmur of the waves he could fancy he heard howlings and whistlings, as of spirits in the air: if he turned his head to the black and wooded masses behind him, they seemed peopled and in motion; and as he again turned it to the shore, phantoms stalked past. Often he cursed himself for the folly of the resolution which had brought him here; often, in the frenzy of fear, he would start up with the horrible determination of suicide; but a rush of softer feeling would come, and then he became calm. At length this gentler state of mind grew habitual; thoughts and impressions which had been familiar to him in childhood again came up; and the years which he had spent with brawling and ferocious shipmates, in the lawless profession of a privateer, were swept out of his memory like a disagreeable dream.

With the return of equanimity, Selkirk began to consider the means of rendering his residence on the island endurable. It was the month of October—a season corresponding in that locality to the middle of spring with us—and all was blooming and fragrant. The possibility of starving was not one of the horrors which his situation presented; and when he recovered calmness of mind sufficient to take a view of his solitary domain, he found himself in the midst of plenty. Beside the fish and seals which swarmed round the shores of the island, there were innumerable fruits and vegetables in the woods, among which was the never-failing cabbage-tree; and hundreds of goats skipped wild among the hills. Almost all the means of ordinary physical comfort were within his reach; and he had only to exert his strength and ingenuity to make the island yield him its resources. How he proceeded to do this; the various shifts and devices which he fell upon to supply his wants, and to add gradually to his store of comforts; the succession of daily steps and contrivances by which, in the course of four years and a half, he raised himself from comparative helplessness to complete dominion over the resources of his little territory; and, along with this, the various stages which his feelings went through, from the agony and stupefaction of the first night which he spent on the island, to the perfect freedom and happiness which he ultimately attained—we have not sufficient materials to be able to describe in detail. It is needless to say that the matchless narrative of Defoe is almost entirely a fiction, so far as the details of his hero's daily life in the desert island are concerned. Alexander Selkirk did not display such a genius for mechanical contrivances as Robinson Crusoe; or, at least, if he did, no record of his contrivances has been preserved. The island was not visited by cannibal savages as is the case in the romance; no faithful Friday appeared to cheer the hours of the solitary; nor is there any journal preserved, from which we learn whether ever such an incident occurred as the discovery of the mysterious foot-print in the sand. All these ornaments of the story the world owes to Defoe, whose object was not to write the history of Selkirk, or any other known castaway, but to describe, by the force of imagination, the life of an ideal hero on an ideal desert island. At the same time, there is no doubt that Defoe's narrative fills up our conception of Selkirk's long residence in his island with details such as must actually be true; and, at all events, there is a correspondence in some points between it and Selkirk's own account of his manner of life, furnished after his return to England to Sir Richard Steele and others, through whom it was made public. The particulars of this narrative, so far as it extends, we proceed to relate.

The stores which Selkirk had brought ashore consisted, beside his clothing and bedding, of a firelock, a pound of gunpowder, a quantity of bullets, a flint and steel, a few pounds of tobacco, a hatchet, a knife, a kettle, a flip-can, a Bible, some books of devotion, and one or two concerning navigation, and his mathematical instruments. Such were the few implements and substances from the great civilized world which Selkirk had to help him in the task of subduing to his own convenience seventy square miles of earth and wood. Yet, in the possession of that small package, what strength lay in his hands, and how superior was he to the savage children of nature! Within the small compass of his chest was wrapped up the condensed skill and wisdom of ages, the ingenuity and industry of hundreds of men who had long gone to their graves. The flint and steel, the firelock, the gunpowder, the knife and hatchet, what power over nature was there not compact in these articles!—the mathematical instruments, of what knowledge were they not the symbols!—and, above all, the Bible, and the books which accompanied it, what wealth of conversation, what health of spirit, did they not bring with them!

The first object that occupied his attention, beside the daily supply of such food as was necessary for his subsistence, was the construction of a dwelling to serve him as a shelter from the weather. Selecting a spot at some distance from the beach, he cut down pimento wood, and in a short time built a hut in which he could reside. To this he afterward added another. They were both constructed during the first eighteen months of his residence; but the task of improving them, and adding to their neatness, was a constant occupation to him during his stay on the island. The larger of his two huts, which "was situated near a spacious wood, he made his sleeping-room, spreading the bedclothes he had brought with him upon a frame of his own construction; and as these wore out, or were used for other purposes, he supplied their places with goat-skins. The smaller hut, which he had erected at some distance from the other, was used by him as a kitchen, in which he dressed his victuals. The furniture was very scanty, but consisted of every convenience his island could afford. His most valuable article was the pot or kettle he had brought from the ship to boil his meat in; the spit was his own handiwork, made of such wood as grew upon the island; the rest was suitable to his rudely constructed habitation. The pimento wood, which burns very bright and clear, served him both for fuel and candle. It gives out an agreeable perfume when burning. He obtained fire, after the Indian method, by rubbing two pieces of pimento wood together until they ignited. This he did, as he was ill able to spare any of his linen for tinder, time being of no value to him, and the labor rather an amusement!" The necessity of providing for his wants had the effect of diverting his thoughts from the misery of his situation; yet every day, for the first eighteen months, he spent more or less time on the beach, watching for the appearance of a sail upon the horizon. At the end of that time, partly through habit, partly through the influence of religion, which here awakened in full force upon his mind, he became reconciled to his situation. Every morning after rising he read a portion of Scripture, sang a psalm, and prayed, speaking aloud, in order to preserve the use of his voice; he afterward remarked that, during his residence on the island, he was a better Christian than he had ever been before, or would probably ever be again. He at first lived much upon turtles and crawfish, which abounded upon the shores—his powder, with which he could shoot the goats of the island, having soon been exhausted, he afterward found himself able to run down the goats, whose flesh he either roasted or stewed, and of which he kept a small stock, tamed, around his dwelling, to be used in the event of his being disabled by sickness. One of the greatest inconveniences which afflicted him for the first few months was the want of salt; but he gradually became accustomed to this privation, and at last found so much relish in unsalted food, that, after being restored to society, it was with equal difficulty that he reconciled himself to take it in any other condition. As a substitute for bread, he had turnips, parsnips, and the cabbage-palm, all of excellent quality, and also radishes, and water-cresses. When his clothes were worn out, he supplied their place with goat-skins, which gave him an appearance much more uncouth than any wild animal. He had a piece of linen, from which he made new shirts by means of a nail and the thread of his stockings; and he never wanted this comfortable piece of attire during the whole period of his residence on the island. Every physical want being thus gratified, and his mind soothed by devotional feeling, he at length began positively to enjoy his existence—often lying for whole days in the delicious bowers which he had formed for himself, abandoned to the most pleasant sensations.

Among the quadruped inhabitants of the isle were multitudes of rats, which at the first annoyed him by gnawing his feet while asleep. Against this enemy he found it necessary to enter into a treaty, offensive and defensive, with the cats, which also abounded in his neighborhood. Having caught and tamed some of the latter animals, he was soon freed from the presence of the rats, but not without some disagreeable consequences in the reflection that, should he die in his hut, his friendly auxiliaries would probably be obliged, for their subsistence, to devour his body. He was, in the meantime, able to turn them to some account for his amusement, by teaching them to dance and perform a number of antic feats, such as cats are not in general supposed capable of learning, but which they might probably acquire, if any individual in civilized life were able to take the necessary pains. Another of his amusements was hunting on foot, in which he at length, through healthy exercise and habit, became such a proficient, that he could run down the swiftest goat. Some of the young of these animals he taught to dance in company with his kittens; and he often afterward declared that he never danced with a lighter heart or greater spirit than to the sound of his own voice in the midst of these dumb companions.

Selkirk was careful, during his stay on the island, to measure the lapse of time, and distinguish Sunday from the other days of the week. Anxious, in the midst of all his indifference to society, that, in the event of his dying in solitude, his having lived there might not be unknown to his fellow-creatures, he carved his name upon a number of trees, adding the date of his being left, and the space of time which had since elapsed. When his knife was worn out, he made new ones, and even a cleaver for his meat, out of some hoops which he found on the shore. He several times saw vessels passing the island, but only two cast anchor beside it. Afraid of being taken by the Spaniards, who would have consigned him to hopeless captivity, he endeavored to ascertain whether these strangers were so or not before making himself known. In both cases he found them enemies; and on one of the occasions, having approached too near, he was observed and chased, and only escaped by taking refuge in a tree.

As Selkirk was only about thirty years of age, and as he found his constitution, which was naturally good, improved and fortified in a wonderful degree by his mode of life, the only cause which he could fear as likely to cut short his days, and prevent him from reaching the old age which he might expect to attain to in his island, provided no ship appeared to carry him off, was the occurrence of some accident, such as might very possibly befall him in his expeditions through the woods. Only one such accident occurred during his stay on the island: it had nearly proved fatal, however. It has already been mentioned that, in many parts of the island, the soil was loose, and undermined by holes, and the rock weathered almost to rottenness. Pursuing a goat once in one of these dangerous places, the bushy brink of a precipice, to which he had followed it, crumbled beneath him, and he and the goat fell together from a great height. He lay stunned and senseless at the foot of the rock for a great while—not less than twenty-four hours, he thought, from the change of position in the sun—but the precise length of time he had no means of ascertaining. When he recovered his senses, he found the goat lying dead beside him. With great pain and difficulty he made his way to his hut, which was nearly a mile distant from the spot; and for three days he lay on his bed, enduring much suffering. No permanent injury, however, had been done him, and he was soon able to go abroad again.

Four years and four months had elapsed since Selkirk was left by Stradling on the island of Juan Fernandez. It was now the month of January, 1709; his reckoning enabled him to know the lapse of time, at least within a week or two. Four times had the January summers of Juan Fernandez passed over his head, and already he was looking forward to the coming of the fifth autumn and winter. The whole island was now familiar to him, with its appearances and productions at various seasons. Custom had reconciled him to it; had almost brought him to regard it as his home; had almost made him cease to remember with regret the world from which he was an outcast. Occasionally, indeed, such thoughts as the poet has supposed must have occurred to him even now, after so long a period of acquaintance with solitude.

"I am monarch of all I survey,
  My right there is none to dispute:
From the center, all round to the sea,
  I am lord of the fowl and the brute.
Oh, solitude! where are the charms,
  That sages have seen in thy face?
Better dwell in the midst of alarms,
  Than reign in this horrible place.

I am out of humanity's reach,
  I must finish my journey alone,
Never hear the sweet music of speech;
  I start at the sound of my own.
The beasts that roam over the plain,
  My form with indifference see;
They are so unacquainted with man,
  Their tameness is shocking to me.

Society, friendship, and love,
  Divinely bestowed upon man,
Oh, had I the wings of a dove,
  How soon would I taste you again!
My sorrows I then might assuage
  In the ways of religion and truth,
Might learn from the wisdom of age,
  And be cheered by the sallies of youth.

Religion! what treasure untold,
  Resides in that heavenly word!
More precious than silver and gold,
  Or all that this earth can afford.
But the sound of the church-going bell
  These valleys and rocks never heard,
Never sighed at the sound of a knell,
  Or smiled when a Sabbath appeared.

Ye winds, that have made me your sport,
  Convey to this desolate shore
Some cordial endearing report
  Of a land I shall visit no more.
My friends, do they now and then send
  A wish or a thought after me?
Oh! tell me I yet have a friend,
  Though a friend I am never to see!

How fleet is a glance of the mind!
  Compared with the speed of its flight,
The tempest itself lags behind,
  And the swift-winged arrows of light!
When I think of my own native land,
  In a moment I seem to be there;
But, alas! recollection at hand
  Soon hurries me back to despair.

But the sea-fowl is gone to her nest,
  The beast is laid down in his lair;
Even here is a season of rest,
  And I to my cabin repair.
There's mercy in every place:
  And mercy, encouraging thought!
Gives even affliction a grace,
  And reconciles man to his lot."

These thoughts, however, were not habitual. Even the idea of dying alone, and leaving his bones stretched out, to be found some day, at the distance of years, by those whom chance might bring to his moldering hut in the woods, ceased to affect him sorrowfully. The religious impressions of his childhood had gained a supreme influence over him; and in communion with his Bible and with his own soul, the solitary man, clad in his goat-skins, became meek, thankful and tender-hearted. How different from the rough young sailor who, not many years before, had been struggling in the grasps of his brother, his sister-in-law, and his old father on the floor of the cottage in Largo! Whether the change of character was permanent, we shall now see, as we are about to relate the circumstances which led to his release from his solitude, and his restoration to society.

One hope of relief for Selkirk, even if other chances had failed, consisted in the probability that intelligence of his situation would reach England through some of the crew of the Cinque Ports, and that some vessel might, in consequence, be induced to pay a passing visit to Juan Fernandez for the purpose of ascertaining his fate. If Selkirk, however, had relied strongly on this probability, he would have been disappointed.

The Cinque Ports never reached England. Old, crank, and worm-eaten, she foundered off the coast of Barbacoa not long after setting sail from Juan Fernandez. Out of the whole crew, only Captain Stradling and six or seven of his men were saved; and these were long detained prisoners among the Spaniards at Lima. They were in captivity during the whole time of Selkirk's residence on his island; and long after he had returned to England, most of them were captives still. Stradling at length obtained his liberty, but his ultimate fate was never known.

Deliverance was to reach Selkirk from another quarter. Dampier who had parted company with the Cinque Ports, about five months before Selkirk had been abandoned by Stradling, had continued his voyage through the South Seas in search of Spanish vessels. Various success nad attended him for several months; a considerable portion of his crew forsook him; and, at length, crossing the Pacific to the East Indies, he and his companions fell into the hands of the Dutch, who seized his ship and all that he had. The expedition planned by him, had turned out a total failure. "Dampier returned naked to his owners, with a melancholy relation of his misfortunes, occasioned chiefly by his own strange temper, which was so self-sufficient and overbearing, that few or none of his officers could endure it. Even in this distress he was received as an eminent man, notwithstanding his failings; and was introduced to Queen Anne, having the honor to kiss her hand, and to give her majesty some account of the dangers he had undergone. The merchants were so sensible of his want of conduct, that they resolved never to trust him any more with a command."

The bad success of Dampier's expedition, however, did not prevent the fitting out of another with similar designs against the Spaniards of the South Seas; and about the middle of the year 1708, two vessels, the *Duke* and the *Duchess*, the property of Bristol merchants, set sail for the Spanish main, having, in all, three hundred and thirty-three men on board. The Duke, a vessel of thirty guns, was commanded by Captain Woodes Rogers, a very able and prudent man; the Duchess, of twenty-six guns, by Captain Stephen Courtney. Poor Dampier, who could not be intrusted with the command, and whose poverty obliged him to accept some occupation of the same kind as that which he had all his life been accustomed to, was glad to sail in the Duke in the capacity of pilot to the expedition. Great care had been taken in the manning of both vessels, and regulations had been drawn up before sailing, to prevent disputes.

Captain Rogers, whose proceedings during the voyage it is not necessary for us to detail, pursued the same track as the former expedition; and after cruising along the Brazilian coast, rounded Cape Horn in the month of December 1708, bearing for Juan Fernandez, to take in water. The crews came in sight of the island on the thirty-first of January, 1709, little anticipating the surprise which awaited them. What occurred as they approached, is thus related by Captain Rogers himself in the account which he published of the voyage:—"About two o'clock, P. M., on the thirty-first of January, we hoisted our pinnace out: Captain Dover, (second captain of the Duke,) with the boat's crew, went in her to go ashore, though we could not be less than four leagues off. As soon as the pinnace was gone, I went on board the Duchess, the crew of which were astonished at our boat attempting to go on shore at so great a distance from land: it was against my inclination, but to oblige Captain Dover, I consented to let her go. As soon as it was dark, we saw a light ashore; our boat was then about a league from the island. She stopped, and bore away again for the ship as soon as she saw the light. We put out lights for the boat, though some were of opinion that the light we saw was not on the island, but the boat's light; but as night came on, it appeared too large for that. We fired one quarter-deck gun and several muskets, showing lights in our mizzen and fore-shrouds, that our boat might find us, while we plied in the lee of the island. About two in the morning our boat came on board the Duchess: we were glad it got well off, because it began to blow. We were all convinced that the light was on the shore, and designed to make oui ships ready to engage, as we believed it to come from French ships at anchor, and that we must either fight them or want water.

"The next day we stood along the south end of the island, in order to lay in with the first southerly wind, which Captain Dampier told us generally blows there all day long. In the morning, being past the island, we tacked, to lay it in close aboard the land; and about ten o'clock, ran close aboard the land that begins to make the north-east side. The flaws came heavy off the shore, and we were forced to reef our topsails when we opened the middle bay, where we expected to find the enemy, but saw all clear, and no ships in that nor the other bay. We guessed there had been ships there, but that they had gone away on sight of us. We sent our yawl ashore about noon with Captain Dover, Mr. Fry, and six men, all armed: meanwhile we and the Duchess kept turning to get in. Our boat did not return, so we sent our pinnace, with the men armed, to see what was the occasion of the yawl's stay; for we were afraid that the Spaniards had a garrison there, and might have seized it. We put out a signal for our boat, and the Duchess showed a French Ensign. Immediately our pinnace returned from the shore, and brought abundance of crawfish, with a man clothed in goat-skins, who looked wilder than the first owners of them."

Selkirk, the man whose appearance caused such surprise, had seen the sails of the vessels at a distance, but had avoided making any signals which could indicate his presence till he ascertained them to be English. As soon as he had assured himself on this point, his joy was extreme. When night came on, he kindled a large fire on the beach, to inform the strangers that a human being was there. It was this signal which had alarmed the crews of the vessels, and deterred the pinnace from landing. During the night, hope having banished all desire of sleep, he employed himself in killing goats, and preparing a feast of fresh meat for those whom he expected to be his deliverers. In the morning he found that the vessels had removed to a greater distance, but ere long he saw the boat leave the side of one of them and approach the shore. Selkirk ran joyfully to meet his countrymen, waving a linen rag to attract their attention; and having pointed out to them a proper landing-place, soon had the satisfaction of clasping them in his arms. Joy at first deprived him of that imperfect power of utterance which solitude had left him, but in a little time he was able to offer and receive explanations. Dover, the second captain, Fry, the lieutenant, and the rest of the boat party, after partaking of Selkirk's hospitality, invited him on board; but so little eager was he to leave his solitude, that he was not prevailed upon to do so till assured that Dampier had no situation of command in the expedition—his former experience of Dampier's mode of conducting a ship having given him no great confidence in him. When he was told that Dampier was only pilot on board, he made no further objection. He was then, as we have seen, brought on board the Duke, along with his principal effects; and on the same day, by the recommendation of Dampier, who said he had been tho best man in the Cinque Ports, he was engaged as a mate. "At his first coming on board us," says Captain Rogers, "he had so much forgot his language, for want of use, that we could scarcely understand him, for he seemed to speak his words by halves. We offered him a dram, but he would not touch it, having drank nothing but water since he came on the island; and it was some time before he could relish our victuals."

For a fortnight the two vessels remained at Juan Fernandez refitting, recruiting their sick, and taking in water and provisions. In this they were greatly assisted by Selkirk, or the "governor," as they used to call him; who, beside giving them all the information necessary respecting the island, made it a daily practice to catch several goats for the use of the sick. "He took them," says Rogers, "by speed of foot; for his way of living, and continual exercise of walking and running, cleared him of all gross humors, so that he ran with wonderful swiftness through the woods, and up the rocks and hills. We had a bulldog, which we sent with several of our nimblest runners to help him in catching goats; but he distanced and tired both the dog and the men, caught the goats, and brought them to us on his back. Being forced to shift without shoes, his feet had become so hard, that he ran everywhere without annoyance; and it was some time before he could wear shoes after we found him; for, not being used to any for so long, his feet swelled when he came first to use them again." Beside giving these particulars, Captain Rogers details at some length Selkirk's mode of life during the four years and four months he had spent on the island, concluding—

"We may perceive, by this story, the truth of the maxim, that necessity is the mother of invention, since this man found means to supply his wants in a very natural manner, so as to maintain his life, though not so conveniently, yet as effectually as we are able to do with the help of our arts and society. It may likewise instruct us how much a plain and temperate way of living conduces to the health of the body and the vigor of the mind, both which we are apt to destroy by excess and plenty, especially of strong liquor, and the variety as well as the nature of our meat and drink; for this man, when he came back to our ordinary method of diet and life, though he was sober enough, lost much of his strength and agility. But these reflections are more proper for a philosopher and divine than a mariner."

In the middle of February, 1709, the Duke and Duchess set sail from the island, to cruise along the western coast of America in quest of prizes, in which they were very successful, taking two prizes in a very short time. The second of these was fitted out as a privateer, to sail in company with the Duke and Duchess; and Selkirk was appointed to command her. During the remainder of the expedition, he acted in a prominent capacity, under Rogers, in the various enterprises, both on sea and on shore, in which the little fleet engaged. The occupation was certainly one by no means calculated to give play to the more amiable qualities of human nature; but even in the sacking of coast towns, and expeditions of plunder into the interior, which for months formed his chief employment, our hero seems to have mingled humanity in as high a proportion as possible with the execution of his duty. The expedition of Rogers was as remarkable for steadiness, resolution, and success, as that of Dampier's had been for quarreling and indecision; and it excites a curious feeling of surprise when we learn that the church of England service was regularly read on the quarter-decks of these piratical vessels, and all hands piped to prayers before every action Selkirk proved himself, by his steadiness, decent manners, and religious turn of mind, a most appropriate member of the corps commanded by Rogers, and was accordingly much valued by his superiors. At the beginning of the ensuing year, the vessels began their voyage across the Pacific, with the design of returning by the East Indies, and in this part of the enterprise Selkirk acted as sailing-master. They did not, however, reach England till October, 1711, when Selkirk had been absent from his country for eight years. Of the enormous sum of £170,000 which Rogers had realised by plundering the enemy, Selkirk seems to have shared to the amount of about eight hundred pounds.

His singular history was soon made known to the public; and immediately after his arrival in London, he became an object of curiosity not only to the people at large, but to those elevated by rank and learning. Sir Richard Steele, some time after, devoted to him an article in the paper entitled "The Englishman," in which he tells the reader that, as Selkirk is a man of good sense, it is a matter of great curiosity to hear him give an account of the different revolutions of his mind during the term of his solitude. "When I first saw him," continues this writer, "I thought if I had not been let into his character and story, I could have discovered that he had been much separated from company, *from his aspect and gesture;* there was a strong but cheerful seriousness in his look, and a certain disregard of the ordinary things about him, as if he had been sunk in thought. When the ship which brought him off the island came in, he received them with the greatest indifference with relation to the prospect of going off with them, but with great satisfaction in an opportunity to refresh and help them. The man frequently bewailed his return to the world, which could not, he said, with all its enjoyments, restore him to the tranquillity of his solitude. 'I am now worth eight hundred pounds,' he said, 'but shall never be so happy as when I was not worth a farthing.' Though I had frequently conversed with him, after a few months' absence he met me in the street, and though he spoke to me, I could not recollect that I had seen him: *familiar converse in this town had taken off the loneliness of his aspect, and quite altered the air of his face.*" What makes this latter circumstance the more remarkable is, the fact of nearly three years having elapsed between his restoration to society and the time when Sir Richard Steele first saw him.

Beside Sir Richard Steele's paper, various short accounts of Selkirk's adventures appeared within a year or two after his return to England. Defoe's romance of Robinson Crusoe was not published till the year 1719, when the original facts on which it was founded must have been nearly forgotten. There is no record of any interview having taken place between Selkirk and Defoe, so that it cannot be decided whether Defoe learnt our hero's story from his own mouth, or from such narratives as those published by Steele and others.

It was a fine Sunday morning in the spring of 1712; the kirk bells of Largo had for some time ceased ringing, and the parishioners were assembled in church, when a handsomely dressed stranger knocked at the door of old John Selkirk's dwelling. No one was within, and the stranger bent his steps toward the parish church. He entered, and sat down in a pew near the door. His late entrance, the fact of his being a stranger, and his fine gold-laced clothes, attracted attention to him, and divided the interest of the congregation with the clergyman's sermon. The service proceeded· not far from the place where the stranger had stationed himself, was the pew where old John Selkirk, his wife, and others of the family were sitting, and toward this pew the stranger continued to direct his eyes. The occupants of the pew returned the glance as discreetly as they could; old Mrs. Selkirk especially several times eyed the stranger with curiosity over her Bible. At length the glances became a fixed gaze; the old woman's face grew pale; and crying, "It's Sandie!—it's Sandie!" she tottered up to the stranger, and flung herself into his arms. The clergyman stopped; the congregation rose in a bustle of excitement, and quiet was not restored until the whole Selkirk family left the church in a body, to give full scope at home to their mutual congratulations and inquiries.

"For a few days," says his biographer, Mr. Howell, who ascertained the particulars by industrious inquiry, "Selkirk was happy in the company of his parents and friends; but from long habit, he soon felt averse to mixing in society, and was most happy when alone. For days his relations never saw his face from the dawn until late in the evening, when he returned to bed. It was his custom to go out in the morning, carrying with him provisions for the day; then would he wander and meditate alone through the secluded and solitary valley of Keil's Den. The romantic beauties of the place, and, above all, the stillness that reigned there, reminded him of his beloved island, which he never thought of but with regret for having left it. When evening forced him to return to the haunts of men, he appeared to do so with reluctance; for he immediately retired to his room, up stairs, in his brother's house, where he resided. Here he was accustomed to amuse himself with two cats that belonged to his brother, which he taught, in imitation of a part of his occupations on his solitary island, to dance and perform many little feats. They were extremely fond of him, and used to watch his return. He often said to his friends, no doubt thinking of himself in his youth, that 'were children as docile and obedient, parents would all be happy in them.' But poor Selkirk himself was now far from being happy, for his relations often found him in tears. Attached to his father's house was a piece of ground, occupied as a garden, which rose in a considerable acclivity backward: here, on the top of the eminence, soon after his arrival in Largo, he constructed a sort of cave, commanding an extensive and delightful view of the Forth and its shores. In fits of musing meditation, he was wont to sit here in bad weather, and even at other times, and to bewail his ever having left his island. This recluse and unnatural propensity, as it appeared to them, was cause of great grief to his parents, who often remonstrated with him, and endeavored to raise his spirits. But their efforts were made in vain; and he sometimes broke out before them in a passion of grief, and exclaimed, 'Oh my beloved island! I wish I had never left thee! I never before was the man I was on thee; I have not been such since I left thee; and I fear never can be again!' Having plenty of money, he purchased a boat for himself, and often, when the weather would permit, he made little excursions, but always alone; and day after day he spent in fishing in the beautiful Bay of Largo, or at Kingscraig Point, where he would loiter till evening among the romantic cliffs catching lobsters—his favorite amusement, as they reminded him of the crawfish of Juan Fernandez. The rock to which he moored his boat is still shown."

Selkirk at length resolved to abandon this mode of life; and the execution of his design was probably hastened by an attachment he had formed to a young girl named Sophia Bruce, whom he often met, tending her mother's cow, in his wanderings through Keil's Den. "He never," says

Mr. Howell, "mentioned the attachment to his friends; for he felt ashamed, after his discourses to them, and the profession he had made of dislike to human society, to acknowledge that he was on the point of marrying. But to marry he was determined, though as firmly resolved not to remain at home to be the subject of their jests. He soon persuaded the object of his choice to elope with him, and bid adieu to the romantic glen. Without the knowledge of their parents, they both set out for London. He left his chest and all his clothes behind; nor did he ever claim them again; and his friends knew nothing and heard nothing of him for many years. At the time of this sudden departure from Largo, Selkirk was nearly forty years of age.

In London Selkirk seems to have lived some time. Nothing, however, is known of his movements till 1717,, in which year we find him executing a will and power of attorney, by the hands of a notary in Wapping, in favor of Sophia Bruce, the object of his affection; being then on the point of again going to sea. The only other known particulars respecting Selkirk's life came to light in the year 1724, when a gaily-dressed lady, named Frances Candis, presented herself at Largo as the widow of Alexander Selkirk, and claimed the property which had been left him by his father, including the house of Craggy Wall, mentioned in the foregoing will. She produced documents which proved her marriage with Selkirk; a will, also, dated the twelfth of December 1720, entitling her to the property; and lastly, an attestation of the death of her husband, Lieutenant Alexander Selkirk, on board his majesty's ship Weymouth in the year 1723. From the second of these documents, it is inferred that Sophia Bruce had died some time between 1717, when the first will was executed in her favor, and 1720, when the second will was drawn up in favor of Frances Candis. Having had her claims adjusted, Selkirk's widow took her departure from Largo after a few days. So far as can be ascertained, Selkirk left no children either by her or by Sophia Bruce.

The house in which Selkirk lived, during his last residence at Largo, is still occupied by the descendants of his brother John, who preserve his chest and his cocoanut shell cup. His flip-can exists in the possession of another relation, and his gun has for some years been the property of Major Lumsden of Lathallan, near Largo. "The flip-can," says Mr. Howell, "holds about a Scottish pint, [two quarts,] and is made of brown stoneware, glazed. On it is the following inscription and posy—sailors being in all ages notoriously addicted to inscribing rhymes on such articles:—

'Alexander Selkirk, this is my one.

When you take me on board of ship,
Pray fill me full with punch or flip.'

The handle of the jug is gone; its mouth is broken in two places; and a crack in the stoneware is patched with pitch, probably put on by Selkirk's own hands."

The island of Juan Fernandez, which may also be considered as a relic of Alexander Selkirk, has passed through the hands of a succession of owners since he quitted it. For upward of thirty years after his departure it remained in the condition in which he had left it—an uninhabited island, where ships, sailing along the western coast of South America, occasionally put in for water and fresh victuals. Once or twice, indeed, the chances of shipwreck gave it one or two inhabitants, who did not remain long. In 1750, the Spaniards again formed a settlement on it, and built a fort. Both were destroyed by an earthquake in the following year; but another town was built at a greater distance from the shore. It continued to be inhabited for about twenty years, but was then abandoned, as the former Spanish settlement in the island had been. Early in the present century, the Chilian government began to use Juan Fernandez as a penal settlement, transporting their state criminals to it; but in consequence of the expense, it was soon given up; and when Lord Cochrane visited the island in 1823, there were but four men stationed on it, apparently in charge of some cattle. The following description is given of the island by a lady who accompanied Lord Cochrane and a party on shore:—"The island is the most picturesque I ever saw, being composed of high perpendicular rocks, wooded nearly to the top, with beautiful valleys, exceedingly fertile, and watered by copious streams, which occasionally form small marshes. The little valley where the town is, or rather was, is exceedingly beautiful. It is full of fruit-trees and flowers, and sweet herbs, now grown wild; near the shore, it is covered with radish and sea-side oats. A small fort was situated on the sea-shore, of which there is nothing now visible but the ditches and part of one wall. Another, of considerable size for the place, is on a high and commanding spot. It contained barracks for soldiers, which, as well as the greater part of the fort, are ruined; but the flag-staff, front wall, and a turret are standing; and at the foot of the flag-staff lies a very handsome brass gun, cast in Spain, A. D. 1614. A few houses and cottages are still in a tolerable condition, though most of the doors, windows, and roofs have been taken away, or used as fuel by whalers and other ships touching here. In the valleys we found numbers of European shrubs and herbs—'where once the garden smiled.' And in the half-ruined hedges, which denote the boundaries of former fields, we found apple, pear, and quince trees, with cherries almost ripe. The ascent is steep and rapid from the beach, even in the valleys, and the long grass was dry and slippery, so that it rendered the walk rather fatiguing; and we were glad to sit down under a large quince-tree on a carpet of balm, bordered with roses, now neglected, and feast our eyes with the lovely view before us. Lord Anson has not exaggerated the beauty of the place, or the delights of the climate. We were rather early for its fruits, but even at this time we have gathered delicious figs, cherries, and pears, that a few days more of sun would have perfected. The landing-place is also the watering-place. There a little jetty is thrown out, formed of the beach pebbles, making a little harbor for boats, which lie there close to the fresh water, which comes conducted by a pipe, so that, with a hose, the casks may be filled without landing with the most delicious water. Along the beach some old guns are sunk, to serve as moorings for vessels, which are all the safer the nearer in shore they lie; as violent gusts of wind often blow from the mountain for a few minutes. The height of the island is about three thousand feet."

The isle of Juan Fernandez, of late years, has been much visited by vessels in the California trade. An American traveler J. Ross Browne, visited the island in 1849, and has given his impressions in a charming little book, half fiction and half truth, under the title of "Crusoe Life, a Narrative of Adventures in the Island of Juan Fernandez," from which we take the following extract.

At the dawn of day I was on deck, looking eagerly toward the island. I may as well confess at once that no child could have felt more delight than I did in the anticipation of something illusive and enchanting. My heart throbbed with impatience to see what it was that cast so strange a fascination about that lonely spot. All was wrapped in mist; but the air was filled with fresh odors of land, and wafts of sweetness more delicious than the scent of new-mown hay. The storm had ceased, and the soft-echoed bleating of goats, and the distant baying of wild dogs were all the sounds of life that broke upon the stillness. It seemed as if the sun, loth to disturb the ocean in its rest, or reveal the scene of beauty that lay slumbering upon its bosom, would never rise again, so gently the light stole upon the eastern sky, so softly it absorbed the shadows of night. I watched the golden glow as it spread over the heavens, and beheld at last the sun in all his majesty scatter away the thick vapors that lay around his resting-place, and each vale was opened out in the glowing light of the morning, and the mountains that towered out of the sea were bathed in the glory of his rays.

Never shall I forget the strange delight with which I gazed upon that isle of romance; the unfeigned rapture I felt in the anticipation of exploring that miniature world in the desert of waters, so fraught with the happiest associations of youth; so remote from all the ordinary realities of life; the actual embodiment of the most absorbing, most fascinating of all the dreams of fancy. Many foreign lands I had seen; many islands scattered over the broad ocean, rich and wondrous in their romantic beauty; many glens of Utopian loveliness; mountain heights weird and impressive in their sublimity; but nothing to equal this in variety of outline and undefinable richness of coloring; nothing so dreamlike, so wrapped in illusion, so strange and absorbing in its novelty. Great peaks of reddish rock seemed to pierce the sky wherever I looked; a thousand rugged ridges swept upward toward the center in a perfect maze of enchantment. It was all wild, fascinating, and unreal. The sides of the mountains were covered with patches of rich grass, natural fields of oats, and groves of myrtle and pimento. Abrupt walls of rock rose from the water to the height of a thousand feet. The surf broke in a white line of foam along the shores of the bay and its measured swell floated upon the air like the voice of a distant cataract. Fields of verdure covered the ravines; ruined and moss-covered walls were scattered over each eminence; and the straw huts of the inhabitants were almost embosomed in trees, in the midst of the valley, and jets of smoke arose out of the groves and floated off gently in the calm air of the morning. In all the shore, but one spot, a single opening among the rocks, seemed accessible to man.

No longer able to control our enthusiasm, we sprang into the boat and pushed off for the landing. We first went up to a bluff, where we spent an hour, in exploring the ruins of the fortifications, built by the Chilians, in 1767. There was nothing left but the foundation and a portion of the ramparts of the principal fort, partly imbedded in banks of clay, and nearly covered with moss and weeds. It was originally strongly built of large stones, which were cast down in every direction, by the terrible earthquake of 1835; and now all that remained perfect was the front wall of the main rampart and the groundwork of the fort. Not far from these ruins we found the convict-cells, which we explored to some extent.

The cells are dug into the brow of a hill, facing the harbor, and extend under ground to the distance of several hundred feet, in the form of passages and vaults, resembling somewhat the Catacombs of Rome. During the penal settlement established here by the Chilian government, the convicts, numbering sometimes many hundreds, were confined in these gloomy dungeons, where they were subjected to the most barbarous treatment. The gates or doors by which the entrances were secured, had all been torn down and destroyed; and the excavations were now occupied only by wild goats, bats, toads, and different sorts of vermin. Rank fern hung upon the sides; overhead was dripping with a cold and deathlike sweat, and slimy drops coursed down the weeds, and the air was damp and chilly: thick darkness was within in the depths beyond; darkness that no wandering gleam from the light of day ever reached—for heaven never smiled upon those dreary abodes of sin and sorrow. A few of the inner dungeons, for the worst criminals, were dug still deeper under ground, and rough stairways of earth led down into them, which were shut out from the upper vaults by strong doors. The size of these lower dungeons was not more than five or six feet in length, by four or five in height; from which some idea may be formed of the sufferings endured by the poor wretches confined in them; shut out from the light of heaven, loaded with heavy irons, crushed down by dank and impenetrable walls of earth, starved and beaten by their cruel guards; with no living soul to pity them in their woe, no hope of release save in death. We saw, by the aid of a torch, deep holes scratched in one of the walls, bearing the impression of human fingers. It might have been that some unhappy murderer, goaded to madness by such cruel tortures of body and terrible anguish of mind, as drive men to tear even their own flesh when buried before the vital spark is extinct, had grasped out the earth in his desperation, and left the marks in his death agonies upon the clay that entombed him, to tell what no human heart but his suffered there, no human ear had heard, no human eye had witnessed. The deep, startling echo breaking upon the heavy air, as we sounded the walls, seemed yet to mingle with his curses, and its last sepulchral throb was like the dying moan of the maniac.

Some time before the great earthquake, which destroyed the fortifications and broke up the penal colony, a gang of convicts, amounting to three hundred, succeeded in liberating themselves from their cells. Unable to endure the cruelties inflicted upon them, they broke loose from their chains, and rushing upon the guards, murdered the greater part of them, and, finally, seized the garrison. For several days, they held complete possession of the island. A whale-ship, belonging to Nantucket, happening to come in at the time for wood and water, they seized the captain, and compelled him to take on board as many of them as the vessel could contain. About two hundred were put on board. They then threatened the captain and officers with instant death, in case of any failure to land them on the coast of Peru, whither they determined to go, in order to escape the vengeance of Chilian government. Desirous of getting rid of them as soon as possible, the captain of the whaler ran over for the first land on the coast of Chili, where he put them ashore, leaving them ignorant of their position until they were unable to regain the vessel. They soon discovered that they were only thirty miles from Valparaiso; but short as the distance was from the Chilian authorities, they evaded all attempts to capture them, and eventually joined the Peruvian army, which was then advancing upon Santiago. The remainder of the prisoners left upon the island, escaped in different vessels, and were scattered over various parts of the world. Only a few out of the entire number engaged in the massacre were ever captured: sentence of death was passed upon them, and they were shot in the public plaza of Santiago.

Turning our steps toward the settlement of the present residents, we passed a few hours very agreeably in rambling about among their rustic abodes. The total number of inhabitants at this period (1849,) is sixteen: consisting of William Pearce, an American, and four or five Chilian men, with their wives and children. No others have lived permanently upon the island for several years. There are in all some six or seven huts, pleasantly surrounded by shrubbery, and well supplied with water from a spring. These habitations are built of the straw of wild oats, interwoven through wattles or long sticks, and thatched with the same; and whether from design or accident, are extremely picturesque. The roofs project so as to form an agreeable shade all round; the doorways are covered in by a sort of projecting porch, in the style of the French cottages along the valley of the Seine; small out-houses, erected upon posts, are scattered about each inclosure; and an air of repose and freedom from worldly care pervades the whole place, though the construction of the houses and mode of living are evidently of the most primitive kind. Seen through the green shrubberies that abound in every direction, the bright yellow of the cottages, and the smoke curling up in the still air, have a very cheerful effect; and the prattling voices of the children, mingled with the lively bleating of the kine, and the various pleasant sounds of domestic life, might well lead one to think, that the seclusion of these islanders from the busy world is not without its charms.

Open at all times to the pleasant breezes from the ocean, without malaria or anything to produce disease, beautifully diversified in scenery, and susceptible of being made a convenient stopping-place for vessels bound to the great Northwestern Continent, it would be difficult to find a more desirable place for a colony of intelligent and industrious people, who would cultivate the land, build good houses, and turn to advantage all the gifts of Providence which have been bestowed upon the island.

THE NARRATIVE

OF

COLONEL ETHAN ALLEN,

THE HERO OF TICONDEROGA, WHO AFTER HE FELL INTO THE HANDS OF THE ENEMY AT MONTREAL, WAS CONFINED, DURING A CONSIDERABLE PERIOD OF HIS CAPTIVITY, A PRISONER ON BOARD OF

BRITISH SHIPS OF WAR.

EVER since I arrived at a state of manhood, and acquainted myself with the general history of mankind, I have felt a sincere passion for liberty; so that the first systematical and bloody attempt at Lexington, to enslave America, thoroughly electrified my mind, and fully determined me to take part with my country.

While I was wishing for an opportunity to signalize myself in its behalf, directions were privately sent to me from the then colony, now State of Connecticut, to raise the Green Mountain Boys; and, if possible, with them to surprise and take the fortress Ticonderoga. This enterprise I cheerfully undertook; and, after first guarding all the several passes that led thither, to cut off all intelligence between the garrison and the country, made a forced march from Bennington, and arrived at the lake opposite Ticonderoga, on the evening of the ninth day of May, 1775, with two hundred and thirty valiant Green Mountain Boys; and it was with the utmost difficulty that I procured boats to cross the lake. However, I landed eighty-five men near the garrison, and sent the boats back for the rear-guard, commanded by Col. Seth Warner; but the day began to dawn, and I found myself under a necessity to attack the fort before the rear could cross the lake; and, as it was viewed hazardous, I harangued the officers and soldiers in the manner following: "Friends and fellow-soldiers you have, for a number of years past, been a scourge and terror to arbitrary power. Your valor has been famed abroad, and acknowledged, as appears by the advice and orders to me from the General Assembly of Connecticut, to surprise and take the garrison now before us. I now propose to advance before you, and in person conduct you through the wicket-gate; for we must this morning either quit our pretensions to valor, or possess ourselves of this fortress in a few minutes; and, inasmuch as it is a desperate attempt, which none but the bravest of men dare undertake, I do not urge it on any contrary to his will. You that will undertake, voluntarily, poise your firelocks."

The men being at this time drawn up in three ranks, each poised his firelock; I ordered them to face to the right, and, at the head of the center file, marched them immediately to the wicket-gate aforesaid, where I found a sentry posted, who instantly snapped his fusee at me. I ran immediately toward him, and he retreated through the covered way into the parade within the garrison, gave a halloo, and ran under a bomb proof. My party, who followed me into the fort, I formed on the parade in such manner as to face the two barracks which faced each other. The garrison being asleep, except the sentries, we gave three huzzas which greatly surprised them. One of the sentries made a pass at one of my officers with a charged bayonet, and slightly wounded him. My first thought was to kill him with my sword; but, in an instant, I altered the design and fury of the blow to a slight cut on the side of the head; upon which he dropped his gun, and asked quarter, which I readily granted him, and demanded of him the place where the commanding officer slept; he showed me a pair of stairs in the front of a barrack, on the west part of the garrison, which led up to a second story in said barrack, to which I immediately repaired, and ordered the commander, Capt. Delaplace, to come forth instantly, or I would sacrifice the whole garrison; at which the captain came immediately to the door with his breeches in his hand, when I ordered him to deliver to me the fort instantly. He asked me by what authority I demanded it. I answered him, "In the name of the great Jehovah and the Continental Congress." The authority of the Congress being very little known at that time, he began to speak again; but I interrupted him, and with my drawn sword over his head, again demanded an immediate surrender of the garrison; to which he then complied, and ordered his men to be forthwith paraded without arms, as he had given up the garrison. In the meantime some of my officers had given orders, and in consequence thereof, sundry of the barrack doors were beat down, and about one third of the garrison imprisoned, which consisted of the said commander, a Lieut. Feltham, a conductor of artillery, a gunner, two sergeants, and forty-four rank and file; about one hundred pieces of cannon, one thirteen-inch mortar, and a number of swivels. This surprise was carried into execution in the gray of the morning of the tenth day of May, 1775. Col. Warner, with the rear guard, crossed the lake, and joined me early in the morning, whom I sent off, without loss of time, with about one hundred men, to take possession of Crown Point, which was garrisoned with a sergeant and twelve men; which he took possession of the same day, as also upward of one hundred pieces of cannon. But one thing now remained to be done, to make ourselves complete masters of Lake Champlain. This was to possess ourselves of a sloop of war, which was then laying at St. John's; to effect which, it was agreed, in a council of war, to arm and man out a certain schooner, which lay at South Bay, and that Captain (now General) Arnold should command her, and that I should command the batteaux. The necessary preparations being made, we set sail from Ticonderoga in quest of the sloop, which was much larger, and carried more guns and heavier metal than the schooner. General Arnold, with the schooner, sailing faster than the batteaux, arrived at St. John's; and by surprise possessed himself of the sloop before I could arrive with the batteaux. He also made prisoners of a sergeant and twelve men, who were garrisoned at that place.

Early in the fall of the year, the little army, under the command of the Generals Schuyler and Montgomery, were ordered to advance into Canada. I was at Ticonderoga when this order arrived; and the General, with most of the field-officers, requested me to attend them in the expedition. I was first ordered by the General to go, in company with Major Brown and certain interpreters, through the woods into Canada, with letters to the Canadians, and to let them know that the design of the army was only against the English garrisons, and not the country, their libert'es, or religion. This was soon accomplished, and on the morning of the 24th day of September, I set out with my guard of about eighty men, from

Longale, to go to Lapraier ; from thence I determined to go to Gen. Montgomery's camp ; but had not advanced two miles before I met with Major Brown, who proposed, that "Provided I would return to Longale, and procure some canoes, so as to cross the river St. Lawrence, a little north of Montreal, he would cross it a little to the south of the town, with near two hundred men, as he had boats sufficient; and that we would make ovrselves masters of Montreal."

This plan was readily approved by me and those in council; and in consequence of which I returned to Longale, collected a few canoes, and added about thirty English Americans to my party, and crossed the river in the night of the 24th. My whole party, at this time, consisted of about one hundred and ten men, near eighty of whom were Canadians. I then reconnoitered the best ground to make a defense, expecting Col. Brown's party were landing on the other side of the town, he having the day before agreed to give three huzzas with his men early in the morning, which signal I was to return, that we might each know that both parties were landed; but the sun by this time being near two hours high, and the sign failing, I began to conclude myself to be in a premunire, and would have crossed the river back again, but I knew the enemy would have discovered such an attempt.

The town of Montreal was in a great tumult. Gen. Carlton and the royal party made every preparation to go on board their vessels as I was afterwards informed. but a spy escaping from my guard to the town, occasioned an alteration in their policy, and emboldened Gen. Carlton to send the force, which he had there collected, out against me. I had previously chosen my ground, but when I saw the number of the enemy as they sallied out of the town, I perceived it would be a day of trouble, if not of rebuke ; but I had no chance to flee, as Montreal was situated on an island, and the river St. Lawrence cut off my communication to Gen. Montgomery's camp. The enemy consisted of not more than forty regular troops, together with a mixed multitude, chiefly Canadians, with a number of English who lived in the town, and some Indians ; in all to the number of near five hundred. The reader will notice that most of my party were Canadians; indeed it was a motley parcel of soldiery which composed both parties. However, the enemy began the attack from wood-piles, ditches, buildings, and such like places, at a considerable distance, and I returned the fire from a situation more than equally advantageous. The fire continued for some time on both sides; and I was confident that such a remote method of attack could not carry the ground provided it should be continued until night, but near half the body of the enemy began to flank round to my right; upon which I ordered a volunteer, by the name of John Dugan, to detach about fifty of the Canadians, and post himself at an advantageous ditch, which was on my right, to prevent my being surrounded. He advanced with the detachment, but instead of occupying the post, made his escape, as did likewise Mr. Young upon the left, with their detachments. The enemy kept closing round me, nor was it in my power to prevent it, by which means my situation, which was advantageous in the first part of the attack, ceased to be so in the last ; and being almost entirely surrounded with such vast, unequal numbers, I ordered a retreat, but found that those of the enemy who were of the country, and their Indians, could run as fast as my men, though the regulars could not. Thus I retreated near a mile, and some of the enemy, with the savages, kept flanking me, and others crowded hard in the rear. In fine I expected in a very short time to try the world of spirits, for I was apprehensive that no quarter would be given to me, and therefore had determined to sell my life as dearly as I could. One of the enemy's officers boldly pressing in the rear, discharged his fusee at me; the ball whistled near me, as did many others that day. I returned the salute and missed him, as running had put us both out of breath. I then saluted him with my tongue in a harsh manner, and told him that inasmuch as his numbers were so far superior to mine, I would surrender, provided I could be treated with honor, and be assured of good quarter for myself and the men who were with me; and he answered I should. Another officer coming up directly after, confirmed the treaty: upon which I agreed to surrender with my party, which then consisted of thirty-one effective men, and seven wounded. I ordered them to ground their arms, which they did. The officer I capitulated with, then directed me and my party to advance toward him, which was done. I handed him my sword, and in half a minute after, a savage, part of whose head was shaved, being almost naked and painted, with feathers intermixed with the hair of the other side of his head, came running to me with an incredible swiftness; he seemed to advance with more than mortal speed; as he approached near me, his hellish visage was beyond all description—snake eyes appear innocent in comparison with his; his features distorted; malice, death, murder and the wrath of devils and damned spirits are the emblems of his countenance; and in less than twelve feet of me, presented his firelock.

At the instant of his present, I twitched the officer to whom I gave my sword between me and the savage; but he flew round with great fury, trying to single me out to shoot me without killing the officer; but by this time I was near as nimble as he, keeping the officer in such a position that his danger was my defense. But in less than half a minute I was attacked by just such another imp of hell. Then I made the officer fly round with incredible velocity for a few seconds of time, when I perceived a Canadian (who had lost one eye, as appeared afterward,) taking my part against the savages; and in an instant an Irishman came to my assistance with a fixed bayonet, and drove away the fiends, swearing "by Jasus he would kill them." This tragic scene composed my mind. The escaping from so awful a death made even imprisonment happy; the more so as my conquerors on the field treated me with great civility and politeness. The regular officers said that they were happy to see Col. Allen. I answered them, that I should rather chose to have seen them at Gen. Montgomery's camp. The gentlemen replied that they gave full credit to what I said, and as I walked to the town, which was, as I should guess, more than two miles, a British officer walked at my right hand, and one of the French noblesse at my left; the latter of which, in the action, had his eyebrow carried away by a glancing shot, but was nevertheless very merry and facetious, and no abuse was offered me till I came to the barrack-yard at Montreal, where I met Gen. Prescott, who asked me my name, which I told him. He then asked me whether I was that Col. Allen who took Ticonderoga. I told him I was the very man. Then he shook his cane over my head, calling many hard names, among which he frequently used the word Rebel, and put himself into a great rage. I told him he would do well not to cane me, for I was not accustomed to it, and shook my fist at him, telling him that that was the beetle of mortality for him, if he offered to strike; upon which Capt. M'Cloud of the British, pulled him by the skirt, and whispered to him (as he afterward told me) to this import: that it was inconsistent with his honor to strike a prisoner. He then ordered a serjeant's command, with fixed bayonets, to come forward and kill thirteen Canadians, which were included in the treaty aforesaid.

It cut me to the heart to see the Canadians in so hard a case, in consequence of their having been true to me; they were wringing their hands, saying their prayers, as I concluded, and expected immediate death. I therefore stepped between the executioners and the Canadians, opened my clothes, and told Gen. Prescott to thrust his bayonet into my breast, for I was the sole cause of the Canadians taking up arms. The guard in the meantime, rolling their eyeballs from the General to me, as though impatient, waiting his dread commands to sheathe their bayonets in my heart. I could, however, plainly discern that he was in a suspense and quandary about the matter. This gave me additional hopes of succeeding, for my design was not to die, but save the Canadians by a finesse. The General stood a minute, when he made me the following reply: "*I will not execute you now: but you shall grace a halter at Tyburn, —— ye.*" General Prescott then ordered one of his officers to take me on board the Gaspee schooner of war, and confine me, hands and feet, in irons, which was done the same afternoon I was taken.

The action continued an hour and three quarters by the watch, and I know not to this day how many of my men were killed, though I am certain there were but few. If I remember right, seven were wounded; the latter were all put into the hospital at Montreal, and those that were not, were put on board of different vessels in the river, and shackled together by pairs, viz., two men fastened together by one handcuff being closely fixed to one wrist of each of them, and treated with the greatest severity, nay, as criminals.

I now come to the desciption of the irons, which were put on me. The handcuff was of a common size and form, but my leg irons, I should imagine, would weigh thirty pounds; the bar was eight feet long, and very substantial; the shackles which encompassed my ancles, were very ight. I was told by the officer who put them on, that it was the king's plate, and I heard other of their officers say, that it would weigh forty weight. The irons were so close upon my ancles, that I could not lie down in any other manner than on my back. I was put into the lowest and most wretched part of the vessel, where I got the favor of a chest to sit on; the same answered for my bed at night; and having procured some little blocks of the guard, who, day and night, with fixed bayonets, watched over me, to lay under each end of the large bar of my leg irons, to preserve my ancles from galling, while I sat on the chest, or lay back on the same, though most of the time, night and day, I sat on it; but at length having a desire to lay down on my side, which the closeness of the irons forbid, I desired the captain to loosen them for that purpose, but was denied the favor. The captain's name was Royal, who did not seem to be an ill-natured man; but oftentimes said, that his express orders were to treat me with such severity, which was disagreeable to his own feelings; nor did he ever insult me, though many others, who came on board, did. One of the officers, by the name of Bradley, was very generous to me; he would often send me victuals from his own table; nor did a day fail, but that he sent me a good drink of grog.

The reader is now invited back to the time I was put into irons. I requested the privilege to write to General Prescott, which was granted. I reminded him of the kind and generous manner of my treatment to the prisoners I took at Ticonderoga; the injustice and ungentleman-like usage, which I had met with from him, and demanded gentleman-like usage, but received no answer from him. I soon after wrote to General Carlton, which met the same success. In the meanwhile many of those who were permitted to see me were very insulting. I was confined in the manner I have related, on board the Gaspee schooner, about six weeks; during which time I was obliged to throw out plenty of extravagant language which answered certain purposes, at that time, better than to grace a history. To give an instance, upon being insulted, in a fit of anger I twisted off a nail with my teeth, which I took to be a ten-penny nail; it went through the mortice of the bar of my handcuff, and at the same time I swaggered over those who abused me; particularly a Doctoı Dace, who told me that I was outlawed by New York, and deserved death for several years past; was at last fully ripened for the halter, and in a fair way to obtain it.

When I challenged him, he excused himself in consequence, as he said, of my being a criminal. But I flung such a flood of language at him that it shocked him and the spectators, for my anger was very great I heard one say, "—— him, can he eat iron?" After that a small padlock was fixed to the handcuff instead of the nail; and as they were mean-spirited in their treatment to me, so it appeared to me, that they were equally timorous and cowardly. I was sent with the prisoners taken with me to an armed vessel in the river, which lay off against Quebec, under the command of Captain M'Cloud of the British, who treated me in a very generous and obliging manner, and according to my rank; in about twenty-four hours I bid him farewell with regret; but my good fortune still continued. The name of the captain of the vessel I was put on board, was Littlejohn; who, with his officers, behaved in a polite, generous, and friendly manner. I lived with them in the cabin, and fared on the best; my irons being taken off, contrary to the order he had received from the commanding officer; but Captain Littlejohn swore that a brave man should not be used as a rascal on board his ship.

Having enjoyed eight or nine days' happiness, from the polite and generous treatment of Captain Littlejohn and his officers, I was obliged to bid them farewell, parting with them in as friendly a manner as we had lived together, which, to the best of my memory, was the eleventh of November. When a detachment of General Arnold's little army appeared on Point Levy, opposite Quebec, who had performed an extraordinary march through a wilderness country, with design to have surprised the capital of Canada, I was then taken on board a vessel called the Adamant, together with the prisoners taken with me, and put under the power of an English merchant from London, whose name was Brook Watson; a man of malicious and cruel disposition, and who was probably excited in the exercise of his malevolence by a junto of tories, who sailed with him to England; among whom were Colonel Guy Johnson, Colonel Closs, and their attendants and associates, to the number of about thirty. A small place in the vessel, enclosed with white oak plank, was assigned for the prisoners, and for me among the rest. I should imagine that it was not more than twenty feet one way and twenty-two the other. Into this place we were all, to the number of thirty-four, thrust and handcuffed, two prisoners more being added to our number, and were provided with two excrement tubs. In this circumference we were obliged to eat and perform the office of evacuation, during the voyage to England; and were insulted by every blackguard sailor and tc y on board, in the cruelest manner; but what is the most surprising is, that not one of us died in the passage. When I was first ordered to go into the filthy enclosure, through a small sort of door, I positively refused, and endeavored to reason the before-named Brook Watson out of a conduct so derogatory to every sentiment of honor and humanity, but all to no purpose, my men being forced in the den already; and the rascal who had the charge of the prisoners, commanded me to go immediately in among the rest. He further added, that the place was good enough for a rebel; that it was impertinent for a capital offender to talk of honor or humanity—that anything short of a halter was too good for me—and that, that would be my portion soon after I landed in England—for which purpose only I was sent thither. About the same time a lieutenant among the tories insulted me in a greivous manner, saying that I ought to have been executed for my rebellion against New York, and spit in my face; upon which, though I was handcuffed, I sprung at him with both hands, and knocked him partly down, but he scrambled along into the cabin, and I after him—there he got under the protection of some men with fixed bayonets, who were ordered to make ready to drive me into the place before mentioned.

I challenged him to fight, notwithstanding the impediments that were on my hands, and had the exalted pleasure to see the rascal tremble for fear. His name I have forgotten, but Watson ordered his guard to get me into the place with the other prisoners, dead or alive; and I had almost as leave die as do it, standing it out till they environed me round with bayonets. Therefore, rather than die, I submitted to their indignities, being drove with bayonets into the filthy dungeon, with the other prisoners, where we were denied fresh water, except a small allowance which was very inadequate to our wants—and in consequence of the stench of the place, each of us was soon followed with a diarrhœa and fever, which occasioned an intolerable thirst. When we asked for water, we were most commonly, instead of obtaining it, insulted and derided—and to add to all the horrors of the place, it was so dark that we could not see each other, and were overspread with body lice. We had, notwithstanding these severities, full allowance of salt provisions, and a gill of rum per day—the latter of which was of the utmost service to us, and probably was the means of saving several of our lives. About forty days we existed in this manner, when the Land's-End of England was discovered from the mast-head—soon after which the prisoners were taken from their gloomy abode, being permitted to see the light of the sun, and breathe fresh air, which to us was very refreshing. The day following we landed at Falmouth. A few days before I was taken prisoner, I shifted my clothes, by which I happened to be taken in a Canadian dress, viz: a short fawn-skin jacket, double-breasted, an under vest and breeches of fagathy, worsted stockings, a decent pair of shoes, two plain shirts, and a red worsted cap. This was all the clothing I had, in which I made my appearance in England. When the prisoners were landed, multitudes of the citizens of Falmouth, excited by curiosity, crowded together to see us, which was equally gratifying to us. I saw numbers of people on the tops of houses, and the rising adjacent grounds were covered with them of both sexes. The throng was so great that the king's officers were obliged to draw their swords, and force a passage to Pendennis Castle, which was near a mile from the town where we were closely confined, in consequence of orders from General Carlton, who then commanded in Canada.

My personal treatment by Lieutenant Hamilton, who commanded the castle, was very generous. He sent me every day a fine breakfast and dinner from his own table, and a bottle of good wine. Another aged gentleman, whose name I cannot recollect, sent me a good supper. But there was no distinction in public support between me and the privates—we all lodged on a sort of Dutch bunks, in one common apartment, and were allowed straw. The privates were well supplied with fresh provisions, and with me took effectual measures to rid ourselves of lice. Among the great numbers of people who came to the castle to see the prisoners, some gentlemen told me that they had come fifty miles on purpose to see me, and desired to ask me a number of questions, and to make free with me in conversation. I gave for answer, that I chose freedom in every sense of the word. Then one of them asked me what my occupation in life had been? I answered him, that in my younger days I had studied divinity, but was a conjuror by profession. He replied that I conjured wrong at the time I was taken; and I was obliged to own, that I mistook a figure at that time, but that I had conjured them out of Ticonderoga This was a place of great notoriety in England, so that the joke seemed to go in my favor. It was a common thing for me to be taken out of close confinement, into a spacious green in the castle, or rather parade, where numbers of gentlemen and ladies were ready to see and hear me. I often entertained such audiences with harangues on the impracticability of Great Britian's conquering the then colonies of America. At one of these times I asked a gentleman for a bowl of punch, and he ordered his servant to bring it, which he did, and offered it to me, but I refused to take it from the hand of his servant. He then gave it to me with his own hand, refusing to drink with me in consequence of my being a state criminal. However, I took the punch and drank it all down at one draught, and handed the gentleman the bowl. This made the spectators as well as myself merry. Two clergymen came to see me, and inasmuch as they behaved with civility, I returned them the same. We discoursed on several parts of moral philosophy and Christianity—and they seemed to be surprised that I should be acquainted with such topics, or that I should understand a syllogism or regular mood of argumentation. I am apprehensive my Canadian dress contributed not a little to the surprise, and excitement of curiosity.

The prisoners were landed at Falmouth a few days before Christmas, and ordered on board of the Solebay frigate, Captain Symonds, the eighth day of January, 1776, when our hand irons were taken off. This remove was in consequence (as I have since been informed) of a writ of habeas corpus, which had been procured by some gentlemen in England, in order to obtain me my liberty. The Solebay, with sundry other men of war, and about forty transports, rendezvoused at the cove of Cork, in Ireland, to take in provisions and water. When we were first brought on board, Captain Symonds ordered all the prisoners, and most of the hands on board, to go on deck, and caused to be read in their hearing a certain code of laws, or rules for the regulation and ordering of their behavior; and then, in a sovereign manner, ordered the prisoners, me in particular, off the deck, and never to come on it again; for, said he, this is a place for gentlemen to walk. So I went off, an officer following me, who told me, that he would show me the place allotted for me, and took me down to the cable tier, saying to me, this is your place. Prior to this I had taken cold, by which I was in an ill state of health, and did not say much to the officer; but stayed there that night, consulted my policy, and found I was in an evil case. I felt myself more desponding than I had done at any time before. However, two days after I shaved and cleaned myself as well as I could, and went on deck The captain spoke to me in a great rage, and said, "Did I not order you not to come on deck?" I answered him, that at the same time he said, that it was the place for gentlemen to walk. That I was Colonel Allen, but had not been properly introduced to him. He replied, "—— you, sir, be careful not to walk the same side of the deck that I do." This gave me encouragement, and ever after that I walked in the manner he had directed, except when he, at certain times afterward, ordered me off in a passion: I would then directly afterward go on again, telling him to command his slaves, that I was a gentleman, and had a right to walk the deck; yet when he expressly ordered me off, I obeyed, not out of obedience to him, but to set an example to his ship's crew, who ought to obey him.

It was but a few nights I lodged in the cable tier, before I gained an acquaintance with the master-of-arms. His name was Gillegan, an Irishman, who was a generous and well disposed man, and in a friendly manner made me a proffer of living with him in a little berth, which was allotted him between decks, and enclosed with canvas; his preferment on board was about equal to that of a serjeant in a regiment. I was comparatively happy in the acceptance of his clemency, and lived with him in friendship, until the frigate anchored in the harbor of Cape Fear, North Carolina, in America.

Nothing of material consequence happened until the fleet rendezvoused at the cove of Cork, except a violent storm which brought old hardy sailors to their prayers. It was soon rumored in Cork that I was on board the Solebay, with a number of prisoners from America—upon which a number of benevolently disposed gentlemen, contributed largely to the relief and support of the prisoners, who were thirty-four in number, and in very needy circumstances. A suit of clothes from head to foot, including an overcoat, or surtout, and two shirts, were bestowed on each of them. My suit I received in superfine broadcloth, sufficient for two jackets, and two pair of breeches, overplus of a suit throughout, eight fine Holland shirts and socks ready made, with a number of pairs of silk and worsted hose, two pair of shoes, two beaver hats, one of which was richly laced with gold. The Irish gentlemen furthermore made a large gratuity of wines of the best sort, old spirits, Geneva, loaf and brown sugar, coffee, tea and chocolate, with a large round of pickled beef, and a number of fat turkies, with many other articles, for my sea-stores, too tedious to mention here. To the privates they bestowed to each man two pounds of tea, and six pounds of sugar. These articles were received on board, at a time when the captain and first lieutenant were gone on shore, by permission of the second lieutenant. To crown all, they sent me by another person fifty guineas, but I could not reconcile the receiving the whole to my own feelings, as it might have the appearance of avarice; and therefore received but seven guineas only.

Two days after the receipt of the aforesaid donations, Captain Symonds came on board, full of envy toward the prisoners, and swore by all that is good, that the damned American rebels should not be feasted at this rate by the damned rebels of Ireland; he therefore took away all my liquors before mentioned, except some of the wine which was secreted, and a two gallon jug of old spirits which was reserved for me, per favor of Lieutenant Douglas. The taking my liquors was abominable in his sight: he therefore spoke in my behalf, until the captain was angry with him, and in consequence, proceeded and took away all the tea and sugar which had been given to the other prisoners, and confiscated it to the use of the ship's crew. Our clothing was not taken away, but the privates were forced to do duty on board. Soon after this there came a boat to the side of the ship, and Captain Symonds asked a gentleman that was in it, in my hearing, what his business was, who answered that he was sent to deliver some sea-stores to Colonel Allen, which, if I remember right, he said were sent from Dublin; but the captain damned him very heartily, ordered him away from the ship, and would not suffer him to deliver the stores. I was furthermore informed, that the gentlemen in Cork requested of Captain Symonds that I might be allowed to come into the city, and that they would be responsible I should return to the frigate at a given time, which was denied them. We sailed from England the eighth day of January, and from the cove of Cork the twelfth day of February. Just before we sailed, the prisoners with me were divided, and put on board three different ships of war.

We had not sailed many days before a mighty storm arose, which lasted twenty-four hours without intermission. The wind blew with relentless fury, and no man could remain on deck, except he was lashed fast, for the waves rolled over the deck by turns, with a forcible rapidity, and every soul on board was anxious for the preservation of their lives. After the storm abated, I could plainly discern that the prisoners were better used for some considerable time. Nothing of consequence happened after this, till we had sailed to the island of Madeira, except a certain favor which I received of Captain Symonds, in consequence of an application I made to him, for the privilege of his tailor to make a suit of clothes of the cloth bestowed on me in Ireland, which he generously granted.

The reader will doubtless recollect the seven guineas I received at the cove of Cork. These would have enabled me to purchase of the purser what I wanted, had not the captain strictly forbid it, though I made sundry applications to him for that purpose ; but his answer to me, when I was sick, was, that it was no matter how soon I was dead, and that he was no ways anxious to preserve the lives of rebels, but wished them all dead ; and indeed that was the language of most of the ship's crew. I expostulated not only with the captain but with other gentlemen on board, on the unreasonableness of such usage ; inferring, that inasmuch as the government in England did not proceed against me as a capital offender, they should not ; for that they were by no means empowered by any authority, either civil or military, to do so; for the English government had acquitted me by sending me back a prisoner of war to America, and that they should treat me as such. I further drew an inference of impolicy on them, provided they should, by hard usage, destroy my life ; inasmuch as I might, if living, redeem one of their officers; but the captain replied, that he needed no directions of mine how to treat a rebel; that the British would conquer the American rebels, hang the Congress, and such as promoted the rebellion, me in particular, and retake their own prisoners; so that my life was of no consequence in the scale of their policy. I gave him for answer, that if they stayed till they conquered America before they hanged me, *I should die of old age*, and desired that till such an event took place, he would at least allow me to purchase of the purser, for my own money, such articles as I greatly needed; but he would not permit it, and when I reminded him of the generous and civil usage that their prisoners in captivity in America met with, he said that it was not owing to their goodness, but to their timidity ; for, said he, they expect to be conquered, and therefore dare not misuse our prisoners, and in fact this was the language of the British officers till General Burgoyne was taken ; and not only of the officers, but of the whole British army. The surgeon of the Solebay, however, whose name was North, was a very humane and obliging man, and took the best care of the prisoners who were sick.

The third day of May we cast anchor in the harbor of Cape Fear, in North Carolina, as did Sir Peter Parker's ship of fifty guns, a little back of the bar, for there was no depth of water for him to come into the harbor. These two men-of-war and fourteen sail of transports and others, came after, so that most of the fleet rendezvoused at Cape Fear, for three weeks. The soldiers on board the transports were sickly, in consequence of so long a passage—add to this, the smallpox carried off many of them: they landed on the main and formed a camp, but the riflemen annoyed them, and caused them to move to an island in the harbor—but such cursing of riflemen I never heard. A detachment of regulars was sent up Brunswick river; as they landed, were fired on by those marksmen, and they came back next day, damning the rebels for their unmanly way of fighting, and swearing that they would give no quarter, for they took sight at them, and were behind timber, skulking about. One of the detachments said they lost one man—but a negro man who was with them, and heard what was said, soon after told me that he helped to bury thirty-one of them.

The prisoners who had been sent on board different men-of-war at the cove of Cork, were collected together, and the whole of them put on board the Mercury frigate, Captain James Montague, who set sail from this port for Halifax, about the twentieth of May. I now found myself under a worse captain than Symonds; for Montague was loaded with prejudices against everybody and everything that was not stamped with royalty; and being by nature underwitted, his wrath was heavier than the others, or at least his mind was in no instance liable to be diverted by good sense, humor or bravery, of which Symonds was by turns susceptible. In this passage the prisoners were infected with the scurvy, some more and some less, but most of them severely. The ship's crew was to a great degree troubled with it, and I concluded that it was catching. Several of the crew died of it on their passage. I was weak and feeble in consequence of so long and cruel a captivity, yet had but little of the scurvy. The purser was again expressly forbid by the captain to let me have anything out of his store—upon which I went on deck, and in the handsomest manner requested the favor of purchasing a few necessaries of the purser, which was denied me. He further told me, that I should be hanged as soon as I arrived at Halifax. I tried to reason the matter with him, but found him proof against reason. He afterward forbid his surgeon to administer any help to the sick prisoners. I was every night shut down in the cable tier, with the rest of the prisoners, and we all lived miserably while under his power. But I received some generosity from several of the midshipmen, who in a degree alleviated my misery. But they were obliged to be private in the bestowment of their favor, which was sometimes good wine bitters, and at others a generous drink of grog. Sometime in the first week of June, we came to anchor at the Hook off New York, where we remained but three days; in which time Governor Tryon, Mr. Kemp, the old Attorney General of New York, and several other perfidious and overgrown tories and land-jobbers came on board. Tryon viewed me with a stern countenance as I was walking on the leeward side of the deck with the midshipmen—and he and his companions were walking with the captain and lieutenant on the windward side of the same, but never spoke to me. What passed between the officers of the ship and these visitors I know not; but this I know, that my treatment from the principal officers was more severe afterward.

We arrived at Halifax not far from the middle of June, where the ship's crew which was infested with the scurvy, were taken on shore, and shallow trenches dug, into which they were put, and partly covered with earth. Indeed every proper measure was taken for their relief. The prisoners were not permitted any sort of medicine, but were put on board a sloop which lay in the harbor, near the town of Halifax, surrounded with several men-of-war and their tenders, and a guard constantly set over them, night and day. The sloop we had wholly to ourselves, except the guard who occupied the forecastle; here we were cruelly pinched with hunger. It seemed to me that we had not more than one third of the common allowance. We were all seized with violent hunger and faintness—we divided our scanty allowance as exact as possible. I shared the same fate with the rest, and though they offered me more than an even share, I refused to accept it, as it was a time of substantial distress, which, in my opinion, I ought to partake equally with the rest, and set an example of virtue and fortitude to our little commonwealth. I sent letter after letter to Captain Montague, who still had the care of us, and also to his lieutenant, but could obtain no answer, much less a redress of grievances; and, to add to the calamity, near a dozen of the prisoners were dangerously ill of the scurvy. I wrote private letters to the doctors, to procure, if possible, some remedy for the sick, but in vain. The chief physician came by in a boat so close that the oars touched the sloop we were in, and I uttered my complaint in the genteelest manner to him, but he never so much as turned his head, or made me any answer, though I continued speaking till he got out of hearing. Our cause then became very deplorable. Still I kept writing to the captain, till he ordered the guards, as they told me, not to bring any more letters from me to him. In the meantime an event happened worth relating. One of the men almost dead of the scurvy, laid by the side of the sloop, and a canoe of Indians coming by, he purchased two quarts of strawberries, and ate them at once, and it almost cured him. The money he gave for them, was all the money he had in the world.

Meanwhile the doctor's mate of the Mercury came privately on board the prison sloop, and presented me with a large vial of smart drops, which proved to be good for the scurvy, though vegetables and some other ingredients were requisite for a cure; but the drops gave at least a check to the disease. This was a well-timed exertion of humanity—and, in my opinion, was the means of saving the lives of several men. The guard which was set over us, was by this time touched with the feelings of compassion; and I finally trusted one of them with a letter of complaint to Governor Arbuthnot, of Halifax, which he found means to communicate, and which had the desired effect—for the governor sent an officer and surgeon on board the prison sloop, to know the truth of the complaint. The officer's name was Russel, who held the rank of lieutenant, and treated me in a friendly and polite manner, and was really angry at the cruel and unmanly usage the prisoners met with; and with the surgeon made a report of matters to Governor Arbuthnot, who, either by his order or influence, took us next day from the prison sloop to Halifax gaol, The sick were taken to the hospital, and the Canadians who were effective, were employed in the king's works; and when their countrymen were recovered from the scurvy, and joined them, they all deserted the king's employ, and were not heard of at Halifax, as long as the remainder of the prisoners continued there, which was till near the middle of October. We were on board the prison sloop about six weeks, and were landed at Halifax near the middle of August. Several of our English American prisoners, who were cured of the scurvy at the hospital, made their escape from thence, and after a long time reached their old habitations. I had now but thirteen with me of those that were taken in Canada, and remained in gaol with me in Halifax, who, in addition to those that were imprisoned before, made our number about thirty-four, who were all locked up in one common large room, without regard to rank; and as sundry of them were infected with the gaol and other distempers, the furniture of this spacious room consisted most principally of excrement tubs.

As to the article of provisions, we were well served, much better than in any part of my captivity. Notwithstanding which I had not been more than three weeks in this place before I lost all appetite for the most delicious food by the gaol distemper, as sundry of the other prisoners. A doctor visited the sick, and did the best, as I suppose, he could for them, to no apparent purpose. I grew weaker and weaker, as did the rest. Several of them could not help themselves. At last I reasoned in my own mind, that raw onion would be good. I made use of it, and found immediate relief by it, as did the sick in general. In a few days after this the prisoners were ordered to go on board of a man-of-war, which was bound for New York. This was about the twelfth of October, and soon after I had got on board, the captain sent for me in particular to come on the quarter-deck. I went, expecting the same rigorous usage I had commonly met with, and prepared my mind accordingly; but when I came on deck, the captain met me with his hand, welcomed me to his ship, invited me to dine with him that day, and assured me that I should be treated as a gentleman, and that he had given orders that I should be treated with respect by the ship's crew. This was so unexpected and sudden a transition that it drew tears from my eyes—which all the ill usage I had before met with was not able to produce—nor could I at first hardly speak, but soon recovered myself, and expressed my gratitude for so unexpected a favor, and let him know that I felt anxiety of my mind in reflecting that his situation and mine was such that it was not probable that it would ever be in my power to return the favor. Captain Smith replied, that he had no reward in view, but only treated me as a gentleman ought to be treated; he said, this is a mutable world, and one gentleman never knows but that it may be in his power to help another.

I dined with the captain agreeable to his invitation, and oftentimes with the lieutenants, in the gun-room, but in general ate and drank with the gentlemen, who were prisoners with me, where I also slept. Captain Burk having been taken prisoner, was added to our company, (he had commanded an American armed vessel,) and was generously treated by the captain and all the officers of the ship. We now had in all near thirty prisoners on board, and as we were sailing along the coast, if I recollect right, off Rhode Island, Captain Burk, with an under officer of the ship, whose name I do not recollect, came to our little berth, proposed to kill Captain Smith and the principal officers of the frigate and take it; adding hat there was 35,000*l* sterling in the same. Captain Burk likewise averred that a strong party out of the ship's crew was in the conspiracy, and urged me and the gentlemen that were with me to use our influence with the private prisoners, to execute the design, and take the ship, with the cash, into one of our own ports. Upon which I replied, that we had

10

been too well used on board to murder the officers; that I could by no means reconcile it to my conscience, and that in fact it should not be done; and while I was yet speaking, my friend Lovel confirmed what I had said, and further pointed out the ungratefulness of such an act; that it did not fall short of murder; and, in fine, all the gentlemen in the berth opposed Captain Burk and his colleague. But they strenuously urged that the conspiracy would be found out, and that it would cost them their lives, provided they did not execute their design. I then interposed spiritedly, and put an end to further arguments on the subject, and told them that they might depend upon it, upon my honor, that I would faith fully guard Captain Smith's life. If they should attempt the assault, I would assist him, for they desired me to remain neuter, and that the same honor that guarded Captain Smith's life, would also guard theirs; and it was agreed by those present not to reveal the conspiracy, to the intent that no man should be put to death in consequence of what had been projected; and Captain Burk and his colleague went to stifle the matter among their associates. I could not help calling to mind what Captain Smith said to me, when I first came on board: "*This is a mutable world, and one gentleman never knows but that it may be in his power to help another.*" Captain Smith and his officers still behaved with their usual courtesy, and I never heard any more of the conspiracy.

We arrived before New York the latter part of October, where we remained several days, and where Captain Smith informed me, that he had recommended me to Admiral Howe and General Sir William Howe, as a gentleman of honor and veracity, and desired that I might be treated as such. Captain Burk was then ordered on board a prison ship in the harbor. I took my leave of Captain Smith, and, with the other prisoners, was sent on board a transport ship, which lay in the harbor, commanded by Captain Craige, who took me into the cabin with him and his lieutenant I fared as they did, and was in every respect well treated in consequence of directions from Captain Smith.

Some of the last days of November, the prisoners were landed at New York, and I was admitted to parole with the other officers. The privates were put into the filthy churches in New York, with the distressed prisoners that were taken at Fort Washington; and the second night serjeant Roger Moore, who was bold and enterprising, found means to make his escape with every one of the remaining prisoners that were taken with me, except three who were soon after exchanged. So that out of thirty-one prisoners, who went with me the round exhibited in these sheets, two only died with the enemy, and three only exchanged: one of them died after he came within our lines; all the rest, at different times, made their escape from the enemy. I now found myself on parole, and restricted to the limits of the city of New York, where I soon projected means to live in some measure agreeable to my rank, though I was destitute of cash. My constitution was almost worn out by such a long and barbarous captivity. The enemy gave out that I was crazy, and wholly unmanned, but my vitals held sound, (nor was I delirous any more than I have been from my youth up; but my extreme circumstances at certain times, rendered it politic to act in some measure the madman,) and in consequence of a regular diet and exercise my blood recruited, and my nerves in great measure recovered their former tone, strength and usefulness, in the course of six months.

I next invite the reader to a consideration of the scene of inhumanity exercised by General Sir William Howe, and the army under his command, toward their prisoners. The private soldiers who were brought to New York were crowded into churches, and sometimes environed with slavish Hessian guards, a people of strange language, who were sent to America for no other design but cruelty and desolation; and at others, by merciless Britons, whose mode of communicating ideas being intelligible in this country, served only to tantalize and insult the helpless and perishing; but above all the hellish delight and triumph of the tories over them, as they were dying by hundreds. This was too much for me to bear as a spectator; for I saw the tories exulting over the dead bodies of their murdered countrymen. I have gone into the churches, and seen sundry of the prisoners in the agonies of death, in consequence of very hunger, and others speechless and near death, biting pieces of chips; others pleading, for God's sake, for something to eat, and at the same time shivering with the cold. Hollow groans saluted my ears, and despair seemed to be imprinted on every one of their countenances. The filth in these churches, in consequence of the fluxes, was almost beyond description. The floors were covered with excrements. I have carefully sought to direct my steps so as to avoid it, but could not. They would beg, for God's sake, for one copper, or morsel of bread. I have seen in one of these churches seven dead at the same time, lying among the excrements of their bodies.

It was a common practice with the enemy to convey the dead from their filthy places in carts, to be slightly buried, and I have seen whole gangs of tories making derision, and exulting over the dead, saying, there goes another load of —— rebels. I have observed the British soldiers to be full of their blackguard jokes and vaunting on those occasions, but they appeared to me less malignant than tories. The provision dealt out to the prisoners was by no means sufficient for the support of life. It was deficient in quantity, and much more so in quality. The prisoners often presented me with a sample of their bread, which I certify was damaged to that degree that it was loathsome and unfit to be eaten. Their allowance of meat, as they told me, was quite trifling, and of the basest sort. I never saw any of it, but was informed, bad as it was, it was swallowed almost as quick as they got hold of it. I saw some of them sucking bones after they were speechless; others who could yet speak, and had the use of their reason, urged me in the strongest and most pathetic manner, to use my interest in their behalf.

I was in one of the churchyards, and it was rumored among those in the church, and sundry of the prisoners came with their usual complaints to me, and among the rest a large-boned, tall young man, as he told me from Pennsylvania, who was reduced to a mere skeleton; said he was glad to see me before he died, which he had expected to have done last night, but was a little revived; he furthermore informed me, that he and his brother had been urged to enlist into the British, but had both resolved to die first; that his brother had died last night, in consequence of that resolution, and that he expected shortly to follow him; but I made the other prisoners stand a little off, and told him with a low voice to list; he then asked, whether it was right in the sight of God? I assured him that it was, and that duty to himself obliged him to deceive the British by enlisting, and deserting the first opportunity. Upon which he answered with transport that he would list. I charged him not to mention my name as his adviser, lest it should get air, and I should be closely confined in consequence of it. The integrity of these suffering prisoners is hardly credible. Many hundreds, I am confident, submitted to death, rather than enlist in the British service, which, I am informed, they most generally were pressed to do.

Near the last of November I was admitted to parole in New York, with many other American officers, and on the 22d day of January, 1777, was with them directed by the British commissary of prisoners to be quartered on the westerly part of Long Island, and our parole continued. On the third day of May, 1778, I was conducted to a sloop in the harbor at New York, in which I was guarded to Staten Island, to General Campbell's quarters, where I was admitted to eat and drink with the general and several other of the British field-officers, and treated for two days in a polite manner. The next day Colonel Archibald Campbell (who was exchanged for me) came to this place conducted by Mr. Boudinot, the then American commissary of prisoners, and saluted me in a handsome manner, saying that he never was more glad to see any gentleman in his life. So we took a glass of wine together, and then I was accompanied by General Campbell, Colonel Campbell, Mr. Boudinot, and a number of British officers, to the boat, which was ready to sail to Elizabethtown Point. I sailed to the Point, and in a transport of joy, landed on liberty ground; and as I advanced into the country, received the acclamations of a grateful people.

In a few days I set out for Bennington, the capital of the Green Mountain Boys, where I arrived the evening of the last day of May to their great surprise; for I was to them as one rose from the dead, and now their joy and mine was complete. Three cannon were fired that evening, and next morning Colonel Herrick gave orders, and fourteen more were discharged, welcoming me to Bennington, my usual place of abode.

INCIDENTS

IN THE

WAR WITH TRIPOLI:

TO WHICH IS ADDED A NARRATIVE OF THE CELEBRATED

CHASE OF THE CONSTITUTION BY A BRITISH SQUADRON.

THE depredations committed on American commerce in the Mediterranean, by the piratical corsairs of the Barbary powers induced Congress to authorize the formation of a naval force for its protection. In the month of August, 1801, Captain Sterrett, of the United States schooner Enterprise, of twelve guns, and ninety men, fell in, off Malta, with a Tripolitan cruiser of fourteen guns, and eighty-five men. In this action the Tripolitans thrice hauled down her colors, and thrice perfidiously renewed the conflict. Fifty of her men were killed and wounded. The Enterprise did not lose a man! Captain Sterrett's instructions not permitting him to make a prize of the cruiser, he ordered her crew to throw overboard all their guns and powder, etc., and to go and tell their countrymen the treatment they might expect from a nation, determined to pay tribute only in powder and ball. On her arrival at Tripoli, so great was the terror produced, that the sailors abandoned the cruisers then fitting out, and not a man could be procured to navigate them.

The Tripolitan cruisers continuing to harass the vessels of the United States, Congress determined, in 1803, to fit out a fleet that should chastise their insolence. The squadron consisted of the Constitution, 44 guns; the Philadelphia, 44; the Argus, 18; the Siren, 16; the Nautilus, 16; the Vixen, 16; and the Enterprise, 12. Commodore Preble was appointed to the command of this squadron, in May, 1803, and on the thirteenth of August, sailed, in the Constitution, for the Mediterranean. Having adjusted the difficulties which had sprung up with the emperor of Morocco, he turned his whole attention to Tripoli. The season was, however, too far advanced for active operations.

On the thirty-first of October, the Philadelphia, being, at nine o'clock in the morning, about five leagues to the westward of Tripoli, discovered a sail in shore, standing before the wind to the eastward. The Philadelphia immediately gave chase. The sail hoisted Tripolitan colors, and continued her course near the shore. The Philadelphia opened a fire upon her, and continued it till half past eleven; when, being in seven fathoms water, and finding her fire could not prevent the vessel entering Tripoli, she gave up the pursuit. In beating off, she ran on a rock, not laid down in any chart, distant four and a half miles from the town. A boat was immediately lowered to sound. The greatest depth of water was found to be astern. In order to back her off, all sails were then laid aback; the topgallant-sails loosened; three anchors thrown away from the bows; the water in the hold started; and all the guns thrown overboard, excepting a few abaft to defend the ship against the attacks of the Tripolitan gunboats, then firing at her. All this, however, proved ineffectual; as did also the attempt to lighten her forward by cutting away her foremast. The Philadelphia had already withstood the attack of the numerous gunboats for four hours, when a large reinforcement coming out of Tripoli, and being herself deprived of every means of resistance and defense, she was forced to strike, about sunset. The Tripolitans immediately took possession of her, and made prisoners of the officers and men, in number three hundred. Forty-eight hours afterward, the wind blowing in shore, the Tripolitans got the frigate off, and towed her into the harbor.

On the seventeenth of December, 1803, Commodore Preble, after making his preparations and disposing of his force in different ways, sailed for Tripoli, with the Enterprise in company, off which place he now appeared for the first time. The twenty-third of the month, the Enterprise 12, Lieutenant Commandant Decatur, fell in with and captured a ketch, called the Mastico, with seventy souls on board.

In a letter of the date of the fifth of December, 1803, Captain Bainbridge suggested the possibility of destroying the Philadelphia, which ship was slowly fitting for sea, there being little doubt of her being sent out as a cruiser, as soon as the mild season should return. Commodore Preble listened to the suggestion, and being much in the society of the commander of the vessel that was most in company with the Constitution, Lieutenant Stephen Decatur, he mentioned the project to that spirited officer. The expedition was just suited to the ardor and temperament of Mr. Decatur, and the possession of the Mastico at once afforded the means of carrying it into effect. The ketch was accordingly appraised, named the Intrepid, and taken into the service, as a tender. About this time, Lieutenant Commandant Stewart, of the Siren, the officer who was then second in command in the Mediterranean, and who had just arrived from below, offered to cut out the Philadelphia with his own brig; but Commodore Preble was pledged to Mr. Decatur, who, at first, had proposed to run in with the Enterprise and carry the ship. The more experienced Preble rejected the propositions of both these ardent young men, substituting a plan of his own.

Although Commodore Preble declined the proposal of Mr. Decatur to carry in the Enterprise, the projected service was assigned to the commander and crew of that schooner. It being necessary, however, to leave some of her own officers and people in her, a selection of a few gentlemen to join in the expedition, was made from the flag-ship, and orders to that effect were issued accordingly. These orders were dated February the third, 1804, and they directed the different gentlemen named to report themselves to Lieutenant Commandant Decatur, of the Enterprise. As it was intended that the crew of the schooner should furnish the entire crew of the ketch, it was not thought proper to add any men to this craft. In short, the duty was strictly assigned to the Enterprise, so far as her complement could furnish the officers required. On the afternoon of the third, according to the orders they had just received, Messrs. Izard, Morris, Laws, Davis, and Rowe, midshipmen of the Constitution, went on board the schooner, and reported themselves for duty to her commander. All hands were now called in the Enterprise, when Lieutenant Commandant Decatur acquainted his people with the destination of the ketch, and asked for volunteers. Every man and boy in the schooner presented himself, as ready, and willing to go. Sixty-two of the most active men were selected, and the remainder, with a few officers, were left to take care of the vessel. As the orders to destroy the frigate, and not to attempt to bring her out, were peremptory, the combustibles, which had been prepared for this purpose, were immediately sent on board the Intrepid, her crew followed, and that evening the ketch sailed, under the convoy of the Siren 16, Lieutenant Commandant Stewart, who was properly the senior officer of the expedition, though, owing to the peculiar nature of the service, Mr. Decatur was permitted to conduct the more active part of the duty, at his own discretion.

The party in the ketch consisted of Lieutenant Commandant Decatur; Lieutenants Lawrence, Bainbridge, and Thorn; Mr. Thomas M'Donough, midshipman, and Dr. Heerman, surgeon; all of the Enterprise;—Messrs. Izard, Morris, Laws, Davis, and Rowe, midshipmen, of the Constitution; and Salvatore Catalano the pilot, with sixty-two petty officers and common men, making a total of seventy-four souls.

On the sixteenth, about noon, calculating that they were abreast of the town, and the wind and weather being, in all respects, favorable, both vessels kept away, the ketch leading some distance, in order that the enemy might not suppose her a consort of the Siren's although the latter was so much disguised, as to render it impossible to recognize her. The wind was fair, but light, and everything looking favorable; Mr. Decatur now seriously made his dispositions for the attack. Apprehensive that they might have been seen, and that the enemy had possibly strengthened the party on board the frigate, Lieutenant Commandant Stewart sent a boat and eight men from the Siren, to the ketch, under the orders of one of his midshipmen, Mr. Anderson, which reinforcement increased the numbers of the intended assailants to eighty-two, all told.

As the ketch drew in with the land, the Philadelphia became visible. She lay not quite a mile within the entrance, riding to the wind, and abreast of the town. Her foremast, which had been cut away while she was on the reef, had not yet been replaced, her main and mizzen-topmasts were housed, and her lower yards were on the gunwales. Her lower standing rigging, however, was in its place, and, as was shortly afterward ascertained, her guns were loaded and shotted. Just within her, lay two corsairs, with a few gun-boats, and a galley or two.

It was a mild evening for the season, and the sea and bay were smooth as in summer. Perceiving that he was likely to get in too soon, when about five miles from the rocks, Mr. Decatur ordered buckets and other drags to be towed astern, in order to lessen the way of the ketch, without shortening sail, as the latter expedient would have been seen from the port, and must have awakened suspicion. In the meantime the wind gradually fell, until it became so light as to leave the ketch but about two knot's way on her, when the drags were removed.

About ten o'clock the Intrepid reached the eastern entrance of the bay, or the passage between the rocks and the shoal. The wind was nearly east, and, as she steered directly for the frigate, it was well abaft the beam. There was a young moon, and as the bold adventurers were slowly advancing into the hostile port, all around them was tranquil and apparently without distrust. For near an hour they were stealing slowly along, the air gradually failing, until their motion became scarcely porceptiblo.

Most of the officers and men of the ketch had been ordered to lie on the deck, where they were concealed by low bulwarks, or weather-boards, and by the different objects that belong to a vessel. As it is the practice of those seas to carry many men even in the smallest craft, the appearance of ten or twelve would excite no alarm, and this number was visible. The commanding officer, himself, stood near the pilot, who was to act as interpreter. The quartermaster at the helm, was ordered to stand directly for the frigate's bows, it being the intention to lay the ship aboard in that place, as the mode of attack which would least expose the assailants to her fire.

The Intrepid was still at a considerable distance from the Philadelphia. when the latter hailed. The pilot answered that the ketch belonged to Malta, and was on a trading voyage; that she had been nearly wrecked, and had lost her anchors in the late gale, and that her commander wished to ride by the frigate during the night. This conversation lasted some time, Mr. Decatur instructing the pilot to tell the frigate's people with what he was laden, in order to amuse them, and the Intrepid gradually drew nearer, until there was every prospect of her running foul of the Philadelphia, in a minute or two, and at the very spot contemplated. But the wind suddenly shifted, and took the ketch aback. The instant the southerly puff struck her, her head fell off, and she got a stern-board, the ship, at the same moment, tending to the new current of air. The effect of this unexpected change was to bring the ketch directly under the frigate's broadside, at the distance of about forty yards, where she lay becalmed, or, if anything, drifting slowly astern, exposed to nearly every one of the Philadelphia's larboard guns.

Not the smallest suspicion appears to have been yet excited on board the frigate, though several of her people were looking over the rails; and, notwithstanding the moonlight, so completely were the Turks deceived, that they lowered a boat, and sent it with a fast. Some of the ketch's men, in the meantime, had got into her boat, and had run a line to the frigate's forechains. As they returned, they met the frigate's boat, took the fast it brought, which came from the after part of the ship, and passed it into their own vessel. These fasts were put into the hands of the men, as they lay on the ketch's deck, and they began cautiously to breast the Intrepid along side of the Philadelphia, without rising. As soon as the latter got near enough to the ship, the Turks discovered her anchors, and they sternly ordered the ketch to keep off, as she had deceived them; preparing, at the same time, to cut the fasts. All this passed in a moment, when the cry of "Amerikanos" was heard in the ship. The people of the Intrepid by a strong pull, brought their vessel along side of the frigate, where she was secured, quick as thought. Up to this moment, not a whisper had betrayed the presence of the men concealed. The instructions had been positive to keep quiet until commanded to show themselves, and no precipitation, even in that trying moment, deranged the plan.

Lieutenant Commandant Decatur was standing ready for a spring, with Messrs. Laws and Morris quite near him. As soon as close enough, he jumped at the frigate's chain-plates, and while clinging to the ship himself, he gave the order to board. The two midshipmen were at his side, and all the officers and men of the Intrepid arose and followed. The three gentlemen named were in the chains together, and Lieutenant Commandant Decatur and Mr. Morris sprang at the rail above them, while Mr. Laws dashed at a port. To the latter would have belonged the honor of having been first in this gallant assault, but wearing a boarding-belt, his pistols were caught between the gun and the side of the port. Decatur's foot slipped in springing, and Mr. Charles Morris first stood upon the quarter-deck of the Philadelphia. In an instant Lieutenant Commandant Decatur and Mr. Laws were at his side, while heads and bodies appeared coming over the rail, and through the ports in all directions.

The surprise appears to have been as perfect, as the assault was rapid and earnest. Most of the Turks on deck crowded forward, and all ran over to the starboard-side, as their enemies poured in on the larboard, A few were aft, but as soon as charged, they leaped into the sea. Indeed, the constant plunges into the water, gave the assailants the assurance that their enemies were fast lessening in numbers by flight. It took but a minute or two to clear the spar-deck, though there was more of a struggle below. Still, so admirably managed was the attack, and so complete the surprise, that the resistance was but trifling. In less than ten minutes Mr. Decatur was on the quarter-deck again, in undisturbed possession of his prize.

There can be no doubt that this gallant officer now felt bitter regrets, that it was not in his power to bring away the ship he had so nobly recovered. Not only were his orders on this point peremptory, however, but the frigate had not a sail bent, nor a yard crossed, and she wanted her foremast. It was next to impossible, therefore, to remove her, and the command was given to pass up the combustibles from the ketch.

The duty of setting fire to the prize, appears to have been executed with as much promptitude and order, as every other part of the service. The officers distributed themselves, agreeably to the previous instructions, and the men soon appeared with the necessary means. Each party acted by itself, and as it got ready. So rapid were they all in their movements, that the men with combustibles had scarcely time to get as low as the cockpit and after store-rooms, before the fires were lighted over their heads. When the officer entrusted with the duty last mentioned, had got through, he found the after-hatches filled with smoke, from the fire in the wardroom and steerage, and he was obliged to make his escape by the forward ladders.

The Americans were in the ship from twenty to twenty-five minutes, and they were literally driven out of her by the flames. The vessel had got to be so dry in that low latitude, that she burnt like pine; and the combustibles had been as judiciously prepared, as they were steadily used. The last party up, were the people who had been in the store-rooms, and when they reached the deck, they found most of their companions already in the Intrepid. Joining them, and ascertaining that all was ready, the order was given to cast off. Notwithstanding the daring character of the enterprise in general, Decatur and his party now ran the greatest risk they had incurred that night. So fierce had the conflagration already become, that the flames began to pour out of the ports, and the head-fast having been cast off, the ketch fell astern, with her jigger flapping against the quarter-gallery, and her boom foul. The fire showed itself in the window, at this critical moment; and beneath, was all the ammunition of the party, covered with a tarpaulin. To increase the risk, the stern-fast was jammed. By using swords, however, for there was not time to look for an ax, the hawser was cut, and the Intrepid was extricated from the most imminent danger, by a vigorous shove. As she swung clear of the frigate, the flames reached the rigging, up which they went hissing, like a rocket, the tar having oozed from the ropes, which had been saturated with that inflammable matter. Matches could not have kindled with greater quickness.

The sweeps were now manned. Up to this moment, everything had been done earnestly, though without noise, but, as soon as they felt that they had got command of their ketch again, and by two or three vigorous strokes had sent her away from the frigate, the people of the Intrepid ceased rowing, and as one man, they gave three cheers for victory. This appeared to arouse the Turks from their stupor, for the cry had hardly ended, when the batteries, the two corsairs, and the galley, poured in their fire. The men lay hold of the sweeps again, of which the Intrepid had eight of a side, and favored by a light air, they went rapidly down the harbor.

The spectacle that followed, is described as having been both beautiful and sublime. The entire bay was illuminated by the conflagration, the roar of cannon was constant, and Tripoli was in a clamor. The appearance of the ship was, in the highest degree, magnificent; and, to add to the effect, as her guns heated, they began to go off. Owing to the shift of wind, and the position into which she had tended, she, in some measure, returned the enemy's fire, as one of her broadsides was discharged in the direction of the town, and the other toward Fort English. The most singular effect of this conflagration was on board the ship, for the flames having run up the rigging and masts, collected under the tops, and fell over, giving the whole the appearance of glowing columns and fiery capitals.

Under ordinary circumstances, the situation of the ketch would still have been thought sufficiently perilous, but after the exploit they had just performed, her people, elated with success, regarded all that was now passing, as a triumphant spectacle. The shot constantly cast the spray around them, or were whistling over their heads, but the only sensation they produced, was by calling attention to the brilliant *jets d'eau* that they occasioned as they bounded along the water. But one struck the Intrepid, although she was within half a mile of many of the heaviest guns for some time, and that passed through her topgallant sail.

With sixteen sweeps, and eighty men elated with success, Decatur was enabled to drive the little Intrepid ahead with a velocity that rendered towing useless. Near the harbor's mouth, he met the Siren's boats, sent to cover his retreat, but their services were scarcely necessary. As soon as the ketch was out of danger, he got into one, and pulled aboard the brig, to report to Lieutenant Commandant Stewart, the result of his undertaking.

The Siren had got into the offing some time after the Intrepid, agreeably to arrangements, and anchored about three miles from the rocks. Here she hoisted out the launch and a cutter, manned and armed them, and sent them in, under Mr. Caldwell, her first lieutenant. Soon after the brig weighed, and the wind having entirely failed outside, she swept into eight fathoms water, and anchored again, to cover the retreat, should the enemy attempt to board the Intrepid, with his gun-boats. It will readily be supposed that it was an anxious moment, and as the moon rose, all eyes were on the frigate. After waiting in intense expectation near an hour, a rocket went up from the Philadelphia. It was the signal of possession, and Mr. Stewart ran below to get another for the answer He was gone only a moment, but when he returned, the fire was seen shining through the frigate's ports, and in a few more minutes, the flames were rushing up her rigging, as if a train had been touched. Then followed the cannonade, and the dashing of sweeps, with the approach of the ketch. Presently a boat was seen coming along side, and a man, in a sailor's jacket, sprang over the gangway of the brig. It was Decatur, himself, to announce his victory!"

After the destruction of the Philadelphia frigate, Commodore Preble was, during the spring and early part of the summer, employed in keeping up the blockade of the harbor of Tripoli, in preparing for an attack upon the town and in cruising.

"When the American commander assembled his whole force before Tripoli, on the twenty-fifth of July, 1804, it consisted of the Constitution 44, Commodore Preble; Siren 16, Lieutenant Commandant Stewart; Argus 16, Lieutenant Commandant Hull; Scourge 14, Lieutenant Commandant Dent; Vixen 12, Lieutenant Commandant Smith; Nautilus 12, Lieutenant Commandant Somers; Enterprise 12, Lieutenant Commandant Decatur; the two bomb-vessels, and six gunboats. In some respects this was a well appointed force for the duty required, while in others it was lamentably deficient. Another heavy ship, in particular, was wanted, and the means for bombarding had all the defects that may be anticipated. The two heaviest brigs had armaments of twenty-four pound carronades; the other brig, and two of the schooners, armaments of eighteen-pound carronades; while the Enterprise retained her original equipment of long sixes, in consequence of her ports being unsuited to the new guns. As the Constitution had a gun-deck battery of thirty long twenty-fours, with six long twenty-sixes, and some lighter long guns above, it follows that the Americans could bring twenty-two twenty-fours and six twenty-sixes to bear on the stone walls of the town, in addition to a few light chase-guns in the small vessels, and the twelve-pounders of the frigate's quarter-deck and forecastle. On the whole, there appears to have been in the squadron, twenty-eight heavy long guns, with about twenty lighter, that might be brought to play on the batteries simultaneously. Opposed to these means of offense, the bashaw had one hundred and fifteen guns in battery, most of them quite heavy, and nineteen gun-boats that, of themselves, so far as metal was concerned, were nearly equal to the frigate. Moored in the harbor were also two large galleys, two schooners, and a brig, all of which were armed and strongly manned. The American squadron was manned by one thousand and sixty persons, all told, while the bashaw had assembled a force that has been estimated as high as twenty-five thousand, Arabs and Turks included. The only advantages possessed by the assailants, in the warfare that is so soon to follow, were those which are dependent on spirit, discipline, and system.

On the third of August, 1804, the squadron ran in and got within a league of the town, with a pleasant breeze at the eastward. The enemy's gun-boats and galleys had come outside of the rocks, and were lying there in two divisions; one near the eastern, and the other near the western entrance, or about half a mile apart. At the same time, it was seen that all the batteries were manned, as if an attack was not only expected, but invited.

At half-past twelve, the Constitution wore with her head off shore, and showed a signal for all vessels to come within hail. As he came up, each commander was ordered to prepare to attack the shipping and batteries. The bomb-vessels and gun-boats were immediately manned, and such was the high state of discipline in the squadron, that in one hour, everything was ready for the contemplated service.

On this occasion, Commodore Preble made the following distribution of that part of his force, which was manned from the other vessels of his squadron:

One bombard was commanded by Lieut. Commandant Dent, of the Scourge. The other bombard by Mr. Robinson, first lieutenant of the Constitution.

FIRST DIVISION OF GUN-BOATS.

No. 1. Lieut. Com. Somers, of the Nautilus.
" 2. Lieut. James Decatur, of the Nautilus.
" 3. Lieut. Blake, of the Argus.

SECOND DIVISION OF GUN-BOATS.

No. 4. Lieut. Com. Decatur, of the Enterprise.
" 5. Lieut. Bainbridge, of the Enterprise.
" 6. Lieut. Trippe, of the Vixen.

At half-past one, the Constitution wore again, and stood toward the town. At two, the gun-boats were cast off, and formed in advance, covered by the brigs and schooners, and half an hour later, the signal was shown to engage. The attack was commenced by the two bombards, which began to throw shells into the town. It was followed by the batteries, which were instantly in a blaze, and then the shipping on both sides opened their fire, with reach of grape.

The eastern, or most weatherly division of the enemy's gun-boats, nine in number, as being least supported, was the aim of the American gun-boats. But the bad qualities of the latter craft were quickly apparent, for, as soon as Mr. Decatur steered toward the enemy, with an intention to come to close quarters, the division of Mr. Somers, which was a little to leeward, found it difficult to sustain him. Every effort was made by the latter officer, to get far enough to windward to join in the attack, but finding it impracticable, he bore up, and ran down alone on five of the enemy to leeward, and engaged them all within pistol-shot, throwing showers of grape, cannister, and musket-balls among them. In order to do this, as soon as near enough, the sweeps were got out, and the boat was backed astern to prevent her from drifting in among the enemy. No. 3 was closing fast, but a signal of recall being shown from the Constitution, she hauled out of the line to obey, and losing ground, she kept more aloof, firing at the boats and shipping in the harbor, while No. 2, Mr. James Decatur, was enabled to join the division to windward. No. 5, Mr. Bainbridge, lost her latine-yard, while still in tow of the Siren, but, though unable to close, she continued advancing, keeping up a heavy fire, and finally touched on the rocks.

By these changes, Lieutenant Commandant Decatur had three boats that dashed forward with him, though one belonged to the division of Mr. Somers, viz. No. 4, No. 6, and No. 2. The officers in command of these three boats, went steadily on, until within the smoke of the enemy. Here they delivered their fire, throwing in a terrible discharge of grape and musket-balls, and the order was given to board. Up to this moment, the odds had been as three to one against the assailants, and it was now, if possible increased. The brigs and schooner could no longer assist. The Turkish boats were not only the heaviest and the best in every sense, but they were much the strongest manned. The combat now assumed a character of chivalrous prowess and of desperate personal efforts, that belongs to the middle ages, rather than to struggles of our own times. Its details, indeed, savor more of the glow of romance, than of the sober severity that we are accustomed to associate with reality.

Lieutenant Commandant Decatur took the lead. He had no sooner discharged his shower of musket-balls, than No. 4 was laid along side the opposing boat of the enemy, and he went into her, followed by Lieutenant Thorn, Mr. M'Donough, and all the Americans of his crew. The Tripolitan boat was divided nearly into two parts, by a long open hatchway, and as the people of No. 4 came in on one side, the Turks retreated to the other, making a sort of ditch of the open space. This caused an instant of delay, and, perhaps, fortunately, for it permitted the assailants to act together. As soon as ready, Mr. Decatur charged round each end of the hatchway, and after a short struggle, a portion of the Turks were piked and bayoneted, while the rest submitted, or leaped into the water.

No sooner had Mr. Decatur got possession of the boat first assailed, than he took her in tow, and bore down on the one next to leeward. Running the enemy aboard, as before, he went into him, with most of his officers and men. The captain of the Tripolitan vessel was a large powerful man, and Mr. Decatur personally charged him with a pike. The weapon, however, was seized by the Turk, wrested from the hands of the assailant, and turned against its owner. The latter parried a thrust, and made a blow with his sword at the pike, with a view to cut off its head. The sword hit the iron, and broke at the hilt, and at the next instant the Turk made another thrust. Nothing was left to the gallant Decatur, but his arm, with which he so far averted the blow, as to receive the pike through the flesh of one breast. Pushing the iron from the wound, by tearing the flesh, he sprang within the weapon, and grappled his antagonist. The pike fell between the two, and a short trial of strength succeeded, in which the Turk prevailed. As the combatants fell, however, Mr. Decatur so far released himself as to lie side by side with his foe on the deck. The Tripolitan now endeavored to reach his poniard, while his hand was firmly held by that of his enemy. [Some accounts state that he had drawn his dirk, and had raised his arm to strike.] At this critical instant, when life or death depended on a moment well employed, or a moment lost, Decatur drew a small pistol from a pocket, passed the arm that was free round the body of the Turk, pointed the muzzle in, and fired. The ball passed entirely through the body of the Musselman, and lodged in the clothes of his foe. At the same instant, Decatur felt the grasp that had almost smothered him relax, and he was liberated. He sprang up, and the Tripolitan lay dead at his feet.

[During the continuance of this terrible struggle, the crews of each vessel impetuously rushed to the assistance of their respective commanders. Such was the carnage in this furious and desperate battle, that it was with difficulty Decatur could extricate himself from the killed and wounded, by which he was surrounded. In this affair an American sailor, Reuben James, of Delaware, manifested the most heroic self-devotion. Seeing a Tripolitan officer, aiming a blow at Decatur's head while he was struggling with his prostrate foe, and which must have proved fatal, had not the generous and fearless tar, who had been deprived of the use of both his hands, by severe wounds, rushed between the saber and his commander, and received the blow on his head, by which his skull was fractured.]

An idea of the desperate nature of the fighting that distinguished this remarkable assault, may be gained from the amount of the loss. The two boats captured by Lieutenant Commandant Decatur, had about eighty men in them, of whom fifty-two are known to have been killed and wounded; most of the latter very badly. As only eight prisoners were made who were not wounded, and many jumped overboard, and swam to the rocks, it is not improbable that the Turks suffered still more severely. Lieutenant

Commandant Decatur himself being wounded, he secured his second prize, and hauled off to rejoin the squadron; all the rest of the enemy's division that were not taken, having, by this time, run into the harbor, by passing through the openings between the rocks.

While Lieutenant Commandant Decatur was thus employed to windward, his brother, Mr. James Decatur, the first lieutenant of the Nautilus, was nobly emulating his example in No. 2. Reserving his fire like No. 4, this young officer dashed into the smoke, and was on the point of boarding, when he received a musket ball in his forehead. The boats met and rebounded; and in the confusion of the death of the commanding officer of No. 2, the Turk was enabled to escape, under a heavy fire from the Americans. It was said, at the time, that the enemy had struck before Mr. Decatur fell, though the fact must remain in doubt. It is, however, believed that he sustained a very severe loss.

In the mean time, Mr. Trippe, in No. 6, the last of the three boats that were able to reach the weather division, was not idle. Reserving his fire, like the others, he delivered it with deadly effect, when closing, and went aboard of his enemy in the smoke. In this instance, the boats also separated by the shock of the collision, leaving Mr. Trippe, with Mr. J. D. Henley, and nine men only, on board the Tripolitan. Here, too, the commanders singled each other out, and a severe personal combat occurred, while the work of death was going on around them. The Turk was young, and of a large atheletic form, and he soon compelled his slighter but more active foe to fight with caution. Advancing on Mr. Trippe, he would strike a blow and receive a thrust in return. In this manner, he gave the American commander no less than eight saber wounds in the head, and two in the breast; when, making a sudden rush, he struck a ninth blow on the head, which brought Mr. Trippe upon a knee. Rallying all his force in a desperate effort, the latter, who still retained the short pike with which he fought, made a thrust that passed the weapon through his gigantic adversary, and tumbled him on his back. As soon as the Tripolitan officer fell, the remainder of his people submitted.

The boat taken by Mr. Trippe, was one of the largest belonging to the bashaw. The number of her men is not positively known, but, living and dead, thirty-six were found in her, of whom twenty-one were either killed or wounded. When it is remembered that but eleven Americans boarded her, the achievement must pass for one of the most gallant on record.

All this time the cannonade and bombardment continued without ceasing. Lieutenant Commandant Somers, in No. 1, sustained by the brigs and schooners, had forced the remaining boats to retreat, and this resolute officer pressed them so hard, as to be compelled to ware within a short distance of a battery of twelve guns, quite near the mole. Her destruction seemed inevitable, as the boat came slowly round, when a shell fell into the battery, most opportunely, blew up the platform, and drove the enemy out, to a man. Before the guns could be again used the boat had got in tow of one of the small vessels.

There was a division of five boats and two galleys of the enemy, that had been held in reserve within the rocks, and these rallied their retreating countrymen, and made two efforts to come out and intercept the Americans and their prizes, but they were kept in check by the fire of the frigate and small vessels. The Constitution maintained a very heavy fire, and silenced several of the batteries, though they re-opened as soon as she had passed. The bombards were covered with the spray of shot, but continued to throw shells to the last.

At half past four, the wind coming round to the northward, a signal was made for the gun-boats and bomb-vessels to rejoin the small vessels, and another to take them and the prizes in tow. The last order was handsomely executed by the brigs and schooners, under cover of a blaze of fire from the frigate. A quarter of an hour later, the Constitution herself hauled off, and ran out of gun-shot.

Thus terminated the first serious attack that was made on the town and batteries of Tripoli. Its effect on the enemy, was of the most salutary kind; the manner in which their gun-boats had been taken, by boarding, having made a lasting and deep impression. The superiority of the Christians in gunnery, was generally admitted before, but here was an instance in which the Turks had been overcome, by inferior numbers, hand to hand, a species of conflict in which they had been thought particularly to excel. Perhaps no instance of more desperate fighting of the sort, without defensive armor, is to be found in the pages of history. Three gun-boats were sunk in the harbor, in addition to the three that were taken, and the loss of the Tripolitans by shot, must have been very heavy. About fifty shells were thrown into the town, but little damage appears to have been done in this way, very few of the bombs, on account of the imperfect materials that had been furnished, exploding. The batteries were a good deal damaged, but the town suffered no essential injury.

On the part of the Americans, only fourteen were killed and wounded in the affair, and all of these, with the exception of one man, belonged to the gun-boats. The Constitution, though under fire two hours, escaped much better than could have been expected. She received one heavy shot through her mainmast, had a quarter-deck gun injured, and was a good deal cut up aloft. The enemy had calculated his range for a more distant cannonade, and generally overshot the ships. By this mistake, the Constitution had her main-royal yard shot away.

Among those who greatly distinguished themselves on this occasion, was Lieutenant Richard Somers, between whom and Decatur existed a noble friendship that was well fitting the chivalrous nature of their dispositions. The mystery connected with his death a month later, has lent a romantic interest to his memory. The circumstances as far as known, are here detailed.

After several unsuccessful enterprises to force the enemy to terms, it was resolved to fit up the ketch "Intrepid" in the double capacity of fire-ship and infernal, and to send her into the inner harbor, of Tripoli, there to explode, in the very center of the vessels of the Turks. As her deck was to be covered with a large quantity of powder, shells, and missiles, it was hoped the town would suffer not less than the shipping The panic created by such an assault, made in the dead of night, it was fondly hoped would produce an instant peace; and more especially the liberation of the frigate Philadelphia, whose officers and crew were thought to have been reduced to extreme suffering by the barbarity of their captors.

The imminent danger of the service forbade the commodore ordering any of his officers upon it; and Somers, with whom the conception of this daring scheme is supposed to have originated, volunteered to take the command.

"On the afternoon of the fourth of September, Somers prepared to leave the Nautilus, with a full determination to carry the ketch into Tripoli that night. Previously to quitting his own vessel, he felt that it would be proper to point out the desperate nature of the enterprise to the four men he had selected, that their services might be perfectly free and voluntary. He told them that he wished no man to accompany him, who would not prefer being blown up to being taken; that such was his own determination, and that he wished all who went with him to be the same way of thinking. The boats now gave three cheers in answer; and each man is said to have separately asked to be selected to apply the match. Once assured of the temper of his companions, Somers took leave of his officers; the boat's crew doing the same, shaking hands, and expressing their feelings, as if they felt assured of their fate in advance. Each of the four men made his will verbally; disposing of his effects among the shipmates, like those about to die. Several of Somers' friends visited him on board the Intrepid before she got under way. Among them were Stewart and Decatur, with whom he had commenced his naval career in the United States. These three young men, then about twenty-six years of age each, were Philadelphia-bred sailors, and had been intimately associated in service for the last six years. They all knew that the enterprise was one of extreme hazard, and the two who were to remain behind felt a deep interest in the fate of him who was to go in. Somers was grave, and entirely without any affectation of levity or indifference; but he maintained his usual tranquil and quiet manner. After some conversation, he took a ring from his finger, and breaking it into three pieces, gave each of his companions one, while he retained the third himself."

Two boats accompanied the ketch to bring off the party just after setting fire to the train. In the whole there were thirteen men, all volunteers.

About nine o'clock in the evening Lieutenant Reed was the last to leave the ketch for his own vessel. "When he went over the side of the Intrepid, all communication between the gallant spirits she contained and the rest of the world ceased. At that time everything seemed propitious. Somers was cheerful, though calm; and perfect order and method prevailed in the little craft. The leave-taking was affectionate and serious with the officers, though the common men appeared to be in high spirits."

The ketch was seen to proceed cautiously into the bay, but was soon obscured by the haze on the water. "It was not long before the enemy began to fire at the ketch, which by this time was quite near the batteries, though the reports were neither rapid or numerous. At this moment, near ten o'clock, Captain Stewart and Lieutenant Carrol were standing in the Siren's gangway, looking intently toward the place where the ketch was known to be, when the latter exclaimed, 'Look! see the light!' At that instant a light was seen passing and waving, as if a lantern were carried by some person in quick motion along a vessel's deck. Then it sunk from view. Half a minute may have elapsed, when the whole firmament was lighted with a fiery glow; a burning mast with its sails was seen in the air; the whole harbor was momentarily illuminated; the awful explosion came, and a darkness like that of doom succeeded. The whole was over in less than a minute; the flame, the quaking of towers, the reeling of ships, and even the bursting of shells, of which most fell in the water, though some lodged on the rocks. The firing ceased, and from that instant Tripoli passed the night in a stillness as profound as that in which the victims of this explosion have lain from that fatal hour to this."

In the American squadron the opinion was prevalent, that Somers and his determined crew had blown themselves up to prevent capture; but subsequent light has rendered it more probable that it was accidental, or occasioned by a hot shot from the enemy. "Thus perished Richard Somers, 'one of the bravest of the brave.' Notwithstanding all our means of reasoning, and the greatest efforts of human ingenuity, there will remain a melancholy interest around the manner of his end, which, by the Almighty will, is forever vailed from human eyes, in a sad and solemn mystery."

THE CHASE OF THE UNITED STATES FRIGATE CONSTITUTION BY A BRITISH SQUADRON.

The Constitution 44, Captain Hull, had gone into the Chesapeake, on her return from Europe, and shipping a new crew, on the twelfth of July, 1812, she sailed from Annapolis, and stood to the northward. So rapidly was her equipment procured, that her first lieutenant joined her only a fortnight before she sailed, and a draft of a hundred men was received on the evening of the eleventh. Friday, July the seventeenth, the ship was out of sight of land, though at no great distance from the coast, with a light breeze from the N. E., and under easy canvas. At one, she sounded in 22 fathoms; and about an hour afterward, four sail were made in the northern board, heading to the westward. At three, the Constitution made sail, and tacked in 18½ fathoms. At four, she discovered a fifth sail to the northward and eastward, which had the appearance of a vessel of war. This ship subsequently proved to be the Guerriere 38, Captain Dacres. By this time, the other four sail were made out to be three ships and a brig; they bore N. N. W., and were all on the starboard tack, apparently in company. The wind now became very light, and the Constitution hauled up her main-sail. The ship in the eastern board, however, had so far altered her position by six, as to bear E. N. E., the wind having hitherto been fair for her to close. But at a quarter past six, the wind came out light at the southward, bringing the American ship to windward. The Constitution now wore round with her head to the eastward, set her light studding-sails and stay-sails, and at half past seven, beat to quarters, and cleared for action, with the intention of speaking the nearest vessel.

The wind continued very light at the southward, and the two vessels were slowly closing until eight. At ten, the Constitution shortened sail, and immediately after she showed the private signal of the day. After keeping the lights aloft near an hour, and getting no answer from the Guerriere, the Constitution, at a quarter past eleven, lowered the signal, and made sail again, hauling aboard her starboard tacks. During the whole of the middle watch the wind was very light, from the southward and westward. Just as the morning watch was called, the Guerriere tacked, then wore entirely round, threw a rocket, and fired two guns. As the day opened, three sail were discovered on the starboard quarter of the Constitution, and three more astern. At five A. M., a fourth vessel was seen astern.

This was the squadron of Commodore Broke, which had been gradually closing with the American frigate during the night, and was now just out of gun-shot. As the ships slowly varied their positions, when the mists were entirely cleared away, the Constitution had two frigates on her lee quarter, and a ship of the line, two frigates, a brig and a schooner astern. The names of the enemy's ships, have already been given; but the brig was the Nautilus, and the schooner another prize. All the strangers had

English colors flying. It now fell quite calm, and the Constitution hoisted out her boats, and sent them ahead to tow, with a view to keep the ship out of the reach of the enemy's shot. At the same time, she whipt up one of the gun-deck guns to the spar-deck, and run it out aft, as a stern-chaser, getting a long eighteen off the forecastle also for a similar purpose. Two more of the twenty-fours below were run out at the cabin windows, with the same object, though it was found necessary to cut away some of the wood-work of the stern frame, in order to make room.

By six o'clock the wind, which continued very light and baffling, came out from the northward of west, when the ship's head was got round to the southward, and all the light canvas that would draw was set. Soon after, the nearest frigate, the Shannon, opened with her bow guns, and continued firing for about ten minutes, but perceiving she could not reach the Constitution, she ceased. At half past six, Captain Hull sounded in 26 fathoms, when finding that the enemy was likely to close, as he was enabled to put the boats of two ships on one, and was also favored by a little more air than the Constitution, all the spare rope that could be found, and which was fit for the purpose, was payed down into the cutters, bent on, and a kedge was run out near half a mile ahead, and let go. At a signal given, the crew clapped on, and walked away with the ship, over-running and tripping the kedge as she came up with the end of the line. While this was doing, fresh lines and another kedge was carried ahead, and, though out of sight of land, the frigate glided away from her pursuers, before they discovered the manner in which it was done. It was not long, however, before the enemy resorted to the same expedient. At half past seven, the Constitution had a little air, when she set her ensign, and fired a shot at the Shannon, the nearest ship astern. At eight, it fell calm again, and further recourse was had to the boats and the kedges, the enemy's vessels having a light air, and drawing ahead, towing, sweeping, and kedging. By nine, the nearest frigate, the Shannon, on which the English had put most of their boats, was closing fast, and there was every prospect, notwithstanding the steadiness and activity of the Constitution's people, that the frigate just mentioned would get near enough to cripple her, when her capture by the rest of the squadron would be inevitable. At this trying moment the best spirit prevailed in the ship. Everything was stoppered, and Captain Hull was not without hopes, even should he be forced into action, of throwing the Shannon astern by his fire, and of maintaining his distance from the other vessels. It was known that the enemy could not tow very near, as it would have been easy to sink his boats with the stern-guns of the Constitution, and not a man in the latter vessel showed a disposition to despondency. Officers and men relieved each other regularly at the duty, and while the former threw themselves down on deck to catch short naps, the people slept at their guns.

This was one of the most critical moments of the chase. The Shannon was fast closing, as has been just stated, while the Guerriere was almost as near on the larboard quarter. An hour promised to bring the struggle to an issue, when suddenly, at nine minutes past nine, a light air from the southward struck the ship, bringing her to windward. The beautiful manner in which this advantage was improved, excited admiration even in the enemy. As the breeze was seen coming, the ship's sails were trimmed, and as soon as she was under command, she was brought close up to the wind, on the larboard tack; the boats were all dropped in along side; those that belonged to the davits were run up, while the others were just lifted clear of the water, by purchases on the spare outboard spars, where they were in readiness to be used at a moment's notice. As the ship came by the wind, she brought the Guerriere nearly on her lee-beam, when that frigate opened a fire from her broadside. While the shot of this vessel were just falling short of them, the people of the Constitution were hoisting up their boats with as much steadiness as if the duty was performing in a friendly port. In about an hour, however, it fell nearly calm again, when Captain Hull ordered a quantity of the water started, to lighten the ship. More than two thousand gallons were pumped out, and the boats were sent ahead again to tow. The enemy now put nearly all his boats on the Shannon, the nearest ship astern; and a few hours of prodigious exertion followed, the people of the Constitution being compelled to supply the place of numbers by their activity and zeal. The ships were close by the wind, and everything that would draw was set, and the Shannon was slowly, but steadily, forging ahead. About noon of this day, there was a little relaxation from labor, owing to the occasional occurrence of cat's-paws, by watching which closely, the ship was urged through the water. But at quarter past twelve, the boats were again sent ahead, and the toilsome work of towing and kedging was renewed.

At one o'clock, a strange sail was discovered nearly to leeward. At this moment the four frigates of the enemy were about one point on the lee-quarter of the Constitution, at long gunshot, the Africa and the two prizes being on the lee-beam. As the wind was constantly baffling, any moment might have brought a change, and placed the enemy to windward. At seven minutes before two, the Belvidera, then the nearest ship, began to fire with her bow-guns, and the Constitution opened with her stern-chasers. On board the latter ship, however, it was soon found to be dangerous to use the main-deck guns, the transoms having so much rake, the window being so high, and the guns so short, that every explosion lifted the upper deck, and threatened to blow out the stern-frame. Perceiving, moreover, that his shot did little or no execution, Captain Hull ordered the firing to cease at half past two.

For several hours, the enemy's frigates were now within gunshot, sometimes towing and kedging, and at others endeavoring to close with the puffs of air that occasionally passed. At seven in the evening, the boats of the Constitution were again ahead, the ship steering S. W. ½ W., with an air so light as to be almost imperceptible. At half past seven, she sounded in 24 fathoms. For hours the same toilsome duty was going on, until a little before eleven, when a light air from the southward struck the ship, and the sails for the first time in many weary hours were asleep. The boats instantly dropped along side, hooked on, and were all run up, with the exception of the first cutter. The topgallant studding-sails and stay-sails were set as soon as possible, and for about an hour, the people caught a little rest.

But at midnight it fell nearly calm again, though neither the pursuers nor the pursued had recourse to the boats, probably from an unwillingness to disturb their crews. At two, A. M., it was observed on board the Constitution that the Guerriere had forged ahead, and was again off their lee-beam. At this time, the topgallant studding-sails were taken in.

In this manner passed the night, and on the morning of the next day, it was found that three of the enemy's frigates were within long gunshot on the lee-quarter, and the other at about the same distance on the lee beam. The Africa and the prizes were much further to leeward.

A little after daylight, the Guerriere, having drawn ahead sufficiently to be forward of the Constitution's beam, tacked, when the latter ship did the same, in order to preserve her position to windward. An hour later the Æolus passed on the contrary tack, so near that it was thought by some who observed the movement, that she ought to have opened her fire; but, as that vessel was merely a twelve-pounder frigate, and she was still at a considerable distance, it is quite probable her commander acted judiciously. By this time, there was sufficient wind to induce Captain Hull to hoist in his first cutter.

The scene, on the morning of this day, was very beautiful, and of great interest to the lovers of nautical exhibitions. The weather was mild and lovely, the sea smooth as a pond, and there was quite wind enough to remove the necessity of any of the extraordinary means of getting ahead, that had been so freely used during the previous eight-and-forty hours. All the English vessels had got on the same tack with the Constitution again, and the five frigates were clouds of canvas, from their trucks to the water. Including the American ship, eleven sail were in sight, and shortly after a twelfth appeared to windward, that was soon ascertained to be an American merchantman. But the enemy were too intent on the Constitution to regard anything else, and though it would have been easy to capture the ships to leeward, no attention appears to have been paid to them. With a view, however, to deceive the ship to windward they hoisted American colors, when the Constitution set an English ensign, by way of warning the stranger to keep aloof.

Until ten o'clock the Constitution was making every preparation for carrying sail hard should it become necessary, and she sounded in 25 fathoms. At noon the wind fell again, though it was found that while the breeze lasted, she had gained on all the enemy's ships; more, however on some, than on others. The nearest vessel was the Belvidera, which was exactly in the wake of the Constitution, distant about two and a half miles, bearing W. N. W. The nearest frigate to leeward, bore N. by W. $\frac{1}{2}$ W. distant three or three and a half miles; the two other frigates were on the lee-quarter, distant about five miles, and the Africa was hull down to leeward, on the opposite tack.

This was a vast improvement on the state of things that had existed the day previous, and it allowed the officers and men to catch a little rest, though no one left the decks. The latitude by observation this day, was 38° 47′ N., and the longitude by dead reckoning 73° 57′ W.

At meridian the wind began to blow a pleasant breeze, and the sound of the water rippling under the bows of the vessel was again heard. From this moment the noble old ship slowly drew ahead of all her pursuers, the sails being watched and tended in the best manner that consummate seamanship could dictate, until four P. M. when the Belvidera was more than four miles astern, and the other vessels were thrown behind in the same proportion, though the wind had again got to be very light.

In this manner both parties kept passing ahead and to windward, as fast as circumstances would allow, profiting by every change, and resorting to all the means of forcing vessels through the water, that are known to seamen. At a little before seven, however, there was every appearance of a heavy squall, accompanied by rain; when the Constitution prepared to meet it with the coolness and discretion she had displayed throughout the whole affair. The people were stationed, and everything was kept fast to the last moment, when, just before the squall struck the ship, the order was given to clew up and clew down. All the light canvas was furled, a second reef was taken in the mizzen-topsail, and the ship was brought under short sail, in an incredibly little time. The English vessels, observing this, began to let go and haul down without waiting for the wind, and when they were shut in by the rain, they were steering in different directions to avoid the force of the expected squall. The Constitution, on the other hand, no sooner got its weight, than she sheeted home and hoisted her fore and main-topgallant sails, and while the enemy most probably believed her to be borne down by the pressure of the wind, steering free, she was flying away from them, on an easy bowline, at the rate of eleven knots.

In a little less than an hour after the squall struck the ship, it had entirely passed to leeward, and a sight was again obtained of the enemy. The Belvidera, the nearest vessel, had altered her bearings in that short period two points more to leeward, and she was a long way astern. The next nearest vessel was still farther to leeward, and more distant, while the two remaining fri ates were fairly hull down. The Africa was barely visible in the horizon!

All apprehensions of the enemy now ceased, though sail was carried to increase the distance, and to preserve the weather-gage. At half past ten the wind backed further to the southward, when the Constitution, which had been steering free for some time, took in her lower studding-sails. At eleven the enemy fired two guns and the nearest ship could just be discovered. As the wind baffled, and continued light, the enemy still persevered in the chase, but at daylight the nearest vessel was hull down astern, and to leeward. Under the circumstances it was deemed prudent to use every exertion to lose sight of the English frigates; and the wind falling light, the Constitution's sails were wet down from the skysails to the courses. The good effects of this care were soon visible, as at six A.M., the topsails of the enemy's nearest vessels were beginning to dip. At a quarter past 8, the English ships all hauled to the northward and eastward, fully satisfied, by a trial that had lasted nearly three days, and as many nights, under all the circumstances that can attend naval maneuvers, from reefed topsails to kedging, that they had no hope of overtaking their enemy.

Thus terminated a chase, that has become historical in the American navy, for its length, closeness, and activity. On the part of the English, there were manifested much perseverance and seamanship, a ready imitation, and a strong desire to get along side of their enemy. But the glory of the affair was carried off by the officers and people of the Constitution. Throughout all the trying circumstances of this arduous struggle, this noble frigate, which had so lately been the subject of the sneers of the English critics, maintained the high character of a man-of-war. Even when pressed upon the hardest, nothing was hurried, confused, or slovenly, but the utmost steadiness, order, and discipline reigned in the ship. A cool, discreet, and gallant commander, was nobly sustained by his officers; and there cannot be a doubt that had the enemy succeeded in getting any one of their frigates fairly under the fire of the American ship, that she would have been very roughly treated. The escape itself, is not so much a matter of admiration, as the manner in which it was effected. A little water was pumped out, it is true; and perhaps this was necessary, in order to put a vessel fresh from port on a level, in light winds and calms, with ships that had been cruising some time; but not an anchor was cut away, not a boat stove, nor a gun lost. The steady and man-of-war like style in which the Constitution took in all her boats, as occasions offered;

the order and rapidity with which she kedged, and the vigilant seamanship with which she was braced up, and eased off, extorted admiration among the more liberal of her pursuers. In this affair, the ship, no less than those who worked her, gained a high reputation, if not with the world generally, at least with those who, perhaps, as seldom err in their nautical criticisms as any people living.

DESCRIPTION BY AN ENGLISH SAILOR BOY, OF THE BATTLE BETWEEN THE AMERICAN FRIGATE UNITED STATES AND THE BRITISH FRIGATE MACEDONIAN.

SAMUEL LEECH, an English sailor boy, who was on board of the British frigate Macedonian at the time of the capture of that vessel by the United States, has left the following vivid sketch of the battle, which, with his subsequent adventures in the American Naval Service here given, forms a few pages rarely equaled in interest by anything in the whole range of maritime narrative.

Sunday (December twenty-fifth, 1812,) came, and it brought with it a stiff breeze. We usually made a sort of holiday of this sacred day. After breakfast it was common to muster the entire crew on the spar-deck, dressed as the fancy of the captain might dictate; sometimes in blue jackets and white trowsers, or blue jackets and blue trowsers; at other times in blue jackets, scarlet vests, and blue or white trowsers; with our bright anchor-buttons glancing in the sun, and our black glossy hats ornamented with black ribbons, and with the name of our ship painted on them. After muster we frequently had church service read by the captain; the rest of the day was devoted to idleness. But we were destined to spend the Sabbath just introduced to the reader in a very different manner.

We had scarcely finished breakfast before the man at the mast-head shouted, "Sail, ho!"

The captain rushed upon deck, exclaiming, "Mast-head there!"

"Sir?"

"Where away is the sail?"

The precise answer to this question I do not recollect, but the captain proceeded to ask,

"What does she look like?"

"A square-rigged vessel, sir," was the reply of the lookout.

After a few minutes, the captain shouted again, "Mast-head there!"

"Sir?"

"What does she look like?"

"A large ship, sir, standing toward us!"

By this time most of the crew were on deck, eagerly straining their eyes to obtain a glimpse of the approaching ship, and murmuring their opinions to each other on her probable character.

Then came the voice of the captain, shouting, "Keep silence fore and aft!"

Silence being secured, he hailed the lookout, who, to his question of "What does she look like?" replied, "A large frigate, bearing down upon us, sir!"

A whisper ran along the crew that the stranger ship was a Yankee frigate. The thought was confirmed by the command of "All hands clear the ship for action, ahoy!" The drum and fife beat to quarters, bulkheads were knocked away, the guns were released from their confinement, the whole dread paraphernalia of battle was produced, and after the lapse of a few minutes of hurry and confusion, every man and boy was at his post, ready to do his best service for his country, except the band, who, claiming exemption from the affray, safely stowed themselves away in the cable-tier. We had only one sick man on the list, and he, at the cry of battle, hurried from his cot, feeble as he was, to take his post of danger. A few of the junior midshipmen were stationed below on the berth-deck, with orders, given in our hearing, to shoot any man who attempted to run from his quarters.

As the approaching ship showed American colors, all doubt of her character was at an end. "We must fight her," was the conviction of every breast. Every possible arrangement that could insure success was accordingly made. The guns were shotted, the matches lighted; for although our guns were all furnished with first-rate locks, they were also provided with matches, attached by lanyards, in case the lock should miss fire. A lieutenant then passed through the ship, directing the marines and boarders—who were furnished with pikes, cutlasses, and pistols—how to proceed if it should be necessary to board the enemy. He was followed by the captain, who exhorted the men to fidelity and courage, urging upon their consideration the well-known motto of the brave Nelson, "England expects every man to do his duty." In addition to all these preparations on deck, some men were stationed in the tops with small arms, whose duty it was was to attend to trimming the sails, and to use their muskets provided we came to close action. There were others, also, below, called sail-trimmers, to assist in working the ship should it be necessary to shift her position during the battle.

My station was the fifth gun on the main-deck. It was my duty to supply my gun with powder, a boy being appointed to each gun in the ship, on the side we engaged, for this purpose. A woolen screen was placed before the entrance to the magazine, with a hole in it, through which the cartridges were passed to the boys; we received them there, and covering them with our jackets, hurried to our respective guns. These precautions are observed to prevent the powder taking fire before it reaches the gun.

Thus we all stood, awaiting orders, in motionless suspense. At last we fired three guns from the larboard side of the main-deck; this was followed by the command, "Cease firing; you are throwing away your shot!"

Then came the order to "wear ship," and prepare to attack the enemy with our starboard guns. Soon after this I heard a firing from some other quarter, which I at first supposed to be a discharge from our quarter-deck guns, but it proved to be the roar of the enemy's cannon.

A strange noise, such as I had never heard before, next arrested my attention; it sounded like the tearing of sails just over our heads. This I soon ascertained to be the wind of the enemy's shot. The firing, after a few minutes' cessation, recommenced. The roaring of cannon could now be heard from all parts of our trembling ship, and mingling as it did with that of our foes, it made a most hideous noise. By and by I heard the shot strike the sides of our ship; the whole scene grew indescribably confused and horrible; it was like some awfully tremendous thunder-storm, whose deafening roar is attended by incessant streaks of lightning, carrying death in every flash, and strewing the ground with the victims of its wrath; only in our case the scene was rendered more horrible than that, by the presence of torrents of blood which dyed our decks. Though the recital may be painful, yet as it will reveal the horrors of war, and show at what a fearful price a victory is won or lost, I will present the reader with things as they met my eye during the progress of this dreadful fight. I was busily supplying my gun with powder, when I saw blood suddenly fly from the arm of a man stationed at our gun. I saw nothing strike him; the effect alone was visible; in an instant the third lieutenant tied his handkerchief round the wounded arm, and sent the poor fellow below to the surgeon.

The cries of the wounded now rang through all parts of the ship. These were carried to the cockpit as fast as they fell, while those more fortunate men who were killed outright were immediately thrown overboard. As I was stationed but a short distance from the main-hatchway, I could catch a glance at all who were carried below. A glance was all I could indulge in, for the boys belonging to the guns next to mine were wounded in the early part of the action, and I had to spring with all my might to keep three or four guns supplied with cartridges. I saw two of these lads fall nearly together. One of them was struck in the leg by a large shot; he had to suffer amputation above the wound. The other had a grape or canister shot sent through his ankle. A stout Yorkshireman lifted him in his arms and hurried with him to the cockpit. He had his foot cut off, and was thus made lame for life. Two of the boys stationed on the quarter-deck were killed. They were both Portuguese. A man who saw one of them killed, afterward told me that his powder caught fire and burnt the flesh almost off his face. In this pitiable situation the agonized boy lifted up both hands, as if imploring relief, when a passing shot instantly cut him in two.

I was an eye-witness to a sight equally revolting. A man named Aldrich had one of his hands cut off by a shot, and almost at the same moment he received another shot, which tore open his bowels in a terrible manner. As he fell, two or three men caught him in their arms, and as he could not live, threw him overboard.

One of the officers in my division also fell in my sight. He was a noble-hearted fellow, named Nan Kivell. A grape or canister shot struck him near the heart. He fell, and was carried below, where he shortly after died.

Mr. Scott, our first-lieutenant, was also slightly wounded by a grummet, or small iron ring, probaly torn from a hammock clew by a shot. He went below, shouting to the men to fight on. Having had his wound dressed, he came up again, shouting to us at the top of his voice, and bidding us fight with all our might.

The battle went on. Our men kept cheering with all their might; I cheered with them, though I confess I scarcely knew for what. Certainly there was nothing very inspiriting in the aspect of things where I was stationed. So terrible had been the work of destruction round us, that it was termed the slaughter-house. Not only had we had several boys and men killed or wounded, but several of the guns were disabled. The one I belonged to had a piece of the muzzle knocked out; and when the ship rolled, it struck a beam of the upper deck with such force as to become jammed and fixed in that position. A twenty-four pound shot had also gone through the screen of the magazine, immediately over the orifice through which we passed our powder. The schoolmaster received a death wound. The brave boatswain, who came from the sick cot to the din of battle, was fastening a stopper on a back-stay which had been shot away, when his head was smashed to pieces by a cannon-ball; another man, going to complete the unfinished task, was also struck down. One of our midshipmen likewise received a severe wound, and the wardroom steward was killed. A fellow named John, who, for some petty offense, had been sent on board as a punishment, was carried past me wounded. I distinctly heard the large blood-drops fall pat, pat, on the deck; his wounds were mortal. Even a poor goat, kept by the officers for her milk, did not escape the general carnage; her hind-legs were shot off, and poor Nan was thrown overboard.

I have often been asked what were my feelings during this fight. I felt pretty much as I suppose every one does at such a time. That men are without thought when they stand amid the dying and the dead, is too absurd an idea to be entertained for a moment. We all appeared cheerful, but I know that many a serious thought ran through my mind; still, what could we do but keep up a semblance, at least of animation? To run from our quarters would have been certain death from the hands of our own officers; to give way to gloom, or to show fear, would do no good, and might brand us with the name of cowards, and insure certain defeat. Our only true philosophy, therefore, was to make the best of our situation, by fighting bravely and cheerfully. I thought a great deal, however, of the other world: every groan, every falling man, told me that the next instant I might be before the Judge of all the earth.

While these thoughts secretly agitated my bosom, the din of battle continued. Grape and canister shot were pouring through our port-holes like leaden rain, carrying death in their train. The large shot came against the ship's side like iron hail, shaking her to the very keel, or passing through her timbers, and scattering terrific splinters, which did a more appalling work than even their own death-giving blows. The reader may form an idea of the effect of grape and canister, when he is told that grape shot is formed by seven or eight balls confined to an iron and tied in a cloth. These balls are scattered by the explosion of the powder. Canister shot is made by filling a powder canister with balls, each as large as two or three musket balls; these also scatter with direful effect when discharged. What, then, with splinters, cannon-balls, grape and canister poured incessantly upon us, the reader may be assured that the work of death went on in a manner which must have been satisfactory even to the King of Terrors himself.

Suddenly the rattling of the iron hail ceased. We were ordered to cease firing. A profound silence ensued, broken only by the stifled groans of the brave sufferers below. It was soon ascertained that the enemy had shot ahead to repair damages; for she was not so disabled but she could sail without difficulty, while we were so cut up that we lay utterly helpless. Our head braces were shot away; the fore and main top-masts were gone; the mizzen-mast hung over the stern, having carried several men over in its fall: we were in the state of a complete wreck.

A council was now held among the officers on the quarter-deck. Our condition was perilous in the extreme; victory or escape was alike hopeless. Our ship was disabled; many of our men were killed, and many more wounded. The enemy would without doubt bear down upon us in a few moments, and, as she could now choose her own position, would doubtless rake us fore and aft. Any further resistance was therefore folly; so, in spite of the hot-brained lieutenant, who advised them not to strike, but to sink along side, it was determined to strike our colors. This was done by the hands of a brave fellow named Watson, whose saddened brow told how severely it pained his lion heart to do it. To me it was a pleasing sight, for I had seen fighting enough for one Sabbath; more than I wished to see again on a week-day. His Britannic Majesty's frigate Macedonian was now the prize of the American frigate United States.

I now went below to see how matters appeared there. The first object I met was a man bearing a limb, which had just been detached from some poor sufferer. Pursuing my way to the wardroom, I necessarily passed through the steerage, which was strewed with the wounded: it was a sad spectacle, made more appalling by the groans and cries which rent the air. Some were groaning, others were swearing most bitterly, a few were praying, while those last arrived were begging most piteously to have their wounds dressed next. The surgeon and his mate were smeared with blood from head to foot; they looked more like butchers than doctors. Having so many patients, they had once shifted their quarters from the cockpit to the steerage; they now removed to the wardroom; and the long table, round which the officers had sat over many a merry feast, was soon covered with the bleeding forms of maimed and mutilated seamen.

I now set to work to render all the aid in my power to the sufferers. Our carpenter, named Reed, had his leg cut off. I helped to carry him to the after wardroom; but he soon breathed out his life there, and then I assisted in throwing his mangled remains overboard. We got out the cots as fast as possible, for most of the men were stretched out on the gory deck. One poor fellow, who lay with a broken thigh, begged me to give him water. I gave him some. He looked unutterable gratitude, drank, and died. It was with exceeding difficulty I moved through the steerage, it was so covered with mangled men, and so slippery with streams of blood. There was a poor boy there crying as if his heart would break. He had been servant to the boatswain whose head was dashed to pieces. Poor boy! he felt that he had lost a friend. I tried to comfort him, by reminding him that he ought to be thankful for having escaped death himself.

Here also I met one of my messmates, who showed the utmost joy at seeing me alive, for he said he had heard that I was killed. He was looking up his messmates, which he said was always done by sailors. We found two of our mess wounded. One was the Swede, Logholm, who fell overboard and was nearly lost, as formerly mentioned. We held him while the surgeon cut off his leg above the knee. The operation was most painful to behold, the surgeon using his knife and saw on human flesh and bones as freely as the butcher at the shambles does on the carcass of a beast! Our other messmate suffered still more than the Swede; he was sadly mutilated about the legs and thighs with splinters. Such scenes of suffering as I saw in that wardroom I hope never to witness again. Could the civilized world behold them as they were, and as they often are, infinitely worse than on that occasion, it seems to me that they would forever put down the barbarous practices of war by universal consent.

Most of our officers and men were taken on board the victor ship. I was left, with a few others, to take care of the wounded. My master, the sailing-master, was also among the officers who continued in the ship Most of the men who remained were unfit for any service, having broken into the spirit-room and made themselves drunk; some of them broke into the purser's room, and helped themselves to clothing; while others. by previous agreement, took possession of their dead messmates' property For my own part, I was content to help myself to a little of the officers provisions, which did me more good than could be obtained from rum. What was worse than all, however, was the folly of the sailors in giving spirits to their wounded messmates, since it only served to aggravate their distress.

The great number of the wounded kept our surgeon and his mate busily employed until late at night, and it was a long time before they had much leisure. I remember passing round the ship the day after the battle. Coming to a hammock, I found some one in it, apparently asleep. I spoke; he made no answer: I looked into the hammock; he was dead. My messmates coming up, we threw the corpse overboard;—that was no time for useless ceremony. The man had probably crawled into his hammock the day before, and, not being perceived in the general distress, bled to death! Oh war, who can reveal thy miseries!

When the crew of the United States first boarded our frigate, to take possession of her as their prize, our men, heated with the fury of the battle, exasperated with the sight of their dead and wounded shipmates, and rendered furious by the rum they had obtained from the spirit-room, felt and exhibited some disposition to fight their captors. But after the confusion had subsided, and part of our men were snugly stowed away in the American ship, and the remainder found themselves kindly used in their own, the utmost good feeling began to prevail. We set to work to cleanse the ship, using hot vinegar to take out the scent of the blood that had dyed the white of our planks with crimson. We also aided in fitting our disabled frigate for her voyage. This being accomplished, both ships sailed in company toward the American coast.

I soon felt myself perfectly at home with the American seamen; so much so, that I chose to mess with them. My shipmates also participated in similar feelings in both ships. All idea that we had been trying to sho: each other so shortly before seemed forgotten. We ate together, drank together, joked, sung, laughed, told yarns; in short, a perfect union of ideas, feelings, and purposes, seemed to exist among all hands. A corresponding state of unanimity existed, I was told, among the officers.

Our voyage was one of considerable excitement. The seas swarmed with British cruisers, and it was extremely doubtful whether the United States would elude the grasp, and reach the protection of an American port with her prize. I hoped most sincerely to avoid them, as did most of my old shipmates: in this we agreed with our captors, who wisely desired to dispose of one conquest before they attempted another. Our former officers, of course, were anxious for the sight of a British flag, but we saw none; and after a prosperous voyage from the scene of conflict, we heard the welcome cry of "Land, ho!" The United States entered the port of New London; but, owing to a sudden shift of the wind, the Macedonian had to lay off and on for several hours. Had an English cruiser found us in this situation, we should have been easily recovered; and as it was extremely probable we should fall in with one, I felt quite uneasy, until, after several hours, we made out to run into the pretty harbor of Newport. We fired a salute as we came to an anchor, which was promptly returned by the people on shore.

While we lay here a few days, several of our men contrived to run away. I would have done so too, but for the vigilance of the prize officers, who were ordered to keep us that we might be exchanged for those Americans who had fallen into British hands. My desire for freedom at length prevailed over prudence, and I made my escape, glad to be rid of the tyranny to which I had been so long exposed. But this step, which, on reflection, I do not commend, brought another evil. I was destitute of any means of support, and after numerous ineffectual efforts to get employment on land, I again took to a seafaring life—this time, however, entering myself on board a United States brig-of-war, the Siren, carrying sixteen guns. I was then in the seventeenth year of my life. I was recommended by acquaintances to ship myself under a false name; but, in defiance of my fears, I entered under my own proper name of Samuel Leech.

My first impressions of the American service were very favorable. The treatment in the Siren was more lenient than in the Macedonian. The captain and officers were kind; while there was a total exemption from that petty tyranny exercised by the upstart midshipmen in the British service. As a necessary effect, our crew was as comfortable and happy as men ever are in a man-of-war.

Our brig had before this taken in her guns, consisting of two long nine-pounders, twelve twenty-four pound carronades, and two forty-two-pounders. Our crew was composed of about one hundred and twenty-five smart active men. We were all supplied with stout leathern caps, something like those used by firemen. These were crossed by two strips of iron, covered with bear-skin, and were designed to defend the head, in boarding the enemy's ship, from the stroke of the cutlass. Strips of bear-skin were likewise used to fasten them on, serving the purpose of false whiskers, and causing us look as fierce as hungry wolves. We were also frequently exercised in the various evolutions of a sea-fight; first using our cannon, then seizing our cutlasses and boarding-pikes, and cutting to the right and left, as if in the act of boarding an enemy's ship. Thus we spent our time from early in the fall until after Christmas, when we received orders to hold ourselves in readiness for sea.

As we lay waiting for our final orders, a report reached us that a large English brig-of-war, called the Nimrod, lay in a cove somewhere near Boston bay. Upon this information, our officers planned a night expedition for the purpose of effecting her capture. Our intended mode of attack was to run close along side, pour a broadside upon her, and then, without further ceremony, board her, cutlass in hand. So we took in our powder, ground up our cutlasses, and toward night got under weigh. A change in the wind, however, defeated our designs, and we put into Salem harbor, with no other result than the freezing of a man's fingers, which happened while we were furling our sails. Thus ended our first warlike expedition in the Siren.

Shortly after this affair we received orders to start on a cruise to the coast of Africa, and, in company with the Grand Turk, a privateer, set sail from Salem. Passing the fort, we received the usual hail from the sentry of, "Brig, ahoy! where are you bound to?"

To this salutation the first-lieutenant jocosely answered, "There and back again, on a man-of-war's cruise." Such a reply would not have satisfied a British soldier; but we shot past the fort unmolested. After two days, we parted company with the Grand Turk, and, by the aid of a fair wind, soon found ourselves in the Gulf stream; where, instead of fearing frozen fingers, we could go barefooted and feel quite comfortable.

We now kept a sharp look-out at the mast-head, but met with nothing until we reached the Canary Islands, near which we saw a boat-load of Portuguese, who, coming along side, talked in their native tongue with great noise and earnestness, but were no more intelligible to us than so many blackbirds.

While off the African coast, our captain died. His wasted body was placed in a coffin, with shot to sink it. After the service had been read, the plank on which the coffin rested was elevated, and it slipped into the great deep. The yards were braced round, and we were under weigh again, when, to our surprise and grief, we saw the coffin floating on the waves. The reason was, the carpenter had bored holes in the top and bottom: he should have made them only in the top.

After the funeral, the crew were called aft, and the first-lieutenant, Mr. Nicholson, told us that it should be left to our decision whether he should assume the command and continue the cruise, or return home. We gave him three hearty cheers, in token of our wish to continue the cruise. He was a noble minded man, very kind and civil to his crew, and the opposite in every respect to the haughty lordly captain with whom I first sailed in the Macedonian. Seeing me one day with rather a poor hat on, he called me aft and presented me with one of his own, but little worn. "Good luck to him," said I, in a sailor phrase, as I returned to my messmates; "he has a soul to be saved." We also lost two of our crew, who fell victims to the heat of the climate.

One morning the cry of "Sail, ho!" directed our attention to a strange sail, which had hove to, with her courses hauled up. At first we took her for a British man-of-war brig. The hands were summoned to quarters, and the ship got ready for action. A nearer approach, however, convinced us that the supposed enemy was no other than our old friend the Grand Turk. She did not appear to know us; for no sooner did she see that our craft was a brig-of-war, than, supposing us to belong to John Bull, she crowded all her canvas, and made the best of her way off. Knowing what she was, we permitted her to escape without further alarm.

The first land we made was Cape Mount. The natives came off to a considerable distance in their canoes, clothed in nothing but a piece of cloth fastened round the waist, and extending downward to the feet. As we approached the shore, we saw several fires burning; this, we were told, in the broken English spoken by our sable visitors, was the signal for trade. We bought a quantity of oranges, limes, cocoanuts, tamarinds, plantains, yams, and bananas. We likewise took in a quantity of cassada, a species of ground root, of which we made tolerable pudding and bread; also a few hogs and some water.

We lay here several days, looking out for any English vessels that might come thither for purposes of trade.

Meanwhile we began to experience the inconvenience of a hot climate. Our men were all covered with blotches or boils, probably occasioned by so sudden a transition from extreme cold to extreme heat. What was worse still, we were in want of a plentiful supply of water. In consequence of this, we were placed on an allowance of two quarts per diem to each man, which occasioned us much suffering; for after preparing our puddings, bread, and grog, we had but little left to assuage our burning thirst. Some, in their distress, drank large quantities of sea water, which only increased their thirst, and made them sick; others sought relief in chewing lead, tea leaves, or anything which would create moisture. Never did we feel more delighted than when our boat's crew announced the discovery of a pool of fine clear water.

While cruising along the coast, we one night perceived a large ship lying at anchor near the shore. We could not decide whether she was a large merchantman or a man-of-war, so we approached her with the utmost caution. Our doubts were soon removed, for she suddenly loosed all her sails, and made chase after us. By the help of their glasses, our officers ascertained her to be an English frigate. Of course it was folly to engage her, so we made all the sail we could carry, beat to quarters, lighted our matches, and lay down at our guns, expecting to be prisoners of war before morning. During the night we hung out false lights, and altered our course: this baffled our pursuer: in the morning she was not to be seen.

The next sail we made was not so formidable. She was an English vessel at anchor in the Senegal river. We approached her, and hailed. Her officer returned an insolent reply, which so exasperated our captain, that he passed the word to fire into her, but recalled it almost immediately. The countermand was too late; for, in a moment, everything being ready for action, we poured a whole broadside into our unfortunate foe. The current carried us away from the stranger. We attempted to beat up again; but our guns had roused the garrison in a fort which commanded the river; and they began to blaze away at us in so expressive a manner, that we found it prudent to get a little beyond the reach of their shot, and patiently wait for daylight.

The next morning we saw our enemy hauled close in shore, under the protection of the fort, and filled with soldiers. At first it was resolved to man the boats and cut her out; but this, after weighing the subject maturely, was pronounced to be too hazardous an experiment, and, notwithstanding our men begged to make the attempt, it was wisely abandoned. How many were killed by our hasty broadside we never learned, but doubtless several poor fellows were hurried to a watery and unexpected grave, affording another illustration of the *beauty* of war. This affair our men humorously styled "the battle of Senegal."

After visiting Cape Three Points, we shaped our course for St. Thomas. On our way we lost a prize through a display of Yankee cunning in her commander. We had hoisted English colors; the officer in command of the stranger was pretty well versed in the secrets of false colors, and in return he ran up the American flag. The bait took: supposing her to be American, we showed the stars and stripes. This was all the merchantman desired. It told him what we were, and he made all possible sail for St. Thomas. We followed, crowding every stitch of canvas our brig could carry; we also got out our sweeps, and swept her along; but in vain. The merchantman was the better sailer, and succeeded in reaching St. Thomas, which, being a neutral port, secured her safety. Her name was the Jane, of Liverpool. The next morning another Liverpool merchantman got into the harbor unseen by our lookout, until she was under the protection of the laws of neutrality.

Our next business was to watch the mouth of the harbor, in the hope of catching them as they left port. But they were too cautious to run into danger, especially as they were expecting a convoy for their protection, which might make us glad to trust more to our canvas than to our cannon.

Shortly after this occurrence we made another sail standing in toward St. Thomas. Hoisting English colors, our officers also donning the British uniform, we soon came near enough to hail her; for not doubting that we were a British brig, the merchantman made no effort to escape us. Our captain hailed her:

"Ship, ahoy!"

"Halloo!"

"What ship is that?"

"The ship Barton."

"Where do you belong?"

"To Liverpool."

"What is your cargo?"

"Red-wood, palm oil, and ivory."

"Where are you bound to?"

"To St. Thomas."

Just at that moment our English flag was hauled down, and to the inexpressible annoyance of the officers of the Barton, the stars and stripes supplied its place.

"Haul down your colors!" continued Captain Nicholson.

The old captain, who up to this moment had been enjoying a comfortable nap in his very comfortable cabin, now came upon deck in his shirt sleeves, rubbing his eyes, and looking so exquisitely ridiculous, that it was scarcely possible to avoid laughing. So surprised was he at the unexpected termination of his dreams, that he could not command skill enough to strike his colors, which was accordingly done by the mate.

After taking out as much of her cargo as we desired, we proceeded to set her on fire. It was an imposing sight to behold the wild antics of the flames, leaping from rope to rope, and from spar to spar, until she looked like a fiery cloud resting on the dark surface of the water. Presently her spars began to fall, her masts went by the board, her loaded guns went off, the hull was burned to the water's edge, and what a few hours before was a fine trim ship, looking like a winged creature of the deep, lay a shapeless charred mass, whose blackened outline, shadowed in the clear still waves, looked like the grim spirit of war lurking for its prey.

This wanton destruction of property was in accordance with our instructions, "to *sink, burn, and destroy*" whatever we took from the enemy. Such is the war-spirit! SINK, BURN, and DESTROY! how it sounds! Yet such are the instructions given by Christian nations to their agents in time of war. What Christian will not pray for the destruction of such a spirit?

The crew of the Barton we carried into St. Thomas, and placed them on board the Jane, excepting a Portuguese and two colored men, who shipped among our crew. We also took with us a fine black spaniel dog, whom the men called by the name of Paddy. This done, we proceeded to watch for fresh victims on which to wreak the vengeance of the war spirit.

The next sail we met was an English brig called the Adventure, which had a whole menagerie of monkeys on board. We captured and burned her just as we did the Barton. Her crew was also disposed of in the same manner. One of them, an African prince, who had acquired a tolerable education in England, and who was remarkably polite and sensible, shipped in the Siren. His name was Samuel Quaqua.

We now remained at St. Thomas several days, carrying on a petty trade with the natives. Our men bought all kinds of fruit, gold-dust, and birds. For these things we gave them articles of clothing, tobacco, knives, etc. For an old vest I obtained a large basketful of oranges; for a handful of tobacco five large cocoanuts—a profitable exchange on my side, since, although I drew my tobacco of the purser, I fortunately never acquired the habit of using it; a loss I never regretted. My cocoanuts were far more gratifying and valuable when we got to sea, parched with thirst, and suffering for water, than all the tobacco in the ship.

From St. Thomas we proceeded to Angola, where we staid long enough to clean, paint, and refit our brig from stem to stern. This was the last port we intended to touch at on the coast of Africa. Our next anchorage was to be in Boston harbor—at least so we purposed; but the events of war frustrated our intention.

To accomplish our object, we had to run the gauntlet through the host of English cruisers that hovered about like birds of prey along both sides of the Atlantic coast. This enterprise appeared so impossible to my mind while we lay at Angola, and the fear of being retaken and hung operated so strongly on my imagination, that more than once I determined to run away and find a refuge among the Africans; but my better judgment prevailed, and I continued at my post.

Still, I used every possible precaution to escape detection in case of of our capture. In accordance with the custom of our navy at that period, I let my hair grow long behind. To change my looks more effectually, instead of tying mine in a cue as the others did, I let it hang in ringlets all round my face and neck. This, together with the effect of time, caused me to appear quite a different lad from what I was when a boy on board the Macedonian. I also adopted that peculiarity of dress practiced by American men-of-war's men, which consisted in wearing my shirt open at the neck, with the corners thrown back. On these corners a device was wrought, consisting of the stars of the American flag with the British flag underneath. By these means I hoped to pass for a genuine Yankee, without suspicion, in case we should fall into English hands.

Having finished our preparations, we left Angola for Boston. We reached the island of Ascension in safety, where was a post-office of a truly patriarchal character. A box is nailed to a post near the shore. Ships that pass send to the box, and deposit or take out letters as the case may be. This is probably the cheapest general post-office establishment in the world.

We had scarcely left this island before the cry of "Sail, ho!" arrested every ear. Supposing her to be a large merchantman, we made toward her; but a nearer approach made it doubtful whether she was an Indiaman or a man-of-war. The captain judged her to be the latter, and tacked ship immediately. He was unwilling to place himself in the situation of an American privateer, who, mistaking a seventy-four for a merchantman, ran his ship close along side, and boldly summoned her to haul down her colors. The captain of the other ship cooly replied, "I am not in the habit of striking my colors." At the same moment the ports of his ship were opened, and disclosed her long ranges of guns yawning over the decks of the privateer. Perceiving his mistake, the privateer, with admirable tact and good humor, said, "Well, if you wont, I will;" and pulling down his bunting, surrendered to his more powerful foe. To avoid such a mistake as this, our captain made all sail to escape the coming stranger, which was now bearing down upon us under a heavy pressure of canvas, revealing, as she gained upon our little brig, that she bore the formidable character of a seventy-four gun ship under English colors.

Of course fighting was out of the question. It would be like the assault of a dog on an elephant, or a dolphin on a whale. We therefore crowded all possible sail, threw our guns, cables, anchors, hatches, etc., overboard, to increase her speed. But it soon became apparent that we could not escape. The wind blew quite fresh, which gave our opponent the advantage: she gained on us very fast. We shifted our course, in hopes to baffle her until night, when we felt pretty sure of getting out of her way. It was of no use; she still gained; until we saw ourselves almost within gunshot of our opponent.

In this extremity the captain ordered the quarter-master, George Watson, to throw the private signals overboard. This was a hard task for the bold-hearted fellow. As he pitched them into the sea, he said, "Good-by, brother Yankee;" an expression which, in spite of their mortifying situation, forced a smile from the lips of the officers.

The sound of a gun now came booming through the air. It was a signal for us to heave to, or to look out for consequences. What might have been, we learned afterward, for a division of the crew of the seventy-four had orders to sink us if we made the least show of resistance. Finding it useless to prolong the chase, our commander reluctantly ordered the flag to be struck. We then hove to, and our foe came rolling down upon us, looking like a huge avalanche rushing down the mountain side to crush some poor peasant's dwelling. Her officers stood on her quarter-deck, glancing unutterable pride, while her captain shouted, "What brig is that?"

"The United States brig Siren," replied Captain Nicholson.

"This is his Britannic majesty's ship Medway!" he answered. "I claim you as my lawful prize."

Boats were then lowered, the little brig taken from us, and our crew transferred to the Medway, stowed away in the cable tier, and put in messes of twelve, with an allowance of only eight men's rations to a mess—a regulation which caused us considerable suffering from hunger. The sight of the marines on board the Medway made me tremble, for my fancy pointed out several of them as having formerly belonged to the Macedonian. I really feared I was destined speedily to swing at the yard-arm: it was, however, a groundless alarm.

This event happened July 12, 1814. Only eight days before, we had celebrated the independence of the United States. Now, we had a fair prospect of a rigorous imprisonment. Such are the changes which constantly occur under the rule of the war-spirit.

The day subsequent to our capture we were marched to the quarter-deck with our clothes-bags, where we underwent a strict search. We were ordered to remove our outside garments for this purpose. They expected to find us in possession of large quantities of gold-dust. What little our crew had purchased was taken from them, with a spirit of rapacity altogether beneath the dignity of a naval commander.

Our short allowance was a source of much discomfort in this our prison-ship. But in the true spirit of sailors, we made even this the subject of coarse jests and pleasant remark. Enduring this evil, we proceeded on our course. When the Medway arrived at Simon's Town, about twenty-one miles from the Cape of Good Hope, we met the Denmark, seventy-four, on her way to England with the prisoners from Cape Town. The captain had hitherto intended to land us at the latter place, but the presence of the Denmark led him to change his purpose, and land us at Simon's Town.

The journey from this place to the Cape was one of great suffering to our crew. We were received on the beach by a file of Irish soldiers. Under their escort we proceeded seven miles, through heaps of burning sand, seeing nothing worthy of notice on the way but a number of men busily engaged in cutting up dead whales on the sea-shore.

After resting a short time, we recommenced our march, guarded by a new detachment of soldiers. Unused to walking as we were, we began to grow excessively fatigued; and after wading a stream of considerable depth, we were so overcome that it seemed impossible to proceed any further. We lay down, discouraged and wretched, on the sand. The guard brought us some bread, and gave half a pint of wine to each man. This revived us somewhat. We were now placed under a guard of dragoons. They were very kind, and urged us to attempt the remaining seven miles. To relieve us, they carried our clothes-bags on their horses; and overtaking some Dutch farmers going to the Cape with broom-stuff and brush, the officer of the dragoons made them carry the most weary among us in their wagons. It is not common for men to desire the inside of a prison, but I can assure my readers we did most heartily wish ourselves there, on that tedious journey. At last, about nine o'clock P. M., we arrived at Cape Town, having left one of our number at Wineburg, through exhaustion, who joined us the next day. Stiff, sore, and weary, we hastily threw ourselves on the hard boards of our prison, where, without needing to be soothed or rocked, we slept profoundly until the next morning, when we took a survey of our new quarters. We found ourselves placed in a large yard surrounded by high walls, and strongly guarded by soldiers. Within this inclosure there was a building or shed composed of three rooms, neither of which had any floor. Round the sidel stood three benches or stages, one above the other, to serve for berths. On these we spread our hammocks and bed-clothes, making them tolerably comfortable places to sleep in. A few of the men preferred to sling their hammocks as they did at sea. Here, also, we used to eat, unless, as was our frequent practice, we did so in the open air.

We remained in prison at the Cape till carried away in the ship Cumberland to England. Stopping by the way at St. Helena, we were removed to the Grampus, a transfer which greatly alarmed me, since the more men who saw me, the greater of course was my chance of detection. Luckily, no one knew me, and I arrived with my companions in safety at Plymouth. I was equally fortunate here, and remained undiscovered till I was transferred with others to a vessel which was to take us in exchange to America. I pass over the circumstances of the voyage, and only mention that we were all landed in due time at New York.

My resolution had been to quit the sea and settle down on land, but on returning to New York all such fancies vanished, as they had done before. I spent my hard-won earnings foolishly like others, and, like them, when reduced to straits, again sought employment as a sailor. On this occasion I shipped on board the Boxer, commanded by Captain Porter, a man, as it proved, of stern disposition. The Boxer was now ready for a cruise, and I prepared to do my duty on board of that vessel as an ordinary seaman.

Formerly, I had been entered only as a boy; but now, as a rated seaman, I had a station assigned me in the foretop, instead of being a servant to any of the officers. I was also appointed to be one of the crew of the captain's gig. This made my lot one of more fatigue and exposure than in any former voyage; a proof of which I very soon experienced. It being now late in the fall, the weather became very cold. One afternoon, the pennant having got foul of the royal mast, an officer ordered me to go up and clear it. I had no mittens on; it took me some time to perform my task; and before I came down, one of my fingers was frozen. Thus it is, however, with the poor tar; and he thinks himself happy to escape with injuries so slight as this. We shortly received sailing orders, and were soon under weigh, bound to the Balize in the Gulf of Mexico. Here we cruised about some time, visiting New Orleans and other places, and keeping an outlook for pirates, with which these seas were then unhappily infested. This was a duty requiring great vigilance, and we were kept constantly at our posts. The most irksome duty of a sailor is to keep watch at night in the tops. Often have I stood for hours on the royal yard, or topgallant yard, without a man to converse with. Here, overcome with fatigue and want of sleep, I have fallen into a dreamy dozing state, from which I was roused by a lee lurch of the ship. Starting up, I have shuddered at the danger I had so narrowly escaped. But notwithstanding this sudden fright, a few minutes had scarcely elapsed before I would be nodding again. This, of course, was a highly punishable offense.

When the weather was rough, we were indulged with permission to stand on the foretopsail yard, or on the topgallant cross-trees; and if the ship rolled heavily, we lashed ourselves to the mast for safety. I can assure my readers there is nothing desirable in this part of a sailor's duty. In whatever the pleasure of a life at sea consists, it is not in keeping a look-out from the mast-head at night. But the most disagreeable of all is, to be compelled to stand on these crazy elevations when half dead with sea-sickness. Some suppose that sailors are never sea-sick after the first time they go to sea. This is a mistake; it is very much with them as with landsmen in respect to being sick in a coach. Those who are of bilious temperament are always affected, more or less, when they ride in a coach or sleigh; while others are never sick on these occasions. So with seamen; some are never sea-sick, others are sick only when going out of port, while some are so in every gale of wind. It is almost needless to say that, for sailors, no allowance is made for sea-sickness; they must in all cases remain at their posts until it is time to be relieved.

Our cruise terminated after a few skirmishes, and we returned to New York, where I left the service, as I trusted, forever. As it occurred, my services as a seaman in a war-vessel would not long have been required. The peace between England and France in 1814, by opening the continent to American commerce, hitherto excluded by British policy naturally removed one of the grounds of quarrel, and opened the way for peace with the United States. On the twenty-fourth of December, 1814, a treaty of peace, accordingly, was effected at Ghent, which left, however, the question of right of search and other matters on the ground on which they had previously stood. The Americans, as is well known, were most successful in their naval warfare; but, after all, that was a trifling compensation for ruined commerce, and for being brought to the very verge of national dismemberment. The losses of the British never made any distinct impression on the nation, otherwise than teaching a tolerably sound lesson in discretion, and leading to many important improvements in naval affairs. I sincerely trust that both nations, united by a thousand inextricable ties, and profiting by experience, will, in all time coming, avoid every description of warlike collision, and exist in the happiest terms of amity and peace.

In taking leave of the sea, it may be expected that I should say a few words respecting the life of a sailor. As I have already mentioned, the profession of a sailor has its hardships, but these were much greater at the time of my service than they are now, after a lapse of twenty years. The duties of the men are now exactly regulated, and their comforts are cared for in many ways. On board of each vessel, in the British navy, there are now means for instruction, a library, and the savings of the men are carefully secured for them, or transmitted to their wives or friends. On shore, also, there are at various ports, establishments called "Sailors'

Homes," where discharged seamen may reside at a moderate expense till engaged in a new vessel. At sea, as on land, steadiness, temperance, good temper, forbearance, and other good qualities, are sure to command respect, notwithstanding the severities of discipline. It is likewise most advantageous for a man to possess a good education; for the more he can make himself useful, and be depended on, the greater is his chance of promotion. A properly bred sailor should, at the very least, be able to *reef and steer*—that is, adapt the sails to the wind whichever way it blows, and govern the vessel by the helm and compass. But beside these comparatively simple duties, he should likewise be able to throw and calculate by the log, to work a reckoning, take an observation, find the longitude, and keep a log-book, in which all necessary particulars of the voyage are daily inscribed. The log is a contrivance for ascertaining the rate of speed at which a vessel goes. It consists of a long cord, having an oblong and loaded piece of wood attached to one end. This wood, when heaved overboard, remains stationary in the water, and consequently, as the vessel advances, the line must be let out from a reel held in the hand. The line is marked by knots and half knots, representing miles and half miles, and the number of these run off indicates the number of miles which the vessel is going at per hour. Every common seaman can cast the log, and calculate the speed of the vessel from it; but few can do any more, because they are contented to remain in ignorance, and inclined to spend their leisure time in trifling amusements rather than in study. Of course such persons cannot expect to rise in their profession.

Having thrown myself adrift, with but slender resources, and far distant from my friends, I experienced the fate of many a disbanded and penniless tar. What hand to turn to for the means of subsistence I knew not. Determined at any rate to make an effort, I went about to different parts of the country seeking employment. I was not successful; and at length my money was all gone, and my shoes more than half worn out. When reduced to this sad extremity, and on the brink of despair, I was so fortunate as to discover an old shipmate; and through his kind influence, his brother-in-law employed me to work in his cloth-dressing establishment. As I was ignorant of the business, and was not really needed, my board was to be my only compensation. I lived here happily for some time, and then got employment of a more lucrative kind in another establishment, where I settled, and have since remained, thankful to have attained a haven of rest after the turmoils and dangers of a sea-life.

THE EXTRAORDINARY SUFFERINGS

OF

DONALD CAMPBELL,

WHO, BEING SHIPWRECKED FELL INTO THE HANDS OF

THE CRUEL HYDER ALI.

It was the eighteenth day of May, 1782, when we sailed from Goa, in Hindoostan, in a Portuguese vessel, bound for Madras. The hemisphere had been, for some days, overcast with clouds: some light showers of rain had fallen, and it did not tend to raise my spirits, or free me from ominous apprehensions, to hear that those circumstances indicated an approaching gale of wind. I observed, moreover, that the vessel was much too deep in the water, being greatly overloaded—that she was, in many respects, defective, and, as the seamen say, ill-found, and, in short, very unfit to encounter a gale of wind of any violence. I scorned, however, to yield to those united impressions, and determined to proceed.

On the nineteenth, the sky was obscured by immense fleeces of clouds, surcharged with inflammable matter; and in the evening the rain fell in torrents, the firmament darkened apace, sudden night came on, and the horrors of extreme darkness were rendered still more horrible by the peals of thunder which rent the air, and the frequent flashes of lightning which served only to show us the horror of our situation, and leave us in increased darkness: meantime, the wind became more violent, blowing on the shore; and a heavy sea, raised by its force, united with it to make our state more formidable.

By daylight, on the morning of the twentieth, the gale had increased to a furious tempest; and the sea, keeping pace with it, ran mountain-high, and as it kept invariably to the same point, the captain and officers became seriously alarmed, and almost persuaded that the south-west monsoon had set in, which, if it were so, would render it absolutely impossible for us to weather the coast. All that day, however, we kept as close as the violence of the weather would allow us, to the wind; but the sea canted her head so to leeward, that she made more lee than headway; and the rigging was so strained with the work that we had little hope of keeping off the shore, unless the wind changed, of which there was not now the smallest probability. During the night, there was no intermission of the storm: many of the sails flew into ribbons; some of the rigging was carried away; and such exertions were made, that, before morning, every stick that could possibly be struck, was down upon the deck.

About seven o'clock on the morning of the twenty-first, I was alarmed by an unusual noise upon the deck, and running up, perceived that every remaining sail in the vessel, the fore-sail alone excepted, was totally carried away. The sight was horrible; and the whole vessel presented a spectacle as dreadful to the feelings, as mortifying to human pride. Fear had produced not only all the helplessness of despondency, but all the mischievous freaks of insanity. In one place stood the captain, raving, stamping, and tearing his hair in handfuls from his head—here some of the crew were cast upon their knees, clapping their hands, and praying, with all the extravagance of horror painted in their faces—there, others were flogging their images, with all their might, calling upon them to allay the storm. One of our passengers, who was purser of an English East Indiaman, had got hold of a case-bottle of rum, and, with an air of distraction and deep despair imprinted on his face, was stalking about in his shirt. I perceived him to be on the point of serving it out, in large tumblers, to the few undismayed people, and well convinced, that, so far from alleviating, it would sharpen the horrors of their minds, I went forward, and with much difficulty prevented him.

Having accomplished this point, I applied myself to the captain, and endeavored to bring him back (if possible) to his recollection, and to a sense of what he owed to his duty as a commander, and to his dignity as a man: I exhorted him to encourage the sailors by his example; and strove to raise his spirits by saying that the storm did not appear to me by any means so terrible as some I had before experienced.

While I was thus employed, we shipped a sea on the starboard side, which, I really thought, would have sent us down. The vessel seemed to sink beneath its weight, shivered, and remained motionless. It was a moment of critical suspense: fancy made me think I felt her gradually descending—I gave myself up as gone, and summoned all my fortitude to bear approaching death with becoming manhood.

Just at this crisis, the water, which rushed with incredible force through all parts of the vessel, brought out floating, and nearly suffocated, another English passenger, who was endeavoring to take a little repose in a small cabin boarded off from the deck: he was a very stout young man, and full of true spirit. Finding that the vessel was not, as I had thought, going immediately down, he joined me in exhorting the captain to his duty; we persuaded him to throw the guns overboard, as well as a number of trunks and packages, with which the vessel was much encumbered, and, with some little exertion, we got the pumps set agoing.

The name of the English passenger who assisted me in getting the captain and mariners to do their duty, was Hall. He and I having, with great difficulty, got some hands to stick to the pumps, stood at the wheel, at once to assist the men, and prevent them from quitting it; and, although hopeless, determined that no effort practicable on our part should be wanting to the preservation of the vessel. The water, however, gained upon the pumps, notwithstanding every effort; and it evidently appeared that we could not keep her long above water.

At ten o'clock the wind seemed to increase, and amounted to a downright hurricane: the sky was so entirely obscured with black clouds, and the rain fell so thick, that objects were not discernable from the wheel to the ship's head. Soon the pumps were choked, and could no longer be worked: then dismay seized on all—nothing but unutterable despair, silent anguish, and horror, wrought up to frenzy, were to be seen; not a single soul was capable of an effort to be useful—all seemed more desirous to extinguish their calamities by embracing death, than willing, by a painful exertion, to avoid it.

At about eleven o'clock, we could plainly distinguish a dreadful roaring noise, resembling that of waves rolling against rocks; but the darkness of the day, and the accompanying rains, prevented us from seeing any distance; and if they were rocks, we might be actually dashed to pieces on them, before we could perceive them. At twelve o'clock, however, the weather cleared up a little, when we discovered breakers and large rocks outside of us; so that it appeared we must have passed quite close to them, and were now fairly hemmed in between them and the land. In this very critical juncture, the captain adopted the dangerous resolution of letting go an anchor, to bring her up with her head to the sea. Though no seaman, my common sense told me that she could never ride it out, but must directly go down. The event nearly justified my judgment: for she had scarcely been at anchor, before an enormous sea, rolling over her, overwhelmed and filled her with water, and every one on board concluded that she was certainly sinking. On the instant, a Lascar, with a presence of mind worthy an old English mariner, took an ax, ran forward, and cut the cable.

On finding herself free, the vessel again floated, and made an effort to right herself; but she was almost completely water-logged, and heeled to larboard so much that the gunwale lay under water. We then endeavored to steer, as fast as we could, for the land, which we knew could not be at any great distance, though we were unable to discover it through the hazy weather. The foresail was loosened; by great efforts in bailing she righted a little; her gunwale was got above water, and we scudded, as well as we could, before the wind, which still blew hard on shore, and at about two o'clock, the land appeared at a small distance ahead.

The love of life countervails all other considerations in the mind of man. The uncertainty we were under with regard to the shore before us, which we had reason to believe was part of Hyder Ali's dominions, (then at war with the English,) where we should meet with the most rigorous treatment, if not ultimate death, was forgotten in the joyful hope of saving life; and we scudded toward the shore in all the exulting transports of people just snatched from the jaws of death.

This gleam of happiness continued not long: a tremendous sea rolling after us, broke over our stern, tore everything before it, stove in the steerage, carried away the rudder, shivered the wheel to pieces, and tore up the very ring-bolts of the deck, conveyed the men who stood at the deck forward, and swept them overboard. I was standing, at the time, near the wheel, and fortunately had hold of the tafferel, which enabled me to resist in part the weight of the wave. I was, however, swept off my feet, and dashed against the main-mast. The jerk from the tafferel, which I held very tenaciously, seemed as if it would have dislocated my arms: however, it broke the impetus of my motion, and, in all probability, saved me from being dashed to pieces against the mast.

I floundered about in the water, at the foot of the mast, till at length I got on my feet, and seized a rope, which I held in a state of great embarrassment, dubious what I should do to extricate myself. At this instant I perceived that Mr. Hall had got upon the capstan, and was waving his hand to me to follow his example: this I wished to do, though it was an enterprise of some risk and difficulty; for, if I lost the hold I had, a single motion of the vessel, or a full wave, would certainly carry me overboard. I made a bold push, however, and fortunately accomplished it. Having attained this station, I could the better survey the wreck, and saw that the water was nearly breast high on the quarter-deck (for the vessel was deep-waisted;) and I perceived the unfortunate English purser standing where the water was most shallow, as if watching with patient expectation its rising, and awaiting death. I called to him to come to us, but he shook his head in despair, and said, in a lamentable tone, "It is all over with us! God have mercy upon us!" then seated himself, with seeming composure, on a chair which happened to be rolling about in the wreck of the deck, and, in a few minutes afterward, was washed into the sea along with it, where he was speedily released from a state ten thousand times worse than death.

During this universal wreck of things, the horror I was in, could not prevent me from observing a very curious circumstance, which, at any other time, would have excited laughter, though it now produced no other emotion than surprise. We happened to be in part laden with mangoes, of which the island of Goa is known to produce the finest in the world; some of them lay in baskets on the poop. A little black boy, in the moment of greatest danger, had got seated by them, devouring them voraciously, and crying all the time most b. erly, at the horrors of his situation. The vessel now got completely water-logged; and Mr. Hall and I were employed in forming conjectural calculations how many minutes she could keep above water, and consoling one another on the unfortunate circumstances under which we met.

As the larboard side of the vessel was gradually going down, the deck, and of course the capstan, became too nearly perpendicular for us to continue on it: we therefore foresaw the necessity of quitting it, and got upon the starboard side, holding fast by the gunwale, and allowing our bodies and legs to yield to the sea as it broke over us. Thus we continued for some time: at length the severity of the labor so entirely exhausted our strength and spirits that our only hope seemed to be a speedy conclusion to our painful death, and we began to have serious intentions of letting go our hold, and yielding ourselves up at once to the fury of the waves. The vessel, which all this time drifted with the sea and wind, gradually approximated the shore, and at length struck the ground, which, for an instant, revived our almost departed hopes, but we soon found that it did not, in the smallest degree, better our situation.

Observing the people consulting together, and resolving to join them, I made an effort to get to the lee-shrouds, where they were standing, or rather clinging; but before I could accomplish it, I lost my hold, fell down the hatchway, (the gratings having been carried away with the long-boat,) and was for some minutes entangled there among a heap of packages, which the violent fluctuations of the water had collected on the lee-side. As the vessel moved with the sea, and the water flowed in, the packages and I were rolled together—sometimes one, sometimes another, uppermost; so that I began to be apprehensive I should not be able to extricate myself: by the merest accident, however, I grasped something that lay in my way, made a vigorous spring, and gained the lee-shrouds. Mr. Hall, who followed me, in seizing the shrouds, came thump against me with such violence, that I could scarcely retain my hold of the rigging. Compelled by the perilous situation in which I stood, I called out to him for God's sake to keep off, that I was rendered quite breathless and worn out: he generously endeavored to make way for me, and, in doing so, unfortunately lost his hold, and went down under the ship's side. Never, never shall I forget my sensations at this melancholy incident—I would have given millions of worlds that I could have recalled the words which made him move; my mind was wound up to the last pitch of anguish, when, as much to my astonishment as to my joy, I saw him borne by a returning wave, and thrown among the very packages from which I had but just before, with such labor and difficulty, extricated myself. In the end, he proved equally fortunate, but after a much longer and harder struggle, and after sustaining much more injury.

I once more changed my station, and made my way to the poop, where I found myself rather more sheltered. I earnestly wished Mr. Hall to be with me, whatever might be my ultimate fate, and beckoned to him to come to me; but he only answered by shaking his head, in a feeble, desponding manner—staring, at the same time, wildly about him: even his spirit was subdued; and despair, I perceived, had begun to take possession of his mind.

Being a little more at ease in my new station than I had been before, I had more time to deliberate, and more power to judge. I recollected that, according to the course of time, the day was far gone, and the night quickly approaching: I reflected, that for any enterprise whatsoever, day was much preferable to night; and, above all, I considered that the vessel could not hold long together. I therefore thought that the best mode I could adopt, would be to take to the water with the first buoyant thing I could see, and, as the wind and water both seemed to run to the shore, to take my chance, in that way, of reaching it. In pursuance of this resolution, I tore off my shirt, having before that thrown off the other parts of my dress. I looked at my sleeve-buttons, in which was set the hair of my departed children, rolled my shirt up, and very carefully thrust it into a hole between decks, with the wild hope that the sleeve-buttons might yet escape untouched. Watching my opportunity, I saw a log of wood floating near the vessel, and, waving my hand to Mr. Hall, as a last adieu, jumped after it. Here, again, I was doomed to aggravated hardships: I had scarcely touched the log when a great sea snatched it from my hold: still, as it came near me, I grasped at it ineffectually, till, at last, it was completely carried away, but not before it had cut, and battered, and bruised me in several places, and in a manner that, at any other time, I should have thought dreadful.

Death seemed inevitable: and all that occurred to me now to do was to accelerate it, and get out of its pangs as speedily as possible; for, though I knew how to swim, the tremendous surf rendered swimming useless, and all hope from that would have been ridiculous. I therefore began to swallow as much water as possible; yet, still rising by the buoyant principle of the waves to the surface, my former thoughts began to recur; and whether it was that, or natural instinct, which survived the temporary impressions of despair, I know not—but I endeavored to swim, which I had not done long, when I again discovered the log of wood I had lost, floating near me, and with some difficulty caught it: hardly had it been an instant in my hands, when, by the same unlucky means, I lost it again. I had often heard it said in Scotland, that if a man will throw himself flat on his back in the water, lie quite straight and stiff, and suffer himself to sink till the water gets into his ears, he will continue to float so forever. This occurred to me now, and I determined to try the experiment; so I threw myself on my back, in the manner I have described, and left myself to the disposal of Providence. Nor was I mistaken; for, in a short time more, without any effort or exertion, and without once turning from off my back, I found myself strike against the sandy beach. Overjoyed, as you may well suppose, to the highest pitch of transport, at my Providential deliverance, I made a convulsive spring, and ran up a little distance on the shore; but was so weak and worn down by fatigue, and so unable to clear my stomach of the salt water with which it was loaded, that I suddenly grew deadly sick, and apprehended that I had only exchanged one death for another; and in a minute or two fainted away.

How long I continued in the swoon into which I had fallen, it is impossible for me to tell; but when I recovered, I found myself surrounded by a guard of armed soldiers, sepoys, and pikemen. I knew them immediately to be the troops of Hyder Ali, and almost wished myself back into the waves again. Looking round, I saw that the people and effects that had been saved from the wreck, were collected all together along with me. In this state, we remained till it was dark. A Lascar belonging to the vessel, perceiving that my nakedness gave me great concern, tore in two a piece of cloth which he had tied round his waist, and gave me one part of it, which afforded a short apron. Of all the acts of beneficence I ever met with, this struck me the most forcibly: it had kindness, disinterestedness and delicacy for its basis; and I have never since thought of it without wishing that I could meet the man, to reward him for his beneficence, with a subsistence for life. The lower order of people of a certain country, I know, would think a man in such circumstances as I was then in, a fitter object of pleasantry than pity.

The vast quantity of salt water I had swallowed, still made me deadly sick in the stomach: however, after some time, I threw it up, and got great relief. I had hardly felt the comfortable effects of this, before I was ordered to march; nine of us, all Lascars except myself, were conveyed to a village at a few miles distance, on the sea-side, where we were, for the night, put into a square place, walled round, open to the inclemency of the weather above and below, and filled with large logs of wood; it blew most violently, and the rain fell in torrents—while not one smooth plank could be found on which to stretch our fatigued and wasted bodies. Thus, naked, sick, exhausted with fatigue and fasting, drenched with wet, and unable to lie down, our misery might be supposed to be incapable of increase. But, alas! where are the bounds we can set to human woe? Thirst, that most dreadful of pains, occasioned by the drenching with salt-water, seized us: we begged, we entreated, we clamored for water, but the inhuman wretches, deaf to the groans and screeches of their fellow-creatures, (for some grew delirious with the agony of thirst,) refused them even the cheap and miserable indulgence of a drop of water!

Indeed, a night of more exquisite horror cannot be imagined. The thought of being a prisoner in the hands of Hyder Ali was, of itself, sufficient to render me completely unhappy: but my utter want of clothes almost put me beside myself; and lying exposed to the open air, where I was glad to sit close to the Lascars, to receive a little heat from their bodies, and to hold open my mouth in order to catch a drop of the descending rain, was a state that might be considered as the highest refinement upon misery.

About four o'clock in the morning, a little cold rice was brought us to eat, and water was dug out of a hole near the spot for us; but as all things in this life are good or bad merely relatively, this wretched fare was some refreshment to us. I was then removed to the ruins of a hut, separated from the rest, and a guard set over me. Here I had full room for reflection. The whole of my situation appeared before me with all its aggravating circumstances of horror; and to any one who considers it, I believe it will appear that it was hardly possible to fill the bitter cup of calamity fuller.

In this state I was, when, to my utter astonishment, and to my no less joy, the companion of my shipwreck, Mr. Hall, appeared before me. I scarcely knew how to think his appearance reality, as I understood that the Lascars then along with me were all that were saved from the wreck, and he was, at the time I parted from him, so exhausted both in body and mind, that I thought he would be the last who could escape. He, however, shook me by the hand; and, sitting down, told me that he had given me up for lost, and remained with the vessel until the tide, having ebbed, left her almost dry: that, immediately on getting ashore, and being taken prisoner, he made inquiries about me; and heard that I had been saved· that, finding this, his joy was such as to make him almost forget his own misfortunes, and, exerting all his entreaties not to be separated from me, they had been so far indulgent to him, and had brought him to me, that we might be companions in bondage. He added, that out of eleven Europeans and fifty-six Lascars, who were on board, only he and I of the former, and fourteen of the latter were saved from the wreck, the rest being drowned in the attempt, excepting some who, overcome with terror, anguish and anxiety, and exhausted with fatigue, had bid a formal adieu to their companions, let go their hold, and calmly and voluntarily given themselves up to the deep.

My pleasure, however, at escaping shipwreck, was by no means as great as the agony my mind underwent, as the prospect now before me was poignant. The unmerciful disposition of Hyder, and all those in authority under him, and the cruel policy of the Eastern chiefs, making the life of any one, particularly a British prisoner, at the best a precarious tenure, I did not know the moment when death might be inflicted upon me, with perhaps a thousand aggravating circumstances. But the abject state of want and nakedness in which it seemed I was likely to remain struck a deep and damp horror to my heart, and almost unmanned me.

For some days we lay in this place, exposed to the weather, without even the slender comfort of a little straw to cover the ground beneath us—our food, boiled rice, served very sparingly twice a day, by an old woman, who just threw a handful or more of it to each, upon a very dirty board, which we devoured with those spoons nature gave us. At the end of that time, we, and along with us the Lascars, were ordered to proceed into the country, and drove on foot to a considerable distance, in order to render up an account of ourselves to persons belonging to Government authorized to take it. It was advanced in the morning when we moved, without receiving any sort of sustenance; and were marched in that wasting climate eight hours, without breaking our fast, during which time we were exposed alternately to the scorching rays of the sun, and heavy torrents of rain, which raised painful blisters on our skin; we had often to stand exposed to the weather, or to lie down, under the pressure of fatigue and weakness, on the bare ground; then wait an hour or more at the door of some insolent, unfeeling monster, until he finished his dinner, or took his afternoon nap; and when this was over, were driven forward with wanton barbarity by the people who attended us.

Two days after this, we were moved again, and marched up the country by a long and circuitous route, in which we underwent every hardship that cruelty could inflict, or human fortitude endure—now blistered with the heat, now drenched with rain, and now chilled with the night-damps—destitute of any place but the bare earth to rest, or lay our heads on, with only a scanty pittance of boiled rice for our support—often without water to quench our thirst, and constantly goaded by the guards, who pricked us with their bayonets every now and then, at once to evince their power entertain the spectators, and mortify us. We arrived at Hydernagur, the metropolis of the province of Biddanore—a fort of considerable strength, mounting upward of seventy guns, containing a large garrison of men, and possessed of immense wealth. It was about two o'clock in the morning when we arrived at Biddanore: the day was extremely hot, and we were kept out, under the full heat of that broiling sun, till six o'clock n the evening before we were admitted to an audience of the Jemadar, or governor of the place, without having a mouthful of victuals offered to us after the fatiguing march of the morning.

While we stood in the court, waiting to be brought before the Jemadar, we presented a spectacle that would have wrung pity, one would think from the heart of a tiger, if a tiger was endowed with reflection. At length we were summoned to appear before him, and brought into his presence. I had made up my mind for the occasion—determined to deport myself in a manly, candid manner—and to let no consideration whatsoever lead me to any thing disgraceful to my real character, or unworthy my situation in life; and, finally, had prepared myself to meet, without shrinking, whatever misfortunes might yet be in store for me, or whatever cruelties the barbarous disposition, or wicked policy, of the tyrant might think proper to inflict.

On entering, we found the Jemadar in full court He was then occupied with the reading of dispatches, and in transacting other public business. We were placed directly opposite to him, where we stood for near an hour, during which time he never cast his eyes toward us. But when at last he had concluded the business in which he was engaged, and deigned to look at us, we were ordered to prostrate ourselves before him: the Lascars immediately obeyed the order, and threw themselves on the ground; but I contented myself with making a salam, in which poor Mr. Hall, who knew not the Eastern manner as I did, followed my example.

As soon as this ceremony was over, the Jemadar (who was no other man than the famous Hyat Sahib,) began to question me. He desired to know who I was?—what my profession was?—what was the cause and manner of my approaching the country of Hyder Ali? To all those questions I gave answers that seemed to satisfy him. Having exhausted his whole string of questions, he turned the discourse to another subject, no less than his great and puissant Lord and Master, Hyder, of whom he had endeavored to impress me with a great if not terrible idea—amplifying his power, his wealth, and the extent and opulence of his dominions, and describing to me, in the most exaggerated terms, the number of his troops—his military talents—his vast, and, according to his account, unrivaled genius — his amazing abilities in conquering and governing nations—and, above all, his many amiable qualities and splendid endowments of heart, no less than understanding. He then vaunted of his sovereign's successes over the English, some of which I had not heard of before, and did not believe; and concluded by assuring me, that it was Hyder's determination to drive all Europeans from Hindoostan, which, he averred he could not fail to do, considering the weakness of the one, and boundless power of the other.

After having expended near half an hour in this manner, he called upon me to come over near him, and caused me to seat myself upon a mat, with a pillow to lean upon—encouraged me, by every means he could, by the most gentle accents, and the most soothing, mollifying language, to speak to him without the least reserve—exhorted me to tell him the truth in everything we spoke of—and hinted to me, that my falling into his hands might turn out the most fortunate event of my life. I was at a loss to what motive to attribute all those singular marks of indulgence; but found that he had learned whose son I was, and knew my father, by reputation, from the prisoners, our sepoys, who were now prisoners at large here: and as rank and office are the chief recommendations in the East, as elsewhere, or rather much more than any where else, the sagacious Hyat Sahib found many claims to esteem and humanity in me, as the son of a Colonel Campbell, which he never would have found in me, had I been the son of a plain, humble farmer, or tradesman in England.

After a full hour's audience, in which Hyat Sahib treated me with distinguished marks of his favor, considering my situation, he dismissed me with the ceremony of beetle-nut, rose-water, and other compliments, which are in that country held as the strongest marks of politeness, respect and good-will. Leaving the Durbar, I was led to the inner fort or citadel: and the officious zeal of those about me, unwilling to let me remain ignorant of that which they conceived to be a most fortunate turn in my affairs, gave the *coup de grace* to my miseries, as I went along, by congratulating me on the favorable opinion which the Jemadar had formed of me, and intimating, at the same time, that I would soon be honored with a respectable command in Hyder's service.

That night, the Jemadar sent me an excellent supper, of not less than six dishes, from his own table; and although I had been so long famishing with the want of wholesome food, the idea of being enlisted in the service of Hyder struck me with such horror, that I lost all appetite, and was scarcely able to eat a mouthful. Mr. Hall and I, however, were separated from the Lascars, who were released and forced to work.

Notwithstanding the favorable intentions manifested toward me by the Jemadar, as I have already mentioned, no mark of it whatsoever appeared in our lodging. This consisted of a small place, exactly the size of our length and breadth, in the zigzag of one of the gates of the citadel. It was open in front, but covered with a kind of shed on the top; and a number of other prisoners were about us. Each of us was allowed a mat and pillow, and this formed the whole of our local accommodations. Upon my remarking it, we were told that in conformity to the custom of the country, we must be treated so for some time, but that our accommodations would afterward be extended, and made more agreeable to our wishes: even this was better than our situation since we landed. In addition to this luxury, we were allowed to the value of four pence halfpenny a day for our maintenance; and a guard of sepoys was put over us and a few more prisoners, one of whom was directed to go and purchase our victuals, and do such offices for us.

In two or three days after this, Hyat Sahib sent for me, treated me with great kindness, gave me some tea, and furnished me with two or three shirts, an old coat, and two pairs of breeches, which were stripped from the dead bodies that were thrown ashore from the wreck—everything that was saved from it being sent to Biddanore. At this interview he treated me great respect—gave me, beside the articles already mentioned, thirty rupees, and, upon my going away, told me that in a few days a very flattering proposal would be made to me, and that my situation would be rendered not only comfortable, but enviable.

On the evening of that day, I was sent for to attend not at the Durbar, but at the house of a man high in office. As I expected to meet Hyat

Sahib himself, and trembled at the thoughts of his expected proposition, I was surprised, and indeed pleased, to find that it was with one of his people only, I was to have a conference. This man, whose name I now forget, received me with great kindness, encouraged me, made me sit down with him, and began to speak of Hyat Sahib, whom he extolled to the skies, as a person endowed with every great and amiable quality; informing me, at the same time, that he was possessed of the friendship and confidence of his master, Hyder Ali, in a greater degree than any other person—Tippoo Sahib, his own son, not excepted.

When he had finished his history of Hyat Sahib, which he overcharged with fulsome panegyric, he told me, with a face full of that triumphant importance which one who thinks he is conferring a great favor generally assumes, that it was the intention of Hyat Sahib, for and on behalf of his master, the Sultan, to give me the command of five thousand men—an offer which he supposed I could not think of declining, and therefore expected no other answer but a profusion of thanks, and strong manifestations of joy, on my part.

It is not possible for me to describe to you my dismay at this formal proposal, or portray to you the various emotions that took possession of my breast. Resentment had its share—the pride of the soldier, not unaccompanied with the pride of family and rank, while it urged me to spurn from me such a base accommodation, made me consider the offer as a great insult. I therefore paused a little to suppress my feelings, and then told him my firm resolution never to accept of such a proposal; and upon his expressing great astonishment at my declining a station so fraught with advantage, I laid down, in the best manner I could, my reasons; and I must say, that he listened to all the objections I started with great patience, but, in the conclusion, said he had little doubt of finding means to overcome my reluctance.

He dismissed me for the present, and I returned to my prison, where I related to my companion, Mr. Hall, everything that passed between us. We canvassed the matter fully, and he agreed with me that it was likely to turn out a most dreadful and cruel persecution. Piqued by the idea, I began to feel a degree of enthusiasm which I was before a stranger to. I looked forward with a kind of gloomy pleasure to the miseries that brutal tyranny might inflict upon me, even to death itself: and already began to indulge in the exultation of martyrdom. Indeed, I had wrought myself up to such a pitch of firmness, that I am persuaded the most exquisite and refined cruelties which the ingenuity of an Iroquois Indian could have inflicted on my body, would have been utterly incapable of bending the stubborn temper of my mind.

On the day succeeding that on which the agent of Hyat Sahib had held the discourse with me, I was again sent for, and brought to the same person, who asked me, whether I had duly considered of the important offer made me by Hyat Sahib, and of the consequences likely to result from a refusal? and he apprised me, at the same time, that the command of five thousand men was an honor which the first rajahs in the Mysorean dominions would grasp at with transport. I told him I was well convinced of the honor such a command would confer on any man but an Englishman, whose country, being then the subject of Hyder's incessant hostility would make the acceptance of it infamy and finally, appealed to the good sense of Hyat Sahib, whether a man who, in such circumstances, had betrayed his country, and sacrified her interests to his own convenience, was such a person as confidence could properly be put in.

Notwithstanding these and a thousand other remonstrances, he still continued to press me, and used every argument, every persuasion, that ingenuity could dictate, or hints of punishment enforce, to shake my purpose—but in vain: attachment to country and family rose paramount to all other considerations; and I gave a peremptory, decisive refusal.

Circumstanced as I was, it was impossible for me to keep an accurate journal of the various incidents that passed, or vicissitudes of thoughts that occurred, during the period of my imprisonment. Indeed, I was scarcely conscious of the length of my captivity, and could not, till I was released, determine exactly how long it had continued. I can only say, in general terms, that I was repeatedly urged on the subject by fair persuasives: they then had recourse to menace; then they withheld the daily pittance allowed for my support; and at length proceeded to coercion—tying a rope round my neck, and hoisting me up to a tree. All this, however, I bore firmly: if it had any effect, it was to confirm me in my resolution, and call in policy to the aid of honor's dictates. As the horrors of my situation thickened round me, I felt my spirits increase; my resolution became more firm, my hopes more sanguine—I even began to look forward, and form projects for the future: whole hours' amusement, every day and every night, arose from the contemplation of my beloved boy. I, in imagination, traced his growth, directed his rising sentiments, formed plans for his future success and prosperity, and indulged by anticipation in all the enjoyment which I now trust I shall yet have in his ripened manhood.

Thus we continued for many months, during which no alteration whatsoever took place in our treatment or situation. The only relief from our sufferings lay in the resources of our own minds, and in our mutual endeavors to please and console one another. The circumstances of aggravation were the necessity of daily bearing witness to the most barbarous punishments he inflicted upon wretched individuals, under the semblance of justice, and the occasional deprivation of our food, either by the fraud of the sepoys who attended us, or the caprice or cruelty of their superiors. It is but justice, however, to say that they were not all alike: some overflowed with mercy, charity, and the milk of human kindness; while others, again, were almost as bad men as the sovereigns they served. We were not allowed the use of pen, ink, or paper; and very seldom could afford ourselves the luxury of shaving or clean linen: nor were we at all sheltered from the inclemency of the weather, till at length a little room was built for us of mud, which, being small and damp, rendered our situation worse than it was before.

Projects and hopes of a new kind now began to intrude themselves on my thoughts; and I conceived a design, which I flattered myself was not entirely impracticable, to effect an escape, and even a revolt in the place, but, while I was settling this much to my own satisfaction, an event occurred which extinguished all my hopes in that way.

Whether the plan was discovered or not, or from what over motive it arose, I have not to this day been able to decide, but so it was, that while my sanguine mind was overflowing with the hope of carrying my project for an escape into effect, Mr. Hall and I were one day unexpectedly loaded with irons, and fastened together, leg by leg, by one bolt. The surprise occasioned by the appearance of the irons, and the precautionary manner in which it was undertaken, was indeed great: still more was I surprised to observe that the person who was employed to see this put in execution, manifested unusual emotions, seemed much affected, and even shed tears as he looked on: and while the suddenness and cautionary mode of doing it, convinced me that some resistance on our part was apprehended, the sorrow which the officer who superintended it disclosed, portended in my mind a fatal, or, at least, a very serious issue. Unfortunately, poor Mr. Hall had for some time been afflicted with a return of his dreadful disorder, the dysentery. From this unlucky event, I received a temporary depression; and his rapidly increasing illness rendered our situation more than ever calamitous. The disease soon fell upon him with redoubled fury: a very scanty portion of boiled rice, with a more scanty morsel of stinking salt fish, or putrid flesh, was a very inadequate support for me, who, though emaciated, was in health—and very improper medicine for a person laboring under a malady such as Mr. Hall's, which required comfort, good medical skill, and delicate, nutritious food. The tea which Hyat Sahib had given me was expended; and we were not allowed to be shaved from the hour we were put in irons, an indulgence of that kind being forbidden by the barbarous rules of the prison: and, to refine upon our tortures, sleep, "that balm of hurt minds," was not allowed us uninterrupted, for, in conformity to another regulation, we were disturbed every half-hour by a noise something resembling a watchman's rattle, and a fellow who, striking every part of our irons with a kind of hammer, and examining them lest they should be cut, broke in upon that kind restorative, and awoke our souls to fresh horrors.

Poor Hall was now approaching to his end with hourly accelerated steps. Every application that I made in his favor was refused, or rather treated with cruel neglect and contemptuous silence. Hyat Sahib, the powerful, the wealthy, the governor of a great opulent province, refused to an expiring fellow-creature a little cheap relief—while a poor sepoy taxed his little means to supply it: one who guarded us, of his own accord, at imminent hazard of punishment, purchased us a lamp and a little oil, which we burned for the last few nights, till my dear friend died, exhausted by disease, neglect, and cruelty.

In the morning a report was made to the commandant of the death of Mr. Hall; and in about an hour afterward he passed me by, but kept his face purposely turned away from me to the other side. I patiently waited for the removal of the dead body till the evening, when I desired the sepoys who guarded me to apply for its being removed. They returned, and told me they could get no answer respecting it. Night came on, but there was no appearance of an intention to unfetter me from the corpse. The commandant was sitting in his court, administering, in the manner I have before described, *justice!* I called out to him myself, with all my might, but could get no answer from him. Nothing could equal my rage and consternation; for, exclusive of the painful idea of being shackled to the dead body of a friend I loved, another circumstance contributed to make it a serious subject of horror. In those climates the weather is so intensely hot, that putrefaction almost instantly succeeds death, and meat that is killed in the morning, and kept in the shade, will be unfit for dressing at night. In a subject, then, on which putrefaction had made advances even before death, and which remained exposed to the open air, the process must have been much more rapid. So far, however, from compassionating my situation, or indulging me by a removal of the body, their barbarity suggested to them to make it an instrument of punishment; and they pertinaciously adhered to the most mortifying silence and disregard of my complaints. For several days and nights it remained attached to me by the irons. I grew almost distracted—wished for the means of putting an end to my miseries by death, and could not move without witnessing some new stage of putrescence it attained, or breathe without inhaling the putrid effluvia that arose from it—while myriads of flies and loathsome insects rested on it, the former of which every now and then visited me, crawling over my face and hands, and lighting in hundreds on my victuals.

At last, when the body had reached that shocking, loathsome state of putrefaction, which threatened that further delay would render removal abominable, if not impossible, the monsters agreed to take it away from me, and I was so far relieved: but the mortification and injury I underwent from it, joined to the agitation of the preceding week, made a visible inroad on my health. I totally lost my spirits; my appetite entirely forsook me: my long nourished hopes fled; and I looked forward to death as the only desirable event that was within the verge of likelihood or possibility. One day I perceived a more than usual bustle in the citadel, while the sepoys informed me that they were ordered on immediate service, and that some events of great importance had taken place. In a day or two the bustle increased to a high pitch, accompanied with marks of consternation: the whole of the troops in the citadel were ordered to march, and the commandant, and a man with a hammer and instrument, came to take off my irons.

I was utterly at a loss to conjecture what this so sudden resolution to release me meant. I endeavored to get some explanation of it from the persons about me; but all I could at the time collect, was that the Jemadar had directed me to be taken out of irons, and ordered me to appear before him. As we proceeded forward, we found, at some distance from the fort, an open dooly, into which the guards forcibly crammed me; and I was carried off, still attended by the same men. As we went along, they gave me to understand that Hyat Sahib, the Jemadar, was at a place ten or a dozen miles distant from Biddanore, I thought it within myself a most extraordinary circumstance, and was at a loss to conjecture for what purpose he required my presence there.

When we had got about a mile from the fort, we met a person attended by three others, all on horseback. He was a man of considerable rank in that country, and I recollected to have seen him at the Jemadar's court, where he had manifested a favorable disposition toward me, looking always graciously, and nodding to me, which, considering my circumstances and his, was not a little extraordinary. The moment he recognized me, he leaped from his horse, apparently in great agitation: then, turning to the guards, ordered them to leave me immediately—saying, at the same time, that he would be answerable for the consequences. They seemed, at first, to hesitate whether to obey him or not: but on his shaking at them his sword, which was all along drawn in his hand, and smeared with blood, and repeating his orders a second time, in a firm and decisive tone of voice and manner, they all ran off.

As soon as we were alone, he revealed to me, that he had all along known who I was—had most heartily pitied my sufferings, and privately entertained the most anxious wishes to serve me, but could not venture to interfere—the least jealousy, when once awakened, being there always followed up by summary vengeance. He then mentioned his name, informing me that he was the son of a Nabob near Vellore, whose dominions had been wrested from him by force, and united to the Carnatic; that his family had received great favors from my father, in return for which he felt himself bound to do me every service in his power; but that, having been, after the misfortunes which befell his family, taken into the service of Hyder, and holding then a place of consequence under him, he was disqualified from demonstrating his gratitude and esteem in the way he wished. Here he stopped, and seemed much agitated; but, recovering himself soon, said in a solemn and alarming manner, "This day I heard Hyat Sahib give orders to bring you before him, in order that he might satiate his revenge by your death! How happy am I in having an opportunity to rescue you! I will carry you back with me, therefore, to Biddanore, and place you in a state of security with my family."

Just as I was on the point of returning with him to Hydernagur, we were startled by the Jemadar's music, which was soon afterward succeeded by the appearance of his guards, advancing toward us at some distance. He seemed confounded and alarmed—lamented, in warm terms, his incapacity to serve me—and pointed to a path which wound through a wood that lay on either side of the road, directed me to strike into it immediately, saying that by following that route I should certainly fall in with the British army. He then rode away, and I followed his advice, and proceeded for some time through the wood without interruption; for, though I did not implicitly believe the assertion that Hyat Sahib meant to have cut me off, I deemed it prudent to avail myself of the opportunity which offered to effect my escape, apprehending a worse fate than death, namely, being sent prisoner to Seringapatam.

The nearest English post to which I could make my escape, was the successful little army under General Matthews—an old friend of my father's, and a person with whom I had served in the cavalry soon after I entered the service. When I arrived he was fast asleep, upon the bare ground, in a tent. His servant, whose name was Snake, recollected me immediately, and was much frightened at my appearance, for it was full five months since my hair and beard were both shaved at the same time, during which period a comb had never touched my head. I had no hat, no stockings, was clad in a pair of very ragged breeches, a shirt which was so full of holes that it resembled rather a net than a web of cloth, and a waistcoat which had been made for a man twice my size—while my feet were defended from the stones only by a pair of Indian slippers. Snake, as soon as he was able to conquer his terror, and stop the loquacious effusions of astonishment, brought me to the General, who expressed great surprise at so unexpected a meeting.

The sudden change of diet which I experienced on my restoration to liberty, had a most sudden and alarming effect upon my constitution; and I was soon seized with the most excruciating internal pains, which were succeeded by a violent vomiting of blood. I felt as if my inside was utterly decayed, and all its functions lost in debility: at the same time my head seemed deranged—I could scarcely comprehend the meaning of what was said; lifting up my head was attended with agonizing pain; and if I had any power of thought, it was to consider myself as approaching fast to dissolution. Tranquillity, kind treatment, and good medical assistance, produced, in the space of two or three weeks, so material a change in my health, that I was soon in a condition to return to my usual duties.

THE CAPTIVITY

OF

THOMAS ANDROS,

SINCE PASTOR OF THE CHURCH AT BERKELEY, MASS., ON BOARD

THE OLD JERSEY PRISON SHIP.

I WAS but in my seventeenth year when the revolutionary struggle commenced, and no politician; but even a schoolboy could see the justice of some of the principles, on the ground of which the country had recourse to arms. The colonies had arrived at the age of manhood. They were fully competent to govern themselves, and they demanded their freedom, or, at least, a just representation in the national legislature. For a power three thousand miles distant to claim a right to make laws to bind us in all cases whatever, and we to have no voice in that legislation, this, it seemed, was a principle to which two millions of freemen ought not tamely to submit. And as all petitions and remonstrances availed nothing, and as the British government, instead of the charter of our liberties and rights, sent her fleets and armies to enforce her arbitrary claims, the colonies had no alternative but slavery or war. Appealing to Almighty God for the justice of their cause, they chose the latter. Whether I approved the motives that led me into the service, is another question, which I shall presently notice.

In the summer of 1781, the ship Hannah, a very rich prize, was captured, and brought into the port of New London. But in this case it was far worse than in common lottery-gambling, for it followed that there were thousands of fearful blanks to this one prize. It infatuated great numbers of young men, who flocked on board our private armed ships, fancying the same success would attend their adventures; but no such prize was ever after brought into that port. But New London became such a nest of privateers, that the English determined on its destruction. They sent an armament and laid it in ashes, took Fort Griswold, on the Groton side of the river, and, with savage cruelty, put the garrison to the sword, after they had surrendered. Another mighty blank to this prize, was, that our privateers so swarmed on the ocean, that the British cruisers, who were everywhere in pursuit of them, soon filled their prisons at New York to overflowing, with captured American seamen.

Among these deluded and infatuated youth, I was one. I entered a volunteer on board a new brig, called the Fair American, built on purpose to prey upon the British commerce. She mounted sixteen carriage guns, and was manned with a crew, whose numbers exceeded what was really her complement. The quarter-deck, tops, and long-boat, were crowded with musketry, so that in action she was a complete flame of fire.

We had not been long at sea, before we discovered and gave chase to an English brig, as long as ours, and, in appearance, mounting as many guns. As we approached her, she saluted us with her stern-chasers, but after exchanging a few shots, we ran directly alongside, as near as we could, and not get entangled in her top-hamper, and with one salute of all the fire we could display, put her to silence. And, thanks be to God, no lives were lost.

I, with others, went on board, to man the prize, and take her into port. But the prize-master disobeyed orders. His orders were, not to approach the American coast till he had reached the longitude of New Bedford, and then to haul up to the northward, and, with a press of sail, to make for that port—but he aimed to make land on the back of Long Island: the consequence was, we were captured on the 27th of August, by the Solebay frigate, and safely stowed away in the old Jersey prison ship, at New York.

This was an old sixty-four gun-ship, which, through age, had become unfit for further actual service. She was stripped of every spar, and all her rigging. After a battle with a French fleet, her lion figure-head was taken away, to repair another ship; no appearance of ornament was left, and nothing remained but an old, unsightly, rotten hulk. Her dark and filthy external appearance, perfectly corresponded with the death and despair that reigned within, and nothing could be more foreign from truth than to paint her with colors flying, or any circumstance or appendage to please the eye. She was moored about three-quarters of a mile to the eastward of Brooklyn Ferry, near a tide-mill on the Long Island shore. The nearest distance to land was about twenty rods. And, doubtless, no other ship in the British navy ever proved the means of the destruction of so many human beings. It is computed that no less than eleven thousand American seamen perished in her. But after it was known that it was next to certain death to confine a prisoner here, the inhumanity and wickedness of doing it was about the same as if he had been taken into the city, and deliberately shot in some public square. Once or twice, by the order of a stranger on the quarter-deck, a bag of apples was hurled promiscuously into the midst of hundreds of prisoners crowded together as thick as they could stand, and life and limbs were endangered by the scramble. This, instead of compassion, was a cruel sport. When I saw it about to commence, I fled to the most distant part of the ship.

On the commencement of the first evening, we were driven down to darkness between decks, secured by iron gratings and an armed soldiery· and a scene of horror, which baffles all description, presented itself. On every side wretched, desponding shapes of men could be seen. Around the well-room, an armed guard were forcing up the prisoners to the winches, to clear the ship of water, and prevent her sinking, and little else could be heard but a roar of mutual execrations, reproaches, and insults. During this operation, there was a small dim light admitted below, but it served to make darkness more visible, and horror more terrific.

When I first became an inmate of this abode of suffering, despair and death, there were about four hundred prisoners on board, but in a short time they amounted to twelve hundred. And, in proportion to our numbers, the mortality increased. All the most deadly diseases were pressed into the service of the King of Terrors, but his prime ministers were dysentery, smallpox, and yellow fever. There were two hospital-ships near to the Old Jersey, but these were soon so crowded with the sick, that they could receive no more. The consequence was, that the diseased and the healthy were mingled together in the main ship. In a short time we had two hundred, or more, sick and dying, lodged in the forepart of the lower gun-deck, where all the prisoners were confined at night. Utter derangement was a common symptom of yellow fever, and to increase the horror of the darkness that shrouded us, (for we were allowed no light between decks,) the voice of warning would be heard, "Take heed to yourselves. There is a madman stalking through the ship with a knife in his hand!" I sometimes found the man a corpse in the morning, by whose side I laid myself down at night. At another time he would become deranged, and attempt, in darkness, to rise and stumble over the bodies that everywhere covered the deck. In this case, I had to hold him in his place by main strength. In spite of my efforts he would sometimes rise, and then I had to close in with him, trip up his heels, and lay him again upon the deck. While so many were sick with raging fever, there was a loud cry for water, but none could be had, except on the upper deck, and but one allowed to ascend at a time. The suffering, then, from the rage of thirst during the night, was very great; nor was it at all times safe to attempt to go up. Provoked by the continual cry fo leave to ascend, when there was already one on deck, the sentry would push them back with his bayonet. By one of these thrusts, which was more spiteful and violent than common, I had a narrow escape of my life. In the morning the hatchways were thrown open, and we were allowed to ascend, all at once, and remain on the upper-deck during the day. But the first object that met our view in the morning, was an appalling spectacle—a boat loaded with dead bodies, conveying them to the Long Island shore, where they were very slightly covered with sand. I sometimes used to stand to count the number of times the shovel was filled with sand to cover a dead body; and certain I am that a few high tides, or torrents of rain, must have disinterred them. And had they not been removed, I should suppose the shore, even now, would be covered with huge piles of the bones of American seamen. There were, probably, four hundred on board who had never had the smallpox—some, perhaps, might have been saved by inoculation.

Now and then an American physician was brought in as a captive, but if he could obtain his parole, he left the ship; nor could we much blame him for this—for his own death was next to certain, and his success in saving others by medicine, in our situation, was small. I remember only two American physicians who tarried on board a few days. No English physician, or any one from the city, ever, to my knowledge, came near us There were thirteen of the crew to which I belonged; but in a short time all but three or four were dead. The most healthy and vigorous were first seized with the fever, and died in a few hours. For them, there seemed to be no mercy. My constitution was less muscular and plethoric, and I escaped the fever longer than any of the thirteen, except one, and the first onset was less violent.

There is one palliating circumstance, as to the inhumanity of the British, which ought to be mentioned. The prisoners were furnished with buckets and brushes to cleanse the ship, and with vinegar to sprinkle her inside. But their indolence and despair were such, that they would not use them, or but rarely. And, indeed, at this time, the encouragement to do it was small. For the whole ship, from the keel to the tafferel, was equally affected, and contained pestilence sufficient to desolate a world—disease and death were wrought into her very timbers. At the time I left, it is to be presumed a more filthy, contagious, and deadly abode for human beings never existed among a Christianized people. It fell but little short of the Black Hole at Calcutta. Death was more lingering, but almost equally certain.

The lower hold and the orlop-deck were such a terror, that no man would venture down into them. Humanity would have dictated a more merciful treatment to a band of pirates, who had been condemned, and were only awaiting the gibbet, than to have sent them here. But, in the view of the English, we were rebels and traitors. Our water was good, could we have had enough of it; our bread was bad in the superlative degree. I do not recollect seeing any which was not full of living vermin; but eat it, worms and all, we must, or starve. The prisoners had laws and regulations among themselves. In severity they were like the laws of Draco—woe to him that dared to trample them under foot. A secret, prejudicial to a prisoner, revealed to the guard, was death. Captain Young, of Boston, concealed himself in a large chest, belonging to a sailor going to be exchanged, and was carried on board the cartel, and we considered his escape as certain; but the secret leaked out, and he was brought back; and one Spicer, of Providence, being suspected as the traitor, the enraged prisoners were about to take his life. His head was drawn back, and the knife raised to cut his throat; but, having obtained a hint of what was going on below, the guard at this instant rushed down, and rescued the man. Of his guilt, at the time, there was to me, at least, no convincing evidence. It is a pleasure now to reflect that I had no hand in the outrage.

If there was any principle among the prisoners that could not be shaken, it was the love of their country. I knew no one to be seduced into the British service. They attempted to force one of our prize brig's crew into the navy; but he chose rather to die than perform any duty, and he was again restored to the prison ship. Another rule, the violation of which would expose the offender to great danger, was, not to touch the provisions belonging to another mess. This was a common cause, and if any one complained that he was robbed, it produced an excitement of no little terror.

As to religion, I do not remember of beholding any trace of it in the ship. I saw no Bible—heard no prayer—no religious conversation—no clergyman visited us, though no set of afflicted and dying men more needed the light and consolations of religion. But the Bethel flag had not yet waved over any ship. I know not that God's name was ever mentioned, unless it was in profaneness and blasphemy; but as every man had almost the certain prospect of death before him, no doubt there were more or less who, in their own minds, like myself, had some serious thoughts of their accountability, of a future state, and of a judgment to come; but, as to the main body, it seemed that when they most needed religion, they treated it with the greatest contempt.

While on board, almost every thought was occupied to invent some plan of escape; but day after day passed, and none presented that I dared to put in execution. But the time had now come when I must be delivered from the ship or die. It could not be delayed even a few days longer; but no plan could I think of that offered a gleam of hope. If I did escape with my life, I could see no way for it but by a miracle. If I continued on board a few days, or even hours longer, the prospect was certain death; for I was now seized with the yellow fever, and should unavoidably take the natural smallpox with it; and who does not know that I could not survive the operation of both these diseases at once? I had never experienced the latter disease in any way, and it was now beginning to rage on board the Old Jersey, and none could be removed. The hospital-ships being already full of the sick, the pox was nearly ripe in the pustules of some; and I not only slept near them, but assisted in nursing those who had the symptoms most violently. In a very short time my doom must have been settled, had I remained in the ship.

The arrival of a cartel, and my being exchanged, would not help the matter, but render my death the more sure. When a list of the names of the prisoners was called for, on board the frigate by which we were captured, I stepped up and gave in my name first, supposing that, in case of an exchange, I should be the sooner favored with this privilege. And the fact, indeed, was, that no exchanges took place but from the port of New London. And former exchanges had left me first on the roll of captives from this port; and I dreaded nothing more than the arrival of a cartel, for numbers would be put on board and sent home from the hospital-ships, whose flesh was ready to fall from their bones in this dreadful disease; and, indeed, I had no sooner made my escape than a cartel did arrive, and such dying men were actually crowded into it; and it was evidently the policy of the English to return, for sound and healthy men sent from our prisons, such Americans as had just the breath of life in them, and were sure to die before they reached home. The guard were wont to tell a man while in health, "You have not been here long enough—you are too well to be exchanged." There was yet one more conceivable method of getting from the ship, and that was, the next night to steal down through a gun-port, which we had managed to open when we pleased, unbeknown to the guard, and swim ashore. But this was a most forlorn hope; for I was under the operation of the yellow fever and but just able to walk, and when well I could never swim ten rods, and would now have at least twenty to swim. Beside, when in the water, there was almost a certainty I should be discovered by the guard and shot as others had been. In this situation what wisdom, or what finite power could save me? If I tarried on board, I must perish! If put on board the cartel, every hour expected, I must perish! If I attempted to swim away, I must be lost!

Mr. Emery, the sailing-master, was just now going ashore after water. Without really considering what I said, and without the least expectation of success, I thus addressed him, "Mr. Emery, may I go on shore with you after water?" My lips seemed to move almost involuntarily, for no such thing to my knowledge had ever been granted to such a prisoner. To the surprise and astonishment of all that heard him, he replied, "Yes, with all my heart." I then descended immediately into the boat, which was in waiting for him. But the prisoners came to the ship's side and queried, "What is that sick man going on shore for?" And the British sailors endeavored to dissuade me from it, but never was counsel so little regarded as theirs, and to put them all to silence I again ascended on board; but even this was an interposition of a kind Providence, for I had neglected to take my great-coat, without which I must have perished in cold and storms. But I now put it on, and waited for the sailing-master, meaning to step down again into the boat just before him, which I did, and turned my face away, that I might not be recognised, and another attempt be made to prevent my going. The boat was pushed off, and we were soon clear of the ship. I took an oar, and attempted to row, but an English sailor took it from me, and very kindly said, "Give me that oar, you are not able to use it; you are too unwell." I resigned it, and gave up myself to the most intense thought upon my situation. I had commenced the execution of a plan, in which, if I failed, my life was gone; but if I succeeded, it was possible I might live. I looked back to the black and unsightly old ship, as an object of the greatest horror. "Am I to escape, or return there and perish," was with me the all-absorbing question. And now we had ascended the creek, and arrived at the spring where the casks were to be filled, and I proposed to the sailors to go in quest of apples. I had before told them that this was my object in coming on shore, but they chose to defer it till the boat was loaded; and they did not exact any labor of me. This was just as I would have it. I thought I could do quite as well without their company as with it.

The sailing-master, passing by me, very kindly remarked, "The fresh air will be of service to you." This emboldened me to ask leave to ascend the bank, a slope of about forty-five degrees and thirty feet in height, terminating in a plain of considerable extent, and to call at a house near by for some refreshment. He said, "Go, but take care and not be out of the way." I replied, "My state of health was such that there was nothing to fear on that score." But here, I confess, I violated a principle of honor for which I could not then, nor can I now entirely excuse myself. I feel a degree of conscious meanness for treating a man thus, who put confidence in me, and treated me in such a manner as showed he was a gentleman of sensibility and kindness. But the love of life was my temptation; but this principle is always too great, when it tempts us to violate any principle of moral rectitude and honor. And should I even now learn that my escape involved him in any trouble, it would be a matter of deep regret. Not long after my arrival at home, I sent him my apology for what I did, by a British officer, who was exchanged, and going directly to New York.

When the boat returned, the inquiry was made by the prisoners, (as I was afterward informed,) "Where is the sick man that went with you?" The English sailors consoled themselves with this reply, "Ah, he is safe enough, he will never live to go a mile." They did not know what the Sovereign of life and death could enable a sick man to do. Intent on the business of escape, I surveyed the landscape all around. I discovered at the distance of a half a mile, what appeared to be a dense swamp of young maples and other bushes. On this I fixed as my hiding-place; but how should I get to it without being discovered and apprehended before I could reach it? I had reason to think the boat's crew would keep an eye upon me; and people were to be seen at a distance in almost every direction. But there was an orchard which extended a good way toward the swamp, and while I wandered from tree to tree, in this orchard, I should not be suspected of anything more than searching after fruit. But at my first entrance into it I found a soldier on sentry, and I had to find out what his business was, and soon discovered he had nothing to do with me, but only to guard a heap of apples; and I now gradually worked myself off to the end of the orchard next to the swamp, and, looking round on every side, I saw no person from whom I might apprehend immediate danger.

The boat's crew being yet at work under the bank of the creek, and out of sight, I stepped off deliberately, (for I was unable to run, and had I been able, it would have tended to excite suspicion in any one that might have seen me, even at a distance,) and having forded the creek once or twice, I reached the swamp in safety. I soon found a place which seemed to have been formed by nature for concealment. A huge log, twenty feet in length, having laid there for many years, was spread over, on both sides, with such a dense covering of green running briers as to be impervious to the eye. Lifting up this covering at one end, I crept in close by the log, and rested comfortably and securely, for I was well defended from the north-east storm, which soon commenced.

When the complete darkness of the night had set in, and while raining in torrents, I began to feel my way out. And though but just able to walk, and though often thrown all along into the water, by my clothes getting entangled with the bushes, yet I reached the dry land, and endeavored to shape my course for the east end of Long Island. In this I was assisted by finding how New York bore from me, by the sound of ship-bells, and the din of labor and activity, even at that late time of night. Here let me remark, how easy it is with God to cause men to do good, when they intend no such thing. Without any great-coat, it would have been scarcely possible to have survived the tempest of rain and cold of this night in the month of October. But had not the prisoners endeavored to prevent my going in the boat and caused me to ascend again into the ship, I should have left it behind. Little did I then think what good heaven meant to bestow on me, by the trouble they then gave me.

I soon fell into a road that seemed to lead the right way, and when, during the night, I perceived I was about to meet any one, my constant plan was to retire to a small distance from the path, and roll myself up as well as I could to resemble a small bunch of bushes, or fern. By this expedient I was often saved from recapture. This road soon brought me into a quiet, populous village, which was resounding with drums and fifes, and full of soldiers; but, in great mercy to me, it rained in torrents, so I passed through, in the midst of the street, in safety. Being sick and greatly exhausted by the adventures of the day and night, it now became absolutely necessary to seek a place of rest, and a barn to me was now the only place in which I dared to enter. I stepped up to the door, of what I took to be such a building, and was just about to open it, when my eye was arrested by a white streak on the threshold, which I found to be the light reflected from a candle, and I heard human voices within. But human voices were now to me the object of the greatest terror, and I fled with all the speed I possessed. Coming to another barn, I discovered a high stack of hay in the yard, covered with a Dutch cap: I ascended and sunk myself down deep in the hay, supposing I had found a most comfortable retreat. But how miserably was I deceived! The weather had now cleared up, and the wind blew strong and cold from the north-west, and the hay was nothing but coarse sedge, and the wind passed into it and reached me as if I had no protection from it. I had not a dry thread in my clothes, and my sufferings from this time, to about eleven o'clock the next day, were great—too great even for health, but I had to encounter them under the operation of a malignant fever, which would have confined me to my room, if not to my bed, had I been at home.

A young woman came into the yard and milked a cow, just at the foot of the tower where I lay concealed: but I had no eye to pity, or kind hand to alleviate my distress. This brought home, with all the tender charities of mother, sister, and brothers, to my recollection, with a sensibility I could feel, but cannot describe. The day was clear and grew more moderate, and the coast being clear, also, I left my cold and wretched retreat, and deliberately made off for the woods, at the distance of half a mile. Before I left the ship I had seen prisoners who had escaped, retaken and carried back. But their mistake was, they would go two, or more, in company. But I would have no companion, it would excite suspicion, and render concealment more difficult, and, under the kind providence of God, I chose to be my own counselor, and to have none to fall out with on the way, as to what course we should pursue.

Having entered the woods, I found a small, but deep, dry hollow, clear of brush in the center, though surrounded with a thicket on every side. Into this the sun shone with a most delightful warmth. Here I stripped myself naked, and spread out my clothes to dry. Being too impatient of delay, I regained the road just as the sun was setting, but it came near proving fatal; for I discovered, just ahead, two light dragoons coming down upon me. At first it seemed escape was impossible. But that God, who gave me a quickness of thought in expedients, that seemed to go quite beyond myself, was present with his kind aid. I now happened to be near a small cottage, and a cornfield adjoining the road, I feigned myself to be the man of that cottage, the owner of that cornfield. And getting over the fence, I went about the field, deliberately picking up the ears of corn that had fallen down, and righting up the cap-sheaf of a stack of stalks. The dragoons came nigh, eyed me carefully, though I affected to take no notice of them, and passed on. They were probably in search of me.

I had lost my hat overboard, when in the Old Jersey, and had henceforward to cover my head with a handkerchief. I deemed it a calamity at the time, but, as an act of Providence, the mystery now began to be unfolded. Having no hat, but a handkerchief about my head, helped to deceive the dragoons, and cause them to think I was the cottager, who owned the corn-field. To lie concealed during the day, and to travel at night, was my practice, till I had got far toward the east end of the island. For several days I had not taken any nourishment, but water and apples. I found late pears, and was pleased with their taste, but they operated as an emetic, quicker than ipecacuanha. A subacid apple sat well on my stomach, and was very refreshing, though had I been sick at home, with the same disease, I should probably have been denied this favor. Indeed, from what I experienced in the free use of water, ripe fruit, unfermented cider, found at the presses, etc., I was led to suspect, that a great deal of the kind nursing of persons in fever, was an unnecessary and cruel kind of self-denial. But I supposed nature would sink without some other kind of aliment. But the first attempt to act upon this principle would have proved fatal, had it not been for a kind providential interference.

Late in the evening, I stepped up to a house on the road, and lifted my hand to rap, but the door folded inward, and evaded my stroke, and a lady appeared with a light in her hand. I besought of her a draught of milk: she replied, "that there was then a guard of soldiers in the house, and they had consumed it all." The business of this guard was to keep a look-out toward the Long Island sound, and their sentries were on the opposite side of the house. Had I rapped and been met by one of this guard, instead of the lady, what would have been the result? And by whose arrangement did the incident so happen that I escaped? Pursuing my journey, I came to a place where the road parted. One branch turned off through a lofty grove of wood; the other ascended a gentle rise toward a house near by. I knew not which to take; but that leading toward the house best suited my general course. But coming up near the house, there issued forth from the out-buildings a greater kennel of dogs than I had ever before seen, and assaulted me with a furious yelling. I stopped short, drew up my hands as far as I could out of their reach, and stood still. They snapped at me very spitefully, with their jaws within a few inches of my body. And now what should I do? To have attacked them, or fled precipitately, would have been instant destruction. I concluded to take no notice of them, but to turn about gently and take the other road, as if there was no such creature in the world as a dog. I did so, and they followed me for about twenty rods, snapping at me, and seeming to say, "You shall not escape; we will have a taste of your blood." And in this design, there seemed to be a perfect union, from the great bow-wow down to the yelping spaniel. But at last they all ceased to roar, bid me a good night and disappeared.

Had I ventured into the habitations of men, instead of those of the horned ox, my escape had been impossible. Soon after escaping the fury of the dogs, in this peaceful abode, I took up my lodgings for the night. A man coming into it in the morning, I made bold to slide down from the hay-loft; and, after making some apology for trespassing upon his premises, I asked him if it was probable I could get some refreshment in the house. He seemed to think I could. I then entered the house, and stated my wants; but as I did not design to be a mean, dishonest beggar, first get what I wanted, and then say I had nothing to pay, or sneak off, and say nothing about pay, I told the family I had but three coppers with me, so that if they gave me meat or drink, it must be done merely on the score of charity. But the woman seemed to be thinking more about providing something for the relief of a wretched sufferer, as I must have appeared to her, than about money. But the old man was troublesome with his questions. He said it was but a few days ago, two men called at his house, and told a story, which was found to be all false; and at last he observed, outright, "I believe *thee* also is a rogue"—but the woman would, now and then, as he pressed hard upon me, check him, and say, "Do let him alone." She had no questions to ask—all she wanted was to feed me; and, had it not been for her, I know not what the crabbed old man would have done with me.

After I had taken my refreshment, I said to the old man, "I thank you for your kindness—here are three coppers, all I have to carry me a long journey." He did not take them, but said, "You may give them to that little girl." She took them; but if she was illiberal and mean, the old man made her so. I left the house, and going a short distance, a spacious plain opened to my view; and on it, by the tents I saw, I concluded there was an encampment of soldiers. I, therefore, turned aside into the field, ascended a stack of rye, covered with a Dutch cap, and here I remained all the day, it being very stormy; but in the evening I looked out from my hiding-place, and behold, a most lovely moonshine had succeeded the storm. The tents had all disappeared, and I took up my journey over the plain. Some time in the latter part of the night, I reached the east end of it, and saw before me a number of buildings, though before this, I had not seen any on the plain. But no sooner had I come up to the first house, than I was drawn into a scene of the utmost peril. In the midst of the road there was a blacksmith's shop; on the north side there was a lane forming a right-angle with the road, and leading up to a house about twelve rods from it. To the westward of the house, about eight rods distant, stood the barn, and a lane leading from the house to it; and the square, three sides of which were formed by the road and these two lanes, was the garden; and, in the corner of this garden, near to the house, I discovered a number of beehives, and I coveted some of the honey. I went first up to the house, and, though the door was open, I saw no light, and heard no noise. But I deemed it prudent not to climb over the fence, just at the door of the house, to get at the bees, but to take the lane down to the barn, and there to get into the garden, and come up, under cover of the fence, to the bee-house. This I did not then call stealing, for I was in an enemy's land, and might make prize of whatever I could lay my hand upon.

Having just stepped into the barn-yard, and not suspecting the least danger, I saw a great number of horses tied all around the yard, with all their manes and docks cut in uniform. I stood motionless for a moment, and began to say to myself, "What does this mean? Can one farmer own so many horses?" But before the thought was finished, and as unexpected as a flash of lightning in a clear day, a dragoon coming out of the barn, with his burnished steel glittering in the bright rays of the moon, stepped up to me, and challenged, "Who comes there?" I answered, "A friend." But before he could say to whom, a plan of escape must be formed, and put in execution. It was formed, and succeeded. Before he could ask the second question, I called out, as if I were angry, "Where is the well? I want to get some water!" Taking me, from this seemingly honest and fearless query, to be one of the party, he showed me the well, and I went to it deliberately, drew water, and escaped out of his hands. The fact was, as I soon found, this was a detachment of horse and foot going out on the island for forage, to be conveyed to the army at New York, and, doubtless, he supposed me to be a person, a wagoner, perhaps, attached to it. And here again I found the great advantage of losing my hat. Having a handkerchief tied about my head, helped me in the deception.

After leaving the well, I went down the lane into the road, near the blacksmith's shop. At this moment four of the party came out from behind the opposite side of the shop, in full view, at the distance of about three rods from me. I stood motionless, and said to myself, "All is now lost." But their attention was taken up with a small dog, with which they were sporting. But as they did not come at once, and seize me in the brightness of the moonlight, I began again to conceive hope, and edged away to the fence, and rolled through between the two lower rails. Soon afterward the men said, "Let us go to the barn, and turn in," and immediately disappeared. Their sporting with the dog, in itself, was a trifling circumstance, but to me it was a great event. It saved my life—to me, in the hour of despair, it brought deliverance.

Stretching along as close as I could lie to the lower rail of the fence, I took a little time to survey my situation on all sides, and to discover, if I could, any opening for escape. If I attempted to save myself by going into the open field, I must be discovered by the sentries, and picked up by a dragoon. If I remained where I was, it would soon be daylight, and I could not be mistaken for one of the party. About thirty rods ahead, I discovered a large house, illuminated from the ground-floor to the garret. This, I was sure, must be the main bivouac of both infantry and horse, and wagons were in numbers passing on to this house. At last I hit upon this plan, when another wagon should pass, I would rise, and lay hold of it behind, and let it carry me forward into the midst of the party, and they would suppose me to belong to it. The driver sitting under cover, forward, could not be able to see me. When the next wagon passed, I attempted to get hold of it, but could not overtake it, and was left alone in the middle of the road, and considerably advanced toward the house just mentioned as the general rendezvous. And now, as no other mode of escape offered, I resolved to walk boldly and leisurely into and through the midst of the throng of men and horses, and wagons and sentries, and pass away if I could. The plan succeeded—I passed fearlessly, with great deliberation, erect and firm, without any shyness, through the midst of them. Some eyed me carefully, yet no one said, "Who art thou?"—and I was soon out of sight, and hid in a dense prim-bush fence, lest a suspicion should arise that a strange man had passed, and a dragoon should pursue me.

Twenty miles further to the eastward, I narrowly escaped falling again into the hands of the same party. Had I not, without any knowledge or intention of my own, happened to take another road, I should have met them in full march on their return; and, being in the day-time, escape would have been next to impossible. As it was, my road brought me on to the ground where, the night before, they had chosen to bivouac, and I found their fires still burning. After leaving my hiding-place in the prim fence, I soon found myself in a large orchard, in quest of fruit. I had examined nearly every tree, and found none. But just as I was about to give up the search, I lit upon a tree where the ground was covered with the fairest and richest species of apple I ever tasted. They refreshed me as if they had been gathered from paradise, having neither eaten nor drank anything for a considerable time. How all the other fruit in the orchard should have been gathered in, and the produce of this uncommonly excellent tree left, struck me as a mystery. It was no miracle, but it was a mercy to a wretched sufferer, then burning up with fever and thirst. I now sought for and took up my lodgings in the birth-place of my Saviour.

Prosecuting my journey on a succeeding evening, I happened to lie opposite to a house standing a little out of the road. Before I was aware of the danger, a dragoon met me, and stopped so near, I could have put my hand on his holsters. Now, thought I to myself, "I am taken"—but what a blessed thing it was I lost my hat! The old dirty handkerchief upon my head saved me again. From this appearance, taking me to be the master of the house near by, he says, "Have you any cider?" "No, sir," was my reply, "but we expect to make next week—call then, and we shall be glad to treat you." This said, we each went his own way.

Commencing my journey at another time, early in the evening, I was accosted by a man of stern appearance and address, standing on the door-step. He wished to know whence I came, and where bound. I told him I had just sailed out of New York, bound to Augustine in Florida, and was driven ashore by an American privateer, a little to the eastward of Sandy Hook, and was making my way down to Huntington, where I belonged. "What?" says he, "you belong to an American privateer? I wonder you have not been taken up before." By this it seems, he would have apprehended me had he known what I was. He was, no doubt, a Long Island tory. But I replied, "Sir, you mistake me, I did not say I belonged, or had belonged, to an American privateer. I meant to say I belonged to an English vessel out of New York, and had been driven ashore by such a privateer." Then, without further ceremony, I passed on, and he did not attempt to stop me. And now again I sought rest and concealment, as it grew late in the evening, and again I found it in a barn. But I had now, by exposure, contracted a violent cough, and could not suppress it, though deep sunk in a hay-mow. The owner coming into the barn, in the morning, heard me, but he offered me no disturbance, and I hoped it would have been my peaceful retreat for the whole day. But some time after the man, who visited the barn, had left it, a number of children came up to it, and placed their hands against the door, and gave it a violent shaking, crying out, at the same time, "Come out, you runaway, you thief, you robber!" and then retreated with great precipitation. But I did not remove out of my bed, hoping they might not give me another such honorable salute. But it was not long before they appeared again, and cried out, "Come out, you old rogue, you runaway, you thief! We know you are here, for daddy heard you cough," and then retreated as before. And I retreated also, fearing some older children might honor me with a visit, and find out in very deed that I was a runaway.

After I had experienced so many narrow escapes, and had now passed, as I supposed, and as proved to be the fact, beyond all further danger from foraging parties, scouts, and patrol of a military character; and though the fever was still upon me, yet it seemed rather to abate than to be aggravated by all the exposure, cold, storms, fatigues, fears, anxieties and privations I endured; I inferred, with great confidence, that it was the design of Almighty God that I should yet again see home; and entering a wood, where no human eye could see me, I fell upon my knees, and, looking up to Heaven, I attributed to Him all my deliverances, and all the understanding, assistance and strength by which I had been sustained; and besought the continuance of his mercy to extricate me from all remaining danger and sufferings, and to complete my deliverance. I arose, and now went forward, more than ever, under a sense of the Divine goodness and protection.

I come now to a day in which various and interesting incidents occurred. I now ventured to travel in open daylight, and no longer to ask protection from the sable honors of an absent sun. Commencing my journey early in the morning, I came to a large and respectable dwelling-house, and thinking it time to seek something to nourish my feeble frame, for appetite I had scarce any, I entered it. Neatness, wealth and plenty seemed to reside there. Among the inmates of it, a decent woman, who appeared to be the mistress of the family, and a tailor, who was mounted upon a large table, and plying his occupation, were all that attracted my notice. To the lady I expressed my wants, telling her, at the same time, which was my invariable practice, if she could impart to me a morsel, it must be a mere act of charity, giving and hoping to receive nothing again. For poverty was a companion of which I could not rid myself. She made no objections, asked no questions, but promptly furnished me with a dish of light food I desired. Expressing my obligations to her, I rose to depart. But, going round through another room, she met me in the front entry, placed a hat upon my head, put an apple-pie in my hand, and said, "You will want this before you get through the woods." I opened my mouth to give vent to the greatful feelings with which my heart was filled, but she would not tarry to hear a word, but instantly vanished out of my sight. The mystery of her conduct, as I suppose, was this: she, her family and property, were under British government. She was, doubtless, well satisfied that I was a prisoner escaping from the hands of the English; and if she granted me any protection or succor, knowing me to be such, it might cost the family the confiscation of all their estate. She did not, therefore, wish to ask me any questions, or hear me explain who I was, within hearing of that tailor. He might turn out to be a dangerous informer. I then departed;

but this mark of kindness was more than I could well bear, and, as I went on for some rods, the tears flowed copiously.

By and by I began to recollect and consider what the lady meant by the woods. I supposed it possible there might be a forest four or five miles in length, through which I might pass; of the real fact I had not the least anticipation. But very soon I came to the woods, and found a narrow road, of deep, loose sand, leading through them. The bushes on both sides, grew hard up to the wagon-ruts, and there was not a step of a side-walk of more solid ground, and the traveling was very laborious. But I pressed on with what strength I had, and, after a few miles, supposed I was nearly through the wilderness, and began to look ahead for cleared land and human dwellings, but none appeared. After I had, with great labor and almost unsupportable distress, traveled a distance I deemed at least nine miles, I met two men pressing on in a direction opposite to my own. They seemed to be in a hurry, and anxious to know how far I had come in these woods. "About nine miles," said I; "how far have you come in them?" They replied, "about the same distance," and immediately pushed forward, asking me no other question. Then said I to myself, "Here I make my grave. My feet were swollen so that the tumefaction hung over the tops of my shoes for three-fourths of an inch, and I was about to seek out a favorable spot to lie down and rise no more. But at this instant, something seemed to whisper to me, "Will it not be just as well, if you must die, to die standing and walking?" I could not say no, and resolved to walk on, till I fell down dead. And this whisper has been of great service to me in after-life, when I have been ready to sink in discouragement under difficulties and troubles, or opposition and persecution. When I say, I have been ready to sink under such trials, I have recollected these woods, and said, "Will it not be as well to die standing up, as lying down?" And thus I have taken courage, and gone forward, and the result has been as auspicious.

The first house I came to, at the east end of these woods, I entered in quest of humanity and pity. But these virtues appeared not to be at home there. Everything without and within, denoted a situation happily above penury, or the trials, vexations, and griefs of poverty. A degree of elegance and neatness appeared. In the kitchen I discovered a number of fish just touched with salt, and hung up and dried. My feverish appetite fixed on a piece of one of these fish, as a rasher that might taste well. I besought the lady of the house, to give me a very small bit; but my request was not granted. I repeated it, again and again. But her denial was irrevocable. Now, thought I, I will try an experiment, and measure the hardness of your heart. So I stated to her my sickly, destitute condition; told her she might judge by my appearance, that I was overwhelmed with misfortune, and had been very unsuccessful at sea. I wished her to consider how she would be delighted, had she a brother, or a dear friend, suffering in a strange land, if any one should stretch out to him the hand of relief, minister to his necessities, wipe away his tears, and console his heart. Indeed, I suggested every thought and plea of which I was master, that could move a heart not made of steel. And what was it all for? For a piece of dried blue-fish, not more than two inches square! And did I succeed? No. All my entreaties were in vain; so without murmuring, or casting on her any reflections, I took my leave.

Passing on but a few rods, I entered another dwelling, and what renders the circumstance that took place, the more to be noticed is, it appeared to be a tavern. I expressed my wants to a lady who, I had no doubt, was the mistress of the house. By the cheerfulness and good nature depicted in her countenance, and her first movements, I knew my suit was granted, and I had nothing more to say, than to apprise her that I was penniless; and if she afforded me any relief, she must do it hoping for nothing again. Now behold the contrast! In a few moments she placed on the table a bowl of bread and milk, the whole of one of those fish roasted, that I had begged for in vain, at the other house, and a mug of cider. And, says she, "Sit down and eat." But her mercy came near to cruelty in its consequences; for although I was aware of the danger, yet I indulged too freely. My fever was soon enraged to violence, and I was filled with alarm.

It was now growing dark, and I went but a short distance further, and entered a house, and begged the privilege of lodging by the fire. My request was granted, and I sat down in silence, too sick and distressed to do or say anything. But I could see and hear. There was no one in the house, but the man and his wife. They appeared to be plain, openhearted, honest people, who never had their minds elated with pride, nor their taste perverted by false refinement, or that education, which just unfits persons to be useful and happy in the common walks of life.

Before it became late in the evening, the man took his Bible, and read a chapter, and that with a tone and air that induced me to think he believed it. He then arose and devoutly offered up his grateful acknowledgments and supplications to God, through the Mediator. By this time I began to think I had gone into a safe, as well as a hospitable retreat. They had before made many inquiries, not impertinent and captious, but such as indicated that they felt tenderly, and took an interest in my welfare; but they evidently obtained no satisfaction from my answers, for I was too weary and distressed, to take pains to form, or relate, anything like a consistent story. But they seemed as if they could not rest till they had drawn from me, the real truth, though they gave not the least hint, that might reproach me for the want of truth and honesty. At last I resolved I would treat them so no longer—I would throw off the mask, risk all consequences, and let them into the real secret of my condition—and said, "You have asked me many questions this evening, and I have told you nothing but falsehoods. Now hear the truth. I am a prisoner, making my escape from the Old Jersey, at New York. Of the horrors of this dreadful prison you may have been informed. There, after many sufferings, I was brought to have no prospect before me, but certain death. By a remarkable and unexpected interposition of Providence, I got on shore, and having had many hair-breadth escapes, I have reached this place, and am now lodged under your hospitable roof. I am loaded with disease, and am in torment from the thousands of vermin which are now devouring my flesh. I have dear and kind friends in Connecticut, and am now aiming to regain my native home. The kindest of mothers is now probably weeping for me, as having, ere this, perished in my captivity, never more expecting to see her child. Thus I have told you the real truth. I have put my life in your hands. Go and inform against me, and I shall be taken back to the prison ship, and death will be inevitable." I ceased to speak, and all was profound silence. It took some time to recover themselves from a flood of tears, in which they were bathed. At last the kind and amiable woman said, "Let us go and bake his clothes." No sooner said, than the man seized a brand of fire and threw it into the oven. The woman provided a clean suit of clothes, to supply the place of mine, till they had purified them by fire. The work done, a clean bed was laid down, on which I was to rest; and rest I did, as in a new world; for I had got rid of a swarm of cannibals, who were without mercy eating me up alive!

In the morning, I took my leave of this dear family, who had enchained and riveted my soul to them by their kindness, in esteem and gratitude, which have for fifty years suffered no abatement. I learned from them a lesson of humanity, I have ever remembered, and ever wished to imitate. The day was clear, and after traveling a short distance, I threw myself down on the sunny side of a stinted pitch-pine, upon a bed of warm sand. I rested as on a bed of down.

In about a week after this, I found myself at Sag Harbor, at the east end of Long Island. Nor did the kind providence of God forsake me. Again I found humanity and pity in a public house. I was permitted to lie by a warm fire, (a great luxury, the weather having become cold,) while two others of my companions on board the same engine of perdition to American seamen, having made their escape, were denied this favor and had to take lodgings in the barn. While lying on my bed of down, (the warm brick hearth,) the door of an adjoining room, where our host and landlady slept, being open, I heard her say, "I could not consent that the other two should lodge in the house, but I pitied this young man." But I could see no cause for this difference of feeling in this woman, but the agency of Him, who hath all hearts in his hand. In a few days an opportunity of crossing the sound presented. A whale-boat, with a commission to make reprisals upon the enemy, came into the harbor. Her crew, as I supposed, were a set of honest, good farmers, who resided at Norwich, in Connecticut, where I was born, and knew my connections. They agreed to give me passage to New London. A sloop also came into the harbor, with a like commission, which belonged on the island. This boat and sloop made sail together, one bound to New London, the other to Saybrook. But the weather being very boisterous, the boat was in danger; so we all went on board the sloop, and the boat was made fast to her by a tow-line. But at no great distance from Plumb Island, a privateer, which proved to be out of Stonington, pounced upon us; and, under the suspicion of our being illicit traders, carried us all into New London. And here a scene of wickedness was developed, of which I could not have supposed my honest friends had been capable. An agent had been sent to New York, had obtained a quantity of dry goods, and brought them to Sag Harbor. Here the cruising whale-boat was to receive and carry them to New London, where they would be libelled; and some of the crew would come into court, and give oath that they were taken from the enemy, by virtue of their commission. And thus a trade was carried on with the enemy to an infinite extent. These goods were put on board the sloop, when the boat was made fast to her. And when the privateer appeared, and we could not escape her, the captain of the sloop agreed to declare the goods were his, and that he had taken them as a lawful prize from the enemy. And the crew of the whale-boat, the purchasers and owners of the goods, were to swear they saw him do it. The goods being condemned, the captain of the sloop was then to act like an honest rogue, and to restore them to the crew of the boat. But after the goods were actually condemned, and the crew of the boat, the real owners, had in open court sworn, that the goods were his by lawful capture, the captain of the sloop thought he had now a fair opportunity, to play on them a profitable trick. Accordingly, he refused to restore them, and went off with the goods, sloop and all, to Connecticut River. But the crew of the boat were not willing thus to quit all claim to the goods, though they had sworn they were not theirs, and contrived to have the sloop with the goods seized. And I, who knew the whole story, was sent for as a witness And by my testimony, and that of one of the whale-boat's crew, who had not testified before, that the goods were captured by the captain of the sloop, the real truth came to light, and both sloop and goods were condemned; so that the crew of the whale-boat ultimately obtained, not only their goods, but the sloop also, as an illicit trader. And thus the treachery of the captain, did not prove so gainful as he intended. He was taken in his own craftiness; an event so common, that it is a matter of wonder, that all rogues do not grow sick of their villainy.

I had now traveled one hundred and fifty miles, and was safely landed at New London. And to me it was a great mercy, that we were captured by the privateer out of Stonington; otherwise I should have been carried into Connecticut River, much further from home. But no sooner did I set my foot down in a land of safety, than I immediately sunk under the power of that disease, which had preyed upon me ever since I left the prison-ship. After arriving at New London, I could travel only about three miles, and all my strength failed, under the reviving power and rage of the fever. But in this, perhaps, the kind hand of woman had some agency. The lady at Sag Harbor, who pressed me in her pity, thought of my welfare after I should leave her house, and, unsolicited, gave me a meat-pie, and a bottle of cider. Though I had not much relish for the pie, yet my thirst tempted me to drink the liquid. I had before drank freely at the press, without injury But here is the difference: the cider in the bottle was fermented. I think it had some hand in producing the relapse.

When I could go no further, I found a man who was kind enough to carry me to Norwich Landing. And I tarried there with a relative, till my friends at Plainfield were informed of my arrival, and my eldest brother came with a carriage, to help me home. The first night I lodged with a brother at Canterbury. This night, I deemed myself to be dying, and going directly to my long home. But the next day, I so revived as to reach the dwelling of my mother—a most affectionate mother, who always seemed willing to live or die for the good of her children, and who had made up her mind to submit to the will of God, and never more to see her son, and a child broken down with sickness, and other calamities. For about three weeks, I was in a state of perfect derangement. But, about ten days later, an unexpected and favorable crisis was formed in my disease. I say unexpected, for my death was looked for as certain. A joiner, who lived near at hand, afterward told me, that having seen me the evening before, and my brother calling at his house the next morning, he did not ask how I did, having no doubt but he had come to speak for my coffin.

Near the close of winter, I so far regained my health, through the great kindness of the God of love, as to engage in the instruction of a school in the town where I resided; and since that period almost my whole life has been devoted to the instruction of youth, and preaching the everlasting gospel.

A SAILOR'S STORY

OF

WHAT HE SAW AND SUFFERED,

IN THE NAVAL SERVICE OF THE UNITED STATES, IN THE

WAR OF THE REVOLUTION.*

DURING the Revolutionary war our coast was lined with British cruisers, which had almost annihilated our commerce; and the state of Massachusetts judged it expedient to build a government vessel, rated as a twenty-gun ship, named the "Protector," commanded by Captain John Foster Williams. She was to be fitted out for service as soon as possible, to protect our commerce, and to annoy the enemy.

All means were resorted to, which ingenuity could devise, to induce men to enlist. A recruiting officer, bearing a flag and attended by a band of martial music, paraded the streets, to excite a thirst for glory and a spirit of military ambition. The recruiting officer possessed the qualifications requisite to make the service appear alluring, especially to the young. He was a jovial, good-natured fellow, of ready wit and much broad humor. When he espied any large boys among the idle crowd around him, he would attract their attention by singing, in a comical manner, the following doggerel:

> "All you that have bad masters,
> And cannot get your due;
> Come, come, my brave boys,
> And join with our ship's crew."

A shout and a huzza would follow, and some would join in the ranks. My excitable feelings were roused; I repaired to the rendezvous, signed the ship's papers, mounted a cockade, and was in my own estimation already more than half a sailor. Appeals continued to be made to the patriotism of every young man to lend his aid, by his exertions on sea or land, to free his country from the common enemy. About the last of February the ship was ready to receive her crew, and was hauled off into the channel, that the sailors might have no opportunity to run away after they were got on board. Upward of three hundred and thirty men were carried, dragged, and driven on board, of all kinds, ages, and descriptions, in all the various stages of intoxication; from that of "sober tipsiness" to beastly drunkenness, with an uproar and clamor that may be more easily imagined than described.

The wind being fair, we weighed anchor and dropped down to Nantasket roads, where we lay till about the first of April; and then set sail for a cruise of six months. We continued to sail along the coast for a few weeks, without meeting with any of the enemy, when, some indications

---

* The narrative here given, is that of Ebenezer Fox, who was born in the vicinity of Boston, Mass., in the year 1763, and was living as late as the year 1838.

of tempestuous weather appearing, our captain judged it expedient to steer for the banks of Newfoundland, that he might have more sea room in case of a gale. On the morning of June 9th, 1780, the fog began to clear away; and the man at the mast-head gave notice that he saw a ship to the westward of us. As the fog cleared up, we perceived her to be a large ship under English colors, to the windward, standing athwart our starboard bow. As she came down upon us, she appeared as large as a seventy-four; and we were not deceived respecting her size, for it afterward proved that she was an old East-Indiaman, of eleven-hundred tons burden, fitted out as a letter-of-marque for the West India trade, mounted with thirty-two guns, and furnished with a complement of one hundred and fifty men. She was called the Admiral Duff, commanded by Richard Strange, from St. Christopher and St. Eustatia, laden with sugar and tobacco, and bound to London. I was standing near our first lieutenant, Mr. Little, who was calmly examining the enemy, as she approached, with his spy-glass, when Captain Williams stepped up and asked his opinion of her. The lieutenant applied the glass to his eye again and took a deliberate look in silence, and replied, "I think she is a heavy ship and that we shall have some hard fighting, but of one thing I am certain, she is not a frigate; if she were, she would not keep yawing, and showing her broadsides as she does; she would show nothing but her head and stern; we shall have the advantage of her, and the quicker we get along side the better." Our captain ordered English colors to be hoisted, and the ship to be cleared for action.

The enemy approached till within musket shot of us. The two ships were so near to each other that we could distinguish the officers from the men; and I particularly noticed the captain on the gangway, a noble looking man, having a large gold-laced cocked hat on his head, and a speaking-trumpet in his hand. Lieutenant Little possessed a powerful voice, and he was directed to hail the enemy; at the same time the quarter master was ordered to stand ready to haul down the English flag and to hoist up the American. Our lieutenant took his station on the after part of the starboard gangway, and elevating the trumpet, exclaimed, "Hallo! whence come you?"—"From Jamaica, bound to London," was the answer. "What is the ship's name?" inquired the lieutenant. "The Admiral Duff," was the reply. The English captain then thought it his turn to interrogate, and asked the name of our ship. Lieutenant Little, in order to gain time, put the trumpet to his ear, pretending not to hear the question. During the short interval, thus gained, Captain Williams called upon the gunner to ascertain how many guns could be brought to bear upon the enemy. "Five," was the answer. "Then fire, and shift the colors," were the orders. The cannons poured forth their deadly contents, and, with the first flash, the American flag took the place of the British ensign at our mast-head.

The compliment was returned in the form of a full broadside, and the action commenced. I was stationed on the edge of the quarter-deck, to sponge and load a six-pounder; this position gave me a fine opportunity to see the whole action. Broadsides were exchanged with great rapidity for nearly an hour; our fire, as we afterward ascertained, produced a terrible slaughter among the enemy, while our loss was as yet trifling. I happened to be looking for a moment toward the main-deck, when a large shot came through our ship's side and killed a midshipman. At this moment a shot from one of our marines killed the man at the wheel of the enemy's ship, and, his place not being immediately supplied, she was brought along side of us in such a manner as to bring her bowsprit directly across our forecastle. Not knowing the cause of this movement, we supposed it to be the intention of the enemy to board us. Our boarders were ordered to be ready with their pikes to resist any such attempt, while our guns on the main-deck were sending death and destruction among the crew of the enemy. Their principal object now seemed to be to get liberated from us, and by cutting away some of their rigging, they were soon clear, and at the distance of a pistol shot.

The action was then renewed, with additional fury; broadside for broadside continued with unabated vigor; at times so near to each other that the muzzles of our guns came almost in contact, then again at such a distance as to allow of taking deliberate aim. The contest was obstinately continued by the enemy, although we could perceive that great havoc was made among them, and that it was with much difficulty that their men were compelled to remain at their quarters. A charge of grape-shot came in at one of our port-holes, which dangerously wounded four or five of our men, among whom was our third lieutenant, Mr. Little, brother to the first.

The action had now lasted about an hour and a half, and the fire from the enemy began to slacken, when we suddenly discovered that all the sails on her mainmast were enveloped in a blaze. The fire spread with amazing rapidity, and, running down the after-rigging, it soon communicated with her magazine, when her whole stern was blown off, and her valuable cargo emptied into the sea. Our enemy's ship was now a complete wreck, though she still floated, and the survivors were endeavoring to save themselves in the only boat that had escaped the general destruction. The humanity of our captain urged him to make all possible exertion to save the miserable, wounded, and burned wretches, who were struggling for their lives in the water. The ship of the enemy was greatly our superior in size, and lay much higher out of the water. Our boats had been much exposed to his fire, as they were placed on spars between the fore and main masts during the action, and had suffered considerable damage. The carpenters were ordered to repair them with the utmost expedition, and we got them out in season to take up fifty-five men, the greater part of whom had been wounded by our shot or burned when the powder magazine exploded. Their limbs were mutilated by all manner of wounds, while some were burned to such a degree that the skin was nearly flayed from their bodies. Our surgeon and his assistants had just completed the task of dressing the wounds of our own crew, and then they directed their attention to the wounded of the enemy. Several of them suffered the amputation of their limbs. Five of them died of their wounds, and were committed to their watery graves. From the survivors we learned, that the British commander had frequently expressed a desire to come in contact with a "Yankee frigate," during his voyage, that he might have a prize to carry to London. Poor fellow! he little thought of loosing his ship and his life in an engagement with a ship so much inferior to his own—with an enemy upon whom he looked with so much contempt.

Our sailors were busily employed in picking up the various articles that were floating, and getting them on board, while the carpenters and riggers were engaged in repairing the damages we had received. The ship was soon in good order and prepared again to meet the enemy, and we continued on our cruise. Our captain, soon finding that sickness was increasing among the crew, and that the wounded were suffering greatly, judged it expedient to leave our cruising ground, and to steer for some eastern port, that we might obtain a supply of wood and water. Some repairs likewise were necessary, which we could not conveniently make at sea. About the twentieth of the month we sailed from the banks of Newfoundland, and arrived at Broad bay in seven or eight days. Having found a good harbor, we dropped anchor, and made immediate preparations to get our sick and wounded men on shore.

Our repairs being completed, and all things ready for sea, we weighed anchor about the last of June, and steered once more for the banks of Newfoundland, where the provisions of the ship beginning to fail, and no prospect of making captures appearing, our captain, with the advice of his officers, concluded to steer for Boston. In a few days we came in sight of Boston lighthouse and anchored in Nantasket roads. In a short time our ship was thoroughly overhauled, her bottom scraped, rigging repaired, and everything was done to put her in perfect order. Wood and water, and various kinds of stores necessary for a cruise of six months, were taken on board; and, having recruited about two hundred men, preparations were made for our immediate departure.

About the last of October, our boats were hoisted on deck and secured, and we dropped down into Nantasket roads, where we remained a few days, and then set sail upon our second cruise; After cruising for some time, and not falling in with anything, our captain concluded to steer for the southern coast of the United States. We arrived off the bar of Charleston, South Carolina; and in the course of a few days fell in with a ship called the Polly, a letter-of-marque, of twenty guns, bound to London. We gave chase late in the afternoon, and, as it soon grew dark, we lost sight of her. A thunder storm came on, and all hands were watching for her; and by the flashes of the lightning we at length discovered her, standing in a different direction from what we had at first seen her pursuing. We accordingly shifted our course, and crowded sail in pursuit. By the aid of the lightning, we kept in her course, and soon came up with her.

"What ship is that, and where from?" roared our lieutenant through his trumpet, in a voice that bore no slight resemblance to the thunder which rolled above our heads, "The ship Polly, from Charleston, bound to London," was the reply. The lightning, flashing upon her colors, showed that they were English; while the enemy had the same means of seeing the American flag flying at our mast-head. We were completely prepared for action; the matches were lighted; the lanterns burning fore and aft; and all anxiously waiting for the commands of the officers. One shot was fired, and our captain ordered the enemy to "Haul down his colors, or he would blow him out of the water." The appearance of our ship being formidable, our captain's demand was instantly complied with. Our boat was lowered, and a prize-master and crew put on board, who took possession of the ship, and she was ordered for Boston.

Our cruise thus far had been prosperous, and we thought the "evil day was afar off." We continued merrily on our course, without seeing friend or foe, during the next day; but, the following morning, the man at the mast-head cried out, "Two sail to the leeward." Mr. Little ascended to the maintop with his glass, and soon ascertained that they were two large ships, closely hauled upon the wind, in full chase of us Our yards were braced, and all sail crowded that the ship could carry. The chase continued, without gaining much upon us till about noon, when, the wind shifting, they fell into our wake, and gained upon us very fast. Our captain, calling all the hands aft, on the quarter-deck, expressed his opinion, that the ships in pursuit of us were English, and that we should be captured. He then distributed among us his money for safe keeping, in sums of fifteen dollars to each, upon condition that it should be returned to him if we were so fortunate as to escape. It was now nearly sunset, and the enemy were gaining upon us rapidly.

To attempt resistance against a force so much our superior would have been unjustifiable; and the flag of thirteen stars and stripes was reluctantly pulled down. The boats of the enemy were manned and sent along side of our ship. Our crew were now permitted by our officers to collect their clothing and their little property together, and secure them in the best manner they could. By this time, the boats had arrived along side, and the enemy had ascended the deck.

Their first exploit was to strike or kick every sailor that came in their way, bestowing a variety of opprobrious epithets, among which "damned rebels" was of the most frequent recurrence; then they commenced searching in every part of the ship for articles of value. Our crew were ordered to pass down the side of the ship into the enemy's boats; but were forbidden to carry anything with them. Some of our crew fastened their bedding upon their backs, and tumbled themselves head foremost down into the boats; and, as it was quite dark, they would unperceived get into the cuddy with their bedding, trusting to future circumstances for opportunity to use or secrete it. We arrived along side, and were ordered on to the quarter-deck of our captors. Some English sailor among our crew, to recommend himself to the favor of the British captain, had given information respecting the money we had secreted about our persons. The sergeant of arms was ordered to search every one of us till the sum of fifteen dollars was found upon each of us. In the capacity of cabin steward I was most of the time in the cabin, and had recommended myself to the favorable notice of the American captain by performing my duties to his satisfaction; and, when the money was distributed among our crew, the captain gave me a double share. I put fifteen dollars in the crown of my hat, which I pressed down upon my head as closely as possible; the remaining fifteen I placed in my shoes, between the soles. At length my turn to be searched came; and I, as the rest of my fellow-prisoners had done, denied having any money. This assertion, however, did not avail; I was seized by the collar, and shaken so violently that my hat fell off, and the dollars rolled out upon the deck. The sum of fifteen dollars being found, it was concluded that I had no more, and I was sent into the ship's hold, where I found those of the crew who had been previously searched. Our accommodations in the hold were not very desirable, especially to those who had not succeeded in getting their bedding into that place. We found nothing to lie upon softer than the ship's ballast, consisting of stones of all shapes and sizes, with here and there a lump of pig-iron by way of variety; and the water-casks, which afforded a surface rather uneven for the comfort and convenience of our weary limbs. Here we spent the first night, and were not allowed to go on deck till the next morning.

Shortly after, we anchored off Sandy Hook, and preparations were made to examine the prisoners, to ascertain what part of them were Englishmen; or rather, who among them would carry the appearance of able-bodied seamen. We were called up from the hold; ordered to the larboard side of the quarter-deck; thence marched, in single file, past a number of British officers on the starboard side; after that to the gangway and down again into the hold. The object of thus moving in procession before the officers was, to give them an opportunity to select such as they chose, to serve on board of their ships. With fear and trembling we passed through this examination. Whenever a healthy, athletic looking man passed by, he was hailed, and accused of being an Englishman. In vain would his comrades attest to the fact of his being a native-born American, tell the place of his birth and the circumstances of his youth, detailed with all the consistency and connection which belong to truth; it was all to no purpose. Sailors they wanted, and have them they would, if they set law and gospel at defiance. In this manner was many an American citizen, in the morning of life, dragged from his country, his friends, and his home; forced on board a ship of war; compelled to fight against his own country; and, if he lived, to fight in battle with other nations, against whom he had no feelings of hostility.

About a third part of our ship's crew were taken on board of their vessels, to serve in the capacity of sailors, without regarding their remonstrances; while the remainder of us were put on board of a wood coaster, to be conveyed on board the noted prison ship called the "Jersey." We wished, if possible, to avoid the hard fate that awaited us; and conceived the design of rising upon the guard, seizing upon the sloop, and running her aground upon the Jersey shore. The plan could have been easily executed had there been any one among us to act as a leader in the enterprise. Our captain with his officers were confined in the cabin, under the watchful care of a number of British officers well armed; while a guard of soldiers stood at the head of the companion-way, to prevent any communication with the prisoners upon the deck. Sailors and soldiers have the courage to execute, but not the skill to plan. Had our captain, in whom we had been in the habit of placing the utmost confidence, been with us, I have no doubt we should have obtained our freedom. As the deck was loaded with wood, we could in a moment have obtained weapons sufficient for our purpose, and, had any one among us been disposed to act as a leader, we should soon have had possession of the vessel. We afterward regretted exceedingly that we did not make the attempt. We proceeded slowly up the river toward our much dreaded place of confinement, and at doubling a point we came in sight of the gloomy looking hulk of the old Jersey, aptly named by the sailors, "The hell afloat." The Jersey was originally a seventy-four gun ship, and, at the commencement of the American Revolution, being found in a state of decay and unfit for service at sea, she was dismantled, moored in the East River, at New York, and used as a store-ship. In the year 1780, she was converted into a prison ship, and continued to be used for that purpose during the remainder of the war.

In consequence of the fears that were entertained that the sickness, which prevailed among the prisoners, might spread to the shore, she was removed, and moored with chain cables at the Wallabout, a lonely and unfrequented place on the shore of Long Island. Her external appearance was forbidding and gloomy. She was dismantled; her only spars were the bowsprit; a derrick, that looked like a gallows, for hoisting supplies on board; and a flag-staff at the stern. The port-holes were closed and secured. Two tiers of holes were cut through her sides, about two feet square and about ten feet apart, strongly guarded by a grating of iron bars. The sloop anchored at a little distance from the Jersey, and two boats were sent along side to receive us. The boats passed and re-passed several times before all of us got on board; and lastly the captain's barge was sent to convey our officers to their place of confinement. Not a great while after we were imprisoned our captain, together with the lieutenant and the sailing-master, Mr. Lemon, were sent to England; the latter, being an Englishman, had the comfortable assurance, that he should be hanged as soon as he arrived. After being detained in the boats along side a little while, we were ordered to ascend to the upper deck of the prison ship. Here our names were registered, and the capacity in which we had served previous to our capture. Each of us was permitted to retain whatever clothing and bedding we had brought, after having been examined to ascertain that they contained no weapons nor money; and then we were directed to pass through a strong door, on the starboard side, down a ladder leading to the main hatchway. I now found myself in a loathsome prison, among a collection of the most wretched and disgusting looking objects that I ever beheld in human form. Here was a motley crew, covered with rags and filth; visages pallid with disease, emaciated with hunger and anxiety, and retaining hardly a trace of their original appearance. Here were men, who had once enjoyed life while riding over the mountain wave or roaming through pleasant fields, full of health and vigor, now shriveled by a scanty and unwholesome diet, ghastly with inhaling an impure atmosphere, exposed to contagion, in contact with disease, and surrounded with the horrors of sickness and death. Here, thought I, must I linger out the morning of my life, in tedious days and sleepless nights, enduring a weary and degrading captivity, till death shall terminate my sufferings, and no friend will know of my departure. A prisoner on board of "the old Jersey!" The very thought was appalling. I could hardly realize my situation.

The first thing we found it necessary to do after our captivity was to form ourselves into small parties, called "messes," consisting of six men each; as, previous to doing this, we could obtain no food. All the prisoners were obliged to fast on the first day of their arrival; and seldom on the second could they procure any food in season for cooking it. No matter how hungry they were, no deviation from the rules of the ship was permitted. All the prisoners fared alike; officers and sailors received the same treatment on board of this old hulk. Our keepers were no respecters of persons. We were all "rebels." The quantity and quality of our fare was the same for all. The only distinction known among us was made by the prisoners themselves, which was shown in allowing those who had been officers previous to their capture, to congregate in the extreme after-part of the ship, and to keep it exclusively to themselves as their places of abode. The various messes of the prisoners were numbered; and nine in the morning was the hour when the steward would deliver from the window in his room, at the after-part of the ship, the allowance granted to each mess. Each mess chose one of their company to be prepared to answer to their number when it was called by the steward, and to receive the allowance as it was handed from the window. Whatever was thrust out must be taken; no change could be made in its quantity or quality. Each mess received daily what was equivalent in weight or measure, but not in quality, to the rations of four men at full allowance: that is, each prisoner received two-thirds as much as was allowed to a seaman in the British navy.

Our bill of fare was as follows: On Sunday, one pound of biscuit, one pound of pork, and half a pint of peas. Monday, one pound of biscuit, one pint of oatmeal, and two ounces of butter. Tuesday, one pound of biscuit, and two pounds of salt beef. Wednesday, one and a half pounds of flour, and two ounces of suet. Thursday was a repetition of Sunday's fare, Friday of Monday's, and Saturday of Tuesday's.

If this food had been of a good quality and properly cooked, as we had no labor to perform, it would have kept us comfortable, at least from suffering. But this was not the case. All our food appeared to be damaged. As for the pork, we were cheated out of it more than half of the time: and, when it was obtained, one would have judged from its motley hues, exhibiting the consistence and appearance of variegated fancy soap, that it was the flesh of the porpoise, or sea-hog, and had been an inhabitant of the ocean rather than of the sty. The peas were generally damaged, and, from the imperfect manner in which they were cooked were about as indigestible as grape-shot. The butter the reader will not suppose was the real "Goshen;" and had it not been for its adhesive properties to retain together the particles of the biscuit, that had been so riddled by the worms as to lose all their attraction of cohesion, we should have considered it no desirable addition to our viands. The flour and the oatmeal were often sour, and when the suet was mixed with it, we should have considered it a blessing to have been destitute of the sense of smelling before we admitted it into our mouths: it might be nosed half the length of the ship. And last, though not the least item among our staples in the eating line—our beef. Its color was of dark mahogany; and it could be pulled into pieces one way in strings, like rope-yarn. It was so completely saturated with salt, that, after having been boiled in water taken from the sea, it was found to be considerably freshened by the process.

Such was our food. But the quality of it was not all that we had reason to complain of. The manner in which it was cooked was more injurious to our health than the quality of the food; and, in many cases, laid the foundation of diseases, that brought many a sufferer to his grave, years after his liberation. The cooking for the prisoners was done in a great copper vessel, that contained between two and three hogsheads of water, set in brick-work. The form of it was square, and it was divided into two compartments by a partition. In one of these, the peas and oatmeal were boiled; this was done in fresh water: in the other, the meat was boiled in salt water taken up from along side of the ship.

The Jersey, from her size and lying near the shore, was imbedded in the mud; and I do not recollect seeing her afloat during the whole time I was a prisoner. All the filth that accumulated among upward of a thousand men was daily thrown overboard, and would remain there till carried away by the tide. The impurity of the water may be easily conceived; and in this water our meat was boiled. It will be recollected, too, that the water was salt, which caused the inside of the copper to become corroded to such a degree that it was lined with a coat of verdigris. Meat thus cooked must in some degree be poisoned; and the effects of it were manifest in the cadaverous countenances of the emaciated beings, who had remained on board for any length of time.

The persons chosen by each mess to receive their portions of food, were summoned by the cook's bell to receive their allowance, and, when it had remained in the boiler a certain time, the bell would again sound, and the allowance must be immediately taken away: whether it was sufficiently cooked or not, it could remain no longer. The food was generally very imperfectly cooked; yet this sustenance, wretched as it was, and deficient in quantity, was greedily devoured by the half-starved prisoners. No vegetables were allowed us. Many times since, when I have seen in the country, a large kettle of potatoes and pumpkins steaming over the fire to satisfy the appetites of a farmer's swine, I have thought of our destitute and starved condition, and what a luxury we should have considered the contents of that kettle on board the Jersey. The prisoners were confined in the two main-decks below. The lowest dungeon was inhabited by those prisoners who were foreigners, and whose treatment was more severe than that of the Americans. The inhabitants of this lower region were the most miserable and disgusting looking objects that can be conceived. Daily washing with salt water, together with their extreme emaciation, caused their skin to appear like dried parchment. Many of them remained unwashed for weeks; their hair long and matted, and filled with vermin; their beards never cut, excepting occasionally with a pair of shears, which did not improve their comeliness, though it might add to their comfort. Their clothes were mere rags, secured to their bodies in every way that ingenuity could devise. Many of these men had been in this lamentable condition for two years, part of the time on board other prison ships; and, having given up all hope of ever being exchanged, had become resigned to their situation. These men were foreigners, whose whole lives had been one continual scene of toil, hardship, and suffering. But far different was the condition of the most numerous class of the prisoners, composed mostly of young men from New England, fresh from home. They had reason to deplore the sudden change in their condition. The thoughts of home, of parents, brothers, sisters, and friends, would crowd upon their minds; till "their desire for home became a madness."

In the morning, the prisoners were permitted to ascend the upper deck, to spend the day, till ordered below at sunset. A certain number, who were for the time called the "working party," performed in rotation the duty of bringing up hammocks and bedding for airing, likewise the sick and infirm, and the bodies of those who had died during the night: of these there were generally a number every morning. After these services it was their duty to wash the decks. Our beds and clothing were allowed to remain on deck till we were ordered below for the night; this was of considerable benefit, as it gave some of the vermin an opportunity to migrate from the quarters they had inhabited. About two hours before sunset, orders were given to the prisoners to carry all their things below; but we were permitted to remain above till we retired for the night into our unhealthy and crowded dungeons. At sunset, our ears were saluted with the insulting and hateful sound from our keepers, of "Down, rebels, down," and we were hurried below, the hatchways fastened over us, and we were left to pass the night amid the accumulated horrors of sighs and groans, of foul vapor, a nauseous and putrid atmosphere, in a stifled and almost suffocating heat. The tiers of holes through the sides of the ship were strongly grated, but not provided with glass; and it was considered a privilege to sleep near one of these apertures in hot weather, for the pure air that passed in at them. But little sleep, however, could be enjoyed even there; for the vermin were so horribly abundant, that all the personal cleanliness we could practice would not protect us from their attacks, or prevent their effecting a lodgment upon us.

When any of the prisoners died in the night, their bodies were brought to the upper deck in the morning, and placed upon the gratings. If the deceased had owned a blanket, any prisoner might sew it around the corpse, and then it was lowered, with a rope tied round the middle, down the side of the ship into a boat. Some of the prisoners were allowed to go on shore, under a guard, to perform the labor of interment. Having arrived on shore, they found in a small hut some tools for digging, and a hand-barrow on which the body was conveyed to the place for burial. Here, in a bank near the Wallabout, a hole was excavated in the sand, in which the body was put, and then slightly covered; the guard not giving time sufficient to perform this melancholy service in a faithful manner Many bodies would, in a few days after this mockery of a burial, be exposed nearly bare by the action of the elements.

"By feeble hands their shallow graves were made:
No stone, memorial of their corpses, laid.
In barren sands, and far from home, they lie,
No friend to shed a tear when passing by—
O'er the mean tombs insulting foemen tread;
Spurn at the sand, and curse the rebel dead."

This was the last resting place of many a son and brother; young and noble spirited men, who had left their happy homes and kind friends to offer their lives in the service of their country; but they little thought of such a termination to their active career. The fate of many of these unhappy victims must have remained forever unknown to their friends; for, in so large a number, no exact account could be kept of those who died, and they rested in a nameless grave; while those who performed the last sad rites were hurried away before their task was half completed, and forbidden to express their horror and indignation at this insulting negligence toward the dead.

The regular crew of the Jersey consisted of a captain, two mates, a steward, a cook, and about a dozen sailors. There was likewise on board a guard of ten or twelve old invalid marines, who were unfit for active service; and a guard of about thirty soldiers, from the different regiments quartered on Long Island, who were relieved by a fresh party every week. The physical force of the prisoners was sufficient at any time to take possession of the ship; but the difficulty was, to dispose of themselves after a successful attempt. Long Island was in possession of the British, and the inhabitants were favorable to the British cause. To leave the ship, and land upon the island, would be followed by almost certain detection. Yet, small as was the chance for succeeding in an undertaking, the attempt to escape was often made, and in not a few instances with success.

Some weeks after our imprisonment on board the Jersey the following successful attempt was made by a number of the prisoners. At sunset the prisoners were driven below, and the main hatchway was closed. In this there was a small trap-door, large enough for a man to pass through, and a sentinel was placed over it with orders to permit but one prisoner at a time to come up during the night. The plan that had been formed was this: one of the prisoners should ascend, and dispose of the sentinel in such a manner that he should be no obstacle in the way of those who were to follow. Among the soldiers was an Irishman who, in consequence of having a head of hair remarkable for its curly appearance, and withal a very crabbed disposition, had been nicknamed "Billy the Ram." He was the sentry on deck this night, for one was deemed sufficient, as the prisoners were considered secure when they were below, having no other place of egress saving the trap-door, over which the sentinel was stationed. Late in the night, one of the prisoners, a bold, athletic fellow, ascended upon deck, and in an artful manner engaged the attention of "Billy the Ram," in conversation respecting the war; lamenting that he had ever engaged in so unnatural a contest; expressing his intention of enlisting in the British service; and requesting Billy's advice as to the course necessary to be pursued to obtain the confidence of the officers. Billy happened to be in a mood to take some interest in his views, and showed an inclination, quite uncommon for him, to prolong the conversation. Unsuspicious of any evil design on the part of the prisoner, and while leaning carelessly on his gun, "Billy" received a tremendous blow from the fist of his entertainer, on the back of his head, which brought him to the deck in a state of insensibility. As soon as he was heard to fall by those below, who were anxiously waiting the result of the friendly conversation of their pioneer with "Billy," and were satisfied that the final knock-down argument had been given; they began to ascend, and, one after another, to jump overboard, to the amount of about thirty.

The noise aroused the guard, who came upon deck, where they found "Billy," not sufficiently recovered from the stunning effects of the blow he had received, to give any account of the transaction. A noise was heard in the water; but it was so dark that no object could be distinguished. The attention of the guard, however, was directed to certain spots, which exhibited a luminous appearance, which salt water is known to assume in the night when it is agitated; and to these appearances they directed their fire, and, getting out the boats, picked up about half of the number that attempted to escape, many of whom were wounded, though no one was killed. The rest escaped. During the uproar overhead, the prisoners below encouraged the fugitives and expressed their approbation of their proceedings in three hearty cheers; for which gratification we suffered our usual punishment—a short allowance of our already short and miserable fare.

Not long after this, another successful attempt to escape was made, which for its boldness is, perhaps, unparalleled in the history of such transactions. One pleasant morning about ten o'clock, a boat came along side, containing a number of gentlemen from New York, who came for the purpose of gratifying themselves with a sight of the miserable tenants of the prison ship: influenced by the same kind of curiosity that induces some people to travel a great distance to witness an execution. The boat, which was a beautiful yawl, and sat like a swan upon the water, was manned by four oarsmen, with a man at the helm. Considerable attention and respect was shown to the visitors, the ship's side being manned when they showed their intention of coming on board, and the usual naval courtesies extended. The gentlemen were soon on board; and the crew of the yawl, having secured her to the fore-chains on the larboard side of the ship, were permitted to ascend the deck.

A soldier, as usual, was pacing with a slow and measured tread the whole length of the deck, wheeling round with military precision when he arrived at the end of his walk; and, whether upon this occasion any one interested in his movements had secretly slipped a guinea into his hand, not to *quicken*, but to retard his progress, was never known; but it was evident to the prisoners that he had never occupied so much time before in measuring the distance with his back to the place where the yawl was fastened. At this time, there were sitting in the forecastle, apparently admiring the beautiful appearance of the yawl, four mates and a captain, who had been brought on board as prisoners a few days previous, taken in some vessel from a southern port. As soon as the sentry had passed these men, in his straight-forward march, they in a very quiet manner lowered themselves down into the yawl, cut the rope, and the four mates taking in hand the oars, while the captain managed the helm, in less time than I have taken to describe it they were under full sweep from the ship. They plied the oars with such vigor, that every stroke they took seemed to take the boat out of the water. In the meantime, the sentry heard nothing and saw nothing of this transaction, till he had arrived at the end of his march, when, in wheeling slowly round, he could no longer affect ignorance, or avoid seeing that the boat was several times its length from the ship. He immediately fired; but, whether he exercised his best skill as a marksman, or whether it was on account of the boat going ahead its whole length at every pull of the rowers, I could never exactly ascertain: but the ball fell harmless into the water. The report of the gun brought the whole guard out, who blazed away at the fugitives, without producing any diminution in the rapidity of their progress.

By this time, the officers of the ship were on deck with their visitors; and, while all were gazing with astonishment at the boldness and effrontery of the achievement, and the guard were firing as fast as they could load their guns, the captain in the yawl left the helm, and, standing erect in the stern, with his back to the Jersey, bending his body to a right angle he exhibited the broadest part of himself to their view, and with a significant gesture directed their attention to it as a proper target for the exercise of their skill. This contemptuous defiance caused our captain to swell with rage; and when the prisoners gave three cheers to the yawl's crew, as expressive of their joy at their success, he ordered all of us to be driven below at the point of the bayonet, and there we were confined the remainder of the day. These five men escaped, greatly to the mortification of the captain and officers of the prison ship. After this, as long as I remained a prisoner, whenever any visitors came on board, all the prisoners were driven below, where they were obliged to remain till the company had departed.

The miseries of our condition were continually increasing: the pestilence on board spread rapidly, and every day added to our bill of mortality. With the hope that some relief might be obtained to meliorate the wretchedness of our situation, the prisoners petitioned Gen. Clinton, commanding the British forces in New York, for permission to send a memorial to General Washington, describing our condition, and requesting his influence in our behalf, that some exchange of prisoners might be effected. Permission was obtained, and the memorial was sent. In a few days, an answer was received from Gen. Washington, containing expressions full of interest and sympathy, but declaring his inability to do anything for our relief by way of exchange, as his authority did not extend to the marine department of the service, and that soldiers could not consistently be exchanged for sailors. He declared his intention, however, to lay our memorial before Congress, and that no exertion should be spared by him to mitigate our sufferings. Gen. Washington at the same time sent letters to Gen. Clinton, and to the British Commissary of Prisoners, in which he remonstrated against their cruel treatment of the American prisoners, and threatened, if our situation was not made more tolerable, to retaliate by placing British prisoners in circumstances as rigorous and uncomfortable as were our own: that "with what measure they meted, the same should be measured to them again."

We experienced after this some little improvement in our food, but no relaxation in the severity of our confinement.

As every principle of justice and humanity was disregarded by the British in the treatment of their prisoners, so, likewise, every moral and legal right was violated in compelling them to enter into their service. We had obtained some information in relation to an expected draught that would soon be made upon the prisoners to fill up a complement of men that were wanted for the service of his Majesty's fleet. One day in the latter part of August, our fears of the dreaded event were realized. A British officer with a number of soldiers came on board. The prisoners were all ordered on deck, placed on the larboard-gangway, and marched in single file round to the quarter-deck, where the officers stood to inspect them and select such ones as suited their fancies, without any reference to the rights of the prisoners, or considering at all the duties they owed to the land of their nativity, or the government for which they had fought and suffered. We continued to march round, in solemn and melancholy procession, till they had selected from among our number about three hundred of the ablest, nearly all of whom were Americans, and they were directed to go below under a guard, to collect together whatever things they wished to take belonging to them. They were then driven into the boats, waiting along side, and left the prison ship, not to enjoy their freedom, but to be subjected to the iron despotism, and galling slavery of a British man-of-war; to waste their lives in a foreign service; and toil for masters whom they hated. Such, however, were the horrors of our situation as prisoners, and so small was the prospect of relief, that we almost envied the lot of those who left the ship to go into the service even of our enemy.

In the midst of our distress, perplexities, and troubles at this period, we were not a little puzzled to know how to dispose of the vermin that would accumulate upon our persons, notwithstanding all our attempts at cleanliness. To catch them was a very easy task, but to undertake to deprive each individual captive of life, as rapidly as they could have been taken, would have been a herculean task. To throw them overboard would have been but a small relief; as they would probably add to the impurities of the boiler, by being deposited in it the first time it was filled up for cooking our unsavory mess. What then was to be done with them? A general consultation was held, and it was determined to deprive them of their liberty. This being agreed upon, the prisoners immediately went to work, for their comfort and amusement, to make a liberal contribution of those migratory creatures, who were compelled to colonize for a time within the boundaries of a large snuff-box appropriated for the purpose. There they lay, snugly ensconced, of all colors, ages, and sizes, to the amount of some thousands, waiting for orders. British recruiting officers frequently came on board, and held out to the prisoners tempting offers to enlist in his Majesty's service; not to fight against their own country, but to perform garrison duty in the island of Jamaica. One day an Irish officer came on board for this purpose, and not meeting with much success among the prisoners who happened to be upon deck, he descended below to repeat his offers. He was a remarkably tall man, and was obliged to stoop as he passed along between the decks. The prisoners were disposed for a frolic, and kept the officer in their company for some time, flattering him with expectations, till he discovered their insincerity, and left them in no very pleasant humor. As he passed along, bending his body, and bringing his broad shoulders to nearly horizontal position, the idea occurred to our minds to furnish him with some recruits from the colony in the snuff-box. A favorable opportunity presented, the cover of the box was removed, and the whole contents discharged upon the red-coated back of the officer. Three cheers from the prisoners followed the migration, and the officer ascended to the deck, unconscious of the number and variety of recruits he had obtained without the formality of an enlistment. The captain of the ship, suspicious that some joke had been practiced, or some mischief perpetrated, from the noise below, met the officer at the head of the gangway, and, seeing the vermin crawling up his shoulders and aiming at his head with the instinct peculiar to them, exclaimed, "Hoot, mon, wha' is the matter wi' yer bock?" The captain was a Scotchman. By this time many of them, in their wanderings, had traveled round from the rear to the front, and showed themselves, to the astonishment of the officer. He flung off his coat in a paroxysm of rage, which was not allayed by three cheers from the prisoners on the deck. Confinement below, with a short allowance, was our punishment for this gratification.

Situated as we were, there appeared to us to be no moral turpitude in enlisting in the British service, especially when we considered that it was almost certain we should soon be impressed into the same. Soon after we had formed this desperate resolution, a recruiting officer came on board to enlist men for the eighty-eighth regiment, to be stationed at Kingston, in the island of Jamaica. We had just been trying to satisfy our hunger upon a piece of beef, which was so tough that no teeth could make an impression on it, when the officer descended between decks, and represented to us the immense improvement that we should experience in our condition, if we were in his Majesty's service; an abundance of good food, comfortable clothing, service easy, and in the finest climate in the world, were temptations too great to be resisted by a set of miserable, half-starved, and almost naked wretches, as we were, and who had already concluded to accept of the proposition even had it been made under circumstances less exciting. The recruiting officer presented his papers for our signature. Again we heard the tempting offers, and again the assurance that we should not be called upon to fight against our government or country; and, with the hope that we should find an opportunity to desert, of which it was our firm intention to avail ourselves when offered —with such hopes, expectations, and motives, we signed the papers, and became soldiers in his Majesty's service.*

But to return to our story, we shortly after, twelve in number, left the Jersey, and were landed upon Long Island and marched under a guard about a mile to an old barn, where we were quartered. Under various pretexts, we frequently went out that night to reconnoiter; but were satisfied that there was no chance for escape then, and must trust to

---

*The reader may have some curiosity to know what became of the "Old Jersey." The prisoners, who were on board of her at the conclusion of the war, in 1783, were liberated. The prison ship was then abandoned, and the dread of contagion prevented any one visiting her. Worms soon destroyed her bottom, and she afterward sunk. It is said that her planks were covered with the names of the captives who had been immured there; a long and melancholy catalogue, as it is supposed that a greater number of men perished on board of her than history informs us of in any other place of confinement in the same period of time.

In the year 1803, the bank at the Wallabout was removed, as preparatory to building a Navy Yard. A vast quantity of bones were found, which were carefully collected and buried under the direction of the Tammany Society of New York.

Providence for some more favorable opportunity. Disappointed in all our hopes and expectations of escape, we were hurried on board of a vessel ready to sail for Jamaica, only waiting for a favorable wind. We entertained a faint hope, that, during our voyage, we might be taken by some American privateer, and consequently obtain our freedom. In the course of six or eight days, we weighed anchor, and hoisted our sail for Jamaica.

The next day we anchored in the harbor of Port Royal, where we lay one day, and sailed for Kingston. We here landed, and with the sergeant at the head marched in single file through Kingston to a place called "Harmony-hall," where the regiment was quartered, and were placed under the care of a drill sergeant. The next morning we were ordered out for drill, and received our uniform and arms, which we were ordered to keep bright and in good order for service. We had but little employment, excepting being drilled to our hearts' content by the sergeant, to make good soldiers of us for the service of his majesty, King George the Third. It appeared to be the object of our officers to reconcile us to the service, by making our duties easy and agreeable. We were often indulged with the privilege of leaving our quarters to visit the town or wander about the country adjacent. In our rambles about the town and country, we visited the grog-shops and taverns, places where sailors generally resort, and had got considerably acquainted with the keepers of these establishments. Our "passes" were signed by a commissioned officer, and they gave us permission to carry our side-arms, that is, a bayonet, and to be absent two hours at a time.

While I and one of my comrades were wandering about the town one day, we stepped into a house where liquors and refreshments were to be obtained. We found one of the seats occupied by an English sailor, to whom we, rather too frankly for prudence, communicated our intentions; or, more correctly speaking, gave him some cause for suspecting our designs from the questions we asked him respecting the probability of obtaining employment on board of some merchant vessel, in case we could get released from our present engagements. The sailor was inclined to be very sociable, and discovered no objections to drinking freely at our expense; telling us that he belonged to an English ship that would sail in a few days; that his captain was in want of hands; and that, at his intercession, he would undoubtedly take us on board. He appeared so friendly, and his manners were so insinuating, that he completely won our confidence. He asked us how we could obtain liberty to leave the garrison, and to pass in and out when we pleased? Taking my "pass" out of my pocket, I showed it to him, and told him that was our authority. He took it into his hand, apparently with an intention of reading it; and, after looking at it for some time, in a sort of careless manner, he put it into his pocket. I felt a little surprised when I saw him do it, and my companion expressed his fears by whispering into my ear, "Blast his eyes, he means to keep the pass."

Having allowed the fellow to get possession of the paper, I felt myself responsible for it, and that it was necessary for me to recover it, even if I were obliged to resort to violent measures. I therefore said to him, "My friend, I must have that paper, as we cannot return to our quarters without it." He replied, "You had better be peaceable about it, for I mean to see your commanding officer."

Matters had now come to a crisis. I saw that it was the sailor's object to inform against us, and to carry the "pass" as an evidence of our conference with him. I immediately drew my bayonet from its scabbard, and thrusting it against his side with force sufficient to inflict a slight wound, put my hand into his pocket and took out the "pass;" and then, giving him a blow upon the head with the butt-end of my bayonet, dropped him senseless on the floor. The noise of this conflict brought the landlord into the room, followed by his wife, with whom a previous acquaintance had made me somewhat of a favorite. The rascal had by this time recovered his senses and had got upon his legs, and began to represent the matter in a light the most favorable to himself.

We vehemently contradicted his assertions, and were stoutly backed up by the landlady, who was considerable of a termagant, and declared that "the sailor was a quarrelsome fellow; that he had made a difficulty once before in the house; and that her husband would be a fool if he did not kick him out of doors." The landlord, to prove that he was "compos mentis," and to appease the wrath of his wife, which waxed warm, complied with her kind wishes, and the sailor was, without much ceremony, hurried through the door, his progress not a little accelerated by a brisk application of the landlord's foot, which sent him spinning into the street in the manner prescribed by the good woman. We were then advised by our friends to return to our quarters as quick as possible, lest the fellow might make some trouble for us. We paid our bill, and gave the landlord many thanks, not forgetting the landlady, to whose kind interference we owed our fortunate escape. About this time I was unexpectedly released from the duties of a soldier. One day I attracted the attention of an officer, by the exercise of my skill as a barber, in the act of shaving a comrade; and was forthwith promoted to the high station of hairdresser and shaver for the officers. I was assiduous in my attentions to my superiors, and thereby gained their confidence, and could, almost whenever I wished, procure a pass to go out when I desired.

To visit my dear native land, my friends, and the scenes of my childhood, was the prevailing wish of my mind; to accomplish this desire I was willing to hazard my life. Many difficulties were to be surmounted before this could be effected. Friends were to be found, in whom confidence could be placed.

I had become acquainted with five soldiers, who had been released from military duty, because they were mechanics, and could make themselves useful in the performance of various mechanical services. They enjoyed considerable liberty, but did not possess the confidence of the officers in so great a degree as I did, having made myself useful and agreeable to them by personal attention in contributing to their comfort and convenience. About this time I had the good fortune to obtain a high degree of confidence, and to find great favor in the sight of the commanding officer, by the exercise of my professional skill in making him wonderfully satisfied with himself upon the occasion of a military ball. He was so much pleased with the improvement I made in his personal appearance, that in the fullness of his heart he gave me a "pass to go out whenever I chose till further orders." The five comrades, with whom I had associated, as I have observed, were mechanics, two of whom were armorers; and they had obtained from the arsenal two pistols and three swords, which were all the weapons we had: these, together with some articles of clothing, we had deposited in the hut of an old negro, whom we had bribed to secrecy.

I had a general pass, as I have before observed, for myself to go out at pleasure; but it was necessary to obtain a special one for my companions, and this duty devolved on me. In the afternoon, soon after dinner, I asked the commanding officer to grant me the favor of a pass for five of my acquaintances to go out to spend the evening, upon condition of returning before nine o'clock. The officer hesitated for a moment; and then, as he signed the pass, said, "I believe I can trust you; but remember that you must not come back without them." This I readily promised, and I faithfully fulfilled the obligation.

About the middle of the week, in the month of July, 1782, our little party of six,—five Americans, and one Irishman, an active, courageous fellow,—left the town, and proceeded to the negro's hut, where we received our weapons and clothing, and some little stores of provisions which we had deposited. That afternoon a soldier had been buried at Rockfort, and part of the regiment had been out to attend the funeral. Seeing these soldiers upon their return, at a distance, and fearing that our bundles might excite their suspicion, we concluded to separate and meet again as soon as the soldiers had passed. We escaped their notice, and fortunately met together a little time after,—all but one, who was missing. We waited some time, and looked in various directions for him, without success.

The man whom we missed was somewhat intoxicated, and the probability was that he had lain down and fallen asleep; or, perhaps, his courage had failed, and he had given up the undertaking, and might have gone back and given information against us. We were satisfied that we could wait no longer for him without exposing ourselves to great danger, and, therefore, concluded to proceed without him. What was his fate I have never been able to ascertain. We pushed rapidly forward till we had got about a mile from Kingston, when we entered a small piece of woodland, and divested ourselves of our uniform, which we had worn with much reluctance, and had never ceased to regret having exposed ourselves to the necessity of putting on; clothed ourselves in the sailor garments, which we had taken care to provide; cut the white binding from our hats; and were soon metamorphosed into much better sailors than we had ever been soldiers. Having loaded our pistols, we again proceeded. We had advanced but a few rods, when we met a sergeant, belonging to a regiment called the Liverpool Blues, who had been to Rockfort to see some of his acquaintance, and was then upon his return. It was near the time for stationing the guard, as usual, at the place called the "Plum-tree." The sergeant hailed us with, "Where are you bound, my lads?" We answered, "To Rockfort." He replied, "I have just come from there and found all well: how goes on the recruiting at New York? and what is the news?"

A ship had arrived the day previous, from New York, and he supposed that we were some of the recruits that she had brought over. We perceived his mistake, and adapted our answers to his questions, so as to encourage his delusion. We told him that the recruiting went on bravely, and we were going to join our regiment at Rockfort. The fellow seemed to be in a very happy mood, and immediately declared his intention of turning back to show us the way to the fort. Our situation was rendered very embarrassing by this kind offer; and to refuse it we feared would excite suspicion. Our generous guide thought he was doing us service, when he was leading us directly to destruction; and the idea of killing him, while he imagined that he was performing a good service for us, was very unpleasant; but it was our only alternative. In a few moments the deed would have been done; self-preservation made it necessary;

but, fortunately for the poor fellow, and much to our satisfaction, he suddenly recollected that his pass required him to be back to Kingston by nine o'clock, and, bidding us good night, and telling us that we could not miss the way, he left us, and pursued his route to Kingston at a rapid pace We thought it important that we should get as far from Kingston that night as possible, as we should undoubtedly be pursued in the morning; and the sergeant, from whom we had just parted, would give information of us, as soon as he arrived and ascertained that we were deserters.

We proceeded at a rapid pace for about half of a mile farther, when we met with an old negro, who hailed us, saying, "Where be you going, massa buckra men? there be a plenty of soldiers a little way ahead; they will take you up, and put you on board of man-of-war." We told him that we had got a pass. The negro replied, "Dey no care for dat, dey put you on board a man-of-war." He mistook us for sailors who were deserting from some ship.

Whatever might be the cause, I always found the negroes in and about Kingston ready to give every facility to a soldier or sailor who wished to desert. We soon agreed with the old fellow for a dollar to guide us into a path through the woods, by following which we should avoid the guard at the "Plum-tree," in whose vicinity we then were. We followed our guide about a mile, when he told us that we had got past the guard, and, giving us directions as to our future course, he left us, after having called God to witness that he never would inform against us. Our anxiety to escape pursuit determined us to use all the expedition we could through the night. About midnight, we came to one of the many rivulets with which Jamaica abounds. As we were unable to determine what its width or depth was, in the darkness, it was necessary to proceed with caution. The tallest of our party was sent forward to try to wade across. The rest followed in single file, according to our respective heights; I, being the shortest, brought up the rear. Holding our arms and provisions and part of our clothing above our heads, we soon arrived on the opposite shore. We traveled in our wet clothes the remainder of the night, and, toward daylight, we looked round for some retired spot, where we could secrete ourselves during the day, as we considered that it would expose us to great hazard, if not to certain detection, to travel by daylight at so little distance from Kingston as we then were.

As soon as it was dark enough to prevent discovery, we left our place of concealment, and proceeded on our second night's journey. After having traveled three or four hours, we unexpectedly found ourselves near a hut, and were alarmed at hearing a negro female voice exclaim, "Here come a whole parcel of buckra man." We immediately started from the spot, and proceeded with all practicable speed till we had traveled three or four miles, when we sat down to rest, and to refresh ourselves with some of our bread and dried herring.

After several hours' rest, we found ourselves considerably refreshed; and as our small stock of provisions was nearly exausted, and we had consumed nearly the time we had anticipated would be required to arrive on the opposite side of the island, we concluded that we would venture to travel by daylight. We traveled without interruption till about three o'clock in the afternoon, and, while ascending a hill, we were alarmed by hearing the sound of voices. We stopped, and collected together to consult upon what course to adopt. In a few moments, we saw, coming over the hill, three stout negroes, armed with muskets, which they immediately presented at us, and ordered us to stop. Our arms, as I have formerly observed, consisted of two pistols and three swords: upon the pistols we could place but little dependence, as they were not in good order; and the swords were concealed under our clothes; to attempt to draw them out would have caused the negroes instantly to fire upon us. They were about ten rods before us, and stood in the attitude of taking a deliberate aim at us. To run would be certain death to some of us; we therefore saw no alternative but to advance. One of our number, a man named Jones, a tall, powerful fellow, took a paper from his pocket, and, holding it up before him, advanced, with great apparent confidence in his manner, and the rest of us imitated his example. As we approached, Jones held out the paper to one of them, telling him that it was our pass, giving us authority to travel across the island. The negroes, as we very well knew, were unable to read; it was therefore immaterial what was written upon the paper,—I believe it was an old letter,—as manuscript or print was entirely beyond their comprehension. While we were advancing, we had time to confer with each other; and the circumstances of the moment, the critical situation in which we were placed, naturally led our minds to one conclusion, to obtain the consent of the negroes that we might pursue our journey; but if they opposed our progress, to resort to violence, if we perished in the attempt.

Our sufferings had made us somewhat savage in our feelings; and we marched up to them with that determination of purpose which desperate men have resolved upon, when life, liberty, and everything they value is at stake;—all depended upon prompt and decisive action. This was a fearful moment. The negroes stood in a row, their muskets still presented, but their attention was principally directed to the paper which Jones held before them; while our eyes were constantly fixed upon them, anxiously watching their motions, and designing to disarm them as soon as a favorable opportunity should be offered. The negroes were large and powerful men, while we, though we outnumbered them, were worn down by our long march, and enfeebled by hunger. In physical power we were greatly their inferiors. But the desperate circumstances in which we were placed inspired us with uncommon courage, and gave us an unnatural degree of strength.

We advanced steadily forward, shoulder to shoulder, till the breasts of three of us were within a few inches of the muzzles of their guns. Jones reached forward and handed the paper to one of the negroes. He took it, and having turned it round several times, and examined both sides, and finding himself not much the wiser for it, shook his head and said, "We must stop you." The expression of his countenance, the doubts which were manifested in his manner of receiving the paper, convinced us, that all hope of deceiving or conciliating them was at an end. Their muskets were still presented, their fingers upon the triggers. An awful pause of a moment ensued, when we made a sudden and desperate spring forward, and seized their muskets; our attack was so unexpected, that we wrenched them from their hands before they were aware of our intention. The negro, whom I attacked, fired just as I seized his gun, but I had fortunately turned the direction of it, and the ball inflicted a slight wound upon my side, the scar of which remains to this day. This was the only gun that was discharged during this dreadful encounter. As soon as it was in my possession, I exercised all my strength, more than I thought I possessed, and gave him a tremendous blow over the head with the breech, which brought him to the ground, from which he never rose. I had no sooner accomplished my work, than I found my companions had been equally active, and had dispatched the other two negroes in the same space of time. None of our party received any injury but myself, and my wound I considered as trifling. The report of the gun we were fearful would alarm some of our enemies' comrades, who might be in the vicinity, and bring them to the spot. We accordingly dragged the bodies to a considerable distance into the woods, where we buried them under a quantity of leaves and brush. In their pockets we found a few biscuit, which were very acceptable to us in our famished condition. The best gun was selected, as we did not think it necessary to burden ourselves with the others, as they had been injured in the conflict. We took what ammunition we thought necessary, and then sought a place of rest for the remainder of the day. The negroes whom we had encountered, belonged to a class called "Cudjoe men." They were encouraged to exercise their vigilance by the promise of receiving a certain sum of money for every fugitive slave they restored to his master, or soldier whom they should arrest as a deserter. We lay down in the woods, languid and exhausted, after the excitement and fatigue from our contest with the negroes, and slept soundly for some hours. As it was now nearly dark, we thought we would venture again upon our journey. Having loaded our musket, the spoils of our victory, we entered the road, and, having looked around with great caution, and finding no obstacles in the way to excite any apprehension, we started forward. We knew not for a certainty where we were; but were satisfied, from the time we had consumed in our journey, that we could not be at a great distance from the northern side of the island. We traveled all night, occasionally stopping to rest, and refresh ourselves with some of the hard biscuit, which we had found in the pockets of the negroes, and a draught of water from the springs by the road-side. As daylight approached, we found ourselves on the summit of a hill, and in sight of the ocean. After we had remained as long as we thought prudent upon the eminence, we retired to the woods, for concealment during the day. We needed rest, and slept the greater part of the day. Before sunset, we left our hiding-place, after eating the remainder of our bread, and proceeded cautiously toward the shore, keeping ourselves concealed as much as possible behind the bushes. The island of Cuba could just be seen in the horizon, at the distance of thirty leagues; between that and us lay the ocean, smooth and unruffled, and not a sail to whiten its surface. To remain where we were long, without starving or being detected, was impossible; but how to get away was the problem to be solved. Undetermined what to do, we left our retreat again, and the first object that met our view upon the water was a sail-boat directing her course to the shore near where we were.

The question now to be decided was, whether we should attempt to make a prize of the boat, and escape to Cuba. The wind was blowing from the shore, and the boat was consequently beating in against the wind. This was a favorable circumstance for us, if we could get possession of the boat. The undertaking was fraught with difficulty and danger, but it was our only chance for escape. We crept cautiously down to the shore, keeping concealed as much as possible behind the bushes, till we arrived near to the point, at which we thought the boat was steering. As she was beating against the wind, we concluded, if the man at the helm could be brought down, the boat would luff, which would bring her near the shore, when we were immediately to spring on board. Jones, being the best marksman, took the musket, and seeing that it was well loaded and primed, crept as close to the edge of the shore as he could without being discovered by the crew, and lay down, to wait for a good opportunity to fire at the man at the helm. The rest of us kept as near to him as possible. Every circumstance seemed to favor our design. The negroes were all in their huts, and everything around was quiet and still.

The boat soon approached near enough for Jones to take a sure aim; and we scarcely breathed as we lay extended on the ground, waiting for him to perform the duty assigned him.

In a few moments, bang went the gun, and down went the negro from the helm into the bottom of the boat; and, as we had anticipated, the helm being abandoned, the boat luffed up in the wind and was brought close to the shore, which was bold, and the water deep enough to float her. The instant the gun was fired, we were upon our feet, and in the next moment up to our waists in the water along side of the boat. No time was lost in shoving her about, and getting her bows from the land. There was a fresh breeze from the shore; the sails filled; and the boat was soon under a brisk headway. I remained in the water the last, and, as I attempted to get on board, my hands slipped from my hold on the gunwale, and I fell into the water. I heard an exclamation, "Good God! Fox is lost!" from one of our party; but as the boat swept by me, I caught with my middle finger in the noose of a rope that hung over the stern, and was seized by the cape of my jacket and drawn into the boat by the powerful arm of Jones, who was managing the helm. All that I have described was apparently the work of a moment. Never did men use greater exertions than we did at this time. The report of Jones' gun alarmed the negroes, and brought them from their huts in all directions down to the shore, armed with muskets and clubs, and full of rage and fury. They waded out after us, up to their chins in the water; and fired volley after volley, as fast as they could load. The bullets fell thickly around us, but fortunately none of us were injured.

Our attention was next directed to the disposal of the crew of the boat we had captured, consisting of three men and a boy. As soon as we sprung into the boat, they fled with terror and amazement into a sort of cabin in the bow, where they still remained. It was no wonder that they were frightened, attacked so suddenly by an enemy, who, as it seemed to them, had arisen all at once from the bowels of the earth or the depths of the ocean. Whether the head of the negro at the helm was bullet-proof, or whether the ball approached so near to it as to frighten him into insensibility, we never knew; but we found him prostrated in the bottom of the boat, when we entered it, apparently dead; but to our gratification, we soon found that he was alive, and not a curl of his wool discomposed. He was soon upon his knees, supplicating mercy, in which attitude and tone he was followed by the rest of the crew as we called them from their hiding-place. We gave them their choice to proceed with us on our voyage, or expose themselves to the hazard of drowning by attempting to swim ashore. They accepted the latter proposition with much gratitude, and were soon swimming lustily for the shore, from which we were at the distance of more than a mile, where we saw them all safely arrive. The negroes collected around them in great numbers after they landed, probably to hear their account of the transaction; and to obtain information concerning our intentions and destination. We felt animated by our success. We found the boat in good order; and, with a fresh breeze, we made rapid progress. We found a plenty of provisions in the boat, with which, for the first time for five days, we abundantly satisfied our hunger. It was now nearly dark, and we had got a considerable distance from the shore; but we continued to watch the movements of the negroes with anxiety, least they should pursue us. After the negroes had held a short consultation together, we saw them all start off with great rapidity toward a point of land, under which we thought we could see something lying, that had the appearance of a vessel. As the negroes ran in that direction, we had no doubt that they had some plan in contemplation in relation to our capture. Our fears and conjectures were soon reduced to a matter of fact; for we had proceeded but a little distance farther, when we came in plain sight of a schooner at anchor. The vessel was soon under weigh, and sailing in a direction to cut us off; but we trusted that the approaching darkness would in a short time conceal us from the sight of our pursuers. As the schooner was a large object, compared with our little boat, we could see her long after we were invisible to them. After being satisfied of the course the schooner was taking, we thought the best way to avoid her would be to put about directly for Jamaica.

We sailed in this direction till we supposed that our enemy had got considerably past the course for us to pursue, when we again put about, and steered as directly as we were able for Cuba. We sailed without interruption through the night, and, from the rapidity with which we had passed through the water, we concluded we could not be a great distance from the land. As soon as daylight approached we espied the shore, and lost no time in making for it. Shortly after, we saw, at a considerable distance, the schooner, apparently steering for Jamaica. They discovered us, and altered their course directly for us. Their approach, however excited no alarm in our minds now, for we were sure that we could run our boat on shore before they could come up with us. Their kind intentions were manifested in the compliment of a few salutes from a swivel, which proved as harmless as the courtesy we endeavored to show them by half a dozen salutes from the musket which had previously done us more faithful service. The schooner soon gave up the chase, "and left us alone in our glory."

In a few days we found a vessel bound for St. Domingo in which we took passage and on our arrival there found the American frigate Flora at anchor. A few hours saw us safe beneath the protection of the stars and stripes.

THE NARRATIVE

OF THE

MUTINY OF THE BOUNTY,

WITH THE ESCAPE OF CAPTAIN BLIGH, AND HIS PERILOUS VOYAGE OF NEAR FOUR THOUSAND MILES IN AN OPEN BOAT TO THE ISLAND OF TIMOR, TOGETHER WITH THE FATE OF FLETCHER CHRISTIAN, THE LEADER OF THE MUTINEERS, AND THE FINAL SETTLEMENT OF THE LATTER AT

PITCAIRN ISLAND, IN THE PACIFIC OCEAN.

His Majesty's ship Bounty was purchased into the service, and placed under the command of Captain Bligh, in 1787. She left England in December of that year, with orders to proceed to Otaheite, and transport the bread-fruit of that country to the British settlements in the West Indies, and to bring also some specimens of it to England. Her crew consisted of forty-four persons, and a gardener. She was ordered to make the passage round Cape Horn, but after contending a long time with adverse gales, in extremely cold weather, she was obliged to bear away for the Cape of Good Hope, where she underwent a refit, and arrived at her destination in October 1788. Six months were spent at Otaheite, collecting and stowing away the fruit, during which time the officers and seamen had free access to the shore, and made many friends, though only one of the seamen formed any alliance there.

In April 1789, they took leave of their friends at Otaheite, and proceeded to Anamooka, where Bligh replenished his stock of water, and took on board hogs, fruit, vegetables, etc., and put to sea again on the 26th of the same month. Throughout the voyage Bligh, who was of an exceedingly tyrannical disposition, had repeated misunderstandings with his officers, and had on several occasions given them and the ship's company just reasons for complaint. Still, whatever might have been the feelings of the officers, Adams declares there was no real discontent among the crew; much less was there any idea of offering violence to their commander. The officers, it must be admitted, had much more cause for dissatisfaction than the seamen, especially the master and the lieutenant, Fletcher Christian. The latter was a protegé of Bligh, and unfortunately was under some obligations to him of a pecuniary nature, of which Bligh frequently reminded him when any difference arose. Christian, excessively annoyed at the share of blame which repeatedly fell to his lot, in common with the rest of the officers, could ill endure the additional taunt of private obligations; and in a moment of excitement told his commander that sooner or later a day of reckoning would arrive. The day previous to the mutiny a serious quarrel occurred between Bligh and his officers, about some cocoa-nuts which were missed from his private stock; and Christian again fell under his commander's displeasure. The same evening he was invited to supper in the cabin, but he had not so soon forgotten his injuries as to accept of this ill-timed civility, and returned an excuse.

Matters were in this state on the 28th of April 1789, when the Bounty, on her homeward voyage, was passing to the southward of Tofoa, one of the Friendly Islands. It was one of those beautiful nights which characterize the tropical regions, when the mildness of the air and the stillness of nature dispose the mind to reflection. Christian, pondering over his grievances, considered them so intolerable, that anything appeared preferable to enduring them, and he determined, as he could not redress them, that he would at least escape from the possibility of their being increased. Absence from England, and a long residence at Otaheite, where new connections were formed, weakened the recollection of his native country, and prepared his mind for the reception of ideas which the situation of the ship and the serenity of the moment particularly favored. His plan, strange as it must appear for a young officer to adopt, who was fairly advanced in an honorable profession, was to set himself adrift upon a raft, and make his way to the island then in sight. As quick in the execution as in the design, the raft was soon constructed, various useful articles were got together, and he was on point of launching it, when a young officer, who afterward perished in the Pandora, to whom Christian communicated his intention, recommended him, rather than risk his life on so hazardous an expedition, to endeavor to take possession of the ship, which he thought would not be very difficult, as many of the ship's company were not well disposed toward the commander, and would all be very glad to return to Otaheite, and reside among their friends in that island. This daring proposition is even more extraordinary than the premeditated scheme of his companion, and, if true, certainly relieves Christian from part of the odium which has hitherto attached to him as the sole instigator of the mutiny.

It however accorded too well with the disposition of Christian's mind, and hazardous as it was, he determined to co-operate with his friend in effecting it, resolving, if he failed, to throw himself into the sea; and that there might be no chance of being saved, he tied a deep sea-lead about his neck, and concealed it within his clothes. Christian happened to have the morning watch, and as soon as he had relieved the officer of the deck, he entered into conversation with Quintal, the only one of the seamen who, Adams said, had formed any serious attachment at Otaheite; and after expatiating on the happy hours they had passed there, disclosed his intentions. Quintal, after some consideration, said he thought it a dangerous attempt, and declined taking a part. Vexed at a repulse in a quarter where he was most sanguine of success, and particularly at having revealed sentiments which, if made known, would bring him to an ignominious death, Christian became desperate, exhibited the lead about his neck in testimony of his own resolution, and taxed Quintal with cowardice, declaring it was fear alone that restrained him. Quintal denied this accusation; and in reply to Christian's further argument, that success would restore them all to the happy island, and the connections they had left behind, the strongest persuasion he could have used to a mind somewhat prepared to acquiesce, he recommended that some one else should be tried—Isaac Martin for instance, who was standing by. Martin, more ready than his shipmate, emphatically declared, "He was for it; it was the very thing." Successful in one instance, Christian went to every man of his watch, many of whom he found disposed to join him, and before daylight the greater portion of the ship's company were brought over.

Adams was sleeping in his hammock, when Sumner, one of the seamen, came to him, and whispered that Christian was going to take the ship from her commander, and set him and the master on shore. On hearing this, Adams went upon deck, and found everything in great confusion; but not then liking to take any part in the transaction, he returned to his hammock, and remained there until he saw Christian at the arm-chest, distributing arms to all who came for them; and then seeing measures had proceeded so far, and apprehensive of being on the weaker side, he turned out again and went for a cutlass. All those who proposed to assist Christian being armed, Adams, with others, was ordered to secure the officers, while Christian and the master-at-arms proceeded to the cabin to make a prisoner of Captain Bligh. They seized him in his cot, bound his hands behind him, and brought him upon deck. He remonstrated with them on their conduct, but received only abuse in return, and a blow from the master-at-arms with the flat side of a cutlass. He was placed near the binnacle, and detained there, with his arms pinioned, by Christian, who held him with one hand, and a bayonet with the other. As soon as the lieutenant was secured, the sentinels that had been placed over the doors of the officers' cabins were taken off; the master then jumped upon the forecastle, and endeavored to form a party to retake the ship; but he was quickly secured, and sent below in confinement.

This conduct of the master, who was the only officer that tried to bring the mutineers to a sense of their duty, was the more highly creditable to him, as he had the greatest cause for discontent, Bligh having been more severe to him than to any of the other officers. About this time a dispute arose, whether the lieutenant and his party, whom the mutineers resolved to set adrift, should have the launch or the cutter; and it being decided in favor of the launch, Christian ordered her to be hoisted out. Martin, who, it may be remembered, was the first convert to Christian's plan, foreseeing that with the aid of so large a boat the party would find their way to England, and that their information would, in all probability, lead to the detection of the offenders, relinquished his first intention, and exclaimed, "If you give him the launch, I will go with him; you may as well give him the ship." He really appears to have been in earnest in making this declaration, as he was afterward ordered to the gangway from his post of command over the lieutenant, in consequence of having fed him with a shaddock, and exchanged looks with him indicative of his friendly intentions. It also fell to the lot of Adams to guard the lieutenant, who, observing him stationed by his side, exclaimed, "And you, Smith, are you against me?"* To which Adams replied that he only acted as the others did—he must be like the rest. Captain Bligh, while thus secured, reproached Christian with ingratitude, reminded him of his obligations to him, and begged he would recollect he had a wife and family. To which Christian replied, that he should have thought of that before.

The launch was by this time hoisted out; and the officers and seamen of Captain Bligh's party having collected what was necessary for their voyage, were ordered into her. Among those who took their seats in the boat was Martin, which being noticed by Quintal, he pointed a musket at him, and declared he would shoot him unless he instantly returned to the ship, which he did. The armorer and carpenter's mates were also forcibly detained, as they might be required hereafter. All those now being in the boat who were intended to accompany their unfortunate commander, Christian addressed him, saying—"Come, Captain Bligh,

*Adams went by the name of Alexander Smith in the Bounty.

your officers and men are now in the boat, and you must go with them; if you attempt to make the least resistance you will instantly be put to death." He was then forced over the side, and his hands unbound. When they were putting him out of the ship, Bligh looked steadfastly at Christian, and asked him, if his treatment was a proper return for the many instances he had received of his friendship? At this question he seemed confused, and answered with much emotion—"That, Captain Bligh, —— that is the thing; —— I am in hell—I am in hell!"

The boat was veered astern, and soon after cast adrift, amid the ridicule and scoffs of these deluded and unthinking men, whose general shout was, "huzza for Otaheite." The armorer and carpenter's mates called on Bligh, and begged him to remember that they had no hand in the transaction, and some others seemed to express by their manner a contrition for having joined in the mutiny.

Before the boat was cast off, Bligh begged that some arms might be handed into her; but these unfeeling wretches laughed at him, and said "he was well acquainted with the people among whom he was going, and therefore did not want them." They, however, threw four cutlasses into the boat. Their whole stock of provisions consisted of one hundred and fifty pounds of bread, sixteen pieces of pork, six quarts of rum, with twenty-eight gallons of water; there were also four empty barrecoes in the boat. The boatswain had been allowed to collect a small quantity of twine, some canvas, lines, and cordage. Mr. Samuel, the clerk, had been also permitted to take a quadrant and compass; but he was forbidden, on pain of death, to touch either chart, ephemeris, book of astronomical observations, sextant, time-keeper, or any of the surveys or drawings which Bligh had been collecting for fifteen years. Mr. Samuel had the good fortune to secure Bligh's journal and commission, with some other material ship papers. And at the time the boat left the ship they were about ten leagues from Tosoa. Bligh's first determination was to steer for this place, to seek a supply of bread-fruit and water, from thence to proceed to Tongataboo, and there to solicit the king to suffer him to equip the boat, and grant them such a supply of water and provisions as might enable them to reach the East Indies. Arriving at Tosoa, they found the natives unfriendly and hostile; and availing themselves of the defenseless state of the English, attacked them violently with stones, so that the supply they got here was very scanty. It was, indeed, with some difficulty they escaped being entirely cut off by the natives; which most probably would have been the case, had not one of the crew (John Norton) resolutely jumped on shore and cast off the stern-fast of the boat; this brave fellow fell a sacrifice to preserve the lives of his companions; he was surrounded and inhumanly murdered by these savages.

It now seemed the general wish of all in the boat, that Bligh should conduct them toward home. He pointed out to them that no hopes of relief remained, excepting what might be found at New Holland, or the island of Timor, which was at the distance of full 1200 leagues; and that it would require the greatest economy to be observed, with regard to the scanty allowance which they had to live upon for so long a voyage. It was therefore agreed by the whole crew, that only an ounce of bread, and a quarter of a pint of water should be issued to each person per day. After Bligh had recommended to them in the most solemn manner not to depart from the promise they had made; he, on the second of May, bore away, and shaped his course for New Holland, across a sea little explored, in a boat only twenty-three feet in length, six feet nine inches in breadth, and two feet nine inches deep, with eighteen persons on board, and heavy laden.

The men were divided into watches, and they returned thanks to God for their miraculous escape. The second day was stormy; and, to lighten the boat, everything was thrown overboard that could be spared, except two suits of clothes to each. A teaspoonful of rum, and a quarter of a bread-fruit, was served out for dinner, with a determination to make their provisions last out eight weeks. The sixth day their allowances were delivered out by a pair of scales made of two cocoanut shells; and the weight of a pistol-ball of bread was served out, making one twenty-fifth part of a pound of sixteen ounces, or two hundred and seventy-two grains, at a meal. The ninth day they were served regularly with one twenty-fifth of a pound of bread, and a quarter of a pint of water at morning, noon, and sunset; and this day with half an ounce of pork for dinner to each, which was divided into three or four mouthfuls. The eleventh day it rained, and was cold; and the men began to be dejected, full of wants, and without the means of relief. Their clothes were wet through, which they stripped off, and wrung through salt water; by which means they felt a warmth which they could not have had while wet with rain.* The fourteenth day they passed by islands they dared not touch at, for fear of the natives, having been in other places pursued; which rather increased their misery. A general run of cloudy wet weather was considered as a great blessing of Providence, as the hot weather would have caused them to have died with thirst. Being so constantly covered with rain or sea, they conceived it protected them from that dreadful calamity.

The nineteenth day the men seemed half dead, and their appearances were horrible. Extreme hunger was now very great. No one suffered from thirst, nor had they much inclination to drink, that desire being satisfied through the skin; and the little sleep they got was in the midst of water. Two spoonfuls of rum were served out this morning, with their usual allowance of bread and water. At noon the sun broke out, which rejoiced every one. In the afternoon they were covered with rain and salt water—the cold was extreme—and every one dreaded the approach of night. Sleep, though longed for, gave but little comfort. Captain Bligh himself almost lived without it. The next morning the weather abated, and a larger allowance of rum was given out. The twenty-second day the weather was bad, and the men in great distress, and in expectation that such another night as their last would put an end to their lives. Several seemed to be no longer able to support their sufferings. Two teaspoonfuls of rum were served out; after which, with wringing their clothes, and their breakfast of bread and water, they became a little refreshed. The weather abated, all hands were rejoiced, and they ate their other scanty meals with more satisfaction than for some time past.

The twenty-third day the fineness of the morning produced cheerful countenances, and they experienced, for the first time, for fifteen days past, comfort from the warmth of the sun. They stripped, and hung up their clothes to dry; which were now so threadbare as to keep neither

---

*Captain Bligh afterward frequently practiced it with great benefit, and states that the preservation of their health during sixteen days of continued heavy rains, was owing to this practice of wringing their clothes out as often as they became filled with rain; and that the men felt a change more like that of dry clothes than could have been imagined; that they often repeated it, and it gave great refreshment and warmth.

cold nor wet out. They saw many birds, a sure sign of being near land The state of their provisions this day, at their usual rate of allowance, would have lasted for nineteen days longer, when they hoped to reach the island of Timor. But as it was possible they might be obliged to go to Java, they reduced their allowance to make their stock hold out for six weeks. The necessity of the case was stated, and every one cheerfully agreed to receive one twenty-fifth of a pound of bread for breakfast, and the same for dinner; and by omitting supper they had forty-three days' allowance. The twenty-fourth day a bird the size of a pigeon was caught, and divided into eighteen portions. They also caught a booby, which was killed for supper, and its blood given to three of those who were most distressed for want of food; and, as a favor, an allowance of bread was given out for supper; and they made a good supper, compared with their usual fare. The twenty-fifth day they caught another booby. The weather was fine; and they thought Providence appeared to be relieving their wants. The men were overjoyed at this addition to their dinner. The blood was given to those who most wanted food. To make their bread a little savory, many dipped it frequently in salt water, while others broke theirs into small pieces, and ate it in their allowance of water, out of a cocoanut shell, with a spoon—economically avoiding to take too large a piece at a time; so that they were as long at dinner as if they had been at a more plentiful meal. The serenity of the weather was not without its inconvenience, and distress now came of another kind. The sun was so powerful that the men were seized with languor and faintness, which made life to some indifferent. The twenty-sixth day they passed by much drifted wood, and caught two boobies, whose stomachs contained several flying-fish and small cuttle-fish. They were considered as valuable prizes, and were divided, with their maws, into eighteen portions, in addition to their common allowance. Captain Bligh was happy to see that with this every person thought he had feasted. In the evening, they saw a gannet; and, as the clouds remained fixed in the west, they had no doubt of being near to land; and they all amused themselves by conversing on the probability of what they should find.

The twenty-eighth day they made an island, in lat. 12° 39′ S., long. (by account) 40° 35′ W. of Tofoa, which they called Restoration Island, where they found plenty of water, and oysters, which were so fast to the rocks that they were obliged to open the shells. They made some excellent stews of them, mixed with bread and a bit of pork, by means of a copper pot which they found on board, and a tinder-box that had been thrown into the boat on turning off. Each person received a full pint. The men, though weak, appeared much refreshed, and in spirits, with a hope of being able to surmount the difficulties they had to encounter. The diseases of the people were, a dizziness in the head, a weakness of joints, and violent tenesmus—few of the men having had an evacuation by stool since they had left the ship;—but the complaints of none were alarming. Every one retained marks of strength that, with a mind possessed of a tolerable share of fortitude, seemed able to bear more fatigue than they imagined they should have in their voyage to Timor. The men were not permitted to expose themselves to the heat of the sun, but to take their short sleep in the shade: they were cautioned about taking berries or fruit, which, unless eaten by birds, were not deemed wholesome. Some suffered by neglecting this caution. The twenty-ninth day, finding themselves discovered by the natives, they said prayers, and embarked. Their stock of bread, according to their last mode of allowance, was a twenty-fifth of a pound at breakfast and at dinner. The thirtieth day they landed on another island, and parties were sent out for supplies. But a spirit of discontent began to discover itself among some, and from one man in particular; but it was instantly checked, and everything became quiet again. Each person got this day a full pint and a half of stewed oysters and clams, thickened with small beans, which the botanists call a species of dolichos.

The thirty-first day, Mr. Nelson, the botanist, was taken very ill with violent pains in his bowels, loss of sight, much drought, and an inability to walk. This was partly owing to heat and fatigue, and not retiring to sleep in the shade, or to improper food. The little wine that remained was of real use. With a few pieces of bread soaked in half a glass of wine occasionally, he continued to mend, and it was found at last not necessary to continue the wine. For six days they coasted along New Holland, and, on landing, got occasionally supplies of oysters, birds, and water. These, though small, with rest, and being relieved from many fatigues, preserved their lives; but, even in their present state, they were deplorable objects. The thirty-third day from their leaving Tofoa, which was the third of June, they again launched into the open ocean for the island of Timor. Bligh was happy to find that no one was so much affected with their miserable situation as himself; but that the men seemed as if they were embarked on a voyage to Timor, in a vessel sufficiently calculated for safety and convenience. This confidence gave him pleasure; and to this cause did he attribute their preservation. Every one was encouraged to believe that eight or ten days would bring them to Timor; and, after prayers, their allowance of water was served out for supper. The thirty-sixth day, the state of stores on hand, at their former rate of serving, was equal to nineteen days' allowance, at three times a day; and there being now every prospect of a quick passage, their suppers were again granted. The thirty-seventh day the sea was high, with much rain, and the night cold. The surgeon and an old hardy seamen appeared to be giving way very fast. They were assisted by a teaspoonful or two of the wine at a time, which had been carefully saved, expecting such a melancholy necessity. The thirty-eighth day they caught a small dolphin, which was their first relief of this kind. Two ounces were delivered out to each man this day, and the remainder was reserved for the next day. The thirty-ninth day the men were beginning to complain generally; and, by the feelings of all, they were convinced they were but too well founded. The surgeon and the old seaman had a little wine given to them; and encouraged with the hopes of reaching Timor in a very few days, on their present fine rate of sailing. The fortieth day, in the morning, after a comfortless night, there was such a visible alteration in many of the people, as to occasion many apprehensions. Extreme weakness, swelled legs, hollow ghastly countenances, a more than common inclination to sleep, and an apparent debility of understanding, seemed to indicate approaching dissolution. The surgeon and the old seaman were the most miserable of objects. A few teaspoonfuls of the little wine that remained, greatly assisted them: hope was their principal support, and birds and rockweed showed they were not far from land.

On the forty-first day every one received his accustomed allowance, and an extra supply of water to those who wanted it. By observation, they found they had now passed the meridian of the eastern part of Timor, which gave great joy. On the forty-second day, the 12th of June, at three in the morning, they discovered Timor, at two leagues' distance. It was impossible to describe the joy it diffused. It appeared scarcely credible to themselves, that in an open boat, so poorly provided, they should have been enabled to reach the coast of Timor in forty-one days after leaving the island of Tofoa; having in that time run the distance of 3,618 miles; and that, notwithstanding their extreme distress, no one should have perished on the voyage.

Some of the natives brought them some Indian corn, and pilots to conduct them to Coupang. They were becalmed, and the men were obliged to try at the oars, which they used with some effect. On the 14th of June they reached Coupang, where they received every attention humanity and kindness could dictate. Nothing but the strictest economy of their provisions, the sacredly keeping to their agreements, and due subordination and perseverance, could have saved Bligh and his men. Such had been their attention to these points, that when they arrived at Timor, there remained on hand eleven days' provisions to have carried them on to Java, if they had missed this island. The quantity of provisions, with which they left the ship was not more than would have been consumed in five days, without such precautions.

In March of the following year, Captain Bligh arrived in England. Out of nineteen who were in the boat, when she was turned adrift by the mutineers, only twelve lived to reach their native country.

We now return to the Bounty, and the adventures of its mutinous crew. Christian, who was the mate, Heywood, Young and Stewart, midshipmen, the master-at-arms, and sixteen seamen, beside the three artificers and the gardener—forming in all twenty-five—made up the entire crew.

The ship having stood for some time to the W.N.W., with a view to deceive the party in the launch, was afterward put about, and her course directed as near to Otaheite as the wind would permit. In a few days they found some difficulty in reaching that island, and bore away for Tobouai, a small island about three hundred miles to the southward of it, where they agreed to establish themselves, provided the natives, who were numerous, were not hostile to their purpose. Of this they had very early intimation, an attack being made upon a boat which they sent to sound the harbor. She, however, effected her purpose; and the next morning the Bounty was warped inside the reef that formed the port, and stationed close to the beach. An attempt to land was next made; but the natives disputed every foot of ground with spears, clubs and stones, until they were dispersed by a discharge of cannon and musketry. On this they fled to the interior, and refused to hold any further intercourse with their visitors. The determined hostility of the natives put an end to the mutineers' design of settling among them at that time; and, after two days' fruitless attempt at reconciliation, they left the island and proceeded to Otaheite. Tobouai was, however, a favorite spot with them, and they determined to make another effort to settle there, which they thought would yet be feasible, provided the islanders could be made acquainted with their friendly intentions. The only way to do this was through interpreters, who might be procured at Otaheite; and in order not to be dependent upon the natives of Tobouai for wives, they determined to engage several Otaheitan women to accompany them. They reached Otaheite in eight days, and were received with the greatest kindness by their former friends, who immediately inquired for the captain and his officers. Christian and his party having anticipated inquiries of this nature, invented a story to account for their absence, and told them that Bligh, having found an island suitable for a settlement, had landed there with some of his officers, and sent them in the ship to procure live stock and whatever else would be useful to the colony, and to bring beside such of the natives as were willing to accompany them. Satisfied with this plausible account, the chiefs supplied them with everything they wanted, and even gave them a bull and a cow which had been confided to their care, the only ones, I believe, that were on the island. They were equally fortunate in finding several persons, both male and female, willing to accompany them; and thus furnished, they again sailed for Toubouai, where, as they expected, they were better received than before, in consequence of being able to communicate with the natives through their interpreters.

Experience had taught them the necessity of making self-defense their first consideration, and a fort was consequently commenced, eight yards square, surrounded by a wide ditch. It was nearly completed, when the natives, imagining they were going to destroy them, and that the ditch was intended for their place of interment, planned a general attack when the party should proceed to work in the morning. It fortunately happened that one of the natives who accompanied them from Otaheite overheard this conspiracy, and instantly swam off to the ship and apprised the crew of their danger. Instead, therefore, of proceeding to their work at the fort, as usual, the following morning, they made an attack upon the natives, killed and wounded several, and obliged the others to retire inland. Great dissatisfaction and difference of opinion now arose among the crew: some were for abandoning the fort and returning to Otaheite; while others were for proceeding to the Marquesas; but the majority were at that time for completing what they had begun, and remaining at Toubouai. At length the continued state of suspense in which they were kept by the natives made them decide to return to Otaheite, though much against the inclination of Christian, who in vain expostulated with them on the folly of such a resolution, and the certain detection that must ensue.

The implements being embarked, they proceeded, therefore, a second time to Otaheite, and were again well received by their friends, who replenished their stock of provisions. During the passage Christian formed his intention of proceeding in the ship to some distant uninhabited island, for the purpose of permanently settling, as the most likely means of escaping the punishment which he well knew awaited him in the event of being discovered. On communicating this plan to his shipmates he found only a few inclined to assent to it; but no objections were offered by those who dissented, to his taking the ship; all they required was an equal distribution of such provisions and stores as might be useful. Young, Brown, Mills, Williams, Quintal, M'Coy, Martin, Adams, and six natives (four of Otaheite and two of Toubouai) determined to follow the fate of Christian. Remaining, therefore, only twenty-four hours at Otaheite, they took leave of their own comrades, and having invited on board several of the women with the feigned purpose of taking leave, the cables were cut and they were carried off to sea.

The mutineers now bade adieu to all the world, save the few individuals associated with them in exile. But where that exile should be passed, was yet undecided: the Marquesas Islands were first mentioned; but Christian, on reading Captain Carteret's account of Pitcairn Island, thought it better adapted to the purpose, and accordingly shaped a course thither. They reached it not many days afterward; and Christian, with one of the seamen, landed in a little nook, which was afterward found very convenient for disembarkation. They soon traversed the island sufficiently to be satisfied that it was exactly suited to their wishes. It possessed water, wood, a good soil, and some fruits. The anchorage in the offing was very bad, and landing for boats extremely hazardous. The mountains were so difficult of access, and the pass so narrow, that they might be maintained by a few persons against an army; and there were several caves, to which, in case of necessity, they could retreat, and where, as long as their provisions lasted, they might bid defiance to their pursuers. With this intelligence they returned on board, and brought the ship to an anchor in a small bay on the northern side of the island, where everything that could be of utility was landed, and where it was agreed to destroy the ship, either by running her on shore, or burning her. Christian, Adams, and the majority, were for the former expedient; but while they went to the forepart of the ship, to execute this business, Matthew Quintal set fire to the carpenter's store-room. The vessel burnt to the water's edge, and then drifted upon the rocks, where the remainder of the wreck was burnt for fear of discovery. This occurred on the twenty-third of January, 1790.

A suitable spot of ground for a village was fixed upon, with the exception of which the island was divided into equal portions, but to the exclusion of the poor blacks, who, being only friends of the seamen, were not considered as entitled to the same privileges. Obliged to lend their assistance to the others in order to procure a subsistence, they thus, from being their friends, in the course of time became their slaves. No discontent, however, was manifested, and they willingly assisted in the cultivation of the soil. In clearing the space that was allotted to the village, a row of trees was left between it and the sea, for the purpose of concealing the houses from the observation of any vessels that might be passing, and nothing was allowed to be erected that might in any way attract attention. Until these houses were finished, the sails of the Bounty were converted into tents; and when no longer required for that purpose, became very acceptable as clothing. Thus supplied with all the necessaries of life, and some of its luxuries, they felt their condition comfortable even beyond their most sanguine expectation, and everything went on peaceably and prosperously for about two years, at the expiration of which, Williams, who had the misfortune to lose his wife about a month after his arrival, by a fall from a precipice while collecting birds' eggs, became dissatisfied, and threatened to leave the island in one of the boats of the Bounty, unless he had another wife; an unreasonable request, as it could not be complied with, except at the expense of the happiness of one of his companions: but Williams, actuated by selfish considerations alone, persisted in his threat, and the Europeans not willing to part with him, on account of his usefulness as an armorer, constrained one of the blacks to bestow his wife upon the applicant. The blacks, outrageous at this second act of flagrant injustice, made common cause with their companion, and matured a plan of revenge upon their aggressor, which, had it succeeded, would have proved fatal to all the Europeans. Fortunately, the secret was imparted to the women, who ingeniously communicated it to the white men in a song, of which the words were, "Why does black men sharpen ax? To kill white men." The instant Christian became aware of the plot, he seized his gun and went in search of the blacks; but with a view only of showing them that their scheme was discovered, and thus by timely interference endeavoring to prevent the execution of it. He met one of them (Ohoo) at a little distance from the village, taxed him with the conspiracy, and, in order to intimidate him, discharged his gun, which he had humanely loaded with powder only. Ohoo, however, imagining otherwise, and that the bullet had missed its object, derided his unskillfulness, and fled into the woods, followed by his accomplice Talaloo, who had been deprived of his wife. The remaining blacks, finding their plot discovered, purchased pardon by promising to murder their accomplices, who had fled; which they afterward performed by an act of the most odious treachery. Ohoo was betrayed and murdered by his own nephew; and Talaloo, after an ineffectual attempt made upon him by poison, fell by the hands of his friend and his wife, the very woman on whose account all the disturbance began, and whose injuries Talaloo felt he was revenging in common with his own.

Tranquillity was by these means restored, and preserved for about two years; at the expiration of which, dissatisfaction was again manifested by the blacks, in consequence of oppression and ill treatment, principally by Quintal and M'Coy. Meeting with no compassion or redress from their masters, a second plan to destroy their oppressors was matured, and, unfortunately, too successfully executed.

It was agreed that two of the blacks, Timoa and Nehow, should desert from their masters, provide themselves with arms, and hide in the woods, but maintain a frequent communication with the other two, Tetaheite and Menalee; and that on a certain day they should attack and put to death all the Englishmen, when at work in their plantations. Tetaheite, to strengthen the party of the blacks on this day, borrowed a gun and ammunition of his master, under the pretence of shooting hogs, which had become wild and very numerous; but instead of using it in this way, he joined his accomplices, and with them fell upon Williams and shot him. Martin, who was at no great distance, heard the report of the musket, and exclaimed, "Well done! we shall have a glorious feast to-day!" supposing that a hog had been shot. The party proceeded from Williams' toward Christian's plantation, where Menalee, the other black, was at work with Mills and M'Coy; and, in order that the suspicions of the whites might not be excited by the report they had heard, requested Mills to allow him (Menalee) to assist them in bringing home the hog they pretended to have killed. Mills agreed; and the four, being united, proceeded to Christian, who was working at his yam-plot, and shot him. Thus fell a man, who, from being the reputed ringleader of the mutiny, has obtained an unenviable celebrity, and whose crime, if anything can excuse mutiny, may, perhaps, be considered as in some degree palliated by the tyranny which led to its commission. M'Coy, hearing his groans, observed to Mills, "there was surely some person dying;" but Mills replied, "It is only Mainmast (Christian's wife) calling her children to dinner." The white men being yet too strong for the blacks to risk a conflict with them, it was necessary to concert a plan, in order to separate Mills and M'Coy. Two of them accordingly secreted themselves in M'Coy's house, and Tetaheite ran and told him that the two blacks who had deserted were stealing things out of his house. M'Coy instantly hastened to detect them, and on entering was fired at; but the ball passed him. M'Coy immediately communicated the alarm to Mills, and advised him to seek shelter in the woods; but Mills, being quite satisfied that one of the blacks whom he had made his friend would not suffer him to be killed, determined to remain. M'Coy, less confident, ran in search of Christian, but finding him dead, joined Quintal (who was already apprised of the work of destruction, and had sent his wife to give the alarm to the others,) and fled with him to the woods. Mills had scarcely been left alone, when the two blacks fell upon him, and he became a victim to his misplaced confidence in the fidelity of his friend. Martin and Brown were next separately murdered by Menalee and Tenina; Menalee effecting with a maul what the musket had left unfinished. Tenina, it is said, wished to save the life of Brown, and fired at him with powder only, desiring him, at the same time, to fall as if killed; but, unfortunately rising too soon, the other black, Menalee, shot him.

Adams was first apprised of his danger by Quintal's wife, who, in hurrying through his plantation, asked why he was working at such a time? Not understanding the question, but seeing her alarmed, he followed her, and was almost immediately met by the blacks, whose appearance exciting suspicion, he made his escape into the woods. After remaining three or four hours, Adams, thinking all was quiet, stole to his yam-plot for a supply of provisions; his movements, however, did not escape the vigilance of the blacks, who attacked and shot him through the body, the ball entering at his right shoulder, and passing out through his throat. He fell upon his side, and was instantly assailed by one of them with the butt-end of the gun; but he parried the blows at the expense of a broken finger. Tetaheite then placed his gun to his side, but it fortunately missed fire twice. Adams, recovering a little from the shock of the wound, sprung on his legs, and ran off with as much speed as he was able, and fortunately outstripped his pursuers, who, seeing him likely to escape, offered him protection if he would stop. Adams, much exhausted by his wound, readily accepted their terms, and was conducted to Christian's house, where he was kindly treated. Here this day of bloodshed ended, leaving only four Englishmen alive out of nine. It was a day of emancipation to the blacks, who were now masters of the island, and of humiliation and retribution to the whites. Young, who was a great favorite with the women, and had, during this attack, been secreted by them, was now also taken to Christian's house. The other two, M'Coy and Quintal, who had always been the great oppressors of the blacks, escaped to the mountains, where they supported themselves upon the produce of the ground about them.

The party in the village lived in tolerable tranquillity for about a week; at the expiration of which, the men of color began to quarrel about the right of choosing the women whose husbands had been killed; which ended in Menalee's shooting Timoa as he sat by the side of Young's wife, accompanying her song with his flute. Timoa not dying immediately, Menalee reloaded, and deliberately dispatched him by a second discharge. He afterward attacked Tetaheite, who was condoling with Young's wife for the loss of her favorite black, and would have murdered him also, but for the interference of the women. Afraid to remain longer in the village, he escaped to the mountains and joined Quintal and M'Coy, who, though glad of his service, at first received him with suspicion. This great acquisition to their force enabled them to bid defiance to the opposite party; and to show their strength, and that they were provided with muskets, they appeared on a ridge of mountains, within sight of the village, and fired a volley which so alarmed the others that they sent Adams to say, if they would kill the black man, Menalee, and return to the village, they would all be friends again. The terms were so far complied with that Menalee was shot; but, apprehensive of the sincerity of the remaining blacks, they refused to return while they were alive.

Adams says it was not long before the widows of the white men so deeply deplored their loss, that they determined to revenge their death, and concerted a plan to murder the only two remaining men of color. Another account, communicated by the islanders, is that it was only part of a plot formed at the same time that Menalee was murdered, which could not be put in execution before. However this may be, it was equally fatal to the poor blacks. The arrangement was, that Susan should murder one of them, Tetaheite, while he was sleeping by the side of his favorite ; and that Young should, at the same instant, upon a signal being given, shoot the other, Nehow. The unsuspecting Tetaheite retired, as usual, and fell by the blow of an ax; the other was looking at Young loading his gun, which he supposed was for the purpose of shooting hogs, and requested him to put in a good charge, when he received the deadly contents.

In this manner the existence of the last of the men of color terminated, who, though treacherous and revengeful, had, it is feared, too much cause for complaint. The accomplishment of this fatal scheme was immediately communicated to the two absentees, and their return solicited. But so many instances of treachery had occurred, that they would not believe the report, though delivered by Adams himself, until the hands and heads of the deceased were produced, which being done, they returned to the village. This eventful day was the third of October, 1793. There were now left upon the island, Adams, Young, M'Coy, and Quintal, ten women, and some children. Two months after this period, Young commenced a manuscript journal, which affords a good insight into the state of the island, and the occupations of the settlers. From it we learn, that they lived peaceably together, building their houses, fencing in and cultivating their grounds, fishing, and catching birds, and constructing pits for the purpose of entrapping hogs, which had become very numerous and wild, as well as injurious to the yam-crops. The only discontent appears to have been among the women, who lived promiscuously with the men, frequently changing their abode.

Young says, March twelfth, 1794, "Going over to borrow a rake, to rake the dust off my ground, I saw Jenny having a skull in her hand: I asked her whose it was? and was told it was Jack Williams's. I desired it might be buried: the women who were with Jenny gave me for answer, it should not. I said it should ; and demanded it accordingly. I was asked the reason why I, in particular, should insist on such a thing, when the rest of the white men did not? I said, if they gave them leave to keep the skulls above ground, I did not. Accordingly when I saw M'Coy, Smith, and Mat. Quintal, I acquainted them with it, and said, I thought that if the girls did not agree to give up the heads of the five white men in a peaceable manner, they ought to be taken by force, and buried." About this time the women appear to have been much dissatisfied ; and Young's journal declares that, "since the massacre, it has been the desire of the greater part of them to get some conveyance, to enable them to leave the island." This feeling continued, and on the fourteenth of April, 1794, was so strongly urged, that the men began to build them a boat; but wanting planks and nails, Jenny, who now resides at Otaheite, in her zeal tore up the boards of her house, and endeavored, though without success, to persuade some others to follow her example.

On the thirteen of August following, the vessel was finished, and on the fifteenth she was launched: but, as Young says, "according to expectation she upset," and it was most fortunate for them that she did so ; for had they launched out upon the ocean, where could they have gone? or what could a few ignorant women have done by themselves, drifting upon the waves, but ultimately have fallen a sacrifice to their folly? However the fate of the vessel was a great disappointment, and they continued much dissatisfied with their condition; probably not without some reason, as they were kept in great subordination, and were frequently beaten by M'Coy and Quintal, who appear to have been of very quarrelsome dispositions; Quintal in particular, who proposed "not to laugh, joke, or give anything to any of the girls." On the sixteenth of August they dug a grave, and buried the bones of the murdered people: and on October third, 1794, they celebrated the murder of the black men at Quintal's house. On the eleventh of November a conspiracy of the women to kill the white men in their sleep was discovered; upon which they were all seized, and a disclosure ensued; but no punishment appears to have been inflicted upon them, in consequence of their promising to conduct themselves properly, and never again to give any cause "even to suspect their behavior." However, though they were pardoned, Young observes "We did not forget their conduct; and it was agreed among us, that the first female who misbehaved should be put to death; and this punishment was to be repeated on each offense until we could discover the real intentions of the women." Young appears to have suffered much from mental perturbation in consequence of these disturbances; and observes of himself on the two following days, that "he was bothered and idle."

The suspicions of the men induced them, on the fifteenth, to conceal two muskets in the bush, for the use of any person who might be so fortunate as to escape, in the event of an attack being made. On the thirtieth of November, the women again collected and attacked them; but no lives were lost, and they returned on being once more pardoned, but were again threatened with death the next time they misbehaved. Threats thus repeatedly made, and as often unexecuted, as might be expected, soon lost their effect, and the women formed a party whenever their displeasure was excited, and hid themselves in the unfrequented parts of the island, carefully providing themselves with firearms. In this manner the men were kept in continual suspense, dreading the result of each disturbance, as the numerical strength of the women was much greater than their own.

On the fourth of May, 1795, two canoes were begun, and in two days completed. These were used for fishing, in which employment the people were frequently successful, supplying themselves with rock-fish and large mackerel.

So little occurred in the year 1796, that one page records the whole of the events; and throughout the following year there are but three incidents worthy of notice. The first, their endeavor to procure a quantity of meat for salting; the next, their attempt to make syrup from the tea-plant (*dracæna terminalis*) and sugarcane; and the third, a serious accident that happened to M'Coy, who fell from a cocoanut tree and hurt his right thigh, sprained both his ancles and wounded his side. The occupations of the men continued similar to those already related, occasionally enlivened by visits to the opposite side of the island. They appear to have been more sociable; dining frequently at each other's houses, and contributing more to the comfort of the women, who, on their part, gave no ground for uneasiness. There was also a mutual accommodation among them in regard to provisions, of which a regular account was taken. If one person was successful in hunting, he lent the others as much meat as they required, to be repaid at leisure; and the same occurred with yams, taros, etc., so that they lived in a very domestic and tranquil state. It unfortunately happened that M'Coy had been employed in a distillery in Scotland; and being very much addicted to liquor, he tried an experiment with the tee-root, and on the twentieth April 1798, succeeded in producing a bottle of ardent spirit. This success induced his companion, Matthew Quintal, to "alter his kettle into a still," a contrivance which unfortunately succeeded too well, as frequent intoxication was the consequence, with M'Coy in particular upon whom at length it produced fits of delirium; in one of which, he threw himself from a cliff and was killed. The melancholy fate of this man created so forcible an impression on the remaining few, that they resolved never again to touch spirits; and Adams, I have every reason to believe, to the day of his death kept his vow.

The journal finishes nearly at the period of M'Coy's death, which is not related in it: but we learned from Adams, that about 1799, Quintal lost his wife by a fall from the cliff while in search of birds' eggs; that he grew discontented and, though there were several disposable women on the island, and he had already experienced the fatal effects of a similar demand, nothing would satisfy him but the wife of one of his companions. Of course neither of them felt inclined to accede to this unreasonable indulgence; and he sought an opportunity of putting them both to death. He was fortunately foiled in his first attempt, but swore he would repeat it. Adams and Young, having no doubt he would follow up his resolution, and fearing he might be more successful in his next attempt, came to the conclusion, that their own lives were not safe while he was in existence, and that they were justified in putting him to death, which they did with an ax.

Such was the melancholy fate of seven of the leading mutineers, who escaped from justice only to add murder to their former crimes; for though some of them may not have actually imbrued their hands in the blood of their fellow-creatures, yet all were accessary to the deed.

As Christian and Young were descended from respectable parents, and had received educations suitable to their birth, it might be supposed that they felt their altered and degraded situation much more than the seamen, who were comparatively well off; but, if so, Adams says, they had thê good sense to conceal it, as not a single murmur or regret escaped them; on the contrary, Christian was always cheerful, and his example was of the greatest service in exciting his companions to labor. He was naturally of a happy. ingenuous disposition, and won the good opinion and respect of all those who served under him; which cannot be better exemplified than by his maintaining, under circumstances of great perplexity, the respect and regard of all who were associated with him up to the hour of his death; and even at the period of our visit, Adams, in speaking of him, never omitted to say "*Mr. Christian.*"

Adams and Young were now the sole survivors out of the fifteen males that landed upon the island. They were both, and more particularly Young, of a serious turn of mind; and it would have been wonderful, after the many dreadful scenes at which they had assisted, if the solitude and tranquillity that ensued had not disposed them to repentance. During Christian's lifetime they had only once read the church service, but since his disease this had been regularly done on every Sunday. They now, however, resolved to have morning and evening family prayers, to add afternoon service to the duty of the Sabbath, and to train up their own children and those of their late unfortunate companions, in piety and virtue. In the execution of this resolution, Young's education enabled him to be of the greatest assistance; but he was not long suffered to survive his repentance. An asthmatic complaint, under which he had for some time labored. terminated his existence about a year after the death of Quintal, and Adams was left the sole survivor of the misguided and unfortunate mutineers of the Bounty. The loss of his last companion was a great affliction to him, and was for some time most severely felt. It was a catastrophe, however, that more than ever disposed him to repentance, and determined him to execute the pious resolution he had made, in the hope of expiating his offenses.

His reformation could not, perhaps, have taken place at a more propitious moment. Out of nineteen children upon the island, there were several between the ages of seven and nine years; who, had they been longer suffered to follow their own inclinations, might have acquired habits which it would have been difficult, if not impossible, for Adams to eradicate. The moment was therefore most favorable for his design, and his laudable exertions were attended by advantages both to the objects of his care and to his own mind, which surpassed his most sanguine expectations. He, nevertheless, had an arduous task to perform. Beside the children to be educated, the Otaheitan women were to be converted; and, as the example of the parents had a powerful influence over their children, he resolved to make them his first care. Here also his labors succeeded; the Otaheitans were naturally of a tractable disposition, and gave him less trouble than he anticipated: the children also acquired such a thirst after Scriptural knowledge, that Adams in a short time had little else to do than to answer their inquiries and put them in the right way. As they grew up, they acquired fixed habits of morality and piety; their colony improved; intermarriages occurred: and they now form a happy and well regulated society, the merit of which, in a great degree, belongs to Adams, and tends to redeem the former errors of his life.

The preceding facts in reference to the mutineers, came gradually to light in the course of years, from the visit of Captain Folger, an American, of the English ship Briton, and of Captain Beechy. Lieutenant Shillibeer of the Briton, gives the following graphic account of his unexpected visit to the island, in the year 1813.

It was in the second watch when we made an island unknown to us. At daylight we proceeded to a more close examination, and soon perceived huts, cultivation, and people; of the latter, some were making signs, others launching their little canoes through the surf, into which they threw themselves with great dexterity, and pulled toward us. They came along side, and for me to picture the wonder which was conspicuous in every countenance, at being hailed in perfect English, what was the name of the ship, and who commanded her, would be impossible—our surprise can alone be conceived. The captain answered, and now a regular conversation commenced. He requested them to come along side, and the reply was, "We have no boat-hook to hold on by." "I will throw you a rope," said the captain. "If you do we have nothing to make it fast to," was the answer. However, they at length came on board, exemplifying not the least fear, but their astonishment was unbounded After the friendly salutation of "Good morrow Sir," from the first man who entered, (Mackey, for that was his name,) "Do you know," said he, "one William Bligh, in England?" This question threw a new light on the subject, and he was immediately asked if he knew one Christian, and the reply was given with so much natural simplicity, that I shall here use his proper words. "Oh yes," said he, "very well; his son is in the boat there coming up, his name is Friday Fletcher October Christian. His father is dead now—he was shot by a black fellow."

The questions which were now put were numerous, among which were the following:

Q. At what age do you marry?

A. Not before nineteen or twenty.

Q. Are you allowed to have more than one wife?

A. No! we can have but one, and it is wicked to have more.

Q. Have you been taught any religion?

A. Yes, a very good religion.

Q. In what do you believe?

A. I believe in God, the Father Almighty, etc. (Here he went through the whole of the Belief.)

Q. Who first taught you this belief?

A. John Adams says it was first by F. Christian's order, and that he likewise caused a prayer to be said every day at noon.

Q. And what is the prayer?

A. It is—"I will arise and go to my Father, and say unto him, Father, I have sinned against Heaven, and before Thee, and am no more worthy of being called thy son."

Q. Do you continue to say this every day?

A. Yes, we never neglect it.

Q. What language do you commonly speak?

A. Always English.

Q. But you understand the Otaheitan?

A. Yes, but not so well.

Q. Do the old women speak English?

A. Yes, but not so well as they understand it, their pronunciation is not good.

Q. What countrymen do you call yourselves?

A. Half English, and half Otaheite.

Q. Who is your king?

A. Why, King George to be sure.

Q. Have you ever seen a ship before?

A. Yes, we have seen four from the island, but only one stopped Mayhew Folger was the captain; I suppose you know him? No we do not know him.

Q. How long did he stay?

A. Two days.

Q. Should you like to go to England?

A. No! I cannot; I am married, and have a family.

Before we had finished our interrogatories the hour of breakfast had arrived, and we solicited our half countrymen, as they styled themselves, to accompany us below, and partake of our repast, to which they acquiesced without much ceremony. The circle in which we had surrounded them being opened, brought to the notice of Mackey, a little black terrier. He was at first frightened, ran behind one of the officers, and looking over his shoulder said, pointing to the dog, "I know what that is, it is a dog; I never saw a dog before—will it bite?" After a short pause he addressed himself to Christian, saying with great admiration, "It is a pretty thing, too, to look at, is it not?"

The whole of them were inquisitive, and in their questions as well as answers, betrayed a very great share of natural abilities. They asked the names of whatever they saw, and the purposes to which it was applied

This, they would say, was pretty—that they did not like, and were greatly surprised at our having so many things which they were not possessed of in the island.

The circumstance of the dog, the things which at each step drew their attention or created their wonder, retarded us on our road to the breakfast table, but arriving there, we had a new cause for surprise. The astonishment which before had been so strongly demonstrated in them, was now become conspicuous in us, even to a much greater degree than when they hailed us in our native language; and I must here confess I blushed when I saw nature in its most simple state, offer that tribute of respect to the Omnipotent Creator, which from education I did not perform, nor from society had been taught its necessity. Before they began to eat; on their knees, and with hands uplifted, did they implore permission to partake in peace what was set before them, and when they had eaten heartily, resuming their former attitude, offered a fervent prayer of thanksgiving for the indulgence they had just experienced. Our omission of this ceremony did not escape their notice, for Christian asked me whether it was not customary with us also. Here nature was triumphant, for I should do myself an irreparable injustice, did I not with candor acknowledge, I was both embarrassed and wholly at a loss for a sound reply, and evaded this poor fellow's question by drawing his attention to the cow, which was then looking down the hatchway, and as he had never seen any of the species before, it was a source of mirth and gratification to him.

The hatred of these people to the blacks is strongly rooted, and which doubtless owes its origin to the early quarrels which Christian and his followers had with the Otaheitans after their arrival at Pitcairn's; to illustrate which I shall here relate an occurrence which took place at breakfast.

Soon after young Christian had begun, a West Indian black, who was one of the servants, entered the gun-room to attend table as usual. Christian looked at him sternly, rose, asked for his hat, and said, "I don't like that black fellow, I must go," and it required some little persuasion, before he would again resume his seat.

After coming along side the ship, so eager were they to get on board, that several of the canoes had been wholly abandoned, and gone adrift. This was the occasion of an anecdote which will show most conspicuously the good nature of their dispositions, and the mode resorted to in deciding a double claim. The canoes being brought back to the ship, the captain ordered that one of them should remain in each, when it became a question to which that duty should devolve; however it was soon adjusted, for Mackey observed that he supposed they were all equally anxious to see the ship, and the fairest way would be for them to cast lots, as then there would be no ill will on either side. This was acceded to, and those to whom it fell to go into the boat, departed without a murmur.

John Adams is a fine looking old man, approaching to sixty years of age. We conversed with him a long time, relative to the mutiny of the Bounty, and the ultimate fate of Christian. He denied being accessary to, or having the least knowledge of the conspiracy, but he expressed great horror at the conduct of Captain Bligh, not only toward his men, but officers also. I asked him if he had a desire to return to England, and I must confess his reply in the affirmative, caused me great surprize.

He told me he was perfectly aware how deeply he was involved; that by following the fortune of Christian, he had not only sacrificed every claim to his country, but that his life was the necessary forfeiture for such an act, and he supposed would be exacted from him was he ever to return; notwithstanding all these circumstances, nothing would be able to occasion him so much gratification as that of seeing once more, prior to his death, that country which gave him birth, and from which he had been so long estranged.

There was a sincerity in his speech, I can badly describe it—but it had a very powerful influence in persuading me these were his real sentiments. My interest was excited to so great a degree, that I offered him a conveyance for himself, with any of his family who chose to accompany him. He appeared pleased at the proposal, and as no one was then present, he sent for his wife and children. The rest of this little community surrounded the door. He communicated his desire, and solicited their acquiescence. Appalled at a request not less sudden than in opposition to their wishes, they were all at a loss for a reply.

His charming daughter although inundated with tears, first broke the silence.

"Oh do not, sir," said she, "take from me my father! do not take away my best—my dearest friend." Her voice failed her—she was unable to proceed—leaned her head upon her hand, and gave full vent to her grief. His wife, too, (an Otaheitan) expressed a lively sorrow. The wishes of Adams soon became known among the others, who joined in pathetic solicitation for his stay on the island. Not an eye was dry—the big tear stood in those of the men—the women shed them in full abundance. I never witnessed a scene so fully affecting, or more replete with interest. To have taken him from a circle of such friends, would have ill become a feeling heart, to have forced him away in opposition to their joint and earnest entreaties, would have been an outrage on humanity.

Those men who came on board, were finely formed, and of manly features. Their height about five feet ten inches. Their hair black and long, generally plaited into a tail. They wore a straw hat, similar to those worn by sailors, with a few feathers stuck into them by way of ornament. I spoke to young Christian, particularly of Adams, who assured me he was greatly respected, insomuch that no one acted in opposition to his wishes, and when they should lose him, their regret would be general. The intermarriages which had taken place among them, have been the occasion of a relationship throughout the colony. There seldom happens to be a quarrel, even of the most trivial nature, and then, (using their own term,) it is nothing more than a word of mouth quarrel, which is always referred to Adams for adjustment.

Twelve years later, these interesting Islanders were visited by Captain Beechy, in the ship Blossom, from whom we derive the following additional information.

The Blossom was so different, or to use the expression of our visitors, "so rich," compared with the other ships they had seen, that they were constantly afraid of giving or committing some injury, and would not even move without first asking permission. This diffidence gave us full occupation for some time, as our restless visitors, anxious to see everything, seldom directed their attention long to any particular object, or remained in one position or place. Having no latches to their doors, they were ignorant of the manner of opening ours; and we were constantly attacked on all sides with "Please may I sit down, or get up, or go out of the cabin?" or, "Please to open or shut the door." Their applications were, however, made with such good nature and simplicity that it was impossible not to feel the greatest pleasure in paying attention to them. They very soon learnt the christian name of every officer in the ship, which they always used in conversation instead of the surname, and wherever a similarity to their own occurred, they attached themselves to that person as a matter of course.

It was many hours after they came on board before the ship could get near the island, during which time they so ingratiated themselves with us that we felt the greatest desire to visit their houses; and rather than pass another night at sea we put off in the boats, though at a considerable distance from the land, and accompanied them to the shore. We followed our guides past a rugged point, surmounted by tall spiral rocks, known to the islanders as St. Paul's rocks, into a spacious iron-bound bay, where the Bounty found her last anchorage. In this bay, which is bounded by lofty cliffs almost inaccessible, it was proposed to land. Thickly-branched evergreens skirt the base of these hills, and in summer afford a welcome retreat from the rays of an almost vertical sun. In the distance are seen several high-pointed rocks which the pious highlanders have named after the most zealous of the Apostles, and outside of them is a square basaltic islet. Formidable breakers fringe the coast, and seem to present an insurmountable barrier to all access.

The difficulty of landing was more than repaid by the friendly reception we met with on the beach from Hannah Young, a very interesting young woman, the daughter of Adams. In her eagerness to greet her father, she had outrun her female companions, for whose delay she thought it necessary in the first place to apologize, by saying they had all been over the hill, in company with John Buffet, to look at the ship, and were not yet returned. It appeared that John Buffet, who was a sea-faring man, ascertained that the ship was a man-of-war, and without knowing exactly why, became so alarmed for the safety of Adams that he either could not or would not answer any of the interrogations which were put to him. This mysterious silence set all the party in tears, as they feared he had discovered something adverse to their patriarch. At length his obduracy yielded to their entreaties; but before he explained the cause of his conduct, the boats were seen to put off from the ship, and Hannah im mediately hurried to the beach to kiss the old man's cheek, which she did with a fervency demonstrative of the warmest affection. Her apology for her companions was rendered unnecessary by their appearance on the steep and circuitous path down the mountain, who, as they arrived on the beach, successively welcomed us to their island, with a simplicity and sincerity which left no doubt of the truth of their professions.

They almost all wore the cloth of the island: their dress consisted of a petticoat, and a mantle loosely thrown over the shoulders, and reaching to the ancles. Their stature was rather above the common height; and their limbs, from being accustomed to work and climb the hills, had acquired unusual muscularity; but their features and manners were perfectly feminine. Their complexion, though fairer than that of the men, was of a dark gipsy hue, but its deep color was less conspicuous, by being contrasted with dark glossy hair, which hung down over their shoulders in long waving tresses, nicely oiled: in front it was tastefully turned back from the forehead and temples, and was retained in that position by a chaplet of small red or white aromatic blossoms, newly gathered from the flower-tree, or from the tobacco plant; their countenances were lively and good-natured, their eyes dark and animated, and each possessed an enviable row of teeth. Such was the agreeable impression of their first appearance, which was heightened by the wish expressed simultaneously by the whole group, that we were come to stay several days with them. As the sun was going down, we signified our desire to get to the village and to pitch the observatory before dark, and this was no sooner made known, than every instrument and article found a carrier.

By the time the tent was up and the instruments secured, we were summoned to a meal, than which a less sumptuous fare would have satisfied appetites rendered keen by long abstinence and a tiresome journey. Our party divided themselves that they might not crowd one house in particular: Adams did not entertain; but at Christian's I found a table spread with plates, knives, and forks; which, in so remote a part of the world, was an unexpected sight. They were, it is true, far from uniform; but, by one article being appropriated for another, we all found something to put our portion upon; and but few of the natives were obliged to substitute their fingers for articles which are indispensable to the comfort of more polished life. A smoking pig, by a skillful dissection, was soon portioned to every guest, but no one ventured to put its excellent qualities to the test until a lengthened *Amen*, pronounced by all the party, had succeeded an emphatic grace delivered by the village parson. "*Turn to*," was then the signal for attack, and as it is convenient that all the party should finish their meal about the same time, in order that one grace might serve for all, each made the most of his time. In Pitcairn's Island it is not deemed proper to touch even a bit of bread without a grace before and after it, and a person is accused of inconsistency if he leaves off and begins again. So strict is their observance of this form, that we do not know of any instance in which it has been forgotten. On one occasion I had engaged Adams in conversation, and he incautiously took the first mouthful without having said his grace; but before he had swallowed it, he recollected himself, and feeling as if he had committed a crime, immediately put away what he had in his mouth, and commenced his prayer.

Welcome, cheer, hospitality, and good humor, were the characteristics of the feast; and never was their beneficial influence more practically exemplified than on this occasion, by the demolition of nearly all that was placed before us. With the exception of some wine we had brought with us, water was the only beverage. This was placed in a large jug at one end of the board, and, when necessary, was passed round the table—a ceremony at which, in Pitcairn's Island in particular, it is desirable to be the first partaker, as the gravy of the dish is invariably mingled with the contents of the pitcher: the natives, who prefer using their fingers to forks, being quite indifferent whether they hold the vessel by the handle or by the spout.

Notwithstanding these deficiencies, we made a very comfortable and hearty supper, heard many little anecdotes of the place, and derived much amusement from the singularity of the inquiries of our hosts. One regret only intruded itself upon the general conviviality, which we did not fail to mention, namely, that there was so wide a distinction between the sexes. This was the remains of a custom very common among the South Sea Islands, which in some places is carried to such an extent, that it imposes death upon the woman who shall eat in the presence of her husband; and though the distinction between man and wife is not here carried to that extent, it is still sufficiently observed to exclude all the women from table, if there happens to be a deficiency of seats. In Pitcairn's Island, they have settled ideas of right and wrong, to which they obstinately adhere; and, fortunately, they have imbibed them generally from the best source.

In the instance in question, they have, however, certainly erred; but of this they could not be persuaded, nor did they, I believe, thank us for our interference. Their argument was, that man was made first, and ought, conseqently, on all occasions, to be served first—a conclusion which deprived us of the company of the women at table, during the whole of our stay at the island. Far from considering themselves neglected, they very good-naturedly chatted with us behind our seats, and flapped away the flies, and by a gentle tap, accidentally or playfully delivered, reminded us occasionally of the honor that was done us. The conclusion of our meal was the signal for the women and children to prepare their own, to whom we resigned our seats, and strolled out to enjoy the freshness of the night. It was late by the time the women had finished, and we were not sorry when we were shown to the beds prepared for us. The mattress was composed of palm-trees, covered with native cloth; the sheets were of the same material; and we knew, by the crackling of them, that they were quite new from the loom or beater. The whole arrangement was extremely comfortable, and highly inviting to repose, which the freshness of the apartment, rendered cool by a free circulation of air through its sides, enabled us to enjoy without any annoyance from heat or insects. One interruption only disturbed our first sleep; it was the pleasing melody of the evening hymn, which, after the lights were put out, was chaunted by the whole family in the middle of the room. In the morning also we were awoke by their morning hymn and family devotion. As we were much tired, and the sun's rays had not yet found their way through the broad opening of the apartment, we composed ourselves to rest again; and on awaking found that all the natives were gone to their several occupations—the men to offer what assistance they could to our boats in landing, carrying burdens for the seamen, or to gather what fruits were in season. Some of the women had taken our linen to wash; those whose turn it was to cook for the day were preparing the oven, the pig, and the yams; and we could hear, by the distant reiterated strokes of the beater, that others were engaged in the manufacture of cloth. By our bedside had already been placed some ripe fruits; and our hats were crowned with chaplets of the fresh blossom of the nono, or flower-tree, which the women had gathered in the freshness of the morning dew. On looking round the apartment, though it contained several beds, we found no partition, curtain, or screens; they had not yet been considered necessary. So far, indeed, from concealment being thought of, when we were about to get up, the women, anxious to show their attention, assembled to wish us a good morning, and to inquire in what way they could best contribute to our comforts, and to present us with some little gift, which the produce of the island afforded. Many persons would have felt awkward at rising and dressing before so many pretty black-eyed damsels assembled in the center of a spacious room; but by a little habit we overcame this embarrassment; and found the benefit of their services in fetching water as we required it, and substituting clean linen for such as we pulled off.

It must be remembered, that with these people, as with the other islanders of the South Seas, the custom has generally been to go naked, the maro with the men excepted, and with the women the petticoat, or kilt, with a loose covering over the bust, which, indeed, in Pitcairn's Island, they are always careful to conceal; consequently, an exposure to that extent carried with it no feeling whatever of indelicacy; or, I may safely add, that the Pitcairn Islanders would have been the last persons to incur the charge.

In this little retreat there is not much variety, and the description of one day's occupation serves equally for its successor. The dance is a recreation very rarely indulged in; but as we particularly requested it, they would not refuse to gratify us. A large room in Quintal's house was prepared for the occasion, and the company were ranged on one side of the apartment, glowing beneath a blazing string of doodœ nuts; the musicians were on the other, under the direction of Arthur Quintal. He was seated upon the ground, as head musician, and had before him a large gourd, and a piece of musical wood (poron,) which he balanced nicely upon his toes, that there might be the less interruption to its vibrations. He struck the instrument alternately with two sticks, and was accompanied by Dolly, who performed very skillfully with both hands upon a gourd, which had a longitudinal hole cut in one end of it; rapidly beating the orifice with the palms of her hands, and releasing it again with uncommon dexterity, so as to produce a tattoo, but in perfect time with the other instrument. A third performed upon the Bounty's old copper fish-kettle, which formed a sort of bass. To this exhilarating music, three *grown-up* females stood up to dance, but with a reluctance which showed it was done only to oblige us, as they considered such performances an inroad upon their usual innocent pastimes. The figure consisted of such parts of the Otaheitan dance as were thought most decorous, and was little more than a shuffling of the feet, sliding past each other, and snapping their fingers; but even this produced, at times, considerable laughter from the female spectators, perhaps from some association of ridiculous ideas, which we, as strangers, did not feel; and, no doubt, had our opinion of the performance been consulted, it would have essentially differed from theirs. They did not long continue these diversions, from an idea that it was too great a levity to be continued long; and only the three before-mentioned ladies could be prevailed upon to exhibit their skill. One of the officers, with a view of contributing to the mirth of the colonists, had obligingly brought his violin on shore, and, as an inducement for them to dance again, offered to play some country dances and reels, if they would proceed; but they could not be tempted to do so. They, however, solicited a specimen of the capabilities of the instrument, which was granted, and, though very well executed, did not give the satisfaction which we anticipated. They had not yet arrived at a state of refinement to appreciate harmony, but were highly delighted with the rapid motion of the fingers, and always liked to be within sight of the instrument when it was played They were afterward heard to say, that they preferred their own simple musical contrivance to the violin. They did not appear to have the least ear for music: one of the officers took considerable pains to teach them the hundredth psalm, that they might not chaunt all the psalms and hymns to the same air; but they did not evince the least aptitude or desire to learn it.

The following day was devoted to the completion of our view of the island, of which the natives were anxious we should see every part. Having accordingly seen every part of the island, we had no further desire to ramble; and as the weather did not promise to be very fair, I left the observatory in the charge of Mr. Wolfe, and embarked, accompanied by old Adams. Soon after he came on board it began to blow, and for several days afterward the wind prevented any communication with the shore. The natives during this period were in great apprehension: they went to the top of the island every morning to look for the ship; and once, when she was not to be seen, began to entertain the most serious doubts whether Adams would be returned to them; but he, knowing we should close the island as soon as the weather would permit, was rather glad of the opportunity of remaining on board, and of again associating with his countrymen; and, although he had passed his sixty-fifth year, joined in the dances and songs of the forecastle, and was always cheerful.

On the sixteenth, the weather permitted a boat to be sent on shore, and Adams was restored to his anxious friends. Previous to quitting the ship, he said it would add much to his happiness if I would read the marriage ceremony to him and his wife, as he could not bear the idea of living with her without its being done. He had long wished for the arrival of a ship-of-war to set his conscience at rest on that point. Though Adams was aged, and the old woman had been blind and bed-ridden for several years, he made such a point of it, that it would have been cruel to refuse him. They were accordingly the next day duly united, and the event noted in a register by John Buffet.

Wives upon Pitcairn Island, it may be imagined, are very scarce, as the same restrictions with regard to relationship exist as in England. George, in his early days, had fallen in love with Polly Young, a girl a little older than himself; but Polly, probably at that time liking some one else, and being at the age when young ladies' expectations are at the highest, had incautiously said, she never would give her hand to George Adams. He, nevertheless, indulged a hope that she would one day relent; and to this end was unremitting in his endeavors to please her. In this expectation he was not mistaken; his constancy and attentions, and, as he grew into manhood, his handsome form, which George took every opportunity of throwing into the most becoming attitudes before her, softened Polly's heart into a regard for him, and, had nothing passed before, she would willingly have given him her hand. But the vow of her youth was not to be got over, and the love-sick couple languished on from day to day, victims to the folly of early resolutions. The weighty case was referred for our consideration; and the fears of the party were in some measure relieved by the result, which was, that it would be much better to marry than to continue unhappy, in consequence of a hasty determination made before the judgment was matured; they could not, however, be prevailed on to yield to our decision, and we left them unmarried.

Another instance of a rigid performance of promise was exemplified in old Adams, who is anxious that his own conduct should form an example to the rising generation. In the course of conversation, he one day said he would accompany me up the mountain, if there was nobody else near; and it so happened, that on the day I had leisure to go, the young men were all out of the way. Adams, therefore, insisted upon performing his engagement, though the day was extremely hot, and the journey was much too laborious, in any weather, for his advanced period of life. He nevertheless set out, adding, "I said I would go, and so I will; beside, without example, precept will have but little effect." At the first valley he threw off his hat, handkerchief and jacket, and left them by the side of the path; at the second his trowsers were cast aside into a bush; and had he been alone, or provided with a maro, his shirt would certainly have followed: thus disencumbered, he boldly led the way, which was well known to him in early days; but it was so long since he had trodden it, that we met with many difficulties. At length we reached the top of the ridge, which we were informed was the place where M'Coy and Quintal appeared in defiance of the blacks. Adams felt so fatigued that he was now glad to lie down. The breeze here blew so hard and cold, that a shirt alone was of little use, and had he not been inured to all the changes of atmosphere, the sudden transition upon his aged frame must have been fatal.

During the period we remained upon the island we were entertained at the board of the natives, sometimes dining with one person, and sometimes with another: their meals, as I have before stated, were not confined to hours, and always consisted of baked pig, yams, and taro, and more rarely of sweet potatoes. The productions of the island being very limited, and intercourse with the rest of the world much restricted, it may be readily supposed their meals cannot be greatly varied. However they do their best with what they have, and cook it in different ways, the pig excepted, which is always baked. There are several goats upon the island, but they dislike their flesh as well as their milk. Yams constitute their principal food; these are boiled, baked, or made into pillihey, (cakes,) by being mixed with cocoanuts; or bruised and formed into a soup. Bananas are mashed, and made into pancakes, or, like the yam, united with the milk of the cocoanut, into pillihey, and eaten with molasses, extracted from the tee-root. The taro root, by being rubbed, makes a very good substitute for bread, as well as the bananas, plantain, and appai. Their common beverage is pure water, but they made for us a tea, extracted from the tee-plant, flavored with ginger, and sweetened with the juice of the sugar-cane. When alone, this beverage and fowl soup are used only for such as are ill. They seldom kill a pig, but live mostly upon fruit and vegetables. The duty of saying grace was performed by John Buffet, a recent settler among them, and their clergyman; but if he was not present, it fell upon the eldest of the company. They have all a great dislike to spirits, in consequence of M'Coy having killed himself by too free an indulgence in it; but wine in moderation is never refused. With this simple diet, and being in the daily habit of rising early, and taking a great deal of exercise in the cultivation of their grounds, it was not surprising that we found them so athletic and free from complaints. When illness does occur, their remedies are as simple as their manner of living, and are limited to salt water, hot ginger tea, or abstinence, according to the nature of the complaint. They have no medicines, nor do they appear to require any, as these remedies have hitherto been found sufficient.

After their noontide meal, if their grounds do not require their attention, and the weather be fine, they go a little way out to sea in their canoes, and catch fish, of which they have several kinds, large and sometimes in abundance; but it seldom happens that they have this time to spare; for the cultivation of the ground, repairing their boats, houses, and making fishing-lines, with other employments, generally occupies the whole of each day. At sunset they assemble at prayers as before, first offering their orison and thanksgiving, and then chaunting hymns. After this follows their evening meal, and at an early hour, having again said their prayers, and chaunted the evening hymn, they retire to rest; but before they sleep, each person again offers up a short prayer upon his bed.

Such is the distribution of time among the grown people; the younger part attend at school at regular hours, and are instructed in reading, writing, and arithmetic. They have, very fortunately, found an able and willing master in John Buffet, who belonged to a ship which visited the island, and was so infatuated with their behavior, being himself naturally of a devout and serious turn of mind, that he resolved to remain among them; and in addition to the instruction of the children, has taken upon himself the duty of clergyman, and is the oracle of the community. During the whole time I was with them I never heard them indulge in a joke, or other levity, and the practice of it is apt to give offense: they are so accustomed to take what is said in its literal meaning, that irony was always considered a falsehood in spite of explanation. They could not see the propriety of uttering what was not strictly true, for any purpose whatever.

The Sabbath-day is devoted entirely to prayer, reading, and serious meditation. No boat is allowed to quit the shore, nor any work whatever to be done, cooking excepted, for which preparation is made the preceding evening. I attended their church on this day, and found the service well conducted; the prayers were read by Adams, and the lessons by Buffet, the service being preceded by hymns. The greatest devotion was apparent in every individual, and in the children there was a seriousness unknown in the younger part of our communities at home. In the course of the Litany they prayed for their sovereign and royal family with much apparent loyalty and sincerity. Some family prayers, which were thought appropriate to their particular case, were added to the usual service; and Adams, fearful of leaving out any essential part, read, in addition, all those prayers which are intended only as substitutes for others. A sermon followed, which was very well delivered by Buffet; and lest any part of it should be forgotten, or escape attention, it was read three times. The whole concluded with hymns, which were first sung by the grown people, and afterward by the children. The service thus performed was very long; but the neat and cleanly appearance of the congregation, the devotion that animated every countenance, and the innocence and simplicity of the little children, prevented the attendance from becoming wearisome. In about half an hour afterward we again assembled to prayers, and at sunset service was repeated; so that, with their morning and evening prayers, they may be said to have church five times on a Sunday.

Marriages and christenings are duly performed by Adams. A ring which has united every person on the island is used for the occasion, and given according to the prescribed form. The age at which this is allowed to take place, with the men, is after they have reached their twentieth, and with the women, their eighteenth year.

All which remains to be said of these excellent people is, that they appear to live together in perfect harmony and contentment; to be virtuous, religious, cheerful, and hospitable, beyond the limits of prudence; to be patterns of conjugal and parental affection; and to have very few vices. We remained with them many days, and their unreserved manners gave us the fullest opportunity of becoming acquainted with any faults they might have possessed.

The Pitcairn islanders are tall, robust, and healthy. Their average height is five feet ten inches; the tallest person is six feet and one quarter of an inch; and the shortest of the adults is five feet nine inches and one eighth. Their limbs are well proportioned, round and straight; their feet turning a little inward. The boys promise to be equally as tall as their fathers; one of them whom we measured was, at eight years of age, four feet one inch; and another, at nine years, four feet three inches. Their simple food and early habits of exercise give them a muscular power and activity not often surpassed. It is recorded among the feats of strength which these people occasionally evince, that two of the strongest on the island, George Young and Edward Quintal, have each carried, at one time, without inconvenience, a kedge anchor, two sledge hammers, and an armorer's anvil, amounting to upward of six hundred weight; and that Quintal, at another time, carried a boat twenty-eight feet in length. In the water they are almost as much at home as on land, and can remain nearly a day in the sea. They frequently swam round their little island, the circuit of which is at least seven miles. When the sea beat heavily on the island they have plunged into the breakers, and swam to sea beyond them. This they sometimes did pushing a barrel of water before them, when it could be got off in no other way, and in this manner we procured several tons of water without a single cask being stove.

Their features are regular and well-looking, without being handsome. Their eyes are bright and generally hazel, though in one or two instances they are blue, and some have white speckles on the iris; the eyebrows being thin, and rarely meeting. The nose, somewhat flat, and rather extended at the nostrils, partakes of the Otaheitan form, as do the lips, which are broad, and strongly sulcated. Their ears are moderately large, and the lobes are invariably united to the cheek; they are generally perforated when young, for the reception of flowers, a very common custom among the natives of the South Sea Islands. The hair, in the first generation, is, with one exception only, deep black, sometimes curly, but generally straight; they allow it to go long, keep it very clean, and always well supplied with cocoanut oil. Whiskers are not common, and the beards are thin. The teeth are regular and white; but are often, in the males, disfigured by a deficiency in enamel, and by being deeply furrowed across. They have generally large heads, elevated in the line of the occiput. Their complexion, in the first generation, is, in general, a dark gipsy hue: there are, however, exceptions to this; some are fairer, and others much darker.

The women are nearly as muscular as the men, and taller than the generality of their sex. Polly Young, who is not the tallest upon the island, measured five feet nine inches and a half. Accustomed to perform all domestic duties, to provide wood for cooking, which is there a work of some labor, as it must be brought from the hills, and sometimes to till the ground, their strength is in proportion to their muscularity; and they are no less at home in the water than the men.

The treatment of their children differs from that of our own country, as the infant is bathed three times a day in cold water, and is sometimes not weaned for three or four years; but as soon as that takes place it is fed upon "popoe," made with ripe plantains and boiled taro rubbed into paste. Upon this simple nourishment children are reared to a more healthy state than in other countries, and are free from fevers and other complaints peculiar to the greater portion of the world. Nothing is more extraordinary in the history of the island than the uniform good health of the children; the teething is easily got over, they have no bowel complaints, and are exempt from those contagious diseases which affect children in large communities.

The women have all learned the art of midwifery: parturition generally takes place during the night time; the duration of labor is seldom longer than five hours, and has not yet in any case proved fatal. There is no instance of twins, nor of a single miscarriage, except from accident.

The number of persons on Pitcairn Island in December, 1825, amounted to sixty-six. The total number of children left by the white settlers was fourteen, of whom two died a natural death; one was seized with fits, to which he was subject, while in the water, and was drowned; and one was killed by accident, leaving ten, as above. Of the grandchildren, or second generation, there was also another male who died an accidental death. There have, therefore, been sixty-two births in the period of thirty-five years, from the 23d January, 1790, to the 23d December, 1825, and only two natural deaths.

Before we close this interesting account, a brief notice should be taken of the fate of that portion of the mutineers, who separated themselves from the ringleader, Christian, at Otaheite.

The intelligence of the mutiny, and the suffering of Bligh and his companions, naturally excited a great sensation in England. Bligh was immediately promoted to the rank of commander, and Captain Edwards was dispatched to Otaheite, in the Pandora frigate, with instructions to search for the Bounty and her mutinous crew, and bring them to England. The Pandora reached Matavai Bay on the twenty-third of March, 1791; and even before she had come to anchor, Joseph Coleman, formerly armorer of the Bounty, pushed off from shore in a canoe, and came on board. In the course of two days afterward, the whole of the remainder of the Bounty's crew, (in number sixteen,) then on the island, surrendered themselves, with the exception of two, who fled to the mountains, where, as it afterward appeared, they were murdered by the natives.

The Pandora, with the mutineers on board, was subsequently wrecked on the west of New Holland—thirty-four of her crew and four of the prisoners perishing in her. The survivors eventually reached England. A court-martial was soon after held, when six of the ten mutineers were found guilty, and condemned to death—the other four were acquitted. Only three of the six, however, were executed.

In consequence of a representation made by Captain Beechy, the British government sent out Captain Waldegrave in 1830, in the Seringapatam, with a supply of sailors' blue jackets and trousers, flannels, stockings and shoes, women's dresses, spades, mattocks, shovels, pickaxes, trowels, rakes, etc. He found their community increased to about seventy-nine, all exhibiting the same unsophisticated and amiable characteristics as we have before described. Other two Englishmen had settled among them; one of them, called Nobbs, a low-bred, illiterate man, a self-constituted missionary, who was endeavoring to supersede Buffet in his office of religious instructor. The patriarch Adams, it was found, had died in March, 1829, aged sixty-five. While on his deathbed, he had called the heads of families together, and urged upon them to elect a chief; which, however, they had not yet done; but the greatest harmony still prevailed among them, notwithstanding Nobbs' exertions to form a party of his own. Captain Waldegrave thought that the island, which is about four miles square, might be able to support a thousand persons, upon reaching which number they would naturally emigrate to other islands.

Such is the account of this most singular colony, originating in crime and bloodshed. Of all the repentant criminals on record, the most interesting, perhaps, is John Adams; nor do we know where to find a more beautiful example of the value of early instruction than in the history of this man, who, having run the full career of nearly all kinds of vice, was checked by an interval of leisurely reflection, and the sense of new duties awakened by the power of natural affections.

HOW THEY LIVE

ON BOARD OF AN

AMERICAN MAN OF WAR:

BEING THE EXPERIENCES OF A SAILOR IN THE

UNITED STATES NAVY.*

"ALL hands up anchor! Man the capstan!"

All was ready; boats hoisted in, stun' sail gear rove, messenger passed, capstan-bars in their places, accommodation-ladder below; and in glorious spirits, we sat down to dinner. In the ward-room, the lieutenants were passing round their oldest Port, and pledging their friends; in the steerage, the *middies* were busy raising loans to liquidate the demands of their laundress, or else—in the navy phrase—preparing to pay their creditors *with a flying fore-topsail.* On the poop, the captain was looking to windward; and in his grand, inaccessible cabin, the high and mighty commodore sat silent and stately, as the statue of Jupiter in Dodona.

It was on the gun-deck that our dinners were spread; all along between the guns; and there, as we cross-legged sat, you would have thought a hundred farm-yards and meadows were nigh. Such a cackling of ducks, chickens, and ganders; such a lowing of oxen, and bleating of lambkins, penned up here and there along the deck, to provide sea repasts for the officers.

"All hands up anchor!"

When that order was given, how we sprang to the bars, and heaved round that capstan—round, round it spun like a sphere, keeping time with our feet to the time of the fifer, till the cable was straight up and down, and the ship with her nose in the water.

"Heave and pull! unship your bars, and make sail!"

It was done:—bar-men, nipper men, tierers, veerers, idlers and all, scrambled up the ladder to the braces and halyards; while like monkeys, the sail-loosers ran out on those broad boughs, or yards; and down fell the sails like white clouds from the ether—topsails, topgallants, and royals; and away we ran with the halyards, till every sheet was distended.

"Once more to the bars!"

"Heave, my hearties, heave hard!"

With a jerk and a yerk, we broke ground; and up to our bows came several thousand pounds of old iron, in the shape of our ponderous anchor.

In merchantmen the seamen are divided into watches—starboard and larboard—taking their turn at the ship's duty by night. This plan is

---

*Abridged from "White Jacket, or the World in a Man-of-war," by Herman Melville, a writer of great ability in his peculiar line. This large 12mo., of 465 pages, gives the most faithful sketches of any work of the kind extant, and to which we take pleasure in referring the reader for those full details foreign to the volume in hand.

followed in all men-of-war. But in all men-of-war, beside this division, there are others, rendered indispensable from the great number of men, and the necessity of precision and discipline. Not only are particular bands assigned to the three *tops*, but in getting under weigh, or any other proceeding requiring all hands, particular men of these bands are assigned to each yard of the tops. Thus, when the order is given to loose the main-royal, a particular individual flies to obey it; and no one but him. Also, in tacking ship, reefing topsails, or "coming to," every man of a frigate's five-hundred-strong, knows his own special place, and is infallibly found there. He sees nothing else, attends to nothing else, and will stay there till grim death or an epaulet orders him away. Were it not for these regulations a man-of-war's crew would be nothing but a mob.

Now the fore, main, and mizzen-top-men of each watch—starboard and larboard — are at sea respectively subdivided into quarter-watches; which regularly relieve each other in the tops to which they may belong; while, collectively, they relieve the whole larboard watch of topmen. Beside these topmen, who are always made up of active sailors, there are sheet-anchor-men—old veterans all—whose place is on the forecastle; the foreyard, anchors, and all the sails on the bowsprit being under their care. They are an old weather-beaten set, culled from the most experienced seamen on board. These are the fellows, who spin interminable yarns about Decatur, Hull, and Bainbridge; and carry about their persons bits of "Old Ironsides," as Catholics do the wood of the true cross. These are the fellows, that some officers never pretend to damn, however much they may anathematize others. These are the fellows, whose society most of the youngster midshipmen much affect; from whom they learn their best seamanship; and to whom they look up as veterans; if so be, that they have any reverence in their souls, which is not the case with all midshipmen.

Then, there is the *after-guard*, stationed on the quarter-deck; who, under the quarter-masters and quarter-gunners, attend to the mainsail and spanker, and help haul the main-brace, and other ropes in the stern of the vessel. The duties assigned to the after-guard's-men being comparatively light and easy, and but little seamanship being expected from them, they are composed chiefly of landsmen; the least robust, least hardy, and least sailor-like of the crew; and being stationed on the quarter-deck, they are generally selected with some eye to their personal appearance. Hence, they are mostly slender young fellows, of a genteel figure and gentlemanly address; not weighing much on a rope, but weighing considerably in the estimation of all foreign ladies who may chance to visit the ship. Then, there are the *Waisters*, always stationed on the gun-deck. These haul aft the fore and main-sheets, beside being subject to ignoble duties; attending to the drainage and sewerage below hatches. These fellows are all sorry chaps, who never put foot in ratlin, or venture above the bulwarks. Inveterate "*sons of farmers*," with the hayseed yet in their hair, they are consigned to the congenial superintendence of the chicken-coops, pig-pens, and potato-lockers. These are generally placed amidships, on the gun-deck of a frigate, between the fore and main-hatches; and comprise so extensive an area, that it much resembles the market-place of a small town. They are the tag-rag and bob-tail of the crew; and he who is good for nothing else is good enough for a *Waister*.

Three decks down — spar-deck, gun-deck, and berth-deck—and we come to a parcel of "*holders*," who burrow, like rabbits in warrens, among the water-tanks, casks, and cables. They are a lazy, lumpish, torpid set;

and when going ashore after a long cruise, come out into the day, like terrapins from their caves, or bears in the spring, from tree-trunks. No one ever knows the names of these fellows; after a three years' voyage, they still remain strangers to you.

Such are the principal divisions into which a man-of-war's crew is divided; but the inferior allotments of duties are endless. We say nothing here of boatswain's mates, gunner's mates, carpenter's mates, sail-maker's mates, armorer's mates, master-at-arms, ship's corporals, cockswains, quarter-masters, quarter-gunners, captains of the forecastle, captains of the foretop, captains of the maintop, captains of the mizzen-top, captains of the after-guard, captains of the main-hold, captains of the fore-hold, captains of the head, coopers, painters, tinkers, commodore's steward, captain's steward, ward-room steward, steerage steward, commodore's cook, captain's cook, officers' cook, cooks of the range, mess-cooks, hammock-boys, messenger boys, cot-boys, loblolly-boys, and numberless others, whose functions are fixed and peculiar. It is from this endless subdivision of duties in a man-of-war, that, upon first entering one, a sailor has need of a good memory, and the more of an arithmetician he is, the better. He is wholly nonplused, and confounded. And when, to crown all, the first lieutenant, whose business it is to welcome all new comers, and assign them their quarters; when this officer—none of the most bland or amiable either—gives him number after number to recollect —246—139—478—351—the poor fellow feels like decamping.

Some account has been given of the various divisions into which our crew was divided; so it may be well to say something of the officers; who they are, and what are their functions. Our ship was the flag-ship; that is, we sported a *broad pennant* or *bougee* at the main, in token that we carried a commodore—the highest rank of officers recognized in the American navy. The bougee is not to be confounded with the *long pennant* or *coach-whip*, a tapering, serpentine streamer, worn by all men-of-war. Owing to certain vague, republican scruples, about creating great officers of the navy, America has thus far had no admirals; though, as her ships of war increase, they may become indispensable. An American commodore, like an English commodore, or the French *Chef d' Escadre*, is but a senior captain, temporarily commanding a small number of ships, detached for any special purpose. He has no permanent rank, recognized by Government, above his captaincy; though once employed as a commodore, usage and courtesy unite in continuing the title. Our commodore was a gallant old man, who had seen service in his time. When a lieutenant, he served in the late war with England; and in the gun-boat actions on the lakes near New Orleans, just previous to the grand land engagements, received a musket-ball in his shoulder; which, with the two balls in his eyes, he carries about with him to this day. On account of this wound in his shoulder, our commodore had a body-servant's pay allowed him, in addition to his regular salary. I cannot say a great deal, personally, of the commodore; he never sought my company at all; never extended any gentlemanly courtesies. One phenomenon about him was the strange manner in which every one shunned him. At the first sign of those epaulets of his on the weather side of the poop, the officers there congregated invariably shrunk over to leeward, and left him alone.

Turn we now to the second officer in rank, almost supreme, however, in the internal affairs of his ship. Captain C—— was a large, portly man, a Harry the Eighth afloat, bluff and hearty; and as kingly in his cabin as Harry on his throne. The captain's word is law; he never speaks but in the imperative mood. When he stands on his quarter-deck at sea, he absolutely commands as far as eye can reach. Only the moon and stars are beyond his jurisdiction. He is lord and master of the sun. It is not twelve o'clock till he says so. For when the sailing-master, whose duty it is to take the regular observation at noon, touches his hat, and reports twelve o'clock to the officer of the deck; that functionary orders a midshipman to repair to the captain's cabin, and humbly inform him of the respectful suggestion of the sailing-master.

"Twelve o'clock reported, sir," says the middy.

"*Make* it so," replies the captain.

And the bell is struck eight by the messenger-boy, and twelve o'clock it is.

As in the case of the commodore, when the captain visits the deck, his subordinate officers generally beat a retreat to the other side; and, as a general rule, would no more think of addressing him, except concerning the ship, than a lackey would think of hailing the Czar of Russia on his throne and inviting him to tea. Perhaps no mortal man has more reason to feel such an intense sense of his own personal consequence, as the captain of a man-of-war at sea.

Next in rank comes the first or senior lieutenant, the chief executive officer. Beside the first lieutenant, the ward-room officers include the junior lieutenants, in a frigate six or seven in number, the sailing-master, purser, chaplain, surgeon, marine officers, and midshipmen's schoolmaster, or "the professor." They generally form a very agreeable club of good fellows; from their diversity of character, admirably calculated to form an agreeable social whole. Of course these gentlemen all associate on a footing of perfect social equality. Next in order come the warrant or forward officers, consisting of the boatswain, gunner, carpenter, and sail-maker. Though these worthies sport long coats and wear the anchor-button; yet, in the estimation of the ward-room officers, they are not, technically speaking, rated gentlemen. The first lieutenant, chaplain, or surgeon, for example, would never dream of inviting them to dinner. In sea parlance, "they come in at the hawse holes;" they have hard hands; and the carpenter and sail-maker practically understand the duties which they are called upon to superintend. They mess by themselves.

In this part of the category now come the "reefers," otherwise "middies" or midshipmen. These boys are sent to sea, for the purpose of making commodores; and in order to become commodores, many of them deem it indispensable forthwith to commence chewing tobacco, drinking brandy and water, and swearing at the sailors. As they are only placed on board a sea-going ship to go to school and learn the duty of a lieutenant; and, until qualified to act as such, have few or no special functions to attend to; they are little more, while midshipmen, than supernumeraries on board. Hence, in a crowded frigate, they are so everlastingly crossing the path of both men and officers, that in the navy it has become a proverb, that a useless fellow is "*as much in the way as a reefer.*"

In a gale of wind, when all hands are called and the deck swarms with men, the little "middies" running about distracted and having nothing particular to do, make it up in vociferous swearing; exploding all about under foot like torpedos. Some of them are terrible little boys, cocking their caps at alarming angles, and looking fierce as young roosters. They are generally great consumers of Macassar oil and the Balm of Columbia; they thirst and rage after whiskers; and sometimes, applying their oint ments, lay themselves out in the sun, to promote the fertility of their chins. The middies live by themselves in the steerage, where, nowadays, they dine off a table, spread with a cloth. They have a castor at dinner· they have some other little boys (selected from the ship's company) to wait upon them; they sometimes drink coffee out of china. But for all these, their modern refinements, in some instances the affairs of their club go sadly to rack and ruin. The china is broken; the japanned coffee-pot dented like a pewter mug in an ale-house; the pronged forks resemble tooth-picks; (for which they are sometimes used;) the table-knives are hacked into hand-saws; and the cloth goes to the sail-maker to be patched.

Having now descended from commodore to middy, we come lastly to a set of nondescripts, forming also a "mess" by themselves, apart from the seamen. Into this mess, the usage of a man-of-war thrusts various subordinates — including the master-at-arms, purser's steward, ship's corporals, marine sergeants, and ship's yeomen, forming the first aristocracy above the sailors. The master-at-arms is a sort of high-constable and schoolmaster, wearing citizen's clothes, and known by his official rattan. He it is whom all sailors hate. His is the universal duty of a universal informer and hunter-up of delinquents. On the berth-deck he reigns supreme; spying out all grease-spots made by the various cooks of the seamen's messes, and driving the laggards up the hatches, when all hands are called. But as it is a heartless, so is it a thankless office. Of dark nights, most masters-of-arms keep themselves in readiness to dodge forty-two pound balls, dropped down the hatchways near them. The ship's corporals are this worthy's deputies and ushers. The marine sergeants are generally tall fellows with unyielding spines and stiff upper lips, and very exclusive in their tastes and predilections. The ship's yeoman is a gentleman who has a sort of counting-room in a tar-cellar down in the fore-hold.

Except the officers above enumerated, there are none who mess apart from the seamen. The "*petty officers*," so called; that is, the boatswain's, gunner's, carpenter's, and sail-maker's mates, the captains of the tops, of the forecastle, and of the after-guard, and of the fore and main holds, and the quarter-masters, all mess in common with the crew, and in the American navy are only distinguished from the common seamen by their slightly additional pay. Thus it will be seen, that the dinner-table is the criterion of rank in our man-of-war world. The commodore dines alone, because he is the only man of his rank in the ship. So, too, with the captain; and the ward-room officers, warrant officers, midshipmen, the master-at-arms' mess, and the common seamen—all of them, respectively, dine together, because they are, respectively, on a footing of equality.

To a common sailor, the living on board a man-of-war is like living in a market; where you dress on the door-steps and sleep in the cellar. No privacy can you have; hardly one moment's seclusion. It is almost a physical impossibility, that you can ever be alone. You dine at a vast *table d'hote*; sleep in commons, and make your toilet where and when you can. Your clothes are stowed in a large canvas bag, generally painted black, which you can get out of the "rack" only once in the twenty-four hours; and then, during a time of the utmost confusion; among five hundred other bags, with five hundred other sailors diving into each, in the midst of the twilight of the berth-deck. In some measure to obviate this inconvenience, many sailors divide their wardrobes between their hammocks and their bags; stowing a few frocks and trowsers in the former; so that they can shift at night, if they wish, when the hammocks are piped down. But they gain very little by this. You have no place whatever but your bag or hammock, in which to put anything in a man-of-war. If you lay any thing down, and turn your back for a moment, ten to one it is gone

From the wild life they lead, and various other causes, sailors, as a class entertain the most liberal notions concerning morality and the Decalogue; or rather, they take their own views of such matters, caring little for the theological or ethical definitions of others concerning what may be criminal, or wrong. Their ideas are much swayed by circumstances. They will covertly abstract a thing from one whom they dislike; and insist upon it, that, in such a case, stealing is no robbing. Or, where the theft involves something funny, they only steal for the sake of the joke; but this much is to be observed nevertheless, i. e., that they never spoil the joke by returning the stolen article. Perhaps it is a thing unavoidable, but the truth is that, among the crew of a man-of-war, scores of desperadoes are too often found, who stop not at the largest enormities. A species of highway robbery is not unknown to them. A *gang* will be informed that such a fellow has three or four gold pieces in the monkey-bag, so called, or purse, which many tars wear round their necks, tucked out of sight. Upon this, they deliberately lay their plans; and, in due time, proceed to carry them into execution. The man they have marked is perhaps strolling along the benighted berth-deck to his mess-chest; when, of a sudden, the foot-pads dash out from their hiding-place, throw him down, and while two or three gag him, and hold him fast, another cuts the bag from his neck, and makes away with it, followed by his comrades. This was more than once done in our frigate. At other times, hearing that a sailor has something valuable secreted in his hammock, they will rip it open from underneath, while he sleeps, and reduce the conjecture to a certainty. To enumerate all the minor pilferings on board a man-of-war would be endless. It is in vain that the officers, by threats of condign punishment, endeavor to instill more virtuous principles into their crew; so thick is the mob, that not one thief in a thousand is detected.

In the American navy, the law allows one gill of spirits per day to every seaman. In two portions, it is served out just previous to breakfast and dinner. At the roll of the drum, the sailors assemble round a large tub, or cask, filled with the liquid; and, as their names are called off by a midshipman, they step up and regale themselves from a little tin measure called a "tot." To many of them, indeed, the thought of their daily *tots* forms a perpetual perspective of ravishing landscapes, indefinitely receding in the distance. It is their great "prospect in life." Take away their grog, and life possesses no further charms for them. It is hardly to be doubted, that the controlling inducement which keeps many men in the navy, is the unbounded confidence they have in the ability of the United States government to supply them, regularly and unfailingly, with their daily allowance of this beverage. I have known several forlorn individuals, shipping as landsmen, who have confessed to me, that having contracted a love for ardent spirits, which they could not renounce, and having by their foolish courses been brought into the most abject poverty, —insomuch that they could no longer gratify their thirst ashore—they incontinently entered the navy; regarding it as the asylum for all drunkards, who might there prolong their lives by regular hours and exercise, and twice every day quench their thirst by moderate and undeviating doses.

The common seamen in a large frigate are divided into some thirty or forty messes, put down on the purser's books as *mess No.* 1, *mess No.* 2, *mess No*. 3, etc. The members of each mess club their rations of provisions, and breakfast, dine, and sup together in allotted intervals between the guns on the main-deck. In undeviating rotation, the members of each mess (excepting the petty-officers) take their turn in performing the functions of cook and steward. And for the time being, all the affairs of the club are subject to their inspection and control. It is the cook's business, also, to have an eye to the general interests of his mess; to see that, when the aggregated allowance of beef, bread, etc., are served out by one of the master's mates, the mess over which he presides receives its full share, without stint or subtraction. Upon the berth-deck he has a chest, in which to keep his pots, pans, spoons, and small stores of sugar, molasses, tea, and flour. But though entitled a cook, strictly speaking, the head of the mess is no cook at all; for the cooking for the crew is all done by a functionary, officially called the "*ship's cook*," assisted by several deputies.

From this it will be seen, that, so far as cooking is concerned, a "*cook of the mess*" has very little to do; merely carrying his provisions to and from the grand democratic cookery. Still, in some things, his office involves many annoyances. Twice a week butter and cheese are served out—so much to each man—and the mess-cook has the sole charge of these delicacies. The great difficulty consists in so catering for the mess, touching these luxuries, as to satisfy all. Some guzzlers are for devouring the butter at a meal, and finishing off with the cheese the same day; others contend for saving it up against *Banyan Day*, when there is nothing but beef and bread; and others, again, are for taking a very small bit of butter and cheese, by way of dessert, to each and every meal through the week. All this gives rise to endless disputes, debates, and altercations. Sometimes, with his mess-cloth—a square of painted canvas—set out on deck between the guns, garnished with pots, and pans, and *kids*, you see the mess-cook seated on a match-tub at its head, his trowsers legs rolled up and arms bared, presiding over the convivial party. "Now, men, you can't have any butter to-day. I'm saving it up for to-morrow. You don't know the value of butter, men. You, Jim, take your hoof off the cloth! Devil take me, if some of you chaps haven't no more manners than so many swines! Quick, men, quick; bear a hand, and '*scoff*' (eat) away.—I 've got my to-morrow's *duff* to make yet, and some of you fellows keep *scoffing* as if I had nothing to do but sit still here on this here tub here, and look on. There, there, men, you've all had enough; so sail away out of this, and let me clear up the wreck." In this strain would one of the periodical cooks of mess No. 15, talk to us. He was a tall, resolute fellow, who had once been a brakeman on a railroad, and he kept us all pretty straight; from his fiat there was no appeal.

To a quiet, contemplative character, averse to uproar, undue exercise of his bodily members, and all kind of useless confusion, nothing can be more distressing than a proceeding in all men-of-war called "*general quarters*." As the specific object for which a man-of-war is built and put into commission is to fight and fire off cannon, it is, of course, deemed indispensable that the crew should be duly instructed in the art and mystery involved. The summons is given by the ship's drummer, who strikes a peculiar beat—short, broken, rolling, shuffling—like the sound made by the march into battle of iron-heeled grenadiers. It is a regular tune, with a fine song composed to it; the words of the chorus, being most artistically arranged, may give some idea of the air:

"Hearts of oak are our ships, jolly tars are our men ;
We are always ready, steady, boys, steady,
To fight and to conquer, again and again."

My station at the batteries was at one of the thirty-two pound carronades, on the starboard side of the quarter-deck. This carronade was known as "Gun No. 5," on the first lieutenant's quarter-bill. Among our gun's crew, however, it was known as *Black Bet.* This name was bestowed y the captain of the gun—a fine negro—in honor of his sweetheart, a colored lady of Philadelphia. Of Black Bet I was rammer and sponger; and ram and sponge I did, like a good fellow. But it was terrible work to help run in and out of the port-hole that amazing mass of metal, especially as the thing must be done in a trice. Then, at the summons of a horrid, rasping rattle, swayed by the captain in person, we were made to rush from our guns, seize pikes and pistols, and repel an imaginary army of boarders, who, by a fiction of the officers, were supposed to be assailing all sides of the ship at once. After cutting and slashing at them awhile, we jumped back to our guns, and again went to jerking our elbows. Meantime, a loud cry is heard of "Fire! fire! fire!" in the fore-top ; and a regular engine, worked by a set of Bowery-boy tars, is forthwith set to playing streams of water aloft. Such a sea-martinet was our captain, that sometimes we were roused from our hammocks at night; when a scene would ensue that it is not in the power of pen and ink to describe. Five hundred men spring to their feet, dress themselves, take up their bedding, and run to the nettings and stow it; then hie to their stations—each man jostling his neighbor—some alow, some aloft; some this way, some that ; and in less than five minutes the frigate is ready for action, and still as the grave ; almost every man precisely where he would be were an enemy actually about to be engaged. The gunner is burrowing down in the magazine under the ward-room, which is lighted by battle-lanterns, placed behind glazed glass bull's-eyes inserted in the bulkhead. The *powder-monkeys*, or boys, who fetch and carry cartridges, are scampering to and fro among the guns ; and the *first and second loaders* stand ready to receive their supplies. These *powder-monkeys*, as they are called, enact a curious part in time of action. The entrance to the magazine on the berth-deck, where they procure their food for the guns, is guarded by a woolen screen ; and a gunner's mate, standing behind it, thrusts out the cartridges through a small arm-hole in this screen. The enemy's shot (perhaps red hot) are flying in all directions; and to protect their cartridges, the powder-monkeys hurriedly wrap tnem up in their jackets ; and with all haste scramble up the ladders to their respective guns, like eating-house waiters hurrying along with hot cakes for breakfast. At *general quarters* the shot-boxes are uncovered ; showing the grape-shot—aptly so called, for they precisely resemble bunches of the fruit; though, to receive a bunch of iron grapes in the abdomen would be but a sorry dessert; and also showing the canister-shot—old iron of various sorts, packed in a tin case, like a tea-caddy.

But if verily going into action, then would the frigate have made still further preparations ; for however alike in some things, there is always a vast difference—if you sound them—between a reality and a sham. Not to speak of the pale sternness of the men at their guns at such a juncture, and the choked thoughts at their hearts, the ship itself would here and there present a far different appearance. Something like that of an extensive mansion preparing for a grand entertainment, when folding-doors are withdrawn, chambers converted into drawing-rooms, and every inch of available space thrown into one continuous whole. For previous to an action, every bulkhead in a man-of-war is knocked down; great guns are run out of the commodore's parlor windows; nothing separates the ward-room officers' quarters from those of the men, but an ensign used for a curtain. The sailors' mess-chests are tumbled down into the hold; and the hospital cots—of which all men-of-war carry a large supply—are dragged forth from the sail-room, and piled near at hand to receive the wounded; amputation-tables are ranged in the *cock-pit* or in the *tiers*, whereon to carve the bodies of the maimed. The yards are slung in chains; fire-screens distributed here and there; hillocks of cannon-balls piled between the guns; shot-plugs suspended within easy reach from the beams; and solid masses of wads, big as Dutch cheeses, braced to the cheeks of the gun-carriages.

No small difference, also, would be visible in the wardrobe of both officers and men. The officers generally fight as dandies dance, namely, in silk stockings; inasmuch as, in case of being wounded in the leg, the silk-hose can be more easily drawn off by the surgeon; cotton sticks, and and works into the wound. But beside these differences between a sham-fight at *general quarters* and a real cannonading, the aspect of the ship, at the beating of the retreat, would, in the latter case, be very dissimilar to the neatness and uniformity in the former. Then our stout masts and yards might be lying about decks, like tree boughs after a tornado in a piece of woodland; our dangling ropes, cut and sundered in all directions, would be bleeding tar at every yarn; and strewn with jagged splinters from our wounded planks, the gun-deck might resemble a carpenter's shop. *Then*, when all was over, and all hands would be piped to take down the hammocks from the exposed nettings, (where they play the part of the cotton bales at New Orleans,) we might find bits of broken shot, iron bolts, and bullets in our blankets. And, while smeared with blood like butchers, the surgeon and his mates would be amputating arms and legs on the berth-deck, an underling of the carpenter's gang would be new-legging and arming the broken chairs and tables in the commodore's cabin; while the rest of his *squad* would be *splicing* and *fishing* the shattered masts and yards. The scupper-holes having discharged the last rivulet of blood, the decks would be washed down; and the galley-cooks would be going fore and aft, sprinkling them with hot vinegar, to take out the shambles' smell from the planks; which, unless some such means are employed, often create a highly offensive effluvia for weeks after a fight.

Then, upon mustering the men, and calling the quarter-bills by the light of a battle-lantern, many a wounded seaman, with his arm in a sling, would answer for some poor shipmate who could never more make answer for himself:

"Tom Brown?"

"Killed, sir."

"Jack Jewel?"

"Killed, sir."

"Joe Hardy?"

"Killed, sir."

And opposite all these poor fellows' names, down would go on the quarter-bills the bloody marks of *red* ink—fitly used on these occasions.

The appearance of the boatswain, with his silver whistle to his mouth, at the main hatchway of the gun-deck, is always regarded by the crew with the utmost curiosity, for this betokens that some general order is about to be promulgated through the ship. What now? is the question that runs on from man to man. A short preliminary whistle is then given by "Old Yarn," as they call him, which whistle serves to collect round him, from their various stations, his four mates. Then Yarn, or Pipes, as leader of the orchestra, begins a peculiar call, in which his assistants join. This over, the order, whatever it may be, is loudly sung out and prolonged, till the remotest corner echoes again. The boatswain and his mates are the town-criers of a man-of-war.

A calm had commenced in the afternoon; and the following morning the ship's company were electrified by a general order, thus set forth and declared: "*D'ye hear there, fore and aft! all hands skylark!* This mandate, nowadays never used except upon very rare occasions, produced the same effect upon the men that exhilarating gas would have done, or an extra allowance of "grog." For a time, the wonted discipline of the ship was broken through, and perfect license allowed. It was a Babel here, a Bedlam there, and a Pandemonium everywhere. The faint-hearted and timorous crawled to their hiding-places, and the lusty and bold shouted forth their glee. Gangs of men, in all sorts of outlandish habiliments, wild as those worn at some crazy carnival, rushed to and fro, seizing upon whomsoever they pleased—warrant-officers and dangerous pugilists excepted—pulling and hauling the luckless tars about, till fairly baited into a genial warmth. Some were made fast to, and hoisted aloft with a will; others, mounted upon oars, were ridden fore and aft on a rail, to the boisterous mirth of the spectators, any one of whom might be the next victim. Swings were rigged from the tops, or the masts; and the most reluctant wights being purposely selected, spite of all struggles, were swung from east to west, in vast arcs of circles, till almost breathless. Hornpipes, fandangoes, Donnybrook-jigs, reels, and quadrilles, were danced under the very nose of the most mighty captain, and upon the very quarter-deck and poop. Sparring and wrestling, too, were all the vogue; *Kentucky bites* were given, and the *Indian hug* exchanged. The din frightened the sea-fowl, that flew by with accelerated wing.

It is worth mentioning that several casualties occurred, of which, however, I will relate but one. While the "skylarking" was at its height, one of the foretop-men—an ugly-tempered devil of a Portuguese, looking on—swore that he would be the death of any man who laid violent hands upon his inviolable person. This threat being overheard, a band of desperadoes coming up from behind, tripped him up in an instant, and in the twinkling of an eye the Portuguese was straddling an oar, borne aloft by an uproarious multitude, who rushed him along the deck at a railroad gallop. The living mass of arms all round and beneath him was so dense, that every time he inclined to one side he was instantly pushed upright, but only to fall over again, to receive another push from the contrary direction. Presently, disengaging his hands from those who held them, the enraged seaman drew from his bosom an iron belaying-pin, and recklessly laid about him to right and left. Most of his persecutors fled; but some eight or ten still stood their ground, and, while bearing him aloft, endeavored to wrest the weapon from his hands. In this attempt, one man was struck on the head, and dropped insensible. He was taken up for dead, and carried below to the surgeon, while the Portuguese was put under guard. But the wound did not prove very serious; and in a few days the man was walking about the deck, with his head well bandaged. This occurrence put an end to the "skylarking," further head-breaking being strictly prohibited. In due time the Portuguese paid the penalty of his rashness at the gangway.

A hint has already been conveyed concerning the subterranean depths of our ship's hold. But there is no time here to speak of the *spirit-room*, a cellar down in the after-hold, where the sailors' "grog" is kept; nor of the *cable-tiers*, where the great hawsers and chains are piled, as you see them at a large ship-chandler's on shore; nor of the grocer's vaults, where tierces of sugar, molasses, vinegar, rice, and flour are snugly stowed; nor of the *sail-room*, full as a sail-maker's loft ashore—piled up with great topsails and topgallant-sails, all ready-folded in their places, like so many white vests in a gentleman's wardrobe; nor of the copper and copper-fastened *magazine*, closely packed with kegs of powder, great-gun and small-arm cartridges; nor of the immense *shot-lockers*, or subterranean arsenals, full as a bushel of apples with twenty-four pound balls; nor of the *bread-room*, a large apartment, tinned all round within to keep out the mice, where the hard biscuit destined for the consumption of five hundred men on a long voyage is stowed away by the cubic yard; nor of the vast iron *tanks* for fresh water in the hold, like the reservoir lakes at Fairmount, in Philadelphia; nor of the *paint-room*, where the kegs of white lead, and casks of linseed oil, and all sorts of pots and brushes, are kept; nor of the *armorer's smithy*, where the ship's forges and anvils may be heard ringing at times; I say I have no time to speak of these things, and many more places of note.

But there is one very extensive warehouse among the rest that needs special mention—*the ship's Yeomen's store-room.* In our vessel it was down in the ship's basement, beneath the berth-deck, and you went to it by way of the *fore-passage*, a very dim, devious corridor, indeed. Entering—say at noonday—you find yourself in a gloomy apartment, lit by a solitary lamp. On one side are shelves, filled with balls of *marline*, *ratlin-stuff*, *seizing-stuff*, *spun-yarn*, and numerous twines of assorted sizes. In another direction you see large cases containing heaps of articles, reminding one of a shoe-maker's furnishing-store—wooden *serving-mallets*, *fids*, *toggles*, and *heavers*; iron *prickers* and *marling-spikes;* in a third quarter you see a sort of hardware shop—shelves piled with all manner of hooks, bolts, nails, screws and *thimbles;* and, in still another direction, you see a block-maker's store, heaped up with lignum-vitæ sheeves and wheels. Through low arches in the bulkhead beyond, you peep in upon distant vaults and catacombs, obscurely lighted in the far end, and showing immense coils of new ropes, and other bulky articles, stowed in tiers, all savoring of tar.

But by far the most curious department of these mysterious store-rooms is the armory, where the pikes, cutlasses, pistols, and belts, forming the arms of the boarders in time of action, are hung against the walls, and suspended in thick rows from the beams overhead. Here, too, are to be seen scores of Colt's patent revolvers, which, though furnished with but one tube, multiply the fatal bullets, as the naval cat-o'-nine-tails, with a cannibal cruelty, in one blow nine times multiplies a culprit's lashes; so that, when a sailor is ordered one dozen lashes, the sentence should read one hundred and eight. All these arms are kept in the brightest order, wearing a fine polish, and may truly be said to *reflect* credit on the yeoman and his mates. Among the lower grade of officers in a man-of-war, that of yeoman is not the least important. His responsibilities are denoted by his pay. While the *petty officers*, quarter-gunners, captains of the tops, and others, receive but fifteen and eighteen dollars a month—but little more than a mere able seaman—the Yeoman in an American line-of-battle ship receives forty dollars, and in a frigate thirty-five dollars per month. He is accountable for all the articles under his charge, and on no account must deliver a yard of twine or a tenpenny nail to the boatswain or carpenter, unless shown a written requisition and order from the senior lieutenant. Indeed, there were several parts of the ship under hatches shrouded in mystery, and completely inaccessible to the sailor. Wondrous old doors, barred and bolted, in dingy bulkheads, must have opened into regions full of interest to a successful explorer. Thus, though for a period of more than a year I was an inmate of this floating box of live-oak, yet there were numberless things in it that, to the last, remained wrapped in obscurity, or concerning which I could only lose myself in vague speculations.

If you begin the day with a laugh, you may, nevertheless, end it with a sob and a sigh. John, Peter, Mark, and Antone—four sailors of the starboard-watch, were charged with violating a well-known law of the ship—having been engaged in one of those tangled, general fights sometimes occurring among sailors. They had nothing to anticipate but a flogging, at the captain's pleasure. Toward evening of the next day, they were startled by the dread summons of the boatswain and his mates at the principal hatchway—a summons that ever sends a shudder through every manly heart in a frigate:

"*All hands witness punishment, ahoy!*"

The hoarseness of the cry, its unrelenting prolongation, its being caught up at different points, and sent through the lowermost depths of the ship; all this produces a most dismal effect upon every heart not calloused by long habituation to it. However much you may desire to absent yourself from the scene that ensues, yet behold it you must; or, at least, stand near it you must; for the regulations enjoin the attendance of the entire ship's company, from the corpulent captain himself to the smallest boy who strikes the bell.

At the summons the crew crowded round the mainmast; multitudes eager to obtain a good place on the booms, to overlook the scene; many laughing and chatting, others canvassing the case of the culprits; some maintaining sad, anxious countenances, or carrying a suppressed indignation in their eyes; a few purposely keeping behind to avoid looking on; in short, among five hundred men, there was every possible shade of character. All the officers—midshipmen included—stood together in a group on the starboard side of the mainmast; the first lieutenant in advance, and the surgeon, whose special duty it is to be present at such times, standing close by his side. Presently the captain came forward from his cabin, and stood in the center of this solemn group, with a small paper in his hand. That paper was the daily report of offenses, regularly laid upon his table every morning or evening, like the day's journal placed by a bachelor's napkin at breakfast. "Master-at-arms, bring up the prisoners," he said. A few moments elapsed, during which the captain, now clothed in his most dreadful attributes, fixed his eyes severely upon the crew, when suddenly a lane formed through the crowd of seamen, and the prisoners advanced—the master-at-arms, rattan in hand, on one side, and an armed marine on the other—and took up their stations at the mast. "You John, you Peter, you Mark, you Antone," said the captain, "were yesterday found fighting on the gun-deck. Have you anything to say?"

Mark and Antone, two steady, middle-aged men, whom I had often admired for their sobriety, replied that they did not strike the first blow; that they had submitted to much before they had yielded to their passions;

but as they acknowledged that they had at last defended themselves their excuse was overruled. John—a brutal bully, who, it seems, was the real author of the disturbance—was about entering into a long extenuation, when he was cut short by being made to confess, irrespective of circumstances, that he had been in the fray. Peter, a handsome lad about nineteen years old, belonging to the mizzen-top, looked pale and tremulous. He was a great favorite in his part of the ship, and especially in his own mess, principally composed of lads of his own age. That morning two of his young messmates had gone to his bag, taken out his best clothes, and, obtaining the permission of the marine sentry at the "brig," had handed them to him, to be put on against being summoned to the mast. This was done to propitiate the captain, as most captains love to see a tidy sailor. But it would not do. To all his supplications the captain turned a deaf ear. Peter declared that he had been struck twice before he had returned a blow. "No matter," said the captain, "you struck at last, instead of reporting the case to an officer. I allow no man to fight on board here but myself. I do the fighting. Now, men," he added, "you all admit the charge; you know the penalty. Strip! Quarter-masters, are the gratings rigged?" The gratings are square frames of barred wood-work, sometimes placed over the hatchways. One of these squares was now laid on the deck, close to the ship's bulwarks, and while the remaining preparations were being made, the master-at-arms assisted the prisoners in removing their jackets and shirts. This done, their shirts were loosely thrown over their shoulders.

At a sign from the captain, John, with a shameless leer, advanced, and stood passively upon the grating, while the bareheaded old quarter-master, with gray hair streaming in the wind, bound his feet to the cross-bars, and, stretching out his arms over his head, secured them to the hammock-nettings above. He then retreated a little space, standing silent. Meanwhile, the boatswain stood solemnly on the other side, with a green bag in his hand, from which taking four instruments of punishment, he gave one to each of his mates; for a fresh "cat," applied by a fresh hand, is the ceremonious privilege accorded to every man-of-war culprit. At another sign from the captain, the master-at-arms, stepping up, removed the shirt from the prisoner. At this juncture a wave broke against the ship's side, and dashed the spray over his exposed back. But though the air was piercing cold, and the water drenched him, John stood still, without a shudder.

The captain's finger was now lifted, and the first boatswain's-mate advanced, combing out the nine tails of his *cat* with his hand, and then, sweeping them round his neck, brought them with the whole force of his body upon the mark. Again, and again, and again; and at every blow, higher and higher rose the long, purple bars on the prisoner's back. But he only bowed over his head, and stood still. Meantime, some of the crew whispered among themselves in applause of their shipmate's nerve; but the greater part were breathlessly silent as the keen scourge hissed through the wintery air, and fell with a cutting, wiry sound upon the mark. One dozen lashes being applied, the man was taken down, and went among the crew with a smile, saying, "—— me! it's nothing when you're used to it! Who wants to fight?" The next was Antone, the Portuguese. At every blow he surged from side to side, pouring out a torrent of involuntary blasphemies. Never before had he been heard to curse. When cut down, he went among the men, swearing to have the life of the captain. Of course, this was unheard by the officers. Mark, the third prisoner, only cringed and coughed under his punishment. He had some pulmonary complaint. He was off duty for several days after the flogging; but this was partly to be imputed to his extreme mental misery. It was his first scourging, and he felt the insult more than the injury. He became silent and sullen for the rest of the cruise. The fourth and last was Peter, the mizzen-top lad. He had often boasted that he had never been degraded at the gangway. The day before his cheek had worn its usual red, but now no ghost was whiter. As he was being secured to the gratings, and the shudderings and creepings of his dazzlingly white back were revealed, he turned round his head imploringly; but his weeping entreaties and vows of contrition were of no avail. "I would not forgive God Almighty!" cried the captain. The fourth boatswain's-mate advanced, and at the first blow, the boy, shouting *"My God! Oh! my God!"* writhed and leaped so as to displace the gratings, and scatter the nine tails of the scourge all over his person. At the next blow he howled, leaped, and raged in unendurable torture. "What are you stopping for, boatswain's-mate?" cried the captain. "Lay on!" and the whole dozen was applied. "I don't care what happens to me now!" wept Peter, going among the crew, with blood-shot eyes, as he put on his shirt. "I have been flogged once, and they may do it again, if they will. Let them look out for me now.' "Pipe down!" cried the captain, and the crew slowly dispersed.

Of all the non-combatants of a man-of-war, the purser, perhaps, stands foremost in importance. Though he is but a member of the gun-room mess, yet usage seems to assign him a conventional station somewhat above that of his equals in navy rank—the chaplain, surgeon, and professor. Moreover, he is frequently to be seen in close conversation with the commodore, who, in our ship, was more than once known to be slightly jocular with our purser. Upon several occasions, also, he was called into the commodore's cabin, and remained closeted there for several minutes together. Nor did I remember that there ever happened a cabinet meeting of the ward-room barons, the lieutenants, in the commodore's cabin, but the purser made one of the party.

Now, under this high functionary of state, the official known as the purser's steward was head clerk of the frigate's fiscal affairs. Upon the berth-deck he had a regular counting-room, full of ledgers, journals, and day-books. His desk was as much littered with papers as any Pearl Street merchant's, and much time was devoted to his accounts. For hours together you would see him, through the window of his subterranean office, writing by the light of his perpetual lamp. In the vicinity of the office of the purser's steward are the principal store-rooms of the purser, where large quantities of goods of every description are to be found. On board of those ships where goods are permitted to be served out to the crew for the purpose of selling them ashore, to raise money, more business is transacted at the office of a purser's steward in one *Liberty-day* morning than all the dry goods shops in a considerable village would transact in a week. Once a month, with undeviating regularity, this official has his hands more than usually full. For once a month, certain printed bills, called mess-bills, are circulated among the crew, and whatever you may want from the purser—be it tobacco, soap, duck, dungeree, needles, thread, knives, belts, calico, ribbon, pipes, paper, pens, hats, ink, shoes, socks, or whatever it may be—down it goes on the mess-bill, which, being the next day returned to the office of the steward, the "slops," as they are called, are served out to the men and charged to their accounts.

Lucky is it for man-of-war's-men that the outrageous impositions to which, but a very few years ago, they were subjected from the abuses in this department of the service, and the unscrupulous cupidity of many of the pursers—lucky is it for them that *now* these things are in a great degree done away. The pursers, instead of being at liberty to make almost what they please from the sale of their wares, are now paid by regular stipends laid down by law. Under the exploded system, the profits of some of these officers were almost incredible. In one cruise up the Mediterranean, the purser of an American line-of-battle ship was, on good authority, said to have cleared the sum of $50,000. Upon that he quitted the service, and retired into the country. Shortly after, his three daughters—not very lovely—married extremely well. No wonder that on board of the old frigate Java, upon her return from a cruise extending over a period of more than four years, one thousand dollars paid off eighty of her crew, though the aggregate wages of the eighty for the voyage must have amounted to about sixty thousand dollars. Even under the present system, the purser of a line-of-battle ship, for instance, is far better paid than any other officer, short of captain or commodore. While the lieutenant commonly receives but eighteen hundred dollars, the surgeon of the fleet but fifteen hundred, the chaplain twelve hundred, the purser of a line-of-battle receives thirty-five hundred dollars. In considering his salary, however, his responsibilities are not to be overlooked; they are by no means insignificant.

To make plain the thing about to be related, it needs to repeat what has somewhere been previously mentioned, that in *tacking ship* every seaman in a man-of-war has a particular station assigned him. What that station is, should be made known to him by the first lieutenant; and when the word is passed to *tack* or *wear*, it is every seaman's duty to be found at his post. But among the various numbers and stations given to me by the senior lieutenant, when I first came on board the frigate, he had altogether omitted informing me of my particular place at those times, and, up to the precise period now written of, I had hardly known that I should have had any special place then at all. For the rest of the men, they seemed to me to catch hold of the first rope that offered, as in a merchantman upon similar occasions. Indeed, I subsequently discovered, that such was the state of discipline—in this one particular, at least—that very few of the seamen could tell where their proper stations were, at *tacking* or *wearing*.

"All hands tack ship, ahoy!" such was the announcement made by the boatswain's mates at the hatchways. It was just eight bells—noon, and springing from my white jacket, which I had spread between the guns for a bed on the main-deck, I ran up the ladders, and, as usual, seized hold of the main-brace, which fifty hands were streaming along forward. When *main-topsail haul!* was given through the trumpet, I pulled at this brace with such heartiness and good-will, that I almost flattered myself that my instrumentality in getting the frigate round on the other tack, deserved a public vote of thanks, and a silver tankard from Congress. But something happened to be in the way aloft when the yards swung round; a little confusion ensued; and, with anger on his brow, Captain C—— came forward to see what occasioned it. No one to let go the weather-lift of the mainyard The rope was cast off, however, by a hand, and the yards, unobstructed, came round. When the last rope was coiled away, the captain desired to know of the first lieutenant who it might be that was stationed at the weather (then the starboard) main-lift. With a vexed expression of countenance the first lieutenant sent a midshipman for the station bill, when, upon glancing it over, my own name was found put down at the post in question. At the time I was on the gun-deck below, and did not know of these proceedings; but a moment after, I heard the boatswain's mate bawling my name at all the hatchways, and along all three decks. It was the first time I had ever heard it so sent through the furthest recesses of the ship, and well knowing what this generally betokened to other seamen, my heart jumped to my throat, and I hurriedly asked Flute, the boatswain's-mate at the fore-hatchway, what was wanted of me.

"Captain wants ye at the mast," he replied. "Going to flog ye, I guess."

"What for?"

"My eyes! you've been chalking your face, hain't ye?"

"What am I wanted for?" I repeated.

But at that instant my name was again thundered forth by the other boatswain's mate, and Flute hurried me away, hinting that I would soon find out what the captain desired of me. I swallowed down my heart in me as I touched the spardeck, for a single instant balanced myself on my best center, and then, wholly ignorant of what was going to be alleged against me, advanced to the dread tribunal of the frigate. As I passed through the gangway, I saw the quarter-master rigging the gratings; the boatswain with his green bag of scourges; the master-at-arms ready to help off some one's shirt. Again I made a desperate swallow of my whole soul in me, and found myself standing before Captain C——. His flushed face obviously showed him in ill humor. Among the group of officers by his side was the first lieutenant, who, as I came aft, eyed me in such a manner, that I plainly perceived him to be extremely vexed at me for having been the innocent means of reflecting upon the manner in which he kept up the discipline of the ship.

"Why were you not at your station, sir?" asked the captain.

"What station do you mean sir?" said I.

It is generally the custom with man-of-war's-men to stand obsequiously touching their hat at every sentence they address to the captain. But as this was not obligatory upon me by the Articles of War, I did not do so upon the present occasion, and previously, I had never had the dangerous honor of a personal interview with Captain C——. He quickly noticed my omission of the homage usually rendered him, and instinct told me, that, to a certain extent, it set his heart against me.

"What station, sir, do you mean?" said I.

"You pretend ignorance," he replied; "it will not help you, sir."

Glancing at the captain, the first lieutenant now produced the station bill, and read my name in connection with that of the starboard main-lift.

"Captain C——," said I, "it is the first time I ever heard of my being assigned to that post."

"How is this, Mr. B——?" he said, turning to the first lieutenant, with a fault-finding expression.

"It is impossible, sir," said that officer, striving to hide his vexation, "but this man must have known his station."

"I have never known it before this moment, Captain C——," said I.

"Do you contradict my officer?" he returned. "I shall flog you."

I had now been on board the frigate upward of a year, and remained unscourged; the ship was homeward-bound, and in a few weeks, at most, I would be a freeman. And now, after making a hermit of myself in some things, in order to avoid the possibility of the scourge, here it was hanging over me for a thing utterly unforeseen, for a crime of which I was as utterly innocent. But all that was as naught. I saw that my case was hopeless; my solemn disclaimer was thrown in my teeth, and the boatswain's mate stood curling his fingers through the *cat.* There are times when wild thoughts enter a man's heart, when he seems almost irresponsible for his act and his deed. The captain stood on the weather-side of the deck. Sideways, on an unobstructed line with him, was the opening of the lee-gangway, where the side-ladders are suspended in port. Nothing but a slight bit of sinnate-stuff served to rail in this opening, which was cut right down to the level of the captain's feet, showing the far sea beyond. I stood a little to windward of him, and, though he was a large, powerful man, it was certain that a sudden rush against him, along the slanting deck, would infallibly pitch him headforemost into the ocean, though he who so rushed must needs go over with him. My blood seemed clotting in my veins; I felt icy cold at the tips of my fingers, and a dimness was before my eyes. But through that dimness the boatswain's mate, scourge in hand, loomed like a giant, and Captain C——, and the blue sea seen through the opening at the gangway, showed with an awful vividness. I cannot analyze my heart, though it then stood still within me. But the thing that swayed me to my purpose was not altogether the thought that Captain C—— was about to degrade me, and that I had taken an oath with my soul that he should not. No, I felt my man's manhood so bottomless within me, that no word, no blow, no scourge of Captain C—— could cut me deep enough for that. I but swung to an instinct in me—the instinct diffused through all animated nature, the same that prompts even a worm to turn under the heel Locking souls with him, I meant to drag Captain C—— from this earthly tribunal of his to that of Jehovah, and let Him decide between us. No other way could I escape the scourge.

"To the gratings, sir!" said Captain C——; "do you hear?"

My eye was measuring the distance between him and the sea.

"Captain C——," said a voice advancing from the crowd. I turned to see who this might be, that audaciously interposed at a juncture like this. It was our remarkably handsome and gentlemanly corporal of marines, Colbrook. "I know that man," said Colbrook, touching his cap, and speaking in a mild, firm, but extremely deferential manner; "and I know that he would not be found absent from his station, if he knew where it was."

This speech was almost unprecedented. Seldom or never before had a marine dared to speak to the captain of a frigate in behalf of a seaman at the mast. But there was something so unostentatiously commanding in the calm manner of the man, that the captain, though astounded, did not in any way reprimand him. The very unusualness of his interference seemed Colbrook's protection. Taking heart, perhaps, from Colbrook's example, Jack Chase interposed, and in a manly but carefully respectful manner, in substance repeated the corporal's remark, adding that he had never found me wanting in the top. The captain looked from Chase to Colbrook, and from Colbrook to Chase—one the foremost man among the seamen, the other the foremost man among the soldiers—then all round upon the packed and silent crew, and, as if a slave to Fate, though supreme captain of a frigate, he turned to the first lieutenant, made some indifferent remark, and saying to me *you may go*, sauntered aft into his cabin; while I, who in the desperation of my soul, had but just escaped being a murderer and a suicide, almost burst into tears of thanksgiving where I stood.

Let us jot down in our memories a few little things pertaining to our man-of-war world. There is no part of a frigate where you will see more going and coming of strangers, and overhear more greetings and gossipings of acquaintances, than in the immediate vicinity of the scuttle-butt, just forward of the main-hatchway, on the gun-deck. The scuttle-butt is a goodly, round, painted cask, standing on end, and with its upper head removed, showing a narrow, circular shelf within, where rest a number of tin cups for the accommodation of drinkers. Central, within the scuttle-butt itself, stands an iron pump, which, connecting with the immense water-tanks in the hold, furnishes an unfailing supply of the much-admired Pale Ale, first brewed in the brooks of the Garden of Eden, and stamped with the brand of our old father Adam, who never knew what wine was. We are indebted to the old vintner Noah for that. The scuttle-butt is the only fountain in the ship; and here alone can you drink, unless at your meals. Night and day an armed sentry paces before it, bayonet in hand, to see that no water is taken away, except according to law.

As five hundred men come to drink at this scuttle-butt; as it is often surrounded by officer's servants drawing water for their masters to wash; by the cooks of the range, who hither come to fill their coffee-pots; and by the cooks of the ship's messes to procure water for their *duffs;* the scuttle-butt may be denominated the town-pump of the ship.

As in all extensive establishments, so in a man-of-war, there are a variety of similar snuggeries for the benefit of decrepit or rheumatic old tars. Chief among these is the office of *mast-man.* There is a stout rail on deck, at the base of each mast, where a number of braces, lifts, and buntlines are belayed to the pins. It is the sole duty of the mastman to see that these ropes are always kept clear, to preserve his premises in a state of the greatest attainable neatness, and every Sunday morning to dispose his ropes in neat *Flemish coils.* The mainmast-man of our ship was a very aged seaman, who well deserved his comfortable berth. He had seen more than half a century of the most active service, and, through all, had proved himself a good and faithful man. He furnished one of the very rare examples of a sailor in a green old age; for, with most sailors, old age comes in youth, and hardship and vice carry them on an early bier to the grave.

There was an old negro, who went by the name of Tawney, a sheet-anchor-man, whom we often invited into our top of tranquil nights, to hear him discourse. He was a staid and sober seaman, very intelligent, with a fine, frank bearing, one of the best men in the ship, and held in high estimation by every one. It seems that, during the last war between England and America, he had, with several others, been "impressed" upon the high seas, out of a New England merchantman. The ship that impressed him was an English frigate, the Macedonian, afterward taken by the United States, the ship in which we were sailing.

It was the holy Sabbath, according to Tawney, and, as the Briton bore down on the American—her men at their quarters—Tawney and his countrymen, who happened to be stationed at the quarter-deck battery, respectfully accosted the captain—an old man by the name of Cardan—as he passed them, in his rapid promenade, his spyglass under his arm. Again they assured him that they were not Englishmen, and that it was a most bitter thing to lift their hands against the flag of that country which harbored the mothers that bore them. They conjured him to release them from their guns, and allow them to remain neutral during the conflict. But when a ship of any nation is running into action, it is no time for argument, small time for justice, and not much time for humanity. Snatching a pistol from the belt of a boarder standing by, the captain leveled it at the heads of the three sailors, and commanded them instantly to their quarters, under penalty of being shot on the spot. So, side by side with his country's foes, Tawney and his companions toiled at the guns, and fought out the fight to the last; with the exception of one of them, who was killed at his post by one of his own country's balls.

At length, having lost her fore and main-topmasts, and her mizzen-mast having been shot away to the deck, and her foreyard lying in two pieces on her shattered forecastle, and in a hundred places having been *hulled* with round shot, the English frigate was reduced to the last extremity. Captain Cardan ordered his signal quarter-master to strike the flag. Tawney was one of those who, at last, helped pull him on board the United States. As he touched the deck, Cardan saluted Decatur, the hostile commander, and offered his sword; but it was courteously declined. Perhaps the victor remembered the dinner parties that he and the Englishman had enjoyed together in Norfolk, just previous to the breaking out of hostilities—and while both were in command of the very frigates now crippled on the sea. The Macedonian, it seems, had gone into Norfolk with dispatches. Then they had laughed and joked over their wine, and a wager of a beaver hat was said to have been made between them upon the event of the hostile meeting of their ships.

Gazing upon the heavy batteries before him, Cardan said to Decatur, "This is a seventy-four, not a frigate; no wonder the day is yours!" This remark was founded upon the United States' superiority in guns. The United States' main-deck batteries then consisted, as now, of twenty-four pounders; the Macedonian's of only eighteens. In all, the American vessel numbered fifty-four guns and four hundred and fifty men; the British, forty-nine guns and three hundred men; a very great disparity, which, united to the other circumstances of this action, deprives the victory of all claims to glory beyond those that might be set up by a river-horse getting the better of a seal.

According to Tawney, when the captain of the Macedonian—seeing that the United States had his vessel completely in her power—gave the word to strike the flag, one of his officers, a man hated by the seamen for his tyranny, howled out the most terrific remonstrances, swearing that, for his part, he would not give up, but was for sinking the Macedonian along side the enemy. Had he been captain, doubtless he would have done so; thereby gaining the name of a hero in this world;—but what would they have called him in the next? But as the whole matter of war is a thing that smites common sense and Christianity in the face; so everything connected with it is utterly foolish, unchristian, barbarous, brutal, and savoring of the Feejee Islands, cannibalism, saltpeter, and the devil. It is generally the case in a man-of-war when she strikes her flag that all discipline is at an end, and the men for a time are ungovernable. This was so on board of the English frigate. The spirit-room was broken open, and buckets of grog were passed along the decks, where many of the wounded were lying between the guns. These mariners seized the buckets, and, spite of all remonstrances, gulped down the burning spirits, ill, as Tawney said, the blood suddenly spirted out of their wounds, and they fell dead to the deck.

The negro had many more stories to tell of this fight; and frequently he would escort me along our main-deck batteries—still mounting the same guns used in the battle—pointing out their inffaceable indentations and scars. Coated over with the accumulated paint of more than thirty years, they were almost invisible to a casual eye; but Tawney knew them all by heart; for he had returned home in the United States, and had beheld these scars shortly after the engagement. One afternoon, I was walking with him along the gun-deck, when he paused abreast of the mainmast. "This part of the ship," said he, "we called the *slaughter-house* on board the Macedonian. Here the men fell, five and six at a time. An enemy always directs its shot here, in order to hurl over the mast, if possible. The beams and carlines overhead in the Macedonian *slaughter-house* were spattered with blood and brains. About the hatchways it looked like a butcher's stall; bits of human flesh sticking in the ring-bolts. A pig that ran about the decks escaped unharmed, but his hide was so clotted with blood, from rooting among the pools of gore, that when the ship struck the sailors hove the animal overboard, swearing that it would be rank cannibalism to eat him." Another quadruped, a goat, lost its fore legs in this fight. The sailors who were killed—according to the usual custom—were ordered to be thrown overboard as soon as they fell; no doubt, as the negro said, that the sight of so many corpses lying around might not appall the survivors at the guns. Among other instances, he related the following. A shot entering one of the port-holes, dashed dead two thirds of a gun's crew. The captain of the next gun, dropping his lock-string, which he had just pulled, turned over the heap of bodies to see who they were; when, perceiving an old messmate, who had sailed with him in many cruises, he burst into tears, and, taking the corpse up in his arms, and going with it to the side, held it over the water a moment, and eying it, cried, "Oh God! Tom!"—"D—— your prayers over that thing! overboard with it, and down to your gun!" roared a wounded lieutenant. The order was obeyed, and the heart-stricken sailor returned to his post.

Among the numerous artists and professors of polite trades in the navy, none are held in higher estimation or drive a more profitable business than the barbers. And it may well be imagined that the five hundred heads of hair and five hundred beards of a frigate should furnish no small employment for those to whose faithful care they may be intrusted. The regular days upon which the barbers shall exercise their vocation are set down on the ship's calender, and known as shaving days. On board of our ship these days are Wednesdays and Saturdays; when, immediately after breakfast, the barbers' shops were opened to customers. They were in different parts of the gun-deck, between the long twenty-four pounders. Their furniture, however, was not very elaborate, hardly equal to the sumptuous appointments of metropolitan barbers. Indeed, it merely consisted of a match-tub, elevated upon a shot-box, as a barber's chair for the patient. These barbers of ours had their labors considerably abridged by a fashion prevailing among many of the crew, of wearing very large whiskers; so that, in most cases, the only parts needing a shave were the upper lip and suburbs of the chin. This had been more or less the custom during the whole three year's cruise; but for some time previous to our weathering Cape Horn, very many of the seamen had redoubled their assiduity in cultivating their beards, preparatory to their return to America. Above all, the captain of the forecastle, old Ushant—a fine specimen of a sea sexagenarian—wore a wide, spreading beard, grizzled and gray, that flowed over his breast, and often became tangled and knotted with tar. This Ushant, in all weathers, was ever alert at his duty; intrepidly mounting the foreyard in a gale, his long beard streaming like Neptune's.

Throughout the cruise, many of the officers had expressed their abhorrence of the impunity with which the most extensive plantations of hair were cultivated under their very noses; and they frowned upon every beard with even greater dislike. They said it was unseamanlike; not *ship-shape*; in short, it was disgraceful to the navy. One evening the ship's company were astounded by an extraordinary announcement made at the main-hatchway of the gun-deck, by the boatswain's mate there stationed. "D'ye hear there, fore and aft? All you that have long hair, cut it short; and all you that have large whiskers, trim them down, according to the navy regulations." The excitement was intense throughout that whole evening. One and all, they resolved not to succumb, and every man swore to stand by his beard and his neighbor. Twenty-four hours after—at the next evening quarters—the captain's eye was observed to wander along the men at their guns—not a beard was shaven! When the drum beat the retreat, the boatswain—now attended by all four of his mates, to give additional solemnity to the announcement—repeated the previous day's order, and concluded by saying, that twenty-four hours would be given for all to acquiesce. But the second day passed, and at quarters, untouched, every beard bristled on its chin. Forthwith Captain C—— summoned the midshipmen, who, receiving his orders, hurried to the various divisions of the guns, and communicated them to the lieutenants respectively stationed over divisions. The officer commanding mine turned upon us, and said, "Men, if to-morrow night I find any of you with long hair, or whiskers of a standard violating the navy regulations, the names of such offenders shall be put down on the report." Though many heads of hair were shorn, and many fine beards reaped that day, yet several still held out, and vowed to defend their sacred hair to the last gasp of their breath. When the proper time arrived, their names were taken down by the officers of divisions, and they were afterward summoned in a body to the mast, where the captain stood ready to receive them. The whole ship's company crowded to the spot, and, amid the breathless multitude, the venerable rebels advanced and unhatted. The rebel beards, headed by old Ushant's, streaming like a commodore's *bougee*, now stood in silence at the mast.

"You knew the order!" said the captain, eying them severely; "what does that hair on your chins?"

"Sir," said the captain of the forecastle, "did old Ushant ever refuse doing his duty? did he ever yet miss his muster? But, sir, old Ushant's beard is his own!"

"What's that, sir? master-at-arms, put that man into the brig."

"Sir," said the old man, respectfully, "the three years for which I shipped are expired; and though I am perhaps bound to work the ship home, yet, as matters are, I think my beard might be allowed me. It is but a few days, Captain C——."

"Put him into the brig!" cried the captain; "and now, you old rascals!" he added, turning round upon the rest, "I give you fifteen minutes to have those beards taken off; if they then remain on your chins, I'll flog you—every mother's son of you—though you were all my own godfathers!" The band of beards went forward, summoned their barbers, and their glorious pennants were no more. In obedience to orders, they then paraded themselves at the mast, and, addressing the captain, said, "Sir, our *muzzle-lashings* are cast off!"

On the morrow, after breakfast, Ushant was taken out of irons, and, with the master-at-arms on one side and an armed sentry on the other, was escorted along the gun-deck and up the ladder to the mainmast. There the captain stood, firm as before. They must have guarded the old man thus to prevent his escape to the shore, something less than a thousand miles distant at the time.

"Well, sir, will you have that beard taken off? you have slept over it a whole night now; what do you say? I don't want to flog an old man like you, Ushant!"

"My beard is my own, sir!" said the old man, lowly.

"Will you take it off?"

"It is mine, sir!" said the old man, tremulously.

"Rig the gratings!" roared the captain. "Master-at-arms, strip him! quarter-master, seize him up! boatswain's-mates, do your duty!"

While these executioners were employed, the captain's excitement had a little time to abate; and when, at last, old Ushant was tied up by the arms and legs, and his venerable back was exposed—that back which had bowed at the guns of the frigate Constitution when she captured the Guerriere—the captain seemed to relent.

"You are a very old man," he said, "and I am sorry to flog you; but my orders must be obeyed. I will give you one more chance; will you have that beard taken off?"

"Captain C——," said the old man, turning round painfully in his bonds, "you may flog me if you will; but, sir, in this one thing I can *not* obey you."

"Lay on! I'll see his backbone!" roared the captain in a sudden fury.

One, two, three, four, five, six, seven, eight, nine, ten, eleven, twelve lashes were laid on the back of that heroic old man. He only bowed over his head, and stood as the dying gladiator lies.

"Cut him down," said the captain.

When the master-at-arms advanced with the prisoner's shirt, Ushant waived him off with the dignified air of a Brahim, saying, "Do you think, master-at-arms, that I am hurt? I will put on my own garment. I am never the worse for it, man; and 'tis no dishonor when he who would dishonor you, only dishonors himself."

"What says he?" cried the captain; "what says that tarry old philosopher with the smoking back? Tell it to me, sir, if you dare! Sentry, take that man back to the brig. Stop! John Ushant, you have been captain of the forecastle; I break you. And now you go into the brig, there to remain till you consent to have that beard taken off."

"My beard is my own," said the old man, quietly. "Sentry, I am ready."

And back he went into durance between the guns; but after lying some four or five days in irons, an order came to remove them; but he was still kept confined. Books were allowed him, and he spent much time in reading. But he also spent many hours in braiding his beard, and enterweaving with it stripes of red bunting, as if he desired to dress out and adorn the thing which had triumphed over all opposition.

He remained a prisoner till we arrived in America; but the very moment he heard the chain rattle out of the hawsehole, and the ship swing to her anchor, he started to his feet, dashed the sentry aside, and gaining the deck, exclaimed, "At home, with my beard!"

Though, as I afterward learned, Ushant was earnestly entreated to put the case into some lawyer's hands, he firmly declined, saying "I have won the battle, my friends, and I do not care for the prize-money."

Years ago there was a punishment inflicted in the English, and I believe in the American navy, called *keel-hauling*—a phrase still employed by man-of-war'smen when they would express some signal vengeance upon a personal foe. The practice still remains in the French national marine, though it is by no means resorted to so frequently as in times past. It consists of attaching tackles to the two extremities of the mainyard, and passing the rope under the ship's bottom. To one end of this rope the culprit is secured; his own shipmates are then made to run him up and down, first on this side, then on that—now scraping the ship's hull under water—anon, hoisted, stunned and breathless, into the air.

But though this barbarity is now abolished from the English and American navies, there still remains another practice which, if anything, is even worse than *keel-hauling*. This remnant of the Middle Ages is known in the navy as "*flogging through the fleet*." It is never inflicted except by authority of a court-martial upon some trespasser deemed guilty of a flagrant offense. Never, that I know of, has it been inflicted by an American man-of-war on the home station. The reason, probably, is, that the officers well know that such a spectacle would raise a mob in any American seaport.

All hands being called "to witness punishment" in the ship to which the culprit belongs, the sentence of the court-martial condemning him is read, when, with the usual solemnities, a portion of the punishment is inflicted. In order that it shall not lose in severity by the slightest exhaustion in the arm of the executioner, a fresh boatswain's mate is called out at every dozen. As the leading idea is to strike terror into the beholders, the greatest number of lashes is inflicted on board the culprit's own ship, in order to render him the more shocking spectacle to the crews of the other vessels. The first infliction being concluded, the culprit's shirt is thrown over him; he is put into a boat—the Rogue's March being played meanwhile—and rowed to the next ship of the squadron. All hands of that ship are then called to man the rigging, and another portion of the punishment is inflicted by the boatswain's mates of that ship. The bloody shirt is again thrown over the seaman; and thus he is carried through the fleet or squadron till the whole sentence is inflicted. In other cases, the launch—the largest of the boats—is rigged with a platform, (like a headsman's scaffold,) upon which halberds, something like those used in the English army, are erected. They consist of two stout poles, planted upright. Upon the platform stand a lieutenant, a surgeon, a master-at-arms, and the executioners with their "cats." They are rowed through the fleet, stopping at each ship, till the whole sentence is inflicted, as before.

In some cases, the attending surgeon has professionally interfered before the last lash has been given, alleging that immediate death must ensue if the remainder should be administered without a respite. But instead of humanely remitting the remaining lashes, in a case like this, the man is generally consigned to his cot for ten or twelve days; and when the surgeon officially reports him capable of undergoing the rest of the sentence, it is forthwith inflicted. Shylock must have his pound of flesh. To say, that after being flogged through the fleet, the prisoner's back is sometimes puffed up like a pillow; or to say that in other cases it looks as if burned black before a roasting fire; or to say that you may track him through the squadron by the blood on the bulwarks of every ship, would only be saying what many seamen have seen. Several weeks, sometimes whole months, elapse before the sailor is sufficiently recovered to resume his duties. During the greater part of that interval he lies in the sick-bay, groaning out his days and nights; and unless he has the hide and constitution of a rhinoceros, he never is the man he was before, but, broken and shattered to the marrow of his bones, sinks into death before his time. Instances have occurred where he has expired the day after the punishment.

Some years ago a fire broke out near the powder magazine in an American national ship, one of a squadron at anchor in the Bay of Naples The utmost alarm prevailed. A cry went fore and aft that the ship was about to blow up. One of the seamen sprung overboard in affright. At length the fire was got under, and the man was picked up. He was tried before a court-martial, found guilty of cowardice, and condemned to be flogged through the fleet. In due time the squadron made sail for Algiers, and in that harbor, once haunted by pirates, the punishment was inflicted—the Bay of Naples, though washing the shores of an absolute king, not being deemed a fit place for such an exhibition of American naval law.

NARRATIVE

OF AN

OLD ENGLISH SAILOR,

YET LIVING, RELATED BY HIMSELF, IN A STYLE OF AMUSING SIMPLICITY, AND SHOWING VIVIDLY THE MANY VICISSITUDES WHICH FORM

LIFE EXPERIENCES ON THE OCEAN.

I AM writing this to show the wonderful mercies the Lord has shown me in fifty years' lifetime at sea, and I hope that whoever may have a chance to look at it, it will teach them not to despair, or give themselves up for lost; for by perseverance, and a firm trust in the Almighty, we can do anything that the giver of all good will allow us to do; for there is a "Sweet little Cherub that sits up aloft, keeps a watch for the life of poor Jack." By accounts that I had from my friends, when I came to the years of recollection, I was informed that I was born at sea, in the year of our Lord 1777, on the 20th of August; my father being master of a brig belonging to Hull, in Yorkshire, and when I was born, he was bound on a voyage from London to Hamburgh; but my mother being very poorly, she and I were left at a place called Cuxhaven, at the entrance of the River Elbe. But my father being obliged to proceed upon his return voyage, my mother and me were left at Hamburgh, at the consul's. And the winter setting in sooner and severer than my father expected—for he expected to make another voyage before the winter set in—me and my mother were left at Hamburgh all the winter; but I being very poorly, and not expected to live, my mother was persuaded to have me christened; and I was christened at St. Catherine's Church at Hamburgh, when I was four months old.

My father was expected to be at Hamburgh in the beginning of the next year; but in the first voyage that he was going to make, in the year 1778, he was cast away, and all hands drowned, at the entrance of the river, near about the same spot where I was born. My mother belonging to Kirkwall, in the Orkneys, she and me went down there, and there I spent my childhood, till my mother died, when I was about eight years old. My mother having a sister who lived at Boston, in Lincolnshire, who was down in Kirkwall when my mother died, she, after all things were settled, took me with her to Boston, where I had a grandmother living, and, between my aunt and my grandmother, I soon became a spoiled child: for as young as I was, I soon found out that they were very fond of me; for my aunt had no children herself, and my grandmother never had any more children but my father; so if I committed a fault at my aunt's, where I lived, I only had to run to my grandmother's, and she was sure to take my part; and the same if I committed myself at my grandmother's, my aunt was sure to take my part. It was my misfortune to lose my parents so soon. I sha'n't say nothing of the many tricks and pranks I played my poor old grandmother and my aunt;

but I passed my time at Boston till the beginning of the year 1790, when I got acquainted with a young man by the name of William Jackson, and his father was mate of a brig belonging to Boston, and they wanted an apprentice, and I persuaded my poor old grandmother to let me go a voyage upon trial, which I did, and it being summer-time, and fine weather, and I liked it so well, that, when we returned to Boston, I was bound apprentice for seven years to Mr. Ingelow; and I was put on board of a brig called the "Joseph and Ann." The master of the brig, a man called William Turner, was a very good man as far as seamanship goes, but he was in other respects a man of very bad morals; and me being young and giddy, I did not gain anything by it, for what good qualities I had belonging to me were soon lost; for I had always been used to say my prayers night and morning, and at my meals; but, seeing no one else do it, I soon forgot it, and I thought within myself I should do as well as the rest.

Our first voyage, after I joined the brig, was from Boston to London with a cargo of oats, and, thanks be to God, we got there safe, as many ships were lost, for it blew a gale of wind nearly the whole three weeks we were on our passage; for it was in the month of November, and I wished myself many times back again in Boston along with my old grandmother; but I soon forgot it all when I came to London; for, when we got there, our captain got a freight to go to Naples, up the Mediterranean, to carry a cargo of pilchards from Falmouth. When I heard that we were going to a foreign country, I forgot all the troubles of my former voyage, and I was glad to go. We proceeded on our voyage to Falmouth, and I got on middling well; we sailed from Falmouth as soon as the convoy was ready, and I left the Land's End of old England the last day of the year 1790, and, thanks be to God, we arrived safe at Naples after a passage of six weeks. I don't wish to trouble the reader with an account of the different places we traded to, but we stood up the Mediterranean, trading from one place to another, till the year 1794, when we got a freight for London, where we arrived safe in August the same year, and, after discharging our cargo, our brig was obliged to go into dock to get repaired, and when that was done, we went down to Boston; when we got there, I found that my grandmother was dead, and my aunt was going to live at Hull. What property my grandmother had left was left to me; but, being young and foolish, I soon got clear of it all; and our brig being bound to London again, where we arrived at the beginning of 1795, and we got a freight to go to Cardiff, in Wales, to get a cargo of iron to take to Gibraltar. We sailed from London in the beginning of March, and we had a strong north-east gale to drive us down the Channel: and when we got to the Land's End of England, the wind was against us, for we were bound up the Bristol Channel; so we were obliged to keep the ship off and on in Mount's Bay till the weather moderated, for it blew a heavy gale of wind from the north north-east.

Now, I forgot to mention how many hands we carried in the brig when we sailed from London; we had eight on board altogether—namely, the master and mate, four men before the mast, and two boys; and we had the misfortune to lose one man overboard when we got under weigh in the Downs; so there were but seven left on board when our misfortune happened, which was on the 17th day of March, about two o'clock in the morning, when, standing off the land, we struck upon a rock called the Randell Stone, which lays in Mount's Bay, about three or four miles off the land; and it blowing a heavy gale of wind, and, at the same time, a heavy sea running, our poor old brig soon went to pieces; but thanks be to God Almighty, who allowed us time enough to get our long-boat out before the mast went out of her, and six of us, out of the seven, got safe into her before the brig went to pieces; the other man must have been knocked overboard when the mast fell, for we could see nothing of him, for it was very dark, and we that were in the boat saved nothing, only what we had on, and I had the misfortune of losing my shoes off my feet in getting into the boat. After we got clear of the wreck, we tried our best to get the boat in shore, but it blowing so hard, we could not hold our own; and, when daylight came, we found ourselves about six or seven miles from the land, and still drifting out as fast as we could. The weather being clear, we could see the islands of Scilly to leeward of us, and our master being a man that had been brought up in the coasting trade, was well acquainted, for he had been several times in the Scilly Islands; so we determined to bear up for a place called Grimsby, and our master intended to go through a place called the Crow Sound; but our misfortune was not complete yet, for it being nearly high water by the time we got near the island, and the rocks being nearly all covered, our master mistook the channel, and we were hove in among the breakers, though we tried our best to get clear of them; and the second sea that struck us capsized our boat, and I found myself hove against a middling steep rock, where, by God's help, I contrived to hold on; and, having no shoes on, I got up to the top of the rock, where I could see my shipmates trying to get; but only one succeeded in getting up, and that was our old mate, a man nearly sixty years of age, and he kicked off his shoes before he succeeded in getting where I was: and here now I had a great cause to be thankful to the Almighty Giver of all mercies for his providential care over me in making me lose my shoes before I left the brig; for what I thought the greatest misfortune to me ten minutes before, proved the only means for me to preserve my life; for if I had been struggling in the water along with my shipmates, I should have had no thought of kicking my shoes off to preserve my life; for I know myself that three men out of the four that we saw struggling for their lives had heavy sea-boots on, and they, being full of water, caused them soon to go down; for the mate told me himself afterward, that the rocks being so slippery, that he would never have got up if he had not hove his shoes away; so here we got on the top of the rock, seeing our poor shipmates drowning one after the other, and we were not able to help them. But, as I said before, that it was near high water when our second misfortune happened; and we soon found that, as the tide ebbed, the water got a good deal smoother, and me and the mate considered it best for us to contrive to get nearer to the island, from which we were about three quarters of a mile. So we waited till about half past two o'clock, for the mate had his watch in his pocket; and then we contrived to get in shore, and a tiresome job we had of it, for we had several places to swim across; and the mate, being an old man, was very much fatigued, being wet and cold such a long time—for a north-east wind blows pretty cold in the month of March. But we contrived to get to the main island about six o'clock that evening, and we both kneeled down to thank the Almighty for his mercy to us.

And now, that through the mercy of the Almighty we got safe landed, what to do next was to be considered; for you may depend that we both were hungry, and night coming on, and in a strange place, where there are no roads to direct you—for I had been upon the highest rock that I could see near us, to see if I could see anything of a house, or any signs of any habitation, but I could not see anything; so we resolved to try to get under the lee of some rock, for we were still on the windward part of the island. But before we left the beach, I went to see if I could find any shell-fish, for I felt hunger pinching me since I came on shore, and, thanks be to God, I found some; and I took them up to my partner in distress, and we ate them; and afterward we went to look for some place to shelter us from the wind and the weather; and, after a little time, we found a place like a cave under the lee of a rock; and close by I found a small puddle of fresh water, which we wanted very much, for we were very thirsty; and, after returning thanks to the Almighty, we laid ourselves down to sleep, and I slept very well till the morning, when my partner called me, for he was very poorly, and could not stand upon his legs. I felt very stiff when I first got up; but I soon got pretty well again. And now we resolved that, as my partner was not able to move, I was to go by myself to see if I could find anybody to help me to bring my partner away, and to get something to eat; for the old mate, as luck would have it, had three shillings and sixpence in his pocket, beside his watch: the money he gave to me, and I parted from him with a heavy heart, for I was afraid I should never see him again alive, for he was very bad; so away I went; and then I found for the first time what it was to be alone in a strange place. I had traveled, I suppose, about two miles, when coming to an open bay, where I saw some ships lying at an anchor; and you may depend I was glad enough at seeing them; and shortly afterward I had the pleasure of seeing some houses, but I was still a good distance from them; but I traveled on till I got pretty near them, when I had the satisfaction of seeing two men. I sung out to them as loud as I could, for fear of losing them again; but they heard me, and they came toward me; and when I came to them, I told them my case, and they very kindly took me home with them, and gave me something to eat and to drink; and I told them of my poor old partner that I had left in the cave, and what state I had left him in. I offered them some money for what they gave me, but they refused it; and as soon as I had finished what they had given me to eat, they took me to a man by the name of Mr. Gilbert, who, I found afterward, was the head man in the place, and a very good man he was; and he sent three men along with me to fetch my old partner from the cave, which, after a great deal of trouble, we found; and glad enough I was to find that he was alive: and, after giving the old man something to eat and to drink, we carried the old man to Grimsby, for that was the name of the place I had been to, where the people used us very kindly; but my poor old partner got worse and worse every day. Though Mr. Gilbert was kind enough to send for a doctor to St. Mary's for him, which is the head town in the island, he died the sixth day after we were wrecked. As for myself, I got pretty well in a few days; and after staying and lending a hand to bury my old shipmate, I shipped myself on board of a brig called the "Hope," belonging to Bridgewater, which was bound to London. But before I left Old Grimsby, I told Mr. Gilbert where the owner of the brig lived that I had been cast away in, so that he might get paid for the trouble and expenses he had been at during our stay there; and as soon as the wind and weather would permit, I sailed for London in my new brig. The master of her was a very good man, and we arrived in London the 17th day of April. My new master liked me very well, and he wrote to Mr. Ingelow, in Boston, about me, to let him know where I was; and Mr. Ingelow, having no ship that wanted an apprentice, sent me my indentures and my wages, after serving him five years out of the seven years that I was bound for; so my new master got me bound apprentice to him for three years. I sailed in the "Hope," of Bridgewater, till the year 1798—chiefly in the coasting trade—and I was very well contented, for our master was a very good man, and the owners had promised me a mate's situation as soon as I got out of my time. And in April, in 1798, we were bound from London to Bridgewater, and getting down the Channel as far as the Lizard, and we being bound off the Bristol Channel, the wind being at that time about north-east, and blowing a strong gale, and our ship being rather light, we got blown off the land; and the gale continuing for eight or ten days, we got drifted a long ways off; and our master not being a navigator, though he was a very good coaster, so that when the gale was over, and we got fine weather, we did not know where we were, but we knew well enough that we had been drifted to the westward. We had to run back to the eastward, and the second day after we had fine weather. We fell in with a Mount's Bay boat, who, like ourselves, had been blown off the land, who was very short of provisions and water, of which, thanks be to God, we had plenty; and we gave them some, and they gave us some brandy and tobacco—for they were smugglers—for the provisions which we gave them; and they directed us what course to steer in for the land, and we parted company. And the next day morning we fell in with the "Brilliant" frigate, who made us heave to, and she sent a boat on board of us to go a pressing; and our master being half drunk, and the rest of the crew being no better, we got a quarreling, when the lieutenant of the frigate came on board, and, through our master being drunk, I got pressed; for I being out of my time two days before this happened, and the master told the lieutenant so when we were mustered; so I was sent on board of the frigate; and a fine large ship I thought she was when I first got on board of her, and I was put in the maintop; but I soon found my mistake out, for the very first night, at reefing topsail, I saw seven men flogged for not being smart enough; and me never seeing a man flogged before, I wished myself back again in my little brig. So here I could see the fruits of drunkenness; for if all hands had been sober aboard of the "Hope" when we fell in with the frigate, I should have been stowed away; but it was my lot, and I was obliged to content myself where I was, for our usage on board of the "Brilliant" was very cruel; for we had nine men doing duty as boatswain's mates on board of her, and there was starting and flogging all day long, and the usage was very little fit to reconcile me to a man-of-war; but being young, and finding it was no use to fret, I made the best I could of it. And our ship being only just come out of Plymouth, and being bound on a six months' cruise in the Bay of Biscay, we went away to the westward on a cruise, and on the 20th of October we fell in with part of a West India convoy, homeward bound, who had been separated in a gale of wind on the banks of Newfoundland, and had lost their commander; and there being no man-of-war along with them, our captain found himself in duty bound to see them safe into port; and away we went along with them for Old England, and in five days we arrived safe in Plymouth Sound, having a strong westerly wind all the way. And one of the masters of one of the ships told our captain, that about a week before they fell in with our ship they had been chased by a French privateer, and that the privateer had taken two ships belonging to London, deeply laden, and he believed that the privateer had taken them into Santa Cruz, a town in the island of Teneriffe, one of the Canary Islands. Our captain acquainting the admiral that was in Plymouth with it, he gave him permission to go to Teneriffe and try to cut them out; and he sent the "Talbot," a sloop of war, along with us; and we sailed from Plymouth in the middle of November, and having nothing but strong westerly winds against us, we were nearly three weeks before we got to Teneriffe; and in our passage we had the good fortune of taking two prizes—the one the very privateer that had taken the two ships that we were going to cut out. She was a fine brigantine, belonging to St. Maloes, and the other a ship belonging to Bristol, that had been taken by the privateer, homeward bound, only two days before we took them again.

And now, having arrived off the island, we arranged everything to go in with the boats to cut the two ships out, and on the 4th day of December we left the ships, about four o'clock in the afternoon. There were seven boats of us altogether—four from our ship, and three from the "Talbot." The boat that I was in was a five-oared boat, half gig and half cutter. She was a very fine boat, and the commanding officer was in her, which was the first lieutenant of our frigate, who pulled backward and forward to the rest of the boats, to encourage the men, and to give his orders. We got into Santa Cruz harbor about ten o'clock in the evening, and we were lucky enough to board one of the ships, and get possession of her without getting any one hurt; but not so with the other ship, for the noise we made in boarding the first ship put them on their guard, and she, being a ship which mounted ten guns, opened her fire on our boats, which were three boats which had to board her; and I belonging to the commanding officer's boat, who was on board of the first ship that had been taken, and who was under weigh by this time, and was going out of the harbor with a light breeze of wind off the land, and our officer seeing how the other boats were likely to be handled, ordered the pinnace and his own boat to go to the assistance of their shipmates; and just as our boat got clear of the quarter of the ship, a shot struck her right in the middle, and killed one man, and wounded two more; and it being very dark by this time, and our boat being very soon full of water, we could not give any assistance to our shipmates, nor could we pull back to the prize; so we were obliged every man to do the best they could for themselves, and I was once more left in a bad situation; but, thanks be to God, I could swim very well, and I seeing a vessel lying pretty close to me, I swum to her, which proved to be an American schooner. I hung on by her cable some time, and the people being all on deck, I could hear them speak English; and at last one of them looking over the bows of the schooner, I spoke to him, and asked him to let me come on board, and he gave me a rope's end, and I soon got on board. When I first got on board of her, I was taken aft to the mate, and I told him how I came there, and he told the captain, who told me that he would be obliged to take me on shore, in the morning, to the governor; but ordered some of the men to give me some dry clothing, and something to eat and to drink; and, in fact, they behaved very well to me. All this time the ship kept firing at the boats, and the boats were obliged to retreat with their one prize; for the forts, getting alarmed by this time, began to open fire; but the boats got their ship safe out, for we could not see anything of her in the morning. When morning was come, and I could see what sort of people I had got amongst, I saw a young man on board of the schooner that I thought I had seen somewhere; and, when I came to inquire, I found that he was an old shipmate of mine, and fellow-apprentice in the "Joseph and Ann," and he was second mate of the schooner, and his name was James Martin. And, when we began to know one another, he told the captain of the schooner that I was a man that served my time to the sea service; and, the schooner being short of hands, the captain of the schooner sent for me, and told me that, as I was a young man that served my time out of Boston—and he had no business to know what Boston it was, whether it was Boston in England or America—and if I had a mind to sign the Articles, he would put me on the schooner's books, and give me thirty dollars a month; and he would take good care no one should know how I got there.

Now you may depend I was not long considering about what to do; for, if I had refused to join the schooner, I should have had to go to a Spanish prison; so I agreed with the captain of the schooner—she was called the "Speedy," of Baltimore. Now this schooner had brought out a new governor, from Cadiz, for the islands, and she was going to carry the old one home again, to any part of Spain or France she might be able to pitch into; and we laid at Teneriffe for nearly two months before the governor was ready to go, and by this time I got quite comfortable on board of her. And we sailed in the latter end of February, 1799, from Teneriffe; and, after being chased by many of the English cruisers, for the "Speedy" sailed remarkably fast, we got into a place called Cordivan, in France, the entrance of the Bordeaux River, by the latter part of March; and we got up to Bordeaux by the beginning of April. And, after the governor was landed, and his things out of the schooner, and there being no freights for the schooner, the captain sold her to the French Government, she being a very fast sailing vessel. And the crew, me in the number, were paid our wages, and sent about our business; and me and my old shipmate, James Martin, went and shipped on board of a large ship, under Hamburgh colors, that was taking in a cargo of wine for Hamburgh; and you may depend that me and my friend were glad to go somewhere, for it was dangerous to be ashore; for if the police knew that you was a sailor, and not belonging to any ship, they took you and sent you on board of one of their frigates; but, thanks be to God, we kept ourselves clear of them; and, by the latter part of April, our ship being loaded, we sailed from the town of Bordeaux, and we got clear of the river by the beginning of May. And, after being at sea some days, our captain called all the men aft, and told them that he was not bound to Hamburgh, but that he expected to go to London, but that his orders were to go to the Island of Guernsey, and wait for orders; and, after a long and tiresome passage, we arrived at Guernsey in the middle part of June. And me and my old shipmate, knowing well enough that if the ship went to London, we should be pressed, and having such a great dread of an English man-of-war, on account of the usage I had received, we went to our master, who was a very good man, and asked him for our discharge from the ship; and, after telling him our reason for doing so, he gave it to us, and paid us our wages; and ashore we went at Guernsey. And, after staying ashore three or four days, me and my shipmate joined a privateer, called the "Blue-Eyed Maid of Guernsey." Our vessel was lugger-rigged, and mounted sixteen guns; and we carried one hundred and twenty men, with six months' protection from the press; and, thanks be to God, we were very lucky in her, for we took a great many prizes and recaptures—the lugger being a very fast sailing vessel; and me and my partner stopped in her till the year 1801.

When peace came, we were paid off, and I had about three hundred and fifty pounds, wages and prize-money, altogether; and me and my friend went from Guernsey to London, intending to go to Boston, where we had served our time, and to see our old friends. But this is the way of the world, for man appoints, and the Almighty disappoints: for the second day after I arrived in London—where we got in June, 1801—I was taken very bad of a fever, and I was obliged to keep my bed for two months; but I soon got better. And my old shipmate, who, during my illness, had gone to Boston, and had promised to return to London again as soon as his business was settled, but he did not; for, poor fellow, he was taken with the same complaint that I had, as soon as he arrived in Boston, and died in a week after he got home. So now, being left to myself again, and being tired of going to sea, I intended to settle myself on shore. With this intent, I went to Mr. Scovel, who was owner of several wharves, where the traders used to discharge and take in their cargoes, and spoke to him, and told him my intention, and likewise to ask him what the best use would be that I could make of my money; and he was very kind to me, and told me that I had best put my money in the bank, and that I should have constant employment at any wharf that he had, that I was a mind to choose. And now, having this point settled, I got to come to another; and that is, that during my illness a young woman that used to attend on me, I found that I had got very fond of her, and I could see, by the attention she paid me, that I was not indifferent to her; and as I was going to stop on shore, I thought I wanted a wife, and, after a little courtship, I gained her consent, and we got married at St. Olave's Church, which is in Tooley Street, in the Borough, on the 27th day of December, 1801.

I had taken a little house in Vine Yard, close to Pickle Herring Stairs; and having money, I set up a little shop to sell cabbages, and potatoes, and wood, and coals; and, thanks be to God, me and my wife we done very well, for I used to go every day to work at the wharves, loading and discharging coasting vessels, and my wife minded the shop. And so things went on quite comfortable till the latter part of July, 1802, when a strange accident occurred which put an end to all my happiness for a long time. The case was this: my wife's mother-in-law was a woman greatly given to drink, and she used to come to my wife and get things upon trust, and go and spend the money in drink; and having run up a pretty good score, my wife spoke to her about it; but she, being half drunk, abused my wife, and struck her.

My landlord, Mr. Bland, seeing the affair, came down and told me of it, for my house was close to the wharf where I was working; and I ran up directly, and ordered her out of the house, and told her not to come there any more; and a good many words passed between us; and at last she told me she would make me sorry for turning her out of doors; but I did not mind her. But I soon had occasion to be sorry for what had happened; for the war between France and England had broke out again, and the press was very hot; and my wife's mother-in-law went to the lieutenant of the press-gang, and informed against me that I was a seafaring man, and served my time at sea; and about half past ten o'clock that same evening, just when I was going to shut my shop up, the press-gang came and took me, too. I had a scuffle for it before I was taken, for I knocked the first two down that came into my house; but I was soon overpowered, and was taken by force, and taken down to the boat which they had brought to Pickle Herring Stairs; and from there I was taken on board the "Enterprise," which lay at Tower Hill Stairs, where I was put, both legs in irons, and my hands tied behind me; and there I laid till the morning, when me and some more pressed men were put on board of a tender, and sent down to the big Nore on board of the "Old Namur," which lay flag-ship there; and next morning I was sent on board of the "Childers," ten-gun brig, to be sent round to Spithead, where we arrived on the 5th of August, 1802. And now having come a little to myself, you may depend my feelings and my mind was none of the best.

The chief thing that grieved me was thinking about my wife; for I knew she was about seven months gone in the family way; but the only way I had left to do her any good was to write to her; and having, by good luck, three guineas in my pocket, which I put there in the evening before I was pressed, to pay for some potatoes, in the morning, which I had bought, I went and bought some paper, and pens, and ink, and I wrote a letter to my landlord, Mr. Bland, and told him where I was; and I told him to go to Mr. Scovel, the gentleman that had my money, for him to get two substitutes for me, which would come to about sixty pounds per man, and to let me know how my wife was, and to be sure not to let my wife's mother-in-law come there. I directed this letter to Mr. Bland, for fear, if I directed it to my own house, it might have been stopped. I remained on board of the "Childers" three days after we arrived at Spithead; and then I was sent on board of the "Royal William," which lay flag-ship at Spithead. And now all my hopes being at an end of getting an answer to my letter, as my letter would be directed to the "Childers," I turned to and wrote again, and told them where I was; but I might have saved myself the trouble, for I was only three days on board of the "Royal William" before I was drafted to the "Albion," of seventy-four guns, and she was bound to the East Indies for to take out a convoy of merchant ships. We sailed from Spithead in the beginning of September, 1802; and I left England with a heavy heart, not having heard from my friends. I often thought that none of my letters had gone; and being very careless of myself I gave way to all sorts of badness, gambling, drunkenness, cursing and swearing, which brought me continually into trouble.

We were obliged to bear up in a heavy gale from the westward, for Plymouth, after being clear of the Land's End; and after having all our defects made good, we sailed from Plymouth the 29th day of September, 1802, with a fine breeze from the north-east, and we had a very fine passage till the 5th of November, when we fell in with two French merchant ships, who did not know that the war had broke out again between England and France, and so they became easy prizes to us; and I had the good luck to be sent on board of one of them, called the "La Favorite." She was from the Isle of France, and was bound to Bordeaux, in France; and after the exchange of the crew, and our captain sending water and provisions on board, we parted company from the fleet for Old England; and you may depend I was glad enough. But the ship that I was in was a very dull sailing vessel, and she was very leaky, so we made very slow progress across the Trade Winds; but by the beginning of December we fell in with a westerly wind, which was a fair wind for England; and you may depend we made the best use we could of it; for we were only complete with six weeks' provisions when we left our ship, and we had now left her a month, and still were a long distance from England.

Now the other prize, our partner, sailed a good deal better than us; and parted company with us the second night after. We had a fair wind, and we never saw any more of her, which was a very rascally trick of them; for they knowing we were very leaky, they ought to have stopped by us. But we having a fair wind and fine weather, we kept on our course till we got into soundings, on the 15th day of December; and the next day, in the morning, it being very hazy, and very little wind, we saw a lugger close to us, which proved to be a French privateer. Now if our partner had been along with us, we might have had a fight for it; but being by ourselves, and only mounting four guns, and being short of provisions, for we had been six upon four for several days, and being continually at the pumps, we were very little fit to fight a vessel mounting sixteen guns, and one hundred and twenty men; so we were boarded, and taken by the privateer; and we found that our other prize had been taken two days before by the same lugger. For, getting information from some of the Frenchmen that there was another ship coming, she laid to for us in our track, and we were taken, and I was sent on board of the French lugger. And now I had a sure prospect before me to be made a prisoner of war at the very commencement of it; but, thanks be to God, I did not stay very long with them; for the Frenchmen on board of the lugger used us very well, and I had not been many days on board of the lugger, when I fell in with a young man on board of her, who was a prisoner like myself, who had been a shipmate of mine in the "Blue-Eyed Maid of Guernsey," who could speak the French language as well as any Frenchman going, and he told me that he would not go to a French prison if he could help it, and I told him the same.

We steered, with the prize in tow, for St. Maloes, and we got into the harbor on the fifth day of January, 1803. Now the captain and the mate of the privateer had both been in an English prison, and they had been used very well in England, and the pair of them spoke very good English, and he told us he was very sorry to see us go to prison; and he told me and the Guernsey man that he would do anything in his power to keep us out of prison.

Now when the privateer and the prizes got into St. Maloes, it was late in the afternoon, and the crew being overjoyed at taking so many prizes, and got them all safe in, and their friends coming to see them, and bringing them something to eat and to drink, that by the time it was dark, there was scarce a sober man on board of the privateer; and the captain not being able to send us on shore in the evening, he kindly told us to look out for ourselves, for he would be obliged to send us on shore in the morning. We thanked him kindly for his good wishes toward us, and me and the Guernsey man said we would make the most of it. Now one of the prizes' boats was towed astern of the privateer, and with her we attempted to make our escape; and the first thing we done after it was dark, was to see how many of our fellow-prisoners we could get to go along with us; and we soon got nine more beside ourselves. And the next thing we done was to haul the boat up along side, and put in her anything that we thought necessary for our voyage, such as provisions and water.

We had the good luck to find two breakers of water, each breaker holding about seven gallons; and, as I told you before, the Frenchmen's friends fetched plenty of bread and other things on board; we found a pretty good stock of it, enough, with care, to last us two or three days, by which time we expected, with God's help, to be in England. And after getting one of the privateer's compasses into the boat, we were all ready; but it would not do for us to start before the rounds had been, which was a guard-boat that pulled round the harbor once a night; so we dropped our boat astern again, and laid down quietly till the guard-boat was past, which came round about ten o'clock in the morning. And our Guernsey man was lucky enough to hear the watchword for the morning; for in going out of the harbor, we had to pass close to a fort on our starboard hand, and the sentry was sure to hail you to ask the countersign. So after the guard-boat was gone, and everything was quiet, we started, and we passed the fort about three o'clock in the morning; and, thanks be to God, we got clear of the mouth of the harbor long before daylight.

Now the wind, when we left the harbor, was about east-south-east, and we being bound to the northward, we had a fair wind, and a fine breeze; and we all expected to have made some part of England by the next day; but our hopes were very soon all frustrated, for toward the middle part of our first day at sea, the wind came round to the north-east, and from there to north-north-east; and it came to blow very hard, and we were obliged to close-reef our sails, and lay as close to the wind as we could: and we made our course nearly north-west, which was four points off our course that we intended to steer for. It blew very hard all night, and it was very cold, and you may depend we were all very glad when it pleased the Almighty to send us daylight once more; but we could not see anything of any ship or land, and we all sat down to eat our scanty breakfast; but before we sat down, we all went to prayers to return thanks to God for preserving us during the night, and hoping that the Almighty would protect us during the day.

After we had done our breakfast, the wind lulling a bit, we shook one reef out of our foresail. But not to tire my reader with everything that we done; we stayed in this condition for four days, the weather being very thick and hazy, and very little wind. We saw a large ship close by us, and being all hands very weak, we got our oars out, and pulled after the ship, which at last we accomplished; and she proved to be a ship belonging to Bremen, with emigrants from Hanover; for the French had drove them out of their country, and they were bound to Baltimore, in America. When we first got along side of the ship, the people on board of her came to the gangway, and seemed quite surprised to see so many poor wretched looking men in so small a boat; for our boat was only twenty-five feet long; and they asked us, in German, where we came from, and what we wanted. Now I being the only one that could understand a little of the German language, which I learned at the time that I belonged to the Hamburgh ship that I mentioned, I told them that we were Englishmen that had run away from a French prison.

As soon as they heard it, they told us to come up; and you may depend we were glad to hear that; and we tried our best to get up, but we could not, for we were so weak, and so cold, that we could not stand upon our legs. So the captain seeing this, he was kind enough to send some of the crew into the boat to help us, and they were obliged to haul us up the ship's side with ropes; and, thanks be to God, we all got safely on board; and a miserable set we were, for we had been nearly five days in a small open boat, and when we started we had scarcely provisions enough to last us two days; and then to be exposed, in the month of January, to a cold north-east wind, and plenty of snow beating about us; so you may depend we were in a very bad state; and if they had given us the ship and all her cargo, we could not stand upon our legs. But the captain and the passengers were very kind to us; and the doctor had us put to bed as soon as he could, and they gave me a little sago and some wine, and I soon fell into a sound sleep, from which I did not awake till the next day; and, thanks be to God, and the good people's care, I was able to come on deck in four or five days' time; but we had the misfortune to lose three of my companions, who died the day after we were picked up.

And now there being only six of us left, and some of them were a long time before they got well; but, in eight or ten days' time, I was as well as ever I was; and I was able to be of some service to my preservers; for we falling in with some very squally weather, we split a good many of our sails, and I being a middling good sail-maker, I was able to repair them, which pleased the captain very much. Now the captain had been kind enough to hoist our boat in, and she being a very good boat, the captain asked me if I would sell the boat to him; for I being the only one that could speak any German, is the reason the captain asked me. I told him that, if he thought the boat was of any use to him, he might have her, and welcome; for, in my opinion, we owed him a great deal more than the value of the boat, for his kindness toward us all. But he said he would not have the boat at that price, for he had done no more than his duty; but, as we were very short of clothing, he would give us a suit of clothes and a couple of shirts a piece out of the slop chest for the boat, to which I agreed at once, and thanked him very kindly for his kind offer; and he gave us our clothes; and, in fact, every one on board of that ship behaved better than if we had been their own brothers; and we all were very comfortable on board of her, till the 16th day of February, when we fell in with an English brig, who had lost her foremast and bowsprit by running foul of an iceberg; and she lost five men overboard when the accident happened, so had only four men left.

Our captain asked us if we would go on board of the brig to assist our countrymen, and we agreed to go on board of the brig; and you may depend we left the Bremen ship with a heavy heart, for they all had been so kind to us; and our old captain was kind enough to give us a spare spar for to rig a jury foremast; and he told the master of the brig to pay the price of the spar to us, if it pleased God to send him safe into port. We all thanked the captain heartily for his kindness toward us, and we parted company.

Now the brig that we got on board of was called the "Spring-flower," belonging to Liverpool; and she was last from Port Royal, Jamaica, bound to Liverpool. She sailed from Port Royal under convoy of a frigate; but being very deeply laden, and a very dull sailer, she lost the convoy in a gale of wind; and a few days afterward she had the misfortune to run foul of an iceberg, and lost her foremast and bowsprit, and five of her men. When we came on board of the brig, we found the master, two men, and a boy, and us six coming on board, made ten altogether; and we turned to with a good will, and got our shears up, and rigged our jury foremast and bowsprit, which, with God's help, we finished the second day; so that we were able to set a maintop-gallant sail for a fore-topsail, and a lower studding-sail for a foresail, and a fore-topmast staysail for a jib.

Now the captain of the brig being well pleased with our work, and seeing we were very short of clothing, and especially when he heard how we got on board of the Bremen ship, was kind enough to give us the men's clothes that had been drowned, for our use; and the mate of the brig being drowned, he made me mate in his stead, for I was the only man out of the whole that could read and write. Now the brig had been out a long time at sea, and though she was bound to England, we could not attempt a passage to England in that time of the year, and the state the vessel was in. The island of Bermuda was the nearest land to us, so we steered for Bermuda, where we arrived safe on the 3d day of March, 1803.

And now being upon my own hands again, and having a little money, and a few clothes, me and my old shipmate, the Guernsey man, shipped on board of a brig called the "Sprightly," about one hundred and twenty tons burden, and she was bound to Barbadoes, one of the West India Islands, and we sailed from Bermuda on the 2d day of April, 1803, and we arrived at the island of Barbadoes, after a pleasant passage, the latter end of April; and I traded, on board of the "Sprightly," from one island to another, till August, 1804. And I had made a good bit of money by this time, when, on the 24th day of August, 1804, we were coming up to windward, and I had the middle watch: it was just after two o'clock in the morning, for I had just been relieved from the helm; the weather being very thick and hazy, we were run down by a large ship, called the "Big Ann," of London. She came down upon us so quick and unawares, that I had only just time to get hold of her bobstays, and I sung out to the rest of them that were on deck; but only one, beside myself, had the good fortune to save himself, and that was the mate of the brig. The rest of the crew, six in number, found a watery grave. The captain of the "Big Ann" tried the best that he could do, for he hove to directly, and lowered two boats down, and pulled about in our direction.

We could not see anything of the brig, or of the unfortunate crew; so, when everything was quiet again on board, and made sail again, the captain called the mate and me, and asked us the particulars about our brig, and we told him all we knew about it. He sent us down below, and told us to lay down till the morning, and he would see what he could do for us; but, for my part, I could not sleep, and I believe my partner in misfortune was the same, for I heard him getting up, every now and then, and singing out for one of his old shipmates, or singing out "Hard a starboard! there she comes!" I went to him and tried to quiet him, but it was of no use, for by the morning he was raving mad; and the captain and some of the passengers did all they could for him, by bleeding him, and giving him what medicines they thought would do him good; but all was of no use, for he died the next day about four o'clock in the afternoon. And now I being the only one that was saved from the "Sprightly's" crew, however all well and hearty only twenty-four hours ago, I knelt down and thanked the Almighty Giver of all good for his wonderful mercy toward me; and I felt greatly relieved afterward.

Now the ship that I was in was from London, bound to Port Royal, Jamaica, and she had a good many passengers on board, and the captain was kind enough to make a collection for me, and he collected forty-seven dollars for me, which he gave me, in the name of the passengers, for the loss of my clothes, and I returned them my sincere thanks for their kindness; and the captain told me that, if I liked, I could stay on board of his ship all the time that the ship lay in Port Royal, or till I got another ship. We arrived in Port Royal on the 28th day of August, 1804; and I was obliged to go on shore the next day to go to the consul, and tell all that I knew about the loss of the "Sprightly" brig. The brig being insured, I received the wages that was due to me to the time she was lost, which amounted to about one hundred and eighty dollars; so I was able to lay myself in a good stock of clothes, which I wanted very much; and I stayed on board the "Big Ann" till the 15th day of September, when I shipped on board of a ship belonging to Liverpool, called the "King George." She was bound to the coast of Africa, for a cargo of slaves; she was a fine ship, mounting eighteen guns, and carried eighty men; and she had a letter-of-marque commission for to fight her own way.

We sailed from Port Royal the latter part of September, and we had a very pleasant passage across the Trades, and we arrived on the coast of Africa, at a place called Anne Bone, the latter part of November; and we traded up and down the coast till we got our cargo, which we completed by the beginning of February, 1805; but just before we sailed, our captain got information, by a ship that arrived there, that two French frigates were cruising in their track, from the coast of Africa to the West Indies; so our captain altered his mind, and, in room of going to the West Indies, we steered for Rio de Janeiro, on the coast of the Brazils, where we arrived on the 15th day of April, 1805; and as soon as we got our cargo of slaves out, and our ship cleaned, we took in a cargo of sugar for Liverpool, and we sailed from Rio de Janeiro the last day of May, and we were bound for Liverpool; and we had a very good passage, though rather a long one, for we were becalmed for twelve days, in what is called the "Horse Latitudes;" that was just after we had crossed the line; but afterward we got a fine breeze across the northeast Trades, till the 17th day of July, when we fell in with a fleet of English men-of-war. The time of our letter-of-marque commission being expired, they came on board of us, and pressed forty men out of us; and I was pressed among the rest, and sent on board of the "Spashot," of seventy-four guns.

So there I was once more on board of an English man-of-war; and I hailed for a foreigner, and I said that I belonged to Hamburgh, in Germany, thinking that I should get clear; but it would not do; they would not let me go; so when I found I could not get clear, I contented myself, and tried to make the best of a bad bargain. We kept cruising at sea, looking out for French or Spanish ships, till the month of October, when Admiral Nelson joined the fleet with some more ships; and then we were stationed off Cadiz, till the glorious twenty-first of October, when we brought the French and Spanish fleet to action; and we had pretty warm work while it lasted, but, thanks be to God, we beat them, and gained the victory. And after the action, I was sent on board of one of the prizes, a Spanish seventy-four; and she had lost her fore and mizzenmast by the board, and it being late in the afternoon before we got on board of her, and got the prisoners secured and exchanged, it was nearly night before we could begin rigging our jury, fore, and mizzenmast; but by daylight next morning we got our fore and mizzen standing; but they proved of very little use to us, for, it coming on a gale of wind, we soon lost our jurymast again, and we were driving as fast as we could toward the Spanish shore. It is bad enough to be on a lee-shore in a gale of wind at any time, but especially when that lee-shore is an enemy's coast; but we found that, if the gale continued, we should have to go on shore before morning; so our commanding officer thought best to run her on shore while it was daylight.

To effect this, we had to get the ship before the wind, which we could not effect without cutting away the mainmast, which we were obliged to do, and then setting a spritsail upon the bowsprit, we got the ship before the wind; and as soon as we got the ship before the wind, we opened the hatches to let our prisoners come up, so that the poor fellows could look out to save their own lives; but the ship run upon a sandy beach, but, thanks be to God, being nearly a new ship, and very strong built, she kept together, and she soon worked herself broadside on; and us on board, heaving all the starboard guns overboard, and rolling all the shot we could get at, or any heavy thing, over to the larboard side, we made shift to give her good list in shore. And the ship having worked herself broadside on, and well into the sand, we contrived to get ashore under her lee, which we did by cutting her port gangway and hammock nettings away, and launching her boom-boats, which we effected after a good deal of trouble, and by which I got my right leg and my arm hurt a good deal, which laid me up for some time afterward. Now, after we got the boats bailed out, we sent the prisoners ashore first, and then followed ourselves afterward; and by four o'clock the next morning—that is to say, the 23d of October—we all got safe on shore.

Now the Spanish prisoners that had come on shore first, some of them had been and seen their friends, and, as daylight came on, they came down to assist us, which they did, for they brought us some bread, and some figs, and some wine, to refresh us, which we wanted very much, for we had scarcely tasted anything the last twenty-four hours; and the Spaniards behaved very kind to us. As for myself, after I had eaten some bread and fruit, and drank some wine, I tried to get up, but I could not; and one of the Spaniards, seeing the state that I was in, was kind enough to get two or three more of his companions, and lifted me up in one of the bullock-carts, in which they had brought down the provisions for us, and covered me up with one of their great ponchos; and he tapped me on the shoulder, and said, "Bono English!" And, being upon the cart, I was out of the wind and rain—for it blew a heavy gale of wind; and I felt myself quite comfortable, only my leg pained me a good deal; but, thanks be to God, I soon fell into a sound sleep; and, as I heard afterward, the French soldiers came down and marched the rest of my shipmates up to Cadiz, and they put them into a Spanish prison. As for my part, I was taken up to Cadiz, in the bullock-cart, and my kind friend took me to his own house, and had me put to bed, where I found myself when I woke.

Now in the house where I was, it happened to be a boarding house, and a good many American sailors boarded there, and when I came te myself, my friend, the Spaniard, brought one of the American sailors to me, for to ask me if I wanted anything. I told the man very kindly that I wanted some one to look at my leg; for I felt my leg very painful. Now this young man was mate of an American ship that was getting repaired at Cadiz, and he spoke very good Spanish, so he told the Spaniard what I wanted, and my friend went away and fetched a doctor, who could speak very good English, who dressed my leg, and assured me there were no bones broken, only he told me that I must keep myself very quiet, and to be sure not to drink any spirits.

I forgot to tell you that the first night that I got on board of the prize, while I was down below, to look for some rope, for to lash the jury foremast to the stump of the old foremast, I picked up a belt; but, being in a hurry, I never looked into it, but put it around me, under my frock, and, being busy at work all the time that I was on board of her, I never hought no more about it till, now I was laying in bed, I felt it uncomfortable round me, and I asked my new friend, the American mate, if he would be kind enough to take it off me. But what was my surprise when, on overhauling of it, I found that there were forty doubloons, ten dollars, and some smaller money in it! My surprise was so great that my young friend perceived it, and I told him the whole truth of it, how I came by it. My friend advised me to keep it quiet, and say nothing about it; I told him I would. And now it came into my thoughts that the money might be serviceable to me, to keep me from going to prison; and I spoke to my young friend about it, and he went down and spoke to the old Spaniard about it, who came up to me directly, and he told the American mate to tell me to make myself quite easy about that; for he had been to the prison to hear if he could find out that I had been missing, and, when I had been missed, that they supposed that I had been drowned; so he said, "It will be your own fault if you go to prison."

You may depend I was very glad to hear what he said, and I offered the old man a doubloon for the kindness he had shown me, which he at first refused; but, after a good deal of persuading, he took it for to pay the doctor. And now this affair being settled, I rested myself quite contented till it pleased the Almighty to restore to me the use of my leg and arm, which got quite well in about a month's time; and me and the American mate got quite friendly together; and, their ship being nearly ready for sea, he persuaded me to join the ship that he belonged to, for they were several hands short, and they would be obliged to ship Spaniards, without they could get any of my former shipmates to run away out of prison and join their ship; so I agreed to go along with him, and I joined the "Matilda," of Boston, on the 1st day of December, 1805. On leaving my old friend, the Spaniard, who had been so kind to me, I made him a present of five Spanish doubloons, which he accepted; and I parted from him with a sorrowful heart.

When I came on board of the "Matilda," I was quite surprised to find four of my old shipmates there before me. They had made their escape out of prison through the assistance of some good Spaniards, and had got on board there before me. But you may depend that their surprise was great to see me, for I was believed, by every one, to be drowned; but we soon reconciled ourselves; and by the 4th day of December we were out at sea, clear of them all; and our ship, the "Matilda," was bound to Boston, in America, where we arrived the 25th day of January, 1806. I liked my ship so well, that I agreed to go along with them another voyage; and we sailed from Boston in the beginning of March; and we went back to Cadiz again, and I had the pleasure of seeing my old friend, the Spaniard, again, who was well and hearty.

And now I must tell my readers that I staid in the "Matilda," of Boston, till, in a voyage from Boston to London, in the beginning of the year 1807, I was pressed out of her, while lying at the Big Nore; and I was taken on board of the "Namur," guard-ship at Sheerness, and from there I was drafted on board of the "Spitfire," sloop-of-war. Although I was on the books as a foreigner, I could not get clear; so I wrote up to my old landlord, Mr. Bland, to hear if I could learn anything of my wife; and I asked him if he would be kind enough to come down to me and see me, and bring my wife along with him. I sent this letter away on Friday, and on Sunday morning Mr. Bland came on board of the "Spitfire" to see me. When we got down below, I asked him how my wife was; and then I heard that my wife was dead; that she died the day after I was pressed; that through the fright she got, she was taken in labor, and she died in childbed, but that the child lived, and was grown a fine boy, and that he would be five years old if he lived till July; and he told me that he had never received only one letter from me, and that was the one I had sent from the "Albion," before I sailed in her; and Mr. Bland told me that he and his wife had taken care of everything; that after my wife was buried, and they got a nurse for the child, they sold everything that I had in the house; and knowing that I had money in Mr. Scovel's hands, he went to him and told him all about it; and Mr. Scovel had allowed him seven shillings a week for to take care of the child and pay the nurse; and he showed me the account of the expenses he had been at, and I found that it amounted to nearly ninety-five pounds; so Mr. Scovel was still a debtor to me.

After we had settled all our accounts, I gave Mr. Bland thirty doubloons, and about one hundred and twenty Spanish dollars, and told him to take them to Mr. Scovel, to put to the rest of my stock; and I told him to be careful of my boy, and whatever he wanted, to get money from Mr. Scovel, and get it for him; and I gave him two doubloons—one for himself, and the other for his wife; and I returned him my kind thanks for the trouble he had been at on my account. And after Mr. Bland was gone, I sat down and had a good cry for the loss of my wife; and I returned my sincere thanks to God for his great mercy to me for raising up friends to look after my child. And now this business being settled, I went on deck to my work, and the next day we sailed for to join a convoy in Yarmouth Roads, and from there we went to Gottenburg, where we arrived in May.

Nothing particular happened to me while in the "Spitfire," sloop-of-war, not till the 1st of August, 1810, when an accident happened to me. We were cruising off the coast of Norway, and the weather being rather thick and hazy, for it had been blowing strong all night, and in the morning, sending our topgallant yards up, a strange sail was reported from the mast-head on the lee-beam; and the hands being turned up to make sail, and I being at the mast-head, binding the topgallant yard; but not getting our jewel-blocks on the yard before we were ordered to loose the sail, and was obliged to put them on after the sail was set; and I being out on the starboard foretop-gallant yardarm, and the slack of the lifts not being taken down, the topgallant halyards carried away, and the slack of the lifts caught me under my rump, and hove me right over the yard; but, as luck would have it, I caught right across the topgallant bowline, and it being slack, I lowered myself down, till I got hold of the leech of the topsail, just before the ship was luffed to the wind. I mention this to show the wonderful mercy and care of God Almighty over us poor mortals; for if I had fell down on deck, I must have been killed upon the spot; but I got safe down on deck without any hurt, and I got the name of the "Flying Dutchman" among my shipmates. During our cruise off the coast of Norway, we took several prizes, and our time passed away merrily enough till the year 1812, when the American war broke out; and the "President," American frigate, Commodore Rogers, was off the North Cape, when our ship, the "Spitfire," sloop-of-war, the "Alexander," thirty-two-gun frigate, and the "Bonne Citoyenne," corvette, were sent off the North Cape to protect our trade, and to see if we could see anything of him.

We arrived off the Cape in the latter part of May, and we found it very cold there; and we kept cruising there till the 10th of June, when, about four o'clock in the afternoon, the weather clearing up, we saw the American frigate, and a large schooner along with her: she was about five or six miles dead to leeward of us, and we made all sail in chase. Now our ship would outsail the other two ships, but our commander would not allow us to go along side of her, for she was too heavy a ship for us to engage; so we chased her till the 14th of June, when both she and us got stuck among the ice; we had chased her as far as eighty-three degrees of north latitude. Now at this time of the year, in this part of the world, there is scarcely any night, but all daylight. We stuck fast among the ice till the 17th day of June, when the ice broke up; but the "President" getting clear of it before we did, he made the best of his way to the southward; and before we got clear, we could see nothing of him, nor any other ship; for the corvette had been sent after the schooner, and the "Alexander" frigate had been drifted off the ice by strong currents, and we did not fall in with the "Alexander" till the 21st of June, and then we kept cruising off the North Cape again.

Now the "President" frigate had taken a great many of our Archangel traders, and a good many Russian vessels, before we came on the coast, and taken them into a place called Colla, which is a large bay, with very good anchorage, and a very good harbor. And when she got them in there, they took the best what they wanted out of the ships, and then set fire to them; and they took one of our Greenland ships, belonging to Hull, and had put all the English prisoners on board of her, and the Russians they had set ashore at Colla, a small town about twenty miles up the river; so the Russians were very much embittered against the Americans. I mention this because it interferes with my story. We and the frigate kept cruising about the North Cape till the latter part of July; and our water getting very short, we put into Colla, for to water, and to get some wood; and our cask and people being sent on shore, we sent them their provisions on shore every day.

Now the second day that we lay off Colla, being the 1st day of August, 1812, I was ordered to go into the boat; and our captain, doctor and purser went ashore to go a shooting. We landed the captain and the rest of the officers on an island, about a quarter of a mile from where our people were at work; and our captain gave me orders to land the provisions, and then come back for them to take them on board to dinner: and accordingly we went, and I delivered what provisions I had to the officer in charge of the working party; and telling him the orders that I had received from the captain, he sent me away to obey them; and we tried to go back the same way we came, but we could not, for the tide run so strong that we could not fetch round the island where our captain was, so we tried to go round the other way; but all our trying was in vain, for the more we pulled, the further we got away from the island; and having no grabbling or anchor in the boat, we resolved to go along side of some of the small vessels which were lying there, to hold on till the tide was down, which we did; and the people on board of them seemed to be glad to receive us. Now these vessels were fishing-vessels, seemingly waiting for the tide to slack before they could go to sea; and the one we got on board of hailed another that lay pretty close to us, but we could not understand a single word they said, and we had no suspicion that they were talking about us.

So we laid ourselves down quite unconcerned, for the weather was warm, and we being rather tired after our long pull; and we might have laid down about two hours, for I could not sleep sound, for I knew that our captain would be very angry for not fetching him to go on board to his dinner. But what was my surprise, on getting up, to see two large boats, with about twenty men in each, close to us. And, coming along side, they took us out of our boat, and tied us back to back, and beat us unmercifully, and called us American spies, for they took us and our ships to be Americans; and they had such a spite against the Americans for burning their ships, that they would not hearken to anything that we had to say if they could have understood us.

So after they were tired of beating and ill-using us, which they did in a cruel manner—for they were a cowardly set of men, for a coward is always cruel when he gets the upper hand of you;—so, after they were tired beating of us, they took our boat in tow, and took us up to Colla, the name of a small town in Russian Lapland; and when we got there, we were put into prison, and they gave us some black bread to eat, and some water to drink, and the next day they put irons on us, and joined two and two together; we had a shackle round one of our legs, and another on our hands, and so we were chained together; and then they sent a sergeant and eight soldiers as a guard along with us to march us to Archangel, which was about one thousand two hundred miles distant. And so we started on our travel in a very helpless condition. Our first fortnight travel was the worst, for we traveled through nothing but woods; and when our stock of black bread got low, they used to feed us upon the bark of trees; for every fir-tree has three different barks or rinds upon it, and the middle rind, when roasted by the fire, makes a good substitute for bread. But this was not the worst misfortune we had to deal with, for, having irons on our legs and arms, we could not pull our clothes off.

And so we traveled on till we got clear of the woods, and we got in among what they called their towns; and here we got a good deal better used, and our traveling was a good deal better, for we used to get horses from place to place; and they tied the two horses' heads together, and when we were mounted on them, chained together as we were, our poor horses had to keep regular step together, or else we were likely to be hauled off our horses, which was very painful to our legs. And sometimes we traveled in boats for whole days together; and the nearer we got to Archangel our food became a good deal better, for they used sometimes to give us some milk, along with our bread, in the room of water; and in this way we kept on traveling till the beginning of September, when we arrived in Archangel, where we were put into prison.

We had been in Archangel prison two or three days, when we found out by the few words of Russian that we had picked up, that we were going to be sent to Siberia along with some more prisoners. And now we thought our fate very hard to be transported without having a trial; but it happened otherwise. For one morning, when I was out in the prison-yard, I heard two gentlemen talking together in German, and me understanding a little of the German tongue, I made bold to speak to one of them as well as I could. I told him what we were, and what ship we belonged to. Now this gentleman that I spoke to happened to be one of the English consul's clerks; and he soon spoke to me in good English, and told me that he would speak to the consul about us; and he was kind enough to put his hand in his pocket and give me a silver ruble, and away he went. And I went to acquaint my shipmates of the news that I had to tell them; and you may depend they were very glad to hear the news, especially when I showed them the silver ruble that the gentleman had been kind enough to give me. And I went and bought something to eat with part of the money; for you may depend we were kept pretty short of provisions, and after we had eaten our bellies full, we all returned thanks to God for his kindness toward us, and waited with patience till about half past ten o'clock, when the turnkey came in and called us, and told us that we were wanted.

When we came into the room where the gentleman was that I had spoken to the day before, he told me that the consul would be there directly; and, when the consul came, he spoke to us, and asked us what ships belonging to England were stationed off the North Cape, and how we came to leave our ship. We told him; and he spoke to the governor, and the next morning we got our discharge from the prison. Now, in the state that we were in, we were not fit to go into a clean house, or among clean people; so the consul put us into an outhouse that he had, and gave us some clean straw to lie on, and two duck frocks and trowsers apiece, for our old clothes were fairly worn out. And he used to send us our provision every day from his own house; and in a week's time we were clear of all vermin, and as clean as anybody need to be. And the English merchants and their ladies who resided at Archangel, when they came to know how we had been served by the Russians, made a subscription for us, and bought us many things that we stood in need of.

We stopped with our good consul till the latter end of September, when the "Oberon," an English gun-brig, arrived at Archangel, to take a convoy home to England; and the captain of her, Captain Young, a very good man, heard about us, and seeing the state that we were in—for the places that the vermin had eaten into us were not quite healed up—he told us that he would take us to England. And on the first day of October we were sent on board of the "Oberon," and the captain and officers behaved very kindly to us; and we sailed from Archangel on the 4th day of October, and on the 17th of October, when nearly off the North Cape, we fell in with our ship, the "Spitfire," and the "Alexander" frigate.

We were sent on board of our ship; and, to our great surprise, we were put in irons. So Captain Young stated to our captain the state he found us in at Archangel, and the punishment that we had received from the Russians. But our captain swore that we intended to run away from the ship, and we were kept in irons till we arrived at Leith Roads, when orders came on board to let us out of irons; for Admiral Young had his flag at Leith Roads, and his son, the captain of the "Oberon," had acquainted his father with the state he had found us in at Archangel. And so now we thought it was all over with this affair; but it was not so, for our ship received orders to go round to Portsmouth to be refitted, and in going round from Leith, as soon as we left the Downs—for we were then under another admiral—our captain turned the hands up, and gave me and a man, named Andrew Paddon, three dozen lashes apiece, for he swore that we two had been ringleaders, and that we intended to run away from the ship. The other two men he forgave: and thus this affair ended.

Now when we arrived at Portsmouth, we refitted our ship, and we were sent to cruise off Cherbourg along with some men-of-war. On the 10th day of February, 1813, it being a fine morning, we chased a French lugger close into the land, and the wind dying away, and what there was coming from the northward, the lugger got clear of us; and we being close in shore, and standing away to the westward, I happened to be at the mast-head to look out. It was about half past ten o'clock in the forenoon, and I was sitting on the maintop-gallant yard, when a little battery, which we had not seen before, opened fire upon us, and the second or third shot they fired carried away our maintop-gallant mast; and me sitting on the maintop-gallant yard, I had a very clumsy fall; but our mainsail being hauled up, I had the good fortune to fall into the belly of the mainsail, where after some time lying there senseless—for I must have struck against the mainyard in my fall, for I was bleeding a good deal—when there were some hands sent to help me out of the mainsail; and when I got on deck, I was obliged to be sent to the doctor, when I soon got well. And by the time that our ship came out to Spithead again, and was ready for sea, we were sent on board of her again, and we hoisted the convoy signal for the coast of Africa; and, on the 20th of April, 1813, we sailed from Spithead with about three hundred sail of ships, all under different convoys.

We staid on the coast till the beginning of May, 1814, when we fell in with an English brig from London, who brought us the news of the peace, and of Bonaparte giving himself up; and the brig brought us some newspapers, and some letters for the captain and officers, for she had been to Sierra Leone. You may depend we were all very glad to hear of the news of peace; and the next morning we went to sea, and shaped our course for Portsmouth, where we arrived on the 20th of July. Now when we got home, an order was issued from the admiralty, that all men that had served eleven years, and all foreigners, were to be discharged. Now I being entered as a foreigner on the ship's books, I claimed my discharge; and I got my discharge from the service on the 2d of August, 1814; and I went to Portsmouth Dockyard to get my pay, and as soon as I got it, I went to the coach-office and booked myself for London.

By six o'clock that evening I was on my journey, and I arrived safe by seven o'clock in the morning, after being away from London a little better than twelve years. I was well and hearty after all my trials and crosses; and, as soon as I got some breakfast, I went to Vine Yard to see Mr. Bland; but, when I got there, Mr. Bland was not at home, but Mrs. Bland was. I soon told her who I was, and asked her where my boy was. She told me that the boy was very well, and that he was at school; but she soon sent for him. And I told her not to tell him who I was, for I wanted to surprise him myself. At last, when he came into the room where I was, I could see a good deal of his mother's face in him, and it was not long before I had him in my arms, for I could not keep myself from him; and the poor boy, when he was told that I was his father, fell a crying; but he still crept close to me, and we soon all got reconciled together. And, when Mr. Bland came in, we passed the day away in talking over past affairs; and the next day me and Mr. Bland settled our accounts together, and I went to Mr. Scovel. I found that I still had better than a hundred pounds in his hands; and, after all that was settled, I thanked Mr. Scovel for the kindness that he had shown me, and I asked his advice what I had best do. He told me that I had best not enter into any sort of business at present, till I saw how things would turn out, for the peace had made a great stagnation in trade; but, if I liked, I might go to work at any of his wharves, and he would allow me twenty-five shillings a week, and I agreed with him.

In the middle of May I fell in with an old shipmate of mine, that had been a master's mate along with me in the "Spitfire," and he was master of a new bark, called the "X. Y. Z.," and he was bound to Riga, and he wanted a second mate; and when I told him my circumstances, he persuaded me to go along with him. So I went. We had a very fine passage across the North Sea, and we arrived at Riga the 10th of July; and, as soon as our cargo was discharged, we commenced taking in our cargo for London.

On the 5th of September, it being Sunday morning, the breeze having nearly died away to a calm, the captain ordered me to call the mate; for he said that he had smelled fire. We all smelled it, too. I advised the captain that the best thing we could do was to get the boats out before we opened any of our hatches. Accordingly we turned the hands up, and got the boats out, and put oars and sails in them, and then we took one hatch off; but no sooner had we done this, but a good deal of smoke came up the hatchway. We roused some of the bales of flax on deck, for we were laden with flax, hemp and tallow; and we mustered all buckets, and began to heave water down the place where the smoke came from. And our mate thinking that if the after hatchway was open, he would be able to heave some water down there; but no sooner were the after hatches taken off, but the flames struck up the after part, and in a very few minutes our main rigging was in a blaze. And now all chance of saving the ship was over, for the fire spread rapidly. The middle part of the ship being on fire, those that were aft could not get forward, and those that were forward could not get aft; so we found it a great blessing that we got our boats out. So all hands got into the boats, and we had a chance to save some of our clothes, and some provision and water, which we put into the long-boat. Now there were fifteen of us, men and boys altogether, and we divided ourselves in the three boats—that is, the long-boat, pinnace, and jolly-boat; and we lay by the ship till she was burnt to the water's edge.

When the accident happened to us, we could see an island in the East Sea that belongs to the Danes, for which we pulled, taking the boats in too. But the people on the island seeing the fire at sea, the governor of the island sent two boats to our assistance, which we met about half way from our ship to the shore, and they very kindly offered us any assistance in their power; but we thanked them kindly, and pulled on shore in company, where we arrived about eight o'clock in the evening, and there was no one hurt. In two days we were sent in a Danish vessel to Copenhagen, where I staid till the 20th of September, when I shipped in a brig, called the "Fame," and arrived in London on the 24th day of November. I found my boy and Mr. and Mrs. Bland well and hearty; and my boy made very good progress in his learning, and I put him apprentice to a sail-maker.

Mr. Scovel, being connected with a great many country bankers, and a great many of them breaking, Mr. Scovel was obliged to stop payment, and I got a shilling in the pound for the little money he had of mine. But my son was bound apprentice to Mr. Mellish for seven years, and

Mr. Mellish told me, when I told him of my misfortune, to make myself quite easy about him; that he had taken a great liking to the boy, and, if he behaved himself, he would be as good as a father to him; and, as Mr. Mellish had a great many South-Seamen, and I wanted to make a long voyage, I had best join one of his ships; and there being a ship of his, called the "Policy," now fitted out, if I liked, he would speak to the captain of her for me; and I, being tired of these short voyages, agreed with the captain. When the captain was gone, he called me to him, and said to me, "Upon account of your late misfortune, losing nearly all, I make you a present of this for to fit you out for the voyage;" and he gave me two five-pound notes. I thanked him very kindly.

On the 20th of June, 1816, we sailed from Gravesend, and we had a very good passage, and we got round Cape Horn by the beginning of October, and we soon had the pleasure of getting into the Pacific Ocean.

On the 20th of May, 1817, we saw the spout of a fish, about four o'clock in the afternoon, and there being very little wind, we lowered our boat, got up to her, and made fast to her. She run us about five or six miles, when she hove to, and we soon killed her; but by the time that she was dead, and we got her in tow, it was past sunset, and we could scarcely see our ship; but we pulled toward her as fast as we could, and the ship, the last time we saw her, was coming toward us; and when it got dark, we hoisted our lantern at our mast-head, so that the ship might see us. We kept pulling away till about twelve o'clock at night, when our candle went out, and being all very tired, the mate ordered us to lay our oars in, and rest ourselves a bit, and told all hands to look out sharp, to see if they could see anything of the ship; but we could not see anything of her.

So, after having a small drop of rum and water, and a bit of biscuit, we got our oars out again, and pulled in the direction where we had seen the ship last; for we could still see a large rock, called Rodondo, and we steered for it, and we kept pulling till daylight; and then, to our great misfortune, we could not see anything of the ship, and we were a long way drifted from Rodondo. And we, finding that our pulling was of little use, laid our oars in, and we had a consultation what was best for us to do; and after different opinions, we agreed that, as there was a little breeze of wind, we should set our sail, and stand to the northward, in hopes to fall in with some ship. For when we started from our own ship, there were six of us in the boat, and all the provisions we had was a breaker of water, which held about six gallons, and about a dozen biscuits, and about a pint of rum, and as we had not been very careful of it, the first night we had very little of it left. So we were not in a very fit state to pull, and we thought by sailing we might have a chance of falling in with some ship. And now we had a hard chance before us, in an open boat, in the great Pacific Ocean, and nearly under the equator, with the sun hot enough to roast us, and scarcely any water to drink, and very little to eat; but it was of no use to fret about it, and we were obliged to make ourselves content, and pray to God to release us out of our calamity.

We staid in this way in the boat for three days, when we had the last cup of water; and you may depend that we were all hungry enough, and some of our men hauled up to the whale, and cut some of his tail off, and broiled it in the sun, and ate it. And I and the mate tried to persuade them from doing it, but they took no notice of it; and the consequence was, that it made them sick, and caused them to heave up what little substance they had on their stomachs. And the next day morning, being the fourth day, we found one of our boat mates lying dead in the boat; and after we said a few prayers over him, we committed his body to the deep with a sorrowful heart; for we were all very weak by this time. And that same day, about four o'clock, another of our boat mates was taken raving mad, and after ill-using himself a good deal, he jumped overboard, and the sharks soon finished him.

Now there were only four of us left, and we suffered a good deal with thirst. I can't say I was very hungry, but I was terribly dry; and the next morning, being the fifth day, we found another of our boat mates dead. It was as much as the three of us could do to heave him overboard, for we were so weak we could not stand upon our feet; but after a good deal of trouble, we got him out of the boat. And after that, we turned to and licked the dew off the oars and the boat, to quench our thirst; and so we passed away the fifth day. And some time during the night our other comrade died; we heard him groan, but we could not help him. And when daylight came, the next morning, we saw a ship quite close to us, but both me and my partner were so weak that we could not get up to show ourselves; but I made shift to hold one of the boat's flags up. The ship, when she came close to us, hove to, and lowered a boat down, and towed us along side of the ship; but which way we got on board of her I can't tell.

When I came to myself, I found that I was on board of a whaler, belonging to London, and that my poor partner, the mate of our ship, had died about four hours after he got on board of her, and the doctor told me that there was no fear of me if the fever only kept off. I found myself very weak, and I could not stand upon my legs. Now the four men that died in the boat were the four men that ate of the whale that we were towing off. The ship that I got on board of was called the "Neptune," bound home, and I was obliged to go home in her.

We arrived safe at Gravesend the 24th day of September, after being away two years and four months. After we got the ship safe into the docks, I went to Mr. Mellish's to see my son; but what was my surprise to find that my son had gone to sea, and that Mr. Bland was dead, and that his widow had gone into the country to live along with her friends Mr. Mellish told me that my son, after hearing of my misfortune, had been continually teasing him to let him go to sea in one of his ships, for he said he wanted to look for his father; and, having a ship ready to sail, he at last consented to let him go, and he sailed in a ship called the "Seringapatam," and was gone from England about five months. And Mr. Mellish told me that he had been a very good lad, and that he was very sorry to lose him from his sail-loft. And now, after our oil was sold, I received my wages, which amounted to ninety-three pounds, for the captain and Mr. Mellish were kind enough to pay me for the whole time that I had been away from the ship. In a South-Seaman the men have no monthly wages, but go by the shares, and they got a good many fish during the time I had been away. And now, having no acquaintance in London, I intended to go in the first ship that was bound to the South Seas, to look after my son.

Mr. Mellish had a ship fitting out, called the "Spring Grove," and I agreed to go as second mate; and we sailed from Gravesend on the 3d of November, 1818, and had a very good passage to James' Island Our passage lay round the south-west point of the island, where there lies a dangerous reef, called the Papases. By going inside of the reef you can fetch your anchorage without making a tack. Now on the evening of the 2d of February, it being a fine night, our captain intended to go inside of the reef. I reasoned against it as much as I could, but it was of no use, for the mate said he had been through the passage a dozen times, and he could take the ship through it; for he said if we went outside of the reef, it would take us a whole day to work up to our anchorage; and accordingly we went. I had the first watch on deck, which is from eight o'clock till twelve at night; but the captain being on deck all my watch, everything went according to his direction.

At twelve o'clock the mate came up and took charge from me, and I went below to my cabin, and I soon went to sleep; but I had not laid long, when I was awoke by the ship striking upon the rocks. I jumped up, and put on my trowsers and my old jacket, and on deck I went; but when I got there, the sea was making a clean breach right over the ship. And as soon as I got clear of the companion hatch, a cross sea took me and hove me against the larboard bulwarks, and carried me, bulwarks and all, away overboard; and I tried to swim a bit, but I still kept hold of the piece of bulwark, till another tremendous sea took me and hove me on shore. But the blow that I received knocked me senseless, and there I lay till about seven or eight o'clock next morning, when I came to myself, and I found our dog Nero standing along side of me, licking my wounds; for my head was cut, and my left side, where I had been hove against the rocks.

When I got up, which I could scarcely do, I looked round to see if I could see anything of the ship, or any of my shipmates; but I could see nothing, only the dog, and he kept running to a short distance from me, and kept barking at something, and then came back to me again—as much as to say, "come here and look." And at last I went to see what it was, though I had a good deal of trouble to get there: and when I got there, I found one of my shipmates lying among the rocks, and you may depend I was glad to see it; but when I tried to get him up, I found he was quite dead, for his head was cut all to pieces. The man that I found was our carpenter, and his name was James Roberts.

Now when I found that he was quite dead, I sat down beside him, and I cried like a child, for I was in great hopes that I should have had a partner in my misfortune; for I could see nothing but starvation before me, and I had a great mind to lie down along side of my shipmate and die; but the dog would not let me, for he kept pulling me by the trowsers for to get up; and the sun was very powerful and hot; so up I got to look for a place to shelter myself, and at last I found one under some trees, where I sat down to rest myself; but I had not sat there long, before I heard my dog barking again very loud, and I got up in hopes of seeing some one alive beside myself, but I could not see anybody; and when I came to my dog, I saw that he had found a land tortoise, which I knew was very good eating, but I had no fire to cook it by; but I knew that the land tortoises have three bladders in them—one full of blood, and two full of water; and, as I was very dry, I killed the tortoise, for I had my knife about me, the only thing then, excepting the clothes I had on, that I had saved from the wreck; and I took one of the bladders of water out of the tortoise, and I drank it, and I found it very good, and I gave the one full of blood to my dog; and I ate some of the lean of the tortoise, and cut it in thin slices, and beat it, and spread it out in the sun to dry for myself to eat, and the rest I gave to my dog;

and the other bladder of water I buried in the sand, close to the trees where I had fixed my present habitation. And after I had eaten, and drank my water, I felt myself a good deal better, and I knelt down to thank the Almighty Giver of all good for his wonderful mercy to me, to send me food in the wilderness that I was in.

My prayer, all alone on the solitary island, made me feel a good deal easier; and I had strength to bury my comrade. I then made my bed, and laid myself down, with my dog along side of me, and soon fell asleep, and I slept very soundly till the next morning.

After I awoke, I went to the beach to see if I could find anything washed on shore from the ship, though I found my side and my head very sore, but I could find nothing that had been washed on shore. And next thing I looked for was to see if I could find anything like a flint; for my chief object was to try to get a fire, for then I should be able to cook my meat for I had found, in my poor shipmate's pockets, a knife and a gimlet, and a few nails, and some chalk; and I tried my knife and his knife on all the stones that looked like flint-stones, to try to strike fire; but I could not find any that would do, so the only thing that I had to do was to try to get two pieces of touch-wood, and rub them together; but now I had nothing but two pocket-knives, but I thought that, with God's help, I should be able to manage it. And I went back to my grove, where I had slept the night before, to get something to eat; but not coming back the same way that I went, I found some sorrel, which has a small leaf, and a big stem, which is a capital thing to quench your thirst; for the stem is full of moisture, of a sourish taste, and it is a very good substitute for water.

At finding this prize, I returned my hearty thanks to God for sending me in the way to find it. Although the water that I got out of the tortoise's bladder was very good, still the sorrel and it made it more pleasant; and, after I and my dog had our breakfast, we went to look for some touch-wood, which, thanks be to God, I found, after a good deal of trouble. And it cost me nearly three month's trouble and hard work before I got a fire, which I did by rubbing the two pieces of wood together; and during this time I lived nearly as I have mentioned, only that I tried several more herbs; and I found a sort of asparagus, which I found contained a good deal of moisture, which was a great help to me; and I tried a good many different barks of trees to make something as a substitute for bread; and, at last, after trying a good many, I found some that, after being baked in the sun, did very well; so, thanks be to God, I got on better and better every day.

Now I must tell you the way I kept an account of my time:—I dug two holes in the earth, and I got thirty small stones, and the day that I was cast away upon the island being the 3d day of February, I counted from that time, and put a stone into the empty hole every day, till the thirty stones were all gone; and then, with my knife, I cut a great notch on a tree that stood close by; so, by these means, I could tell how many days I had been on the island. And now, after I got a fire, I used to cook my meat, and make myself as comfortable as my circumstances would allow me to be. But you might, perhaps, wish to know what I did for a pot or a frying-pan?—why, I used the top shell of the tortoise for a pot, and the under shell for a frying-pan. And I took great care that my fire should not go out, for there was plenty of cork or match-wood on the island; and I knew, by former trials, that the wood would keep alight while there was a bit of it left, but it would never come to a blaze; and, to prevent my fire from going out, I always had two or three pieces alight.

Being busy the chief part of the time that I had been on the island in making a fire, I had scarcely gone any distance from the beach, and from my grove. I resolved now to go into the interior of the island, and, with this intent, I lighted a couple of large pieces of match-wood, that I knew would last two or three days, and away I and my dog started for the middle part of the island; and we traveled on a good while, when my dog fell a barking at something; and, to my great surprise, what should it be but two wild goats, that had been laying down, when the dog came close to them. Now my seeing these goats, put a desire into my head, that I should like to get some of them; for I thought that I might get some goat's milk, which would be a great addition to me.

I began to get tired of walking, and I went and got a small tortoise, and killed him; and I found plenty of sorrel here, so I gave my dog something to eat and to drink. I had some myself; for I had taken care to bring a piece of match-wood along with me, and there being plenty of dry brushwood, I soon made a fire, and roasted my meat; and after I had my dinner, and returned thanks to God, I and my dog went on our travels again; and we traveled a good distance, and we saw plenty more goats. And by tracing the goats, I found a small spring of water, and you may depend that I shall never forget how sweet the first drop of water tasted, that I had; and after having a good drink, I returned thanks to the Almighty for his wonderful mercy to me. And now, as it was beginning to be late, I resolved to stop where I was for the night; so, on that account, I began to look out for a place to shelter from the dew; and when I had found one, I gathered some leaves and some moss, and made myself a bed.

As it was early yet, I looked round to see what sort of place I had got to; but I soon found that I had nearly got to the north-east part of the island, for I had not walked far from my new habitation, when I could see the sea: and finding the place so convenient to the sea, and more cool than the lee-side of the island, I resolved to shift my habitation round to this part of the island; and, with this intention, I went to my new lodging; and after I had some supper, and given some to my dog, and returned my sincere thanks to God for the many blessings he had showered down upon me, I laid myself down to sleep; but I could not sleep for a long time, for my thoughts were occupied how I should be able to make myself master of some of the goats that I had seen. At length I came to the resolution to make myself a bow and some arrows; and I thought that if I was able to wound a goat, my dog would be able to catch him. And, with this thought, I went to sleep, and I slept very soundly till the next morning, when, after returning my thanks to God for preserving me during the night, I made a fire, and cooked myself some breakfast; and after I and my dog had done, we traveled on to my old habitation, and soon packed up my all.

When I counted my stones, I found that I had been one hundred and fifteen days on the island. And away I and my dog went, back to my new lodgings; and we got back before sunset, for we had taken a nearer road than we did the first day. And after I had put all my store in my new house, I went to bed, for I was tired; and the first thing I did, next morning, was to regulate my time-keeper, in digging two more holes, and put my stones in them, and cutting my notches in a tree that stood close by. And now I began to work at my bow and arrows; for that purpose I killed a large tortoise, to get his gut to make a string for my bow; and after getting a piece of wood, fit for a bow, I made it; and I found my gimlet that I found in my poor shipmate's trowsers' pocket very handy. And after my bow was done, I went to work to make the arrow, and I finished my weapon in three days, which I don't think very long, considering I had nothing but my knife to do it with, and I had everything to look for before I could use it.

I was soon repaid for my trouble; for the fourth day that I was out with my bow and arrow, and my dog, I wounded an old she-goat, and my dog soon caught it; and as he and I were bringing the goat home, I found that two young ones followed the old one; and as the old goat was only wounded in the leg, I tied her up outside my grove; and I had the pleasure of seeing them come to the old one, and sucking her. After they were tired of sucking, they laid down beside the old dam.

My next trouble was to make a place to keep my goats in; and I turned to, and fenced a piece of ground all round, which cost me a good deal of trouble; but I completed a piece in four days, and I put my goats into it: and now, keeping the young ones by themselves, I had some milk to drink, which was a great help to me; and I returned the Almighty God thanks for his wonderful mercy to me. And now that I saw I had made a good job of the fence, that I had made for my goats, I intended to make a sort of fence round my dwelling-place, and to try to cover it more from the sun, for rain is scarcely ever known in these islands, for I had been here now one hundred and eighty-four days, and I had no rain all that time; so to work I went, and finished my job in about thirty days, and I found myself a good deal more comfortable than I was before.

I had not long finished my job, when one night, which I believed to be nearly the latter end of September, it came on to blow and rain as if heaven and earth were coming together, and very heavy lightning and thunder along with it. It was a night such as I had not experienced since I had been on the island, and I thanked the Lord Almighty for putting it into my head to put my house to rights, in order to shelter me from the weather. But about midnight, as near as I could guess, the roof, and everything that I had put on my house, was blown off, and I was exposed to the open air. The only thing that I was fretting about was, that the rain would put my fire out, which I had been at so much trouble in getting; but about four or five o'clock next morning, the rain ceased, and the wind died away, and by sunrise it was quite a fine morning. And, thanks be to God, my fire was not gone out; but on looking round me, to see the destruction which the wind and lightning had caused, and still I was saved among the living to praise the Lord, which I did, I hope, with a true heart, I had the misfortune to find that one of my young goats had been killed by lightning, for he was black and blue all over; my house was much damaged, and my bed soaking with rain.

Repairing my house and bed cost me a good deal of trouble and time, for I had never been properly well since the night the hurricane swept over the island, and I found myself getting worse every day. My legs began to swell very much, so that I was scarcely able to go to the spring to fetch my water, or able to catch a tortoise; but my dog, my only companion, used to fetch them to me. But at last I got that bad, that I was not able to get up out of my bed-place, and I nearly gave myself up for lost.

I had lain in this state two or three days, when one day, as I was nearly famishing with thirst, I heard my dog barking a good deal more than he used to do. I tried to get up, but I could not. I called my dog, "Nero! Nero!" as loud as I could, but still he kept on barking, but I could hear that he was getting nearer to my habitation. But what was my surprise when I heard a human voice singing out to some one, "Come along, Jack, I must go and see where this dog is going to!" I cannot express my feelings at the first sound of a human voice. Joy and fear overcame me, so that I was nearly fainting away when my dog came in, and two men close to him. They were quite surprised at finding me there, and they asked me several questions, which I was scarcely able to answer; but after a little while, I asked one of them to give me a drink of water, which I had in my hat, and after I got a little revived, I asked them how they came there.

They told me they belonged to an American schooner, called the "Flying Fish," of Baltimore, and that they came on shore there to get some wood, and to try if they could find any water, and that, on landing, they had seen the dog; and being surprised at seeing a dog upon the island, which they knew was uninhabited, the second mate and one man had followed the dog till they found me; and I told them, as well as I was able, how I came on the island, and how long I had been there. The second mate, who was talking to me, told me that he would go on board of the schooner directly, and acquaint the captain of the schooner of my condition; but I begged of him to allow his shipmate to stop along with me while he was gone, to which he agreed, and away he went; but my feelings during the time he was gone I can't express, for hope and fear were mixed together.

I asked the man that was left along with me to make my fire up, and fry some tortoise, for the dog had dragged a large one close to my hut, and my new companion soon killed him, and cooked the best part of it, and before it was quite done, the captain of the schooner came up to my hut, and he brought four men along with him, to carry me down to the boat, and he brought some rum, and some water, and some biscuit along with them, for me to have something to eat and to drink before they took me away; and the captain and the men had some of my tortoise that their shipmate had cooked, and they liked it very well. But the first morsel of bread that I tasted I could scarcely get down, for it was now two hundred and seventy days since I had tasted a bit of bread; and still the Lord had been kind enough to preserve me, and send me help when I was in the greatest distress, and could not help myself; and how wonderful that the dog should be the means of my deliverance! It was a long time before I came to again, when I got on board the schooner; and the people on board told me afterward that they could not keep the dog from me during the time that I was lying senseless; and as soon as he saw that I moved and spoke again, he ran fore and aft the decks like as if he was mad.

When I came on board of the "Flying Fish," it was the 29th day of October, 1820, and I was cast away on the 3d day of February, which made exactly two hundred and seventy days that I had been on James' Island. Now the schooner lay there eight or ten days after I had been on board, to get wood and tortoises on board; and then we sailed from the island, and the schooner being bound to Baltimore, in America, we went to windward. In the beginning of January, 1821, but a few days after we got round Cape Horn, and being off the Falkland Islands, a sad misfortune befell me: I lost my dog, who died through eating some porpoise liver. Some of the crew of the schooner had caught a porpoise, and the dog, being used so long to live upon raw meat, ate too greedily of the liver, and he died on the 15th day of January, and you may depend that I was very sorry for it; but he was gone, and all the fretting about him would do no good; so we kept on our course, and arrived in Baltimore on the 2d of March, 1821. Now the captain and the crew had given me a good many clothes on the passage, for what I had on the island were all worn out, and my legs were a good deal better; and the captain of the schooner took me up to the owners, and told them what state he had found me in; and the owners were kind enough to send me to a boarding-house, where I was to stay till I got well, and they made me a present of twenty dollars, for which, and all the other kindnesses which I had received from them, I thanked them kindly.

I staid in Baltimore till the 20th day of April, when I found myself quite well, and shipped on board of a brig, called the "Buck," of Boston, and she was bound to New Orleans, where we arrived on the 16th day of May. I forgot to mention that before I left Baltimore I sent a letter to Mr. Mellish, in an English ship bound to Liverpool, to acquaint him with the loss of the "Spring Grove," and I acquainted him that the ship had one thousand three hundred barrels of oil in her when she was lost, and every other particular about her; and I told him that I intended to come to London myself as soon as I had an opportunity.

Now when we arrived at New Orleans, our brig was found unfit for sea, for she was very leaky, and we, the crew, were discharged from her; and I being in a strange place, and having very little money, I was obliged to look out for another ship as soon as I could; and I shipped myself in a steamboat, called the "Olive Branch," to go from New Orleans up the Mississippi to the Falls of Ohio; and I got twenty-five dollars per month. I went up in the "Olive Branch" as far as a place called Shipping Point, close to the Falls of the Ohio; but it now being the latter part of June, and the river being very low, our steamer was laid up, and I was paid off. I got back to New Orleans on the 10th of December, but I had the misfortune to hurt my leg on the passage down; and when we got to New Orleans, and our cargo discharged, I found my leg so bad that I was obliged to take my discharge from the "Lafayette," and go on shore under the doctor's hands; and I was obliged to go to a boarding-house; but, thanks be to God, I had saved a little money.

Now the house that I was recommended to was kept by a widow woman, and she seemed to be a very industrious woman, but she was obliged to keep a bar-keeper, or a man to look after the business. Now after I had been in the house for about two months, she asked me, one day, if I could read and write; I told her yes. She asked me if I would be kind enough to have a look at her books, for she was pretty well sure that the man that she had for a bar-keeper had cheated her. I told her that I would do it with pleasure; for my leg was getting nearly well; and, on overhauling her book, I found a great many frauds. And when the man was asked about it, he said that he would settle everything in the morning; but that night he ran away, and took nearly fifty dollars, that he had received from different people, along with him; and we never saw no more of him.

Now my leg, as I told you before, was nearly well; and she asked me if I would be kind enough to look after her bar; and, after a little consideration, I consented. And I showed her what money I had of my own before I had anything to do with her money; and she agreed to give me twenty dollars a month, and my board; and I went and took charge of everything. But, to make a long story short, before I had been her bar-keeper two months, I became her husband; for I married her the 5th of April, 1822; and, thanks be to God, a very good wife she proved to be. And I began to look upon myself as settled; and I wrote a letter to my son and to Mr. Mellish, telling Mr. Mellish that, if he thought my son deserved it, or stood in need of it, to let him have the sixty pounds that I put in his hands when I was paid off from the "Policy."

I was beginning to do very well; but we appoint, and the Almighty disappoints; for, the sickly season setting in very severe, my wife, my dearest Martha, caught the fever, and died in three days after she was taken bad; and I buried her on the 25th of July, 1822. I had not been long at home before I was taken bad, and the doctor advised me to go to the hospital, which I accordingly did; but, before I went to the hospital, I had my house shut up, and I left what goods there were, in charge of my late wife's sister; and I took about two hundred dollars, in notes, along with me in the hospital. I staid in the hospital about six weeks, when it pleased God to let me recover, and get to my senses again; for I had been out of my mind nearly all the time that I had been there. And when I came to inquire after my late wife's sister, I was obliged to hear that she died about four days after I had gone into the hospital. But I soon got better, and I came out of the hospital on the 1st day of October; and I felt myself very weak when I came out into the fresh air.

When I got home to where I had lived, I found an empty house; for, after my sister-in-law died, everything was taken out of the house, and was ordered to be burnt. So here I was again, nearly as bad as I was when I first came to New Orleans; and I began to take a dislike to the place, and I intended to leave it as soon as I could; and the very next day I shipped myself on board the "Friendship;" and we sailed from New Orleans, the 10th day of October, for Campeachy, to take in a cargo of logwood, to take to London; and, thanks be to God, I got quite well again. And we soon got our cargo; and we sailed from Campeachy the 2d of November, and we had a very good passage home, as far as the English Channel, when the wind got round to the eastward, which delayed us three or four weeks. Our provisions got very short, and especially our water; and, our ship being very leaky, we were obliged to put into Falmouth harbor, where we discharged all her cargo; and the owners came down to Falmouth, and, finding that the ship wanted a great deal of repair, they paid the crew their wages, and I was discharged on the 5th day of January, 1823.

Now it being the dead of the winter, and knowing that there would be very few ships, in London, to be got at that time of the year, I shipped myself on board of a brig, belonging to Bangor, in Wales, called the "Jane Ellen;" and she was bound up the Straits, to Smyrna, with a cargo of pilchards. And we sailed from Falmouth the 12th of January; and, thanks be to God, we had a very good passage out to Smyrna, and we arrived there the 3d day of March; and we kept trading from one place to another till the latter part of 1824; and nothing particular happened during that time. And, thanks be to God, I was in good health, when, on the 10th of October, 1824, when we were lying at Cephalonia, our captain got a freight for London, to take a cargo of currants there; and, when we got our cargo in, we sailed from Cephalonia on the 24th of

October. And we had a very good passage down as far as the rock of Gibraltar, where we were obliged to lay wind-bound for several days, for it blew a very heavy gale of wind; but we held on, though a great many ships parted from their anchors, and were driven on shore; but on the 10th of December it moderated, and we got under weigh, and, thanks be to God, we arrived safe at the Downs on the 24th of December.

Our master being eager to get something fresh on board for Christmas day, for dinner, he sent me on shore, in one of the Deal boats, to get something; for the master himself was very poorly, and he was not able to go. And I had been mate of the brig for about eighteen months, for we lost our mate, that came out from England with us, at Smyrna, by sickness; so ashore I went. And when I left the brig, the weather looked very fair, for the time of the year, and the wind was about west by south; but we scarcely got on shore, when the wind shifted round to the south-south-east, and it came on to blow tremendous hard, and a heavy sea came tumbling in upon the beach. And I wanted the watermen to go off at once, but they refused to go off till low water, which was about three o'clock in the afternoon, and when I landed, it was about eleven o'clock in the forenoon; and the weather came on in thick snow showers; and two of the Deal boats tried to get off, but both boats were swamped, and two of the Deal men, belonging to the boats, were drowned. Now here I was on shore in a heavy gale of wind, and my poor shipmates out there by themselves; for our captain, as I told you before, was very poorly, and had been so ever since we left Gibraltar; and there were only three men and two boys on board beside himself; but I could not help them, if I had given a hundred guineas.

I could not get a boat to take me on board of the "Jane Ellen." When I found that none of the boats could go off with me, I went to Lloyd's agents, and acquainted them how I was situated, for I knew that the brig and cargo were insured; but they told me that I must content myself till the weather moderated, and they would take care to send me on board as soon as possible. But as night came on, the gale was still increasing, and there were no hopes of me getting on board that night. But I could not sleep, though several people offered me a bed, and I staid on the beach till daylight next morning. But it was still blowing very hard, but the weather was clearer, and we could see no vessel in the Downs, only one large ship, and that was a man-of-war, and the poor "Jane Ellen" was nowhere to be seen. What to do, or what to think, I did not know; but I concluded that the brig was lost, and all hands perished. I went to Lloyd's agents again, and asked them what they thought of it. They told me that they expected she was lost; and they told me that I ought to think myself very lucky that I was on shore out of her; but still the captain of the brig was to blame to send any of his crew on shore out of the ship, while she was lying in an open roadstead, and especially this time of the year; and that was all the satisfaction I could get from them.

Now I was on shore, but scarce any money in my pocket; for I had nearly been two years in this brig, and had no occasion to draw any money from the captain; for, when I joined her, I had my pay from the "Friendship" to fit me out, and I had money on board, beside my clothes. But here I was hove upon the wide world once more; and I staid in Deal for one week, to try if I could hear anything concerning the "Jane Ellen;" but hearing nothing by New Year's day, I intended to travel up to London, and go and see if my son was alive or not. Now all the money I had in my pocket when I started from Deal, which is seventy-two miles from London, was three shillings and sixpence; and it was bitter cold weather, for I started from Deal on the 2d day of January, 1825; and, thanks be to God and good friends, I arrived in London on the 6th of the month; and tired enough I was; and all the money that I had left was twopence. I had middling good clothes on my back, and I went to Mr. Mellish to inquire after my son; and when I told Mr. Mellish of my new misfortune, he told me that I was a wonderful man; but when I asked him concerning my son, he told me that he was married to his housekeeper, and that they were doing very well; and that he had paid the sixty pounds to my son, according to my wish. I thanked him very kindly; and he told me that my son, in coming home in the "Seringapatam," had the misfortune to fall out of the maintop, and broke his left arm, and it not being properly set, he had partly lost the use of it; and when he came home, having a very good character, Mr. Mellish made him wharfinger at his wharf, and after a little time he got married.

I told Mellish how I was situated in regard to money, and he was kind enough to give me five pounds; and he told me, that if my circumstances would ever allow me to pay him, I might, but he should never ask me for it. I thanked him very kindly for it, and I asked him if he would be kind enough to send for my son, which he did; and when my son came in, he was quite surprised at seeing me, and he and I went home to his house. And when I came to tell him how I was situated, he called his wife in, and told her that I should have to stay along with them a few days, and that I was his father; but I could see by the first appearance of her actions that I was an unwelcome guest, for she said she did not know how to make room for me.

I told my son; "Francis," said I, "seemingly your wife, whom I thought to embrace as a daughter, is not agreeable for me to stay here. Give me a few shillings, so that I can go and get a lodging somewhere for the night;" for I did not let him know that Mr. Mellish had given me five pounds. He told me he would try what he could do, and away he went; and I heard him and his wife having very high words outside of the room, and between other words that passed, I heard her calling me a beggar. My temper, at that present time, could not stand that, and I got up and went out, and wished them a good night, and I left the house, and I have never seen her since; and away I went down to Tooley street, in the Borough, and there I got a lodging.

In a few days I got pretty well round again, and I went to Lloyd's office to report the loss of my brig, and likewise to see if I could recover any of my wages; for I was sent on shore on duty, and certainly I ought to be entitled to my wages to the time we sailed from the last port; and they told me that as I gave in my claim for wages due to me for the "Jane Ellen," that as soon as they had returns from Sierra Leone, they would pay me what was due to me.

I staid in London till the middle of March, when I shipped on board of a brig called the "Intrepid" packet, and she was bound from London to Gibraltar, and from there to Buenos Ayres. And we sailed from London the 2d day of April, 1825, and, thanks be to God, we had a very good passage to Gibraltar, where we arrived the 1st day of May, and sailed from there the 5th of June for Buenos Ayres, where we arrived on the 30th day of July.

Now at this present time the Buenos Ayreans were at war with the Brazilians, and the River Plate was blocked up; so we were obliged to go and lay in a place called Helsinado, about seven miles from Buenos Ayres, and there we laid till March, 1826, when our captain got a freight for Gibraltar, to carry some of the old Spaniards home to their own country; and we sailed from Helsinado on the 5th of April, 1826. But coming from Helsinado, down the River Plate, we were caught in a very heavy Pampiro, and were very near losing the brig; for our mate that came from England with us, had left us at Buenos Ayres; and the young man that we got in the room of him was not experienced with the country he was sailing in; and at twelve o'clock, when I came on deck, he told me to clear away the flying jib, and I told him, "You had better shorten sail as fast as you can, or else you will lose every stitch of canvas that you have got set, for I see it arising;" and I showed it to him; but he said, "Never mind, do as you are told." And I told him that for the safety of myself and the brig, I could not do it; but if he would not shorten sail, I should be obliged to call Captain Gordon, which I accordingly did. And when he came on deck, we began to shorten sail; but it was too late then, for the Pampiro struck the brig, and she was hove on her beam-ends, and every stitch of canvas that we had set blew into ribbons.

I advised our captain to let go both anchors, so as to fetch the ship's head to wind, that she might righten; and accordingly I went forward, and got some of the men to lend me a hand; and I let go the best bower anchor, which brought her head to wind; and the brig rightened, for she had then been nearly a quarter of an hour on her beam-ends; but still she would not bring up; and, with a good deal of trouble, I got the small bower anchor clear, and let it go. And she took the chain to the beam-end, but still she would not bring up, but still kept drifting; and we were afraid we should drive on a sand called the English bank. So, after a good deal of trouble, we got our stream anchor clear, and let it go; and after she got the best part of the stream cable, she brought up in five fathoms water. But all this time neither the captain nor I could see anything of the mate, and we were afraid that he had gone overboard, and had been drowned; but after we got everything middling snug, we found our mate stowed away down in the fore-hold, among the water-casks; and he said that he was knocked down the fore-hatchway when the squall first struck the ship. We did not believe his story; but the captain had been obliged to make him mate, for he was one of the owners' nephews.

Now after we got everything pretty snug, we set the watch again, and next morning it turned out to be very fine, and we went to work to bend a fresh set of sails, for our old ones were all blown to pieces; and after getting our anchors up, and stowing them, which took us two days, we went down to Monte Video, where we arrived on the 12th day of April. And after putting everything to rights, we sailed for Rio de Janeiro, where we arrived on the 1st of May. Now as I told you that we had lost all our canvas in the Pampiro, and bent all new ones, except what we called our fore and aft spencer, and the brig having only one on board, I was obliged to make a new one, for the captain knew that I was able to do it; and accordingly the captain bought the canvas, and I cut the sail out; and on the 18th of May I and the mate were working about the sail, and I saw him putting a piece of canvas the wrong way; and I said, "Mr. Middleton, you are putting that piece in the wrong way."

He told me to mind my own business; and words arose between him and me, and at last he jumped up and struck me. I was obliged to stand in my defense, and I gave him a good beating, so that he was obliged to go below. Now I knew well enough that when the captain came on board, he would take the mate's part, and I should have to go on shore to go to prison, which I did not like at all.

Knowing the "Ranger" frigate wanted hands, I hailed the "Ranger's" boat, and she came along side, and I told the officer of the boat what had happened, and that I intended to enter for his Majesty's service, upon which he told me to get into the boat; and so I got once more on board of a man-of-war. My old captain tried all that he could do to get me back again; but I found that a man-of-war was quite different from what it was when I was in them in war time; for there was no starting, or fears of any flogging; and if a man was only attentive and clean, and did what he was told, he never needed to be afraid of getting himself into trouble. So, after I got settled on board of the "Ranger," the captain was kind enough to give me the rate of gunner's mate; and I did very well. And we sailed from Rio de Janeiro the latter part of May, bound to Callao, on the coast of Peru. We had a long and tedious passage round the Cape, but arrived safe at Valparaiso on the 19th of June, after a passage of seventy-seven days. We staid on the coast of Peru till the beginning of 1828; and on the 5th of February a sad accident happened to me—for I was both shot and drowned on that day!

To explain this, I must go to some particulars that occurred when we were lying at a place called Coquimbo, the last place we were going to touch at before we went round the Horn. And the governor of the place and his suite being on board to take their farewell of our captain and officers, and our ship being hove short, and all ready for starting, and our captain intended to salute the governor when he left the ship, and in getting the ship under weigh, I was sent to look out for the buoy. And I being in the larboard fore-chains, when the anchor was up to the bows, and after the anchor was settled and fixed, I went forward upon the anchor, to try to get the buoy-rope clear of the anchor-stock; and while in the act of going forward, they fired the forecastle gun, which was a long nine-pounder; and the whole charge reached me, and hove me away from the ship, and knocked the senses out of me, so that I laid upon the water like one dead; but I soon began to go down. But there was an English brig lying there, called the "Mediæval," of London, and her boat had been on board of our ship, to put some letters on board, for us to take home; and she shoving off from the ship when the accident happened, they saw my hat, and they picked it up, and then they saw the wake I made in going down, and they hooked me with a boat-hook, for I was going down as fast as I could; and they hauled me into the boat, and brought me on board of my ship. But I was senseless to the whole of it; so I did not come to myself again, not till next day, about dinner time. And I was told that our doctor said that I was dead, and that they were going to heave me overboard; but a young gentleman, a doctor's mate, a passenger, said that I was not dead; and he, with God's help, saved my life. If anybody should doubt my tale about being shot and drowned, I could bring plenty of witnesses that saw it, both officers and men.

The next day, when I came to my senses, I felt very weak; but I soon got better, and I was able to go to my duty in about a fortnight's time. And we had a very good passage round Cape Horn; and we arrived in

Rio de Janeiro in the beginning of April; and after we completed our water, we sailed for England; and we arrived at Spithead on the 10th of June, 1828.

When I came back, I went on board of the "Castor" frigate, and I was shipped as able seaman, for she had no vacancy for a petty officer, but I was promised the first vacancy that occurred. We went to join the experimental squadron in the North Sea, under the command of Sir Pulteney Malcom, and there we cruised till the beginning of August; and then the fleet went to the Cove of Cork, and from there we went a cruising off the Land's End. On the 5th of February, 1833, we were ordered to go to Chatham to refit; and while at Chatham, fitting out, I got married to an old widow woman, who was nearly my own age, and a very good wife I found she was; and I married her on account that she had a heavy family to bring up, and I thought I could do no better with my money than to assist the widow and the fatherless; and, thanks be to God, I have never missed it.

Now, after our ship was fitted out, we were ordered to go to Lisbon, where we arrived on the 12th of June, and from there we were ordered to go to Oporto to lay off the bar; and our captain, God bless him, was kind enough to make me quarter-master. And on the 13th of September, I having the middle watch on deck, that is, from twelve o'clock at night till four o'clock next morning, our butcher—his name was Henry Ellis—was very bad in the sick bay; and the sick bay men came to me, about two o'clock, telling me that Ellis, the butcher, was very bad, and that he wanted to see me; and after asking permission from the officer of the watch, I went down to the sick bay, and I found Ellis very bad, for the doctor did not expect he would live till the morning.

Ellis asked me to grant him one favor, and he being in the state that he was in, I could not well refuse him; and I told him that anything that laid in my power I would do for him; and he asked me to speak to the captain to have him buried on shore, for "I know I can't live much longer." And then, getting hold of my hand, he said to me, "Swear that, if it ever lay in your power, you will protect my wife and children." I promised it to him; for I being a married man at that time, I had little thought that it would ever be in my power to perform it, for my wife lived at Chatham, and his at Portsmouth, and I only promised him to satisfy his mind; and, poor soul, he died very shortly after I had left him. And the next morning, the first thing I did was to acquaint the captain of poor Ellis's last wish, and the captain very kindly granted it; and we took him on shore in the bar-boat, and he was buried in the English burial-ground at Oporto.

We staid off Portugal till March, when orders came out from England for our ship to proceed to Plymouth, to refit our ship, to attend upon the Queen, who was going that summer to the Continent to see her friends. We arrived in Plymouth by the latter part of April; and after we had refitted our ship, we went round to Portsmouth, to take the state barge on board, in order to attend upon Queen Adelaide; and from Portsmouth we went to the Nore, where we laid till the Queen came down from London in her yacht. And from there we went to Helvoëtsluys, on the coast of Holland; and after landing the Queen, we went back to Sheerness, where we took in stores for the flag-ship at Lisbon. And on the 23d day of August we sailed from the Nore, and went down to the Downs; and on the 26th day of August, at three o'clock in the morning, we got under weigh from the Downs, with the wind about north-north-east. And a little after six o'clock in the morning, being just below Dover, we had the misfortune to run the "Chameleon," revenue-cutter, down; and out of seventeen men and officers on board of her, we could only save two men and two boys. Though our ship was hove to instantly, and our quarter boats down, we could not save more; so there were thirteen poor souls drowned.

We staid by the spot some time afterward, but we could see no more of anything belonging to her. And we proceeded down to Plymouth, and there we had a court-martial upon our captain and officers, and our captain was honorably acquitted; but our third lieutenant was dismissed the service, and all hands on board were very sorry for it, for he was a very good man. And after the court-martial was over, we sailed for Santander, on the coast of Spain, where we arrived on the 1st of October; but it being a very bad roadstead for ships to lay in, in winter time, we went down to a place called Passages, and there we got our ship in, and moored her. But we found that our ship struck at low water, and we were obliged to go from there to Santander again; and we went into Santander harbor, and there we lay snug enough.

One of my shipmates that came out of the "Castor" along with me, got married, and he lived at Gosport; and he asked me to come over with him, one night, before I left the ship, to spend the evening with him and his wife, and I agreed; and enjoying ourselves till it was too late for me to go on board, I was obliged to get a bed somewhere for the night; and my shipmate's wife took me to a widow woman who let beds. What was my surprise when I found this woman to be the widow of my old shipmate Ellis, our butcher in the "Castor" frigate! All my promises that I made to him came fresh in my mind; and after paying her for my bed, I gave her half the money that I had in my pocket, which was no great deal; and when I left the "North Star," I took my chest and things to her house, and she washed my clothes for me, while we were fitting out; for my wife lived round at Chatham; and after the "Princess Charlotte" was ready for sea, we sailed from Spithead on the 3d day of July; and we were bound up the Mediterranean, to relieve the "Caledonia;" and we relieved her on the 2d day of August.

We kept cruising about at sea, for we could not go into Malta, for it was very sickly. We arrived at Malta the latter part of October; and I had not been there long, when I received a letter from Chatham, acquainting me of my wife's death. She died the same day that I sailed from Spithead, after being bad only twenty-four hours. We lay in Malta all the winter; and the latter part of January, 1838, I was taken very bad; and I was obliged to be invalided on the 14th day of February, from Malta hospital. As soon as I was able to be moved, I was sent home in the "Portland" frigate; and she took me and some more invalids as far as the Rock of Gibraltar, where we were sent on board of the "Bellerophon," and she took us to Portsmouth; and we arrived at Spithead on the 8th day of April. And from her I was sent on board of the flag-ship, and from there I was discharged. And after I got my pay from the "Princess Charlotte," I went up to London, to pass the Board of Admiralty, for my pension; but all that they gave me was seventeen pounds, four shillings, per annum. And from there I went to Chatham, to see my late wife's family; but I found that they had made away with everything that belonged to me. And when I found how things were, I came back again to Gosport, with a full intent to fulfill my oath, that I swore to Henry Ellis, when he was dying. And accordingly I told Ellis's widow all that had happened between me and her late husband; and I told her that I would do anything in my power for her and her children; and that, if she was a mind to wait till my last wife had been dead a twelvemonth, I would marry her; and, after a little consideration, she consented. And we were married on the 26th day of July, 1838, in Stoke Church.

On the 15th of August, 1844, I was discharged, and the Admiralty granted me a pension of twenty-one pounds per annum for life; and, with what little I can earn, I live as comfortable as circumstances will allow me to be: and I hope that I am truly thankful to the Lord for the many blessings and mercies that I have received at his hands through life. Oftimes, when I see a poor man or woman going along without any shoes on them, or scarcely any clothes to cover them, how thankful I am to feel that I have got a bed to lie on, and clothes to cover me, and a house to shelter me from the weather. Have I deserved to be thus favored any more than them? No; but it is God's mercy that provides for me; and I hope that the Lord will grant me one prayer, and that is, contentment with the lot the Almighty has been pleased to give me. And I find every day new blessings and mercies to be thankful for; and especially for health, which is one of the greatest blessings we can enjoy; for here I am, a man seventy-three years old, and knocked about at sea better than fifty years, in which time I experienced some hard trials; and still, thanks be to God, some days I walk above twenty miles, which is a great deal for a man of my age. But I know that the Lord fits the back to the burden.

DESTRUCTION

OF THE

OCEAN STEAMER ARCTIC,

BY COLLISION WITH THE VESTA, A FRENCH PROPELLER, ON THE BANKS OF NEWFOUNDLAND, ON WEDNESDAY, THE 27TH OF SEPTEMBER, 1854, BY WHICH DISASTER

MORE THAN THREE HUNDRED PERSONS PERISHED.

THE Ocean Steamer Arctic formed one of the Collins' line of American steamers, plying between New York and Liverpool, so called in contradistinction to those of the Cunard or British line, the latter having been built in England, and owned and controlled by an English company. The Arctic was built in New York, in 1850, at an expense of nearly one million of dollars, and was one of the largest and noblest steamships in the world. Of beautiful proportions and great speed, she was the pride of her countrymen, as a specimen of their attainments in marine architecture.

On her homeward bound passage, at noon, on the 27th of September, 1854, she came in collision with the French propeller Vesta, on the banks of Newfoundland; and a few hours thereafter the last vestige of her noble form, together with more than three hundred of her passengers and crew, disappeared beneath the waters. The fate of the smaller vessel was more fortunate. Provided by her more cautious builders with bulkheads, or water-tight partitions, between her different sections, she succeeded in gaining port in safety.

When tidings of this awful event reached our country, a profound sensation was created. The people of the city of New York, the most mercurial and impulsive of any in America, the earliest to be aroused by, and the earliest to forget, any startling event, were most intensely excited. The Arctic was a New York vessel; the pride of the great commercial metropolis; and numbers of her prominent citizens were known to have been on board of her. To give an idea of the effect there, we make brief extracts from a city paper of the day.

"The sorrow and excitement in New York, on the reception of the sad tidings, were beyond expression. Thousands of our citizens are bereaved of relatives, and tens of thousands have lost friends and acquaintances. Early in the morning the newspaper offices, and the office of the steamship company, were thronged with anxious inquirers for further news, and all day long the crowds were kept up by fresh arrivals. The flags on the City Hall, on the hotels, and the shipping in the harbor, were at half-mast through the day. Business was neglected, and the whole town bore on its outward features evidences of the sorrow within. There were hundreds of persons crowding Adams & Co.'s Office, waiting their several turns to see Mr. Burns, one of the saved; and each concerned to ascertain whether there was not some possible chance that a beloved brother, or sister, or friend, in the Arctic, had escaped. Old men, as well as young, were sobbing like children, and telling their grief to the passers-by, with that absence of all reserve which so overpowering a misfortune is apt to produce.

In the office of E. K. Collins & Co., the proprietors of the line, a similar scene was being enacted. A large crowd had collected to hear the report of Mr. Brennan, an *attache* of the enginery department, whose careworn looks, and marks of excessive fatigue, showed that he was one of the survivors of the sad catastrophe. A deep feeling of anxiety seemed to pervade the minds of all present, and eager questions were propounded to Mr. Brennan in rapid succession. Some described the personal appearance of absent ones, bound to them by affinities and deep friendship, some by ties of consanguinity, and others bound by nearer and dearer ties, and inquired if he had seen them enter any of the boats which left the vessel previous to the last one, on which he was saved. His words were anxiously waited for, and in some instances they were sufficient to buoy up an expiring hope, but in others to lead them to despair of ever meeting the loved ones again on earth.

At brief intervals, the announcement of the arrival of an installment of the telegraphic dispatch from Halifax would draw all to another part of the room, and, with feelings of mingled hope and fear, they listened in breathless silence to the words of the dispatch read by a gentleman connected with the office. When the reading of the installments was finished, many were the impatient exclamations because the names of the saved, in the boats which had arrived, were not forwarded first, instead of Mr. Baalham's account of the catastrophe; and when, at last, the concluding portion of the dispatch contained the list of the names of those who were safe in Halifax, near a hundred hearts beat heavily and rapidly as they stood in expectation of the announcement of a name which was to make them rejoice, or drive them into a despairing gloom. The reading of the list was commenced. The announcement of several names was received with exclamations of deep joy, accompanied with words of thankfulness to heaven for the mercy extended to them. As the end of the list was approached, deeper sighs were drawn, and when it was announced that the names had been all read, '*Oh God!*' '*Oh God!*' were the words that many uttered in the deep anguish that wrung their hearts. The list was again read, but it only confirmed their worst fears; and after the announcement that no more dispatches would be received, those present left the apartment which had been the scene of such exciting interest, and its doors were closed for the balance of the day."

After the announcement by telegraph that Captain Luce, and several of his companions in suffering, had arrived safely in Quebec, the entire city was on the *qui vive*, waiting for the least word in confirmation of the intelligence, and fearing the next announcement would be that the statement was premature, and was not justified by the facts. But as another and another dispatch arrived, each one stating explicitly the safety of the noble captain, who chose to stand by the wreck and make himself his last thought in his efforts to save, a feeling of joy amounting to enthusiasm seemed to animate all; and when it was announced that Captain Luce's statement was being forwarded by telegraph, the most intense anxiety was manifested to know his words. The following is Captain Luce's statement to E. K. Collins, Esq., and dated at Quebec Saturday, October 14, 1854:

"It becomes my painful duty to inform you of the total loss of the Arctic, under my command, with many lives; and I fear among them must be included your own wife, daughter and son, *of whom I took a last leave the moment the ship was going down*, without ever expecting to see the light of another day, to give you an account of the heart-rending scene.

The Arctic sailed from Liverpool on Wednesday, September 20th, at eleven A. M., with two hundred and thirty-three passengers, and a crew of about one hundred and fifty. Nothing of special note occurred during the passage until Wednesday, September 27th, when, at noon, we were on the Banks, in latitude 46° 45′ north, and longitude 52° west, steering west by compass.

The weather had been foggy during the day; generally a distance of half to three quarters of a mile could be seen, but at intervals of a few minutes a very dense fog, followed by being sufficiently clear to see one or two miles. At noon I left the deck for the purpose of working out the position of the ship. In about fifteen minutes I heard the cry of "Hard starboard" from the officer of the deck. I rushed on deck, and had just got out, when I felt a crash forward, and at the same moment saw a steamer under the starboard-bow; at the next moment she struck against our guards, and passed astern of us. The bows of the strange vessel seemed to be literally cut or crushed off for full ten feet, and seeing that she must, probably, sink in a few minutes, and taking a hasty glance at our own ship, and believing that we were comparatively uninjured, my first impulse was to endeavor to save the lives of those on board the sinking vessel. The boats were cleared, and the first officer and six men left with one boat, when it was found our own ship was leaking fearfully.

The engineers were set to work, being instructed to put on the steam pumps, and the four deck pumps were worked by the passengers and crew, and the ship headed for the land, which I judged to be about fifty miles distant. I was compelled to leave my boat with the first officer and crew to take care of themselves.

Several ineffectual attempts were made to stop the leak by getting sails over the bows; but finding the leak gaining on us very fast, notwithstanding all our very painful efforts to keep her free, I resolved to get the boats ready, and as many ladies and children placed in them as possible; but no sooner had the attempt been made *than the firemen and others rushed into them in spite of opposition.*

Seeing this state of things, I ordered the boats astern to be kept in readiness until order could be restored, when, to my dismay, I saw them *cut the ropes in the bow, and soon disappear astern in the fog.* Another boat was broken down by persons rushing at the davits, and many were precipitated into the sea and drowned. This occurred while I had been engaged in getting the starboard guard-boat ready, and placed the second officer in charge, *when the same fearful scene as with the first boat was being enacted—men leaping from the top of the rail, twenty feet, crushing and maiming those who were in the boat.* I then gave orders to the second officer to let go, and row after the ship, keeping under or near the stern, to be ready to take on board women and children, as soon as the fires were out, and the engines stopped. My attention was then drawn to the other quarter-boat, which I found broken down, but hanging by one tackle. *A rush was made for her also, and some fifteen got in, and cut the tackle, and were soon out of sight.* I found that not a seaman was left on board, nor a carpenter, and we were without any tools to assist us in building a raft, as our only hope. The only officer left was Mr. Dorian, the third mate, who aided me, with the assistance of many of the passengers, who deserve great praise for their coolness and energy in doing all in their power up to the very latest moment before the ship sunk.

The chief engineer, with a part of his assistance, had taken our smallest deck-boat, and before the ship went down, pulled away with about fifteen persons.

We had succeeded in getting the fore and main-yard and two topgallant-yards overboard, and such other small spars and material as we could collect, when I was fully convinced that the ship must go down in a very short time, and not a moment was to be lost in getting the spars lashed together to form a raft, to do which it became necessary to get the life-boat, (our only remaining boat,) into the water.

This being accomplished, I saw Mr. Dorian, the third officer, in charge of the boat, taking care to keep the oars on board to prevent them from leaving the ship, hoping still to get most of the women and children in this boat. At last they had made considerable progress in collecting the spars, when an alarm was given that the ship was sinking, and the boat was shoved off without oars or anything to help themselves with; and when the ship sunk, the boat had got clear, probably an eighth of a mile, to leeward.

In an instant, about four and three quarters P. M., *the ship went down, carrying every soul on board with her.*

I soon found myself on the surface, after a brief struggle, with my own helpless child in my arms, when again I felt myself impelled downward to a great depth, and before I reached the surface a second time, had nearly perished, and *lost the hold of my child.* As I again struggled to the surface of the water, a most awful and heart-rending scene presented itself to my view—*over two hundred men, women and children struggling together amidst pieces of wreck of every kind,* calling on each other for help, and imploring God to assist them. Such an appalling scene may God preserve me from ever witnessing again.

I was in the act of trying to save my child, when a portion of the paddle-box came rushing up edgewise, just grazing my head, falling with its whole weight upon the head of my darling child. Another moment, I beheld him lifeless in the water. I succeeded in getting on to the top of the paddle-box, in company with eleven others; one, however, soon left for another piece, finding that it could not support so many. Others remained until they were one by one relieved by death. We stood in water at a temperature of 45°, up to our knees, and frequently the sea broke directly over us. We soon separated from our friends on other parts of the wreck, and passed the night, each one of us expecting every hour would be our last.

At last the wished for morning came, surrounding us with a dense fog—not a living soul to be seen but our own party—seven men being left. In the course of the morning, we saw some water-casks and other things belonging to our ship, but nothing that we could get to afford us any relief. Our raft was rapidly settling, as it absorbed water.

About noon, Mr. S. M. Woodruff, of New York, was relieved by death. All the others now began to suffer very severely for want of water, except Mr. George F. Allen and myself. In that respect we were very much favored, although we had not a drop on the raft. The day continued foggy, except just at noon, as near as we could judge, we had a clear horizon for about half an hour, and nothing could be seen but water and sky. Night came on, thick and dreary, with our minds made up that neither of us would again see the light of another day. Very soon three more of our suffering party fell down from exhaustion, and were washed off by the sea, leaving Mr. Allen, a boy, and myself. Feeling myself getting exhausted, I now sat down, for the first time, about eight o'clock in the evening, on a trunk, which providentially had been found on the wreck. In this way I slept a little throughout the night, and became somewhat refreshed.

Young Keyn, the German boy who was with us, suffered intensely. He happened to have some biscuit with him which had become soaked with the salt-water, and eating these only increased his thirst, and to make matters still worse, he drank some of the sea-water. His sufferings were beyond all description. Twice he jumped overboard, saying he would rather die than suffer as he was doing; and each time we pulled him back on the wreck. At one time he cut open a vein in his arm and sucked his blood.

About an hour before daylight—now Friday, the 29th—we saw a vessel's light near to us. We all three of us exerted ourselves to the utmost of our strength in hailing her, until we became quite exhausted. In about a quarter of an hour the light disappeared to the east of us. Soon after daylight a bark hove in sight to the north-west, the fog having lightened a little, steering apparently for us; but in a short time she seemed to have changed her course, and again we were doomed to disappointment; yet I felt hope that some of our fellow-sufferers might have been seen and rescued by them.

Shortly after we had given up all hopes of being rescued by the bark, a ship was discovered to the east of us, steering directly for us. We now watched her with the most intense anxiety as she approached. The wind changing, caused her to alter her course several points. About noon they fortunately discovered a man on a raft near them, and succeeded in saving him by the second mate jumping over the side, and making a rope fast around him, when he was got on board safely. This man saved proved to be a Frenchman, who was a passenger on board the steamer which we came in collision with.

He informed the captain that others were near, on pieces of the wreck; and, going aloft, he saw us and three others. We were the first to whom the boat was sent, and safely taken on board about three P. M. The next was Mr. James Smith, of Mississippi, second-class passenger. The others saved were five of our firemen. The ship proved to be the Cambria, of this port, from Glasgow, bound to Montreal, Captain John Russell.

From the Frenchman who was picked up, we learned that the steamer with which we came in collision was the screw steamer Vesta, from St. Pierre, bound for and belonging to Grenville, France, and having on board one hundred and forty passengers and twenty seamen. As near as we could learn, the Vesta was steering east-south-east, and was crossing our course two points, with all sails set, wind west by south. Her anchor stock, about seven by four inches square, was driven through the bows of the Arctic, about eighteen inches above the water line, and an immense hole had been made, at the same instant, by the fluke of the anchor, about two feet below the water line, raking fore and aft the plank, and finally breaking the chains, leaving the stock remaining in and through the side of the Arctic; or it is not unlikely, as so much of her bows had been crushed in, that some of the heavy longitudinal pieces of iron running through the ship may have been driven through our side, causing the loss of our ship, and, I fear, hundreds of most valuable lives."

To this account of Captain Luce, we annex that of a passenger, Mr. James Smith, a native of Scotland, now a citizen of Mississippi. It contains some facts not given in any other narrative, and is enhanced by the pious emotions disclosed by the narrator:

"During the day, up to the time of the accident, the weather had been quite foggy, and I was somewhat astonished and alarmed several times when on deck, seeing the weather so thick, that I fancied not more than three or four of the ship's lengths ahead could be seen, and she going on at full speed, without any alarm bell, steam whistle, or other signal being sounded at intervals, in some such manner as I had been accustomed to in a fog on other vessels. At about fifteen minutes after the meridian, eight bells had been struck, and while sitting in my stateroom in the forward cabin, the earnest cry of a voice on deck (who I at the moment took to be the man on the lookout) to "stop her, stop her, a steamer ahead," was heard with alarm by myself and all others in the cabin; at the same time the man giving the alarm could be heard running off toward the engine-room.

I stepped out of my stateroom, and while endeavoring, with Mr. Cook, my room-mate, to calm the excitement among the ladies in the cabin, and before the man giving the alarm on deck had reached the engine-room, we were made aware of the concussion by a somewhat slight jar to our ship, accompanied by a crashing against the starboard bow. It was a moment of awe and suspense, but I think we all seemed to satisfy ourselves that the shock was slight, and that, as we were on so large and strong a vessel, no serious damage had happened or could well happen to such a ship, in an occurrence of such a nature. With such a reliance on my own mind, at any rate, I was very quickly on deck, and in detached accounts from other passengers, learned that a screw steamer, with all sail set, had struck us on the starboard bow, and glancing aft our starboard wheel and wheel-house, struck her again, and she passed off astern of us out of sight immediately in the thick fog. I saw on the first glance at our bulwarks that all was right *with us*, but instantly began to get alarmed from our careening over on the side we had been struck, as well as from the call for the passengers to keep on the port-side. I understood, also, at this time, that one of our boats had been cleared away and lowered with our first officer and six of the men, to render assistance to the other vessel, and that our ship was making round in search of her also.

I saw Captain Luce on the paddle-box, giving orders in one way and another, and most of the officers and men running here and there on the deck, getting into an evident state of alarm, without seeming to know what was to be done or applying their energies to any one thing in particular, except in getting the anchors and other heavy articles over to the port-side of the ship. I looked over the starboard bow and saw several large breaks in the side of our ship, from eight to twelve or fourteen feet abaft of the cut-water, and I was convinced that in the ten or fifteen minutes' time our wheels were further submerged in the water than usual. Our ship seemed to right herself somewhat after getting the deck weight upon the larboard, but it was too evident that

Captain Luce himself, as well as all hands, was becoming aware of our danger; and, from the tremendous volume of water being thrown out from our steam pumps, I was convinced we were making water at a fearful rate.

Then came in full view before us the other vessel, presenting a most heart-rending spectacle; the whole of her bow, for at least ten feet abaft her cut-water, was literally crushed away, leaving, to all appearance, an open entrance to the sea; and how she had remained above water for so many minutes seemed a mystery. Her decks were covered with people, and all her sails on all three of her masts were set. We merely passed her again, and she was in less than a minute hid in the fog, but scarcely out of sight when we heard arise from her deck a loud and general wail of mourning and lamentation. It was just previous to, or at the same time that we thus came in sight of and passed her, that our wheels went over two or three separate individuals in the water, as well as a boat and crew, who had evidently left the other ship for safety on ours. One man, only, we picked up, an old weather-beaten French fisherman, who, having leaped from the small boat before she went under our wheel, caught a rope hanging from our ship, and was finally pulled on board of us, and from whom we learned something of the other vessel. Captain Luce had, by the time of our coming in sight of the Vesta, become so convinced of our own critical situation, that our only or best chance was to keep under headway as fast as possible toward the land.

A deep-seated, thoughtful look of despair began to settle upon every countenance — no excitement, but ladies and children began to collect on deck with anxious and inquiring looks; receiving no hope or consolation, wife and husband, father and daughter, brother and sister, would weep in each other's embrace, or kneel together imploring Almighty God for help. Men would go about the decks in a sort of bewilderment as to what was best to be done; now laying hold of the hand pumps with redoubled energy, or with sickening effort applying their power to the hauling up of freight out of the forward hold, already floating in water before the lower hatches were opened. System of management or concentration of effort was never commenced or applied to any one object. Two separate ineffectual attempts to stop the leaking by dropping a sail down over the bow, were made, and the engines were kept working the ship ahead toward the land; but in the course of an hour, I should think, from the time of the collision, the lower furnaces were drowned out and the steam pumps stopped. Then it seemed to become only a question of how many hours or minutes we would be above water. The first officer with his boat's crew we had left behind from the first. The second officer, with a lot of the sailors, had lowered another boat and left the ship, and a general scrambling seemed to be going on as to who should have places in the only two remaining boats that I saw on deck. The stern tackling of another had given way from the weight of persons in it while it was swinging over the side, and I think several must have been lost with that. I saw one lady hanging to the bow tackle of it after the stern had broken loose. One of those still remaining was a large one, on the quarter-deck, occupied by ladies and children and some few gentlemen. The other was on the upper deck forward, and in the possession of a lot of firemen. Things were in this condition at about two hours after the accident. Captain Luce was superintending the lowering of spars and yards, aided mostly by passengers, for the purpose of making a raft, and complaining that all his officers and men had left him. Most of the women and children were collected round the boat on the quarter-deck seemingly resigned to their fate.

Some few gentlemen exerted all their powers to prevail on others to work on the pumps, but all to no purpose, the ship kept on gaining in quantity as steadily as time progressed. The engines had stopped working, and I, seeing that the chief engineer, with some of his assistants and firemen, had got the forward boat in the water over by the bow, under the pretense I saw of working at the canvas, which was hanging over the bow, so as to sink it down over the leaking places, but seeing, as I thought, symptoms of their real intention to get off from the ship without too many in the boat, I dropped myself down near by them on a small raft of three planks about a foot wide each, and ten or twelve feet long and an inch in thickness, lashed together with some rope and four handspikes, and which I had just previously helped to lower into the water for the purpose of working from about the bow of the ship. Finding it bore me up, I shoved off, intending to get along side of the engineer's boat, but as I shoved off several firemen and one or two passengers dropped down into the boat, the engineer protesting against their doing so, and at the same time pushed off, and pulled well away from the ship, with about twelve or fifteen persons in his boat, declaring to those on board, at the same time, that he was not going off, but would stay by the ship to the last. At the same time, he, or those in the boat with him, continued to pull away in what I considered was the direction of the land, and were in a few minutes lost in the fog.

I now saw there was no probable chance for me but to remain where I was, on my frail little raft, until I could see some better chance after or before the ship went down. She had now settled down to the wheelhouses. The upper furnaces had for some time been drowned out. People on board were doing nothing but firing signal guns of distress, trying to get spars overboard, and tearing doors off the hinges, nothing else seemed to present itself, as the means of saving the lives of some three hundred souls still on board.

I have crossed the Atlantic nine times now, and nearly every previous time have had in charge one or more of my family or near relatives, but now, I thanked my God that I had not even an acquaintance with me in this my adversity. I tightened up my little raft as well as I could, so as to make it withstand the buffetings and strainings of the heavy rolling sea, and, with the aid of a long narrow piece of plank, which I tore up off the others, using it as a paddle, I kept hovering within two or three hundred yards of the sinking ship, watching operations there, and keeping myself from being drifted out of sight, so as to have what company there might be left on rafts like my own after our doomed vessel had sunk beneath the surface. In this position, I saw three different small rafts like my own leave the ship, one of them with three and another with two of the firemen standing erect on them, the third with the old Frenchman we had already picked up, and one of the mess boys of the ship sitting on it. Those three rafts all drifted close by me, so near that I was hailed by one and another of them with the request for us all to keep near together, to which I assented, but told them that we had all better try and keep by the ship till she went down. At this time, I noticed that the large boat, which had been on the quarter-deck, was in the water, and was being freighted pretty fully, to all appearance, with several females and a good number of males, and that the raft of spars was at the same time being lashed together, and several getting on it. I noticed also a couple of large empty water-casks, lashed together, with five men on them, apparently passengers, leave the ship and drifting toward me, while within about fifty yards they capsized with the force of a heavy swell, giving their living freight an almost immediate watery grave. Three of them, I noticed, regained the top side of the casks only to be immediately turned over again, and the casks separating, I saw no more of them. My heart sickened at so much of immediate death, and still I almost longed to have been one of them, for at the same instant, and, as near as I can judge, at about four and a half o'clock, the ship began to disappear—stern foremost she entered under the surface, her bow rising a little as she slowly went under; and I distinctly heard the gurgling and rushing sound of the water filling her cabins, from stem to stern, as she went under; taking, I should think, from thirty seconds to a minute in disappearing, with a large number of people still upon her deck.

Thus went down the noble steamer Arctic, leaving nothing behind but a mixture of fragments of the wreck and struggling human beings. I saw one large half-round fragment burst above the surface, and several of the struggling fellow-mortals get on it; this, and the raft of spars, with several on it, and the boat full of people, were all that I could distinctly make out as being left in the neighborhood of where the ship went down to windward; and the three small rafts to leeward, along with my own, were left to pass the night now beginning to close in upon, and hide away from my sight, I wish I could say from my memory, this dreadful day; but such a night of extreme melancholy, despair, and utter loneliness, I hope I shall never again experience. I had, it is true, become familiarized with death, and felt as if it would be great relief to go immediately like the rest; and, for this end, I, with somewhat of satisfaction, thought of the vial of laudanum in my pocket, previously intended for a better use—but, oh! how unprepared was I to see my God, and for my family's sake how necessary I felt it was for me still to live a while longer, else would I have emptied that vial or rolled over the side of my plank most willingly.

The night was cold and chilly, the dense fog was saturating my already wet clothing. I was standing to the ankles in the water, with the the waves every now and then washing me above the knees, no hope in my mind of being drifted to the land, and in a part of the ocean where it is expected a thick fog continually hangs over the surface, precluding the hope of any chance vessel, in passing near us, being aware of our situation—all circumstances seemed to say, it is but a question of how long the physical frame can endure this perishing state, or how long before a more boisterous sea turns over or separates the slightly fastened planks. Thus reflecting, I offered up to Him who ruleth the winds and waves—to Him unto whom we all flee in our deepest distress—a sincere petition for mercy, that, as I had now been called to account, I might, notwithstanding my unworthiness, find an acceptance through the merits of Him who suffered for us, and who stands ready to aid, and who says, Knock and it shall be opened unto you — unto whom can we look, oh, our God! but unto thee?—our whole life is, after all, as this hour, a mere question of a few short days, and what are all the mere vanities transpiring during an ambitious but short existence, compared to an assurance which maketh our latter end a fearless one. Relieved and consoled by this my last petition, I was somewhat calmly resigning myself to await my time, as long as my strength and power of endurance could hold out, when I discovered a large square basket, lined with tin, floating lightly by me — one of the steward's dish baskets it proved to be — and, paddling up to it, I got it aboard, and, with the help of a small piece of rope I had round my shoulders, I lashed it pretty firmly on the top of the plank; thus, not only tending to make my raft more secure, but affording me a comparatively dry place to sit on the edge of it, and, with my feet inside, forming a shelter for my legs up as high as my knees. After getting this all arranged, and while sitting watching the water every now and then dashing over the top of it, and becoming convinced that it would soon be partly filled and add to my discomfort, as well as to the weight of the raft, I was again surprised to hear a distinct rattle against the side of the raft, which, proving to be a small air-tight tin can, a part of a set of such used as life-preservers, I seized hold of it, as an additional token of the presence of a protecting Providence. I cut out one end of it with my pocket-knife, and found it to answer the purpose of what, above anything else, I then needed—a bailing-pot—and by which I was enabled to keep my little shelter clear of water; and so acceptable, as a protection from the cold, damp blast, did I find this little willow house, that I soon found myself cramped down into the inside, thus keeping not only my feet and legs, but the lower part of my body somewhat warm. In this sort of situation, I wore away the tedious night, and the breaking dawn revealed to my sight nothing but thick mist, the unceasing rolling waves, and my own little bark — not a single vestige of all else that the night closed upon was now to be seen.

About midday the sun cleared away the mist, and the heat of his rays was truly grateful; but, oh! how desolate in its very cheerfulness, seemed the prospect he thus unfolded. Over the whole broad expanse of waters, not a sail could be seen, not a thing save the figures of the two firemen, about half a mile distant, still standing erect, and showing themselves at intervals, as every heavy swell raised them on its crest. I had not yet felt either hunger or thirst, for which I was truly thankful, for I had but a handful of dry broken crackers in my hat, which I felt determined to save to the last, and of course no water. I dreaded the craving of either. The day wore on still clear until about an hour before nightfall, when the two firemen (within hailing distance of whom I had worked my way again) discovered a ship under full sail, broadside toward us; but it was with faint hopes of success that I hoisted my handkerchief, tied to the end of the strip of wood I was using as a paddle, the firemen doing the same with a shorter piece of wood in their possession. The ship, at one time, we noticed, laid to or altered her course for a moment, giving us a hope that she had discovered something, but the night closed in again, and with it all our hopes of a rescue.

I passed through this night in a dozing, dreary, shivering, half sensible sort of state, with all sorts of fancies before my drowsy and somewhat disordered mind, and all sorts of pictures in my wakeful moments, both of a pleasing and of a revolting character, floating before me on the dark surface of the water. Now and then, during the night, I fancied myself hailed by various surrounding parties, convinced, as I was, at the same time, that none others were within hailing distance but the two firemen. My disordered fancy, however, kept me for more than half the night, in an agreeable state of excitement, under the firm belief that companies of boats' crews were on the search for us, and most lustily did I answer every fancied or real signal. The morning dawned again, and with it a horrid scene of despair at the gloomy prospect of the same dense, foggy atmosphere, now and then fully developing to view the same two erect figures dancing about on the rolling surf; and, in my selfish liberality, I bargained with myself that I would endure still during this day, seeing that my two companions, who were obliged to be on their feet, supporting each other in a very precarious looking back-to-back attitude, were able to still exist. I felt a little hungry this morning, and ate half a biscuit. While warming myself by about two hours' paddling up toward them, during which the fog partially cleared away, and while close to them, we all became excited at the sight of a sail far to the south, as I thought, but broadside toward us. Like the one on the previous day, I had little hope of her coming much nearer; but, being determined to leave no effort untried which might possibly attract their notice, I stript myself, and taking off my shirt, tied it by the sleeves to the end of my paddle, and, with my handkerchief on a small strip of wood tied on above it, I thought I had a tolerably conspicuous signal, and waved it to and fro for more than an hour, until the ship was nearly out of sight—and just as I had lowered it, in utter hopelessness, we all descried, at the same instant, in the opposite direction, another sail—and on to us—just entering, as it were, into our grand amphitheater, through a cloud of mist that seemed to rise and clear away above the vessel, forming a grand triumphal archway around, our Eureka, like a tower of promise, in the center. Feeling sure, at first sight, that this one was standing toward us, I did not long remain undeceived, for she began to increase in size as time wore slowly on; and, although she was falling to leeward considerably, as she advanced, still I felt sure, if she kept on the same tack, she would undoubtedly see our signals before passing beyond. My large signal, too, continued to drift me nearer to her track, and took me almost out of sight of my two companions.

When within about two or three miles of us, and about an hour and a half after she first hove in sight, we were relieved by her backing her sails, altering her course, and lying-to for awhile; then, hoisting a signal on her spanker-gaff, she put about and bore away, on and on, far in the distance, on the opposite tack, until my heart began to fail again, doubting whether she was beating to windward for us, or had gone on her way, rejoicing in the discovery and rescue of only a portion of the unfortunate wretches within range of her. But, again, how light and buoyant was the joy, as she at last put about, and stood directly for us; and on and on she advanced, like a saving angel, until we could see her noble looking hull distinctly rise and fall, within little over a mile distant from us, when she backed her sails again, and waited for some time in the prosecution of her mission of mercy, no doubt, relieving some of our scattering companions from a like precarious state. Soon, she filled away again; and, at last, lying-to close by the two firemen, I saw her boat lowered with five men in it, who, picking up the two firemen in their course, came dashing along direct for my raft, and soon bouncing alongside, I allowed myself to tumble aboard of them, unable, physically, to adopt anything of a grateful action, and, morally, overpowered with gratitude to God and to those his instruments.

I remained speechless until I got on board the ship. Before getting on board, however, the boat went away off some distance to windward, and picked up the three other firemen, whom I had seen leave the Arctic, but who had been ever since out of view. We all got huddled upon the deck, somehow, although rather awkwardly, and making my way down to her neat little cabin, as well as my stiff feet and legs would allow, I had the pleasure of paying my respects to Captain John Russell, and found myself on board the ship Cambria, of Greenock, bound from Glasgow to Quebec. Captain Russell, the Reverend Mr Walker, of the Free Church of Scotland, and his very kind and attentive lady, Mr. Sutherland, of Caithnesshire in Scotland, Mr. John McNaught, and several of the passengers of the steerage, paid us every attention that I could have desired; Captain Russell giving me up the berth which he had been using himself, and putting everything on board in requisition that might tend in the least to relieve and make us comfortable. I was surprised to learn that the old Frenchman, whom we had picked up from the Vesta, was our good genius on this occasion; being directly in the track of the approaching Cambria, he was picked up by the second mate of the Cambria, Mr. Ross, jumping overboard, with a line, and, seizing hold of the old man, they were both pulled on board; and the rescued Frenchman, in the best English he could muster, made Captain Russell aware that others were near, who then went to the mast-head, and, with his glass, made out the other four pieces of wreck, which we were all on, and, making his long tack to windward, came back in the midst of us, picking up first, from that half-round piece of wreck that I saw burst above the surface at the time of the ship going under, Captain Luce, Mr. George Allen, of the Novelty Works, and a young German, a passenger on the Arctic, by the name of Ferdinand Keyn.

They, along with eight others of those who went down with the ship, had gained this piece of wreck, which turned out to be a segment of one of the paddle-boxes—and, singular as it seems, Captain Luce, who had stuck by his sinking ship to the last minute, was thus saved at last on the very boards, which, as commander, were his post of duty. The same thing, however, had caused the death of an interesting son, by striking or falling on him as it burst above water. The eight others, who had gained it with them, had, from time to time, perished on it; and Mr. Keyn was on the point of making the ninth, when the Cambria hove in sight. Mr. Allen, too, although saved himself, lost his wife and several other relatives, who were on board with him, and whom he saw placed on the raft of spars before the ship went under. I found those three my companions in the cabin of the Cambria, and being attended to like myself. The old Frenchman and the five firemen were comfortably quartered away in the forecastle, all suffering much; and the old man having lost his 'compagnon de voyage,' the mess boy, who held out as long as he could, but finally rolled overboard. In the course of a few days, we all began to get around and feel pretty well, with the exception of the severe pains in our feet, which continued with very little intermission; and, at the same time, it was most congenial to our feelings, that, through the leadership of Mr. Walker, we had the daily opportunity of rendering praises and thanksgiving to a gracious God for his mercy and goodness toward us. Captain Russell feels the circumstance of his instrumentality in the matter with great gratification, on account of Captain Nye, of the Collins' steamer Pacific, having, some years ago, run great risk in saving him and his crew from off the sinking Jessie Stevens, in a severe gale on the Atlantic."

Of the five boats that left the Arctic, only two were ever heard from, the one commanded by Mr. Francis Dorian, the third mate, the other by Mr. William Baalham, the second mate. The remainder, doubtless, sunk in the storm of the succeeding Saturday. The persons in these boats, with eight or ten more on the rafts or fragments of the wreck, comprised all of the survivors of the catastrophe. Not a single female on board was saved—all perished!

Mr. Dorian's conduct, during these trying scenes, was noble. He was the only one of all the principal officers that remained faithful to the orders of his superior to the last. The recital of Peter McCabe, a waiter in the cabin, the solitary survivor of the large raft, which Mr Dorian worked to construct with much zeal, unfolds to us other terrible incidents of this calamity. In common with the rest of the crew and passengers, McCabe seemed at first to have had no idea that the ship had encountered serious damage by the collision, but when he came on deck, he was soon undeceived. He was busy at work on the raft, when there came a dull rushing sound, and a long wail, and the Arctic went down. He was himself ingulfed in the vortex of the sinking ship, and gave himself up for lost. The waters had closed over him, but presently he perceived, as it were, a dim light over his head, and he rose to the surface. He caught hold of a door, then of a barrel, then he swam to the raft, to which the seventy poor creatures were clinging. The sea was rough—*not* strong; but, in the confusion, the raft had been so imperfectly constructed, that the waves dashed over it, and the miserable passengers were swept from their hold. What follows, we will not attempt to paraphrase. Has human eye ever witnessed a scene of more awful and protracted agony?

"Those who had life-preservers did not sink, but floated with their ghastly faces upward, reminding those who still remained alive of the fate that awaited them. In the midst of all this, thank heaven, I never lost hope, but retained my courage to the last. One by one, I saw my unfortunate companions drop off; some of them floated off, and were eaten and gnawed by fishes, while others were washed under the raft and remained with me till I was rescued. I could see their faces in the openings, as they were swayed to and fro by the waves, which threatened every moment to wash me off. The raft, at one time, was so crowded that many had to hold on by one hand. Very few words were spoken by any, and the only sound that we heard was the splash of the waters, or the heavy breathing of the poor sufferers, as they tried to recover their breath after a wave had passed over them. Nearly all were submerged to their arm-pits, while a few could with great difficulty keep their heads above the surface. The women were the first to go; they were unable to stand the exposure more than three or four hours. They all fell off the raft without a word, except one poor girl, who cried out in intense agony, 'Oh, my poor mother and sisters!' When I had been a few hours on the raft, there were not more than three or four left."

One of these three or four gave to Peter McCabe a paper, which he describes as like a "small map," and which, as he thought, was some kind of title-deed. A few minutes after he had given it, as though all energy had been exhausted in the preservation of that precious document, which he had at length been compelled to consign to the custody of another, his grasp gave way, and the owner of the title-deed was washed away. It is strange enough that McCabe, despite of all his efforts, could not succeed in preserving that precious paper; he made ineffectual efforts to get it into his pocket; he swam with it some time between his teeth, but all was in vain; the deed, which had been so dearly prized, was carried away from his mouth, and added for a moment to the relics of the wreck—then seen no more. A little incident of this kind seems to bring the scene before one's eyes with a more vivid reality even than the recital of the greater and more sweeping destruction. Before eight and a half o'clock that evening, every soul on the raft with McCabe were either dead or washed off; and "I," says he, "*was left alone!* But a few minutes before the last man went, I asked him the time. He told me, and *died in five minutes afterward!*"

Nothing could have been more exemplary on this occasion, than the resignation of the women, or the ready obedience displayed by the passengers. If all had acted as they did upon that fatal day, we should now be commenting upon a far less distressing tale; but the flight of the seamen and officers in the boats, full two hours before the vessel sunk, was the cause of all the multiplied horrors of the disaster.* Individuals, however, displayed undaunted courage. The good conduct of one young man, who fired the cannon, an engineer learning under instructions, named Stewart Holland, was more conspicuous than that of any other person on board. "A more brave, courageous and self-sacrificing being," says Captain Luce, "I never saw." He tried to save all, without seeming to think anything about his own safety, never attempting to get into a boat. His end was heroic. Unmoved by the base desertion of others, he continued firing the signal gun, that, like a death-knell, boomed over the waters; and when the wreck sunk to its gloomy grave, he, too, became numbered with the dead. Was death ever more noble?

Holland was from Washington City. His father, on first learning of the event, still clung to the hope that his son had escaped the perils of the wreck, by some such miracle as saved Captain Luce. He exclaimed: "My son is *not* lost; I will not give him up; but," he continued, "better a thousand times that he should perish in the manly discharge of his duty, than have saved a craven life by such cowardice and selfishness as marked the conduct of many of the crew." Such sentiments show a father worthy of such a son. Soon after his arrival in New York, Mr. Dorian addressed the following letter to Mr. Isaac Holland:

"I am a stranger and can offer no apology for addressing you, further than my desire of adding my humble testimony to the merits of your noble boy. He was in the habit of daily coming to my room, telling me funny stories, etc., and, in this way, I had the pleasure of forming an intimate acquaintanceship with him. Believing that anything connected with him in the last scene might possess a dear, though painful, interest to you, I send you all I know. I regret it is so exceedingly scanty.

About two hours after the Arctic was struck, the firing of the gun

---

* A larger part of the seamen were foreigners, the offscourings of the marine service of many countries. Had they been of that class of brave, hardy, right-principled men that years ago composed the crews of our merchant vessels, their conduct might have been more like that exhibited on board the British steamer Birkenhead, which was lost on the coast of Africa a few years since. That vessel struck on a hidden rock, stove a plank at the bow, and went down in half an hour's time. A regiment of troops was on board. As soon as the alarm was given, and it was apparent that the ship's doom was sealed, the roll of the drum called the soldiers to arms on the upper deck. That call was promptly obeyed, though every gallant heart knew that it was his death summons. The women and children were placed in the boats, and nearly all saved. There were no boats for the troops, but there was no panic, no blanched, quivering lips among them. Down went the ship, and down went the heroic band, shoulder to shoulder, firing a *feu de joie* as they sunk beneath the waves.

attracted my attention; and I recollect that, when I saw Mr. Holland, it struck me as remarkably strange that he alone, of all belonging to the engineering department, should be there. He must have had a good chance to go in the chief engineer's boat and be saved, but he did not, it seems, make the slightest exertion to save himself. His whole conduct can be accounted for by the simple word *duty*, and nothing else.

I recollect that, about an hour before the ship sunk, I was hurriedly searching for spikes, to help to form a raft. I had just passed through the saloon; on the sofas were men who had fainted—and there were many of them, too—the ladies were in little groups, clasped together; and they seemed to me to be strangely quiet and resigned. As I emerged from the saloon, the scene that presented itself was one I hope never to see again. The passengers had broken up the bar; the liquors were flowing down the scuppers. Here and there were strong, stout-looking men on their knees, in the attitude of prayer; others, when asked to do anything, were immovable, perfectly stupefied.

In the midst of this scene, Stewart came running up to me; his words were: 'Dorian, my powder is out; I want more; give me the key.' 'Never mind the key,' I replied; 'take an ax and break open the door.' He snatched one close behind me, and down into the ship's hold he dived, and I went over the ship's side to my raft. Half an hour later, when busy at the raft, a voice hailed me, and, on looking up, I again saw Stewart, when he hurriedly asked: 'Dorian, have you a compass in your boat?' 'No,' I replied; and off he went. He knew that any chance I had would be shared with him; and I have often thought how strange it was that that young man should, for a moment, quit his gun to inquire after my safety, and never, for a moment, think of his own. But such was Stewart Holland. I recollect distinctly his appearance as he hailed me from the deck. The right side of his face was black with powder, and two large spots on the left side. When he spoke, his countenance seemed lighted up with something like a quiet smile."

The clergy of our large cities preached discourses upon the loss of the Arctic. We conclude this article by a pathetic extract from a sermon by the Rev. Henry Ward Beecher, delivered in his church of the Pilgrims, at Brooklyn, the power of which will strike every heart. The text was the forty-sixth Psalm, first three verses: "God is our refuge and strength, a very present help in time of trouble: therefore will not we fear, though the earth be removed and the mountains be carried into the midst of the sea; though the waters thereof roar and be troubled, though the mountains shake with the swelling thereof."

"It was autumn. Hundreds had wended their way from pilgrimages; from Rome and its treasures of dead art, and its glory of living nature, from the sides of Switzer's mountains, from the capitals of various nations; all of them saying in their hearts, we will wait for the September gales to have done with their equinoctial fury, and then we will embark; we will slide across the appeased ocean, and in the gorgeous month of October we will greet our longed-for native land, and our heart-loved homes. And, so, the throng streamed along from Berlin, from Paris, from the Orient, converging upon London, still hastening toward the welcome ship, and narrowing every day the circle of engagements and preparations. They crowded aboard. Never had the Arctic borne such a host of passengers, nor passengers so nearly related to so many among us. The hour was come. The signal ball fell at Greenwich. It was noon also at Liverpool. The anchors were weighed; the great hull swayed to the current; the national colors streamed abroad, as if themselves instinct with life and national sympathy. The bell strikes; the wheels revolve; the signal gun beats its echoes in upon every structure along the shore, and the Arctic glides joyfully forth from the Mersey, and turns her prow to the winding channel, and begins her homeward run.

The pilot stood at the wheel, and men saw him. Death sat upon the prow, and no eye beheld him. Whoever stood at the wheel in all the voyage, *Death was the pilot* that steered the craft, and none knew it. He neither revealed his presence nor whispered his errand. And so, hope was effulgent, and lithe gayety disported itself, and joy was with every guest. Amid all the inconveniences of the voyage, there was still that which hushed every murmur—*home is not far away.* And every morning, it was still one night nearer home, and at evening, one day nearer home! Eight days had passed. They beheld that distant bank of mist that forever haunts the vast shallows of Newfoundland. Boldly they made at it, and plunging in, its pliant wreaths wrapped them about. They shall never emerge. The last sunlight has flashed from that deck. The last voyage is done to ship and passengers. At noon, there came noiselessly stealing from the north that fated instrument of destruction. In that mysterious shroud, that vast atmosphere of mist, both steamers were holding their way with rushing prow and roaring wheels, but invisible. At a league's distance, unconscious, and at nearer approach, unwarned; within hail and bearing right toward each other, unseen, unfelt, until, in a moment more, emerging from the gray mists, the ill-omened Vesta dealt her deadly stroke to the Arctic. The death-blow was scarcely felt along the mighty hull. She neither reeled nor shivered. Neither commander nor officers deemed that they had suffered harm.

Prompt upon humanity, the brave Luce (let his name be ever spoken with admiration and respect) ordered away his boat with the first officer to inquire if the stranger had suffered harm. As Gourlie went over the ship's side, oh, that some good angel had called to the brave commander, in the words of Paul, on a like occasion, "*except these abide in the ship ye cannot be saved!*" They departed, and with them the hope of the ship—for now, the waters gaining upon the hold and rising up upon the fires, revealed the mortal blow. Oh! had now that stern, brave mate, Gourlie, been on deck, whom the sailors were wont to mind—had he stood to execute efficiently the commander's will—we may believe that we should not have to blush for the cowardice and recreancy of the crew, nor wept for the untimely dead. But, apparently, each subordinate officer lost all presence of mind, then courage, and so honor.

In a wild scramble, that ignoble mob of firemen, engineers, waiters, and crew, rushed for the boats, and abandoned the helpless women, children, and men, to the mercy of the deep! Four hours there were from the catastrophe of the collision to the catastrophe of sinking. In that time, near two hundred able-bodied men, well directed, might have built an ample raft, stored it for present necessity, filled the boats with discretion, and put off from the sinking ship with a flotilla, that ere many hours would have been hailed by some of the many craft that pass and repass that ill-fated spot. It was not so to be. All command was lost. The men heeded but one impulse, and that the desperate selfishness of an aroused and concentrated *love of life.* They abandoned their posts They deserted their duty. They betrayed their commander. They yielded up to death more than two hundred helpless souls committed to their trust. And yet, even for these, let there be some thought of charity. Let us not forget the weakness of the flesh ; the absence of the first mate, whom they were wont to obey; the terrible force of panic, even upon brave men ; the sense of the hopelessness of effort to save so many, and the instinctive desire of self-preservation. All this is but a little.

But so much extenuation as there may be, let them have its benefit who certainly need every cover of charity, to save them from the indignation of a grieved and outraged community. Let it be remembered, also, that *individuals* among them acted most nobly, and, because the multitude were base, let not the exceptional cases be forgotten. Let that single officer, who did cling to the last manfully to his duty—the third mate, Dorian—be remembered; and that man who was set to fire the signal gun of distress, young Holland, who stood by his post until the ship sunk, and was in the very act of firing as the last plunge was made ; and that engineer, who had a boy under his care, but refused to leave in the first boat, where a place was offered him, because he could not find his ward, and would not go without him. Let us charitably hope that many more such individual acts occurred, unnoticed and unreported, to redeem the crew and engineers from such disgrace as weighs heavily upon them. Many a poor fellow lies beneath the waves, unable to defend himself, who may have lost his life because he *was* faithful to the last; and his heroism may be without a witness, his name without a defender.

How nobly, in the midst of weakness and terror, stood that worthy man, Luce, in this terrible scene—calm, self-sacrificing, and firm to the end. Of all the witnesses, but *one* has disparaged his exertions. *He* says, that this noble commander '*seemed like a man whose judgment was paralyzed.*' Yet this man says, that when *he* was rushing desperately for the boat, Captain Luce withstood him, and tore the very raiment from his back, exclaiming: '*Let the passengers go in the boat;*' and with disgraceful naivette he says: '*No more attention was paid to the captain than to any other man on board. Life was as sweet to us as to others.*'—(Patrick Tobin.) Without doubt such a man would think his judgment was paralyzed who would not run; whose life was not so sweet as his duty; who could die, but could not abandon a trust as sacred as was ever committed to human hands. Nor do I remember, in all my reading, any Roman heroism that can compare with one incident recorded by one witness. When Captain Luce was urged to enter one of the boats, he declined utterly. He was urged to let his son go in—that son whom, afterward, sinking, he carried in his arms—that son that, rising from the wave, was slain in his bosom by the stroke of a piece of the wreck. But should a man give precedence to anything that belonged to him, over the hundred helpless creatures that clung to him? His thrice heroic reply was: 'My son shall share his father's fate!'

Now, all over the deck, was there displayed every frantic form of fear, of anguish, of bitter imploration, of transfixed despair. Some, with insane industry, strove at the pumps; others rushed headlong over the sides of the ship; the raft was overburdened ; the sea was covered with men struggling for a little time against their fate. But let us remember that there were other scenes than these. There were scores there who had long known that, by death, heaven was to be entered. There were those who had rested the burden of their sin upon Him who came to take away the sin of the world. Not in vain had they prayed every day, for years, that they might be ready whenever the Son of Man should come. There were mothers there, that, when the first shock was over, settled their face to die, as if it were to dream in peaceful sleep. Maidens were there, who looked up in that tremendous hour as the bride for her bridegroom. Oh! in the dread crisis, upon that mournful sea, which mists covered, that the tragedy of the waters might not be seen of the sun, how many were there that could say, '*God is our refuge and strength, a very present help in trouble!*' There, friends exchanged their last embraces; they determined to die, holding in their arms those best beloved, and to yield up together their lives to the hands of God. Oh, noble loves! that in such an hour triumph over all fear, and crown the life with true grandeur! Oh, noble trust! that, in the shock of such a sudden death, could mount up above the waves, and behold the Redeemer, and *rest* in him, to the taking away of all fear! In such an hour, every one was tried by infallible tests. *Then*, the timid became heroic, and the heroic became timed. Then it was neither wealth, nor honors, nor station, nor pretense, that could give help. Strength, and skill, and foresight, were all useless. Nothing was of worth, except a clear-eyed piety that could behold the Invisible—a faith that could rest the very soul in the hands of its Creator, and a hope that could behold so much in heaven, that it willingly let go its hold upon the earth. I will not doubt that, in those staterooms, many a prayer was uttered, which attending angels wafted to heaven; in that cabin, there were men and women who waited calmly for the event, as one waits for the morning. At length the time was ended. That great ship, treacherously stabbed, and drinking in the ocean at its wounds, gave her last plunge. With one last outcry, the devoted company were whelmed; and, high above all other sounds, there came a roaring from the black, uplifted chimney, as if the collected groans of all were mingled with the last groan of the ship itself.

Oh, what a burial was here! Not as when one is borne from his home, among weeping throngs, and gently carried to the green fields and laid peacefully beneath the turf and the flowers. No priest stood to pronounce a burial service. It was an ocean grave. The mists alone shrouded the burial-place. No spade prepared the grave, nor sexton filled up the hollowed earth. Down, down they sunk, and the quick returning waters, smoothed out every ripple, and left the sea as if it had not been."

THE

LOST RUSSIAN SAILORS,

WHO WERE ABANDONED ON THE DESERT ISLAND OF EAST SPITZBERGEN: TO WHICH IS ADDED THE NARRATIVE OF THE MISFORTUNES OF THE CREW OF THE

RUSSIAN SHIP ST. PETER.

IN THE year 1743, Jeremiah Okladmkoff, a merchant of Mesen, in the province of Jugovia, and the government of Archangel, fitted out a vessel carrying fourteen men. She was destined for Spitzbergen, to be employed in the whale and seal-fishery. For eight successive days after they had sailed, the wind was fair; but on the ninth it changed, so that instead of getting to the west of Spitzbergen, the usual place of rendezvous for the Dutch ships, and those of other nations annually employed in the whale-fisheries they were driven eastward of those islands; and, after some days, they found themselves at a small distance from one of them, called East Spitzbergen.

Having approached this island within about three wersts, or two English miles, their vessel was suddenly surrounded by ice, and they found themselves in an extremely dangerous situation. In this alarming state a consultation was held, when the mate, Alexis Himkof, declared, he recollected he had heard that some of the people of Mesen, having some time before, formed a resolution of wintering on this island, had accordingly carried from that town timber proper for building a hut, and had actually erected one at some distance from the shore.

This information induced the whole company to resolve on wintering there; if, as they hoped, the hut still existed: for they clearly perceived the imminent danger in which they were, and that they must inevitably perish if they continued in the ship. They, therefore, dispatched four of the crew in search of the hut, or any other succor they could meet with. These were Alexis Himkof, the mate; Iwan Himkof, his godson; Stephen Scharapof, and Feoder Weregin. As the shore on which they were to land was uninhabited, it was necessary that they should make some provision for their expedition. They had almost two miles to travel over loose bridges of ice, which being raised by the waves, and driven against each other by the wind, rendered the way equally difficult and dangerous. Prudence, therefore, forbade their loading themselves too much, lest being overburdened, they might sink between the pieces of ice and perish.

Having thus maturely considered the nature of their undertaking, they provided themselves with a musket, a powder-horn, containing twelve charges of powder, with as many balls; an ax, a small kettle, a bag with about twenty pounds of flour, a knife, a tinder-box and tinder, a bladder filled with tobacco, and every man his wooden pipe. Thus equipped these four sailors arrived on the island, little suspecting the misfortune that was about to befal them. The first thing they did was to explore the country, and soon discovered the hut they were in search of, about a mile and a half from the shore. It was thirty-six feet in length, eighteen in breadth, and as many high. It contained a small antechamber, about twelve feet broad, which had two doors, one to shut out the exterior air, the other to communicate with the inner room. This contributed greatly to keep the larger room warm when once heated. In the large room was an earthen stove, constructed in the Russian manner; that is, a kind of oven without a chimney; which serves occasionally either for baking, for heating the room, or, as is customary among the Russian peasants in very cold weather, to sleep upon.

This discovery gave our adventurers great joy. The hut had, however, suffered much from the weather, having now been built a considerable time. They passed the night in it, and early the next morning hastened to the shore, impatient to inform their comrades of their success, and also to procure from the vessel such provisions, ammunition, and other necessaries as might better enable the crew to winter on the island. Their astonishment and agony of mind, when, on reaching the place where they had landed, they saw nothing but an open sea, free from ice, which but the day before had covered the ocean, may more easily be conceived than described. A violent storm which had arisen during the preceding night, had been the cause of this disastrous event. But they could not tell whether the ice which had before hemmed in the vessel, had been driven by the violence of the waves against the ship, and shattered her to pieces; or whether she had been carried out to sea by the current, a circumstance which frequently happens in those seas. Whatever accident had befallen her, they saw her no more; and as no tidings were ever afterward received of her, it is most probable that she sunk, and that all on board of her perished.

This unfortunate event deprived the wretched mariners of all hope of ever being able to quit the island, and they returned to the hut full of horror and despair. Their first attention was employed, as may easily be imagined, in devising the means of providing subsistence and repairing their hut. The twelve charges of powder which they had brought with them, soon procured them as many reindeer, with which animals the island abounds.

It has already been observed that the hut discovered by the sailors had sustained some damage. There were cracks in many places between the boards of the building, which allowed free admission to the air. This inconvenience was, however, easily remedied; as they had an ax, and the beams were still sound, it was an easy matter to make the boards join again very tolerably; beside, as moss grew in great abundance all over the island, there was more than sufficient to fill up the crevices, to which wooden houses must always be liable. Repairs of this kind cost the unhappy men the less trouble, as they were Russians, for all Russian peasants are good carpenters, building their own houses, and being, in general, very expert in handling the ax.

The intense cold which makes those climates habitable to so few species of animals, renders them equally unfit for the production of vegetables. No species of tree, or even shrub, is found on any of the islands of Spitzbergen, a circumstance of the most alarming nature to our sailors. Without fire it was impossible to resist the severity of the climate; and without wood how was that fire to be produced or supported? Providence has, however, so ordered it, that in this particular the sea supplies the defects of the land. In wandering along the beach they collected plenty of wood, which had been driven ashore by the waves. It consisted at first of the wrecks of ships, and afterward of whole trees with their roots, the produce of some more hospitable, but to them unknown, country.

During the first year of their exile, nothing proved of more essential service to these unfortunate men, than some boards they found on the beach, having a long iron hook, some nails about five or six inches in length and proportionably thick, together with other pieces of old iron fixed in them, the melancholy relics of some vessels cast away in those remote parts. These were thrown on shore by the waves, at a time when the want of powder gave our men reason to apprehend that they must fall a prey to hunger, as they had nearly consumed the reindeer they had killed. This circumstance was succeeded by another equally fortunate; they found on the shore the root of a fir-tree, which nearly approached to the figure of a bow.

As necessity has ever been the mother of invention, so, with the help of a knife, they soon converted this root into a good bow; but they still wanted a string and arrows. Not knowing how to procure these at present, they resolved upon making a couple of lances to defend themselves against the white bears, the attacks of which animals, by far the most ferocious of their kind, they had great reason to dread. Finding they could neither make the heads of their lances, nor of their arrows, without the help of a hammer, they contrived to form the large iron hook mentioned above into one, by heating it, and widening a whole it happened to have about its middle, with the assistance of one of the largest nails. This received the handle, and a round knob at one end of the hook served for the face of the hammer. A large stone supplied the place of the anvil, and tongs were formed of a couple of reindeer's horns. With these tools they made two spear-heads, and after polishing and sharpening them on stones, they tied them as fast as possible with thongs of reindeer skin, to sticks about the thickness of a man's arm, which they got from some branches of trees that had been cast on shore. Thus equipped with spears, they resolved to attack a white bear; and after a most dangerous encounter, they killed the formidable creature, and thus obtained a fresh supply of provisions. The flesh of this animal they relished exceedingly, and they thought it much resembled beef in flavor. They perceived, with great pleasure, that the tendons might, with little or no trouble, be divided into filaments as fine as they pleased. This was, perhaps, the most fortunate discovery these men could have made; for beside other advantages, they were thus furnished with strings for their bow.

The success our unfortunate islanders had experienced in making the spears, and the great utility of the latter encouraged them to proceed, and to forge some pieces of iron into heads of arrows of the same shape, though somewhat smaller than those of the spears. Having ground and sharpened these like the former, they tied them with the sinews of the white bears to pieces of fir, to which, by means of sinews, also of the white bear, they fastened feathers of sea-fowl, and thus became possessed of a complete bow and arrows. Their ingenuity in this respect was crowned with success far beyond their expectation; for, during the time of their continuance upon the island, they killed with these arrows no less than 250 reindeer, beside a great number of blue and white foxes. The flesh of these animals served them also for food, and their skins for clothing, and other necessary preservatives against the intense cold of a climate so near the pole.

They, however, killed only ten white bears in all, and these not without the utmost danger; for these animals being prodigiously strong, defended themselves with astonishing vigor and fury. The first they attacked designedly, but the other nine they killed in their own defense; for some of these creatures even ventured to enter the outer room of their hut in order to devour them. All the bears did not, it is true, show an equal degree of fury; either because some were less pressed by hunger, or were naturally of a less ferocious disposition; for several which entered the hut immediately betook themselves to flight on the first attempt of the sailors to drive them away. A repetition of these formidable attacks threw the men into great terror and anxiety, as they were in almost perpetual danger of being devoured. The reindeer, the blue and white foxes, and the white bears, were the only food these wretched mariners tasted during their continuance in that dreary abode.

In their excursions through the island, they had found, nearly in the middle of it, a slimy loam or a kind of clay. Out of this they found means to form a utensil to serve for a lamp, and they proposed to keep it constantly burning with the fat of the animals they might kill. To have been destitute of light, in a country where, in winter, darkness reigns for several months together, would have greatly increased their other calamities. Having, therefore, fashioned a kind of lamp, they filled it with some reindeer's fat, and stuck in it some linen twisted into the shape of a wick. But they had the mortification to find that, as soon as the fat melted, it not only soaked into the clay, but fairly ran through it on all sides. It was, therefore, necessary to contrive some method of preventing this inconvenience, which did not proceed from cracks, but from the substance of which the lamp was made being too porous. They made another one, dried it thoroughly in the air, then heated it red-hot, and afterward quenched it in their kettle, in which they had boiled down a quantity of flour to the consistence of starch. The lamp being then dried and filled with melted fat, they now found, to their great joy, that it did not leak. But, for greater security, they dipped linen rags in their paste, and with them covered it all over on the outside. Having succeeded in this attempt, they immediately made another lamp for fear of an accident, that at all events they might not be destitute of a light; upon which they determined to reserve the remainder of their flour for similar purposes.

As they had carefully collected whatever happened to be cast on shore to supply themselves with fuel, they had found among the wrecks of vessels some cordage and a small quantity of oakum, which served them to make wicks for their lamp. When these stores began to fail, their shirts and trowsers were employed to make good the deficiency. By these means they kept their lamp burning, without intermission, from the day they first made it, which was soon after their arrival on the island, until that of their embarkation for their native country.

The necessity of converting the most essential parts of their clothing, such as their shirts and drawers, to the use above specified, exposed them the more to the rigor of the climate. They also found themselves in want of shoes, boots, and other articles of dress; and as winter was approaching, they were again obliged to have recourse to that ingenuity which necessity suggests, and which seldom fails in the trying hour of distress.

They had abundance of skins of foxes and reindeer, that had hitherto served them for bedding, and which they now thought of employing to some more essential service, but they were at a loss how to tan them. After some deliberation, they resolved to adopt the following method: They soaked the skins for several days in fresh water, till they could pull off the hair pretty easily; they then rubbed the wet skin with their hands till it was nearly dry, when they spread some melted reindeer fat over it, and again rubbed it well. By this process the leather was rendered soft, pliant and supple, and proper for every purpose for which they wanted to employ it. Those skins that were designed for furs, they soaked only one day to prepare them for being wrought, and then proceeded in the manner before mentioned, excepting only that they did not remove the hair. Thus they soon provided themselves with the necessary materials for all the parts of dress they wanted.

They made a curious needle out of a piece of wire; and the sinews of the bear and reindeer, which they split into several threads, served them to sew with.

Excepting the uneasiness which generally accompanies an involuntary solitude, these people having thus, by their ingenuity, so far overcome their wants, might have had reason to be contented with what Providence had done for them in their distressful situation. But that melancholy reflection, to which each of these forlorn persons could not help giving way, that perhaps he might survive his companions, and then perish for want of subsistence, or become a prey to the wild beast, incessantly disturbed their minds. The mate, Alexis Himkof, more particularly suffered: having left a wife and three children behind, he was deeply afflicted at his separation from them. He declared, after his return, that they were constantly in his mind, and that the thought of never more seeing them rendered him very unhappy.

When our four mariners had passed nearly six years in this dreary place, Feodor Weregin, who had from the first been in a languid condition, died, after suffering excruciating pains during the latter part of his life. Though they were relieved by that event from the trouble of attending him, and the pain of witnessing without being able to alleviate his misery, yet his death affected them not a little. They saw their numbers diminished, and each of the survivors wished to be the next to follow him.

As he died in winter, they dug a grave in the snow as deep as they could, in which they laid the corpse, and then covered it to the best of their power, that the white bears might not get at it. The melancholy reflections occasioned by the death of their comrade were still fresh in their minds, and each expected to pay this last duty to his remaining companions in misfortune, or to receive it from them, when, on the fifteenth of August, 1749, a Russian ship unexpectedly appeared in sight.

The vessel belonged to a trader, who had come with it to Archangel, intending that it should winter in Nova Zembla, but, fortunately for our poor exiles, the director of the whale-fishery proposed to the merchant to let his vessel winter at West Spitzbergen, to which, after many objections, he at length agreed.

The contrary winds they met with on their passage made it impossible for them to reach the place of their destination. The vessel was driven toward East Spitzbergen, directly opposite to the residence of our mariners, who, as soon as they perceived her, hastened to light fires upon the hills nearest their habitation, and then ran to the beach, waving a flag made of reindeer's skin, fastened to a pole. The people on board, perceiving these signals, concluded that there were men upon the island, who implored their assistance, and therefore came to an anchor near the shore. It would be in vain to attempt to describe the joy of these poor people, at seeing the moment of their deliverance so near. They soon agreed with the master of the ship to work for him during the voyage, and to pay him eighty rubels on their arrival, for taking them on board with all their riches, which consisted of fifty pud or 2000 pounds weight of rein-deer fat; beside many hides of those animals, skins of blue and white foxes, and those of the ten white bears they had killed. They took care not to forget their bow and arrows, their spears, their knife and ax, which were almost worn out, their awls and their needles, which they carefully kept in a bone-box, very ingeniously made with their knife only; and in short, everything they possessed.

Our adventurers arrived safe at Archangel on the twenty-eighth of September, 1749, having spent six years and three months in their dreary solitude. The moment of their landing was near proving fatal to the loving and beloved wife of Alexis Himkof, who being present when the vessel came into port, immediately knew her husband, and ran with such eagerness to his embraces, that she slipped into the water, and very narrowly escaped being drowned.

All three on their arrival were strong and healthy; but having lived so long without bread, they could not reconcile themselves to the use of it, and complained that it filled them with wind; nor could they bear any spiritous liquors, and therefore drank nothing but water.

LOSS OF THE RUSSIAN SHIP ST. PETER,

On the coast of Beerings' Island, in the Sea of Kamtschatka, and subsequent distresses of the Crew.

The Russians, though of all the European nations the most interested in making discoveries in the north, were not, however, roused to any undertaking of that nature till long after the attempts of the English to discover a north-west passage to China and India. The Czar Peter, was the first to project an expedition for that purpose, and himself drew up the instructions for those who were to conduct it.

The celebrated Beerings, a native of Denmark, but who had served ever since 1707 in the Russian navy, was appointed to head this expedition. He was an officer who to extensive knowledge united fortitude and great experience. His lieutenants were a German, named Martin Spanberg, and Tschirikoff, a Russian. Beerings and his officers spent almost five years in making the necessary preparations and in the voyage itself.

In 1727 they landed in Kamtschatka, surveyed the coast, and wintered in that country. The ensuing year they discovered the Island of St. Lawrence, and three smaller ones not far from the east coast of Asia. The approach of winter and the fear of being blocked up by the ice, obliged Beerings to think of returning; and on the eighteenth of September he again reached the river of Kamtschatka. They quitted a second time the inhospitable coast of that country on the fifth of June, 1729, but the wind blew from E. N. E., with such violence that they could not get out farther than sixty-eight leagues from it. As they found no land in that space, they altered their course, doubled the southermost Cape of Kamtschatka, and cast anchor at Ochotzk. From that place Beerings traveled over land to Irkutzk in Siberia, and proceeded to Petersburgh, where he arrived on the first of March, 1730.

On his return Beerings declared that, in the course of his navigation, being in the latitude of between 50 and 60 degrees, he had observed signs which seemed to indicate that there was some coast or land toward the east. This declaration was confirmed by the testimony of his lieutenants Spanberg and Tschirikoff, and they proposed a second expedition to Kamtschatka, to explore the regions which separated the Asiatic continent from the north of America. The Russian Government, sensible of the importance of the project, acquiesced in the proposal of Beerings, who was appointed to conduct the new enterprise, with the rank of commodore, while his two lieutenants were nominated captains under him.

Commodore Beerings went on board the St. Peter, and Captain Tschirikoff took the command of the St. Paul. Two other vessels carried the provisions, and another had on board two academicians, sent out by the Russian Academy of Sciences, and their baggage. A few days previous to their departure, Beerings called a council, in which it was resolved, first to go in quest of the land laid down in the chart as having been seen by John de Gama. On the fourth of June, 1741, the two captains set sail, steering the direction which had been agreed upon till the twelfth of that month, when, being in the latitude of forty-six degrees, they were convinced that Gama's land did not exist, as they had met with none during that run. They immediately put the ships about, and stood to the northward, to the fifteenth degree, without making any discovery. They then agreed to steer eastward for the American continent, but on the twentieth the ships were separated by a violent storm, succeeded by a thick fog.

Nothing of consequence occurred till the eighteenth of July, when Beerings, still hoping to meet with the St. Paul, and continuing to steer to the northward, perceived the continent of America. Having cast anchor, the commodore sent Chitroff, the master, with a few armed men, to survey the coast, while another shallop was dispatched in quest of water. Steller went on board the latter, and in an island on which they landed he found several empty huts, whence it was conjectured that the natives of the continent visited it for the purpose of fishing. These huts were of wood, wainscoted with planks well joined together. They here found a box of poplar wood, a hollow ball of earth containing a small pebble, as if to serve for a child's plaything, and a whetstone, on which were visible the marks of copper knives that had recently been whetted on it.

Steller made several observations in the huts. He found, among other things, a cellar containing smoked salmon and a sweet herb, ready dressed for eating, in the same manner as vegetables are prepared in Kamtschatka. There were likewise cords, grindstones, and utensils of various kinds. Having approached a place where the savages had been dining, they betook themselves to flight as soon as they perceived him. He there found a dart, and an instrument for producing fire, of the same form as those made use of in Kamtschatka. It consists of a board perforated in several places; the end of a stick being put into one of these holes, the other extremity is turned backward and forward between the palms of the hands till, with the rapidity of the motion, the board takes fire, on which the sparks are received upon some matter that is easily inflamed.

The watering party related that they had passed two places where fires appeared to have been recently made, that they had observed wood which had been cut, and the track of human feet in the grass. They had likewise seen five red foxes, which showed no shyness or timidity on meeting them. They carried nothing with them from the huts but a few smoked fish resembling carp, and which proved very good eating. To convince the natives that they had nothing to fear from the strangers who had landed on their coast, the commodore sent on shore a few presents for them, consisting of a piece of green cloth, two iron pots, two knives, twenty gross of glass beads, and a pound of tobacco, which he presumed would prove extremely acceptable to the savages.

The Russians now stood out to sea, and having been several days without seeing land, they, on the thirtieth of July discovered an island, to which, from the thickness of the weather, they gave the name of Foggy Island. The whole month of August was spent in standing off and on; in the meantime the crew began to be attacked with scurvy, and the commodore himself was in a worse situation than any other. Fresh water beginning to run short, the Russians, on the twenty-ninth of August, stood to the north, and soon discovered the continent. The coast in this part is extremely steep, and lined with a multitude of islands, among which the St. Peter came to an anchor. On the thirtieth the pilot, Andrew Hasselberg, was sent to one of the largest of these islands in quest of fresh water. He soon returned with two specimens, taken out of different lakes, which were more or less salt. But, as there was no time to be lost, it was judged prudent to take in a quantity of this water rather than be left completely without, as it would serve for cooking, and thus the remaining fresh water might be made to last till they could procure a supply. All the empty casks were accordingly filled with it. To the use of this water Steller attributed the redoubled attacks of the scurvy, which at length proved fatal to a great part of the crew.

In the morning the Russians heard the cries of men on one of the islands, and likewise saw a fire there. Soon afterward, two savages, each in a canoe resembling those of the Greenlanders, approached the ship within a certain distance. By their words and gestures they invited the Russians to land, and the latter, by signs and presents which they threw toward them, endeavored, but without success, to entice them into the ship. After looking some time at the Russians, they returned to the island.

Beerings and his officers resolved to venture to land, and for this purpose the great shallop was hoisted overboard. Lieutenant Waxel, accompanied by Steller and nine men well armed, went into the boat, and proceeded toward the island. The savages, to the number of nine, appeared on the shore, and were invited by signs to come to the shallop. But, as they could neither be tempted by the signs that were made, nor the presents which were offered them, and still continued to invite the Russians to land, Waxel put on shore three men, among whom was a Tschutski or Koriak interpreter. They moored the shallop to one of the rocks, as they had been ordered.

These men were kindly received by the savages, but being unable to understand each other, they were obliged to converse by signs. The latter, with a view to regale the Russians, presented them with whale's flesh, which was the only provisions they had with them. It appeared that their residence here was only for the purpose of catching whales, for on the shore was observed as many boats as men, but no hut, and not a woman among them; so that, probably they had no permanent habitation but on the continent. They had neither arrows nor any other arms that could give umbrage to the Russians, and at length one of them had the courage to go into the boat to Waxel. He appeared to be the oldest person, and the chief of the party. Waxel presented him with a glass of brandy, but that liquor appeared equally disagreeable and strange to him. After spitting it out of his mouth, he began to cry out, as if complaining to his countrymen that the Russians were using him ill. It was found impossible to appease him; needles, glass beads, an iron pot, and pipes, were offered him, but he refused them all. He immediately returned to the island, and Waxel did not judge it prudent to detain him any longer. At the same time he called off the three men who had been put on shore.

The savages at first showed a disposition to detain them all. At length they suffered two of the Russians to return, but kept the interpreter. Some of them even seized the cable by which the shallop was moored, thinking no doubt she was as easily managed as one of their canoes, or hoping to dash her to pieces against the rocks. To prevent their design, Waxel cut the cable. The interpreter meanwhile entreated not to be left behind. The savages disregarding all the signs that were made them to let him go, Waxel ordered two muskets to be fired, with a view to frighten them only. The success answered his expectation; the report, re-echoed by a neighboring mountain, terrified them to such a degree that they fell down on the ground, and the interpreter immediately made his escape. The savages soon recovered from their panic, and, by their cries and gestures, appeared highly irritated. Waxel did not think proper to remain there any longer, as the night was coming on, the sea grew very rough, and the vessel was at the distance of a mile and a half.

Leaving the island, the Russians steered to the south, in order to get off the coast. From this time till far in the autumn, the wind scarcely varied, excepting between W. S. W. and W. N. W. This was a great obstacle to the speedy return of the ship. Beside this, the weather was almost always foggy, so that they were sometimes two or three weeks without seeing either sun or stars, and, consequently, without being able to take the altitude or correct their reckoning. It is easy to conceive the inquietude which they must have experienced, wandering in such uncertainty in an unknown sea. "I know not (says one of the officers) if there be a situation in the world more disagreeable than that of navigating an unknown sea. I speak from experience, and I can say with truth, that during the five months of our voyage I had very few hours of tranquil sleep, being incessantly involved in danger and anxiety in regions heretofore unknown."

The crew struggled with contrary winds and tempests till the twenty-fourth of September, when they again came in sight of the land. A brisk gale from the south rendering it dangerous for them to remain near the coast, they resolved to keep the ship to the wind, which soon turned to the west, increased to a violent storm, and drove the vessel very far to the south-west. This tempest continued seventeen days without intermission, and was so furious, that Andrew Hasselberg, the pilot, acknowledged that, during the forty years in which he had served at sea, in various parts of the world, he had never seen anything equal to it. They shortened sail as much as possible, that they might not be carried too far; but, notwithstanding this precaution, they lost much way till the twelfth of October, when the tempest abated.

The disease which already prevailed among the crew became worse, and the scurvy extended its ravages more and more. A day seldom passed without a death, and scarcely men enough were left in health to navigate the vessel. In this melancholy situation they were undecided whether to return to Kamtschatka, or to seek some port in which they might winter on the American coast. The lateness of the season, the want of fresh water, and the great distance from Petropawlowska, appeared to render the latter measure indispensable. In a council held on board, it was, however, resolved to attempt the former.

They were, however, unable to discover the coast of Kamtschatka, and they had no hope of reaching any port in such an advanced season. The crew, exposed to the most intense cold and incessant rain, continued to labor without intermission. The scurvy had made such ravages that the man who guided the helm was obliged to be supported in his station by two of his comrades, who still possessed sufficient strength to keep their legs. When he became unable either to sit up or to steer, another, who was in a situation very little better, took his place. They durst not carry a press of sail, because, in case of necessity, there was no person to lower those which might be too much. The sails themselves were so worn out that the first gale would have torn them to pieces, and there were not hands sufficient to hoist the spare sails which they had taken out with them.

The incessant rain, which had fallen till now, was succeeded by hail and snow. The nights grew longer and darker, and their dangers were consequently increased, because they every moment had reason to apprehend that the ship would strike. At the same time their fresh water was entirely consumed. The excessive labor became insupportable to the few hands who still remained in health, and when summoned to their duty, they declared themselves incapable of any farther exertions. They impatiently expected death, which appeared inevitable, to deliver them from their misery.

During several days the vessel remained without a steersman, and as if motionless on the water; or if she had any movement she received it only from the impulse of the winds and waves, to which she was consigned. It would have been in vain to resort to vigorous measures with a crew driven to despair. In this extremity Waxel adopted a more prudent method, spoke with kindness to the seamen, exhorting them not to despair entirely of the assistance of the Almighty, and rather to make a last effort for their common deliverance, which was, perhaps, much nearer than they expected. With this kind of language he persuaded them to keep on deck and work the ship as long as they were able.

Such was the dismal situation of the crew, when, on the fourth of November, they again began to sail westward, without knowing either in what latitude they were, or at what distance from Kamtschatka. They knew, however, that it was only by steering west, they could hope to reach that country. What was the joy of the Russians, when, about eight in the morning, they discovered land!

At this so much wished for sight the seamen mustered up the little strength they had left. They endeavored to approach it, but it was still at a great distance, for they could only perceive the snow-covered summits of the mountains; and when they had come pretty near it, night arrived. The officers judged it prudent to stand off, in order not to risk the loss of the ship. The next morning the greatest part of the rigging on the starboard side of the vessel was found broken to pieces. Nothing more was necessary to render their misfortunes complete.

Waxel having made his report of this new disaster to the commodore, received orders to assemble all the officers and to consult with them what was best to be done. A council was accordingly held. They considered the danger to which they were all exposed in a crazy ship which it was no longer possible to navigate. They knew that the cordage which remained whole was as much worn as that which had broken, as the rigging was heard snapping every moment, and even during the time of their deliberation. The water diminished every day, and the sickness grew worse; they had before suffered from the rain, but they now felt much greater inconvenience from the cold, which, instead of becoming more moderate, grew every day more intense. They determined, in consequence of all these considerations, to disembark on the land which they had discovered, as their lives would at least be safer there, and probably they might find some method of getting the ship into a place of safety.

The Russians, conformably to the decision of the council, steered for the land, but only under the small sails, on account of the weak condition of their masts. At five at night they came into twelve fathoms of water, where they cast anchor, and veered away three-fourths of the cable. At six the cable gave way, and the waves, which were of prodigious size, drove the ship against a rock, on which she twice struck, and yet the lead indicated five fathoms of water. At the same time the sea broke with such fury against the sides of the vessel that she shook to her very keel. A second anchor was thrown out, but the cable broke even before the anchor appeared to have taken hold. Fortunately the remaining one was not in readiness, otherwise, in this extremity, that also would have been thrown overboard, and thus they would have lost all their anchors. At the moment when they were busily employed in getting ready the third anchor, a prodigious sea took the ship and drove her clear off the rock. The Russians suddenly found themselves in calm water, and anchored in four fathoms and a half, and about three hundred fathoms from the shore.

On the sixth of November, at one o'clock, Lieutenants Waxel and Steller went on shore, and found the land sterile, and covered with snow. A stream which issued from the mountains and fell into the sea not far from the spot, was not yet frozen; its water was limpid and very good. No trees were to be seen, nor even any brushwood for fuel; the sea had, however, thrown some upon the beach, but being concealed beneath the snow, it could not easily be found. This account was not calculated to produce the most favorable impressions. Where were they to procure the materials necessary for constructing habitations? where could the sick be placed in comfort? and how could they be preserved from the cold? Man, however, should never abandon himself to despair; for the more forlorn his situation, the more ingenious is he rendered by necessity. Between the sand-hills, bordering the stream above mentioned, were holes of considerable depth; these it was proposed to clean out at the bottom, to cover them with sails, and thus take shelter in them till they could collect a sufficient quantity of drift-wood to erect huts. In the evening Waxel and Steller returned to the ship to make their report to the commodore.

Immediately upon their return a council was called, and it was resolved to send on shore, the next day, all those of the crew who were still in health, to prepare some of the holes for the reception of the sick. This being done, on the eighth of November the weakest were carried on shore. Some expired as soon as they were exposed to the air, even before they reached the deck, others upon deck, or in the boat, and several after they had reached the land. The country swarmed with a species of foxes, called in the Russian language *Pestzi*. Steller has given a very interesting account of these animals, which the reader will find introduced at the conclusion of this article, in order to prevent the interruption of the narrative. On the ninth of November the commodore, well covered against the external air, was carried on shore by four men, on a kind of litter formed of two poles crossed with cords. A separate hole had been prepared for his reception. The business of removing the sick continued every day, and not a day passed without several of them dying. None of those who had kept their beds on board the ship recovered; they were principally those who, out of indifference to life, or rather pusillanimity, had suffered the disease to get the upper hand.

The sea-scurvy begins with extreme lassitude, which seizes the whole body, renders the man indolent, disgusts him with everything, entirely dejects his spirits, and gradually forms a kind of asthma, which manifests itself on the slightest movement. It usually happens that the patient prefers lying down to walking, and in this case he is inevitably lost. All the members are soon afflicted with acute pains, the legs swell, the complexion becomes yellow, the body is covered with livid spots, the mouth and gums bleed, and teeth grow loose. The patient then feels no inclination to stir, and it is indifferent to him whether he lives or dies. These different stages of the disease and their effects were observed on board. It was likewise remarked that some of the sick were seized with a panic, and were startled at the least noise, and at every call that was given in the ship. Others ate with a very hearty appetite, and did not imagine themselves in danger. The latter no sooner heard the order given for the removal of the sick, than they quitted their hammocks and dressed themselves, not doubting but that they should speedily recover. But coming up from below, saturated with humidity, and out of a corrupted atmosphere, the fresh air which they inhaled on deck soon put a period to their lives.

Those only recovered who were not so far overcome by the disease as to be obliged continually to keep their beds, who remained as long as possible on their legs, and in motion. It was owing to their vivacity and their natural gayety that they were not dejected like the others. A man of this disposition served at the same time for an example, and encouraged by his conversation those who were in the same condition. The good effects of exercise were particularly apparent in the officers, who were constantly employed in giving orders, and obliged to be on deck the greatest part of the time, to keep an eye on what passed. They were always in action, and could not lose their spirits, for they had Steller with them. Steller was a physician of the soul as well as of the body; cheerfulness was his constant companion, and he communicated it to all around him. Among the officers, the commodore was the only person who sunk beneath the disease; his age and his constitution rendered him more disposed to rest than to activity. He at length became so suspicious, and was so impressed with the idea that every one was his enemy, that at last even Steller, whom he had before regarded as his best friend, durst not appear in his presence.

Waxel and Chitroff remained in tolerable health as long as they were at sea. They remained in the ship till the last, resolving that all the crew should be put on shore before they repaired thither themselves. They likewise had better accommodations on board. This situation, however, had nearly proved fatal to them, either because they no longer had so much exercise, or were exposed to the noxious vapors which ascended from the hold. In a few days they were taken so ill that they were obliged to be carried from the ship to the shore, and with proper precautions on their removal into the air, they both recovered.

Beerings died the eighth of December, 1741, and the island was called after his name. It may almost be said that he was buried alive. Having been carried on shore with the greatest precaution, he was placed in the largest and least incommodious hole, and a covering was carefully erected over him in the form of a tent. The sand soon began to fall down from the sides of the hole in which he lay, and every moment covered his feet. It was immediately removed by those who attended him; but, at last, he would not suffer it to be taken away, thinking he felt some warmth from it, the vital heat having already forsaken the other parts of his body. The sand gradually accumulated, till it covered him up to the belly; and when he had expired, his people were obliged to dig him out, in order to give him a decent interment.

A few days before the death of the commodore, the Russians had the misfortune to lose their vessel, the only resource capable of extricating them from their forlorn situation. She was at anchor, as we have seen above, and exposed to the violence of a tempestuous sea, when, in the night, between the twenty-eighth and twenty-ninth, a furious storm arose, the cable parted, and the vessel was driven ashore, very near the dens of the Russians. She was found in the morning buried in the sand to the depth of eight or ten feet. Upon inspection, the keel and sides were found to be broken to pieces. The water, which entered the ship and ran off below, had washed away or spoiled the greatest part of the remaining provisions, consisting of flour, oatmeal, and salt.

Situated as the unfortunate mariners were, this loss was extremely afflicting: but appeared much less when they reflected that the vessel, though much damaged, had been thrown upon the sand at their feet, and not carried out to sea; they still entertained hopes that, even if she could not be got afloat again, they might with the materials build a bark capable of carrying them to Kamtschatka.

The events which had occurred since their shipwreck had diverted the attention of the Russians from two important objects in their situation; in the first place, to take a survey of the country in which they had landed, and, in the second, to provide for their subsistence. After reconnoitering the island, they proceeded to examine the provision which had been saved from the ship. Having first deducted and stowed away eighteen hundred pounds of flour to serve them on their passage from the island to Kamtschatka, the remainder was divided into equal portions. Though these were very scanty, and thirty of their number died during their stay on the island, yet they would not have been sufficient, but for the seasonable supply which the marine animals afforded.

The first which served them for food were the otters. Their flesh was hard, but they were obliged to put up with it till they could procure some less disagreeable in its stead. After they had ceased to use them for food, the Russians killed a great number of these animals for the sake of their beautiful skins, nine hundred of which they collected during their residence on the island. In the month of March the otters disappeared, and were succeeded by another animal, called the sea-cat, and afterward by seals. Their flesh was exceedingly disgusting to the Russians, who fortunately, now and then, surprised a young sea-lion. The latter are excellent eating; but they never durst venture to attack them excepting when asleep.

The sea-cow likewise proved of great utility to the Russians. One of these animals which they took, weighed eight thousand pounds, and furnished them with food for a fortnight. Their flesh may be compared to beef, and the fat, with which it is covered to the depth of three or four inches, resembles that of pork. This they melted down and used instead of butter. They likewise salted a considerable quantity of the flesh and filled several casks, which they added to the provision already destined for their voyage to Kamtschatka. During their residence on the island two whales were likewise cast on shore, and these furnished them with an abundant supply when other marine animals failed.

On the melting of the snow, about the end of March, 1742, the Russians began to think seriously of their return. Being all assembled, to the number of forty-five, they took into consideration the means of returning to Kamtschatka. The state of perfect equality in which they had lived since their landing on the island produced a variety of opinions, which were warmly supported by those with whom they originated. Waxel, to whom the command by right devolved, conducted himself under these circumstances with great art and prudence. Without giving offense to the authors of the different plans, he opposed them to each other, and destroyed them by means of a third, which he again overthrew by objections which appeared unanswerable. At length he and Chitroff, who acted in concert, proposed their opinion, which was to take the vessel to pieces, and to construct another of a smaller size, but sufficiently spacious to hold all the crew and the provisions. In discussing the business, they laid great stress on the consideration that all those who had suffered together would not be separated; that none would be left behind; that if a new misfortune occurred, they would be together, and that none of them would be exempted from it. This opinion being unanimously approved of, a paper was drawn up to the effect, and signed by all the crew. The favorable weather at the beginning of April permitted them to put it in execution. The whole month was employed in breaking up the ship, and the officers, by their diligence, set a laudable example to the rest.

On the sixth of May they began to work upon their new vessel, which was forty feet in length and thirteen wide. She had but one mast and one deck, with a cabin at the stern, and a kitchen at the head. At the same time they likewise built a boat capable of holding nine or ten persons.

The vessel being completed, was launched on the tenth of August, and named the St. Peter, after the ship from the remains of which she had been constructed. The balls and superfluous iron-work served for ballast. A calm, which continued six days, enabled them to fix the mast, rudder and sails, and to take on board the provisions.

On the sixteenth they put to sea; and, with the help of oars, got clear of the rocks and shallows near the island. They then set their sails to take advantage of a breeze which sprung up. They had the satisfaction to find that their vessel was an excellent sailer, and might be managed with the greatest facility. On the eighteenth they were overtaken by a contrary wind, which blew with great violence at south-west. Being apprehensive of a tempest, they resolved to lighten the vessel, by throwing overboard part of their ballast. On the twenty-fifth they came in sight of Kamtschatka, and, on the twenty-seventh, came to an anchor in the harbor of Petropawlowska. It is scarcely possible to express the transports of the Russians when they again found themselves in the midst of comfort and abundance.

After passing the winter at Petropawlowska, they again embarked in the month of May, and arrived at Ochotzk. Waxel repaired to Jakutsk, where he resided during the winter. In October, 1744, he arrived at Jeniseisk, at which place he found Captain Tschirikoff, who soon afterward received an order from the senate to repair to Petersburgh; on which Waxel succeeded him in the command of the crews of both vessels. With these he proceeded to the same city, where he arrived in the month of January, 1749, which may be considered as the conclusion of the second expedition to Kamtschatka, after a period of sixteen years from its commencement.

The Arctic fox, of which the Russians found such numbers in Beerings' Island, is of a bluish gray color. The hair is very thick, long and soft, the nose sharp, and the ears short, and almost hid in the fur. The tail is shorter, but more bushy than that of the common fox. The following is the account given by Steller of the habits and manners of this extraordinary animal.

"During my unfortunate abode on Beerings' Island I had opportunities more than enough of studying the nature of this animal, which far exceeds the common fox in impudence, cunning, and roguery.

"They forced themselves into our habitations by night as well as by day, stealing all that they could carry off; even things that were of no use to them, such as knives, sticks, and clothes. They were so inconceivably ingenious as to roll down our casks of provisions, several pounds in weight, and then steal the meat out of them so ably, that at first we could not bring ourselves to ascribe the theft to them. As we have stripped an animal of its skin, it has often happened that we could not avoid stabbing two or three foxes, from their rapacity in taking the flesh out of our hands.

"If we buried it ever so carefully, and even added stones to the weight of earth that was upon it, they not only found it out, but with their shoulders shoved away the stones, lying under them and helping one another with all their might. If, in order to secure it, we put an animal on the top of a high post in the air, they either dug up the earth at the bottom, and thus tumbled the whole down, or one of them clambered up, and with incredible artifice and dexterity threw down what was upon it.

"They watched all our motions, and accompanied us in whatever we were about to do. If the sea threw up an animal of any kind, they devoured it before we could get up to rescue it from them; if they could not consume the whole of it at once, they dragged it in portions to the mountains, where they buried it under stones before our eyes, running to and fro as long as anything remained to be conveyed away. While this was doing others stood on guard and watched us. If they saw anything coming at a distance, the whole troop would combine at once and begin digging all together in the sand, till a beaver or sea-bear would be so completely buried under the surface that not a trace of it could be seen. In the night, when we were asleep, they came and pulled off our nightcaps, and stole our clothes from under our heads, with the beaver coverings and the skins we lay upon. In consequence of this we always slept with our clubs in our hands, so that if they awoke us we might drive them away or knock them down.

When we made a halt to rest by the way, they gathered around us and played a thousand tricks in our view, and when we sat still they approached so near that they gnawed the thongs of our shoes. If we lay down, as intending to sleep, they came and smelt at our noses, to try whether we were dead or alive; if we held our breath they gave us such a tug by the nose as if they would bite it off. On our first arrival they bit off the toes, fingers, and noses of the dead while we were preparing the grave, and thronged in such a manner about the infirm and sick, that it was with difficulty we could keep them off.

"Every morning we saw these audacious animals patrolling about among the sea-lions and sea-bears lying on the strand, smelling at such as were asleep, to discover whether some one of them might not be dead, if that happened to be the case, they proceeded to dissect him immediately, and soon afterward all were at work in dragging the parts away: because the sea-lions in their sleep overlay their young, they every morning examined, as if conscious of this circumstance, the whole herd of them, one by one, and immediately dragged away the dead cubs from their dams.

"As they would not suffer us to be at rest either by night or day, we became so exasperated at them that we killed young and old, and plagued them in every way we could devise. When we awoke in the morning there always lay two or three that had been knocked on the head in the night; and I can safely affirm that during my stay in the island I killed above two hundred of these animals with my own hands. On the third day after my arrival I knocked down upward of seventy of them with a club, within the space of three hours, and made a covering to my hut of their skins. They were so ravenous, that with one hand we could hold to them a piece of flesh, and with a stick or ax in the other could knock them on the head.

"From all the circumstances that occurred during our stay, it was evident that these animals could never before have been acquainted with mankind, and that the dread of man is not innate in brutes, but must be grounded on long experience."

EXPERIENCES

OF A

BRITISH NAVAL OFFICER,

AS GIVEN BY CAPTAIN BASIL HALL, OF THE

ROYAL NAVY.

Various circumstances conspired to give me, very early in life, what is called a taste for the sea. In the first place, I came into the world in the midst of a heavy gale of wind; when such was the violence of the storm, and the beating of the rain, that there were some thoughts of removing the whole party to a less rickety corner of the old mansion, which shook from top to bottom. So strong, indeed, was the impression made on the imagination of those present, by the roaring of the surf, close at hand, the whistling of the wind in the drenched forest, and the obvious rocking of the house, under the heavy gusts of that memorable gale, that, as soon as I was old enough to understand anything at all, the association between the events of my future life, and those of my birth-night, began to be sown in my mind. Thus, long before I shipped a pair of trowsers, I felt that a salt-water destiny was to be mine; and as everybody encouraged me to cherish these early predilections for the sea, I grew up with the certainty of becoming a sailor.

It is clear enough that no boy, instruct him as we will, can form correct ideas of what he is likely to meet with in any profession. The incipient difficulties and discomforts of all professions are, probably, pretty much alike; and the boy who has not energy enough to set his face resolutely against the early discouragements of any particular calling, will, in all probability, be successful in no other. It is, however, so great an advantage to have a young person's own feelings, and his point of honor heartily engaged in the cause in which he has embarked, that, if circumstances render such a thing at all expedient, or not quite unreasonable, the choice of a profession may often be conceded with advantage. But such free choice ought to be afterward burdened, with a positive interdict against change. In the case of a sea life, this appears to be quite indispensable; for the contrast is so striking, in most cases, between the comforts of home and the discomforts of a ship—to say nothing of rough fare, hard work, sea-sickness, and strict discipline—that, if an opening be constantly presented for escape, few youngsters will have resolution enough to bear up against those trials to which they must be exposed, and which they ought to hold themselves prepared to meet with cheerfulness.

Perhaps the naval profession owes a good deal of its peculiar character to these very disadvantages, as they are called; and though we may often regret to see young men, of good abilities, dropping out of the navy, who, if they had only cast on the right tack, might have done the service and themselves much honor—yet there is no denying that their more vigorous minded and sterner framed companions, whom they leave afloat, are, upon the whole, better fitted to make useful public servants.

In many other professions, it is possible to calculate beforehand, with more or less precision, the degree and kind of work which a young man is likely to be called upon to perform; but there is peculiar difficulty in coming to any just conclusion upon these points, even in a vague way, in the life of a sailor. His range of duties includes the whole world; he may be lost in the wilderness of a three-decker, or be wedged into a cock-boat; he may be fried in Jamaica, or frozen in Spitzbergen; he may be cruising, or be in action during six days of the week, in the midst of a fleet, and flounder in solitude on the seventh; or he may waste his years in peaceful idleness, the most fatal to subordination; or be employed on the home station, and hear from his friends every day; or he may be fifteen months, as I have been, at a time, without getting a letter, or seeing a newspaper. He may have an easy-going commander, which is a very great evil; or his captain may be one of those tight hands, who, to use the slang of the cock-pit, keeps every one on board "under the fear of the Lord and a broomstick." In short, a man may go to sea for twenty years, and find no two men, and hardly two days alike.

All this, which is delightful to some minds, and productive in them of every kind of resource, is utterly distracting, and very often ruinous to others. Weak frames generally sink under its severity; and weak minds become confused with its complication, and the intensity of its action. But, on the other hand, the variety of its objects is so boundless, that if a young man has only strength of body, to endure the wear and tear of watching, and other inevitable fatigues, and has also strength of character enough to persevere, in the certainty of openings occurring, sooner or later, by which his talents or his industry may find profitable employment, there can be little doubt that the profession of a sailor might be made suitable to most of those who, on entering it, are positively cut off from retreat.

I must own that, in spite of all my enthusiasm, when the actual time came for fairly leaving friends and home, and plunging quite alone and irrevocably into a new life, I felt a degree of anxiety and distrust of myself, which, as these feelings were quite strange, I scarcely knew how to manage. I had been allowed to choose my own profession, it is true, and was always eager to be off; yet I almost wished, when the actual moment arrived, that I had not been taken at my word. I can well remember my heart sunk within me, and I felt pretty much as if I were on the verge of death, when the carriage that was to convey me away drove up to the door.

I remember, as well as if the incidents had occurred yesterday, most of the details which are stated in the following letter, written only the day after I was left to my fate—among strangers—in the unknown world of a man-of-war. I certainly was far from happy, and might easily have made my friends wretched by selecting chiefly what was disagreeable. I took a different course.

"H. M. Ship Leander, June 12, 1802.

"Dear Father:—After you left us, I went down into the mess-room; it is a place about twenty feet long, with a table in the middle of it, and wooden seats, upon which we sit. When I came down, there were a great many cups and saucers upon the table. A man came in and poured hot water into the teapot. There are about fourteen of us mess at the same time. We were very merry in this dark hole, where we had only two candles.

"We come down here, and sit when we like; and at other times go upon deck. At about ten o'clock we had supper upon bread and cheese, and a kind of pudding, which we liked very much. Some time after this I went to a hammock, which was not my own, as mine was not ready, there not being enough of clues at it, but I will have it to-night. I got in at last. It was very queer to find myself swinging about in this uncouth manner, for there was only about a foot of space between my face and the roof; so, of course, I broke my head a great many times on the different posts in the cock-pit, where all the midshipmen sleep. After having got in, you may be sure I did not sleep very well, when all the people were making such a noise, going to bed in the dark, and the ship in such confusion.

"I fell asleep at last, but was always disturbed by the quarter-master coming down to awake the midshipmen who were to be on guard during the night. He comes up to their bedsides and calls them; so I, not being accustomed to it, was always awaked too. I had some sleep, however, but early in the morning was again roused up by the men beginning to work.

"There is a large hole which comes down from the decks, all the way through to the hold, where they let down the casks. The foot of the hammock that I slept in was just at the hole, so I saw the casks all coming down close by me. I got up at half past seven, and went into the berth, (our mess-room,) and we were all waiting for breakfast till eight, when the man who serves and brings in the dishes for the mess came down in a terrible passion, saying that as he was boiling the kettle at the stove, the master-at-arms had thrown water upon the fire and put it out. All this was because the powder was coming on board. So we had to want our breakfast for once. But we had a piece of bread and butter; and as we were eating it, the master-at-arms came down, and said that our candles were to be taken away; so we had to eat our dry meal in the dark."

MIDSHIPMENS' PRANKS.

During the long winters of our slothful discontent at Bermuda, to which island our ship had been sent, caused by the Peace of Amiens, the grand resource, both of the idle and busy, among all classes of the Leander's officers, was shooting. The midshipmen were generally obliged to content themselves with knocking down the blue and red birds with the ship's pistols, charged with his majesty's gun-powder, and, for want of small shot, with slugs formed by cutting up his majesty's musket-bullets. The officers aimed at higher game, and were, of course, better provided with guns and ammunition. Several of these gentlemen had brought from England some fine dogs—high-bred pointers; while the middies, also, not to be outdone, must needs have a dog of their own: they recked very little of what breed; but some sort of animal they said they must have.

I forget how we procured the strange-looking beast whose services we contrived to engage; but, having once obtained him, we were not slow in giving him our best affections. It is true he was as ugly as anything could possibly be. His color was a dirty, reddish yellow; and while a part of his hair twisted itself up in curls, a part hung down quite straight, almost to the ground. He was utterly useless for all the purposes of real sport, but quite good enough to furnish the mids with plenty of fun when they went on shore—in chasing pigs, barking at old white-headed negresses, and other amusements, suited to the exalted taste and habits of the rising generation of officers.

People will differ as to the merits of dogs; but we had no doubts as to the great superiority of ours over all the others on board, though the name we gave him certainly implied no such confidence on our part. After a full deliberation, it was decided to call him Shakings. Now it must be explained that shaking is the name given to small fragments of rope-yarns, odds and ends of cordage, bits of oakum, old lanyards—in short, to any kind of refuse arising out of the wear and tear of the ropes. This odd name was, perhaps, bestowed on our beautiful favorite in consequence of his color not being very dissimilar to that of well-tarred Russia hemp; while the resemblance was increased by many a dab of pitch, which his rough coat imbibed from the seams between the planks of the deck, in the hot weather.

If old Shakings was no great beauty, he was, at least, the most companionable of dogs; and though he dearly loved the midshipmen, and was dearly beloved by them in return, he had enough of the animal in his composition to take a still higher pleasure in the society of his own kind. So that, when the high-bred, showy pointers belonging to the officers came on board, after a shooting excursion, Mr. Shakings lost no time in applying to them for the news. The pointers, who liked this sort of familiarity very well, gave poor Shakings all sorts of encouragement. Not so their masters; they could not bear to see such an abominable cur, as they called our favorite, at once so cursedly dirty, and so utterly useless, mixing with their sleek and well-kept animals. At first their dislike was confined to such insulting expressions as these; then it came to an occasional kick, or a knock on the nose with the butt-end of a fowling-piece; and lastly, to a sound cut with the hunting-whip.

Shakings, who instinctively knew his place, took all this, like a sensible fellow, in good part; while the mids, when out of hearing of the higher powers, uttered curses, both loud and deep, against the tyranny and oppression exercised against an animal which, in their fond fancy, was declared to be worth all the dogs in the ward-room put together. They were little prepared, however, for the stroke which soon fell upon them, perhaps in consequence of these very murmurs. To their great horror and indignation, one of the lieutenants, provoked at some liberty which Master Shakings had taken with his newly-polished boot, called out, one morning,—

"Man that jolly-boat, and land that infernal, dirty, ugly beast of a dog, belonging to the young gentlemen!"

"Where shall I take him to, sir?" asked the strokesman of the boat.

"Oh, any where; pull to the nearest part of the shore, and pitch him on the rocks. He 'll shift for himself, I have no doubt." So off went poor dear Shakings!

If a stranger had come into the midshipmens' berth at that moment, he might have thought his majesty's naval service was about to be broken up. All allegiance, discipline, or subordination seemed utterly canceled by this horrible act. Many were the execrations hurled upward at the offending "knobs," who, we thought, were combining to make our lives miserable. Some of our party voted for writing a letter of remonstrance to the admiral against this unheard-of outrage; and one youth swore deeply that he would leave the service, unless justice were obtained. But as he had been known to swear the same thing half a dozen times every day since he joined the ship, no great notice was taken of this pledge. Another declared, upon his word of honor, that such an act was enough to make a man turn Turk, and fly his country! At last, by general agreement, it was decided that we should not do a bit of duty, or even stir from our seats, till we obtained redress for our grievances. However, while we were in the very act of vowing mutiny and disobedience, the hands were turned up to "furl sails!" upon which the whole party, totally forgetting their magnanimous resolution, scudded up the ladders, and jumped into their stations with more than usual alacrity; wisely thinking that the moment for actual revolt had not yet arrived.

A better scheme than throwing up the service, or writing to the admiral, or turning Musselmen, was afterward concocted. The midshipmen, who went on shore in the next boat, easily got hold of poor Shakings, who was howling on the steps of the watering-place. In order to conceal him, he was stuffed, neck and crop, into the captain's cloak-bag, brought safely on board, and restored once more to the bosom of his friends.

In spite of all we could do, however, to keep Master Shakings below, he presently found his way to the quarter-deck, to receive the congratulations of the other dogs. There he was soon detected by the higher powers, and very shortly afterward trundled over the gangway, and again tossed on the beach. Upon this occasion he was honored by the presence of one of his own masters, a middy, sent upon this express duty, who was specially desired to land the brute, and not bring him on board again. Of course this particular youngster did not bring the dog off; but before night, somehow or other, old Shakings was snoring away, in grand chorus, with his more fashionable friends, the pointers, and dreaming no evil, before the door of the very officer's cabin whose beautifully polished boot he had brushed so rudely in the morning; an offense that had led to his banishment.

This second return of our dog was too much. The whole posse of us were sent for on the quarter-deck, and, in very distinct terms, positively ordered not to bring Shakings on board again. These injunctions having been given, this wretched victim, as we termed him, of oppression was once more landed among the cedar groves. This time he remained a full week on shore; but how or when he found his way off again no one ever knew; at least no one chose to divulge. Never was there anything like the mutual joy felt by Shakings and his two dozen masters. He careered about the ship, barked and yelled with delight, and, in his raptures, actually leaped, with his dirty feet, on the milk-white duck trowsers of the disgusted officers, who heartily wished him at the bottom of the anchorage! Thus the poor beast unwittingly contributed to accelerate his hapless fate, by this ill-timed show of confidence in those who were then plotting his ruin. If he had kept his paws to himself, and staid quietly in the dark recesses of the cock-pit, wings, cable-tiers, and other wild regions, the secrets of which were known only to the inhabitants of our sub-marine world, all might yet have been well.

We had a grand jollification on the night of Shakings' restoration; and his health was in the very act of being drunk, with three times three, when the officer of the watch, hearing an uproar below, the sounds of which were conveyed distinctly up the windsail, sent down to put our lights out; and we were forced to march off growling to our hammocks

Next day, to our surprise and horror, old Shakings was not to be seen or heard of. We searched every where, interrogated the coxswains of all the boats, and cross-questioned the marines who had been sentries, during the night, on the forecastle, gangways and poop; but all in vain—no trace of Shakings could be found.

At length the opinion began to gain ground among us, that the poor beast had been put an end to by some diabolical means, and our ire mounted accordingly. This suspicion seemed the more natural, as the officers said not a word about the matter, nor even asked us what we had done with our dog. While we were in this state of excitement and distraction for our loss, one of the midshipmen, who had some drollery in his composition, gave a new turn to the expression of our thoughts.

This gentleman, who was more than twice as old as most of us, say about thirty, had won the affections of the whole of our class, by the gentleness of his manners, and the generous part he always took on our side. He bore among us the pet name of Daddy; and certainly he was like a father to those among us who, like myself, were quite adrift in the ship, without any one to look after them. He was a man of talents and classical education, but he had entered the navy far too late in life ever to take to it cordially. His habits, indeed, had become so rigid, that they could never be made to bend to the mortifying kind of discipline which, it appears, every officer should run through, but which only the young and light-hearted can brook. Our worthy friend, accordingly, with all his abilities, taste and acquirements, never seemed at home on board ship; and unless a man can reach this point of liking for the sea, he is better on shore. At all events, old Daddy cared more about his books than about the blocks, and delighted much more in giving us assistance in our literary pursuits, and trying to teach us to be useful, than in rendering himself a proficient in those professional mysteries, which he never hoped to practice in earnest himself.

What this very interesting person's early history was we never could find out; nor why he entered the navy; nor how it came that a man of his powers and accomplishments should have been kept back so long. Indeed, the youngsters never inquired too closely into these matters, being quite contented to have the advantage of his protection against the oppression of the oldsters, who occasionally bullied them. Upon all occasions of difficulty, we were in the habit of clustering round him, to tell our grievances, great and small, with the certainty of always finding in him that great desideratum in calamity—a patient and friendly listener.

It will easily be supposed that our kind Daddy took more than usual interest in this affair of Shakings, and that he was applied to by us at every stage of the transaction. He was sadly perplexed, of course, when the dog was finally missing; and for some days he could give us no comfort, nor suggest any mode of revenge which was not too dangerous for his young friends to put in practice. He prudently observed, that, as we had no certainty to go upon, it would be foolish to get ourselves into any serious scrape for nothing at all.

"There can be no harm, however," he continued, in his dry and slightly sarcastic way, which all who knew him will recollect as well as if they saw him now, drawing his hand slowly across his mouth and chin; "there can be no harm, my boys, in putting the other dogs in mourning for their dear departed friend Shakings; for, whatever is come of him, he is lost to them as well as to us, and his memory ought to be duly respected."

This hint was no sooner given than a cry was raised for crape, and every chest and bag ransacked, to procure badges of mourning. The pointers were speedily rigged up with a large bunch of crape, tied in a handsome bow, upon the left leg of each, just above the knee. The joke took immediately. The officers could not help laughing; for, though we considered them little better than fiends at that moment of excitement, they were, in fact, except in this instance, the best natured and most indulgent men I remember to have sailed with. They, of course, ordered the crape to be instantly cut off from the dogs' legs; and one of the officers remarked to us, seriously, that as we had now had our piece of fun out, there were to be no more such tricks.

Off we scampered, to consult old Daddy what was to be done next, as we had been positively ordered not to meddle any more with the dogs.

"Put the pigs in mourning," he said.

All our crape was expended by this time; but this want was soon supplied by men whose trade it is to discover resources in difficulty. With a generous devotion to the cause of public spirit, one of these juvenile mutineers pulled off his black handkerchief, and, tearing it in pieces, gave a portion to each of the circle, and away we all started to put into practice this new suggestion of our director-general of mischief.

The row which ensued in the pig-sty was prodigious—for in those days, hogs were allowed a place on board a man-of-war, a custom most wisely abolished of late years, since nothing can be more out of character with any ship than such nuisances. As these matters of taste and cleanliness were nothing to us, we did not intermit our noisy labor till every one of the grunters had his armlet of such crape as we had been able to muster. We then watched our opportunity, and opened the door so as to let out the whole herd of swine on the main-deck just at a moment when a group of the officers were standing on the fore part of the quarter-deck. Of course the liberated pigs, delighted with their freedom, passed, in review, under the very nose of our superiors, each with his mourning knot displayed, grunting or squealing along, as if it was their express object to attract attention to their domestic sorrow for the loss of Shakings. The officers were excessively provoked, as they could not help seeing that all this was affording entertainment, at their expense, to the whole crew; for, although the men took no part in this touch of insubordination, they were ready enough, in those idle times of the weary, weary peace, to catch at any species of distraction or deviltry, no matter what, to compensate for the loss of their wonted occupation of pommeling their enemies.

The matter, therefore, necessarily became rather serious; and the whole gang of us being sent for on the quarter-deck, we were ranged in a line, each with his toes at the edge of a plank, according to the orthodox fashion of these gregarious scoldings, technically called "toe-the-line matches." We were then given to understand that our proceedings were impertinent, and, after the orders we had received, highly offensive. It was with much difficulty that either party could keep their countenances during this official lecture, for, while it was going on, the sailors were endeavoring, by the direction of the officers, to remove the bits of silk from the legs of the pigs. If, however, it be difficult—as most difficult we found it—to put a hog into mourning, it is a job ten times more troublesome to take him out again. Such, at least, is the fair inference from these two experiments; the only one, perhaps, on record—for it cost half the morning to undo what we had effected in less than an hour—to say nothing of the unceasing and outrageous uproar which took place along the decks, especially under the guns, and even under the coppers, forward in the galley, where two or three of the youngest pigs had wedged themselves, apparently resolved to die rather than submit to the degradation of being deprived of their mourning.

All this was very creditable to the memory of poor Shakings; but, in the course of the day, the real secret of this extraordinary difficulty of taking a pig out of mourning was discovered. Two of the mids were detected in the very act of tying on a bit of black bunting to the leg of a sow, from which the seamen declared they had already cut off crape and silk enough to have made her a complete suit of black.

As soon as these fresh offenses were reported, the whole party of us were ordered to the mast-head as a punishment. Some were sent to sit on the topmast cross-trees, some on the topgallant yard-arms, and one small gentleman being perched at the jib-boom end, was very properly balanced abaft by another little culprit at the extremity of the gaff. In this predicament we were hung out to dry for six or eight hours, as old Daddy remarked to us with a grin, when we were called down as the night fell.

Our persevering friend, being rather provoked at the punishment of his young flock, now set to work to discover the real fate of Shakings. It soon occurred to him, that if the dog had really been made away with, as he shrewdly suspected, the butcher, in all probability, must have had a hand in his murder; accordingly he sent for the man in the evening, when the following dialogue took place:

"Well, butcher, will you have a glass of grog to-night?"

"Thank you, sir, thank you. Here 's your honor's health?" said the other, after smoothing down his hair, and pulling an immense quid of tobacco out of his mouth.

Old Daddy observed the peculiar relish with which the butcher took his glass; and mixing another, a good deal more potent, placed it before the fellow, and continued the conversation in these words:

"I tell you what it is, Mr. Butcher—you are as humane a man as any in the ship, I dare say; but, if required, you know well that you must do your duty, whether it is upon sheep or hogs?"

"Surely, sir."

"Or upon dogs either?" suddenly asked the inquisitor.

"I do n't know about that," stammered the butcher, quite taken by surprise, and thrown all aback.

"Well, well," said Daddy, "here 's another glass for you—a stiff north-wester. Come, tell us all about it now. How did you get rid of the dog?—of Shakings, I mean?"

"Why, sir," said the peaching rogue, "I put him in a bag—a bread bag, sir."

"Well—what then?"

"I tied up the mouth, and put him overboard—out of the midship lower-deck port, sir."

"Yes; but he would not sink?" said Daddy.

"Oh, sir," cried the butcher, now entering fully into the merciless spirit of his trade, "I put a four-and-twenty-pound shot into the bag along with Shakings."

"Did you?—Then, Master Butcher, all I can say is, you are as precious a rascal as ever went about unhanged. There, drink your grog, and be off with you!"

Next morning when the officers were assembled at breakfast in the ward-room, the door of the captain of marines' cabin was suddenly opened, and that officer, half shaved, and laughing through a collar of soap-suds, stalked out, with a paper in his hand.

"Here," he exclaimed, "is a copy of verses, which I found just now in my basin. I can't tell how they got there, nor what they are about—but you shall judge."

So he read the two following stanzas of doggerel:

"When the Northern Confed'racy threatened our shores,
And roused Albion's Lion, reclining to sleep,
Preservation was taken of all the King's Stores,
Nor so much as a *Rope Yarn* was launched in the deep.

"But now it is Peace; other hopes are in view,
And all active service as light as a feather;
The Stores may be ——, and humanity, too,
For SHAKINGS and *Shot* are thrown o'erboard together!"

I need hardly say in what quarter of the ship this biting morsel of cock-pit satire was concocted, nor, indeed, who wrote it, for there was no one but our good Daddy who was equal to such a flight. About midnight, an urchin, who shall be nameless, was thrust out of one of the after-ports of the lower-deck, from which he clambered up to the marine officer's port, and the sash happening to have been lowered down on the gun, the epigram, copied by another of the youngsters, was pitched into the soldier's basin.

The wisest thing would have been for the officers to have said nothing about the matter, and let it blow by. But angry people are seldom judicious; so they made a formal complaint to the captain, who, to do him justice, was not a little puzzled how to settle the affair. The reputed author, however, was called up, and the captain said to him:

"Pray, sir, are you the writer of these lines?"

"I am, sir," he replied, after a little consideration.

"Then all I can say is," remarked the captain, "they are clever enough in their way—but take my advice, and write no more such verses."

So the affair ended. The satirist took the captain's hint in good part, and confined his pen to topics below the surface of the water.

KEEPING WATCH.

With a few exceptions, every person on board a man-of-war keeps watch in his turn: and as this is one of the most important of the wheels which go to make up the curious clock-work of a ship's discipline, it seems to deserve a word or two in passing.

The officers and midshipmen are generally divided into three watches—first, second and third. As the senior lieutenant does not keep watch, the officer next in rank takes the first, the junior lieutenant the second, and the master the third watch, in ships where there are not more than three lieutenants. Under each of these chiefs there is placed a squad of midshipmen; the principal one of whom is mate of the watch, the next in seniority is stationed on the forecastle, and after him comes the poop mid. The youngsters remain on the lee-side of the quarter-deck, along with the mate of the watch. For it must be observed, that no one but the captain, the lieutenants, the master, surgeon, purser, and marine officer is ever allowed, upon any occasion whatsoever, to walk on the weather-side. This custom has become so much a matter of course, that I hardly remember asking myself before, what may have been the origin of the regulation? The chief purpose, no doubt, is to draw a strong line of distinction between the different ranks; although, independently of this, the weather-side is certainly the most convenient to walk upon when the ship is pressed with sail: it is also the best sheltered from wind and rain; and the view, both low and aloft, is more commanding than it is from the leeward.

Every person, also, not excepting the captain, when he comes on the quarter-deck, touches his hat; and as this salutation is supposed to be paid to this privileged spot itself, all those who at the moment have the honor to be upon it are bound to acknowledge the compliment. Thus, even when a midshipman comes up, and takes off his hat, all the officers who are walking the deck, the admiral included, if he happens to be of the number, touch their hats likewise.

So completely does this form grow into a habit, that in the darkest night, and when there may not be a single person near the hatchway, it is invariably attended to with the same precision. Indeed, when an officer of the navy happens to be on board a merchant ship, or a packet, he finds it difficult to avoid carrying his hand to his hat every time he comes on deck. I, for one, at least, can never get over the feeling that it is rude to neglect this ceremony, and have often, when on board passage vessels, wondered to see gentlemen so deficient in good breeding, as to come gaping up the hatchway, as if their hats were nailed to their heads, and their hands sewed into their breeches-pockets!

Of course, each person in the watch has a specific duty to attend to, as I shall endeavor to describe presently; but, first, it may be well to mention the ingenious arrangement of the hours by which the periods of watching are equally distributed to all.

In speaking of the three watches, it will, perhaps, avoid confusion, and rather simplify the description, to call them, for a moment, not first, second and third, as they are named on board ship, but to designate them by the letters A, B and C.

Let us begin then by supposing that A's watch commences at eight o'clock in the evening; the officer and his party remain on deck till midnight, four hours being one period. This is called the first watch. B is next roused up, and keeps the middle watch, which lasts from midnight till four o'clock. C now comes up, and stays on deck till eight, which is the morning watch. A then returns to the deck, where he walks till noon, when he is relieved by B, who stays up till four. If C were now to keep the watch from four to eight, of course A would again have to keep the first watch on the second night, as he did it first starting; and all the others, in like manner, would have to keep over again exactly the same watches, every night and day. In order to break this uniform recurrence of intervals, an ingenious device has been hit upon to produce a constant and equitable rotation. When or where this plan was invented, I do not know, but I believe it exists in the ships of all nations.

The period from four o'clock in the afternoon till eight in the evening, instead of constituting one watch, is divided into two watches, of a couple of hours each. These, I don't know why, are called the "dog watches." The first, which lasts from four to six o'clock, belongs, on the second day, according to the order described above, to C, who is, of course, relieved at six o'clock by A. This alteration, it will be observed, gives the first watch (from eight to midnight) to B, on the second night; the middle watch (from midnight to four) to C; and the morning watch (from four to eight) to A; the forenoon watch (from eight to noon) to B; and the afternoon (from noon to four) to C. The first dog watch (from four to six) will now be kept by A, the second dog watch (from six to eight) by B, and so on, round and round. By this mechanism, it will easily be perceived, the officers, on each succeeding day, have a watch to keep, always one stage earlier than that which they kept on the day before. Thus if A has the morning watch one night, he will have the middle watch on the night following, and the first watch on the night after that again. The distribution of time which this produces is very unequal, when the short period of twenty-four hours only is considered; but the arrangement rights itself in the course of a few days. On the first day, A has ten hours' watch to keep out of the twenty-four, B eight, and C only six. But on the next day, A has only six hours, while B has ten, and C eight; while on the third day, A has eight, B six, and C ten hours' watching; and so on, round and round, from year's end to year's end.

This variety, to a person in health and spirits, is often quite delightful. Each watch has its peculiar advantages; and I need hardly add that each likewise furnishes an ample store of materials for complaining, to those discontented spirits whose chief delight is to coddle up grievances, as if, forsooth, the principal object of life was to keep ourselves unhappy, and to help to make others so.

The first watch (eight o'clock to midnight) which comes after the labor of the day is done, and when everything is hushed and still, carries with it this great recommendation, that, although the hour of going to bed is deferred, the night's rest is not afterward broken in upon. The prospect of "turning in" at midnight, and being allowed to sleep till seven in the morning, helps greatly to keep us alive and merry during the first watch, and prevents the excitement of the past day from ebbing too fast. On the other hand, your thorough-bred growlers are apt to say, it is a grievous task to keep the first watch, after having gone through all the toil of the day, and, in particular, after having kept the afternoon watch, (noon to four o'clock,) which, in hot climates, is always a severe trial upon the strength. Generally speaking, however, I think the first watch is the least unpopular; for, I suppose, no mortal, whatever he might think, was ever found so Quixotic as to profess openly that he really liked keeping watch. Such a paradox would be famously ridiculed on board ship!

The middle watch is almost universally held to be a great bore; and certainly it is a plague of the first order, to be shaken out of a warm bed at midnight, when three hours of sound sleep have sealed up our eyelids all the faster, and steeped our senses in forgetfulness, and in repose, generally much needed. It is a bitter break, too, to have four good hours sliced out of the very middle of the night's rest, especially when this tiresome interval is to be passed in the cold and rain, or, which is often still more trying, in the sultry calm of a smooth, tropical sea, when the sleepy sails, as wet with dew as if they had been dipped overboard, flap idly against the masts and rigging, but so very gently as barely to make the reef points patter-patter along the canvas, with notes so monotonous, that the bare recollection of their sound almost sets me to sleep now.

Nevertheless the much abused middle watch has its advantages, at least for those ardent young spirits who choose to seek them out, and whose habit it is to make the most of things. There are full three hours and a half of sound snooze before it begins, and as long a "spell of sleep" after it is over. Beside which, the mind, being rested as well as the body, before the middle watch begins, both come to their task so freshly, that if there be any hard or anxious duties to execute, they are promptly and well attended to. Even if there be nothing to do but pace the deck, the thoughts of an officer of any enthusiasm may contrive to find occupation either in looking back, or in looking forward, with that kind of cheerfulness which belongs to youth and health usefully employed. At that season of the night every one else is asleep, save the quartermaster at the con, the helmsman at the wheel, and the lookout-men at their different stations on the gangways, the bows, and the quarters, and except, of course, the different drowsy middies, who, poor fellows! keep tramping along the quarter-deck, backward and forward, counting the half-hour bells with anxious weariness; or looking wistfully at the sand-glass, which the sentry at the cabin door shakes ever and anon, as if the lazy march of time, like that of a tired donkey, could be accelerated by jogging.

But the joyous morning watch is very naturally the universal favorite It is the beginning of a new day of activity and enterprize. The duties are attacked, too, after a good night's rest; so that, when the first touches of the dawn appear, and the horizon, previously lost in the black sky, begins to show itself in the east, there comes over the spirits a feeling of elasticity and strength, of which even the dullest are not altogether insensible. In war time, this is a moment when hundreds of eyes are engaged in peering all round into the twilight; and happy is the sharp-sighted person who first calls out with a voice of exultation:

"A sail, sir, a sail!"

"Whereabouts?" is the eager reply.

"Three or four points on the lee-bow, sir."

"Up with the helm!" cries the officer. "Set the topgallant and royal studding-sails—rig out the foretopmast studding-sail boom! Youngster, run down and tell the captain there is a stranger on the lee-bow—and say that we are making all sail. She looks very roguish."

As the merry morning comes dancing gloriously on, and other vessels hove in sight, fresh measures must be taken, as to the course steered, or the quantity of sail to be set. So that this period of the day, at sea, in a cruising ship, gives occasion, more, perhaps, than any other time, for the exercise of those stirring qualities of prompt decision, and vigor in the execution of every purpose, which, probably, form the essential characteristics of the profession.

The morning watch, also, independent of the active employment it hardly ever fails to afford, leaves the whole day free, from eight o'clock till four in the afternoon. Many a previously broken resolution is put off to this period, only to be again stranded. To those, however, who choose to study, the certainty of having one clear day in every three, free from the distraction of all technical duties, is of the greatest consequence; though, it must be owned that at the very best, a ship is but a wretched place for reading. The eternal motion, and the infernal noise, almost baffle the most resolute students.

For a hungry midshipman (when are they not hungry?) the morning watch has attractions of a still more tender nature. The mate, or senior man among them, is always invited to breakfast with the officers at eight o'clock; and one or two of the youngsters, in turn, breakfast with the captain at half past eight, along with the officer of the morning watch and the first lieutenant, who, in many ships, is the constant guest of the captain, both at this meal and at dinner.

I have already mentioned that the first watch begins, nominally, at eight, and ends at midnight; but people are much mistaken, who suppose that a sleepy-headed midshipman, with the prospect of a cold middle watch before him, and just awakened out of a sound nap, is disposed to jump up at once, dress himself, and run upon deck. Alas! it is far from this; and no one who has not been exposed to the trial can conceive the low ebb to which patriotism, zeal, public spirit—call it what you please—sinks at such an hour in the breast of the unhappy wretch who, in the midst of one of those light and airy dreams, which render the night season of young people such a heaven of repose, is suddenly roused up. After being awakened by a rude tug at the clues of his hammock, he is hailed, after the following fashion, by the gruff old quarter-master:

"Mr. Doughead!"

No answer. Another good tug at the hammock.

"Mr. Doughead! it's twelve o'clock, sir!"

"Very well, very well; you need not shake me out of bed, need you? What sort of a night is it?"

"It rains a little, sir, and is just beginning to blow. It looks very black, sir."

"Oh, plague take it! Then we shall have to take in a reef, I suppose?"

"It seems very like it, sir. It is beginning to snuffle."

With this, Mr. Doughead gives himself a good shrug in his blanket, turns half round, to escape the glare of light from the quarter-master's lantern, hung up within six inches of his face, expressly to keep him awake, and in ten seconds he is again tightly clasped in the arms of Morpheus, the presiding deity of the cock-pit at that hour. By and by comes down the quarter-master of the middle watch, who, unlike the young gentleman, has relieved the deck twenty minutes before.

"Mr. Doughead! it's almost one bell, sir."

"Indeed!" exclaims the youth. "I never knew anything of it. I never was called."

"Oh, yes, you were, sir. The man I relieved said you asked him what sort of weather it was, and whether we should have to take in a reef."

"I ask about the weather! That's only one of the lies he always tells, to get me into a scrape."

While they are speaking, the bell strikes one, indicating that half an hour has elapsed since the first conversation took place, touching the weather; and presently, before Mr. Doughead has got his second foot over the side of his hammock, the mid who is to be relieved by him comes rattling down the cock-pit ladder, as wet as a shag, cold, angry, and more than half asleep.

"I say, Master Doughy, do you mean to relieve the deck to-night? Here it 's almost two bells, and you have hardly shown a leg yet. I 'll be hanged if it is not too bad! You are the worst relief in the whole ship. I am obliged to keep all my own watch, and generally half of yours. I 'll not stand it any more; but go to the first lieutenant to-morrow morning, and see whether he cannot find ways and means of making you move a little faster. It 's a disgrace to the service!"

To all this Duffy has only one pettish dogged reply, "I tell you, again, I was not called."

The appeal to the first lieutenant, however, is seldom made; for all the parties concerned are pretty much alike. But the midshipmen are not slow, at times, to take the law of these cases into their own hands, and to execute summary justice, according to their own fashion, on any particularly incorrigibly "bad relief," as these tardy gentlemen are aptly termed.

One of the most common punishments, on these occasions, is called "cutting down," a process not quite so fatal as might be imagined from the term. Most people, I presume, know what sort of a thing a hammock is. It consists of a piece of canvas, five feet long by two wide, suspended to the deck overhead by means of two sets of small lines, called clues, made fast to grummets, or rings of rope, which again are attached by a lanyard to the battens stretching along the beams. In this sacking are placed a small mattress, a pillow, and a couple of blankets, to which a pair of sheets may or may not be added. The degree of nocturnal room and comfort enjoyed by these young gentlemen may be understood, when it is mentioned that the whole of the apparatus just described occupies less than a foot and a half in width, and that the hammocks touch one another. Nevertheless, I can honestly say, that the soundest sleep, by far, that I have ever known, has been found in these apparently uncomfortable places of repose; and though the recollection of many a slumber broken up, and the bitter pang experienced on making the first move to exchange so cozy a nest for the snarling of a piercing north-west gale, on the coast of America, will never leave my memory; yet I look back to those days and nights with a sort of evergreen freshness of interest, which only increases with years.

The wicked operation of "cutting down" may be managed in three ways. The mildest form is to take a knife and divide the foremost lanyard, or suspending cord. Of course that end of the hammock instantly falls, and the sleepy-headed youth is pitched out, feet foremost, on the deck. The other plan, which directs the after lanyard to be cut, is not quite so gentle, nor so safe, as it brings down the sleeper's head with a sharp bang on the deck, while his heels are jerked into the air. The third is to cut away both ends at once, which has the effect of bringing the round stern of the young officer in contact with the edge of any of the chests which may be placed so as to receive it. The startled victim is then rolled out of bed with his nose on the deck; or, if he happens to be sleeping in the tier, he tumbles on the hard bends of the cable coiled under him. This flooring is much more rugged, and not much softer than the planks, so that his fall is but a choice of miserable bumps.

The malice of this horse-play is sometimes augmented by placing a line round the middle part of the hammock, and fastening it to the beams overhead, in such a way that, when the lanyards at the ends are cut the head and tail of the youth shall descend freely; but the nobler part of him being secured by the belly-band, as it is called, the future hero of some future Trafalgar remains suspended ingloriously, in mid air, like the golden fleece over a wollen-draper's shop.

These are but a few of the tricks played off upon those who will not relieve the deck in proper time. I remember an incorrigible snoozer, who had been called three or four times, but still gave no symptoms of any intention of "showing a leg," the only allowable test of sincerity in the process called "turning out." About five o'clock, on a fine tropical morning, when the ship was cruising off the Mono Passage, in the West Indies, and just before the day began to dawn, it was resolved, in a full conclave of the middies of his own watch, assembled on the lee-side of the quarter-deck, that an example should forthwith be made of the sleeper.

A detachment, consisting of four stout hands, was sent to the hammock of the culprit. Two of them held the youth firmly down, while the others wrapped the bed-clothes round him, and then lashed him up—that is, strapped him tightly in by means of the lashing, a long cord with which the hammocks are secured when brought upon deck in the day-time. No part of the unfortunate wight was left exposed except his face. When he was fairly tied in, the lanyards of his hammock were cast off, and the bundle, half midshipman, half bedding, was dragged along, like a log of wood, to the square of the hatchway.

When all was secure, the word "haul up" was given from below, upon which the party on deck hoisted away. The sleeper awakened, vanished from the cock-pit, only to make his appearance, in a few seconds, at the mouth of the windsail, half way between the quarter-deck and the mizzen-stay. Of course, the boys watched their opportunity, when the officer of the watch had gone forward on the gangway, to see how the head-yards were trimmed; but long before he came aft again, their victim was lowered down, and the signal halyards unbent. What to do with the wretch next was a great puzzle, till one of them said, "Oh! let us stick him up on his end, between two of the guns on the weather-side of the deck, and, perhaps, the officer of the watch may take him for an Egyptian mummy, and have him sent to the British Museum, as a present to the king." This advice was instantly followed; and the enraged, mortified and helpless youngster, being placed so that the first rays of the sun should fall on his countenance, there was no mistaking his identity.

JACK'S ALLOWANCE.

The moment of noon is the most important of all the grand epochs which mark the progress of time on board ship. It commences our day in nautical astronomy, and is ushered in by a number of ceremonies, some of which never fail to excite the ridicule of our "shore going" friends who may happen to be on board; and who, from not well understanding the drift of what they see, are apt to fancy much of it unnecessary. Nothing is so easy, indeed, as to quiz those punctilious formalities with which naval discipline abounds. But if experience has taught that many of the most valuable fruits of good order can be traced to the exact observance of these very forms, they surely lose none of their importance from having been so long established that their origin is forgotten—still less from being laughed at by persons not having had the happiness of being brought up at sea, and, therefore, by no means the best judges of the utility of these refinements.

As the hour of noon approaches, the cooks of the messes may be seen coming up the fore and main hatchways, with their mess-kids in their hands, the hoops of which are kept as bright as silver, and the wood-work as neat and clean as a pail of the most tidy dairy-maid. The grog, also, is now mixed in a large tub, under the half-deck, by the quarter-masters of the watch below, assisted by other leading and responsible men among the ship's company, closely superintended, of course, by the mate of the hold, to see that no liquor is abstracted, and also by the purser's steward, who regulates the exact quantity of spirits and of water to be measured out. The seamen whose next turn it is to take the wheel, or heave the lead, or who have to mount to the mast-head to look out, as well as the marines who are to be planted as sentries at noon, are allowed to take both their dinner and their grog beforehand. These persons are called "seven-bell men," from the hour at which they have their allowance served to them.

Long before twelve o'clock, all these, and various other minor preparations, have been so completely made, that there is generally a remarkable stillness over the whole ship just before the important moment of noon arrives. The boatswain stands near the break of the forecastle, with his bright silver call, or whistle, in his hand, which ever and anon he places just at the tip of his lips, to blow out any crumbs which threaten to interfere with its melody, or to give a faint "too weet! too weet!" as a preparatory note, to fix the attention of the boatswain's mates, who being, like their chief, provided with calls, station themselves at intervals along the main-deck, ready to give due accompaniment to their leader's tune.

The boatswain keeps his eye on the group of observers, and well knows when the "sun is up," by the stir which takes place among the astronomers, or by noticing the master working out his latitude with a pencil, on the ebony bar of his quadrant, or on the edge of the hammock-railing; though if he be one of your modern neat-handed navigators, he carries his little book for this purpose. In one way or other the latitude is computed, as soon as the master is satisfied that the sun has reached his highest altitude in the heavens. He then walks aft to the officer of the watch, and reports twelve o'clock, communicating, also, the degrees and minutes of the latitude observed. The lieutenant proceeds to the captain, wherever he may be, and repeats that it is twelve, and that so and so is the latitude. The same formal round of reports is gone through, even if the captain be on deck, and has heard every word spoken by the master, or even if he has himself assisted in making the observation.

The captain now says to the officer of the watch, "Make it twelve."

The officer calls out to the mate of the watch, "Make it twelve."

The mate — ready primed — sings out to the quarter-master, "Strike eight bells!"

And lastly, the hard-a-weather old quarter-master, stepping down the ladder, grunts out to the sentry at the cabin door, "Turn the glass, and strike the bell!"

By this time the boatswain's call has been in his mouth for several minutes, his elbow in the air, and his little finger on the stop, ready to send forth the glad tidings of a hearty meal. Not less ready or less eager are the groups of listeners seated at their snow-white deal tables below, or the crowd surrounding the coppers, with their mess-kids acting the part of drums to their impatient knuckles. At the first stroke of the bell, which, at this particular hour, is always sounded with peculiar vivacity, the officer of the watch exclaims to the boatswain, "Pipe to dinner!"

These words, followed by a glorious burst of shrill sounds, "long drawn out," are hailed with a murmur of delight by many a hungry tar, and many a jolly marine. The merry notes are nearly drowned, next instant, in the rattle of tubs and kettles, the voice of the ship's cook and his mates, bawling out the numbers of the messes, as well as by the sound of feet trampling along the decks, and down the ladders, with the steaming, ample store of provisions—such as set up and brace the seaman's frame, and give it vigor for any amount of physical action.

A SEAMAN'S GRAVE.

Independently of any personal interest, sailors are always very desirous that no one should die on board—or rather, they have a great objection to the body of any one who has died remaining among them. This is a superstition easily accounted for among men whose whole lives are passed, as it were, on the very edge of the grave, and who have quite enough, as they suppose, to remind them of their mortality, without the actual presence of its effects. An idea prevails among them, that sharks will follow a ship for a whole voyage which has a corpse on board; and the loss of a mast, or the long duration of a foul wind, or any other inconvenience, is sure to be ascribed to the same influence. Accordingly, when a man dies on board ship, there is an obvious anxiety among the crew to get rid of their late shipmate as speedily as possible.

It need not be mentioned that the surgeon is in constant attendance upon the dying man, who has generally been removed from his hammock to a cot, which is larger and more commodious, and is placed within a screen on one side of the sick bay, as the hospital of the ship is called. It is usual for the captain to pass through this place, and to speak to the men, every morning; and I imagine there is hardly a ship in the service in which wine, fresh meat, and any other supplies recommended by the surgeon, are not sent from the tables of the captain and officers to such of the sick men as require a more generous diet than the ship's stores provide. After the carver in the gun-room has helped his messmates, he generally turns to the surgeon, and says, "Doctor, what shall I send to the sick?" But, even without this, the steward would certainly be taken to task were he to omit inquiring, as a matter of course, what was wanted in the sick bay. The restoration of the health of the invalids by such supplies is, perhaps, not more important, however, than the moral influence of the attention on the part of the officers.

I have generally observed, also, a most valuable effect produced on the minds of the survivors, by the captain attending the death-bed of any of his crew. It is astonishing, indeed, how far such well timed notice, however small, goes with the sailors; and it is of importance to remember that this is only one of numberless means by which a judicious officer may always strengthen his hands, and improve the discipline of his ship, at an extremely small sacrifice of time, and none at all of his true dignity. For the men are vastly easier managed when they have reason to believe their superiors enter into and respect their feelings, than when, as sometimes happens, they see them act as if they scarcely considered themselves of the same species. Sailors, indeed, will submit cheerfully to much greater hardships, and work with double energy, at the word of an officer, however strict, provided they are made sensible that while he is regulated by a sense of justice in his severity, he likewise considers an attention to their comforts and happiness a part of his duty.

I would, accordingly, strongly recommend every captain to be seen (no matter for how short a time) by the bedside of any of his crew whom the surgeon may report as dying. Not occasionally, and in the flourishing style with which we read of great generals visiting hospitals, but uniformly, and in the quiet sobriety of real kindness, as well as hearty consideration for the feelings of a man falling at his post in the service of his country. The éclat of such a death is inferior, no doubt, to that which is bestowed in battle; but we should recollect that on this very account the sacrifice deserves more attention at our hands. A man who is killed in action has a brilliant Gazette to record his exploits, and the whole country may be said to attend his death-bed. But the merit is not less—or may even be much greater—of the soldier or sailor who dies of a fever in a distant land—his story untold, and his sufferings unseen. In warring against climates unsuited to his frame, he may have encountered, in the public service, enemies often more formidable than those who handle pike and gun. There should be nothing left undone, therefore, at such a time, to show, not only to the dying man, but to his shipmates, and his family at home, that his services are appreciated.

I remember, on one occasion, hearing the captain of a ship say to a poor fellow who was almost gone, that he was glad to see him so cheerful at such a moment; and begged to know if he had anything to say.

"I hope, sir," said the expiring seaman, with a smile, "I have done my duty to your satisfaction?"

"That you have, my lad," said his commander, "and to the satisfaction of your country, too."

"That is all I wanted to know, sir," replied the man.

These few common-place words cost the captain not five minutes of his time, but were long recollected with gratitude by the people under his orders, and contributed, along with many other graceful acts of considerate attention, to fix his authority as firmly as he could desire.

If a sailor who knows he is dying has a captain who pleases him, he is very likely to send a message by the surgeon to beg a visit—not often to trouble his commander with any commission, but merely to say something at parting. No officer, of course, would ever refuse to grant such an interview, but it appears to me it should always be volunteered; for many men may wish it whose habitual respect would disincline them to take such a liberty, even at the moment when all distinctions are about to cease.

Very shortly after poor Jack dies, he is prepared for his deep sea grave by his messmates, who, with the assistance of the sail-maker, and in the presence of the master-at-arms, sew him up in his hammock, and having placed a couple of cannon-shot at his feet, they rest the body (which now not a little resembles an Egyptian mummy) on a spare grating. Some portion of the bedding and clothes are always made up in the package — apparently to prevent the form being too much seen. It is then carried aft, and, being placed across the after hatchway, the union jack is thrown over all. Sometimes it is placed between two of the guns, under the half-deck; but generally, I think, he is laid where I have mentioned, just abaft the mainmast.

I should have mentioned before that as soon as the surgeon's ineffectual professional offices are at an end, he walks to the quarter-deck, and reports to the officer of the watch that one of his patients has just expired. At whatever hour of the day or night this occurs, the captain is immediately made acquainted with the circumstance. At the same time the master-at-arms is ordered by the officer of the watch to take possession of the dead man's clothes; and his messmates, soon afterward, proceed to dress and prepare the body for burial.

Next day, generally about eleven o'clock, the bell on which the half hours are struck is tolled for the funeral by one of the quarter-masters of the watch below, or by one of the deceased's messmates; and all who choose to be present assemble on the gangways, booms, and round the mainmast, while the forepart of the quarter-deck is occupied by the officers.

In some ships—and it ought, perhaps, to be so in all—it is made imperative on the officers and crew to attend this ceremony. If such attendance be a proper mark of respect to a professional brother—as it surely is—it ought to be enforced, and not left to caprice. There may, indeed, be times of great fatigue, when it would harass men and officers needlessly to oblige them to come on deck for every funeral, and upon such occasions the watch on deck may be sufficient. Or, when some dire disease gets into a ship, and is cutting down her crew by its daily and nightly, or it may be hourly, ravages, and when two or three times in a watch, the ceremony must be repeated, those only whose turn it is to be on deck need be assembled. In such fearful times, the funeral is generally made to follow close upon the death.

While the people are repairing to the quarter-deck, in obedience to the summons of the bell, the grating on which the body is placed, being lifted from the main-deck by the messmates of the man who has died, is made to rest across the lee gangway. The stanchions for the man-ropes of the side are unshipped, and an opening made at the after-end of the hammock netting sufficiently large to allow a free passage.

The body is still covered by the flag already mentioned, with the feet projecting a little over the gunwale, while the messmates of the deceased range themselves on each side. A rope, which is kept out of sight in these arrangements, is then made fast to the grating, for a purpose which will be seen presently.

When all is ready, the chaplain, if there be one on board, or, if not, the captain, or any of the officers he may direct to officiate, appears on the quarter-deck, and commences the beautiful service, which, though but too familiar to most ears, I have observed, never fails to rivet the attention even of the rudest and least reflecting. Of course, the bell has ceased to toll, and every one stands in silence and uncovered as the prayers are read. Sailors, with all their looseness of habits, are well disposed to be sincerely religious; and when they have fair play given them, they will always, I believe, be found to stand on as good vantage ground, in this respect, as their fellow-countrymen on shore. Be this as it may, there can be no more attentive, or apparently reverent auditory, than assembles on the deck of a ship of war, on the occasion of a shipmate's burial.

There is no material difference in the form of this service from that used on shore, excepting in the place where allusion is made to the return of the body to its parent earth. Perhaps it might have been as well as to have left this unchanged—for the ocean may well be taken, in this sense, as a part of the earth—but since an alteration of the words was thought necessary, it could not have been made in better taste.

The land service for the burial of the dead contains the following words:—

"Forasmuch as it hath pleased Almighty God, of his great mercy, to take unto himself the soul of our dear brother here departed, we therefore commit his body to the ground; earth to earth, ashes to ashes, dust to dust; in sure and certain hope," etc.

Every one, I am sure, who has attended the funeral of a friend—and who will this not include?—must recollect the solemnity of that stage of the ceremony, where, as the above words are pronounced, there are cast into the grave three successive portions of earth, which, falling on the coffin, send up a hollow, mournful sound, resembling no other that I know.

In the burial service at sea, the part quoted above is varied in the following very striking and solemn manner:—

"Forasmuch as it hath pleased Almighty God, in his wise providence, to take out of this world the soul of our deceased brother, we therefore commit his body to the deep, to be turned into corruption, looking for the resurrection of the body, when the sea shall give up her dead," etc.

At the commencement of this part of the service, one of the seamen stoops down, and disengages the flag from the remains of his late shipmate, while the others, at the words, "we commit his body to the deep," project the grating right into the sea. The body being loaded with shot at one end, glances off the grating, plunges at once into the ocean, and—

"In a moment, like a drop of rain,
He sinks into its depths with bubbling groan,
Without a grave, unknelled, uncoffined, and unknown."

This part of the ceremony is rather less impressive than the correspondent part on land; but still there is something solemn, as well as startling, in the sudden splash, followed by the sound of the grating, as it is towed along, under the main-chains.

In a fine day at sea, in smooth water, and when all the ship's company and officers are assembled, the ceremony just described, although a melancholy one, as it must always be, is often so pleasing, all things considered, that it is calculated to leave even cheerful impressions on the mind.

Occasions, however, as gloomy as any sad heart could conceive, do sometimes occur for a sea funeral, sufficient to strike the sternest natures. The most impressive which I recollect, of the numbers I have witnessed, was in the flag-ship, on the coast of North America.

There was a poor little middy on board, so delicate and fragile, that the sea was clearly no fit profession for him; but he or his friends thought otherwise; and as he had a spirit for which his frame was no match, he soon gave token of decay. This boy was a great favorite with everybody; the sailors smiled whenever he passed, as they would have done to a child; the officers petted him, and coddled him up with all sorts of good things; and his messmates—in a style which did not altogether please him, but which he could not well resist, as it was meant most kindly—nicknamed him Dolly. Poor fellow!—he was long remembered afterward. I forget what his particular complaint was, but he gradually sunk; and at last went out just as a taper might have done, exposed to such gusts of wind as blew in that tempestuous region. He died in the morning; but it was not until the evening that he was prepared for a seaman's grave.

I remember, in the course of the day, going to the side of the boy's hammock, and on laying my hand upon his breast, was astonished to find it still warm—so much so, that I almost imagined I could feel the heart beat. This, of course, was a vain fancy; but I was much attached to my little companion, being then not much taller myself; and I was soothed and gratified, in a childish way, by discovering that my friend, though many hours dead, had not yet acquired the usual revolting chillness.

In after years I have sometimes thought of this incident, when reflecting on the pleasing doctrine of the Spaniards, that as soon as children die, they are translated into angels, without any of those "cold obstructions" which, they pretend, intercept and retard the souls of other mortals. The peculiar circumstances connected with the funeral which I am about to describe, and the fanciful superstitions of the sailors upon the occasion, have combined to fix the whole scene in my memory.

Something occurred during the day to prevent the funeral taking place at the usual hour, and the ceremony was deferred till long after sunset. The evening was extremely dark, and it was blowing a treble-reefed topsail breeze. We had just sent down the topgallant yards, and made all snug for a boisterous winter's night. As it became necessary to have lights to see what was done, several signal lanterns were placed on the break of the quarter-deck, and others along the hammock railings on the lee gangway. The whole ship's company and officers were assembled, some on the booms, others in the boats, while the main rigging was crowded half way up to the cat-harpings. Overhead, the mainsail, illuminated as high as the yard by the lamps, was bulging forward under the gale, which was rising every minute, and straining so violently at the main-sheet, that there was some doubt whether it might not be necessary to interrupt the funeral in order to take sail off the ship. The lower-deck ports lay completely under water, and several times the muzzles of the main-deck guns were plunged into the sea; so that the end of the grating on which the remains of poor Dolly were laid, once or twice nearly touched the tops of the waves, as they foamed and hissed past. The rain fell fast on the bare heads of the crew, dropping also on the officers, during all the ceremony, from the foot of the mainsail, and wetting the leaves of the prayer-book. The wind sighed over us among the wet shrouds, with a note so mournful, that there could not have been a more appropriate dirge.

The ship—pitching violently—strained and creaked from end to end: so that, what with the noise of the sea, the rattling of the ropes, and the whistling of the wind, hardly one word of the service could be distinguished. The men, however, understood, by a motion of the captain's hand, when the time came, and the body of our dear little brother was committed to the deep.

So violent a squall was sweeping past the ship at this moment, that no sound was heard of the usual splash, which made the sailors allege that their young favorite never touched the water at all, but was at once carried off in the gale to his final resting-place!

THE CHASE.

On the 8th of November, 1810, when we were lying in that splendid harbor the Cove of Cork, and quietly refitting our ship, an order came for us to proceed to sea instantly, on a cruise of a week off Cape Clear, in quest of an enemy's vessel, reported to have been seen from some of the signal towers on the west coast. We were in such a predicament that it was impossible to start before the next morning, though we worked all night. Off we went at last; but it was not till the 11th that we reached our appointed station. Toward evening it fell dead calm, at which time there were two strange sails in sight; one of them a ship, which we "calculated" was an American, from the whiteness of his sails; the other a very suspicious, roguish-looking brig; but as both of them were hull down, much of this was guess-work.

As the night fell, a light breeze sprung up, and we made all sail in the direction of the brig, though she was no longer visible. In the course of the middle watch, we fortunately got sight of her with our night-glasses, and by two in the morning were near enough to give her a shot. The brig was then standing on a wind; while we were coming down upon her, right before it, or nearly so. The sound of our bow-chaser could hardly have reached the vessel it was fired at before her helm was up; and in the next instant her booms were rigged out, and her studding-sails, low and aloft, seen dangling at the yard-arms. The most crack ship in his majesty's service, with everything prepared, could hardly have made sail more smartly.

For our parts, we could set nothing more, having already spread every stitch of canvas; but the yards were trimmed afresh, the tacks hauled closer out, and the halyards sweated up till the yards actually pressed against the sheeve-holes. The best helmsman on board was placed at the wheel; and the foot of the foresail being drawn slightly up by the bunt slab-line, he could just see the chase clear of the foremast, and so keep her very nearly right ahead. The two forecastle guns, long nine-pounders, were now brought to bear on the brig; but as we made quite sure of catching her, and did not wish needlessly to injure our prize, or to hurt her people, orders were given to fire at the sails, which, expanded as they now were before us, like the tail of a peacock in his fullest pride, offered a mark which could not well be missed. Nevertheless, the little fellow would not heave to for all we could do with our fore-castle guns. At four o'clock, therefore, we managed to get one of the long eighteen-pounders on the main-deck, to bear upon him from the bridle-port. Still we could not stop him, though it was now bright moonlight, and there was no longer any tenderness about hurting his people, or injuring his hull. The vessel, however, at which we were now peppering away with round and grape shot, as hard as we could discharge them from three good smart guns, was so low in the water, that she offered, when seen end on, scarcely any mark. How it happened that none of her yards or masts came rattling down, and that none of her sails flew away, under the influence of our fire was quite inexplicable.

The water still continued quite smooth, though the breeze had freshened, till we went along at the rate of six or seven knots. When the privateer got the wind, which we had brought up with us, she almost kept her own, and it became evident that she was one of that light and airy description of vessels which have generally an advantage over larger ships when there is but little wind. We, therefore, observed, with much anxiety, that about half past four the breeze began gradually to die away, after which the chase rather gained than lost distance. Of course, the guns were now plied with double care, and our best marksmen were straining their eyes, and exerting their utmost skill, confident of hitting her, but all apparently to no purpose. One or two of the officers, in particular, who piqued themselves on knowing how to level a gun on principles quite unerring, in vain tried their infallible rules to bring our persevering chase to acknowledge himself caught.

By this time, of course, every man and boy in the ship was on deck, whether it was his watch or not; even the marine officer, the purser and the doctor left their beds—a rare phenomenon. Every one was giving his opinion to his neighbor; some said the shot went over her, some that they fell short; and the opinion that she was a witch, or the Flying Dutchman, or some other phantom, was current among the sailors, while the marines were clicking their flints, and preparing to give our little gentleman a taste of the small arms when within their reach.

While things were in this anxious, but very pleasurable state, our foresail flapped slowly against the mast—a sure indication that the breeze was lulling. The quadruple rows of reef-points were next heard to rattle along the topsails—sounds too well known to every ear as symptoms of an approaching calm. The studding-sails were still full, and so were the royals; but, by and by, even their light canvas refused to belly out, so faint was the air which still carried us, but very gently, along the water, on the surface of which not a ripple was now to be seen in any direction. As the ship, however, still answered her helm, we kept the guns to bear on the chase without intermission, and with this degree of effect, that all her sails, both low and aloft, were soon completely riddled, and some of them were seen hanging in such absolute rags, that the slightest puff of wind must have blown them away like so many cobwebs. By five o'clock it was almost entirely calm, and we had the mortification to observe that the chase, whose perseverance had kept him thus long out of our clutches, was putting in practice a maneuver we could not imitate. He thrust out his sweeps, as they are called, huge oars, requiring five or six men to each. These, when properly handled, by a sufficiently numerous crew, in a small light vessel, give her the heels of a large ship, when so nearly calm as it now was with us. We were not going more than a knot through the water, if so much, which was barely enough to give us steerage way.

The Frenchman got out, I suppose, about fifteen or twenty of these sweeps, and so vigorously were they plied, that we could see by the moonlight, and still more distinctly when the dawn appeared, that the foam was made to fly in sheets at each stroke of these gigantic oars, which were worked together, by their looms being united by a hawser stretching fore and aft. Our chief anxiety now was to pitch a shot among his sweeps, as one successful hit there would have sent half his crew spinning about the decks. But we were not so fortunate; and in less than an hour he was out of shot, walking off from us in a style which it was impossible not to admire, though our disappointment and vexation were excessive. By mid-day he was at least ten miles ahead of us; and at two o'clock we could just see his upper sails above the horizon. We had observed, during the morning, that our indefatigable little chase, as soon as he had rowed himself from under the relentless fire of our guns, was busily employed in bending a new suit of sails, fishing his splintered yards, shifting his topgallant-masts, and rigging out fresh studding-sail booms—all wounded, more or less, by our shot. As the severe labor of the sweeps was never intermitted, we knew, to a certainty, that the chase, though small, must be full of hands, and, consequently, it was an object of great importance for us to catch him. Of this, however, there now seemed but very little chance; and many were the hearty maledictions he received, though shared, it is true, by our own crack marksmen, now quite crest-fallen, or driven to the poor excuse of declaring that the moonlight on the water had deceived them as to the distance.

It really seemed as if every one on board had been seized with a fever—nothing else was thought of, or talked of, but the French brig; every glass, great and small, was in requisition, from the pocket spy-glass of the youngest midshipman, to the forty-inch focus of the captain. Each telescope in its turn was hoisted to the cross-trees, and pointed, with a sort of sickening eagerness, toward the lessening speck on the distant horizon. One might also have thought that the ship was planted in a grove of trees, in the height of spring time, so numerous were the whistlers. This practice of whistling for a wind is one of our nautical superstitions, which, however groundless and absurd, fastens insensibly on the strongest minded sailors at such times. Indeed, I have seen many an anxious officer's mouth take the piping form, and have even heard some sounds escape from lips which would have vehemently disclaimed all belief in the efficacy of such incantation.

But it would be about as wise a project to reason with the gales themselves as to attempt convincing Jack that, as the wind bloweth only when and where it listeth, his invoking it can be of no sort of use one way or the other. He will still whistle on, I have no doubt, in all time to come, when he wants a breeze, in spite of the march of intellect; for, as long as the elements remain the same, a sailor's life, manage it as we will, cannot be materially altered. It must always be made up of alternate severe labor and complete indolence, of the highest imaginable excitement, and of the most perfect lassitude. If I were not anxious at this moment to get back to my chase, I think I could show how these causes, acting upon such strange stuff as sailors are made of, leads to the formation of those superstitious habits by which they have always been characterized.

In the course of the afternoon, we perceived from the mast-head, far astern, a dark line along the horizon, which some of our most experienced hands pronounced the first trace of a breeze coming up. In the course of half an hour, this line had widened so much that it could easily be perceived from the deck. Upon seeing this, the whistlers redoubled their efforts; and whether, as they pretended, it was owing to their interest with the clerk of the weather office, or whether the wind, if left alone, would have come just as soon, I do not venture to pronounce; but certain it is, that, long before sunset, our hearts were rejoiced by the sight of those numerous flying patches of wind, scattered over the calm surface of the sea, and called by seamen, cat's-paws—I presume from the stealthy, timorous manner in which they seem to touch the water, and straightway vanish again. By and by the true wind, the ripple from which had marked the horizon astern of us, and broken the face of the mirror shining brightly everywhere else, indicated its approach, by fanning out the skysails, and other flying kites, generally supposed to be superfluous, but which, upon such occasions as this, do good service, by catching the first breath of air that seems always to float far above the water. One by one the sails were filled; and as the ship gathered way, every person marked the glistening eye of the helmsman, when he felt the spokes of the wheel pressing against his hand, by the action of the water on the rudder. The fire engine had been carried into the tops, and, where its long spout could not reach, buckets of water were drawn up, and thrown on the sails, so that every pore was filled, and the full effect of the wind was exerted on the canvas.

The ship now began to speak, as it is termed; and looking over the gangway, we could see a line of small hissing bubbles, not yet deserving the name of spray, but quite enough to prove to us that the breeze was beginning to tell. It was near the middle of November, but the day was as hot as if it had been summer; and the wind, now freshening at every second, blew coolly and gratefully upon us, giving assurance that we should have no more calms to trouble us, whatever might be our other difficulties in capturing Monsieur Frenchman.

Of these difficulties, the greatest by far was that of keeping sight of the brig after it became dark. We overhauled him, however, so fast that we had great hopes of being able to command him with our night-glasses, in which case we made pretty sure of our prize. The night-glass, it may be right to explain, is a telescope of small power, increasing the diameter of objects only about eight times. It has a large field-glass; and, in order to save the interception of light, has one lens fewer than usual, which omission has the effect of inverting the object looked at. But this, though inconvenient, is of little consequence, in cases where the desideratum is merely to get sight of a vessel, without seeking to make out the details.

Meanwhile, as we spanked along, rapidly accelerating our pace, and rejoicing in the cracking of the ropes, and the bending of the lightest and loftiest spars—that butterfly sort of gear which a very little wind soon brushes away—we had the malicious satisfaction of observing that the poor little privateer had not yet got a mouthful of the charming wind, which, like the well known intoxicating gas, was by this time setting us all a-skipping about the decks. The greater part of the visible ocean was now under the influence of the new-born breeze; but, in the spot where the brig lay, there occurred a belt or splash of clear white light, within which the calm still lingered, with the privateer sparkling in its center. Just as the sun went down, however, this spot was likewise melted into the rest, and the brig, like a poor hare roused from her seat, sprang off again. We were soon near enough to see her sweeps rigged in—to the delight, no doubt, of her weary crew, whose apprehensions of an English prison had probably kept up their strength to a pitch rarely equalled.

As the twilight—the brief twilight of winter—galloped away, a hundred pairs of eyes were almost jumping out of their sockets, in their attempts to pierce the night; while those who had glasses kept scrubbing them without mercy, as if they imagined more light would be let into the tube the more they injured the lenses. One person, and only one, continued, as he asserted, to see the chase, faintly strung, like a bead, on the horizon. I need not say that this sharp-sighted gentleman was nailed to his post, and ordered on no account to move his head, fatigue or no fatigue. There happened to be a single star, directly over the spot to which this fortunate youth was directing his view, with as much anxiety as ever Galileo peered into the heavens in search of a new planet. This fact being announced, a dozen spy-glasses were seen wagging up and down, between this directing star and that part of the horizon, now almost invisible, which lay immediately below it. Many were the doubts expressed of the correctness of the first observation, and many the tormenting questions put to the observer, as to which way the brig was standing? what sail was set? whether we were drawing up with her or not? as if the poor youngster had been placed along side of the vessel. These doubts and fears were put an end to, or nearly so, by bidding the boy keep his eye fixed on what he took to be the chase, and then, without acquainting him with the change, altering the ship's course for half a minute. This experiment had scarcely been commenced before he cried out, "I have lost sight of her this very moment! I saw her but an instant ago!" And when the ship's head was brought back to the original course, he exclaimed, "There she is again, by jingo! just to the right of the star."

This star served another useful purpose at the same time. The man at the wheel could see it shining between the leech of the foretop-sail and that of the topmast-studding-sail, and was thus enabled to steer the ship with much greater steadiness than he could possibly have done by the compass alone. Before midnight, as the breeze had freshened greatly, and we were going at the rate of nine knots an hour, we had drawn up so much with the privateer, that every one could see her with the naked eye, and the gunner, with his mates, and the marksmen who had lost their credit on the preceding night, were fidgeting and fussing about the guns, eager to be banging away at the prize, as they now began, rather prematurely, to call her—little knowing what a dextrous, persevering, and gallant little fellow they had to deal with, and how much trouble he was yet to give us.

It was not till about two o'clock that we once more came within good shot of him; and as it had been alleged that the guns were fired too quickly the night before, and without sufficient care in pointing, the utmost attention was now paid to laying them properly; and the lanyard of the trigger never pulled till the person looking along the gun felt confident of his aim. The brig, however, appeared to possess the same witch-like, invulnerable quality as ever; for we could neither strike her hull, so as to force her to cry "peccavi," nor bring down a yard, nor lop off a mast or a boom. It was really a curious spectacle to see a little bit of a thing skimming away before the wind, with such a huge monster as the Endymion tearing and plunging after her, like a voracious dolphin leaping from sea to sea in pursuit of a flying-fish.

In time, this must have ended in the destruction of the brig; for, as we gained upon her rapidly, some of our shot must by and by have taken effect, and sent her to the bottom. She was destined, however, to enjoy a little longer existence. The proper plan, perhaps, would have been to stand on, firing at her sails, till we had reached within musket-shot, and then to have knocked down the helmsman and every one else on her deck. This, however, was not our captain's plan—or perhaps he became impatient—at all events he gave orders for the whole starboard broadside to be got ready, and then, giving the ship a yaw, poured the whole discharge, as he thought, right into his wretched victim!

Not a mortal on board the frigate expected ever to see the poor brig again. What, then, was our surprise, when the smoke blew swiftly past, to see the intrepid little cocky gliding away more merrily than before. As far as good discipline would allow, there was a general murmur of applause at the Frenchman's gallantry. In the next instant, however, this sound was converted into hearty laughter, over the frigate's decks, when, in answer to our thundering broadside, a single small gun, a six-pounder, was fired from the brig's stern, as if in contempt of his formidable antagonist's prowess.

Instead of gaining by our maneuver, we had lost a good deal, and in two ways. In the first place, by yawing out of our course, we enabled the privateer to gain several hundred yards upon us; and secondly, his funny little shot, which had excited so much mirth, passed through the lee foretop-sail yardarm, about six feet inside the boom iron. Had it struck on the windward side, where the yard was cracking and straining at a most furious rate, the greater part of the sails on the foremast might have been taken in quicker than we could have wished—for we were now going at the rate of eleven and a half, with the wind on the quarter.

Just as we made out where his first shot had struck us, another cut through the weather main-topgallant sheet, and so he went on, firing away briskly till most of our lofty sails were fluttering with the holes made in them. His own sails, I need scarcely add, were by this time so completely torn up by our shot, that we could see the sky through them all; but still he refused to heave to—and, by constantly firing his single stern-chaser, was evidently resolved to lose no possible chance of escape. Had one or two of his shot struck either of our topmasts, I really believe he might have got off. It therefore became absolutely necessary that we should either demolish or capture him without further loss of time. The choice we left to himself, as will be seen. But such a spirited cruiser as this was an enemy worth subduing at any cost; for there was no calculating the mischief a privateer so admirably commanded might have wrought in a convoy. There was a degree of discretion, also, about this expert privateersman, which was very remarkable, and deserving of such favor at our hands as we had to spare. He took care to direct his stern-chaser so high that there was little chance of his shot striking any of our people. Indeed, he evidently aimed solely at crippling the masts, knowing right well that it would answer none of his ends to kill or wound any number of his enemy's crew, while it might irritate their captain to show him less mercy at the last moment, which, as will be seen, was fast approaching.

The breeze had now freshened nearly to a gale of wind, and when the log was hove, out of curiosity, just after the broadside I have described, we were going nearly twelve knots, (or between thirteen and fourteen miles an hour,) foaming and splashing along. The distance between us and the brig was now rapidly decreasing, for most of his sails were in shreds, and we determined to bring him, as we said, to his senses at last. The guns were reloaded, and orders given to depress them as much as possible—that is, to point their muzzles downward—but not a shot was to be fired till the frigate came actually along side of the chase. Such was the poor privateer's sentence of death: severe, indeed, but quite necessary, for he appeared resolved never to yield.

On we flew, right down upon our prey, like the enormous rockbird of the Arabian Nights. We had ceased firing our bow-chasers, that the smoke might not stand between us and the lesson we meant to read to our resolute pupil, so that there was "silence deep as death" along our decks, and doubtless on his; for he likewise had intermitted his firing, and seemed prepared to meet his fate, and go to the bottom like a man. It was possible, also, we thought, that he might only be watching, even in his last extremity, to take advantage of any negligence on our part, which should allow him to haul suddenly across our bows, and, by getting on a wind, have a chance of escaping. This chance, it is true, was very small, for not one of his sails was in a condition to stand such a breeze as was now blowing, unless when running nearly before it. But we had seen enough, during the two days we had been together, to apprehend that his activity was at least a match for ours; and as he had already shown that he did not care a fig for shot, he might bend new sails as fast as we could.

At all events, we were resolved to make him surrender, or run him down: such was our duty, and that the Frenchman knew right well. He waited, however, until our flying jib-boom end was almost over his taffrail; and the narrow space between us was filled with a confused, boiling heap of foam, partly caused by his bows, and partly by ours. Then, and not till then, when he must have seen into our ports and along the decks, which were lighted up fore and aft, he first gave signal of surrender.

The manner in which this was done by the captain of the privateer was as spirited and characteristic as any part of his previous conduct. The night was very dark; but the ships were so near to one another that we could distinguish the tall figure of a man mount the weather main-rigging of the brig, where he stood erect, with a lantern in his hand, held out at right-angles from his body. Had this light not been seen, or its purpose not understood, or had it been delayed for twenty seconds, the frigate must, almost in spite of herself, have gone right over him, and the salvo of a double-shotted broadside would have done the last and fitting honors over the Frenchman's grave.

Even as it was, it cost us some trouble to avoid running him down for, although the helm was put over immediately, our lee quarter, as the ship flew up in the wind, almost grazed his weather gangway. In passing, we ordered him to bring-to likewise. This he did as soon as we gave him room; though we were still close enough to see the effect of such a maneuver at such a moment. Every stitch of sail he had set was blown, in one moment, clean out of the bolt-ropes. His halyards, tacks, and sheets had been all racked aloft, so that everything not made of canvas remained at its place—the yards at the mast-heads, and the booms rigged out—while the empty leech and foot-ropes hung down in festoons where, but a minute before, the tattered sail had been spread.

We fared, comparatively speaking, not much better; for although the instant the course was altered, the order was given to let fly the topsail halyards, and every other necessary rope; and although the down-haul tackles, clewlines, and buntlines, were all ready manned, in expectation of this evolution, we succeeded with great difficulty in saving the fore or main-topsails; but the topgallant-sails were blown to pieces. All the flying kites went off in a crack, whisking far away to leeward, like dried forest leaves in autumn.

It may be supposed that the chase was now completely over; and that we had nothing further to do than to take possession of our prize. Not at all! It was found next to impossible to board the brig, or, at least, it seemed so dangerous, that our captain was unwilling to hazard a boat and crew, till daylight came. The privateer, having no sail set to keep her steady, became so unmanageable, that the sea made a clean breach over all, rendering it out of the question to board her on the weather side. Nor was she more easily approachable to leeward, where a tangled network of broken spars, half-torn sails, shattered booms, and smacking rope's-ends formed such a line of "chevaux-de-frise" from the cat-head to the counter, that all attempts to get near her on that side were useless.

The gale increased, before morning, to such a pitch, that, as there was still a doubt if any boat could live, the intention of boarding our prize was of course further delayed. But we took care to keep close to her, a little to windward, in order to watch her proceedings as narrowly as possible. It did not escape our notice, in the meantime, that our friend, (he was no longer our foe, though not yet our prisoner,) went on quietly, even in the height of the gale, shifting his wounded yards, reefing new ropes, and bending fresh sails. This caused us to redouble our vigilance during the morning, and the event showed that we had good need for such watchfulness. About three o'clock in the afternoon, the brig having fallen a little to leeward, and a furious squall of wind and rain coming on at the same moment, she suddenly bore up, and set off once more, right before the wind. At the height of the squall, we totally lost sight of our prize; and such a hubbub I rarely recollect to have heard in my life before.

"Where is she? — Who was looking out? — Where did you see her last?" — and a hundred similar questions, reproaches, scolds, and the whole of the ugly family of oaths, were poured out in abundance; some on the privateer, whose adroitness had thus over-reached our vigilance; some upon those who, by their neglect, had given him the opportunity; and many imprecations were uttered merely to express the depth of anger and disappointment at the stupid loss of a good thing, which had cost so much trouble to catch. All this passed over in the first burst — sail was made at once — the topsails, close reefed, were sheeted home like lightning — and off we dashed, into the thick of the squall, in search of our lost treasure. At each mast-head, and at every yard-arm, there was planted a look-out man, while the forecastle hammock-netting was filled with volunteer spyglasses. For about a quarter of an hour a dead silence reigned over the whole ship, during which anxious interval every eye was strained to the utmost, for no one knew exactly where to look. There was, indeed, no certainty of our not actually running past the privateer, and it would not have surprised us much, when the squall cleared up, had we seen him a mile or two to windward, far beyond our reach. These fears were put on end to by the sharp-eyed captain of the foretop, who had perched himself on the jib-boom end, calling out, with a voice of the greatest glee—

"There he goes! there he goes! right ahead! under his topsails and foresail!"

And, sure enough, there we saw him, springing along from wave to wave, with his masts bending forward like reeds, under the pressure of sail enough to have laid him on his beam-ends, had he broached to. In such tempestuous weather, a small vessel has no chance whatever with a frigate; indeed, we could observe that, when the little brig fell between two high seas, her foresail flapped to the mast, fairly becalmed by the wave behind her.

In a very few minutes, we were again along side, and doubtless the Frenchman thought we were at last going to execute summary vengeance upon him for his treachery, as we called it. Nothing daunted, however, by the style in which we bore down upon him, the gallant commander of this pretty little eggshell of a vessel placed himself on the weather-quarter, and with a speaking trumpet in his hand, indicated, by gesticulations, a wish to be heard. This could not well be refused; and we steered as close as we could pass along without bringing the two vessels in contact, or risking the entanglement of the yards, when we rolled toward one another.

"I have been compelled to bear up," he called out in French, "otherwise the brig must have gone to the bottom. The sea broke over us in such a way that I have been obliged, as you may perceive, to throw all my guns, boats and spars overboard. We have now several feet of water in the hold, in consequence of your shot, which you may likewise observe have nearly destroyed our upper works. If, therefore, you oblige me to heave to, I cannot keep the vessel afloat one hour in such weather."

"Will you make no further attempt to escape?" asked the captain of the Endymion.

"As yet I have made none," he replied, firmly; "I struck to you already. I am your prize, and, feeling as a man of honor, I do not consider myself at liberty to escape, even if I had the power. I bore up, when the squall came on, as a matter of necessity. If you will allow me to run before the wind, along with you, till the weather moderates, you may take possession of the brig when you please—if not, I must go to the bottom."

Such was the substance of a conversation, very difficult to keep up across the tempest, which was now whistling at a great rate. To have brought the ships again to the wind, after what had been said, would have been to imitate the celebrated "Noyades," of Nantes; for the privateer must have been swamped instantly. Although we distrusted our companion, therefore, most grievously, we sailed along most lovingly together, as if we had been the best possible friends, for about sixty or seventy miles; during the greater part of this interval, the frigate had scarcely any sail set at all; and we sometimes expected to see our little friend pop fairly under the water, and so elude us by foundering, or escape by witchcraft, by the protection of which, in the opinion of the Johnnies, he had been so long kept from us.

At eight o'clock in the evening, it began to moderate, and by midnight we succeeded in getting on board the prize, after a run of between three and four hundred miles. Such is the scale of nautical sport!

And where, I now beg to ask, is the fox-hunting, or the piracy, or anything else more exciting than this noble game?

The brig proved to be the Milan privateer, from St. Malo, of fourteen guns, and eighty men, many of whom were unfortunately wounded by our shot, and several were killed. She had been at sea eighteen days, but had made no captures. The guns, as I have already mentioned, had been thrown overboard to lighten her. In the morning we stopped the leaks, exchanged the prisoners for a prize crew, and put our heads toward the Cove of Cork again, chuckling at our own success in having nabbed the very vessel we were sent after. But this part of the exploit, it seemed, we had no title to claim merit for, since the Milan had not seen the land, nor been within many miles of it. This was a trifle, however; and we returned right merrily to tell our long story of the three days' chase.

The captain's name was Lepelletier—I have pleasure in recording it—M. Pierre Lepelletier, of St. Malo; and wherever he goes I will venture to say he can meet no braver or more resolute man than himself. Long before he came on board he had well earned the respect of his captors, high and low; and his manners and information, after we became personally acquainted with him, raised him still more in general estimation.

NARRATIVE

OF

A SAILOR AMONG SAVAGES,

BEING THE ADVENTURES OF JOHN R. JEWETT, SURVIVOR OF THE CREW OF THE SHIP BOSTON, DURING A CAPTIVITY OF NEARLY THREE YEARS, AMONG THE SAVAGES OF NOOTKA SOUND, BY WHOM HIS

COMRADES WERE MASSACRED.

I WAS born in Boston, a considerable borough town in Lincolnshire, in Great Britain, on the twenty-first of May, 1783. My father, Edward Jewitt, was by trade a blacksmith, and esteemed among the first in his line of business in that place.

When a child I was always fond of being in the shop, among the workmen, endeavoring to imitate what I saw them do. I was at length introduced into the shop, and my natural turn of mind corresponding with the employment, I became, in a short time, uncommonly expert at the work to which I was set. About a year after I had commenced this apprenticeship, my father, finding that he could carry on his business to more advantage in Hull, removed thither with his family. Among his principal customers at Hull, were the Americans who frequented that port, and from whose conversation, my father, as well as myself, formed the most favorable opinion of that country, as affording an excellent field for the exertions of industry, and a flattering prospect for the establishment of a young man in life. In the summer of the year 1802, during the peace between England and France, the ship Boston, belonging to Boston, in Massachusetts, and commanded by Captain John Salter, arrived at Hull, whither she came to take on board a cargo of such goods as were wanted for the trade, with the Indians on the north-west coast of America, from whence, after having taken in a lading of furs and skins, she was to proceed to China, and from thence home to America. The ship, having occasion for many repairs and alterations, necessary for so long a voyage, the captain applied to my father to do the smith-work, which was very considerable. That gentleman, who was of a social turn, used often to call at my father's house, where he passed many of his evenings.

In the hours that he passed at my father's, Captain Salter, who had for a great number of years been at sea, and seen almost all parts of the world, used sometimes to speak of his voyages, and observing me listen with much attention to his relations, he one day when I had brought him some work, said to me, in rather a jocose manner, "John, how should you like to go with me?" I answered that it would give me great pleasure, that I had for a long time wished to visit foreign countries, particularly America, which I had been told so many fine stories of, and that if my father would give his consent and he was willing to take me with him, I would go. "I shall be very glad to do it," said he, "if your father can be prevailed on to let you go, and as I want an expert smith for an armorer, the one I have shipped for that purpose not being sufficiently master of his trade, I have no doubt that you will answer my turn well, and on my return to America, I shall probably be able to do something much better for you in Boston. I will take the first opportunity of speaking to your father about it, and try to persuade him to consent." He accordingly, the next evening that he called at our house, introduced the subject: my father at first would not listen to the proposal. But on Captain Salter's telling him of what benefit it would be to me to go the voyage with him, and that it was a pity to keep a promising and ingenious young fellow, like myself, confined to a small shop in England, when if I had tolerable success, I might do so much better in America, where wages were much higher, and living cheaper, he at length gave up his objections and consented that I should ship on board the Boston as an armorer, at the rate of thirty dollars per month.

The ship having undergone a thorough repair and been well coppered, proceeded to take on board her cargo, which consisted of English clothes, Dutch blankets, looking-glasses, beads, knives, razors, etc., which were received from Holland, some sugar and molasses, about twenty hogsheads of rum, including stores for the ship, a great quantity of ammunition, cutlasses, pistols, and three thousand muskets and fowling-pieces. The ship being loaded and ready for sea, as I was preparing for my departure, my father came to me, and taking me aside, said to me with much emotion, "John, I am now going to part with you, and heaven only knows if we shall ever again meet. But in whatever part of the world you are, always bear it mind, that on your own conduct will depend your success in life. Be honest, industrious, frugal, and temperate, and you will not fail, in whatsoever country it may be your lot to be placed, to gain yourself friends. Let the Bible be your guide, and your reliance in any fortune that may befall you, that Almighty Being who knows how to bring forth good from evil, and who never deserts those who put their trust in him." He repeated his exhortations to me to lead an honest and Christian life, and to recollect that I had a father, a mother, a brother, and sister, who could not but feel a strong interest in my welfare, enjoining me to write him by the first opportunity that should offer to England, from whatever part of the world I might be in, more particularly on my arrival in Boston. This I promised to do, but long unhappily was it before I was able to fulfill this promise. I then took an affectionate leave of my worthy parent, whose feelings would hardly permit him to speak, and bidding an affectionate farewell to my brother, sister, and step-mother, who expressed the greatest solicitude for my future fortune, went on board the ship, which proceeded to the Downs to be ready for the first favorable wind. I found myself well accommodated on board as regarded my work, an iron forge having been erected on deck; this my father had made for the ship on a new plan, for which he afterward obtained a patent; while a corner of the steerage was appropriated to my vice bench, so that in bad weather I could work below.

On the third day of September, 1802, we sailed from the Downs with a fair wind, in company with twenty-four sail of American vessels, most of which were bound home. During the first part of our voyage we saw scarcely any fish, excepting some whales, a few sharks, and flying fish; but after weathering Cape Horn we met with numerous shoals of sea porpoises, several of which we caught, and as we had been for some time without fresh provisions, I found it not only a palatable but really a very excellent food. With a fair wind and easy weather from the twenty-eighth of December, the period of our passing Cape Horn, we pursued our voyage to the northward until the twelfth of March, 1803, when we made Woody Point, in Nootka Sound, on the north-west coast of America. We immediately stood up the Sound for Nootka, where Captain Salter had determined to stop, in order to supply the ship with wood and water before proceeding up the coast to trade. The ship accordingly came to anchor in this place, at twelve o'clock at night, in twelve fathom water, muddy bottom, and so near the shore that to prevent the ship from winding we secured her by a hawser to the trees. On the morning of the next day, the thirteenth, several of the natives came on board in a canoe from the village of Nootka, with their king, called Maquina, who appeared much pleased on seeing us, and with great seeming cordiality, welcomed Captain Salter and his officers to his country. As I had never before beheld a savage of any nation, it may readily be supposed that the novelty of their appearance, so different from any people that I had hitherto seen, excited in me strong feelings of surprise and curiosity. I was, however, particularly struck with the looks of their king, who was a man of a dignified aspect, about six feet in height and extremely straight and well proportioned; his features were in general good, and his face was rendered remarkable by a large Roman nose, a very uncommon form of feature among these people; his complexion was of a dark copper hue, though his face, legs, and arms, were on this occasion, so covered with red paint, that their natural color could scarcely be perceived; his eyebrows were painted black, in two broad stripes, like a new moon, and his long black hair, which shone with oil, was fastened in a bunch on the top of his head, and strewed or powdered all over with white down, which gave him a most curious and extraordinary appearance. He was dressed in a large mantle or cloak of the black sea-otter skin, which reached to his knees, and was fastened around his middle by a broad belt of the cloth of the country, wrought or painted with figures of several colors; this dress was by no means unbecoming, but, on the contrary, had an air of savage magnificence.

From his having frequently visited the English and American ships that traded to the coast, Maquina had learned the signification of a number of English words, and in general could make himself pretty well understood by us in our own language. He was always the first to go on board such ships as came to Nootka, which he was much pleased in visiting, even when he had no trade to offer, as he almost always received some small present, and was in general extremely well treated by the commanders. He remained on board of us for some time, during which the captain took him into the cabin and treated him with a glass of rum; these people being very fond of distilled spirits, and some biscuit and molasses which they prefer to any kind of food that we can offer them.

As there are seldom many furs to be purchased at this place, and it was not fully the season, Captain Salter had put in here not so much with an expectation of trading as to procure an ample stock of wood and water for the supply of the ship on the coast, thinking it more prudent to take it on board at Nootka, from the generally friendly disposition of the people, than to endanger the safety of his men in sending them on shore for that purpose among the more ferocious natives of the north. With this view, we immediately set about getting our water-casks in readiness, and the next and two succeeding days part of the crew were sent on shore to cut pine timber and assist the carpenter in making it into yards and spars for the ship, while those on board were employed in refitting the rigging, repairing the sails, etc., when we proceeded to take in our wood and water as expeditiously as possible, during which time I kept myself busily employed in repairing the muskets, making knives, tomaxes, etc., and doing such iron work as was wanted for the ship. Meantime more or less of the natives came on board of us daily, bringing with them fresh salmon with which they supplied us in great plenty, receiving in return some trifling articles. Captain Salter was always very particular before admitting these people on board to see that they had no arms about them, by obliging them indiscriminately to throw off their garments, so that he felt perfectly secure from any attack. On the fifteenth the king came on board with several of his chiefs; he was dressed, as before, in his magnificent otter skin robe, having his face highly painted, and his hair tossed off with the white down which looked like snow; his chiefs were dressed in mantles of the country cloth of its natural color, which is a pale yellow; these were ornamented with a broad border, painted or wrought in figures of several colors, representing men's heads, various animals, etc., and secured around them by a belt like that of the king, from which it was distinguished only by being narrower. The dress of the common people is of the same fashion, and differs from that of the chiefs in being of a coarser texture, and painted red, of one uniform color.

Captain Salter invited Maquina and his chiefs to dine with him, and it was curious to see how these people, when they eat, seat themselves, in their country fashion, upon our chairs, with their feet under them, crossed like Turks. They cannot endure the taste of salt, and the only thing they would eat with us was the ship-bread, which they were very fond of, especially when dipped in molasses; they had also a great liking for tea and coffee, when well sweetened. As iron weapons and tools of almost every kind are in much request among them, whenever they came on board they were always very attentive to me, crowding around me at the forge, as if to see in what manner I did my work, and in this way became quite familiar; a circumstance, as will be seen in the end, of great importance to me. On the nineteenth, the king came again on board and was invited by the captain to dine with him. He had much conversation with Captain Salter, and informed him that there were plenty of wild ducks and geese near Friendly Cove, on which the captain made him a present of a double-barreled fowling-piece with which he appeared to be greatly pleased and soon after went on shore.

On the twentieth, we were nearly ready for our departure, having taken in what wood and water we were in want of. The next day Maquina came on board with nine pair of wild ducks, as a present, at the same time he brought with him the gun, one of the locks of which he had broken, telling the captain that it was *peshak*, that is bad. Captain Salter was very much offended at this observation, and considering it as a mark of contempt for his present, he called the king a liar, adding other opprobrious terms, and taking the gun from him tossed it indignantly into the cabin and calling me to him said, "John, this fellow has broken this beautiful fowling-piece, see if you can mend it:" on examining it I told him that it could be done.—As I have already observed, Maquina knew a number of English words, and, unfortunately, understood but too well the meaning of the reproachful terms that the captain addressed to him.—He said not a word in reply, but his countenance sufficiently expressed the rage he felt, though he exerted himself to suppress it, and I observed him, while the captain was speaking, repeatedly put his hand to his throat and rub it upon his bosom, which, he afterward told me, was to keep down his heart, which was rising into his throat and choking him. He soon after went on shore with his men, evidently much discomposed.

On the morning of the twenty-second, the natives came off to us, as usual, with salmon, and remained on board, when about noon Maquina came along side with a considerable number of his chiefs and men in their canoes, who, after going though the customary examination were admitted into the ship. He had a whistle in his hand, and over his face a very ugly mask of wood representing the head of some wild beast, appeared to be remarkably good humored and gay, and while his people sung and capered about the deck, entertaining us with a variety of antic tricks and gestures, he blew his whistle to a kind of tune which seemed to regulate their motions. As Captain Salter was walking on the quarter-deck amusing himself with their dancing, the king came up to him and inquired when he intended to go to sea?—he answered, to-morrow.—Maquina then said, "You love salmon—much in Friendly Cove, why not go then and catch some?"—The captain thought that it would be very desirable to have a good supply of these fish for the voyage, and on consulting with Mr. Delouisa, the first mate, it was agreed to send part of of the crew on shore after dinner with the seine in order to procure a quantity—Maquina and his chiefs staid and dined on board, and after dinner the chief mate went off with nine men in the jolly-boat and yawl to fish at Friendly Cove, having set the steward on shore at our watering place to wash the captain's clothes. Shortly after the departure of the boats I went down to my vice-bench in the steerage, where I was employed in cleaning muskets. I had not been there more than an hour when I heard the men hoisting in the long-boat, which, in a few minutes after, was succeeded by a great bustle and confusion on deck. I immediately ran up the steerage stairs, but scarcely was my head above deck, when I was caught by the hair by one of the savages, and lifted from my feet; fortunately for me, my hair being short, and the ribbon with which it was tied slipping, I fell from his hold into the steerage. As I was falling, he struck at me with an ax, which cut a deep gash in my forehead, and penetrated the skull, but in consequence of his losing his hold, I luckily escaped the full force of the blow; which, otherwise, would have cleft my head in two. I fell, stunned and senseless, upon the floor—how long I continued in this situation I know not, but on recovering my senses the first thing that I did, was to try to get up; but so weak was I, from the loss of blood, that I fainted and fell.

I was, however, soon recalled to my recollection by three loud shouts or yells from the savages, which convinced me that they had got possession of the ship. It is impossible for me to describe my feelings at this terrific sound.—Some faint idea may be formed of them by those who have known what it is to half awaken from a hideous dream and still think it real. Never, no, never, shall I lose from my mind, the impression of that dreadful moment. I expected every instant to share the wretched fate of my unfortunate companions; and when I heard the song of triumph, by which these infernal yells was succeeded, my blood ran cold in my veins. Having at length sufficiently recovered my senses to look around me, after wiping the blood from eyes, I saw that the hatch of the steerage was shut. This was done, as I afterward discovered, by order of Maquina, who, on seeing the savage strike at me with the ax, told him not to hurt me, for I was the armorer, and would be useful to them in repairing their arms; while, at the same time, to prevent any of his men from injuring me, he had the hatch closed. But to me this circumstance wore a very different appearance, for I thought that these barbarians had only prolonged my life in order to deprive me of it by the most cruel tortures.

I remained in this horrid state of suspense for a very long time, when at length the hatch was opened, and Maquina, calling me by name, ordered me to come up. I groped my way up as well as I was able, being almost blinded with the blood that flowed from my wound, and so weak as with difficulty to walk. The king, on perceiving my situation, ordered one of his men to bring a pot of water to wash the blood from my face, which having done, I was able to see distinctly with one of my eyes, but the other was so swollen from my wound that it was closed. But what a terrific spectacle met my eyes: six naked savages, standing in a circle around me, covered with the blood of my murdered comrades, with their daggers uplifted in their hands, prepared to strike. I now thought my last moment had come, and recommended my soul to my Maker. The king, who, as I have already observed, knew enough of English to make himself understood, entered the circle, and placing himself before me, addressed me nearly in the following words—"John—I speak—you no say no—You say no—daggers come!" He then asked me if I would be his slave during my life—If I would fight for him in his battles—If I would repair his muskets and make daggers and knives for him—with several other questions, to all of which I was careful to answer, yes. He then told me that he would spare my life, and ordered me to kiss his hands and feet to show my submission to him, which I did. In the meantime his people were very clamorous to have me put to death, so that there should be none of us left to tell our story to our countrymen and prevent them from coming to trade with them; but the king, in the most determined manner opposed their wishes, and to his favor am I wholly indebted for my being yet among the living.

As I was busy at work at the time of the attack, I was without my coat, and what with the coldness of the weather, my feebleness from loss of blood, the pain of my wound, and the extreme agitation and terror that I still felt, I shook like a leaf, which the king observing, went into the cabin, and bringing up a great-coat that belonged to the captain, threw it over my shoulders, telling me to drink some rum from a bottle which he handed me at the same time, giving me to understand that it would be good for for me and keep me from trembling as I did. I took a draught of it, after which, taking me by the hand, he led me to the quarter-deck, where the most horrid sight presented itself that ever my eyes witnessed—the heads of our unfortunate captain and his crew, to the number of twenty-five, were all arranged in a line, and Maquina ordering one of his people to bring a head, asked me whose it was: I answered, the captain's; in like manner the others were showed me, and I told him the names, excepting a few that were so horribly mangled that I was not able to recognize them. I now discovered that all our unfortunate crew had been massacred, and learned that, after getting possession of the ship, the savages had broke open the arm chest and magazine, and supplying themselves with ammunition and arms, sent a party on shore to attack our men who had gone thither to fish, and being joined by numbers from the village, without difficulty overpowered and murdered them, and cutting off their heads, brought them on board, after throwing their bodies into the sea. On looking upon the deck, I saw it entirely covered with the blood of my poor comrades, whose throats had been cut with their own jack-knives the savages having seized the opportunity while they were busy hoisting in the boat to grapple with them and overpower them by their numbers; in the scuffle the captain was thrown overboard, and dispatched by those in the canoes, who immediately cut off his head. What I felt on this occasion, may be more readily conceived than expressed.

After I had answered his questions, Maquina took my silk handkerchief from my neck and bound it around my head, placing over the wound a leaf of tobacco, of which we had a quantity on board. This was done at my desire, as I had often found, from personal experience, the benefit of this application to cuts.

Maquina then ordered me to get the ship under weigh for Friendly Cove. This I did by cutting the cables and sending some of the natives aloft to loose the sails, which they performed in a very bungling manner. But they succeeded so far in loosing the jib and topsails, that, with the advantage of a fair wind, I succeeded in getting the ship into the Cove, where, by order of the king, I run her ashore, on a sandy beach, at eight o'clock at night. We were received by the inhabitants of the village, men, women, and children, with loud shouts of joy, and a most horrible drumming with sticks upon the roofs and sides of their houses, in which they had also stuck a great number of lighted pine torches, to welcome their king's return and congratulate him on the success of his enterprize.

Maquina then took me on shore to his house—which was very large and filled with people—where I was received with much kindness by the women, particularly those belonging to the king, who had no less than nine wives, all of whom came around me expressing much sympathy for my misfortune, gently stroking and patting my head in an encouraging and soothing manner, with words expressive of condolence.

In the meantime, all the warriors of the tribe, to the number of five hundred, had assembled at the king's house to rejoice for their success. They exulted greatly in having taken our ship, and each one boasted of his own particular exploits in killing our men, but they were in general much dissatisfied with my having been suffered to live, and were very urgent with Maquina to deliver me to them to be put to death, which he obstinately refused to do, telling them that he had promised me my life, and would not break his word; and that beside, I knew how to repair and to make arms, and would be of great use to them.

The king then seated me by him and ordered his women to bring him something to eat, when they set before him some dried clams and train oil, of which he ate very heartily, and encouraged me to follow his example, telling me to eat much and take a great deal of oil which would make me strong and fat; notwithstanding his praise of this new kind of food, I felt no disposition to indulge in it, both the smell and taste being loathsome to me; and had it been otherwise, such was the pain I endured, the agitation of my mind, and the gloominess of my reflections, that I should have felt very little inclination for eating. Not satisfied with his first refusal to deliver me up to them, the people again became clamorous that Maquina should consent to my being killed, saying that not one of us ought to be left alive to give information to others of our countrymen and prevent them from coming to trade, or induce them to revenge the destruction of our ship, and they at length became so boisterous that he caught up a large club in a passion and drove them all out of the house. During this scene a son of the king, about eleven years old, attracted no doubt by the singularity of my appearance came up to me: I caressed him; he returned my attentions with much apparent pleasure, and considering this as a fortunate opportunity to gain the good will of the father, I took the child on my knee, and cutting the metal buttons from off the coat I had on, I tied them around his neck. At this he was highly delighted, and became so much attached to me that he would not quit me.

The king appeared much pleased with my attention to his son, and telling me that it was time to go to sleep, directed me to lie with his son next to him, as he was afraid lest some of his people would come while he was asleep and kill me with their daggers. I lay down as he ordered me, but neither the state of my mind nor the pain I felt would allow me to sleep. About midnight I was greatly alarmed by the approach of one of the natives, who came to give information to the king that there was one of the white men alive, who had knocked him down as he went on board the ship at night. This Maquina communicated to me. giving me to understand that as soon as the sun rose he should kill him. I endeavored to persuade him to spare his life, but he bade me be silent and go to sleep. I said nothing more, but lay revolving in my mind what method I could devise to save the life of this man. What a consolation, thought I, what a happiness would it prove to me in my forlorn state among these heathen, to have a Christian and one of my own countrymen for a companion, and how greatly would it alleviate and lighten the burden of my slavery. As I was thinking of some plan for his preservation, it all at once came into my mind that this man was probably the sail-maker of the ship, named Thompson, as I had not seen his head among those on deck, and knew that he was below, at work upon the sails, not long before the attack. The more I thought of it the more probable it appeared to me, and as Thompson was a man nearly forty years of age, and had an old look, I conceived it would be easy to make him pass for my father, and by this means prevail on Maquina to spare his life. Toward morning I fell into a doze, but was awakened with the first beams of the sun by the king, who told me that he was going to kill the man who was on board the ship, and ordered me to accompany him. I rose and followed him, leading with me the young prince his son.

On coming to the beach I found all the men of the tribe assembled. The king addressed them, saying that one of the white men had been found alive on board the ship, and requested their opinion as to saving his life or putting him to death. They were unanimously for the first: this determination he made known to me. Having arranged my plan, I asked him, pointing to the boy whom I still held by the hand, if he loved his son, he answered that he did; I then asked the child if he loved his father, and on his replying in the affirmative, I said "And I also love mine." I then threw myself on my knees at Maquina's feet, and implored him, with tears in my eyes, to spare my father's life, if the man on board should prove to be him, telling him that if he killed my father it was my wish that he should kill me too, and that if he did not I would kill myself—and that he would thus lose my services; whereas, by sparing my father's life he would preserve mine, which would be of great advantage to him by my repairing and making arms for him. Maquina appeared moved by my entreaties and promised not to put the man to death if he should be my father. He then explained to his people what I had said, and ordered me to go on board and tell the man to come on shore. To my unspeakable joy on going into the hold, I found that my conjecture was true, Thompson was there, he had escaped without any injury, excepting a slight wound in the nose, given him by one of the savages with a knife, as he attempted to come on deck, during the scuffle. Finding the savages in possession of the ship, as he afterward informed me, he secreted himself in the hold, hoping for some chance to make his escape—but that the Indian who came on board in the night approaching the place where he was, he supposed himself discovered, and being determined to sell his life as dearly as possible, as soon as he came within his reach, he knocked him down, but the Indian immediately springing up, ran off at full speed.—I informed him in a few words that all our men had been killed; that the king had preserved my life, and had consented to spare his on the supposition that he was my father, an opinion which he must be careful not to undeceive them in, as it was his only safety. After giving him his cue, I went on shore with him and presented him to Maquina, who immediately knew him to be the sail-maker and was much pleased, observing that he could make sails for his canoe.—He then took us to his house and ordered something for us to eat.

On the twenty-fourth and twenty-fifth, the natives were busily employed in taking the cargo out of the ship, stripping her of her sails and rigging, cutting away the spars and masts, and, in short, rendering her as complete a wreck as possible; the muskets, ammunition, cloth, and all the principal articles taken from her, being deposited in the king's house.

While they were thus occupied, each one taking what he liked, my companion and myself being obliged to aid them, I thought it best to secure the accounts and papers of the ship, in hopes that on some future day I might have it in my power to restore them to the owners. With this view I took possession of the captain's writing-desk which contained the most of them, together with some paper and implements for writing. I had also the good fortune to find a blank account book, in which I resolved, should it be permitted me, to write an account of our capture and the most remarkable occurrences that I should meet with during my stay among these people, fondly indulging the hope that it would not be long before some vessel would arrive to release us. I likewise found in the cabin, a small volume of sermons, a Bible, and a common prayer-book of the Church of England, which furnished me and my comrade great consolation in the midst of our mournful servitude, and enabled me, under the favor of Divine Providence, to support, with firmness, the miseries of a life which I might otherwise have found beyond my strength to endure. As these people set no value upon things of this kind, I found no difficulty in appropriating them to myself, by putting them in my chest, which, though it had been broken open and rifled by the savages, as I still had the key, I without much difficulty secured. In this I also put some small tools belonging to the ship, with several other articles, particularly a journal kept by the second mate, Mr. Ingraham, and a collection of drawings and views of places taken by him, which I had the good fortune to preserve, and on my arrival at Boston, I gave them to a connection of his, the honorable Judge Dawes, who sent them to his family in New York.

On the twenty-sixth, two ships were seen standing in for Friendly Cove. At their first appearance the inhabitants were thrown into great confusion, but soon collecting a number of muskets and blunderbusses, ran to the shore, from whence they kept up so brisk a fire at them, that they were evidently afraid to approach nearer, and after firing a few rounds of grape-shot which did no harm to any one, they wore ship and stood out to sea. These ships, as I afterward learned, were the Mary and Juno of Boston. They were scarcely out of sight when Maquina expressed much regret that he had permitted his people to fire at them, being apprehensive that they would give information to others in what manner they had been received, and prevent them from coming to trade with him. A few days after hearing of the capture of the ship, there arrived at Nootka a great number of canoes filled with savages from no less than twenty tribes to the north and south.

Maquina, who was very proud of his new acquisition, was desirous of welcoming these visitors in the European manner. He accordingly ordered his men, as the canoes approached, to assemble on the beach with loaded muskets and blunderbusses, placing Thompson at the cannon which had been brought and laid upon two long sticks of timber in front of the village, then taking a speaking-trumpet in his hand he ascended with me the roof of his house, and began drumming or beating upon the boards with a stick most violently. Nothing could be more ludicrous than the appearance of this motley group of savages collected on the shore, dressed as they were, with their ill-gotten finery, in the most fantastic manner, some in women's smocks, taken from our cargo, others in *Kotsacks*, (or cloaks,) of blue, red or yellow broadcloth, with stockings drawn over their heads, and their necks hung round with numbers of powder-horns, shot-bags, and cartridge-boxes; some of them having no less than ten muskets a piece on their shoulders, and five or six daggers in their girdles. Diverting, indeed, was it to see them all squatted upon the beach, holding their muskets perpendicularly, with the butt pressed upon the sand instead of against their shoulders, and in this position awaiting the order to fire. Maquina, at last, called to them with his trumpet to fire, which they did in the most awkward and timid manner, with their muskets hard pressed upon the ground as above mentioned. At the same moment the cannon was fired by Thompson, immediately on which they threw themselves back and began to roll and tumble over the sand as if they had been shot, when suddenly springing up they began a song of triumph, and running backward and forward upon the shore, with the wildest gesticulations, boasted of their exploits and exhibited as trophies what they had taken from us. When the ceremony was concluded, Maquina invited the strangers to a feast at his house, consisting of whale blubber, smoked herring spawn, and dried fish and train oil, of which they ate most plentifully. The feast being over, the trays out of which they ate, and other things, were immediately removed to make room for the dance which was to close the entertainment.

On this occasion Maquina gave away no less than one hundred muskets, the same number of looking-glasses, four hundred yards of cloth, and twenty casks of powder, beside other things. After receiving these presents, the strangers retired on board their canoes, for so numerous were they that Maquina would not suffer any but the chiefs to sleep in the houses; and in order to prevent the property from being pillaged by them, he ordered Thompson and myself to keep guard, during the night, armed with cutlasses and pistols. In this manner tribes of savages from various parts of the coast, continued coming for several days, bringing with them, blubber, oil, herring spawn, dried fish and clams, for which they received in return, presents of cloth, etc., after which they in general immediately returned home.

Early on the morning of the eighteenth, the ship was discovered to be on fire. This was owing to one of the savages having gone on board with a firebrand at night for the purpose of plunder, some sparks from which fell into the hold, and communicating with some combustibles soon enveloped the whole in flames. The natives regretted the loss of the ship the more as a great part of her cargo still remained on board. To my companion and myself it was a most melancholy sight, for with her disappeared from our eyes every trace of a civilized country; but the disappointment we experienced was still more severely felt, for we had calculated on having the provision to ourselves, which would have furnished us with a stock for years, as whatever is cured with salt, together with most of our other articles of food, is never eaten by these people. I had luckily saved all my tools, excepting the anvil, and the bellows which were attached to the forge, and from their weight had not been brought on shore. We had also the good fortune, in looking over what had been taken from the ship, to discover a box of chocolate and a case of Port wine, which, as the Indians were not fond of it, proved a great comfort to us for some time, and from one of the natives I obtained a nautical almanac, which had belonged to the captain, and which was of great use to me in determining the time.

About two days after, on examining their booty, the savages found a tierce of rum, with which they were highly delighted, as they have become very fond of spirituous liquors since their intercourse with the whites. This was toward evening, and Maquina, having assembled all the men at his house, gave a feast, at which they drank so freely of the rum, that in a short time they became so extremely wild and frantic that Thompson and myself, apprehensive for our safety, thought it prudent to retire privately into the woods, where we continued till past midnight. On our return, we found the women gone, who are always very temperate, drinking nothing but water, having quitted the house and gone to the other huts to sleep, so terrified were they at the conduct of the men, who all lay stretched out on the floor in a state of complete intoxication. How easy, in this situation, would it have been for us to have dispatched or made ourselves masters of our enemies, had there been any ship near to which we could have escaped, but as we were situated, the attempt would have been madness.

The burning of our ship, which we had lamented so much, as depriving us of so many comforts, now appeared to us in a very different light, for had the savages got possession of the rum, of which there were nearly twenty puncheons on board, we must inevitably have fallen a sacrifice to their fury in some of their moments of intoxication. This cask, fortunately, and a case of gin, was all the spirits they obtained from the ship. To prevent the recurrence of similar danger, I examined the cask, and finding still a considerable quantity remaining, I bored a small hole in the bottom with a gimblet, which, before morning, to my great joy, completely emptied it.

By this time the wound in my head began to be much better, so that I could enjoy some sleep, which I had been almost deprived of by the pain, and, though I was still feeble from the loss of blood and my sufferings, I found myself sufficiently well to go to work at my trade, in making for the king and his wives bracelets and other small ornaments of copper or steel, and in repairing the arms, making use of a large square stone for the anvil, and heating my metal in a common wood fire This was very gratifying to Maquina and his women particularly, and secured me their good will.

In the meantime great numbers from the other tribes kept continually flocking to Nootka, bringing with them, in exchange for the ship's plunder, such quantities of provision, that, notwithstanding the little success that

Maquina met with in whaling this season, and their gluttonous waste, always eating to excess when they have it, regardless of the morrow, seldom did the natives experience any want of food during the summer. As to myself and companion, we fared as they did, never wanting for such provision as they had, though we were obliged to eat it cooked in their manner and with train oil as a sauce, a circumstance not a little unpleasant, both from their uncleanly mode of cooking, and many of the articles of their food which, to a European, are very disgusting, but, as the saying is, hunger will break through stone walls; and we found, at times, in the blubber of sea animals and the flesh of the dog fish, loathsome as it in general was, a very acceptable repast.

But much oftener would poor Thompson, who was no favorite with them, have suffered from hunger had it not been for my furnishing him with provision.—This I was enabled to do from my work, Maquina allowing me the privilege, when not employed for him, to work for myself in making bracelets and other ornaments of copper, fish-hooks, daggers, etc., either to sell to the tribes who visited us, or for our own chiefs, who, on these occasions, beside supplying me with as much as I wished to eat, and a sufficiency for Thompson, almost always made me a present of a European garment taken from the ship, or some fathoms of cloth, which were made up by my comrade, and enabled us to go comfortably clad for some time, or small bundles of penknives, razors, scissors, etc., for one of which we could almost always procure from the natives two or three fresh salmon, cod, or halibut; or dried fish, clams and herring spawn from the stranger tribes; and had we only been permitted to cook them after our own way, as we had pots, and other utensils belonging to the ship, we should not have had much cause of complaint in this respect; but so tenacious are these people of their customs, particularly in the article of food and cooking, that the king always obliged me to give whatever provisions I bought to the women to cook—and one day finding Thompson and myself on the shore employed in boiling down sea-water into salt, on being told what it was, he was very much displeased, and taking the little we had procured, threw it into the sea. In one instance alone, as a particular favor, he allowed me to boil some salmon in my own way, when I invited him and his queen to eat with me; they tasted it, but did not like it, and made their meal of some of it that I had cooked in their country fashion.

My health being at length re-established, and my wound healed, Thompson became very importunate for me to begin my journal, and as I had no ink, proposed to cut his finger to supply me with blood for the purpose whenever I should want it On the first of June I accordingly commenced a regular diary, but had no occasion to make use of the expedient suggested by my comrade, having found a much better substitute in the expressed juice of a certain plant, which furnished me with a bright green color, and after making a number of trials I at length succeeded in obtaining a very tolerable ink, by boiling the juice of the blackberry with a mixture of finely powdered charcoal and filtering it through a cloth. This I afterward preserved in bottles and found it answer very well, so true is it that "necessity is the mother of invention." As for quills I found no difficulty in procuring them, whenever I wanted, from the crows and ravens with which the beach was almost always covered, attracted by the offal of whales, seals, etc., and which were so tame that I could easily kill them with stones, while a large clam-shell furnished me with an inkstand.

The extreme solicitude of Thompson, that I should begin my journal, might be considered as singular in a man who neither knew how to write or read—a circumstance, by the way, very uncommon in an American—were we less acquainted with the force of habit, he having been for many years at sea, and accustomed to consider the keeping of a journal as a thing indispensable. This man was born in Philadelphia, and when eight years old, ran away from his friends, and entered as a cabin boy on board a ship bound to London; on his arrival there, finding himself in distress, he engaged as an apprentice to the captain of a Collier, from whence he was impressed on board an English man-of-war, and continued in the British naval service about twenty-seven years, during which he was present at the engagement under Lord Howe with the French fleet in June, 1794; and when peace was made between England and France, was discharged. He was a very strong and powerful man, an expert boxer, and perfectly fearless; indeed so little was his dread of danger, that, when irritated, he was wholly regardless of his life. Of this the following will furnish a sufficient proof:

One evening, about the middle of April, as I was at the house of one of the chiefs, where I had been employed on some work for him, word was brought me that Maquina was going to kill Thompson. I immediately hurried home, where I found the king in the act of presenting a loaded musket at Thompson, who was standing before him with his breast bared, and calling on him to fire. I instantly stepped up to Maquina, who was foaming with rage, and addressing him in soothing words, begged him, for my sake, not to kill my father, and at length succeeded in taking the musket from him and persuading him to sit down. On inquiring into the cause of his anger, I learned that while Thompson was lighting the lamps in the king's room, Maquina having substituted our's for their pine torches, some of the boys began to teaze him, running around him and pulling him by the trowsers; among the most forward of whom was the young prince. This caused Thompson to spill the oil, which threw him into such a passion, that, without caring what he did, he struck the prince so violent a blow in his face with his fist as to knock him down. The sensation excited among the savages by an act which was considered as the highest indignity, and a profanation of the sacred person of majesty may be easily conceived. The king was immediately acquainted with it, who, on coming in and seeing his son's face covered with blood, seized a musket and began to load it, determined to take instant revenge on the audacious offender; and had I arrived a few minutes later than I did, my companion would certainly have paid with his life for his rash and violent conduct. I found the utmost difficulty in pacifying Maquina, who, for a long time after, could not forgive Thompson, but would repeatedly say, "John, *you* die—Thompson kill." But to appease the king was not all that was necessary. In consequence of the insult offered to their prince, the whole tribe held a council, in which it was unanimously resolved that Thompson should be put to death in the most cruel manner. I, however, interceded so strenuously with Maquina for his life, telling him that if my father was killed, I was determined not to survive him, that he refused to deliver him up to the vengeance of his people, saying, that for John's sake they must consent to let him live. The prince, who, after I had succeeded in calming his father, gave me an account of what had happened, told me that it was wholly out of regard to me, as Thompson was my father, that his life had been spared; for that if any one of the tribe should dare to lift a hand against him in anger, he would most certainly be put to death.

Yet even this narrow escape produced not much effect on Thompson, or induced him to restrain the violence of his temper. For not many weeks after, he was guilty of a similar indiscretion, in striking the eldest son of a chief, who was about eighteen years old, and, according to their custom, was considered as a Tyee, or chief himself, in consequence of his having provoked him by calling him a white slave. This affair caused great commotion in the village, and the tribe was very clamorous for his death, but Maquina would not consent. I used frequently to remonstrate with him on the imprudence of his conduct, and beg him to govern his temper better, telling him it was our duty, since our lives were in the power of these savages, to do nothing to exasperate them; but all I could say on this point availed little; for so bitter was the hate he felt for them, which he was no way backward in manifesting, both by his looks and actions, that he declared he never would submit to their insults; and that he had much rather be killed than be obliged to live among them; adding, that he only wished he had a good vessel and some guns, and he would destroy the whole of the cursed race; for to a brave sailor like him, who had fought the French and Spaniards with glory, it was a punishment worse than death to be a slave to such a poor, ignorant, despicable set of beings.

As for myself, I thought very differently. I had determined from the first of my capture to adopt a conciliating conduct toward them, and conform myself, as far as was in my power, to their customs and mode of thinking, trusting that the same divine goodness that had rescued me from death would not always suffer me to languish in captivity among these heathen. With this view, I sought to gain their good will by always endeavoring to assume a cheerful countenance, appearing pleased with their sports and buffoon tricks, making little ornaments for the wives and children of the chiefs, by which means I became quite a favorite with them, and fish-hooks, daggers, etc., for themselves. As a farther recommendation to their favor, and what might eventually prove of the utmost importance to us, I resolved to learn their language, which, in the course of a few months residence, I so far succeeded in acquiring, as to be able in general to make myself well understood. I likewise tried to persuade Thompson to learn it as what might prove necessary to him. But he refused, saying, that he hated both them and their cursed lingo, and would have nothing to do with it.

By pursuing this conciliatory plan, so far did I gain the good will of the savages, particularly the chiefs, that I scarcely ever failed experiencing kind treatment from them, and was received with a smile of welcome at their houses, where I was always sure of having something given me to eat, whenever they had it; and many a good meal have I had from them, when they themselves were short of provisions and suffering for the want of them.

But to return to our unhappy situation. Though my comrade and myself fared as well, and even better than we could have expected among these people, considering their customs and mode of living, yet our fears lest no ship would come to our release, and that we should never more behold a Christian country, were to us a source of constant pain. Our principal consolation in this gloomy state was to go on Sundays, whenever the weather would permit, to the borders of a fresh water pond, about a mile from the village, where, after bathing, and putting on clean clothes, we would seat ourselves under the shade of a beautiful pine, while I read some chapters in the Bible, and the prayers appointed by our Church for the day, ending our devotions with a fervent prayer to the Almighty that he would deign still to watch over and preserve our lives, rescue us from the hands of the savages, and permit us once more to behold a Christian land. In this manner were the greater part of our Sundays passed at Nootka; and I felt grateful to heaven, that amidst our other sufferings, we were at least allowed the pleasure of offering up our devotions unmolested; for Maquina, on my explaining to him, as well as was in my power, the reason of our thus retiring at this time, far from objecting, readily consented to it.

In July, we at length thought that the hope of delivery we had so long anxiously indulged, was on the point of being gratified. A ship appeared in the offing; but, alas! our fond hopes vanished almost as soon as formed; for, instead of standing in for the shore, she passed to the northward and soon disappeared.

On the third of September, the whole tribe quitted Nootka, according to their constant practice, in order to pass the autumn and winter at Tashees and Cooptee, the latter lying about thirty miles up the sound in a deep bay, the navigation of which is very dangerous from the great number of reefs and rocks with which it abounds. On these occasions, everything is taken with them, even the planks of their houses, in order to cover their new dwellings.

Tashees is pleasantly situated, and in a most secure position from the winter storms, in a small vale or hollow, on the south shore, at the foot of a mountain. The principal object in coming to this place, is the facility it affords these people of providing their winter stock of provisions, which consists principally of salmon, and the spawn of that fish; to which may be added herring and sprats, and herring spawn. The salmon are taken at Tashees principally in pots or wears. This pot or wear is placed at the foot of a fall or rapid, where the water is not very deep, and the fish, driven from above with long poles, are intercepted and caught in the wear, from whence they are taken into the canoes. In this manner, I have seen more than seven hundred salmon caught in the space of fifteen minutes. I have also sometimes known a few of the striped bass taken in this manner, but rarely.

At such times, there is great feasting and merriment among them; the women and female slaves being busily employed in cooking, or in curing, the fish for their winter stock; which is done by cutting off the heads and tails, splitting them, taking out the backbone, and hanging them up in their houses to dry. They also dry the halibut and cod, but these, instead of curing whole, they cut up into small pieces for that purpose, and expose to the sun. Such is the immense quantity of these fish, and they are taken with such facility, that I have known upward of twenty-five hundred brought into Maquina's house at once, and, at one of their great feasts, have seen one hundred or more cooked in one of their largest tubs.

I was, however, very apprehensive, soon after our arrival at this place, that I should be deprived of the satisfaction of keeping my journal, as Maquina one day, observing me writing in it, inquired of me what I was doing; and, when I endeavored to explain it, by telling him that I was keeping an account of the weather, he said it was not so, and that I was speaking bad about him, and telling how he had taken our ship and killed the crew, so as to inform my countrymen, and that if he ever saw me writing in it again, he would throw it into the fire. I was much rejoiced that he did no more than threaten, and became very cautious afterward not to let him see me write.

Not long after, I finished some daggers for him, which I polished highly; these pleased him much, and he gave me directions to make a cheetoolth, in which I succeeded so far to his satisfaction, that he gave me a present of cloth sufficient to make me a complete suit of raiment, beside other things. Thompson, also, who had become rather more of a favorite than formerly, since he had made a fine sail for his canoe, and some garments for him out of European cloth, about this time, completed another, which was thought by the savages a most superb dress. This was a *kootsuk*, or mantle, a fathom square, made entirely of European vest patterns of the gayest colors. These were sewed together, in a manner to make the best show, and bound with a deep trimming of the finest otter skin, with which the arm-holes were also bordered; while the bottom was further embellished with five or six rows of gilt buttons, placed as near as possible to each other. Nothing could exceed the pride of Maquina when he first put on this royal robe, decorated, like the coat of Joseph, with all the colors of the rainbow, and glittering with the buttons, which, as he strutted about, made a tinkling, while he repeatedly exclaimed, in a transport of exultation, *Klew shish katsuk—wick kum atack Nootka.*—A fine garment—Nootka can't make him.

The king, finding that I was desirous of learning their language, was much delighted, and took great pleasure in conversing with me. On one of these occasions, he explained to me his reasons for cutting off our ship, saying that he bore no ill will to my countrymen, but that he had been several times treated very ill by them. The first injury of which he had cause to complain, was done him by a Captain Tawnington, who commanded a schooner which passed a winter at Friendly Cove, where he was well treated by the inhabitants. This man, taking advantage of Maquina's absence, who had gone to the Wickinninish to procure a wife, armed himself and crew, and entered the house where there were none but women, whom he threw into the greatest consternation, and, searching the chests, took away all the skins, of which Maquina had no less than forty of the best; and that, about the same time, four of their chiefs were barbarously killed by a Captain Martinez, a Spaniard. That, soon after, Captain Hanna, of the Sea-Otter, in consequence of one of the natives having stolen a chisel from the carpenter, fired upon their canoes, which were along side, and killed upward of twenty of the natives, of whom several were *tyees* or chiefs; and that he himself, being on board the vessel, in order to escape, was obliged to leap from the quarter-deck, and swim for a long way under water.

These injuries had excited in the breast of Maquina, an ardent desire of revenge, the strongest passion of the savage heart, and though many years had elapsed since their commission, still they were not forgotten; and the want of a favorable opportunity alone prevented him from sooner avenging them. Unfortunately for us, the long wished for opportunity presented itself in our ship, which Maquina, finding not guarded with the usual vigilance of the north-west traders, and feeling his desire of revenge rekindled by the insult offered by Captain Salter, formed a plan of attacking, and, on his return, called a counsel of his chiefs, and communicated it to them, acquainting them with the manner in which he had been treated. No less desirous of avenging this affront offered their king, than the former injuries, they readily agreed to his proposal which was to go on board without arms, as usual, but under different pretexts, in greater numbers, and wait his signal for the moment of attacking their unsuspecting victims. The execution of this scheme, as the reader knows, was unhappily too successful.

On the thirty-first of December, all the tribe quitted Tashees for Cooptee, whither they go to pass the remainder of the winter, and complete their fishing, taking off everything with them in the same manner as at Nootka. The natives now began to take the herring and sprat in immense quantities, with some salmon, and there was nothing but feasting from morning until night.

On the twenty-fifth of February, we quitted Cooptee, and returned to Nootka. With much joy did Thompson and myself again find ourselves in a place where, notwithstanding the melancholy recollections which it excited, we hoped before long to see some vessel arrive to our relief. Not long after our return, a son of Maquina's sister, a boy about eleven years old, who had been for some time declining, died. Tootoosch, his father, was esteemed the first warrior of the tribe, and was one who had been peculiarly active in the destruction of our ship, having killed two of our poor comrades whose names were Hall and Wood. About the time of our removal to Tashees, while in the enjoyment of the highest health, he was suddenly seized with a fit of delirium, in which he fancied that he saw the ghosts of those two men constantly standing by him, and threatening him, so that he would take no food, except what was forced into his mouth.

When Maquina was first informed by his sister of the strange conduct of her husband, he immediately went to his house, taking us with him; suspecting that his disease had been caused by us, and that the ghosts of our countrymen had been called thither by us, to torment him. We found him raving about Hall and Wood, saying that they were *peshak*, that is, bad. Maquina then placed some provision before him, to see if he would eat. On perceiving it, he put forth his hand to take some, but instantly withdrew it, with signs of horror, saying that Hall and Wood were there, and would not let him eat. Maquina then, pointing to us, asked if it was not John and Thompson who troubled him. *Wik*, he replied, that is, no; *John klushish — Thompson klushish* — John and Thompson are both good; then, turning to me, and patting me on the shoulder, he made signs to me to eat. I tried to persuade him that Hall and Wood were not there, and that none were near him but ourselves: he said, I know very well you do not see them, but I do. At first, Maquina endeavored to convince him that he saw nothing, and to laugh him out of his belief; but, finding that all was to no purpose, he at length became serious, and asked me if I had ever seen any one affected in this manner, and what was the matter with him. I gave him to understand, pointing to his head, that his brain was injured, and that he did not see things as formerly. Being convinced by Tootoosch's conduct, that we had no agency in his indisposition, on our return home, Maquina asked me what was done in my country in similar cases. I told him that such persons were closely confined, and sometimes tied up and whipped, in order to make them better. After pondering for some time, he said that he should be glad to do anything to relieve him, and that he should be whipped; and immediately gave orders to some of his men to go to Tootoosch's house, bind him, and bring him to his, in order to undergo the operation. Thompson was the person selected to administer this remedy, which he undertook very readily, and for that purpose provided himself with a good number of spruce branches, with which he whipped him most severely, laying it on with the best will imaginable, while Tootoosch displayed the greatest rage, kicking, spitting, and attempting to bite all who came near him. This was too much for Maquina, who, at length, unable to endure it longer, ordered Thompson to desist, and Tootoosch to be carried back, saying that, if there was no other way of curing him but by whipping, he must remain mad. The application of the whip produced no beneficial effect on Tootoosch, for he afterward became still more deranged; in his fits of fury sometimes seizing a club, and beating his slaves in a most dreadful manner, and striking and spitting at all who came near him, until, at length, his wife, no longer daring to remain in the house with him, came with her son to Maquina's.

Early in June, Tootoosch, the crazy chief, died. As soon as he was dead, the body, according to their custom, was laid out on a plank, having the head bound round with a red bark fillet, which is, with them, an emblem of mourning and sorrow. After laying some time in this manner, he was wrapped in an otter skin robe, and three fathoms of I-whaw being put about his neck, he was placed in a large coffin, or box, about three feet deep, which was ornamented on the outside with two rows of the small white shells. In this, the most valuable articles of his property were placed with him, among which were no less than twenty-four prime sea-otter skins. The place of burial was a large cavern on the side of a hill, at a little distance from the village, in which, after depositing the coffin carefully, all the attendants repaired to Maquina's house, where a number of articles belonging to the deceased, consisting of blankets, pieces of cloth, etc., were burned by a person appointed by Maquina for that purpose, dressed and painted in the highest style, with his head covered with white down, who, as he put in the several pieces, one by one, poured upon them a quantity of oil to increase the flame, in the intervals between making a speech and playing off a variety of buffoon tricks, and the whole closed with a feast and dance from Sat-sat-sak-sis, the king's son.

The man who performed the ceremony of burning, on this occasion, was a very singular character, named *Kinneclimmets.* He was held in high estimation by the king, though only of the common class, probably from his talent for mimicry and buffoonry, and might be considered as a kind of king's jester, or rather as combining in his person the character of a buffoon with that of master of ceremonies and public orator to his majesty, as he was the one who, at feasts, always regulated the place of the guests, delivered speeches on receiving or returning visits, beside amusing the company at all their entertainments, with a variety of monkey pranks and antic gestures, which appeared to these savages the height of wit and humor, but would be considered as extremely low by the least polished people.

This man *Kinneclimmets*, was particularly odious to Thompson, who would never join in the laugh at his tricks, and when he began, would almost always quit the house with a very surly look, and an exclamation of, cursed fool! which Maquina, who thought nothing could equal the cleverness of his *Climmer-habbee*, used to remark with much dissatisfaction, asking me, why Thompson never laughed, observing that I must have had a very good tempered woman indeed for my mother, as my father was so very ill-natured a man. Among those performances that gained him the greatest applause, was his talent of eating to excess, for

I have known him devour, at one meal, no less than seventy-five large herring; and, at another time, when a great feast was given by Maquina, he undertook, after drinking three pints of oil by way of a whet, to eat four dried salmon, and five quarts of spawn, mixed up with a gallon of train oil, and actually succeeded in swallowing the greater part of this mess, until his stomach became so overloaded, as to discharge its contents in the dish.

Our situation had now become unpleasant in the extreme. The summer was so far advanced, that we nearly despaired of a ship arriving to our relief; and, with that expectation, almost relinquished the hope of ever having it in our power to quit this savage land. We were treated, too, with less indulgence than before, both Thompson and myself being obliged, in addition to our other employments, to perform the laborious task of cutting and collecting fuel, which we had to bring on our shoulders from nearly three miles distant, as it consisted wholly of dry trees, all of which near the village had been consumed. Another thing which, to me in particular, proved an almost constant source of vexation and disgust, and which living among them had not in the least reconciled me to, was their extreme filthiness, not only eating fish, especially the whale, when in a state of offensive putridity, but, while at their meals, of making a practice of taking the vermin from their heads or clothes, and eating them, by turns thrusting their fingers into their hair, and into the dish, and spreading their garments over the tubs in which the provision was cooking, in order to set in motion their inhabitants. Fortunately for Thompson, he regarded this much less than myself; and, when I used to point out to him any instances of their filthiness in this respect, he would laugh and reply, Never mind, John; the more good things, the better. I must, however, do Maquina the justice to state, that he was much neater, both in his person and eating, than were the others, as was likewise his queen, owing, no doubt, to his intercourse with foreigners, which had given him ideas of cleanliness, for I never saw either of them eat any of these animals; but, on the contrary, they appeared not much to relish this taste in others. Their garments, also, were much cleaner, Maquina having been accustomed to give his away when they became soiled, until after he discovered that Thompson and myself kept ours clean by washing them, when he used to make Thompson do the same for him.

In the latter part of July, Maquina informed me that he was going to war with the *A-y-charts*, a tribe living about fifty miles to the south, on account of some controversy that had arisen the preceding summer, and that I must make a number of daggers for his men, and cheetoolths for his chiefs, which having completed, he wished me to make for his own use a weapon of quite a different form, in order to dispatch his enemy by one blow on the head—it being the calculation of these nations, on going to war, to surprise their adversaries while asleep. This was a steel dagger, or more properly a spike, of about six inches long, made very sharp, set at right angles in an iron handle fifteen inches long, terminating, at the lower end, in a crook or turn, so as to prevent its being wrenched from the hand, and at the upper end, in a round knob or head, from whence the spike protruded. This instrument I polished highly, and, the more to please Maquina, formed on the back of the knob the resemblance of a man's head, with the mouth open, substituting for eyes black beads, which I fastened in with red sealing-wax. This pleased him much, and was greatly admired by his chiefs, who wanted me to make similar ones for them, but Maquina would not suffer it, reserving for himself alone this weapon. When these people have finally determined on war, they make it an invariable practice, for three or four weeks prior to the expedition, to go into water five or six times a day, where they wash and scrub themselves from head to foot with bushes, intermixed with briars, so that their bodies and faces will often be entirely covered with blood. Maquina, having informed Thompson and myself that he should take us with him, was very solicitous that we should bathe and scrub ourselves in the same way with them, telling me that it would harden our skins, so that the weapons of the enemy would not pierce them, but as we felt no great inclination to amuse ourselves in this manner, we declined it.

The expedition consisted of forty canoes, carrying from ten to twenty men each. Thompson and myself armed ourselves with cutlasses and pistols, but the natives, although they had a plenty of European arms, took with them only their daggers and cheetoolths, with a few bows and arrows, the latter being about a yard in length, and pointed with copper, muscle-shell, or bone; the bows are four feet and a half long, with strings made of whale sinew.

To go to A-y-chart, we ascended, from twenty to thirty miles, a river about the size of that of Tashees, the banks of which are high and covered with wood. At midnight, we came in sight of the village, which was situated on the west bank, near the shore, on a steep hill, difficult of access, and well calculated for defense. It consisted of fifteen or sixteen houses, smaller than those at Nootka, and built in the same style, but compactly placed. By Maquina's directions, the attack was deferred until the first appearance of dawn, as he said that was the time when men slept the soundest.

At length, all being ready for the attack, we landed with the greatest silence, and, going around so as to come upon the foe in the rear, clambered up the hill; and while the natives, as is their custom, entered the several huts, creeping on all-fours, my comrade and myself stationed ourselves without, to intercept those who should attempt to escape, or come to the aid of their friends. I wished, if possible, not to stain my hands in the blood of any fellow creature, and, though Thompson would gladly have put to death all the savages in the country, he was too brave to think of attacking a sleeping enemy. Having entered the houses, on the war-whoop being given by Maquina, as he seized the head of the chief, and gave him the fatal blow, all proceeded to the work of death. The A-y-charts, being thus surprised, were unable to make resistance, and, with the exception of a very few, who were so fortunate as to make their escape, were all killed, or taken prisoners, on condition of becoming slaves to their captors. I, also, had the good fortune to make four captives, whom Maquina, as a favor, permitted me to consider as mine, and occasionally employ them in fishing for me; as for Thompson, who thirsted for revenge, he had no wish to take any prisoners, but with his cutlass, the only weapon he would employ against them, succeeded in killing seven stout fellows who came to attack him, an act which obtained him great credit with Maquina and the chiefs, who, after this, held him in much higher estimation, and gave him the appellation of *Chehiel-suma-har*, it being the name of a very celebrated warrior of their nation in ancient times, whose exploits were the constant theme of their praise. After having put to death all the old and infirm of either sex, as is the barbarous practice of these people, and destroyed the buildings, we re-embarked, with our booty in our canoes, for Nootka, where we were received with great demonstrations of joy by the women and children, accompanying our war-song with a most furious drumming on the houses. Repeated applications had been made to Maquina, by a number of kings or chiefs, to purchase me, especially after he had shown them the harpoon I had made for him, which he took much pride in, but he constantly refused to part with me on any terms.

With hearts full of dejection, and almost lost to hope, no ship having appeared off Nootka this season, did my companion and myself accompany the tribe, on their removal in September, to Tashees; relinquishing, in consequence, for six months, even the remotest expectation of relief. Soon after our establishment there, Maquina informed me that he and his chiefs had held council, both before and after quitting Nootka, in which they had determined that I must marry one of their women, urging a reason to induce me to consent, that, as there was now no probability of a ship coming to Nootka to release me, I must consider myself as destined to pass the remainder of my life with them, that the sooner I conformed to their customs the better, and that a wife and family would render me more contented and satisfied with their mode of living. I remonstrated against this decision, but to no purpose, for he told me that should I refuse, both Thompson and myself would be put to death, telling me, however, that if there were none of the women of his tribe that pleased me, he would go with me to some of the other tribes, where he would purchase for me such a one as I should select. Reduced to this sad extremity, with death on the one side, and matrimony on the other, I thought proper to choose what appeared to me the least of the two evils, and consented to be married, on condition, that, as I did not fancy any of the Nootka women, I should be permitted to make choice of one from some other tribe.

This being settled, the next morning, by daylight, Maquina, with about fifty men, in two canoes, set out with me for A-i-tiz-zart, taking with him a quantity of cloth, a number of muskets, sea-otter skins, etc., for the purchase of my bride. With the aid of our paddles and sails, being favored with a fair breeze, we arrived some time before sunset at the village. Our arrival excited a general alarm, and the men hastened to the shore, armed with the weapons of their country, making many warlike demonstrations, and displaying much zeal and activity. We, in the meantime, remained quietly seated in our canoes, where we remained for about half an hour, when the messenger of the chief, dressed in their best manner, came to welcome us, and invite us on shore to eat. We followed him, in procession, to the chief's house, Maquina at our head, taking care to leave a sufficient number in the boats to protect the property. When we came to the house, we were ushered in with much ceremony, and our respective seats pointed out to us, mine being next to Maquina, by his request.

After having been regaled with a feast of herring spawn and oil, Maquina asked me if I saw any among the women who were present that I liked. I immediately pointed out to him a young girl of about seventeen, the daughter of *Upquesta*, the chief, who was sitting near him by her mother. On this, Maquina, making a sign to his men, arose, and, taking me by the hand, walked into the middle of the room, and sent off two of his men to bring the boxes containing the presents from the canoes. In the meantime, Kinneclimmets, the master of ceremonies, made himself ready for the part he was to act, by powdering his hair with the white down. When the chests were brought in, specimens of the several articles were taken out, and showed by our men, one of whom held up a musket, another a skin, a third a piece of cloth, etc. On this, Kinneclimmets stepped forward, and, addressing the chief, informed him that all these belonged to me, mentioning the number of each kind, and that they were offered him for the purchase of his daughter *Eu-stoch-ee-exqua*, as a wife for me. As he said this, the men who held up the various articles, walked up to the chief, and with a very stern and morose look, the complimentary one on these occasions, threw them at his feet. Immediately on which, all the tribe, both men and women, who were assembled on this occasion, set up a cry of, Klack-ko-tyee, that is, Thank ye, chief. His men, after this ceremony, having returned to their places, Maquina, rose, and, in a speech of more than half an hour, said much in my praise to the A-i-tiz-zart chief, telling him that I was as good a man as themselves, differing from them only in being white; that I was, beside, acquainted with many things of which they were ignorant; that I knew how to make daggers, cheetoolths, and harpoons, and was a very valuable person, whom he was determined to keep always with him; praising me, at the same time, for the goodness of my temper, and the manner in which I had conducted since I had been with them, observing that all the people of Nootka, and even the children loved me.

When he had ceased, the A-i-tiz-zart chief arose amidst the acclamations of his people, and began with setting forth the many good qualities and accomplishments of his daughter; that he loved her greatly, and, as she was his only one, he could not think of parting with her. He spoke in this manner for some time, but finally concluded by consenting to the proposed union, requesting that she might be well used and kindly treated by her husband. When Upquesta had finished his speech, he directed his people to carry back the presents, which Maquina had given him, to me, together with two young male slaves to assist me in fishing. These, after having been placed before me, were, by Maquina's men, taken on board the canoes. After this, our company returned to lodge at Upquesta's, except a few who were left on board the canoes to watch the property. In the morning, I received from the chief his daughter, with an earnest request that I would use her well, which I promised him; when, taking leave of her parents, she accompanied me with apparent satisfaction on board of the canoe.

At about five in the morning, we reached Tashees, where we found all the inhabitants collected on the shore to receive us. We were welcomed with loud shouts of joy, and exclamations of Wocash, and the women, taking my bride under their charge, conducted her to Maquina's house, to be kept with them for ten days; it being a universal custom, as Maquina informed me, that no intercourse should take place between the new married pair during that period.

The term of my restriction over, Maquina assigned me, as an apartment, the space in the upper part of his house, between him and his elder brother, whose room was opposite. Here, I established myself with my family, consisting of myself and wife, Thompson, and the little Sat-sat-sak-sis, who had always been strongly attached to me, and now solicited his father to let him live with me, to which he consented. This boy was handsome, extremely well formed, amiable, and of a pleasant, sprightly disposition. I used to take a pleasure in decorating him with rings, bracelets, ear-jewels, etc., which I made for him of copper, and ornamented and polished them in my best manner. I was also very careful to keep him free from vermin of every kind, washing him and combing his hair every day. These marks of attention were not only very pleasing to the child, who delighted in being kept neat and clean, as well as in being dressed off in his finery, but were highly gratifying both to Maquina and his queen, who used to express much satisfaction at my care of him.

In making my domestic establishment, I determined, as far as possible, to live in a more comfortable and cleanly manner than the others. For this purpose, I erected, with planks, a partition about three feet high, between mine and the adjoining rooms, and made three bedsteads, of the same, which I covered with boards, for my family to sleep on, which I found much more comfortable than sleeping on the floor amidst the dirt.

Fortunately, I found my Indian princess both amiable and intelligent, for one whose limited sphere of observation must necessarily give rise to but a few ideas. She was extremely ready to agree to anything that I proposed relative to our mode of living, was very attentive in keeping her garments and person neat and clean, and appeared, in every respect, solicitous to please me. She was, as I have said, about seventeen; her person was small, but well formed, as were her features; her complexion was, without exception, fairer than any of the women, with considerable color in her cheeks; her hair long, black, and much softer than is usual with them, and her teeth small, even, and of a dazzling whiteness, while the expression of her countenance indicated sweetness of temper and modesty. She would, indeed, have been considered as very pretty in any country, and, excepting Maquina's queen, was by far the handsomest of any of their women.

With a partner possessing so many attractions, many may be apt to conclude, that I must have found myself happy, at least comparatively so; but far otherwise was it with me—a compulsory marriage with the most beautiful and accomplished person in the world, can never prove a source of real happiness, and, in my situation, I could not but view this connection as a chain that was to bind me down to this savage land, and prevent my ever again seeing a civilized country; especially, when, in a few days after, Maquina informed me that there had been a meeting of his chiefs, in which it was determined that, as I had married one of their women, I must be considered as one of them, and conform to their customs; and that, in future, neither myself nor Thompson should wear our European clothes, but dress in Kutsaks like themselves. This order was to me most painful, but I persuaded Maquina, at length, so far to relax in it as to permit me to wear those I had at present, which were almost worn out, and not to compel Thompson to change his dress, observing that, as he was an old man, such a change would cause his death.

Though, in some respects, my situation was rendered more comfortable since my marriage, as I lived in a more cleanly manner, and had my food better and more neatly cooked, of which, beside, I had always a plenty, my slaves generally furnishing me, and Upquesta never failing to send me an ample supply by the canoes that came from A-i-tiz-zart; still, from my being obliged, at this season of the year, to change my accustomed clothing, and to dress like the natives, with only a piece of cloth about two yards long, thrown loosely around me, my European clothes having been for some time entirely worn out, I suffered more than I can express from the cold, especially as I was compelled to perform the laborious task of cutting and bringing the fire-wood, which was rendered still more oppressive to me, from my comrade, for a considerable part of the winter, not having it in his power to lend me his aid, in consequence of an attack of the rheumatism in one of his knees, with which he suffered for more than four months, two or three weeks of which he was so ill as to be unable to leave the house. On the twentieth of February, we returned to our summer quarters at Nootka, but, on my part, with far different sensations than the last spring, being now almost in despair of any vessel arriving to release us, or our being permitted to depart if there should. Soon after our return, as preparatory to the whaling season, Maquina ordered me to make a good number of harpoons for himself and his chiefs, several of which I had completed, with some lances, when, on the sixteenth of March, I was taken very ill with a violent cholic, caused, I presume, from my having suffered so much from the cold in going without proper clothing. For a number of hours, I was in great pain, and expected to die; and, on its leaving me, I was so weak as scarcely to be able to stand, while I had nothing comforting to take, nor anything to drink but cold water. The feebleness in which the violent attack of my disorder had left me, the dejection I felt at the almost hopelessness of my situation, and the want of warm clothing and proper nursing, though my Indian wife, as far as she knew how, was always ready, and even solicitous, to do everything for me she could, still kept me very much indisposed, which Maquina perceiving, he finally told me, that, if I did not like living with my wife, and that was the cause of my being so sad, I might part with her. This proposal I readily accepted, and the next day Maquina sent her back to her father. On parting with me, she discovered much emotion, begging me that I would suffer her to remain until I had recovered, as there was no one who would take so good care of me as herself. But when I told her that she must go, for that I did not think I should ever recover, which, in truth, I but little expected, and that her father would take good care of her, and treat her more kindly than Maquina, she took an affectionate leave, telling me that she hoped I should soon get better, and left her two slaves to take care of me.

Though I rejoiced at her departure, I was greatly affected with the simple expressions of her regard for me, and could not but feel strongly interested for this poor girl, who, in all her conduct toward me, had discovered so much mildness and attention to my wishes; and, had it not been that I considered her as an almost insuperable obstacle to my being permitted to leave the country, I should, no doubt, have felt the deprivation of her society a real loss. After her departure, I requested Maquina, that, as I had parted with my wife, he would permit me to resume my European dress; for, otherwise, from not having been accustomed to dress like them, I should certainly die. To this he consented, and I once more became comfortably clad. Change of clothing, but, more than all, the hopes which I now began to indulge, that, in the course of the summer, I should be able to escape, in a short time restored me to health, so far, that I could again go to work in making harpoons for Maquina, who, probably, fearing that he should have to part with me, determined to provide himself with a good stock.

It was now past mid-summer, and the hopes we had indulged of our release, became daily more faint; for, though we had heard of no less than seven vessels on the coast, yet none appeared inclined to venture to

Nootka. The destruction of the Boston, the largest, strongest, and best equipped ship, with much the most valuable cargo, of any that had ever been fitted out for the north-west trade, had inspired the commanders of others with a general dread of coming thither, lest they should share the same fate; and, though in the letter I wrote (imploring those who should receive them, to come to the relief of two unfortunate Christians who were suffering among heathen,) I stated the cause of the Boston's capture, and that there was not the least danger in coming to Nootka, provided they would follow the directions I laid down; still I felt very little encouragement that any of these letters would come to hand, when, on the morning of the nineteenth of July, a day that will be ever held by me in grateful remembrance of the mercies of God, while I was employed with Thompson in forging daggers for the king, my ears were saluted with the joyful sound of three cannon, and the cries of the inhabitants, exclaiming, Weena, weena, Mamethlee—that is, strangers, white men.

Soon after, several of our people came running into the house, to inform me that a vessel, under full sail, was coming into the harbor. Though my heart bounded with joy, I repressed my feelings, and, affecting to pay no attention to what was said, told Thompson to be on his guard, and not betray any joy, as our release, and perhaps our lives, depended on our conducting ourselves so as to induce the natives to suppose we were not very anxious to leave them. We continued our works as if nothing had happened, when, in a few minutes after, Maquina came in, and, seeing us at work, appeared much surprised, and asked me if I did not know that a vessel had come. I answered, in a careless manner, that it was nothing to me. How, John, said he, you no glad go board. I replied that I cared very little about it, as I had become reconciled to their manner of living, and had no wish to go away. He then told me that he had called a council of his people respecting us, and that we must leave off work and be present at it.

The men having assembled at Maquina's house, he asked them what was their opinion should be done with Thompson and myself, now a vessel had arrived, and whether he had not better go on board himself to make a trade, and procure such articles as were wanted. Each one of the tribe who wished, gave his opinion. Some were for putting us to death, and pretending to the strangers that a different nation had cut off the Boston; while others, less barbarous, were for sending us fifteen or twenty miles back into the country until the departure of the vessel. These, however, were the sentiments of the common people, the chiefs opposing our being put to death, or injured, and several of them were for immediately releasing us; but this, if he could avoid it, by no means appeared to accord with Maquina's wishes.

With regard, however, to Maquina's going on board the vessel, which he discovered a strong inclination to do, there was but one opinion, all remonstrating against it, telling him that the captain would kill him, or keep him a prisoner, in consequence of his having destroyed our ship. When Maquina had heard their opinions, he told them that he was not afraid of being hurt from going on board the vessel, but that he would, however, in that respect, be guided by John, whom he had always found true. He then turned to me, and asked me if I thought there would be any danger in his going on board. I answered, that I was not surprised at the advice his people had given him, unacquainted as they were with the manners of the white men, and judging them by their own; but, if they had been with them as much as I had, or even himself, they would think very different; that he had almost always experienced good and civil treatment from them, nor had he any reason to fear the contrary now, as they never attempted to harm those who did not injure them; and, if he wished to go on board, he might do it, in my opinion, with security. After reflecting a few moments, he said, with much apparent satisfaction, that, if I would write a letter to the captain, telling him good of him, that he had treated Thompson and myself kindly since we had been with him, and to use him well, he would go. It may readily be supposed that I felt much joy at this determination; but, knowing that the least incaution might annihilate all my hopes of escape, I was careful not to manifest it, and to treat his going or staying as a matter perfectly indifferent to me. I told him, that, if he wished me to write such a letter, I had no objection, as it was the truth, otherwise I could not have done it. The letter which I wrote was nearly in the following terms:—

NOOTKA, *July* 19, 1805.

To Captain ———, *of the brig* ———:

Sir—The bearer of this letter is the Indian king by the name of Maquina. He was the instigator of the capture of the ship Boston, of Boston, in North America, John Salter, captain, and of the murder of twenty-five men of her crew, the two only survivors being now on shore; wherefore, I hope you will take care to confine him according to his merits, putting in your dead lights, and keeping so good a watch over him, that he cannot escape from you. By so doing, we shall be able to obtain our release in the course of a few hours.

JOHN R. JEWETT, *Armorer of the Boston, for himself and*
JOHN THOMPSON, *Sail-maker of said ship.*

I have been asked how I dared to write in this manner: my answer is, that, from my long residence among these people, I knew that I had little to apprehend from their anger on hearing of their king being confined, while they knew his life depended upon my release, and that they would sooner have given up five hundred white men, than have had him injured. This will serve to explain the little apprehension I felt at their menaces afterward; for, otherwise, sweet as liberty was to me, I should hardly have ventured on so hazardous an experiment.

On my giving the letter to Maquina, he asked me to explain it to him. This I did, line by line, as he pointed them out with his finger, but in a sense very different from the real, giving him to understand that I had written to the captain, that, as he had been kind to me since I had been taken by him, that it was my wish that the captain should treat him accordingly, and give him what molasses, biscuit, and rum he wanted. When I had finished, placing his finger, in a significant manner, on my name at the bottom, and eyeing me with a look that seemed to read my inmost thoughts, he said to me, "John, you no lie?" Never did I undergo such a scrutiny, or ever experience greater apprehensions than I felt at that moment, when my destiny was suspended on the slightest thread, and the least mark of embarrassment on mine, or suspicion of treachery on his part, would probably have rendered my life the sacrifice. Fortunately, I was able to preserve my composure, and my being painted in the Indian manner, which Maquina had, since my marriage, required of me, prevented any change in my countenance from being noticed, and I replied, with considerable promptitude, looking at him in my turn, with all the confidence I could muster, "Why do you ask me such a question, Tyee? Have you ever known me to lie?" "No." "Then how can you suppose I should tell you a lie now, since I have never done it?" As I was speaking, he still continued looking at me, with the same piercing eye, but, observing nothing to excite his suspicion, he told me that he believed what I said was true, and that he would go on board, and gave orders to get ready his canoe. His chiefs again attempted to dissuade him, using every argument for that purpose, while his wives crowded around him, begging him on their knees not to trust himself with the white men. Fortunately for my companion and myself, so strong was his wish of going on board the vessel, that he was deaf to their solicitations, and, making no other reply to them, than "John no lie," left the house, taking four prime skins with him as a present to the captain.

Scarcely had the canoe put off, when he ordered his men to stop, and, calling to me, asked me if I did not want to go on board with him. Suspecting this as a question merely intended to ensnare me, I replied, that I had no wish to do it, not having any desire to leave them. On going on board the brig, Maquina immediately gave his present of skins and my letter to the captain, who, on reading it, asked him into the cabin, where he gave him some biscuit and a glass of rum, at the same time privately directing his mate to go forward and return with five or six of the men armed. When they appeared, the captain told Maquina that he was his prisoner, and should continue so, until the two men, whom he knew to be on shore, were released, at the same time ordering him to be put in irons, and the windows secured, which was instantly done, and a couple of men placed as a guard over him. Maquina was greatly surprised and terrified at this reception; he, however, made no attempt to resist, but requested the captain to permit one of his men to come and see him. One of them was accordingly called, and Maquina said something to him, which the captain did not understand, but supposed to be an order to release us, when the man, returning to the canoe, it was paddled off, with the utmost expedition, to the shore. As the canoe approached, the inhabitants, who had all collected upon the beach, manifested some uneasiness at not seeing their king on board; but when, on its arrival, they were told that the captain had made him a prisoner, and that John had spoken bad about him in a letter, they all, both men and women, set up a loud howl, and ran backward and forward upon the shore, like so many lunatics, scratching their faces, and tearing the hair in handfuls from their heads.

After they had beat about in this manner for some time, the men ran to their huts for their weapons, as if preparing to attack an invading enemy; while Maquina's wives and the rest of the women came around me, and, throwing themselves on their knees, begged me with tears to spare his life; and Sat-sat-sak-sis, who kept constantly with me, taking me by the hand, wept bitterly, and joined his entreaties to theirs, that I would not let the white men kill his father. I told them not to afflict themselves, that Maquina's life was in no danger, nor would the least harm be done to him.

The men were, however, extremely exasperated with me, more particularly the common people, who came running, in the most furious manner, toward me, brandishing their weapons, and threatening to cut me in pieces no bigger than their thumb nails, while others declared they would burn me alive, over a slow fire, suspended by my heels. All this fury, however, caused me but little alarm, as I felt convinced they would not dare to execute their threats while the king was on board the brig. The chiefs took no part in this violent conduct, but came to me and inquired the reason why Maquina had been thus treated, and if the captain intended to kill him. I told them that, if they would silence the people, so that I could be heard, I would explain all to them. They immediately put a stop to the noise, when I informed them that the captain, in confining Maquina, had done it of his own accord, and only in order to make them release Thompson and myself, as he well knew we were with them, and, if they would do that, their king would receive no injury, but be well treated; otherwise, he would be kept a prisoner. As many of them did not appear to be satisfied with this, and began to repeat their murderous threats—Kill me, said I to them, if it is your wish, throwing open the bear skin which I wore; here is my breast, I am only one among so many, and can make no resistance; but, unless you wish to see your king hanging by his neck to that pole, pointing to the yard-arm of the brig, and the sailors firing at him with bullets, you will not do it. Oh, no! was the general cry; that must never be; but what must we do? I told them, that their best plan would be to send Thompson on board, to desire the captain to use Maquina well, until I was released, which would be soon. This they were perfectly willing to do, and I directed Thompson to go on board; but he objected, saying that he would not leave me alone with the savages. I told him not to be under any fear for me, for that, if I could get him off, I could manage well enough for myself; and that I wished him, immediately on getting on board the brig, to see the captain, and request him to keep Maquina close until I was released, as I was in no danger while he had him safe.

When I saw Thompson off, I asked the natives what they intended to do with me. They said I must talk to the captain again, in another letter, and tell him to let his boat come on shore with Maquina, and that I should be ready to jump into the boat at the same time Maquina should jump on shore. I told them, that the captain, who knew that they had killed my shipmates, would never trust his men so near the shore, for fear they would kill them too, as they were so much more numerous; but that, if they would select any three of their number to go with me in a canoe, when we came within hail, I could desire the captain to send his boat with Maquina, to receive me in exchange for him.

This appeared to please them, and, after some whispering among the chiefs, who, from what words I overheard, concluded, that if the captain should refuse to send his boat with Maquina, the three men would have no difficulty in bringing me back with them, they agreed to my proposal, and selected three of their stoutest men to convey me. Fortunately, having been for some time accustomed to see me armed, and suspecting no design on my part, they paid no attention to the pistols that I had about me.

As I was going into the canoe, little Sat-sat-sak-sis, who could not bear to part with me, asked me, with an affecting simplicity, since I was going away to leave him, if the white men would not let his father come on shore, and not kill him. I told him not to be concerned, for that no one should injure his father, when, taking an affectionate leave of me, and again begging me not to let the white men hurt his father, he ran to comfort his mother, who was at a little distance, with the assurances I had given him. On entering the canoe, I seated myself in the prow, facing the three men, having determined, if it was practicable, from the moment I found Maquina was secured, to get on board the vessel before he was released, hoping, by that means, to be enabled to obtain the restoration of what property belonged to the Boston still remaining in the possession of the savages, which, I thought, if it could be done, a duty that I owed to the owners. As we came within hail of the brig, they at once ceased paddling, when, presenting my pistols at them, I ordered them instantly to go on, or I would shoot the whole of them. A proceeding so wholly unexpected threw them into great consternation, and resuming their paddles, in a few moments, to my inexpressible delight, I once more found myself along side of a Christian ship, a happiness which I had almost despaired of ever again enjoying. All the crew crowded to the side to see me, as the canoe came up, and manifested much joy at my safety. I immediately leaped on board, where I was welcomed by the captain, Samuel Hill, of the brig Lydia of Boston, who congratulated me on my escape, informing me, that he had received my letter off Klaiz-zart, from the chief Mackee Ulatilla, who came off himself in his canoe to deliver it to him, on which he immediately proceeded hither to aid me. I returned him my thanks, in the best manner I could, for his humanity, though I hardly knew what I said, such was the agitated state of my feelings at that moment, with joy for my escape, thankfulness to the Supreme Being, who had so mercifully preserved me, and gratitude to those whom he had rendered instrumental in my delivery, that I have no doubt, that what with my strange dress, being painted with red and black from head to foot, having a bear skin wrapped around me, and my long hair, which I was not allowed to cut, fastened on the top of my head in a large bunch, with a sprig of green spruce, I must have appeared more like one deranged, than a rational creature; as Captain Hill afterward told me, that he never saw anything in the form of man look so wild as I did when I first came on board.

The captain then asked me into the cabin, where I found Maquina in irons, with a guard over him. He looked very melancholy, but, on seeing me, his countenance brightened up, and he expressed his pleasure with the welcome of "Wocash, John;" when, taking him by the hand, I asked the captain's permission to take off his irons, assuring him, that as I was with him, there was no danger of his being the least troublesome. He accordingly consented, and I felt a sincere pleasure in freeing from fetters a man, who, though he had caused the death of my poor comrades, had, nevertheless, always proved my friend and protector, and whom I had requested to be thus treated only with a view of securing my liberty. Maquina smiled, and appeared much pleased at this mark of attention from me. When I had freed the king from his irons, Captain Hill wished to learn the particulars of our capture, observing that an account of the destruction of the ship and her crew had been received at Boston before he sailed, but that nothing more was known, except that two of the men were living, for whose rescue the owners had offered a liberal reward; and that he had been able to get nothing out of the old man, whom the sailors had supplied so plentifully with grog, as to bring him too much by the head to give any information.

I gave him a correct statement of the whole proceeding, together with the manner in which my life and that of my comrade had been preserved. On hearing my story, he was greatly irritated against Maquina, and said he ought to be killed. I observed, that, however ill he might have acted in taking our ship, yet that it would, perhaps, be wrong to judge an uninformed savage with the same severity as a civilized person, who had the light of religion and the laws of society to guide him; that Maquina's conduct in taking our ship arose from an insult that he thought he had received from Captain Salter, and from the unjustifiable conduct of some masters of vessels who had robbed him, and, without provocation, killed a number of his people; beside, that a regard for the safety of others ought to prevent his being put to death, as I had lived long enough with these people to know that revenge of an injury is held sacred by them, and that they would not fail to retaliate, should he kill their king, on the first vessel or boat's crew that should give them an opportunity; and that, though he might consider executing him as but an act of justice, it would probably cost the lives of many Americans.

The captain appeared to be convinced from what I said of the impolicy of taking Maquina's life, and said that he would leave it wholly with me whether to spare or kill him, as he was resolved to incur no censure in either case. I replied, that I most certainly should never take the life of a man who had preserved mine, had I no other reason; but, as there was some of the Boston's property still remaining on shore, I considered it a duty that I owed to those who were interested in that ship, to try to save it for them, and, with that view, I thought it would be well to keep him on board until it was given up. He concurred in this proposal, saying, if there was any of the property left, it most certainly ought to be got.

During this conversation, Maquina was in great anxiety, as from what English he knew, he perfectly comprehended the subject of our deliberation, constantly interrupting me to inquire what we had determined to do with him; what the captain said; if his life would be spared; and if I did not think that Thompson would kill him. I pacified him as well as I was able, by telling him that he had nothing to fear from the captain, that he would not be hurt, and that if Thompson wished to kill him, which was very probable, he would not be allowed to do it. He would then remind me that I was indebted to him for my life, and that I ought to do by him as he had done by me. I assured him that such was my intention, and I requested him to remain quiet, and not to alarm himself, as no harm was intended him. But I found it extremely difficult to convince him of this, as it accorded so little with the ideas of revenge entertained by them. I told him, however, that he must restore all the property still in his possession, belonging to the ship. This he was perfectly ready to do, happy to escape on such terms; but, as it was now past five, and too late for the articles to be collected and brought off, I told him that he must content himself to remain on board with me that night, and in the morning he should be set on shore as soon as the things were delivered. To this he agreed, on condition that I would remain with him in the cabin. I then went on deck, and the canoe that brought me having been sent back, I hailed the inhabitants, and told them that their king had agreed to stay on board until the next day, when he would return; but that no canoes must attempt to come near the vessel during the night, as they would be fired upon. They answered, *Woho, woho*—very well, very well, I then returned to Maquina, but so great were his terrors, that he would not allow me to sleep, constantly disturbing me with his questions, and repeating, "John, you know when you was alone, and more than five hundred men were your enemies, I was your friend, and prevented them from putting you and Thompson to death, and now I am in the power of your friends, you ought to do the same by me." I assured him that he would be detained on board no longer than the property was released, and that, as soon as it was done. he would be set at liberty.

At day-break, I hailed the natives, and told them that it was Maquina's order that they should bring off the cannon and anchors, and whatever remained with them of the cargo of the ship. This they set about doing with the utmost expedition, transporting the cannon and anchors by lashing together two of their largest canoes, and covering them with planks; and, in the course of two hours, they delivered everything on board that I could recollect, with Thompson's and my chest, containing the papers of the ship, etc.

When everything belonging to the ship had been restored, Maquina was permitted to return in his canoe, which had been sent for him, with a present of what skins he had collected, which were about sixty, for the captain, in acknowledgment of his having spared his life and allowed him to depart unhurt; such was also the transport he felt, when Captain Hill came into the cabin and told him that he was at liberty to go, that he threw off his mantle, which consisted of four of the very best skins, and gave it to him, as a mark of his gratitude; in return for which, the captain presented him with a new great-coat and hat, with which he appeared much delighted. The captain then desired me to inform him that he should return to that part of the coast in November, and that he wished him to keep what skins he should get, which he would buy of him. This Maquina promised, saying to me at the same time, "John, you know I shall be then at Tashees; but, when you come, make *pow*, (which means, fire a gun,) to let me know, and I will come down." When he came to the side of the brig, he shook me cordially by the hand, and told me that he hoped I would come to see him again in a big ship, and bring much plenty of blankets, biscuit, molasses, and rum, for him and his son, who loved me a great deal, and that he would keep all the furs he got for me, observing, at the same time, that he should never more take a letter of recommendation from any one, or ever trust himself on board a vessel unless I was there; then, grasping both my hands, with much emotion, while the tears trickled down his cheeks, he bade me farewell, and stepped into the canoe, which immediately paddled him on shore.

The brig being under weigh, immediately on Maquina's quitting us, we proceeded to the northward, constantly keeping the shore in sight, and touching at various places for the purpose of trading. After a period of nearly four months from our leaving Nootka, we returned from the northward to Columbia river, for the purpose of procuring masts, etc., for our brig, which had suffered considerably in her spars during a gale of wind. Here, after providing ourselves with spars, we sailed for Nootka, where we arrived in the latter part of November. The tribe being absent, the agreed signal was given, by firing a cannon, and in a few hours after, a canoe appeared, which landed at the village, and, putting the king on shore, came off to the brig. Inquiry was immediately made by Kinneclimmets, who was one of the three men in the canoe, if John was there, as the king had some skins to sell them if he was. I then went forward and invited them on board, with which they readily complied, telling me that Maquina had a number of skins with him, but that he would not come on board unless I would go on shore for him. This I agreed to, provided they would remain in the brig in the meantime. To this they consented, and the captain taking them into the cabin, treated them with bread and molasses. I then went on shore in the canoe, notwithstanding the remonstrances of Thompson and the captain, who, though he wanted the skins, advised me by no means to put myself in Maquina's power; but I assured him that I had no fear as long as those men were on board. As I landed, Maquina came up and welcomed me with much joy: on inquiring for the men, I told him that they were to remain until my return. "Ah, John," said he, "I see you are afraid to trust me; but, if they had come with you, I should not have hurt you, though I should have taken good care not to let you go on board of another vessel." He then took his chest of skins, and stepping into the canoe, I paddled him along side of the brig, where he was received and treated by Captain Hill with the greatest cordiality, who bought of him his skins. He left us much pleased with his reception, inquiring of me how many moons it would be before I should come back again to see him and his son; saying that he would keep all his furs for me.

As soon as Maquina had quitted us, we got under weigh and stood again to the northward. We had a prosperous passage to China, arriving at Macao in December, from whence the brig proceeded to Canton. There I had the good fortune to meet a townsman and an old acquaintance, in the mate of an English East-Indiaman, named John Hill, whose father, a wealthy merchant in Hull, in the Baltic trade, was a next door neighbor to mine. Shortly after our arrival, the captain being on board the English ship, and mentioning his having had the good fortune to liberate two men of the Boston's crew from the savages, and that one of them was named Jewett, my former acquaintance immediately came on board the brig to see me.

Words can ill express my feelings on seeing him. Circumstanced as I was, among persons who were entire strangers to me, to meet thus, in a foreign land, with one between whom and myself a considerable intimacy had subsisted, was a pleasure that those alone who have been in a similar situation can properly estimate. He appeared, on his part, no less happy to see me, whom he supposed to be dead, as the account of our capture had been received in England some time before his sailing, and all my friends supposed me to have been murdered.

He supplied me with a new suit of clothes and a hat, a small sum of money for my necessary expenses, and a number of little articles for sea-stores on my voyage to America. I also gave him a letter for my father, in which I mentioned my wonderful preservation and escape, through the humanity of Captain Hill, with whom I should return to Boston. This letter he inclosed to his father, by a ship that was just sailing, in consequence of which it was received much earlier than it otherwise would have been.

We left China, in February, 1807, and after a pleasant voyage of one hundred and fourteen days, arrived at Boston. My feelings on once more finding myself in a Christian country, among a people speaking the same language with myself, may be more readily conceived than expressed. In the post-office in that place, I found a letter for me from my mother, acknowledging the receipt of mine from China, expressing the great joy of my family on hearing of my being alive and well, whom they had for a long time given up for dead.

ADVENTURES

OF

PHILIP ASHTON,

OF MASSACHUSETTS, WHO WAS TAKEN BY PIRATES, ESCAPED FROM THEM, AND DWELT FOR SIXTEEN MONTHS

IN SOLITUDE ON A DESOLATE ISLAND.

On Friday, the fifteenth of June, 1722, after being out some time in a schooner with four men and a boy, off Cape Sable, I stood in for Port Rossaway, designing to lie there all Sunday. Having arrived about four in the afternoon, we saw, among other vessels which had reached the port before us, a brigantine supposed to be inward bound from the West Indies. After remaining three or four hours at anchor, a boat from the brigantine came along side, with four hands, who leaped on deck, and suddenly drawing out pistols, and brandishing cutlasses, demanded the surrender both of ourselves and our vessel. All remonstrance was vain, nor, indeed, had we known who they were before boarding us, could we have made any effectual resistance, being only five men and a boy, and were thus under the necessity of submitting at discretion. We were not single in misfortune, as thirteen or fourteen fishing-vessels, were, in like manner, surprised the same evening.

When carried on board the brigantine, I found myself in the hands of Ned Low, an infamous pirate, whose vessel had two great guns, four swivels, and about forty-two men. I was strongly urged to sign the articles of agreement among the pirates, and to join their number, which I steadily refused, and suffered much bad usage in consequence. At length being conducted, along with five of the prisoners, to the quarter-deck, Low came up to us with pistols in his hand, and loudly demanded, "Are any of you married men?" This unexpected question, added to the sight of the pistols, struck us all speechless; we were alarmed lest there was some secret meaning in his words, and that he would proceed to extremities, therefore none could reply. In a violent passion he cocked a pistol, and clapping it to my head, cried out, "You dog, why don't you answer?" swearing vehemently at the same time that he would shoot me through the head. I was sufficiently terrified by his threats and fierceness, but rather than lose my life in so trifling a matter, I ventured to pronounce, as loud as I durst speak, that I was not married. Hereupon he seemed to be somewhat pacified, and turned away.

It appeared that Low was resolved to take no married men whatever, which often seemed surprising to me until I had been a considerable time with him. But his own wife had died lately before he became a pirate, and he had a young child at Boston, for whom he entertained such tenderness, on every lucid interval from drinking and reveling, that, on mentioning it, I have seen him sit down and weep plentifully. Thus I concluded, that his reason for taking only single men, was, probably, that they might have no ties, such as wives and children, to divert them from his service, and render them desirous of returning home. The pirates finding force of no avail in compelling us to join them, began to use persuasion instead of it. They tried to flatter me into compliance, by setting before me the share I should have in their spoils, and the riches which I should become master of; and all the time eagerly importuned me to drink along with them. But I still continued to resist their proposals, whereupon Low, with equal fury as before, threatened to shoot me through the head; and though I earnestly entreated my release, he and his people wrote my name, and that of my companions, in their books.

On the nineteenth of June, the pirates changed the privateer, as they called their vessel, and went into a new schooner belonging to Marblehead, which they had captured. They then put all the prisoners, whom they designed sending home, on board of the brigantine, and sent her to Boston, which induced me to make another unsuccessful attempt for liberty; but though I fell on my knees to Low, he refused to let me go; thus I saw the brigantine depart, with the whole captives, excepting myself and seven more. Very short time before she departed, I had nearly effected my escape; for a dog belonging to Low being accidentally left on shore, he ordered some hands into a boat to bring it off. Thereupon two young men, captives, both belonging to Marblehead, rapidly leaped into the boat, and I, considering that if I could once get on shore, means might be found of effecting my escape, endeavored to go along with them. But the quarter-master, called Russell, catching hold of my shoulder, drew me back. As the young men did not return, he thought I was privy to their plot, and, with the most outrageous oaths, snapped his pistol, on my denying all knowledge of it. The pistol missing fire, however, only served to enrage him the more: he snapped it three times again, and as often it missed fire; on which he held it overboard, and then it went off. Russel on this drew his cutlass, and was about to attack me in the utmost fury, when I leaped down into the hold and saved myself.

Off St. Michael's, the pirates took a large Portuguese pink, laden with wheat, coming out of the road; and being a good sailer, and carrying fourteen guns, transferred their company into her. It afterward became necessary to careen her, whence they made three islands, called Triangles, lying about forty leagues to the eastward of Surinam. In heaving down the pink, Low had ordered so many men to the shrouds and yards, that the ports, by her heeling, got under water, and the sea rushing in, she overset: he and the doctor were then in the cabin, and as soon as he observed the water gushing in, he leaped out of the stern-port, while the doctor attempted to follow him. But the violence of the sea repulsed the latter, and he was forced back into the cabin. Low, however, contrived to thrust his arm into the port, and dragging him out, saved his life. Meanwhile, the vessel completely overset. Her keel turned out of the water; but as the hull filled, she sunk, in the depth of about six fathoms The yard-arms striking the ground, forced the masts somewhat above the water; as the ship overset, the people got from the shrouds and yards, upon the hull, and as the hull went down, they again resorted to the rigging, rising a little out of the sea.

Being an indifferent swimmer, I was reduced to great extremity; for, along with the other light lads, I had been sent up to the maintop-gallant yard; and the people of a boat, who were now occupied in preserving the men refusing to take me in, I was compelled to attempt reaching the buoy. This I luckily accomplished, and, as it was large, secured myself there until the boat approached. I once more requested the people to take me in, but they still refused, as the boat was full. I was uncertain whether they designed leaving me to perish in this situation; however, the boat being deeply laden, made way very slowly, and one of my comrades, captured at the same time with myself, calling to me to forsake the buoy and swim toward her, I assented, and reaching the boat, he drew me on board. Two men, John Bell, and Zana Guordon, were lost in the pink. Though the schooner in company was very near at hand, her people were employed mending their sails under an awning, and knew nothing of the accident until the boat full of men, got along side.

The pirates having thus lost their principal vessel, and the greatest part of their provisions and water, were reduced to great extremities for want of the latter. They were unable to get a supply at the Triangles; nor, on account of calms and currents, could they make the island of Tobago. Thus they were forced to stand for Grenada, which they reached, after being on short allowance for sixteen days together. Grenada was a French settlement, and Low, on arriving, after having sent all his men, except a sufficient number to maneuver the vessel below, said he was from Barbadoes; that he had lost the water on board, and was obliged to put in here for a supply. The people entertained no suspicion of his being a pirate, but afterward, supposing him a smuggler, thought it a good opportunity to make a prize of his vessel. Next day, therefore, they equipped a large sloop of seventy tons, and four guns, with about thirty hands, as sufficient for the capture, and came along side, while Low was quite unsuspicious of their design. But this being evidently betrayed by their number and actions, he quickly called ninety men on deck, and, having eight guns mounted, the French sloop became an easy prey.

Provided with these two vessels, the pirates cruised about in the West Indies, taking seven or eight prizes, and at length arrived at the island of Santa Cruz, where they captured two more. While lying there, Low thought he stood in need of a medicine chest, and, in order to procure one, sent four Frenchmen, in a vessel he had taken, to St. Thomas's, about twelve leagues distant, with money to purchase it; promising them liberty, and the return of all their vessels for the service. But he declared, at the same time, if it proved otherwise, he would kill the rest of the men, and burn the vessels. In little more than twenty-four hours, the Frenchmen returned with the object of their mission, and Low punctually performed his promise by restoring the vessel.

Having sailed for the Spanish American settlements, the pirates descried two large ships, about half way between Carthagena and Portobello, which proved to be the Mermaid, an English man-of-war, and a Guineaman. They approached in chase until discovering the man-of-war's great range of teeth, when they immediately put about, and made the best of their way off. The man-of-war then commenced the pursuit, and gained upon them apace, and I confess that my terrors were now equal to any that I had previously suffered; for I concluded that we should certainly be taken, and I should no less certainly be hanged for company's sake: so true are the words of Solomon, "A companion of fools shall be destroyed." But the two pirate vessels finding themselves outsailed, separated, and Farrington Spriggs, who commanded the schooner in which I was, stood in for the shore. The Mermaid observing the sloop with Low himself to be the larger of the two, crowded all sail, and continued gaining still more, indeed until her shot flew over; but one of the sloop's crew showed Low a shoal, which he could pass, and in the pursuit the man-of-war grounded. Thus the pirates escaped hanging on this occasion. Spriggs and one of his chosen companions, dreading the consequences of being captured and brought to justice, laid their pistols beside them in the interval, and pledging a mutual oath in a bumper of liquor, swore, if they saw no possibility of escape, to set foot to foot, and blow out each other's brains. But standing toward the shore, they made Pickeroon Bay, and escaped the danger.

Next we repaired to a small island called Utilla, about seven or eight leagues to leeward of the island of Roatan, in the Bay of Honduras, where the bottom of the schooner was cleaned. There were now twenty-two persons on board, and eight of us engaged in a plot to overpower our masters, and make our escape. Spriggs proposed sailing for New England, in quest of provisions, and to increase his company; and we intended on approaching the coast, when the rest had indulged freely in liquor, and fallen sound asleep, to secure them under the hatches, and then deliver ourselves up to government.

Although our plot was carried on with all possible privacy, Spriggs had, somehow or other, got intelligence of it; and having fallen in with Low on the voyage, went on board his ship to make a furious declaration against us. But Low made little account of his information, otherwise it might have been fatal to most of our number. Spriggs, however, returned raging to the schooner, exclaiming, that four of us should go forward to be shot, and to me in particular he said, "You dog, Ashton, you deserve to be hanged up at the yard-arm, for designing to cut us off." I replied, "that I had no intention of injuring any man on board; but I should be glad if they would allow me to go away quietly." At length this flame was quenched, and, through the goodness of God, I escaped destruction. Roatan harbor, as all about the Bay of Honduras, is full of small islands, which pass under the general name of Keys; and having got in here, Low, with some of his chief men, landed on a small island, which they called Port Royal Key. There they erected huts, and contined carousing, drinking and firing, while the different vessels, of which they now had possession, were repairing.

On Saturday, the ninth of March, 1723, the cooper, with six hands, in the long-boat, was going ashore for water; and coming along side of the schooner, I requested to be of the party. Seeing him hesitate, I urged that I had never hitherto been ashore, and thought it hard to be so closely confined, when every one beside had the liberty of landing as there was occasion. Low had before told me, on requesting to be sent away in some of the captured vessels which he dismissed, that I should go home when he did, and swore that I should never previously set my foot on land. But now I considered, if I could possibly once get on terra-firma, though in ever such bad circumstances, I should account it a happy deliverance, and resolved never to embark again.

The cooper at length took me into the long-boat, while Low, and his chief people, were on a different island from Roatan, where the watering-place lay; my only clothing was an Osnaburgh frock and trowsers, a milled cap, but neither shirt, shoes, stockings, nor anything else. When we first landed, I was very active in assisting to get the casks out of the boat, and in rolling them to the watering-place. Then taking a hearty draught of water, I strolled along the beach, picking up stones and shells;

but on reaching the distance of a musket-shot from the party, I began to withdraw toward the skirts of the woods. In answer to a question by the cooper of whither I was going? I replied, "for cocoanuts, as some cocoa-trees were just before me;" and as soon as I was out of sight of my companions, I took to my heels, running as fast as the thickness of the bushes and my naked feet would admit. Notwithstanding I had got a considerable way into the woods, I was still so near as to hear the voices of the party if they spoke loud, and I lay close in a thicket where I knew they could not find me.

After my comrades had filled their casks, and were about to depart, the cooper called on me to accompany them; however, I lay snug in the thicket, and gave him no answer, though his words were plain enough At length, after hallooing loudly, I could hear them say to one another, "The dog is lost in the woods, and cannot find the way out again;" then they hallooed once more, and cried "he has run away and wont come to us;" and the cooper observed, that, had he known my intention, he would not have brought me ashore. Satisfied of their inability to find me among the trees and bushes, the cooper at last, to show his kindness, exclaimed, "If you do not come away presently, I shall go off and leave you alone." Nothing, however, could induce me to discover myself; and my comrades seeing it vain to wait any longer, put off without me.

Thus I was left on a desolate island, destitute of all help, and remote from the track of navigators; but, compared with the state and society I had quitted, I considered the wilderness hospitable, and the solitude interesting. When I thought the whole were gone, I emerged from my thicket, and came down to a small run of water, about a mile from the place where our casks were filled, and there sat down to observe the proceedings of the pirates. To my great joy, in five days their vessels sailed, and I saw the schooner part from them to shape a different course.

I then began to reflect on myself and my present condition: I was on an island which I had no means of leaving; I knew of no human being within many miles; my clothing was scanty, and it was impossible to procure a supply. I was altogether destitute of provision, nor could tell how my life was to be supported. This melancholy prospect drew a copious flood of tears from my eyes; but as it had pleased God to grant my wishes in being liberated from those whose occupation was devising mischief against their neighbors, I resolved to account every hardship light. Yet Low would never suffer his men to work on the Sabbath, which was more devoted to play; and I have even seen some of them sit down to read in a good book.

In order to ascertain how I was to live in time to come, I began to range over the island, which proved ten or eleven leagues long, and lay in about sixteen degrees north latitude. But I soon found that my only companions would be the beasts of the earth, and fowls of the air; for there were no indications of any habitations on the island, though every now and then I found some shreds of earthenware scattered in a lime walk, said by some to be remains of Indians formerly dwelling here. The island was well watered, full of high hills and deep vallies. Numerous fruit trees, such as figs, vines, and cocoanuts are found in the latter; and I found a kind larger than an orange, oval-shaped, of a brownish color without, and red within. Though many of these had fallen under the trees, I could not venture to take them, until I saw the wild hogs feeding with safety, and then I found them very delicious fruit.

Stores of provisions abounded here, though I could avail myself of nothing but the fruit; for I had no knife or iron implement, either to cut up a tortoise on turning it, or weapons wherewith to kill animals; nor had I any means of making a fire to cook my capture, even if I were successful. Sometimes I entertained thoughts of digging pits, and covering them over with small branches of trees, for the purpose of taking hogs or deer; but I wanted a shovel and every substitute for the purpose, and I was soon convinced that my hands were insufficient to make a cavity deep enough to retain what should fall into it. Thus I was forced to rest satisfied with fruit, which was to be esteemed very good provision for any one in my condition.

In process of time, while poking among the sand with a stick, in quest of tortoise eggs, which I had heard were laid in the sand, part of one came up adhering to it; and, on removing the sand, I found nearly a hundred and fifty, which had not lain long enough to spoil. Therefore, taking some, I ate them, and strung others on a strip of palmetto, which, being hung up in the sun, became thick and somewhat hard; so that they were more palatable. After all, they were not very savory food, though one, who had nothing but what fell from the trees, behoved to be content. Tortoise lay their eggs in the sand, in holes about a foot or a foot and a half deep, and smooth the surface over them, so that there is no discovering where they lie. According to the best of my observation, the young are hatched in eighteen or twenty days, and then immediately take to the water.

Many serpents are on this and the adjacent islands; one, about twelve or fourteen feet long, is as large as a man's waist, but not poisonous. When lying at length, they look like old trunks of trees, covered with short moss, though they usually assume a circular position. The first time I saw one of these serpents, I had approached very near before discovering it to be a living creature; it opened its mouth wide enough to have received a hat, and breathed on me. A small black fly creates such annoyance, that even if a person possessed ever so many comforts, his life would be oppressive to him, unless for the possibility of retiring to some small quay, destitute of wood and bushes, where multitudes are dispersed by the wind. To this place, then, was I confined during nine months, without seeing a human being. One day after another was lingered out, I know not how, void of occupation or amusement, except collecting food, rambling from hill to hill, and from island to island, and gazing on sky and water. Although my mind was occupied by many regrets, I had the reflection that I was lawfully employed when taken, so that I had no hand in bringing misery on myself: I was also comforted to think that I had the approbation and consent of my parents in going to sea, and trusted that it would please God, in his own time and manner, to provide for my return to my father's house. Therefore, I resolved to submit patiently to my misfortune.

It was my daily practice to ramble from one part of the island to another, though I had a more special home near the water-side. Here I built a hut to defend me against the heat of the sun by day, and the heavy dews by night. Taking some of the best branches which I could find fallen from the trees, I contrived to fix them against a low hanging bough, by fastening them together with split palmetto leaves; next I covered the whole with some of the largest and most suitable leaves that I could get Many of these huts were constructed by me, generally near the beach, with the open part, fronting the sea, to have the better look-out, and the advantage of the sea-breeze, which both the heat and the vermin required. But the insects were so troublesome, that I thought of endeavoring to get over to some of the adjacent keys, in hopes of enjoying rest. However, I was, as already said, a very indifferent swimmer; I had no canoe, nor any means of making one. At length, having got a piece of bamboo, which is hollow like a reed, and light as cork, I ventured, after frequent trials with it under my breast and arms, to put off for a small key about a gun-shot distant, which I reached in safety. My new place of refuge was only about three or four hundred feet in circuit, lying very low, and clear of woods and brush; from exposure to the wind, it was quite free of vermin, and I seemed to have got into a new world, where I lived infinitely more at ease. Hither I retired, therefore, when the heat of the day rendered the insect tribe most obnoxious; yet I was obliged to be much on Roatan, to procure food and water, and at night on account of my hut.

When swimming back and forward between the two islands, I used to bind my frock and trowsers about my head, and if I could have carried over wood and leaves, whereof to make a hut, with equal facility, I should have passed more of my time on the smaller one. Yet these excursions were not unattended with danger. Once, I remember, when passing from the larger island, the bamboo, before I was aware, slipped from under me; and the tide, or current, set down so strong, that it was with great difficulty I could reach the shore. At another time, when swimming over to the small island, a shovel-nosed shark, which, as well as alligators, abound in those seas, struck me in the thigh, just as my foot could reach the bottom, and grounded itself, from the shallowness of the water, as I suppose, so that its mouth could not get round toward me. The blow I felt some hours after making the shore. By repeated practice, I at length became a pretty dextrous swimmer, and amused myself by passing from one island to another, among the keys.

I suffered very much from being barefoot; so many deep wounds were made in my feet from traversing the woods, where the ground was covered with sticks and stones, and on the hot beach, over sharp broken shells, that I was scarce able to walk at all. Often, when treading with all possible caution, a stone or shell on the beach, or a pointed stick in the woods, would penetrate the old wound, and the extreme anguish would strike me down as suddenly as if I had been shot. Then I would remain, for hours together, with tears gushing from my eyes, from the acuteness of the pain. I could travel no more than absolute necessity compelled me, in quest of subsistence; and I have sat, my back leaning against a tree, looking out for a vessel during a complete day. Once, while faint from such injuries, as well as smarting under the pain of them, a wild boar rushed toward me. I knew not what to do, for I had not strength to resist his attack; therefore, as he drew nearer, I caught the bough of a tree, and suspended myself by means of it. The boar tore away part of my ragged trowsers with his tusks, and then left me. This, I think, was the only time that I was attacked by any wild beast, and I considered myself to have had a very great deliverance.

As my weakness continued to increase, I often fell to the ground insensible, and then, as also when I laid myself to sleep, I thought I should never awake again, or rise in life. Under this affliction I first lost count of the days of the week; I could not distinguish Sunday, and, as my illness became more aggravated, I became ignorant of the month also. All this time I had no healing balsam for my feet, nor any cordial to revive my drooping spirits. My utmost efforts could only now and then procure some figs and grapes. Neither had I fire; for, though I had heard of a way to procure it by rubbing two sticks together, my attempts in this respect, continued until I was tired, proved abortive. The rains having come on, attended with chill winds, I suffered exceedingly While passing nine months in this lonely, melancholy, and irksome condition, my thoughts would sometimes wander to my parents; and I reflected that, notwithstanding it would be consolatory to myself if they knew where I was, it might be distressing to them. The nearer my prospect of death, which I often expected, the greater my penitence became.

Some time in November, 1723, I descried a small canoe approaching, with a single man; but the sight excited little emotion. I kept my seat on the beach, thinking I could not expect a friend, and knowing that I had no enemy to fear, nor was I capable of resisting one. As the man approached, he betrayed many signs of surprise; he called me to him, and I told him he might safely venture ashore, for I was alone, and almost expiring. Coming close up, he knew not what to make of me; my garb and countenance seemed so singular, that he looked wild with astonishment. He started back a little, and surveyed me more thoroughly; but, recovering himself again, came forward, and, taking me by the hand, expressed his satisfaction at seeing me. This stranger proved to be a native of North Britain; he was well advanced in years, of a grave and venerable aspect, and of a reserved temper. His name I never knew, he did not disclose it, and I had not inquired during the period of our acquaintance. But he informed me he had lived twenty-two years with the Spaniards who now threatened to burn him, though I know not for what crime; therefore he had fled hither as a sanctuary, bringing his dog, gun, and ammunition, as also a small quantity of pork, along with him. He designed spending the remainder of his days on the island, where he could support himself by hunting.

I experienced much kindness from the stranger; he was always ready to perform any civil offices, and assist me in whatever he could, though he spoke little: and he gave me a share of his pork. On the third day after his arrival, he said he would make an excursion in his canoe among the neighboring islands, for the purpose of killing wild hogs and deer, and wished me to accompany him. Though my spirits were somewhat recruited by his society, the benefit of the fire, which I now enjoyed, and dressed provisions, my weakness and the soreness of my feet, precluded me; therefore he set out alone, saying he would return in a few hours. The sky was serene, and there was no prospect of any danger during a short excursion, seeing he had come nearly twelve leagues in safety in his canoe. But, when he had been absent about an hour, a violent gust of wind and rain arose, in which he probably perished, as I never heard of him more.

Thus, after having the pleasure of a companion almost three days, I was as unexpectedly reduced to my former lonely state, as I had been relieved from it. Yet, through the goodness of God, I was myself preserved from having been unable to accompany him; and I was left in better circumstances than those in which he had found me, for now I had about five pounds of pork, a knife, a bottle of gunpowder, tobacco, tongs and flint, by which means my life could be rendered more comfortable. I was enabled to have fire, extremely requisite at this time, being the rainy months of winter. I could cut up a tortoise, and have a delicate broiled meal—Thus, by the help of the fire, and dressed provisions, through the blessing of God, I began to recover strength, though the soreness of my feet remained. But I had, beside, the advantage of being able now and then to catch a dish of crayfish, which, when roasted, proved good eating. To accomplish this I made up a small bundle of old broken sticks, nearly resembling pitch-pine, or candle-wood, and having lighted one end, waded with it in my hand, up to the waist in water. The cray-fish, attracted by the light, would crawl to my feet, and lie directly under it, when, by means of a forked stick, I could toss them ashore.

Between two and three months after the time of losing my companion, I found a small canoe, while ranging along the shore. The sight of it revived my regret for his loss, for I judged that it had been his canoe; and, from being washed up here, a certain proof of his having been lost in the tempest. But, on examining it more closely, I satisfied myself that it was one which I had never seen before. Master of this little vessel, I began to think myself admiral of the neighboring seas, as well as sole possessor and chief commander of the islands. Profiting by its use, I could transport myself to the places of retreat more conveniently than by my former expedient of swimming.

In process of time, I projected an excursion to some of the larger and more distant islands, partly to learn how they were stored or inhabited, and partly for the sake of amusement.—Laying in a small stock of figs and grapes, therefore, as also some tortoise to eat, and carrying my implements for fire, I put off to steer for the island of Bornacco, which is about four or five leagues long, and situated five or six from Roatan. In the course of the voyage, observing a sloop at the east end of the island, I made the best of my way to the west, designing to travel down by land, both because a point of rocks ran far into the sea, beyond which I did not care to venture in the canoe, as was necessary to come ahead of the sloop, and because I wished to ascertain something concerning her people before I was discovered. Even in my worst circumstances, I never could brook the thoughts of returning on board of any piratical vessel, and resolved rather to live and die in my present situation. Hauling up the canoe, and making it fast as well as I was able, I set out on the journey. My feet were yet in such a state, that two days, and the best part of two nights were occupied in it. Sometimes the woods and bushes were so thick that it was necessary to crawl half a mile together on my hands and knees, which rendered my progress very slow. When within a mile or two of the place where I supposed the sloop might be, I made for the water side, and approached the sea gradually, that I might not too soon disclose myself to view; however, on reaching the beach, there was no appearance of the sloop, whence I judged that she had sailed during the time spent by me in traveling. Being much fatigued with the journey, I rested myself against the stump of a tree, with my face toward the sea, where sleep overpowered me. But I had not slumbered long before I was suddenly awakened by the noise of firing.—Starting up in affright, I saw nine pirogues, or large canoes, full of men, firing upon me from the sea; whence I soon turned about and ran among the bushes as fast as my sore feet would allow, while the men, who were Spaniards, cried after me, "O Englishman! we will give you good quarter." However, my astonishment was so great, and I was so suddenly roused from my sleep, that I had no self-command to listen to their offers of quarter, which, it may be, at another time, in my cooler moments, I might have done. Thus I made into the woods, and the strangers continued firing after me, to the number of one hundred and fifty bullets at least, many of which cut small twigs off the bushes close by my side. Having gained an extensive thicket beyond reach of the shot, I lay close several hours, until observing, by the sound of their oars, that the Spaniards were departing, I crept out. I saw the sloop under English colors sailing away with the canoes in tow, which induced me to suppose she was an English vessel which had been at the Bay of Honduras, and taken there by the Spaniards. Next day I returned to the tree, where I had been so nearly surprised, and was astonished to find six or seven shot in the trunk, within a foot or less of my head. Yet through the wonderful goodness of God, though having been as a mark to shoot at, I was preserved.

After this I traveled to recover my canoe at the western end of the island, which I reached in three days, but suffering severely from the soreness of my feet, and the scantiness of provisions. This island is not so plentifully stored as Roatan, so that during the five or six days of my residence, I had difficulty in procuring subsistence; and the insects were, beside, infinitely more numerous and harassing than at my old habitation. These circumstances deterred me from further exploring the island; and having reached the canoe very tired and exhausted, I put off for Roatan, which was a royal palace to me, compared with Bonacco, and arrived at night in safety. Here I lived, if it may be called living, alone, for about seven months, after losing my North British companion.—My time was spent in the usual manner, hunting for food, and ranging among the islands.

Some time in June, 1724, while on the small quay, whither I often retreated to be free from the annoyance of insects, I saw two canoes making for the harbor. Appoaching nearer, they observed the smoke of a fire which I had kindled, and at a loss to know what it meant, they hesitated on advancing.—What I had experienced at Bonacco, was still fresh in my own memory, and loth to run the risk of such another firing, I withdrew to my canoe, lying behind the quay, not above a hundred yards distant, and immediately rowed over to Roatan. There I had places of safety against an enemy, and sufficient accommodation for any ordinary number of friends.

The people in the canoes observed me cross the sea to Roatan, the passage not exceeding a gun-shot over; and being as much afraid of pirates as I was of Spaniards, approached very cautiously toward the shore. I then came down to the beach, showing myself openly; for their conduct led me to think that they could not be pirates, and I resolved before being exposed to the danger of their shot, to inquire who they were. If they proved such as I did not like, I could easily retire. But before I spoke, they, as full of apprehension as I could be, lay on their oars, and demanded who I was, and from whence I came? to which I replied, that "I was an Englishman, and had run away from pirates." On this they drew somewhat nearer, inquiring who was there beside myself? when I assured them, in return, that I was alone. Next, according to my original purpose, having put similar questions to them, they said they had come from the Bay of Honduras; their words encouraged me to bid them row ashore, which they accordingly did, though at some distance, and one man landed, whom I advanced to meet. But he started back at the sight of a poor ragged, wild, forlorn, miserable object so near him. Collecting himself, however, he took me by the hand, and we began embracing each other, he from surprise and wonder, and I from a sort of ecstacy of joy. When this was over, he took me in his arms, and carried me down to the canoes, when all his comrades were struck with astonishment at my appearance; but they gladly received me, and I experienced great tenderness from them.

I gave the strangers a brief account of my escape from Low, and my lonely residence for sixteen months, all excepting three days, the hardships I had suffered, and the dangers to which I had been exposed They stood amazed at the recital; they wondered I was alive, and expressed much satisfaction at being able to relieve me. Observing me very weak and depressed, they gave me about a spoonful of rum to recruit my fainting spirits; but even this small quantity, from my long disuse of strong liquors, threw me into violent agitation, and produced a kind of stupor, which at last ended in privation of sense. Some of the party perceiving a state of insensibility come on, would have administered more rum, which those better skilled among them prevented; and after lying a short time in a fit, I revived. Then I ascertained, that the strangers were eighteen in number, the chief of them named John Hope, an old man, called Father Hope, by his companions, and John Ford, and all belonging to the Bay of Honduras. The cause of their coming hither, was an alarm for an attack from the sea, by the Spaniards, while the Indians should make a descent by land, and cut off the Bay; thus they had fled for safety. On a former occasion, the two persons above named, had for the like reason, taken shelter among these islands, and lived four years at a time on a small one, named Barbarat, about two leagues from Roatan. There they had two plantations, as they called them; and now they brought two barrels of flour, with other provisions, fire-arms, dogs for hunting, and nets for tortoise; and also an Indian woman to dress their provisions. Their principal residence was a small key, about a quarter of a mile round, lying near to Barbarat, and named by them the Castle of Comfort, chiefly because it was low and clear of woods and bushes, so that the free circulation of wind could drive away the pestiferous musquitoes and other insects. From hence they sent to the surrounding islands for wood, water and materials to build two houses, such as they were, for shelter.

I now had the prospect of a much more agreeable life than what I had spent during the sixteen months past; for, beside having company, the strangers treated me with a great deal of civility in their way; they clothed me, and gave me a large wrapping gown as a defense against the nightly dews, until their houses were erected; and there was plenty of provisions. Yet after all, they were bad society; and as to their common conversation, there was but little difference between them and pirates. However, it did not appear that they were now engaged in any such evil design as rendered it unlawful to join them, or be found in their company. In process of time, and with the assistance afforded by my companions, I gathered so much strength as sometimes to be able to hunt along with them. The islands abounded with wild hogs, deer and tortoise; and different ones were visited in quest of game. This was brought home, where, instead of being immediately consumed, it was hung up to dry, in smoke, so as to be a ready supply at all times. I now considered myself beyond the reach of danger from an enemy, for, independent of supposing that nothing could bring any one here, I was surrounded by a number of men with arms constantly in their hands. Yet, at the very time that I thought myself most secure, I was very near again falling into the hands of pirates.

Six or seven months after the strangers joined me, three of them, along with myself, took a four-oared canoe, for the purpose of hunting and killing tortoise on Bonacco. During our absence the rest repaired their canoes, and prepared to go over to the Bay of Honduras, to examine how matters stood there, and bring off their remaining effects, in case it were dangerous to return. But before they had departed, we were on our voyage homeward, having a full load of pork and tortoise, as our object was successfully accomplished. While entering the mouth of the harbor, in a moonlight evening, we saw a great flash, and heard a report much louder than that of a musket, proceeding from a large pirogue, which we observed near the Castle of Comfort. This put us in extreme consternation, and we knew not what to consider; but in a minute we heard a volley of eighteen or twenty small arms, discharged toward the shore, and also some returned from it. Satisfied that the enemy, either Spaniards or pirates, was attacking our people, and being intercepted from them by pirogues lying between us and the shore, we thought the safest plan was trying to escape. Therefore, taking down our little mast and sail, that they might not betray us, we rowed out of the harbor as fast as possible, toward an island about a mile and a half distant, to retreat undiscovered. But the enemy either having seen us before lowering our sail, or heard the noise of the oars, followed with all speed, in an eight or ten oared pirogue. Observing her approach, and fast gaining on us, we rowed with all our might to make the nearest shore. However, she was at length enabled to discharge a swivel, the shot from which passed over our canoe. Nevertheless, we contrived to reach the shore before being completely within the range of small arms, which our pursuers discharged on us while landing.

They were now near enough to cry aloud that they were pirates, and not Spaniards, and that we need not dread them, as we should get good quarter; thence supposing that we should be the easier induced to surrender. Yet nothing could have been said to discourage me more from putting myself in their power; I had the utmost dread of a pirate, and my original aversion was now enhanced, by the apprehension of being sacrificed for my former desertion. Thus, concluding to keep as clear of them as I could, and the Honduras Bay men having no great inclination to do otherwise, we made the best of our way to the woods. Our pursuers carried off the canoe, with all its contents, resolving, if we would not go to them, to deprive us, as far as possible, of all means of subsistence where we were. But it gave me, who had known both want and solitude, little concern, now that I had company, and there were arms among us to procure provision, and also fire wherewith to dress it. Our assailants were some men belonging to Spriggs, my former commander, who had thrown off his allegiance to Low, and set up for himself at the head of a gang of pirates, with a good ship of twenty-four guns, and a sloop of twelve, both presently lying in Roatan harbor. He had put in for fresh water, and to refit, at the place where I first escaped; and, having discovered my companions at the small island of their retreat, sent a pirogue full of men to take them. Accordingly they carried all ashore, as also a child and an Indian woman; the last of whom they shamefully abused. They killed a man after landing, and throwing him into one of the canoes containing tar, set it on fire, and burnt his body in it. Then they carried the people on board of their vessels, where they were barbarously treated. One of them turned pirate, however, and told the others that John Hope had hid many things in the woods; therefore, they beat him unmercifully to make him disclose his treasure, which they carried off with them.

After the pirates had kept these people five days on board of their vessels, they gave them a flat of five or six tons, to carry them to the Bay of Honduras, but no kind of provision for the voyage; and further, before dismissal, compelled them to swear that they would not come near me and my party, who had escaped to another island. While the vessels rode in the harbor, we kept a good look-out, but were exposed to some difficulties, from not daring to kindle a fire to dress our victuals, lest our residence should be betrayed. Thus we lived for five days, on raw provisions.—As soon as they sailed, however, Hope, little regarding the oath extorted from him, came and informed us of what had passed; and I could not, for my own part, be sufficiently grateful to Providence for escaping the hands of the pirates, who would have put me to a cruel death.

Hope and all his people, except John Symonds, now resolved to make their way to the Bay. Symonds, who had a negro, wished to remain some time for the purpose of trading with the Jamaica men on the main. But thinking my best chance of getting to New England was from the Bay of Honduras, I requested Hope to take me with him. The old man, though he would gladly have done so, advanced many objections, such as the insufficiency of the flat to carry so many men seventy leagues; that they had no provisions for the passage, which might be tedious; and the flat was, beside, ill calculated to stand the sea; as also, that it was uncertain how matters might turn out at the Bay: thus he thought it better for me to remain; yet rather than I should be in solitude, he would take me in. Symonds, on the other hand, urged me to stay and bear him company, and gave several reasons why I should more likely obtain a passage from the Jamaica men to New England, than by the Bay of Honduras. As this seemed a fairer prospect of reaching my home, which I was extremely anxious to do, I assented; and, having thanked Hope and his companions for their civilities, I took leave of them, and they departed. Symonds was provided with a canoe, fire-arms, and two dogs, in addition to his negro, by which means he felt confident of being able to provide all that was necessary for our subsistence. We spent two or three months after the usual manner, ranging from island to island, but the prevalence of the winter rains precluded us from obtaining more game than we required.

When the season for the Jamaica traders approached, Symonds proposed repairing to some other island to obtain a quantity of tortoise shell which he could exchange for clothes and shoes; and, being successful in this respect, we next proceeded to Bonacco, which lies near the main, that we might thence take a favorable opportunity to run over. Having been a short time at Bonacco, a furious tempest arose, and continued for three days, when we saw several vessels standing in for the harbor. The largest of them anchored at a great distance, but a brigantine came over the shoals opposite to the watering-place, and sent her boat ashore with casks. Recognizing three people who were in the boat, by their dress and appearance, for Englishmen, I concluded they were friends, and showed myself openly on the beach before them. They ceased rowing immediately on observing me, and, after answering their inquiries of who I was, I put the same questions, saying they might come ashore with safety. They did so, and a happy meeting it was for me. I now found that the vessels were a fleet, under convoy of the Diamond man-of-war, bound for Jamaica; but many ships had parted company in the storm. The Diamond had sent in the brigantine to get water here, as the sickness of her crew had occasioned a great consumption of that necessary article.

Symonds, who had kept at a distance, lest the three men might hesitate to come ashore, at length approached to participate in my joy, though, at the same time, testifying considerable reluctance at the prospect of my leaving him. The brigantine was commanded by Captain Dove, with whom I was acquainted, and she belonged to Salem, within three miles of my father's house. Captain Dove not only treated me with great civility, and engaged to give me a passage home, but took me into pay, having lost a seaman, whose place he wanted me to supply. Next day, the Diamond having sent her long-boat with casks for water, they were filled; and after taking leave of Symonds, who shed tears at parting, I was carried on board of the brigantine.

We sailed along with the Diamond, which was bound for Jamaica, on the latter end of March, 1725, and kept company until the first of April. By the providence of Heaven we passed safely through the Gulf of Florida, and reached Salem Harbor on the first of May, two years, ten months and fifteen days after I was first taken by pirates; and two years and two months, after making my escape from them on Roatan Island. That same evening I went to my father's house, where I was received as one risen from the dead.

SHIPWRECK

OF THE

FRENCH FRIGATE MEDUSA:

AS RELATED BY MADEMOISELLE PICARD; ADDED TO WHICH IS THE NARRATIVE OF TWO OF THE OFFICERS, WHO SHARED THE UNSPEAKABLE MISERIES OF A RAFT FULL OF HER SAILORS AND PASSENGERS WHO WERE REDUCED TO THE NECESSITY OF

FEEDING UPON THE CORPSES OF THEIR COMPANIONS.

Early on the morning of the 22d of June, 1816, we were on our way to the boats that were to convey us on board the Medusa, which was riding at anchor off the island of Aix, on the western coast of France. We soon arrived at the place of embarkation, where we found some of our fellow passengers, who, like myself, seemed casting a last look to heaven while we were yet on the French soil. When we got on board we found our berths not provided for us, consequently were obliged to remain indiscriminately together till next day. Our family, which consisted of nine persons, was placed in a berth near the main-deck. As the wind was still contrary, we lay at anchor for several days.

On the 17th of June, at four in the morning, we set sail, as did the whole expedition, which consisted of the Medusa frigate, the Loire store-ship, the Argus brig, and the Echo corvette. The wind being very favorable, we soon lost sight of the green fields of l'Aunis. At six in the morning, however, the island of Rhe still appeared above the horizon. We fixed our eyes upon it with regret, to salute for the last time our dear country. Now, imagine the ship borne aloft, and surrounded by huge mountains of water, which at one moment tossed it in the air, and at another plunged it into the profound abyss. The waves, raised by a stormy northwest breeze, came dashing in a horrible manner against the sides of our ship. I know not whether it was a presentiment of the misfortune which menaced us that had made me pass the preceding night in the most cruel inquietude. In my agitation I sprung upon deck and contemplated with horror the frigate winging its way upon the waters. The winds pressed against the sails with great violence, strained and whistled among the cordage, and the great hulk of wood seemed to split every time the surge broke upon its sides. On looking a little out to sea I perceived, at no great distance on our right, all the other ships of the expedition, which quieted me much. Toward ten in the morning the wind changed; immediately an appalling cry was heard, concerning which the passengers, as well as myself, were equally ignorant. The whole crew were in motion. Some climbed the rope ladders, and seemed to perch on the extremities of the yards; others mounted to the highest parts of the masts; these bellowing and pulling certain cordages in cadence; those crying, swearing, whistling, and filling the air with barbarous and unknown sounds. The officer on duty, in his turn, roared out these words, starboard! larboard! hoist! luff! tack! which the helmsman repeated in the same tone. All this hubbub, however, produced its effect: the yards were turned on their pivots, the sails set, the cordage tightened, and the unfortunate sea-boys having received their lesson, descended to the deck. Everything remained tranquil, except that the waves still roared, and the masts continued their creaking. However, the sails were swelled, the winds less violent, though favorable, and the mariner, while he carolled his song, said he had a noble voyage.

On the 28th of June, at six in the morning, we discovered the Peak of Teneriffe toward the south, the summit of whose cone seemed lost among the clouds. We were then distant about two leagues, which we made in less than a quarter of an hour. At ten o'clock we brought to before the town of St. Croix. Several officers got leave to go on shore to procure refreshments. While these gentlemen were away, a certain passenger, member of the self-instituted Philanthropic Society of Cape Verd, suggested that it was very dangerous to remain where we were, adding that he was well acquainted with the country, and had navigated in all these latitudes. M. Le Roy Lachaumareys, captain of the Medusa, believing the pretended knowledge of the intriguing Richefort, gave him the command of the frigate. Various officers of the navy represented to the captain how shameful it was to put such confidence in a stranger, and that they would never obey a man who had no character as a commander. The captain despised these wise remonstrances; and, using his authority, commanded the pilots and the crew to obey Richefort; saying he was king, since the orders of the king were that they should obey him. Immediately the impostor, desirous of displaying his great skill in navigation, made them change the route for no purpose but that of showing his skill in maneuvering a ship. Every instant he changed the tack, went, came, and returned, and approached the very reefs, as if to brave them. In short, he beat about so much that the sailors at length refused to obey him, saying boldly that he was a vile impostor. But it was done. The man had gained the confidence of Captain Lachaumareys, who, ignorant of navigation himself, was doubtless glad to get some one to undertake his duty. But it must be told, that this blind and inept confidence was the sole cause of the loss of the Medusa frigate, as well as of all the crimes consequent upon it.

Toward three in the afternoon, those officers who had gone on shore in the morning, returned on board loaded with vegetables, fruits and flowers. They laughed heartily at the maneuvers that had been going on during their absence, which doubtless did not please the captain, who flattered himself he had already found in this pilot Richefort *a good and able seaman;* such were his words. At four in the afternoon he took a southerly direction. M. Richefort then beaming with exultation for having, as he said, saved the Medusa from certain shipwreck, continued to give his pernicious counsels to Captain Lachaumareys, persuaded him he had been often employed to explore the shores of Africa, and that he was perfectly well acquainted with the Arguine Bank. On the 1st of July we recognized Cape Bojador, and then saw the shores of Sahara. Toward ten in the morning they set about the frivolous ceremony which the sailors have invented for the purpose of exacting something from those passengers who have never crossed the line. During the ceremony the frigate doubled Cape Barbas, hastening to its destruction. Captain Lachaumareys very good humoredly presided at this species of baptism, while his dear Richefort promenaded the forecastle, and looked with indifference upon a shore bristling with danger. However that may be, all passed on well; nay, it may be even said that the farce was well played off. But the route which we pursued soon made us forget the short-lived happiness we had experienced. Every one began to observe the sudden change which had taken place in the color of the sea, as we ran upon a bank in shallow water. A general murmur rose among the passengers and officers of the navy—they were far from partaking in the blind confidence of the captain.

On the 2d of July, at five in the morning, the captain was persuaded that a large cloud, which was discovered in the direction of Cape Blanco, was that cape itself. After this pretended discovery, they ought to have steered to the west, for about fifty leagues, to have gained sea-room to double with certainty the Arguin bank; moreover, they ought to have conformed to the instructions which the Minister of Marine had given to the ships which set out for Senegal. The other part of the expedition, from having followed these instructions, arrived in safety at their destination. During the preceding night the Echo, which had hitherto accompanied the Medusa, made several signals, but being replied to with contempt abandoned us. Toward ten in the morning, the danger which threatened us was again represented to the captain, and he was strongly urged, if he wished to avoid the Arguin bank, to take a westerly course; but the advice was again neglected, and he despised the predictions. One of the officers of the frigate, from having wished to expose the intriguing Richefort, was put under arrest. My father, who had already twice made the voyage to Senegal, and who, with various persons, was persuaded they were going right upon the bank, also made his observations to the unfortunate pilot. His advice was no better received than that of others. Richefort, in the sweetest tone, replied. "My dear, we know our business; attend to yours, and be quiet. I have already twice passed the Arguin bank: I have sailed upon the Red Sea, and you see I am not drowned." What reply could be made to such a preposterous speech? My father, seeing it was impossible to get our route changed, resolved to trust to providence to free us from our danger, and descended to our cabin, where he sought to dissipate his fears in the oblivion of sleep.

At noon, on the 2d of July, soundings were taken. M. Maudet, ensign of the watch, was convinced we were upon the edge of the Arguin bank. The captain said to him, as well as to every one, that there was no cause of alarm. In the meanwhile, the wind blowing with great violence, impelled us nearer and nearer to the danger which menaced us. A species of stupor overpowered all our spirits, and every one preserved a mournful silence, as if they were persuaded we would soon touch the bank. The color of the water entirely changed, a circumstance even remarked by the ladies. About three in the afternoon, a universal cry was heard upon deck. All declared they saw sand rolling among the ripples of the sea. The captain in an instant ordered to sound. The line gave eighteen fathoms; but on a second sounding it only gave six. He at last saw his error, and hesitated no longer on changing his route, but it was too late. A strong concussion told us the frigate had struck. Terror and consternation were instantly depicted on every face. The crew stood motionless; the passengers in utter despair. In the midst of this general panic, cries of vengeance were heard against the principal author of our misfortunes, wishing to throw him overboard; but some generous persons interposed, and endeavored to calm their spirits by diverting their attention to the means of our safety. The confusion was already so great, that M. Poinsignon commandant of a troop, struck my sister Caroline a severe blow, doubtless thinking it was one of his soldiers. At this crisis my father was buried in profound sleep, but he quickly awoke, the cries and the tumult upon deck having informed him of our misfortunes. He poured out a thousand reproaches on those whose ignorance and boasting had been so disastrous to us. However, they set about the means of averting our danger. The officers, with an altered voice, issued their orders, expecting every moment to see the ship go in pieces. They strove to lighten her, but the sea was very rough and the current strong. Much time was lost in doing nothing; they only pursued half measures, and all of them unfortunately failed.

When it was discovered that the danger of the Medusa was not so great as was at first supposed, various persons proposed to transport the troops to the island of Arguin, which was conjectured to be not far from the place where we lay aground. Others advised to take us all successively to the coast of the Desert of Sahara by the means of our boats, and with provisions sufficient to form a caravan, to reach the island of St. Louis, at Senegal. M. Schmaltz, the governor, suggested the making of a raft of sufficient size to carry two hundred men, with provisions: which latter plan was seconded by the two officers of the frigate, and put in execution. The fatal raft was then begun to be constructed, which would, they said, carry provisions for every one. Masts, planks, boards, and cordage, were thrown overboard. Two officers were charged with the framing of these together. Large barrels were emptied and placed at the angles of the machine, and the workmen were taught to say that the passengers would be in greater security there, and more at their ease, than in the boats. However, as it was forgotten to erect rails, every one supposed, and with reason, that those who had given the plan of the raft, had no design of embarking upon it themselves. When it was completed, the two chief officers of the frigate publicly promised, that all the boats would tow it to the shores of the Desert; and, when there, stores of provisions and firearms would be given us to form a caravan to take us all to Senegal. If these promises had been fulfilled, every one would have been saved, and humanity would not now have had to deplore the scenes of horror consequent on the wreck of the Medusa! On the third of July the efforts were renewed to disengage the frigate, but without success. We then prepared to quit her. The sea became very rough, and the wind blew with great violence. Nothing now was heard but the plaintive and confused cries of a multitude, consisting of more than four hundred persons, who, seeing death before their eyes, deplored their hard fate in bitter lamentations. On the 4th there was a glimpse of hope. At the hour the tide flowed, the frigate, being considerably lightened by all that had been thrown overboard, was found nearly afloat; and it is very certain, if on that day they had thrown the artillery into the water, the Medusa would have been saved; but M. Lachaumareys said he could not thus sacrifice the king's cannon, as if the frigate did not belong to the king also. However, the sea ebbed, and the ship sinking into the sand deeper than ever, made them relinquish that on which depended our last ray of hope. On the approach of night the fury of the winds redoubled, and the sea became very rough. The frigate then received some tremendous concussions, and the water rushed into the hold in the most terrific manner, but the pumps would not work. We had now no alternative but to abandon her for the frail boats, which any single wave would overwhelm. Frightful gulfs environed us; mountains of water raised their liquid summits in the distance. How were we to escape so many dangers? Whither could we go? What hospitable land would receive us on its shores?

My father perceived my distress, but how could he console me? What words could calm my fears, and place me above the apprehension of those dangers to which we were exposed? How, in a word, could I assume a serene appearance, when friends, parents, and all that was most dear to me, were, in all human probability, on the very verge of destruction? Alas! my fears were but too well founded. For I soon perceived that, although we were the only ladies, beside the Misses Schmaltz, who formed a part of the governor's suite, they had the barbarity of intending our family to embark upon the raft, where were only soldiers, sailors, planters of Cape Verd, and some generous officers, who had not the honor (if it could be accounted one) of being considered among the ignorant confidants of MM. Schmaltz and Lachaumareys. My father, indignant at a proceeding so indecorous, swore we would not embark upon the raft, and that, if we were not judged worthy of a place in one of the six boats, he would himself, his wife and children, remain on board the wreck of the frigate. The tone in which he spoke these words was that of a man resolute to avenge any insult that might be offered to him. The governor of Senegal, doubtless fearing the world would one day reproach him for his inhumanity, decided we should have a place in one of the boats. This having in some measure quieted our fears concerning our unfortunate situation, I was desirous of taking some repose, but the uproar among the crew was so great I could not obtain it.

Toward midnight a passenger came to inquire of my father if we were disposed to depart; he replied, we had been forbidden to go yet. However we were soon convinced that a great part of the crew and various passengers were secretly preparing to set off in the boats. A conduct so perfidious could not fail to alarm us, especially as we perceived among those so eager to embark unknown to us, several who had promised, but a little while before, not to go without us.

M. Schmaltz, to prevent that which was going on upon deck, instantly rose to endeavor to quiet their minds; but the soldiers had already assumed a threatening attitude, and holding cheap the words of their commander, swore they would fire upon whosoever attempted to depart in a clandestine manner. The firmness of these brave men produced the desired effect, and all was restored to order. The governor returned to his cabin, and those who were desirous of departing furtively were confused and covered with shame. The governor, however, was ill at ease; and as he had heard very distinctly certain energetic words which had been addressed to him, he judged it proper to assemble a council. All the officers and passengers being collected, M. Schmaltz there solemnly swore before them not to abandon the raft, and a second time promised that all the boats would tow it to the shore of the desert, where they would all be formed into a caravan. I confess this conduct of the governor greatly satisfied every member of our family; for we never dreamed he would deceive us, nor act in a manner contrary to what he had promised.

About three in the morning, some hours after the meeting of the council, a terrible noise was heard in the powder-room; it was the helm which was broken. All who were sleeping were roused by it. On going on deck every one was more and more convinced that the frigate was lost beyond all recovery. Alas! the wreck was, for our family, the commencement of a horrible series of misfortunes; the two chief officers then decided, with one accord, that all should embark at six in the morning, and abandon the ship to the mercy of the waves. After this decision followed a scene the most whimsical, and, at the same time, the most melancholy that can be well conceived. To have a more distinct idea of it, let the reader transport himself in imagination to the midst of the liquid plains of the ocean, then let him picture to himself a multitude of all classes, of every age, tossed about at the mercy of the waves upon a dismasted vessel, foundered, and half submerged; let him not forget these are thinking beings, with the certain prospect before them of having reached the goal of their existence.

Separated from the rest of the world by a boundless sea, and having no place of refuge but the wreck of a grounded vessel, the multitude addressed at first their vows to Heaven, and forgot, for a moment, all earthly concerns. Then, suddenly starting from their lethargy, they began to look after their wealth, the merchandise they had in small ventures, utterly regardless of the elements that threatened them. The miser thinking of the gold contained in his coffers, hastened to put it into a place of safety, either by sewing it into the lining of his clothes, or by cutting out for it a place in the waistband of his trowsers. The smuggler was tearing his hair at not being able to save a chest of contraband which he had secretly got on board, and with which he had hoped to have gained two or three hundred per cent. Another, selfish to excess, was throwing overboard all his hidden money, and amusing himself by burning all his effects. A generous officer was opening his portmanteau, offering caps, stockings, and shirts, to any who would take them. These had scarcely gathered together their various effects, when they learned that they could not take anything with them; those were searching the cabins and store-rooms to carry away every thing that was valuable. Ship-boys were discovering the delicate wines and fine liquors which a wise foresight had placed in reserve. Soldiers and sailors were penetrating into the spirit-room, broaching casks, staving others, and drinking till they fell exhausted. Soon the tumult of the inebriated made us forget the roaring of the sea which threatened to ingulf us. At last the uproar was at its height; the soldiers no longer listened to the voice of their captain. Some knit their brows and muttered oaths; but nothing could be done with those whom wine had rendered furious. Next, piercing cries, mixed with doleful groans, were heard—this was the signal of departure.

At six o'clock on the morning of the fifth, a great part of the military was embarked upon the raft, which was already covered with a large sheet of foam. The soldiers were expressly prohibited from taking their arms. A young officer of infantry, whose brain seemed to be powerfully affected, put his horse beside the barricadoes of the frigate, and then, armed with two pistols, threatened to fire upon any one who refused to go upon the raft. Forty men had scarcely descended when it sunk to the depth of about two feet. To facilitate the embarking of a greater number, they were obliged to throw over several barrels of provisions which had been placed upon it the day before. In this manner did this furious officer get about one hundred and fifty heaped upon that floating tomb; but he did not think of adding one more to the number by descending himself, as he ought to have done, but went peaceably away, and placed himself in one of the best boats. There should have been sixty sailors upon the raft, and there were but about ten. A list had been made out on the 4th, assigning each his proper place; but this wise precaution being disregarded, every one pursued the plan he deemed best for his own preservation. The precipitation with which they forced one hundred and fifty unfortunate beings upon the raft was such that they forgot to give them one morsel of biscuit. However, they threw toward them twenty-five pounds in a sack, while they were not far from the frigate; but it fell into the sea, and was with difficulty recovered.

During this disaster, the governor of Senegal, who was busied in the care of his own dear self, effeminately descended in an arm-chair into the barge, where were already various large chests, all kinds of provisions, his dearest friends, his daughter, and his wife. Afterward the captain's boat received twenty-seven persons, among whom were twenty-five sailors, good rowers. The shallop, commanded by M. Espiau, took forty-five passengers and put off. The boat called the Senegal took twenty-five, the pinnace thirty-three, and the yawl, the smallest of all the boats, took only ten.

Almost all the officers, the passengers, the mariners, and supernumeraries, were already embarked—all but our weeping family, who still remained on the boards of the frigate till some charitable souls would kindly receive us into a boat. Surprised at this abandonment, I instantly felt myself roused, and calling with all my might to the officers of the boat, besought them to take our unhappy family along with them. Soon after, the barge, in which were the governor of Senegal and all his family, approached the Medusa, as if still to take some passengers, for there were but few in it. I made a motion to descend, hoping that the Misses Schmaltz, who had, till that day, taken a great interest in our family, would allow us a place in their boat; but I was mistaken: those ladies, who had embarked in a mysterious incognito, had already forgotten us; and M. Lachaumareys, who was still on the frigate, positively told me they would not embark along with us. Nevertheless I ought to tell, what we learned afterward, that the officer who commanded the pinnace had received orders to take us in, but, as he was already a great way from the frigate, we were certain he had abandoned us. My father, however, hailed him, but he persisted on his way to gain the open sea. A short while afterward we perceived a small boat upon the waves, which seemed desirous to approach the Medusa; it was the yawl. When it was sufficiently near, my father implored the sailors who were in it to take us on board, and carry us to the pinnace, where our family ought to be placed. They refused. He then seized a firelock, which lay by chance upon deck, and swore he would kill every one of them if they refused to take us into the yawl, adding that it was the property of the king, and that he would have advantage from it as well as another. The sailors murmured, but durst not resist, and received all our family, which consisted of nine persons, viz: four children, our stepmother, my cousin, my sister Caroline, my father, and myself. A small box, filled with valuable papers, which we wished to save, some clothes, two bottles of ratafia, which we had endeavored to preserve amid our misfortunes, were seized and thrown overboard by the sailors of the yawl, who told us we would find in the pinnace everything which we could wish for our voyage. We had then only the clothes which covered us, never thinking of dressing ourselves in two suits; but the loss which affected us most was that of several manuscripts, at which my father had been laboring for a long while. Our trunks, our linen, and various chests of merchandise of great value; in a word, everything we possessed was left in the Medusa. When we boarded the pinnace the officer who commanded it began excusing himself for having set off without forewarning us, as he had been ordered, and said a thousand things in his justification. But, without believing half of his fine protestations, we felt very happy in having overtaken him; for it is most certain that they had no intention of encumbering themselves with our unfortunate family. I say encumber, for it is evident that four children, one of whom was yet at the breast, were very indifferent beings to people who were actuated by a selfishness beyond all parallel. When we were seated in the long-boat, my father dismissed the sailors with the yawl, telling them he would ever gratefully remember their services. They speedily departed, but little satisfied with the good action they had done. My father hearing their murmurs and the abuse they poured out against us, said, loud enough for all in the boat to hear, "We are not surprised sailors are destitute of shame, when their officers blush at being compelled to do a good action." The commandant of the boat feigned not to understand the reproaches conveyed in these words, and to divert our minds from brooding over our wrongs, endeavored to counterfeit the man of gallantry.

All the boats were already far from the Medusa, when they were brought to, to form a chain in order to tow the raft. The barge, in which was the governor of Senegal, took the first tow, then all the other boats in succession joined themselves to that. M. Lachaumareys embarked, although there yet remained upon the Medusa more than sixty persons. Then the brave and generous M. Espiau, commander of the shallop, quitted the line of boats, and returned to the frigate, with the intention of saving all the wretches who had been abandoned. They all sprung into the shallop; but as it was very much overloaded, seventeen unfortunates preferred remaining on board rather than expose themselves as well as their companions to certain death. But, alas! the greater part afterward fell victims to their fears or their devotion. Fifty-two days after they were abandoned, no more than three of them were alive, and these looked more like skeletons than men. They told that their miserable companions had gone afloat upon planks and hen-coops, after having waited in vain forty-two days for the succor which had been promised them; and that all had perished.

The shallop carrying with difficulty all those she had saved from the Medusa, slowly rejoined the line of boats which towed the raft. M. Espiau earnestly besought the officers of the other boats to take some of them along with them; but they refused, alleging to the generous officer that he ought to keep them in his own boat, as he had gone for them himself. M. Espiau, finding it impossible to keep them all without exposing them to the utmost peril, steered right for a boat which I will not name. Immediately a sailor sprung from the shallop into the sea, and endeavored to reach it by swimming; and when he was about to enter it, an officer, who possessed great influence, pushed him back, and drawing his sabre, threatened to cut off his hands if he again made the attempt. The poor wretch regained the shallop, which was very near the pinnace, where we were. Various friends of my father supplicated M. Laperere, the officer of our boat, to receive him on board. My father had his arms already out to catch him, when M. Laperere instantly let go the rope which attached us to the other boats, and tugged off with all his force. At the same instant every boat imitated the execrable example; and wishing to shun the approach of the shallop, which sought for assistance, stood off from the raft, abandoning, in the midst of the ocean, and to the fury of the waves, the miserable mortals whom they had sworn to land on the shores of the desert. Scarcely had these cowards broken their oath, when we saw the French flag flying upon the raft. The confidence of these unfortunate persons was so great, that when they saw the first boat, which had the tow, removing from them, they all cried out, The rope is broken! the rope is broken! But when no attention was paid to their observation, they instantly perceived the treachery of the wretches who had left them so basely. Then cries of *Vive le Roi* arose from the raft, as if the poor fellows were calling to their father for assistance; or as if they had been persuaded that, at the rallying word, the officers of the boats would return, and not abandon their countrymen. The officers repeated the cry of *Vive le Roi*, without a doubt to insult them; but more particularly M. Lachaumareys, who, assuming a martial attitude, waved his hat in the air. Alas! what availed these false professions? Frenchmen, menaced with the greatest peril, were demanding assistance with the cries of *Vive le Roi;* yet none were found sufficiently generous, nor sufficiently French, to go to aid them. After a silence of some minutes, horrible cries were heard; the air resounded with the groans, the lamentations, the imprecations of these wretched beings. The raft already appeared to be buried under the waves, and its unfortunate passengers immersed. The fatal machine was drifted by currents far behind the wreck of the frigate; without cable, anchor, mast, sail, oars, in a word, without the smallest means of enabling them to save themselves. Each wave that struck it made them stumble in heaps on one another. Their feet getting entangled among the cordage, and between the planks, bereaved them of the faculty of moving. Maddened by these misfortunes, suspended, adrift upon the merciless ocean, they were soon tortured between the pieces of wood which formed the scaffold on which they floated The bones of their feet and their legs were bruised and broken every time the fury of the waves agitated the raft; their flesh covered with contusions and hideous wounds, dissolved, as it were, in the briny waves, while the roaring flood around them was colored with their blood.

As the raft, when it was abandoned, was nearly two leagues from the frigate, it was impossible these unfortunate persons could reach it; they were soon after far out at sea. These victims still appeared above their floating tomb; and, stretching out their supplicating hands toward the boats which fled from them, seemed yet to invoke, for the last time, the names of the wretches who had deceived them. My father, exasperated to excess, and bursting with rage at seeing so much cowardice and inhumanity among the officers of the boats, began to regret that he had not accepted the place which had been assigned for us upon the raft. "At least," said he, "we would have died with the brave, or we would have returned to the wreck of the Medusa; and not have had the disgrace of saving ourselves with cowards." Although this produced no effect upon the officers, it proved very fatal to us afterward; for, on our arrival at Senegal, it was reported to the governor; and, very probably, was the principal cause of all those evils and vexations which we endured in that colony.

Let us now turn our attention to the several situations of all those who were endeavoring to save themselves in the different boats, as well as to those left upon the wreck of the Medusa. We have already seen that the frigate was half sunk when it was deserted, presenting nothing but a hulk and a wreck. Nevertheless, seventeen still remained upon it, and had food, which, although damaged, enabled them to support themselves for a considerable time; while the raft was abandoned to float at the mercy of the waves, upon the vast surface of the ocean. One hundred and fifty wretches were embarked upon it, sunk to the depth of at least three feet on its fore-part, and on its poop immersed even to the middle. What victuals they had were soon consumed, or spoiled by the salt water; and perhaps some, as the waves hurried them along, became food for the monsters of the deep. Two only of all the boats which left the Medusa, and these with very few people in them, were provisioned with every necessity; these struck off with security and dispatch. But the condition of those who were in the shallop was but little better than those upon the raft; their great distance from the shore gave them the most melancholy anticipations of the future. Their worthy commander, M. Espiau, had no other hope but of reaching the shore as soon as possible. The other boats were less filled with people, but they were scarcely better provisioned; and, as by a species of fatality, the pinnace, in which were our family, was destitute of everything. Our provisions consisted of a barrel of biscuit and a tierce of water; and, to add to our misfortunes, the biscuit being soaked in the sea, it was almost impossible to swallow one morsel of it. Each passenger in our boat was obliged to sustain his wretched existence with a glass of water, which he could get only once a day. To tell how this happened, how this boat was so poorly supplied, while there was abundance left upon the Medusa, is far beyond my power. But it is at least certain that the greater part of the officers, commanding the boats, the shallop, the pinnace, the Senegal boat, and the yawl, were persuaded, when they quitted the frigate, that they would not abandon the raft, but that all the expedition would sail together to the coast of Sahara; that when there, the boats would be again sent to the Medusa, to take provisions, arms, and those who were left there; but it appears the chiefs had decided otherwise.

After abandoning the raft, although scattered, all the boats formed a little fleet, and followed the same route. All who were sincere hoped to arrive the same day at the coast of the desert, and that every one would get on shore; but MM. Schmaltz and Lachaumareys gave orders to take the route for Senegal. This sudden change in the resolutions of the chiefs was like a thunderbolt to the officers commanding the boats. Having nothing on board but what was barely necessary to enable us to allay the cravings of hunger for one day, we were all sensibly affected. The other boats, which, like ourselves, hoped to have got on shore at the nearest point, were a little better provisioned than we were; they had at least a little wine, which supplied the place of other necessaries. We then demanded some from them, explaining our situation; but none would assist us, not even Captain Lachaumareys, who, drinking to a kept mistress, supported by two sailors, swore he had not one drop on board. We were next desirous of addressing the boat of the governor of Senegal, where we were persuaded were plenty of provisions of every kind, such as oranges, biscuits, cakes, comfits, plums, and even the finest liqueurs; but my father opposed it, so well was he assured we would not obtain anything.

We will now turn to the condition of those on the raft, when the boats left them to themselves. If all the boats had continued dragging the raft forward, favored as we were by the breeze from the sea, we would have been able to have conducted them to the shore in less than two days. But an inconceivable fatality caused the generous plan to be abandoned When the raft had lost sight of the boats, a spirit of sedition began to manifest itself in furious cries. They then began to regard one another with ferocious looks, and to thirst for one another's flesh. Some one had already whispered of having recourse to that monstrous extremity, and of commencing with the fattest and youngest. A proposition so atrocious filled the brave Captain Dupont and his worthy lieutenant, M L'Heureux, with horror; and that courage which had so often supported them in the field of glory, now forsook them. Among the first who fell under the hatchets of the assassins was a young woman who had been seen devouring the body of her husband. When her turn was come, she sought a little wine, as a last favor, then rose, and without uttering one word, threw herself into the sea. Captain Dupont being proscribed for having refused to partake of the sacrilegious viands on which the monsters were feeding, was saved, as by a miracle, from the hands of the butchers. Scarcely had they seized him to lead him to the slaughter, when a large pole, which served in place of a mast, fell upon his body; and believing that his legs were broken, they contented themselves by throwing him into the sea. The unfortunate captain plunged, disappeared, and they thought him already in another world.

Providence, however, revived the strength of the unfortunate warrior. He emerged under the beams of the raft, and clinging with all his might, holding his head above water, he remained between two enormous pieces of wood, while the rest of his body was hid in the sea. After more than two hours of suffering, Captain Dupont spoke in a low voice to his lieutenant, who by chance was seated near the place of concealment. Dupont was instantly drawn from the water, and L'Heureux obtained for his unfortunate comrade again a place upon the raft. Those who had been so inveterate against him, touched at what Providence had done for him in so miraculous a manner, decided, with one accord, to allow him entire liberty upon the raft.

The sixty unfortunates who had escaped from the first massacre, were soon reduced to fifty, then to forty, and at last to twenty-eight. The least murmur, or the smallest complaint, at the moment of distributing the provisions, was a crime punished with immediate death. In consequence of such a regulation, it may easily be presumed the raft was soon lightened. In the meanwhile the wine diminished sensibly, and the half rations very much displeased a certain chief of the conspiracy. On purpose to avoid being reduced to that extremity, the *executive power* decided it was much wiser to *drown thirteen people*, and to get full rations, than that twenty-eight should have half rations. After the last catastrophe, the chiefs of the conspiracy, fearful doubtless of being assassinated in their turn, threw all the arms into the sea, and swore an inviolable friendship with the heroes which the hatchet had spared. On the 17th of July, in the morning, Captain Parnajon, commandant of the Argus brig, still found fifteen men on the raft. They were immediately taken on board, and conducted to Senegal.

On the 5th of July, at ten in the morning, one hour after abandoning the raft, and three after quitting the Medusa, M. Laperere, the officer of our boat, made the first distribution of provisions. Each passenger had a small glass of water and nearly the fourth of a biscuit. Each drank his allowance of water at one draught, but it was found impossible to swallow one morsel of our biscuit, it being so impregnated with sea-water. It happened, however, that some was not quite so saturated. Of these we ate a small portion, and put back the remainder for a future day. Our voyage would have been sufficiently agreeable, if the beams of the sun had not been so fierce. On the evening we perceived the shores of the desert; but as the two chiefs (MM. Schmaltz and Lachaumareys) wished to go right to Senegal, notwithstanding we were still one hundred leagues from it, we were not allowed to land. Several officers remonstrated, both on account of our want of provisions and the crowded condition of the boats for undertaking so dangerous a voyage. Others urged with equal force, that it would be dishonoring the French name if we were to neglect the unfortunate people on the raft, and insisted we should be set on shore, and while we waited there, three boats should return to look after the raft, and three to the wreck of the frigate, to take up the seventeen who were left there, as well as a sufficient quantity of provisions to enable us to go to Senegal by the way of Barbary. But MM. Schmaltz and Lachaumareys, whose boats were sufficiently well provisioned, scouted the advice of their subalterns, and ordered them to cast anchor till the following morning. They were obliged to obey these orders, and to relinquish their designs.

On the morning of the 6th of July, at five o'clock, all the boats were under way on the route to Senegal. The boats of MM. Schmaltz and Lachaumareys took the lead along the coast, and all the expedition followed. About eight, several sailors in our boat, with threats, demanded to be set on shore; but M. Laperere, not acceding to their requests, the whole were about to revolt and seize the command; but the firmness of this officer quelled the mutineers. In a spring which he made to seize a firelock which a sailor persisted in keeping in his possession, he almost tumbled in the sea. My father fortunately was near him, and held him by his clothes, but he had instantly to quit him for fear of losing his hat, which the waves were floating away. A short while after this slight accident, the shallop, which we had lost sight of since the morning, appeared desirous of rejoining us. We plied all hands to avoid her, for we were afraid of one another, and thought that that boat, encumbered with so many people, wished to board us, to oblige us to take some of its passengers, as M. Espiau would not suffer them to be abandoned like those upon the raft. That officer hailed us at a distance, offering to take our family on board, adding, he was anxious to take about sixty people to the desert. The officer of our boat, thinking that this was a pretence, replied, we preferred suffering where we were. It even appeared to us that M. Espiau had hid some of his people under the benches of the shallop. But, alas! in the end we deeply deplored being so suspicious, and of having so outraged the devotion of the most generous officer of the Medusa. A second distribution of provisions was now made; each received a small glass of water and about the eighth part of a biscuit. Notwithstanding our meager fare, every one seemed content, in the persuasion we would reach Senegal by the morrow. But how vain were all our hopes, and what sufferings had we yet to endure!

At half past seven the sky was overcast with stormy clouds. The serenity we had admired a little while before entirely disappeared, and gave place to the most gloomy obscurity. Suddenly a frightful noise was heard from the west, and all the waves of the sea rushed to founder our frail bark. A fearful silence succeeded to the general consternation. Every tongue was mute, and none durst communicate to his neighbor the horror with which his mind was impressed. At intervals the cries of the children rent our hearts. At that instant a weeping and agonized mother bared her breast to her dying child, but it yielded nothing to appease the thirst of the little innocent who pressed it in vain. Having full before our eyes the prospect of inevitable death, we gave ourselves up to our unfortunate condition, and addressed our prayers to Heaven. The winds growled with the utmost fury; the tempestuous waves arose exasperated. In their terrific encounter a mountain of water was precipitated into our boat, carrying away one of the sails and the greater part of the effects which the sailors had saved from the Medusa. Our bark was nearly sunk; the females and the children lay rolling in its bottom, drinking the waters of bitterness; and their cries, mixed with the roaring of the waves and the furious north wind, increased the horrors of the scene.

Every soul in the boat was seized with the same perturbation, but it manifested itself in different ways. One part of the sailors remained motionless, in a bewildered state; the other cheered and encouraged one another; the children, locked in the arms of their parents, wept incessantly. Some demanded drink, vomiting the salt water which choked them; others, in short, embraced as for the last time, entwining their arms and vowing to die together. In the meanwhile the sea became rougher and rougher. Our boat, beset on all sides by the winds, and at every instant tossed on the summit of mountains of water, was very nearly sunk, in spite of our every effort in bailing it when we discovered a large hole in its poop. It was instantly stuffed with everything we could find: old clothes, sleeves of shirts, shreds of coats, shawls, useless bonnets, everything was employed, and secured us as far as it was possible. During the space of six hours we rowed, suspended alternately between hope and fear, between life and death. At last, toward the middle of the night, Heaven, which had seen our resignation, commanded the floods to be still. Instantly the sea became less rough, the vail which covered the sky became less obscure, the stars again shone out, and the tempest seemed to withdraw. A general exclamation of joy and thankfulness issued at one instant from every mouth.

The day at last, the day so much desired, entirely restored the calm; but it brought no other consolation. During the night the currents, the waves, and the winds had taken us so far out to sea, that on the dawning of the 7th of July we saw nothing but sky and water, without knowing whither to direct our course; for our compass had been broken during the tempest. In this hopeless condition we continued to steer sometimes to the right and sometimes to the left, until the sun arose, and at last showed us the east. On the morning of the 7th of July we again saw the shores of the desert, notwithstanding we were yet a great distance from it. The sailors renewed their murmurings, wishing to get on shore, with the hope of being able to get some wholesome plants and some more palatable water than that of the sea; but as we were afraid of the Moors, their request was opposed. However, M. Laperere proposed to take them as near as he could to the first breakers on the coast, and when there, those who wished to go on shore should throw themselves into the sea and swim to land. Eleven accepted the proposal; but when we had reached the first waves, none had the courage to brave the mountains of water which rolled between them and the beach. Our sailors then betook themselves to their benches and oars, and promised to be more quiet for the future. A short while after, a third distribution was made since our departure from the Medusa; and nothing more remained than four pints of water and one half dozen biscuits. What steps were we to take in this cruel situation? According to the calculation of our commanding officer, we could arrive at Senegal on the morrow. Deceived by the false account, we preferred suffering one day more, rather than to be taken by the Moors of the desert, or perish among the breakers. We had now no more than a small half glass of water and the seventh of a biscuit. Exposed as we were to the heat of the sun, which darted its rays perpendicularly on our heads, that ration, though small, would have been a great relief to us; but the distribution was delayed to the morrow. We were then obliged to drink the bitter sea-water, ill as it was calculated to quench our thirst. Must I tell it? thirst had so withered the lungs of our sailors that they drank salter water than that of the sea! Our numbers diminished daily, and nothing but the hope of arriving at the colony on the following day sustained our frail existence. My young brothers and sisters wept incessantly for water. The little Laura, aged six years, lay dying at the feet of her mother. Her mournful cries so moved the soul of my unfortunate father, that he was on the eve of opening a vein to quench the thirst which consumed his child; but a wise person opposed his design, observing that all the blood in his body would not prolong the life of his infant child one moment.

The freshness of the night-wind procured us some respite. We anchored pretty near to the shore, and, though dying of famine, each got a tranquil sleep. On the morning of the 8th of July, at break of day, we took the route of Senegal. A short while after, the wind fell, and we had a dead calm. We endeavored to row, but our strength was exhausted. A fourth and last distribution was made, and in the twinkling of an eye, our last resources were consumed. We were forty-two people who had to feed upon *six biscuits* and about *four pints* of water, with no hope of a farther supply. Then came the moment for deciding whether we were to perish among the breakers which defended the approach to the shores of the desert, or to die of famine in continuing our route. The majority preferred the last species of misery. We continued our progress along the shore, painfully pulling our oars. Upon the beach were distinguished several downs of white sand, and some small trees. We were thus creeping along the coast, observing a mournful silence, when a sailor suddenly exclaimed, "Behold the Moors!" We did, in fact, see various individuals upon the rising ground, walking at a quick pace, and whom we took to be the Arabs of the Desert. As we were very near the shore, we stood farther out to sea, fearing that these pretended Moors, or Arabs, would throw themselves into the sea, swim out, and take us. Some hours after, we observed several people upon the eminence, who seemed to make signals to us. We examined them attentively, and soon recognized them to be our companions in misfortune. We replied to them by attaching a white handkerchief to the top of our mast. Then we resolved to land, at the risk of perishing among the breakers, which were very strong toward the shore, although the sea was calm. On approaching the beach we went toward the right, where the waves seemed less agitated, and endeavored to reach it, with the hope of being able more easily to land. Scarcely had we directed our course to that point, when we perceived a great number of people standing near to a little wood surrounding the sand-hills. We recognized them to be the passengers of that boat, who, like ourselves, were deprived of provisions.

The helm of the boat was again given to the old pilot, who had already so happily steered us through the dangers of the storm. He instantly threw into the sea the mast, the sails, and everything that could impede our proceedings. When we came to the first landing point, several of our shipwrecked companions, who had reached the shore, ran and hid themselves behind the hills, not to see us perish; others made signs not to approach at that place; some covered their eyes with their hands:

others, at last despising the danger, precipitated themselves into the waves to receive us into their arms. We then saw a spectacle that made us shudder. We had already doubled two ranges of breakers; but those which we had still to cross raised their foaming waves to a prodigious height, then sunk with a hollow and monstrous sound, sweeping along a long line of the coast. Our boat, sometimes greatly elevated, and sometimes ingulfed between the waves, seemed now given up to utter ruin. Bruised, battered, tossed about on all hands, it turned of itself, and refused to obey the kind hand which directed it. At that instant a huge wave rushed from the open sea and dashed against the poop; the boat plunged, disappeared, and we were all among the waves. Our sailors, whose strength had returned at the presence of danger, redoubled their efforts, uttering mournful sounds. Our bark groaned, the oars were broken; it was thought aground, but it was stranded; it was upon its side. The last sea rushed upon us with the impetuosity of a torrent. We were up to the neck in water; the bitter sea-froth choked us. The grapnel was thrown out. The sailors threw themselves into the sea; they took the children in their arms; returned, and took us upon their shoulders; and I found myself seated upon the sand on the shore, by the side of my step-mother, my brothers and sisters, almost dead. Every one was upon the beach except my father and some sailors; but that good man arrived at last, to mingle his tears with those of his family and friends.

After we had a little recovered from the fainting and fatigue of our getting on shore, our fellow-sufferers told us they had landed in the forenoon, and had cleared the breakers by the strength of their oars and sails; but they had not all been so lucky as we were. One unfortunate person, too desirous of getting quickly on shore, had his legs broken under the shallop, and was taken and laid on the beach, and left to the care of Providence. M. Espiau, commander of the shallop, reproached us for having doubted him when he wished to board us to take our family along with him. It was most true he had landed sixty-three people that day. A short while after our refusal, he took the passengers of the yawl, who would infallibly have perished in the stormy night of the 6th and 7th. The boat named the Senegal, commanded by M. Maudet, had made the shore at the same time with M. Espiau. The boats of MM. Schmaltz and Lachaumareys were the only ones which continued the route for Senegal, while nine-tenths of the Frenchmen intrusted to these gentlemen were butchering each other on the raft, or dying of hunger on the burning sands of Sahara.

About seven in the morning a caravan was formed to penetrate into the interior, for the purpose of finding some fresh water. We did accordingly find some at a little distance from the sea, by digging among the sand. Every one instantly flocked round the little wells, which furnished enough to quench our thirst. This brackish water was found to be delicious, although it had a sulphurous taste: its color was that of whey. As all our clothes were wet and in tatters, and as we had nothing to change them, some generous officers offered theirs. My step-mother, my cousin, and my sister were dressed in them; for myself, I preferred keeping my own. We remained nearly an hour beside our beneficient fountain, then took the route for Senegal; that is, a southerly direction, for we did not know exactly where that country lay. It was agreed that the females and children should walk before the caravan, that they might not be left behind. The sailors voluntarily carried the youngest on their shoulders, and every one took the route along the coast. Notwithstanding it was nearly seven o'clock, the sand was quite burning, and we suffered severely, walking without shoes, having lost them while landing. As soon as we arrived on the shore, we went to walk on the wet sand, to cool us a little. Thus we traveled during all the night, without encountering anything but shells, which wounded our feet.

In the forenoon of the next day, two officers of marine complained that our family incommoded the progress of the caravan. It is true, the females and the children could not walk so quickly as the men. We walked as fast as it was possible for us, nevertheless we often fell behind, which obliged them to halt till we came up. These officers, joined with other individuals, considered among themselves whether they would wait for us, or abandon us in the desert. I will be bold to say, however, that but few were of the latter opinion. My father being informed of what was plotting against us, stepped up to the chiefs of the conspiracy and reproached them in the bitterest terms for their selfishness and brutality. The dispute waxed hot. Those who were desirous of leaving us drew their swords, and my father put his hand upon a poniard, with which he had provided himself on quitting the frigate. At this scene we threw ourselves in between them, conjuring him rather to remain in the desert with his family, than seek the assistance of those who were, perhaps, less humane than the Moors themselves. Several people took our part, particularly M. Bregnere, captain of infantry, who quieted the dispute by saying to his soldiers, "My friends, you are Frenchmen, and I have the honor of being your commander; let us never abandon an unfortunate family in the desert, so long as we are able to be of use to them." This brief, but energetic speech, caused those to blush who wished to leave us. All then joined with the old captain, saying they would not leave us, on condition we would walk quicker. M. Bregnere and his soldiers replied, they did not wish to impose conditions on those to whom they were desirous of doing a favor; and the unfortunate family of Picard were again on the road with the whole caravan. Some time after this dispute M. Rogery, member of the Philanthropic Society of Cape Verd, secretly left the caravan, striking into the middle of the desert, without knowing very well what he sought. That intrepid traveler had not time to find that after which he searched; for, a few days after, he was captured by the Moors, and taken to Senegal, where the governor paid his ransom.

About noon hunger was felt so powerfully among us that it was agreed upon to go to the small hills of sand, which were near the coast, to see if any herbs could be found fit for eating; but we only got poisonous plants, among which were various kinds of euphorbium. Convolvuluses of a bright green carpeted the downs; but on tasting their leaves we found them as bitter as gall. The caravan rested in this place, while several officers went farther into the interior. They came back in about an hour, loaded with wild purslain, which they distributed to each of us. Every one instantly devoured his bunch of herbage without leaving the smallest branch; but as our hunger was far from being satisfied with this small allowance, the soldiers and sailors betook themselves to look for more. They soon brought back a sufficient quantity, which was equally distributed, and devoured upon the spot, so delicious had hunger made that food to us. For myself, I declared I never ate anything with so much appetite in all my life. Water was also found in this place, but it was of an abominable taste. After this truly frugal repast we continued our route. The heat was insupportable in the last degree. The sands on which we trod were burning; nevertheless, several of us walked on these scorching coals without shoes; and the females had nothing but their hair for a cap. When we reached the sea-shore we all ran and lay down among the waves. After remaining there some time, we took our route along the west beach. On our journey we met with several large crabs, which were of considerable service to us. Every now and then we endeavored to slake our thirst by sucking their crooked claws. About nine at night we halted between two pretty high sand-hills. After a short talk concerning our misfortunes, all seemed desirous of passing the night in this place, notwithstanding we heard on every side the roaring of leopards. We deliberated on the means of securing ourselves, but sleep soon put an end to our fears. Scarcely had we slumbered a few hours when a terrible roaring of wild beasts awoke us, and made us stand on our defense. It was a beautiful moonlight night, and, in spite of my fears and the horrible aspect of the place, nature never appeared so sublime to me before. Instantly something was announced that resembled a lion. This information was listened to with the greatest emotion. Every one being desirous of verifying the truth, fixed upon something he thought to be the object; one believed he saw the long teeth of the king of the forest; another was convinced his mouth was already open to devour us; several, armed with muskets, aimed at the animal, and advancing a few steps, discovered the pretended lion to be nothing more than a shrub fluctuating in the breeze. However, the howlings of ferocious beasts had so frightened us, being yet heard at intervals, that we again sought the sea-shore, on purpose to continue our route toward the south.

Our situation had been thus perilous during the night; nevertheless at the break of day we had the satisfaction of finding none missing. About sunrise we held a little to the east to get farther into the interior to find fresh water, and lost much time in a vain search. The country which we now traversed was a little less arid than that which we had passed the preceding day. The hills, the valleys, and a vast plain of sand were strewed with mimosa, or sensitive plants, presenting to our sight a scene we had never before seen in the desert. The country is bounded as it were by a chain of mountains, or high downs of sand, in the direction of north and south, without the slightest trace of cultivation.

Toward ten in the morning some of our companions were desirous of making observations in the interior, and they did not go in vain. They instantly returned and told us they had seen two Arab tents upon a slight rising ground. We instantly directed our steps thither. We had to pass great downs of sand, very slippery, and arrived in a large plain, streaked here and there with verdure; but the turf was so hard and piercing we could scarcely walk over it without wounding our feet. Our presence in these frightful solitudes put to flight three or four Moorish shepherds, who herded a small flock of sheep and goats in an oasis. At last we arrived at the tents after which we were searching, and found in them three Mooresses and two little children, who did not seem in the least frightened by our visit. A negro servant, belonging to an officer of marine, interpreted between us and the good women, who, when they had heard of our misfortunes, offered us millet and water for payment. We bought a little of that grain at the rate of thirty pence a handful; the water was got for three francs a glass; it was very good, and none grudged the money it cost. As a glass of water, with a handful of millet, was but a poor dinner for famished people, my father bought two kids, which they would not give him under twenty piasters. We immediately killed them, and our Mooresses boiled them in a large kettle. While our repast was preparing, my father, who could not afford the whole of the expense, got others to contribute to it; but an old officer of marine, who was to have been captain of the port of Senegal, was the only person who refused, notwithstanding he had about him nearly three thousand francs, which he boasted of in the end. Several soldiers and sailors had seen him count it in round pieces of gold, on coming ashore on the desert, and reproached him for his sordid avarice; but he seemed insensible to their reproaches, nor ate the less of his portion of kid with his companions in misfortune.

When about to resume our journey, we saw several Moors approaching to us armed with lances. Our people instantly seized their arms, and put themselves in readiness to defend us, in case of an attack. Two officers, followed by several soldiers and sailors, with our interpreter, advanced to discover their intentions. They instantly returned with the Moors, who said, that, far from wishing to do us harm, they had come to offer us their assistance, and to conduct us to Senegal. This offer being accepted of with gratitude by all of us, the Moors, of whom we had been so afraid, became our protectors and friends, verifying the old proverb, *there are good people everywhere!* As the camp of the Moors was at some considerable distance from where we were, we set off all together to reach it before night. After having walked about two leagues through the burning sands, we found ourselves again upon the shore. Toward night our conductors made us strike again into the interior, saying we were very near their camp, which is called, in their language, Berkelet. But the short distance of the Moors was found very long by the females and the children, on account of the hills of sand which we had to ascend and descend every instant, also of prickly shrubs over which we were frequently obliged to walk. Those who were barefooted felt most severely, at this time, the want of their shoes. I myself lost among the bushes various shreds of my dress, and my feet and legs were all streaming with blood. At length, after two long hours of walking and suffering, we arrived at the camp of that tribe to which belonged our Arab conductors. We had scarcely got into the camp, when the dogs, the children, and the Moorish women began to annoy us. Some of them threw sand in our eyes, others amused themselves by snatching at our hair, on pretence of wishing to examine it. This pinched us, that spit upon us; the dogs bit our legs, while the old harpies cut the buttons from the officers' coats, or endeavored to take away the lace. Our conductors, however, had pity on us, and chased away the dogs and the curious crowd, who had already made us suffer as much as the thorns which had torn our feet. The chiefs of the camp, our guides, and some good women, at last set about getting us some supper. Water in abundance was given us without payment, and they sold us fish dried in the sun, and some bowlfuls of sour milk, all at a reasonable price.

We found a Moor in the camp who had previously known my father in Senegal, and who spoke a little French. As soon as he recognized him, he cried, "Tiens toi, Picard! ni a pas connaitre moi Amet? (Hark ye, Picard, know you not Amet?) We were all struck with astonishment at these French words coming from the mouth of a Moor. My father recollected having employed, long ago, a young goldsmith at Senegal, and discovering the Moor Amet to be the same person, shook him by the hand. After that good fellow had been made acquainted with our shipwreck, and to what extremities our unfortunate family had been reduced, he could not refrain from tears. Amet was not satisfied with deploring our hard fate; he was desirous of proving that he was generous and humane, and instantly distributed among us a large quantity of milk and water, free of any charge. He also raised for our family a large tent of the skins of camels, cattle and sheep, because his religion would not allow him to lodge with Christians under the same roof. The place appeared very dark, and the obscurity made us uneasy. Amet and our conductors lighted a large fire to quiet us; and at last bidding us good night, and retiring to his tent, said: "Sleep in peace; the God of the Christians is also the God of the Mussulmans."

We had resolved to quit this truly hospitable place early in the morning, but, during the night, some people, who had probably too much money, imagined the Moors had taken us to their camp to plunder us. They communicated their fears to others, pretending that the Moors, who walked up and down among their flocks, and cried, from time to time, to keep away the ferocious beasts, had already given the signal for pursuing and murdering us. Instantly a general panic seized all our people, and they wished to set off forthwith. My father, although he knew well the perfidy of the inhabitants of the desert, endeavored to assure them we had nothing to fear, because the Arabs were too much frightened by the people of Senegal, who would not fail to avenge us if we were insulted; but nothing could quiet their apprehensions, and we had to take the route during the middle of the night. The Moors being soon acquainted with our fears, made us all kinds of protestations; and seeing we persisted in quitting the camp, offered us asses to carry us as far as the Senegal. My father was able to hire only two asses for the whole of our family; and as it was numerous, my sister Caroline, my cousin and myself, were obliged to crawl along, while my unfortunate father followed in the suit of the caravan, which, in truth, went much quicker than we did.

A short distance from the camp, the brave and compassionate Captain Begnere, seeing we still walked, obliged us to accept of the ass he had hired for himself, saying he would not ride when young ladies, exhausted with fatigue, followed on foot. During the remainder of the night we traveled in a manner sufficiently agreeable, mounting alternately the ass of Captain Begnere. At five in the morning of the 11th of July we regained the sea-shore. Our asses, fatigued with the long journey among the sands, ran instantly and lay down among the breakers, in spite of our utmost exertions to prevent them. This caused several of us to take a bath we wished not: I was myself held under one of the asses in the water, and had great difficulty in saving one of my young brothers who was floating away. But, in the end, as this incident had no unfortunate issue, we laughed, and continued our route, some on foot, and some on the capricious asses. Toward ten o'clock, perceiving a ship out at sea, we attached a white handkerchief to the muzzle of a gun, waving it in the air, and soon had the satisfaction of seeing it was noticed. The ship having approached sufficiently near the coast, the Moors who were with us threw themselves into the sea and swam to it. It must be said we had wrongfully supposed that these people had a design against us, for their devotion could not appear greater than when five of them darted through the waves to endeavor to communicate between us and the ship; notwithstanding, it was still a good quarter of a league distant from where we stood on the beach. In about half an hour we saw these good Moors returning, making float before them three small barrels. Arrived on shore, one of them gave a letter to M. Espiau from M. Parnajon. This gentleman was the captain of the Argus brig, sent to seek after the raft, and to give us provisions. This letter announced a small barrel of biscuit, a tierce of wine, a half tierce of brandy, and a Dutch cheese. We were very desirous of testifying our gratitude to the generous commander of the brig, but he instantly set out and left us. We staved the barrels which held our small stock of provisions, and made a distribution. Each of us had a biscuit, about a glass of wine, a half glass of brandy, and a small morsel of cheese. Each drank his allowance of wine at one gulp; the brandy was not even despised by the ladies. I however preferred quantity to quality, and exchanged my ration of brandy for that of wine. To describe our joy, while taking this repast, is impossible. Exposed to the fierce rays of a vertical sun; exhausted by a long train of suffering; deprived for a long while of the use of any kind of spiritous liquors; when our portions of water, wine and brandy, mingled in our stomachs, we became like insane people. Life, which had lately been a great burden, now became precious to us. Foreheads, lowering and sulky, began to unwrinkle; enemies became most brotherly; the avaricious endeavored to forget their selfishness and cupidity; the children smiled for the first time since our shipwreck; in a word, every one seemed to be born again from a condition melancholy and dejected.

About six in the evening, my father, finding himself extremely fatigued, wished to rest himself. We allowed the caravan to move on, while my step-mother and myself remained near him, and the rest of the family followed with their asses. We all three fell asleep. When we awoke we were astonished at not seeing our companions. The sun was sinking in the west. We saw several Moors approaching us, mounted on camels; and my father reproached himself for having slept so long. Their appearance gave us great uneasiness, and we wished much to escape from them, but my step-mother and myself felt quite exhausted. The Moors, with long beards, having come quite close to us, one of them alighted and addressed us in the following words: "Be comforted, ladies; under the costume of an Arab you see an Englishman, who is desirous of serving you. Having heard at Senegal that Frenchmen were thrown ashore on these deserts, I thought my presence might be of some service to them, as I was acquainted with several of the princes of this arid country." Recovering from our fright, we rose and expressed to the philanthropic Englishman the gratitude we felt. Mr. Carnet, the name of the generous Briton, told us that our caravan, which he had met, waited for us at about the distance of two leagues. He then gave us some biscuit, which we ate; and we then set off together to join our companions. Mr. Carnet wished us to mount his camels, but my step-mother and myself, being unable to persuade ourselves we could sit securely on their hairy haunches, continued to walk on the moist sand, while my father, Mr. Carnet, and the Moors who accompanied him, proceeded on the camels. At last, having walked about an hour, we rejoined our companions, who had found several wells of fresh water. It was resolved to pass the night in this place, which seemed less arid than any we saw near us.

We passed a very good night, and at four in the morning continued our route along the shore. At noon, the heat became so violent that even the Moors themselves bore it with difficulty. We then determined on finding some shade behind the high mounds of sand which appeared in the interior; but how were we to reach them? The sands could not be hotter. We had been obliged to leave our asses on the shore, for they would neither advance nor recede. The greater part of us had neither shoes nor hats; notwithstanding, we were obliged to go forward almost a long league to find a little shade The heat reflected by the sands of the desert could be compared to nothing but the mouth of an oven at the moment of drawing out the bread ; nevertheless, we endured it, but not without cursing those who had been the occasion of all our misfortunes. Arrived behind the heights for which we searched, we stretched ourselves under the mimosa gumtree, (the acacia of the desert;) several broke branches from the asclepias (swallow-wort) and made themselves a shade. But, whether from want of air, or the heat of the ground on which we were seated, we were nearly all suffocated. I thought my last hour was come. Already my eyes saw nothing but a dark cloud, when a person by the name of Borner, who was to have been a smith at Senegal, gave me a boot containing some muddy water, which he had the precaution to keep. I seized the elastic vase, and hastened to swallow the liquid in large draughts. One of my companions equally tormented with thirst, envious of the pleasure I seemed to feel, and which I felt effectually, seized it in his turn, but it availed him nothing, the water which remained was so disgusting that he could not drink it and spilled it on the ground. Captain Begnere, who was present, judging by the water which fell, how loathsome must that have been which I had drank, offered me some crumbs of biscuit which he had kept most carefully in his pocket. I chewed that mixture of bread, dust, and tobacco, but I could not swallow it, and gave it, all masticated, to one of my younger brothers, who had fallen from inanition.

We were about to quit this furnace, when we saw our generous Englishman approaching, who brought us provisions. At this sight I felt my strength revive, and ceased to desire death, which I had before called on, to release me from my sufferings. Several Moors accompanied Mr. Carnet, and every one was loaded. On their arrival we had water, with rice and dried fish in abundance. Every one drank his allowance of water, but had not ability to eat, although the rice was excellent. We were all anxious to return to the sea, that we might bathe ourselves, and the caravan put itself on the road to the breakers of Sahara. After an hour's march of great suffering, we regained the shore, as well as our asses, which were lying in the water. We rushed among the waves, and after a bath of half an hour, we reposed ourselves upon the beach. My cousin and I went to stretch ourselves upon a small rising ground, where we were shaded with some old clothes which we had with us. My cousin was clad in an officer's uniform, the lace of which strongly attracted the eyes of Mr. Carnet's Moors. Scarcely had we lain down, when one of them, thinking we were asleep, came to endeavor to steal it ; but seeing we were awake, contented himself by looking at us very steadfastly.

Such is the slight incident which it has pleased MM. Correard and Savigny to relate, in their account of the shipwreck of the Medusa, in a totally different manner. Believing, doubtless, to make it more interesting or amusing, they say that one of the Moors who were our guides, either through curiosity or a stronger sentiment, approached Miss Picard while asleep, and, after having examined her form, raised the covering which concealed her bosom, gazing awhile like one astonished; at length drew near, but durst not touch her, then, after having looked a long while, he replaced the covering, and returning to his companions related in a joyous manner what he had seen. Several Frenchmen having observed the proceedings of the Moor, told M. Picard, who, after the obliging offers of the officers, decided in clothing the rest of the ladies in the military dress, on purpose to prevent their being annoyed by the attentions of the inhabitants of the desert. Mighty well ! I beg pardon of MM. Correard and Savigny, but there is not one word of truth in all this. How could these gentlemen see from the raft, that which passed during the 12th of July, on the shores of the Desert of Sahara? And supposing that this was reported to them by some one of our caravan, and inserted in their work, which contains various inaccuracies, I have to inform them they have been deceived.

About three in the morning, a north-west wind having sprung up, and a little refreshed us, our caravan continued its route, our generous Englishman again taking the task of procuring us provisions. At four o'clock the sky became overcast, and we heard thunder in the distance. We all expected a great tempest, which happily did not take place. Near seven we reached the spot where we were to wait for Mr. Carnet, who came to us with a bullock he had purchased. Then quitting the shore, we went into the interior to seek a place to cook our supper. We fixed our camp beside a small wood of acacias, near to which were several wells or cisterns of fresh water. Our ox was instantly killed, skinned, cut to pieces, and distributed. A large fire was kindled, and each was occupied in dressing his meal. At this time I caught a smart fever; notwithstanding, I could not help laughing at seeing every one seated round a large fire holding his piece of beef on the point of a bayonet, a saber, or some sharp-pointed stick. The flickering of the flames on the different faces, sunburned and covered with long beards, rendered more visible by the darkness of the night, joined to the noise of the waves and the roaring of ferocious beasts which we heard in the distance, presented a spectacle at once laughable and imposing.

While these thoughts were passing across my mind, sleep overpowered my senses. Being awaked in the middle of the night, I found my portion of beef in the shoes which an old sailor had lent me for walking among the thorns. Although it was a little burned, and smelled strongly of the dish in which it was contained, I ate a good part of it, and gave the rest to my friend the sailor. That seaman, seeing I was ill, offered to exchange my meat for some which he had the address to boil in a small tin box. I prayed him to give me a little water, if he had any; and he instantly went and fetched some in his hat. My thirst was so great that I drank it out of this nasty cap without the slightest repugnance.

A short while after, every one awoke, and again took the route for Senegal at an early hour. At nine o'clock we met upon the shore a large flock herded by young Moors. These shepherds sold us milk, and one of them offered to lend my father an ass for a knife which he had seen him take from his pocket. My father having accepted the proposal, the Moor left his companions to accompany us as far as the river Senegal, from which we were yet two good leagues.

There happened a circumstance in the forenoon which had like to have proved troublesome, but it turned out pleasantly. The steersman of the Medusa was sleeping upon the sand, when a Moor found means to steal his saber. The Frenchman awoke, and as soon as he saw the thief escaping with his booty, rose and pursued him with horrid oaths. The Arab, seeing himself followed by a furious European, returned, fell upon his knees, and laid at the feet of the steersman the sabre which he had stolen; who, in his turn, touched with this mark of confidence or repentance, voluntarily gave it to him to keep. During this scene we frequently stopped to see how it would terminate, while the caravan continued its route. Suddenly we left the shore. Our companions appearing quite transported with joy, some of us ran forward, and having gained a slight rising ground, discovered the Senegal at no great distance from them. We hastened our march, and for the first time since our shipwreck, a smiling picture presented itself to our view. We could not satiate our eyes with gazing on the beauties of this place, verdure being so enchanting to the sight, especially after having traveled through the desert. Before reaching the river, we had to descend a little hill covered with thorny bushes. My ass stumbling, threw me into the midst of one, and I tore myself in several places; but was easily consoled, when I at length found myself on the banks of a river of fresh water. Everyone having quenched his thirst, we stretched ourselves under the shade of a small grove, while the beneficent Mr. Carnet and two of our officers set forward to Senegal, to announce our arrival, and to get us boats.

At two in the afternoon we saw a small boat beating against the current of the stream with oars. It soon reached the spot where we were. Two Europeans landed, saluted our caravan, and inquired for my father. One of them said he came on the part of MM. Artigue and Laboure, inhabitants of Senegal, to offer assistance to the boats which were getting ready for our family; the other added, that he had not waited for us at the island of St. Louis, knowing too well what would be our need. They placed before us large baskets containing several loaves, cheese, a bottle of Madeira, a bottle of filtered water, and dresses for my father. Every one, who, during our journey, had taken any interest in our unfortunate family, and especially the brave Captain Begnere, had a share of our provisions. We experienced a real satisfaction in partaking with them, and giving them this small mark of our gratitude. A young aspirant of marine, who had refused us a glass of water in the desert, pressed with hunger, begged of us some bread; he got it, also a small glass of Madeira. It was four o'clock before the boats of the government arrived, and we all embarked. Biscuit and wine were found in each of them, and all were refreshed.

That in which our family were was commanded by M. Artigue, captain of the port, and one of those who had sent us provisions. My father and he embraced as two old friends who had not seen one another for eight years, and congratulated themselves that they had been permitted to meet once more before they died.

Immediately the town of St. Louis presented itself to our view. At the distance its appearance is fine; but in proportion as it is approached the illusion vanishes, and it looks as it really is—dirty, very ill built, poor, and filled with straw huts black with smoke. At six in the evening we arrived at the port of St. Louis. It would be in vain for me to paint the various emotions of my mind at that delicious moment. I am bold to say, all the colony, if we except MM. Schmaltz and Lachaumareys, were at the port to receive us from our boats. M. Artigue going on shore first to acquaint the English governor of our arrival, met him coming to us on horseback, followed by our generous conductor, Mr. Carnet, and several superior officers. We went on shore carrying our brothers and sisters in our arms. My father presented us to the English governor, who had alighted; he appeared to be sensibly affected with our misfortunes, the females and children chiefly exciting his commiseration. And the native inhabitants and Europeans tenderly shook the hands of the unfortunate people; the negro slaves even seemed to deplore our disastrous fate.

The following is the substance, abridged from MM. Correard and Savigny, of what took place on the raft during thirteen days before the sufferers were taken up by the Argus brig.

After the boats had disappeared, the consternation became extreme. All the horrors of thirst and famine passed before our imaginations; beside, we had to contend with a treacherous element, which already covered the half of our bodies. The deep stupor of the soldiers and sailors instantly changed to despair. All saw their inevitable destination, and expressed by their moans the dark thoughts which brooded in their minds. Our words were at first unavailing to quiet their fears, which we participated with them, but which a greater strength of mind enabled us to dissemble. At last, an unmoved countenance and our proffered consolations quieted them by degrees, but could not entirely dissipate the terror with which they were seized.

When tranquillity was a little restored, we began to search about the raft for the charts, the compass, and the anchor, which we presumed had been placed upon it, after what we had been told at the time of quitting the frigate. These things, of the first importance, had not been placed upon our machine. Above all, the want of a compass the most alarmed us, and we gave vent to our rage and vengeance. M. Correard then remembered he had seen one in the hands of one of the principal workmen under his command; he spoke to the man, who replied, "Yes, yes, I have it with me." This information transported us with joy, and we believed that our safety depended upon this futile resource: it was about the size of a crown-piece, and very incorrect. The compass was given to the commander of the raft, but an accident deprived us of it forever: it fell, and disappeared between the pieces of wood which formed our machine. We had kept it but a few hours, and, after its loss, had nothing to guide us but the rising and setting of the sun.

We had all gone afloat without taking any food. Hunger beginning to be imperiously felt, we mixed our paste of sea-biscuit (which had fallen into the sea, and was with difficulty recovered,) with a little wine, and distributed it thus prepared. Such was our first meal, and the best we had during our stay upon the raft.

An order, according to our numbers, was established for the distribution of our miserable provisions. The ration of wine was fixed at three quarters a day. We will speak no more of the biscuit, it having been entirely consumed at the first distribution. The day passed away sufficiently tranquil. We talked of the means by which we would save ourselves; we spoke of it as a certain circumstance, which reanimated our courage; and we sustained that of the soldiers, by cherishing in them the hope of being able, in a short while, to revenge themselves on those who had so basely abandoned us. This hope of vengeance, it must be avowed, equally animated us all; and we poured out a thousand imprecations against those who had left us a prey to so much misery and danger.

The officer who commanded the raft being unable to move, M. Savigny took upon himself the duty of erecting the mast. He caused them to cut in two one of the poles of the frigate's masts, and fixed it with the rope which had served to tow us, and of which we made stays and shrouds. It was placed on the anterior third of the raft. We put up for a sail the main-topgallant, which trimmed very well, but was of very little use, except when the wind served from behind; and to keep the raft in this course, we were obliged to trim the sail as if the breeze blew athwart us. In the evening, our hearts and our prayers, by a feeling natural to the unfortunate, were turned toward Heaven. Surrounded by inevitable dangers, we addressed that invisible Being who has established, and who maintains the order of the universe. Our vows were fervent, and we experienced from our prayers the cheering influence of hope.

One consoling thought still soothed our imagination. We persuaded ourselves that the little division had gone to the isle of Arguin, and that, after it had set a part of its people on shore, the rest would return to our assistance; we endeavored to impress this idea on our soldiers and sailors, which quieted them. The night came without our hope being realized; the wind freshened, and the sea was considerably swelled. M. Savigny, seconded by some people who still preserved their presence of mind amid the disorder, stretched cords across the raft, by which the men held, and were better able to resist the swell of the sea; some were even obliged to fasten themselves. In the middle of the night the weather was very rough; huge waves burst upon us, sometimes overturning us with great violence. The cries of the men mingled with the roaring of the flood, while the terrible sea raised us at every instant from the raft, and threatened to sweep us away. This scene was rendered still more terrible by the horrors inspired by the darkness of the night. Suddenly we believed we saw fires in the distance, at intervals. We had the precaution to hang at the top of the mast, the gunpowder and pistols which we had brought from the frigate. We made signals by burning a large quantity of cartridges; we even fired some pistols; but it seems the fire we saw was nothing but an error of vision, or, perhaps, nothing more than the sparkling of the waves.

We struggled with death during the whole of the night, holding firmly by the ropes, which were made very secure. Tossed by the waves from the back to the front, and from the front to the back, and sometimes precipitated into the sea; floating between life and death, mourning our misfortunes, certain of perishing; we disputed, nevertheless, the remainder of our existence with that cruel element which threatened to ingulf us. Such was our condition till day-break. At every instant we heard the lamentable cries of the soldiers and sailors; they prepared for death, bidding farewell to one another, imploring the protection of Heaven, and addressing fervent prayers to God. Everyone made vows to him, in spite of the certainty of never being able to accomplish them.

Toward seven in the morning the sea fell a little, the wind blew with less fury; but what a scene presented itself to our view! Ten or twelve unfortunates, having their legs fixed in the openings between the pieces of the raft, had perished by being unable to disengage themselves; several others were swept away by the violence of the sea. At the hour of repast we took the numbers anew; we had lost twenty men. We will not affirm that this was the exact number; for we perceived some soldiers who, to have more than their share, took rations for two, and even three; we were so huddled together that we found it absolutely impossible to prevent this abuse.

In the midst of these horrors a touching scene of filial piety drew our tears. Two young men raised and recognized their father, who had fallen, and was lying, insensible, among the feet of the people. They believed him, at first, dead, and their despair was expressed in the most afflicting manner. It was perceived, however, that he still breathed, and every assistance was rendered for his recovery in our power. He slowly revived, and was restored to life, and to the prayers of his sons, who supported him, closely folded in their arms. While our hearts were softened by this affecting episode in our melancholy adventures, we had soon to witness a dark contrast. Two ship-boys and a baker feared not to seek death, and threw themselves into the sea, after having bid farewell to their companions in misfortune. Already the minds of our people were singularly altered; some believed they saw land; others ships, which were coming to save us; and talked aloud of their fallacious visions. The day was fine, and the most perfect tranquillity reigned all the while on our raft. The evening came, and no boats appeared. Despondency began to seize our men, and then a spirit of insubordination manifested itself in cries of rage. The voice of the officers was entirely disregarded. Night fell rapidly in, the sky was obscured by dark clouds; the wind, which, during the whole of the day, had blown rather violently, became furious, and swelled the sea, which, in an instant, became very rough. The men, from the violence of the sea, were hurried from the back to the front; we were obliged to keep to the center, the firmest part of the raft, and those who could not get there almost all perished. Before and behind the waves dashed impetuously, and swept away the men in spite of all their resistance. At the center the pressure was such that some unfortunates were suffocated by the weight of their comrades, who fell upon them at every instant. The officers kept by the foot of the little mast, and were obliged every moment to call to those around them, to go to the one or the other side, to avoid the wave; for the sea coming nearly athwart us, gave our raft nearly a perpendicular position, to counteract which they were forced to throw themselves upon the side raised by the sea.

The soldiers and sailors, frightened by the presence of almost inevitable danger, doubted not that they had reached their last hour. Firmly believing they were lost, they resolved to soothe their last moments by drinking until they lost their reason. We had no power to oppose this disorder. They seized a cask which was in the center of the raft, made a hole in the end of it, and, with small tin cups, took each a pretty large quantity; but they were obliged to cease, for the sea-water rushed into the hole they had made. The fumes of the wine failed not to disorder their brains, already weakened by the presence of danger and want of food. Thus excited, these men became deaf to the voice of reason. They wished to involve in one common ruin all their companions in misfortune. They avowedly expressed their intention of freeing themselves from their officers, who, they said, wished to oppose their design, and then to destroy the raft, by cutting the ropes which united its different parts. Immediately after they resolved to put their plans in execution, one of them advanced upon the side of the raft with a boarding-ax, and began to cut the cords. This was the signal of revolt. We stepped forward to prevent these insane mortals, and he who was armed with a hatchet, with which he even threatened an officer, fell the first victim: a stroke of the saber terminated his existence.

This man was an Asiatic, and a soldier in a colonial regiment. Of a colossal stature, short hair, a nose extremely large, an enormous mouth, dark complexion, he made a most hideous appearance. At first he placed himself in the middle of the raft, and, at each blow of his fist, knocked down everyone who opposed him; he inspired the greatest terror, and none durst approach him. Had there been six such, our destruction would have been certain.

Some men, anxious to prolong their existence, armed and united themselves with those who wished to preserve the raft; among this number were some subaltern officers and many passengers. The rebels drew their sabers, and those who had none armed themselves with knives. They advanced in a determined manner upon us; we stood on our defense; the attack commenced. Animated by despair, one of them aimed a stroke at an officer; the rebel instantly fell, pierced with wounds. This firmness awed them for an instant, but diminished nothing of their rage. They ceased to advance, and withdrew—presenting to us a front bristling with sabers and bayonets—to the back part of the raft, to execute their plan. One of them feigned to rest himself on the small railings on the sides of the raft, and with a knife began cutting the cords. Being told by a servant, one of us sprang upon him. A soldier, wishing to defend him, struck at the officer with his knife, which only pierced his coat; the officer wheeled round, seized his adversary, and threw both him and his comrade into the sea.

There had been as yet but partial affairs: the combat now became general. Some one cried to lower the sail; a crowd of infuriated mortals threw themselves in an instant upon the halyards, and shrouds, and cut them. The fall of the mast almost broke the thigh of a captain of infantry, who fell insensible. He was seized by the soldiers, who threw him into the sea. We saved him and placed him on a barrel, whence he was taken by the rebels, who wished to put out his eyes with a penknife. Exasperated by so much brutality, we no longer restrained ourselves, but rushed in upon them, and charged them with fury. Sword in hand, we traversed the line which the soldiers formed, and many paid with their lives the errors of their revolt. Various passengers, during these cruel moments, evinced the greatest courage and coolness.

M. Correard fell into a sort of swoon; but hearing at every instant the cries, *To arms! with us, comrades; we are lost!* joined with the groans and imprecations of the wounded and dying, was soon roused from his lethargy. All this horrible tumult speedily made him comprehend how necessary it was to be upon his guard. Armed with his saber, he gathered together some of his workmen on the front of the raft, and there charged them to hurt no one, unless they were attacked. He almost always remained with them; and several times they had to defend themselves against the rebels, who, swimming round to the point of the raft, placed M. Correard and his little troop between two dangers, and made their position very difficult to defend. At every instant he was opposed to men armed with knives, sabers, and bayonets. Many had carabines, which they wielded as clubs. Every effort was made to stop them, by holding them off at the point of their swords; which, in spite of the repugnance they experienced in fighting with their wretched countrymen, they were compelled to use without mercy. Many of the mutineers attacked with fury, and they were obliged to repel them in the same manner. Some of the laborers received severe wounds in this action. Their commander could show a great number received in the different campaigns. At last their united efforts prevailed in dispersing this mass who had attacked them with such fury.

During this combat, M. Correard was told by one of his workmen who remained faithful, that one of their comrades, named Dominique, had gone over to the rebels, and that they had seized and thrown him into the sea. Immediately forgetting the fault and treason of this man, he threw himself in at the place whence the voice of the wretch was heard calling for assistance, seized him by the hair, and had the good fortune to restore him on board. Dominique had got several saber wounds in a charge, one of which had laid open his head. In spite of the darkness, we found out the wound, which seemed very large. One of the workmen gave his handkerchief to bind and stop the blood. Our care recovered the wretch; but when he had collected strength, the ungrateful Dominique, forgetting at once his duty and the signal service which we had rendered him, went and rejoined the rebels. So much baseness and insanity did not go unrevenged; and soon after he found, in a fresh assault, that death from which he was not worthy to be saved, but which he might, in all probability, have avoided, if, true to honor and gratitude, he had remained among us.

Just at the moment we finished dressing the wounds of Dominique, another voice was heard. It was that of the unfortunate female who was with us on the raft, and whom the infuriated beings had thrown into the sea, as well as her husband, who had defended her with courage. M. Correard, in despair at seeing two unfortunates perish, whose pitiful cries, especially the woman's, pierced his heart, seized a large rope, which he found on the front of the raft, which he fastened round his middle, and throwing himself a second time into the sea, was again so fortunate as to save the woman, who invoked, with all her might, the assistance of our Lady of Land. Her husband was rescued at the same time by the head workman, Lavilette. We laid these unfortunates upon the dead bodies, supporting their backs with a barrel. In a short while they recovered their senses. The first thing the woman did was to acquaint herself with the name of the person who saved her, and to express to him her liveliest gratitude. Finding, doubtless, that her words but ill expressed her feelings, she recollected she had in her pocket a little snuff, and instantly offered it to him—it was all she possessed. Touched with the gift, but unable to use it, M. Correard gave it to a poor sailor, which served him for three or four days. But it is impossible for us to describe a still more affecting scene—the joy this unfortunate couple testified, when they had sufficiently recovered their senses, at finding they were both saved.

The rebels being repulsed, as it has been stated above, left us a little repose. The man and wife, who had been but a little before stabbed with swords and bayonets, and thrown both together into a stormy sea, could scarcely credit their senses when they found themselves in one another's arms. The woman was a native of the Upper Alps, which place she had left twenty-four years before, and during which time she had followed the French armies in the campaigns in Italy, and other places, as a sutler. "Therefore preserve my life," said she to M. Correard, "you see I am a useful woman. Ah! if you knew how often I had ventured upon the field of battle, and braved death to carry assistance to our gallant men! Whether they had money or not, I always let them have my goods. Sometimes a battle would deprive me of my poor debtors; but after the victory, others would pay me double or triple for what they had consumed before the engagement. Thus I came in for a share of their victories." Unfortunate woman! she little knew what a horrible fate awaited her among us! They felt, they expressed so vividly that happiness which they, alas! so shortly enjoyed, that it would have drawn tears from the most obdurate heart. But in that horrible moment when we scarcely breathed from the most furious attack—when we were obliged to be continually on our guard, not only against the violence of the men, but a most boisterous sea, few among us had time to attend to scenes of conjugal affection.

After this second check, the rage of the soldiers was suddenly appeased, and gave place to the most abject cowardice. Several threw themselves at our feet and implored our pardon, which was instantly granted. Thinking that order was re-established, we returned to our station on the center of the raft, only taking the precaution of keeping our arms. We, however, had soon to prove the impossibility of counting on the permanence of any honest sentiment in the hearts of these beings. It was nearly midnight; and, after an hour of apparent tranquillity, the soldiers rose afresh. Their mind was entirely gone: they ran upon us in despair, with knives and sabers in their hands. As they yet had all their physical strength, and beside were armed, we were obliged again to stand on our defense. Their revolt became still more dangerous, as, in their delirium, they were entirely deaf to the voice of reason. They attacked us, we charged them in our turn, and immediately the raft was strewed with their dead bodies. Those of our adversaries who had no weapons, endeavored to tear us with their sharp teeth. Many of us were cruelly bitten. M. Savigny was torn on the legs and shoulder; he also received a wound on the right arm, which deprived him of the use of his fourth and little finger for a long while. Many others were wounded; and many cuts were found in our clothes, from knives and sabers. Some short while after, in a fresh attack of the rebels, Sub-lieutenant Lozach fell into their hands. In their delirium they had taken him for Lieutenant Danglas, of whom we have formerly spoken, and who had abandoned the raft at the moment when we were quitting the frigate. The troop, to a man, eagerly sought this officer, who had seen little service, and whom they reproached for having used them ill during the time they garrisoned the Isle of Rhe. We believed this officer lost, but hearing his voice, we soon found it still possible to save him. Immediately a number of our men, formed themselves into small platoons, and rushed upon the insurgents with great impetuosity, overturning everyone in their way, and retook M. Lozach, and placed him on the center of the raft. Every moment the soldiers demanded he should be delivered to them, designating him always by the name of Danglas. We endeavored to make them comprehend their mistake, and told them that they themselves had seen the person for whom they sought, return on board the frigate. They were insensible to everything we said; everything before them was Danglas; they saw him perpetually, and furiously and unceasingly demanded his head. It was only by force of arms we succeeded in repressing their rage and quieting their cries of death.

We had also to tremble for the life of M. Coudin. Wounded and fatigued by the attacks which he had sustained with us, and in which he had shown a courage superior to everything, he was resting himself on a barrel, holding in his arms a young sailor boy of twelve years of age, to whom he had attached himself. The mutineers seized him, with his barrel, and threw him into the sea with the boy, whom he still held fast. In spite of his burden, he had the presence of mind to lay hold of the raft, and to save himself from extreme peril. We cannot yet comprehend how a handful of men should have been able to resist such a number so monstrously insane. We are sure we were not more than twenty to combat all these madmen. Let it not, however, be imagined that in the midst of all these dangers we had preserved our reason entire. Fear, anxiety, and the most cruel privations, had greatly changed our intellectual faculties. But being somewhat less insane than the unfortunate soldiers, we energetically opposed their determination of cutting the cords of the raft. Permit us now to make some observations concerning the different sensations with which we were affected. During the first day, M. Griffin entirely lost his senses. He threw himself into the sea, but M. Savigny saved him with his own hands. His words were vague and unconnected. A second time he threw himself in, but, by a sort of instinct, kept hold of the cross pieces of the raft, and was again saved.

The following is what M. Savigny experienced in the beginning of the night. His eyes closed in spite of himself, and he felt a general drowsiness. In this condition the most delightful visions flitted across his imagination. He saw around him a country covered with the most beautiful plantations, and found himself in the midst of objects delightful to his senses. Nevertheless, he reasoned concerning his condition, and felt that courage alone could withdraw him from this species of non-existence. He demanded some wine from the master gunner, who got it for him, and he recovered a little from this state of stupor. If the unfortunates who were assailed with these primary symptoms had not strength to withstand them, their death was certain. Some became furious; others threw themselves into the sea, bidding farewell to their comrades with the utmost coolness. Some said—"Fear nothing; I am going to get you assistance, and will return in a short while." In the midst of this general madness some wretches were seen rushing upon their companions, sword in hand, demanding *a wing of a chicken and some bread*, to appease the hunger which consumed them; others asked for their hammocks, to go, they said, *between the decks of the frigate to take a little repose.* Many believed they were still on the decks of the Medusa, surrounded by the same objects they there saw daily. Some saw ships, and called to them for assistance, or a fine harbor, in the distance of which was an elegant city. M. Correard thought he was traveling through the beautiful fields of Italy. An officer said to him—"I recollect we have been abandoned by the boats; but fear nothing. I am going to write to the governor, and in a few hours we shall be saved." M. Correard replied in the same tone, and as if he had been in his ordinary condition —"Have you a pigeon to carry your orders with such celerity?" The cries and the confusion soon aroused us from this languor; but when tranquillity was somewhat restored, we again fell into the same drowsy condition. On the morrow we felt as if we had awoke from a painful dream, and asked our companions if, during their sleep, they had not seen combats and heard cries of despair. Some replied that the same visions had continually tormented them, and that they were exhausted with fatigue. Everyone beleived he was deceived by the illusions of a horrible dream.

After these different combats, overcome with toil, with want of food and sleep, we laid ourselves down and reposed till the morrow dawned and showed us the horror of the scene. A great number in their delirum had thrown themselves into the sea. We found that sixty or sixty-five had perished during the night. A fourth part at least, we supposed, had drowned themselves in despair. We only lost two of our number, neither of whom were officers. The deepest dejection was painted on every face; each, having recovered himself, could now feel the horrors of his situation; and some of us, shedding tears of despair, bitterly deplored the rigor of our fate.

A new misfortune was now revealed to us. During the tumult, the rebels had thrown into the sea two barrels of wine, and the only two casks of water which we had upon the raft. The casks of wine had been consumed the day before, and only one was left. We were more than sixty in number, and we were obliged to put ourselves on half-rations

At break of day the sea calmed, which permitted us again to erect our mast. When it was replaced, we made a distribution of wine. The unhappy soldiers murmured and blamed us for privations which we equally endured with them. They fell exhausted. We had taken nothing for forty-eight hours, and we had been obliged to struggle continually against a strong sea. We could, like them, hardly support ourselves; courage alone made us still act. We resolved to employ every possible means to catch fish, and collecting all the hooks and eyes from the soldiers, made fish-hooks of them; but all was of no avail. The currents carried our lines under the raft, where they got entangled. We bent a bayonet to catch sharks; one bit at it, and straightened it, and we abandoned our project. Something was absolutely necessary to sustain our miserable existence, and we tremble with horror at being obliged to tell that of which we made use. We feel our pen fall from our hands; a mortal cold congeals all our members, and our hair bristles erect on our foreheads. Reader! we implore you, feel not indignant toward men already loaded with misery. Pity their condition, and shed a tear of sorrow for their deplorable fate.

The wretches whom death had spared during the disastrous night we have described, seized upon the dead bodies with which the raft was covered, cutting them up by slices, which some even instantly devoured. Many nevertheless refrained. Almost all the officers were of this number. Seeing that this monstrous food had revived the strength of those who had used it, it was proposed to dry it to make it a little more palatable. Those who had firmness to abstain from it, took an additional quantity of wine. We endeavored to eat shoulder-belts and cartouch-boxes, and contrived to swallow some small bits of them. Some ate linen; others, the leathers of the hats, on which was a little grease, or rather dirt. We had recourse to many expedients to prolong our miserable existence, to recount which would only disgust the heart of humanity.

The day was calm and beautiful. A ray of hope beamed for a moment to quiet our agitation. We still expected to see the boats, or some ships, and addressed our prayers to the Eternal, on whom we placed our trust. The half of our men were extremely feeble, and bore upon their faces the stamp of approaching dissolution. The evening arrived, and we found no help. The darkness of the third night augmented our fears, but the wind was still, and the sea less agitated. The sun of the fourth morning since our departure shone upon our disaster, and showed us ten or twelve of our companions stretched lifeless upon the raft. This sight struck us most forcibly, as it told us we would be soon extended in the same manner in the same place. We gave their bodies to the sea for a grave, reserving only one to feed those who, but the day before, had held his trembling hands, and sworn to him eternal friendship. This day was beautiful. Our souls, anxious for more delightful sensations, were in harmony with the aspect of the heavens, and got again a new ray of hope. Toward four in the afternoon an unlooked for event happened, which gave us some consolation. A shoal of flying-fish passed under our raft, and as there was an infinite number of openings between the pieces that composed it, the fish were entangled in great quantities. We threw ourselves upon them, and captured a considerable number. We took about two hundred and put them in an empty barrel; we opened them as we caught them, and took out what is called their milt. This food seemed delicious; but one man would have required a thousand. Our first emotion was to give God renewed thanks for this unhoped for favor. An ounce of gunpowder having been found in the morning, was dried in the sun during the day, which was very fine; a steel, gun-flints, and tinder made also a part of the same parcel. After a good deal of difficulty we set fire to some fragments of dry linen. We made a large opening in the side of an empty cask, and placed at the bottom of it several wet things, and upon this kind of scaffolding we set our fire; all of which we placed on a barrel, that the sea might not extinguish it. We cooked some fish and ate them with extreme avidity; but our hunger was such, and our portion so small, that we added to it some of the sacrilegious viands, which the cooking rendered less revolting. This some of the officers touched for the first time. From this day we continued to eat it but we could no longer dress it, the means of making a fire having been entirely lost; the barrel having caught fire, we extinguished it, without being able to preserve anything to rekindle it on the morrow. The powder and tinder were entirely done. This meal gave us all additional strength to support our fatigues. The night was tolerable, and would have been happy, had it not been signalized by a new massacre.

Some Spaniards, Italians, and negroes, had formed a plot to throw us all into the sea. The negroes had told them that they were very near the shore, and that, when there, they would enable them to traverse Africa without danger. We had to take to our arms again; the sailors, who had remained faithful to us, pointing out to us the conspirators. The first signal for battle was given by a Spaniard, who, placing himself behind the mast, holding fast by it, made the sign of the cross with one hand, invoking the name of God, and with the other held a knife. The sailors seized him and threw him into the sea. An Italian, servant to an officer of the troops, who was in the plot, seeing all was discovered, armed himself with the only boarding-ax left on the raft, made his retreat to the front, enveloped himself in a piece of drapery he wore across his breast, and, of his own accord, threw himself into the sea. The rebels rushed forward to avenge their comrades; a terrible conflict again commenced; both sides fought with desperate fury; and soon the fatal raft was strewed with dead bodies and blood, which should have been shed by other hands, and in another cause. In this tumult we heard them again demanding, with horrid rage, the head of Lieutenant Danglas! In this assault the unfortunate sutler was again thrown into the sea. M. Coudin, assisted by some workmen, saved her, to prolong for awhile her torments and her existence.

In this terrible night Lavillette failed not to give proofs of the rarest intrepidity. It was to him and some of those who have survived the sequel of our misfortunes, that we owed our safety. At last, after unheard of efforts, the rebels were once more repulsed, and quiet restored. Having escaped this new danger, we endeavored to get some repose. The day at length dawned upon us for the fifth time. We were now no more than thirty in number. We had lost four or five of our faithful sailors, and those who survived were in the most deplorable condition. The sea-water had almost entirely excoriated the skin of our lower extremities; we were covered with contusions or wounds, which, irritated by the salt water, extorted from us the most piercing cries. About twenty of us only were capable of standing upright or walking. Almost all our fish were exhausted; we had but four days supply of wine: in four days, said we, nothing will be left, and death will be inevitable. Thus came the seventh day of our abandonment. In the course of the day two soldiers had glided behind the only barrel of wine that was left, piercing it, and were drinking by means of a reed. We had sworn that those who used such means should be punished with death; which law was instantly put in execution, and the two transgressors were thrown into the sea.

The same day saw the close of the life of a child named Leon, aged twelve years. He died like a lamp which ceases to burn for want of aliment. All spoke in favor of this young and amiable creature, who merited a better fate. His angelic form, his musical voice, the interest of an age so tender, increased still more by the courage he had shown and the services he had performed, for he had already made, in the preceding year, a campaign in the East Indies, inspired us all with the greatest pity for this young victim, devoted to so horrible and premature a death. Our old soldiers and all our people in general did everything they could to prolong his existence, but all was in vain. Neither the wine which they gave him without regret, nor all the means they employed, could arrest his melancholy doom, and he expired in the arms of M. Coudin, who had not ceased to give him the most unwearied attention. While he had strength to move he ran incessantly from one side to the other, loudly calling for his mother, for water and food. He trod indiscriminately on the feet and legs of his companions in misfortune, who, in their turn, uttered sorrowful cries, but these were very rarely accompanied with menaces; they pardoned all which the poor boy had made them suffer. He was not in his senses, consequently could not be expected to behave as if he had the use of his reason.

There now remained but twenty-seven of us. Fifteen of that number seemed able to live yet some days; the rest, covered with large wounds, had almost entirely lost the use of their reason. They still, however, shared in the distributions, and would, before they died, consume thirty or forty bottles of wine, which to us were inestimable. We deliberated, that by putting the sick on half allowance was but putting them to death by halves; but after a council, at which presided the most dreadful despair, it was decided they should be thrown into the sea. This means, however repugnant, however horrible it appeared to us, procured the survivors six days' wine. But after the decision was made, who durst execute it? The habit of seeing death ready to devour us; the certainty of our infallible destruction without this monstrous expedient; all, in short, had hardened our hearts to every feeling but that of self-preservation. Three sailors and a soldier took charge of this cruel business. We looked aside and shed tears of blood at the fate of these unfortunates. Among them were the wretched sutler and her husband. Both had been grievously wounded in the different combats. The woman had a thigh broken between the beams of the raft, and a stroke of a saber had made a deep wound in the head of her husband. Everything announced their approaching end. We consoled ourselves with the belief that our cruel resolution shortened but a brief space the term of their existence. Ye who shudder at the cry of outraged humanity, recollect that it was other men, fellow-countrymen, comrades, who had placed us in this awful situation!

This horrible expedient saved the fifteen who remained: for when we were found by the Argus brig, we had very little wine left, and it was the sixth day after the cruel sacrifice we have described. The victims, we repeat, had not more than forty-eight hours to live, and by keeping them on the raft we would have been absolutely destitute of the means of existence two days before we were found. Weak as we were, we considered it as a certain thing, that it would have been impossible for

30

us to have lived only twenty-four hours more, without taking some food. After this catastrophe we threw our arms into the sea; they inspired us with a horror we could not overcome. We only kept one saber, in case we had to cut some cordage or some pieces of wood.

A new event, for everything was an event to wretches to whom the world was reduced to the narrow space of a few feet, and for whom the winds and waves contended in their fury as they floated above the abyss; an event happened which diverted our minds from the horrors of our situation. All on a sudden a white butterfly, of a species common in France, came fluttering above our heads and settled on our sail. The first thought this little creature suggested was that it was the harbinger of approaching land, and we clung to the hope with a delirium of joy. It was the ninth day we had been upon the raft; the torments of hunger consumed our entrails; and the soldiers and sailors already devoured with haggard eyes this wretched prey, and seemed to dispute about it. Others looking upon it as a messenger from Heaven, declared that they took it under their protection, and would suffer none to do it harm. It was certain we could not be far from land, for the butterflies continued to come on the following days and flutter about our sail. We had also, on the same day. another indication, not less positive, by a Goeland which flew around our raft. This second visitor left us not a doubt that we were fast approaching the African soil, and we persuaded ourselves we would be speedily thrown upon the coast by the force of the currents.

This same day a new care employed us. Seeing we were reduced to so small a number, we collected all the little strength we had left, detached some planks on the front of the raft, and, with some pretty long pieces of wood, raised on the center a kind of platform, on which we reposed. All the effects we could collect were placed upon it, and rendered to make it less hard; which also prevented the sea from passing with such facility through the spaces between the different planks; but the waves came across, and sometimes covered us completely.

On this new theater we resolved to meet death in a manner becoming Frenchmen, and with perfect resignation. Our time was almost wholly spent in speaking of our happy country. All our wishes, our last prayers, were for the prosperity of France. Thus passed the last days of our abode upon the raft. Soon after our abandonment, we bore with comparative ease the immersions during the nights, which are very cold in these countries; but latterly, every time the waves washed over us we felt a most painful sensation, and we uttered plaintive cries. We employed every means to avoid it. Some supported their heads on pieces of wood, and made, with what they could find, a sort of little parapet to screen them from the force of the waves; others sheltered themselves behind two empty casks. But these means were very insufficient; it was only when the sea was calm that it did not break over us.

An ardent thirst, redoubled in the day by the beams of a burning sun, consumed us. An officer of the army found by chance a small lemon, and it may be easily imagined how valuable such a fruit would be to him. His comrades, in spite of the most urgent entreaties, could not get a bit of it from him. Signs of rage were already manifested, and had he not partly listened to the solicitations of those around him, they would have taken it by force, and he would have perished the victim of his own selfishness. We also disputed about thirty cloves of garlic which were found in the bottom of a sack. These disputes were, for the most part, accompanied with violent menaces, and if they had been prolonged, we might have come to the last extremities. Three days passed in inexpressible anguish. So much did we despise life, that many of us feared not to bathe in sight of the sharks which surrounded our raft; others placed themselves naked upon the front of our machine, which was under water. These expedients diminished a little the ardor of our thirst. On the 16th, reckoning we were very near the land, eight of the most determined among us resolved to endeavor to gain the coast. Accordingly a second raft, of smaller dimensions, was formed for transporting them thither; but it was found insufficient, and they at length determined to await death in their present situation. Meanwhile night came on, and its somber vail revived in our minds the most afflicting thoughts. We were certain there were not above a dozen or fifteen bottles of wine in our barrel. We began to have an invincible disgust at the flesh which had till then scarcely supported us; and we may say that the sight of it inspired us with feelings of horror, doubtless produced by the idea of approaching destruction. On the morning of the 17th the sun appeared free from clouds. After having addressed our prayers to the Eternal, we divided among us a part of our wine. Each with delight was taking his small portion, when a captain of infantry, casting his eyes on the horizon, perceived a ship, and announced it to us by an exclamation of joy. We knew it to be a brig, but it was at a great distance; we could only distinguish the masts. The sight of this vessel revived in us emotions difficult to describe. Each believed his deliverance sure, and we gave a thousand thanks to God. Fears, however, mingled with our hopes. We straightened some hoops of casks, to the ends of which we fixed handkerchiefs of different colors. A man, with our united assistance, mounted to the top of the mast, and waved these little flags. For more than half an hour we were tossed between hope and fear. Some thought the vessel grew larger, and others were convinced its course was from us. These last were the only ones whose eyes were not blinded by hope, for the ship disappeared.

From this delirium of joy we passed to that of despondency and sorrow. We envied the fate of those whom we had seen perish at our sides; and we said to ourselves, "When we shall be in want of everything, and when our strength begins to forsake us, we will wrap ourselves up as well as we can, and will stretch ourselves on this platform, the witness of the most cruel sufferings, and there await death with resignation." At length, to calm our despair, we sought for consolation in the arms of sleep. The day before we had been scorched by the beams of a burning sun; to-day, to avoid the fierceness of his rays, we made a tent with the mainsail of the frigate. As soon as it was finished, we laid ourselves under it; thus all that was passing without was hid from our eyes. We proposed then to write upon a plank an abridgment of our adventures, and to add our names at the bottom of the recital, and fix it to the upper part of our mast, in the hope that it would reach the government and our families.

After having passed two hours, a prey to the most cruel reflections, the master gunner of the frigate, wishing to go to the front of the raft, went out from below the tent. Scarcely had he put out his head when he turned to us, uttering a piercing cry. Joy was painted upon his face; his hands were stretched toward the sea; he breathed with difficulty. All he was able to say was: *Saved! see the brig upon us!* and in fact it was not more than half a league distant, having every sail set, and steering right upon us. We rushed from our tent; even those whom enormous wounds in their inferior extremities had confined for many days, dragged themselves to the back of the raft, to enjoy a sight of the ship which had come to save us from certain death. We embraced one another with a transport which looked much like madness, and tears of joy trickled down our cheeks, withered by the most cruel privations. Each seized handkerchiefs, or some pieces of linen, to make signals to the brig, which was rapidly approaching us. Some fell on their knees and fervently returned thanks to Providence for this miraculous preservation of their lives. Our joy redoubled when we saw at the top of the foremast a large white flag, and we cried, "It is then to Frenchmen we will owe our deliverance." We instantly recognized the brig to be the Argus; it was then about two gunshots from us. We were terribly impatient to see her reef her sails, which at last she did, and fresh cries of joy arose from our raft. The Argus came and lay to on our starboard, about a half pistol shot from us. The crew, ranged upon the deck and on the shrouds, announced to us, by the waving of their hands and hats, the pleasure they felt at coming to the assistance of their unfortunate countrymen. In a short time we were all transported on board the brig, where we found the lieutenant of the frigate, and some others who had been wrecked with us. Compassion was painted on every face, and pity drew tears from every eye which beheld us. We found some excellent broth on board the brig, which they had prepared, and when they had perceived us, they added to it some wine, and thus restored our nearly exhausted strength. We had scarcely escaped, when some became again delirious. An officer of infantry wished to throw himself into the sea to look for his pocket-book, and would have done it had he not been prevented; others were seized in a manner not less frenzied.

The commander and officers of the brig watched over us, and kindly anticipated our wants. They snatched us from death by saving us from the raft; their unremitted care revived within us the spark of life. The surgeon of the ship, M. Renaud, distinguished himself for his indefatigable zeal. He was obliged to spend the whole of the day in dressing our wounds; and during the two days we were on board the brig, he bestowed on us all the aid of his art, with an attention and gentleness which merit our eternal gratitude. In truth, it was time we should find an end of our sufferings; they had lasted thirteen days in the most cruel manner. The strongest among us might have lived forty-eight hours or so longer. M. Correard felt that he must die in the course of the day; he had, however, a presentiment that we would be saved. He said that a series of events so unheard of would not be buried in oblivion; that Providence would at least preserve some of us to tell the world the melancholy story of our misfortunes.

Such is the faithful history of those who were left upon the memorable raft. Of one hundred and fifty, fifteen only were saved. Five of that number never recovered of their fatigue, and died at St. Louis. Those who yet live are covered with scars; and the cruel sufferings to which they have been exposed, have materially shaken their constitutions.

THE STORY

OF

ROBERT DRURY,

A SAILOR BOY, WHO WAS SHIPWRECKED, CAPTURED AND HELD IN SLAVERY FOR FIFTEEN YEARS, BY

THE SAVAGES OF MADAGASCAR.

I WAS born on the 24th of July, 1687, in Crutched Friars, London, where my father then lived; but soon after he removed to the Old Jewry, near Cheapside, where he kept, for several years afterward, that noted house called the King's Head, a famous beef steak house in its day, and a great resort of merchants and other gentlemen. Reared in London, and often about the Thames, I acquired an unconquerable desire to go to sea; and though my parents did everything in their power to give me a good education, and promised to push me on in the world, if I would abandon this notion, I persevered in my obstinate resolution. Not all the entreaties of my poor dear mother, though she once begged me on her knees, nor the persuasions of my father, or any other friends, could make the least impression on me.

When they found their endeavors were ineffectual, they formed a new scheme to wean me from a sea-life. This was to procure me a short voyage, hoping that the many dangers and hardships to which I should be exposed, and should see others undergo, would deter me from persevering in that course of life.

As willful persons never want woe, such was my obstinacy, that nothing would content me but what contributed to my ruin; and Providence justly frustrated all my hopes, by indulging me in the choice I had so foolishly and ungratefully made, in direct opposition to my duty to my affectionate parents. When it was proposed that I should take a short voyage, I insisted that nothing but a voyage to the East Indies would please me; for no other reason that I can think of, than that I had a cousin in the East India Company's service at Calcutta. It was accordingly resolved to gratify this whim. My father, however, showed a due concern for my comfort and welfare, by the manner in which he fitted me out. He supplied me plentifully with provisions, clothes, and other necessaries for the voyage; beside which I had a cargo to trade on, to the value of a hundred pounds, which was a large trust for a boy of not yet fourteen years of age. I went as a passenger, well recommended to Captain William Younge, with whom my passage, and the freight of my cargo, were agreed for, and we soon after embarked.

The vessel Captain Younge commanded was the Degrave, of 700 tons burden, and carrying 52 guns. She was a regular India trader, and, like all others of her class, required to be well armed for the sake of defense. The parting with my mother was not without pain; but I was a giddy boy, and soon recovered my spirits. The ship dropped pleasantly down the Thames to the Nore, and passed through the Downs on February 19, 1701. Nothing remarkable occurred during the outward-bound voyage. In our route we stopped a week at the Canaries, and arrived at Fort George, in the East Indies, in three months and twenty days from the Downs. Two days after we weighed anchor, and sailed to Mastapatan, where we stayed a month, and then proceeded to complete our voyage to Bengal.

On arriving at Calcutta, my cousin came on board, and offered to assist in disposing of my goods; but the captain discovering that he was far from being trustworthy, took charge of my cargo, and sold the whole to good advantage, taking in exchange the commodities of the country. While lying at this port, we lost many of our crew by fever; and, worst of all, at length Captain Younge also died, leaving his son, who was second mate, to take charge of the ship. This was a serious disaster, for our new commander was an inexperienced young man, not fit for so important a trust. The number of deaths on board, caused us to wait a considerable time to recruit the ship's company. During this period of inaction, I learned to swim, and frequently amused myself by swimming in the Hoogly. I became so exceedingly expert in this art, that I could swim several miles up or down the river.

Our business being finished at Bengal, and our crew greatly renewed, we sailed on our homeward voyage, having on board 120 hands, some of them Lascars, beside two women and myself, and a few other passengers. As we were going down the river, our ship ran aground, and stuck fast; but there being a very strong tide, it turned her round, and we got off the next high water without any damage, as we imagined. This accident proved the cause of the sad misfortune, which soon after overtook us. On getting out to sea, the vessel was found to have sprung a leak, and we were obliged to keep two chain-pumps continually at work. We were two months in this distressing condition, every man taking his turn at the severe labor of pumping. It was a joyful sight to see the island of Mauritius rising on the horizon, and we were all still more delighted to arrive at the island, which lies about 600 miles to the east of Madagascar. This fine island was inhabited by the Dutch, who treated us with great kindness and humanity, assisting us with whatever was in their power. We made a tent on shore, in which we stowed great part of our cargo, in order to lighten the ship, and discover the leak. In this search, which could not have been properly performed, the sailors were unsuccessful, and the captain gave it up as hopeless. A month was spent on the island. Having taken on board plenty of good fish, turtle, and goats, with some beef, we departed, shaping our course directly for the Cape of Good Hope.

The infatuation of going to sea with a leaky vessel, is more than I can possibly account for. Whatever motive urged the captain to do such an act of folly, he and all of us were severely punished for it. When we had been gone a few days from the Mauritius, the leak gained on us more and more, and it was with great difficulty the ship could be kept above water. Young as I was, I saw that we were on the verge of destruction, and now repented in tears, the madness of putting myself in the way of such a catastrophe. It was dreadful to see the exertions which the men made to keep the vessel from sinking. They worked incessantly at the pumps; but the water came in as quickly as it was pumped and bailed out, and gained gradually, in spite of every effort. All were spent with fatigue, and despair settled on every countenance. According to our reckoning, we were a hundred leagues southward of Madagascar; and to lighten the ship, several guns, and much of the heavy goods, were heaved overboard. The captain was for continuing our course to the Cape, 600 leagues distant, but the ship's company in general opposed it, being of opinion that they could not keep her above water long enough, and were in favor of running to Madagascar, which was the nearest land.

The peril we were in did not admit of delay, and, by urgent persuasion, the captain ordered 'bout ship, and put back for Madagascar. The wind favoring us, the water-logged vessel got on somewhat better in its new course, and on the third day, I was sent, along with the captain's boy, up to the mast-head to look out for land, since nobody else could be so well spared. In such apparent danger, my being a passenger was no excuse. Accordingly I went up, and sat there two hours and a half, looking across the broad ocean for the much desired land. At length a speck seemed to rise on the horizon, and I asked my comrade if that were land; for I feared to call out, and inspire men in such desperate circumstances with groundless hopes: they were not, I knew, in a frame of mind to be trifled with. I therefore did not call out till I could plainly discover a white cliff, and a smoke at a distance from it, whereupon I boldly shouted, *Land! land!*

At this joyful news several sailors immediately ran up the shrouds, and even the captain himself, to make his observations. One among them knew the land, and said it was Port Dauphine, and that the king of that part of the island—all the people being negroes, in a savage state—was an enemy to all white men, and treated all the Europeans who fell into his hands in a barbarous manner. This king, he said, was called Samuel, and he advised us by all means to avoid landing on his territories. This information put us into the utmost confusion and despair, and proved indeed our ruin. The man who made the discouraging report, spoke his real sentiments; but he labored under a mistake, as we afterward discovered. King Samuel had, it appears, received an affront from the crew of a French vessel, and he ever afterward attacked all French without mercy, who put into his dominions; he had, however, no animosity against any other white nation, but the reverse; so that, had we put in there, we had at least saved our lives, and some of our cargo. Under the erroneous impression made by the sailor, we unfortunately steered westward along the coast, to see if a proper landing-place could be found.

Crawling onward in this wretched condition, we kept a look-out for some safe spot to run the vessel aground. Nothing of the kind was to be seen; and the ship, staggering in the water, threatened every instant to be swamped. The men now went to the captain and asked him what he proposed to do, for the ship could swim no longer. He asked them if they approved of his running the vessel on shore at all risks, to which they all agreed, crying out, "Anything to save our lives." It would have been of great importance to get ashore in an orderly manner; but this could not be done, in consequence of another blunder of the captain.

We had lost our long-boat and pinnace at Bengal, and the captain not taking the trouble to replace them, we had but one small boat left. In this juncture, an attempt was made to ease the vessel by cutting away the masts, and throwing everything overboard, hoping she would drive high on the beach. This failed, and now our only chance of getting through the breakers that dashed on the shore was by the small boat, and a raft made with some planks and yards.

While engaged making the raft, some of the natives, who were fishing saw our distress, and made a smoke to guide us to the shore ; but although this looked like kindness, we entertained a poor opinion of the intentions of the savages. The raft was finished that night, and it was arranged that the attempt to land should be made in the morning.

After a dismal night, day dawned, and all prepared to leave the ill-fated vessel. The first thing done was to send Mr. Pratt, our chief mate, and four men in the boat, with a long rope for a warp, to fasten on the land. A great sea constantly runs here upon the rocks, and before they got to land, their boat was staved in pieces; however, being pretty near it, by the help of some of the natives, who were negroes, they saved that part of the boat to which the rope was fastened. We had two English women on board; one of them would not venture on the raft, nor would the captain; but the other woman and about forty or fifty of us did: I stripped off all my clothes, but took two purses of money, and a silver cup, and tied them fast round my middle. We hauled by the rope toward the shore, but were no sooner among the breakers, than the first sea upset the raft, and washed us off: some swum to the raft again, but were soon washed off; and though the woman was drowning just by me, yet I could not save her. I sunk under every wave, and with great difficulty got on shore, as did every one else on the raft, except the woman. There was such a surf running, and the sea broke so high, that we durst not venture out with the raft again, which the captain perceiving, ordered the cable to be cut, and let the ship drive nearer the land, where she soon beat to pieces. The captain got on shore with his father's heart in his hand, which according to his request when dying, was put into a bottle, in order to be brought to England and buried at Dover.

At length they all got on shore on pieces of the ship, planks, etc., two men only excepted, who were drowned, and the woman before mentioned: the other woman escaped, though she was so full of water, as well as some others, that we were obliged to roll and rub them well, to make them disgorge the water: we laid them also before a great fire, made for that purpose, and in a little time they revived. We were in all above one hundred and sixty, including the Lascars.

The country now began to be alarmed, and we had already two or three hundred negroes flocking round us, picking up several pieces of silk and fine calicoes: the muslin they had little or no regard for. Our goods were driven ashore in whole bales; for what with saltpetre and other things, we reckoned there might be 300 tons left, after all that was thrown overboard at sundry times before.

One of the negroes brought an ox to us, and intimated by signs that we should kill him ; but we made signs to them again to shoot him for us, we having no ammunition. When one of them perceived this, he lent us his gun, ready charged, and with it one of our men shot the bullock dead on the spot.

It was extremely shocking to see the negroes cut the beast, skin and flesh together, then toss them into the fire, or ashes, as it happened, and eat them half-roasted. I shuddered for fear they should devour us in like manner; for they seemed to me to be a kind of cannibals, of whom I had heard very dreadful stories: everything, in short, appeared horrible to nature, and excited in us the most dismal apprehensions.

Being very much at the mercy of the barbarians, into whose hands we had fallen, they used no ceremony in taking possession of every article that had belonged to the ship. While some were busily engaged in opening our bales, and taking what they liked best, I observed that several of them regarded the iron they found much more than all those goods we usually look on as valuable, and took great pains to break all such pieces of timber as had iron in them. I broke open my chest, and took out only one suit of clothes, leaving the rest to those who had most mind for them.

Our shipwreck had been conducted with so little regard to future proceedings, or even the preservation of our lives against the attacks of the natives, that the whole company were now exposed to any fresh misery that might ensue. As I was a mere boy, and had no right to advise one way or another, I necessarily submitted to the decision of others. Our captain, whose rashness and folly had caused all our disasters, proved equally incompetent in this new posture of affairs. He could give no directions; and two days and nights were spent very miserably on the shore, without coming to any resolution, or knowing what to do.

On the third evening, about nine o'clock, we heard a man call out Hollo! at a great distance, like an Englishman, who, being immediately answered, came nearer, and asked who we were. Having given him the required information, he sat down with us by our fire, and told us the object of his visit. He was one of the crew of an English vessel, commanded by Captain Drummond, a Scotchman, which had been two months before wrecked on the island, and the captain and crew, including a Captain Steward, were now detained by the king of this part of the country, and would gladly make their escape. He, our visitant, whose name was Sam, had been deputed by the king to bring information as to who we were, and what we wanted. Sam further gave us an idea of the condition of things in Madagascar. The whole island, he said, which was as large as Great Britain, was altogether inhabited by negroes, forming a great many petty kingdoms, which were almost continually at war with each other. All were much on a level as to barbarism, but they were generally acquainted with the use of firearms and gunpowder, which, with other articles, they got from English, Dutch, and other traders, in exchange principally for slaves. The capturing of slaves, in order to carry on this trade, was a main cause of the numerous wars between the different kings and chiefs. The only king who possessed the inclination to help distressed English sailors was king Samuel, a man who had once been in Europe, and acquired some civilized habits; and although he had a great enmity to the French, he would have succored us had we put into Port Dauphine. Sam having made an end of his story, to which everybody listened with the utmost attention, we parted, and went with heavy hearts to our respective quarters, which were under the bushes. It was very late, and we endeavored to repose ourselves as well as we could. The pieces of muslin served us to spread on the ground for beds; but as for my own part, I could not close my eyes to rest. I now began to reflect on my former obstinacy and perverseness. The thought of my tender mother's begging me on her knees not to go to sea, gave me the most distracting torture. I could now see my error, and repent, but who could I blame but myself? Here were many poor men, who had no other way to live, but I was reduced to no such necessity: I ran headlong into misery, and severely felt the effects of it. Tears I shed in plenty, but could not with any justice complain of fate or Providence, for my punishment was but the natural result of my own ill conduct. We were all up by daylight, and most of my fellow-sufferers got as little rest as I; for the man's relation had made us give over all hopes of relief, and nothing but sorrow, distress, and despair, appeared in all its dismal forms in each man's face, according to his different constitution. We had saved neither arms nor ammunition, the want of which completed our ruin; for nearly one hundred and seventy of us would have made our way through that part of the country we wanted to travel, had we but wherewithal to defend ourselves.

About one o'clock in the afternoon, the king came down with about two hundred negroes. They brought no firearms with them, lest we should seize them by force, but they were armed with lances. As soon as we saw them approaching us, we all stood together in a body, with our captain at the head of us. When they drew near, he called Sam and asked him who was our captain. As soon as he was informed, he came up to him, and took him by the hand, and said in a familiar manner, Salamonger, captain; which is a term of salutation, much like our saying, Your servant, sir. The captain returned the compliment, Sam having informed him before in what manner he should behave himself to the king. His majesty brought with him four large bullocks, six calabashes of toake,(a kind of drink,) ten baskets of potatoes, and two pots of honey, all which he presented to our captain; and gave us, moreover, two or three earthen pots to dress our victuals in. We immediately roasted the potatoes. The king stayed two hours with us, before he withdrew to the cottage where he proposed to lodge that night, and asked several questions about our ship, and the manner of her being lost. He told the captain he was heartily sorry for his misfortune, though in my opinion, that was nothing but a compliment; for, as I found afterward, he was more brutish and dishonest than most of the other kings on the island; and his whole nation were clothed for many years out of the effects they saved from our wreck.

The next morning he paid us another visit, and then he told us that he expected we should prepare to go along with him to his town, and there we should remain till some ships should come to trade, when we might return to our own country. The captain suspecting this to be a mere artifice, told Sam to say that he would think of the proposal. Upon this the king departed, and gave us no further trouble at that time. As soon as he was gone, the captain called us all together, and in a very pathetic speech, addressed us as follows:—I am now on an equality with the meanest man here present; my fortune is as low, and my life is as little to be regarded; I do not pretend, therefore, to command, but to consult with you what is most expedient to be done in the present unhappy situation of our affairs. However, said he, I am happy in this, that though my own life and liberty are lost as well as yours, yet this misfortune is not any ways chargeable on me, for I would rather have kept on my course to the Cape of Good Hope in a leaky ship, than put in here; but you strenuosly opposed it; for death in my opinion is to be preferred to our present and prospective condition. In death, our sorrows would have ended; but now, who can tell the troubles and torments we shall yet undergo? (At this the tears stood in his eyes.) Consider, gentlemen, said he, we have neither arms nor ammunition wherewith to defend ourselves, and I have endeavored to prevail on the king to give us a passage through his country to a seaport, but in vain. Think of it, therefore, and consult your own safety as well as you can: be but of one mind, and I am ready to comply with anything you would have me do. As for my own life, I set no value upon it; it would not now be worth preserving, but for the hopes I have of being serviceable to my friends. Remember, I must return an answer to-morrow morning, and I will advise nothing, nor do anything without your concurrence.

We went together and consulted, as the captain advised, and came soon to an agreement, for the matter in debate lay within a small compass The king had refused to give us leave to go to a seaport, and we had no arms to fight and force our way, if we could have found it. We therefore determined to go quietly up the country with the king, to his place of residence, where we were in hopes of seeing and conversing with Captain Drummond, Captain Steward, and the other people, who, being gallant and courageous men, and by this time somewhat acquainted with the natives, might probably be capable of giving us some proper and seasonable advice.

Next morning the king paid the captain a visit; they saluted each other in the usual manner, and sat down together upon the sand, while we all stood round them. Soon after, the king ordered Sam to ask the captain if he was ready to go, for it would be best to walk in the cool of the morning, and rest at noon. The captain observed that he did not ask whether he was inclined to go or not, as might reasonably have been expected, since he pretended to give him time to consider of it, but peremptorily asked if he was ready to go. The captain answered that we were. At this the king seemed fully satisfied, and ordered Sam to tell us he would breakfast first, and advised us to do so too, that we might be the better enabled to perform our journey. We had little satisfaction, however, in eating and drinking, especially since the hour was come in which we were obliged to leave the seaside; and it galled us severely to think how we were forced up the country, like a flock of sheep, at the pleasure of a parcel of barbarous negroes, without any power to make terms for ourselves like men. The king having sent, the word was given to march. I was ready in an instant, for I carried nothing with me but what I brought ashore; but many of our people took pieces of silk and fine calico. We assembled together, and went to the place where the king's tent was pitched. We were no sooner come than he was for marching. We left the sea with heavy hearts, looking very wishfully back as long as we could discern it; and as often as we did, we observed the negroes hard at work breaking up our bales, and enriching themselves with the plunder of our goods. In short, they were so busy, that but few went back with the king. Our people were but ill disposed for traveling, since everybody was tired with working and want of rest. Many were lamed with hurts received in getting on shore; some were also without shoes, and most of us had but bad ones. Then, again, the country near the seaside, and some few miles further, is full of short underwood and thorny shrubs, which tore our clothes to rags; for the path was very narrow, and, before this accident, but little frequented; the ground also was sandy, so that when the sun was advanced pretty high, it scorched our feet to that degree that we were scarcely able to walk.

About noon we came to one of their small, mean villages, consisting of about eight or ten houses, or rather huts; for they were not above six or seven feet high, and about eight or nine feet in length, and their doors not above three or four feet high. Our people crept into these hovels to rest, and to see what they could meet with to refresh themselves. Some found honey, others milk, and others beef; for the king had given us free permission to take what eatables soever came to hand. The inhabitants were all absent, the men at the seaside taking advantage of the wreck, and the women and children fled into the woods at our approach. We passed several of these poor villages, but saw few of the people. Here we reposed till the heat was abated, when we made ourselves but a poor compensation by robbing them of their trifles, while they were enriching themselves with our most valuable commodities.

In the cool of the evening we marched again, and in a little time came to a more open and better road. As we were now some miles from the sea, the king left us, and went before to his seat, leaving us to march at our leisure, having taken care that we should not want provisions, and left his chief officer strict orders to supply us with whatever we wanted, and what the country could afford.

At night we came to another of these little villages, where we killed a bullock, and got a few earthen pots to cook our meat in. The water was very thick and nasty, they having none but what they brought from a great distance, out of holes and pits in the woods, and kept in calabashes, or long tubs, which hold about four or five gallons each: however, it served our purpose, for at that time we were not very curious. We reposed ourselves on the ground in the best manner we could, and rose the next morning by daylight. We had beef for our breakfast, without any bread, or roots, in the place of it, and our meat was full of sand: however, eating and drinking was the least of our concern at that time. We passed this day much after the same manner as the one before, with this difference only, that those who wanted shoes were sadly harassed in the woods.

On the third day of our march, we came to our journey's end. We were obliged to walk much faster than either of the two former, having more ground to traverse, and less time to do it in ; for we were ordered to be at the king's town before sunset. I missed one of my purses in this day's journey: the loss of it was not of any great importance to me at that time, for it would have been of little service to me had I kept it; but the loss of a medal afterward, which my dear mother had presented me with, as a testimony of her love, and a token to remember her, was no small addition to my other misfortunes.

The residence of this king is about fifty miles from the seaside; for I reckon we might travel sixteen or seventeen miles a day. It stands in a wood, secured with trees all round, which seem to have been planted there when very young: they grow very regular and tall, and so close together, that a small dog cannot pass between them. The outworks are likewise armed with large, strong thorns, so that there is no breaking through, or climbing over them. There are but two passages, or gates, which are so narrow that two only can go abreast. One of these is to the northward, and the other to the southward: the whole is about a mile in circumference.

When we came near our journey's end, we halted, while Sam went to inform the king of our arrival. We were ordered to wait till he was ready for our reception; our captain, too, put us into the best form he could, ordering all our baggage, and such things as our people brought with them, to be lodged under a tamarind tree, and three or four Lascars to look after them. The king soon sent for us, and we marched in order by fours. He was sitting on a mat, cross-legged, in the open air, just before the door of his palace, with a gun leaning on his shoulder, and a brace of pistols lying by his side ; his sons and kinsmen sat in the same manner on the ground, on each hand of him, armed with guns and lances ; the natives joined them on both sides, and formed together a semicircle ; most of these were likewise furnished with guns and lances. There were mats spread from one end of the people to the other for us to sit on ; so that when we had joined them, the assembly assumed a circular form. We were somewhat concerned to see them all thus in arms, till Sam informed us that they never go from one house to another without them. As soon as we were seated, the king (by Sam) assured the captain he was welcome, and sent for ten calabashes of toake; six he gave to our people, three to his own, and one he reserved for our captain and himself. He also sent for Captain Drummond, Captain Steward, and the rest of their company. Captain Younge arose to salute them; and after the usual compliments were passed, the captains sat down together. The king ordered a servant to pour out some toake into a clean earthen cup, which he kept for his own use, and drank it up without drinking to anybody, but ordered some more to be poured out for our captain in another cup; but as it was dirty, he refused it: the king asked Sam the reason of it, who told him the truth, so he sent a man immediately to wash it. The captain, indeed, expected to be served out of the king's cup, but Sam informed him that neither black nor white nor even his wives or children, ever drank out of his cup; and this is the general custom of the country.

When I saw the servant returning with the cup our captain had refused, I took out my silver one and presented it to him. After we had all drank out of it, the king wished to see it, and was so wonderfully pleased with it, that he desired to keep it; but the captain informed him that it was none of his, but belonged to a lad who was behind him. I called to Sam, and desired him to acquaint the king, that since so many people had drank out of it, I humbly conceived it could not be fit for his use. At this he and the people round him laughed heartily. He ordered me to stand up, that he might see me; however, I saved my cup this time. Night drawing on, he withdrew, ordering us a bullock for our supper. Notwithstanding his courteous reception of us, he would not trust us all to lie within the gates of the town. Our captain, Mr. Pratt, our chief mate, Mr. Bembo, our second mate, and myself, were the only persons who were so far indulged. We had a hutch ordered us next to that of Captain Drummond and his companions; but the rest of the people lay without the gates under the trees. In this manner we lived for some few days.

Every morning we went, as was expected, in a body to visit the king; but one morning he ordered Sam to inform us that he had an inveterate enemy to the westward, who had hitherto proved too powerful for him, but since his gods had been so indulgent as to send some white men into his dominions, he would embrace so favorable an opportunity once more to try his strength with our assistance. But in the meantime he should be obliged to distribute us among his sons, who lived at distant towns, not only for the convenience of providing for such a number of us, (there not being room enough in this town,) but to ease himself of a charge which was too great and burdensome for him to support alone. He also sent to me this night to beg the silver cup before mentioned, with which request (knowing it was in his power to take it by force, if he thought fit,) I readily complied. This unexpected separation was a terrible blow to us, and we returned to our cottages with heavy hearts, well knowing if we could not find out some way to prevent it, there were no hopes of ever getting off the island.

Hereupon the three captains, namely, Drummond, Steward, and Younge, with some of the chief of our people, entered immediately into a consultation about what was proper to be done in this emergency, and to make some bold attempt for our lives and liberty. Captain Drummond, as I heard afterward, was the person who proposed to take the king prisoner, and by that means to make their own terms with the natives.

Now Captain Drummond and some others were men of experience and undaunted resolution: our captain, indeed, had courage enough, but he was too young. However, the proposition was universally approved of, and the time and manner of the execution was fixed. I was too young to be admitted as one of the council, therefore I shall not pretend to relate what reasons were produced either for or against the proposal. I observed Captain Younge and Mr. Bembo to talk with great earnestness, but in whispers, and with the utmost precaution. As I was then a stranger to that design, I slept sound, till I was roused in the morning by a great and sudden noise in the town, occasioned by the plot being put in execution. Our people went as usual betimes in the morning to pay their compliments to the king; and while some of them were at the prince's house, the signal was given by one of Captain Drummond's men firing a pistol, at which the king was seized, and his son at the same time.

This instantly alarmed the whole town: I started up without my shoes, being frightened at the sudden outcry. Not knowing what was the matter, and seeing the negroes flocking out of the town, I ran with them, till I was taken notice of by one of our men, who called me back; and I was as much amazed as the natives to see the king, his consort, and one of his sons, with their hands tied behind them, under the guard of our people. They presently rifled the king's mansion-house, and every other place where they could find any agreeable plunder. We happened to find about thirty small arms, a small quantity of powder and shot, and a few lances. The natives, as I observed before, ran out of the town, but they did it with no other view than to procure assistance; for they soon alarmed the country, and returned with great numbers from all the adjacent towns, and immediately besieged us. They fired in upon us, and wounded one of our men in the groin, on which Captain Younge ordered Sam to tell the king if they fired any more, they would kill him that very moment. The king, hearing their resolution, called to his men, and desired them to desist, if they had a mind to save his life.

This attempt, indeed, was bold and hazardous, and some, perhaps, may censure it as criminal. I shall not say much in its defense: but since I have come to years of maturity, I cannot forbear reflecting that if nature, even in a Christian country, will rebel against principle, what will it not do for life and liberty, under the tyranny and oppression of a barbarous and savage nation? Be this as it may, we put ourselves in a posture of defense, and marched out of the town; six men under arms marched in the front; and in the body, where the king was, six went armed before him, and six behind; three before his son, and three behind; and six brought up the rear, in which were the Lascars. Captain Younge, out of compassion, would have released the queen, and let her go wherever she pleased, but she would not abandon her husband.

We had not gone above four miles on our march, before our wounded companion fainted, and not being able to carry him off, we were forced to leave him by the side of a pond of water, where, as I was afterward informed, they soon put him out of pain, by striking their lances into several parts of his body. Having marched about two or three miles farther, we got out of the woods, and found ourselves in a spacious, open plain, where we could see all around us, and soon found that our enemies were not only near, but numerous, and threatened immediately to attack us. We faced toward them, our armed men being in the front, with the king bound before them. Sam was ordered at the same time to tell him that our design was not to hurt either him or his son, nor to carry them into their enemies' country, but only to detain them as hostages for our safeguard while we passed through his dominions; and that as soon we came to the borders of Port Dauphine, we would let them go again, and give them back the arms and ammunition we had taken from them; but if the least violence was offered to us, we should sacrifice them both; and this we desired him to tell his people.

Hereupon he called one of his generals to him, assuring him that he should receive no harm. Accordingly he left his gun and lance behind him, and came to us, where he was informed, both by us and the king, of our resolution; upon which he told us there should not be a gun fired while we preserved the king alive, and gave him civil treatment.

This parley being over, we continued our march through the plain till near evening; many of us without shoes, as well as myself, and some sick, which obliged us to take up our quarters sooner than we would otherwise have done; so that every one was almost faint, and glad of rest. The king ordered Sam to tell us that an ox should be sent to us forthwith. We made a trench like a ring, in the midst whereof we planted the black king and his son: our captain and some few others were appointed as a guard over them: our armed men were divided into four parties, in order to secure us in the best manner they could. We had just finished our camp, when the officer who had been with us before, and three other men, brought us a bullock. He brought likewise some roasted meat in his hand, and a horn of water for the king; so we loosed our royal prisoners' hands, that they might feed themselves. They ate some small matter, and gave the remainder to Captain Younge.

While we were employed in killing the ox, we desired the king to send some of his people into the woods for some fuel to dress it, which he readily did; and they soon brought us sufficient for our purpose. But all this time we wanted water, and complained thereof to the king, who assured us that there was none to be got near that place by several miles, and that what small quantity was given him in the horn, was taken from that very pond where we left the wounded man, which could not be less than ten miles distant. This very much disheartened us; for we were parched with thirst, which was the more increased by the fatigue of our long march and the heat of the country. However, there was no help for us, and patience was the only remedy. When the king and his son had supped, we bound their hands before them, that they might sleep as easy as they could; so, after we had cut up our bullock, and divided it amongst us, we broiled and ate it, though with but little satisfaction, for want of water; and when we had made as good a supper as our unhappy circumstances would well admit of, we also used our best endeavors to repose ourselves. The three captains, however, agreed to watch alternately, and divided our people into three parties for that purpose. The king entreated his wife to go home and comfort his children, but more particularly recommended his beloved daughter to her care. She went at his request, but shed tears when departing, as did also the king and his son. Such of us as were not on the watch lay down; but we had a wretched night; for the ground was stony, and there was but little grass; and, what was still a greater affliction, we were excessively dry, and had nothing to quench our thirst.

At dawn of day we arose, which was the second day of our travel, and the better to support ourselves under the fatigue of it, we ate part of the remains of our beef; but it was a miserable repast, as we had nothing to drink. However, we put ourselves in the same order as we had done the day before, and went forward. The natives perceiving us in motion, moved too, but kept at a greater distance, and went into our camp after we had quitted it, to see what they could find; and their labor was not altogether lost, for many of our people thought proper to leave half those India goods they had brought out of the town behind them, that they might travel with less fatigue. We walked with more ease half this day than we did the day before, it proving cloudy weather, and cool. About noon, the general who had been with us before came with some roasted meat and a horn of water for the king and his son: as we did not loosen their hands, we were forced to feed them. The general ordered Sam to ask the captains if they would release the king for six guns. I perceived there was a debate between them and Mr. Bembo; some thinking the six guns would be of great service to us, especially as we should still have the king's son: others were of opinion that it would be more for our safety to keep the king: however, it was agreed at last that he should be dismissed. We informed the general, that if they would give us six very good guns, and promise on their honor not to follow us, but return with their king, we would let him go; and that as soon as we came to the river Manderra, which divided his dominions from those of Port Dauphine, we would release the king's son, and leave all their arms behind us.

The general was startled at this unexpected condescension of our people, and dispatched one of his attendants to the king's other sons, who were not far off with their army, to acquaint them with our proposal; and in half an hour's time, returned to us with six of the best guns. They made the more haste, lest our minds should alter: we kept them no longer in suspense than while we took the guns to pieces, to see whether they were in good condition or not; and finding them better than we could reasonably have expected in such a country, we released their king, and sent him away with the general. He took his leave of the prince, and went directly to the army. We were so near as to see the ceremony of his meeting with his sons, who fell down and embraced his knees, and, with all the earnestness imaginable, shed tears for joy. After they had kissed and licked his knees and legs for about five or six minutes, they arose to give his head officers an opportunity of paying the like homage; and after them, some others of an inferior station, who in general expressed a most sincere and passionate affection to his person, and showed all the demonstrations of joy imaginable on account of his return. This ceremonial being over, they all hallooed and fired their guns, as a public testimony of their joy and satisfaction.

We now walked away on our toilsome march, still retaining the prince a prisoner as a hostage. In the course of the day we were disconcerted to observe that a crowd still hung on our rear, and that this party came to a pause when we encamped for the night. Our sufferings were at this point considerably increased. We could find neither victuals nor water, and were so parched with thirst, that we crawled on the ground to lick the dew; and this was all the refreshment we could then meet with.

On the third day of our march we rose early, and put forward as well as we could. The negroes, who strictly observed our motions, were as ready as we; but we placed our armed men in the front, determined to make a bold push for it if they attempted to obstruct our passage. They divided, and let us proceed without molestation; and though we traveled all the morning, yet we met with nothing remarkable, till we arrived at a little round hill, whereon there stood a prodigious large tub, about six feet high, which held near a hundred gallons, and was full of toake. Our people were going immediately to drain it dry; but Sam threw it down, and spilt all the liquor, asking us, with some warmth, if we were so blind as not to see the plot that was laid for our destruction; for it was planted there to tempt us to drink, with no other intention than to poison us all, or, at least, to intoxicate us to that degree that they might rescue their prince without opposition, and murder us at their pleasure.

While we were reflecting on this extraordinary action, the general and two or three more came up to us, and asked Sam what reason he could offer for spilling the toake; to which he made no regular reply, but bid him be gone about his business. The general desired to speak with the young prince; and after a little discourse with him, directed Sam to acquaint Captain Younge, that if he should think fit to release the prince, they would give him three of the head men of the country in exchange. Under the delusive idea that they followed us only on account of the prince, and that, if we should release him, they would all return back, our captain complied with the general's proposition, and, in a short time, three men were delivered in exchange for the prince.

All arrangements for securing the three new hostages being made, we proceeded on our journey as well as men could without provisions, and were too soon convinced of Captain Younge's mistake; for the negroes, instead of retiring, approached nearer, and some marched before us, so that we expected every minute they would attack us. We had a young lad in our company, who lost his leg in Bengal. Notwithstanding he was well recovered, and supplied with a wooden one well fitted, yet it cannot be imagined that he should be able to keep up with us: for, being now surprised by their surrounding us, we doubled our pace, and, in short, were obliged to leave this poor lad behind us. We saw the barbarians come up with him, take off his wooden leg, and first insult him; then they thrust their lances into his body, and left him wallowing in his blood Being eyewitnesses of this act of inhumanity, and apprehensive of the like treatment, we hurried on as fast as our feeble limbs would carry us till sunset, when we came to a large tamarind tree, the leaves whereof, as they were sour, we chewed, to moisten our mouths. The fruit itself was not then in season.

The three negroes whom we had taken as hostages, observing what had passed, and thinking their lives in danger, called to Sam and the captains, and told them they had a scheme to propose, which would be for the safety of us all; which was this, that as soon as it was dark, we should keep marching on, as silently as possible, all night. The captains approved of this proposal, and ordered none of us to sleep, but to be ready as soon as the watchword was given. This was very grievous, considering how tired we were the day before; but we submitted cheerfully to anything that gave us hopes of escaping from the violent hands of those bloodthirsty barbarians. As soon as it was dark enough to conceal our flight, we assembled together, and took a considerable quantity of muslins and calicoes and hung them upon the bushes, that the spies, who we knew watched us, might not anywise mistrust our sudden removal.

We walked off accordingly undiscovered by them. Captain Drummond, however, being taken so ill that he could not walk at all, none of us being strong enough to carry him, we resolved to make the three negroes perform that office by turns. After we had thus traveled most part of the night, we came to a thicket among some cotton trees, where the man who had the charge of Captain Drummond threw him upon the ground, ran away into the wood, and we never saw him more. Upon this we had a more watchful eye over the other two, and led him whose turn it was to carry the captain with a rope about his neck.

Weak as we were, we traveled a great many miles that night, and were glad when the day broke upon us; for the negroes had told us before, that if we walked hard all night, we should be at Manderra river betimes in the morning. And their information was correct; for as soon as we came to a little hill, the sun then just rising, we had a prospect of the river, though at a considerable distance; however, the hopes we had of coming to it in a short time, and of getting water to quench our thirst, gave us no small pleasure, and our spirits began to revive at the very sight of it. It was some comfort, likewise, to think that the king's dominions extended no farther, notwithstanding there were no inhabitants to protect us within several miles on the other side. Some of our people who were more tired than the rest, took liberty to sit down to refresh themselves, as taking it for granted that the negro army would never come in sight of us again.

But this vain notion of being safe and secure too quickly vanished; for as soon as they missed us in the morning, they pursued us like so many beagles, and before we got within a mile of Manderra river, overtook us. Thereupon they began to butcher our men then resting under the trees, striking their lances into their sides and throats. Though I was one of those who could not travel well, yet there were twenty behind me: the woman whose life was preserved in our ship was next to me. I, seeing them kill our people in this barbarous manner, threw off my coat and waistcoat, and trusted to my heels; for the foremost of our people having passed the river, and I not being far off, took courage; but hearing the report of a gun, I looked back, and saw the poor woman fall, and the negroes sticking their lances in her sides. My turn was next, for the same negroes pursued me, and before I reached the brink of the river, they fired a gun at me, but I jumped in. Our men who had got safe over made a stand, in order to defend those who were behind; and notwithstanding the negroes followed me so close, I could not refrain from drinking two or three times.

Those who had got over now marched forward, and I kept up with them as well as I could. We had a wood to pass through, and the negroes, as soon as they saw us quit the banks, immediately crossed and pursued us. They got into the woods, and, firing behind the trees every now and then, they killed three or four of our men. We had not traveled above two miles in this wood, before we came to a large, sandy plain, to which we could see no end; and here they determined to stop our progress, since, if we went much farther, we should be within hearing of king Samuel's subjects, who were their mortal enemies, and would readily assist us. They divided themselves, therefore, into several bodies, in order to break in upon us on all sides; and we, being apprised of their designs, were resolved to sell our lives and liberties as dear as possible. Hereupon our captains put us in as good a posture of defense as they could, and divided the men who bore arms into four classes; one under the command of each of our three captains, and the other under Mr. John Bembo: such as had no arms, or were disabled, were covered in a little valley, and with them were the two negro hostages.

We had not above thirty-six firearms among us all, and not many more persons fit to fight, so that we were a poor handful to withstand an army of two or three thousand. When they found we made a stand, they did so too, and according to their wonted manner, where it could be done, three or four of them in a place threw up the sand before them, and being also beneath us, we could see only their heads. Their shot flew very fast over us, and we kept them in play from noon till six in the evening, by which time all our ammunition was spent. Those of us who had money made slugs of it; our next shift was to take the middle screws out of our guns, and charge our pieces with them. When we had used all these means, we knew not what to do further: now we began to reflect on those who advised us to deliver up first the king, and afterward his son, since the keeping of them would have been our principal safeguard. The two negroes in our custody expected no doubt every minute to be killed, as very justly they might; but as their death would be of no service to us, we did them no injury.

At length it was unanimously agreed that Dudey and her husband should be sent to the enemy with a flag of truce, not only to prolong the time, but to know what they further wanted; so we tied a piece of red silk to a lance, and sent them away. They kept firing at us all this time, not knowing what we meant by not returning it. They shot at those who carried the flag; but perceiving that they were not armed, the prince ordered them to cease. Dudey was interpreter, and told them that our captain was inclined to make peace with them, and to deliver up the two hostages, with the guns and ammunition we took with us, as soon as we were advanced a little further into the country. They said they would suffer us to go in the morning, in case we would deliver up our arms and the men, but not that evening, because it was dark. Their true reason was this: they knew, if we got away that night, we should send some of King Samuel's people, who were their bitter enemies, to be revenged on them for the ill-treatment we had met with.

With the vain idea of appeasing them, it was resolved that next morning we should give up our arms, Captain Drummond and some of his friends, however, protesting against the folly which the party were about to commit. Morning dawned, after a dismal night, bringing with it a day of sorrow. As soon as we could see, we missed Captain Drummond, Captain Steward, Mr. Bembo, Dudey, and her husband, and four or five more, who deserted in the night, without communicating their intentions to us. Now we plainly saw destruction before us, and the end of this miserable journey, which, after so bold an attempt, we undertook for the preservation of our lives and liberty: and a tragical one it was; for no sooner was it broad daylight than the negroes came up to us, and the prince had a short conference with Sam. Captain Younge asked him the purport of their discourse; he answered, they wanted to know what was become of Captain Drummond and the rest. The words were no sooner out of his mouth than one of the princes took hold of me, and delivered me to one of his attendants. There were three or four lads like myself, and much about my age, who were seized at the same time, and delivered to their people in the same manner, who bound our hands with cords.

There now ensued a scene of horrid butchery, every one of our unfortunate company, including Captain Younge, being killed on the spot. The bodies were next stripped of their clothing, and every article carried off as spoil. Little time was consumed in this tragical affair; for the savages expected that the subjects of King Samuel, roused by Captain Drummond, would soon be down upon them; and I afterward learned that such a friendly force actually came soon after our departure. In the attack which had been made on us, Sam contrived to escape, and returned with the negroes; whether he was ever sincere in his friendship for us, is doubtful; however, by our infatuated simplicity, we had been our own worst enemies.

I was now the captive of a naked savage, and was led away like a calf to the shambles, galled with cords, and not knowing what should be my fate. Other two lads were treated in the same manner, and soon we were parted by our respective masters. My master, or proprietor, as I may call him, was named Mevarrow; he was a chief of some consequence, or rather the king of a tribe, and his design was now to return home with his booty.

All the way we went, I was shocked in observing the mangled bodies of our men, which lay exposed under the broiling sun. When we reached the river we had crossed, I was so faint for want of victuals, having had no sustenance for three days, that I could scarcely stand on my legs. Though my master expressed some little concern for me, yet he would not bait till he was past the river; however, he ordered his people to stop at the first commodious place and make a fire; and now I was in hopes of some agreeable refreshment, for some of his servants had carried beef on their backs for that purpose. Though they cut it in two long pieces, with the hide, and dressed and ate it half roasted, according to their custom, and gave it to me in the same manner, yet I thought this contemptible food—and what a beggar in England would not have touched—the most delicious entertainment I ever met with. We rested here about an hour, when he to whose care I was intrusted made signs to know if I could walk; and as I was a little refreshed, I got up, and traveled the remainder of the day with more ease than I expected, since they walked but slowly, as I perceived, on purpose to indulge me.

At night, we came to a wood, the place appointed for our lodging, and there we met with three or four men whom my master had sent out a foraging, and they brought in with them two bullocks, one of which my master sent to his brother, for the use of him and his people, and the other was killed for us; for the army was now disbanded, and all were marching home with their respective chiefs to their own habitations. Here my master came to me and gave me a lance, intimating that I might cut out as much as I thought proper. I cut about a pound, without any part of the hide, which he perceiving, imputed it to my ignorance, and so cut a slice with the hide, and dressed it for me, which I ate with seeming thankfulness, not daring to refuse it. As soon as supper was over, each man pulled as much grass as was sufficient for himself to lie on: my guardian, however, provided enough for himself and me: I then reposed myself accordingly, and he lay by me; but his black skin smelled so rank, that I was forced to turn my back on him all night long. I had very little rest, for the ghastly spectacle of my massacred friends was ever before me, and made me start from sleep as soon as I closed my eyes.

At break of day we arose, and, after a short repast, marched on till noon, when we baited among some shady trees near a pond of water. While some employed themselves in kindling a fire, others were busy in digging up and down amongst the grass. I could not at first conceive what they were doing, but I soon observed one of them pulling out of the ground a long white root, which I found was a yam, having seen many of them at Bengal. They soon furnished themselves with a sufficient quantity. I perceived they grew wild, without any cultivation. Some of them were eighteen inches long at least, and about six or seven inches in circumference. They gave me some of them, which I roasted, and ate, with a great deal of pleasure, instead of bread with my beef. They are very agreeable to the taste, as well as wholesome food. We arrived that evening at a small town, which we no sooner entered, than the women and children flocked round about me, pinched me, struck me on the back with their fists, and showed several other tokens of their derision and contempt, at which I could not forbear weeping, as it was not in my power to express my feelings any other way; but when my guardian observed it, he came to my assistance, and freed me from my persecutors. All the houses that were empty were taken up by my master, his brother, and other head men, so that my guardian and I lay exposed to the open air. The ill treatment I met with from the women and children put a thousand distracting thoughts into my head: sometimes I imagined that I might be preserved alive for no other purpose than to be carried to the king and his son, who would, in all probability, be fired with resentment at our late seizing of them, and making them prisoners; then again I thought, that, to gratify their pleasure and revenge, they would order me to be put to death before their faces, by slow degrees, and the most exquisite torments. Such melancholy reflections as these so disordered me, that when once, through weariness, I fell into a slumber, I had a dream which so terrified me, that I started upright, and trembled in every joint; in short, I could not get one wink of sleep all the night long.

When it was broad daylight we marched homeward—for now I must call it so—and in three or four hours' time we arrived at a considerable town, with three or four tamarind trees before it. One of the negroes carried a large shell, which, when he blew, sounded like a postboy's horn. This brought the women to a spacious house in the middle of the town, about twelve feet high, which I soon perceived was my master's. No sooner had he seated himself at the door, than his wife came out, crawling on her hands and knees till she came to him, and then licked his feet; and when she had thus testified her duty and respects, his mother paid him the like compliment; and all the women in the town saluted their husbands in the same manner; then each man went to his respective habitation, my master's brother only excepted, who, though he had a house, had no wife to receive him, and so he stayed behind.

My mistress intimated by her motions that she would have me go in and sit down. Much serious discourse passed between my master and her; and though I knew nothing of what they said, yet, by her looking so earnestly at me while he was talking, I conjectured he was relating to her our tragical tale, and I perceived that the tears frequently stood in her eyes. This conference over, she ordered some carravances to be boiled for our dinner—a kind of pulse much like our gray peas: she gave me some, but as they had been boiled in dirty water, I could not eat them. She, perceiving I did not like them, strained them off the water, and put some milk to them, and after that I made a tolerable meal of them. She gave me not only a mat to lie down upon, but likewise a piece of calico, about two yards in length, to cover me. She intimated that she wanted to know my name, which I told her was Robin. Having received so much civility from my mistress, I began to be much better satisfied than I was at first, and then laid me down and slept, without any fear or concern, about four hours, as near as I could guess by the sun. When I waked, my mistress called me by my name, and gave me some milk to drink. She talked for some considerable time to me, but I could not understand one word she said. My master was all this time with his brother at the door, regaling themselves with toake.

Through the kindness of my mistress, who had herself been taken captive, and brought as a slave to my master's camp, I was less harshly treated than any of the other slaves in the establishment, of whom there were upward of two hundred. Perhaps, also, I was indebted to my want of bodily strength for not being put to excessive labor. Nevertheless, my fate was most distressing and hopeless. At night I slept in a hut without any furniture, and my clothes being taken from me, the only covering which I wore was a piece of cloth round the middle, like that worn by all the people in the country. Thus stripped of my apparel, and almost entirely naked, I was a miserable looking object; but I suffered less from the cold than heat. The sun beat on my body, blistering the skin, and covering it with freckles, while I was exposed at the same time to the bites and stings of insects, of which there is a vast variety in Madagascar.

I was first tried by my master as a laborer to hoe the weeds in the fields of carravances; but being awkward at that kind of work, I was made to attend on the cattle, drive them to water, and see that they did not break into any of the plantations. Beside this, I was obliged to drag home every night a tub of water for the use of the family, there being no water near my master's house. In my employment as a neat-herd, I had the society of other boys, also attendants on their master's cattle, and from these companions, who were natives of the country, as well as from others, I picked up a knowledge of the language, and was soon able to speak it so as to be understood.

After being some months in this kind of service, my master departed, with a numerous band of followers, on a warlike expedition. He was absent for more than a fortnight, and, at his return, made a triumphant entry into the town, amidst the firing of guns and blowing of horns. After Mevarrow, came his brother Sambo and the attendants, followed by the cattle which had been taken from the enemy; the prisoners of war, now become slaves, brought up the rear. The great man, my master, having halted, and seated himself in front of his house, his consort, attended by the women of the neighborhood, came as usual and licked his feet.

During this ceremonial my master, casting his eyes around, saw me at a distance, and called me to him. I approached him in a manner considered respectful, with my hands lifted up, as in a praying posture; but did not kneel down, as all the others did, having a conscientious reluctance to perform such an act. Whereupon my brutal owner flew into a rage, and reproached me for not paying him the same respect as his wife, mother, and others about him. However, I peremptorily refused, and told him I would obey all his lawful commands, and do whatever work he thought proper to employ me in, but this act of divine homage I could never comply with.

On this he fell into a violent passion, upbraided me with being ungrateful, and insensible of his saving me from being killed among my countrymen, and urged, moreover, that I was his slave, etc.; but notwithstanding all this, I still continued resolute and firm to my purpose. Whereupon he arose from his seat, and, with his lance, made a stroke at me with all his might; but his brother, by a sudden push on one side, prevented the mischief he intended. He was going to repeat his blow, but his brother interposed, and entreated him to excuse me; but he absolutely, and in the warmest terms, refused to forgive me unless I would lick his feet. His brother begged he would give him a little time to talk with me in private, which he did; and after he had told me the danger of not doing it, and that, in submitting to it, I did no more than what many great princes were obliged to do when taken prisoners, I found at length it was prudence to comply; so I went in, asked pardon, and performed the ceremony as others had done before me. He told me he readily forgave me, but would make me sensible I was a slave. I did not much regard his menaces; for, as I had no prospect of ever returning to England, I set but little value on my life. The next day I incurred his displeasure again, and never expected to escape from feeling the weight of his resentment.

My master then performed the ceremony of thanksgiving to God for his happy deliverance from all the hazards of war, and for the success of his arms; which is done by some silly adoration before a kind of household altar, accompanied with ridiculous ceremonies. Having performed his devotions, my master would have me do the same; but this I also firmly refused, and he was now more savage than ever. Taking hold of me by one hand, and with his lance in the other, he threatened instantly to sacrifice me. I expected nothing but death, and waited every moment in an agony for the mortal blow. Sambo, at this crisis, again humanely interfered, along with many others, all using their utmost endeavors to persuade him against so rash an action; but to no purpose; till his brother at last very warmly told him he would that minute depart, and see his face no more, if he offered to be guilty of such an act of inhumanity; and rose up to be gone accordingly. When my master saw his brother was going in good earnest, he called him back, and promised to spare my life, but assured him he would punish me very severely for my contempt of his orders. Sambo told him he should submit that to his own discretion; all he begged of him was, not to kill me. Upon this, by a secret sign, he advised me to kneel down and lick his feet, which I readily complied with, and asked his pardon. When I got up, I kneeled down to Dean Sambo of my own accord, and licked his feet, as a testimony of my gratitude and respect for thus saving my life a second time.

As soon as this storm was blown over, I was remanded to my former post of cow-keeper. I had a great deal of trouble sometimes with these cattle, for they are very unruly; and notwithstanding they are larger beasts than any I ever saw elsewhere of the kind, they are so nimble, that they will leap over high fences like a greyhound. They have an excrescence between their shoulders, somewhat like that of camels, all fat and flesh, some of which will weigh about three or fourscore pounds. They are also beautifully colored: some are streaked like a tiger, others, like a leopard, are marked with various spots. Here are, likewise, some sheep, with large heavy tails, like Turkish sheep—not woolly as ours, but more like a goat; and also a small number of goats, resembling those of other countries. There are, beside, plenty of hogs in the country, and immense swarms of bees. These bees produce a vast abundance of honey, from which the natives make their drink called toake.

[What with cow-herding, gathering honey, helping to build huts with wood and clay, and going sometimes, greatly against his will, on warlike or cattle-stealing expeditions, beside doing much thankless drudgery of a miscellaneous kind, Drury informs us that twelve years were consumed. Often in his hut, in the silence of night, he thought of his father, mother, and friends in England, and wept when he reflected on the hopelessness of his lot. He, however, felt more than he could well express, even by tears. Twelve years of slavery had changed him in a remarkable manner. He had forgotten his own language, and could no longer converse in English. The words stuck half-expressed on his tongue. From being a handsome English boy, he had grown to be a brown-skinned savage.

His feelings had been changed as well as his person; and in some of his habits he was little superior to the lower animals. Yet, as has been said, he sometimes wept, and never forgot his home. The recollection of his mother's tenderness could not be obliterated from his memory. It survived all the horrors of his hapless condition, and stimulated him to attempt his escape from an odious bondage.

He pondered long on the means of absconding; and, at length, by the friendly aid of a fellow-servant, he took to flight. His plan was in the first place, to reach the territory of a chief, called Afferrer, friendly to the whites, before his absence was discovered; and although this required great dexterity and toil, he effected the journey. Still, he was scarcely safe. His enraged master sent messengers to request that he should be delivered up as a runaway slave, and poor Drury trembled for the result. Afferrer appeared to be shocked at the proposal. He said that the idea of making a white man a slave was ridiculous, and that the refugee should remain with him as long as he pleased, or go wherever he thought proper. The men were therefore obliged to return disconcerted, and Drury was in the meantime secure. In this new home he was certainly not compelled to work as a slave, but neither was he altogether a freeman. The chief with whom he had taken refuge was pretty constantly at war, and his object was to make use of him in his expeditions. Constrained to appear satisfied, Drury lived with Afferrer two months, going with him on two excursions against his enemies. As this, however, was an employment not at all to the mind of the refugee, he took an opportunity of once more escaping. We continue the narrative chiefly in his own language.]

With a bundle of dried meat, which I had contrived to conceal, I set off on my journey, walking briskly all night, and keeping in a south-easterly direction, with the hope of reaching Port Dauphine. A great river, called the Oneghaloyhe, issuing in St. Augustine's bay, I was told had to be crossed on the journey. In the morning I saw certain mountains that had been mentioned to me; by this I perceived I had made considerable progress, and therefore would not conceal myself, as at first I proposed, but proceeded on my journey, looking sharply about me, in case of any lurking enemy. With little to fear, I went merrily on, singing Madagascar songs, for I had forgotten all my English ones. The bellowing of the wild cattle would now and then make me start, imagining they were my pursuers. When I came to a pleasant brook, I baited there, and at sunset I looked out for a covert in a thicket to lie in; but I could not find one near at hand, so I was contented to repose myself in the open plain, pulling up a sufficient quantity of grass for a bed and a pillow, and making a small fire to warm my beef. I did not think proper to make a great one, lest it should be discerned at a distance, for in the afternoon I observed some fires to the eastward of the mountain. I was disturbed in my sleep by night-walkers, whom I imagined were my pursuers, and accordingly I took up my lances in order to defend myself; but when I was thoroughly awake, I found they were only some cattle that snorted at the smell of my fire, and ran away much more afraid of me than I was of them.

The second day, in the morning, I stayed till the sun appeared before I moved forward, that I might not be deceived in my course. Nothing remarkable happened this day. I looked out early this evening for a lodging, the clouds gathering very black, and soon found a large thick tree, where I kindled a fire, warmed some meat, and hung up the remainder, to keep it as dry as I could, for I had nothing else that could be injured by the rain. At length it poured down, as I expected, in a violent manner, attended with thunder and lightning. It soon penetrated my roof; however, I crowded myself up together, with my head on my knees, my hands between my legs, and my little body-covering over my ears. The rain ran down like a flood, but, as it was warm, I did not so much regard it. In three or four hours it was fair weather again, and I laid me down and took a comfortable nap.

The next morning I dried my beef at a fire, which I made for that purpose, for it was the third day after it was killed; but I was very careful of it, not knowing how to kill more at that time; so I put it up in clean grass, and marched forward. The mountains over which I was to pass seemed very high, craggy, and thick with wood, and no path nor opening could I find. It looked dismal enough, but I was determined to run all hazards. Those mountains seemed to me to traverse the island, and appeared, as we call it at sea, like double land—one hill behind another. I saw nothing all this day but a few wild cattle, and now and then a wild dog. The weather was fair, and I slept sound all this night.

The fourth day I walked till noon, at which time I baited; my beef was now but very indifferent. In the afternoon, as I was walking, I saw about a dozen men before me; upon this I skulked in a bush, peeping to observe whether they had discovered me; but I was soon out of my pain, for they were surrounding some cattle, a good way to the westward, on a hill. I was likewise on another hill, so that I could see them throw their lances, and kill three beeves, which I was well assured were more than they could carry away with them at once. I stayed where I was, proposing, when they were gone, to have some beef. To work they fell immediately, cutting up the beasts, and each man made up his burden, hanging the remainder up in a tree, that the wild dogs might not get it, and went home to the eastward. As soon as they were gone, and I had looked well about me, I threw away my bad meat, made up to the tree, and took as much as I could well carry. Away I marched with my booty toward the mountains, not daring to rest, lest they should return and discover me. In less than an hour I reached the foot of the hills in the thick woods, and finding no path, nor track of men, nor any hopes of any, not knowing what to do, I determined to go through all; but as I happened on a run of water, I took up my quarters near it, made a fire, cut some wooden spits, and roasted my beef. I kept my fire burning all night, lest the foxes should come and attack me.

The next morning I made up my package with grass, binding it with the bark of trees, and moved forward up the hill. My burden was now much lighter. In an hour, though I could find no path but what some swine had made, I got to the top of it. I climbed a high tree to take a survey; but could discover no entrance, nothing but hills and vales, one beyond another; a cragged, dismal desert was all that presented itself to my view. I would have descended, had I not been in danger of being seen by the hunters; beside, I could not tell which way to look, whether east or west, for the proper pass; so setting a lance up on end, I turned the way it fell, though I imagined it was due north, or rather somewhat to the eastward. However, superstition prevailed where reason was nowise concerned, for I was as likely to be right one way as another; and in case I went to the northward, so long as I knew it, I must go as often as I could to the westward, as sailors are forced to do, run their latitude first, and their longitude afterward. I went down this hill, and up another, which was about an hour's walk; but when I came to descend this, it was right up and down. Without due thought, I threw down my lances, hatchet, and burden, thinking to descend by a very tall tree, whose top branches reached close to the brow; but I could not do it. However, I made ropes of the bark of a tree, and fixing them to the strongest branches, I slid down, I dare say, no less than thirty feet, rather than I would lose my lances and other materials. I passed over a fine spring and run of water in the vale. Though the hill on the other side was a craggy, steep rock, I found a way to ascend it; and on the top, climbed another to take my view; but had the same dismal prospect. Here I dug faungidge, it being sunset, and seeing a hole in a large rock, I had thoughts of taking up my lodging there; but peeping in, on a sudden I heard such an outcry, which, with the echo in the rock, made so confused a noise, that I knew not what it could be. My fears prevailed, and I imagined it might be pursuers, for it drew nearer and nearer; so, setting my back to a tree, with a lance in each hand, I waited for the murderers, when instantly came squeaking toward me a herd of wild swine, which ran away more terrified than myself. After I was well recovered from my fright I made two fires, for fear of the foxes, and then laid me down on my stony bed, for here was no grass.

The next morning, which was the sixth day, I made a hearty meal on roots and beef, and, the hill extending north and south, I went straight on till it declined gradually into a valley, in which was a small river that ran westward. By the time I arrived at the top of the next hill it drew toward evening, for I was not much less than two hours in ascending it; and yet, considering my burden, though it was not very heavy now, I went at a good pace. As I was looking out for a commodious lodging—that is to say, a place with the fewest stones in it—I discovered a swarm of bees; this was a joyful sight, for it was food that would not spoil with keeping. I soon cut down a tree, and smoked them out.

I made such a hearty meal this night of honey and beef, that I slept too sound, insomuch that I was waked with a severe mortification for my thoughtless security. A fox caught hold of my heel, and would have dragged me along; whereupon I started, and catching up a firebrand, gave him such a blow as staggered him; but as soon as he recovered he flew at my face. By this time I was upon my feet, and recovered one of my lances, with which I prevented him from ever assaulting me more; but his hideous howling brought more about him. I saw three, whose eyes sparkled like diamonds: however, they kept at a distance; for, with some light, dry wood, that lay near me, I made a blaze directly, in order to keep a flame all night; but did not wake to renew it, as I ought to have done; so that both my fires being almost reduced to ashes, one of them boldly ventured between them; and it was very happy for me that he did not seize upon my throat, for when men have negligently slept where they haunt, I have known them meet with such a mischance. After I had made up my fires, and put my enemies to flight, I examined my heel, and found two large holes on each side where his teeth had entered. I bound it up in the best manner I could, and making a great fire, threw the fox upon it by way of resentment. I had not that pleasure in eating my breakfast this morning I had in my last night's supper; beside, my beef was now a little too tender; however, as I had honey enough for a week, and here were good roots in plenty, I did not concern myself much about it.

I walked on the seventh day, and though I favored my lame foot as much as I could, yet I rested but once all day. This way happened to be plain and easy. At evening I came to a place where lay several bodies of trees which were dead and dry. Thinking this, therefore, a proper lodging, I made four very large fires, sat me down to supper, and afterward ventured to go to sleep with all those fires round me. But my heel now became so painful, and was swelled to that degree, that I could not go forward the next day; but as there was faungidge enough within twenty or thirty yards of me, I dug up several, and determined to continue here till my foot grew better. My beef was soon gone, but faungidge was both meat and drink to me. I saved part of my beef-fat to dress my heel with, which, as I gave it six days' rest, took down all the swelling During this time I made such large fires every night, that, could they have been seen, were like those of an army. I had not far to go for wood, or anything else that I wanted, or at least that I could anywise expect in such a place.

Proceeding on my journey, and exposed, day after day, to accidents, fatigue, and often hunger, I at length, on the morning of the twenty-third day, had the joyful sight of the Oneghaloyhe, a river as broad as the Thames at London. All day I spent in contriving how I should cross so broad a stream without a canoe, and lay down at night still uncertain what I should do. In the morning I thought of looking out for some old trees, or branches that were fallen; and in a short time I met with several that were fit for my purpose—not only great arms, but trunks of trees broken off by tempests: these I dragged to the river-side. In the next place, I made it my business to find out a creeper, which is as large as a withy, but, twining round trees, is very pliant. I lopped off the superfluous branches from six long and thick arms of trees, and placing three at bottom and three at top, I bound them together, making what we call in the East Indies a catamarran. I built it afloat in the water, for otherwise I could not have launched it, and moored it to a lance, which I stuck in the shore for that purpose. I then fixed my package, in order to preserve it as dry as I possibly could, as also my hatchet and my other lance; after that I made a paddle to row with. Then I pulled up my lance, and kept it in my hand to defend myself against the alligators, in case any of them should assault me; for I was informed they were very numerous and very fierce here. It blew a fresh gale at west against the stream, which in the middle made a sea, and gave me no small concern; for I was in great danger of being overset, and becoming a prey to the alligators. It pleased God, however, to protect me, and I landed safely on the other shore. This being a pretty good day's work, I determined not to go much further that evening before I took up my lodging.

[Traveling in the manner he describes, Drury had at length the good fortune to fall in with different tribes friendly to the English, among whom he lived for some time, but still watched by his jealous entertainers. The great man with whom he latterly lived was named Rer Moume, and by him he was kept two years and a half, during which an incident occurred that led to his removal from the island. The court of Rer Moume being visited by a person named William Thornbury, connected with the trade carried on upon the coast, Drury endeavored to interest him in his behalf; nor was he unsuccessful. After a lapse of many months, two ships arrived at a place called Yong-Owl to trade.] This (continues Drury) I was overjoyed to hear, and flattered myself that William Thornbury had not forgotten me. They stayed there for several days, and slaves were sent to be sold, and guns and other goods were returned for them. I was at a loss how to break my mind to Rer Moume, hoping he would say something to me of his own accord; but as I was sitting with him one evening, two men came in with a basket of palmetto leaves sewed up, and delivered it to the prince, who opened it, and, finding a letter, asked the men what they meant by giving him that. The captain, they said, gave it to us for your white man, but we thought proper to let you see it first. Rer Moume now handed me the packet, which, to my great surprise, contained a letter from Captain William Macket, directed *To Robert Drury, on the island of Madagascar.* I opened it, and the contents were to the following effect:—"That he had a letter on board from my father, with full instructions, as well from him as his owners, to purchase my liberty, let it cost what it would; and in case I could not possibly come down myself, to send him word the reason of it, and what measures he should take to serve me."

Rer Moume perceived that my countenance changed while I was reading the letter, and asked me what was the matter. I told him that the captain desired to speak with me, and that my father had sent for me home, and hoped he would be pleased to give his consent. How do you know all this? says the prince, can you conjure? Then, turning to the messengers, Have you, pray, heard anything like this? Yes, said they, it is all the discourse at the seaside, that Robin's father sent both these ships for him. Rer Moume took the letter, and turning it over and over, said he had heard of such methods of conveying intelligence to one another, but never actually saw it before, and could not conceive what way it could be done without conjuration. I endeavored to demonstrate to him, as well as I could, how we learnt in our infancy the characters first, and then we put them together. But, says he, I presume you have no inclination to leave us now, since you live here so much at your ease? You have several cattle and a slave, and if you shall want more, you shall have them. These offers I of course put aside, and besought him to let me go. I said that if he thought proper to demand any consideration of the captain for my freedom, it should be paid. Rer Moume answered, that if I wished to go, he should take nothing for my release; but that if my friends would make him a present of a good gun, he should accept of the favor, and call it *Robin*, in remembrance of me. This generous answer gave me such joy, that I immediately kneeled down and licked his feet with the utmost sincerity, as justly thinking I could never sufficiently express my gratitude. He would not dismiss me instantly, but did in a day or two after, and ordered the messengers to be taken care of in the meantime.

How joyful were my feelings when I at length departed, and came in sight of the seacoast, with the huts which had been erected for trading with the commanders of the vessels. At these huts, or factory, as I may call it, I met Mr. Hill, the steward of the Drake, Captain Macket's ship, and two or three more of the crew, who took me for a wild man; and in a letter which Hill sent off by a canoe to the captain, he told him the wild Englishman was come. I desired him to say I could speak but little English; and for several days I was frequently puzzled for words to express my meaning.

[A few days after this, Drury was taken on board of their vessel, which sailed for England; on his arrival he had been absent from his native country about seventeen years, of which fifteen had been spent in captivity. His pleasure was greatly damped by the intelligence of the death of his father and mother, grief for his loss having for years preyed upon their spirits.]

INCIDENTS

IN THE

LIFE OF A YANKEE SAILOR,

AS DETAILED BY WILLIAM NEVENS, IN HIS

FORTY YEARS AT SEA.

I WAS born in Danville, Maine, A.D. 1781, and spent the time of my youth to the age of seventeen, much in the manner of other children. While young, the peculiar cast of my mind was displayed by the pleasure which I felt in listening to stories of the sea, in reading accounts of distant countries, and probably the earnest desire which I had of seeing and knowing all these things, influenced me in my course.

Being by trade a carpenter, I one day went to Bath to purchase some tools. While rambling about the wharves to see the shipping, I was accosted by a gentleman, who proved to be the captain of a new brig, just from Liverpool. He inquired of me if I would like to take a trip to sea. Not feeling much inclined to drop my former occupation for another upon so short notice, I answered in the negative. Not satisfied with this answer, he continued his persuasions, peppering them occasionally with fine stories of a seafaring life—many of which I found quite the reverse in subsequent years—and in conclusion offered me ten dollars to go to Boston by the run. As money was then a *cash* article with me, this *argument* was not to be withstood; I therefore closed the bargain, went on board, and, all things being ready, we set sail June 15th, 1799. And the next day, at ten o'clock, A. M., we were in Boston harbor. This was my first trip, and little did I, a thoughtless boy, think that it would lead to such a result. I was then paid off, and was immediately offered one dollar per day, to stay and cook for the crew, while discharging the cargo, which I accepted, and remained here eight days, at the end of which I found myself the possessor of eighteen dollars, which I had earned in less than ten days. The next morning, as I was proceeding leisurely along, at the head of Long Wharf, fingering my change, and thinking how I might expend it to the best advantage, I was aroused from my reveries by a call from the opposite side of the street. Turning my head, I beheld an old tar, leaning against a grog-shop for his mainstay, who, on looking up, roared out at the top of his voice, "Hello! shipmate, heave to." Upon this, I crossed the street, and asked him what he wanted. After some *palaver*, he asked me if I wanted to ship. I answered that I had not thought of it. In return, he stated that wages were good, and that I could not do better than to take a trip to the West Indies, in the brig Daniel and Mary, of Newburyport. The desire of seeing these picturesque islands, and of visiting that land which first greeted the eyes of the immortal Columbus, at once overpowered my doubts, and I answered that I would go, provided I could get wages to suit me.

He now took me to the counting-house of the owners, and introduced me to the captain in the following words: "Here is a fine chubby fellow for you, who thinks he should like to take a trip to the land of sharks, and he looks like a right chap."

"What do you ask a month, my lad?" said the captain.

I told him I did not know how much I could earn.

"Well," said he, "Perkins," (which was my conductor's name,) "I will leave it to you, if the young man is willing." To which I readily assented. After eyeing me closely, fore and aft, he said that I could earn eighteen dollars.

"Will you go for that?" the captain asked.

I replied in the affirmative, and having pocketed a month's pay in advance, signed the shipping papers of the brig Daniel and Mary, Newburyport, of the firm of Sweet and Parley, and bound to the West Indies.

You may be assured that I was well satisfied with this turn in my affairs: eighteen dollars, and an opportunity to see the world, being much more satisfactory than nine dollars per month, which was all that I could command as a carpenter. After having dispatched a letter to my parents, informing them where I was, and what were my intentions, I proceeded to lay in a stock of summer clothing, a trunk, bed, blankets, and other necessary articles, and then went on board, in company with the captain, whose name was McFarly. The brig was then lying at anchor, well up the south side of Long Wharf, with no soul on board. The captain having unlocked the cabin, told me to put my trunk in there, the floor of which was completely covered with the ship's stores, such as rum, molasses, tea, coffee, etc. He then directed me to make up my berth in the steerage, and, having struck a light, went on shore, and left me to *fix* things as I could. After I had made arrangements, as I thought, satisfactory to the captain, I resolved to satisfy myself, and helped myself to bread, cheese, and other eatables, not forgetting a glass of '*snap-eye*,' to wash it down with. My external and internal condition having been thus duly considered, I had nothing to do but meditate upon the "change that had come o'er the spirit of my dreams," in the short space of ten days.

Nothing worthy of notice occurred, until our arrival at Port-au-Prince, July 26th. The Island of St. Domingo—now Hayti—was at this time convulsed by civil commotions. It was but a short period after the massacre of the whites, the horrors of which are too well known to be recapitulated. A war of extermination raged between the blacks and mulattoes, the former occupying the north side of the Island, and the latter the south side. An embargo had been laid upon the ports occupied by the blacks, in order to starve them into submission; and this had just been taken off.

While lading here, I had frequent opportunities of seeing the barbarity of the blacks toward their prisoners. Fears were entertained that the mulattoes would attack the city of Port-au-Prince, therefore we lay at anchor a short distance from the shore, with the stern warped in and moored. Beyond us, lay an old French frigate, converted into a prison-ship, which received a body of prisoners every day. When this prison became crowded, they were taken out, the oath of allegiance administered to such as would receive it, and the remainder were shot. Being on shore one morning, I witnessed the execution of ten in this manner. A few days after, several were executed in a different way. A lighter was hove out, and an old twenty-four pounder hoisted out over the side, about five feet above the wale, to which eighteen or twenty victims were triced, when the tackle was cut, and the gun tumbled into the sea, dragging with it the unfortunate prisoners. This took place immediately before our brig, and the water was so clear that I could see the miserable beings laying upon the bottom. Having at length completed our cargo, which consisted of coffee and sugar, we set sail in company with several other vessels, under convoy of the United States frigate Washington; and September 15, arrived at Boston, after a passage of twenty-one days.

I then bought me a suit of clothes, and resolved to act the gentleman; but found the business duller than I had supposed—moreover, I found that there still reigned in my breast the same ardent desire of seeing the world. I therefore, in a few days, shipped on board the Essex, bound on a whaling voyage to the South Sea. The crew was shipped on shares, with fifty dollars paid in advance, and consisted of forty hands. About the last of October, 1799, all things being ready, we put to sea, with a fair wind, and flattering prospects of a fine voyage. Our captain was Joseph Kilby, a fine, gentlemanly appearing person, and a thorough seaman. The first mate was named Haskell, a Scotchman, who had formerly been a lieutenant in the British navy, and master of a Guineaman, and was, in my estimation, one of the greatest villains that ever trod a deck. The ship was armed, on account of the war between the United States and France. Still, we were obliged to keep a sharp look-out for French privateers, and were trained to the guns every day, in complete man-of-war style. Nothing of a hostile appearance, however, troubled us, and as we were now drawing near the line, preparations were made to introduce about fifteen green hands to his majesty, Neptune, the sovereign of the ocean. For this purpose, the day before crossing the line, about twenty barrels of apples were hoisted on deck, overhauled, and the rotten ones thrown into some flour barrels, while those that were sound were returned below. The next day, about one o'clock, P. M., all the green hands were sent below to clean the forecastle, where they were immediately secured by closing the hatches. One of the whale-boats was then hoisted out of the launch, lashed to the starboard side, and filled with water. In the meantime, the gunner, who personified old Neptune, the ruler of the deep, horribly disguised, proceeded over the head of the vessel, and after having been thoroughly drenched with water, appeared coming in over the bows, as well soaked as if he had just sprung from the bottom.

Armed with a trident in one hand and a speaking trumpet in the other, he addressed the captain in the following terms:

"Ship ahoy! from whence came you?"

"From Boston, and bound to the South Pacific Ocean, on a whaling voyage. Pray, what do you wish here?" replied the Captain.

"I came on board to see if any of my children here have not been initiated."

"There are none here."

His majesty, however, was not to be deceived, but soon smelt them out, and one by one they were hauled forward, and shaved with the hoop of an old barrel for a razor, and a precious mixture of tar, pitch, lime, and whitewash for soap-suds. As soon as this ceremony was over, about a dozen sailors, with each a bucket of water, proceeded to wet the officers, as is customary on such occasions, who heeled it for the cabin; but in their haste, the captain, two mates, and steward, got completely jammed up in the companion-way, and before the snarl could be well cleared, their capital extremities were smoothed down with about fifty bucketsfull of the trident king's element, much to the glee of the sailors, who delighted in this spargefaction of their officers.

The rotten apples were next called into requisition, which flew in all directions, until the vessel and crew were as completely bedaubed as one could wish. But as all visits must come to an end, so must Neptune's. Therefore the head pumps were set to work, and soon all things looked trim again. The rest of the afternoon, it being calm, was spent in drinking lemon-punch, singing songs, and spinning yarns. [There are records of this custom of the "baptism of the line" as far back as 1712. It probably originated in the love of fun and frolic, for which sailors are so peculiar, and may have been designed with a view to relieve the tedium and monotony of a long sea-voyage, amid the calms which prevail in the region of the equator. The observance is now gradually falling into disuse.] The next morning, a favorable breeze springing up, we shaped our course for the Cape de Verde Islands, and the first land we made was St. Jago. From here we took our departure, and steered for St. Augustine.

Soon after our arrival at St. Augustine, the ship was overhauled and condemned. She had formerly been a whale-ship belonging to Salem, and after lying in port about two years, had been fitted up with a new deck and bulwarks, brought to Boston, and sold. Being now about to separate, the crews of the American vessels in the harbor resolved to have a grand supper on shore. I had in my chest one hundred and ten dollars, five of which I took to defray the expenses of the night; and about dark we were all assembled, each armed with a club to keep off press-gangs. Having passed the greater part of the evening merry making, myself, with three others, walked down on the beach, to enjoy the cool sea-breeze, and drive off the effects of our tamarind punch, where we were suddenly surrounded by an officer and ten or twelve armed men, who very unceremoniously bundled us into a boat and pulled off. There were eight or ten more in the boat, who appeared to be conditioned like ourselves. After winding our way among the different vessels in the harbor, we were pulled along side of an armed ship, and ordered on board. Inquiring, I found that I was on board his Britannic majesty's sloop-of-war Cayenne, and that they had, according to the principles of John Bullism, taken me, without inquiring as to the character I sustained, into his majesty's service.

In the morning, we were all taken aft and overhauled; and here you may see a specimen of every day tyranny exercised, at that time, upon American citizens. The captain of the Cayenne asked me my name, and on answering that I was an American, he demanded to see my protection. I took it from my pocket, and gave it to him. After looking at it, he said, "You are an Irishman. What business have you with a protection? There are plenty of Nevenses in Ireland, but there never was one *born* in America." He then tore up my protection, and threw it overboard, stating that he wanted men, and should keep me. When I found that right was of no avail against might, I sent, by a bum-boat, a note to Captain Kilby, stating my situation, and asking his assistance. Accordingly, about eleven o'clock, he came on board, and demanded me as an American citizen; but the British Captain swore that he knew my father in Ireland, that I was a —— Irish rebel, and ordered Captain Kilby into his boat. Finding that he was determined to retain me, I requested Captain Kilby to take home my chest and bedding, and if, at the expiration of a year, I did not return, to send them to my parents. Having made these dispositions, I bade adieu to liberty, and settled myself to the consoling prospect of serving Great Britain a few years for nothing.

Cases of impressment were not then of rare occurrence. Beside myself, there were eight or ten American born citizens in this same sloop-of-war; and there was not a vessel in the British Navy but what had more or less on board. Many escaped; but many more were obliged to endure servitude until the commencement of the late war, when thousands surrendered themselves as prisoners of war, rather than fight against their native land. But some were not allowed this, and were compelled to serve the enemy under the ignominious lashes of that instrument of torture, the cat-o'-nine-tails.

Completely disheartened, about one o'clock in the afternoon I heard the coarse tones of the boatswain, calling, "All hands up anchor, ahoy!" and went aft to help man the capstan bars, and heave up the anchor. We were soon under weigh—the Cayenne, having the leeward station, was bound to Surinam. When about ten days out, we fell in with the American sloop-of-war Moreland, Commodore Rogers, under the following circumstances. About sunset, saw a ship running from us, and the captain expressed his fear that it was a French frigate that was cruising in this quarter, since we could not muster more than ninety men. Commodore Rogers was cruising for this same Frenchman, and had seen us long before we saw him, and to give us no alarm had run from us. As soon as it was dark, he tacked ship and stood for us; and while we were gogging on, in a comfortable drizzle of rain, about ten, what should we see but a large ship sweeping down across our bows, with her ports up, lanterns lighted, and men at their quarters, all ready to give us a broadside.

The lieutenant, in a fright, ran down and called the captain, who came up and ordered the boatswain to pipe all hands to their quarters; but before this could be done, Commodore Rogers hailed, "What ship is that?" To which the captain of the Cayenne answered, in true Yankee style, by asking who he was. "The United States ship Moreland." This answer calmed the fears of our heroic captain, since he was intimately acquainted with the American commodore. He now had his gig lowered, and was pulled on board of the American vessel, and stopped the remainder of the night. About sunrise, the lookout on board the Moreland discovered a sail right ahead, and in two minutes her canvas was spread, and she was darting along, with a fresh breeze, in full chase, leaving our captain to make his way on board in his gig. We also made sail, but at eight o'clock the Moreland was hull down ahead of us. The captain of the Cayenne observed to the first lieutenant, "These Yankees have deuced fine ships for sailing, but they do not know how to work them." "Don't know 'bout that," replied the lieutenant, who was willing to give every one his due; "if we had been an enemy, he would have shown us, last night, how to work ship, and would have blown us out of the water before we could have brought a gun to bear." The stranger was soon out of sight, and we saw no more of her until we had brought to anchor in Surinam river, when she came in, and anchored close by us.

After lying here about a month, we set sail, and on the 20th of April arrived at St. Kitts, and cast anchor about three miles from the shore. This was done to prevent the crew from deserting. About half way between us and the shore lay the American sloop-of-war Baltimore. I here resolved to seize the first opportunity to attempt an escape. I considered myself quite a swimmer, but had never swum any great distance. There were also plenty of sharks, but I thought it no worse to be eaten by the sharks than to spend my life in British servitude. At length, one dark, stormy night, when no one was on deck but a sentinel, I crept into the head, divested myself of my clothing, threw over the swab rope, let myself down, and struck off for the Baltimore. The wind was fresh, and on my starboard beam, so that instead of making the sloop, I found that I was half a mile to the leeward, and to reach her I would be necessitated to beat up against wind and tide. I therefore abandoned my original intention, and put for the shore. After I had been in the water for more than two hours, and was almost exhausted, I came along side of a London brig, and climbed up her cable on board. There was but one man on deck, who, after listening to my recital, gave me a jacket and pantaloons, and also a glass of grog, which refreshed me much. He then informed me that I was not safe there, for his captain had been an officer in the British Navy, and that, but a short time previous, two sailors had swum on board, whom he had taken in his boat, and returned to the vessel from which they had deserted.

Under these considerations, I thought proper to find some other shelter; therefore, after resting about half-an-hour, I threw off the clothes which he had so kindly given me, and once more committed myself to the waves. At length, when almost exhausted, I reached another brig, with a boat moved under her stern, into which I climbed, and from thence went upon deck, where I found the foremast men sitting on the main-hatch, drinking and singing, although it was near twelve o'clock. The mate, who was walking the deck, upon discovering me sung out, "Who's there?" "A friend," I responded. "A friend in distress, I should think," he returned, "since you are scudding under bare poles." He then gave me his jacket, and ordered one of the men to bring more clothing for me. In the meantime, he mixed a pint of weak sling, and told me to drink it, a little at a time. When I was somewhat revived, I related my story, and found that I was among friends.

On the following morning, I was called into the cabin by the captain, who, after inquiring into my affairs, told me that, as he had a full crew, he did not want me, but that his brother had written to him from Tetollen. to ship a couple of hands for him, and if I would go, he would take me to that place. The vessel in which I then was, was the Sally, of Greenock, Scotland, Captain Walker, and was about to join the convoy for home. In three days we sailed for Tetollen, and on our arrival I found that the captain's brother had shipped all his crew, and did not want me. Here now was a *pickle*. The captain was unwilling to take me, but said he would set me on shore; and this I did not at all relish, for there were several men-of-war in the harbor; and as I had no protection, I should be impressed. The brig lay about four miles from the town, in the passage between two small rocky islands. As the captain expected every moment to hear the signal gun from the commodore, for getting under weigh, and refused to take me with him, I told him to land me on one of these islands, and that I would run the risk of being taken off after the fleet had sailed. I was rowed to the island by two stout, kind hearted Scotchmen, who appeared to have a good deal of compassion for me, particularly when we came to the island, which was about an acre over, sprinkled with lime bushes, and not a drop of water to be found

This, I thought a little harder than anything I had yet seen; for if I was not soon taken off, I must inevitably perish by hunger or thirst. A length, the boat returned to the vessel, and when the sailors on board had learned my situation, they refused to leave unless I was taken on board. Presently, the admiral fired the signal for getting under weigh, but the sailors would not budge an inch to heave up the anchor, until a boat had been sent and taken me off, when they appeared as willing as ever.

Soon after we had cleared the harbor, a small brig ran along side, which the captain hailed, and found her bound to New York. Seeing but few men on deck, our captain told them of my case, in answer to which he said, that, if I would go with him he would give me twenty-two dollars per month. This good fortune relieved my mind of an incubus which had weighed upon it ever since I had suffered impressment.

The next thing was to get on board. Each of the vessels had but one boat, both of which were safely stowed on deck, and it seemed too much trouble to hoist them out. Therefore the little brig sheered up, as near as was safe, an oar was made fast to a line, and thrown under our bows. I then went into the forechains, threw off my clothes—thus leaving the vessel as naked as I entered it—seized the oar, and was dragged along side, from whence I crept into the main-chains, and there received some articles of dress before making my *debut* on deck. Just as I had reached the main-chains, a huge shark made his appearance from under the brig, who eyed me very wishfully, but happened to be a little too late "for tea," for I was out of his reach. I found myself on board of the brig Sally, Captain Evans, and a few weeks later in New York.

During my intercourse with the English at this period, and in later years, I had taken many dry jokes in silence, upon the faint-heartedness of the Americans. A British officer once remarked to me that the Yankees were great cowards, or great fools, to stand all the *sauce* that the English government had given them. I replied that brother Jonathan was remarkable for his good nature, but that there was that in him, when roused, which would humble the British lion on anything like terms of equality; that we had suffered a great deal of imposition from Great Britain, but such things, I told him, would not last long, and when war did come, they would find as brave hearts and strong arms in our insulted country, as in their own boasted land. He said he did not doubt the bravery of the people, but that would avail nothing while the policy of the government remained the same. "I know," said he, "that we have violated the law of nations, but they dare not declare war against us, and all they can do is to remonstrate. Our naval power, at one sweep, would annihilate your force at sea, thus leaving your extensive coast open, and exposed to our attacks. Your government perceives this, and they will not venture into the contest. They will rather suffer in silence." I excused this, by saying that it was much better to have a good and sufficient cause to make a war, than, at the first insult, to rush headlong into hostilities, without resources or preparation; but rather go calmly and deliberately to work, and at one swoop wipe out a long catalogue of insults and aggressions. I frequently remarked to them, that I myself had once suffered impressment on board his Majesty's sloop-of-war Cayenne, and that I should yet see myself revenged, by seeing the American stars and stripes waving at her mast-head, which was afterward so fully verified. To be sure, my assertions would sometimes raise a laugh at my expense, but there was generally some American near. who would join me in a hearty cheer for our own native land. Indeed, when war was declared, a large portion of the English were opposed to the movement, and would cheer as loud as I could, when they heard of any disaster to themselves. When the loss of the Guerriere was ascertained, it gave me a fine opportunity of throwing back the insinuations against the bravery of my countrymen.

Once, during the late war, while at Portsmouth, I was standing on the wharf, and viewing a beautiful frigate lying at anchor a short distance from me, an officer accosted me, by saying, "There is another of our frigates going to be cut in pieces by the Yankees; and," he continued, "I hope that they will send every such one to the bottom. Then the Admiralty will learn to send such ships as will be able to cope with the American frigates. The metal of your frigates is too heavy for such nutshells as these, and the Board will find it out when they have lost a few more of them." The disposition and feeling of the British officers were very much changed after the first successes of the Americans. The boastful manner of Captain Dacres, and his deep humiliation, were before them, and acted as a caution to these hitherto invincible heroes of the ocean, and they gave due allowance to the fineness of our ships and the skill of our marksmen.

Before the close of the war, great caution was taken in the appointment of officers known for coolness and courage, and great care taken in giving instructions not to engage an American vessel on anything less than terms of equality, The feeling of the English toward our country, was much changed by this war, and although many of them said that they had lost nothing, yet they would be as ready to admit that they had not gained much.

My next trip was for St. Thomas, on board the schooner Seaflower, of Boston. We cleared the harbor of that city, June 11th, 1800, and bowled along for six days, under a smacking breeze from the north-west. Our captain was a very pleasant man, had been a sailor himself, and knew and appreciated the merits of every man on board. The name of the mate was Joshua Sweet, of Newburyport, a thorough seaman, knew his own place and duties, the captain's, and the place of every man in the ship. Nothing of importance occurred, until we judged ourselves to be in the neighborhood of land, when, at daylight one morning, we found ourselves close along side of a French privateer of ten guns. As we had no means of escape or resistance, the frog-eaters took possession, manned her, and sent her to Gaudaloupe. The mate and myself, with another sailor, were put on board of the Frenchman. They were very polite, and permitted us to take our clothes and bedding. She was bound to Point Petre, where she arrived July 5th. As soon as she came to anchor, a large lighter came along side, into which we were all put, to the number of thirty, and landed. We asked permission to step into a small grocery, and take a throat seasoning, which was granted, when we were hurried to our prison, a small stone building, about twenty feet square, where we were all crowded in together. There was but one window, which was grated on the outside, affording but a small circulation of air, and the heat was excessive. Here we were obliged to remain all night, without water, crowded to suffocation, and deprived of sleep, from the smallness of our prison, and the noisomeness of the air. This night seemed the longest that ever I had experienced, and never did I hail the morning with greater pleasure. At length, our horrid den was unlocked, and we were once more permitted to taste the sweetness of fresh air. Nearly exhausted with thirst, I ran to the pickets, called to a black woman, and gave her twenty cents for a junk-bottle full of water, which I turned off at a draught. About eight o'clock, our provisions were served out for the day, and four casks of water rolled into the yard, so that we suffered no more from thirst. Not long after, they took us to Basse-Terre, and confined us in an old church, where we remained about twenty days before we were exchanged.

While we were there, several prizes were brought in, and the owner came to the prison to hire some of the prisoners to discharge the cargoes. He offered us one dollar per day, and several of us went. I was sent to assist in discharging an English brig, laden with teas. Some of the chests were found broken open, and some were broken while hoisting them out of the hold, so that, in a short time, the tea was a foot deep under the main hatch. Knowing that it would be wasted, I asked permission to carry some of it away. In order to do this, the next morning I put on two pairs of pantaloons, and when I got into the hold, took off one pair, tied up the legs, broke open a chest of the best imperial, and filled them up. At night, I lugged it up to my prison, emptied the flocks out of my bed, and put the tea into it. I continued in this way until I had filled my bed with about eighty-five pounds of tea. My mess-mates frequently laughed at me, telling me that I should "get my labor for my pains," but I persisted in my course, telling them that "we should see who was right."

At length we were exchanged, and a cartel carried us to St. Kitts, where we went to the American consul and received a joe (eight dollars) a-piece, to support us a few days, until we could find a passage home. After I had found me a boarding house, I went to the American coffee-house and disposed of my tea for one dollar per pound, receiving eighty-five dollars, which I thought fine "potatoes" for a prisoner of war to earn.

[The next event which Nevens relates of prominent interest, is the narrative of his shipwreck, which occurred many years later. We here make the extract referred to.]

I now thought I would take what means and stores I had, and draw from the bank what cash I had then deposited, and retire from a seafaring life forever. While making the necessary arrangements so to do, I fell in, at a public house at Boston, with Captain Joseph Crosby, of North Carolina, with whom I had sailed before the mast some years before, always having supposed him to be an Englishman until he made me acquainted with his early history.

As was perfectly natural, we boarded for several days at the same house, and had frequent conversations respecting seafaring life, the voyages we had made, the perils we had endured, the narrow escapes we had met with, and, also, as to our future prospects and calculations. He informed me there was a brig to be sold in a few days, of one hundred and ninety tons burden, a good vessel, and that, if I would buy one third of her, he would take the rest, and we would freight her for some foreign port, and so make at least one more voyage together. I told him plainly that I had determined, in my own mind, not to go to sea any more; that it was a hard and dangerous life to lead, and my inclination strongly led me to seek for a livelihood on shore. "But," said he, "make one voyage with me, and when we return, if you wish to buy me out, and own her alone, I will sell out to you; or if you wish to sell out what you own, I will buy you out, for I have money enough to buy the whole, but it is too much to risk at once." For a long time I held back. But he represented, in such glowing colors, the pleasures of life upon the ocean that I at last consented to buy one third of the brig, for which I paid, in cash, two thousand dollars. After making some slight repairs, and re-painting her, we advertised for freight to some port in Europe. In the course of eight or ten days, we were freighted with fish for Bilboa, in Spain.

Our brig was now to be manned and victualed for a foreign voyage, which, for the state of my funds, was rather a serious job. However, we made out to manage it; and as I had two hundred and fifty dollars left, I invested it in fish, and placed it on board. All things were now in readiness, and on the 26th of November, 1822, we weighed anchor and sailed for Spain.

Captain Crosby and myself had thought it best not to have our vessel insured, as it was a time of general peace, and the owners of the cargo, for the same reason, concluded to get no insurance. But we made arrangements with the owners, that if the weather grew bad, or the times uncertain and dangerous, to effect an insurance on vessel and cargo. But after we sailed, peace continued, the weather held firm, and no insurance was effected. Here, then, I was, with my little world around me, my all invested—and the fruits of the toil, privation and care of years committed to a frail bark upon the treacherous wave.

The weather continued fine, and the winds fair, until we had passed the Western Islands, and then heavy gales from almost every point of compass made our progress slow and dangerous; but no serious misfortune occurred till we had arrived in latitude forty-four, and longitude sixteen, when a very heavy gale from the south-west obliged us to lay to for twenty-eight hours; she rode out the gale like a gull. From evening till morning, the gale seemed gradually to abate in its violence. I had the morning watch, and the two men in my watch were on deck with me. The rest of the crew, with the captain, were below. About seven o'clock in the morning, I saw to windward a very heavy sea rolling along in the wake of the vessel, directly upon us. As soon as I saw the danger, I sung out to the men to look out for themselves, and jumped into the main rigging followed by the two men in my watch. When the sea struck the brig, it was with such force as to bury her yards in the water; she, however, partly righted, when a second sea struck her, and buried her masts under water. The companion-way and forecastle were now four feet under water. Our only hope was now to cut away the masts and clear the deck; we had two sharp axes, but both were in the cabin, and could not be got at. All hope, therefore, of saving either vessel or cargo being now vain, our next thought was of our own condition. The only chance we had of saving our own lives, was by getting the long boat afloat. How to do this was now the question. After some time, I succeeded in cutting with my knife a piece of rigging, which I fastened around me in such a way, that my two companions lowered me down, and I at length succeeded in cutting some of the ropes, and giving her a shake, she slid out of the slings without filling. After some difficulty, we cleared her from the rigging of the vessel, got her under our lee quarter, and put into her two oars, and the cook's draw bucket, these being the only articles we could get at. We staid by the brig as long as we dared, and when we left her, we were in momentary expectation that she would go down. We shoved off about a cable's length from her, and after wait ing about half of an hour, she sunk, and with her the captain and crew and a valuable cargo. Though we were alone upon the mighty deep, nearly four hundred miles from land, yet we had strong hopes of being picked up by some vessel, as we were in the track of all European vessels going to and returning from the West Indies. I therefore tried to comfort my companions in affliction with hopes, that I dared not indulge myself. But they tauntingly asked me to serve out their rations to them! "Provisions," said I. "Yes! where is our bread! our water! our meat? What are we to eat? what are we to drink?"

These were questions I could not answer; for water we had none, and our whole stock of provisions consisted of but three potatoes and a small dry fish, which were by chance in the stern of the boat. These I divided equally among us, and tried to encourage them, but they were frightened, and gave up all for lost. The weather was favorable, the wind came in light breezes from the north-west, and a smooth sea. We had but to keep the boat before the wind, and let her drift as she would, for all hope of reaching land was vain. The fourth day of our suffering I shall never forget—our distress and suffering were great; more, however, from thirst than hunger. A sickly, gnawing sensation was all from hunger that we suffered. But from thirst! reader, may you never know the dreadful feeling. It is beyond all imagination, and far, very far, beyond all description. Think of it, as you drink your fill from the bubbling brook or sparkling fountain: think of it as the plentiful shower descends to refresh and enliven nature: yes, think of it as you awake at midnight, parched with the thirst of burning fever, and reflection tells you that parching, burning, firing thirst will never be appeased until death sets his cold seal upon you. The eighth day, one man laid down and died without a groan. We laid his body in the stern sheets, to devour when nature could hold out no longer. Horrible alternative, to starve or devour dead humanity! That same night, the other man became crazy, laid down upon the bottom of the boat, and soon became insensible. He, too, was dead. And here I was alone, with the dead around me; the shoreless waters stretching their vast expanse around me—not an object to be seen, and no sound to be heard but the sullen dash of the waves upon the side of the boat. I was exhausted—I was discouraged—I was in despair. Horrible whisperings, cursings, and blasphemies sounded in my ears; ghastly, grinning faces seemed to mock my misery; my imagination mistook the dull hoarse murmur of the sea, for fearful shrieks and groans. My hunger was gone, and the dead rested as securely as though I had been feasting; but I was parching, drying, crackling, consuming; my vitals were on fire, and nature could bear no more. I sank down upon the stern-sheets beside the dead, and prayed for death to cure my pains. Soon I fell into a drowsy stupor; my pains were gone, and my fears removed. The days of my boyhood had returned, and I was playing in the flowery meadow, wandering over green fields, roaming through the wild wood, slaking my thirst at the sparkling rill, as it gushed from the moss-covered rock. Again the scene changed, and I was in the school-room of my childhood, and it seemed to me that the long, long summer day would never pass; as lesson after lesson was heard, and noon came not, the hum still went on with youthful impatience. I longed to be at my dinner, and, casting a furtive glance at the stern master of "the birch," I eagerly seized a tempting morsel, and——but again the scene changed, and I dreamed that I was by my own father's fireside, a boy, spending the evening of a glorious New England thanksgiving, and had eaten to fullness—and as the apples, cider, and nuts went round, so did the merry jest: and the laugh, loud and boisterous, made the old kitchen walls echo again. At length, the old clock told the hour of nine, and sleep stole gently upon me; their voices and glee grew fainter—the fire, a few moments before blazing so brightly, grew dim—the lights danced a moment, and all was dark and still—forgetfulness and insensibility now held undisputed reign.

How long I continued in this state, I know not. I was suddenly aroused by a sound that seemed familiar, like that of a ship going in stays. I got up as well as I was able, and looked around, but my eyes were so dim I could see nothing. Everything around me was shrouded in green, but no object could I distinguish. After rubbing my eyes some time, I saw, a little to windward of me, a large brig in the act of lowering a boat. The exertion had been too much for my exhausted powers, and I fell upon the stern-sheets again, perfectly insensible. My first recollection on coming to, is of finding myself sitting upon the cabin floor, and being fed with something warm by a French lady. I heard her remark, "He has been drinking." I could not speak for a long time. When I recovered the faculty of speech, my first inquiry was for my dead friends in the boat! They told me they had been buried, and the boat hoisted on deck. The captain then prepared me a glass of warm wine and water, after drinking of which I soon recovered my faculties and thoughts, though it was a long time before I recovered from the shock my system had received. The vessel which had picked me up proved to be a French brig, bound from Havana to France.

[In the course of his life, Nevens had considerable experience on board of whalers, and describes, in his narrative, the different kinds of whales, and how they are caught.]

It may not be improper to speak of the different kinds of whales usually met with, and the manner of taking them. These animals so closely resemble fish in their outward form and developments, that they are generally considered as such by the mass of mankind. Upon an examination of their structure, however, we shall find that they differ from quadrupeds only in their organs of motion. They are warm-blooded, and, by means of lungs, breathe atmospheric air, and that only. Like quadrupeds, they bring forth and suckle their young; and indeed, in all the details of their organization, they are the same as in this class of animals. The head of the whale is very large and long, forming about one third of the whole length of the animal. The opening of the mouth is of corresponding magnitude. The nostrils are situated upon the top of the head, and are usually denominated "blow holes;" through these the air finds its way to the lungs, when the whale rises to the surface of the water. The skin is destitute of outward covering, and beneath it is a covering of oily fat, called "blubber," from six to twelve inches in thickness. Their senses are not very acute, and they do not seem to possess much intelligence. Their ordinary speed in the water is about four miles an hour, which, however, they sometimes increase to twelve or fifteen. The common or Greenland whale is destitute of teeth, but instead of them the upper jaw is furnished with transverse layers of a horny substance, called baleen or whalebone. This species is timid and inactive, and yields more oil than any other—consequently, they are more easily captured than any other. When fully grown, its length is from fifty to sixty-five feet, and its circumference from thirty to forty The ordinary weight is about seventy tons. They make a loud noise when breathing or "blowing," and often eject water to the height of six or eight yards, which, when seen in the distance, appears like a puff of smoke. They usually remain at the surface about two minutes, and "blow" eight or nine times, and then descend into the water, where they remain five, ten, and, when feeding, fifteen or twenty minutes, and then return to the surface to breathe. In thus rising, they ascend, at times, with such velocity as to throw themselves completely out of the water.

The Razor or "Fin Back" whale is the most bulky and powerful of its tribe. It "blows" with such violence, that in calm weather it may be heard a mile. Its length is about one hundred feet. It is much more swift and active in its motions than any other kind, and is by no means a timid animal. When harpooned, or otherwise wounded, it exerts all its energies. It is difficult and dangerous taking them, and the small quantity of inferior oil it affords offers but little inducement to the whalemen The Spermaceti whale differs from the one described in many important particulars. The mouth is destitute of whalebone, but the lower jaw is armed, on each side, with about twenty strong, conical teeth, which shut into corresponding cavities in the upper jaw. The head is very large, with a very abrupt termination in front; the upper part of the head is composed of cavities, separated by cartilaginous partitions filled with oil, which, on cooling, crystalizes, forming the substance known as "spermaceti." The males of this species are known among whalers as "bulls," and the females as "cows." This is the kind most sought for, and most valuable.

A whale-ship, properly fitted and manned, has three or four boats, and from thirty to forty men on board, according to the number of boats. The weapons used in securing and killing the whale are but two. First the harpoon. This is an instrument of iron, about three feet in length, with an arrow-shaped head, the two branches of which have internally a reversed barb, like a fish-hook. When this instrument, to which a line is fastened, is forced, by a well-directed blow, into the fat of the whale, and the line drawn, the principal barb seizes the strong fibers of the blubber, and it cannot be withdrawn.

The lance is used for killing the whale, when secured. It consists of a spear of iron six feet in length, terminating in a head of steel, made very thin and sharp.

These two instruments, with the lines, boats and oars, form all the apparatus for capturing the whale. When the ship arrives on whale-ground, two men are kept at mast-head continually, on the look-out—the boats ready to lower at a moment's warning.

The whale is discovered sometimes by the "spout," and sometimes by the breach of the waves over it. When the "mast-head" sings out, "There she blows," the captain asks, "Where away?" When it is ascertained to be a "sperm whale," the word is, "All hands on deck, see all clear for lowering the boats." All is now bustle and excitement. Each man is interested, as his wages depend upon the success of the cruise. The "lay" is one barrel of oil out of such a number. The master may have, perhaps, one in twenty; mate, one in fifty; ship's keeper one in one hundred; boat steerer one in one hundred and fifty; and a common hand, one in two hundred, according to the "lay" on which they engaged. The captain supplies all their wants while out, from the ship's stores, and it is deducted from their wages when they arrive home. Thus every one is anxious of success. When the ship arrives within about half a mile of the whale, she is hove-to, and the ship's keeper goes to the mast-head with a spy-glass, to watch the operation, and give directions to the man at the helm how to work the ship. The boats being lowered, each with its own crew, row for the whale. Care and skill are requisite to approach the whale before it has its "blow" out. The boat which is nearest the whale, approaches the whale at the right moment, and some expert workman throws the harpoon, and "fastens" to the whale. Sometimes, when the whale has done blowing, and is about going down, the harpoon is thrown a distance of ten yards, and made to "fasten." But usually the boat is run directly upon the animal, and the harpoon buried in its back. This is a critical moment, and requires presence of mind in an officer, and perfect obedience in the boat's crew. The instant she is fast, the word is, "Stern all." The boat now moves rapidly astern till out of the reach of the fluke or tail of the whale. The tail of the whale lying horizontally or flat in the water, enables him to dive almost instantaneously and with great power. When the whale feels the wound made by the harpoon, it makes a convulsive effort to escape. This is a moment of danger, the men and boats are exposed to instant destruction from the violent blow of the ponderous tail. The whale now goes down, sometimes to the depth of a mile, and the utmost care and order are requisite on the part of the crew, while the line is running out. Should the line meet with any obstruction while running, the boat would be instantly drawn down. Their stay down is from five to forty minutes, the longer time they are down the greater their exhaustion when they rise, owing to the pressure of the water upon them. When it rises, a second harpoon is fastened to it, and then the lance is used for killing him. The officer of the boat goes forward to do this; the lance, which has a long shank of wood, is forced into the vitals just back of the fin. This being done two or three times, the whale is seen to be dying by the blood mingled with his spout, and, after a short time, rolls over upon the side or back, and the job is done.

A signal is now made, and the ship comes along side, the boats are hoisted, and a strong chain, called the "fluke-chain," is put round the tail, a little above where it begins to spread. A good "stiff throat seasoning" is now expected by every man, and willingly given by the officers. Two men now get upon the whale, each armed with a straight, sharp blubber-spade, with which they begin to cut near the fin. They cut lengthways of the whale about five feet, then, standing face to face they cut round, as far as they can, down on the side. A hole is now made through this "blanket-piece," near the end, into which a blubber-hook, weighing about sixty pounds, is forced; this hook, being connected with a very strong purchase and fall, the end of which is fastened to the windlass, then the word is, "Haul taut." Eighteen or twenty hands, with handspikes, now heave away at the windlass, and the blanket-piece begins to rise, peeling off from the carcass as fast as the men on the whale can cut. As they cut spirally, and the whale rolls in the water and fluke-ropes, the blanket continues to rise till it reaches the mainyard, and then another hole is cut down near the whale, into which another hook is fastened, and the operation goes on till the blubber is all in. These blanket-pieces are swung in over the main-hatch and lowered into the blubber room, where they are cut up into thin slices for the kettle. The head is now cut from the body, and divided into two pieces, called the "case" and the "junk," the last of which is brought on deck and lashed; the "case" is then raised as high as the plankshire of the ship, and a large hole cut in it, from which head matter is taken, from ten to fifteen barrels in quantity. The "junk," when tried out, goes in with this, and it is called head oil, or "spermaceti."

Thus the whale is "cut in." It now has to be "tried out," and even the head oil must be boiled, to keep it from spoiling. The scraps made in trying out the blubber are used to feed the fires, and after being first kindled, they require no other fuel.

The oil is then stowed away, where it remains, unless some of the casks leak, which is discovered by the pumps. If they bring up oil and water, the whole of it has to be trimmed, that is, overhauled, and the leaky casks taken out, emptied, and repaired, and the whole stowed away again.

[Captain Scoresby, in his works on the Whale Fishery, gives some interesting anecdotes illustrative of the perils and disasters to which whalemen are subject, some of which we here annex, in addition to what Nevens has given us of the peculiarities of this occupation.]

The most extensive source of danger to the whale-fisher, when actively engaged in his occupation, arises from the object of his pursuit. Excepting when it has young under its protection, the whale generally exhibits remarkable timidity of character. A bird perching on its back alarms it; hence, the greater part of the accidents which happen in the course of its capture, must be attributed to adventitious circumstances on the part of the whale, or to mismanagement or fool-hardiness on the part of the fishers.

A harpooner belonging to the Henrietta, of Whitby, when engaged in lancing a whale, into which he had previously struck a harpoon, incautiously cast a little line under his feet, that he had just hauled into the boat, after it had been drawn out by the fish. A painful stroke of his lance induced the whale to dart suddenly downward; his line began to run out from beneath his feet, and in an instant caught him, by a turn, round his body. He had but just time to cry out, "Clear away the line!" "Oh, dear!" when he was almost cut asunder, dragged overboard, and never seen afterward. The line was cut at the moment, but without avail. The fish descended a considerable depth, and died, from whence it was drawn to the surface by the lines connected with it, and secured.

While the ship Resolution navigated an open lake of water, in the eighty-first degree of north latitude, during a keen frost and strong north wind, on the 2d of June, 1806, a whale appeared, and a boat put off in pursuit. On its second visit to the surface of the sea it was harpooned. A convulsive heave of the tail, which succeeded the wound, struck the boat at the stern, and by its reaction projected the boat-steerer overboard. As the line in a moment dragged the boat beyond his reach, the crew threw some of their oars toward him for his support, one of which he fortunately seized. The ship and boats being at a considerable distance, and the fast-boat being rapidly drawn away from him, the harpooner cut the line, with the view of rescuing him from his dangerous situation. But no sooner was this act performed, than, to their extreme mortification, they discovered, that in consequence of some oars being thrown toward their floating comrade, and others being broken or unshipped by the blow from the fish, one oar only remained, with which, owing to the force of the wind, they tried in vain to approach him. A considerable period elapsed before any boat from the ship could afford him assistance, though the men strained every nerve for the purpose. At length, when they reached him, he was found with his arms stretched over an oar, almost deprived of sensation. On his arrival at the ship, he was in a deplorable condition His clothes were frozen like mail, and his hair constituted a helmet of ice. He was immediately conveyed into the cabin, his clothes taken off, his limbs and body dried and well rubbed, and a cordial administered to him, which he drank. A dry shirt and stockings were then put upon him, and he was laid in the captain's bed. After a few hours' sleep, he awoke and appeared considerably restored, but complained of a painful sensation of cold. He was, therefore, removed to his own berth, and one of his messmates ordered to lie on each side of him, whereby the diminished circulation of the blood was accelerated, and the animal heat restored. The shock on his constitution, however, was greater than was anticipated. He recovered in the course of a few days, so as to be able to engage in his ordinary pursuits; but many months elapsed before his countenance exhibited its wonted appearance of health.

The Aimwell, of Whitby, while cruising the Greenland seas, in the year 1810, had boats in chase of whales on the 26th of May. One of them was harpooned. But instead of sinking immediately on receiving the wound, as is the most usual manner of the whale, this individual only dived for a moment, and rose again beneath the boat, struck it in the most vicious manner with its fins and tail, stove it, upset it, and then disappeared. The crew, seven in number, got on the bottom of the boat; but the unequal action of the lines, which for some time remained entangled with the boat, rolled it occasionally over, and thus plunged the crew repeatedly into the water. Four of them, after each immersion, recovered themselves, and clung to the boat; but the other three, one of whom was the only person acquainted with the art of swimming, were drowned before assistance could arrive. The four men on the boat being rescued and conveyed to the ship, the attack on the whale was continued, and two more harpoons struck. But the whale, irritated instead of being enervated by its wounds, recommenced its furious conduct. The sea was in a foam. Its tail and fins were in awful play; and, in a short time, harpoon after harpoon drew out, the fish was loosened from its entanglements, and escaped.

In the fishery of 1812, the Henrietta, of Whitby, suffered a similar loss. A fish, which was struck very near the ship, by a blow of its tail stove a small hole in the boat's bow. Every individual shrinking from the side on which the blow was impressed, aided the influence of the stroke, and upset the boat. They all clung to it while it was bottom up; but the line having got entangled among the thwarts, suddenly drew the boat under water, and with it part of the crew. Excessive anxiety among the people in the ship occasioned delay in sending assistance; so that, when the first boat arrived at the spot, two survivors only, out of six men, were found.

During a fresh gale of wind, in the season of 1809, one of the Resolution's harpooners struck a sucking whale. Its mother being near, all the other boats were disposed around, with the hope of entangling it. The old whale pursued a circular route round its cub, and was followed by the boats; but its velocity was so considerable, that they were unable to keep pace with it. Being in the capacity of harpooner on this occasion myself, I proceeded to the chase, after having carefully marked the proceedings of the fish. I selected a situation, in which I conceived the whale would make his appearance, and was in the act of directing my crew to cease rowing, when a terrible blow was struck on the boat. The whale I never saw, but the effect of the blow was too important to be overlooked. About fifteen square feet of the bottom of the boat were driven in; it filled, sunk, and upset in a moment. Assistance was providentially at hand, so that we were all taken up without injury, after being but a few minutes in the water. The whale escaped; the boat's lines fell out and were lost, but the boat was recovered.

A remarkable instance of the power which the whale possesses in its tail, was exhibited, within my own observation, in the year 1807. On the 29th of May, a whale was harpooned by an officer belonging to the Resolution. It descended a considerable depth, and, on its reappearance, evinced an uncommon degree of irritation. It made such a display of its fins and tail, that few of the crew were hardy enough to approach it. The captain, observing their timidity, called a boat, and himself struck a second harpoon. Another boat immediately followed, and unfortunately advanced too far. The tail was again reared into the air, in a terrific attitude. The impending blow was evident—the harpooner, who was directly underneath, leaped overboard, and the next moment the threatened stroke was impressed on the center of the boat, which it buried in the water. Happily no one was injured. The harpooner, who leaped overboard, escaped certain death by the act—the tail having struck the very spot on which he stood. The effects of the blow were astonishing. The keel was broken, the gunwales, and every plank, excepting two, were cut through, and it was evident that the boat would have been completely divided, had not the tail struck directly upon a coil of lines. The boat was rendered useless.

Instances of disasters of this kind, occasioned by blows from the whale, could be adduced in great numbers—cases of boats being destroyed by a single stroke of the tail are not unknown—instances of boats having been stove or upset, and their crews wholly or in part drowned, are not unfrequent—and several cases of whales having made a regular attack upon every boat which came near them, dashed some in pieces, and killed or drowned some of the people in them, have occurred within a few years, even under my own observation.

The Dutch ship Gort-Moolen, commanded by Cornelius Gerard Ouwekaas, with a cargo of seven fish, was anchored in Greenland, in the year 1660. The captain, perceiving a whale ahead of his ship, beckoned his attendants, and threw himself into a boat. He was the first to approach the whale, and was fortunate enough to harpoon it before the arrival of the second boat, which was on the advance. Jacques Vienkes, who had the direction of it, joined his captain immediately afterward, and prepared to make a second attack on the fish, when it should remount again to the surface. At the moment of its ascension, the boat of Vienkes happening, unfortunately, to be perpendicularly above it, was so suddenly and forcibly lifted up by a stroke of the head of the whale, that it was dashed to pieces before the harpooner could discharge his weapon. Vienkes flew along with the pieces of the boat, and fell upon the back of the animal. This intrepid seaman, who still retained his weapon in his grasp, harpooned the whale on which he stood; and, by means of the harpoon and and the line, which he never abandoned, he steadied himself firmly upon the fish, notwithstanding his hazardous situation, and regardless of a considerable wound that he received in his leg, in his fall along with the fragments of the boat. All the efforts of the other boats to approach the whale, and deliver the harpooner, were futile. The captain, not seeing any other method of saving his unfortunate companion, who was in some way entangled with the line, called to him to cut it with his knife, and betake himself to swimming. Vienkes, embarrassed and disconcerted as he was, tried in vain to follow this council. His knife was in the pocket of his drawers, and, being unable to support himself with one hand, he could not get it out. The whale, meanwhile, continued advancing along the surface of the water with great rapidity, but fortunately never attempted to dive. While his comrades despaired of his life, the harpoon by which he held at length disengaged itself from the body of the whale. Vienkes, being thus liberated, did not fail to take advantage of this circumstance; he cast himself into the sea, and, by swimming, endeavored to regain the boats which continued the pursuit of the whale. When his shipmates perceived him struggling with the waves, they redoubled their exertions. They reached him just as his strength was exhausted, and had the happiness of rescuing this adventurous harpooner from his perilous situation.

Captain Lyons, of the Raith, of Leith, while prosecuting the whale-fishery on the Labrador coast, in the season of 1802, discovered a large whale at a short distance from the ship. Four boats were dispatched in pursuit, and two of them succeeded in approaching it so closely together that two harpoons were struck at the same moment. The fish descended a few fathoms in the direction of another of the boats, which was on the advance, rose accidentally beneath it, struck it with his head, and threw the boat, men and apparatus about fifteen feet in the air. It was inverted by the stroke, and fell into the water with its keel upward. All the people were picked up alive by the fourth boat, which was just at hand, excepting one man, who, having got entangled in the boat, fell beneath it, and was unfortunately drowned. The fish was soon afterward killed.

Perhaps one of the most remarkable instances of the destruction of a vessel by a whale, is that of the ship Essex, which sailed from Nantucket about the year 1820. She was commanded by Captain Pollard, and had entered the Pacific Ocean, where she was employed some time in catching whales. One day the seamen harpooned a young whale. In this species, the affection of the mother toward its young is very strong, as was evinced in a remarkable manner on this occasion. When the mother of the young whale found that her progeny was killed, she went to some distance from the ship, and then, rushing through the water, came against the stern of the vessel with the greatest violence. So tremendous was the force of the shock, that several of the timbers were loosened, and the vessel pitched and reeled on the water, as if struck by a whirlwind. Nor was the whale satisfied with this. Again she went to the distance of more than a mile, and then, shooting through the waves with incredible swiftness, came like a thunderbolt upon the bow of the vessel. The timbers were instantly beaten in, and the ship began to fill with water. Scarcely had the crew sufficient time to get into their boat before she went down. In this sudden and frightful situation, the poor seamen now found themselves. They were upon the wide-heaving and perilous ocean, in an open boat, and far from any land. If the whale had come upon them in the condition they were now in, they must have inevitably perished. But they saw no more of the monster. Captain Pollard and his men for several days suffered severe hardships from the weather, and from a want of water and food. At length, the delightful vision of another ship broke upon their sight. They were all taken on board, and finally reached their native country in safety.

In 1822, two boats belonging to the ship Baffin went in pursuit of a whale. John Carr was harpooner and commander of one of them.

The whale they pursued led them into a vast shoal of his own species; they were so numerous that their blowing was incessant, and they believed that they did not see fewer than a hundred. Fearful of alarming them without striking any, they remained for awhile motionless. At last, one rose near Carr's boat, and he approached, and, fatally for himself, harpooned it. When he struck, the fish was approaching the boat, and, passing very rapidly, jerked the line out of its place over the stern, and threw it upon the gunwale. Its pressure, in this unfavorable position, so careened the boat, that the side was pulled under water, and it began to fill. In this emergency, Carr, who was a brave, active man, seized the line, and endeavored to relieve the boat, by restoring it to its place; but, by some circumstance which was never accounted for, a turn of the line flew over his arm, dragged him overboard in an instant, and drew him under the water, never more to rise. So sudden was the accident, that only one man, who was watching him, saw what had happened; so that, when the boat righted, which it immediately did, though half full of water, the whole crew, on looking round, inquired what had become of Carr. It is impossible to imagine a death more awfully sudden and unexpected. The invisible bullet could not have effected more instantaneous destruction. The velocity of the whale, at its first descent, is from thirteen to fifteen feet per second. Now, as this unfortunate man was adjusting the line at the water's very edge, where it must have been perfectly tight, owing to its obstruction in running out of the boat, the interval between the fastening the line about him, and his disappearance, could not have exceeded the third part of a second of time, for in one second only he must have been dragged ten or twelve feet deep. Indeed, he had not time for the least exclamation; and the person who saw his removal, observed that it was so exceeding quick, that, though his eye was upon him at the moment, he could scarcely distinguish his figure as he disappeared.

As soon as the crew recovered from their consternation, they applied themselves to the needful attention which the lines required. A second harpoon was struck, from the accompanying boat, on the raising of the whale to the surface, and some lances were applied, but this melancholy occurrence had cast such a damp on all present, that they became timid and inactive in their subsequent duties. The whale, when nearly exhausted, was allowed to remain some minutes unmolested, till, having recovered some degree of energy, it made a violent effort, and tore itself away from both harpoons. The exertions of the crews thus proved fruitless, and were attended with serious loss.

[We again skip over many years in Nevens' history. In the meantime, he had arisen to the command of a vessel, and had frequently sailed to the remotest parts of the world. He was now an old man: age, with its infirmities, had begun to do their work upon his constitution, and he had made up his mind to go to sea no more, but to gather his little all together, and settle down, he did not care much where. The relation of the subsequent misfortunes that befell the honest-hearted old sailor, and his return to the scenes of his boyhood, after the lapse of nearly half a century, is very affecting.]

Having some business to transact at Providence, I took stage, and, in a tremendous snow-storm, landed in that place, at the house of an old acquaintance, where I was received as one from the dead. The storm continued for several days, I was forced to stay longer in the place than I at first intended. I now wrote to Mr. Stevens, my agent in Boston, requesting him to draw what funds I had from the bank, and forward the same to me at Providence. But day after day passed on, and I heard nothing from him, and began to grow rather uneasy, when his son entered my room, one evening, with the money. His father delayed sending it, until a safer opportunity than by mail should occur, when unexpected business called the young man to Providence. I now found myself in possession of thirteen hundred and twenty-one dollars.

It was necessary for me to lay out immediately between two and three hundred dollars, for clothing and other necessary articles. Having thus supplied my most pressing necessities, I concluded to go to Boston, and find out if any of my father's family were yet alive, having heard nothing from any of them for most twenty years. I therefore began to look about myself for some kind of conveyance. Here were the railroad cars, which run from Providence to Boston weekly, but as the snow was very deep, I was told that it was dangerous traveling in them, as they were likely to run off the track, on account of the snow. As I was ignorant about them, I did not know but this might be the case, and as a sailor always feels safest on the water, I engaged a passage on board a small schooner. I thought, as the weather had now become moderate and pleasant, there would be little risk in so short a voyage.

I asked the captain when he should sail. He told me he was all ready, and waited only for the tide. I accordingly lost no time in getting my baggage on board, together with many curiosities, and some valuable articles, which I had collected in the course of my seafaring life. All things being now ready, we sailed down river, with a fair wind and pleasant sky. The next day, however, the wind shifted round to the eastward, while we were off Block Island, and there came on a fog so dense that for some time we could not see the length of the schooner, and then the fog would lift a little, and give us a momentary glimpse of our bearings. About two o'clock in the afternoon, it looked so likely for squalls, that the captain said he would put back and go into Newport, and wait for fair weather. We then wore the vessel round, and hauled her close on the wind, so as to weather the north-east point of the island. At this critical moment, a squall struck us, and being closer in to the shore than we thought, for we were not able to weather the point, the sea was running very high, and before we were aware of our danger, the vessel struck, with a tremendous crash, upon a reef of rocks. She rebounded and struck the second time, and in a moment, seemingly, she was full of water. The sea now broke over us with great fury, and washed our deck from one end of the schooner to the other. At this moment, a pilot-boat, which was driven in by the gale, came near to us, and seeing our helpless condition, the pilot sung out to us to stand ready to jump on board, one at a time, when the boat should come near enough to enable us so to do.

The pilot-boat tacked and stood off a little, then wore round and came close to the weather-quarter of the schooner, when I jumped and caught by the rigging. She then tacked again, and wore round in the same way, until all were taken from the wreck. The boat now stood away for Newport, and before we had sailed five rods from the schooner, she went down. When we hauled into the wharf, we were as wet as drowned rats, though our clothes were fast freezing to us, and it was piercingly cold. We all went to a public house, and stopped that night, though sleep was a stranger that I could not woo to my pillow. I spent the night in reviewing my past life, and the strange reverses I had met with, and now the scanty pittance I had saved with so much care, to build my hopes in old age upon, was swallowed up in a moment, and I was left destitute in the world. Before retiring to my bed, I took everything from my pockets. I had a knife, a piece of tobacco, the key of my trunk, in which my thousand dollars were snugly laid away, which was now in the bottom of the ocean, about a dollar in small change, and one poor, solitary five dollar bill. Here was the whole, my all — my forty years of toil, of danger, of strife with the elements, of hardship and suffering, for all this I had six dollars to show. The bill was in my pocket by mere accident, as I put all my money into my trunk, as I supposed, excepting a little change for present use, which was loose in my pocket. The next morning, I concluded to take the stage for Swanzey, and from thence I traveled on foot to Taunton. It was a very cold day; the whole face of the country was covered with snow; the roads were all ice, which the horses' feet had so cut up as to make traveling very loose and difficult. However, I arrived at Taunton very much fatigued in body, and discouraged at heart; I had hardly money enough to carry me to Boston, and when I got there I was not certain of finding a soul living that cared anything for me. Indeed, I never, in my moments of greatest peril, felt so cast down as at this time; my health was gone, my constitution broken down, my friends dead, as I supposed, myself without means to gain a living. I sat down and wept like a child. But again, the thought came to mind, that I had nothing to reproach myself with; I had not foolishly squandered my money in drunkenness and riotous living, but it had been taken from me by the "hand that tempers the wind to the shorn lamb." I had ever adhered to the strictest principles of temperance and morality, and I know not that I have ever spent a dollar to feed an unworthy appetite, or gratify a wrong passion. I had now

> "No wife nor babes to hold me here,
> No cottage in the wilderness."

It was about dark, when I stopped at Mr. Willmouth's tavern in Taunton. I had traveled from daylight till this time without eating a mouthful of anything, fearing to spend any money, lest I should not have enough to bear my expenses to Boston. I was, or had been, well acquainted with the landlord, and was received as an old friend. After supper I went to bed, but it was a long time before I could rest.

The scenes of peril, hardship and suffering through which I had recently passed, had made so deep an impression on my mind, that my imagination was wandering among them still. At one time, I was in the crater of a volcano, and as I was reposing my wearied limbs, I sunk into a dreamy state of forgetfulness, from which I was suddenly awakened by the rumbling of the earth, and I saw, with terror, smoke and flame issuing from the cracks and fissures in the rocks around me. In alarm, I made an effort to escape from the fearful spot, when I found that I was bound down by numerous yellow silken cords, and huge spiders were running over me. A tremendous crash changed the "spirit of my dreams," and I found myself sinking in the fathomless ocean. The boiling flood was gurgling in my ears, huge, slimy monsters were all around me, and eyes of fire seemed peering at me from the dark caverns, while cold, serpentine coils seemed to draw their folds with deathly tightness around me. Again the scene changed, and I was in an open boat upon a wide expanse of waters; the boat was filled with the dead, and huge monsters of the deep, with fiery eye-balls, dashed along the main, scenting their prey; they seemed to threaten my frail bark with instant destruction. To divert them from their fearful purpose, I had to feed out to them my dead companions. At length, the dead were all fed out, and still I was followed by a fearful-looking monster, who, with wide-extended jaws, seized the boat, and in an instant crushed it to atoms. With a shriek of agony I made one spring, and I awoke. I was lying upon the floor of my chamber, bedewed with a cold sweat of agony. At this moment, the landlord entered the room with a light, to learn what the trouble was. I told him what a fearful dream I had, and he said he would prepare me something that would make me sleep. He left the room, and, in a few minutes, returned with an opiate, which I drank, and in five minutes my senses were steeped in forgetfulness. I knew nothing more till morning, when the landlord entered my room, and, after much shaking, aroused me to a sense of my situation. After breakfast, I went to the depot, to ascertain what time the train started for Boston, and what the fare would be. I found that I must be on hand at three o'clock in the afternoon, and ready in disposition to fork over nine shillings of my little fortune, for my passage. After dinner I called for my bill, when Mr. Willmouth told me he asked nothing, and should be happy to have me stay with him longer. At three o'clock, I was at the depot, and took my place in the cars, and about dark arrived at Boston. The "shot in my locker" had now got so low that I could not afford to go to a public house; and I began to cast about in my mind, to know where to stow myself away for the night. Seeing a bright light in a large wooden building, I went in, and found it to be an Irish boarding-house. I found I could have lodgings for twelve and a half cents, and a supper for a shilling. I slept soundly that night, and early the next morning I went down to a packet bound to Portland, Captain Dyer. I asked the fare to Portland. "Three dollars," said the captain. But when informed of my situation, he offered to carry me for two dollars. I accordingly paid my fare, and went on shore again, after learning the time he would sail. I then went to see if I could find my old boarding place. But the house was torn down, and in its place stood a large brick store. I entered the store, and asked the man in attendance if he knew where the family was who formerly resided there. He said the woman had been dead eight years, and he knew nothing about the rest of the people.

I then went down to the packet, and about twelve o'clock at night, we sailed for Portland. The harbor was slightly frozen over, so that we were two hours getting down as far as the castle. We had a fine passage, and the next day got into Portland. Captain Dyer invited me to dine with him. After dinner, he made me a present of half a dollar, as did one of the passengers. I now went out into the market, to see if I could find any person from Danville. As I was passing down one of the streets, I went into a shop to purchase some tobacco, and observing the kind, benevolent look of the shop-keeper, I made bold to ask him if he was acquainted with any people from that place. He said he was not; but there was a man "higher up," whose name was James True, who had married his wife in Danville, and could probably give me any information I desired. I soon found True, and found he was well acquainted with my father's family. He told me that my father and oldest brother had both been dead several years. "But," said he, "your mother is still living, and that is some consolation to you."

I felt that it was indeed so. "Have I any other relations?" I asked, with anxiety.

"Yes," said he, "you have three brothers and three sisters."

"But," said I, "I never had so many to my knowledge."

"Well," said he, "you have to my knowledge; after you went to sea you had one brother and three sisters born, who were alive and well the last time I heard from them."

I now made True fully acquainted with my adventures and present situation. He told me to give myself no uneasiness — that he would let me have money to bear my expenses home, and find me a passage in the stage. He told me that one of my brothers kept a tavern in Poland, and my mother lived with him. He said that he would see that the stage called for me the next morning at sunrise, and I returned to the boarding-house. I went to bed at an early hour, that I might be up in time for the stage the next morning. My slumbers were quiet and refreshing, and I was up at the first sign of the morning, before the family were any of them moving, and had just got out of my chamber, when up drove the stage, and I was forced to start immediately and without my breakfast. It was one of the coldest days I ever knew, and I suffered much from the cold; still my head was continually out of the stage, I was so anxious to fix my eye upon some familiar object; but it was of no use. I had been gone so long, and the face of the country had undergone such changes and alterations, and being covered with snow, no spot looked familiar, or awakened any remembrance of the past.

About nine o'clock, we arrived at what is now called Gray corner, and after taking some refreshment we proceeded to New Gloucester. Here some things upon which my eye rested awakened my sleeping memory, and I began to feel that I was getting on "old ground" again. We arrived at the house of my brother, in Poland, about half past eleven o'clock. My brother, who was in the stable, saw me when I entered the house, and soon came in, He was much changed in his personal appearance, and instead of the light, elastic form he once possessed, he was now a stout, portly looking man. Indeed, I could hardly discover anything about him that reminded me of former days. As it was a very cold day, I was much chilled with my ride, and it was some time before I had got "thawed out," so as to be any ways comfortable. Finding that he had no recollection of me, I entered into conversation with him upon the state of the weather, badness of the roads, business of the country, and such topics as are commonly first broached between strangers. After some time, I asked him if he had ever followed the sea. He answered that he never had. "But," said I, "there is one of your name, who is a seafaring man, that went from these parts somewhere." "Yes," said he, "I had a brother William, who followed the sea for a great many years; but as I have heard nothing from him for a number of years, I suppose he must be dead—probably lost at sea."

During this conversation, I could occasionally see something that reminded me of "by-gone days." Some peculiar glance of the eye or turn of the head assured me that I was indeed holding conversation with my own brother. He had several times, while I was talking, fixed his eyes keenly and earnestly upon me, and then, as if disappointed, again dropped them. I could govern my feelings no longer, and burst into tears. He looked at me in much surprise, and suddenly exclaimed, "Is it possible? Is this William?" I told him we were brothers, and we were instantly in each other's arms. "This is an unexpected happinesss," said he. "I will call the family," he continued, and left the room. In a few minutes an old lady came in, exclaiming, "Where is William?"

It is useless for me to attempt to portray the scene that followed my recognition. For more than forty years I had been roaming, and now returned, an old man, to crave again a mother's blessing. That mother was now about ninety years of age, and is still living. Many were the questions that were asked and answered that night. I began to inquire after my old associates—the companions of my boyhood. But they were gone, some to the west, and some to the south. Some few had settled down in that vicinity, while many had "gone to that bourne from whence no traveler returns." I staid in Poland a few weeks, and then left for the eastward, to visit other relations, with whom I am still living. And now, kind reader, I must take my leave of you. I feel that I am an old man, fast approaching my narrow resting-place, and my desire is that my last hours may be peaceful.

FLOGGING SCENE ON AN AMERICAN MERCHANT VESSEL.

"For several days, the captain seemed very much out of humor. Nothing went right or fast enough for him. He quarreled with the cook, and threatened to flog him for throwing wood on deck; and had a dispute with the mate about reefing a Spanish burton; the mate saying that he was right, and had been taught how to do it by a man *who was a sailor*.

This the captain took in dudgeon, and they were at sword's points at once. But his displeasure was chiefly turned against a large, heavy-molded fellow from the Middle States, who was called Sam. This man hesitated in his speech, and was rather slow in his motions, but was a pretty good sailor, and always seemed to do his best; but the captain took a dislike to him, thought he was surly and lazy; and "if you once give a dog a bad name," as the sailor phrase is, "he may as well jump overboard." The captain found fault with everything this man did, and hazed him for dropping a marline-spike from the main-yard, where he was at work. This, of course, was an accident, but it was set down against him. The captain was on board all day Friday, and everything went on hard and disagreeably. "The more you drive a man the less he will do," was as true with us as with any other people. We worked late Friday night, and were turned to, early Saturday morning. About ten o'clock, the captain ordered our new officer, Russell, who, by this time, had become thoroughly disliked by all the crew, to get the gig ready to take us ashore.. John, the Swede, was sitting in the boat along side, and Russell and myself were standing by the main hatchway, waiting for the captain, who was down in the hold, where the crew were at work, when we heard his voice raised in violent dispute with somebody, whether it was with the mate or one of the crew I could not tell; and then came blows and scuffling. I ran to the side and beckoned to John, who came up, and we leaned down the hatchway; and though we could see no one, yet we knew that the captain had the advantage, for his voice was loud and clear.

"You see your condition! You see your condition! Will you ever give me any more of your *jaw?*" No answer, and then came wrestling and heaving, as though the man was trying to turn him. "You may as well keep still, for I have got you," said the captain. Then came the question, "Will you ever give me any more of your jaw?"

"I never gave you any," said Sam; for it was his voice that we heard, though low and half choked.

"That 's not what I asked you. Will you ever be impudent to me again?"

"I never have been, sir," said Sam.

"Answer my question, or I 'll make a spread eagle of you! I 'll flog you, by G—."

"I 'm no negro slave," said Sam.

"Then I 'll make you one," said the captain, and he came to the hatchway and sprang on deck, threw off his coat, and, rolling up his sleeves, called out to the mate, "Seize that man up, Mr. A——! Seize him up! Make a spread eagle of him! I 'll teach you all who is master aboard!"

The crew and officers followed the master up the hatchway, and, after repeated orders, the mate laid hold of Sam, who made no resistance, and carried him to the gangway.

"What are you going to flog that man for?" said John, the Swede, to the captain.

Upon hearing this, the captain turned upon him, but knowing him to be quick and resolute, he ordered the steward to bring the irons, and, calling Russell to help him, went up to John.

"Let me alone," said John; "I am willing to be put in irons. You need not use any force," and putting out his hands, the captain slipped the irons on, and sent him aft to the quarter-deck. Sam was by this time seized up, as it is called, that is, placed against the shrouds, with his wrists made fast to them, his jacket off, and his back exposed. The captain stood on the break of the deck, a few feet from him, and a little raised, so as to have a good swing at him, and held in his hand the bight of a thick, heavy rope. The officers stood round, and the crew grouped together in the waist.

All these things made me sick and almost faint, angry and excited as I was. A man, a human being made in God's likeness, fastened up and flogged like a beast! A man, too, whom I had lived with and eaten with for months, and knew almost as well as a brother. The first and almost uncontrollable impulse was resistance. But what was to be done? The time for it had gone by. The two best men were fast, and there were only two beside myself and a small boy, of ten or twelve years of age. And then there were, beside the captain, three officers, steward, agent, and clerk. But beside the numbers, what is there for sailors to do? If they resist, it is mutiny; if they succeed and take the vessel, it is piracy. If they ever yield again, their punishment must come; and if they do not yield, they are pirates for life. If a sailor resists his commander, he resists the law, and piracy or submission are his only alternatives, Bad as it is, it must be borne. It is what a sailor ships for.

Swinging his rope over his head, and bending his body, so as to give it full force, the captain brought it down upon the poor fellow's back. Once, twice, six times. "Will you ever give me any more of your jaw?" The man writhed with pain, but said not a word. Three times more. This was too much, and he muttered something which I could not hear, this brought as many more as the man could stand, when the captain ordered him to be cut down, and to go forward.

"Now for you," said the captain, making up to John, and taking his irons off. As soon as he was loose, he ran forward to the forecastle.

"Bring that man aft," shouted the captain.

The second mate, who had been a shipmate of John's, stood still in the waist, and the mate walked slowly forward; but our third officer, anxious to show his zeal, sprang forward over the windlass, and laid hold of John; but he soon threw him from him. At this moment I would have given worlds for the power to help the poor fellow; but it was all in vain. The captain stood on the quarter-deck, bare-headed, his eyes flashing with rage, and his face as red as blood, swinging the rope, and calling out to his officers: "Drag him aft! Lay hold of him! I'll sweeten him!" etc., etc.

The mate now went forward, and told John quietly to go aft; and he, seeing resistance in vain, threw the blackguard third mate from him—said he would go aft himself—that they should not drag him—and went up to the gangway, and held out his hands; but, as soon as the captain made him fast, the indignity was too great, and he began to resist; but the mate and Russell holding him, he was soon seized up. When he was made fast, he turned to the captain, who stood rolling up his sleeves, and getting ready for the blow, and asked him what he was to be flogged for. "Have I ever refused my duty, sir? Have you ever known me to hang back, or be insolent, or not to know my work?"

"No," said the captain; "it is not that I flog you for; I flog you for your interference—for asking questions?"

"Can't a man ask questions here without being flogged?"

"No," shouted the captain, "nobody shall open his mouth aboard this vessel but myself," and began laying the blows upon his back, swinging half round, between each blow, to give it full effect. As he went on, his passion increased, and he danced about the deck, calling out, as he swung the rope,

"If you want to know what I flog you for, I'll tell you. It's because I like to do it!—because I like to do it! It suits me! That's what I do it for!"

The man writhed under the pain, until he could endure it no longer, when he called out with an exclamation, more common among foreigners than with us: "Oh, Jesus Christ! Oh, Jesus Christ!"

"Don't call on Jesus Christ," shouted the captain, "*he can't help you. Call on Captain T——!* He's the man! He can help you! Jesus Christ can't help you now!"

At these words, which I never shall forget, my blood ran cold. I could look on no longer. Disgusted, sick, and horror-struck, I turned away and leaned over the rail, and looked down into the water. A few rapid thoughts of my own situation, and of the prospect of future revenge, crossed my mind; but the falling of the blows, and the cries of the man called me back at once. At length they ceased, and turning round I found that the mate, at a signal from the captain, had cut him down. Almost doubled up with pain, the man walked slowly forward, and went down into the forecastle. Every one else stood still at his post, while the captain, swelling with rage, and with the importance of his achievement, walked the quarter-deck, and, at each turn, as he came forward, called out to us:

"You see your condition! you see where I have got you all, and you know what to expect."—"You have been mistaken in me: you didn't know what I was! Now you know what I am!"—"I'll make you toe the mark, every sort of you, or I'll flog you all, fore and aft, from the boy up!"—"You've got a driver over you! Yes, a *slave-driver! a negro-driver!* I'll see who'll tell me he isn't a negro slave!"

With this and the like matter, equally calculated to quiet us, and to allay any apprehension of any future trouble, he entertained us for about ten minutes when he went below. Soon after, John came aft, with his bare back covered with stripes and wales in every direction, and dreadfully swollen, and asked the steward to ask the captain to let him have some salve or balsam to put upon it. "No," said the captain, who heard him from below, "tell him to put his shirt on, that's the best thing for him; and pull me ashore in the boat. Nobody is going to lay up on board of this vessel."

He then called to Mr. Russell, to take those two men and two others in the boat, and pull him ashore. I went for one. The two men could hardly bend their backs, and the captain called out to them to "give way! give way!" but finding they did their best, he let them alone. The agent was in the stern-sheets, but during the whole pull—a league or more—not a word was spoken. We landed; the captain, agent, and officer went up to the house, and left us with the boat. I and the man with me staid near the boat, while John and Sam walked slowly away, and sat down on the rocks. They talked some time together, but at length separated, each sitting alone. I had some fears of John. He was a foreigner, and violently tempered, and under suffering; and he had his knife with him, and the captain was to come down alone to the boat. But nothing happened, and we went quietly on board. The captain was probably armed, and if either of them had lifted a hand against him, they would have had nothing before them but flight and starvation in the woods of California, or capture by the soldiers and Indian bloodhounds, whom the offer of twenty dollars would have set upon them.

After the day's work was done, we went down into the forecastle, and ate our plain supper; but not a word was spoken. It was Saturday night, but there was no song, no "sweethearts and wives." A gloom was over everything. The two men lay in their berths, groaning with pain, and we all turned in, but for myself not to sleep. A sound coming now and then from the berths of the two men, showed that they were awake, as awake they must have been, for they could hardly lie in one posture a moment; the dim, swinging lamp of the forecastle shed its light over the dark hole in which we lived, and many and various reflections and purposes coursed through my mind. I thought of our situation, living under a tyranny, of the character of the country we were in; of the length of the voyage, and of the uncertainty attending our return to America; and then, if we should return, of the prospect of obtaining justice and satisfaction for these poor men; and vowed that if God should ever give me the means, I would do something to redress the grievances, and relieve the sufferings of that poor class of beings of whom I then was one.*

The excitement which immediately followed the flogging scene soon passed off; but the effect of it upon the crew, and especially upon the two men themselves, remained. The different manner in which these two men were affected, corresponding to their different characters, was not a little remarkable. John was a foreigner, and high-tempered, and

---

* Well has this resolution been observed. R. H. Dana, Esq., of Boston, author of Two Years Before the Mast, from which the above is extracted, is widely known for his philanthropic advocacy in behalf of seamen who have suffered from the tyranny of brutal officers.

though mortified, as any one would be at having the worst of an encoun ter, yet his chief feeling seemed to be anger; and he talked much of satisfaction and revenge, if he ever got back to Boston. But with the other it was very different. He was an American, and had had some education, and this thing coming upon him, seemed completely to break him down. He had a feeling of the degradation that had been inflicted upon him, which the other man was incapable of. Before that he had a good deal of fun, and amused us often with queer negro stories, (he was from a slave State;) but afterward he seldom smiled, seemed to lose all life and elasticity, and appeared to have but one wish, and that was, for the voyage to come to an end. I have often known him to draw a long sigh when he was alone, and he took but little part or interest in John's plans of satisfaction and retaliation.

The flogging was seldom, if ever, alluded to by us in the forecastle. If any one was inclined to talk about it, the others, with a delicacy I hardly expected to find among them, always stopped him, or turned the subject. But the behavior of the two men who were flogged toward one another, showed a delicacy, and a sense of honor which would have been worthy of admiration in the highest walks of life. Sam knew that the other had suffered solely on his account, and in all his complaints he said that if he alone had been flogged, it would have been nothing, but that he never could see that man without thinking what had been the means of bringing that disgrace upon him; and John never, by word or deed, let anything escape him to remind the other that it was by interfering to save his shipmate, that he had suffered.

ADVENTURES

OF

A SLAVE-TRADER,

WHO WAS ENGAGED FOR MANY YEARS IN THE

AFRICAN SLAVE-TRADE.

THEODORE CANOT, the son of a captain in the army of Napoleon, was born in the interior of Italy, in the year 1807. When twelve years of age, his mother, a native of Italy, who had become a widow by the battle of Waterloo, allowed him to follow the bent of his inclinations, and with a liberal outfit, he embarked at Leghorn, as an apprentice, upon the American ship Galatia, of Boston.

For several years he sailed out of the port of Salem, Massachusetts, on voyages to all quarters of the globe. At this period he looked upon slaves for the first time in his life. It was in India, at the disembarking of a cargo of slaves, when he saw a Malay drag a young and beautiful female by the hair. Indignant at the outrage, he felled the savage to the earth with his boat-hook—an act more honorable to his humanity than to his judgment, as it compelled their vessel to leave the port in haste, to avoid popular retaliation. A disappointment of a tender nature caused him to forsake his American employers, and he made several voyages from European ports; but, having grown reckless, his hard-earned wages at sea were always spent on shore in dissipation: wine, women, and gambling were the chief attractions of this fast young man. At length we find him on board of a Dutch galiot, bound for Havana. This was in 1824, at which time the West Indies were infested with those scourges of the sea—pirates. When near the termination of their voyage, their vessel was wrecked at night upon one of those hidden reefs of coral which render navigation in those seas so full of peril. Day dawned, to show them the blue mountains of Cuba rising in beauty in the distance, while near they discovered a low, sandy, and apparently deserted key. Suddenly there shot out from this barren islet a boat containing several ill-looking fellows, in the garb of fishermen, who approached and boarded their vessel. An arrangement was made, that if their vessel did not float off by the next rise of tide, these men, with their companions on shore, should the next day give their assistance to lighten her by carrying her cargo to land. On the second morning, the wreckers proceeded to assist the crew in discharging the cargo; but by sunset very little had been effected. From various circumstances, Canot had his suspicions aroused in regard to these men; but his fears only excited the ridicule of his companions. Fatigued with the labors of the day, he retired to his state-room to sleep. The night being very calm and the vessel near the land, he found his berth filled with musquitoes, and took refuge in the stay-sail nettings, and, notwithstanding a sort of nervous apprehension, was soon buried in sleep. A little past midnight, he was aroused by a piercing shriek Although the moon had set, sufficient light was had to dimly show the decks behind him crowded with men. On being thus suddenly aroused from sleep, Canot at first thought he was laboring under a dreadful nightmare; but in a moment more, the screams of the wounded and the dying, and the appeals for mercy that arose, convinced him that a terrible tragedy was enacting. The vessel had been boarded by pirates, who were then massacring the crew.

With his usual presence of mind, Canot seized the gasket, and gently dropping into the water, boldly struck out for land. He was, in spite of his care, overheard, and had swum but a short distance, when he was ordered in harsh tones and in Spanish, to return or be shot. Anticipating what was to follow, he turned over on his back, and the moment he saw the expected flash from a pistol, he dodged, like a duck, under the water, and the ball passed harmlessly over his body. Several times the same plan was resorted to, until the increasing distance placed him out of the danger. Half an hour was then spent industriously in swimming, in which art he was an adept, and by which he managed to escape both pistol-bullets and the sharks ever numerous in those waters, and reaching land, he secreted himself in a dense growth of mangroves. Destitute of all clothing except trowsers, he had been in this dismal jungle but a short time when swarms of musquitoes lighted upon him, and he was obliged to run and plunge into the water to avoid the torture of their stings; and so it continued alternately through the night. At the gray of morning, Canot climbed the tallest tree he could find, which rose but a few feet above the sand, and casting his eye over the water, saw his vessel surrounded by numerous boats, which the pirates were busy loading with their ill-gotten booty. All the morning he watched the movements of the ruffians with no pleasurable emotions. To add to his distress, the sun poured down upon his naked body with an intensity known only to the tropics, and he suffered greatly from burning thirst, which he vainly endeavored to assuage by chewing bitter berries that grew around him. Late in the afternoon, the pirates towed the vessel in a south-eastern direction, until it was lost to view behind a headland. As the galiot disappeared, and all traces of his companions had vanished, he felt for the first time the utter loneliness and destitution of his condition, and gave vent to his feelings in a copious flood of tears.

The sun had sunk in the west, when Canot, exhausted in body from hunger and thirst, and his nervous system shocked by the dreadful scenes he had witnessed, commenced arrangements to pass the night. To escape the swarms of musquitoes, he was about to bury his body in the sand, and cover his head with his trowsers, when he was startled by a noise in the adjacent bushes. Looking in that direction, he saw a bloodhound quickly moving to and fro, his nose to the earth, snuffing out his prey. Instantly divining his errand, Canot sprang into a tree, just in time to escape the fangs of the ferocious beast, which came bounding on with yells of rage, followed by two armed men. These proved to have been men sent out by the pirate leader in search of any of the crew of the galiot that might have escaped.

Canot was conducted by his captors to a hut at no great distance, made of planks and sails from wrecks, where the whole piratical community had assembled. A council was had upon his fate, and he would doubtless have been sacrificed, upon the principle that dead men tell no tales, were it not that their leader had taken an interest in the young sailor, and interposed in his behalf. Don Rafael, for so he was called, was originally an officer in the French army, who, after the close of the career of Napoleon at Waterloo, found his way to the New World, and had drawn his sword in behalf of the revolutionists of Mexico; but, as is common with similar adventurers, had been buffeted by fortune until circumstances had changed him into a leader of wrecker-pirates—the very vilest of their kind, who never strike until their foe is crippled.

The band of villains who made this island their head-quarters ostensibly followed the occupation of fishing for the market of Havana. But their position was chosen with a view to committing depredations upon the many unfortunate vessels which were wrecked, from time to time, by the dangerous navigation in its vicinity. Canot was duly installed as assistant cook to the band—no unimportant office, as to men who lead a mere animal existence a tickled palate is one of the great chief ends of life. His stay with them was but brief. In a few weeks thereafter, Don Rafael furnished him with a letter to Signor Carlo, a friend in Havana, who was engaged in the slave-trade. He had been in the Cuban city but a few weeks, when Signor Carlo bought a pilot-boat of forty tons, named her "El Areostatico," from her great speed, placed a culverin amidships, and furnished her with all the requisites of a slave vessel, not omitting several kegs of specie, wherewith to purchase her return cargo of human beings. It was on the second of September, 1826, that the "El Areostatico" sailed from the port of Havana, carrying Canot as a sort of supernumerary. The crew consisted of twenty-one scamps—the offscourings of various nations. The captain, a native of the island of Majorica, was but a poor sailor, and the want of discipline and utter worthlessness and ignorance of the men under him, rather astonished Canot, himself a thorough-bred sailor. On the thirteenth of October, they reached the Rio Pongo, on the African coast, and anchored at Bengalong. This place was the residence and slave factory of Mr. Ormond, or, as he was called by the natives, Mongo John—the word "Mongo" signifying chief.

The Areostatico, in a few days, was in complete order to receive her cargo; was well supplied with wood, water and provisions; and being small, without any slave-deck, soft mats were placed among and over the firewood and casks in her hold, to make an even surface for the stowage of a living freight. This task completed, Canot was invited by Mongo John to regale himself ashore. He was shown the town, the baracoons or pens for slaves, the stores, and the harem or wifery of his entertainer. He had been but a few days on shore, when the chief offered and he accepted the situation of a clerk. His compensation was, a private establishment, a seat at his table, and a negro per month, or his equivalent value on his native soil, forty dollars. The runners into the interior having filled the complement of the Areostatico's cargo, Canot went aboard, just previous to her sailing, to see it stowed. It was composed of children, boys and girls, all under sixteen years of age. One hundred and eight of these young people were packed in the hold of this little vessel, which was but one foot and ten inches in height; yet, strange of belief, all but three survived the miseries of their passage to Havana!

The quarters assigned to Canot at Bengalong, consisted of a cane house, plastered with mud and thatched, with an earthen floor and a broad projecting veranda, shade and shelter being the chief points required within the tropics. His employer was a fair specimen of the African slave merchant. He was the mulatto son of a rich English slave-trader, by the daughter of a negro chief. When a youth, he was sent to England to be educated. His father dying a few years after, he was thrown upon his own resources, and became a sailor, following that business for five years, sometimes before the mast, and sometimes as a dandy waiter in the cabin. Hoarding his earnings, he returned to Africa to claim his father's property, and there found his mother yet alive. The sable matron recognized her first-born; "a grand palaver" was had of all his relations, when Ormond was duly reinstated, according to coast law, in possession of all his father's property in houses, lands, and slaves. Thus raised to comparative opulence, he embarked in the profession of his deceased parent, under the name of "Mongo," or Chief of the River. Trade poured in upon him; his stores were supplied with the fabrics of Europe and America, and the native products of hides, wax, palm-oil, ivory and gold, while his overflowing slave-pens were from time to time emptied by vessels which drove a thriving trade with Cuba and Brazil. In a few years, he was a wealthy merchant, and a great man among the petty chiefs of the Foulah and Mandingo tribes of the back country, who flattered his vanity by the title of "king," and evinced their desire to cultivate his good-will by stocking his harem with their prettiest daughters.

One of the first acts of Canot was to take an inventory of the Mongo's property. This showed a large deficiency, the result of the chief's negligence, growing out of his debasing, voluptuous habits. On presenting this to Ormond, he viewed it with indifference, and evinced such petulance, that Canot felt satisfied he knew that his affairs were in a disastrous condition. On re-entering the warehouse, Canot met an old hag, Ungagolah by name, the manager of the Mongo's harem, who went to the cloth-chest, and took out several yards of calico. Canot, upon this, gave her to understand by signs, for he could not speak a word of the dialect, he should not allow such liberties without a written order from the chief. She thereat flew into a violent passion, her horrid face lit up with a devilish ferocity, never seen excepting among savages, and with violent contortions of the body, flashing eyes and awful screams, she poured upon him torrents of abuse.

Ormond received the relation of this petty larceny with a laugh of indifference. That night, while meditating on his pallet, Canot was aroused by a gentle tap at his door. Extinguishing the light, to avoid treachery, he grasped his pistols, and cautiously opened the door. A female stood before him, whom he recognized in the starlight as one of the pearls of Mongo's harem—a beautiful quadroon. She was the child of a mulatto by a white man, and having been born at Sierra Leon could converse in English. She came on an errand of mercy—to warn Canot of the wrath of Ungagolah, never to take anything that a Mandingo offered him, to eat exclusively from the Mongo's table, or else Ungagolah, who knew all the Mandingo *ju-jus*, (poisons,) would soon put him where she could again have free access to the keys of the warehouse.

The wifery or harem of the Mongo was a primitive establishment, formed by a square of mud huts. In his more early days, Mongo governed his harem with the usual decorum of such establishments. But now, as age stole over him, he became a worn-out *debaucheé*, his mind and body weak from licentiousness, ardent spirits and opium. His harem was kept up from fashion; and his wives had generally each a lover in Bengalong. Womanly quarrels sometimes took place, especially if two of these black beauties happened to fancy the same lover. On these occasions, they would sometimes strip, and a regular battle ensue. Sometimes their lovers would have a set-to to determine these matters. The usual form of the duel was to decide by lot, for the first chance, when the lover stripped and received a certain number of blows from his antagonist, from a cowhide. And so on in turn, the one who stood the greatest number of blows without flinching was declared the victor. To show a back well marked with the stripes of such conflicts, was a point of great pride with those chivalrous youths.

At the close of the rainy season, the caravans were looked for, with slaves from the interior. A number of messengers were dispatched through the trails among the dense forests back from the coast, to meet and welcome the traders of the back country. A few days after their departure, the report of musketry signaled the approach of a caravan, which was replied to by the Mongo's people with firing of cannon. In a few minutes, a long caravan entered the village, headed by a band of singers praising their chief and leader—the great Ahmah-de-Bellah. The train consisted of about seven hundred persons, leading captive forty negroes, bound with bamboo withes. Beside the slaves, were large quantities of the usual articles of produce of the interior—hides, ivory, gold, rice, bullocks, sheep, goats, beeswax, etc.

Mr. Ormond received the Mohammedan strangers, with great pomp, in the piazza of his receiving house—the ceremony of presentation to the traders of the caravan occupying about an hour. The trading lasted several days, each day being devoted to one especial article. Each morning a crier went through the town, to give information of the special trade of the day. One day it was in rice, another in cattle, another in slaves, and so on.

Ahmah-de-Bellah was the son of the Ali-Mami, or King of Footha-Yallon, who, having arrived at the age of "twenty-four rainy seasons," was invested with the honor of leading a caravan to the coast, which to form requires time and skill. When the wet season is finished, the chieftain goes out with bands of armed men, and lays in ambush on all the trails which lead to the sea-side, until enough of small traders are secured to form a large caravan, which gives consequence to the leader, and enhances his property, by his per centage on the amount of sales at the towns or factories on the coast.

Eight of the slaves of this caravan were rejected by the Mongo. One of them Ahmah insisted should be shipped, as he could neither *kill* nor keep him. This slave had been guilty of the murder of his son, and was sentenced to be sold *a slave to the Christians*, a punishment ranked worse than death. It was interesting to watch the examination of the slaves when brought before the Mongo for purchase. Disregardful of sex, he examined each from head to foot, handled the principal muscles, the arm-pits, groins, cracked the joints, peered into their mouths to note the missing teeth, scanned the eyes, voice, lungs, fingers, and even toes, so as to be assured of their soundness. To Canot's astonishment, the Mongo rejected one apparently powerful man, whose full muscles and sleek skin evinced high health. He had been subjected to the usual jockey tricks of the dealers: they had medicated him with bloating drugs, and given him a glossy skin by sweating him with powder and lemon-juice. A few days after, Canot saw him abandoned in a neighboring hut, a mere wreck of a man. Whenever a slave in the interior evinces an impaired constitution, he is sold to a peddler or broker, who, with the aid of a quack, repairs him for sale to greenhorns; but the old slavers detect the ruse by the yellow eye, swollen tongue and feverish skin.

Canot eventually left the employment of Mongo John, and took up his residence with a slave-trader, named Edward Joseph. While a guest with him, a great event occurred in his history. This was on the fifth of March, 1827, when a Spanish slaver, the *La Fortuna*, from Regla, the Havana grocer, arrived, which, to the astonishment of Canot, was consigned to him, with all the materials with which to purchase an "assorted cargo of slaves." Thus suddenly elevated to the position of "a trader," but destitute of a baracoon or pen of slaves, he called in requisition all the traders of the river, and offering unusually high terms, soon collected the required number; so that, at the appointed day, the vessel sailed with two hundred and twenty human beings packed in her hold. She arrived safely at Cuba: the voyage yielded a profit of over forty thousand dollars, which was more than one hundred per cent. profit, over all the expenses. Canot was now fairly embarked in the slave-trade, and in the history of his life gives a detail of the customs of this commerce, some of which we here subjoin.

An African trader of reputation selects his cargo with great care, so as to avoid sending to his employers any that are not able-bodied, or that are afflicted with any contagious disease, that may be communicated to other slaves on the voyage. Previous to the shipment, the heads of every male and female are shaved, and the initials of their respective owners burnt on their bodies. This is omitted, when the cargo is consigned to but one proprietor. The last day is signalized by a feast given to the slaves in their baracoons. When over, they are taken to the vessel in canoes, and there stripped entirely *naked*, perfect nudity being considered indispensable to health and cleanliness during the voyage. The men are placed in the hold, the women in the cabin, and the children on deck—the latter protected at night by a sail. They take their meals in messes of ten, and in olden times, when the trade was lawful, it was a universal custom of the Spanish captains to say grace and return thanks. Nowadays, the ceremony is substituted for a "Hurrah for Havana!" accompanied by a clapping of hands. Before eating, the slaves wash their hands in buckets of salt water, and then kids of either rice, farina, yams or beans are given to each squad. As a preventive against greediness, each mouthful is dipped up at a signal from a monitor. Whenever a slave refuses to eat, he is duly reported by the guard, and if from illness, he is cared for, and if from a desire to commit suicide by starvation, as is sometimes the case, a good appetite is stimulated by a few blows from a cat-o'-nine tails, well laid on. The slaves are fed twice a day—at ten in the morning, and four in the afternoon, and a pint and a half of water allowed them during the twenty-four hours. Aside from this they are occasionally indulged in a few whifs of tobacco, each in rotation, from pipes passed round by boys. Every alternate day their mouths are rinsed with vinegar, and each morning a dram is given them to keep off the scurvy. The sexes, although separated, are permitted during the day to converse on deck, and when punishment is inflicted, it is for some fault, and is done only by an order from an officer. Weekly they are shaved, without lathering, by a barber, and their nails pared, so that they need not harm each other in those nightly contests in which they battle for room on their plank beds. In pleasant weather, they are permitted to unite their voices in singing their native melodies, mixed with various drummings, or *tom-toms*, on reversed tubs or tin-kettles

The greatest care is taken to keep the vessel clean: chloride of lime is freely distributed, the decks often washed, scraped and holystoned, so that in neatness and in discipline a well-conducted slaver is only equaled by a man-of-war. At sunset, the slaves are stowed for the night; the officers, with whip in hand, ranging the slaves—those on the right side of the vessel facing the bows, those on the left facing the stern, so as to bring each negro on his right side, and thus allow better action for the heart. The tallest are placed in the center and broadest part of the vessel, the shortest near the bows and stern. *Strict* discipline is required for the nightly stowage, lest the living freight should take upon themselves the airs of passengers. To insure silence and order, every tenth slave is provided with a whip, and if any of those under his charge are noisy, he dextrously uses his weapon, and finds his reward in a present of an old shirt or tar-besmeared trowsers. Ventilation is well provided for, and when among the suffocating calms of the tropics, a portion of the slaves sleep on deck under an armed watch. In the baracoons, and while being shipped, slaves are chained in gangs of ten; but at sea they are fastened in pairs, by irons at their ankles.

From this account of Canot, it would appear that no unnecessary severity is or ever has been resorted to: the slavers manifesting about the same degree of interest in the welfare of their cargo, as the commander of a Connecticut horse jockey evinces in his cargo of four-limbed quadrupeds, which he wishes to land on one of the Bermudas in as salable a condition as is possible. Our own countryman, Captain Andrew H. Foote, of the U. S. Navy, in his work on Africa and the American Flag, has accumulated evidence which gives a very different account from that drawn by Canot, and from which we subjoin some statements.

The slave-trade is now carried on by comparatively small and ill-found vessels, watched by the cruisers incessantly. They are, therefore, induced, at any risk of loss of life, to crowd and pack their cargoes, so that a successful voyage may compensate for many captures. In olden times, when the trade was legal, large vessels were fitted expressly for the business—Indiamen or whalers. It has been objected to the employment of squadrons to exterminate that trade, that their interference has increased its enormity. This, however, is not true, for if there ever was anything on earth, which, for revolting, filthy, heartless atrocity might make the devil wonder and hell recognize its own likeness, then it was on the decks of any one of the old slavers. The sordid cupidity of the older, as it is meaner, was also more callous than the hurried ruffianism of the present age. In fact, a slaver now has but one deck; in the last century they had two or three, the number of decks rendering the suffocating and pestilential hold a scene of unparalleled wretchedness.

Here are some instances of this, collected from evidence taken before the British House of Commons, in 1792. James Morley, gunner of the Medway, states: "He has seen them under great difficulty of breathing. The women often, particularly, got upon the beams to get air, but they were driven down because they take air from the rest. He has known rice held in the mouths of sea-sick slaves, until they were almost strangled. He has seen the surgeon's mate force the panniken between their teeth, and throw the medicine over them, so that not half of it went into their mouths—the poor wretches wallowing in their blood, hardly having life, and this with blows of the cat." Dr. Thomas Trotter, surgeon of the Brookes, says: "He has seen the slaves drawing their breath with all those laborious and anxious efforts for life, which are observed in expiring animals, subjected, by experiment, to foul air, or in the exhausted receiver of an air-pump. Has also seen them, when the tarpaulins have inadvertently been thrown over the gratings, attempt to heave them up, crying out: '*Kickeraboo! kickeraboo!!*' — i.e., '*We are dying! we are dying!!*' On removing the tarpaulin and gratings, they would fly to the hatchways with all the signs of terror and dread of suffocation; many of those whom he has seen in a dying state have recovered by being brought upon deck; others, who were previously well, perished by suffocation." In regard to the *Garland's* voyage in 1788, the testimony is: "The slaves, both when ill and well, were frequently forced to eat against their inclination, and were whipped with a cat if they refused. The parts on which their shackles are fastened, are often excoriated by the violent exercise they are forced to take. Fell in with the *Hero*, which had lost over three hundred, mostly by the smallpox—the surgeon stating, that when removed from one place to another, they left marks of their skin and blood upon the deck, and that it was the most horrid sight he had ever seen."

Even at that time, when the trade was under systematic regulations, the slaves were obliged to lie upon their backs, and were shackled by their ankles, the left of one being fastened close by the right of the next; so that the whole number, in one line for the length of the deck, formed a single living chain. When one died, the body remained during the night; and in bad weather, when the hatches were necessarily closed, suffocation would occur. It can, therefore, be understood that the strong strangled the weak intentionally, to procure more space, and that when striving to get near some aperture affording air to breathe, many would be injured or killed in the struggle. Such were "the horrors of the middle passage." We subjoin some extracts, giving the condition in which slave vessels have been found in our time. The first is from a report of Captain Hayes to the Admiralty, of a representation made to him respecting a slaver, in 1832:

"The master, having a large cargo of these human beings chained together, with more humanity than his fellows, permitted some of them to come on deck for the benefit of the weather, but still chained together, when they immediately commenced jumping overboard, hand in hand, and drowning in couples. They had just been brought from between decks, to which they knew they must return, where the scalding perspiration was running from one to the other, men dying and living, and dead bodies chained together; and the living, in addition to all their torments, laboring under the most famishing thirst. These unfortunate people had just been torn from their country, their families, their all!—men from their wives, women from their husbands, children from their parents; and yet, in this man's eye, there was no cause whatever for jumping overboard and drowning. The men are chained in pairs, and as a proof they are intended so to remain until the end of the voyage, their fetters are not locked but riveted by the blacksmith; and as deaths are frequently occurring, living men are often for awhile confined to dead bodies, the latter sometimes in a putrid state."

The notorious Spanish slaver, the *Velos Passagueiro*, was captured by the North Star, after a long chase and a battle, and was found full of slaves. Behind her foremast was an enormous gun, turning on a broad circle of iron, and enabling her to act as a pirate, if her slave speculation had failed. She had taken in 562 slaves, and had been out seventeen days, dr ing which she had thrown overboard fifty-five.

The slaves were all inclosed under grated hatchways between decks. The space was so low that they sat between each other's legs, and were stowed so close together that there was no possibility of their lying down, or at all changing their position by day or night. As they were shipped on account of different individuals, they were all branded like sheep, with the owner's marks, of different forms. These were impressed under their hearts, or on their arms, and as the mate informed me, with perfect indifference, "burnt with the red-hot iron." Over the hatchway, stood a ferocious-looking fellow, with a scourge of many twisted thongs in his hand, who was the slave-driver of the ship.

As soon as the poor creatures saw us looking down at them, their dark and melancholy visages brightened up. They perceived something of sympathy and kindness in our looks, to which they had been unaccustomed; and feeling instinctively that we were friends, they immediately began to shout and clap their hands. One or two had picked up a few Portuguese words, and cried out, Viva! viva! The women were particularly excited. They all held up their arms, and when we bent down and shook hands with them, they could not restrain their delight: they endeavored to scramble up on their knees, stretching up to kiss our hands, and we understood that they knew we were coming to liberate them. Some, however, hung their heads in apparently hopeless dejection; some were greatly emaciated, and some, particularly children, seemed dying. But the circumstance which struck us most forcibly, was, how it was possible for such a number of human beings to exist, packed up and wedged together as close as they could cram, in low cells three feet high. In one part of the hold, the average sitting space to each woman was not more than thirteen inches. The heat of these horrid places was so great, and the odor so offensive, that it was quite impossible to enter them, even had there been room. The officers insisted that the poor suffering creatures should be admitted on deck to get air and water.

On looking into the places where they had been crammed, there were found some children next the sides of the ship, in the places most remote from the air and light; they were lying in nearly a torpid state, after the rest had been turned out. The little creatures seemed indifferent as to life and death; and when carried on deck, many of them could not stand. After enjoying, for some time, the unusual luxury of air, some water was brought; it was then that the extent of their sufferings was exposed in a fearful manner. They all rushed like maniacs toward it; no entreaties, or threats, or blows, could restrain them; they shrieked, and struggled, and fought with one another, for a drop of this precious liquid, as if they grew rabid at the sight of it. There is nothing slaves in the mid-passage suffer so much from as the want of water. It is sometimes usual to take out casks filled with sea-water, as ballast, and when the slaves are received on board, to start the casks and refill them with fresh. On one occasion, a ship from Bahia neglected to change the casks, and on the mid-passage found, to their horror, that they were filled with nothing but salt water. All the slaves on board perished. At the time of this seizure of the Velos Passaguiro, Brazil was precluded from the slave-trade north of the equator; but the time had not arrived when, by treaty, the Southern trade was to be extinguished. The Captain of this slaver had papers which exhibited an apparent uniformity to the law, and which, false as they may have been, could in no way be absolutely disproved. The accounts of the slaves themselves, that they had originally come from parts of Africa north of the line, the course which the slaver was steering, her flight from the English cruiser—were circumstances raising suspicions the most violent; but the reader will not be a little disappointed to learn that, with all this, the case was too doubtful, in point of legal proof, to bear out a legal detention; and the slaver, therefore, after nine hours of close investigation, was finally set at liberty, and suffered to proceed. It was dark when we separated, and the last parting sounds we heard from the unhallowed ship, were the cries and shrieks of slaves, suffering under some bodily infliction."

We now return to the story of Canot, who had grown to such sudden importance, that the neighboring kings and chiefs sent him various presents, to propitiate the good graces of the young and enterprising slave-dealer. In the month of November, he received and accepted an invitation, by a messenger, from Ahmah-de-Bellah, to visit him in his own country, the land of the Fellahs, several weeks' journey into the interior. This journey was undertaken with an eye to the advancement of the business interests of Canot, in the merchandise of human flesh. He left Bengalong with a caravan of about forty-five. Ten of his servants were assigned to carry his baggage, merchandise, and provisions. Ali Ninpha, the guide, two interpreters, two servants, and a hunter, formed his immediate guard. As the best of African roads are mere paths, the train marched in single file, preceded by two men, armed with cutlasses and muskets, who, by loud cries, warned the caravan when approaching bee-trees, ant-hills, hornet-nests, reptiles, or any of those perils common in African forests. Behind, came women, children, and guards, and, last of all, Canot and the chiefs, with whip in hand, to spur up the stragglers. For a few days, they passed through a rolling country; with alternate forests and cultivated fields and villages, where they were welcomed by the head men. The time was beguiled by jokes and songs, and chanting praises to Allah. Occasionally the masters would relieve their slaves of their burdens; at night, the women brought the water, cooked the food, and distributed it to the men. The fourth night was passed at Kya, a fortified town of the Mandingoes, where they were feasted by the chief with the best of the land, and whose hospitality Canot reciprocated by such abundance of the white man's strong water, that the next morning he was unable to leave his couch to bid farewell to his guests.

Traveling into the interior of Africa would be a mere rural jaunt, were it not for the perils of war. The African, in his life, is a half shepherd and half warrior. Though uncivilized, his country is not absolutely wild, and Mohammedanism, descending from the north, in its southward journeyings, has, in the course of centuries, much altered and improved the negro character. The humanizing influence of the Koran upon the interior tribes is evident. But with all these changes, external nature is ever magnificent. Shade and shelter is all the climate requires, and so great the fertility, that trifling labor, united to the abundance of tropical fruits, yields ample support. Amid such oppressive heats, with so little occasion for effort, it does not seem as though the African could ever be stimulated to the industry which develops all that is noble in man in more inhospitable climes.

For the six hundred miles that Canot traversed, his course was through an almost continuous forest, and so dense the foliage, that often for hours not a glimpse of the sun was had; but when they entered the bare vallies the suffering from heat was intense. Everything was all glare: the reflected rays from every surrounding object pierced them like lances, and it seemed as if their very eyes were simmering and drying up in their sockets. When the highlands were reached, the temperature became invigorating, and the scenery always beautiful, and frequently grand. In their rear, gently-rounded hills, checkered here and there by native huts, with patches of sward and cultivation amid the forest, swelled up in surpassing beauty of contour; while to the north and east, lofty hills and mountains rose up in continuous succession, until, in the far distance, the blue of land and sky met and mingled in the same ethereal tint. The next principal town reached was Tamisso, which the caravan entered with great pomp, the women being particularly careful in adorning their persons. "Wool was combed to its utmost rigidity; skins were greased until they shone like polished ebony; ankles and arms were restrung with beads, and loins were girded with snowy waist-cloths." Mounted on a beautiful horse, Canot rode with his motley group into the town, amid the discharge of fire-arms, the noise of tom-toms, and the melody of the unctuous women. Crowds of men, women and children, rushed forward to gaze upon the white man, the Mongo of the coast. He pressed on to the palace of Mohamedo, which, like all royal palaces in Africa, consisted of a collection of mud huts, with shady verandas, in the midst of a quadrangular court. On a couch covered with leopard skins reclined in state the chief Mohamedo, in half-Turkish costume. He was a fat old man, with a long, flowing, snowy beard, in strange contrast to his ebony skin. The old sinner being informed that Canot was on a trading tour for the purchase of slaves for numerous vessels hovering on the coast, with immense cargoes of red cloth, beads, and other gew-gaws of savage desire, rose, and in a loud voice presented him to his people as his "beloved son!"

That evening, Canot, jaded out with the dust, heat, and crowd of this noisy African town, retired to a court behind his lodgings to take a bath. But his modesty was shocked by the presence of a bevy of the sable damsels of the harem, who, on learning that the "Furtoo" was about to bathe, crowded around him as he commenced to disrobe. When he pulled off his shirt, but leaving his lower garment untouched, several of them fled to call their companions to see "the peeled Furtoo," whose snowy back and breast had excited their wonder. One old hag run her fingers over his chest, and then, as if he were reeking with leprosy, wiped them on the wall. With great difficulty, he got rid of the chattering crowd, and finished his preparations for his ablutions,

Tamisso, like many of the interior towns, was completely inclosed by two lines of high fence, a few feet apart, the space between being filled with upright staves, their sharp points hardened by fire. Admittance to the town was through gates, with winding passages.

It was not many days before the caravan arrived at their journey's end, the town of Timbo, the capital of the kingdom of Footha-Yallon. The king, Ali-Mami, Canot found a gouty, inquisitive old Mussulman, who greeted him with most affectionate hugs, then stretched out his arms to Heaven, and exclaimed, "God is great! God is great! and Mohammed is his prophet!" He then plied him with questions about his history—"Who was his father? who was his mother? how many brothers had he? were they warriors? were they book men?" etc., etc. The next day, a grand palaver was had with the chiefs, in a beautiful grove of trees. His friend, Ahmah-de-Bellah, presented him to the great men, stating that he was a rich trader from the Rio Pongo, who was entitled to most courteous treatment from Fellahs, for he had penetrated to their distant country to purchase slaves on most generous terms—an interesting communication, which they received with shouts of joy. Canot, in return, made a sort of stump speech, and then unfolded to their view a quantity of presents he had brought for them, consisting of gaudy calicoes, scarlet cloth, powder, muskets, tobacco, and beads, not omitting a gilded sword, and a package of *cantharides* for the king.

During his sojourn at Timbo, Canot made several incursions into the neighboring villages, but the poor people, knowing that the object of his journey was to obtain slaves, fled in the greatest terror before him, Panic-stricken, they would leave their pots of rice, vegetables and meat, boiling in their huts, and fly in the greatest terror from the presence of the notorious slaver. War-parties and scouts were sent out in the meantime, to collect slaves for Canot, and even the town itself was not spared, so that the more common people regarded him as a sort of devil incarnate.

Timbo was a town of narrow streets, low houses, mud walls, cul-de-sacs, and mosques. The people appeared to be industrious. Peddlers supplied them with fruit, vegetables, and meat. The females kept themselves busy with their spinning-wheels, and occasionally an old lady, devoutly disposed, was seen poring over the pages of the Koran. The men wore cotton, worked in leather, fabricated iron from the bar, and when at leisure, studied the Koran, or occupied themselves in writing.

Canot, on his return to Bengalong, headed a caravan of near a thousand strong, the greater part of which were slaves collected by his friends in Timbo. For a change of scene, he soon after took command of one of his vessels, and set sail on a visit to Cuba. He had scarce got out of sight of land, when the slaver fell into the hands of a British cruiser, and Canot was taken prisoner. He managed to escape in a small boat, and, with a slave for a companion, reached Bengalong in safety. He there found the Felix at anchor, a vessel which had been consigned to him from Cuba, with remittances in money and merchandise to cover the purchase of 350 slaves. Unable to procure in season a full cargo, he made a short journey to a village in the interior, to obtain the additional fifty required. A grand "palaver" was had with the chief and head men, when he made known his wants and announced his terms. His merchandise, his scarlet-cloth, bits of looking-glass, beads, etc., had their usually magical effects. Jealous husbands suddenly recollected their wives' infidelity. Young folks, who had never dreamed of being made slaves, were captured and brought in. The whole place was in a turmoil. Every man was ready to accuse his neighbor of some crime, that he might kidnap him, and obtain a share of the spoils. And when Canot left the town, he carried with him the eternal remembrances of some forty or fifty of its families, whom he had deprived of some one of their members. The capture of his former vessel rendered it necessary that Canot should visit Cuba in the Felix. This voyage was successful. From Cuba he sailed for Jamaica, for a cargo of merchandise, with the intention of returning and refitting for slaves. The trip was disastrous, the vessel being wrecked, by which Canot was so reduced in fortune, as gladly to accept the situation of sailing-master in the San Pablo, a slaver which was fitting out at St. Thomas. This vessel was armed with sixteen guns, and the entire crew and officers arrayed in the uniform of the French navy, so as to convey the deception that she was a French man-of-war. Her destination was a town in the Mozambique

Channel, on the eastern coast of Africa. Eight hundred negroes were obtained and shipped, and the vessel had arrived off the Cape of Good Hope when the smallpox broke out. A council was held, and it was determined at first to destroy the sick by laudanum, to preserve the living; but the examination showed that too many were infected to render this of any avail. A series of tremendous gales springing up, rendered the closing of the hatches imperative. When, at its termination, the gratings were removed, it was found that nearly all the slaves were sick or dead. Twelve of the stoutest survivors, together with a part of the crew, armed with tarred mittens, went into the hold, dragged out and threw overboard more than three hundred corpses, men, women, and children, in a most disgusting state of putrefaction.

Twelve thousand dollars fell to the share of Canot, as the result of this voyage, which he applied to the fitting out of the Conchita, a Baltimore clipper. He was no sooner ready for sea than his vessel was seized for a fraud practiced upon the Cuban authorities, and Canot barely escaped a prison, by fleeing to and remaining in the interior for several weeks. He was too valuable a man for the slave-dealers to allow to remain idle. He was speedily put in command of the Estrella, and steered for Ayudah, on the Gold Coast, with a sufficient supply of rum, powder, English muskets, and rich cottons from Manchester, to purchase 450 slaves.

The Estrella was consigned to Senor da Sousa, one of the most notorious and successful of those infamous merchants known in coast annals. This man was a mulatto, born in Rio Janeiro. How he reached Africa is unknown; but when there, he deserted his master, and eventually made his way into the interior, to the court of Dahomey. At this period the Brazilian slave-trade was in full vigor, and the adventurous refugee managed with great skill in his dealings, as a broker, among the natives; from small beginnings, he gradually grew up into an opulent trader. His mixed blood helped him on. He learned to speak like a native, became an African among Africans, and among the whites assumed the easy, winning address of his country. Chief after chief became his friend, and he finally obtained the summit of his influence, in being made the favorite of the powerful king of Dahomey. So great was the estimation in which this man was held by the Dahomians, that when he died, in 1849, a boy and girl were beheaded and buried with him, and three men offered up in sacrifice. For months the funeral honors to his memory were continued. The town was kept in a continual ferment. Three hundred of the women who compose the Dahomian army daily paraded, and fired, and danced in his honor. Bands of people paraded the streets, headed by guinea-fowls, ducks, goats, pigeons and pigs, on poles, alive for sacrifice. Much rum was distributed, and nightly there was shouting, firing, and dancing. Such were the hellish orgies occasioned by the death of this infamous wretch.

At the time of Canot's arrival, da Sousa was at the summit of his career. He had built him a magnificent dwelling at Ayudah, and surrounded himself with all the luxuries of an animal existence. "Wines, food, delicacies and raiment were brought from Paris, London and Havana. The most beautiful women of the country were lured to his settlement. Billiard-tables and gambling halls spread their wiles for detained navigators. And here this horrible man had surrounded himself with all that could corrupt virtue, gratify passion, tempt avarice, betray weakness, satisfy sensuality, and complete a picture of incarnate slavery in Dahomey.

When he sallied forth, an officer preceded him to clear the path; a fool or buffoon hopped beside him; a band of native musicians, and a couple of singers, screamed, at the top of their voices, the most fulsome praises of the mulatto. Numbers of vessels were of course required to feed this African nabob with doubloons and merchandise. Sometimes commanders from Cuba or Brazil would be kept months in his perilous nest, while their craft cruised along the coast, in expectation of human cargoes. At such seasons, no expedient was left untried for the entertainment and pillage of wealthy or trusted idlers. If da Sousa's board and wines made them drunkards, it was no fault of his. If *rouge-et-noir* or *monte* won their doubloons and freight at his saloon, he regretted, but dared not interfere with the amusement of his guests. If the syrens of his harem betrayed a cargo for their favor, over cards, a convenient fire destroyed the frail warehouse *after* the merchandise was removed." Canot, by avoiding the wiles of da Sousa and his dissipated sons, won the respect of the great man, so that, at the end of two months, he had secured a cargo of 480 prime negroes in the bowels of the Estrella.

While at Ayudah, da Sousa received an invitation from the king of Dahomey to visit his court, with his guests, at the yearly sacrifice of human beings. Canot did not accompany the party; but the English traveler, Duncan, some years later, (in 1845,) visited the court of Dahomey, and in his travels gives an interesting account of his presentation to this most powerful of all the monarchs of the Negro tribes. His experiences there we give in his own language:

"We arrived at Abomey, the capital of Dahomey, at three minutes past one o'clock, amid crowds of spectators, and were guided to an excellent house prepared for me by Mayho, the king's prime minister, an excellent old man, and very different to the generality of uncivilized Africans, not having that covetous and selfish disposition usual with them. On the following morning, after an early breakfast, I was fully equipped, and rode, attended by some of the king's principal men, to the market-place, or parade-ground, in front of his palace or house. On our march to the market-place, we passed along part of the walls of the palace, which covers an immense space. The walls as well as houses are made of red, sandy clay, and on top of the walls, at intervals of thirty feet, human skulls were placed along their whole extent. On approaching nearer the market-place we beheld, on an elevated pole, a man fixed in an upright position, with a basket on his head, apparently holding it with both his hands. A little farther on we saw two more men, now in a state of decomposition, hung by the feet from a thick pole, placed horizontally on two upright poles, about twenty feet high.

On the opposite side of the market were two more human bodies, in the same position as those I have just mentioned, with the exception that the bodies had been mutilated. This excited my curiosity, for decapitation is the favorite mode of execution in Abomey. I was informed that these men had been guilty of adulterous intercourse with one of the king's wives, in consequence of which they were sentenced to be put to death by being beaten with clubs, and after death mutilated. The king had not yet arrived at the appointed place, where a high stool and footstool were placed for him under a huge umbrella, surrounded by about twenty more of nearly the same dimensions, forming a crescent—his own being in the center. He had requested, through Mayho, that I would salute him as I would the Queen of England, for he was anxious to become acquainted with European manners and customs.

Accordingly, upon a nearer approach, I saluted his Majesty according to military regulation, with which he seemed much pleased, and returned the compliment in a much more graceful manner than I expected. He then requested me to dismount and come to him. Upon which his prime minister, and four others next in rank, who were conducting me to his Majesty's presence, desired me to halt till they paid their compliment to his Majesty. Forming in line in front of me, they completely prostrated themselves at full length, rubbing both sides of their faces on the ground, and kissing it. They then raised themselves on their knees, where they remained till they had completely covered themselves with dust, and rubbed their arms over with dirt as high as the shoulders.

I was much surprised as well as disgusted with such absurd, abject humiliation. Their robes, which a few minutes before looked clean and respectable, were now, as well as their persons, smeared with dirt. Myself and the governor of Whydah fort were the only persons who did not observe the same degrading form. Even the soldiers, male and female, although under arms, observe the same humiliation. After this ceremony, we stepped forward to the king, and he descended from his stool or throne, and shook me cordially by the hand, declaring his great satisfaction at having an Englishman in his country. He then proposed to drink my health. A table having already been prepared for me, a liquor-case was placed thereon, containing numerous different sorts of flasks and decanters, with as many sorts of liquors, namely, Hollands, rum, brandy, aniseed, claret, cherry brandy, and other cordials. During the time the king is drinking, his face is always concealed from observation by a number of handkerchiefs, held up round his head. At this moment a firing of muskets and beating of gong-gongs and hurrahing takes place.

I was ushered to a seat close to the king, who paid me great attention, and showed every anxiety to give me information, and explain everything to me. It may be well, before proceeding further, to state that all his attendants and soldiers on guard near his person, sit down cross-legged; the soldiers with the butt-end of the musket resting on the ground, between their legs, in a perpendicular position. During this time, troop after troop of female soldiers arrived, preceded by a band of very barbarous music, similar to sheep-bells and drums, made from part of the trunk of a hollow tree, with some bullock or sheep-skin covered over the top of it.

The king is a tall, athletic man, about forty-three years of age, with a pleasing expression and good features, but the top of his forehead falling back rather too much to meet the views of a phrenologist. His voice is good and manner graceful, in comparison with the barbarous customs of the country.

In all directions, troops of female soldiers were now arriving, and taking their stations at a distance, lying down or squatted, until they are called upon to come before his Majesty. No particular discipline is observed. The regiments severally form up in an irregular column, and the principal, or commanding officer, calls out the officers, who kneel on both knees, and cover their heads and bodies with dust. The commander then introduces, one after the other, each officer of this female regiment; and if any one has in any way distinguished herself, it is commented upon, and the party complimented and rewarded for her valor. This regiment belonged to the king's son, in the government of a country bearing an ensign or flag, ornamented with the figure of a lion.

After all the ceremony of compliments and boasting of valor is gone through, the officers fall in, and the whole regiment sing a song in compliment to the king. After that, any individual who chooses is allowed to step to the front, and declare her fidelity to his majesty, and as soon as one retires another takes her place, so that the ceremony becomes irksome. Sometimes the ceremony of one regiment passing occupies three hours. After all is over, the whole of the regiment kneel down, with the butt of their muskets on the ground and the barrel slanting back over the shoulder, and with both hands scrape up the dust and cover themselves with it. The dust being of a light red color, gives them a very singular appearance. Many have their heads entirely shaved, except a tuft resembling a cockade; others only shave a breadth of two inches from the forehead to the poll. After this ceremony, they all rise up from the stooping position, still on their knees, but body otherwise erect, and poising their muskets horizontally on their two hands, all join in a general hurrah. Suddenly, then, they rise up, throwing the musket sharply into one hand, holding it high in the air, at the same time giving another hurrah. The whole then shoulder muskets, and run off at full speed. Each individual runs as fast as she is able, so that it is a race with the whole regiment of six hundred women. It would surprise a European to see the speed of these women, although they carry a long Danish musket and a short sword each, as well as a sort of club.

It may be well to give some account of the dress and equipments of these Amazons. They wear a blue and white striped cotton surtout—the stripes about one and a half inch wide—of stout native manufacture, *without sleeves*, leaving freedom for the arms. The skirt or tunic reaches as low as the kilt of the Highlanders. A pair of short trowsers is worn underneath, reaching two inches below the knee. The cartouch-box, or *agbwadya*, forms a girdle, and keeps all their dress snug and close. The cartouch-box contains twenty cartridges, about four times the quantity of that used in England, owing to the inferiority of the powder. It is very conveniently placed, being girded round the loins. These women certainly make a very imposing appearance, and are very active. From their constant exercise of body, (for the women in all cases do the principal part of both domestic and agricultural labors here, as well as at other places,) they are capable of enduring much fatigue.

Next came the king's second son's female soldiers, from a part called Kakagee's country, in consequence of having the government of that country. These soldiers, about six hundred, went through the same ceremony as the others. His Majesty always anxiously explained everything to me, and sent to the palace for paper for me to make notes upon. During the day, about six thousand women-soldiers passed successively before the king, who frequently introduced the principal officers of this corps to me, relating their achievements. This seemed to give them great satisfaction. Among them, he introduced me to one of his principal wives, a stout, noble-looking woman, of a light brown complexion. She commanded the whole of the king's wives, who are all soldiers, amounting to six hundred, present on this occasion.

Next morning, June 12th, as early as seven o'clock, I was again summoned to attend the review. Some of the principal ministers came with me, to show me where to stand, to allow the passing soldiery to have a full view of king's visitor, or king's stranger, as they called me. The soldiers were now fast arriving from all quarters; each regiment preceded by its band, whose instruments produced the most discordant sounds that can be imagined—drums, elephants' teeth, bullock's horns, and a sort of triangular iron tube, which they beat with a small stick, and which gave forth sounds like a sheep-bell.

The commander rides in the center of his regiment, if provided with a horse, (which is not stronger than a Shetland pony,) with two men holding him on. Others, who have no horses, are carried in hammocks. After about four thousand men had passed me, marching without any discipline or form, I returned to the king's canopy, to await the commencement of the review. In a short time, the female soldiers made their appearance, in full marching order, with provisions, amounting to about seventeen hundred. This corps was preceded by its band. The drum is carried on the head, one end to the front and the other to the rear; the person beating it walks behind the carrier. The drum belonging to the corps was ornamented with twelve human skulls. Seven standards are carried with this regiment, the tops of which are ornamented with human skulls. This regiment belongs to Megah, the king's principal jailor.

About two hundred marched past, as I have described, followed in succession by the king's women, to-day amounting to six hundred, all from the king's palace. These were headed by Dagbyweka. The drum was also ornamented by twelve skulls of traitors, or men caught in arms against the king. This corps observed certain regulations on the march, not customary with the others: nine women and an officer marched in front, as an advance guard; at a short interval fifty supporters; then followed the main body. One individual officer is always appointed to lead the attack, who is distinguished by a sword of different pattern. An attack is, if possible, always made in the night, or very early in the morning. Next followed the female soldiers from Apadomey, commanded by Knawie, (or white man's mother.) Next, Icandee people, a country distant one day's journey to the W.N.W. of Abomey.

After this procession, which consisted altogether of about eight thousand women, well-armed and clothed, had passed, the king asked me to go and see what his women soldiers were about to perform. I was accordingly conducted to a large space of broken ground, where fourteen days had been occupied in erecting three immense prickly piles of green bush. These three clumps, or piles, of a sort of strong briar or thorn, armed with the most dangerous prickles, were placed in line, occupying about four hundred yards, leaving only a narrow passage between them, sufficient merely to distinguish each clump appointed to each regiment. These piles are about seventy feet wide, and eight feet high. Upon examining them, I could not persuade myself that any human being, without boots or shoes, would, under any circumstances, attempt to pass over so dangerous a collection of the most efficiently armed plants I had ever seen. Behind these piles already mentioned, were yards, or large pens, at the distance of three hundred yards, fenced with piles seven feet high, thickly matted together with strong reeds. Inclosed therein were several hundred slaves belonging to the king.

It may be well to state that this affair was entirely got up to illustrate an attack upon a town, and the capture of prisoners, who are of course made slaves. After waiting a short time, the Apadomey soldiers made their appearance at about two hundred yards from, or in front of the first pile, where they halted with shouldered arms. In a few seconds, the word for attack was given, and a rush was made toward the pile with a speed beyond conception, and in less than one minute the whole body had passed over this immense pile, and had taken the supposed town. Eacn of the other piles was passed with equal rapidity, at intervals of twenty minutes, after which we again returned to our former station in the market-place. Here we found his Majesty waiting for us. He anxiously inquired how I was pleased with the performance of his female soldiers, and asked if I thought the same number of Englishwomen would perform the same. I, of course, answered *no:* we had no female soldiers in England, but we had females who had, individually and voluntarily, equally distinguished themselves.

In a short time after our return, the Apadomey regiment passed, on their return, in single file—each leading, in a string, a young male or female slave, carrying also the dried scalp of one man supposed to have been killed in the attack. On all such occasions, when a person is killed in battle, the skin is taken from the head, and kept as a trophy of valor. I counted seven hundred scalps pass in this manner. The captains of each corps, in passing, again presented themselves before his Majesty, and received the king's approval of their conduct. After all had passed each regiment again formed in column before the king, and each officer was presented to me, and their deeds of valor recorded for which they were promoted. No promotion takes place unless merited on account of some act of distinguished merit. When the king's household troop or regiment formed up, his Majesty asked me if I observed the form of an animal worn on the white cotten skull-cap of this corps. I replied in the affirmative. This animal, he informed me, was killed by some of his women when in the bush, during the last war, a few months ago; and he had ordered the figure to be worn on the cap as a badge of distinction.

One officer of this corps of king's soldier-wives was introduced to me. Her name was Adadimo. This female had, during the two last years' war, taken, successively, each year a male prisoner, for which she was promoted, and his Majesty had also presented her with two female slaves. Adadimo is a tall, thin woman, about twenty-two years of age, and good-looking for a black, and mild and unassuming in appearance. The king also introduced her to an Ashantee prince and some attendants, who were here on a visit. After presenting Adadimo to the Ashantees, he addressed her and the regiment to the following effect, the regiment being now on their knees:—He told them I was one of the Queen of England's soldiers, sent on a friendly mission or visit, to collect information respecting his kingdom; and he himself felt proud and much gratified to be able to inform them all of the circumstance, more especially as he could assure them that the Queen of England was the greatest and most powerful sovereign in the world, and far surpassed all countries in war, as well as in the manufacture of guns and cloth, the two British articles best known in the country. He repeated that the highest possible compliment was paid to Adadimo, by her being introduced to me, and having her name registered in my book. During this speech, she remained on her knees, and returned me repeated thanks. The same example was followed by the whole regiment.

Next came a regiment belonging to a country called Ginoa, commanded by a female of the same name. This regiment consisted only of three hundred women. This corps make no prisoners, but kill all. After all this ceremony was over, the principal male officers prostrated themselves, and went through the regular form of harangue, as if this review had been actual service. They informed his Majesty that they were happy to congratulate him upon the return of his victorious army, and capture of a great number of slaves.

His Majesty, then turning to me, addressed me in a loud voice, to the following effect: "You come from the greatest and richest country in the world, and I am truly gratified at seeing you in my country. The only thing I regret is that so few Englishmen come to see me. I should at all times feel proud to do anything in my power to accommodate an Englishman, and endeavor to make him comfortable in my country. I am aware," he added, "that I have not in my power all the necessaries required by Englishmen, but if I were more frequently visited by them, I would take care to procure everything necessary for their comfort. You have traveled much in Africa, and from what you have seen you are now aware that I am as far superior in Africa, as England is to Spain or Portugal."

Before breaking up, the king assembled all his principal officers, and introduced them to me, describing their rank and office. After many introductions, the principal officers were desired to drink the Queen of England's health. This was to be drunk out of a human skull: apparently, not long before, it had been useful to the original possessor. However, as this was considered the highest compliment that can be paid to any person, I drank my sovereign's health from the bony goblet. The king also joined. I then proposed his Majesty's health, which was drunk from the same vessel. This concluded the second day's performance.

I may be permitted to make a few remarks on the army of women. It is certainly a surprising sight in an uncivilized country. I had, it is true, often heard of the king's female soldiers, but now I have seen them, all well armed, and generally fine, strong, healthy women, and doubtless capable of enduring great fatigue. They seem to use the long Danish musket with as much ease as one of our grenadiers does his firelock, but not, of course, with the same quickness, as they are not trained to any particular exercise, but, on receiving the word, make an attack like a pack of hounds, with great swiftness. Of course they would be useless against disciplined troops, if at all approaching to the same numbers. Still, their appearance is more martial than the generality of the men; and if undertaking a campaign, I should prefer the females to the male soldiers of this country. From all I have seen of Africa, I believe the King of Dahomey possesses an army superior to any sovereign west of the Great Desert.

June 13th.—To-day I attended at the king's house or palace. After passing through two quadrangles of about sixty yards by thirty, we entered the principal square. This square is formed, of three sides, of houses, or long sheds, and on the opposite side to the principal part or side is a high wall of clay, with human skulls placed at short intervals on the top. All the quadrangles were filled with a mob of armed men, some sitting, some lying down asleep, others walking about smoking.

After I was comfortably seated, his Majesty advanced toward me to drink my health, which was accompanied with loud hurrahs from his people. After I had partaken of some eatables, the day's amusements commenced. All the principal men in his Majesty's service were ordered to the front. They were all dressed in their most gaudy dresses, of various shapes and colors, according to the taste of the wearer; but all of the head men wore silver gauntlets, and a profusion of beads and anklets, generally made of a common small iron chain, in substance similar to a horse-collar chain used in England, but the links merely closed, not welded. Others of lower rank, or second, as they are called, (for each head man has his second,) were dressed in their military dress. Several of the principal men were also disguised in masks and clown's dresses, who performed antics and all manner of buffoonery. Some had on masks resembling the head of a bear, others that of a monkey, Some also displayed a pair of silver horns, fixed on the forehead by a bandeau. About ten yards in front of the place where his Majesty lay, three skulls were placed on the ground, forming an equilateral triangle, about three feet apart. At a little distance from the three last named skulls, a calabash was placed, containing several skulls of distinguished men taken or killed in war.

Near the king were placed several large staffs, or walking-sticks, with a skull fixed on the upper end of each, the stick passing through the skull so as to leave about seven inches of the stick above the skull, for the hand when walking. In a short time his Majesty expressed his wish to dance, which was approved of by all the people, by loud yells and the firing of muskets. The king then came forward to the open space in front, where the three skulls were placed, and commenced a dance, or rather elephantine motion, the movement being all in the hips and shoulders. After moving in this way about one minute, his Majesty took one of the staffs and skulls, and recommenced dancing among the three skulls, which lay on the ground. He then ordered a cigar to be lighted for him, and began smoking; at the same time he folded his arms, with the staff under his arms, resting with his breast on the top of the skull, and displaying all the indifference possible. He then advanced toward me and gave me a cigar, and again desired me to drink his health. He asked me if I should like to be present on the following day to witness the execution of four (men) traitors, and proffered me the honor of being the executioner. This honor, however, I declined; but he pressed me, observing he should like to see the capability of my sword, which he admired much. I told him I would rather save a man's life than take it, unless in my own defense. This he admitted was all very good, but asked me whether I should like to save the life of a person who had attempted the life of my Queen? I, of course, replied, Certainly not. Then he told me that the crime of these men was similar.

14th.—Again I visited the palace, at half-past eight o'clock. The ceremonies of this day were nearly a repetition of those of yesterday, till the time arrived, (an hour before sunset,) when the four traitors were brought into the square for execution. They marched through the mob, or assembled crowd, apparently as little concerned as the spectators, who seemed more cheerful than before the prisoners made their appearance, as if they were pleased with the prospect of a change of performance. They were all young men of the middle size, and appeared to be of one family, or at least of the same tribe of Mahees, who are much better looking than the people of the coast. Each man was gagged with a short piece of wood, with a small strip of white cotton tied round each end of the stick, and passed round the pole. This was to prevent them from speaking. They were arranged in line, kneeling before the king. The head gong-gong man then gave four beats on the gong, as one—two, and one—two, the upper part of the gong being smaller than the lower, and thus rendering the sounds different, similar to our public clocks in England, when striking the quarters.

After the four beats, the gong man addressed the culprits upon the enormity of their crime and the justice of their sentence. During this lengthened harangue the gong-gong was struck at short intervals, which gave a sort of awful solemnity to the scene. After this, the men were suddenly marched some distance back from his Majesty, who on this occasion refused to witness the execution. The men were then ordered to kneel in line about nine feet apart, their hands being tied in front of the body, and the elbows held behind by two men, the body of the culprit bending forward. Poor old Mayho, who is an excellent man, was the proper executioner. He held the knife or bill-hook to me, but I again declined the honor; when the old man, at one blow on the back of the neck, divided the head from the body of the first culprit, with the exception of a small portion of the skin, which was separated by passing the knife underneath. Unfortunately, the second man was dreadfully mangled, for the poor fellow, at the moment the blow was struck having raised his head, the knife struck in a slanting direction, and only made a large wound; the next blow caught him on the back of the head, when the brain protruded. The poor fellow struggled violently. The third stroke caught him across the shoulders, inflicting a dreadful gash. The next caught him on the neck, which was twice repeated. The officer steadying the criminal, now lost his hold on account of the blood which rushed from the blood-vessels on all who were near. Poor old Mayho, now quite palsied, took hold of the head, and after twisting it several times round, separated it from the still convulsed and struggling trunk. During the latter part of this disgusting execution the head presented an awful spectacle, the distortion of the features, and the eyeballs completely upturned, giving it a horrid appearance.

The next man, poor fellow, with his eyes partially shut and head drooping forward near to the ground, remained all this time in suspense; casting a partial glance on the head which was now close to him, and the trunk dragged close past him, the blood still rushing from it like a fountain. Mayho refused to make another attempt, and another man acted in his stead, and at one blow separated the spinal bone, but did not entirely separate the head from the body. This was finished in the same manner as the first. However, the fourth culprit was not so fortunate, his head not being separated till after three strokes. The body afterward rolled over several times,when the blood spurted over my face and clothes. The most disgusting part of this abominable and barbarous execution was that of an old ill-looking wretch, who, like the numerous vultures, stood with a small calabash in his hand, ready to catch the blood from each individual, which he greedily devoured before it had escaped one minute from the veins. The old wretch had the impudence to put some rum in the blood and ask me to drink; at that moment I could with good heart have sent a bullet through his head.

From this period I passed my time heavily, rarely taking any exercise, on account of the ridiculous custom of being obliged to turn out of the road if any of the king's wives should meet you. They are in all parts of the town and neighborhood, employed on different domestic occupations, but principally in carrying food in immense gourds or calabashes on the head, containing provisions for the king's ministers and principal men, who, although they live in their own houses with their families, yet are all furnished with food by the king, which is prepared in the palace.

The approach of the king's wives is always announced by the ringing of a small bell, which is carried by a female servant or slave, who invaribly precedes them. The moment this bell is heard all persons, whether male or female, turn their backs, but the males must retire to a certain distance. In passing through the town this is one of the most intolerable nuisances. Several other customs exist, one or two of which it may be well to mention. On passing many different places, either in hammock or on horseback, the traveler is obliged to get out and walk, and upon passing out of the town from Dahomey toward the coast, are a sort of custom-houses, where your pass is demanded. This is all very well, but the nuisance does not end here. Should you have a number of fowls as presents in Dahomey, (which is mostly the case,) and should any one of the cocks crow in passing, or while you wait to be interrogated by the appointed officer, the cock is seized as the king's property; or if more than one crow, the offenders, as many as they may be, are seized.

We now return to Canot, who regretted that when he left Ayudah, on the return voyage, that he had no interpreter to make the necessary communications with the slaves. They soon became discontented, one threw himself into the sea, and another choked himself to death, and apprehensions soon began to be felt that the slaves would revolt. One afternoon, when a part of the slaves were on deck, a sudden squall arose, and all hands were summoned by the boatswain's whistle to take in sail. Seizing the opportunity amid the confusion of the gale, they poured upon the deck, and about forty stout fellows armed with staves of broken water-casks, or clubs of wood, found in the hold, with savage yells and passion-excited visages, rushed upon the crew. A terrible fight occurred; several of the sailors were laid prostrate, bleeding upon the deck, and the contest for awhile seemed doubtful; but firearms in the hands of white men fighting for life, were too much for ignorant savages with clubs only, and the latter, after several discharges, were driven into the hold. The crew now had leisure to attend to the vessel, which was in peril of foundering in the squall—the sails, ropes, tacks and sheets were in the greatest disorder, flapping and dashing about in wild confusion. As soon as below, a battle took place among the slaves, which was with difficulty quelled by firing in among them, and pouring scalding water on the combatants through holes bored for the purpose in the deck. A part only of the slaves had engaged in the rising, otherwise this bold stroke for liberty would have been successful.

Canot now felt as if he lived with a pent up volcano. Terror reigned over all, and the lash was used with unmitigated severity. To add to his anxiety, a slave-boy, of a gentle nature, who had been drilled as a waiter in the cabin, was seized with that dreadful pestilence the smallpox. To prevent the disease from spreading, he was murdered by laudanum, and his body was thrown to its final resting-place in the depths of the ocean. As they approached the termination of their voyage, continuous storms and adverse winds prevailed. On the last two days they were chased by a British vessel of war, and only escaped capture by running the Estrella on to the beach, and with such force that the mainmast snapped like a pipe-stem. They were obliged in their haste to leave a part of their slaves to their pursuers, so close were they at their heels.

Canot's next voyage was taken in the Golden Eagle, a Baltimore clipper of elegant proportions. The voyage was disastrous. While in the river Salem, the Golden Eagle, with all her crew, was unexpectedly pursued and taken by a French war-vessel, and Canot was carried to France, and thrown into prison at Brest, where, after remaining a year or two, he was pardoned out by Louis Philippe, in consequence of some illegality in his condemnation. True to his education, he was no sooner liberated than he made his way to the African coast, and entered the employment of the celebrated Pedro Blanco, at Gallinas. This man Blanco, the monarch of slave-traders, was a native of Spain. Carrying into the business in which he was engaged, all the far-reaching acumen of the most thorough merchant, he selected, for his seat of trade, a spot upon the African coast, where a short sluggish river empties into the Atlantic, by a perfect labyrinth of low, reed-covered islands, fronted by a bar perilous to navigation, and off which no vessel of war could, except in the most perilous weather, watch in safety this dismal spot, which slavery had selected for her recruiting station. Blanco's factories and barracoons were scattered about among the islands, and here and there, to the height of seventy-five or a hundred feet, rose telegraph stations, shaded by the sun and rain, on which lookouts were constantly sweeping the horizon with telescopes, to descry the approach of cruisers or slavers.

Blanco lived in barbaric splendor, with his seraglio of favorites, and surrounded by the luxuries of every land. His ten or twelve barracoons contained each from one hundred to five hundred slaves. These slave-pens were formed of piles driven into the ground, strongly united by iron bands, thatched overhead, and closely guarded by armed Spaniards or Portuguese, whom dissipation and the malaria had given an aspect little less wretched than that of corpses.

The advent of Canot at Gallinas, was in the year 1836. Blanco, a man of slender figure, swarthy face, and most graceful manners, had then passed fifteen years upon this spot. Three years later he left it for Cuba, a millionaire. The drafts of this Rothschild of man-merchants upon Europe or America, were as good as gold in Sierra Leone and Monrovia.

A few years after the establishment of Blanco, the thousands of slaves sent away began to exhaust the vicinity; but the appetite for plunder was stimulated to such a degree, that the neighboring blacks supplied with powder by the factories, and enticed by their tempting merchandize, carried their hunts far inland. The multitudes, too ignorant to combine, by fighting them singly, fell an easy prey, and yet the demand continued until Don Pedro and his myrmidons established numerous branches along the coast, north and south, offshoots from the parent-den, and reaped a harvest greater than that of Californian gold. Various tribes were stimulated by avarice, to war upon each other, with all the wild ferocity of African savages; so that down in the hold of many a slaver, as it steered its way across the broad Atlantic, have been shackled to the same bolt, two deadly enemies, while others have met in the same horrid union a long-lost son or brother, or, perhaps, parent, taken in war. In these wars among the natives, their soothsayers were ever consulted. The story is told of Amarar, a native chief of the Gallinas, who was besieged, and wished to make a sally, that his oracle informed him the moment would be propitious, as soon as he had stained his hands in the blood of his own son. Amarar, upon this, snatched his infant from its mother's arms, cast it into a rice mortar, and with a pestle mashed it to death! Such is man in his wild state, left to the instincts of his own perverted nature.

The familiarity of Canot with the slave-trade, in all its branches, was such that Blanco engaged him to establish a branch factory at New Seostris, an independant principality, under the control of Prince Freeman, a Bassa chief. Having erected a house and surrounded it with palisades, he purchased about seventy slaves, of an inferior quality, at an exorbitant price; and then sent for the chief to assist in shipping them, on a slave-vessel that lay off the spot. To this request an impudent reply was borne to Canot by the son of the king, a lad of sixteen, which so enraged the former, that he gave the lad a blow that sent him bleeding and howling home. Shortly the whole black hive was in a great ferment; and, by a second messenger, word was sent Canot he must leave the place. Anticipating trouble, Canot landed some whites from his schooner, to assist in his defense. At evening, he placed a number of loaded muskets in a long trade-chest, which he used as a sofa, put an open keg of powder upon a table, concealed beneath a blanket, and then, laying a pair of double-barrelled pistols under his broad-brimmed hat, set a guard, and threw himself into his hammock for the night. In the morning, he was aroused by the war-drum and village bells, announcing the approach of the people. In a few moments his palisades were filled with armed and chattering savages. The Prince strutted pompously into the presence of Canot, attired only in the red coat of a British drummer, but without any trowsers. Canot received him cordially, and conducted him into his house. With some few preliminary words, Canot jerked off the blanket from the open powder, and aiming one pistol at the keg and the other at the Prince, defied him to order him off. At this, Freeman gave a sudden bound out of the house, followed by his body-guard, all in the extremest consternation. He subsequently, cringing as a whipped puppy, swore eternal fidelity to Canot. The oath was ratified over New England rum, and by sunset the slaves were duly shipped in the canoes of his people.

Canot, when securely established, erected permanent buildings. The main structure was a large two story house, surrounded by broad verandahs, on the summit of which was a watch-tower, commanding a broad view of the ocean. Beside this, were stores, a private kitchen, one for slaves, a rice-house, servant's-houses, a water depot, huts for single men, and slave-pens, guarded by cannon. The whole was surrounded by a lofty fence, with double gates. The center of the place was an open square, where, after their meals, the slaves, sometimes to the number of six or seven hundred, guarded by a few armed men, were accustomed to recreate themselves by dancing, singing, and drumming on tom-toms.

New Seostris grew wonderfully under the new system of things. Two populous towns arose as if by magic, on the sandy beach, supplied with merchandize and employment by the factory. Prince Freeman's memory of past grievances, and of old debts due his ancestors, received a sudden quickening, and expedition followed expedition to settle these old affairs.

On Canot's first arrival, the people were basely superstitious, and all classes liable to be accused upon any pretext, by the *ju-ju-men* or priests, who tested their innocence or guilt by giving the *saucy-wood* potion. Often when the removal of a sick wife, a superanuated parent, or a rich relative was desired, they would be accused of witchcraft, and as the potion could be graduated by the priest, death ensued when desired. As large numbers of innocent people were, by these means, constantly falling victims to avarice or malice, Canot determined to stop this abominable practice. He respectfully requested that the next person operated upon, should be brought to his barracoon. Shortly a Krooman accused of the death of his nephew by witchcraft, was delivered to Canot, and while the ju-ju-man was preparing the poisonous drink over a slow fire, he bribed him to make it of unusual strength, "for," said he, "my own ju-ju says he is innocent, and I wish to ascertain the relative truth of our soothsayers." Just before the administration of the poison, Canot privately gave to the accused a strong dose of tartar-emetic, which caused him to throw up the venomous drink, almost the instant it was given. This established the innocence of the drinker, and overwhelmed the ju-ju-man with confusion. This result was soon noised about, and to the astonishment of the superstitious Africans. Ever after that, those who were to be subjected to this ordeal, were brought to Canot. He thus succeeded in saving many lives, ending eventually in a complete abandonment of the practice.

Along the African coast, for a distance of many hundred miles, commerce has given rise to a peculiar class of men, known as Kroomen and Fishmen. These are the native boatmen, without whose skill and boldness, merchandize could not be landed, nor slaves shipped from this part of Africa, on account of the terrific surf, which, even in the calmest weather, rolls in such tremendous combing waves, that a European or American boat could not live in it. Their canoes are made of logs of trees, hollowed out and sharpened at the ends: so indispensable are the services of the boatmen, that it is the aim of all slavers, traders, and men-of-war in these waters, to propitiate their favor. Among the first steps of Canot, when he went to New Seostris, was to obtain a little fleet of Kroomen, with whose aid it was seldom that the condition of the surf was such as to prevent him from shipping his cargoes. Off the more dangerous bar of Gallinas, all the skill of these boatmen, could not, at times, prevent boat load after boat load of slaves, from falling a prey to ravenous sharks. On one occasion while loading a single vessel, over one hundred slaves met this terrible death.

At one period, Canot had been greatly annoyed by the continuous blockade of a cruiser. Finally, getting short of provisions, she steered for Sierra Leone, for a fresh supply. Canot dispatched a messenger, with the news, to his friend Don Pedro, at Gallinas; and in about two days thereafter, a clipper brig, sent with dispatch by him, with the well-known signal for a cargo, appeared in the offing. The moon was now at the full, and the surf so terrible as to render an attempt at shipment exceedingly perilous. But the absent cruiser was hourly expected, and there was no alternative, as the barracoons were literally crammed with slaves. By the stimulus of an extra reward, Canot persuaded the Kroomen to make the attempt, with the smallest boats, and the best rowers, while on shore stood a large number of the most expert swimmers, ready for a plunge whenever a canoe was upset by the breakers. They commenced with the females, and had shipped seventy, when a strong wind set in from the ocean, and rolled in the breakers with such fury, that almost every other boat was upset, and negro after negro was rescued. Night now approaching, left still one-third of his slaves unembarked. Canot ran to and fro on the beach, in great excitement, encouraging, coaxing, and refreshing the boatmen and swimmers; but neither words, nor rum were of any avail, the exhausted boatmen were immovable. He was on the point of despair, when he suddenly thought of a quantity of false coral beads among his goods, just then all the rage with the Kroo girls. "The smile of a lip has the same magical power in Africa, as elsewhere; and the offer of a coral bunch for each head embarked, brought all the dames and damsels of Seostris to his aid. Such a shower of chatter was never heard out of a canary cage. Mothers, sisters, daughters, wives, sweethearts, took charge of the embarkation, by coaxing or commanding their respective gentlemen; and before the sun's rim dipped below the horizon, a few strands of false coral, or the kiss of a negro girl, sent one hundred more of the Africans into Spanish slavery." The brig took flight in the darkness, and the next morning the cruiser appeared off the place, when Canot sent a Krooman aboard with his compliments, and an offer of his services if required!

In one of his business visits to Digby, Canot was a witness of the fiendish ferocity of the native African, under the excitement of war. He had established a slave-factory at one of the two Digby towns, which was productive of a fatal quarrel between the respective chiefs, who were cousins, and had previously lived in harmony. Canot, on this occasion, had landed at sunset, at the neglected town, with a lot of merchandize, with a view to supply its chief with goods, and to establish a factory if the opening appeared favorable. Some time past midnight, he was aroused from his sleep by shrieks and volleys of musketry, and then in rushed the negro chief with an appeal to him, to rise and fly for life, that they had all been betrayed, and resistance was in vain. Canot remained where he was, knowing that he was in no personal danger; that he only would suffer a brief detention, and that if he attempted to escape, he might be slaughtered by mistake. The shouts of the savages grew nearer and nearer, as they rushed onward, murdering all they met. On coming to the door of the house in which Canot was, they battered it in, and Jenkin, their leader, with a lighted flambeau entered, and made his party their prisoners. "Of course," says Canot, in relating the history of this transaction, "we submitted without resistance, for, although fully armed; the odds were so great in those anti-revolver days, that we would have been overwhelmed by a single wave of the infuriated crowd. The barbarian chief instantly selected our house for his head-quarters, and dispatched his followers to complete their task. Prisoner after prisoner was thrust in. At times, the heavy mash of the war-club, and the cry of strangling women, gave notice that the work of death was not yet ended. But the night of horror wore away. The gray dawn crept through our hovel's bars, and all was still, save the groans of wounded captives, and the wailings of women and children.

"By degrees, the warriors dropped in around their chieftain. A *palaver-house*, immediately in front of my quarters, was the general rendezvous; and scarcely a *bushman* appeared without the body of some maimed and bleeding victim. The mangled, but living captives were tumbled on a heap in the center, and soon every avenue to the square was crowded with exulting savages. Rum was brought forth in abundance for the chiefs. Presently, slowly approaching from a distance, I heard the drums, horns, and war-bells; and in less than fifteen minutes a procession of women, whose naked black limbs were besmeared with white and yellow paint, poured into the palaver house, to join the beastly rites. Each of these devils was armed with a knife, and bore in her hand some cannibal trophy. Jenkin's wife, a corpulent wench of forty-five, dragged along the ground, by a single limb, the slimy corpse of an infant, ripped alive from its mother's womb. As her eyes met those of her husband, the two fiends yelled forth a shout of mutual joy, while the lifeless babe was tossed in the air, and caught as it descended on the point of a spear. Then came the *refreshment*, in the shape of rum, powder, and blood, which was quaffed by the brutes, till they reeled off, with linked hands in a wild dance, around the pile of victims. As the women leaped and sang, the men applauded and encouraged. Soon the ring was broken, and with a yell each female leaped on the body of a wounded prisoner, and commenced the final sacrifice, with a mockery of lascivious embraces. In my wanderings in African forests, I have often seen the tiger pounce upon its prey, and with instinctive thirst, satiate its appetite for blood, and abandon the drained corpse; but these African negresses were neither as decent nor as merciful as the beasts of the wilderness. Their malignant pleasure seemed to consist in the invention of tortures that would agonize, but not slay. There was a devilish spell in the tragic scene, that fascinated my eyes to the spot. A slow, lingering, tormenting mutilation was practiced on the living, as well as on the dead; and, in every instance, the brutality of the women exceeded that of the men. I cannot picture the hellish joy with which they passed from body to body, digging out eyes, wrenching off lips, tearing the ears, and slicing the flesh from the quivering bones; while the queen of the harpies crept amid the butchery, gathering the brains from each severed skull, as a *bonne bouche* for the approaching feast. After the last victim yielded his life, it did not require long to kindle a fire, produce the requisite utensils, and fill the air with the odor of *human flesh!* Yet, before the various messes were half-broiled, every mouth was tearing the dainty morsels with shouts of joy, denoting the combined satisfaction of usage and appetite! In the midst of this appalling scene, I heard a fresh cry of exultation, as a pole was borne into the apartment, on which was impaled the living body of the conquered chieftain's wife. A hole was quickly dug, the stave planted, and fagots supplied; but before a fire could be kindled, the wretched woman was dead, so that the barbarians were defeated in their hellish scheme of burning her alive! I do not know how long these brutalities lasted, for I remember very little after this last attempt, except that the bushmen packed in plaintain leaves whatever flesh was left from the orgie, to be conveyed to their friends in the forest. The butchery made me sick, dizzy, paralyzed. I sank on the earth benumbed with stupor; nor was I roused until nightfall, when my Kroomen bore me to the conqueror's town, and negotiated our redemption for the value of twenty slaves."

Canot remained at New Seostris several years, carrying on an extensive business. He was finally compelled by the English cruisers to break up his establishment; and, after various adventures, he sunk all he had acquired from his ill-spent years of labor. The same talents and zeal applied to any of the ordinary avocations, which inure to the benefit of man at large, might have yielded him an ample competence, and the sweet solace in old age, of a well-spent life. His memoirs edited by Brantz Mayer, of which this fragmentary and scattered abridgment, can give but an inadequate idea, is a work full of instruction in African aboriginal life, and in the characteristics of those atrocious men, who live by trade in human blood.

Singular as it may seem, the slave-trade at the present hour is extensively carried on, though not near so much as it was a few years since. It was the cessation of the last great European war, which assembled the matured villainy of the world on the African coast, to re-establish the slave-trade. This traffic had been suspended during the later years of the contest, as England and the United States had abolished it; the former, too, swept almost the whole European marine from the ocean. About twenty years since, England, by treaties with different slave-trading powers, obtained permission to capture vessels outward bound for Africa, when fitted for the slave-trade, as well as after they had taken in their cargoes. This, however, did not apply to American vessels, or those protected by the American flag. If a vessel, other than American, was found on the African coast with slave-irons, and with a slave-deck laid for packing slaves, she was seized and condemned. By this arrangement, with a vigorous squadron, over a thousand slavers were captured in the course of the ten years ensuing.

The efforts of the British squadron were seconded by those of France and the United States. "France had withdrawn from the treaty, stipulating the *right of search*, and sent a squadron of her own to prevent French vessels from engaging in the slave-trade; and the United States which never has surrendered and never will surrender the *inviolability of her own flag* to a foreign power, guaranteed in 1842, to keep a squadron on the coast. These with other *subsidiary means*, in 1849, had reduced the exportation of slaves from 105,000 to 37,000 annually. And since that period the trade has lessened, until in Brazil, the greater slave mart, it has became almost extinct; although, at times, it has been carried on briskly with Cuba.

"The subsidiary means alluded to, arose out of the presence of the squadrons, and would have had no effect without them. They consist in arrangements on the part of England, with some of the native powers, to join in checking the evil, and in substituting the legal trade; and in conversion of the old slave-factories and forts, into positions defensive against their former purpose. These measures have also prepared the way for the establishment of Christian missions, as well as permitted to legitimate traffic, its full development. As the missions grow, the slave-trade diminishes, and legitimate trade advances."

"Trade of all kinds was originally an adjunct to the slave-trade. Cargoes were to be sold where they could find a purchaser. Gold, ivory, dye-stuffs and pepper, were the articles procured on the coast. All of these are from exhaustible sources. The great vegetable productions of the country, constituting heavy cargoes, have but lately come into the course of commerce. The heavier articles now in demand, require more industry with hands, and a settled life. Trade thus becomes inconsistent with slavery, and hostile to it; and the more so, as it becomes more dependent on the collection of oil, ground-nuts, and other produces of agriculture. Covering the coast now with trading establishments excludes the slaver. The efforts of the squadrons were necessary to carry out this proceeding, for commerce needed to be protected against the piracies of the slaver afloat, and robbery by the slaver on shore.

Exposure to capture, gave origin to the barracoons. A slaver could no longer leisurely dispose of her cargo, at different points, in return for slaves, who happened to be there. The crime now required concealment and rapidity. Wholesale dealers on shore, had to collect sufficient victims for a cargo, to be taken on board at a moment's notice. This required that the slaver should arrive at the station, with arrangements previously made with the slave-factor, ready to "take in;" or that she should bring over a cargo of goods in payment for slaves.

"In the case of falling in with British cruisers, an American slaver was inviolate, on presenting her register or sea-letter, as a proof of nationality, and could not be searched or detained. But the risk of falling in with American cruisers, especially if co-operating with the British, led to the disguise of legal trading; with a cargo corresponding to the manifest, and all the ship's papers in form.

The American flag became in these ways deeply involved in the slave traffic. In the presence of British, or other foreign cruisers, only vessels known to be slavers, to this day, run but little danger of capture, for the Star Spangled Banner is a protection against the *search* necessary for proof. In 1844 our minister to Brazil, stated: "It is a fact not to be disguised or denied, that the slave-trade is almost entirely carried on under our flag, in American built vessels, sold to slave-traders here, chartered for the coast of Africa, and there sold, or sold here—delivered on the African coast. And, indeed, the scandalous traffic could not be carried on to any great extent, were it not for the use made of our flag, and the facilities given for the chartering of our vessels, to carry to the coast of Africa, the outfit for the trade, and the material for purchasing slaves."

"Captain Smith, a slave-trader, who was arrested in New York, in 1854, for being engaged in this traffic, has made the astonishing statement, that twenty or thirty slavers annually sail from that port—*that New York is the chief port in the world for the slave-trade:* there are strong grounds for believing in the truth of these allegations. An officer of an American war-vessel, writing from off Sierra Leone, in 1845, says: "The English are doing everything in their power to prevent the slave-trade; and keep a force of thirty vessels on this coast, all actively cruising. It is extremely difficult to get up these rivers to the places where the slavers are. In these streams, almost concealed by the trees, the vessels lie, and often elude the strictest search; but when they have taken on board their living cargo, and are getting out to sea, the British are very apt to seize them, except, alas! when they are *protected by the banner of the United States.*"

As the right of search can never be given up by the United States, and as our cruisers have not the right to search suspected vessels, sailing under foreign flags, the only course for the complete suppression of the traffic, is for the vessels of the two principal maritime nations, the United States and Great Britain, to cruise in company for the detection of slavers; and this, to some extent, is at the present time practiced.

"Civilized governments are now very generally united in measures for the suppression of the slave-trade. The coast of Africa is rapidly closing against it. The American and English colonies secure a vast extent of sea coast against its revival. Christian missions at many points are inculcating the doctrines of divine truth, which by its power upon the hearts of men, is the antagonist to such cruel unrighteousness.

"The present is an interesting period in the history of the world. Changes are rapid and irrevocable. Circumstances illustrative of the condition of our race, as it has been, are disappearing rapidly. The helplessness, and artlessness, and the make shifts of barbarism, are becoming things of the past. There is, perhaps, no region of the earth which is now altogether beyond the reach of civilized arts. Shells, and flints, and bows, and clubs, and bone-headed spears are everywhere giving way to more useful or more formidable implements. Improvements in dress, and tools, and furniture, will soon be universal. The history of man as he has been, requires, therefore, to be written now, while the evidence illustrative of it, has not altogether vanished.

"The changes of the last three centuries have, to only a slight degree, influenced the African races. An inaccessible interior, and a coast bristling with slave-factories, and bloody with slaving cruelties, probably account for this. The slight progress made, shows the obduracy of the degradation to be removed, and the difficulty of the first steps needed for its removal. Wherever the slave-trade or its effects penetrated, there, of course, peace vanished, and prosperity became impossible. This evil affected not only the coast, but spread warfare, to rob the country of its inhabitants, far into the interior regions. There were tribes, however, uninfluenced by it, and some of these have gained extensive, although but temporary authority. Yet nowhere has there been any real civilization. It is singular that these people should have rested in this unalloyed barbarism for thousands of years, and that there should have been no native-born advancement, as in Mexico, or Peru, or China; and no flowing in upon its darkness, of any glimmering of light, from the brilliant progress and high illumination of the outside world. It has been considered worthy of notice, that a few years ago, one of the Veys had contrived a cumbrous alphabet to express the sounds of his language; but it is surely, to an incomparable degree, more a matter of surprise, that centuries passed away in communication with Europeans, without such an attempt having been made by any individual, of so many millions, during so many generations of men.

"The older state of negro society, therefore, still continues. With the exception of civilized vices, civilized arms, and some amount of civilized luxuries, life on the African coast, or at no great distance from it, remains now much the same as the first discoverers found it."

Christian commerce is, however, destined to effect great changes, even in the remotest parts of the African continent, and by creating new wants to open up avenues to industry, which will eventually develop and civilize her now degraded and barbarian people. Every part of our globe is to be, in time, penetrated by enlightened christianized industry, and wherever man may be, its surface is to be dotted with happy, virtuous homes.

CONVICT

LIFE IN AUSTRALIA.

HOW THEY GET THERE, AND WHAT THEY GET WHEN THERE, TOGETHER WITH A NARRATIVE OF CONVICT LIFE IN NORFOLK ISLAND, THE PLACE FOR THOSE

TOO BAD FOR BOTANY BAY.

When a ragged boy, (says O'Connell,) lounging around the London Docks, Captain Salmon, of the ship Phœnix, took a fancy to me, and without the knowledge or consent of any of my friends, I shipped as cabin-boy on board his vessel. A short time after I joined her at Deptford, she moved down to Woolwich, to take in live freight; being chartered by Government for the transportation of female convicts to Botany Bay. The ship's company, including the two extremes, officers and boys, numbered about thirty-five. And her passengers were rising two hundred in number.

No crime or worthlessness of character can destroy all feeling of pity, on the part of the philanthropist, for such unfortunates as render themselves amenable to the laws of their country. Indeed, as the worst conduct calls down the severest punishment, perhaps the vilest characters command more pity than those who are less guilty, and, consequently, liable to punishment less severe. But pity for women embarking for Port Jackson seems a waste of sympathy, as, just taken from jail, they seem rather giddily to rejoice in the anticipation of a change of scene, than to feel sorrow at the prospect of punishment. Taken from the very lowest haunts of vice and misery; generally entirely destitute of self-respect, and apparently careless of everything but mere bodily comfort and ease; incapable, by habit, of appreciating anything but pleasure of the senses, they wore the outward seeming of careless indifference, or thoughtless merriment. Occasionally, among the crowd, there was a face the index of remorse, and a consciousness of degradation; or, perchance, of the remembrance of friends, and bitter grief at the loss of respectable standing. Such, however, were rare; in the chatter of the convicts, flash, obscenity, and profanity were the principal features. In dress they varied from the beggars' rags of St. Giles', to the tawdry finery of the aristocracy in vice: and there was not wanting even an occasional neat dress, which bespoke the wearer not all degraded. Over the faces of the whole there was more or less of the "prison aspect," a wanness, the effect of trial and confinement.

After receiving her passengers, the Phœnix laid three or four days at Woolwich. The acquaintances and connections of the convicts were on board in crowds, bidding farewell, and bringing trifles to minister to the comfort of their erring friends during a long passage. Weeping, embracing, hysteric laughter, snatches of flash songs, ribaldry, affected mirth, and unaffected despondence, soon took the place of the general appearance of cheerfulness with which the convicts came from their places of confinement. The anchor is weighed, and the steamboat takes us in tow down the river. Handkerchiefs of all complexions are waving to the people who swarm in boats in our wake;—"Hip—hip—hip—hurra!"—three cheers for Botany Bay from the convicts, and a response from the watermen and the banks of the river. In a few hours the steamer left us; we were in the channel. Two hundred female convicts, a little million to appearance in the snug quarters of the vessel, are not missed from among the swarms of the vile in modern Babylon. They are as a bucket from the ocean; and yet every one of these despised beings has friends; low, and probably vicious, but still affectionate. Feelings and sensibility they have too; blunted it may be, but still human. Their disappearance may be unnoticed by the spectator of the mass, but each of them leaves a void in the circle in which she has moved, though that may have been none of the purest. Weeping eyes follow the departure of the convict ship; aching hearts yearn after the guilty beings whom it is bearing to a distant and degrading place of exile.

At Spithead we lay two days, and on the third weighed again, and made no harbor, till at the end of a five months' passage we came to, in Sydney Cove. The convicts were divided into three general divisions, according to their sentences;—the sentenced for seven, those for fourteen, and those for life. The crew of the vessel lived in the steerage, the short sentenced convicts under the main hatch, the "lifers" forward; and forward of them, in what is, on board of merchant ships, the forecastle, is the "sick bay," or hospital. The berths, in tiers at the sides, accommodated six persons each; and the inmates of each berth formed a mess. The women were all compelled to muster, in divisions, on deck, at least once a day, in tolerable weather, one division at a time; and to insure this airing, necessary to health, female "boatswains" were appointed. It was the duty of these petticoat officers to compel cleanliness also. The provisions were similar in quality and kind to those furnished vessels of the navy. In lieu of "grog" a cheap wine was served out, which the prisoners were obliged to drink at the tub, to prevent hoarding, or selling to one another, The usual punishment for minor offenses was cutting off this allowance of wine; for the more refractory, a machine was contrived, similar in operation to the stocks, but more resembling a very straight sentry-box. The offender was locked into it, standing erect, and when it was closed upon her she could hardly move a limb.

The passengers, after the first fortnight, were generally healthy, and, notwithstanding they were sentenced convicts, happy. The majority of them had been in England as poor as vicious; no change could, with them, have been for the worse, and the temperate and regular manner of living, attention to cleanliness, and relief from squalid poverty, made them happy even under what are usually thought the privations of the vessel.

Land ho! from the foretop-gallant yard; land ho! on deck; and land ho! the hearts of two hundred women responded. It was four or five days after making the land before we could fetch the harbor. The first joy at the sight of land had changed, on the part of the women, to impatience, and from impatience to a sort of careless half despair, which did not a whit abate at sight of the rocky heads of Sydney Cove. When the headland was doubled, and the romantic situations of gentlemen's country seats, and then the settlement at Sydney, were spread before them, hope and expectation were awake again, and there was nothing in their deportment to remind the observer that they were unwilling emigrants. Vessels which have sickness on board are ordered to the quarantine ground; those which, as was our case, have no apparent sickness, other than the usual effects of a long passage, ride out a half quarantine outside the usual range of anchorage. People are not allowed to come on board, but all communication is by no means cut off, as boats are continually along side, selling fresh provisions, bread, etc., to the convicts. It may be well here to remark, that if a convict is discovered to have money to any considerable amount, it is taken from him or her, and deposited in a Savings Institution at Sydney, where it accumulates till the time of sentence expires. The conversations of the passengers with the boats along side are peculiar, and have a character which no greetings away from New South Wales can resemble. "Lord love 'ee, Sal! is that you? and how long are ye lagged for?" "Only for seven years." An Irish girl among our passengers was hailed by her mother, who had preceded her to this land of promise about two years. "Och, Mary!" cried the parent, "is it here I see you? and how long are ye lagged for?" "Only eighty-four months, mother." "Och, my child, avourneen machree! It's glad I am that you're not lagged for seven years. "An' where did ye l'ave Jemmy, my son?" "He's hanged, mother, the assize before they lagged me. An' thin we brought him to St. Giles', an a beauthiful corpse he made, only he had the black stroke roun' his neck."

In about ten days after our arrival, the convicts were landed at the dock-yard, where they were inspected. Upon the arrival of a convict ship at Port Jackson, it is usual for such free residents as need domestics to make application at the superintendent's office for them. These applications are first answered, then the unappropriated residue are sent to the factory at Paramatta, if females, if males, to the prisoners' barracks.

The Phœnix was condemned at Port Jackson, as unworthy, purchased by Government, and made a receiving ship for double convicts, sentenced to penal settlements. This discharged the crew, and I was taken into the employment of Mr. Charles Smith, with whom I remained about a year. Mr. Smith's history was that of many of the free residents in New South Wales. Originally,

"He left his country for that country's good."

Correct behavior procured him, at the end of three years, a "ticket of leave," and at the end of his sentence he had collected a pretty little capital to commence the world with anew. Enterprise, shrewdness and industry, made him one of the wealthiest men in the colony. He was a large contractor for the supply of butcher's meat to the government, for the soldiers and prisoners, and was one of the first, if not the very first, who succeeded in packing beef in New Holland; the climate, prior to his giving proof to the contrary, having been supposed an insuperable objection.

Mr. Smith's intercourse, as contractor, with the convicts, gave me unusual advantages for becoming acquainted with their discipline and situation, and, beside these, there were not wanting excellent opportunities of observing the general character of the colony. There cannot be a better place than this to introduce notices of some other of the freedmen of the colony, who at the time of my residence there, 1820 to 1826, were prominent members of society. No secret is attempted to be made of the cause of one's sojourn at Sydney. If two strangers meet in any situation where conversation seems necessary, almost the first question exchanged is, "Are you free, or a transport?" The next may be,

"What were you lagged for, and for how long?" Freemen are sometimes foolish enough to take offense at a Botany Bay greeting. I was at first, but soon learned the folly of permitting any such sensitiveness to appear, and becoming acclimated, I ceased to feel it.

Mr. Samuel Terry paid a pig for his passage from England to Sydney—that is to say, the pig purchased his passage. It is to be presumed however, that the simple feat of "going a whole pig," though reported as the ostensible cause of his transportation, could not have been the whole cause, Previous convictions and character must have affected his sentence, as it was, in flash phraseology, a *winder*. Nor did his acquisitive propensities cease upon his arrival, as it is in the memory of some of the colonists that the rich Samuel Terry has been whipped for stealing poultry. Growing, however, after awhile, to see the evil of his ways, he obtained by good conduct a ticket of leave; put his acquisitiveness under restraint, and became one of the wealthiest men in the colony. There was upon him the nominal restraint of a convict, but with his ticket of leave, and ticket of exemption, he was in effect free, excepting the single condition of remaining in Australia. To this however he had a stronger tie than government restriction, the proprietorship of one of the largest estates in the possession of any individual. He married, and sons and daughters were born unto him. Although his children may not be particularly anxious to perpetuate the family history, and care nothing about heraldry, they are not a whit the less respectable in Sydney from the slight circumstance that their father is a *winder*. Mr. Terry is, or was, also connected with the whale fishery.

Mr. Thomas Cooper was a sort of aristocrat among convicts. He was transported for fourteen years, his crime being purchasing stolen goods. The articles upon which he was convicted, were stolen from the wardrobe of the Prince of Wales. Upon gaining a ticket of leave, he commenced the manufacture of a sort of gin from Indian corn, and his name is identified with the grocer's vocabulary, "Cooper's best" being as readily understood as Cogniac or Jamaica. Mr. Haynes, a proprietor of whale ships, a principal stay of the Methodist Church, and a local preacher, was a convict.

Paramatta factory, situate about fourteen miles from Sydney, is the depot for female convicts before they are assigned as servants, and the place to which assigned servants are sentenced for punishment for light offenses, upon complaint of their masters; and wives upon complaint of their husbands. The manufacture of the cloth which makes the uniform of the convicts, male and female, and the making of it up into garments, supplies the convicts at Paramatta with employment. The factory is about two miles from the town of Paramatta. The convicts in the factory are divided into three classes; arranged, not with reference to their crimes before transportation, but to their conduct in the factory. All convicts, upon entering, are placed in the first class, in which their employment is needlework, and other comparatively light occupations. Infraction of the rules, or disobedience and disrespect to the government of the factory, degrades the convict to the next class. Here she is employed in carding, weaving, and other laborious employment. When convicts are degraded from the second to the third class, employment suited to their sex ceases; their heads are shaved, and they are set to breaking stone, wheeling earth, and cultivating the grounds about the factory. The government of the convicts at this institution is intrusted principally to a female, whose title is "The Matron."

When a *lady* (these women always speak of each other as "*ladies*") is, in the third class, incorrigible, solitary confinement in a cell, or a visit to the treadmill, is imposed as a punishment. Freed women, married *ladies*, and assigned servants, when recomitted to the factory, are placed in either class, as their offenses merit. Spirits and tobacco are forbidden the convicts in the factory. Wine, allowed as a cordial on the passage out, is also withdrawn, but the food is wholesome, and abundant. Indian corn meal stirred in boiling water, called in America hasty pudding, or mush, in Australia hominy, makes the breakfast. At dinner they have animal food and vegetables, and at supper "Scotch coffee," i. e. burned corn. Convicts are discharged from the factory by three methods—tickets of leave at the expiration of half their time of sentence, tickets of exemption upon the arrival of their husbands in the colony, and tickets of exemption upon the application of a suitor, who must marry, forthwith, the damsel whose liberty he seeks. Sailors who have conceived a penchant for lady passengers on the voyage out, and are, also, upon their arrival in the country, so in love with it as to wish to remain, and *legitimate* settlers who have served out their sentences and taken grants of land, are usually the applicants for wives at the factory. Applications are often made by persons who come without any particular damsel in view; and obtaining a wife is pretty easy, from among a set of women who are ready to take anything for a husband, rather than remain at the factory. The exchange, on the part of the woman, is, however, only the exchange of a mild government for a despotic, as the husband can at any time turn her back to the factory by preferring a complaint. Consequently, the most frequent result of matches formed by a mere freak, or love not the most refined, on the one part, and the acceptance of any offer, rather than remaining in durance, on the other, is the remanding of the bride back to the factory and a shaved head. The advantage is altogether on the side of the husband, the wife's sentence to the colony being standing evidence against her to corroborate his testimony. Grey-bearded old settlers, who have served out their sentences, and are ready to recommence the world on an Australian farm, need a wife to take care of the homestead. Debarred by character, ill personal appearance, and other disagreeables, from obtaining an assigned or freed woman to wife, these gentry seek in the factory a wife who will shut her eyes to the defects of a husband, be they ever so glaring, when by marriage she can again obtain "a home of her own." Quarrels soon follow the tying of the nuptial knot, and a large proportion of the police cases are complaints preferred by husbands against wives, who have too soon let the motives of their marriage become apparent by their conduct.

When an assigned servant woman is married, the consent of her master or mistress is first to be obtained. The form of proclaiming the bans in church is also, in such matches, adhered to. They are in every way more respectable, as the parties know each other some *weeks* at least. In such matches, the husband has also the right of turning his wife into the factory again; but in all cases he is bound to take her out when her term of punishment has expired. If he does not, her board is generally charged to him.

Of a female convict ship I have spoken from observation. The ships used for the transportation of males are managed in like manner, except the additional precautions necessary for restraining men. The usual number of females conveyed in one ship is about ninety. Male convicts are usually ironed, or a majority of them, on the passage. At night a strong grating separates each berth from the center of the hold, and a guard of about thirty men are always on duty. I believe the only instance on record of the capture of a convict ship, is that of the Jane Shore That vessel carried female convicts who instigated the sailors to rise upon the officers. They took the vessel into Monte Video, but the usual fate of mutineers and runaways overtook them there. In addition to the security afforded by the presence of soldiers and other precautions, on board a male convict ship, the appointment of boatswains, or captains, to each mess, from among the convicts, is a farther assurance of safety. The jealousy thus created prevents concert among the prisoners; the performance of his duty makes the convict officer unpopular, and the creation of such a state of feud begets a jealousy which renders him vigilant. The food allowed the prisoners is good and abundant; lime juice, vinegar, and three or four gills of Spanish wine per week, are allowed for the prevention of scurvy. Under good officers, amusements are permitted as preventives of disease; sometimes *private theatricals*, and more frequently dancing. The convicts upon landing are marched to the prisoners' barracks. There, such as are not immediately assigned to answer applications for servants or laborers, don the livery—a Paramatta suit, adorned with the initials "P. B." and the broad arrow.

The prisoners in direct custody of the government are employed about trades, if they are fortunate enough to have them, if not, in road gangs, and in breaking stone. Saturday is allowed to each prisoner to keep his person and clothing in order, and to earn money for himself, if he chooses to labor. Upon this day the weekly rations are served out; articles which bear keeping, sufficient for the next week, and tickets to obtain butcher's meat and other perishable necessaries, at the stores of the contractors. At Wellington Valley, about a hundred and fifty miles from Sydney, is a station to which are sent convicts from the better classes of society; well educated men, convicted of such offenses as forgery, genteel swindling, or a single departure from rectitude, sufficient, indeed, to transport them, but not to sink them to a level with the representatives of St. Giles and Ratcliffe High Way. They are employed in agriculture, till such time as they have given evidence of reformation, or proof of the fact that the crime for which they were transported was an exception to their habitual mode of life. As opportunities offer, they are placed at the head of schools, and employed as clerks in the government offices. Thus are those who are supposed to possess some self-respect, allowed, as far as is compatible with punishment, to retain it; instead of being degraded to the standing of those who are known to be utterly vile. Appointment to schools, or secretaryships, makes them, in a manner, their own masters, and is a reposal of confidence which appeals to, while it nourishes their self-respect. Should one, however, despite these favorable circumstances, transgress by inebriation, theft, or other crime, all the respect at first paid to their circumstances is forfeited. They are more rigorously punished than common convicts, as they are supposed to sin against superior light and knowledge. Of the low rogues transgression is expected, and they are treated as if constant oversight and rigorous discipline was necessary as a thing of course; lighter peccadillos being winked at. The favored prisoners who abuse the privileges extended to them are punished for ingratitude, as well as the bare infraction of the law. They get longer sentences to the treadmill, to the iron-gang, and to the penal settlements, than more ignoble offenders, while their previous habits of life render any sentence to severe labor a double punishment. Labor on the road, which to a common convict is considered no extra punishment, is such to them. No system of human invention is without its defects. The reader will perceive that to carry out all the machinery of the colony, and the discipline of prisoners, a very large number of sub-overseers are necessary

Wherever the experiment has been tried, it has been found that promoted bondsmen make cruel task-masters. The tyranny of these sub-agents of power overdoes the purposes of punishment, rendering men desperate, and driving them to attempt elopement, or, in the country phrase, to "take to the bush." The first steps in an escape are by no means difficult, except to members of a chain-gang; as these, in addition to their irons, are watched by soldiers. Goaded by the arrogance and cruelty of their overseers, two or three prisoners, or more, concert an escape. There are constables' lodges outside the town, which the fugitives avoid by avoiding the highroad. This first difficulty surmounted, the runaways meet at an appointed rendezvous, and the first move is burglary. They surprise the house of some settler, or stock-keeper, and plunder it of such movables as can be most conveniently carried off; always taking care, if possible, to seize firearms. When armed, the fugitives organize themselves with others who have preceded, or who follow them to the bush, into banditti, robbing the market carts for food, and finding the little shelter which the climate renders necessary in caves and bark huts, like the natives. Some probably have method and wisdom enough to betake themselves into unfrequented parts of the interior, where they make clearings, build more substantial houses, and till the earth, upon which very little labor is necessary to produce sufficient for subsistence, and remain undiscovered.

To return to the more usual fate of fugitives: in order to secure their apprehension, it is a standing rule that the apprehension, or the giving of information which shall lead to the apprehension, of four runaways, entitles a seven years convict to a ticket of leave; six entitles a fourteen years'; and eight, a life transport to the same reward. In some cases a handbill is issued, offering a ticket of leave, or a gratuity in money, to the person who shall bring in a notorious highwayman, burglar, or murderer, *dead or alive*. The reward is of course adapted to the situation of the person who apprehends the culprit, as a ticket of leave could not be given a free man. Sometimes a free pardon and passage to England is held out as an inducement.

Trusty natives are created "bush constables." These are about the only blacks who have guns and ammunition. The majority of the natives are incapable of using them, and as they have no articles to offer in traffic, they could not obtain arms if they wished. The guns of the black constables are given them by government, and they wear a brass plate, on which is inscribed the name of the wearer, the tribe he belongs to, and the certificate of his office. These fellows pretended to follow a man by the scent, like a dog, and I have known several circumstances which would seem to prove their possession of some such faculty. The capture of a prisoner, and the surrender of him at the barracks, creates the black captor a bush constable, and he is presented his musket and brass plate. They get also a gratuity of some sort for each prisoner surrendered. Still another method of arresting runaways is, to disguise soldiers, and send them, in such squads as not to alarm suspicion, into the interior. It is however dangerous service. Bushrangers who have plundered a house, or a market cart, are burglars, or highway robbers, and of course liable, upon conviction, to death. Murder of their pursuers can subject them to no worse punishment, and may procure their escape. The sale or gift of arms or ammunition to a bushranger is punishable by transportation to a penal settlement, or other heavy penalty; yet the fugitives provide themselves in some way with arms, and encounters with them are by no means trifles, after they have been absent long enough to become desperate. The dead bodies of fugitives who fall in defending themselves are frequently brought into Sydney to be identified. Where a prisoner is retaken, if no robbery or murder is proved against him upon trial, and no attempt at forcible escape by the use of deadly weapons, he gets a sentence to a penal settlement, for the crime of running away. After this sentence is completed, he is returned to the barracks, on his original sentence, and serves out that; the time spent in the woods and in the penal settlement counting him nothing. If he has resisted the soldiers, or officers, with weapons, or if he be proved to have committed burglary, or highway robbery, he is hung.

A "ticket of leave," is a conditional pardon, granted to convicts after a series of years of good behavior in the colony. Those sentenced originally for seven years, if convicted of no crime in New Holland, receive a ticket of leave at the end of three years; fourteen years' transports at the end of six; and *lifers* at the end of eight or ten. Sometimes these tickets give the possessor the liberty of the whole continent, but more generally, only particular towns or districts. Unconditional pardon, or emancipation, seldom precedes the expiration of the sentence. "Ticket of leave" men are permitted to employ their time as they please, and are exempted from the spotted livery, as also are assigned servants. A "ticket of exemption" may be obtained by a male convict after two years of good behavior. This allows the receiver, if a barrack prisoner, to live out of the barracks with his wife. No extra ration is allowed him for her support, but only four days in the week are required of him for labor, the day extra being supposed, with his wife's industry, sufficient for her support. In the discipline and punishment of convicts, the intervention of a magistrate is always customary. Complaint must be preferred to the police authorities, particularly in the case of assigned servants. One magistrate may inflict fifty lashes; a bench of two or more punish at discretion, by lashes, or the stocks, or the treadmill. Crimes of character meriting severer penalties, go before the higher court, at the quarter sessions, for final trial and sentence.

For the offenses which come before the quarter sessions, the convicts are sentenced to iron-gangs, to penal settlements, and to death. "Penal settlements," to which frequent allusion has been made, are the places to which criminals are sent after conviction, before a colonial court, of offenses which degrade them even below the Botany Bay standard. The life-sentenced double convicts are usually sent to Norfolk Island. This island has no harbor, and the residents upon it are allowed no communication with the world, except such as is afforded by the arrival of new exiles. A strong guard prevents the landing of boats from any vessel, except those of the government. Prisoners sent here are, with few exceptions, sentenced to a perpetual and irremediable exile from the world; tickets of leave and other indulgences are unknown, and I verily believe that many of the prisoners brought to Sydney from penal settlements for trial, commit crime to obtain that deliverance which is only reached by the gallows. The employment of the prisoners at penal settlements is calculated exclusively for punishment. Most of the males labor with irons on their legs. Indeed, the discipline of iron-gangs and of settlers at penal stations differs only in name, and in the duration of the punishment. Impatient of control, and regardless of all consequences, they eagerly seize upon every opportunity of making their escape—with what fatal consequences let the following narrative, written by a gentleman for some time resident in Norfolk Island, bear witness: the whole may be relied upon as a true relation of facts.

"On the northern side of Norfolk Island the cliffs rise high, and are crowned by woods, in which the elegant whitewood and gigantic pine predominate. A slight indentation of the land affords a somewhat sheltered anchorage ground, and an opening in the cliffs has supplied a way to the beach by a winding road at the foot of the dividing hills. A stream of water, collected from many ravines, finds its way by a similar opening to a ledge of rock in the neighborhood, and, falling over in feathery spray, has given the name of Cascade to this part of the island. Off this bay, on the morning of the 21st of June 1842, the brig *Governor Philip* was sailing, having brought stores for the use of the penal establishment. It was one of those bright mornings which this hemisphere alone knows, when the air is so elastic that its buoyancy is irresistibly communicated to the spirits. At the foot of the cliff, near a group of huge fragments of rock fallen from the overhanging cliffs, a prisoner was sitting close to the sea, preparing food for his companions, who had gone off to the brig the previous evening with ballast, and who were expected to return at daylight with a load of stores. The surface of the sea was smooth, and the brig slowly moved on upon its soft blue waters. Everything was calm and still, when suddenly a sharp but distant sound as of a gun was heard. The man, who was stooping over the fire, started on his feet, and looked above and around him, unable to distinguish the quarter from whence the report came. Almost immediately he heard the sound repeated, and then distinctly perceived smoke curling from the vessel's side. His fears were at once excited. Again he listened; but all was hushed, and the brig still stood steadily in toward the shore. Nearer and nearer she approached; until, alarmed for her safety, the man ran to summon the nearest officer. By the time they returned, the vessel had wore, and was standing off from the land; but while they remained in anxious speculation as to the cause of all this, the firing was renewed on board, and it was evident that some deadly fray was going on. At length a boat was seen to put off from the brig, and upon its reaching the shore, the worst fears of the party were realized. The misguided prisoners on board had attempted to seize the vessel. They were but twelve in number, unarmed, and guarded by twelve soldiers and a crew of eighteen men; yet they had succeeded in gaining possession of the vessel, had held it for a time, but had been finally overpowered, and immediate help was required for the wounded and dying.

June 21, 1842—My duty as a clergyman called me to the scene of blood. When I arrived on the deck of the brig, it exhibited a frightful spectacle. One man, whose head was blown to atoms, was lying near the forecastle. Close by his side a body was stretched, the face of which was covered by a cloth, as if a sight too ghastly to be looked upon; for the upper half of the head had been blown off. Not far from these, a man badly wounded was lying on the deck, with others securely handcuffed. Forward, by the companion-hatch, one of the mutineers was placed, bleeding most profusely from a wound which had shattered his thigh; yet his look was more dreadful than all—hate, passion, and disappointed rage rioted in his breast, and were deeply marked in his countenance. I turned away from the wretched man, and my eye shrunk from the sight which again met it. Lying on his back in a pool of blood, the muscular frame of a man whom I well knew was stretched, horribly mutilated. A ball had entered his mouth, and passing through his skull, had scattered his brains around. My heart sickened at the extent of carnage, and I was almost sinking with the faintness it produced, when I was roused by a groan so full of anguish and pain, that for a long time afterward its echo seemed to reach me. I found that it came from a man lying farther for ward, on whose face the death-dew was standing, yet I could perceive no wound. Upon questioning him, he moved his hand from his breast, and I then perceived that a ball had pierced his chest, and could distinctly hear the air rushing from his lungs through the orifice it had left. I tore away the shirt, and endeavored to hold together the edges of the wound until it was bandaged. I spoke to him of prayer, but he soon grew insensible, and within a short time died in frightful agony. In every part of the vessel evidences of the attempt which had ended so fatally presented themselves; and the passions of the combatants were still warm. After attending those who required immediate assistance, I received the following account of the affair:—

The prisoners had slept the previous night in a part of the vessel appropriated for this purpose; but it was without fastening, or other means of securing them below. Two sentries were, however, placed over the hatchway. The prisoners occasionally came on deck during the night, for their launch was towing astern, and the brig was standing off and on until the morning. Between six and seven o'clock in the morning the men were called to work. Two of them were up some time before the rest. They were struck by the air of negligence which was evident on deck, and instantly communicated the fact to one or two others. The possibility of capturing the brig had often been discussed by the prisoners, among their many other wild plans for escaping from the island, and recently had been often proposed by them. The thought was told by their looks, and soon spread from man to man. A few moments were enough; one or two were roused from sleep, and the intention was hurriedly communicated to them. It was variously received. One of them distrusted the leader, and intreated his companions to desist from so mad an attempt. It was useless; the frenzied thirst for liberty had seized them, and they were maddened by it. Within a few minutes they were all on deck; and one of the leaders rushing at the sentry nearest to him, endeavored to wrest from him his pistols, one of which had flashed in the pan as he rapidly presented it, and threw him overboard; but he was subsequently saved. The arms of the other sentry were demanded, and obtained from him without resistance. A scuffle now took place with two other soldiers who were also on the deck, but not on duty, during which one of them jumped over the vessel's side, and remained for some time in the main chains; but upon the launch being brought along side, he went down into it. The other endeavored to swim ashore (for by this time the vessel was within a gun-shot of the rocks;) but, encumbered by his great-coat, he was seen, when within a few strokes of the rock, to raise his hands, and uttering a faint cry to Heaven for mercy he instantly sunk. In the meanwhile, the sergeant in charge of the guard hearing the scuffling overhead, ran upon deck, and seeing some of the mutineers struggling with the sentry, shot the nearest of them dead on the spot. He had no sooner done so than he received a blow on the head, which rendered him for some time insensible. Little or no resistance was offered by the sailors; they ran into the forecastle, and the vessel was in the hands of the mutineers. All the hatches were instantly fastened down, and every available thing at hand piled upon them. But now, having secured their opponents, the mutineers were unable to work the brig; they therefore summoned two of the sailors from below, and placed one of them at the wheel, while the other was directed to assist in getting the vessel off. The coxswain, a free man in charge of the prisoners, had the first onset taken to the rigging, and remained in the maintop with one of the men who refused to join in the attack. At this moment a soldier who had gone overboard, and endeavored to reach the shore, had turned back, and was seen swimming near the vessel. Woolfe, one of the convicts, immediately jumped into the boat along side, and saved him. While this was the state of things above, the soldiers had forced their way into the captain's cabin, and continued to fire through the gratings overhead as often as any of the mutineers passed. In this manner several of them received wounds. To prevent a continuance of this, a kettle of hot water was poured from above, and shortly afterward a proposal was made to the captain from the prisoners to leave the vessel in the launch, provided he handed up to them the necessary supplies. This he refused, and then all the sailors were ordered from below into the launch, with the intention of sending them ashore. Continuing to watch for the ringleaders, the captain caught a glimpse of one them standing aft, and, as he supposed, out of the reach. He mounted the cabin table, and almost at a venture fired through the woodwork in the direction he supposed the man to be standing. The shot was fatal; the ball struck him in the mouth, and passed through his brain. Terrified at the death of their comrades, the remainder were panic-struck, and instantly ran below. One of the leaders sprung over the taffrail, and eventually reached the launch. The sailor at the wheel, now seeing the deck almost cleared, beckoned up the captain, and without an effort the vessel was again in their possession. In the confusion, a soldier who had been in the boat, and was at this moment with the sailors returning on deck, was mistaken for one of the mutineers, and shot by tbe sergeant. The prisoners were now summoned from their place of concealment. They begged hard for mercy; and upon condition of their quietly surrendering, it was promised to them. As the first of them in reliance upon this assurance, was gaining the deck, by some unhappy error he received a ball in his thigh, and fell back again. The res refused to stir; but after a few moment's hesitation, another of them ventured up, was taken aft by the captain, and secured. A third followed, and as he came up, he extended his arms, and cried, 'I surrender; spare me.' Either this motion was mistaken by the soldiers, or some of them were unable to restrain their passion, for at this instant the man's head was literally blown off. The captain hastened to the spot and received the others, who were secured without further injury.

When we reached the vessel, the dying, dead, and wounded were lying in every direction. In the launch astern, we saw the body of one wretched man who had leaped over the taffrail, and reached the boat badly wounded; he was seen lying in it when the deck was regained, and was then pierced through with many balls. Nothing could be more horrible than his appearance; the distortion of every feature, his clenched hands, and the limbs which had stiffened in the forms of agony into which pain had twisted them, were appalling. The countenance of every man on board bore evidence of the nature of the deadly conflict in which he had been engaged. In some, sullenness had succeeded to reckless daring, and exultation to alarm in others. Nothing could have been more desperate than such an attempt to seize the vessel. The most culpable neglect could alone have encouraged it; and it is difficult to conceive how it could have succeeded, if anything like a proper stand had been made by those in charge of her when it commenced. The wounded were immediately landed, and conveyed to the hospital, and the dead bodies were afterward brought on shore. The burial-ground is close to the beech. A heavy surf rolls mournfully over the reef. The moon had just risen, when, in deep and solemn silence, the bodies of these misguided men were lowered into the graves prepared for them. Away from home and country, they had found a fearful termination of a miserable existence. Perhaps ties had still bound them to the world; friends whom they loved were looking for their return, and, prodigals though they had been, would have blessed them, and forgiven their offenses. Perhaps even at that sad moment mothers were praying for their lost ones, whom in all their infamy they had still fondly loved. Such thoughts filled my mind; and when a few drops of rain at that moment descended, I could not help thinking that they fell as tears from heaven over the guilt and misery of its children.

On the morning following the fatal occurrence, I visited the jail in which the mutineers were confined. The cells are small, but clean and light. In the first of them I found George Beavers, Nicholas Lewis, and Henry Sears. Beavers was crouching in one corner of the cell, and looking sullen, and in despair. Lewis, who was walking the scanty space of the cell, seemed to glory in the rattle of his heavy chains; while Sears was stretched apparently asleep upon a grass mat. They were all heavily ironed, and every precaution had evidently been taken to prevent escape. The jail is small, and by no means a secure one. It was once a public house; and notwithstanding every effort to adapt it to its present purpose, it is not a safe or proper place of confinement. It is little calculated to resist any attempt to rescue the men, whose daring conduct was the subject of high encomium among their fellow-prisoners, by whom any attempt to escape is considered a meritorious act. In the other cell I found Woolfe and Barry, the latter in great agony from an old wound in the leg, the pain of which had been aggravated by the heavy irons which galled it. All the prisoners, except Barry and Woolfe, readily acknowledged their participation in the attempt to seize the brig; but most solemnly denied any knowledge of a preconcerted plan to take her; or that they, at least, had attempted to throw the soldiers overboard. They were unwilling to be interrupted, and inveighed in the bitterest manner against some of their companions who had, they seemed to think, betrayed them; or, at least, had led them on, and at the moment of danger had flinched. The names of the surviving mutineers were John Jones, Nicholas Lewis, Henry Sears, George Beavers, James Woolfe, Thomas Whelan, and Patrick Barry.

The depositions against them having been taken, all the men I have mentioned, with the exception of Jones and Whelan, who were wounded, were brought out to hear them read. The listened with calm attention, but none of them appeared to be much excited. Once only during the reading, Beavers passionately denied the statements made by one of the witnesses present, and was with difficulty silenced. His countenance at that moment was terribly agitated; every bad feeling seemed to mingle in its passionate expression. They were all young, powerful, and, with one or two exceptions, not at all ill-looking men. From the jail I proceeded to the hospital, where the wounded men were lying. They had each received severe wounds in the thigh, and were in great agony.

The violence of Jones was excessive. Weakened in some degree by an immense loss of blood, the bitterness of his spirit, nevertheless, exhibited itself in passionate bursts of impatience. He was occasionally convulsed with excessive pain; for the nerves of the thigh had been much lacerated, and the bone terribly shattered. His features were distorted with pain and anger, and occasionally bitter curses broke from his lips; yet there was something about his appearance which powerfully arrested my attention—an evident marking of intellect and character, repulsive in its present development, yet in many respects remarkable. His history had been a melancholy one, and, as illustrative of many thousand others, I give it as I afterward received it from his lips.

At eleven years of age he was employed in a warehouse in Liverpool as an errand-boy. While following this occupation, from which by good conduct he might have risen to something better, he was met in the street one day by the lad whom he had succeeded in this employment, and was told by him how he might obtain money by robbing the warehouse, and then go with him to the theater. He accordingly took an opportunity of stealing some articles which had been pointed out, and gave them to his companion, who, in disposing of them, was detected, and of course criminated Jones. After remaining some weeks in jail, Jones was tried and acquitted; but his character being now gone, he became reckless, and commenced a regular career of depredation. In attempting another warehouse robbery, he was detected, and sentenced to twelve months' imprisonment. By the time he was released from this, he was well tutored in crime, and believed that he could now adroitly perform the same robbery in which he had previously failed. He made the attempt the very night of his release from jail, and with temporary success. Subsequently, however, he was detected, and received sentence of transportation for seven years. He underwent this sentence, and an additional one in Van Diemen's Land, chiefly at Port Arthur, the most severe of the penal stations there. From this place he, with Lewis, Moss, (who was shot on board the brig,) and Woolfe, having seized a whale-boat, effected their escape. During three months they underwent the most extreme hardships from hunger and exposure. Once they had been without food for several days, and their last hook was over the boat's side; they were anxiously watching for a fish. A small blue shark took the bait, and in despair one of them dashed over the boat's side to seize the fish; his leg was caught by one of the others, and they succeeded in saving both man and hook. They eventually reached Twofold Bay, on the coast of New South Wales, and were then apprehended, conveyed to Sydney, and thence sent back to Van Diemen's Land; tried, and received sentence of death; but this was subsequently commuted to transportation for life to Norfolk Island. Jones often described to me the intense misery he had undergone during his career. He had never known what freedom was, and yet incessantly longed for it. All alike confessed the unhappiness of their career. Having made the first false step into crime, they acknowledged that their minds became polluted by the associations they formed during imprisonment. Then they were further demoralized by thinking of the *glory*—such miserable glory!—attending a trial; and the hulks and the voyage out gave them a finished criminal training. The extent of punishment many of them have undergone during the period of transportation is almost incredible. I have known men whose original sentence of seven years has been extended over three times that period, and who, in addition to other punishment, have received five thousand or six thousand lashes

After many solemn interviews with the mutineers, I found them gradually softening. They became more communicative, and extremely anxious to receive instruction. I think I shall never forget one of the earliest of these visits to them. I first saw Sears, Beavers, and Jones. After a long and interesting conversation with them, we joined in that touching confession of sin with which the liturgy of the Church of England commences. As we knelt together, I heard them repeat with great earnestness—'We have erred and strayed from Thy ways like lost sheep,' etc. When we arose, I perceived that each of them had been shedding tears. It was the first time I had seen them betray any such emotion, and I cannot tell how glad I felt; but when I proceeded afterward to read to them the first chapter of Isaiah, I had scarcely uttered that most exquisite passage in the second verse—'I have nourished and brought up children, and they have rebelled against me'—when the claims of God, and *their* violation and rejection of them; His forbearance, and *their* ingratitude, appeared to overwhelm them; they sobbed aloud, and were thoroughly overpowered.

For a considerable time we talked together of the past; the wretched years they had endured; the punishments, and the crimes which had led to them; until they seemed to feel most keenly the folly of their sad career. We passed on to contrast the manner in which their lives had been spent, with what God and society required from them; their miserable perversion of God's gifts, with the design for which He gave them, until we were led on to speak of hope and of faith; of Him who 'willeth not the death of a sinner, but rather that he should turn from his wickedness and live;' and then the Saviour's remonstrance seemed to arrest them—'Ye will not come to me that ye might have life;' until at length the influences of the Holy Spirit were supplicated with earnestness and solemnity. These instructions, and such conversation, were daily repeated; and henceforth each time I saw them I perceived a gradual but distinct unfolding of the affections and the understanding.

August.—The wounded men are much recovered, and the whole of the mutineers are now confined together in a large ward of the jail. They have long received extreme kindness from the commandant, and are literally bewildered at finding that even this last act has not diminished the exercise of his benevolence. That anybody should care for them, or take such pains about them, after their violent conduct, excited surprise—at first almost amounting to suspicion; but this at length gave place to the warmest gratitude. They were, in fact, subdued by it. They read very much, are extremely submissive, and carefully avoid the slightest infringement of the prison regulations. At first, all this was confined to the three men I have mentioned; but their steady consistency of conduct, and the strange transformation of character so evident in them, gradually arrested the attention of the others, and eventually led to a similar result.

They will be detained here until the case has been decided by the authorities in Sydney. They will probably be tried by a commission sent from thence to the island for the purpose. Formerly, however, prisoners charged with capital offenses here were sent up for trial; but (it is a horrible fact) this was found to lead to so much crime, that, at much inconvenience and expense, it was found absolutely necessary to send down a judicial commission on each important occasion, in order to prevent it. The mere excitement of a voyage, with the chances connected with it, nay, merely a wish to get off the island even for a time, led many men to commit crimes of the deepest dye in order to be sent to Sydney for trial.

Two months, therefore, at least, must intervene between the perpetration of the offense and their trial; and this interval is usually employed in similar cases in arranging a defense but too commonly supported by perjury. In the present instance, I found not the slightest attempt to follow such a course. They declare that they expect death, and will gladly welcome it. Of their life, which has been a course of almost constant warfare with society, ending in remorseful feelings, they are all thoroughly weary, although only one of them exceeds thirty years of age.

In addition to the ordinary services, Captain Maconochie each Sunday afternoon has read prayers to them, and has given permission to a few of their friends to be present. Singular good has resulted from it, both to the men and those who join in their devotions. At the conclusion of one of these services Sears stood up, and with his heart so full as scarcely to allow him utterance, to the surprise of every person there, he addressed most impressively the men who were present. 'Perhaps,' said he, 'the words of one of yourselves, unhappily circumstanced as I am, may have some weight with you. You all know the life I have led; it has, believe me, been a most unhappy one; and I have, I hope not too late, discovered the the cause of this. I solemnly tell you that is because I have broken God's laws. I am almost ashamed to speak, but I dare not be silent. I am going to tell you a strange thing. I never before was happy; I begin now, for the first time in my life, to *hope*. I am an ignorant man, or at least I was so; but I thank God I begin to see things in their right light now. I have been unhappily placed from my childhood, and have endured many hardships. I do not mention this to excuse my errors; yet if I had years since received the kindness I have done here, it might have been otherwise. My poor fellows, do turn over a new leaf; try to serve God, and you, too, will be happier for it.' The effect was most thrilling; there was a death-like silence; tears rolled down many cheeks, which I verily believe never before felt them; and without a word more, all slowly withdrew.

This man's story is also a common, but painful one. At fifteen years of age he was transported for life as an accomplice in an assault and alleged robbery, of which, from circumstances which have since transpired, I have little doubt he was entirely innocent. During a long imprisonment in Horsham jail, he received an initiation in crime, which was finished during the outward voyage. Upon his arrival in New South Wales, he was assigned to a settler in the interior, a notoriously hard and severe man, who gave him but a scanty supply of food and clothing, and whose aim seemed to be to take the utmost out of him at the least possible expense. Driven at length to desperation, he, with three fellow-servants, absconded; and when taken, made a complaint to the magistrate before whom they were brought almost without clothes. Their statements were found to be literally correct; but for absconding they were sent to Newcastle, one of the penal stations of New South Wales, where Sears remained nearly two years. At the expiration of that time he was again assigned, but unfortunately to a man, if possible, worse than his former employer, and again absconded. For this offense he was sent to Moreton Bay, another penal settlement, and endured three years of horrible severity, starvation, and misery of every kind. His temper was by this time much soured; and, roused by the conduct of the overseers, he became brutalised by constant punishment for resisting them. After this he was sent to Sydney, as one of the crew in the police-boat, of which he was soon made assistant coxswain. For not reporting a theft committed by one of the men under his charge, he was sentenced to a road party; and attempting to escape from it, he was apprehended, and again ordered to Moreton Bay for four years more. There he was again repeatedly flogged for disobedience and resistance of overseers, as well as attempting to escape; but having most courageously rendered assistance to a vessel wrecked off the harbor, he attracted the attention of the commandant, who afterward showed him a little favor. This was the first approach to kindness he had know since, when years before, he had left his home; and it had its usual influence. He never was again in a scrape there. His good conduct induced the commandant to recommend him for a mitigation of sentence, which he received, and he was again employed in the police-boat. The free coxswain of the boat was, however, a drunkard, and intrusted much to Sears. Oftentimes he roused the men by his violence, but Sears contrived to subdue his passion. At length, one night returning to the hut drunk, the man struck at one of crew with his cutlass, and the rest resisted and disarmed him. But the morning came; the case was heard; their story was disbelieved;. and upon the charge and evidence of the aggressor, they were sent to an ironed gang, to work on the public roads. When Sears again became eligible for assignment, a person whom he had known in Sydney applied for him. The man must be removed within a fixed period after the authority is given. In this case, application was made a day beyond the prescribed time, and churlishly refused. The disappointment roused a spirit so untutored as his, and once again he absconded; was of course apprehended, tried, and being found with a man who had committed robbery, and had a musket in his possession, was sent to Norfolk Island for life. This sentence has, however, for meritorious conduct, been reduced to fourteen years; and his ready assistance during a fire which recently broke out in the military garrison here, might possibly have helped to obtain a still further reduction. He never, during those abscondings, was absent for any long period, and never committed any act of violence. His constant attempt seems to have been to reach Sydney, in order to affect his escape from the scene of so much misery.

For some time past I have noticed his quiet and orderly conduct, and was really sorry when I found him concerned in this unhappy affair. His desire for freedom was, however, most ardent, and a chance of obtaining it was almost irresistible. He has since told me that a few words kindly spoken to himself and others by Captain Maconochie, when they landed, sounded so pleasantly to him—such are his own words—that he determined from that moment he would endeavor to do well. He assures me that he was perfectly unconscious of a design to take the brig, until awoke from his sleep a few minutes before the attack commenced; that he then remonstrated with the men; but finding it useless, he considered it a point of honor not to fail them. His anxiety for instruction is intense; he listens like a child; and his gratitude is most touching. He, together with Jones, Woolfe, and Barry, were chosen by the commandant as a police-boat's crew; and had, up to this period, acted with great steadiness and fidelity in the discharge of the duties required from them. Nor did I think they would, even now, tempting as the occasion was, have thought of seizing it, had it not been currently reported that they were shortly to be placed under a system of severity such as they had already suffered so much from.

Woolfe's story of himself is most affecting. He entered upon evil courses when very young; was concerned in burglaries when only eleven years of age. Yet this was from no natural love of crime. Enticed from his home by boys older than himself, he soon wearied of the life he led, and longed to return to his home and his kind mother. Oftentimes he lingered near the street she lived in. Once he had been very unhappy, for he had seen his brother and sister that day pass near him, and it had rekindled all his love for them. They appeared happy in their innocence; he was miserable in his crime. He now determined to go home and pray to be forgiven. The evening was dark and wet, and as he entered the court in which his friends lived, his heart failed him, and he turned back; but, unable to resist the impulse, he again returned, and stole under the window of the room. A rent in the narrow curtain enabled him to see within. His mother sat by the fire, and her countenance was so sad that he was sure she thought of him; but the room looked so comfortable, and the whole scene was so unlike the place in which he had lately lived, that he could no longer hesitate. He approached the door; the latch was almost in his hand, when shame and fear, and a thousand other vile and foolish notions, held him back; and the boy who in another moment might have been happy—*was lost.* He turned away, and I believe has never seen them since. Going on in crime, he, in due course of time, was transported for robbery. His term of seven years expired in Van Diemen's Land. Released from forced servitude, he went a whaling voyage, and was free nearly two years. Unhappily, he was then charged with aiding in a robbery, and again received a sentence of transportation. He was sent to Port Arthur, there employed as one of the boat's crew, and crossing the bay one day with a commissariat officer, the boat was capsized by a sudden squall. In attempting to save the life of the officer, he was seized by his dying grasp, and almost perished with him; but extricating himself, he swam back to the boat. Seeing the drowning man exhausted, and sinking, he dashed forward again, diving after him, and happily succeeded in saving his life. For this honorable act he would have received a remission of sentence; but ere it could arrive, he and five others made their escape. He had engaged with these men in the plan to seize the boat, and although sure of the success of the application in his favor, he could not now draw back. The result I have already shown. There were two more men concerned in the mutiny, who, with those I have mentioned, and those killed on board the brig, made up the number of the boat's crew. But neither of these men came under my charge, being both Roman Catholics.

At length the brig, which had been dispatched with an account of the affair, returned, and brought the decision of the governor of New South Wales. He had found it extremely difficult, almost impossible, to obtain fitting members for the commission, who would be willing to accept the terms proposed by the government, or trust themselves in this dreadful place, and therefore he had determined that the prisoners should be sent up for trial. The men were sadly disappointed at this arrangement. They wished much to end their days here, and they dreaded both the voyage and the distracting effect of new scenes. They clung, too, with grateful attachment to the commandant's family, and the persons who, during their long imprisonment, had taken so strong an interest in their welfare. I determined to accompany them, and watch for their perseverance in well-doing, that I might counsel and strengthen them under the fearful ordeal I could not doubt they would have to pass. The same steady consistency marked the conduct of these men to the moment of their embarkation. There was a total absence of all excitement; one deep serious feeling appeared to possess them, and its solemnity was communicated to all of us. They spoke and acted as men standing on the confines of the unseen world, and who not only thought of its wonders, but, better still, who seemed to have caught something of its spirit and purity.

November.—The voyage up was a weary, and, to the prisoners, a very trying one. In a prison on the lower deck of a brig of one hundred and eighty-two tons, fifty-two men were confined. The place itself was about twenty feet square, of course low, and badly ventilated. The men were all ironed, and fastened to a heavy chain drove through iron rings let into the deck, so that they were unable, for any purpose, to move from the spot they occupied; scarcely, indeed, to lie down. The weather was also unfavorable. The vessel tossed and pitched most fearfully during a succession of violent squalls, accompanied by thunder and lightning. I cannot describe the wretchedness of these unhappy convicts: sick, and surrounded by filth, they were huddled together in the most disgusting manner. The heat was at times unbearable. There were men of sixty—quiet and inoffensive old men—placed with others who were as accomplished villains as the world could produce. These were either proceeding to Sydney, their sentences on the island having expired, or as witnesses in another case, (a bold and wicked murder,) sent there also for trial. The sailors on board the brig were for the most part the cowardly fellows who had so disgracefully allowed the brig to be taken from them; and they, as well as the soldiers on guard, (some of them formed a part of the former one,) had no very kindly feeling toward the mutineers. It may be imagined, therefore, that such feelings occasioned no alleviation of their condition. In truth, although there was no actual cruelty exhibited, they suffered many oppressive annoyances; yet I never saw more patient endurance. It was hard to bear, but their better principles prevailed. Upon the arrival of the vessel in Sydney, we learned that the case had excited an unusual interest. Crowds assembled to catch a glimpse of the men as they landed; and while some applauded their daring, the great majority very loudly expressed their horror at the crime of which they stood accused. I do not think it necessary to describe the trial, which took place in a few days after landing. All were arraigned except Barry. The prisoner's counsel addressed the jurors with powerful eloquence; but it was in vain: the crime was substantiated; and the jury returned a verdict of guilty against all the prisoners, recommending Woolfe to mercy.

During the whole trial, the prisoners' conduct was admirable; so much so, indeed, as to excite the astonishment of the immense crowd collected by curiosity to see men who had made so mad an attempt for liberty They scarcely spoke, except once to request that the wounded man, who yet suffered much pain, might be allowed to sit down. Judgment was deferred until the following day. When they were then placed at the bar, the judge, in the usual manner, asked whether they had any reason to urge why sentence should not be pronounced upon them? It was a moment of deep solemnity; every breath was held; and the eyes of the whole court were directed toward the dock. Jones spoke in a deep clear voice, and in a deliberate harangue pointed out some defects in the evidence, though without the slightest hope, he said, of mitigating the sentence now to be pronounced on himself and fellows. Three of the others also spoke. Whelan said, 'that he was not one of the men properly belonging to the boat's crew, but had been called upon to fill the place of another man, and had no knowledge of any intention to take the vessel, and the part he took on board was forced upon him. He was compelled to act as he had done; he had used no violence, nor was he in any way a participator in any that had been committed.' At the conclusion of the address to them, Jones, amid the deep silence of the court, pronounced a most emphatic prayer for mercy on his own soul and those of his fellow-prisoners, for the judge and jury, and finally for the witnesses. Sentence of death was then solemnly pronounced upon them all; but the judge informed Woolfe that he might hold out to him expectations that his life would be spared. They were then removed from the bar, and sent back to the condemned cells.

I cannot say how much I dreaded my interview with them that day; for although I had all along endeavored to prepare their minds for the worst result, and they had themselves never for a moment appeared to expect any other than this, I feared that the realization of their sad expectation would break them down. Hitherto there might have been some secret hope sustaining them. The convulsive clinging to life, so common to all of us, would now, perhaps, be more palpably exhibited. Entering their cells, I found them, as I feared, stunned by the blow which had now fallen on them, and almost overpowered by mental and bodily exhaustion. A few remarks about the trial were at length made by them; and from that moment I never heard them refer to it again. There was no bitterness of spirit against the witnesses, no expression of hostility toward the soldiers, no equivocation in any explanation they gave. They solemnly denied many of the statements made against them; but, nevertheless, the broad fact remained, that they were guilty of an attempt to violently seize the vessel, and it was useless debating on minor considerations.

In the meantime, without their knowledge, petitions were prepared and forwarded to the judges, the governor, and executive council. In them were stated various mitigatory facts in their favor; and the meliorated character of the criminal code at home was also strongly urged. Every attention was paid to these addresses, following each other to the last moment. But all was in vain. The council sat, and determined that five of the men should be hanged on the following Tuesday. Whelan, who could have no previous knowledge of a plan to seize the vessel, together with Woolfe, was spared. The remaining four were to suffer. The painful office of communicating this final intelligence to these men was intrusted to me, and they listened to the announcement not without deep feeling, but still with composure.

It would be very painful for me to dwell on the closing scene. The unhappy and guilty men were attended by the zealous chaplain of the jail, whose earnest exhortations and instructions they most gratefully received. The light of truth shone clearly on the past, and they felt that their manifold lapses from the path of virtue had been the original cause of the complicated misery they had endured. They entreated forgiveness of all against whom they had offended; and in the last words to their friends were uttered grateful remembrances to Captain Maconochie, his family, and others. At the place of execution, they behaved with fortitude and a composure befitting the solemnity of the occasion. Having retired from attendance upon them in their last moments, I was startled from the painful stupor which succeeded in my own mind, by the loud and heavy bound of the drop as it fell, and told me that their spirits had gone to God who gave them."

Our reverend informant, in closing his narrative, adds some reflections on the painful nature of the tragedy in which he was called to lend his professional assistance. He laments the general harshness of penal discipline, and attributes the last fatal crime of these men to the recent arrival of orders which shut out all hope of any improvement being effected in their circumstances, however well they might behave. Previously, he says, while hope was permitted to them, they had conducted themselves well. While agreeing in his humane views, we would, at the same time avoid appearing as the apologists of crime under any circumstances.

It may be seen from the history of the unhappy men before us, that transportation is, at the best, equivalent to going into slavery—that the convict loses, for the time, his civil rights. Torn from his family, his home, and his country, he is placed at the disposal of the crown and its functionaries; can be put to any kind of labor, however repugnant to his feelings; dressed in the most degrading apparel; chained like a wild beast if refractory; and on the commission of any new offense, while in this state of servitude, he is liable to fresh punishment by transportation to such penal settlements as Norfolk Island. It might almost be said that no man in his senses would voluntarily commit crimes which would expose him to the risk of so terrible an infliction as that of transportation, even for the limited period of seven years. But, alas! men who have entered on a course of error, forgetful of every duty which they owe to themselves and society, can scarcely be said to be in possession of a sound mind; and they go on floundering from one degree of vice to another.

THE

HORRORS OF A FIRE AT SEA,

AS SHOWN BY THE ACCOUNT OF THE BURNING OF THE PRINCE, A FRENCH VESSEL, RELATED BY LIEUTENANT FONDA, ONE OF HER OFFICERS, TO WHICH IS ANNEXED A SERIES OF ARTICLES

ILLUSTRATING LIFE ON THE DEEP.

Our vessel, the Prince, was in the service of the French East India Company. She was commanded by M. Morin, and left the harbor of L'Orient, bound to Pondicherry, on the 19th of February, 1752.

After a fortunate navigation, we met with a disaster, of which the strongest expressions can convey but a faint idea. In this narrative, I shall confine myself to a brief detail, as it is impossible to recollect all the circumstances. The 26th of July, 1752, being in the latitude of 8° 30′ south, and in longitude 5° west, the wind being south-west, just at the moment of taking the observation of the meridian, I had repaired to the quarter where I was going to command, when a man informed me that a smoke was seen to issue from the pannel of the greater hatchway.

Upon this information, the first lieutenant, who kept the keys of the hold, opened all the hatchways to discover the cause of an accident, the slightest suspicion of which frequently causes the most intrepid to tremble. The captain, who was at dinner in the great cabin, went upon deck, and gave orders for extinguishing the fire. I had already directed several sails to be thrown overboard, and the hatchways to be covered with them, hoping by these means to prevent the air from penetrating into the hold. I had even proposed, for the greater security, to let in the water between decks to the height of a foot, but the air, which had already obtained a free passage through the openings of the hatchways, produced a very thick smoke that issued forth in abundance, and the fire continued gradually to gain ground. The captain ordered sixty or eighty of the soldiers under arms to restrain the crew, and prevent the confusion likely to ensue in such a critical moment. These precautions were seconded by M. de la Touche, with his usual fortitude and prudence. That hero deserved a better opportunity of signalizing himself, and had destined his soldiers for other operations more useful to his country. All hands were now employed in getting water; not only the buckets, but likewise the pumps were kept at work, and pipes were carried from them into the hold; even the water in the jars was emptied out. The rapidity of the fire, however, baffled our efforts and augmented the general consternation. The captain had already ordered the yawl to be hoisted overboard, merely because it was in the way; four men, among whom was the boatswain, took possession of it. They had no oars, but called out for some, when three sailors jumped overboard and carried them what they stood so much in need of. These fortunate fugitives were required to return; they cried out that they had no rudder, and desired a rope to be thrown them; perceiving that the progress of the flames left them no other resource, they endeavored to remove to a distance from the ship, which passed them in consequence of a breeze that sprung up.

All hands were still busy on board; the impossibility of escaping, seemed to increase the courage of the men. The master boldly ventured down into the hold, but the heat obliged him to return; he would have been burnt, if a great quantity of water had not been thrown over him. Immediately afterward, the flames were seen to issue with impetuosity from the great pannel. The captain ordered the boats overboard, but fear had exhausted the strength of the most intrepid. The jolly-boat was fastened at a certain height, and preparations were made for hoisting her over; but, to complete our misfortunes, the fire, which increased every moment, ascended the mainmast with such violence and rapidity as to burn the tackle; the boat pitching upon the starboard guns, fell bottom upward, and we lost all hope of raising her again. We now perceived that we had nothing to hope from human aid, but only from the mercy of the Almighty. Dejection filled every mind; the consternation became general; nothing but sighs and groans were heard; even the animals we had on board, uttered the most dreadful cries. Every one began to raise his heart and hands toward heaven; and in the certainty of a speedy death, each was occupied only with the melancholy alternative between the two elements ready to devour us.

The chaplain, who was on the quarter-deck, gave the general absolution, and went into the gallery to impart the same to the unhappy wretches who had already committed themselves to the mercy of the waves. What a horrible spectacle! Every one was occupied only in throwing overboard whatever promised a momentary preservation; coops, yards, spars, everything that came to hand, was seized with despair, and disposed of in the same manner. The confusion was extreme; some seemed to anticipate death by jumping into the sea, others, by swimming, gained the fragments of the vessel; while the shrouds, the yards, and ropes, along the side of the ship, were covered with the crew, who were suspended from them, as if hesitating between two extremes equally imminent and equally terrible.

Uncertain for what fate Providence intended me, I saw a father snatch his son from the flames, embrace him, throw him into the sea, then following himself, they perished in each other's embrace. I had ordered the helm to be turned to starboard; the vessel heeled, and this maneuver preserved us for some time on that side, while the fire raged on the larboard side, from stem to stern. Till this moment I had been so engaged, that my thoughts were directed only to the preservation of the ship; now, however, the horrors of a twofold death presented themselves; but, through the kindness of heaven, my fortitude never forsook me. I looked round and found myself alone upon the deck. I went into the round-house, where I met M. de la Touche, who regarded death with the same heroism that procured him success in India. "Farewell, my brother and my friend," said he, embracing me. "Why, where are you going?" replied I. "I am going (said he) to comfort my friend Morin." He spoke of the captain, who was overwhelmed with grief at the melancholy fate of his female cousins, who were passengers on board his ship, and whom he had persuaded to trust themselves to sea in hen-coops, after having hastily stripped off their clothes, while some of the sailors, swimming with one hand, endeavored to support them with the other. The yards and masts floating around the ship, were covered with men struggling with the waves; many of them perished every moment by the balls discharged by the guns, in consequence of the flames, a third species of death that augmented the horrors by which we were surrounded. With a heart oppressed with anguish, I turned my eyes away from the sea. A moment afterward, I entered the starboard gallery, and saw the flames rushing with a horrid noise through the windows of the great cabin and round-house. The fire approached, and was ready to consume me; my presence was then entirely useless for the preservation of the vessel, or the relief of my fellow-sufferers.

In this dreadful situation, I thought it my duty to prolong my life a few hours, in order to devote them to my God. I stripped off my clothes with the intention of rolling down a yard, one end of which touched the water; but it was so covered with unfortunate wretches, whom the fear of drowning kept in that situation, that I tumbled over them and fell into the sea, recommending myself to the mercy of Providence. A stout soldier, who was drowning, caught hold of me at this extremity; I employed every exertion to disengage myself from him, but without effect. I suffered myself to sink under the water, but he did not quit his hold; I plunged a second time, and he still held me firmly in his grasp; he was incapable of reflecting that my death would rather hasten his own than be of service to him. At length, after struggling a considerable time, his strength was exhausted in consequence of the quantity of water he had swallowed, and perceiving that I was sinking the third time, and fearing lest I should drag him to the bottom along with me, he loosed his hold. That he might not catch me again, I dived and rose a considerable distance from the spot.

This first adventure rendered me more cautious in future; I even shunned the dead bodies, which were so numerous, that, to make a free passage, I was obliged to push them aside with one hand, while I kept myself above water with the other. I imagined that each of them was a man who would assuredly seize me and involve me in his own destruction. My strength began to fail, and I was convinced of the neccssity of resting, when I met a piece of the flag-staff. To secure it, I put my arm through the noose of the rope, and swam as well as I was able. I perceived a yard floating before me, when I approached and seized it by the end. At the other extremity, I saw a young man scarcely able to support himself, and speedily relinquished this feeble assistance that amounted to a certain death. The sprit-sail yard next appeared in sight; it was covered with people, and I durst not take a place upon it without asking permission, which my unfortunate companions cheerfully granted. Some were quite naked, and others in their shirts; they expressed their pity at my situation, and their misfortune put my sensibility to the severest test.

M. Morin and M. de la Touche, both so worthy of a better fate, never quitted the vessel, and were doubtless buried in its ruins. Whichever way I turned my eyes, the most dismal sights presented themselves. The mainmast, burnt away at the bottom, fell overboard, killing some, and affording to others a precarious resource. This mast I observed covered with people, and abandoned to the impulse of the waves; at the same moment, I perceived two sailors upon a hen-coop with some planks, and cried out to them, "My lads, bring the planks and swim to me." They approached me, accompanied by several others; and each taking a plank, which we used as oars, we paddled along upon the yard, and joined those who had taken possession of the mainmast. So many changes of situation presented only new spectacles of horror

I fortunately here met with our chaplain, who gave me absolution. We were in number about eighty persons, who were incessantly threatened with destruction by the balls from the ship's guns. I saw likewise on the mast two young ladies, by whose piety I was much edified; there were six females on board, and the other four were, in all probability, already drowned or burned. Our chaplain, in this dreadful situation, melted the most obdurate hearts by his discourse, and the example he gave of patience and resignation. Seeing him slip from the mast and fall into the sea, as I was behind him, I lifted him up again. "Let me go," said he, "I am full of water, and it is only a prolongation of my sufferings." "No, my friend," said I, "we will die together, when my strength forsakes me." In his pious company, I awaited death with perfect resignation. I remained in this situation three hours, and saw one of the ladies fall off the mast with fatigue and perish; she was too far distant for me to give her any assistance. When I least expected it, I perceived the yawl close to us; it was then five o'clock, P. M. I cried out to the men in her that I was their lieutenant, and begged permission to share our misfortune with them. They gave me leave to come on board, upon condition that I would swim to them. It was their interest to have a conductor, in order to discover land; and for this reason my company was too necessary for them to refuse my request. The condition they imposed upon me was perfectly reasonable; they acted prudently not to approach, as the others would have been equally anxious to enter their little bark, and we should all have been buried together in a watery grave. Mustering, therefore, all my strength, I was so fortunate as to reach the boat. Soon afterward, I observed the pilot and master, whom I had left on the mainmast, follow my example; they swam for the yawl, and we took them in. This little bark was the means of saving the ten persons who alone escaped out of nearly three hundred.

The flames still continued to consume our ship, from which we were not more than half a league distant; our too great proximity might prove pernicious, and we, therefore, proceeded a little to windward. Not long after, the fire communicated to the powder-room, and it is impossible to describe the noise with which our vessel blew up. A thick cloud intercepted the light of the sun; amid this horrid darkness we could perceive nothing but large pieces of floating wood projecting into the air, and whose fall threatened to dash to pieces, numbers of unhappy wretches still struggling with the agonies of death. We, ourselves, were not quite out of danger; it was not impossible but that one of the flaming fragments might reach us, and precipitate our frail vessel to the bottom. The Almighty, however, preserved us from that misfortune; but what a spectacle now presented itself! The vessel had disappeared; its fragments covered the sea to a great distance, and floated in all directions with our unfortunate companions, whose despair and whose lives had been terminated together by their fall. We saw some completely suffocated, others mangled, half-burned, and still preserving sufficient life to be sensible of the accumulated horrors of their fate.

Through the mercy of heaven I retained my fortitude, and proposed to make toward the fragments of the wreck, to seek provisions and to pick up any other articles we might want. We were totally unprovided, and were in danger of perishing with famine; a death more tedious and more painful than that of our companions. We found several barrels, in which we hoped to find a resource against this pressing necessity, but discovered, to our mortification, that it was part of the powder which had been thrown overboard during the conflagration. Night approached, but we providentially found a cask of brandy, about fifteen pounds of salt pork, a piece of scarlet cloth, twenty yards of linen, a dozen of pipe-staves, and a few ropes. It grew dark, and we could not wait till daylight, in our present situation, without exposing ourselves a hundred times to destruction among the fragments of the wreck, from which we had not yet been able to disengage ourselves. We therefore rowed away from them as speedily as possible, in order to attend to the equipment of our new vessel. Every one fell to work with the utmost assiduity; we employed everything, and took off the inner sheathing of our boat, for the sake of the planks and nails; we drew from the linen what thread we wanted; fortunately one of the sailors had two needles; our scarlet cloth served us for a sail, an oar for a mast, and a plank for a rudder. Notwithstanding the darkness, our equipment was in a short time as complete as circumstances would permit. The only difficulty that remained, was how to direct our course; we had neither charts nor instruments, and were nearly two hundred leagues from land. We resigned ourselves to the Almighty, whose assistance we implored in fervent prayers.

At length we raised our sail, and a favorable wind removed us forever from the floating corpses of our unfortunate companions. In this manner we proceeded eight days and eight nights without perceiving land, exposed, stark naked, to the burning rays of the sun by day, and to intense cold by night. The sixth day a shower of rain inspired us with the hope of some relief from the thirst by which we were tormented; we endeavored to catch the little water that fell in our mouths and hands. We sucked our sail, but having been before soaked in sea-water, it communicated the bitter taste of the latter to the rain which it received. If, however, the rain had been more violent, it might have abated the wind that impelled us, and a calm would have been attended with inevitable destruction.

That we might steer our course with greater certainty, we consulted every day the rising and setting of the sun and moon; and the stars showed us what wind we ought to take. A very small piece of salt pork furnished us one meal in the twenty-four hours; and from this even, we were obliged to desist on the fourth day, on account of the irritation of blood which it occasioned. Our only beverage was a glass of brandy from time to time; but that liquor burned our stomachs, without allaying our thirst. We saw abundance of flying fish, but the impossibility of catching them rendered our misery still more acute; we were, therefore, obliged to be contented with our provisions. The uncertainty with respect to our fate, the want of food, and the agitation of the sea, combined to deprive us of rest, and almost plunged us into despair. Nature seemed to have abandoned her functions; a feeble ray of hope alone cheered our minds and prevented us from envying the fate of our deceased companions. I passed the eighth night at the helm; I remained at my post more than ten hours, frequently desiring to be relieved, till at length I sunk down with fatigue. My miserable comrades were equally exhausted, and despair began to take possession of our souls. At last, when just perishing with fatigue, misery, hunger, and thirst, we discovered land by the first rays of the sun, on Wednesday, the 3d of August, 1752. Only those who have experienced similar misfortunes, can form an adequate conception of the change which this discovery produced in our minds. Our strength returned, and we took precautions not to be carried away by the currents. At two P. M., we reached the coast of Brazil, and entered the bay of Tresson, in latitude 6°.

Our first care, upon setting foot on shore, was to thank the Almighty for his favors; we threw ourselves upon the ground, and in the transports of our joy rolled ourselves in the sand. Our appearance was truly frightful, our figures preserved nothing human that did not most forcibly announce our misfortunes. Some were perfectly naked, others had nothing but shirts that were rotten and torn to rags, and I had fastened round my waist a piece of scarlet cloth, in order to appear at the head of my companions. We had not yet, however, arrived at the end of our hardships; although rescued from the greatest of our dangers, that of an uncertain navigation, we were still tormented by hunger and thirst, and in cruel suspense whether we should find this coast inhabited by men susceptible of sentiments of compassion. We were deliberating which way we should direct our course, when about fifty Portuguese, most of whom were armed, advanced toward us, and inquired the reason of our landing. The recital of our misfortunes was a sufficient answer, at once announced our wants, and strongly claimed the sacred rights of hospitality. Their treasures were not the object of our desire, the necessities of life were all that we wanted. Touched by our misfortunes, they blessed the power that had preserved us, and hastened to conduct us to their habitations. Upon the way, we came to a river, into which all my companions ran to throw themselves, in order to allay their thirst; they rolled in the water with extreme delight, and bathing was in the sequel, one of the remedies of which we made the most frequent use, and which, at the same time, contributed most to the restoration of our health.

The principal person of the place came and conducted us to his house, about half a league distant from the place of our landing. Our charitable host gave us linen shirts and trowsers, and boiled some fish, the water of which, served us for broth, and seemed delicious. After this frugal repast, though sleep was equally necessary, yet we prepared to render solemn thanks to the Almighty. Hearing that at the distance of half a league, there was a church dedicated to St. Michael, we repaired thither, singing praises to the Lord, where we presented the homage of our gratitude to Him to whom we were so evidently indebted for our preservation. The badness of the road had fatigued us so much, that we were obliged to rest in the village; our misfortunes, together with such an edifying spectacle, drew all the inhabitants around us, and every one hastened to fetch us refreshments. After resting a short time, we returned to our kind host, who at night furnished us with another repast of fried fish. As we wanted more invigorating food, we purchased an ox, which we had in exchange for twenty-five quarts of brandy. We had to go to Paraiba, a journey of fifteen leagues, barefooted, and without any hope of meeting with good provisions on the way; we therefore took the precaution of smoke-drying our meat, and adding to it a provision of flour. After resting three days, we departed under an escort of three soldiers. We proceeded seven leagues the first day, and passed the night at the house of a man who received us kindly. The next evening a sergeant, accompanied by twenty-nine soldiers, came to meet us for the purpose of conducting and presenting us to the commander of the fortress; that worthy officer received us graciously, gave us an entertainment, and a boat to go to Paraiba. It was midnight when we arrived at that town; a Portuguese captain was waiting to present us to the governor, who gave us a gracious reception, and furnished us with all the comforts of life. We there reposed for three days; but being desirous of reaching Pernambuco, to take advantage of a Portuguese fleet that was expected to sail every day, in order to return to Europe, the governor ordered a corporal to conduct us thither. My feet were so lacerated that I could scarcely stand, and a horse was therefore provided for me.

At length, after a journey of four days, we entered the town of Pernambuco. My first business was to go with my people to present myself to the general, Joseph de Correa, who condescended to give us an audience; after which, Don Francisco Miguel, a captain of a king's ship, took us in his boat to procure us the advantage of saluting the admiral of the fleet, Don Juan d'Acosta de Porito. During the fifty days that we remained at Pernambuco, that gentleman never ceased to load me with new favors and civilities. His generosity extended to all my companions in misfortune, to some of whom, he even gave appointments in the vessels of his fleet.

On the 5th of October we set sail, and arrived without any accident at Lisbon, on the 17th of December. On the 2d of January, our consul, M. du Vernay, procured me a passage in a vessel bound to Morlaix. The master and myself went on board together, the rest of my companions being distributed among the ships. I arrived at Morlaix on the 2d of February. My fatigues obliged me to take a few days' rest in that place, from whence I repaired, on the 10th, to L'Orient, overwhelmed with poverty, having lost all that I possessed in the world, after a service of twenty-eight years, and with my health greatly impaired by the hardships I had endured.

A SAILOR'S LIFE AND DUTIES.

As we had now a long spell of fine weather, without any incident to break the monotony of our lives, I will describe the duties, regulations, and customs of an American merchantman, of which ours was a fair specimen.

The captain, in the first place, is lord paramount. He stands no watch, comes and goes when he pleases, and is accountable to no one, and must be obeyed in everything without a question even from his chief officer. He has the power to turn his officers off duty, and to even break them and make them do duty as sailors in the forecastle. Where there are no passengers and no supercargo, he has no companion but his own dignity, and no pleasures, unless he differs from most of his kind, but the consciousness of possessing supreme power, and occasionally the exercise of it.

The prime minister, the official organ, and tho activo and superintend ing officer, is the chief mate. He is first lieutenant, boatswain, sailing master, and quartermaster. The captain tells him what he wishes to have done, and leaves to him the care of overseeing, of allotting the work, and also the responsibility of its being well done. *The* mate (as he is always called, *par excellence*,) also keeps the log-book, for which he is responsible to the owners and insurers, and has the charge of the stowage, safe keeping, and delivery of the cargo. He is also, ex-officio, the wit of the crew; for the captain does not condescend to joke with the men, and the second mate no one cares for, so that when "the mate" thinks to entertain "the people" with a coarse joke, or a little practical wit, every one feels bound to laugh. The second mate's, is proverbially a dog's berth. He is neither officer nor man. The men do not respect him as an officer, and he is obliged to go aloft to furl and reef the topsails, and to put his hands into the slush and tar with the rest. The crew call him the "sailor waiter," as he has to furnish them with spun-yarn, marline, and all other stuffs that they need in their work, and has charge of the boatswain's locker, which includes serving-boards, marline-spikes, etc., etc. He is expected by the captain, to maintain his dignity, and to enforce obedience, and still is kept at a great distance from the mate and obliged to work with the men. He is one to whom little is given, and of whom much is required. His wages are usually double those of a common sailor, and he eats and sleeps in the cabin; but he is obliged to be on deck nearly all his time, and eats at the second table, that is, makes a meal out of what the captain and chief mate leave.

The steward is the captain's servant, and has charge of the pantry, from which every one, even the mate himself, is excluded. These distinctions usually find him an enemy in the mate, who does not like to have any one on board who is not entirely under his control; the crew do not consider him as one of their number, so he is left to the mercy of the captain.

The cook is the patron of the crew, and those who are in his favor, can get their wet mittens and stockings dried, or light their pipes at the galley in the night watch. These two worthies, together with the carpenter and sail-maker, if there be one, stand no watch, but being employed all day, are allowed to "sleep in" at night, unless all hands are called.

The crew are divided into two divisions as equally as may be, called *the watches*. Of these, the chief mate commands the larboard, and the second mate the starboard. They divide the time between them, being on and off duty, as it is called, on deck and below every other four hours. If, for instance, the chief mate with the larboard watch have the first night watch from eight to twelve, at the end of the four hours, the starboard watch is called, and the second mate takes the deck, while the larboard watch and the first mate go below until four in the morning, when they come on deck again and remain until eight, having what is called the morning watch. As they will have been on deck eight hours out of the twelve, while those who had the middle watch—from twelve to four—will have been up only four hours, they have what is called "a forenoon watch below," that is, from 8 A. M., until noon. In a man-of-war, and in some merchantmen, this alternation of watches is kept up throughout the twenty-four hours; but our ship, like most merchantmen, had "all hands" from twelve o'clock till dark, except in bad weather, when we had "watch and watch."

An explanation of the "dog-watches" may, perhaps, be of use to one who has never been at sea. They are to shift the watches each night, so that the same watch need not be on deck at the same hour. In order to effect this, the watch from *four* to *eight* P. M. is divided into two half or dog-watches, one from four to six, and the other from six to eight. By this means, they divide the twenty-four hours into *seven* watches instead of *six*, and thus shift the hours every night. As the dog-watches come during twilight, after the day's work is done, and before the night watch is set, they are the watches in which everybody is on deck. The captain is up walking on the weather side of the quarter-deck; the chief mate is on the lee side, and the second mate about the weather gangway. The steward has finished his work in the cabin, and has come up to smoke his pipe with the cook in the galley. The crew are sitting on the windlass or lying on the forecastle, smoking, singing, or telling long yarns. At eight o'clock, eight bells are struck, the log is hove, the watch set, the wheel relieved, the galley shut up, and the other watch goes below.

The morning commences with the watch on deck "turning to" at daybreak, and washing down, scrubbing, and swabbing the decks. This, together with filling the scuttle-butt with fresh water, and coiling up rigging, usually occupies the time until seven bells, (half past seven,) when all hands go to breakfast. At eight, the day's work begins, and lasts until sundown, with the exception of an hour for dinner.

Before I end my explanations, it may be well to define a *day's work*, and to correct a mistake prevalent among landsmen about a sailor's life. Nothing is more common than to hear people say "Are not sailors very idle at sea? What can they find to do?" This is a very natural mistake, and being very frequently made, it is one which every sailor feels interested in having corrected. In the first place, the discipline of the ship requires every man to be at work upon *something* when he is upon deck, except at night and on Sundays. Except at these times, you will never see a man on board a well ordered vessel, standing idle on deck, sitting down, or leaning over the side. It is the officers' duty to keep every one at work, even if there is nothing to be done but to scrape the rust from the chain cables. In no state prison are the convicts more regularly set to work, and more closely watched. No conversation is allowed among the crew at their duty, and though they frequently do talk when aloft, or when near one another, yet they always stop when an officer is nigh.

With regard to the work upon which the men are put; it is a matter which probably would not be understood by one who has not been at sea. When I first left port, I found that we were regularly employed for a week or two. I supposed that we were getting the vessel into sea trim, and that it would soon be over and we should have nothing to do but to sail the ship, but I found that it continued so for two years, and at the end of the two years, there was as much to be done as ever. As has often been said, a ship is like a lady's watch, always out of repair. When first leaving port, studding-sail gear is to be rove, all the running rigging to be examined, that which is unfit for use to be got down, and new rigging rove in its place; then the standing rigging is to be overhauled, replaced, and repaired in a thousand different ways, and wherever any of the numberless ropes are wearing or chafing upon it, there "chafing gear," as it is called, is to be put on. This chafing gear consists of worming, parceling, roundings, battons, and service of all kinds—both rope-yarns, spun-yarn, marline, and seizing stuffs. Taking off, putting on and mending the chafing gear alone, upon a vessel would find constant employment for two or three men during working hours, for a whole voyage.

The next point to be considered, is, that all the "small stuffs" which are used on board a ship—such as spun-yarn, marline, seizing stuff, etc.,

etc.—are made on board. The owners of a vessel buy up incredible quantities of "old junk," which the sailors untwist, and after drawing out the yarns, knot them together, and roll them up in balls. These "rope yarns" are constantly used for various purposes, but the greater part is manufactured into spun-yarn. For this purpose every vessel is furnished with a "spun-yarn winch," which is very simple, consisting of a wheel and spindle. This may be heard constantly going on deck in pleasant weather; and we had employment during a great part of the time, for three hands in drawing and knotting yarns, and making spun-yarn.

Another method of employing the crew is "setting up" rigging. Whenever any of the standing rigging becomes slack, (which is constantly happening,) the seizings and coverings must be taken off, tackles got up, and after the rigging is bowsed, well taut, the seizings and coverings replaced, which is a very nice piece of work. There is also such a connection between different parts of a vessel, that one rope can seldom be touched without altering another. You cannot stay a mast aft by the back-stays without slacking up the head-stays, etc., etc. If we add to all this the tarring, greasing, oiling, varnishing, painting, scraping and scrubbing, which is required in the course of a long voyage, and also remember that this is to be done in *addition* to watching at night, steering, reefing, furling, bracing, making and setting sail, and pulling, hauling and climbing in every direction, one will hardly ask, "What can a sailor find to do at sea?"

If after all this labor, after exposing their lives and limbs in storms, wet and cold, the merchants and captains think they have not earned their twelve dollars a month—out of which they clothe themselves—and their salt beef and hard bread, they keep them picking oakum—*ad infinitum.* This is the moral resource upon a rainy day, for then it will not do to work upon rigging; and when it is pouring down in floods, instead of letting the sailors stand about in sheltered places and talk, and keep themselves comfortable, they are separated to different parts of the ship, and kept at work picking oakum. I have seen oakum stuff placed about in different parts of the ship, so that the sailors might not be idle in the *snatches* between the frequent squalls upon crossing the equator. Some officers have been so driven to find work for the crew in a ship ready for sea, that they have set them to pounding the anchors—often done—and scraping the chain-cable.

This kind of work, of course, is not kept up off Cape Horn, Cape of Good Hope, and in extreme north and south latitudes; but I have seen the decks washed down and scrubbed when the water would have frozen if it had been fresh; and all hands kept at work upon the rigging when we had on our pea-jackets, and our hands were so numb that we could hardly hold our marline-spikes. Before leaving this description, I would state, in order to show landsmen how little they know of the nature of a ship, that a *ship-carpenter* is kept in constant employ, during good weather, on board vessels which are in what is called perfect sea-order.

On Sabbaths, when the weather is fine, the decks are washed down, the rigging coiled up, and everything put in order; and throughout the day only one watch is kept on deck at a time. The men are all dressed in their best white duck trowsers, and red or checked shirts, and have nothing to do, but to make the necessary changes in the sails. They employ themselves in reading, talking, smoking, and mending their clothes. If the weather is pleasant, they bring their work and their books upon deck, and sit down upon the forecastle and windlass. This is the only day on which these privileges are allowed them. When Monday comes, they put on their tarry trowsers again, and prepare for six days of labor.

To enhance the value of the Sabbath to the crew, they are allowed on that day a pudding, or, as it is called, a "duff." This is nothing more than flour boiled with water and eaten with molasses. It is very dark and clammy, yet it is looked upon as a luxury, and really forms an agreeable variety with salt beef and pork. Many a rascally captain has made friends of his crew by allowing them duff twice a week on the passage home.

SCENES ON A MAN-OF-WAR IN A HURRICANE.

Among the most vivid descriptions of a hurricane at sea is that given by Lieutenant Archer, in a letter to his mother. He was on board of his majesty's ship Phœnix in a hurricane in the West Indies, in the year 1780. This ship was lost, together with twelve others, comprising the British fleet on that station. The narrative is so powerful that the reader seems almost transported to the decks of the Phœnix, and to be an eye witness of the awful events which are transpiring on the occasion.

"It happened to be my middle watch, and about three o'clock, when the man upon the forecastle bawls out:

'Breakers ahead, and land upon the lee bow!'

I looked out, and it was so, sure enough.

'Ready about! Put the helm down! Helm a lee!'

Sir Hyde Parker, hearing me put the ship about, jumped upon deck.

'Archer, what's the matter? you are putting the ship about without my orders!'

'Sir, 'tis time to go about; the ship is almost ashore; there is the land.'

'Good God! so it is. Will the ship stay?'

'Yes, sir; I believe she will, if we don't make any confusion; She is all aback—forward now?'

'Well,' says he, 'work the ship; I will not speak a single word.'

The ship stayed very well.

'Then heave the lead! see what water we have.'

'Three fathom.'

'Keep the ship away, W. N. W.'

'By the mark, three.'

'This won't do, Archer.'

'No, sir; we had better haul more to the northward; we came S. S. E., and had better steer N. N. W.'

'Steady, and a quarter three.'

'This may do, as we deepen a little.'

'By the deep, four.'

'Very well, my lad; heave quick.'

'Five fathom.'

'That's a fine fellow; another cast nimbly.'

'Quarter less eight.'

'That will do. Come, we shall get clear by and by.'

'Mark under water, five.'

'What's that?'

'Only five fathom, sir.'

'Turn all hands up; bring the ship to an anchor, boy! Are the anchors clear?'

'In a moment, sir—all clear.'

'What water have you in the chains now?'

'Eight, half, nine.'

'Keep fast the anchors until I call you.'

'Ay, ay, sir; all fast.'

'I have no ground with this line.'

'How many fathoms have you out? pass along the deep-sea line!'

'Ay, ay, sir.'

'Heave away—watch! watch! bear away! veer away.'

'No ground, sir, with a hundred fathom.'

'That 's clever! Come, Madam Phœnix, there is another squeak in you yet. All down but the watch; secure the anchors again; heave the maintopsail to the mast; luff, and bring her to the wind!'

"I told you, Madam, you should have a little sea jargon; if you can understand half of what is already said, I wonder at it, though it is nothing to what is to come yet, when the old hurricane begins. As soon as the ship was a little to rights, and all quiet again, Sir Hyde came to me in the most friendly manner, the tears almost starting from his eyes:

'Archer, we ought all to be much obliged to you for the safety of the ship, and, perhaps, of ourselves. I am particularly so; nothing but that instantaneous presence of mind and calmness saved her; another ship's length, and we should have been fast on shore; had you been the least diffident, or made the least confusion, so as to make the ship haulk in her stays, she must have been inevitably lost.'

'Sir, you are very good, but I have done nothing that I suppose anybody else would not have done in the same situation. I did not turn all the hands up, knowing the watch able to work the ship; beside, had it spread immediately about the ship that she was almost ashore, it might have created a confusion that was better avoided.'

'Well,' says he, ''tis well, indeed.'

"At daylight we found that the current had set us between the Colladora rocks and Cape Antonio, and that we could not have got out any other way than we did; there was a chance; but Providence is the best pilot. We had sunset that day twenty leagues to the south-east of our reckoning by the current.

After getting clear of this scrape, we thought ourselves fortunate, and made sail for Jamaica; bnt misfortune seemed to follow misfortune. The next night, my watch upon deck, too, we were overtaken by a squall, like a hurricane while it lasted; for though I saw it coming, and prepared for it, yet, when it took the ship, it roared and laid her down so that I thought she would never get up again. However, by keeping her away, and clueing up everything, she righted. The remainder of the night we had very heavy squalls, and in the morning found the mainmast sprung half the way through: one hundred and twenty-three leagues to the leeward of Jamaica, the hurricane months coming on, the head of the mainmast almost off, and at a short allowance; well, we must make the best of it. The mainmast was well finished, but we were obliged to be very tender of carrying the sail.

Nothing remarkable happened for ten days afterward, when we chased a Yankee man-of-war for six hours, but could not get near enough to her, before it was dark, to keep sight of her; so that we lost her because unable to carry any sail on the mainmast. In about twelve days more made the island of Jamaica, having weathered all the squalls, and put into Montego Bay for water: so that we had a strong party for kicking up a dust on shore, having found three men-of-war lying there. Dancing, etc., etc., till two o'clock every morning; little thinking what was to happen in four days' time: for out of the four men-of-war that were there, not one was in being at the end of that time, and not a soul alive but those of our crew. Many of the houses where we had been so merry, were so completely destroyed that scarcely a vestige remained to mark where they stood. Thy works are wonderful, O God! praised be thy holy name!

September the 30th, weighed; bound for Port Royal, round the eastward of the island; the Barbadoes and Victor had sailed the day before, and the Scarborough was to sail the next. Moderate weather until October the 2d. Spoke to the Barbadoes, off Port Antonio, in the evening. At eleven at night it began to snuffle, with a monstrous heavy bill from the eastward. Close reefed the topsails.

Sir Hyde sent for me: 'What sort of weather have we, Archer?'

'It blows a little, and has a very ugly look; if in any other quarter but this, I should say we were going to have a gale of wind.'

'Ay, it looks so very often here when there is no wind at all; however, don't hoist the topsails till it clears a little, there is no trusting any country.'

'At twelve I was relieved; the weather had the same rough look. however, they made sail upon her, but had a very dirty night. At eight in the morning I came up again, found it blowing hard from the E. N. E. with close reefed topsails upon the ship, and heavy squalls at times.

'Sir Hyde came upon deck: 'Well, Archer, what do you think of it?'

'Oh, sir, 't is only a touch of the times; we shall have an observation at twelve o'clock; the clouds are beginning to break; it will clear up at noon, or else blow very hard afterward.'

'I wish it would clear up, but I doubt it much. I was once in a hurricane in the East Indies, and the beginning of it had much the same appearance as this. So take in the topsails, we have plenty of sea-room.'

At twelve, the gale still increasing, wore ship, to keep as near mid channel between Jamaica and Cuba as possible; at one the gale increasing still; at two harder! Reefed the courses, and furled them; brought to under a foul mizzen-staysail, head to the northward. In the evening no sign of the weather taking off, but every appearance of the storm increasing, prepared for a proper gale of wind; secured all the sails with spare gaskets; good rolling tackles upon the yards; squared the booms; saw the boats all made fast; new lashed the guns; double breeched the lower deckers; saw that the carpenters had the tarpaulins and batins all ready for hatchways; got the topgallant-mast down upon the deck; jib-boom and sprit-sail-yard fore and aft; in fact, everything we could think of to make a snug ship.

The poor devils of birds now began to find the uproar in the elements, for numbers, both of sea and land kinds, came on board of us. I took notice of some, which happening to be to leeward, turned to windward like ship, tack and tack: for they could not fly against it. When they came over the ship they dashed themselves down upon the deck, without attempting to stir till picked up; and when let go again, they would not leave the ship, but endeavored to hide themselves from the wind.

At eight o'clock a hurricane; the sea roaring, but the wind still steady to a point; did not ship a spoonful of water. However, got the hatchways all secured, expecting what would be the consequences should the wind shift; placed the carpenters by the mainmast, with broad-axes, knowing from experience, that at the moment you may want to cut it away to save the ship, an ax may not be found. Went to supper: bread, cheese, and porter. The purser frightened out of his wits about his bread-bags; the two marine officers as white as sheets, not understanding the ship's working so much, and the noise of the lower deck guns; which, by this time, made a pretty screeching to the people not used to it; it seemed as if the whole ship's side was going at each roll. *Wooden,* our carpenter, was all this time smoking his pipe and laughing at the doctor; the second lieutenant upon deck, and the third in his hammock.

At ten o'clock I thought to get a little sleep: came to look into my cot; it was full of water; for every seam, by the straining of the ship, had begun to leak. Stretched myself, therefore, upon deck between two chests, and left orders to be called, should the least thing happen.

At twelve a midshipman came to me: 'Mr. Archer, we are just going to wear ship, sir!'

'Oh, very well, I'll be up directly; what sort of weather have you got?'

'It blows a hurricane.'

Went upon deck, found Sir Hyde there. 'It blows hard, Archer.'

'It does, indeed, sir.'

'I don't know that I ever remember its blowing so hard before; but the ship makes a very good weather of it upon this tack, as she bows the sea; but we must wear her, as the wind has shifted to the S. E. and we are drawing right upon Cuba; so do you go forward, and have some hands stand by; loose the lee yard-arm of the foresail, and when she is right before the wind, whip the clew-garnet close up and roll up the sail.'

'Sir, there is no canvas that can stand against this a moment; if we attempt to loose him he will fly into ribbons in an instant, and we may lose three or four of our people; she'll wear by manning the fore shrouds.'

'Oh, I don't think she will.'

'I'll answer for it, sir; I have seen it tried several times on the coast of America with success.'

'Well, try it; if she does not wear, we can only loose the foresail afterward.'

This was a great condescension from such a man as Sir Hyde. However, by sending about two hundred people into the fore-rigging, after a hard struggle she wore; found she did not make so good weather on this tack as on the other; for, as the sea began to run across, she had not time to rise from one sea before another dashed against her. Began to think we should lose our masts, as the ship lay very much along by the pressure of the wind constantly upon the yards and masts alone; for the poor mizzen-staysail had gone in shreds long before, and the sails began to fly from the yards through the gaskets into coach whips. My God! to think that the wind could have such force! Sir Hyde now sent me to see what was the matter between decks, as there was a good deal of noise. As soon as I was below, one of the marine officers calls out:

'Good God! Mr. Archer, we are sinking; the water is up to the bottom of my cot.'

'Pooh, pooh! as long as it is not over your mouth you are well off; what the d——l do you make so much noise for?'

I found there was some water between decks, but nothing to be alarmed at; we scuttled the deck and run it into the well; found she made a good deal of water through the sides and decks; turned the watch below to the pumps, though only two feet of water in the well; but expected to be kept constantly at work now, as the ship labored much, with scarcely a part of her above water but the quarter-deck, and that but seldom.

'Come, pump away, my boys. Carpenters, get the weather chain-pump rigged.'

'All ready, sir.'

'Then man it, and keep both pumps going.'

At two o'clock the chain-pump being choked, we set the carpenters at work to clear it; the two head-pumps at work upon deck; the water gained upon us while our chain-pumps were idle; in a quarter of an hour they were at work again, and we began to gain upon it. While I was standing at the pumps cheering the people, the carpenter's mate came running to me with a face as long as my arm.

'Oh, sir! the ship has sprung a leak in the gunner's room.'

'Go, then, and tell the carpenter to come to me, but do not speak a word to any one else. Mr. Goodinoh, I am told there is a leak in the gunner's room; go and see what is the matter, but do not alarm any body, and come and make your report privately to me.'

In a short time he returned; 'Sir, there is nothing there; it is only the water washing up between the timbers that this booby has taken for a leak.'

'Oh, very well; go upon deck and see if you can keep any of the water from washing down below.'

'Sir, I have had four people constantly keeping the hatchways secure, but there is such a weight of water upon the deck that nobody can stand when the ship rolls.'

The gunner soon afterward came to me, saying, 'Mr. Archer, I should be glad to have you step this way into the magazine for a moment.'

I thought something was the matter, and ran directly. 'Well, what is the matter here?'

He answered. 'The ground tier of the powder is spoiled, and I want to show you that it is not out of carelessness in me in stowing it, for no powder in the world could be better stowed. Now, sir, what am I to do? If you do not speak to Sir Hyde, he will be angry with me.'

I could not forbear smiling to see how easy he took the danger of the ship, and said to him, 'Let us shake off this gale of wind first, and talk of the damaged powder afterward.' At four we had gained upon the ship a little, and I went upon deck, it being my watch. The second lieutenant relieved me at the pumps. Who can attempt to describe the appearance of things upon deck? If I was to write for ever, I could not give you an idea of it — a total darkness all above; the sea on fire, running as if it were in the Alps, or Peaks of Teneriffe; (mountains are too common an idea;) the wind roaring louder than thunder, (absolutely no flight of imagination,) the whole made more terrible, if possible, by a very uncommon kind of blue lightning; the poor ship very much pressed, yet doing what she could, shaking her sides and groaning at every stroke. Sir Hyde upon deck lashed to windward! I soon lashed myself along side of him, and told him the situation of things below, saying the ship did not make more water than might be expected in such weather, and that I was only afraid of a gun breaking loose.

'I am not in the least afraid of that; I have commanded her six years, and have had many a gale of wind in her; so that her iron work, which always gives way first, is pretty well tried. Hold fast! that was an ugly sea; we must lower the yards, I believe, Archer; the ship is much pressed.'

'If we attempt it, sir, we shall lose them, for a man can do nothing; beside, their being down would ease the ship very little; the mainmast is a sprung mast; I wish it was overboard without carrying anything else along with it; but that can soon be done, the gale cannot last forever; 'twill soon be daylight now.'

Found by the master's watch that it was five o'clock, though but a little after four by ours; I was glad it was so near daylight, and looked for it with much anxiety. Cuba, thou art much in our way! Another ugly sea: sent a midshipman to bring news from the pumps; the ship was gaining on them very much, for they had broken one of their chains, but it was almost mended again. News from the pump again.

'She still gains! a heavy lee!'

Back-water from leeward, half way up the quarter-deck; filled one of the cutters upon the booms, and tore her all to pieces; the ship lying almost on her beam ends, and not attempting to right again. Word from below that the ship still gained on them, as they could not stand to the pumps, she lay so much along.

I said to Sir Hyde: 'This is no time, sir, to think of saving the masts, shall we cut the mainmast away?'

'Ay! as fast as you can.'

I accordingly went into the weather-chains with a pole-ax, to cut away the lanyards; the boatswain went to leeward, and the carpenters stood by the masts. We were all ready, when a very violent sea broke right on board of us, carried everything upon deck away, filled the ship with water, the main and mizzen-masts went, the ship righted, but was in the last struggle of sinking under us. As soon as we could shake our heads above water, Sir Hyde exclaimed:

'We are gone, at last, Archer! foundered at sea!'

'Yes, sir, farewell, and the Lord have mercy upon us!'

I then turned about to look at the ship, and thought she was struggling to get rid of some of the water; but all was in vain, she was almost full below.

'Almighty God! I thank thee, that now I am leaving this world, which I have always considered as only a passage to a better, I die with a full hope of thy mercies through the merits of Jesus Christ, thy Son, our Saviour!'

I then felt sorry that I could swim, as by that means I might be a quarter of an hour longer dying than a man who could not, and it is impossible to divest ourselves of a wish to preserve life. At the end of these reflections I thought I heard the ship thump and grinding under our feet; it was so.

'Sir, the ship is ashore!'

'What do you say?'

'The ship is ashore, and we may save ourselves yet!'

By this time the quarter-deck was full of men who had come up from below; and the "Lord have mercy upon us," flying about from all quarters.

The ship now made everybody sensible that she was ashore, for every stroke threatened a total dissolution of her whole frame; we found she was stern ashore, and the bow broke the sea a good deal, though it was washing clean over at every stroke, Sir Hyde cried out:

'Keep to the quarter-deck, my lads; when she goes to pieces it is your best chance!'

Providentially got the foremast cut away, that she might not pay round broadside. Lost five in cutting away the foremast, by the breaking of a sea on board just as the mast went. That was nothing; every one expected it would be his own fate next; looked for daybreak with the greatest impatience. At last it came; but what a scene did it show us! The ship upon a bed of rocks, mountains of them on one side, and Cordilleras of water on the other; our poor ship grinding and crying out at every stroke between them; going away by piece-meal. However, to show the unaccountable workings of Providence, that which often appears to be the greatest evil, proves to be the greatest good! That unmerciful sea lifted and beat us up so high among the rocks, that at last the ship scarcely moved. She was very strong, and did not go to pieces at the first thumping, though her decks tumbled in. We found afterward that she had beat over a ledge of rocks almost a quarter of a mile in extent beyond us, where, if she had struck, every soul of us must have perished.

I now began to think of getting on shore, so I stripped off my coat and shoes for a swim, and looked for a line, to carry the end with me. Luckily I could not find one, which gave me time for recollection: 'This won't do for me, to be the first man out of the ship, and first lieutenant; we may get to England again, and people may think I paid a great deal of attention to myself, and did not care for anybody else. No, that won't do; instead of being the first, I'll see every man, sick and well, out of her before me.'

I now thought there was no probability of the ship's soon going to pieces, therefore had not a thought of instant death: took a look round with a kind of philosophic eye, to see how the same situation affected my companions, and was surprised to find the most swaggering, swearing bullies in fine weather, now the most pitiful wretches on earth, when death appeared before them. However, two got safe; by which means, with a line we got a hawser on shore, and made fast to the rocks, upon which many ventured and arrived safe. There were some sick and wounded on board, who could not avail themselves of this method; we therefore got a spare topsail yard from the chains and placed one end ashore and the other on the cabin window, so that most of the sick got ashore this way.

As I had determined, so I was the last man out of the ship; this was about ten o'clock. The gale now began to break. Sir Hyde came to me, and taking me by the hand, was so affected that he was scarcely able to speak.

'Archer, I am happy beyond expression to see you on shore, but look at our poor Phœnix!'

I turned about, but could not say a single word, being too full; my mind had been too intensely occupied before; but everything now rushed upon me at once, so that I could not contain myself, and I indulged for a full quarter of an hour. By twelve it was pretty moderate; got some nails on shore and made tents; we found great quantities of fish driven up by the sea into holes of the rocks: knocked up a fire and had a most comfortable dinner. In the afternoon we made a stage from the cabin windows to the rocks, and got out some provisions and water, lest the ship should go to pieces, in which case we must all have perished of hunger and thirst; for we were upon a desolate part of the coast, and under a rocky mountain that could not supply us with a single drop of water.

Slept comfortably this night; and the next day the idea of death vanishing by degrees, the prospect of being prisoners, during the war, at Havana, and walking three hundred miles to it through the woods, was rather unpleasant. However, to save life for the present, we employed this day in getting more provisions and water on shore, which was not an easy matter, on account of decks, guns, and rubbish, and ten feet of water that lay over them. In the evening I proposed to Sir Hyde to repair the remains of the only boat left, and to venture in her to Jamaica myself; and in case I arrived safe to bring vessels to take them all off; a proposal worthy of consideration. It was next day agreed to; therefore we got the cutter on shore, and set the carpenters to work on her; in two days she was ready, and at four o'clock in the afternoon I embarked with four volunteers and a fortnight's provision; hoisted English colors as we put off from shore, and received three cheers from the lads left behind, and set sail with a light heart; having not the least doubt that, with God's assistance, we should come and bring them all off. Had a very squally night, and a very leaky boat, so as to keep two buckets constantly bailing. Steered her myself the whole night by the stars, and in the morning saw the coast of Jamaica, distant twelve leagues. At eight in the evening arrived at Montego Bay.

I must now begin to leave off, particularly as I have but half an hour to conclude; else my pretty little short letter will lose its passage, which I should not like, after being ten days, at different times, writing it, beating up with the convoy to the northward, which is a reason that this epistle will never read well; for I never sat down with a proper disposition to go on with it; but as I knew something of the kind would please you, I was resolved to finish it; yet it will not bear an overhaul; so do not expose your son's nonsense.

But to proceed—I instantly sent off an express to the Admiral, another to the Porcupine man-of-war, and went myself to Martha Bray to get vessels; for all their vessels here, as well as many of their houses, were gone to *Moco*. Got three small vessels, and set out back again to Cuba, where I arrived the fourth day after leaving my companions. I thought the ship's crew would have devoured me on my landing; they presently whisked me up on their shoulders and carried me to the tent where Sir Hyde was.

A MAN OVERBOARD.

MONDAY, November 19th, was a black day in our calendar. At seven o'clock in the morning, it being our watch below, we were aroused from a sound sleep by the cry. "All hands ahoy! a man overboard!"

This unwonted cry sent a thrill through the heart of every one; and hurrying on deck, we found the vessel hove flat aback, with all her studding-sails set; for the boy who was at the helm, left it to throw something overboard, and the carpenter, who was an old sailor, knowing that the wind was light, put the helm down, and hove her aback. The watch on deck were lowering away the quarter-boat, and I got on deck just in time to heave myself into her as she was leaving the side; but it was not until out upon the wide Pacific, in our little boat, that I knew whom we had lost. It was George Ballmer, a young English sailor, who was prized by the officers as an active and willing seaman, and by the crew as a lively, hearty fellow, and a good shipmate. He was going aloft to fit a strap round the main-top-mast-head, for ring-tail halyards, and had the strap and block, a coil of halyards, and a marline-spike about his neck. He fell from the starboard futtock shrouds, and not knowing how to swim, and being heavily dressed, with all those things around his neck, he probably sunk immediately. We pulled astern, in the direction in which he fell, and though we knew that there was no hope of saving him, yet no one wished to speak of returning, and we rowed about for nearly an hour, without the hope of doing anything, but unwilling to acknowledge to ourselves that we must give him up. At length we turned the boat's head and made toward the vessel.

Death is at all times solemn, but never so much so as at sea. A man dies on shore; his body remains with his friends, and, "the mourners go about the streets;" but when a man falls overboard at sea and is lost, there is a suddenness in the event, and a difficulty in realizing it, which give to it an air of awful mystery. A man dies on shore — you follow his body to the grave, and a stone marks the spot. You are often prepared for the event. There is always something which helps you to realize it when it happens, and to recall it when it has passed. A man is shot down by your side in battle, and the mangled body remains an *object*, and a *real evidence;* but at sea, the man is near you — at your side — you hear his voice, and in an instant he is gone, and nothing but a *vacancy* shows his loss. Then, too, at sea — to use a homely but expressive phrase — you *miss* a man so much. A dozen men are shut up together in a little bark, upon the wide, wide sea, and for months and months see no forms and hear no voices but their own, and one is taken suddenly from among them, and they miss him at every turn. It is like losing a limb. There are no new faces, or new scenes to fill up the gap. There is always an empty berth in the forecastle, and one man wanting when the small night watch is mustered. There is one less to take the wheel, and one less to lay out with you on the yard. You miss his form, and the sound of his voice, for habit had made them almost necessary to you, and each of your senses feels the loss.

All these things make such a death peculiarly solemn, and the effect of it remains upon the crew for some time. There is more kindness shown by the officers to the crew, and by the crew to one another. There is more quietness and seriousness. The oath and the loud laugh are gone. The officers are more watchful, and the crew go more carefully aloft. The lost man is seldom mentioned, or is dismissed with a sailor's rude eulogy. "Well, poor George is gone! His cruise is up soon! He knew his work, and did his duty, and was a good shipmate." Then usually follows some allusion to another world, for sailors are almost all believers; but their notions and opinions are unfixed and at loose ends. They say,—"God wont be hard upon the poor fellow," and seldom get beyond the common phrase which seems to imply that their sufferings and hard treatment here will excuse them hereafter,—

"*To work hard, live hard, die hard, and go to hell after all, would be hard indeed!*" Our cook, a simple hearted old African, who had been through a good deal in his day, and was seriously inclined, always going to church twice a day when on shore, and reading his Bible on a Sunday in the galley, talked to the crew about spending their Sabbaths badly, and told them that they might go as suddenly as George had, and be as little prepared.

Yet a sailor's life is at best but a mixture of a little good with much evil, and a little pleasure with much pain. The beautiful is linked with the revolting, the sublime with the common-place, and the solemn with the ludicrous.

We had hardly returned on board with our sad report, before an auction was held of the poor man's clothes. The captain had first, however, called all hands aft and asked them if they were satisfied that everything had been done to save the man, and if they thought there was any use in remaining there any longer. The crew all said that it was in vain, for the man did not know how to swim, and was very heavily dressed. So we filled away and kept her off to her course.

The laws regulating navigation make the captain answerable for the effects of a sailor who dies during the voyage, and it is either a law or universal custom, established for convenience, that the captain should immediately hold an auction of his things, in which they are bid off by the sailors, and the sums which they give are deducted from their wages at the end of the voyage.

In this way the trouble and risk of keeping his things through the voyage are avoided, and the clothes are usually sold for more than they would be worth on shore. Accordingly, we had no sooner got the ship before the wind, than his chest was brought up upon the forecastle; and the sale began. The jackets and trowsers in which we had seen him dressed but a few days before, were exposed and bid off while the life was hardly out of his body, and his chest was taken aft and used as a store-chest, so that there was nothing left that could be called his. Sailors have an unwillingness to wear a dead man's clothes during the same voyage, and they seldom do unless they are in absolute want.

As is usual after a death, many stories were told about George. Some heard him say that he repented never having learned to swim, and that he knew that he should meet his death by drowning. Another said that he never knew any good to come of a voyage made against the will, and the deceased man shipped and spent his advance, and was afterward very unwilling to go, but not being able to refund, was obliged to sail with us. A boy, too, who had become quite attached to him said that George talked to him during most of the watch on the night before, about his mother and family at home, and this was the first time that he had mentioned the subject during the voyage.

NARRATIVE

OF THE

MUTINY ON THE SOMERS,

A BRIG OF WAR IN THE AMERICAN NAVAL SERVICE, ALEXANDER SLIDELL MACKENZIE COMMANDER; AND OF THE

EXECUTION OF SPENCER, CROMWELL, AND SMALL.

THE UNITED STATES brig-of-war "Somers" sailed from New York on the twelfth of September, 1842, with dispatches for the United States sloop-of-war "Vandalia," at Liberia, on the coast of Africa. The Somers had on board A. S. Mackenzie, commander, with seven officers in the steerage, and four in the wardroom, making in all twelve; together with twelve petty officers—four rated as seamen; nine ordinary seamen, six landsmen, and seventy-four apprentices, rated as boys.

Early in October the brig arrived at Madeira, and from thence proceeded, according to orders, via Teneriffe, and Porto Prayo, to Liberia. But, upon arriving there, the commander learned that the Vandalia had sailed, on the fifth of October, for the United States. The dispatches with which he was entrusted, being thus rendered of no use, were left with the United States agent. On the eleventh of November, Captain Mackenzie sailed for the United States by the way of St. Thomas, where he thought it would be necessary to take in a supply of bread, water, and other refreshments.

"On Saturday, the twenty-fifth of November," states Captain Mackenzie, "Lieutenant Gansevoort came into the cabin and informed me that he had learned from Mr. Wales that a conspiracy existed on board to capture the vessel, murder the captain, bring over as many of the crew as possible, murder the rest, and convert the vessel into a pirate; and that Midshipman Spencer, [a son of the Honorable John C. Spencer, United States Secretary of War,] was at the head of the conspiracy. This, Lieutenant G. said, had been told him by Mr. Wales, whose narrative was as follows:—On the night of the — of November, betwen six and eight o'clock in the evening, Wales said he was roused by Spencer, who asked him to go upon the booms, as he had something to say to him. He got up, and, upon arriving at the booms, he was asked by Spencer, 'Do you fear death? do you fear a dead man? do you fear to kill a man?' Wales, with admirable coolness, induced Spencer to go on, took the oath of secrecy, and entered into all his plans. Spencer told him that he had about twenty men in his plot; that they would easily get possession of the ship, murder the commander and officers, and commence piracy. He gave Wales all the details of his plan, which were admirably suited for his purpose, and arranged much better, Mr. Wales said, than he could have done it himself. As an inducement to embark in the enterprise, Spencer said that a large box of wine on board contained a large amount of gold and other treasure. Spencer's object was to go to the Isle of Pines, where one of his associates, who had been a pirate before, had a confederate He said he would attack no vessels that he could not capture, and would destroy all that he captured; that he would select from them such females as were proper, use them, and then dispose of them; that he had all the details of the plan drawn out on paper, which was in the back of his cravat. He showed money to Mr. Wales, and, before separating, threatened him with instant death if he ever revealed what he had told him." Such, says Captain Mackenzie, was the purport of the information which I received from Lieutenant Gansevoort.

Captain M. further said, that to him the whole affair seemed so monstrous that he at first treated it with ridicule, believing that Spencer had been amusing himself and Wales with some story of piracy he had learned from some novel or tale of murder; still he (Captain M.) could not help feeling that it was sporting with a serious subject, and he resolved to be on his guard and watch closely the movements of Spencer. During that day Spencer was much in the wardroom, examining a chart of the West Indies, and made some inquiries in regard to the Isle of Pines; he passed the day sullenly, and was often observed to be looking over a paper and writing with a pencil. He was frequently seen engaged in holding secret conferences with Cromwell and Small, and was known to have given money to different persons of the crew. He had also incited the steward to steal brandy, which he had given to some of the men, and with which he had once or twice got drunk himself.

Spencer had the faculty of throwing his lower jaw out of joint, and thus playing with it a variety of musical airs; and he was repeatedly found to be thus amusing the crew. In his intercourse with Captain Mackenzie (*vide Captain M.'s narrative*,) he was servile to the last degree; but among the crew he was loudly and blasphemously vituperative against him, and the captain was informed of his declaration that it would give him pleasure to roll him overboard from the round-top. Captain Mackenzie discovered that he had drawn a representation of a *black flag*, and asked members of the crew what they thought of it; and that he had often said the vessel could be easily taken.

"These things," continues Captain Mackenzie's narrative, "induced me to look back over all I had heard or observed of Spencer. When he first reported himself to me for duty on board my vessel, I gave him my hand and welcomed him on board. I heard, not long after, that he had been involved in difficulty when on the Brazil station, and that he had been dismissed for drunkenness. Upon hearing this, I earnestly desired his removal from my vessel—principally on account of the young men I had with me; two of whom were connected with me by blood, two by alliance, and four were entrusted to my especial care. The circumstance of his connexion with a high and distinguished officer of the Government, by enhancing, if possible, his baseness, increased my desire to get rid of him.

"I desired Lieutenant Gansevoort to state to Mr. Spencer that if he would apply to Commodore Perry to detach him from the Somers, I would second his application. The application was accordingly made and I seconded it, earnestly urging that it might be granted in order to secure the comfort of the young officers. Commodore Perry, however, declined to detach Midshipman Spencer, but said he would consent to detach Midshipman Rogers. I could not, however, consent to part with Mr. Rogers, whom I had long known to be an accomplished seaman, a gentleman, and an officer of the highest attainments both in and beyond his profession. The Somers accordingly sailed with seven in the steerage; they could not all sit down together at the table; two of them had no lockers, but slept upon the steerage deck, and subjected themselves to considerable inconvenience, to all which, however, they readily submitted without the slightest murmur or complaint, and performed every duty which fell to them, to the perfect satisfaction of all the officers.

"All these things I called to recollection, and endeavored carefully to review the whole conduct of Spencer. I had treated him precisely as I treated other midshipmen; though I had, perhaps, reproved him somewhat less than the others for slight deviations from the strict line of his duty. This arose from my conviction that there could be but little hope of essentially serving one who had proved to be so decidedly his own enemy. I observed that he was in the habit of associating but little with the other officers, but that he was continually intimate with the crew. He was often in the habit of joking with them and smiling whenever he met them, with a smile never known but on such occasions; and I had frequently observed in him a strange flashing of the eye."

Captain Mackenzie goes on to say that he observed a marked feeling of disrespect toward himself and other officers of the vessel, which seemed to be gaining ground daily. *Samuel Cromwell* seemed especially surly and disobedient. He was a large muscular man, and apparently of a rough and vindictive disposition. When the vessel first sailed from New York he was very tyrannical toward the apprentices, having no conversation with them, and keeping aloof from them altogether, and when called upon to inflict punishment, he would strike with all his might, as though it was pléasing to him to whip them. His manner toward them changed; he endeavored by every means to please them, would laugh and joke with them, allowed them to pull him about, and appeared anxious to secure their favor. He also grew negligent in his duty, evincing no desire, when orders were given him, to see them carried out, but repeating them lazily to the men, and without any attempt to urge their execution. His manner at times was disrespectful to the officers of the brig; and once, when Captain Mackenzie asked why some rigging had not been attended to, he burst into a fit of rage and heaped curses upon the commander as soon as his back was turned. He said he did not care a —— about the rigging; that Captain Mackenzie wanted too much work out of the crew, and he wished "the commander and the brig farther in —— than they were out!" Soon after the brig left New York, he told Wales that Spencer had given him $15, he mentioned no purpose, though he said something about its being a "pretty good present." Spencer also drew from $15 to $20 worth of tobacco and cigars during the cruise, which he distributed to the crew—the tobacco rather to the boys than the men. He gave Cromwell a bunch or two of cigars at one time, and also to Small.

Recalling these matters, in addition to what had been revealed, Captain Mackenzie resolved at once to make himself sure of Spencer's person. In the evening he gave orders to Mr. Perry, his clerk, to have all the officers come aft upon the quarter-deck. Midshipman M. C. Perry was ordered to take the wheel, and all the officers, except Mr. Hays, assembled on the starboard of the after-deck. Captain Mackenzie then addressed Spencer:

"I understand, sir, that you aspire to the command of this vessel?"

With a deferential air he replied, "Oh, no, sir!"

"Did you not," said the commander, "tell Mr. Wales that you had a mutinous project on foot—that you intended to kill the commander and the officers of the Somers, and such of the crew as you could not seduce to your plans, and to enter upon a course of piracy!"

"I *may* have told him something like it," Spencer replied, but it was *only in joke*."

"You admit, then, that you told him of such a plan?"

"Yes, sir, but it was all in joke."

"This, sir, you must know is joking upon a forbidden subject. This joke, sir, may cost you your life. Be pleased to remove your neck handkerchief."

Spencer did so. Captain Mackenzie opened it, but there was nothing in it.

"What have you done with the paper that was in it?"

"The paper," he said, "which had been in it, contained my day's work; and I destroyed it."

"It is a strange place, sir, to keep your accounts!"

Spencer acquiesced with an air of the greatest deference and blandness.

Captain Mackenzie said to him: "Your design was to make yourself commander of this vessel. You must have been aware that you could compass it only by passing over my dead body and over the dead bodies of all the officers of the Somers. You had laid out for yourself, sir, a great deal to do. It is my duty to confine you."

Turning to Lieutenant Gansevoort, Captain Mackenzie said, "Arrest Mr. Spencer, and place him in double irons."

Lieutenant Gansevoort stepped forward and received from Mr. Spencer his sword. Mr. Spencer was then ordered to sit down: he did so. Lieutenant Gansevoort was directed to place a watch over Spencer, and to give orders to put him to instant death if he was detected in speaking or holding any communication with any of the crew. The nature of these orders was told to Mr. Spencer. At the same time Lieutenant G. was directed to allow him every possible indulgence consistent with his safe keeping. The task was executed by Lieutenant Gansevoort with the greatest kindness and humanity. While he watched with an eagle eye over all his movements, and was ready at a moment's warning to take his life upon a violation of those conditions on which his safety depended, he attended to all his wants, and covered him with his own garment from the squalls of rain by which they were visited.

The officers were then remanded to quarters; the crew and batteries were inspected, the orders were repeated, and the retreat was beaten. The officers of the watch were all directed to be fully armed with cutlasses and pistols, with rounds of ammunition, and everything was put in order for the night.

On searching the locker of Spencer, a razor case was found in it, which he had recently drawn from the purser. On opening it, there was no razor within, but in its stead a piece of paper in which was rolled another. On the inner paper was written a string of characters, afterward found to be Greek letters, with which Spencer was known to be familiar. It fortunately happened that there was on board another individual who was well acquainted with the Greek—one whose knowledge of this, as of everything else, was devoted wholly to the service of his country. The Greek characters, on being converted into our own language by Mr. Henry Rogers, proved to contain the plan for the proposed mutiny. There was a list of the different members of the crew, some of whom were marked certain, and others doubtful; some were marked to be *kept* at all events, and others to be destroyed. Those were designated who were to do the work of murder in the various apartments; others were to open the arm-chest, and the stations of all were assigned.

The following day was Sunday, and all were to be inspected at ten o'clock. Captain Mackenzie took his station aft, for the purpose of observing Cromwell and Small, as they should come along on the quarter-deck. The persons of both were faultlessly clean and neat. *Cromwell* stood up to his full stature, carrying his battle-ax firmly and steadily; his cheeks pale, but his eyes fixed to starboard. He wore a determined and dangerous air. *Small* presented a very different figure. His appearance was ghastly, his manner uneasy; he shifted his weight from side to side, and his battle-ax from hand to hand. His eye was never for a moment fixed, but always averted from Captain Mackenzie. "I then attributed his conduct to fear," says the captain, "though I now believe the business upon which he had entered was repugnant to his nature, but that his love for money and rum was too strong for his fidelity." Five bells, or ten o'clock, was the time for divine service. The roll was called—crew all present—unusually attentive, and their responses more than ordinarily full and audible. In the afternoon the sky-sails and studding-sails were set. Gazely, one of the best of the apprentices, was sent aloft on the royal yard to make some alteration in the rigging. At once a sudden jerk was given to the brace by Small and another, who has not been discovered, and the fore-topmast, with the topsail, gallant stay-sail, and head gaff-topsail, came down. Captain Mackenzie says, "I scarcely dared to look to see the spot where the boy should fall. The next moment his shadow appeared at the mast-head, and I presently discovered him examining with admirable coolness what was to be done. I did not dare to believe this carrying away of the topmast the work of treachery; but I knew that an occasion of this sort, such as the loss of the boy, which should create confusion, and interrupt the duty of the officers, would be sought by them, if they were bent on the prosecution of the enterprise. All possible measures were taken to prevent confusion. The rigging was immediately restored and the sails bent afresh. Every member of the crew was employed, and all things were made to go on with regularity. To my astonishment, upon the occurrence of this disaster all the conspirators who were named in the programme of Spencer no matter in what part of the vessel they were engaged at the time, im mediately mustered at the mainmast—whether animated by some new-born zeal to serve their country, or intending to carry out their designs, I cannot say. This circumstance at once confirmed my belief in the continued existence of the danger. The eye of Spencer traveled continually to the mast-head, and he cast quick and stealthy glances about, as he had not done before."

The wreck was soon cleared away and supper piped. After supper the same persons mustered at the mast-head, and the sails were set. After quarters they dispersed. Still Captain M. did not think it safe to leave Cromwell at liberty during the night, which was emphatically the season of danger. After consulting with Lieutenant Gansevoort, he determined to arrest Cromwell. An officer was sent to guard the rigging. As soon as Cromwell came upon the Jacob's ladder, Lieutenant Gansevoort met him, cocked his pistol and pointed it at him, and when he got on deck told him that the captain wanted to see him. When he came to where Captain M. stood, he was commanded to sit down. The captain interrogated him about the conversation he had had with Spencer. He said

"It was not me, sir; it was Small." (Cromwell was the tallest man on board and Small the shortest.) Cromwell was immediately put in irons. Small, being thus accused by an associate, was ordered before the captain.

"Spencer has talked with you about the plot?" said the captain.

Small acquiesced. He was then ironed, and given to understand that he would be confined as the others were, brought home, and tried. The utmost vigilance was then enjoined upon the officers. All were armed, and either Lieutenant Gansevoort or Captain Mackenzie was constantly on deck.

The next morning, which was Monday, the twenty-sixth of November, two crimes of considerable magnitude came to light. One of the men had been detected in stealing from a boat, and the steward had stolen money and given some of it to Spencer. This was no time to relax the discipline of the ship, and both the men were punished to the extent of the law. It was soon after found that a man named Waltham had told M'Kinley where three bottles of wine were placed, and offered them to him. M'Kinley was stationed near the arm-chest and reported this to the first lieutenant. Punishment of Waltham, however, was postponed till the next day. Punishment of the other two being over, the commander deemed it a fit opportunity to make an impression upon the crew. He had good reason to think that the danger of the conspiracy was not over; he believed that a majority of the crew might be said to be in general disaffected, and disposed to resist discipline. Some mysterious agency had evidently been at work since the departure of the Somers from New York, and this was now disclosed.

Captain Mackenzie explained to the crew the general nature of Spencer's plot, and the atrocious character of the designs he had formed. He took especial care not to betray a suspicion that he thought any particular one of them was deeply implicated, but exhorted all of them to repent of their intentions and attend faithfully to their duty. He took good care to assure them that the majority of the crew must at all events share the fate of the officers. He strove to divert their minds from the pictures of successful vice which Spencer had presented to them. He brought up before them images of friends at home; he endeavored to impress upon their minds the endearing nature of those ties of kindred from which Spencer had sought to sever them forever, and expressed the hope that within three weeks they should all be again among their friends. He thanked God that he had provided them all with dear friends who were deeply interested in their welfare, and that they had the prospect of so soon being once more among them.

The effect of his address upon them was various. Many of them seemed delighted at their narrow delivery, and others seemed struck with horror at the thought of the terrible danger they had escaped. Some seemed overwhelmed with terror at the anticipation of punishment that awaited them. Others were overcome by thoughts of returning home, and wept profusely at the mention of the friends they hoped so soon to see. He could not help believing that all the crew were now tranquil, and that the vessel was again safe. Having observed that Spencer was endeavoring to hold intelligence with some of them, he directed the faces of all the prisoners to be turned aft, and that no tobacco should be allowed them when the supply they had upon their persons at the time of their arrest should be exhausted. He told them that he would see that they had everything necessary for their comfort; that each should have his ration; that they should be abundantly supplied with everything necessary for their health and convenience. But he told them that tobacco was only a stimulant, and that, as he wished their minds to become as quiet and tranquil as possible, he could not allow them to use it.

The day after Spencer's tobacco was stopped, his spirit gave way. He would sit for a long time with his face buried in his cloak, and when he raised his head, his face was bathed in tears. He was touched by the kind attention of Mr. Gansevoort. He told him that he was not then in a state to speak of anything, but that he would the next day tell him all—would answer any question that might be put to him.

On Tuesday, after quarters, all hands were again called to witness punishment, and Waltham was punished to the extent of the law, for offering three bottles of wine to M'Kinley. Captain Mackenzie then spoke to the crew of the necessity of conforming in all particulars to the orders of the vessel, which were known. He told them that every punishment on board must be made known to the Secretary of the Navy, and that the less they were in amount, the greater would be the credit that would attach to the commander and crew.

But he soon discovered that the whole crew were far from tranquil. They collected in knots upon the deck—seditious words were heard among them—and they assumed an insolent and menacing tone. Some of the petty officers were examined and found to be true to the colors, but there was reason to fear that on that very night a rescue would be attempted. The commander obtained from time to time intelligence of various conferences among the disaffected; and individuals not before supposed to be deeply implicated, were now found in close association with those who were.

During the first watch, while Midshipman Perry had charge of the deck, the boon-tackle was carried away. The officer of the deck told the boy at the wheel to get hold of the weather-sheet, and sung out "Some of you come aft." In similar cases, it had before been difficult to get enough aft to do the duty required, but now some fifteen or eighteen rushed aft; three were ordered to remain and the rest to go forward. Throughout the vessel there was strong evidence of an intention to attempt a rescue. The men talked together in an under tone. In the morning, while the crew were holystoning the deck, Wales being officer in charge of the prisoners, observed signs passing between Spencer, Wilson and M'Kinley; they put their hands to their chins, and Cromwell, who was lying on the arm-chest, rose up. Wales told him that his orders were to shoot him down if he made the least attempt to escape, and he should do so if he did not lie still. He then lay down. Wales then went back, with his pistol cocked, to the launch, where Wilson was looking about, and found that he had a number of the holystones out, and that he was taking out a handspike. Wales told him if he saw him making any further signs he would blow his brains out. He said nothing; did not put the handspike back, but went to draw some water. Wales expressed his fears to Commander Mackenzie and the first lieutenant, telling them he thought it dangerous to leave the holystones about, as they might be offensively used. While Spencer was in irons, near the battle-ax rack, he was observed trying how he could work an ax with his irons on, moving it up and down. After this was told to the first lieutenant, he told it to the captain, and the battle-axes were removed to the arm-chest.

Rendered apprehensive by these indications upon the part of the crew, the commander felt more anxious than he had before done, and remained continually on deck. At twelve o'clock, when the watch was called

M'Kinley, Green, and others, seriously implicated, missed their muster they could not be asleep, and why they should be absent just at that time, when they never had been before, was not easy to be seen. When they appeared, they all had some lame excuse. They probably had agreed to meet at the time, and to commence some act of violence. Green said he could not get aft. The commander rejected his excuse with an exclamation of impatience, and ordered him to take the forward look-out for four hours.

"At four o'clock others missed their muster," continues the narrative of the captain. "I heard of this with the greatest uneasiness. Where, I asked, was this to end? If the men upon a bright night like this seem mutinous and disposed to undertake the rescue of those confined; on a bad night, in a storm, in the midst of utter darkness, how much greater will be the probability of a rescue? If all suspected should be ironed, would the danger be over? What sympathy might not be felt for the prisoners? These matters crowded upon my mind. I considered the imminent peril which hung over the lives of the officers and crew; I thought of the seas traversed in every direction by merchantmen, unarmed and defenseless; I thought of what was due to the interests of commerce, to the safety of the lives of thousands upon the deep, to the sanctity of the American flag, entrusted to my care, and to my own honor. All these considerations impressed me with the absolute necessity of adopting some further means of security for the vessel which had been given to my charge.

"I took council with the first lieutenant, and was fortified in my purposes by finding his opinion identical with my own. In so grave a case, involving so many interests and such high responsibilities, I felt desirous of having the opinion of all my officers upon the matter, though not a shadow of doubt remained in my mind of the guilt of the prisoners, should their execution be deemed necessary. I did not forget that the officers were still boys, and that all the responsibility of the proceeding must rest upon the older and higher officers. Still I felt desirous to have their opinion, and accordingly addressed them the following letter.

"U. S. Brig Somers, *November* 30*th*, 1842.

"Gentlemen: I am desirous of availing myself of your counsel in the very responsible position in which I find myself placed. You are aware of the circumstances which resulted in the confinement of Midshipman Spencer, of Boatswain's-mate Cromwell, and of Seaman Small; and I purposely abstain from entering into details concerning them. Necessarily ignorant, as I am, of the extent of disaffection among the crew who have so long been tampered with, and knowing the suspicion which attaches to some of the crew who are at large, I address you and ask your united counsel as to the best course now to be pursued; and I call upon you to take into deliberate and dispassionate consideration, the conduct which will be necessary for a safe continuance of the remainder of our course, and to enlighten me with your opinion as to the proper method to be pursued.

I am, your obedient servant,

Alex. Slidell Mackenzie,

Commander.

"Lieut. Gansevoort, and others."

After I had written this letter, but before I had sent it, at about nine o'clock, Wilson being foiled in his attempt to get up an outbreak at night, and feeling that he was narrowly watched and was no longer left at liberty, came forward and made some lame and worthless confession, and requested that he might not be put in irons. I told him that if he had made any *real* confession, in sincerity and truth, he should not be molested; but that it was an insult to his officer to offer him so lame a story as that he had told. Nothing more could be got out of him, and he was immediately put in irons.

While on the African coast I knew that he had procured an extraordinary knife, broad in the middle, and running to a point. He had made it very sharp on both sides. It was a singular weapon, of no use except to kill. He had been seen also the day before sharpening his battle-ax with a file, and had brought one part of it to an edge. This was a thing never allowed or known before on board. M'Kinley was now arrested. He was evidently the individual in every way the most formidable of all concerned.—M'Kee was also put in irons. They were made to sit down; and when the irons were put on I walked around the batteries, followed by Lieutenant Gansevoort, and made a careful inspection.

On the receipt of my letter the officers immediately assembled and entered upon the examination of witnesses, who were sworn and their testimony written down. In addition to this each witness signed the evidence he gave. In this employment the officers passed the whole day without interruption, and without taking the least food. I remained, myself, in charge of the deck. The officers were excused from watch duty, and the watches were so arranged that two in succession fell to me. On the first of December the first lieutenant presented me with the following letter:

"U. S. Brig Somers, *December* 1*st*, 1842.

"Sir: In answer to your letter requiring our counsel as to the best course to be pursued with regard to the prisoners, Spencer, Cromwell and Small, we have the honor to state, that the evidence which has come to our knowledge after the most careful, deliberate and dispassionate consideration which the exigency would allow, is of such a nature as to call for the most decided action. We are convinced that in the existing state of things, it will be impossible to carry the prisoners to the United States. We think that the safety of our lives, and honor of the flag entrusted to our charge, require that the prisoners be put to death, as the course best calculated to make a salutary impression upon the rest of the crew. In this decision we trust we have been guided by our duty to our God, to our country, and to the service.

Respectfully, your obedient servants,

Lieut. Gansevoort, and others.

"Com. Mackenzie."

I at once concurred in the justice of this opinion, and made preparations to carry the recommendation into effect. Two other conspirators were almost as guilty as the three singled out for execution: they could be kept confined without extreme danger to the ultimate safety of the vessel. The three chief mutineers were the only ones capable of navigating and sailing the vessel. By their removal, all motive to capture the vessel and carry out their original design would be at once taken away. Their lives were justly forfeited, and the interests of the country, the safety of the sea, and the honor of the flag, required the sacrifice.

In the necessity of my position I found my law; and *in that necessity I trust for justification.* I thought it best to arm the petty officers; on this point only the first lieutenant differed from me; and I found that he was of the same opinion with some of the petty officers themselves;—they said that since I could not tell whom to trust, it would be best to trust no one. I made up my mind, and judged of the characters whom I could trust, and determined to arm them. I ordered to be issued to each a cutlass, a pistol, and cartridges. I ordered preparation also to be made for execution of the three. All hands were called to witness punishment. The whips were arranged, the officers were stationed about the deck, and the petty officers were directed to cut down every one who should let go his whip or fail to haul when ordered.

I put on my full uniform, came on deck, and proceeded to execute the most painful duty that ever devolved upon any officer in the American Navy—the announcement to the prisoners of the fate that awaited them. I approached Spencer and said to him, You were about to take my life, Mr. Spencer, without provocation, without cause or the slightest offense. You intended to kill me suddenly, in the night, while I was buried in sleep, without giving me a single moment to send one word of affection to my wife, one prayer to God for her welfare. Your life is now forfeited; and the necessity of the case compels me to take it. I do not intend, however, to imitate you in the mode of claiming the sacrifice. If there be in your breast one feeling true to nature, you will be grateful for the premature disclosure of your horrible designs. You surely ought to be thankful that you have been prevented from the terrible deeds you meditated If you have any word to send to your father, any satisfaction to express to him that you were not allowed to become a pirate, as you ought to do, you will have ten minutes granted in which to write it. Midshipman Thompson was then directed to note the time and inform us when it had expired.

Spencer seemed overcome with emotion. He burst into a flood of tears, sank on his knees, and said he was not fit to die. I repeated to him his catechism, and begged him to offer sincere prayers for the divine forgiveness. I recommended to him the English Prayer Book, assuring him that he would find in it something suited to all his necessities. Cromwell fell upon his knees, protesting his innocence, and invoking the name of his wife. Spencer declared that Cromwell was innocent, and begged that this might be believed. This, I confess, staggered me; but the evidence of his guilt was conclusive. Lieutenant Gansevoort said that there was not a shadow of doubt of it.

The petty officers said he was the one man from whom real apprehension was entertained. He was at first the accomplice of Spencer, and was then urged on by him, and had been by him turned to his account. I tried to show him how Spencer had endeavored to use him, and told Spencer that he had made remarks about him he would not consider flattering. He expressed great anxiety to know what they were. I told him Cromwell had said of him and another person that 'there was a —— fool on one side, and a —— knave on the other,' and told him that Cromwell would have allowed him to live only so long as he could have made him useful to himself. This roused him, and from that time he said no more of Cromwell's innocence

Subsequent circumstances made me believe that Spencer wished to save him, probably from the hope that he would yet get possession of the vessel and carry out his original design; and, perhaps, that Cromwell would in some way effect his rescue. He endeavored, at the same time, to persuade me that Small was only an alias for some one else on his list, though this was proved to be false. Small alone was the one we had set down as the poltroon of the three; yet he received the announcement of his fate with great composure. He was asked what preparation he wished to make. He said he had none: 'Nobody cares for me,' said he, 'but my poor old mother, and I would rather she would not know what has become of me.'

I returned to Spencer. I asked him what message he had to send to his friends. He said, 'None. Tell them that I die wishing them every blessing and happiness. I deserve death for this and my other crimes. There are few crimes I have not committed. I am sincerely penitent for them all. I only fear my repentance is too late.' I asked him if there was any one whom he had injured to whom he could make reparation—any one who was suffering obloquy on his account. He said, 'No; but this will kill my poor mother.' I did not know before that he had a mother, and was touched by his allusion to her. I asked him if it would not have been far more dreadful if he had succeeded in his attempt—if it were not much better to die as he would, than to become a pirate and steep himself so terribly in blood and guilt. He said, 'I do not know what would have become of me if I had succeeded.'

I told him that Cromwell would soon have made away with him, and that M'Kinley would probably have destroyed them both. He said he feared this would injure his father. Had you succeeded, I replied, the injury you would have done him would have been much greater. If it had been possible to take him home, as I first intended, I told him that he would have got clear, as in America a man with money and influential friends would always be cleared;* that the course I was taking would injure his father less than if he should go home and be condemned, yet again escape. He said that he had attempted the same thing on board the John Adams and the Potomac, but had been unsuccessful. He asked if I had not exaggerated the danger. I told him No; that his attempts to corrupt the crew had been too widely successful; that I knew of the existence of the conspiracy, but did not know how extensive it was. I recapitulated to him his acts. He was startled when I told him of his stealing brandy. He admitted the justice of his fate, but asked me if I was not going too far and too fast. 'Does the law justify you?' said he. I replied that his opinion was not unprejudiced; that I had consulted all the officers and they had given their opinion that it was just—that he deserved death.

He asked what would be the manner of his death. I explained it to him. He requested that he might be shot. I told him that it could not be—that he must be hung. He admitted that it was just. He objected to the shortness of the time, and requested that an hour might be given to prepare. I made no answer to this, but allowed much more than the hour he asked for to elapse. He requested that his face might be covered. I granted his request and asked him what it should be covered with. He said a handkerchief. In his locker was found a black one, which

* Perhaps this is an extreme and erroneous opinion, and not just. But I am merely stating facts—what passed on the occasion.

was put on his face. Cromwell and Small made the same request, and frocks were taken from their lockers with which their heads were covered.

Spencer asked for a Bible and Prayer Book—they were given to him. He said 'I am a believer—but do you think that my repentance will be accepted?' I called to his mind the thief on the cross, and told him that God's mercies were equal to all his wants. He kneeled down and read from the Prayer Book, and asked again if I thought his repentance would be accepted, saying that his time was short. I told him God not only understood his case but could suit his grace to it. He begged that I would forgive him. I told him I did, most sincerely and cordially, and asked him if I had done anything which made him seek my life, or whether his hatred was unfounded. He said he thought it was only fancy. 'Perhaps,' he added, 'there was something in your manner which offended me.' I read over to him what I had written down. He wished me to alter the passage in which I said that he 'offered *as an excuse*,' that he had attempted the same thing on the John Adams and Potomac. He only mentioned it as a fact, he said.

More than an hour had now elapsed. Spencer, as he met Cromwell, paused and asked to see Mr. Wales. As he passed Cromwell, he said not a word of his innocence, nor did he make any appeal in his favor. Spencer said, 'Wales, I hope you will forgive me for tampering with your fidelity.' Wales replied, overcome with emotion, 'I do forgive you from the bottom of my heart, and I hope God will forgive you also.' Wales was weeping; and Spencer, in passing, met Small at the gangway. He extended his hand and said, 'Small, forgive me for having brought you into trouble.' Small answered, 'No, —— Spencer, I cannot forgive you.' Spencer repeated his request. Small said, 'How can you ask that of me after having brought me to this? We shall soon be before God, and shall there know all about it.' Spencer said, 'You must forgive me—I cannot die without it.' I went to Small and asked him not to cherish any resentment at such a time, and asked him to forgive him. He relented—held out his hand to Spencer and said, 'I do forgive you—and may God forgive you also.'

Small then asked my forgiveness. I took his hand and expressed my forgiveness in the strongest terms. I asked him what I had done that he should seek my life; if I had been harsh either in deed or word to him. He exclaimed, 'What have you done to me? Nothing—but treated me like a man.' I told him of the high responsibilities under which I acted; of the duty I owed my Government and the ship with which it had entrusted me; of his offense to his commander and the boys he intended to put to death; and of the high duty I owed to the flag of my country. Right! he exclaimed; 'God bless that flag and prosper it! Now,' said he, 'give me a quick and easy death.' Spencer said to Lieutenant Gansevoort that his courage had been doubted; but he wished him to bear witness that he died like a brave man.

He asked what would be the signal for his execution. I told him that I was desirous of hoisting colors at the instant, to show that the flag of the Somers was fixed at the mast-head; and that I intended to beat the call to hoist colors and then roll off; and at the third roll a gun would be fired as the signal. He asked leave to give the signal. I at once acceded. He asked if it was the gun under him. I told him it was but one removed. He asked if it would be fired by a lock and wafer. I was told that preparations had been made to fire it with a match; and immediately ordered a supply of live coals, and fresh coals to be passed constantly; and then assured him that there should be no delay. The time was now wearing away. Small requested leave to address the crew. Spencer having had leave to give the signal, was asked if he would give Small the leave he asked. He said yes. Small then said:

'*Shipmates and topmates*—Take warning by my example. I never killed a man, but only said that I would do it, and for that I am about to die. Going in a Guineaman [a slaver] brought me to this. Take warning, and never go in a Guineaman.' Turning to Spencer, he said, 'I am ready to die; are you?'

Cromwell's last words were, 'Tell my wife that I die innocent; I die an innocent man.' From the appearance of this man in assuming to be innocent, it would seem that Spencer took all the risk of the affair, and Cromwell intended to profit by it.

I placed myself where I could take in the whole deck with my eye. No word was given by Spencer. He finally said he could not give the word, and wished me to do it. The word was accordingly given and the execution took place.

The crew were ordered aft, when I addressed them. I called their attention to the fate of the young men who had just been hung in their presence. I spoke of the distinguished social position Spencer had held at home, and held up before them the career of usefulness and professional honor to which a course of faithful duty would have raised him. After having been but a few months at sea, he had criminally aspired to supplant me in a command I had earned by thirty years' faithful service. Their own future fortunes, I told them, were within their own control. I opened to them the stations of respectability and of future honor to which they might rise, but told them it could only be step by step, in a regular course. I called their attention also to Cromwell's course. He had received a handsome education, and his handwriting was even elegant; but he had also failed through his love for gold. The first $15 he had received from Spencer had bought him, and the hope of great plunder had secured the purchase. An anecdote had been told to me by Collins of Cromwell, which carried its own moral with it, and which I desired Collins to repeat. He did so: he told them that he once went to India with Cromwell, and that they took on board there a keg of doubloons for Mr. Thorndike. Collins alone knew of its being aboard, and kept it a secret till they went ashore. He then told Cromwell of it, who laughed at him, and said that if 'he had known about it, he would have run away with the keg.' I told the crew they had only to choose between the two—Collins and Cromwell. Small also had been brought up to better things, but had not been able to resist temptation, and had died invoking blessings on the flag of his country.

All hands were then called to cheer ship, and gave three hearty cheers. Three *heartier* cheers never went up from the deck of an American ship! In that electric moment I verily believe the purest and loftiest patriotism burst forth from the breasts even of the worst conspirators. *From that moment I felt that I was again completely master of my vessel, and that I could do with her whatever the honor of my country required.*

Dinner was piped, and I noticed with feelings of pain that some of the boys, as they passed the bodies, laughed and sneered at them. I still desired that Spencer should be buried in a coffin, and gave orders to have one built. But Lieutenant Gansevoort offered to relinquish a mess chest he had, for that purpose, which was soon converted into a substantial coffin. The watch was set, and the bodies were lowered. They were received by their messmates, to be decently laid out for burial. The midshipmen assisted in the duty. Spencer was laid out clothed in his complete uniform, except his sword, which he had forfeited the right to wear. I noticed that upon the hands of one of the others a seaman had tied a ribbon, with the name upon it of that Somers who so distinguished himself by his gallantry, patriotism, and skill. On Cromwell's face a saber-cut was visible, and on removing his hair four or five more were discovered; which showed that he had been where wounds were given. He was said to have been in a slaver, and in Moro Castle in Havana; and it was the general impression that he had been a pirate.

A squall of rain soon sprung up, which rendered it necessary to cover the bodies with tarpaulins. They were arranged according to their rank, and all hands were called to bury the dead. The American Ensign was lowered to half-mast. Night had now set in. All the lamps were lit and distributed among the crew and placed in the bows, in the gangway, and in the quarter boat. The service for the dead was read, and the bodies were committed to the deep. The offices were closed by reading that beautiful prayer, so suitable to the occasion, 'Preserve us from the dangers of the seas and the violence of enemies. Bless the United States:—watch over all that are upon the deep, and protect the inhabitants of the land in peace and quiet, through Jesus Christ our Lord.'

In reading this I sincerely thanked God for the protection of the Somers, and felt a firm faith that he would sanction the deed of that day. On the following Sunday, the fourth of December, after the laws for the government of the navy had been read, according to invariable custom on board the Somers, I took occasion to allude to the lessons to be drawn from the fate of those who had suffered. I led the minds of the crew back to their youthful days, and showed them how they had trampled under foot the wise counsel and admonitions of their friends. In Small's locker were letters from his mother, expressing the joy she felt that he was so happy on board the Somers. (This was before Spencer had joined.) There was also a Bible, in the leaves of which he had copied some verses from the Sailor's Magazine, in praise of its holy precepts. These verses I read to the crew. I thus showed them how Small valued his Bible, but that he did not resist temptation. I urged them to read it closely and attend faithfully to its precepts. I endeavored to show that there could be no such thing as honest Atheism. I held up before them how Spencer had injured many people, and especially his parents. He had lacked filial piety and piety toward God—two principles which would never have suffered him to go astray. In conclusion, I called on them as they had given three cheers for their country, now to give three cheers for God—as they would do by singing his praise. The colors were then hoisted, and above the American Ensign was raised the Banner of the Cross—the only flag that ever floats above it from any vessel under my command. The hundredth Psalm was sung, after which the crew dispersed. I could not help, on that day of peaceful Sabbath worship, contrasting the condition of my vessel with that she would have presented had she fallen into pirates' hands. Nor could I avoid observing the marked effect produced upon the ship's company by the proceedings. I was satisfied at once that all danger was past, and the mutiny broken forever.

On the fourteenth of December the Somers arrived at New York, and in a day or two the sad catastrophe was communicated to the world. Captain Mackenzie sent a narrative of the affair to the seat of government, and a court of inquiry was appointed by Mr. Upshur, the Secretary of the Navy, to examine the facts connected with the mutiny.

This court, consisting of Commodore Charles Stewart, President; Commodore A. J. Dallas; Commodore Jacob Jones; Hon. Ogden Hoffman, *Judge Advocate*, met on board the United States ship North Carolina, lying in the harbor at New York, on Wednesday, December the twenty-eighth, 1842, at eleven o'clock. Many distinguished persons were present, and Captain Mackenzie appeared in full uniform. "He is," says the New York Tribune, "a man of medium height, with a fine head covered rather thinly by light auburn hair, a high forehead, and an amiable and pleasing rather than stern and commanding presence."

The examination of witnesses commenced, and nineteen days were taken up in the inquiry. The president then stated that the testimony being now closed, the court would be cleared, which was accordingly done. The court then deliberated and framed their decision in secret, and sent it on to Washington for approval.

The authorities at Washington subsequently ordered a court martial, which was accordingly opened, a re-examination of the witnesses took place, and after a protracted trial Captain Mackenzie and Lieutenant Gansevoort were acquitted.

Thus was crushed, by a vengeance swifter and more terrible than human laws usually allot to human crimes, the first, as we fervently trust it will be the last, regularly organized attempt at mutiny on board a vessel intrusted with the honor and interests of the United States Navy. If the attempt had succeeded, imagination shudders at the black pall of horror and dread that would have fallen upon the sea.

All the officers examined, solemnly declared that they believed *necessity* demanded the course pursued—that if the execution of Spencer, Cromwell, and Small, had not been resorted to, the Somers would never have reached any port under the command of her officers, but would have been a Pirate, scouring the ocean with destructive fury, making it a highway of blood and terror to the world. If this belief be well founded, we should rejoice that so terrible a calamity, so black a disgrace, was not suffered to stain the escutcheon of our navy!

Under the impulse of thankfulness for what was regarded as a great danger escaped, and a great ignominy avoided, the country, generally, applauded the act of Captain Mackenzie as justified by the emergency of the case, and by the crimes of the victims. Commerce and trade, from their very nature, are timid, and it is not strange that the great commercial cities of the Atlantic should have given way to the impulse of the moment, and have justified the doubtful act instead of remembering the sanctity of every human life, until such life has been pronounced forfeited according to the form, and by the authority of the law.

But now that years have elapsed since the painful occurrence, it is probable that the more thoughtful of the mercantile as of other classes, cherish serious doubts, to say the least, of the necessity or expediency of the course pursued. The great law of humanity, as well as the law of the Lord, demands that every man accused of crime, shall be tried not by hurried and frightened courts, but by the calm deliberate judgment of his peers. Hardly any necessity can arise in time of general peace to justify a departure from this salutary requirement.

ABSTRACT OF AMERICAN NAUTICAL LAWS.

Shipping articles are required to be signed by every mariner, declaring the voyage and the term of the time for which the seamen are shipped, and when they are to render themselves on board. Seamen are liable to imprisonment for desertion. But if the master sails and leaves a seaman in imprisonment abroad, he will be entitled to his wages till his return to the United States, deducting the time of imprisonment. Provision is made for the prompt recovery of seamen's wages, by admiralty process against the ship, if the wages be not paid within ten days.

It is the duty of the American consuls and commercial agents, to relieve American seamen who may be found destitute in foreign ports, and to provide for their passage to some port in the United States, at the expense of the United States. American vessels are bound to take them, not exceeding two for every hundred tons, at a rate not exceeding ten dollars per man.

If an American vessel be sold in a foreign port, or a seaman discharged with the master's consent, the master is obliged to pay the consul three months' wages beside the amount then due, two months to be paid to the seamen when they engage again, and one month's pay to the fund for the return of American seamen.

The master has the right to discharge a seaman for just cause in a foreign port, but is responsible in damages if he does it without just cause. The master must be supreme in the ship. The French law affords peculiar protection to seamen, and prohibits the master from discharging a seaman, for any cause, in a foreign country.

The expense of curing a sick seaman in the course of the voyage is a charge upon the ship; and this rule recommends itself as much by its intrinsic equity and sound policy, as by the sanction of general authority. Such an expense is in the nature of additional wages during sickness, and it constitutes a material ingredient in the just remuneration of seamen for their labor and services. This claim, equally with a claim for wages, may be enforced in a court of admiralty.

Every seaman engaged to serve on board a ship, is bound, from the nature and terms of the contract, to do his duty to the utmost of his ability, and, therefore, a promise made by the master when the ship is in distress, or when some of the crew are sick, or the like, to pay extra wages, as an inducement to extraordinary exertion, is illegal and void. It requires some service not within the scope of the original contract, as by becoming a hostage, or the like, to create a valid claim for extra wages. No wages can be recovered for an illegal voyage, for the law will not countenance such a contract, nor permit any one to claim the wages of iniquity.

A seaman is entitled to his wages for the whole voyage, even though he is unable to render his service by sickness, or bodily injury, happening in the course of the voyage, and while in the performance of his duty; or if wrongfully discharged by the master in the course of the voyage, or forced to quit the ship by the cruelty of the master. In this case the voyage is ended as to him, and he is immediately entitled to his wages for the whole voyage.

The general principle of the marine law is, that freight is the mother of wages, and if no freight be earned, no wages are due. If the ship perish by the perils of the sea, as tempest, fire, enemies, etc., the mariners lose their wages. Otherwise they might not use their endeavors to save the ship. But the seamen do not lose their wages, if the freight is lost by the misconduct of the master.

When a seaman dies on the voyage, his wages are due to his representatives, up to the time of his death. The seamen's wages on the outward voyage are due when the ship delivers her outward cargo. And if the owners and the charterer agree to consider the voyages out and home as one entire voyage, they cannot, by this, deprive the seamen, without their consent, of the rights belonging to them by the general principles of the marine law. Capture by an enemy extinguishes the seamen's contract for wages, but if by recapture, the owner recovers his freight, the seamen recover their wages, for freight is the parent of wages. And this holds for those seamen who remain prisoners and render no assistance in the recapture, or afterward; because they are suffering in the service. And in case of shipwreck, if any portion of freight is paid for the cargo saved, the wages of the seamen are due in the same proportion.

Every agreement that goes to separate the demand for wages, from the fact of freight being earned, is viewed with distrust by the court, as an encroachment on the rights of seamen. "The courts of maritime law extend to them a peculiar protecting favor, and treat them as wards of the admiralty; and though they are not incapable of making valid contracts, they are treated by the courts in the same manner that courts of equity are accustomed to treat young heirs dealing with their expectancies, wards with their guardians, etc. They are considered as placed under the influence of men who have naturally acquired a mastery over them. Every deviation from the terms of the common shipping paper is rigidly inspected, and if additional burdens are imposed upon the seamen, without adequate remuneration, the courts will interfere, and moderate or annul the stipulation."

Mariners are bound to contribute out of their wages for embezzlement of the cargo, or injuries produced by the misconduct of any of the crew. But the individual criminal must be unknown, and circumstances must be such as clearly to fix and prove the wrong upon some of the crew; and then those of the crew upon whom the presumption of guilt rests, must stand sureties for each other, and contribute rateably to the loss. If an individual can free himself from suspicion, he does not contribute. And if no reasonable presumption lies against any of the crew, the loss falls upon the owner or master.

In case of shipwreck, and there are materials of the ship saved, the seamen by whose exertions they are saved, are entitled to their wages out of the proceeds of the fragments, even although no freight was earned to the owners. Chancellor Kent, however, thinks that in such a case, the allowance to seamen out of the wreck ought to be called salvage. "Wages, in such cases, would be contrary to the great principle in marine law, that freight is the mother of wages, and the safety of the ship the mother of freight."

The wages of seamen constitute a lien upon the ship, which does not, like other liens, depend on possession. Seamen's wages are hardly earned, and liable to many contingencies, by which they may be entirely lost, without any fault on their part. Few claims are so highly favored by law, and when due, the vessel, owners, and master, are all liable for them. Their demand takes precedence of all bottomry bonds, and is good against even a subsequent *bona fide* purchaser. It is a sacred claim, and as long as a single plank of the ship remains, the sailor is entitled, as against all other persons, to the proceeds, as security for his wages. The wages of seamen do not contribute to the general average when a loss of goods, masts, or the like, is voluntarily incurred at sea for the common safety, except in the single instance of the ransom of the ship. They are exempted here, lest the fear of personal loss should restrain them from making the requisite sacrifice; and the hardships and perils they endure, well entitle them to an exemption from further distress.

Desertion from a ship without just cause, or the justifiable discharge of a seaman by the master for bad conduct, will work a forfeiture of the wages previously earned. This is the rule of justice and of policy. But if the seaman quits the vessel involuntarily, or is driven ashore by reason of cruel usage, and for personal safety, the wages are not forfeited. On the other hand, it is the duty of the seamen to abide by the vessel as long as reasonable hope remains; and if they desert the ship in the perils of the sea, when they might have prevented damage, or saved the vessel, they forfeit their wages and are answerable in damages.

So liberal and kind is the care which our laws have taken for the interests of seamen in the merchant service. It would seem that nothing more is wanting for *their* benefit, excepting a more effectual security for the *kind* of provision which is to be made for them when they fall into sickness or distress in a foreign port, and some arrangement for their comfortable support, when worn out and decrepit at home.

MEN AND THINGS

IN THE

NAVY OF THE UNITED STATES.

AS DESCRIBED BY THE REV. CHAS. ROCKWELL, LATE CHAPLAIN IN THE

AMERICAN NAVAL SERVICE.

As THE condition and character of our Navy, and the reputation and conduct of its officers and men abroad, are matters of national interest and concern, it may not be amiss, briefly to allude to these and other kindred topics. To enter fully upon them, and give at length the results of years of free daily intercourse with seafaring men of all classes, as suggested by a close and constant observation of their peculiar habits and modes of thought and feeling, and a sincere and heartfelt sympathy with them and their friends, under the severe and varied trials of their lot—fully to present these points, would indeed require a volume.

With a view to aid us in forming a correct estimate of our navy, as also to furnish with important facts, those illustrious orators who are wont to speak of our ships of war as fully able to sweep the vessels of all other nations from the face of the ocean, it may be well to give the following statement of the naval forces of the United States, Great Britain, and France, as they were some few years since, and which have not since relatively materially changed. Including those in commission, as also those building and afloat, there were belonging to the Navy of the United States, 68 vessels of war; to that of France, 486; to Great Britain, 702.

In speaking of those who man our ships of war, I shall begin with such as are rated as boys. Of these, we had nearly thirty on board our ship, many of whom were taken from the House of Refuge, in New York, or were the sweepings of the streets of our large cities. Some were children of poor parents, who had been placed under the care of some sailor of their acquaintance, to take their first lesson in shipcraft, and, I may add, in devilcraft, too, on board a man-of-war; for surely a boy must be a dull scholar, who, in such a place, would not learn far more evil than good. These boys were from ten to sixteen or seventeen years of age, and some of them, from having been familiar, from their earliest years, with vice and crime, in almost every form, were among the most hardened, hopeless vagabonds in the world; and yet, they had so much shrewdness and intelligence, and such perfect self-possession in all circumstances, that one could not but feel a peculiar interest in them.

In turning from the boys to the men on board our ships of war, let us first notice the marines. These are soldiers who dress in uniform, are placed as sentries in different parts of the ship, and are not required to go aloft on sailor's duty, but aid in pulling the ropes on deck. They have their own officers, distinct from those of the ship; and as they know but little of sea-life, and are placed on board as a restraint upon the sailors, the latter do not like them, are fond of playing tricks upon them, and especially of palming off upon them all sorts of improbable stories as true. Hence the common proverb, "Tell that to the marines," which is used when one listens to a doubtful or incredible story.

We had on board our ship fifty-two marines, of whom twenty-two were foreigners; thirteen of this number being Swiss. They had an efficient commander, and were under excellent discipline. On one occasion, when off the coast of Africa, some oranges and bananas, which hung where sentries had charge of them, were stolen, and hence some one of the six marines, who had been on duty there during the night, must have connived at the theft. But as all denied being guilty, they were all whipped, that thus the right one might be punished, and all collusion as to screening each other in future might be prevented. This was indeed summary justice; and yet, among men in whose word you cannot confide, you must either lump matters in this way, or crime will thrive and pass unpunished. As it was, no more fruit was stolen.

Among the marines there are often men of education and intelligence, who, as merchants that have failed in business, or the profligate sons of respectable parents, or professional men, who have become dissipated, have seen better days; but having fallen from their former condition, have fled to a man-of-war as a place of refuge from trouble or disgrace. Not to dwell on other cases, we had with us a young man, who had come from a foreign country to obtain an education. While a senior at Yale College, he became involved in a fracas, for which he was dismissed from the institution; and thinking that he was not kindly treated by his guardian in this country, he enlisted as a marine. Such men like to dwell upon their brighter days; and where they find one who will listen to and sympathize with them, they take a kind of melancholy pleasure in minutely describing the scenes of trial and disgrace through which they have passed. There are many such, as well among the seamen as the marines, on board a ship of war; and often has my heart been deeply pained, when listening to the story of their woes. When in port, marines are stationed at every accessible entrance to the ship, to prevent men from deserting, and ardent spirits from being smuggled on board. Next to the officers of the ship, the marines are the main reliance for quelling a mutiny, and sustaining rightful authority on board our men-of-war.

In a crew of from five hundred to a thousand men, as collected together on board our larger ships, one meets with seamen of every class and condition, and of almost every nation under heaven. Most common sailors are of no nation, but change from the employ of one to that of another, just as convenience, or caprice, or higher wages may induce them to do so. We have many English seamen on board our ships of war; and it is said, that there are some thousand American sailors in the English Navy. That by desertion, or otherwise, men are constantly passing from one service to the other, is well known.

As those who ship seamen often receive so much a head for all they furnish, no very close inquiries are made as to whether a seaman's protection, as it is called, that is, the legal paper which certifies to what nation he belongs, tells the truth about him or not; for, aside from false swearing, at which few common sailors would hesitate, there are other ways in which seamen obtain new papers, and a new name. For example, we had on board our ship a foreigner by the name of John Cole, a Swede, or a Dane, if I mistake not. He spoke English in a very broken manner, and this led me to ask him, one day, how he came to have such a regular built Yankee name.

"I bought it of a landlord in Portland," was his reply.

"What did you give for it?"

"Fifty cents," he said; "but I've got most sick of it, and shall change it for another before long." And thus it is often true that sailor-landlords sell the papers of seamen who have died in their houses, or have gone to sea leaving them behind. Many of the seamen in our navy, ship by a new name almost every cruise.

But few officers and men of the old school now remain in our navy. By this I mean those who were trained amid scenes of war and carnage, and were more distinguished for their rough and reckless manners and habits, and their noisy, dare-devil bravery, than for improvement of mind, or a desire so to shape their course as to please those around them. The fact that many of the officers of our navy were formerly taken from the merchant service, with more regard to their energy of character and good seamanship than to their education and refinement of manners, together with the exciting influence of war, and the demoniac power of ardent spirits, gave a far ruder and more turbulent cast to our navy in former days than now belongs to it. By raising the standard of education among our naval officers, by limiting their power of inflicting punishment, and by promoting temperance among the men, a tranquilizing, elevating influence has been exerted on board our ships of war; so that now they deserve, far less than formerly, the appellation of "floating hells." Still much remains to be done, as will be seen when I come to speak of the prevailing vices of seamen. An old man-of-war's man is a very different being from a merchant-sailor. From mingling with so large a mass, he has been able to select such associates as pleased him, and thus to retain and strengthen his own peculiar tastes, feelings and habits. He has also been led to look well to his own rights, and to guard with jealous care against the encroachments of others.

From the rigid discipline to which seamen in our navy are subjected, as also from the fact that they are closely pressed upon by the mass around them, they become peculiarly sensitive and selfish as to what they regard as their rights, and are greatly given to grumbling when they fancy themselves misused. As to seamanship, too, from being confined to a narrow round of duties, such as handling the ropes and sails in a given part of the ship, as, for example, on the forecastle, or in one of the tops, they become very skillful in performing these duties, but know little of anything else. Hence, a good merchant-sailor, who knows a little of everything, and not much of anything, about a ship, may not succeed well on board a man-of-war; while, on the other hand, a good navy sailor may know but little of many things required to be done on board a merchant vessel. Merchant-sailors, too, have to labor much harder, and bear more exposure to the weather, than seamen in our navy; and they are apt, withal, to be much more filthy in their habits, and slovenly in their dress, than they would be permitted to be on board a man-of-war. These remarks show, in one point of view, the importance of training men expressly for our naval service.

There are several distinct classes of seamen to be met with on board our men-of-war. Of these, the first and most numerous are sailors by profession, who, from the poverty of their parents, or some other cause, have early entered on a seafaring life, without such an education as would fit them to rise above the grade of common seamen, and in this condition they remain for life. A few of these have families, and are frugal, honest and trustworthy. By far the greater number, however, are reckless, profligate, intemperate and profane. Cut off at an early age from all correct moral and religious influence, and exposed to temptation to vice in almost every form, they become the mere creatures of impulse, slaves to the will of despotic masters at sea, and the dupes of rapacious landlords and greedy harpies on shore. With no high and commanding motives to effort, in the hope of improving their condition, they yield themselves up to the pleasures of the moment, without regard to the future; and though, from the dangers of the sea, and exposure to corroding vices, and in sickly climes, they are in daily peril of their lives, yet, drowning reflection with reckless gayety, with sensual pleasure, or the drunkard's cup of woe, they rush madly on in the way to death. "Let us eat and drink, for to-morrow we die," seems to be their motto. We had on board our ship an old sailor, who ran away from his parents in Boston when nine years of age, and had been at sea, almost without cessation, forty-five years. In the year 1800, he was on board the English frigate Austria, on the coast of Egypt, where he had the plague, of which two hundred out of two hundred and fifty on board died. He had been shipwrecked seven times. The year before he joined our ship, he was cast away on the Scylla rocks, and was in the water two hours and a half. He lost his wife and two children by the cholera in New York; and, though himself one of thirteen children, he has now no near relative living. He was broken down with the rheumatism, and his lot was sad and cheerless indeed. Such is too often the condition of the few weather-beaten sailors, who are spared, almost by a miracle, to reach the period of old age. With no friends to care for them, and no means of support, they float like a weed torn from its native rock, where wind and wave may bear them. Perhaps they find a refuge in some naval hospital, or, cast forth on the cold charities of the world, they beg a humble pittance from door to door.

Another class of seamen are those who are ruined in character or property, or both, by a course of vice, or by some single act of folly or of crime, but who have seen better days. Of many a commander of a man-of-war, as of King David when he gathered his bandit forces at the cave of Adullam, may it be truly said, "And every one that was in distress, and every one that was in debt, and every one that was discontented, gathered themselves unto him, and he became a captain over them." Among these are merchants and others, who have failed in business, broken down play-actors, and sometimes professional men, the wayward and profligate sons of wealthy and respectable parents, convicts from State prisons, who have been guilty of forgery, counterfeiting, house-breaking, or other gentlemanly crimes, with now and then a pirate, and one who has been engaged in the slave-trade, to say nothing of old sailors who were pressed into the English service during the last war, and are as familiar with Dartmoor prison and its usages as with the district school in which they spent their boyhood. We had one who had lived among the natives of one of the South Sea islands, and conformed, for many months, to their savage modes of life; another who had been with Major Ashley to the Rocky Mountains, and had many amusing stories of the Flathead and other tribes of Indians; and another still who had been in the service of the fur-traders in the region of Hudson's Bay, traveling hundreds of miles over the snow, with a heavy burden on his back.

Seamen are perfectly accessible; and, from the free, social intercourse in which they indulge, will rarely refuse to answer a question of the most personal nature, if your manner is such as to gain their confidence. Indeed, they take peculiar pleasure in dwelling even on the darker portions of their past history, when they meet with one who will kindly listen to and sympathize with them. Many an hour have I spent, during the night watches, in listening to their singular narrations; and often have I thought, in reviewing the sketches of these stories in my journal, that, were one to collect an account of the most striking characters on board a man-of-war, as given by themselves, it would make a book of peculiar variety and effect.

There was one man on board our ship who had fled from domestic troubles, but whose mind was oppressed with a sadness which nothing could remove. He was the son of an elder of one of the first churches in the city of New York, and having married a beautiful woman whom he tenderly loved, and by whom he had several children, he removed to Illinois, where he purchased a farm of several hundred acres. For some time he had suspected the fidelity of his wife; when returning from hunting one night, sooner than he was expected, he found her with her guilty paramour, a man of wealth, in the vicinity. Highly excited, he aimed his rifle at them, intending to shoot them both, when he was seized by his hired man, who thus prevented a fatal deed. Having obtained a divorce from his wife, she married again, and he, feeling wretched where he was, and fearing that, should he meet the ruthless destroyer of his happiness alone, he should, in a moment of excited wrath and anguish, be led to murder him, he leased his farm to one in whose care he left his children, and sought a refuge from his troubles on board a man-of-war.

The most hopeless class of seamen, so far as moral reformation is concerned, are those who, like the squatters and others on the outskirts of civilization on land, have broken away from virtuous society, because they have forfeited the protection of the laws, by their crimes, or could not brook the restraints of religion, morality and law, or were unable, elsewhere than on board a man-of-war, to gratify their love of strong drink, or were conscious of being such helpless slaves of vice as to be wholly unfit to take care of themselves, and have, therefore, placed themselves in "durance vile," just as some men on shore wish to be imprisoned for the same reason.

There is another small class of seamen, sons of respectable parents, who have become so from a love of adventure, an attachment to a seafaring life, a strong desire to see foreign lands, or with a view to improve their health, or a wish, on the part of their friends, to check, by means of the rigid discipline of a ship, an unsubdued and refractory spirit.

In treating of the peculiar characteristics of seamen, and the vices to which they are most addicted, I shall notice, first, their superstition. The old idea that Sunday is a lucky and Friday an unlucky day, because on one Christ was crucified, and on the other he rose from the dead, has a strong hold on the minds of most seamen. There are commanders, even in our navy, who would not sail from port on Friday if they could avoid it, and who would make peculiar efforts to do so on the Sabbath. There are still many vessels, on the masts of which a horse-shoe is nailed, as a protection against the devil; and ship owners will rarely purchase a vessel which, by meeting with repeated accidents at sea, has proved to be unlucky.

Sailors have a peculiar superstition with regard to cats, especially black ones. Some years since, two men fell from the mast-head on board one of the ships in our navy, in a single day, of whom one was killed, and the other had his arm broken. Finding that one of the crew had killed a cat the night before, his shipmates regarded that as the cause of these accidents, and could not be appeased until the man was severely whipped; and then, as no one would mess with him, it was necessary to send him on shore. Clergymen have, in times past, been regarded as bringing ill luck to a ship on board which they sail, on the ground that the devil owes them a spite, and, as prince of the power of the air, strives, by means of tempests, to destroy them. This superstition may, however, have owed its origin to the story of Jonah, and the troubles which he brought upon his shipmates.

There are those who regard the playing of a death-march as a sure sign that some one on board is soon to die; and I have known a highly intelligent officer who would punish a man for such an act as soon as for a gross crime, on the ground, as he said, that he never knew it fail of being soon followed by a death. When lying in the bay of Gibraltar, during a violent storm, two of our massive anchors were broken, and we were driven rapidly out to sea. There was, at the time, on board, the body of one of the crew, lying in a coffin, with a view to his being buried on shore. Being compelled, however, to inclose him in his hammock, and bury him at sea, the carpenter was compelled to cut the coffin up into small pieces, and throw it overboard, because the men were superstitious and fearful as to its remaining on board.

The credulity of seamen as to ghosts and apparitions, good and bad signs, lucky and unlucky days, and the like, are owing, in part, to the peculiarly dangerous and exciting mode of life which they lead, to the many marvelous stories that are told in order to astonish the young and inexperienced, or to beguile the tedium of the night watches; but, more than all, to their being, from an early age, cut off from religious instruction. There are seamen who most religiously believe that when a man has been hung from the fore-yard-arm, two voices always reply when the man who is stationed there by night is hailed, one being that of him who has been hung; nor would the wealth of the world induce them to keep watch there.

That seamen have commonly much wit and humor, all know who have had intercourse with them. They have a great number of pithy expressions at ready command, and are very quick at repartee. This is owing to the fact that their mode of life is so peculiarly varied and exciting, that their minds act much more rapidly than those of most other men, as also to their being in such close and constant contact and collision with those around them, to which we may add the attention and applause secured by such as, by their ready wit, can aid in cheering the spirits of those around them, and thus relieve the monotony of a long and tedious voyage at sea. The craving for social excitement, on the part of seamen, leads them also to be very attentive hearers on the Sabbath, and few congregations on shore will follow a plain, but condensed and rapid, logical argument with so full an understanding of it as will a body of seamen on board our men-of-war. The wit and the songs of seamen are, for the most part, however, of a low, vulgar, and licentious cast.

This is the more to be regretted, as seamen are fond of the excitement of music, and, where a sailor has a fine voice, his songs are often called for, as well by officers as by the men.

As most seamen are, from an early age, cut off from kind parental restraint, and from moral and religious instruction, and exposed to the hardening and debasing influence of vice, it is not strange that, among other bad habits, they should form that of lying. Fear of punishment, too, leads them to resort to falsehood to conceal their guilt, when charged with it; nor dare they disclose the evil deeds of their shipmates, for fear of reproach and personal injury from them. Hence, most common sailors are inveterate liars, where their interest leads them to be so; nor is their word or oath, in such cases, regarded as of much value by those who know them well. One of our ship's boats, with ten or twelve rowers, had been ashore at a port where we were lying at anchor, and the midshipman who had charge of it, as is often done, had given the men a bottle of ardent spirits to drink, with a view to gain favor with them. As the men came on board, the officer of the deck saw that they had been drinking, and charged them with it. They all, to a man, stoutly denied the charge, and persevered in doing so, even after the officer of the boat had admitted before them that he had given them the spirits, and, in thus doing, had violated the rules of the ship. Events of this kind are of frequent occurrence on shipboard. It is, indeed, true that we hear much of the noble frankness of seamen, in freely confessing their faults, just as if there was some merit in it. The amount of it is, however, that such is the standard of morals to which they have conformed themselves, that they feel no guilt as to those things of which they so freely speak, but rather take pride in them.

Thieves are in very ill odor on shipboard, mainly because every one is exposed to suffer from them. When detected and brought up for punishment, the boatswain's mate always whips them with a relish. Still there is much thieving on board a man-of-war, and no small article of value is safe if exposed where it may be taken. Another prominent vice of seamen is selfishness. Many will, doubtless, be surprised at this statement. They have so often heard, in anniversary addresses and the like, that seamen are the most liberal, noble hearted and generous men in the world, that they really believe it to be true. But let us look, for a moment, at facts in the case. Seamen, on shipboard, are under such despotic rule, and are, in so many ways, checked and restrained, that they become peculiarly selfish and sensitive as to what they regard as their rights; and, where they dare to be so, are noisy and obstinate in defending them.

Much of the apparent liberality of seamen is shown when, from the influence of ardent spirits, they are hardly moral agents. I have known a seaman on shore, in a foreign port, buy a donkey with its load of fresh meat on the way to market, and, taking out his jack-knife, he cut up the meat, and divided it among the poor who thronged around him, and then, turning the donkey adrift, he went on his way. He was so drunk, however, that he hardly knew what he was doing. Money, too, has not the same value to a sailor, who has no one to provide for but himself, that it has to others. When a seaman gives three or five dollars to a disabled shipmate, the only difference it makes with him is that he has three or five dollars less in two or three hundred dollars of which to be robbed, when drunk, or otherwise defrauded of, at the end of his cruise. Sailors are often tired of the land before they have spent all their money, and are anxious to ship again. They feel much more at home to sit down on the deck, cut up their victuals with a jack-knife, and drink their tea out of a quart-cup, than to conform to table usages on shore. The same is true also of their clothes; while the unrighteous way in which they are fleeced by landlords and others, leads them to regard those around them as a set of landsharks, and to hasten on shipboard for safety.

We had on board our ship an old quarter-master, who had been to sea from childhood. He said that once, after a long cruise, he was seven days on shore before he spent all his money, and that when he went to the rendezvous to ship again, they scolded at him for having been gone so long. On one occasion he was paid off at Pensacola, and finding it difficult to get rid of his money, he hired a house for a month, with a man servant, and a yellow girl for a housekeeper. Having staid a few days, and paid all his bills, he had sixty-five dollars left, and not knowing how else to get rid of it, he had it all changed into silver half dollars, when, going to a plantation near, he gave each negro one of these coins, and then went and shipped for another cruise.

Licentiousness, of the lowest and most debasing character, is the habitual and easily besetting sin of most common seamen. That a sailor has a wife in every port he visits is an axiom in their creed and practice; and, so far are they from being ashamed of this fact, that they will most resolutely argue in favor of this indulgence as right, on the ground that such is their course of life, that they cannot, like other men, well sustain the social and domestic relations, and perform the duties of the marriage connection. And this unblushing advocacy of the grossest vice, must, forsooth, be regarded as a specimen of the noble frankness of the sailor, of which we hear so much. Allurements to licentiousness are among the surest and most common means of enticing seamen into those snares, which greedy and rapacious landlords so often spread for them. When the agent of these landsharks visits a ship just returning from a distant voyage, he excites the passions of his wretched dupes by offering his services as a guide to her whose "house is the way to hell, leading down to the chambers of death."

In times past, it has been customary with our naval commanders, when in foreign ports, both of savage and of so-called civilized and Christian nations, to permit hundreds of abandoned females to spend nights on board our national ships; thus converting them into floating brothels, and deeply disgracing the land from whence they came. The experiment was tried on a limited scale by a base and profligate commander, on board two ships belonging to the station where we cruised; the one just before our arrival, and the other while we were lying in the same port. So decided, however, was the opposition of many of the officers to this vile profanation of our country's flag, that the evil was soon checked, and did not spread to the other vessels in the squadron. So gross and brutal are most common seamen in this respect, that the most serious difficulties which occur on board our national ships arise, from opposing their wishes for liberty to go on shore in foreign ports, mainly with a view to gratify their lower passions and appetites.

The known corruption, in principle and practice, of many of the younger and some of the older officers in the navy, as to licentiousness, is a serious obstacle to efforts for the reformation of the common seamen. What good can be hoped for, in this respect, when the commander of a ship or squadron, when wintering in a foreign port, openly hires a house, and keeps a mistress as an undisguised member of his household, inviting his youngest officers to his table, and sending home in a national ship the illegitimate offspring of a former cruise? For an unmarried officer in our navy, from the youngest to the oldest, to be notoriously and habitually licentious when abroad, is not considered seriously disreputable, or a matter to be concealed in common conversation; and this because so few are without sin in that respect, that no correct public sentiment is embodied against this form of vice. Where young officers are first corrupted by low and gross conversation when at sea, and then with passions strong and reckless, and far removed from home and its virtuous and wholesome restraints, are exposed in foreign ports to the most seductive influences, and enticed along in the pathway to ruin by debased companions, who would reduce all around them to their own degraded level of infamy and vice—young officers, thus placed, are almost sure to fall; and should they afterward chance to reform, the oppressive consciousness of their own past misdeeds, fully known as they are to those who associate with them, will commonly restrain them from any strong and decided efforts to check the onward flow of corruption and vice around them.

Gambling is a vice to which our naval officers are too much addicted when in foreign ports, and especially when confined for the winter at such places as Mahon, where there is but little in the way of social intercourse, or of literary and intellectual amusements, to interest and attract them. In such places, sharpers assemble, and open their gambling-shops, with no other object than, by the thousand frauds and tricks of play, to fleece those wretched dupes who place themselves in their power. It is said that when our ships of war wintered some years since at Smyrna, Spanish gamblers repaired there, with their implements of trade; thus making a voyage of several hundred miles, rather than lose a golden harvest.

As these gambling places are open to all, the young officer visits them at first merely as a spectator. He wishes, he says, to study human nature, and see the world. He gazes upon the scene with lively interest. He watches the play of absorbing passions, as they glow in the faces of those around him—the rapid succession of hope and despair, of deep depression and lively transport. In a moment, as if by some magic spell, the shining heaps of gold become the spoil of him who, but just before, was almost penniless. Alas! the temptation is too strong for him. He begins by staking a small amount, and thus the fever grows upon him. If, for a time, successful, he is injured by spending in reckless dissipation the wealth so easily acquired. If stripped of his own means, he is tempted to borrow all he can of others, that, by staking it, he may indulge his love of play, or feed the momentary and delusive hope of regaining what he has lost. Unless taught by sad experience, he early breaks away from this seductive course; the love of play becomes a desperate and engrossing passion, which absorbs the soul, and destroys his relish for all minor excitements. Literary pursuits, and the purer and more elevated social pleasures, lose their relish, and he gives himself fully up to the influence of this feverish excitement.

Well do I remember my feelings, when conversing with a foreign merchant of uncommon intelligence and worth, speaking of a commander who had left the place several thousand dollars in debt. He said that he came to him, just before he left for home, and begged him, with tears in his eyes, to become his security for a year for one thousand dollars, most solemnly pledging himself that he would pay the debt within that time, and that his bondman should suffer no inconvenience for it. Since that time he had received several letters from the officer in question, in which he did not even allude to this debt, and the merchant had been compelled to pay it, though he knew not how to spare the funds for the purpose. He then asked me if such were the principles, and such the value of the word of honor of the highest officers of our navy. Such acts of unprincipled swindling leave a stain of infamy on our national flag, and their corrupting influence extends, in the way of example, from the higher to the lower grades of our naval officers.

One form of imposition, from which seamen in our navy suffer, is connected with their half-pay tickets. There is a rule, by which, when they go abroad, they can receive a certificate, which entitles the holder of it to draw half his wages, as they become due, from the navy agent of the station at home, where it is given. Of these, sailors are often defrauded by landlords and other sharpers, but especially by their so called wives. These women, who are often the lowest and most abandoned harpies in our large cities, manage to secure the confidence of the seamen of our navy, when they are on shore for a spree, and thus secure to themselves the benefit of a half-pay ticket for years. It is said of one of them at New York, that the disbursing officer noticed that she came quite often for pay, and, on inquiry, he found that she had been married to two seamen, whose cruises commenced and ended at different times, so that one was sure to be at sea while the other was at home. By thus entertaining each of them a week or two, once in two or three years, she received full seamen's pay, equal, perhaps, to one hundred and fifty dollars a year.

Intemperance in the use of ardent spirits, is to the seaman literally the mother of abominations, and the prolific source of most of his degradation and deep and bitter woe. When our ship was taking in stores at the navy-yard, before leaving home, one of the crew managed to whitewash a barrel filled with whisky, and, thus passing it on board as a tar-barrel, he rolled it forward on deck, and at night, having broken in the head, and using an old shoe for a cup, all helped themselves, and twenty-eight were found drunk the next morning. We had on board a man who, in going out to the Mediterranean, in one of our national ships, a short time before, had become intoxicated, and being confined for it, and deprived of his grog, so strong was his thirst for ardent spirits, that he drank a quantity of paint in which whisky had been mixed, though he knew that it was rank poison.

A common way of bringing ardent spirits on board, is in what are called snakes; that is, in the skins of the intestines of animals, which sailors, who have been on shore, wind around their legs under their large trowsers. When they come on board, they are always examined by passing the hand over every part of their bodies. Boatmen who bring on board articles to sell, often manage to conceal ardent spirits, and smuggle it on board, knowing, as they do, that a sailor will give almost any price for it. In one case, a man used to take bladder-skins, and putting them, when empty, into a large earthern jug, would fill them with spirits, and then, tying a string around the mouth, dropped them. Having thus filled the jug, he poured in a little milk among them, so that, when he came on board, he would open his jug, and show his milk, and was permitted to pass on, when by breaking the jug, or piercing the skins, he came at the liquor, and sold it At the island of Malta, ardent spirits are smuggled on board in cigar-boxes, lined with parchment, those who bring them having one box of cigars open, which they show, in passing, to the officer of the deck.

The most singular means, however, I have ever known of obtaining ardent spirits, was the following: When we reached Mahon, most of the crew of the Delaware 74, were at the hospital on an island in the harbor, with the cholera among them. Some of the stronger ones were employed, from time to time, to cover the walls of the hospital with a wash, made of Spanish white, olive oil, and whisky. The lieutenant in command, perceiving that, when he was absent, but little was done, concealed himself, and, unseen by the men, watched their movements. He found that they waited until the oil in their paint-tub had collected together on the top, with the whisky next below, and the Spanish white at the bottom, when, running a quill through the oil, they sucked out the whisky and drank it.

Many of our crew told me, that the great number of merchant ships which sail on the temperance plan, led them to go on board a man-of-war, where they could have their grog. Their allowance was half a pint of whisky a day, which, on board our ship, was put in a large tub, and mingled freely with water, and served out to them three times a day. Thus, the time taken up in serving out this poison is nearly equal to that taken up by their meals, to say nothing of the space occupied by it on shipboard, which, in long voyages, is needed for water and provisions.

Those who relinquish their allowance of spirits for any period of not less than three successive months, receive in the place of it one dollar and eighty cents a month. Of about five hundred on board our ship, less than one hundred had, at the end of the first year of our cruise, drawn their grog the whole time; and by thus saving their money, they were able to supply themselves with many little comforts in the way of provision and clothing, of which they must otherwise have been destitute. In one case, the whole crew of one of our sloops of war stopped their grog for two months, that thus they might have money with which to buy a sword to present to a favorite officer, and then returned to their old courses again.

We had on board an old man whose life, from his youth up, had been a truly eventful one. He had, among other things, been impressed into the English navy during the last war; his papers, proving him an American citizen, had been torn to pieces before his face by a British officer; he had escaped from his ship, and lived for some time among the natives in the East Indies; had for a long time been an inmate of Dartmoor Prison, where, being one of the shrewdest of the universal Yankee nation, he had carried on an active trade in selling beer. Having returned to Boston, at the close of the war, after an absence of eight or nine years, some of his friends came a distance of forty miles to see him, furnished him with money with which to clothe himself and go home. This he spent in a spree, and shipped on board a man-of-war for a foreign cruise of four years, and sailed without seeing his wife and children. When with us, his children were respectable and prosperous, and would have provided well for him at home, or he might at any time have had command of a vessel, if he would have consented to sign the temperance pledge. This, however, he had refused, and, during the early part of our cruise, his allowance of whisky so addled his brain, that he was almost an idiot, being stupid and silly in the extreme. Having been persuaded to give up his grog, he suffered severely by the change; and such were the fears for the result, enfeebled as his constitution had been by long indulgence, that the surgeon, the captain, and other officers advised him to commence drinking again. He replied, that he had bound himself not to do so, and he would not, if he died. At length his health, strength, and vigor of mind returned, and, as a petty officer, he was one of the shrewdest and most diligent and useful men on board The change seemed almost miraculous, and one could hardly believe him to be the same man as before.

A sore evil connected with issuing spirit rations on board our men-of war, is found in the fact, that seamen often lose their lives by neglecting to report themselves until disease has such a hold upon them, that they cannot be cured, and this, merely, because they cannot have their grog when they are on the sick-list. I had a shipmate, who, from this cause, suffered under a raging fever, without medical treatment, until within three days of his death, when he was past all hope. Another of our crew was sick for several months, during which time, his character seemed to have undergone a radical religious change. As he began to recover and come on deck, the surgeon strictly charged him not to taste of ardent spirits, as, in the state he was, it would surely kill him. Led by the force of appetite, however, and the persuasions of his shipmates, to take a drink of grog, he died a day or two afterward. When we first reached Mahon, twenty-three men belonging to the Delaware had just died of the cholera. Commodore P—— told me, that not one of them would have been lost, had they obeyed orders as to reporting themselves early to the surgeon of the ship, and that the love of strong drink prevented them from doing so.

Two men on board our ship, were one night engaged in a drunken quarrel, when, in falling, one of them had his own knife thrust into his groin, by which the femoral artery was severed so as soon to end his life. Both of these men had respectable connexions in the vicinity of Boston, and the one who was killed had been a merchant in that city.

I overheard one of our men at breakfast, lamenting the degradation and ruin which intemperance had brought upon him, and with strong feeling, telling his messmates of the efforts which a pious father had made to reclaim him, and how he revered and loved the good old man, and how often he thought of him, though many years had passed since he had seen him. With burning shame, he compared his own wretched and degraded state with the high standing and success in life of his brothers, who were virtuous men. Soon after this, I went and pressed him with the folly of his course, and he saw and felt that it was worse than madness. At noon I saw him again, and oh, it was enough to break one's heart to see him. To drown the voice of conscience, he had drained the cup of woe. Confined, and in irons, he rolled about upon the deck, a drunken, raving maniac. He howled and prayed, and cursed and blasphemed the name of his God, all in a single breath. And oh, that unearthly howl! it made my blood run cold, as it rung through the ship, it seemed so like the voice of wailing from the pit of woe. It was no stupid, brutal cry: it had in it the soul of a man, and was filled with the anguish of a deathless spirit. It came, too, from one of warm heart, and fine feelings, who, but for this single curse, might have been a man indeed, wearing the image of his God. Then I thought, that could this man, sunken as he was, but be placed within the halls of Congress, where those who make our laws could see and hear him, it would do more than any human eloquence, to lead them, as one man, to rise up and refuse longer to furnish the poor sailor with this liquid fire. I have blushed for shame when I have seen those who, as seamen, wore our naval uniform, and such even as had the badge of petty officers, reeling, raving, and belching forth their curses in the streets of a foreign city, or lying dead drunk upon the pavement, the objects of pity, or scoffed and sneered at by hundreds who were passing every hour, and exposed when night came on, to be robbed even to the very clothes they wore. I have also heard little children, when at play, freely using the vilest and most wicked oaths, which were the only English words they knew, and which had been fixed in their memory by hearing them so often used by our seamen. They did not know the meaning of these words, and when I have told them that what they said was bad and wicked, they said that they did not know it, and would say so no more.

I have one charge more to bring against intemperance, as it exists in our navy: it is the crime of murder, and the guilt of shedding human blood. So far as I could learn by observation and inquiry, not a winter passes at Mahon, in which one or more of our seamen is not murdered, either in drunken quarrels with each other when on shore, or with the natives there. The witnesses of these deeds of blood, too, are commonly so far intoxicated that their evidence is good for nothing, and hence justice cannot be done. The guilty do not, however, always escape detection and punishment, as the following case will show.

Among those who went on shore on liberty, the last winter we were in Mahon, were two young men who were shipmates and friends, and about twenty-one years of age. Instead of returning, as commanded to do, at the end of twenty-four hours, they were on shore a week, when one of them came on board, and was confined for being drunk, and disobeying orders. The next morning, having slept off the stupor caused by drinking, as one of the lieutenants of the ship was passing near him, he rushed toward him and, shaking with violence the irons which bound him, exclaimed, "I am a murderer!" "For God's sake, then, keep your hands off from me," said the lieutenant, shrinking back, startled at the guilty horror of the man. He then confessed that he had killed his friend, and offered to go and point out where the body was. An officer with a guard of marines, was sent with him, when he led them to a retired place, where the body was lying in a natural position, as if sleeping, with a small switch in its hand, and a pair of shoes beside it. The head was badly broken and mashed, and the work of death had evidently been instantaneous.

The story told by the murderer was, that he and his friend, during their absence, had every day carried a supply of ardent spirits with them, to some retired place in the fields, and there remained, more or less intoxicated, until night, when they returned to the city to lodge. At length, when in a kind of drunken stupor, he had tried to awaken his friend, who was sleeping; and, failing to do it readily, he took a large stone, weighing about fifty pounds, and raising it some feet, let it fall upon the head of the sleeping man. This he did twice, though the first stroke must have caused instant death. The body was removed, and I performed over it the rites of Christian burial, when it was laid in the grave. The murderer was tried by a court-martial, and sentenced to be hung from the foreyard-arm of the ship, to which he belonged, six weeks from time of his trial.

Were we to turn from the seamen to the officers on board our men-of-war, a volume might be written in tracing the various causes which unite in forming their characters and directing their conduct, and in making them what they should, or what they should not be. I can, however, only glance, in closing, at a few peculiarities of the singular, unnatural, and highly artificial state of society, under the influence of which, as existing in our naval service, the minds and morals of our officers are shaped. Midshipmen ought, before receiving a warrant, to be closely examined as to their habits, moral character, and health. Many a reprobate and ungovernable son has, as a last resort, been placed in the navy with a view to subdue him, when, perhaps, his constitution has been impaired by vicious indulgence, or undermined by disease; and thus, physically weak and morally debased and depraved, has become a burden to the service, and a curse to all around him. Unable to endure the exposure and fatigue of duty, beneath the scorching sun, or chilling night-air, or drenching rain, or amid the howling tempest, he hangs upon the sick-list, and the duties he should do fall heavily upon others. Delicate boys, transferred, at a tender age, from the school-room, or luxurious parlor, to the steerage of a man-of-war, with its coarse fare and hard accommodations, its noise and riot, its loss of rest and fatiguing duty on deck, are full apt to wilt and wither, like the tender plant torn from its native earth and placed in harder and more ungenial soil. These causes, with youthful intemperance and licentiousness, have not only driven many from our navy, but have undermined or seriously injured the health and constitutions of large numbers still connected with it. I once heard a number of lieutenants give it as their united and deliberate opinion, that were there an invalid list formed in our navy, of those who were permanently diseased, it would embrace one half the officers of the grade of lieutenant and upward. Most of these, it is true, are engaged in active duty, but a little extra exposure to the weather, or over exertion, or undue indulgence of some of the animal appetites, brings them upon the sick-list, and the burden of their duties rests severely on others.

The late increase of pay, in our navy, has a tendency to encourage and enable the younger officers to appear and dress like gentlemen. Compel a young man to live on coarse fare and dress poorly, to use his sheets for a table-cloth, to borrow clothes of his messmates and be meanly served, and you humble and degrade him, and greatly lessen his pride of character and self-respect. A man's conduct and language are affected not a little by the dress and style of living of himself and those around him. An increase of pay furnishes the means of an earlier and better settlement in married life than could otherwise be hoped for; and no one, who has not witnessed the fact referred to, can know how much is effected by a devoted and honorable attachment to a lovely and virtuous woman, in restraining from vice wild and reckless young men, when peculiarly exposed to temptation, and cut off from all moral and religious restraint.

I am happy to state, that there is an increasing number of officers in our navy, who, by their virtues and their moral and religious worth, are a credit to the service, and would grace any circle in which they might be placed. There are others, however, and sorry am I that it is so, who, though wearing swords and epaulets, and claiming to be gentlemen, are so in dress alone; their conduct and their language grossly belying their outward appearance and their vaunted claims to gentility. Some of this class are so lost to all sense of decency, that their common conversation at the mess-table and elsewhere, is most loathsome and offensive to every virtuous mind, and such, withal, as should forever exclude them from all decent society. There are some prominent evils connected with the system of promotion to rank and office, existing in our navy. Where reference is had in promotion to the time one has been in the service alone, and not to merit, each one being elevated to a higher rank when his turn comes, it will, of course, happen that some, and it may be many, will reach the highest grade of office, who, by their want of self-control, of natural talent, of courage, of good morals or education, are wholly unfit for the station they occupy. It is often true, also, that the weakest and most worthless officers, have the most influential friends and connexions to stand by them in the hour of trouble, and shield them from their just deserts. A commander, convicted of theft and other base crimes, has been freed from the sentence of a court-martial, by the discovery, on the part of a learned friend, of a slight informality in the proceedings of the court; and the wretch, guilty, but unharmed, has been sent back to his station, to tyrannize over those by whose means he had been brought to trial.

A weak and timid commander may not only disgrace his country in time of action, but, when sailing in warm and sickly latitudes, may fear to run near enough to the coast to secure the benefit of the land breezes, or to avail himself, so far as it is prudent to do so, of the breath of the tornado to bear him onward, instead of putting his ship directly before it, and permitting it to carry him in a direction opposite to that in which he should go. Thus may the cowardice of a single man endanger the lives of scores or hundreds, by detaining them where the deadly breath of the pestilence reaches them. Such a man may, through natural weakness of character, be scarcely a moral agent, and the guilt and blame in the case must rest upon the government which employs such wretched tools.

It has been said by one long familiar with our navy, that there are many intimacies, but few friendships, among the officers. The reason of this, is found in the frequent collisions of feelings, arising from conflicting claims to rank and honor, and the jealousy with which officers of the lower grades regard the standing and authority of those above them. The eager thirst for rank and promotion, attended as they are by higher authority, increased pay, and better fare and accommodations on shipboard or elsewhere, leads the younger officers to feel anything but unmingled grief for the death of those above them; nor is the chance of promotion connected with war, or the cruise of a ship or squadron in sickly climes, viewed without interest by the eager aspirants for rank and office. This, surely, is a gross perversion of the moral feelings and sympathies of our nature.

Though seamen often meet with incidents which excite the feelings, far more than anything which occurs on land would do, yet, they not unfrequently sacrifice, in a great degree, the religious benefit they might derive from impressive dispensations of the providence of God, by their unrestrained indulgence of wit and humor. Examples of this occur in the epitaphs which they compose for their deceased shipmates. Of these, the following, copied from monuments in the graveyard where our seamen are buried, at Mahon, may serve as a specimen. Over the inscription which follows, the outlines of a cask are drawn. The epitaph reads thus:

"In memory of William Mulloy, a native of Troy, state of New York, a cooper on board the United States ship Delaware 74. His adze becoming edgeless, his staves worm-eaten, his hoops consumed, his flags expended, and his bungs decayed, he yielded up his trade, with his life on the twenty-ninth of April, 1829." The following explains itself:

> " Although his skin's of dusky hue,
> His heart was pure, his friendship true:
> His glass upon this earth is run,
> He 'll rise again in kingdom come.
> His duty he performed with care,
> As captain's cook of Delaware."

Another,—

> " The bark is waiting,
> I must be ready ;
> Charon put off,
> Steer small and steady."

There has been a change for the better, great and strongly marked, in the general character and deportment of the officers and men of our navy, within a few years past; and, in repeated instances, chaplains have been cheered and encouraged amid the peculiarly trying and self-denying labors of their office, by a general seriousness among those who sailed with them, and the commencement, on the part of many, of a sober, devout, and religious course of life. Some, who were formerly officers in the navy, are now able, pious, and successful preachers of the Gospel; and there are others still, who are now connected with the naval service, whose education, talents, piety, and knowledge of the world are such as would fit them for peculiar usefulness in the clerical profession.

www.ingramcontent.com/pod-product-compliance
Lightning Source LLC
LaVergne TN
LVHW021102110826
845150LV00001B/147

* 9 7 8 1 4 2 5 5 6 5 7 7 0 *